T0180298

Lecture Notes in Artificial Intelligence   11888

Subseries of Lecture Notes in Computer Science

Series Editors

Randy Goebel
University of Alberta, Edmonton, Canada
Yuzuru Tanaka
Hokkaido University, Sapporo, Japan
Wolfgang Wahlster
DFKI and Saarland University, Saarbrücken, Germany

Founding Editor

Jörg Siekmann
DFKI and Saarland University, Saarbrücken, Germany

More information about this series at http://www.springer.com/series/1244

Jianxin Li · Sen Wang · Shaowen Qin · Xue Li ·
Shuliang Wang (Eds.)

Advanced Data Mining and Applications

15th International Conference, ADMA 2019
Dalian, China, November 21–23, 2019
Proceedings

 Springer

Editors
Jianxin Li ⓘ
Deakin University
Burwood, VIC, Australia

Sen Wang
The University of Queensland
St. Lucia, QLD, Australia

Shaowen Qin ⓘ
Flinders University
Bedford Park, SA, Australia

Xue Li
Dalian Neusoft University of Information
Dalian, China

Shuliang Wang
Beijing Institute of Technology
Beijing, China

ISSN 0302-9743   ISSN 1611-3349 (electronic)
Lecture Notes in Artificial Intelligence
ISBN 978-3-030-35230-1   ISBN 978-3-030-35231-8 (eBook)
https://doi.org/10.1007/978-3-030-35231-8

LNCS Sublibrary: SL7 – Artificial Intelligence

This Springer imprint is published by the registered company Springer Nature Switzerland AG
The registered company address is: Gewerbestrasse 11, 6330 Cham, Switzerland

Preface

The 15th International Conference on Advanced Data Mining and Applications (ADMA 2019) was held during November 21–23, 2019, in Dalian, China. As the tradition of a leading international forum continued, it brought together researchers and practitioners, ranging from young to experienced, from many countries around the world to share innovative ideas, original research findings, case study results as well as experience-based insights in Advanced Data Mining and Applications – an area of growing importance in the current data-rich era. Indeed, ADMA has become a flagship conference in the field of data mining and applications.

The conference received 170 submissions. All papers were peer-reviewed by at least three members of the Program Committee (PC) composed of international experts in relevant research fields. 39 regular research papers (acceptance rate of 23%) and 26 short research papers (of more than 8 pages) were accepted for presentation at the conference and publication in these proceedings. The selected papers covered a wide variety of important topics in the area of data mining, including parallel and distributed data mining algorithms, mining on data streams, graph mining, spatial data mining, multimedia data mining, Web mining, the Internet of Things, health informatics, and biomedical data mining. The ADMA 2019 conference program was complemented by four outstanding keynote presentations given by Prof. Vincent S. Tseng, Prof. Osamr Zaiane, Prof. Guoren Wang, and Dr. Hongzhi Yin. The conference also included demonstrations of new tools for advanced data mining and applications, a competition on "Robust Automated Event Detection for Multi-Camera Streaming Video Environment", as well as tutorials given by Yong Xiang, Ming Zhong, Changdong Wang, Senzhang Wang, Guojie Song and Fuzhen Zhuang.

We would like to take this opportunity to thank all authors who submitted papers to this conference, and express our gratitude to all individuals, institutions, and sponsors that supported ADMA 2019. This high-quality program would not have been possible without the expertise and dedication of our PC members. We thank the PC members for completing the review process and providing valuable reports under a tight schedule constraint.

We are grateful for the guidance of the general chair Xue Li and co-chair Shuliang Wang, the time and effort of the publication chair Shaowen Qin, the publicity chair Weitong Chen, the demo co-chairs Ye Yua and Guodong Long, the tutorial co-chairs Tanmoy Chakraborty and Chuan Shi, the competition chair Xin Wang, the workshop co-chairs Yongfeng Dong and Hua Wang, the special issue co-chairs Mohammed Eunus Ali and Tarique Anwar, and the local organization chair Yingqiu Li. We also would like to acknowledge the support of the members of the conference Steering

Committee. All of them helped to make ADMA 2019 a success. Finally, we would like to thank all researchers, practitioners, and students who contributed their work and participated in the conference. We believe that many colleagues will find this collection of papers exciting and useful for advancing their own research.

November 2019   Jianxin Li
                                                                                                      Sen Wang

Organization

Organizing Committee

General Chair

Xue Li — Dalian Neusoft University of Information, China

General Co-chair

Shuliang Wang — Beijing Institute of Technology, China

Program Co-chairs

Jianxin Li — Deakin University, Australia
Sen Wang — The University of Queensland, Australia

Proceedings (Publication) Chair

Shaowen Qin — Flinders University, Australia

Publicity Chair

Weitong Chen — The University of Queensland, Australia

Local Chair

Yingqiu Li — Dalian Neusoft University of Information, China

Demo Co-chairs

Ye Yuan — Dalian Neusoft University of Information, China
Guodong Long — University of Technology Sydney, Australia

Tutorial Co-chairs

Tanmoy Chakraborty — Indraprastha Institute of Information Technology Delhi (IIIT-D), India
Chuan Shi — Beijing University of Posts and Telecommunications, China

Competition Chair

Xin Wang — Tianjin University, China

Workshop Co-chairs

Yongfeng Dong — Hebei University of Technology, China
Hua Wang — Victoria University, Australia

Special Issue Co-chairs

Mohammed Eunus Ali   Bangladesh University of Engineering and Technology,
                       Bangladesh
Tarique Anwar   Indian Institute of Technology, India

Web Chair

David Yang   Dalian Neusoft Institute of Information, China

Program Committee

Noha Alduaiji   Majmaah University, Saudi Arabia
Tarique Anwar   Indian Institute of Technology Ropar, India
Taotao Cai   Deakin University, Australia
Tanmoy Chakraborty   Indraprastha Institute of Information Technology Delhi,
                       India
Hongxu Chen   The University of Queensland, Australia
Liang Chen   Sun Yat-sen University, China
Lu Chen   Swinburne University of Technology, Australia
Tong Chen   The University of Queensland, Australia
Yurong Cheng   Beijing Institute of Technology, China
Farhana Choudhury   The University of Melbourne, Australia
Ningning Cui   Northeastern University, China
Ke Deng   RMIT University, Australia
Hong Fang   Shanghai Polytechnic University, China
Longxiang Gao   Deakin University, Australia
Yunjun Gao   Zhejiang University, China
Yanhui Gu   Nanjing Normal University, China
Bin Guo   Télécom SudParis, France
Sung Ho Ha   Kyungpook National University, South Korea
Guangyan Huang   Deakin University, Australia
Md. Saiful Islam   Griffith University, Australia
Jing Jiang   University of Technology Sydney, Australia
Wang Jianming   Tianjin Polytechnic University, China
Peiquan Jin   University of Science and Technology of China, China
Xiangjie Kong   Dalian University of Technology, China
Jianxin Li   Deakin University, Australia
Li Li   Southwest University, China
Yingqiu Li   Dalian Neusoft University of Information, China
Yukun Li   Tianjin University of Technology, China
Alan Wee-Chung Liew   Griffith University, Australia
Luyao Liu   The University of Queensland, Australia
Wei Liu   The University of Western Australia, Australia
Guodong Long   University of Technology Sydney, Australia

Zongmin Ma	CUAA, China
Yasuhiko Morimoto	Hiroshima University, Japan
Quoc Viet Hung Nguyen	Griffith University, Australia
Bo Ning	Dalian Maritime University, China
Xueping Peng	University of Technology Sydney, Australia
Dechang Pi	Nanjing University of Aeronautics and Astronautics, China
Wenjie Ruan	Lancaster University, UK
Michael Sheng	Macquarie University, Australia
Chuan Shi	Beijing University of Posts and Telecommunications, China
Lukui Shi	Hebei University of Technology, China
Shaoxu Song	Tsinghua University, China
Eiji Uchino	Yamaguchi University, Japan
Sayan Unankard	Maejo University, Thailand
Can Wang	CSIRO, Australia
Chang-Dong Wang	Sun Yat-sen University, China
Forest Wang	Griffith University, Australia
Hongzhi Wang	Harbin Institute of Technology, China
Meng Wang	Southeast University, China
Sen Wang	The University of Queensland, Australia
Weiqing Wang	Monash University, Australia
Xianzhi Wang	University of Technology Sydney, Australia
Xiaofei Wang	Tianjin University, China
Xin Wang	Tianjin University, China
Feng Xia	Dalian University of Technology, China
Junchang Xin	Northeastern University, China
Jiajie Xu	Soochow University, China
Shan Xue	Macquarie University, Australia
Yajun Yang	Tianjin University, China
Lina Yao	The University of New South Wales, Australia
Hongzhi Yin	The University of Queensland, Australia
Yongxin Yu	Tianjin University, China
Weiwei Yuan	Nanjing University of Aeronautics and Astronautics, China
Ye Yuan	Northeastern University, China
Peng Yuwei	Wuhan University, China
Guang Lan Zhang	Boston University, USA
Mingwei Zhang	Northeastern University, China
Wei Emma Zhang	The University of Adelaide, Australia
Xiaowang Zhang	Tianjin University, China
Xiuzhen Zhang	RMIT University, Australia
Xuyun Zhang	The University of Auckland, New Zealand

Contents

Data Mining Foundations

Mining Emerging High Utility Itemsets over Streaming Database 3
   Acquah Hackman, Yu Huang, Philip S. Yu, and Vincent S. Tseng

A Methodology for Resolving Heterogeneity and Interdependence
in Data Analytics 17
   *Han Han, Yunwei Zhao, Can Wang, Min Shu, Tao Peng, Chi-Hung Chi,
and Yonghong Yu*

Learning Subgraph Structure with LSTM for Complex Network
Link Prediction. 34
   Yun Han, Donghai Guan, and Weiwei Yuan

Accelerating Minimum Temporal Paths Query Based
on Dynamic Programming 48
   Mo Li, Junchang Xin, Zhiqiong Wang, and Huilin Liu

Multiple Query Point Based Collective Spatial Keyword Querying 63
   Yun Li, Ziheng Wang, Jing Chen, Fei Wang, and Jiajie Xu

Unsupervised Feature Selection for Noisy Data. 79
   Kaveh Mahdavi, Jesus Labarta, and Judit Gimenez

Tri-Level Cross-Domain Sign Prediction for Complex Network 95
   Jiali Pang, Donghai Guan, and Weiwei Yuan

An Efficient Mining Algorithm of Closed Frequent Itemsets
on Multi-core Processor. 107
   Huan Phan

TSRuleGrowth: Mining Partially-Ordered Prediction Rules From
a Time Series of Discrete Elements, Application to a Context
of Ambient Intelligence 119
   *Benoit Vuillemin, Lionel Delphin-Poulat, Rozenn Nicol,
Laetitia Matignon, and Salima Hassas*

HGTPU-Tree: An Improved Index Supporting Similarity Query
of Uncertain Moving Objects for Frequent Updates. 135
   Mengqian Zhang, Bohan Li, and Kai Wang

Robust Feature Selection Based on Fuzzy Rough Sets
with Representative Sample 151
*Zhimin Zhang, Weitong Chen, Chengyu Liu, Yun Kang, Feng Liu,
Yuwen Li, and Shoushui Wei*

Classification and Clustering Methods

HUE-Span: Fast High Utility Episode Mining...................... 169
Philippe Fournier-Viger, Peng Yang, Jerry Chun-Wei Lin, and Unil Yun

Clustering Noisy Temporal Data............................... 185
Paul Grant and Md Zahidul Islam

A Novel Approach for Noisy Signal Classification Through the Use
of Multiple Wavelets and Ensembles of Classifiers 195
Paul Grant and Md Zahidul Islam

Recommender Systems

Reminder Care System: An Activity-Aware Cross-Device
Recommendation System..................................... 207
*May S. Altulyan, Chaoran Huang, Lina Yao, Xianzhi Wang,
Salil Kanhere, and Yunajiang Cao*

Similar Group Finding Algorithm Based on Temporal Subgraph Matching... 221
Yizhu Cai, Mo Li, and Junchang Xin

Traditional PageRank Versus Network Capacity Bound 236
Robert A. Kłopotek and Mieczysław A. Kłopotek

RecKGC: Integrating Recommendation with Knowledge
Graph Completion... 250
*Jingwei Ma, Mingyang Zhong, Jiahui Wen, Weitong Chen,
Xiaofang Zhou, and Xue Li*

PRME-GTS: A New Successive POI Recommendation Model
with Temporal and Social Influences............................ 266
Rubai Mao, Zhe Han, Zitu Liu, Yong Liu, Xingfeng Lv, and Ping Xuan

Social Network and Social Media

Precomputing Hybrid Index Architecture for Flexible Community
Search over Location-Based Social Networks 277
Ismail Alaqta, Junhu Wang, and Mohammad Awrangjeb

Expert2Vec: Distributed Expert Representation Learning in Question
Answering Community 288
Xiaocong Chen, Chaoran Huang, Xiang Zhang, Xianzhi Wang, Wei Liu,
and Lina Yao

Improving the Link Prediction by Exploiting the Collaborative
and Context-Aware Social Influence 302
Han Gao, Yuxin Zhang, and Bohan Li

A Causality Driven Approach to Adverse Drug Reactions
Detection in Tweets. 316
Humayun Kayesh, Md. Saiful Islam, and Junhu Wang

Correlate Influential News Article Events to Stock Quote Movement. 331
Arun Chaitanya Mandalapu, Saranya Gunabalan, Avinash Sadineni,
Taotao Cai, Nur Al Hasan Haldar, and Jianxin Li

Top-N Hashtag Prediction via Coupling Social Influence and Homophily. . . . 343
Can Wang, Zhonghao Sun, Yunwei Zhao, Chi-Hung Chi,
Willem-Jan van den Heuvel, Kwok-Yan Lam, and Bela Stantic

Unfolding the Mixed and Intertwined: A Multilevel View of Topic
Evolution on Twitter 359
Yunwei Zhao, Can Wang, Han Han, Willem-Jan van den Heuvel,
Chi-Hung Chi, and Weimin Li

Behavior Modeling and User Profiling

DAMTRNN: A Delta Attention-Based Multi-task RNN
for Intention Recognition 373
Weitong Chen, Lin Yue, Bohan Li, Can Wang, and Quan Z. Sheng

DeepIdentifier: A Deep Learning-Based Lightweight Approach for User
Identity Recognition 389
Meng-Chieh Lee, Yu Huang, Josh Jia-Ching Ying, Chien Chen,
and Vincent S. Tseng

Domain-Aware Unsupervised Cross-dataset Person Re-identification 406
Zhihui Li, Wenhe Liu, Xiaojun Chang, Lina Yao, Mahesh Prakash,
and Huaxiang Zhang

Invariance Matters: Person Re-identification by Local Color Transfer 421
Ying Niu, Chunmiao Yuan, Kunliang Liu, Yukuan Sun, Jiayu Liang,
Guanghao Jin, and Jianming Wang

Research on Interactive Intent Recognition Based on Facial Expression
and Line of Sight Direction 431
   Siyu Ren, Guanghao Jin, Kunliang Liu, Yukuan Sun, Jiayu Liang,
   Shiling Jiang, and Jianming Wang

Text and Multimedia Mining

Mining Summary of Short Text with Centroid Similarity Distance 447
   Nigel Franciscus, Junhu Wang, and Bela Stantic

Children's Speaker Recognition Method Based
on Multi-dimensional Features 462
   Ning Jia, Chunjun Zheng, and Wei Sun

Constructing Dictionary to Analyze Features Sentiment of a Movie
Based on Danmakus 474
   Jie Li and Yukun Li

Single Image Dehazing Algorithm Based on Sky Region Segmentation 489
   Weixiang Li, Wei Jie, and Somaiyeh Mahmoudzadeh

Online Aggregated-Event Representation for Multiple Event
Detection in Videos... 501
   Molefe Vicky Mleya, Weiqi Li, Jiayu Liang, Kunliang Liu, Yunkuan Sun,
   Guanghao Jin, and Jianming Wang

Standard Deviation Clustering Combined with Visual Psychological
Test Algorithm for Image Segmentation......................... 516
   Zhenggang Wang, Jin Jin, and Zhong Liu

Fast Video Clip Retrieval Method via Language Query 526
   Pengju Zhang, Chunmiao Yuan, Kunliang Liu, Yukuan Sun, Jiayu Liang,
   Guanghao Jin, and Jianming Wang

Research on Speech Emotional Feature Extraction Based
on Multidimensional Feature Fusion 535
   Chunjun Zheng, Chunli Wang, Wei Sun, and Ning Jia

Improved Algorithms for Zero Shot Image Super-Resolution
with Parametric Rectifiers 548
   Jiayi Zhu, Senjian An, Wanquan Liu, and Ling Li

Spatial-Temporal Data

Spatial-Temporal Recurrent Neural Network for Anomalous
Trajectories Detection 565
    Yunyao Cheng, Bin Wu, Li Song, and Chuan Shi

Spatiotemporal Crime Hotspots Analysis and Crime
Occurrence Prediction 579
    Niyonzima Ibrahim, Shuliang Wang, and Boxiang Zhao

Medical and Healthcare Data/Decision Analytics

Fast Bat Algorithm for Predicting Diabetes Mellitus Using Association
Rule Mining. 591
    Hend Amraoui, Faouzi Mhamdi, and Mourad Elloumi

Using a Virtual Hospital for Piloting Patient Flow
Decongestion Interventions. 605
    Shaowen Qin

Deep Interpretable Mortality Model for Intensive Care
Unit Risk Prediction 617
    Zhenkun Shi, Weitong Chen, Shining Liang, Wanli Zuo, Lin Yue,
    and Sen Wang

Causality Discovery with Domain Knowledge for Drug-Drug
Interactions Discovery 632
    Sitthichoke Subpaiboonkit, Xue Li, Xin Zhao, Harrisen Scells,
    and Guido Zuccon

Personalised Medicine in Critical Care Using Bayesian
Reinforcement Learning. 648
    Chandra Prasetyo Utomo, Hanna Kurniawati, Xue Li,
    and Suresh Pokharel

TDDF: HFMD Outpatients Prediction Based on Time Series
Decomposition and Heterogenous Data Fusion in Xiamen, China 658
    Zhijin Wang, Yaohui Huang, Bingyan He, Ting Luo, Yongming Wang,
    and Yingxian Lin

Other Applications

Efficient Gaussian Distance Transforms for Image Processing. 671
    Senjian An, Yiwei Liu, Wanquan Liu, and Ling Li

Tourist's Tour Prediction by Sequential Data Mining Approach 681
    Lilia Ben Baccar, Sonia Djebali, and Guillaume Guérard

TOM: A Threat Operating Model for Early Warning of Cyber
Security Threats   696
    Tao Bo, Yue Chen, Can Wang, Yunwei Zhao, Kwok-Yan Lam,
    Chi-Hung Chi, and Hui Tian

Prediction for Student Academic Performance Using SMNaive
Bayes Model   712
    Baoting Jia, Ke Niu, Xia Hou, Ning Li, Xueping Peng, Peipei Gu,
    and Ran Jia

Chinese Sign Language Identification via Wavelet Entropy and Support
Vector Machine   726
    Xianwei Jiang and Zhaosong Zhu

An Efficient Multi-request Route Planning Framework Based
on Grid Index and Heuristic Function   737
    Jiajia Li, Jiahui Hu, Vladislav Engel, Chuanyu Zong, and Xiufeng Xia

Nodes Deployment Optimization Algorithm Based on Fuzzy Data
Fusion Model in Wireless Sensor Networks   750
    Na Li, Qiangyi Li, and Qiangnan Li

Community Enhanced Record Linkage Method for Vehicle
Insurance System   761
    Christian Lu, Guangyan Huang, and Yong Xiang

COEA: An Efficient Method for Entity Alignment
in Online Encyclopedias   777
    Yimin Lv, Xin Wang, Runpu Yue, Fuchuan Tang, and Xue Xiang

Efficient Deployment and Mission Timing of Autonomous Underwater
Vehicles in Large-Scale Operations   792
    Somaiyeh MahmoudZadeh

MLCA: A Multi-label Competency Analysis Method Based
on Deep Neural Network   805
    Guohao Qiao, Bin Wu, Bai Wang, and Baoli Zhang

MACCA: A SDN Based Collaborative Classification Algorithm for QoS
Guaranteed Transmission on IoT   815
    Weifeng Sun, Zun Wang, Guanghao Zhang, and Boxiang Dong

DataLearner: A Data Mining and Knowledge Discovery Tool
for Android Smartphones and Tablets   828
    Darren Yates, Md Zahidul Islam, and Junbin Gao

Prediction of Customer Purchasing Power of Google Merchandise Store   839
    ZhiYu Ye, AiMin Feng, and Hang Gao

Research on Short-Term Traffic Flow Forecasting Based on KNN
and Discrete Event Simulation   853
   Shaozheng Yu, Yingqiu Li, Guojun Sheng, and Jiao Lv

Application of Weighted K-Means Decision Cluster Classifier
in the Recognition of Infectious Expressions of Primary School
Students Reading   863
   Dongqing Zhang and Zhenyu Liu

An Anti-fraud Framework for Medical Insurance Based on Deep Learning . . .   871
   *Guoming Zhang, Shucun Fu, Xiaolong Xu, Lianyong Qi, Xuyun Zhang,
   and Wanchun Dou*

Demos

BSI: A System for Predicting and Analyzing Accident Risk   881
   Xinyu Ma, Yuhao Yang, and Meng Wang

KG3D: An Interactive 3D Visualization Tool for Knowledge Graphs   886
   *Dawei Xu, Lin Wang, Xin Wang, Dianquan Li, Jianpeng Duan,
   and Yongzhe Jia*

Author Index   891

Data Mining Foundations

Mining Emerging High Utility Itemsets over Streaming Database

Acquah Hackman[1], Yu Huang[2], Philip S. Yu[3], and Vincent S. Tseng[2(✉)]

[1] Department of EECS-IGP, National Chiao Tung University, Hsinchu, Taiwan, ROC
ahackman.cs03g@nctu.edu.tw
[2] Department of Computer Science,
National Chiao Tung University, Hsinchu, Taiwan, ROC
yuvisu.cs04g@nctu.edu.tw, vtseng@cs.nctu.edu.tw
[3] Department of Computer Science, University of Illinois at Chicago, Chicago, USA
psyu@cs.uic.edu

Abstract. *HUIM (High Utility Itemset Mining)* is a classical data mining problem that has gained much attention in the research community with a wide range of applications. The goal of HUIM is to identify all itemsets whose utility satisfies a user-defined threshold. In this paper, we address a new and interesting direction of high utility itemsets mining, which is mining temporal emerging high utility itemsets from data streams. The temporal emerging high utility itemsets are those that are not high utility in the current time window of the data stream but have high potential to become a high utility in the subsequent time windows. Discovery of temporal emerging high utility itemsets is an important process for mining interesting itemsets that yield high profits from streaming databases, which has many applications such as proactive decision making by domain experts, building powerful classifiers, market basket analysis, catalogue design, among others. We propose a novel method, named *EFTemHUI (Efficient Framework for Temporal Emerging HUI mining)*, to identify *Emerging High Utility Itemsets* better. To improve the efficiency of the mining process, we devise a new mechanism to evaluate the high utility itemsets that will emerge, which has the ability to capture and store the information about potential high utility itemsets. Through extensive experimentation using three datasets, we proved that the proposed method yields excellent accuracy and low errors in the prediction of emerging patterns for the next window.

Keywords: High utility itemset · Utility pattern mining · Emerging patterns · Data stream · Data mining

1 Introduction

In the last decade, there has been a rapid increase in the generation of large-scale temporal data in various real-world domains such as transaction, internet of things, and social media. As a result, this has triggered and placed emphases on

© Springer Nature Switzerland AG 2019
J. Li et al. (Eds.): ADMA 2019, LNAI 11888, pp. 3–16, 2019.
https://doi.org/10.1007/978-3-030-35231-8_1

the importance of pattern analysis for various applications. Over the years, *High Utility Itemset Mining (HUIM)* has gained grounds and become a classical data mining problem in the research community. The problem of HUIM states that given user defined minimum threshold and a transaction dataset, what are the itemsets whose utility are greater than or equal to the minimum threshold. Due to the interesting challenges that HUIM poses, there have been numerous [1–3] mining algorithms that have been developed to address these challenges. These challenges include but not limited to; the absence of the downward closure property, and large candidate generation, among others. However, regardless of its challenges, HUI also has notable applications like market basket analysis, decision making and planning in retail, and product catalog design. The challenges of HUIM have led to several branches [4–6] in the HUIM communities.

An important research direction extended from the HUIM is the discovery of high utility itemsets in data streams environment due to the wide applications on various domains. For time-variant data streams, there is a strong demand to develop an efficient and effective method to mine various temporal patterns. Previous work [7,8] used the growth rate as the main indicating factor for emergence. An emerging itemset is an itemset i over two datasets D_1 and D_2 whose *growth rate* in favor of D_1 is defined as $\frac{supportD_1(i)}{supportD_2(i)}$. In other words, a positive change in the support of an item (itemsets) from dataset D_1 to D_2 is considered emerging itemset if the threshold set by the user is satisfied. Mining temporal emerging high utility itemsets are by no doubt equally insightful and in some cases preferred patterns over the traditional HUI output. For instance, if a user plans to purchase stock items in the next coming days, HUI output may not result in the most informed decision making. In this case, emerging high utility itemsets will be useful and interesting patterns to be considered. However, most methods designed for the traditional databases cannot be directly applied for mining temporal high utility itemsets in data streams.

In this paper, we address the problems of mining temporal emerging high utility itemsets over streaming database. As aforementioned, there are two major issues in this problem: (1) how to mine temporal emerging high utility itemsets correctly and efficiently, and (2) how to set the minimum utility threshold that satisfies all windows. To deal with these two issues, we propose a novel method named *EFTemHUI (Efficient Framework for Temporal Emerging HUI mining)*, which offers high accuracy on mining temporal emerging high utility itemsets. To enhance the efficiency of the mining process, we devise a new mechanism to identify the high utility itemsets that will emerge in the future, which has the ability to capture and store the information about potential high utility itemsets.

The contributions of this paper are the following:

1. We propose a novel method that efficiently mines emerging high utility itemsets mining over streaming transaction databases.
2. To capture emerging high utility itemsets efficiently, we define a new class of itemsets, called *Nearest High Utility Itemsets (NHUI)*.

3. In order to improve the accuracy of mining emerging high utility itemsets, we devise a novel mechanism that adopts regression-based predictive model to incorporate into our method.
4. Through a series of experiments, we prove the excellent performance of our proposed method. To the best of our knowledge, this is the first work that considers the topic of mining emerging high utility itemsets over streaming databases.

The rest of this paper is as follows: Sect. 2 highlights the related work of this research. In Sect. 3, we formally present the problem and other definitions. Section 4 gives detailed information of our proposed method. Finally, in Sects. 5 and 6, we present the results of our experimental evaluation based on the method, and the summary respectively.

2 Related Work

The background of this research encompasses a number of key research directions in data mining; Streaming data mining, high utility itemset mining, emerging patterns, and regression models which are well-studied techniques in both data mining and machine learning. Since this is the first work that considers the mining of emerging high utility itemsets, our related work will center around and highlight the advancements in both HUIM and emerging pattern mining research. We will also introduce some challenges in working with streaming data, which is the type of transaction data used in this research.

The research of high utility itemset (HUI) mining [1–3,6,9] has focused on the development of efficient algorithms that identify itemsets with high utility values based on user's threshold. HUIM algorithms can be categorized into two main groups depending on whether there is a candidate generation (two-phase type) or no candidate generation (one-phase type). The latter of the two groups of algorithms performs best in terms of execution time and memory management [1]. [10] highlights some of the challenges encountered in mining over streaming data. Mining over streaming data posses the challenges of storage, data inconsistency, the arrival of data at high speeds, and a few others. As a result of these challenges, the traditional data mining algorithms are not sufficient for dealing with this type of data. Regardless of the challenges in mining over streaming data, there has been some pioneering [4,11] as well as state-of-the-art algorithms that address these challenges in other directions [5] of high utility itemset mining over streaming data. Algorithms that are designed to mine HUI over stream data typically falls into two paradigms: (1) Time-fading [11] and (2) Sliding window [4] paradigm.

In 1999, Dong et al. [7] first introduced the idea of emerging patterns (EPs). EPs were described as patterns that show significant increment in terms of support from one dataset to another. Dong et al. [7] then introduced a border-based algorithm to solve this problem. Over the years there have been numerous publications on emerging patterns. Depending on the strategy adopted in a given algorithm, EP algorithm may fall under one of these four groups [12]; constraint-based [13], border-based [7], tree-based [8] and evolutionary fuzzy system-based [14].

3   Problem Definitions

In this section, we formally define the problem statement. In addition to the problem statement, we also introduce some preliminary definitions which are essential to our problem statement. For clarity, we will use Table 1 which is our streaming data, and Table 2 which is the external utility as our running example.

3.1   Definitions

Our streaming data is processed using the sliding window method. According to our running example in Table 1, here is the description of the table's annotation; A window (W) represents the size of the portion of the data that is already captured and is being processed. From Table 1 a window's size is measured in terms of batch, W_1 contains two batches (B_1 and B_2). A batch is a number of transactions that arrives in a window together. B_1 contains three transactions (T_1, T_2, and T_3). Note that the window slides one batch at a time.

Table 1. Streaming data

TID	Transaction
T1	(a,2),(c,3),(d,2)
t2	(b,1),(c,2),(d,4)
t3	(a,5),(b,1),(c,12)
t4	(a,3),(c7)
t5	(c,8),(d,5)
t6	(b,5),(c,4),(d,9)
t7	(a,4),(d,8)
t8	(a,2),(b,1),(c,9),(d,5)
t9	(a,6),(b,4),(c,1)

Definition 1. *Utility:*
The utility of an itemset i in a given transaction T from a streaming dataset S_D is denoted as $u(i, T_{S_D})$, is defined as the product of its internal utility (quantity) denoted as $q(i, T_{S_D})$ and the external utility (unit profit) denoted as $p(i)$. Example, $u(a, T_7) = 4 \times 6 = 24$.

Definition 2. *Utility of an Itemset in a Window:*
The utility of an itemset in a given window w is the sum of the given itemset's utility over all transactions in the given w, $U(i_w) = \sum u(i_n, T_w)$. For example $U(\{c, d\}_{w_1}) = u(\{c, d\}, t_1) + u(\{c, d\}, t_2) + u(\{c, d\}, t_5) + u(\{c, d\}, t_6) = 40 + 40 + 105 + 85 = 270$.

Table 2. External utility values

Items	a	b	c	d
Utility	6	8	10	5

Definition 3. *High Utility Itemset in a window*
Given a Window w, and a user-specified minimum threshold mu, an itemset is considered high utility iff its utility in current w is no less than or equal to mu. For example, if mu = 100 and window = w_1, {c, d} is a HUI whereas {a, d} isn't.

Definition 4. *Nearest High Utility Itemset (NHUI)*
Given a current window w, user-specified minimum utility threshold mu, and a tolerance threshold in percentage, m%, a nearest HUI is an itemset whose utility value is less than mu but greater than m% of mu. For example, from Definition 3, {d} in w_1 is not an HUI but an NHUI if m% = 75% and mu = 130.

Definition 5. *Growth Rate*
According to [15] as shown in Eq. 1, we redefine growth rate as the utility of and itemset x in window i over utility x in window i − 1. See Eq. 1.

$$
GR(x) = \begin{cases} 0, & if\ Util_{W_i}(x) = Util_{W_i-1}(x) = 0, \\ \infty, & if\ Util_{W_i-1}(x) \neq 0 \wedge Util_{W_i}(x) = 0, \\ \frac{Util_{W_i-1}(x)}{Util_{W_i}(x)} & other\ case \end{cases} \quad (1)
$$

3.2   Problem Statement

Given a streaming data S_D, user-specified minimum utility threshold *mu*, and tolerance threshold *m%* the goal is to identify all high utility itemsets that will emerge in a future given window w_f.

4   Proposed Method

Figure 1 illustrates the *EFTemHUI (Efficient Framework for Temporal Emerging HUI mining)* which incorporates regression model into the mining of emerging high utility itemsets. The following subsections highlight the different components of the EFTemHUI method.

4.1   Method Input - Streaming Transaction Data

Our datasets are streaming data which are the benchmark datasets used in HUIM research. The key features about streaming data are; (1) they are continuous (streaming), (2) there is a limitation in terms of data arrival (speed factor), and (3) Storage and memory consideration needs to be handled well. In today's

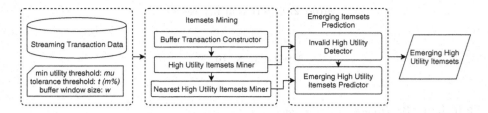

Fig. 1. EFTemHUI (Efficient Framework for Temporal Emerging HUI mining)

world, there are numerous sources of streaming data, some of which includes; RFID data, Web clicks, Telecommunication network data, Media data, Sensor network, Retail transaction, as well as many others.

In this section, we need to pre-process the dataset to fit the right format to be used by HUIM algorithms in the next stage of the method. The standard HUIM algorithms takes input in the form of this example; $a, b, c : 150 : 100, 25, 25$. This format is also true for HUIM over streaming transaction data. Table 3 shows a quick summary of some of the benchmark datasets used in HUIM research [16].

The parameters required for the mining of the emerging high utility itemsets are *minimum utility threshold (mu), tolerance threshold (t) and buffer window size (w)*. The parameter w indicates the amount of data to be captured for analysis at any given time.

Table 3. Dataset summary

Dataset	No. transactions	No. distinct items	Average transaction length
Accidents	340,183	468	33.8
ChainStore	1,112,949	46086	7.2
Foodmart	4,141	1,559	4.4
Mushroom	8,124	119	23.0

4.2   Itemsets Mining

This section of the method is subdivided into three main components, the *buffer transaction constructor, high utility itemsets miner, and nearest high utility itemsets miner*. The two mining components utilizes the minimum utility threshold and the tolerance threshold to mine two types of *High Utility Itemsets (HUI)*. These HUIs are (1) HUI, and (2) Nearest HUI (see Definition 4).

Buffer Transaction Constructor: The buffered transaction constructor component is used to identify the portion of the streaming data that should be captured for analysis by the method. Table 1 illustrates the window size and batch size mechanisms used in this component.

High Utility Itemsets (HUI) Miner: In short definition, a high utility itemset is a group of items that are sold together, and their combined utility meets a minimum utility threshold set by the user. Below is a definition by [1].

> The problem of high-utility itemset mining is defined as follows. Let I be a finite set of items (symbols). An itemset X is a finite set of items such that $X \subseteq I$. A transaction database is a multiset of transactions $D = \{T_1, T_2, ..., T_n\}$ such that for each transaction $T_c, T_c \subseteq I$ and T_c has a unique identifier c called its TID (Transaction ID). Each item $i \in I$ is associated with a positive number $p(i)$, called its external utility (e.g. unit profit).Every item i appearing in a transaction T_c has a positive number $q(i, T_c)$, called its internal utility (e.g. purchase quantity)

The correctly mined HUI are the direct input of the *Invalid High Utility Detector* in the next section of the method.

Nearest High Utility Itemsets Miner: Nearest HUI is a new terminology that is introduced by this framework. A nearest HUI is an item/itemset that doesn't meet the minimum utility requirement set by the user; however, it is close enough to satisfy $m\%$ of the minimum threshold set by the user.

For example, given a minimum threshold of 100 and a minimum nearest (tolerance threshold) percentage of 75%, any itemset whose utility is greater than or equal to 100 is considered HUI while any itemset whose utility is greater than or equal 75, but less than 100 is considered as an NHUI (see Definition 4). The NHUI are the input for the *Emerging High Utility Itemets Predictor*. Since their utility does not meet the mu, the predictor component is used to predict their value in the next future window.

4.3 Emerging Itemsets Prediction

In this section, two main operations are performed here. The NHUI is quite important at this level of the framework because it is the input of the regression model. The two main operations of this stage are; (1) Purge HUI, and (2) Regression model implementation.

Invalid High Utility Detector: Since we will be moving to the next window, it is essential to get rid of the older batch of transaction in preparation for the newer batch of transactions from the upcoming transaction stream. The *Invalid High Utility Detector* is used to identify itemsets that will not meet the mu threshold in the next window. We call this class of itemsets a Purge HUI (P-HUI). An itemset is considered a P-HUI if it's utility is greater than or equal to minimum utility after the utility of the older batch has been removed, but newer ones are not added yet. For example $U(\{c\}_{w_1}) = u(\{c\}, t_1) + u(\{c\}, t_2) + u(\{c\}, t_3) + u(\{c\}, t_4) + u(\{c\}, t_5) + u(\{c\}, t_6) = 30 + 20 + 120 + 70 + 80 + 40 = 360$. However, after purge in transition to w_2, utility of P-HUI $\{c\}$ will become $U(\{c\}_{w_1}) = u(\{c\}, t_4) + u(\{c\}, t_5) + u(\{c\}, t_6) = 70 + 80 + 40 = 190$. 190 is still a high utility itemset in the next time window if the $mu = 100$.

Emerging High Utility Itemsets Predictor: We tested and compared the performance of three different regression models. The models used for comparison (see Fig. 3) are: Linear Regression, Lasso Regression, and Random Forest Regression. The component of the framework responsible for utility prediction is the *Emerging High Utility Itemsets Predictor*, and it takes the NHUI as input. The task of a prediction model is to predict or estimate the utility of the NHUIs for the upcoming time window. When the estimated value is greater than or equal to the minimum utility threshold, it is considered as a potential HUI that could emerge in the next time window.

4.4   Emerging Itemsets

With a 100% certainty, all the outputs from the *Invalid High Utility Detector* will eventually emerge in the next time window. This observation is valid because their utility already satisfies the minimum requirement and as such, they are *high utility itemsets*. However, for the outputs from the *Emerging High Utility Itemsets Predictor* component, since the utility values are estimates, they need to be confirmed at this stage to evaluate the accuracy of the method. An optimal accuracy of the framework depends on the regression model used for the utility estimation.

5   Experimental Evaluation

We conduct a series of experiments for evaluating the performance of our framework by the semi-synthetic data under various system conditions. All experiments were performed on an Intel Xeon CPU E5-2630 2.20 GHz machine with 128 GB of memory running Ubuntu 14.04. Two programming languages (Java and Python) are utilized for implementing our framework, each processing a section of the framework.

5.1   Experimental Setup

Our evaluation is separated into two parts, which are internal observation and external comparison. In the first part, we adjust the threshold of minimum utility to observe the effect of the execution time on our framework. Moreover, we analyze the effect of window size and accuracy on three different regression models. The regression models were to predict which of the NHUI will emerge as HUI in the next time window. In the external comparison, we developed a baseline algorithm (see Algorithm 1) that implements the basic rule for emerging itemset identification. We then compared the accuracy of both the baseline and our framework's method of itemset identification.

Dataset: In the experiment, we use three different datasets. One of the dataset is the chainstore (Table 3), which is a real dataset in HUIM research. The accidents (Table 3) dataset which is a semi-real dataset is also obtained from the

HUIM datasets. The accident is considered semi-real because the utility value of the dataset is synthetic values which were generated following the same normal distribution formula in [1]. The third dataset is a full simulation data that was generated using the spmf [16] toolkit. However, to simulate and ensure trendiness in the dataset, we used the same technique by [17]. Table 4 describes the datasets used for our experiments.

Table 4. Description of datasets used for experiment.

Dataset	Number of transactions	Number of distinct items	Average transaction length
Accidents	340, 183	468	33.8
ChainStore	1, 112, 949	46086	7.2
spmf150k_200di_75ipt (spmf)	150, 000	468	33.8

Algorithm 1. GR-Based Algorithm

---

1 function GR-Based Algorithm $(D, \mathcal{W}, \delta)$;
    Input   : D: streaming transaction database, W: selected window
    Output: A set of temporal emerging high utility itemsets
2 Initialize $\Omega \leftarrow \{\}$;
3 Initialize $GR \leftarrow 0$;
4 **foreach** *itemset* $\alpha \in \mathcal{D}$ **do**
5   Initialize $Utility_1 \leftarrow Util(\alpha, w_{i-1})$;
6   Initialize $Utility_2 \leftarrow Util(\alpha, w_i)$;
7   **if** $Utility_1 = Utility_2$ **then**
8          $GR \leftarrow 0$;
9   **else if** $Utility_1 \neq 0 \wedge Utility_2 = 0$ **then**
10          $GR \leftarrow \infty$;
11   **else**
12          $GR \leftarrow Utility_1/Utility_2$;
13   **end**
14   **if** $GR <1$ **then**
15          $\Omega \leftarrow \{\alpha\}$
16   **end**
17 **end**
18 return Ω;

Growth Rate-Based Algorithm: Our growth rate algorithm is implemented using the growth rate evaluation method in Definition 5. The algorithm takes streaming database D, window W, and minimum utility δ as input. The output of this algorithm is list of high utility itemsets that according to Eq. 1 could be

emerging itemsets. The growth rate function has three main evaluation outputs;
(1) $GR = 0$ if $Util_{W_i}(x) = Util_{W_{i-1}}(x)$, (2) $GR = \infty$ if $Util_{W_{i-1}}(x) \neq 0 \wedge$
$Util_{W_i}(x) = 0$ (3) GR could be a negative value, or a positive value.

5.2   Internal Observation

We evaluated our framework based on some observed parameters that need to
be considered carefully when mining emerging high utility itemsets. The most
obvious parameter is the minimum utility. The value of the minimum utility
determines how many itemsets will be generated and consequently how fast the
entire framework performs.

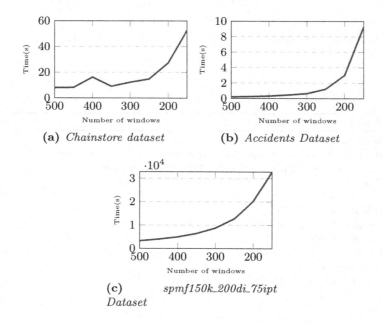

(a) *Chainstore dataset*   (b) *Accidents Dataset*

(c)   *spmf150k_200di_75ipt*
Dataset

Fig. 2. The execution time for the mining of NHUI

The minimum utility value for the chainstore dataset is 52 times the average
transaction utility per window. The accident and the spmf150k_200di_75ipt are
400 and 350 respectively. In Fig. 2, the value of the minimum utility contributes
to longer execution time. The second contribution factor for higher execution
time is the number of windows; the smaller number of windows takes more time
for execution. This trend is possible because as the number of windows decreases,
the size of windows increases thereby more NHUI can be generated from each
window.

We also tested and compared the performance of the three different regression
models. The models we used were *linear regression, lasso regression, and random*

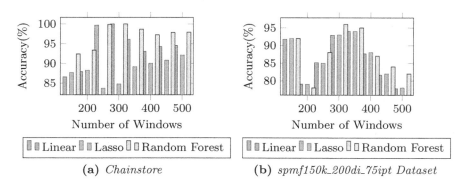

Fig. 3. Performance of regression models with respect to window size

forest regression. According to the performance of these models, each model consumes a significant amount of time depending on the average number of NHUI. On average, random forest performed well on almost all datasets proving the highest accuracy which can be seen in Fig. 3.

As described above, we used three different datasets to implement our framework for the mining of emerging high utility itemsets. It is crucial to set the right minimum utility value as this will either result in a very high number of NHUI generated or a very low NHUI generated. For instance, if an absolute minimum utility is set for all windows, the minimum utility phenomenon previously mentioned will surface. To circumvent this, we used the relative minimum utility. In all the three datasets, the minimum utility is set relatively as the product of n (arbitrarily set value) and the average utility of the given window.

In Fig. 4, we also observed that the number of NHUI generated increases as the number of windows decreases. Again, this is because the window sizes are much more significantly larger as the number of windows decreases; therefore many NHUI and HUI can be mine from such large-sized windows. We can, therefore, conclude that both the execution time and the number of NHUI generated are inversely proportional to the number of windows.

5.3   External Comparison

In Table 5, we compared the performance of our framework with the baseline algorithm. We used three different datasets, each of which had two number of windows settings. In all the datasets used, our proposed framework outperformed the baseline algorithm. One of the key advantages of our framework over the GR-Based algorithm was the ability to keep utility values of the NHUI list over several windows. The GR-Based algorithm, on the other hand, uses information from the current window and the immediate previous window. Using only the immediate previous window makes the GR-Based algorithm lose a lot of essential patterns, such is the case of accidents 500 in Table 5.

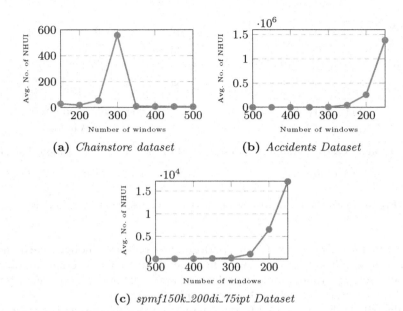

(a) *Chainstore dataset*   (b) *Accidents Dataset*

(c) *spmf150k_200di_75ipt Dataset*

Fig. 4. The average number of NHUIs mined per window

Table 5. Performance of our proposed framework in comparison to GR-Based method. Accuracy is measured in percentage (%)

Dataset	GR-based	Our framework
chainstore250	92.31	**98.25**
chainstore300	77.78	**99.90**
accidents450	100	**100**
accidents500	0	**35.71**
spmf300	61.86	**100**
spmf450	63.04	**66.66**

It is also worth noticing that even though our regression-based method outperformed the baseline in all the datasets used; however, in some cases the difference is not quite significant, or both achieved the same performance. This observation is attributed to the dataset that is used. The weakness of the baseline model is missing itemsets when the immediate previous window had a value of 0. On the other hand, the weakness of our model is when there are several previous windows with 0 values. When there are several 0 or missing values, this causes the regression model to make less accurate predictions. The strength of our framework depends on the ability of the regression model used as well as the dataset used.

6   Conclusion

In this work, we introduced a promising research problem, named mining *Temporal Emerging High Utility Itemsets* over streaming database, which is extended by the classical high utility itemsets mining problem. To solve this problem, we designed and implemented a novel method to unearth these interesting itemsets correctly and efficiently. For ensuring the efficiency of our method, we devised a new mechanism that utilizes proven predictive model to evaluate high utility itemsets that will emerge, which has ability to capture and store the information about these potential high utility itemsets. We evaluated our proposed method using three different large public datasets and the experimental results show that EFTemHUI outperforms the GR-based algorithm in terms of accuracy. To conclude, EFTemHUI validated as promising solution that offers high accuracy and efficiency for mining temporal emerging high utility itemsets.

Temporal emerging high utility itemsets are essential and insightful patterns to mine as they help to give information about what might happen in the future. This type of pattern is particularly useful for applications that require prior planning like the stock market, retail store inventory management, etc as well as other applications that require prior planning. For our future work, we plan to incorporate and experiment with other powerful predictive models for the mining of emerging high utility itemsets. We also hope to obtain more real datasets that can help us to expand the applications of emerging HUI in domains such as biomedicine, retail market, and the stock market.

Acknowledgements. This research was partially supported by Ministry of Science and Technology, Taiwan, under grant no. 108-2218-E-009-051.

References

1. Zida, S., Fournier-Viger, P., Lin, J.C.W., Wu, C.W., Tseng, V.S.: EFIM: a fast and memory efficient algorithm for high-utility itemset mining. Knowl. Inf. Syst. **51**(2), 595–625 (2017)
2. Chan, R., Yang, Q., Shen, Y.D.: Mining high utility itemsets. In: Proceedings of the Third IEEE International Conference on Data Mining, ICDM 2003, Washington, DC, USA, p. 19. IEEE Computer Society (2003)
3. Liu, J., Wang, K., Fung, B.C.M.: Direct discovery of high utility itemsets without candidate generation. In: Proceedings of the 2012 IEEE 12th International Conference on Data Mining, ICDM 2012, Washington, DC, USA, pp. 984–989. IEEE Computer Society (2012)
4. Shie, B.E., Yu, P.S., Tseng, V.S.: Efficient algorithms for mining maximal high utility itemsets from data streams with different models. Expert Syst. Appl. **39**(17), 12947–12960 (2012)
5. Dam, T.L., Li, K., Fournier-Viger, P., Duong, Q.H.: An efficient algorithm for mining top-k on-shelf high utility itemsets. Knowl. Inf. Syst. **52**(3), 621–655 (2017)
6. Dawar, S., Sharma, V., Goyal, V.: Mining top-k high-utility itemsets from a data stream under sliding window model. Appl. Intell. **47**(4), 1240–1255 (2017)

7. Dong, G., Li, J.: Efficient mining of emerging patterns: discovering trends and differences. In: Proceedings of the Fifth ACM SIGKDD International Conference on Knowledge Discovery and Data Mining, KDD 1999, pp. 43–52. ACM, New York (1999)
8. Bailey, J., Manoukian, T., Ramamohanarao, K.: Fast algorithms for mining emerging patterns. In: Elomaa, T., Mannila, H., Toivonen, H. (eds.) PKDD 2002. LNCS, vol. 2431, pp. 39–50. Springer, Heidelberg (2002). https://doi.org/10.1007/3-540-45681-3_4
9. Song, W., Liu, Y., Li, J.: BAHUI: fast and memory efficient mining of high utility itemsets based on bitmap. Int. J. Data Warehous. Min. **10**(1), 1–15 (2014)
10. Ikonomovska, E., Loskovska, S., Gjorgjevik, D.: A survey of stream data mining. In: Proceedings of 8th National Conference with International Participation, ETAI, pp. 19–21 (2007)
11. Manike, C., Om, H.: Time-fading based high utility pattern mining from uncertain data streams. In: Kumar Kundu, M., Mohapatra, D.P., Konar, A., Chakraborty, A. (eds.) Advanced Computing, Networking and Informatics-Volume 1. SIST, vol. 27, pp. 529–536. Springer, Cham (2014). https://doi.org/10.1007/978-3-319-07353-8_61
12. Ventura, S., Luna, J.M.: Supervised Descriptive Pattern Mining. Springer, Cham (2018). https://doi.org/10.1007/978-3-319-98140-6
13. Zhang, X., Dong, G., Ramamohanarao, K.: Exploring constraints to efficiently mine emerging patterns from large high-dimensional datasets. In: KDD, pp. 310–314 (2000)
14. García-Vico, A.M., Montes, J., Aguilera, J., Carmona, C.J., del Jesus, M.J.: Analysing concentrating photovoltaics technology through the use of emerging pattern mining. In: Graña, M., López-Guede, J.M., Etxaniz, O., Herrero, Á., Quintián, H., Corchado, E. (eds.) ICEUTE/SOCO/CISIS -2016. AISC, vol. 527, pp. 334–344. Springer, Cham (2017). https://doi.org/10.1007/978-3-319-47364-2_32
15. García-Vico, A., Carmona, C., Martín, D., García-Borroto, M., del Jesus, M.: An overview of emerging pattern mining in supervised descriptive rule discovery: taxonomy, empirical study, trends, and prospects. Wiley Interdisc. Rev. Data Min. Knowl. Discovery **8**(1), e1231 (2018)
16. Fournier-Viger, P., Gomariz, A., Gueniche, T., Soltani, A., Wu, C.W., Tseng, V.S.: SPMF: a Java open-source pattern mining library. J. Mach. Learn. Res. **15**(1), 3389–3393 (2014)
17. Hackman, A., Huang, Y., Tseng, V.S.: Mining trending high utility itemsets from temporal transaction databases. In: Hartmann, S., Ma, H., Hameurlain, A., Pernul, G., Wagner, R.R. (eds.) DEXA 2018. LNCS, vol. 11030, pp. 461–470. Springer, Cham (2018). https://doi.org/10.1007/978-3-319-98812-2_42

A Methodology for Resolving Heterogeneity and Interdependence in Data Analytics

Han Han[1], Yunwei Zhao[1], Can Wang[2(✉)], Min Shu[1], Tao Peng[3], Chi-Hung Chi[4], and Yonghong Yu[5]

[1] CNCERT/CC, Beijing, China
[2] School of ICT, Griffith University, Gold Coast, Australia
`can.wang@griffith.edu.au`
[3] Dongguan University of Technology, Dongguan, China
[4] CSIRO, Hobart, Australia
[5] Nanjing University of Posts and Telecommunications, Nanjing, China

Abstract. The big data analytics achieves wide application in a number of areas due to its capability in uncovering hidden patterns, correlations and insights through integrating multiple data sources. However, the interdependence and heterogeneity features of these data sources pose a big challenge in managing these data sources to support "last mile" analytics in decision making and value co-creation which are usually with multiple perspectives and at multiple granularities. In this paper, we propose a unified knowledge representation framework, namely, Cyber-Entity (Cyber-E) modeling, to capture and formalize selected behaviors of real entities in both the social and physical worlds to the cyber analytic space. Its special features include not only the stateful, intra- properties of a Cyber-E, but also the inter-relationship and dependence among them. A grouping mechanism, called Cyber-G, is also introduced to support flexible granularity adjustment in the knowledge management. It supports rapid on-demand self-service analytics. An illustrating example of applying this approach in academic research community is given, followed by a case study of two top conferences in service computing area–ICSOC and ICWS– to illustrate the effectiveness and potentials of our approach.

Keywords: Heterogeneity and inter-dependence · Big data analytics · Knowledge representation

1 Introduction

Due to the interactiveness nature of big data analytics [1], i.e. the analytics is not conducted in a one-time end-to-end fashion, instead it is a demand-driven process and usually with several rounds of trials. The data heterogeneity and the interdependence issue pose great challenges in supporting the varying analytic

© Springer Nature Switzerland AG 2019
J. Li et al. (Eds.): ADMA 2019, LNAI 11888, pp. 17–33, 2019.
https://doi.org/10.1007/978-3-030-35231-8_2

needs, in particular, the people conducting the big data analytics are comprised of more and more "non-IT" professionals.

While the traditional knowledge extraction techniques [2] mainly focus on the data distribution, the recent work demonstrates a trend with the interdisciplinary (i.e. psychology, sociology and economics) efforts where domain knowledge is resorted to tackle the interdependence issue. Examples include large-scale measurement of happiness based on tweets [3], stock market prediction [4], etc. However, these models adopt an "end-to-end" approach. That is, when applied to data sets with high heterogeneity and interdependence, and faced with various analytic requirements, these approaches suffer from the following: (i) the modeling techniques are tightly coupled with data and analytic requirements; when new data arrives or new analytic techniques are put forward, it usually requires a re-computation from scratch; (ii) the factors considered are limited and difficult to extend.

More specifically, the interdependence in analytics [5] usually refer to the following three categories:

- Intra-personal effect indicates the temporal non-independence of the behavior of the subject under analysis, as the temporal order of behaviors always has an irreversible effect. E.g., a reviewer's score given to the current paper may be influenced by the previous paper.
- Inter-personal effect indicates the behavior of the subject under analysis is not independent of other subjects. E.g., in non-double blind review process, a reviewer's decision may be influenced by other reviewers.
- Inter-group effect indicates the subject under analysis is not independent of the groups it belongs. E.g., a person's belief may be influenced by family, culture, etc.

Based on these considerations, in this paper, we propose a Cyber-Entity (Cyber-E) modelling approach with a hierarchical structure to capture and formalize the heterogeneity and interdependence in the cyber analytic space. In this model, one behavioral view of the targeted entity to be studied is modeled as properties. Property is the basic analytic unit, and Cyber-E is can be viewed a set comprised of properties characterizing its existential modalities (e.g. behaviors, relational connectivity with other entities, etc.). A graphical representation is also introduced to facilitate the discussion. With introducing the notion of "Influence Set" and "Coverage Set", the interdependence and heterogeneity in analytics can be formalized in this model.

The contribution of this paper can be summarized as follows:

1. We propose a unified Cyber-Entity (Cyber-E) modelling approach with a conceptual framework and methodology to formalize the interdependence and heterogeneity in analytics.
2. We propose a hierarchical model of Cyber-E, named as Cyber-Group (Cyber-G) to support the on-demand and flexible granularity adjustment in the knowledge management of entity behaviors in data analytics.

3. We apply our Cyber-E and Cyber-G model to the academic research community analysis and conduct a case study of two top conferences in the service computing area, ICWS and ICSOC, to demonstrate the effectiveness of the proposed methodology.

The rest of the paper is as follows: we briefly describe the previous related research in Sect. 2. Sections 3 and 4 introduce the proposed Cyber-E modeling framework and methodology, respectively. Next, an illustrative case study in comparing two top conferences (i.e. ICSOC and ICWS) in the service area is presented in Sect. 5. Section 6 closes this paper with concluding remarks, and suggestions for future research directions.

2   Related Work

Due to the interactiveness nature of big data analytics [1], i.e. the analytics is not conducted in an one-time end-to-end fashion, instead it is a demand-driven process with varying analytic needs. The data heterogeneity and interdependence issue poses great challenges in this process [5]. In this section, we will briefly review three main strands of literature: (i) Big data analytics, (ii) knowledge representation and knowledge accumulation, and (iii) knowledge management.

Firstly, existing efforts mainly focuses on data fusion and data integration, i.e., corresponding to "Volume" and "Variety". However, the data source for integration and analytics is expanding to cover from single source to multiple sources with different types and formats, the data heterogeneity and interdependence issue is of critical importance is providing big data analytics, in particular, in most cases, the analysts are not-IT professionals conducting "last-mile" self-service analytics [1].

Secondly, even though there has been a wide variety of knowledge representation models proposed in knowledge management, e.g. Frames, semantic networks [6]. It is noted that systematic accumulation and various adaptations of knowledge are critical issues in the knowledge management field [6].

Thirdly, in the knowledge management part, we note that with human behaviors monitored and recorded more conveniently, interests in human-centric analytics have increased dramatically [7]. While traditional knowledge extraction techniques [2] mainly focus on data distribution, recent work demonstrates a trend with interdisciplinary (psychology, sociology and economics) efforts where domain knowledge is resorted to tackle the interdependence issue. Examples include large-scale measurement of happiness based on tweets [3], stock market prediction [4], etc. However, these models adopt an "end-to-end" approach, when applied to data sets with high heterogeneity and interdependence, and faced with various analytic requirements, these approaches suffer from the following: (i) the modeling techniques are tightly coupled with data and analytic requirements; When new data arrives or new analytic techniques are put forward, it usually requires a re-computation from scratch; (ii) the scope of factors considered is narrow and difficult to extend.

3 Conceptual Framework

Definition 1. Cyber Analytics Space (CAS) is the universe where all analytics related activities takes place, $CAS = (ES, FS, DS)$, where $DS = d_1, d_2, \ldots, d_{nd}$ represents the data service set, $FS = caf_1, caf_2, \ldots, caf_{nf}$ the cyber analytic function set supported, and $ES = ce_1, ce_2, \ldots, ce_{ne}$ the Cyber-Entity set.

3.1 Cyber-Entity Structure

Cyber-E is a set of properties describing an entity in the cyber analytic space; and its computation is based on data service(s) d_i and cyber analytic function service(s) caf_j.

Definition 2 (Property). A property of a Cyber-E ce_i, denoted as $p_j(ce_i)$ is a modality describing how the action or state of ce_i is conceived in the given CAS.

Definition 3 (Cyber Entity). A Cyber Entity (Cyber-E) $c_e \in ES$ is a set of n properties $\{p_i(c_e)\}$ (where $1 \le i \ge n$) describing the behavioral statuses of an entity. That is, $c_e = \{p_i(c_e)\}$.

Based on this definition, each property of a Cyber-E actually describes one behavioral view of the targeted entity; and its computation is based on data service(s) d_i and cyber analytic function service(s) caf_j. That is, CAF transforms raw data into properties, the output of CAF is property.

Furthermore, the properties of Cyber-E have two important dimensions that are key to the interdependence analysis. The first one is the temporal aspect, see Definition 4. The second one is existential relationship of properties of one Cyber-E with those of other Cyber-E(s), see Definition 5. For example, in e-commerce domain, happiness could be reasonably defined as both a person's overall experience and a particular relation between a person and a product, and this is time-sensitive; satisfaction could be defined as feedback from a single customer or a group of customers, this is less time-sensitive and more stable. These two dimensions will incur different levels of complicacy in the interdependence analysis (see Sect. 4).

Definition 4 (Temporality of Property). For a given property p_i, if $p_i(t) = p_i(t')$ (where $t' < t$), then p_i is a permanent property, otherwise it is a variant property.

Definition 5 (Connectivity of Property). For a given property p_i, the connectivity of p_i, denoted as $Con(p_i)$, is the number of Cyber-Es included in the definition of p_i.

3.2   Hierarchical Structure

The concept of "Cyber-Group" includes (i) the constitutional group, e.g. countries, companies, universities, etc., and (ii) similarity-driven ad-hoc group, e.g. people with different tastes, education levels, etc. In short, commonalities between Cyber-Es lead to the formation of a Cyber-G. The definition is given below,

Definition 6 (Cyber Group). For a specific Cyber-E ce_i, if its $Mem(ce_i) \neq \emptyset$, and $\forall e \in Mem(ce_i)$, $e \in ES$, then ce_i is said to be a Cyber-Group (Cyber-G), $ce_i \in Group(e)$. If a Cyber-E ce_i is a Cyber-G, it could also be represented as cg_i, to distinguish that it is a group entity. Let $GS = cg_i$, then $GS \subset ES$.

On one extreme side, for each entity there is at least one Cyber-E in CAS. Cyber-G may or may not exist, e.g. personalized recommendation in online-shopping. On the other extreme side, there is only one Cyber-E that is an invisible group entity maintained in CAS, e.g., the government agencies may be interested in only the overall happiness of all the citizens.

The hierarchical structure helps retain the hierarchical recognition relation and allows a multiple-granularity view of intelligence analysis. It enables to zoom in or out between coarser and finer granularities in an easy and tractable way.

4   Methodology

The methodology that we propose for coping with data heterogeneity and interdependence issue comprises of the following four steps:

4.1   Identify the Properties and Entities in the Given Domain w.r.t Analytic Aim

Despite the infinite number of views that can be possibly be modeled as properties of an entity, the selection should be driven first by the user requirements, and then the cost of computation and maintenance, and real time constraints. Below are some suggested guidelines.

Guideline 1. The modalities that are the core analytic concerns supporting the most of the analytic aims.

In research community scenario (see Sect. 5), examples include "Paper Quality", "Author Authority" and "Publishing Venue Authority" which are the core fundamental properties supporting the analytics in this area.

Guideline 2. The modalities that enable multi-perspective and multi-granularity analytics are modeled as properties.

Guideline 2 complements Guideline 1 by enabling various analytic perspectives and adjusting analytic granularities flexibly. Without Guideline 1, some analytic aim is unable to achieve due to the missing property; it will be a partial coverage. Without Guideline 2, it is less convenient to achieve the various analytic needs.

Following the research community scenario, examples include "Research Area", "Title", "Abstract" and "Year" for papers. Among these properties, "Research Area" might enable an automatic detection of researchers or papers with similar interests, which further facilitate detecting potential collaborators, and the middle two enable extracting paper focus, thereby to predict the future trends research in related areas.

Guideline 3. The modalities that are behavioral statistics are good candidates to be modeled as properties.

Examples include "Citation Count" and "Publication Count" for authors and publishing venues. These serve as the components to calculate the core fundamental properties obtained through Guideline 1.

Guideline 4. The modalities that explicate the relational connectivity between entities are modeled as properties.

Examples include "InVenue", "ByAuthor", "CitedByPaper", based on which different network structure can be constructed. Thus, different inter-dependence types can be specified.

4.2   Determine the Interdependence Types Through "Influence Set"

To define interdependence types of a CAF, we define the "Influence set" of CAS components:

Definition 7 (Influence Set of Property, Data Source, CAF). For a specific data source d_i, a function caf_i, a property p_i, its influence set, denoted as $IS(d_i)$, $IS(caf_i)$, $IS(p_i)$ respectively, is the set of any caf_j and property p_k that computationally depends on d_i, caf_i, and p_i, that is $IS(d_i) = \{caf_j, p_k | caf_j, p_k \to d_i\}$, $IS(caf_i) = \{caf_j, pk | caf_j, p_k \to caf_i\}$, $IS(p_i) = \{caf_j, p_k | caf_j, p_k \to p_i\}$.

To facilitate the discussion and have an intuitive understanding, we introduce graphical notations of CAS and its components, as shown in Fig. 1:

1. A CAS is represented as a rectangle.
2. A data source is represented as a concentric circle with solid border located outside the CAS rectangle, showing that its provisioning mechanism is out of the interest of CAS.
3. A CAF is represented as a bar with input arrows pointing to the bar and output arrows pointing away from the bar. The output arrow pointing to the property it models[1].
4. A property is represented as a hollow circle with solid border, while a Cyber-entity is represented as a hollow ellipse with dashed border.

---

[1] The CAF can take multiple inputs and gives one single output. More specifically, we have (a) the input of caf can be raw data, can also be property output of the same or other CAF, (b) different CAF can share the same input, (c) an algorithm of multiple outputs could be decomposed into multiple single-output algorithms. Correspondingly, the number of the input arrows could be 1 or many, while the number of output arrows could only be 1.

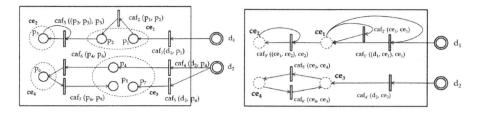

Fig. 1. Graphical representation of CAS.

Let $InE(caf_i)$ denote the set of data sources and Cyber-Es that the input properties belong to, and $OutE(caf_i)$ the only one Cyber-E to which the output property of caf_i belongs to. Then, the three types of inter-dependences, namely, intra-entity, inter-entity, and inter-group[2] can be defined as follows,

Definition 8 (Intra-entity CAF). A cyber analytic function caf_i with $\mathrm{Out}(caf_i) = p_j(ce_k)$ is an intra-entity CAF, iff: $In(caf_i) \cap ce_k \neq \emptyset$.

Definition 9 (Inter-entity CAF). A cyber analytic function caf_i with $\mathrm{Out}(caf_i) = p_j(ce_k)$ is an inter-entity CAF, iff: $In(caf_i) \cap ce_{l(l \neq k)} \neq \emptyset$, $ce_l \in ES$.

Definition 10a (Inter-group CAF-Type I). A cyber analytic function caf_i with $\mathrm{OutE}(caf_i) = cg_{k_1} \in GS$ is an inter-group CAF, iff: $\exists cg_{k_2} \in InE(caf_i)$, $cg_{k_2} \in GS$, and $k_1 \neq k_2$.

Definition 10b (Inter-group CAF-Type II). A cyber analytic function caf_i with $\mathrm{OutE}(caf_i) = ce_{l_1}$, $ce_{l_1} \in ES - GS$ and $ce_{l_1} \in Mem(cg_{k_1})$, $cg_{k_1} \in GS$. caf_i is an inter-group CAF, iff: $InE(caf_i) \cap G \neq \emptyset$, but $InE(caf_i) \cap ES \neq \emptyset$, i.e. $\exists ce_{l_2} \in ES - GS$ that has $ce_{l_2} \in InE(caf_i)$ and $ce_{l_2} \in Mem(cg_{k_2})$, $cg_{k_2} \in GS$, and $k_1 \neq k_2$.

We can easily tell from Fig. 1 (Fig. 1b is the equivalent representation of Fig. 1a) that $caf_1((d_1, p_1), p_1)$ and $caf_2(p_1, p_2)$ are intra-entity functions, while $caf_3((p_2, p_3), p_3)$ is both an intra-entity and inter-entity function. With this definition, we can see that the temporality and connectivity of a property is simply reflected as the intersection relation of the input set and output set of the property's CAF. For example, a varying property, its CAF will take its own as the input, therefore, it will be an intra-entity CAF. Similarly, for connectivity ≥ 2, it will be inter-entity (or inter-group) CAF.

4.3 Determine the Heterogeneity Through "Coverage Set"

The above defined "Influence Set" is approached from the "active" viewpoint of a CAF component, i.e. the elements that are influenced by it. From the "passive"

---

[2] There are two situations for the output of a potential inter-group CAF: (i) a property of a Cyber-G, or (ii) a property of a Cyber-E which belongs to certain Cyber-G. Suppose $GS \neq \emptyset$, for each situation, the definition is given in Definition 10

viewpoint, the concept of coverage set, i.e. components that contribute to its computation, is given in Definition 11.

Definition 11a (Coverage Set of Property). For a specific property p_i, the coverage set, denoted as $CS(p_i)$, is the set of any caf_j and property p_k and data source d_l that p_i depends on, i.e., $CS(p_i) = \{caf_j,\ p_k,\ d_l\}$. $CS(p_i) = CS\_CAF(p_i) \cup CS\_P(p_i) \cup CS\_D(p_i)$, where $CS\_CAF(p_i) = \{caf_j|p_i \rightarrow caf_j\}$, $CS\_P(p_i) = \{p_k|p_i \rightarrow p_k\}$, $CS\_D(p_i) = \{d_l|p_i \rightarrow d_l\}$.

Definition 11b (Coverage Set of Cyber-E). For a specific cyber-entity ce_i, the coverage set, denoted as $CS(ce_i)$, is the set of any caf_j and cyber-entity ce_k and data source d_l that ce_i depends on, i.e., $CS(ce_i) = CS\_E(ce_i) \cup CS\_CAF(ce_i) \cup CS\_D(ce_i)$, where $CS\_E(ce_i) = \{ce_k|ce_i \rightarrow ce_k\}$, $CS\_CAF(ce_i) = \{caf_j|ce_i \rightarrow caf_j\}$, $CS\_D(ce_i) = \{d_l|ce_i \rightarrow d_l\}$.

For example, in Fig. 1, $CS(p_3) = \{caf_3, d_1\}$. We can see that "Coverage Set" enables a clear view of the boundaries of current analysis, i.e. the factors taken into consideration, the heterogeneity of the analysis is reflected as the size of the "Coverage Set".

4.4   Conduct Multi-perspective and Multi-granularity "last-mile" Analytics Through Leveraging Cyber-E(G) Properties

In this fourth step, the "last-mile" analysis could be easily done by non-IT people through leveraging the CAS components, either with self-defined algebraic operations (or with existing algorithms repositories). Moreover, the analytics granularity can be adjusted through grouping a set of Cyber-E and a property assigned to the newly formed Cyber-G with a newly designed caf, which is typically comprised of basic algebraic operations (or with existing algorithms repositories) so that can be easily handled by non-IT people.

5   An Illustrating Example in Research Community

Research community is an environment with complex inter-relationships between researchers, papers and publishing venues. Participants with different roles are with different analytic needs. For researchers, they need to decide on the publishing venue to submit their manuscripts to and the potential collaborators to work with; for publishing venues, they need to invite publications from the authoritative researchers to achieve a higher impact; for research funding agencies, when a multi-country multi-group research project ends, to guide their future funding decisions, they are interested in evaluating the collaborative degree of the involved research groups and the probability of future collaboration among these groups or subgroups continuing to push forward science and technology improvements. Based on these considerations, we will use it as an illustrating example of our proposed methodology in this paper.

Table 1. Identified Cyber-E and properties in research community.

Property(p_i)	Through Guideline	Temporal Char.	Connectivity (p_i)
Paper Cyber-E			
Paper Quality	1	Variant	1
Citation Count	3	Variant	1
Cited By Paper	4	Variant	2
Reference Count	3	Permanent	1
Research Area	2	Permanent	1
Title	2	Permanent	1
Abstract	2	Permanent	1
Year	2	Permanent	1
Published In Venue	4	Permanent	2
Cited By Author	4	Permanent	2
Author Cyber-E			
Author Authority	1	Variant	1
Productivity in Publishing Venue	2	Variant	2
Citation count	3	Variant	1
Publishing Venue Cyber-G			
Publishing Venue Authority	1	Variant	1
Citation count	3	Variant	1
Publication count	3	Variant	1

5.1 Identified Entities and Properties

In research community scenario, CAS is comprised of the analytic activities revolving around the behaviors of the three main types of entities: researchers, papers and publishing venues, with raw data from academic database, review record, etc. We identify the following properties, as shown in Table 1.

5.2 Interdependence and Heterogeneity Analysis

Figure 2 illustrates the interdependence analysis of cyber analytics functions of "Publishing venue authority", "Researcher authority", and "Paper quality" in literature. In this figure, Journal/Conference Cyber-G include: cg_1, cg_2 with its authority property denoted as p_1 are colored red, Paper Cyber-E include: ce_3, ce_4, ce_5 with its quality property denoted as p_1 are colored green. Author Cyber-E include: ce_6, ce_7, with its authority property, p_1 are colored blue. Example CAFs are listed in Table 2. In this table, the analytic perspective and the interdependence types are analyzed.

Table 2. Example CAF in research community.

Example CAF of Fig. 2 in literature	Analytic perspective	CAF type
$caf_1 \in$ {ISI IF, Eigen Factor [8], PageRank [9], Y-factor [10], H-Index [11]}	"Publishing venue authority" considering its published papers	Inter-entity, Intra-group
$caf_2 \in$ {Reading Factor [12,13], Program Committee Characteristics [14], Centrality Metrics [9]}	"Publishing venue authority" considering involved researchers with regard to their different roles: authors, reviewers, and audience	Inter-entity, Intra-group
$caf_3 \in$ {Authority of the publishing venue, a rule of thumb in practice.}	"Researcher authority" considering the publication venue	Inter-entity, Inter-group
$caf_4 \in$ {Author Rank [15], h-index [11], g-index [16], Centrality Metrics [15], Affiliation Prestige}	"Researcher authority" considering their publications	Intra-entity, Inter-entity, Inter-group
$caf_5 \in$ {PageRank [17]}	"Paper quality" considering paper citation	Inter-entity, Inter-group
$caf_5 \in$ {P-Rank [18], MMRQ [19], Tri-rank [20]}	"Paper quality" considering paper citation, paper-researcher authorship, and paper-venue publishing relation	Inter-entity, Inter-group

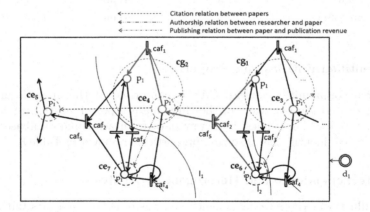

Fig. 2. Interdependence analysis of cyber analytics functions in research community. (Color figure online)

Figure 3 illustrates through two common journal indicators, namely, h-index [11], and SJR2 [21]. Through the coverage set, we can clearly see the factors taken into consideration in evaluating a publishing venue's authority.

5.3 Case Study: Comparison Between ICSOC and ICWS

ICSOC and ICWS are both top conferences in service area: while ICWS is slightly larger in terms of conference size, both conferences provide high quality papers. It poses a problem for a researcher in making submission decisions with maximum potential acceptance chance and maximum benefits attending the conference. The information provided by Microsoft Academic Search only include h-Index and Citation Counts, see Table 3, which is insufficient for a researcher to get to know the two conferences. Other key information includes: the top papers distribution within these two conferences, the authority of the main contributing authors of each conference, etc.

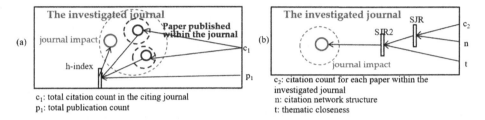

Fig. 3. An illustration of heterogeneity analysis with coverage set via journal impact indicators.

Data Collection. We collect the data of ICWS and ICSOC from Microsoft Academic Search[3], ACM DL[4] and IEEE Xplore[5], with only main conference papers taken into consideration from 2003–2011. Table 3 shows the statistics of the collected data. The authority of the authors published within these two conferences, and the authority of the papers citing the publications within these two conferences are also collected.

Table 3. Statistics of ICWS and ICSOC in Microsoft Academic Search, ACM DL and IEEE Xplore.

	Microsoft Academic Search		ACM DL		IEEE Xplore	
	ICSOC	ICWS	ICSOC	ICWS	ICSOC	ICWS
Paper Count	669	1336	387	841	–	841
Author count	1534	2693	1006	1892	–	1892
Citation count	5324	8329	1013	2102	–	3175
H-Index	33	38	–	–	–	–

---

[3] https://www.microsoft.com/en-us/research/project/academic/
[4] https://dl.acm.org/
[5] https://ieeexplore.ieee.org/Xplore/home.jsp

Multi-perspective "last-mile" Decision Analytics. Compared with Fig. 2 (in this case, cg_2 represents ICSOC or ICWS)[6], we can see the contribution through the citing publishing venue and citing author is missing, as indicated by caf_5 in Fig. 2. Thus, the analytic gap can be clearly specified. The publishing venue authority is estimated with the paper quality of the papers published within the venue, i.e. caf_1 as given by Eq. (1). The paper quality is estimated from two perspectives below: (i) considering both the citing author authority and the citing publishing venues authority (see Eq. (2)), (ii) simply considering the citing venue authority (see Eq. (3)).

$$Aut_1(v) = f(Q(p_i)), f(Q(p_i)) \in \{ \sum_{i=1...N_v} Q(p_i), \frac{1}{N_v} \sum_{i=1...N_v} Q(p_i) \} \quad (1)$$

where $Q(p_i)$ denotes the quality of the ith paper, N_v denotes the number of papers published in publishing venue v. Both the cumulative and average paper quality are considered in evaluating $Aut_1(v)$.

$$Q(p_i) = \sum_j \sum_k Aut(a_{i,j}^k) \times Aut(v_{i,j}), Aut(a_{i,j}^k) \in \{C, CPP, P\}, Aut(v_{i,j}) \in \{h\} \quad (2)$$

where $Aut(a_{i,j}^k)$ denotes the authority of the kth author in the jth venue citing paper p_i and is measured with "C", "P" and "CPP", which stand for "Total Cites", "Total publications", and "Average cites (Citation Per Publication)", respectively. $Aut(v_{i,j})$ denotes the authority of the jth venue citing paper p_i and is measured with h-index.

$$Q(p_i) = \sum_j Aut(v_{i,j}), Aut(v_{i,j}) \in h \quad (3)$$

where $Aut(v_{i,j})$ denotes the authority of the jth venue citing paper p_i and is measured with h-index.

In Eq. (2), the paper quality $Q(p_i)$ is measured by the sum of the product of its citing authors and citing publishing venues. From which we can see that it is comprised of only two kinds of operations: addition and multiplication. Therefore in total we have three models for authors and one model for publishing venue, then through combinations, we have three perspectives studying these two conferences. The results are shown in the first three rows of Table 4. We can see that ICSOC has average better paper quality than ICWS, while ICWS wins over for its quantity.

As mentioned above, some other users may be only interested in citing publishing venue, an example of the CAF designed can be given by Eq. (3). The results are shown in the last two rows of Table 4. It further strengthens our previous findings that ICSOC has average better paper quality than ICWS.

---

[6] Due to data limitations, the propagation through the relational properties (i.e., "Published In Venue", "Cited By Author", "Cited By Paper") is broken as illustrated by line l_1 and l_2, as shown in Fig. 2.

Table 4. A multi-perspective comparative analysis of the impact of ICSOC and ICWS.

Measurement of interior dimension and data sources				$Aut_1(ICSOC)$		$Aut_1(ICWS)$	
Paper Citation Relation Data Source	Paper Quality $Q(p_i)$	Citing Author Authority $Aut(a)$	Citing Venue Authority	Cumulative Paper Quality	Avg Paper Quality	Cumulative Paper Quality	Avg Paper Quality
ACM	Equation (2)	Average cites (CPP)	h-index	12.47	0.03	19.05	0.02
ACM	Equation (2)	Total publications (P)	h-index	24.88	0.06	44.86	0.05
ACM	Equation (2)	Total Cites (C)	h-index	12.53	0.03	17.27	0.02
ACM	Equation (3)	–	h-index	99.34	0.26	193.17	0.23
IEEEXplore	Equation (3)	–	h-index	–	–	272.259	0.27

Adjustable Multi-granularity "last-mile" Self-service Analytics. As mentioned above, the hierarchical structure of basic Cyber-Es modeled in CAS enables a convenient multi-granularity analysis. In this section, we illustrate the comparison analysis of ICOSC and ICWS with two Cyber-Gs: top n high quality papers and top m main contributing authors, see Fig. 4.

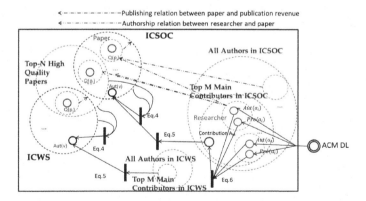

Fig. 4. "Top-N High Quality Papers" Cyber-G and "Top-M Main Contributors" Cyber-G for ICSOC and ICWS.

Top n High Quality Papers. The first grouping view is from the top n high quality papers among all the publishing venues. Let $Aut_2(v, n)$ denote the authority of publishing venue v when considering top n high quality papers, see Eq. (4). Here $f(Q(p_i, n))$ is estimated from two perspectives: (i) the percentage the high quality papers a publishing venue occupies in the top n papers, (ii) the percentage the number of papers published in publishing venue v that belong to top n papers over the number of total papers publishing within the publishing venue.

$$Aut_2(v,n) = f(Q(p_i),n), f(Q(p_i,n)) \in \{N_v^n/n, N_v^n/N_v\} \tag{4}$$

where $Q(p_i)$ denotes the quality of the ith paper, N_v^n denotes the number of papers published in publishing venue v that belong to top n papers, and N_v denotes the number of papers published in publishing venue v.

The results are shown in Fig. 5 with top n varying from 1–100 at an interval of 10 (the two conferences have 1228 papers in total). Figure 5(a) shows the proportion of the ICSOC (Blue Line) or ICWS (Red Line) papers belonging to top n papers, while Fig. 5(b) shows the proportion of ICSOC or ICWS papers belonging to top n over all the papers in ICSOC or ICWS, respectively. The top n papers are determined with paper quality calculated using Eq. (2), here, $Aut(a_{i,j}^k) = CPP$, $Aut(v_{i,j}) = h$. From Fig. 5(a), we can see that the percentage of the high quality papers in ICSOC occupies in the n top papers investigated is decreasing as n increases. The percentage of the high quality papers in ICWS increases. When only top 10 papers are considered, ICSOC wins over ICWS. When top 20 papers are considered, then, ICWS wins over ICSOC through top 30 to top 100. This leads us to conclude that ICSOC provides more very high quality papers, while ICWS provides more medium high quality papers. However, from Fig. 5(b), we can see that within each conference, when different n is considered, the percentage of the high quality papers from ICSOC always surpasses that of ICWS. This means if the two conferences publish the same number of papers, ICSOC will also win in numbers, that is, the previous advantage ICWS has is due to its larger base number of papers.

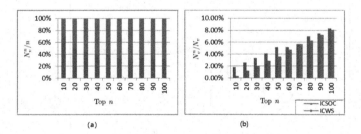

Fig. 5. Comparison of ICSOC and ICWS based on top n papers distribution. (Color figure online)

Top m Main Contributors. The second grouping view is from the top m main contributors within each publishing venue. The authority of publishing venue v w.r.t its top m main contributors $Aut_3(v,m)$ is evaluated considering both the productivity and authority of the main m authors, see Eq. (5).

$$Aut_3(v,m) = f(Contr(A_m)) = \sum_{i=1...m} Contr(a_i) \tag{5}$$

where $A_m = \{a_i | i = 1 \dots m\}$ denotes the set of top m main contributors, $Contr(a_i)$ denotes the contribution of author a_i, and is the product of his authority and his productivity within a publishing venue, see Eq. 6.

$$Contr(a_i) = Pro(a_i) \times Aut(a_i), Aut(a_i) \in \{C, CPP, P\} \tag{6}$$

where $Pro(a_i)$ denotes the productivity of author a_i, $Aut(a_i)$ the authority of author a_i, and is measured with "C(Total Cites)", "P(Total Publications)" and "CPP(Average Cites, or Citation Per Publication)".

The results are shown in Fig. 6. The contribution of an author is the product of his normed productivity in this ICSOC/ICWS and his normed authority is approximated by "Average Cites (CPP)" in (a) and (b), by "Total Publications (P)" in (c) and (d), and by "Total Cites (C)" in (e) and (f). We can see that the most contributing authors in ICSOC are more authoritative than those in ICWS, whether the authority is measured by average cites, total publications or total cites. However, through comparison between (a), (c), (e), and (b), (d), (f), we can also see that the authors in both conferences are more or less the same (see Fig. 6(c) and (d)), when $Aut(a_i)$ is measured with "Total Publication (P)". The difference is most evident (see Fig. 6(a) and (b)), when $Aut(a_i)$ is measured with "Average Cites (CPP)".

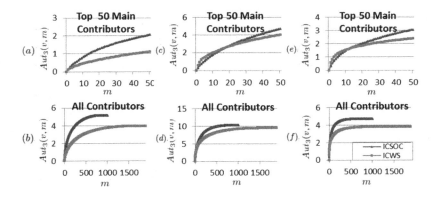

Fig. 6. Comparison of ICSOC and ICWS based on top m main contributions.

6   Conclusion

The main contributions include (i) a unified knowledge representation framework, namely, Cyber-Entity (Cyber-E) modeling, to capture and formalize the interdepence and heterogeneity in data analytics; (ii) a flexible model that enables the adjustment of different analytic granularities. To demonstrate the effectiveness, we have conducted a comparative analysis of two top conferences in the service area: ICSOC and ICWS. The results show that ICSOC has better paper quality than ICWS, and its main contributing authors receive more citations than those of ICWS, while the productivity of the authors from those two conferences are similar. Our future work will focus on improving the Cyber-E model, in particular, refine the cyber analytic functions modelling w.r.t. temporal factors, to support the incremental analytics, and etc.

References

1. Lustig, I., Dietrich, B., et al.: The analytics journey. Analytics Mag. (2010)
2. Rutkowski, L.: Computational Intelligence: Methods and Techniques, 1st edn. Springer, Heidelberg (2008). https://doi.org/10.1007/978-3-540-76288-1
3. Miller, G.: Social scientists wade into the tweet stream. Science **333**(6051), 1814–1815 (2011)
4. Johan, B., Huina, M.: Twitter mood as a stock market predictor. IEEE Comput. **44**(10), 91–94 (2011)
5. Kenny, D.A., Cook, W.L.: Dyadic Data Analysis. The Guilford Press, New York (2006)
6. Brachman, R., Levesque, H.: Knowledge Representation and Reasoning. Morgan Kaufmann, San Francisco (2004)
7. Zhang, D., Guo, B., Yu, Z.: The emergence of social and community intelligence. IEEE Comput. **44**(7), 21–28 (2011)
8. Bergstrom, C.: Eigenfactor: measuring the value and prestige of scholarly journals. College Res. Libr. News **68**(5), 314–316 (2007)
9. Cheang, B., Chu, S., et al.: A multidimensional approach to evaluating management journals: refining pagerank via the differentiation of citation types and identifying the roles that management journals play. J. Am. Soc. Inform. Sci. Technol. **65**(12), 2581–2591 (2014)
10. Bollen, J., Rodriguez, M.A., et al.: Journal status. Scientometrics **69**(3), 669–687 (2006)
11. Alonso, S., Cabrerizo, F.J., et al.: h-index: a review focused in its variants, computation and standardization for different scientific fields. J. Inf. **3**(4), 273–289 (2009)
12. Guerrero-Bote, V.P., Moya-Anegon, F.: Relationship between downloads and citations at journal and paper levels, and the influence of language. Scientometrics **101**(2), 1043–1065 (2014)
13. Aduku, K.J., ThelWall, M., et al.: Do Mendeley reader counts reflect the scholarly impact of conference papers? An investigation of computer science and engineering. Scientometrics **112**(1), 1–9 (2017)
14. Zhuang, Z., Elmacioglu, E., et al.: Measuring conference quality by mining program committee characteristics. In: Proceedings of the 7th ACM/IEEE-CS Joint Conference on Digital Libraries, Vancouver, BC, Canada (2007)
15. Yan, E., Ding, Y.: Discovering author impact: a PageRank perspective. Inf. Process. Manage. **47**(1), 125–134 (2011)
16. Egghe, L.: Theory and practise of the g-index. Scientometrics **69**(1), 131–152 (2006)
17. Ma, N., Guan, J., et al.: Bringing PageRank to the citation analysis. Inf. Process. Manage. **44**(2), 800–810 (2008)
18. Yan, E., Ding, Y., et al.: P-rank: an indicator measuring prestige in heterogeneous scholarly networks. J. Am. Soc. Inform. Sci. Technol. **62**(3), 467–477 (2011)

19. Mu, D., Guo, L., et al.: Query-focused personalized citation recommendation with mutually reinforced rankingk. IEEE Access, 3107–3119 (2018)
20. Liu, Z., Huang, H., et al.: Tri-rank: an authority ranking framework in heterogeneous academic networks by mutual reinforce. In: 2014 IEEE 26th International Conference on Tools with Artificial Intelligence, pp. 493–500 (2014)
21. Guerrero-Bote, V.P., Moya-Anegón, F.: A further step forward in measuring journals' scientific prestige: the SJR2 indicator. J. Inf. **6**(4), 674–688 (2012)

Learning Subgraph Structure with LSTM for Complex Network Link Prediction

Yun Han[1], Donghai Guan[1,2], and Weiwei Yuan[1,2(✉)]

[1] Department of Computer Science and Technology,
Nanjing University of Aeronautics and Astronautics, Nanjing, China
hanyunnuaa@126.com, {dhguan,yuanweiwei}@nuaa.edu.cn
[2] Collaborative Innovation Center of Novel Software Technology
and Industrialization, Nanjing 210093, China

Abstract. Link prediction is a hot research topic in complex network. Traditional link prediction is based on similarities between nodes, such as common neighbors and Jaccard index. These methods are easy to understand and widely used. However, most existing works use a single relationship between two target nodes, lacking the use of information around the two target nodes. Due to the poor scalability of these methods, the performances of link prediction are not good. In this paper, we propose a novel link prediction method, learning Subgraph structure with Long-Short Term Memory network (SG-LSTM), which uses a recurrent neural network to learn the subgraph patterns to predict links. First, we extract the enclosing subgraph of the target link. Second, we use a graph labeling algorithm called the hash-based Weisfeiler-Lehman (HWL) algorithm to re-label the extracted closed subgraphs, which maps the subgraphs to the sequential data that reflects the subgraph structure. Finally, these sequential data are trained using long-short term memory network (LSTM) to learn the link prediction model. This learned LSTM model is used to predict the link. Large-scale experiments verify that our proposed method has superior link prediction performances to traditional link prediction methods.

Keywords: Subgraph structure · Graph labeling · Link prediction · Recurrent neural network

1 Introduction

Link prediction [1] is used to predict whether two nodes in the network have links. In the field of data mining and machine learning, it has attracted widespread attention from many researchers. Link prediction has many applications in real world, such as friend recommendations in social networks [2], product recommendation in e-commerce [2], knowledge graph completion [3], finding associations between proteins [4], and recovering missing reactions in metabolic networks [4, 6]. Some classic link prediction methods, such as Common Neighbor (CN) [1, 4], have a wide range of applications and are easy to understand. The key idea of CN is that if two nodes have more common neighbors, the probability that these two nodes have a link is greater. Other popular algorithms for calculating the similarity of two nodes include Adamic-Adar (AA) [5], Resource Allocation (RA) [8], Jaccard Index (JC) [8], etc.

© Springer Nature Switzerland AG 2019
J. Li et al. (Eds.): ADMA 2019, LNAI 11888, pp. 34–47, 2019.
https://doi.org/10.1007/978-3-030-35231-8_3

However, the classical link prediction algorithms ignore the high-order network topology information and lack scalability in different networks. For example, CN may work well when predicting friendships in social networks or predicting partnerships in collaborative networks, but has proven to be poorly performing on grids and bio-networks [8]. These existing link prediction methods are less robust. Therefore, we consider the enclosing subgraph of the link and using the long-short term memory network (LSTM) [7] to learn the subgraph pattern that constitutes the network. A large number of experiments have proved that our method achieves good link prediction performance on different datasets. Our method learn subgraph structure with LSTM, namely SG-LSTM, studying the structure that constitutes the link from the overall perspective of the subgraph. Specifically, for each target link, SG-LSTM first extracts a subgraph in its neighborhood, which is called an enclosing subgraph. The SG-LSTM then maps the extracted enclosing subgraphs into a sequence of nodes. Finally, these nodes sequence are used to train the LSTM to learn the link prediction model. Figure 1 shows the framework of the proposed method.

There are two key issues in our proposed approach. One is to provide the LSTM learning machine with a sequence of nodes associated with the subgraph topology, and the other is the node embedding input associated with it. The goal of a graph labeling is to assign nodes of two different enclosing subgraphs to similar positions of the corresponding node sequence, if and only if they have similar structural roles in the respective graphs. Since LSTM read data sequentially, stable ordering based on vertex structure roles is critical to learning meaningful models. When training a long-short term memory recurrent network with node sequences, we use node embedding based on random walks, node2vec [9] and deepwalk [10], as inputs to each time point of the LSTM.

The Weisfeiler-Lehman (WL) algorithm [11] is a graph labeling algorithm that determines the order of nodes based on the topology of the graph. We use an improved WL algorithm called hashing-based Weisfeiler-Lehman (HWL) [12] to sort nodes of the extracted enclosing subgraph. And the subgraph is mapped to a node sequence. A LSTM is trained on these node sequences to learn a link prediction model. Our experiments show that SG-LSTM can achieve better link prediction performance than traditional link prediction algorithms.

Our work has two main contributions:

1. We propose a link prediction model based on the enclosing subgraph of links, which maps the enclosing subgraph to a node sequence of nodes that the recurrent neural network can read;
2. A large number of experiments show that our method can effectively improve link prediction performance.

The rest of the paper is organized as follows: Sect. 2 presents definition used in this work; Sect. 3 introduces the related works; Sect. 4 presents our proposed methods in details; Sect. 5 gives the experimental results of our proposed method, which are compared with the performances of existing works; Sect. 6 summarizes this paper.

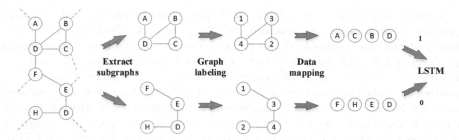

Fig. 1. The illustration of the proposed method. SG-LSTM first samples a set of positive links (B, D), and negative links (E, H) as training links, and extracts an enclosing subgraph for each link. Graph labeling is used to decide the node ordering and node sequence. The resulting (sequence, tag) pairs are fed into a LSTM for link predicton.

2 Definitions

In this section, we will introduce some background knowledge about graph theory and LSTM recurrent neural networks, which are essential for understanding our proposed model.

Graphs. A graph $G = (V, E)$ can represent s network, where $V = \{v_1, \cdots, v_n\}$ is the set of nodes and $E \subseteq V \times V$ is the set of links. We use $N^1(v)$ to denote the set of 1-hop neighbors of a node $v \in V$. And $N^d(v)$ is used to denote the set of nodes, whose distance to v is less than or equal to d, $d = 1, 2, 3, \cdots$. In the paper, We research undirected and connected networks.

Long Short-Term Memory (LSTM). The long-short term memory network [7] is an improved recurrent neural network that can solve the long-distance dependence problem that RNN cannot handle in sequential data. We denote the input vector at time t by x_t. And we use h_t to represent the hidden layer vector at time t. At each step, the LSTM calculates a memory cell vector c_t, an input gate vector i_t, an forgetting gate vector f_t, and an output gate vector o_t. The following function is the mathematical expression of LSTM at time t:

$$
\begin{aligned}
i_t &= \sigma(W_i x_t + U_i h_{t-1} + K_i c_{t-1} + b_i) \\
f_t &= \sigma(W_f x_t + U_f h_{t-1} + K_f c_{t-1} + b_f) \\
o_t &= \sigma(W_o x_t + U_o h_{t-1} + K_o c_{t-1} + b_o) \\
c_t &= f_t \otimes c_{t-1} + i_t \otimes \tanh(W_c x_t + U_c h_{t-1} + b_c) \\
h_t &= o_t \otimes \tanh(c_t),
\end{aligned}
\tag{1}
$$

where $\otimes$ denotes elementwise multiplication, σ is the logistic sigmoid function, each W is a weight matrix connecting inputs to particular gates (denoted by subscripts), each U is an analogous matrix connecting hidden vectors to gates, each K is a diagonal matrix connecting cell vectors to gates, and each b is a bias [16]. In this paper, the enclosing subgraphs we extracted are mapped to the node sequence by the HWL algorithm, which is used to train the weight matrix and bias of the long short-term memory network. Then, the LSTM model is used to predict links.

3 Related Works

A common method to predict the link between two nodes is to measure the similarity between these two nodes. The more similar these two nodes are, the more likely there exists a link between these two nodes [13]. Some classic link prediction algorithms based on node similarity include Common Neighbors (CN), Adamic-Adar index (AA), Resource Allocation (RA) and Jaccard index (JC) [14]. We summarize several most popular methods as follows: If two nodes v_i and v_j share more common neighbors, they are regarded to have more topology similarity in the network [15], and it is more likely that there exists a link between these two nodes. CN is defined as (2). where $|\bullet|$ represents the number of $\bullet$. Unlike CN, the AA measure assumes that two nodes v_i and v_j whose common neighbors have more neighbors tend to have lower link probability [14].

$$CN(v_i, v_j) = \left| N^1(v_i) \cap N^1(v_j) \right|. \tag{2}$$

AA is formally defined as

$$AA(v_i, v_j) = \sum\nolimits_{z \in N^1(v_i) \cap N^1(v_j)} \frac{1}{\log D(z)}, \tag{3}$$

where $D(z)$ is degree of the selected common neighbor. RA [5] is similar as AA, while changes the degree on how the number of two nodes' common neighbors influence the existence of the link, is defined as

$$RA(v_i, v_j) = \sum\nolimits_{z \in N^1(v_i) \cap N^1(v_j)} \frac{1}{D(z)}. \tag{4}$$

After that, JC is also often used to measure the similarity between two nodes. The larger the Jaccard index between two nodes, the more likely there is a link., JC is defined as

$$JC(v_i, v_j) = \frac{\left| N^1(v_i) \cap N^1(v_j) \right|}{\left| N^1(v_i) \cup N^1(v_j) \right|}. \tag{5}$$

These link prediction methods based on first-order or second-order neighbors similarity between two nodes tend to lose a large amount of network topology information, resulting in poor prediction performance and poor scalability [17]. We research subgraph structure that promote the formation of links in the paper. We build a predictive model from the perspective of the enclosing subgraph of the target link, namely SG-LSTM. Experiments have proved that predicting the formation of links from the global perspective of the entire subgraph can achieve better performance.

4 The Proposed Method

The proposed method is to extract the enclosing subgraph for the target link and map the extracted subgraph into sequential data. The LSTM is trained by acquired sequential data to learn link prediction model. The algorithm we proposed is shown in workflow 1. The proposed method mainly includes three phases: Enclosing Subgraph Generation phase, which generates a k-enclosing subgraph for the target link, k is the number of nodes in the subgraph; Enclosing subgraph encoding phase, which encodes the extracted k-enclosing subgraph into sequential data processed by LSTM; LSTM training phase, which obtain the link prediction model by training the LSTM with node sequence that subgraph is mapped into and the tag of the target link.

4.1 Enclosing Subgraph Generation

In our proposed method, we first extract the k-enclosing subgraph for each target link. The T_{ij} is used to represent the target link, and the two nodes that make up the target link are v_i and v_j. The k-enclosing subgraph of a link is a subgraph composed by the neighbor nodes of this link, and the size of the neighbor nodes is k. The k-enclosing subgraph describes the topology information surrounding the target link. It discovers the local patterns promoting the existence of links between nodes. For a T_{ij}, its enclosing subgraph is represented as $SG(T_{ij})$ is generated by adding the neighborhood nodes iteratively, as shown in Algorithm 1:v_i and v_j are firstly added to $SG(T_{ij})$; the d-order neighbor nodes of v_i and v_j, which are represented by $N_d(v_i)$ and $N_d(v_j)$, $d \in N$, are then added to $SG(T_{ij})$ according to the ascending order of d until $|SG(T_{ij})| \geq k$. After executing Algorithm 1, when $|SG(T_{ij})| > k$, nodes lastly added to $SG(T_{ij})$ are removed until $|SG(T_{ij})| = k$. The k-enclosing subgraph of T_{ij} is represented as $SG^k(T_{ij})$.

Workflow 1: The proposed method

1. Extract k-enclosing subgraph for target link

2. Encode k-enclosing subgraph into sequential data

3. Train LSTM model by sequential data

4. Predict link with LSTM model

4.2   Enclosing Subgraph Encoding

A graph labeling function is a map $f:V \rightarrow C$ from nodes V to an ordered set C, conventionally called **colors** in literature [6]. If f is injective, the obtained C can be used to uniquely determine the order of the nodes in the sequence. In this paper, we adopt the set of integer colors starting from 1. The Weisfeiler-Lehman (WL) algorithm [11] is a newly proposed graph labeling algorithm which has been verified to be effective in the real applications. Algorithm 2 illustrates the details of the WL algorithm. The key idea of WL is to iteratively augment the vertex color using their neighbor's color and compress the augmented color into new color before convergence [11]. Specifically, we first initialize the color of all nodes in a graph to 1; For each node in the graph, its own color is concatenated with its neighbor's color as new string; The nodes are reassigned to color 1, 2, 3 according to the ascending order of their corresponding strings.

For example, assume vertex v_i has color 1 and its neighbors have color $\{2, 1, 2\}$ respectively. At the same time, v_j has color 1 and its neighbors have color $\{1, 1, 2\}$. The signature strings for v_i and v_j are $<1, 122>$ and $<1, 112>$ respectively. Because $<1, 112>$ is smaller than $<1, 122>$ lexicographically. v_j is assigned a smaller color than v_i in the next iteration. Figure 2 gives an example.

Algorithm 1: Enclosing Subgraph Generation

Input: the network G , the target link T_{ij}

Output: the enclosing subgraph $SG(T_{ij})$ of T_{ij}

Parameter: subgraph size k

1: $SG(T_{ij}) = \{v_i, v_j\}$

2: $border = \{v_i, v_j\}$

3: **while** $\left| SG(T_{ij}) \right| < k$ **do**

4: $\quad border = (\cup_{v \in border} N^1(v)) - SG(T_{ij})$

5: $\quad SG(T_{ij}) = SG(T_{ij}) \cup border$

6: **end while**

7: **return** $SG(T_{ij})$

Algorithm 2 The Weisfeiler-Lehman Algorithm

Input: Initial color $c_0(v) = 1$ for all nodes $v \in V$, graph $G = (V, E)$

Output: Final color $c(v)$ for all $v \in V$

1: Let $c(v) = c_0(v)$ for all $v \in V$

2: **while** $c(v)$ has not converged **do**

3:      **for** each $v \in V$ **do**

4:            Assign a multiset-color $M(v')$ which consists of its neighbors' color $\{c(v') \mid v' \in N_1(v)\}$

5:            Sort elements in $M(v')$ in an ascending order and concatenate them into a string $s(v')$

6:            Add $c(v)$ as a prefix to $s(v')$ and call the resulting string $s(v) = [c(v), s(v')]$

7:      **end for**

8:      Resort all of the strings $s(v)$ for all v from $G = (V, E)$ in lexicographical ascending order

9:      Relabel all $s(v)$ to new color 1,2,3,... sequentially; same strings will get the same color

10: **end while**

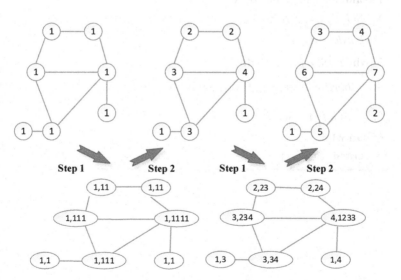

Step 1: generate signature strings.   Step 2: sort signature strings and relabel.

Fig. 2. The executive process of WL with two iterations.

One of the main advantages of the WL algorithm is that the final color encodes the structural roles of the nodes in the graph and defines the relative ordering of the nodes. This allows the LSTM to learn a meaningful node sequence that is related to the subgraph structure. We give the result of another graph relabeled by the WL algorithm, as shown in Fig. 3. Comparing Figs. 2 and 3, it shows that if vertices have similar structural roles in their respective graphs, they will have similar relative positions in their respective rankings.

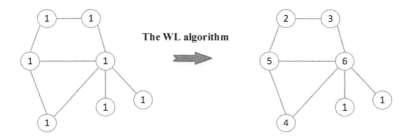

Fig. 3. Another similar graph relabeled by the WL algorithm

In our proposed method, the WL algorithm is a valid graph labeling algorithm. However, the WL algorithm requires a lot of storage to process the strings generated in the algorithm execution, which usually takes a lot of resources. In our paper, we use a hash-based WL(HWL) algorithm that using a hash function $h(x)$ to maps a single string to a single real number [6]. In the WL algorithm iteration process, it is proved that it is more efficient to use $h(x)$ to map the string into a real number. The hash function used is as follows:

$$h(v) = c(v) + \sum_{z \in N^1(v)} \log(P(c(z))), \tag{6}$$

where $c(v)$ and $c(z)$ are integer colors, P is the list of all primes, where $P(n)$ is the nth prime number. In SG-LSTM, we use the HWL algorithm to map the k-enclosing subgraphs into node sequences. For target link T_{ij}, the node sequence corresponding to its k-enclosing subgraph is represented as $seq^k(T_{ij})$.

4.3   LSTM Training

After acquiring the node sequences mapped by the subgraph, we use LSTM to learn the subgraph pattern of the target link. For a given network G, we select a certain number of positive samples from $T_{ij} \in E$, and select some negative samples from $v_i, v_j \in V$ and $T_{ij} \notin E$. For our training links, we first extract the k-enclosing subgraphs for links, and then map the subgraph to a sequential data related to the subgraph structure. The training set $D = \{(seq^k(T_1), y_1), (seq^k(T_2), y_2), \cdots, (seq^k(T_n), y_n)\}$ is obtained from the node sequence corresponding to the target link and their tags, T_i represents the

i^{th} target link of the training set D, and y_i is the tags of T_i in D. $y_i \in \{0, 1\}$, in which 1 means T_i exists in positive samples, while 0 means T_i exist in negative samples, $i = 1, 2, \cdots, n$. A LSTM is trained onto learn link prediction model. For a target link T_{xy}, its tag is predicted as

$$y(T_{xy}) = LSTM(seq^k(T_{xy})),\qquad(7)$$

where $y(T_{xy}) \in \{0, 1\}$, and LSTM is the link prediction model trained on D.

5 Experiments

In this section, in order to validate the link prediction performance of our proposed method, we compared SG-LSTM with six methods on five different datasets.

Datasets. These real-world networks include: (1) USAir traffic network [18] (UTN): nodes represent airports or service centers, and links represent routes between airports or service centers; (2) Power network [20] (PWN): nodes represent generators, transformators or substations of the power grid, and links represent power supply lines between nodes; (3) E.coli network [21] (ECN): nodes are metabolites, and links are reactions between nodes; (4) Router network [21] (RTN): nodes represent routers of the Internet connected autonomous system, and links represents the communications between routers; (5) Political blog network [19] (PBN): nodes represent US political blogs, and links represent hyperlinks between blogs. The detailed information of these experimental networks are given in Table 1.

Table 1. Detailed information of the experimental datasets

	UTN	PWN	ECN	RTN	PBN
Number of nodes	500	4941	1805	5022	1222
Number of edges	2980	6594	14660	6258	16714

Baselines. We compare our method with some classical link prediction methods that have been introduced in the Sect. 2. These methods measure the neighborhoods of links for link prediction. The neighborhood measured in these methods is the subset of the subgraph used in the proposed methods. These methods include Common neighbors (CN), Resource Allocation (RA), Adamic-Adar index (AA), Jaccard index (JC). A LSTM is trained on node sequences, the input vector x_t at each time t in the sequence is the node embedding. We use node2vec [10] and deepwalk [9] based on random walk to get node embedding, which is used as the input vector for each node. In our experiments, the link prediction method based on node2vec and deepwalk was also added to baselines, which predicts links based on the embedding relationship of the two nodes. After that, Accuracy is used to evaluate the link prediction performances of these methods.

Experimental Setup. For the proposed method, we choose the subgraph size $k = 15$. When training LSTM, the input vector x_t of a sequence at time t is 32 dimensions, that is, in the node sequence, the 32-dimensional node embedding is used. And we chose the number of negative samples to be twice the number of positive samples as experimental data. The experimental data was divided into different test ratio, and the performance of the link predictions of different methods was measured by *accuracy*. For LSTM model, the input layer relies on pre-trained node embeddings, SG-LSTM-NV and SG-LSTM- DW respectively represent the SG-LSTM method of relying on Node2vec and Deepwalk to get node embedding. We train the LSTM-RNN with ADAM optimizer with a learning rate of 0.001 and a mini-batch size of 128 and using binary cross entropy loss function. We set the number of training epochs to be 100. The model parameters with the best results on 10% validation splits of the training set are used to predict the testing links [6]. The neural network is implemented using Tensorflow. For baselines, Logistic Regression (LR) is used as a classifier, LR is implemented by LibLinear and L1-regularization. Tables 2, 3, 4, 5 and 6 shows the experimental results on five datasets. The bold font in the table indicates that the *accuracy* of our proposed method is higher than the baseline.

Results. From Table 2, we can observe the following. The better link prediction performance obtained by SG-LSTM-NV is compared with the six baselines under all different test ratios. SG-LSTM-DW has also better link prediction performance than baseline. The link prediction performance of SG-LSTM-NV is better than node2vec that uses only embedding of two target nodes. Similarly, SG-LSTM-DW's performance is better than deepwalk. More generally, from Tables 3, 4, 5 and 6, SG-LSTM-NV has the higher *accuracy* than other baselines under different test ratio on five datasets. Experimental results show that our method can effectively improve the accuracy of link prediction. This suggests that SG-LSTM can learn subgraph structure which other baselines cannot express with LSTM to construct link prediction model. Another interesting finding is that, for all the six baseline methods, none of them can perform well on all datasets. For example, JC has higher *accuracy* than the other five baselines on the UTN datasets, but JC has poor prediction performance on the ECN datasets, that is, its *accuracy* is lower than 0.700. Comparatively speaking, our proposed methods shows scalability.

Table 2. Accuracy of link prediction for various methods on the UTN

Methods	Test ratio				
	10%	20%	30%	40%	50%
SG-LSTM-NV	**0.810**	**0.816**	**0.816**	**0.824**	**0.824**
SG-LSTM-DW	**0.809**	0.792	**0.808**	**0.813**	0.800
Node2vec	0.800	0.784	0.800	0.792	0.784
Deepwalk	0.792	0.776	0.784	0.768	0.776
CN	0.793	0.804	0.781	0.786	0.798
RA	0.805	0.805	0.782	0.786	0.802
AA	0.798	0.805	0.790	0.792	0.799
JC	0.800	0.810	0.795	0.804	0.813

Table 3. Accuracy of link prediction for various methods on the PWN

Methods	Test ratio				
	10%	20%	30%	40%	50%
SG-LSTM-NV	**0.713**	**0.727**	**0.720**	**0.717**	**0.705**
SG-LSTM-DW	0.707	**0.720**	**0.723**	**0.715**	0.693
Node2vec	0.700	0.707	0.693	0.713	0.680
Deepwalk	0.708	0.635	0.612	0.631	0.618
CN	0.695	0.710	0.685	0.697	0.700
RA	0.707	0.711	0.685	0.697	0.700
AA	0.700	0.711	0.690	0.697	0.700
JC	0.705	0.708	0.683	0.687	0.654

Table 4. Link prediction accuracy with various methods on ECN

Methods	Test data ratio				
	10%	20%	30%	40%	50%
SG-LSTM-NV	**0.789**	**0.804**	**0.800**	**0.796**	**0.793**
SG-LSTM-DW	0.780	**0.793**	**0.789**	**0.797**	**0.790**
Node2vec	0.671	0.680	0.683	0.685	0.672
Deepwalk	0.650	0.656	0.641	0.649	0.648
CN	0.763	0.760	0.774	0.790	0.782
RA	0.785	0.761	0.767	0.771	0.758
AA	0.715	0.698	0.686	0.693	0.684
JC	0.685	0.678	0.680	0.682	0.685

Table 5. Link prediction accuracy with various methods on RTN

Methods	Test data ratio				
	10%	20%	30%	40%	50%
SG-LSTM-NV	**0.700**	**0.733**	**0.707**	**0.693**	**0.688**
SG-LSTM-DW	**0.693**	**0.727**	**0.713**	**0.700**	**0.680**
Node2vec	0.689	0.671	0.636	0.652	0.655
Deepwalk	0.682	0.664	0.652	0.650	0.656
CN	0.682	0.678	0.647	0.657	0.659
RA	0.689	0.674	0.645	0.655	0.658
AA	0.682	0.674	0.647	0.657	0.658
JC	0.689	0.668	0.640	0.652	0.654

Table 6. Link prediction accuracy with various methods on PBN

Methods	Test data ratio				
	10%	20%	30%	40%	50%
SG-LSTM-NV	**0.780**	**0.790**	**0.795**	**0.793**	**0.800**
SG-LSTM-DW	0.733	**0.753**	**0.760**	**0.753**	0.747
Node2vec	0.740	0.720	0.725	0.713	0.733
Deepwalk	0.720	0.748	0.753	0.750	0.745
CN	0.755	0.723	0.716	0.727	0.726
RA	0.768	0.751	0.729	0.750	0.754
AA	0.755	0.728	0.714	0.730	0.730
JC	0.702	0.664	0.670	0.674	0.676

Parameter Sensitivity Analysis. The parameter sensitivity is further analyzed for the proposed model. An important parameter that can affect the performance of our proposed method is the node embedding's dimension, represented as di, and the subgraph size k. In the parameter sensitivity experiment, the ratio of the test set is set to 20%. We assign subgraph size $k = 15$, we observe the link prediction results obtained by SG-LSTM-NV and SG-LSTM-DW in different nodes embedding's dimensions di, $di = \{16, 32, 64, 128\}$. Figures 4 and 5 shows the link prediction results. It is not difficult to see that the link prediction accuracy of our proposed method is relatively close on the respective datasets. Similarly, we set node embedding dimension $di = 32$, we research the link prediction results obtsained by SG-LSTM-NV and SG-LSTM-DW in different subgraph sizes k,$k = \{10, 15, 20, 25\}$. As shown in Figs. 4 and 5, We also find that our proposed method is robust under the variation of k. Its performance is similarly good for $k = \{10, 15, 20, 25\}$ on five datasets.

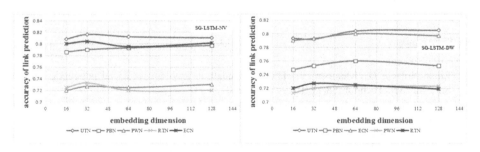

Fig. 4. SG-LSTM-NV and SG-LSTM-DW link prediction accuracy with different node embedding dimensions.

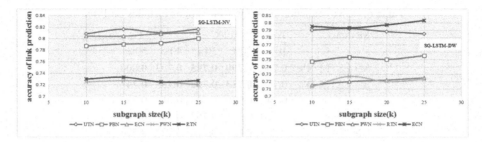

Fig. 5. SG-LSTM-NV and SG-LSTM-DW link prediction accuracy with different subgraph sizes

6   Conclusions

In this paper, we propose to learn the subgraph pattern that constitutes the link with LSTM, namely SG-LSTM, for link prediction task. Specifically, we first extract the local enclosing subgraph for the links. Then, an efficient graph labeling algorithm called HWL is used to imposes an order on the subgraph vertices according to the structural roles of the nodes in the subgraph.. So that the subgraph are mapped to a sequential data that the LSTM can process. After that, a LSTM is trained on the sequence to learn subgraph features for link prediction. A large number of experimental results show that our proposed method has better performance than other link prediction methods on different datasets.

Acknowledgement. This research was supported by Nature Science Foundation of China (Grant No. 61672284), Natural Science Foundation of Jiangsu Province (Grant No. BK20171418), China Postdoctoral Science Foundation (Grant No. 2016M591841), Jiangsu Planned Projects for Postdoctoral Research Funds (No. 1601225C).

References

1. Liben-Nowell, D., Kleinberg, J.: The link-prediction problem for social networks. J. Am. Soc. Inf. Sci. Technol. **58**(7), 1019–1031 (2007)
2. Adamic, L.A., Adar, E.: Friends and neighbors on the web. Soc. Networks **25**(3), 211–230 (2003)
3. Lin, Y., Liu, Z., Sun, M., Liu, Y., Zhu, X.: Learning entity and relation embeddings for knowledge graph completion. In: Proceedings of AAAI (2015)
4. Lü, L., Zhou, T.: Link prediction in complex networks: a survey. Phys. A **390**, 1150–1170 (2011)
5. Zhou, T., Lü, L., Zhang, Y.-C.: Predicting missing links via local information. Eur. Phys. J. B **71**(4), 623–630 (2009)
6. Zhang, M., Chen, Y.: Weisfeiler-lehman neural machine for link prediction. In: Proceedings of the 23rd ACM SIGKDD International Conference on Knowledge Discovery and Data Mining, pp. 575–583. ACM (2017)

7. Hochreiter, S., Schmidhuber, J.: Long short-term memory. Neural Comput. **9**, 1735–1780 (1997)
8. Hasan, M., Chaoji, V., Salem, S., Zaki, M.: Link prediction using supervised learning. In: Proceedings of the Workshop on Link Discovery: Issues, Approaches and Applications (2005)
9. Perozzi, B., Al-Rfou, R., Skiena, S.: Deepwalk: online learning of social representations. In: Proceedings of KDD, pp. 701–710 (2014)
10. Grover, A., Leskovec, J.: node2vec: Scalable feature learning for networks. In: Proceedings of KDD, pp. 855–864 (2016)
11. Shervashidze, N., et al.: Weisfeiler-lehman graph kernels. J. Mach. Learn. Res. **12**, 2539–2561 (2011)
12. Kersting, K., Mladenov, M., Garnett, R., Grohe, M.: Power iterated color refnement. In: AAAI, pp. 1904–1910 (2014)
13. Yuan, W., He, K., Guan, D., Zhou, L., Li, C.: Graph kernel based link prediction for signed social networks. Inf. Fusion **46**, 1–10 (2019)
14. Liu, Z., Dong, W., Fu, Y.: Local degree blocking model for missing link prediction in complex networks. Chaos **25**, 013115 (2015)
15. Barabási, A.-L., Albert, R.: Emergence of scaling in random networks. Science **286**(5439), 509–512 (1999)
16. Taheri, A., Gimpel, K., Berger-Wolf, T.: Learning graph representations with recurrent neural network autoencoders. In: KDD DL Day (2018)
17. Zhang, M., Chen, Y.: Link prediction based on graph neural networks. In: Advances in Neural Information Processing Systems, pp. 5165–5175 (2018)
18. Wilkinson, S., Dunn, S., Ma, S.: The vulnerability of the European air traffic network to spatial hazards. Nat. Hazards **60**(3), 1027–1036 (2012)
19. Watts, D.J., Strogatz, S.H.: Collective dynamics of 'small-world' networks. Nature **393**(6684), 440–442 (1998)
20. Spring, N., Mahajan, R., Wetherall, D., Anderson, T.: Measuring ISP topologies with rocketfuel. IEEE/ACM Trans. Networking **12**(1), 2–16 (2004)
21. Meraz, S.: Using time series analysis to measure intermedia agenda-setting influence in traditional media and political blog networks. Journalism Mass Commun. Q. **88**(1), 176–194 (2011)

Accelerating Minimum Temporal Paths Query Based on Dynamic Programming

Mo Li[1], Junchang Xin[1(✉)], Zhiqiong Wang[2], and Huilin Liu[1]

[1] School of Computer Science and Engineering, Northeastern University,
Shenyang, China
xinjunchang@mail.neu.edu.cn
[2] Sino-Dutch Biomedical and Information Engineering School, Northeastern
University, Shenyang, China

Abstract. Temporal path is a fundamental problem in the research of
temporal graphs. The solutions [19] in existing studies are not efficient
enough since they spend more time to scan temporal edges which reflects
connections between two vertices in every time instants. Therefore, in
this paper, we first propose efficient algorithms including FDP and SDP,
using dynamic programming to calculate the shortest path and fastest
path respectively. Then we define a restricted minimum temporal path
for some special requirements, including the restricted earliest-arrival
path and restricted latest-departure path, and present REDP and RLDP
algorithms to solve them. Finally, extensive experiments have demonstrated that our proposed algorithms are effective and efficient over massive real-world temporal graphs.

1 Introduction

In recent years, graph data management and analysis are attracting much attention due to the increasing complexity of online social networks, communication
networks and traffic networks. Existing researches have mainly focus on static
networks, where the edges between vertices are independent on time [8,14]. However, most networks in the real world are actually temporal graphs, where a
vertex communicates with others during a specific time interval. For example,
assume that Fig. 1 is a traffic network, where there is a path with length 1 from
a to b during the period of $[1, 2]$, and a path with length 2 from a to b during
the period of $[3, 4]$.

There are many applications in the real world that can be represented in
temporal graphs [3,6,9,11]. For example, A calls B during time interval $[t_1, t_2]$
in telephone call networks, A works with B during time period $[t_1, t_2]$ in collaboration networks, the road is unimpeded from A to B during time interval $[t_1, t_2]$
in traffic networks. Such examples show that the study of temporal networks is
essential for social networks, gene regulatory networks, transport networks, etc.

In the study of temporal graphs, the "shortest" path is an fundamental
research in advanced graph analysis such as subgraph mining and subgraph

© Springer Nature Switzerland AG 2019
J. Li et al. (Eds.): ADMA 2019, LNAI 11888, pp. 48–62, 2019.
https://doi.org/10.1007/978-3-030-35231-8_4

matching. Meanwhile, there are many application requirements for the shortest path in the real world. Take the traffic networks for example, It is vital for the path to plan how to find the path with least traversal time and least distance from source to the destination. In addition, special requirements for the path planning may be emerged, such as given a necessary path, which also called a restricted path, we are told to calculate the path via the restricted path starting from the source and arriving at the destination earliest, or the path via the restricted path starting from the source and arriving at the destination latest during the specific time interval.

Therefore, we focus on the shortest path of the graph in this paper, and define two types of paths, including **minimum temporal path** and **restricted minimum temporal path**. There are two kinds of paths in minimum temporal path, namely: (1) the fastest path (i.e. the path which costs the minimum elapsed time starting from a given source u, and arriving at the target v); (2) the shortest path (i.e. the path which costs the minimum traversal time starting from a given source u, and arriving at the target v). While in the restricted minimum temporal path, it includes two kinds of temporal paths, namely: (1) the restricted earliest-arrival path (i.e. the path which arrives at the target v earliest leaving from a given source u via a restricted temporal edge); (2) the restricted latest-departure path (i.e. the path which leaves the source u latest arriving at target v via a restricted temporal edge during a specific time interval).

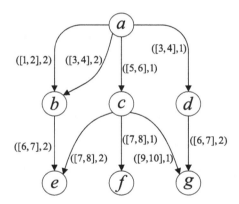

Fig. 1. Temporal graph G

Example 1. Figure 1 shows a temporal graph G. Assume that G is a traffic network, then each vertex represents a site, and the numbers on each edge represent the smoothness time interval and the traversal time of each road. For instance, $([1, 2], 2)$ on the edge from a to b indicates that one can leave a during $[1, 2]$, and the traversal time is 2.

Wu et al. in [19] proposed efficient algorithms to solve the minimum temporal paths with time complexity $O(N + M \log d_{max})$, where N is the number of vertices and M is the number of temporal edges which indicates the connection between two vertices at a specific time point, and d_{max} represents the maximum degree of vertices in temporal graphs. However, in many temporal graphs, such as telephone networks and social networks, most vertices continuously connect with others for a period of time, not just for a time instant, which will lead to the increasing number of temporal edges and the degree of nodes. In that case, the algorithms proposed in [19] are not efficient enough. In order to overcome these shortcomings, we use a new model to store the interactive information of vertices for a time interval rather than a time instant. And then we propose improving algorithms based on dynamic programming to compute the minimum temporal paths with the time complexity $O(|E|)$, where $|E|$ is the number of the temporal edges we defined. In addition, we also define the problem of restricted minimum temporal path, adding restriction on the temporal path, and present efficient algorithms to solve it with time complexity $O(|E|)$. Finally, extensive experiments over real-world datasets prove that our proposed algorithms are more efficient than that of [19].

To summarize, the contributions of our paper are,

- We propose SDP and FDP algorithms to compute the minimum temporal path than that proposed in [19], involving the shortest path and fastest path.
- We also define the problem of restricted minimum temporal path, including the restricted earliest-arrival path and restricted latest-departure path, and devise efficient algorithms to solve them.
- Extensive experiments show that the performance of our proposed algorithms are better than that of [19], and also verify the efficiency and scalability of our proposed algorithms.

2   Problem Definition

Let $G = (V, E)$ be a temporal graph, where V is the set of vertices and E is the set of edges of G. For any edge $e \in E$ can be represented by a 5-tuple $(a, b, t^1, t^2, \lambda)$, where $a, b \in V$, $[t^1, t^2]$ is the time interval in which edge e is active, λ is the traversal time to go from a to b, and $[t^1 + \lambda, t^2 + \lambda]$ is the arrival time.

If the edges in the temporal graphs are undirected, then the leaving time interval $[t^1, t^2]$, the traversal time λ from a to b are the same as these from b to a. For simplicity, we just focus on the directed temporal graphs in this paper since the undirected temporal graphs can be easily to be transferred.

We use the adjacency list to store the temporal edges, and its order follows the order of the starting time t^1. When the starting time of two temporal edges are the same, it follows the order of the ending time t^2.

The temporal path P can be denoted by a set of every nodes in the temporal path, that is $P = < v_1, v_2, ..., v_k >$, where $(v_i, v_{i+1}, t^i, \lambda_i)$ is the i-th edge in the temporal path, and $(t^i + \lambda_i) < t^{i+1}$ are met for each $1 < i < k$. In addition, we also define the starting time of the temporal path P as $start(P) = t^1$, the ending time as $end(P) = t^k + \lambda_k$, the duration time as $dura(P) = end(P) - start(P)$, and the distance as $dist(P) = \sum_{i=1}^{k} \lambda_i$.

In the following, we formally define the concept of minimum temporal paths.

Definition 1 (Minimum Temporal Path). *Given a temporal graph* $G =$ (V, E)*, a source vertex* a*, a target vertex* b *and a query time interval* $[t^\alpha, t^\omega]$*, let* $\mathbf{P}(a, b)$ *be a set of all paths from* a *to* b *within* $[t^\alpha, t^\omega]$*, then we can define the* ***minimum temporal paths****, including:*

Shortest Path: *If* $dist(P') = \min\{dist(P') : P' \in \mathbf{P}(a, b)\}$*, then* P' *is the shortest path, where array dist calculates the total traversal time on all edges in the path.*

Fastest Path: *If* $dura(P') = \min\{dura(P') : P' \in \mathbf{P}(a, b)\}$*, then* P' *is the fastest path where array dura calculates the sum of total traversal time on all edges and total waiting time on all vertices in the path.*

Definition 2 (Restricted Minimum Temporal Path). *Given a temporal graph* $G = (V, E)$*, a source vertex* a*, a target vertex* b*, a query time interval* $[t^\alpha, t^\omega]$*, and a restricted edge* $e_r = (v_j, v_{j+1}, t_j^1, t_j^2, \lambda)$*, let* $\mathbf{P}(a, b)$ *be a set of all paths from* a *to* b *via* e_r *within* $[t^\alpha, t^\omega]$*, then we can define the* ***restricted minimum temporal paths****, including:*

Restricted Earliest-arrival Path: *If* $start(P') = \min\{start(P') : P' \in \mathbf{P}(a, b)\}$*, then* P' *is the shortest path, where array start calculates arrival time on all vertices in the path.*

Restricted Latest-departure Path: *If* $end(P') = \min\{end(P') : P' \in \mathbf{P}(a, b)\}$*, then* P' *is the shortest path, where array end calculates departure time from* u *to arrive every vertices in given time intervals in the path.*

3   Computing Minimum Temporal Paths

3.1   Shortest Path

In order to solve the single-source shortest path problem, this subsection will introduce a SDP method based on two-dimensional dynamic programming, taking into account the shortest path from the source to the rest of the vertices at all times instants. The main idea of SDP algorithm is to use the queue for storing temporal edges, using dynamic programming algorithm to update the shortest path of the target vertex of the top element in queue at different time instants. This process is repeated until the queue is empty.

More concretely, first, the nodes that adjoin to the source vertex in adjacency list are added to the queue, then the nodes are asked to come out of the queue in order, where each element can be represented by $(a, b, t^1, t^2, \lambda)$. In the process of coming out of the queue, we use two-dimensional dynamic programming to update the shortest path from source u to the end-point b of current temporal edge. If the shortest path has changed, then we need to add the unvisited nodes that are adjoined to the start-point a of current temporal edge into the queue. This process is executed repeatedly, until the queue is empty.

In the process of the dynamic programming, in order to avoid updating the shortest path every time, we propose an optimization strategy. When updating the shortest path from source u to b using temporal edge $e = (a, b, t^1, t^2, \lambda)$, only the shortest path in time $[t^1 + \lambda, t^2 + \lambda]$ is updated, meanwhile, the corresponding time of the latest shortest path changes is recorded, instead of updating the entire time period $[t^1 + \lambda, t^\omega]$.

For simplicity, $S[v][j]$ is used to describe the shortest path from source u to target v at time j, the recursion formula of the two-dimensional dynamic programming is shown as Eq. (1).

$$S[b][j] = \min(S[b][j], S[a][j - \lambda] + \lambda), \forall t^1 \leq j \leq t^2 \qquad (1)$$

Equation (1) shows that the shortest path from source u to b at time j is the smaller value between the original outcome and the shortest path from source u via node a to b.

The SDP algorithm is shown as Algorithm 1. First, we use array $S[v][j]$ to save the shortest path from source u to v at time j, then conduct initialization (Line 1). Initialize $L_u = 0, \forall u \in V$, which means the last changing time of shortest path of every vertices (Line 2). Meanwhile, we use a queue Q to save temporal edges (Line 3). In the initial state, we add the nodes that adjoined to the source u to Q (Line 4). After that, if Q is not empty, then we conduct the dynamic programming process (Line 5–14). In the process of dynamic programming, we dequeue the top element of Q and use it to update the shortest path from source u to b in time interval $[t^1 + \lambda, t^2 + \lambda]$. During the process, we first update the shortest path from source u to b at current time $S[b][j]$ according to the shortest path $S[b][L_b]$ at the latest changing time L_b, and record the new last changing time (Lines 7–10). Then we will decide whether the value of $S[b][j]$ need to be updated based on Eq. (1). If the value is updated, the latest changing time is recorded and the unvisited node adjoined to a is added to Q (Lines 11–14). This process is executed repeatedly until Q is empty, then the shortest paths from source u to each vertex at every moments are returned (Line 15).

Time Complexity: This algorithm scans all the edges and this process consumes $O(|E|)$. In the process of scanning each edge, the shortest path in the time interval $[t^1 + \lambda, t^2 + \lambda]$ from source u to the end-point of the temporal edge is updated, which takes $O(|I_{avg}|)$, where $|I_{avg}|$ is the average length of time interval. So the complexity of the entire algorithm is $O(|E| |I_{avg}|)$. Note that $|I_{avg}|$ is always a small constant in practice.

3.2 Fastest Path

In order to solve the problem of single-source fastest path, this section introduces a FDP algorithm based on a two-dimensional dynamic programming method, taking into account the fastest path from the source u to the rest of the vertices at all time instants. The main idea of FDP algorithm is similar to SDP algorithm, the difference lies in the dynamic programming process. Specifically, during the entire dynamic programming, each temporal edge $e = (a, b, t^1, t^2, \lambda)$, the fastest

---

Algorithm 1: SDP: computing shortest path

---

    input : A temporal Graph $G = (V, E)$, source vertex u, time interval $[t^\alpha, t^\omega]$

    output: the shortest path from source u to every other vertex within time
              interval $[t^\alpha, t^\omega]$

1 Initialize $S[u][j] = 0, \forall j \leq t^\omega$, and $S[v][j] = 0, \forall v \in V \backslash u, j \leq t^\omega$

2 Initialize $L_u = 0, \forall u \in V$

3 Initialize a queue Q

4 Push the adjacency with u during the time interval $[t^\alpha, t^\omega]$ into Q

5 **while** Q *is not empty* **do**

6   Pop the top element in Q assigning to P, which can be denoted by
        $(a, b, t_1, t_2, \lambda)$

7   **for** $i = t^1 + \lambda ... t^2 + \lambda$ **do**

8   **if** $S[b][j] > S[b][L_b]$ **then**

9            $S[b][j] = S[b][L_b]$

10           $L_b = j$

11   **if** $S[b][j] > S[a][j - \lambda][\lambda]$ **then**

12            $S[b][j] = S[a][j - \lambda][\lambda]$

13           $L_b = j$

14   Push the unvisited adjacency with a during the time interval $[t^\alpha, t^\omega]$
          into Q

15 **return** $S[v][j]$ for all $v \in V$

---

path from source u to b can be updated by the path from source u via a to b. For
simplicity, $F[v][j]$ is used to represent the fastest path from source u to v at time
j. The recursion formula in dynamic programming is as shown in formula (2).

$$F[b][j] = \min(F[b][j], F[a][j - \lambda] + \lambda), \forall t^1 \leq j \leq t^2 \qquad (2)$$

Equation (2) shows the length of fastest path from source u to b at time j is
the minimum of the length of its original calculation and the fastest path length
from source u to target b through a.

In addition, after the fastest path from source u to target b at time j is
determined, the fastest path at each subsequent time is equal to the fastest path
at the previous time plus 1, i.e. $F[b][j] = F[b][j-1]+1, \forall j > t^2$, so as to perform
a new fastest path update later. This is because the fastest path calculates the
elapsed time from source u to each vertex, which includes not only the time
spent on the path, but also the latency at the vertex.

However, it takes a lot of time to traverse the entire query time each
time, so we adopt an optimization strategy to replace scanning sequentially
the entire query time by recording the last changing time of the fastest path.
Specifically, when the fastest path of b is updated by using the temporal edge
$e = (a, b, t^1, t^2, \lambda)$, only need update the fastest path in the time interval
$[t^1 + \lambda, t^2 + \lambda]$, and record the last changing time, instead of updating the
entire time period $[t^1 + \lambda, t^\omega]$. When computing the fastest path from u to b
by $(a, b, t^1, t^2, \lambda)$, the original fastest path from u to b at current time j should

---

Algorithm 2: FDP: computing fastest path

---

    input : A temporal Graph $G = (V, E)$, source vertex u, time interval $[t^\alpha, t^\omega]$
    output: the fastest path from source u to every other vertex within time
           interval $[t^\alpha, t^\omega]$

  1 Initialize $F[u][j] = 0, \forall j \leq t^\omega$, and $F[v][j] = 0, \forall v \in V\backslash u, j \leq t^\omega$
  2 Initialize $L_u = 0, \forall u \in V$
  3 Initialize a queue Q
  4 Push the adjacency with u during the time interval $[t^\alpha, t^\omega]$ into Q
  5 **while** Q *is not empty* **do**
  6   Pop the top element in Q assigning to P, which can be denoted by
        $(a, b, t_1, t_2, \lambda)$
  7   **for** $i = t^1 + \lambda...t^2 + \lambda$ **do**
  8   **if** $F[b][j] > (F[b][L_b] + L_b - j)$ **then**
  9 $F[b][j] = (F[b][L_b] + L_b - j)$
 10 $L_b = j$
 11   **if** $F[b][j] > F[a][j - \lambda][\lambda]$ **then**
 12 $F[b][j] = F[a][j - \lambda][\lambda]$
 13 $L_b = j$
 14   Push the unvisited adjacency with a during the time interval $[t^\alpha, t^\omega]$
                into Q

 15 **return** $S[v][j]$ for all $v \in V$

---

be calculated by the fastest path of b at last changing time L_b and the waiting time, which is the difference between j and last changing time L_b. The specific algorithm is shown in Algorithm 2. In addition, the time complexity of FDP algorithm is similar to that of SDP algorithm.

4 Computing Restricted Minimum Temporal Paths

4.1 Restricted Earliest-Arrival Path

In this subsection, we first present an EDP algorithm to solve the earliest-arrival path problem, then we devise a REDP algorithm to compute the restricted earliest-arrival path.

The main idea of EDP algorithm is to use the queue for storing temporal edges, updating the earliest-arrival path from the source to each node during dequeuing process. Specifically, we can compute the earliest-arrival path by scanning all the temporal edges $(a, b, t^1, t^2, \lambda)$, and the earliest-arrival path from source u to b can be updated by the path from source u via a to b.

The whole algorithm is shown in Algorithm 3. Firstly, an initialized array **e** is used to record the earliest-arrival path from u to each node (Line 1). Then we initialize a queue Q for storing the temporal edges (Line 2) and join the adjacency nodes with u to the Q (Line 3). If Q is not empty, dequeue the head element which is a temporal edge $(a, b, t^1, t^2, \lambda)$ (Line 5). We also use t to record

---

Algorithm 3: EDP Algorithm

---

input : $G = (V, E)$, source node u, time interval $[t^\alpha, t^\omega]$

output: the earliest-arrival time from u to every other vertex within $[t^\alpha, t^\omega]$

1 Initialize $e[u]=0$, and $e[v] = \infty$ for all $v \in V\backslash\{u\}$

2 Initialize a queue Q

3 push the adjacency with u during the time interval $[t^\alpha, t^\omega]$ into Q

4 **while** Q *is not empty* **do**

5 $\quad$ Pop the top element in Q assigning to P, denoted by $(a, b, t^1, t^2, \lambda)$

6 $\quad$ t is the minimum number larger than t^α within $[t^1, t^2]$

7 $\quad$ **if** $t \geq e[a]$ *and* $t + \lambda < e[b]$ **then**

8 $\quad\quad$ $e[b] = t + \lambda$

9 $\quad\quad$ Push the unvisited node adjacency with a within $[t^\alpha, t^\omega]$ into Q

10 **return** $e[v]$ for all $v \in V$

---

the minimum number larger than t^α within $[t^1, t^2]$ (Line 6). Then, we continue to judge whether the current earliest-arrival time from source u to b is greater than that from source u via a to b. If so, update the earliest-arrival path from source u to b and add the unvisited vertices adjoining with a into the Q (Line 7–9). This process is repeated until the queue is empty. Finally, we get the earliest-arrival path of each vertex leaving from the source u (Line 10). Obviously, the time complexity is $O(|E|)$ since all the edges will be scanned once.

Algorithm 4: REDP Algorithm

---

input : $G = (V, E)$, source node u, time interval $[t^\alpha, t^\omega]$, a restricted edge
$\quad\quad e_r = (v_j, v_{j+1}, t_j^1, t_j^2, \lambda)$

output: the restricted earliest-arrival time from u to every other vertex within
$\quad\quad [t^\alpha, t^\omega]$

1 Initialize $e[u]=0$, and $e[v] = \infty$ for all $v \in V\backslash\{u\}$

2 **if** $t_j^1 < t^\alpha$ *or* $t_j^2 > t^\omega$ **then**

3 $\quad$ **return** $e[v]$ for all $v \in V$

4 $\mathbf{E}=EDP(G, u, [t^\alpha, t_j^1])$

5 **if** $E[v_j] = \infty$ **then**

6 $\quad$ **return** $e[v] = \infty$ for all $v \in V\backslash\{u\}$

7 Initialize $e[u]=0$, and $e[v] = \infty$ for all $v \in V\backslash\{u\}$

8 $\mathbf{E}=EDP(G, v_{j+1}, [t_j^2, t^\omega])$

9 **return** $e[v]$ for all $v \in V$

The main idea of the REDP algorithm is to take the restricted edge $e_r = (v_j, v_{j+1}, t_j^1, t_j^2, \lambda)$ as the key point of the restricted earliest-arrival path, judge whether u can arrive at the starting point of restricted edge v_j no later than t_j^1, and then compute the single-source earliest-arrival path from v_{j+1} later than

t_j^2. The whole algorithm is shown as Algorithm 4. Firstly, we use an initialized array **e** to record the restricted earliest-arrival path from u to each node (Line 1). Then we judge whether the lasting time of the restricted edge is within time interval $[t^\alpha, t^\omega]$, if not, the process is break and return the initialized array **e** (Line 2–3). After that, the EDP algorithm is invoked to calculate the earliest-arrival time from u to v_j (Line 4). If there is no path from u to v_j with its arriving time less than t_j^1, the process will be interpreted and return infinity for the reversed earliest-arrival time of all the nodes (Line 5–6). Otherwise, the restricted earliest-arrival time from u to every other nodes within $[t^\alpha, t^\omega]$ will be transferred to a solved problem that the earliest-arrival from v_{j+1} to every other nodes within $[t_j^2, t^\omega]$, so we also invoke the EDP algorithm to calculate it (Line 7-8). Finally, the restricted earliest-arrival time from u will be returned (Line 9). Obviously, the time complexity is $O(|E|)$ since all the edges will be only scanned once.

4.2   Restricted Latest-Departure Path

In order to solve the restricted latest-departure path problem, this subsection introduces a LDP algorithm to compute the latest-departure path and a RLDP algorithm to compute the restricted latest-departure path. Due to the space limitation, we just introduce the main ideas of these algorithms.

The main idea of LDP algorithm is similar to that of EDP algorithm. We use a stack for storing temporal edges, updating the latest-departure path that arrives at each vertex during the process of poping up the top element until the stack is empty. Meanwhile, the current latest-departure time from source u to b will be updated by the latest-departure time from u to b via a if it can get a larger figure.

The main idea of the RLDP algorithm takes after that of REDP algorithm. It also takes the restricted edge $e_r = (v_j, v_{j+1}, t_j^1, t_j^2, \lambda)$ as the key point of the restricted latest-departure path, calculate the latest-departure path from u to every other nodes within $[t^\alpha, t_j^1]$, and then computes the latest-departure time from v_{j+1} to every other nodes in the temporal graph.

5   Experimental Evaluation

5.1   Experimental Environment and Datasets

The algorithms are implemented in C++, and the experiments are performed on a Windows 10 machine with Inter Core i7-6700 3.40 GHz CPU and 8 GB memory. The time costs reported here are calculated by system clock.

The data used in this experiment are obtained from the Koblenz Large Network Collection[1], and 12 real data sets are selected as the subjects of this experiment, which are the similar with that of [19]. Table 1 summarizes the parameters of the experimental data, respectively labeled with the number of vertices $|V|$,

---

[1] http://konect.uni-koblenz.de/.

and the number of edges $|E|$ in the temporal network G and the number of edges $|E_s|$ of the corresponding static graph G_s. In addition, $|T_G|$ represents the number of distinct time instances, $|I_{avg}|$ represents the average of the duration of temporal edges.

Table 1. Real temporal graphs (K $= 10^3$)

Dataset	$|V|$	$|E_s|$	$|E|$	$|T_G|$	$|I_{avg}|$	$|E_s^{1-pass}|$	$|E^{1-pass}|$
arxiv	28K	63K	92K	2337	100	6297K	9194K
dblp	1103K	845K	1196K	70	10	8451K	11957K
elec	8K	520	535	101012	200	104K	107K
enron	87K	1600	5675	213218	200	320K	1135K
epin	132K	17K	17K	939	50	841K	841K
fb	64K	4K	6K	736675	200	817K	1270K
flickr	2303K	1657K	1657K	134	20	33140K	33140K
digg	30K	850	860	8261	100	85K	86K
slash	51K	650	700	89862	200	130K	140K
conflict	118K	10K	15K	273909	200	2054K	2918K
growth	1871K	400K	400K	2198	100	39953K	39953K
youtube	3224K	469K	611K	203	20	9377K	12224K

To evaluate the performance of our proposed algorithms for computing single-source minimum temporal paths, we compare the methods in [19] called one-pass algorithms. Since the duration of temporal edges doesn't exist, the experimental data should be modified to apply to one-pass algorithm, and the number of edges are shown in column 7 and column 8. Meanwhile, the algorithm in [19] cannot be used to solve the restricted minimum temporal path problem, so we modify it and compare with it.

Since the shortest paths and the fastest paths are influenced by the different input time interval $[t^\alpha, t^\omega]$, in order to further test the stability of our algorithms, the experiment will query the shortest paths and fastest paths on five different time intervals, I_1 to I_5. We set $I_1 = [0, |T_G|]$, where $|T_G|$ is shown in Table 1. For each I_i, $\forall 1 \leq i \leq 4$, we divide I_i into two equal sub-intervals so that $I_i + 1$ is the first sub-interval of I_i.

5.2   Results

Taken the average of the many groups of experiments, the results obtained on the real data sets are shown in Table 2. Table 2 shows the running time that our proposed algorithms, one-pass algorithms and transformation methods in [19] spend on computing the shortest path and fastest path, restricted earliest-arrival

Table 2. Running time in seconds

Datasets	Shortest			Fastest			Earliest		Latest	
	1-pass	Trans	SDP	1-pass	Trans	FDP	1-pass	REDP	1-pass	RLDP
arxiv	0.1673	0.1433	**0.1059**	0.3969	**0.0565**	0.1013	0.0119	**0.0003**	0.0121	**0.0005**
dblp	0.6706	1.671	**0.2635**	0.7842	0.4654	**0.2794**	0.0449	**0.0005**	0.0407	**0.0009**
elec	0.0013	0.0313	**0.0009**	0.0017	0.0048	**0.0008**	0.0003	**0.0001**	0.0003	**0.0001**
enron	0.0329	0.3469	**0.0103**	0.1093	0.1053	**0.0194**	0.0023	**0.0008**	0.0023	**0.0010**
epin	0.0102	0.0928	**0.0077**	0.0155	0.0302	**0.0071**	0.0014	**0.0002**	0.0019	**0.0003**
fb	0.0400	0.4816	**0.0155**	0.0531	0.1558	**0.0104**	0.0038	**0.0015**	0.0041	**0.0017**
flickr	1.2522	5.1928	**0.9810**	2.6368	1.7497	**1.0010**	0.0907	**0.0059**	0.1356	**0.0067**
digg	0.0008	0.0177	**0.0004**	**0.0009**	0.0018	0.0013	0.0002	**0.0001**	0.0002	**0.0001**
slash	0.0032	0.0487	**0.0016**	0.0041	0.0125	**0.0016**	0.0006	**0.0003**	0.0006	**0.0003**
conflict	**0.0520**	0.7887	0.0614	**0.1013**	0.3264	0.1519	0.0055	**0.0018**	0.0057	**0.0021**
growth	2.8376	20.6097	**1.5571**	4.5404	7.718	**1.8468**	0.1794	**0.0961**	0.1936	**0.0986**
youtube	0.612	3.1188	**0.2243**	0.8317	0.8199	**0.1563**	0.0559	**0.0016**	0.061	**0.0018**

path and restricted latest-departure path leaving from the randomly selected source point arriving at the rest of vertices in given time interval.

By comparing the running time that our proposed DP algorithms and one-pass algorithms spend on computing the shortest path and fastest path, restricted earliest-arrival path and restricted latest-departure path, it is obvious that the algorithms we proposed takes less time than one-pass algorithms. This is because the time complexity of our algorithm is $O(|E|\,|I_{avg}|)$. The time complexity is closed to one-pass algorithms, but our algorithms is using a time interval, rather than a time instant, therefore the value of $|E|$ is much smaller than that of one-pass algorithm. Meanwhile, $|I_{avg}|$ is also a very small constant, so our proposed algorithms cost less time.

By comparing the running time taken by our algorithms and the transformation methods in calculating minimum temporal paths, we can find that the transformation methods sometimes are slightly faster than our algorithms, but the memory costs by the transformation methods are much larger. Table 3 shows the memory costs comparison between our algorithms and the transformation methods when storing the temporal graphs. It can be found that although the our algorithms are slightly slower than the transformation methods sometimes, it can save a lot of memory space.

Since SDP and FDP algorithms are affected by the length of the query time interval $[t^\alpha, t^\omega]$ to some extent, we respectively use different input time intervals to test our algorithms and one-pass algorithms. The experimental results are shown in Tables 4 and 5. By comparing the running time of the two algorithms, we can find that they are both affected by the length of the time interval, and when the length of input time interval becomes smaller, the running time is significantly reduced. This can be explained that with the reduction of length time interval, the number of temporal edges $|E|$ are decreased. Comparing our algorithms and one-pass algorithms, it can be easily found that the time costs of SDP and FDP algorithms are shorter than one-pass algorithms, which supports the stability and value of promotion for the proposed algorithm.

Table 3. Size of the storage model (K $= 10^3$)

Datasets	Trans		DP	
	$|V|$	$|E|$	$|V|$	$|E|$
arxiv	433K	9759K	28K	92K
dblp	5553K	16977K	1103K	1196K
elec	212K	313K	8K	535
enron	1367K	2505K	87K	5675
epin	482K	1219K	132K	17K
fb	1637K	3037K	64K	6K
flickr	12600K	44358K	2303K	1657K
digg	172K	233K	30K	860
slash	273K	381K	51K	700
conflict	3191K	6009K	118K	15K
growth	34815K	77196K	1871K	400K
youtube	11498K	21140K	3224K	611K

Table 4. Running time for varying intervals (shortest path)

Datasets	I_1		I_2		I_3		I_4		I_5	
	1-pass	SDP	1-pass	SDP	1-pass	SDP	1-pass	SDP	1-pass	SDP
arxiv	0.1158	0.0543	0.0037	0.0019	0.0002	0	0	0	0	0
dblp	0.144	0.0965	0.0004	0.0001	0	0	0	0	0	0
elec	0.0006	0.0004	0.0002	0.0001	0.0001	0	0	0	0	0
enron	0.0075	0.0041	0.0031	0.0014	0.0011	0.0002	0.0004	0	0.0001	0
epin	0.004	0.0019	0.003	0.0014	0.0024	0.0015	0.0018	0.001	0.0015	0.0001
fb	0.0095	0.0054	0.0042	0.0023	0.0024	0.0014	0.0017	0.0008	0.0013	0.0001
flickr	0.4711	0.3126	0.2307	0.1754	0.1405	0.0807	0.0496	0.0107	0.0422	0.0098
digg	0.0003	0.0002	0.0001	0.0001	0.0001	0	0	0	0	0
slash	0.001	0.0008	0.0003	0.0002	0.0001	0	0	0	0	0
conflict	0.0176	0.0127	0.006	0.0028	0.002	0.0009	0.0005	0.0001	0.0002	0
growth	1.3652	1.0008	0.0176	0.0095	0.0018	0.0009	0.0001	0.0001	0	0
youtube	0.1172	0.0807	0.0291	0.0108	0.0194	0.0057	0.0099	0.0009	0.0087	0.0037

6 Related Work

Temporal graphs have become an advanced research hotspot in recent years. One of the hottest topic in temporal graphs is the problem of computing temporal paths [12]. Xuan et al. [21] proposed graph theoretic model to compute shortest journeys, foremost journeys and fastest journeys by adoption of Dijkstra's strategy. Huang et al. [19] focused on traversal problems in a temporal graph, and proposed efficient algorithms to compute the temporal DFS and BFS.

Table 5. Running time for varying intervals (fastest path)

Datasets	I_1		I_2		I_3		I_4		I_5	
	1-pass	SDP	1-pass	SDP	1-pass	SDP	1-pass	SDP	1-pass	SDP
arxiv	0.0978	0.0512	0.0036	0.002	0.0002	0	0	0	0	0
dblp	0.152	0.0917	0.0004	0.0002	0	0	0	0	0	0
elec	0.0006	0.0004	0.0002	0.0001	0.0001	0	0	0	0	0
enron	0.0069	0.0043	0.0031	0.0017	0.0012	0.0003	0.0004	0	0.0001	0
epin	0.0049	0.0021	0.0036	0.0016	0.0027	0.0014	0.0019	0.0011	0.0015	0.0001
fb	0.0093	0.0059	0.0043	0.0028	0.0024	0.0013	0.0016	0.0009	0.0013	0.0001
flickr	0.5015	0.3751	0.2362	0.1864	0.1431	0.0813	0.0494	0.0111	0.0421	0.0099
digg	0.0003	0.0002	0.0001	0.0001	0.0001	0	0	0	0	0
slash	0.0011	0.0009	0.0003	0.0002	0.0001	0	0	0	0	0
conflict	0.0227	0.0134	0.0072	0.0031	0.0022	0.0009	0.0006	0.0001	0.0002	0
growth	1.4803	1.001	0.0177	0.0096	0.0018	0.0009	0.0001	0.0001	0	0
youtube	0.1204	0.0856	0.0292	0.0109	0.0195	0.058	0.01	0.0009	0.0088	0.0038

Wu et al. [19] studied on the "shortest path" in temporal graphs, and formally defined the minimum temporal graphs, and proposed one-pass algorithms to compute them. The one-pass algorithms are not efficient enough, since are influenced by the number of temporal edges and the degree of nodes, as the temporal edges reflecting the interaction of every two vertices at specific time points, the algorithms are inefficient when there are enormous temporal edges. To overcome these shortcomings, our paper have proposed a new temporal storage model, using the temporal edges reflecting the interaction of every two vertices during time intervals. At the same time, algorithms based on dynamic programming are proposed to compute minimum temporal paths with linear time complexity.

We also briefly discuss many other applications of temporal paths. In [13], a temporal notion of "distance" in the underlying social network is proposed, which is similar to the definition of latest-departure (without the information of λ for the temporal edges). Tang et al. [17] applied earliest-arrival time to define a new temporal distance metrics to quantify and compare the speed of information diffusion processes in temporal graphs. Tang et al. [18] focused on the temporal distance metrics to capture characteristic of time-varying graphs. Meanwhile, network reachability were also computed. In [16], the existence of a path during some time intervals are used to ask the historical reachability of evolving graphs. In [20], temporal paths were applied to study the reachability and time-based path queries in a temporal graph. Three kinds of temporal queries were proposed in social networks, aiming to explore temporal dimension in users, relationships and social activities [7].

However, the advanced applications based on temporal paths are also attracting lot of attentions. The problem of finding the highest-scoring temporal subgraphs in a dynamic network, called Heaviest Dynamic Subgraph (HDS) were explored in [4]. In [23], they investigate how to query temporal graphs and treat query formulation as a discriminative temporal graph mining problem. The problem of mining a set of diversified temporal subgraph patterns from a temporal graph based on temporal paths were studied in [22]. A fast incremental approach for continuous frequent subgraph mining problem on a single large evolving graph was proposed in [1]. More comprehensive surveys on temporal graphs are investigated in [2,5,10,15].

7   Conclusion

We present improving algorithms based on DP with linear time complexity to solve the shortest path and fastest path in temporal graph. Moreover, we also define the problem of restricted minimum temporal path, including restricted earliest-arrival path and restricted latest-departure path, and devise efficient algorithms to calculate them. Finally, experiments on a wide range of real-world temporal graphs show that our algorithms are more efficient than the existing algorithms in [19].

Acknowledgement. This work was supported in part by the National Natural Science Foundation of China (Nos. 61472069, 61402089 and U1401256), China Postdoctoral Science Foundation (Nos. 2019T120216 and 2018M641705), the Fundamental Research Funds for the Central Universities (Nos. N161602003, N180408019 and N180101028), the Open Program of Neusoft Institute of Intelligent Healthcare Technology, Co. Ltd. (No. NIMRIOP1802) and the fund of Acoustics Science and Technology Laboratory.

References

1. Abdelhamid, E., Canim, M., Sadoghi, M., Bhattacharjee, B., Chang, Y.C., Kalnis, P.: Incremental frequent subgraph mining on large evolving graphs. TKDE **29**(12), 2710–2723 (2017)
2. Aggarwal, C., Subbian, K.: Evolutionary network analysis: a survey. ACM Comput. Surv. (CSUR) **47**(1), 10 (2014)
3. Alduaiji, N., Datta, A., Li, J.: Influence propagation model for clique-based community detection in social networks. IEEE Trans. Comput. Soc. Syst. **5**(2), 563–575 (2018)
4. Bogdanov, P., Mongiovì, M., Singh, A.K.: Mining heavy subgraphs in time-evolving networks. In: ICDM, pp. 81–90 (2011)
5. Casteigts, A., Flocchini, P., Quattrociocchi, W., Santoro, N.: Time-varying graphs and dynamic networks. Int. J. Parallel Emergent Distrib. Syst. **27**(5), 387–408 (2012)
6. Chen, L., Liu, C., Zhou, R., Li, J., Yang, X., Wang, B.: Maximum co-located community search in large scale social networks. PVLDB **11**(10), 1233–1246 (2018)
7. Chen, X., Zhang, C., Ge, B., Xiao, W.: Temporal social network: Storage, indexing and query processing. In: EDBT/ICDT Workshops (2016)
8. Chen, Y., Chen, Y.: An efficient algorithm for answering graph reachability queries. In: ICDE, pp. 893–902 (2008)

9. Ghosh, B., Ali, M.E., Choudhury, F.M., Apon, S.H., Sellis, T., Li, J.: The flexible socio spatial group queries. PVLDB **12**(2), 99–111 (2018)
10. Holme, P., Saramäki, J.: Temporal networks. Phys. Rep. **519**(3), 97–125 (2012)
11. Kong, X., Li, M., Li, J., Tian, K., Hu, X., Feng, X.: CoPFun: an urban co-occurrence pattern mining scheme based on regional function discovery. World Wide Web J., 1–26 (2018)
12. Kosmatopoulos, A., Giannakopoulou, K., Papadopoulos, A.N., Tsichlas, K.: An overview of methods for handling evolving graph sequences. In: Karydis, I., Sioutas, S., Triantafillou, P., Tsoumakos, D. (eds.) ALGOCLOUD 2015. LNCS, vol. 9511, pp. 181–192. Springer, Cham (2016). https://doi.org/10.1007/978-3-319-29919-8_14
13. Kossinets, G., Kleinberg, J., Watts, D.: The structure of information pathways in a social communication network. In: SIGKDD, pp. 435–443 (2008)
14. Maleki, S., Nguyen, D., Lenharth, A., Padua, D., Pingali, K.: DSMR: a shared and distributed memory algorithm for single-source shortest path problem. In: ACM SIGPLAN Symposium on Principles and Practice of Parallel Programming, p. 39 (2016)
15. Müller-Hannemann, M., Schulz, F., Wagner, D., Zaroliagis, C.: Timetable information: models and algorithms. In: Geraets, F., Kroon, L., Schoebel, A., Wagner, D., Zaroliagis, C.D. (eds.) Algorithmic Methods for Railway Optimization. LNCS, vol. 4359, pp. 67–90. Springer, Heidelberg (2007). https://doi.org/10.1007/978-3-540-74247-0_3
16. Semertzidis, K., Pitoura, E., Lillis, K.: TimeReach: historical reachability queries on evolving graphs. In: EDBT, pp. 121–132 (2015)
17. Tang, J., Musolesi, M., Mascolo, C., Latora, V.: Temporal distance metrics for social network analysis. In: Proceedings of the 2nd ACM Workshop on Online Social Networks, pp. 31–36 (2009)
18. Tang, J., Musolesi, M., Mascolo, C., Latora, V.: Characterising temporal distance and reachability in mobile and online social networks. ACM SIGCOMM Comput. Commun. Rev. **40**(1), 118–124 (2010)
19. Wu, H., Cheng, J., Huang, S., Ke, Y., Lu, Y., Xu, Y.: Path problems in temporal graphs. PVLDB **7**(9), 721–732 (2014)
20. Wu, H., Huang, Y., Cheng, J., Li, J., Ke, Y.: Reachability and time-based path queries in temporal graphs. In: ICDE, pp. 145–156 (2016)
21. Xuan, B.B., Ferreira, A., Jarry, A.: Computing shortest, fastest, and foremost journeys in dynamic networks. Int. J. Found. Comput. Sci. **14**(02), 267–285 (2003)
22. Yang, Y., Yan, D., Wu, H., Cheng, J., Zhou, S., Lui, J.: Diversified temporal subgraph pattern mining. In: SIGKDD, pp. 1965–1974 (2016)
23. Zong, B., et al.: Behavior query discovery in system-generated temporal graphs. PVLDB **9**(4), 240–251 (2015)

Multiple Query Point Based Collective Spatial Keyword Querying

Yun Li[1](✉), Ziheng Wang[1], Jing Chen[1], Fei Wang[2], and Jiajie Xu[1]

[1] Soochow University, GanJiang East Road, Suzhou 215006, China
sglxx4206@126.com
[2] Siemens Corporate Technology, Suzhou, China

Abstract. Spatial keyword search is a useful technique to enable users find the spatial web object they prefer. Since they objects spatially close to the query point may not fulfill all query objectives, collective spatial keyword query aims to retrieve a group of objects that can cover all required query keywords while properly located in spatial. However in some cases, the querying may be subject to several people in different locations together, and the returned group of objects should not only cover all of their objectives, but also optimal regarding to all of the related people. To this end, this paper studies the problem of multiple query point based collective spatial keyword querying (MCSKQ). Two novel algorithms, HCQ and BCQ, are proposed to support efficient collective query processing w.r.t. multiple query points. The experimental results and related analysis show that MCSKQ has good efficiency and accuracy performance.

Keywords: Spatial textual object · CSKQ · Multiple queries · Location-based services · Collaborative search

1 Introduction

Spatial keyword query is known as a basic query for location based services. It takes a user location and a set of user specified keywords as input, and returns the spatial web objects that have high spatial and textual relevance to these arguments. In recent years, the study of spatial keyword query has received great attention from both industry and research communities.

Collective spatial keyword query (CSKQ), which aims to retrieve a set of the objects that collectively cover users queried keywords with the minimum cost, has attracted lots of attention from academia [3,10] more recently. However CSKQ considers one query point only, but in many cases, the query may subject to several users in different locations (i.e. multiple query points). This problem needs to find a set V of spatial keyword objects which should meet the following two requirements: (1) all returned objects are supposed close to each other, so that users can visit all of them with less travel cost; (2) the returned objects are supposed to be close to the query points for the same reason.

© Springer Nature Switzerland AG 2019
J. Li et al. (Eds.): ADMA 2019, LNAI 11888, pp. 63–78, 2019.
https://doi.org/10.1007/978-3-030-35231-8_5

Example 1. Figure. 1(a) shows the spatial distribution of the set of objects marked as green points and the queries q1, q2 and q3 marked as yellow triangles, and Table 1 describes the keyword corresponding to objects in Fig. 1(a). As shown in Fig. 1(a), there are three users in q1 and q2 and q3 position respectively who need to gather together and go to restaurants, markets and banks. We want to find a set of objects as a candidate for their goals. If three people query through the existing CSKQ technology respectively, the result sets of the people in position q1, q2 and q3 are $\{o_2, o_5, o_7\}$, $\{o_5, o_6, o_9\}$ and $\{o_5, o_8, o_9\}$ respectively. The query processing is carried out w.r.t. each query location independently. But for all users as a group together, none of them are acceptable result for users as a group, since at least one user would have very high travel cost to visit the places. From Fig. 1(a) and Table 1, it can be observed that $\{o_4, o_5, o_7\}$ and $\{o_2, o_3, o_6\}$ can meet all the query requirements of multiple users. The set $\{o_4, o_5, o_7\}$ can guarantee that all three users travel less distances, spend less time to reach their destinations. Obviously, such a result set is more reasonable.

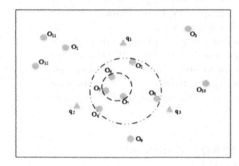 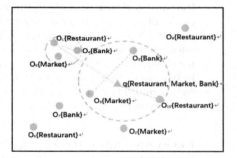

Fig. 1. MCSKQ and CSKQ (Color figure online)

In the above example we used the CSKQ method. Give a simple example ofCSKQ. As shown in Fig. 1(b), both result sets $\{o_3, o_9, o_{10}\}$ and $\{o_1, o_4, o_5\}$ are able to satisfy the query q, but objects in $\{o_3, o_9, o_{10}\}$ are more dispersed. The objects in returned are supposed to have high spatial coherence (meaning less travel cost to visit all locations of the objects), the set $\{o_1, o_4, o_5\}$ should have higher priority to be returned.

However, query processing of MCSKQ also faces many technical challenges. First, because of the size of dataset and explosive growth in the number of combinations, the query will face a huge search space; secondly, due to the combination of the two dimensions of spatial and textual, the management of spatial keyword objects requires an appropriate hybrid index structure. Besides, the distance measure is supposed to find a good balance of several factors, such as the spatial distance to query point, keyword similarity and spatial coherence of objects in result set. In addition, since multiple query points are involved in MCSKQ, it

Table 1. The keyword description of objects

Object	Keyword	Object	Keyword
o_1	Market	o_2	Market
o_3	Market	o_4	Restaurant
o_5	Market	o_6	Bank
o_7	Bank	o_8	Bank
o_9	Restaurant	o_{10}	Restaurant
o_{11}	Bank	o_{12}	Restaurant

is more difficult to find a collect of objects to be close to all query points while preserving high spatial coherence. All above issues causes pruning to be difficult and thus incurs high computational overhead for MCSKQ processing.

To solve this problem, we design a query-sensitive algorithm based on existing knowledge. This multi-query-sensitive algorithm retrieves IR-Tree with multiple locations as entrances to prune the search space and taking the problem of result sets combination into account. This algorithm aims to find a spatial keyword object set with minimal distance cost.

In brief, the key contributions of this paper are threefold:

- We propose a new type of query, called multiple query point based collective spatial keyword queries, that find groups of objects that collectively satisfy queries.
- We propose three kinds of query algorithms. These algorithms use the spatial keyword index structure to prune the search space, and finally get the result set that can meet all the queries conditions.
- We conduct comprehensive experiments on real datasets to verify the accuracy and efficiency of our algorithms.

The rest of this paper is organized as follows. Section 2 reviews related work. Section 3 formalizes our problem, and presents the index structure employed to store the objects. In Sect. 4, we elaborate three algorithms. Considerable experimental results and our findings are reported in Sect. 5. Finally, Sect. 6 concludes the paper.

2 Related Work

In this section, we survey the existing work related to spatial keyword queries and query models for spatial keyword query.

2.1 Spatial Keyword Queries

Spatial keyword query is a core technology in LBS [3,4,6,18], which has been intensively studied and applied in recent years. Many types of spatial keyword queries have been proposed in the literature. Three of them which are namely the Boolean kNN query, the top-k kNN query, and the Boolean range query received particular attention. There are some comprehensive surveys [1,5].

The Boolean kNN query aims to retrieve the k objects nearest to the user's current location (represented by a point) such that each object's text description contains the query keywords. The query keywords in the Boolean kNN queries are used as a hard constraint. The top-k kNN query [11,12] aims to retrieve the k objects with the highest ranking scores, measured as a combination of their distance to the query location and the relevance of their text description to the query keywords. The query keywords in the top-k kNN queries are used as a soft constraint. The IR-tree index structure adopted by us for NN queries and range queries was proposed in [6]. And it considers both the spatial proximity and the textual information of the objects. The Boolean range query aims to retrieve all objects whose text description contains the query keywords and whose location is within a given query region of the query location. The query keywords in the Boolean Range queries are used as a hard constraint.

It is worth noting that most of them are different from MCSKQ studied in this paper, since they use a single object to cover all keywords specified in queries but MCSKQ uses multiple objects collectively for the same purpose.

2.2   Query Models for Spatial Keyword Queries

Various forms of spatial keyword queries have also been explored intensively [13,17]. A collective spatial keyword query (CSKQ) [3,10,15,16] finds a set of the objects that collectively cover the queried keywords. Cao et al. [3] consider two cost functions to handle this query, and prove that both are NP-complete. They propose approximate algorithms with provable approximation bounds, and exact algorithms for two sub-problems.

In [10], Long et al. present two improved algorithms for such query including one exact algorithm and one approximate algorithm. The exact algorithm is more scalable than Cao's exact algorithm. The approximate algorithm improves the constant approximation factor without incurring a higher worst-case time complexity. Besides, they also investigate a new instantiation of the CSKQ.

Last but not least, there are still many variations of spatial keyword queries, such as preference-based top-k spatial keyword query [16], direction-aware spatial keyword search [9], a spatial keyword query on a road network [2,8,14] to name just a few.

In recent years, researchers have investigated various types of spatial keyword queries, such as interactive query [22–24], trip based query [25,26], semantic based query [21,28], and multi-objective query [27]. Nevertheless, it is worth mentioning that all the aforementioned works are fundamentally different from our studied problem.

3   Problem Definition and Preliminaries

In this section, we formalize the problem of this paper and introduce index structure.

3.1   Problem Definition

Definition 1. *Spatial Keyword Object. A spatial keyword object o is a point of interest (POI) in LBS systems, and it is formalized as $o = (o.\lambda, o.\psi)$ where $o.\lambda$ represents the position of o and $o.\psi$ represents the textual description of o.*

Definition 2. *Spatial Keyword Query. Given an object set $D = \{o_1, o_2, \cdots, o_n\}$ of spatial keyword objects and a query $q = (q.\lambda, q.\psi)$, where $q.\lambda$ represents a geographical location which contains longitude and latitude and $q.\psi$ represents textual description for query q used to choose object, such as "market". The spatial keyword query returns a result set $V = \{o_1, o_2, \cdots, o_m\}$ of text-related objects that are close to the query. Each object in V should cover all query keywords.*

Definition 3. *Collective Spatial Keyword Query (CSKQ). Given an object set $D = \{o_1, o_2, \cdots, o_n\}$ of spatial keyword objects and a query $q = (q.\lambda, q.\psi)$, the CSKQ problem is to find a set $V = \{o_1, o_2, \cdots, o_m\}$ of objects in D such that V covers $q.\psi$ and the cost of V is minimized. The cost may have different definitions in different applications.*

Definition 4. *Distance Cost. Cost of result set Cost (V) can be defined as follow:*

$$Cost(V) = \alpha \cdot max_{o \in V}(\bigcup_{i=1}^{n} min_{q_i \in Q} dist(o, q_i)) + (1-\alpha) \cdot max_{o, o_j \in V} dist(o, o_j)(1)$$

The first part of this equation can be regards as two steps, (1) get minimum distances between o and Q as a set $Dist_D$; (2) get the maximum distance in $Dist_D$. The second part represents the maximum distance between objects in V. For example, for the result set $\{o_4, o_5, o_7\}$ in Fig. 1(a), the first part is dist(o_7, q_3) and another part is dist (o_4, o_7). Among them, the spatial distance between q_i and o is measured by $dist(o, q_i) = \frac{2}{1+e^{-\|q_i.\lambda, o.\lambda\|}} - 1$ The distance varies from 0 to 1 by normalization. Similarly, the distance between two spatial keyword objects in the result set can be obtained.

Problem Statement Given a set $D = \{o_1, o_2, \cdots, o_n\}$ of spatial keyword objects and a set $Q = \{q_1, q_2, \cdots, q_l\}$ of queries where $q_i = (q.\lambda, q.\psi), i \in [0, l], l \in N+$. Each query q_i has the same query keywords, namely $q_i.\psi = q_j.\psi, (i, j \leq l) \wedge (i \neq j)$. The multiple query point based collective spatial keyword querying(MCSKQ) problem aims to find a set $V = \{o_1, o_2, \cdots, o_m\}$ of objects in D such that $\forall o \in V, o.\psi \supseteq q_i.\psi, i \leq n$, and the distance cost of V is minimized.

3.2   IR-Tree

In order to improve the efficiency of data retrieval, we choose IR-Tree index structure [6,19,20] which is a hybrid index structure obtained by adding an inverted file for each node of R-Tree [7]. IR-Tree can manage data including both spatial and textual dimensions. The structure of IR-Tree is shown in Fig. 2.

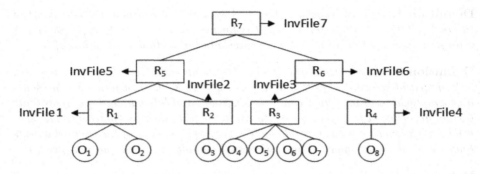

Fig. 2. index structure of IR-tree

IR-Tree use the inverted file for text indexing. An inverted file has a vocabulary of keywords, and each keyword is associated with an inverted list. Each inverted list comprises a sequence of postings, each of which normally contains the identifier of an object o whose description $o.\psi$ contains the keyword (Table 2).

Table 2. InvertedList of IR-tree

Keyword	InvFile1	InvFile2	InvFile3	InvFile4	InvFile5	InvFile6	InvFile7
Market	o_1	–	–	o_8	o_1	o_8	o_1, o_8
Restaurant	o_2	–	o_4, o_6, o_7	–	o_2	o_4, o_6, o_7	o_2, o_4, o_6, o_7
Bank	–	o_3	o_5	–	o_3	o_5	o_3, o_5

4   Query Processing

In this section, we propose three algorithms for MCSKQ, namely LO algorithm, HCQ algorithm and BCQ algorithm.

,

4.1 LO Algorithm

An intuitive idea can be solving MCSKQ on top of CSKQ methods directly. We know that CSKQ targets one query point, and returns a set of objects that can cover all required keywords and have optimal spatial locality w.r.t. the single query point. The baseline method, called Local Optimization (LO) algorithm, means to find and compare the local optimized results w.r.t. all query points in MCSKQ.

Algorithm 1. LO algorithm

Input: Spatial keyword objects data set D; Query set Q
Output: Result set V
1: $Q=\{q_1, q_2, \cdots, q_n\}$;U.Enqueue(irTree,0);
2: initialize distance cost $Cost_V = \infty$
3: **for** $q_i \in Q$ **do**
4:     V' = Type2Appro2(q_i, irTree);
5:     Calculate CostV' = Cost(V');
6:     **if** $Cost_{V'} \leq Cost_V$ **then**
7:         V = V'
8:         $Cost_V = Cost_{V'}$
9:     **end if**
10: **end for**
11: **return** V

In the LO algorithm, we fetch each query q_i, and to derive the result V_i such that (1) cover the keywords of all queries in MCSKQ to ensure capability; (2) the spatial distribution of objects in result set is optimal w.r.t. the location of q_i only. CSKQ processing is carried out for query points one by one. In this procedure, we maintain the top-k results to return.

Although LO algorithm makes full use of the existing CSKQ method, the final result still cannot satisfy the condition of multiple queries in some cases. As shown in Fig. 3, there are three queries q_1, q_2 and q_3. After performingCSKQ, these queries get $\{o_2, o_4, o_8\}$, $\{o_5, o_6, o_9\}$ and $\{o_2, o_8, o_{10}\}$ respectively. From these three result sets, the set $\{o_5, o_6, o_9\}$ with the lowest distance cost is selected as the LO search result. Learn from Fig. 3, for q_2 and q_3, it is obviously unreasonable to take $\{o_5, o_6, o_9\}$as the result set due to highly distance cost. LO algorithm does not take the closeness between the result set V and the multiple queries Q into account. The influence of multiple query points should be considered collaboratively in the query process.

4.2 HCQ Algorithm

We can learn from LO algorithm that only when the result set is close to the whole query set Q can we find a reasonable result. Therefore, it is necessary to

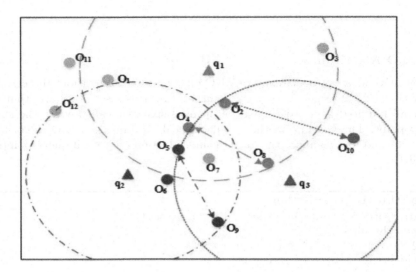

Fig. 3. LO algorithm

propose an efficient, multi-query sensitive algorithm. So we propose the Heuristic Collective Querying (HCQ) algorithm.

HCQ algorithm will consider the position correlation between the objects and the multiple query points in the query process, and update the uncovered keyword set to ensure the correctness of the result. The uncovered keyword set contains all keywords in queries but not in result. HCQ algorithm can get the set of spatial keyword objects that covers all the query keywords and satisfy the query conditions. The basic idea of the HCQ algorithm is to continuously search for a spatial keyword object o that satisfies the following conditions: (1) contains any query keywords, namely $o.\psi \land q_i.\psi \neq \emptyset$; (2) minimize the maximum spatial distance between o and query set Q, namely, $min(max(\| o.\lambda, q_i.\lambda \|))$. Continuously adding o that satisfies the conditions into the result set V until all the query keywords are covered by V, which means the query ends when the uncovered keyword set is empty.

Learn from HCQ algorithm that in the query process, if the inverted file of the node in the IR-Tree does not include any uncovered query keyword, then the node and its subtree need not to be visited. If the node contains an uncovered query keyword, then visit its subtree and add the corresponding spatial keyword object to the priority queue. The cost of visiting an object o is $\frac{dist(q_i,o)}{|o.\psi \cap q_i.\psi|}$ and the cost of visiting a node n is $\frac{min(dist(q_i,n))}{|o.\psi \cap q_i.\psi|}$ where $min(dist(q_i, n))$ is the minimum distance from a query to a node.

Theorem 1. *Given a query set $Q = \{q_1, q_2, \cdots, q_n\}$ and the IR-Tree of spatial keyword objects dataset D. The cost of visiting each node n in the IR-Tree is the lower bound of the cost of all the child nodes n_i of n.*

Algorithm 2. HCQ algorithm

Input: Spatial keyword objects data set D; Query set Q
Output: Result set V
 1: U.Enqueue(irTree, 0);
 2: invoke Algorithm 1:
 3: $Cost_v = Cost(V)$;
 4: $t_s = argmax_t(dist(Q, o_i))$
 5: **while** $U \neq \emptyset$ **do**
 6:     e = U.Dequeue();
 7:     **if** e instanceof Object **then**
 8:         V.Enqueue();
 9:         Keyword = Keyword-e.ψ;
10:         **if** $Keyword \neq \emptyset$ **then**
11:             Break;
12:         **end if**
13:     **else**
14:         **for** $e' \in e$ **do**
15:             **if** $e' \cap Keyword \neq \emptyset$ **then**
16:                 **if** e' is leaf node **then**
17:                     U.Enqueue(e', maxD(Q,e'));
18:                 **else**
19:                     U.Enqueue(e', maxD(Q,o));
20:                 **end if**
21:             **end if**
22:         **end for**;
23:     **end if**
24: **end while**
25: **return** V;

Proof. The minimum distance from a node to multiple queries must be less than or equal to the minimum distance from its children to multiple queries, namely, $\forall q_j \in Q, min(dist(q_j, n)) \leq min(dist(q_j, n_i))$. And for the nodes that need to visit, there are $| n.\psi \cap q_j.\psi | \geq | n_i.\psi \cap q_j.\psi |$. Therefore, the cost of node n is the lower bound of the cost of its child nodes.

Theorem 2. *Nodes that have been visited can be ignored during query processing.*

Proof. An uncovered keywords set is a subset of all keywords. For a visited node, all child nodes or spatial keyword objects that have intersections with the keywords set in the subtree of this node have been added to the priority queue, so all uncovered keywords of this node have also been added to the priority queue. Therefore, there is no need to access the nodes that have been visited in the IR-Tree.

Therefore, in the query process, if the cost of visiting a node is greater than the current minimum distance cost Cost(V), then we need not to visit its subtree. Thus the query efficiency is greatly improved.

The uncovered keyword set contains all queries keywords at the beginning. The HCQ algorithm first adds the root node to the priority queue U. Then, when U is visited, the values in U are fetched one by one. If a spatial keyword object is fetched and this object contains an uncovered query keyword, then add the object to the result set and update the uncovered keyword set (line 5). If a node is fetched, then scan the inverted file of this node and add all the child nodes which contain the corresponding query keyword to U.

If an object is added to U, the maximum distance between this object and multiple queries should be added at the same time, $max(D(Q, o)) = max_{1 \leq i \leq n}(\parallel q_i.\lambda, o.\lambda \parallel)$; If the node n is added to U, the weight distance between n and the query set Q should be added too. The weight distance is defined as $Score(n) = max(min_{1 \leq i \leq n; 1 \leq j \leq n}(\parallel q_i.\lambda, n_j.\lambda \parallel))$, which is the maximum distance of the minimum distances between each child node of n and multiple queries. The upper bound of the distance between the result set V and queries Q is $UB = max_{o \in V, q_i \in Q}(\parallel q_i.\lambda, o.\lambda \parallel)$; and the upper bound of the distance cost of V is as follows:

$$Cost_{UB}(V) = \alpha \cdot UB + (1 - \alpha) \cdot max_{o_i, o_j \in O}(dist(o_i, o_j)) \quad (2)$$

Constantly update the uncovered keywords set until the set is empty or unable to find spatial keyword object with the remaining keywords in the dataset.

However, the result set found by HCQ algorithm is still irrational. For example, the HCQ algorithm finds $\{o_2, o_6, o_8\}$ in Fig. 1(a). It can be seen that although each object has the minimum distance to the query set, the objects in the result set are too scattered. In the result set $\{o_4, o_5, o_7\}$, although the distance from each object to the query set is not the minimum, the distance cost of the result set is smaller due to the close combination of the result objects. In general, the query performance of the HCQ algorithm is high, but the accuracy of the candidate set cannot be sufficiently ensured because of the small space of the combination of the candidate sets.

4.3   BCQ Algorithm

In this section, we propose Bounded Collective Querying(BCQ) algorithm to find a more accurate result. The basic idea of the BCQ algorithm is based on the result set obtained by the HCQ algorithm, and an update strategy is found to continuously update the result set, and finally obtain a more accurate result. The algorithm is shown as Algorithm 3.

Firstly, the BCQ algorithm takes the result set found in the HCQ algorithm as the initial result set V and treats its distance cost as the initial distance cost $Cost_v$. Then, BCQ algorithm update V in the query progress by finding an object $o \in V$ where $o = argmax_{o \in V}(\bigcup_{i=1}^{n} min_{q_i \in Q} dist(o.q_i))$, and take o as a new queryq_i, $(q_i.\lambda = o.\lambda) \wedge (q_i.\psi = o.\psi)$. The distance cost of a spatial keyword object o changes within a certain range, which can be proved by theorem 3. Use q_v to find a new result set V', if the distance cost of V' less than V, then replace V by V' and $Cost_v$ by $Cost_{v'}$. The above process is repeated until $Cost_v$ is no longer updated. Finally, return V as the final result set of the BCQ algorithm.

Algorithm 3. BCQ algorithm

Input: Spatial keyword objects data set D; Query set Q
Output: Result set V
 1: U.Enqueue(irTree,0);
 2: invoke Algorithm 2:
 3: $Cost_v = Cost(V)$;
 4: $t_s = argmax_t(dist(Q, o_i))$
 5: **while** $U \neq \emptyset$ **do**
 6:     e = U.Dequeue();
 7:     **if** e instanceof Node **then**
 8:         **if** $Cost(V) < minDist(Q, e')$ **then**
 9:             Break;
10:         **end if**
11:         **for** $e' \in e$ **do**
12:             **if** $e' \cap Keyword \neq \emptyset$ **then**
13:                 **if** e' is leaf node **then**
14:                     U.Enqueue(e', maxminD(Q,e'));
15:                 **else**
16:                     U.Enqueue(e', maxD(Q,o));
17:                 **end if**
18:             **end if**
19:         **end for**;
20:     **else**
21:         **if** $Dist(Q, e') > Cost(V)$ **then**
22:             Break;
23:         **end if**
24:         $q_i.\lambda = e.\lambda$;
25:         $Cost_{v'} = Cost(V')$;
26:         **if** $Cost_{v'} < Cost_V$ **then**; V = V';
27:         **end if**
28:     **end if**
29: **end while**
30: **return** V;

Theorem 3. *Given a spatial keyword object o. Assuming that the distance cost of the result set containing o is Cost(o), the range of Cost(o) is* $\bigcup min_{i \leq m} dist(q_i, o) + dist(o, o_{max}) \leq Cost(o) \leq \bigcup min_{i \leq m} dist(q_i, o) + 3 \cdot dist(o, o_{max})$, *where o_{max} is the object that is the furthest from the result set.*

Proof. (1) When o is determined, the minimum distance cost of the result set containing o is $\bigcup min_{i \leq m} dist(q_i, o) + dist(o, o_{max})$ (2) The result set is in the circle with o as the center and dist(o, o_{max}) as the radius. Thus the maximum distance between objects will not exceed 2 dist(o, o_{max}). Therefore, the upper bound of the distance cost is $\bigcup min_{i \leq m} dist(q_i, o) + 3 \cdot dist(o, o_{max})$.

5 Experiments

In this section, we evaluate the performance of our proposed algorithms in terms of both efficiency and accuracy.

5.1 Experimental Setup

We use three real datasets, namely, Hotel, Web and GN. Table 3 is a specific description of these datasets. Table 4 is the default value and the range of the parameters.

Table 3. Dataset properties

Performance	Hotel	Web	GN
Number of objects	20790	579727	1868821
Number of non repeating words	602	2899175	222409
Number of words	80845	249132883	18374228

All codes are implemented by Java and run under Intel (R) Core (TM) i5-3470 CPU @ 3.20 GHz environment.

Table 4. Experimental parameters

Name	Symbol	Default value	Variation
Number of keywords	K	3	3–15
Number of queries	Q	3	3–10
Weight parameter	α	0.5	0–1

5.2 Performance Evaluation

Effect of K. We investigate the effect of K on the efficiency and accuracy of the proposed algorithms. Figure 4(a) shows the LO algorithm has much more time consumption than both BCQ algorithm and HCQ algorithm. Different from the steady increase of query time of HCQ and BCQ, the query time of LO algorithm increases rapidly with the increase of K. These can be explained by the fact that only the LO executes CSKQ for each query and performing a CSKQ is time-consuming. Besides, BCQ takes a longer query time than HCQ cause BCQ constantly updates the current result while HCQ stops querying once it finds a result set. As shown in Fig. 4(b), in different datasets, BCQ obtains the minimum distance cost which means the highest query accuracy. LO has the lowest accuracy because the result set found by LO is often clustered next to a query and farther from other queries. It is easy to understand that as K increases,

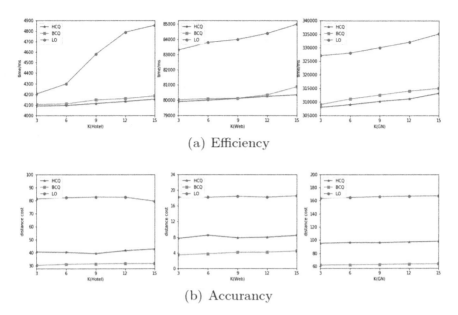

(a) Efficiency

(b) Accurancy

Fig. 4. Effect of K

the distance cost of the corresponding result set also increases. **Effect of Q.** We proceed to examine the effect of Q by plotting query time and distance cost to queries. As shown in Fig. 5(a), the query time of these algorithms increases linearly with the increase of Q. The query time of BCQ is always greater than the HCQ but less than the LO which have the same reason as above. As shown in Fig. 5(b), the result set of BCQ algorithm has the minimum distance cost, and the result set of the LO algorithm has the maximum distance cost. The increase of queries has a lower impact on distance cost.

Effect of α**.** The parameter α determines the order of the spatial keyword object to be accessed, so it can affect query time indirectly. As can be seen from Fig. 6(a), α has little effect on the query time of HCQ. Because the HCQ does not update the result set, so the query time is almost a constant. However, the query time for both BCQ and LO grows in parabolic increments cause both of them update the result set by the distance cost. As shown in Fig. 6(b), it can be seen that the distance cost of HCQ is higher than that of BCQ but lower than LO. To sum up, compared the BCQ algorithm with the LO algorithm and the HCQ algorithm, the BCQ algorithm can achieve a relatively high quality collective object set within short time in all settings.

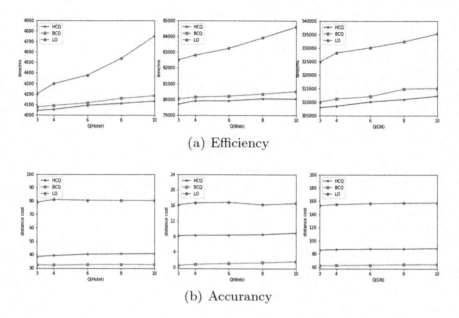

(a) Efficiency

(b) Accurancy

Fig. 5. Effect of Q

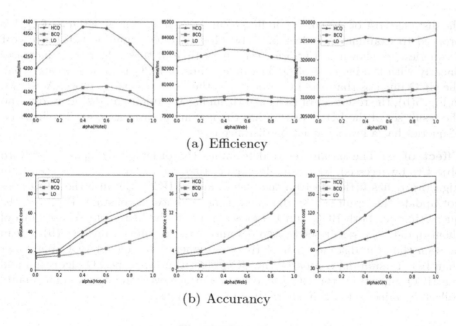

(a) Efficiency

(b) Accurancy

Fig. 6. Effect of α

6   Conclusion

In this paper, we design an collective spatial keyword query algorithm for group queries, which called MCSKQ, to solve the problem that multiple users at different locations cooperate to make collective queries. This algorithm enables the collaboration between query and result set to be realized. In this paper, IR-Tree is chosen to manage spatial text data, and an effective pruning strategy is presented. In addition, three query algorithms are proposed, namely LO, HCQ and BCQ. Through the demonstration and analysis of the experimental results, we can see that the accuracy of BCQ algorithm is high, which ensures the accuracy and rationality of the query results.

References

1. Cao, X., et al.: Spatial keyword querying. In: Atzeni, P., Cheung, D., Ram, S. (eds.) ER 2012. LNCS, vol. 7532, pp. 16–29. Springer, Heidelberg (2012). https://doi.org/10.1007/978-3-642-34002-4_2
2. Cao, X., Chen, L., Gao, C., Xiao, X.: Keyword-aware optimal route search. VLDB **5**(11), 1136–1147 (2012)
3. Cao, X., Cong, G., Jensen, C.S., Ooi, B.C.: Collective spatial keyword querying. In: SIGMOD 2011, pp. 373–384 (2011)
4. Chen, L., Lin, X., Hu, H., Jensen, C.S., Xu, J.: Answering why-not questions on spatial keyword top-k queries. In: ICDE 2015, pp. 279–290 (2015)
5. Chen, L., Cong, G., Jensen, C.S., Wu, D.: Spatial keyword query processing: an experimental evaluation. VLDB **6**(3), 217–228 (2013)
6. Cong, G., Jensen, C.S., Wu, D.: Efficient retrieval of the top-k most relevant spatial web objects. VLDB **2**(1), 337–348 (2009)
7. Guttman, A.: R-trees: a dynamic index structure for spatial searching. In: SIGMOD 1984, pp. 47–57 (1984)
8. Rocha-Junior, J.: Top-k spatial keyword queries on road networks. In: ICEDT 2012, pp. 168–179 (2012)
9. Li, G., Feng, J., Xu, J.: DESKS: direction-aware spatial keyword search. In: ICEDT 2012, pp. 474–485 (2012)
10. Long, C., Wong, C.W., Wang, K., Fu, W.C.: Collective spatial keyword queries: a distance owner-driven approach. In: SIGMOD 2013, pp. 689–700 (2013)
11. Lu, J., Lu, Y., Cong, G.: Reverse spatial and textual k nearest neighbor search. In: SIGMOD 2011, pp. 349–360 (2011)
12. Wu, D., Man, L.Y., Jensen, C.S., Cong, G.: Efficient continuously moving top-k spatial keyword query processing. In: ICDE 2011, pp. 541–552 (2011)
13. Yao, B., Tang, M., Li, F.: Multi-approximate-keyword routing in GIS data. In: ACM SIGSPATIAL 2011, pp. 201–210 (2011)
14. Zhang, C., Zhang, Y., Zhang, W., Lin, X.: Inverted linear quadtree: efficient top-k spatial keyword search. In: ICDE 2013, pp. 901–912 (2013)
15. Zhang, D., Chee, Y.M., Mondal, A., Tung, A.K.H., Kitsuregawa, M.: Keyword search in spatial databases: towards searching by document. In: ICDE 2009, pp. 688–699
16. Zhang, D., Ooi, B.C., Tung, A.K.H.: Locating mapped resources in web 2.0. In: ICDE 2010, pp. 521–532 (2010)

17. Zhang, L., Sun, X., Hai, Z.: Density-based spatial keyword querying. Future Gener. Comput. Syst. **32**(1), 211–221 (2014)
18. Zheng, K., et al.: Interactive top-k spatial keyword queries. In: ICDE 2015, pp. 423–434 (2015)
19. Zhou, Y., Xie, X., Wang, C., Gong, Y., Ma, W.Y.: Hybrid index structures for location-based web search. In: ACM CIKM 2005, pp. 155–162 (2005)
20. Zobel, J., Moffat, A.: Inverted files for text search engines. ACM Comput. Surv. (2006)
21. Qian, Z., Jiajie, X., Zheng, K., Zhao, P., Zhou, X.: Semantic-aware top-k spatial keyword queries. World Wide Web **21**(3), 573–594 (2018)
22. Sun, J., Xu, J., Zheng, K., Liu, C.: Interactive spatial keyword querying with semantics. In: CIKM 2017, pp. 1727–1736 (2017)
23. Zheng, K.: Interactive top-k spatial keyword queries. In: ICDE 2015, pp. 423–434 (2015)
24. Chen, X., et al.: S2R-tree: a pivot-based indexing structure for semantic-aware spatial keyword search. Geoinformatica (2019). https://doi.org/10.1007/s10707-019-00372-z
25. Xu, J., Chen, J., Zhou, R., Fang, J., Liu, C.: On workflow aware location-based service composition for personal trip planning. Future Gener. Comput. Syst. (2019). https://doi.org/10.1016/j.future.2019.03.010
26. Liu, H., Xu, J., Zheng, K., Liu, C., Du, L., Wu, X.: Semantic-aware query processing for activity trajectories. In: WSDM 2017, pp. 283–292 (2017)
27. Chen, J., Xu, J., Liu, C., Li, Z., Liu, A., Ding, Z.: Multi-objective spatial keyword query with semantics. In: Candan, S., Chen, L., Pedersen, T.B., Chang, L., Hua, W. (eds.) DASFAA 2017. LNCS, vol. 10178, pp. 34–48. Springer, Cham (2017). https://doi.org/10.1007/978-3-319-55699-4_3
28. Qian, Z., Xu, J., Zheng, K., Sun, W., Li, Z., Guo, H.: On efficient spatial keyword querying with semantics. In: Navathe, S.B., Wu, W., Shekhar, S., Du, X., Wang, X.S., Xiong, H. (eds.) DASFAA 2016. LNCS, vol. 9643, pp. 149–164. Springer, Cham (2016). https://doi.org/10.1007/978-3-319-32049-6_10

Unsupervised Feature Selection for Noisy Data

Kaveh Mahdavi[1,2(✉)], Jesus Labarta[1,2], and Judit Gimenez[1,2]

[1] Barcelona Supercomputing Center (BSC), Jordi Girona. 29, Barcelona, Spain
{kaveh.mahdavi,jesus,judit}@bsc.es
[2] Universitat Politcnica de Catalunya, Campus Nord, Barcelona, Spain

Abstract. Feature selection techniques are enormously applied in a variety of data analysis tasks in order to reduce the dimensionality. According to the type of learning, feature selection algorithms are categorized to: supervised or unsupervised. In unsupervised learning scenarios, selecting features is a much harder problem, due to the lack of class labels that would facilitate the search for relevant features. The selecting feature difficulty is amplified when the data is corrupted by different noises. Almost all traditional unsupervised feature selection methods are not robust against the noise in samples. These approaches do not have any explicit mechanism for detaching and isolating the noise thus they can not produce an optimal feature subset. In this article, we propose an unsupervised approach for feature selection on noisy data, called Robust Independent Feature Selection (RIFS). Specifically, we choose feature subset that contains most of the underlying information, using the same criteria as the Independent component analysis (ICA). Simultaneously, the noise is separated as an independent component. The isolation of representative noise samples is achieved using factor oblique rotation whereas noise identification is performed using factor pattern loadings. Extensive experimental results over divers real-life data sets have showed the efficiency and advantage of the proposed algorithm.

Keywords: Feature selection · Independent Component Analysis · Oblique rotation · Noise separation

1 Introduction

Data is often represented by high dimensional feature vectors in many areas, such as face recognition, image possessing and text mining. In practice, not all features are relevant and important to the learning task, many of them are often correlated, redundant, or even noisy sometimes, which may result in adverse effects such as over-fitting, low efficiency and poor performance. Moreover, high dimensionality significantly increases the time and space requirements for processing the data. Feature selection is one effective means to identify relevant features for dimension reduction [11]. Once a reduced feature subset is chosen, conventional data analysis techniques can then be applied.

© Springer Nature Switzerland AG 2019
J. Li et al. (Eds.): ADMA 2019, LNAI 11888, pp. 79–94, 2019.
https://doi.org/10.1007/978-3-030-35231-8_6

From the perspective of label availability, feature selection algorithms can also be classified into supervised feature selection and unsupervised feature selection. Supervised feature selection methods, such as Pearson correlation coefficients [16], Fisher score [3], and Information gain [4], are usually able to effectively select good features since labels of training data, which contain the essential discriminative information for classification that can be used. However, in practice, there is usually no shortage of unlabeled data but labels are expensive. Hence, it is a great significance to develop unsupervised feature selection algorithms which can make use of all the data points. In this paper, we consider the problem of selecting features in unsupervised learning scenario which is more challenging task because of the lack of label information that would guide the search for relevant features.

Fig. 1. Gaussian noisy versions of the image sample from COIL20 data set with different σ^2. From left to right σ^2 is: 0, 0.1, 0.4 and 0.7.

Another important factor which affects the performance of feature selection is the consideration of outliers and noise. Real data is not usually ideally distributed and outliers or noise often appear in the data, thus the traditional feature selection approach may work well on clean data. However, it is very likely to fail in noisy data sets. [15]. As an example, various types of noise are arisen during the image transmission and acquisition that Gaussian noise is one of them. It means noisy image pixel is the sum of the actual pixel value and a random Gaussian distributed noise value [18]. Figure 1 shows noisy versions of sample image from COIL20[1] data set with different σ^2 values. It can be seen that indeed, as the σ^2 value increases, the picture gets more and more ambiguous. In experimental part of this work we aim at applying our robust feature selection on cropped data set by Gaussian noise with $\sigma^2 \leq 0.7$.

In this paper, we introduce a new unsupervised feature selection algorithm, called Robust Independent Feature Selection (RIFS). We perform noise separation, isolation and robust feature selection simultaneously to select the most important and discriminative features for both unsupervised and supervised learning. Specifically, our purposed method exploits the structure of the latent independent components of a feature set and separates the noise as a component. By using independent component analysis, RIFS suggests a principled way to

---

[1] http://www.cad.zju.edu.cn/home/dengcai/Data/MLData.html.

measure the similarity between different features and to rank each of them without label information. Thus, it imposes an oblige rotation on the independent factor indicator matrix to isolate the noise.

The rest of the paper is as follow: in Sect. 2, we present a brief review of the related work. Our proposed method, which we name Robust Independent Feature Selection (RIFS), is described in Sect. 3. The experimental results are illustrated in Sect. 4, followed by a summary in Sect. 5.

2   Related Work

Feature selection algorithms can be grouped into two main families: filter and wrapper. Filter methods [7,20] select a subset of features by evaluating statistical properties of data. For wrapper methods [6], feature selection is wrapped in a learning algorithm and the performance on selected features is taken as the evaluation criterion. Wrapper methods couples feature selection with built-in mining algorithm tightly, which lead to less generality and extensive computation. In this paper, we are particularly interested in the filter methods which are much more affordable.

The majority of the existing filter methods are supervised. Perhaps, Max variance [5] is the simplest yet effective unsupervised assessing criterion for selecting features. This measure principally projects the data points along the dimensions of maximum variances. Although the maximum variance metrics detect features that are purposeful for descriptive analysis, there is no reason to assume that these features must be useful for discriminating between data in distinct classes.

The Principal Component Analysis (PCA) algorithm shares the same principle of maximizing variance. Thus, some feature selection algorithms [12,14] are available for selecting the features by means of Principal Component Analysis. However, its orthogonal constraint on the feature selection projection matrix is unreasonable since feature vectors are not necessarily orthogonal with each other in nature.

Currently, the Laplacian Score algorithm [7] and its extensions [2,20] have been proposed to select features by leverage of manifold learning. Laplacian Score algorithm utilizes a spectral graph to extract the local geometric structure of the data then it selects feature subset which is mapped perfectly to the graph.

Another important factor which affects the performance of feature selection is the consideration of outliers and noise. In reality, outliers and noise are corrupting the distribution of the data, thus it is important or even necessary to consider noise robustness for unsupervised feature selection. Zhai [15] purposed RUFS method which jointly performs robust label learning via local learning regularized robust orthogonal non-negative matrix factorization and robust feature learning via joint $l_{1,2}$-norms minimization. A remarkable drawback of the algorithm is that its performance is relatively sensitive to the number of selected features.

The intention of our work is to purpose an unsupervised feature selection technique that can choose better features subset across a noisy data set; thereby, we are proposing a hybrid algorithm to utilize feature selection along with the noises separation and isolation.

3   Background

We consider the canonical problem of unsupervised feature selection is the following. We use X to indicate a data set of N data points $X = (x_1, x_2, ..., x_N)$, $x_i \in R^M$. The objective is to find a feature subset with size d which includes the majority informative features. In preference to, the points $[x'_1, x'_2, ..., x'_N]$ mirrored in the reduced d–dimensional space $x'_i \in R^d$ can perfectly maintain the original geometric structure of data in M–dimensional space.

In the remaining part of this section, we discuss the main data mining techniques that we utilize in our feature selection approach.

Independent Component Analysis (ICA). To detect the latent structure of data, Independent Component Analysis (ICA) [9] tries to unmix some different sources (includes noise) that have been collected together. ICA is a statistical and computational technique for revealing the hidden sources/components that underlie sets of random variables, measurements or signals. The main ICA problem assumes that the observation X is an unknown linear mixture A of the M' unknown sources S:

$$X = AS, \qquad X \in \Re^M, \qquad S \in \Re^{M'}, \qquad A \in \Re^{M \times M'}$$

We assume that each component s_i of S is zero-mean, mutually independent $p(s_i, s_j) = p(s_i)p(s_j)$ and drawn from different probability distribution which is not Gaussian except for at most one. The goal of ICA is to find an approximation W (demixing matrix) of A^{-1} such that:

$$\hat{S} = WX \approx S, \qquad W \in \Re^{M' \times M}$$

ICA is a generative model since the model describes how X could be generated from A and S. ICA tries to find A by estimating the matrices of its SVD decomposition $A = U\Sigma V^T$ [17]. Ideally, W should be:

$$W = A^{-1} = V\Sigma^{-1}U^T$$

FastICA [19] is an algorithm that searches the optimal value of W, which estimates the sources S by approximating statistical independence. The algorithm starts from an initial condition, for example, random demixing weights w_0. Then, on each iteration step, the weights w_0 are first updated by:

$$w_0{}^+ = E\{x(w_0{}^T x)^3\} - 3||w_0||^2 w_0$$

so that the corresponding sources become more independent, and then $w_0{}^+/norm$ (normalized), so that w_0 stays orthonormal. The iteration is continued until the weights converge $|w_0{}^T w_0{}^+| \approx 1$. The w_0 is an optimal approximation of W.

$$\hat{S} = w_0 X \approx S \tag{1}$$

When one tries to perform feature analysis of the data, each row of S can reflect the data distribution on the corresponding hidden source. Thus, if the data is cropped by noise, the noise is remarked as an independent source.

Oblique Rotation. Preliminary result from a factor analysis is not easy to post-process (i.e. clustering, classification). Simply, rotation has been developed not long after factor analysis to help us to clarify and simplify the results of a factor analysis. Two main types of rotation are used: orthogonal when the new axes are also orthogonal to each other, and oblique when the new axes are not required to be orthogonal to each other. The Promax [8] is an oblige rotation technique which has the advantage of being fast and conceptually simple. Promax rotation has three distinct steps.

First, it extracts the Varimax [10] orthogonal rotated matrix $\Lambda_R = \{\lambda_{ij}\}$.

Second, a target matrix is contrived to power matrix $P = (p_{ij})_{p \times m}$ by raising the factor structure coefficients to the power of Promax rotation $k > 1$,

$$p_{ij} = \left| \frac{\lambda_{ij}}{\sqrt{(\sum_{j=1}^{m} \lambda_{ij}^2)}} \right|^{k+1} \left(\frac{\sqrt{\sum_{j=1}^{m} \lambda_{ij}^2}}{\lambda_{ij}} \right)$$

Finally, it uses the matrix P to rotate the original matrix X by two levels approximation. Level one, it calculates the matrix $L = (\Lambda_R' \Lambda_R)^{-1} \Lambda_R' P$. Then, it normalizes the L by column to a transformation matrix $Q = LD$, where $D = 1/\sqrt{diag(L'L)}$ is the diagonal matrix that normalizes the columns of L. So, the preliminary rotated matrix is

$$f_{promax-temp} = Q^{-1} f_{varimax}$$

by reason of, $Var(f_{promax-temp}) = (Q'Q)^{-1}$ and the diagonal elements do not equal 1.

Level two, the rotated matrix is modified by matrix $C = \sqrt{diag((Q'Q)^{-1})}$ to $f_{promax} = C f_{promax-temp}$ the rotated factor pattern is

$$\Lambda_{Promax} = \Lambda_R Q C^{-1} \tag{2}$$

The coefficients in the rotated data is smaller, but the absolute distance between them significantly increased. It improves the quality of posterior analysis (i.e. clustering, classification).

4   RIFS Algorithm Description

In the this section, we will introduce our Robust Independent Feature Selection (RIFS) algorithm.

First of all, the independent components are computed from the X. Let $\mathbb{S}$ be a matrix whose rows are the independent decomposition vector of the matrix X and $V = [v_1, v_2, ..., v_M]$, $v_i \in R^{M'}$ is the columns of $\mathbb{S}$. Each vector

v_i represents the projection of the $i'th$ feature (variable) of the vector X to the new dimensional space, that is, the M' elements of v_i correspond to the weights of the $i'th$ factor on each axis of the new subspace. The key observation is that features that are highly correlated or have high mutual information will have extremely similar weight (changing the sign has no statistical significance). On the two extreme sides, two independent features have maximally separated weight vectors; while two fully correlated features have identical similar absolute weights vectors.

Technically, the ICA method decomposes a multivariate data into independent latent sources and white noise is an underlying source that is also drawn out as an independent component by ICA. Let $S = [s_1, s_2, ..., s_{m'}]$, $s_i \in R^M$ be the rows of $\mathbb{S}$. The s_{wn} is representing white noise when the M elements of s_{wn} have much the same absolute value with finite variance, because the white noise is randomly having equal intensity at different features [13].

In order to isolate the noise, we use the Promax method to rotate the projected feature vectors v_is to $RV = [rv_1, rv_2, ..., rv_m]$, $rv_i \in R^{M'}$ with power k. It forces the structure of the factors loadings to become bipolar that subsequently facilitates the noise isolation from the main hidden sources. It quite mitigates the drawback of the noise during discriminative analysis by uniforming the factors load of s_{wn}.

To find the best subset, we look for the profoundly cross-correlated features subset by using the underlying factor structure of the RV_i and k_mean. The features of random vector X are clustered to $C = [c_1, ..., c_d]$ when c_j represents $j'th$ cluster. We consider selecting d feature from M feature candidates.

In continue, the centroid of any cluster is computed:

$$C_j = \frac{1}{m_j} \sum_{rv_i \in c_j} rv_i \tag{3}$$

where m_j is the size of $j'th$ cluster.

Then, in any cluster the feature vectors rv_i are ranked based on their similarity with cluster centroid:

$$similarity(rv_i, C_j) = \frac{rv_i.C_j}{\|rv_i\| \times \|C_j\|} \tag{4}$$

Where values range between -1 and 1, where -1 is perfectly dissimilar and 1 is perfectly similar.

We select the highest ranked rv_i for each cluster as a corresponding vector and the corresponding feature x_i is chosen as an independent representative feature. The selected features depute each cluster properly in terms of escalated spread, independence and restoration.

We summarize the complete RIFS algorithm for feature selection in Algorithm 1.

Algorithm 1: RIFS for Feature Selection

Require: N data points with M features;
             $d < M$: the number of selected features ;
             k : the power of Promax rotation;

Ensure: d selected features

1: Compute the Independent Components as discussed in Section 3.1. Let $V = [v_1, v_2, ..., v_M]$, $v_i \in R^{M'}$ contain feature decomposition vectors and M' is the number of hidden independent components.

2: Rotate the V to RV as discussed in Section 3.2, with power coefficient set to k. We get $RV = [rv_1, rv_2, ..., rv_M]$, $v_i \in R^{M'}$.

3: Cluster the vectors rv_i to d categories $C = [c_1, ..., c_d]$ by K-Means algorithm. Let C_j be the centroid of cluster c_j according to Eq. (3).

4: Compute the ***similarity*** score for each feature vectors rv_i according to Eq.(4)

5: Return the corresponding feature x_i of the most similar feature vector rv_i to the cluster's centroids for each d cluster.

4.1   Computational Complexity Analysis

The computational cost for the main steps of our algorithm can be computed as follows:

- The ICA computational cost is $O(NM(1 + M)d')$ where M is the number of features/dimensions, N is the number of samples, and d' is the number of iterations in fastICA algorithm.
- The K-Means and Promax algorithms are utilized on just lower dimension including M points with $M' - dimensional$ vectors, so their computational costs are negligible.

Therefor, where $M' \ll N$ and d' is customarily fixed as a constant 200, the total computational cost of RIFS is roughly corresponding to the performance of fastICA. So the total cost of our RIFS algorithm is $O(NM(1 + M)d')$.

5   Empirical Study

In this section, we have carried out several experiments to show the robustness, efficiency and effectiveness of our proposed RIFS method for unsupervised feature selection. The experiments consider both unsupervised (clustering) and supervised (classification) study. In the experiments, we have compared the RIFS, Laplacian Score and Maximum Variance. Laplacian Score and Maximum Variance are both state-of-the-art feature selection algorithms (filter methods), so this comparison makes possible to examine the efficacy of our proposed RIFS method.

5.1   Parameter Selection

Our RIFS has only one parameter, which is the k in performing the Promax rotation. We carried out different experiments in order to estimate the optimum value of k. RIFS achieves stable good performance with the k between 2 and 4 on all the four data sets. When k is less than 2, the performance slightly decreases as the k decreases. We assume $k = 4$ entire all experiments (both unsupervised and supervised study), in order to bring into uniformity.

Table 1. Summary of four benchmark data sets

Data set	Instance	Feature	Classes
YALE	165	1024	15
ISOLET	1560	617	26
USPS	9298	256	10
COIL20	1440	1024	20

5.2   Data Sets

We used four real world data sets in our experiments. The basic statistics of these data sets are outlined below in Table 1:

– The first one is **YALE**[2] face database which contains 165 grayscale images in GIF format of 15 individuals. There are 11 images per subject, one per different facial expression or configuration: center-light, w/glasses, happy, left-light, w/no glasses, normal, right-light, sad, sleepy, surprised, and wink. The original images are normalized (in scale and orientation) in order that the two eyes have been aligned at the same level. Then, we have cropped the face area into the final images for processing. The size of each cropped image is 32×32 pixels, with 256 gray levels per pixel. Thus, each face image can be represented by a 1024-dimensional vector.
– The second one is **ISOLET**[3] spoken letter recognition data. It contains 150 subjects who spoke the name of each letter of the alphabet twice. The speakers are grouped into sets of 30 speakers each, and are referred to as isolet1 through isolet5. In our experimentation, we use isolet1 which consists 1560 examples with 617 features.
– The third one is the **USPS** (see Footnote 3) handwritten digit database. A famous subset contains 9298 16×16 hand written digit images in total.
– The fourth one is **COIL20** (see Footnote 3) image library from Columbia which contains 20 objects. The images of each object were taken $5°$ apart as the object is rotated on a turntable and each object has 72 images. The size of each image is 32×32 pixels, with 256 gray levels per pixel.

---

[2] http://www.cad.zju.edu.cn/home/dengcai/Data/FaceData.html.
[3] http://www.cad.zju.edu.cn/home/dengcai/Data/MLData.html.

5.3 Study of Unsupervised Cases

In this subsection, we apply our feature selection algorithm to clustering. The k-means clustering is performed by using the selected features subset and compare the results of both different algorithms and noise varieties.

Evaluation Metric. We evaluate the clustering result by informative overlapping between the obtained label of each data point using clustering algorithms and the label provided by the data set. We use the normalized mutual information metric (NMI) [7] as a performance measure. Let C indicate the set of clusters collected from the ground truth and C' obtained from a clustering algorithm. Their mutual information metric $MI(C, C')$ is defined as follows:

$$MI(C, C') = \sum_{c_i \in C, c'_j \in C'} p(c_i, c'_j).log_2 \frac{p(c_i, c'_j)}{p(c_i).p(c'_j)} \tag{5}$$

where $p(c_i)$ and $p(c'_j)$ are the probabilities that a data point arbitrarily selected from the data set belongs to the clusters c_i and c'_j, respectively, and $p(c_i, c'_j)$ is the joint probability that the arbitrarily selected data point belongs to the clusters c_i as well as c'_j at the same time. In our experiments, we use the normalized mutual information NMI as follows:

$$NMI(C, C') = \frac{MI(C, C')}{max(H(C), H(C'))} \tag{6}$$

where $H(C)$ and $H(C')$ are the entropies of C and C', respectively. It is easy to check that $NMI(C, C')$ ranges from 0 to 1. $NMI = 1$ if the two sets of clusters are identical, and $NMI = 0$ if the two sets are independent.

Clustering Results. In order to randomize the experiments, we evaluate the clustering performance with different number of clusters (K = 7, 11, 13, 15 on YALE; K = 3, 5, 7, 10 on USPS; K = 5, 10, 15, 20 on COIL20 and K = 10, 15, 20, 26 on ISOLET). For each given cluster number K (except using the

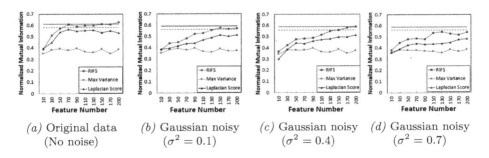

(a) Original data   (b) Gaussian noisy   (c) Gaussian noisy   (d) Gaussian noisy
    (No noise)   ($\sigma^2 = 0.1$)   ($\sigma^2 = 0.4$)   ($\sigma^2 = 0.7$)

Fig. 2. Clustering performance vs. the number of selected features on YALE.

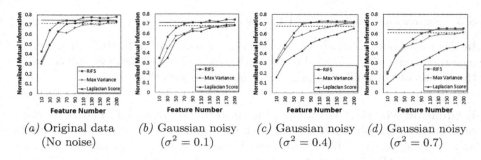

(a) Original data   (b) Gaussian noisy   (c) Gaussian noisy   (d) Gaussian noisy
(No noise)   ($\sigma^2 = 0.1$)   ($\sigma^2 = 0.4$)   ($\sigma^2 = 0.7$)

Fig. 3. Clustering performance vs. the number of selected features on Isolet.

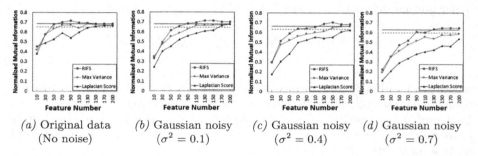

(a) Original data   (b) Gaussian noisy   (c) Gaussian noisy   (d) Gaussian noisy
(No noise)   ($\sigma^2 = 0.1$)   ($\sigma^2 = 0.4$)   ($\sigma^2 = 0.7$)

Fig. 4. Clustering performance vs. the number of selected features on USPS.

entire data set), 10 tests were conducted on different randomly chosen clusters. Then, for each data set, the overall average performance as well as the standard deviation was computed over all tests with different cluster number K. In each test, we applied different algorithms to select d features and applied k-means for clustering. In order to initiate the k-mean starting point, we applied the Hierarchical Clustering algorithm [1] then the obtained d clusters centroids are used as k-mean starting points. In principal, we performed the above procedure on clean data sets. Then, we added different Gaussian noise ($\sigma^2 = 0.1, 0.4, 0.7$)

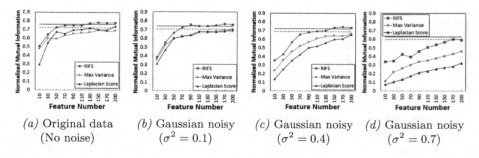

(a) Original data   (b) Gaussian noisy   (c) Gaussian noisy   (d) Gaussian noisy
(No noise)   ($\sigma^2 = 0.1$)   ($\sigma^2 = 0.4$)   ($\sigma^2 = 0.7$)

Fig. 5. Clustering performance vs. the number of selected features on COIL20.

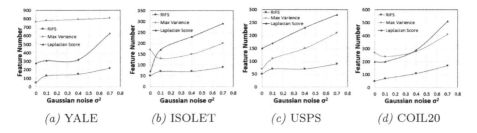

(a) YALE   (b) ISOLET   (c) USPS   (d) COIL20

Fig. 6. The noise level vs. the number of selected feature that is needed to achieve the 95% of clustering performance with all features.

Table 2. The proportion of features (# selected features/# all features%) that is needed to achieve the 95% of clustering performance with all features.

	Method	No noise	$\sigma^2 = 0.1$	$\sigma^2 = 0.4$	$\sigma^2 = 0.7$	Average
YALE	RIFS	**4.9 ± 3.8**	**12.7 ± 3.2**	**14.6 ± 3.7**	**21.5 ± 2.5**	**13.4**
	Laplacian Score	27.3 ± 2.3	30.3 ± 3.9	31.3 ± 5.1	61.5 ± 8.6	37.6
	Max Variance	74.7 ± 1.1	76.2 ± 3.2	77.4 ± 3.1	79.1 ± 1.4	76.9
ISOLET	RIFS	**8.1 ± 2.2**	**11.3 ± 3.1**	**11.3 ± 4.3**	**14.6 ± 4.4**	**11.3**
	Laplacian Score	11.3 ± 3.6	27.6 ± 11.2	37.3 ± 7.8	47.0 ± 9.0	30.8
	Max Variance	27.6 ± 8.1	21.1 ± 6.2	24.3 ± 4.3	32.4 ± 11.1	26.3
USPS	RIFS	**19.5 ± 1.7**	**27.3 ± 2.3**	**27.3 ± 1.8**	**35.2 ± 4.6**	**27.3**
	Laplacian Score	58.6 ± 8.1	66.4 ± 17.2	89.8 ± 9.8	100.0 ± 0.0	78.7
	Max Variance	27.3 ± 5.2	43.0 ± 7.9	58.6 ± 15.1	82.0 ± 12.0	52.7
COIL20	RIFS	**4.9 ± 3.3**	**6.8 ± 2.3**	**10.7 ± 5.1**	**16.6 ± 7.7**	**9.8**
	Laplacian Score	19.5 ± 8.8	19.5 ± 6.3	28.3 ± 9.1	50.0 ± 12.8	29.3
	Max Variance	26.4 ± 5.4	23.4 ± 6.2	27.3 ± 8.7	40.0 ± 3.2	29.3

to the original data sets and repeated the above clustering producer. For each σ^2 value, 10 random noise generated and tests executed, and both the average performance and standard deviation recorded over these 10 tests.

Figures 2, 3, 4 and 5 present the plots of clustering performance versus the number of selected features d on ISOLET, USPS, COIL20 and YALE, successively, without and with different level of Gaussian noises. As shown in the plots, our proposed RIFS algorithm persistently surpasses both competitors on all the four data sets and noise levels. From the plot (a) of each Figs. 2, 3, 4 and 5 (noise less), we can see RIFS converges to the best result in double quick time, with approximately 50 features. Meanwhile, both other methods mostly require more than 100 features (in average) to achieve 95% of the best result. When we add Gaussian noise with higher standard variance, we need to select more features to achieve reasonable clustering performance, as it can be seen in the plot $(b \sim c)$ of each Figs. 2, 3, 4 and 5. However, in RIFS case, this trend is very slightly pronounced when the performance of the other methods is reduced quickly by increasing the Gaussian noise standard variance, as it can be seen in Fig. 6. It would be worth mentioning that, on the ISOLET data set, our proposed RIFS algorithm performs strangely robust against the noise by selecting few more features. For example, in $\sigma^2 = 0.4$ case only 70 features are selected by RIFS and the clustering normalized mutual information is 70.3%, which is almost equal to the clustering result by using all the 617 features (71.7%). However, the Max Variance and Laplacian Score perform comparably to one another on original ISOLET data set but the Laplacian Score shows higher sensitivity to the noisy data. On COIL20 data set the Max Variance and Laplacian Score perform comparably to one another while Max Variance becomes obviously better than Laplacian Score On USPS data set. On YALE data set, Laplacian Score completely performs better than Max Variance, roughly, Max Variance does not have any function on YALE data set, possibly, due to the fact that sample size is small. The most surprising aspect of the result is that Max Variance slightly performs worse on original than data with light noise ($\sigma^2 = 0.1$) on COIL2 and ISOLET data sets.

The main objective of our experiment is to reduce the dimensionality of the data by taking to account the robustness against the noise, in Table 2, we report the selected feature proportion for achieving to at least 95% of the best clustering performance by using all features for each algorithm and Gaussian noise standard variance. The last column of each table records the average selected feature proportion over different standard variance of Gaussian noise. As it can be seen, RIFS significantly outperforms both other methods on all the four data sets. Laplacian Score performs the second best on YALE data set. Max Variance performs the second best on USPS and ISOLET data sets. Max Variance and Laplacian Score perform comparably to one another on COIL20 data set. Comparing with the second best method, RIFS selects 24.2%, 15.0%, 25.4% and 19.5% less proportion of features in average for reaching to the at least 95% of clustering performance with all features, when measured by normalized mutual information on the YALE, ISOLET, USPS and COIL20 data sets, respectively.

5.4   Study of Supervised Cases

In this experiment, we examine the discriminating capability of the different feature selection methods. The 1-Nearest Neighbor (1NN) classifier is used and we assume that well-selected feature subset should yield more accurate classifier [2]. We perform leave-one-out cross validation as follows: For each data point x_i, we find its nearest neighbor x_i'. Let $c(x_i)$ be the class label of x_i. The nearest neighbor classification accuracy rate (AR) is thus defined as

$$AR = \frac{1}{N} \sum_{i=1}^{N} \delta(c(x_i), c(x_i')) \tag{7}$$

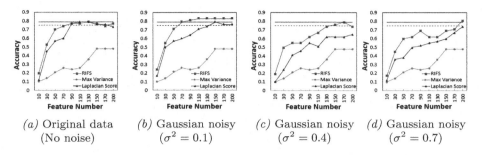

(a) Original data
(No noise)

(b) Gaussian noisy
($\sigma^2 = 0.1$)

(c) Gaussian noisy
($\sigma^2 = 0.4$)

(d) Gaussian noisy
($\sigma^2 = 0.7$)

Fig. 7. Classification accuracy vs. the number of selected features on YALE.

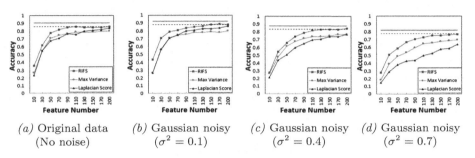

(a) Original data
(No noise)

(b) Gaussian noisy
($\sigma^2 = 0.1$)

(c) Gaussian noisy
($\sigma^2 = 0.4$)

(d) Gaussian noisy
($\sigma^2 = 0.7$)

Fig. 8. Classification accuracy vs. the number of selected features on Isolet.

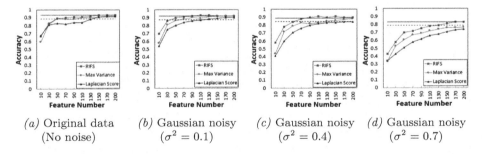

(a) Original data
(No noise)

(b) Gaussian noisy
($\sigma^2 = 0.1$)

(c) Gaussian noisy
($\sigma^2 = 0.4$)

(d) Gaussian noisy
($\sigma^2 = 0.7$)

Fig. 9. Classification accuracy vs. the number of selected features on USPS.

where N is the number of data points and $\delta(a, b) = 1$ if $a = b$ and 0 otherwise. All results reported in this paper are obtained by averaging the accuracy from 10 trials of experiments. Figures 7, 8, 9 and 10 represent the plots of 1-nearest neighbor classification accuracy rate versus the number of selected features. As it can be seen, roughly on all the four data sets, RIFS at every turn goes one better than both other methods. Almost identical to clustering or even better, RIFS converges to the best result quickly on original (No noise) data set, with less than 90 features (in average) and it shows strange robustness against the noises. For example in case of $\sigma^2 = 0.7$, RIFS selects approximately 100 more

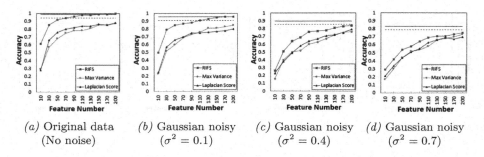

(a) Original data   (b) Gaussian noisy   (c) Gaussian noisy   (d) Gaussian noisy
     (No noise) $(\sigma^2 = 0.1)$ $(\sigma^2 = 0.4)$ $(\sigma^2 = 0.7)$

Fig. 10. Classification accuracy vs. the number of selected features on COIL20.

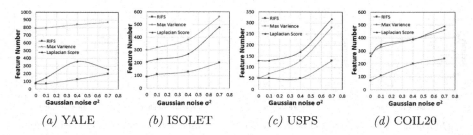

(a) YALE   (b) ISOLET   (c) USPS   (d) COIL20

Fig. 11. The noise level vs. the number of selected feature that is needed to achieve the 95% of classification accuracy with all features.

features in average to converge to the best result on all data sets, as it can be seen in Fig. 11. Remarkably, on the USPS data set with moderate additive Gaussian noise $(\sigma^2 \leqslant 0.4)$, RIFS consistently can achieve 95% of the best classification accuracy by using no more than 50 features. On this data set, the Max Variance algorithm performs comparably to our algorithms and much better than Laplacian Score, and Laplacian Score's performance is defected more by additive noise. On the COIL20 data set, the Laplacian Score and Max Variance algorithms perform comparably to each other. On the ISOLET data set, the Laplacian Score and Max Variance algorithms perform comparably to each other, and Laplacian Score performs the worst. Surprisingly, on the YALE data sets, Max Variance algorithm performs quite bad in both with and without noise, unless selecting approximately 80% of features and Laplacian Score performs better on noisy data with Gaussian noise $\sigma^2 = 0.7$ than $\sigma^2 = 0.4$, possibly, due to the fact that sample size is small. The same as unsupervised study, in Table 3, we report the average (over all Gaussian noise $\sigma^2 \in \{0, 0.1, 0.4, 0.7\}$) selected feature proportion for achieving to at least 95% of the best classification performance by using all features for each algorithm. As it can be seen, RIFS achieves to the 95% of the best classification performance with approximately two times less numbers of features than the second best competitor on all data sets.

Table 3. The average proportion of features (# selected features/# all features%) that is needed to achieve the 95% of classification accuracy rate with all features.

	YALE	ISOLET	USPS	COIL20
RIFS	**11.7**	**21.5**	**27.3**	**15.1**
Laplacian Score	21.0	48.2	67.4	36.4
Max Variance	80.4	63.2	51.8	35.6

5.5 Conclusion

In this paper, we present a new robust unsupervised feature selection approach called, *Robust Independent Feature Selection* (RIFS). We propose to make the best use of the independent components structure of a set of features, which is defined on the mixing matrix, both to select the feature subset and to decouple the noise as an latent independent source, simultaneously. Thus, RIFS isolates the noise by rotating the mixing matrix obliquely. When we have compared our RIFS method with two state-of-the-art methods, namely, Laplacian Score and Max Variance, the empirical results on different real world data sets validate that the proposed method obtains considerably higher effectiveness for both clustering and classification. Our proposed RIFS algorithm performs well on original data and it is strongly resists noises.

Acknowledgements. We thankfully acknowledge the support of the Comision Inter-ministerial de Ciencia y Tecnologa (CICYT) under contract No. TIN2015-65316-P which has partially funded this work.

References

1. Arai, K., Barakbah A. R.: Hierarchical K-means: an algorithm for centroids initialization for K-means. Reports of the Faculty of Science, Saga University, **36**(1), pp. 25–31 (2007)
2. Cai, D., Zhang, C., He, X.: Unsupervised feature selection for multi-cluster data. In: Proceedings of the 16th ACM SIGKDD (2010). https://doi.org/10.1145/1835804.1835848
3. Cover, T.M., Thomas, J.A.: Elements of Information Theory, 2nd edn., p. 394. Wiley-Interscience (2005). https://doi.org/10.1002/047174882x
4. Duda, R.O., Hart, P.E., Stork, D.G.: Pattern Classification, 2nd edn., pp. 400–401. Wiley-Interscience, Hoboken (2000)
5. Dy, J.G., Brodley, C.: Feature selection for unsupervised learning. JMLR **5**, 845–889 (2004)
6. Guyon, I., Elisseeff, A.: An introduction to variable and feature selection. JMLR **3**, 1157–1182 (2003)
7. He, X., Cai, D., Niyogi, P.: Laplacian score for feature selection. In: Advances in Neural Information Processing System, vol. 18, pp. 507–514 (2005)
8. Hendrickson, A.E., White, P.O.: PROMAX: a quick method for rotation to oblique simple structure. J. Stat. Psychol. **17**(1), 65–70 (1964). https://doi.org/10.1111/j.2044-8317.1964.tb00244.x

9. Hyvrinen, A., Oja, E.: Independent component analysis: algorithms and applications. Neural Netw. **13**(4–5), 411–430 (2000)
10. Kaiser, H.F.: The varimax criterion for analytic rotation in factor analysis. Psychometrika **23**(3), 187–200 (1958). https://doi.org/10.1007/bf02289233
11. Liu, H., Yu, L.: Toward integrating feature selection algorithms for classification and clustering. IEEE Trans. Knowl. Data Eng. **17**(4), 491–502 (2005). https://doi.org/10.1109/tkde.2005.66
12. Lu, Y., Cohen, I., Zhou, X.S., Tian, Q.: Feature selection using principal feature analysis. In: Proceedings of the 15th ACM International Conference on Multimedia, pp. 301–304 (2007). https://doi.org/10.1145/1291233.1291297
13. Mancini, R., Carter, B.: Op Amps for Everyone. Texas Instruments, pp. 10–11 (2009). https://doi.org/10.1016/b978-1-85617-505-0.x0001-4
14. McCabe, G.P.: Principal variables. Technometrics **26**(2), 137–144 (1984)
15. Qian, M., Zhai, C.: Robust unsupervised feature selection. In: Proceedings of the 23rd International Joint Conference on Artificial Intelligence, pp. 1621–1627 (2013)
16. Rodgers, J.L., Nicewander, W.A.: Thirteen ways to look at the correlation coefficient. Am. Stat. **42**(1), 59–66 (1988). https://doi.org/10.2307/2685263
17. Shlens, J.: A tutorial on principal component analysis. ArXiv preprint arXiv: 1404.2986 (2014)
18. Shukla, H., Kumar, N., Tripathi, R.P.: Gaussian noise filtering techniques using new median filter. IJCA **95**(12), 12–15 (2014). https://doi.org/10.5120/16645-6617
19. Zarzoso, V., Comon, P., Kallel, M.: How fast is FastICA? In: Proceedings of the 14th European Signal Processing Conference, pp. 1–5 (2006)
20. Zhao, Z., Liu, H.: Spectral feature selection for supervised and unsupervised learning. In: Proceedings of the 24th ICML, pp. 1151–1157 (2007). https://doi.org/10.1145/1273496.1273641

Tri-Level Cross-Domain Sign Prediction
for Complex Network

Jiali Pang[1], Donghai Guan[1,2], and Weiwei Yuan[1,2(✉)]

[1] Department of Computer Science and Technology,
Nanjing University of Aeronautics and Astronautics, Nanjing, China
{jialipang,dhguan,yuanweiwei}@nuaa.edu.cn
[2] Corroborative Innovation Center of Novel Software Technology
and Industrialization, Nanjing 210093, China

Abstract. Sign prediction is a fundamental research issue in complex network mining, while the high cost of data collection leads to insufficient data for prediction. The transfer learning method can use the transferable knowledge in other networks to complete the learning tasks in the target network. However, when the inter-domain differences are large, it is difficult for existing methods to obtain useful transferable knowledge. We therefor propose a tri-level cross-domain model using inter-domain similarity and relativity to solve the sign prediction problem in complex networks (TCSP). The first level pre-classifies the source domain, the second level selects the key instances of the source domain, and the third level calculates the similarity between the source domain and the target domain to obtain the pseudo-labels of the target domain. These "labeled" instances are used to train the sign classifier and predict the sign in the target network. Experimental results on real complex network datasets verify the effectiveness of the proposed method.

Keywords: Sign prediction · Transfer learning · Complex networks

1 Introduction

The insufficiency of the labeled data for sign classifier training is the main challenge of existing works. A trained classifier is used to predict the signs of unlabeled links in the complex network. Since the cost of labelling instances is often expensive and time consuming, it is not always possible to get the labelled instances in the real applications. Transfer learning can be used in sign prediction to address this challenge. Transfer learning transfers knowledge from an available domain (named source domain) to an information-insufficient domain (named target domain). The target domain can use the transferred knowledge to perform the different learning task.

Existing transfer learning based sign prediction method [1] cannot predict signs for unlabeled target domains because it needs known labels in the target domain. Besides, the sparse coding based method [2] has knowledge loss because of its sparse solution in the optimization course, adversarial network based method [3] has negative transfer because the generated fake instances are quite different from original instances.

© Springer Nature Switzerland AG 2019
J. Li et al. (Eds.): ADMA 2019, LNAI 11888, pp. 95–106, 2019.
https://doi.org/10.1007/978-3-030-35231-8_7

Structured based methods [4] uses triangle structure features of networks, which is heavily influenced by the noisy instances.

To solve the problems of existing works, a novel cross-domain tri-level based sign prediction model (TCSP) is proposed in this paper. TCSP solves problems of three levels: the lower level is the problem of source domain pre-classification; the second level problem is the key instances selection; the third level problem is node similarity measurement. The first level problem classifies the source domain according to sign distribution and returns a sign-significant source domain. Then the key instances can be extracted from the sign-significant source domain and target domain in the intermediate level. Finally, in the upper level, the similarity and relativity between the source domain and the target domain is measured. The main contributions of this paper are as follows:

- We propose a novel tri-level transfer learning based sign prediction model which can predict signs without any known sign knowledge.
- We solve three key problems of transfer learning based sign prediction by the proposed TCSP model. It can obtain the optimal solution in the knowledge transfer, so that the knowledge in the source domain can be efficiently utilized.

The rest of this paper is organized as follows: Sect. 2 introduces the related works, Sect. 3 introduces some necessary definitions. The proposed method in detail is given in Sect. 4. The Sect. 5 is the experimental results, and the last section concludes this paper and points out the future work.

2   Related Works

Sign prediction is a crucial unsupervised classification problem. But the labels of the networks that we are interested in is always very few even missing. Therefore, transfer learning is a suitable tool to help us to construct the latent relationship that is difficult to find for clustering or other unsupervised methods. Following this plan, the relative works displayed as two parts: unsupervised classification and transfer learning.

Unsupervised Classification
Because of the difficulty of getting real labels for each instance in complex networks, it is unavoidable to research the weakly supervised learning or unsupervised learning in classification task. The existing types of unsupervised methods mainly contains unsupervised-based transfer learning [5], deep learning [6], feature learning [7], and ensemble learning [8]. These approaches facing the same challenge: it is difficult to combine the global and local knowledge among source domain and target domain. Besides, [9] needs deep neural network or CNN to train the classifier which may facing dimension explosion problem. [10] extract the adjacency matrix in networks as the feature which will time-consuming when deal with large networks. And the ensemble methods [11] can be easily influenced by noise inference.

Transfer Learning
Facing up to the reality of insufficient labels in real complex networks, a reasonable solution is to translate unsupervised leaning into weakly supervised learning or

semi-transfer learning. According to existing advantaged non-deep-learning knowledge transfer methods [12, 13], they calculated similarity via mapping the features from source domain and target domain into a new common space. However, this procedure may increase the uncertainty of the whole prediction process and may also generate the new noise in data sets. Some deep learning methods such as [14] reconstruct the feature vectors among source domain and target domain by autoencoder, whose problem is the difficulty of matching the domain dimensions facing to complex networks and this impacts seriously the prediction performance of those models.

3   Problem Definitions

Complex networks can be described as a directed graph $\mathbf{G} = (\mathbf{V}, \mathbf{E}, \mathbf{W})$, $\mathbf{V}$ represents the nodes set in this network, $\mathbf{E}$ means a set including the edges between nodes existing in this network, $\mathbf{W}$ is the set of weight for each edges in $\mathbf{G}$. For each $w(i,j) \in \mathbf{W}$. $w(i,j) = 1$ represents the relationship is positive (e.g. agree, trust, and so on) and $w(i,j) = -1$ notes the negative relationship (e.g. disagree, distrust and so on). And all the value of $\forall w(i,j) \in \mathbf{W}$, $\exists v_i, v_j \in \mathbf{V}$ belongs to $\{-1, 1\}$. In this paper, a signed network is equal to a complex network in literal meaning. Here a link (or an edge) with its weight in $\mathbf{G}$ can be represented as a triplet $e(i,j) = \{v_i, v_j, w(i,j)\}$.

For a complex network $\mathbf{G}$, assuming that $\mathbf{W}$ is unavailable, and $\mathbf{G}$'s feature vector set is noted as $\mathbf{X}$. Sign prediction aims to how to design a function F to get a proper training instance set for the sign classifier that predicts $\mathbf{W}'$ of $\mathbf{G}$ as similar to $\mathbf{W}$ as possible is the aim to this problem. Usually, $\mathbf{X}$ is some available information that are the input of F and the output of F is $\mathbf{W}'$. Specifically, this problem can be formulized as:

$$F : \text{Function} (\mathbf{X}) \rightarrow \mathbf{W}'$$

$$\text{s.t. min } Sim(\mathbf{W}', \mathbf{W}),$$

where $Sim(.)$ represents the similarity measurement function that measures the error between prediction $\mathbf{W}'$ and ground-truth $\mathbf{W}$.

Transfer learning is a learning method that transfers available knowledge from source domain to target domain when the data is insufficient in target domain. For unsupervised classification task, a domain is a data set that noted as $\mathbf{D} = \{\mathbf{X}, \mathbf{Y}\}$, $\mathbf{X}$ is the extracted feature vector set and $\mathbf{Y}$ is the label set of instances. Each instance can be represented as $(\mathbf{x_i}, y_i), \mathbf{x_i} \in \mathbf{X}, y_i \in \mathbf{Y}, i = 1, 2, \dots, |\mathbf{X}|$. And the source domain can be noted as $\mathbf{D_S} = \{(\mathbf{x_1}, y_1), (\mathbf{x_2}, y_2), \dots, (\mathbf{x_m}, y_m)\}, m = |\mathbf{X_S}|, \mathbf{X_S}$ is the feature matrix for D_S and $\mathbf{Y_S}$ is the label set for source domain. Similarly, the target domain can be represented as $\mathbf{D_T} = \{(\mathbf{x_1}, y_1), (\mathbf{x_2}, y_2), \dots, (\mathbf{x_n}, y_n)\}, n = |\mathbf{X_T}|, \mathbf{X_T}$ is the feature matrix for $\mathbf{D_T}$, $\mathbf{Y_T}$ is the label set for target domain. For unsupervised sign prediction in complex network, a domain is also called a network. In this learning task, $\mathbf{Y_T}$ is unknown and $\mathbf{X_S}$, $\mathbf{Y_S}$ are abundant, $\mathbf{X_T}$ is available but not sufficient.

Trilevel program is a novel optimization problem proposed in this paper. There are three parts in a trilevel program: lower problem, intermediate problem and upper problem. The optimal solution of lower problem is the constraints or necessary conditions of intermediate problem and the solution of intermediate problem is the constraint of upper problem. A general tri-level program is formulized as:

$$Upper(\mathbf{X})$$
$$\text{s.t. } \text{Cons}_{intermediate}(\mathbf{X_I}) \cap \mathcal{U}(\mathbf{X_U})$$
$$Intermediate\ (\mathbf{X_I})$$
$$\text{s.t. } \text{Cons}_{lower}(\mathbf{X_L}) \cap \mathcal{I}(\mathbf{X_I})$$
$$Lower(\mathbf{X_L})$$
$$\text{s.t. } \mathcal{L}(\mathbf{X_L}),$$

where $Upper(.)$, $Intermediate(.)$, $Lower(.)$ are the objective functions in upper problem, intermediate problem and lower problem respectively. $\mathbf{X_U}$, $\mathbf{X_I}$ and $\mathbf{X_L}$ are the corresponding optimal solution in each level problem. $\text{Cons}_{intermediate}(.)$ and $\text{Cons}_{lower}(.)$ represent the constraints on different solution in intermediate level and lower level. $\mathcal{L}(.)$, $\mathcal{I}(.)$ and $\mathcal{U}(.)$ are the constraints in lower problem, intermediate problem and upper problem respectively.

4 The Proposed Model

The proposed model is a tri-level based program cross-domain sign prediction model (TCSP) that consists of three programs. In the lower problem, we use the topological features in [1] to extract feature vectors $\mathbf{X_S}$ and $\mathbf{X_T}$ in the $\mathbf{D_S}$ and $\mathbf{D_T}$ respectively. And the source domain needs to be pre-classified and then return the instance sets with a discriminate distribution difference; in the intermediate problem, key instances in $\mathbf{D_S}$ are selected via measuring the distribution distance between instances and the classification plane; in the upper problem, calculating the similarity of source domain key instances and target instances and then assigning the pseudo-labels to the most similar target instances with source domain labels according to source domain key instances. Therefore, the sign classifier can be trained with labeled source domain key instances and some of target instances with pseudo-labels and then predict the rest of target domain instances. The framework of TCSP is shown as Fig. 1.

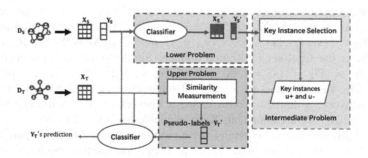

Fig. 1. The framework of TCSP.

4.1   Lower Problem: Pre-classification in Source Domain

To get the most distinctive feature distribution for D_S, the instances are classified firstly. For classification task, it is reasonable to learn a plane function P to divide each kind of instances as discriminate as possible:

$$\text{P}: \min_{\mathbf{W},b} \|\mathbf{W}\|^2 + C \sum_{i=1}^{m} \mathbf{L}_* \left(\mathbf{W}\mathbf{X}_i^T + b, y_i \right), \tag{1}$$

where each $\mathbf{X}_i^T \in \mathbf{X}$ represents the transposition of an instance vector and $y_i \in \{-1, 1\}$ is the labels of instance $\mathbf{X}_i$. $\mathbf{W} \in \mathbf{R}^{m \times n}$ is a matrix, $b \in \mathbf{R}$ is a real number. $\mathbf{L}_*(.)$ is the loss function to measure the knowledge loss of pre-classification in source domain. C is a parameter to set the scale of magnitude of $\mathbf{W}$ and loss function value. And m is the number of instances in D_S, n is the dimension of the features in the data set.

For sign prediction problem, $\mathbf{L}_*(.)$ is square loss function to calculate structure features and content features, so (1) can be concreted defined as:

$$\min_{\mathbf{W},b} \frac{1}{2} \|\mathbf{W}\|^2 + C \sum_{i=1}^{m} \left(1 - y_i \left(\mathbf{W}\mathbf{X}_i^T + b \right) \right)^2. \tag{2}$$

After we get $\mathbf{W}$ and b by the theory support of SVM [15], the classification plane P can be determined uniquely. And the $\mathbf{X}_S$ can be classified with the most distinctive feature distribution.

4.2   Intermediate Problem: Key-Instances Selection in D_S

The aim of this section is to obtain the most valuable instances in $\mathbf{D}_S$ to transfer the characteristic distribution knowledge, which have excluded the interference of noises from source domain to $\mathbf{D}_T$. The solution for intermediate problem is the key instances in $\mathbf{D}_S$. They are key instances, which help transfer the advantaged knowledge from $\mathbf{D}_S$ to $\mathbf{D}_T$. For binary classification learning task, we just use $\mathbf{X}^+$ to express positive key instances and $\mathbf{X}^-$ to express the negative key instance. The objective function of the intermediate problem is designed as:

$$\max_{\mathbf{x},\mathbf{y}} \sum_{i=1}^{m} \sum_{\substack{j=1 \\ i \neq j}}^{m} \left\| x_i^+ - \boldsymbol{P}\left(x_i^+\right) \right\|_F^2 y_i - \left\| x_j^- - \boldsymbol{P}\left(x_j^-\right) \right\|_F^2 y_j + \alpha \left\| x_i^+ \right\|_1 + \beta \left\| x_j^- \right\|_1, \tag{3}$$

where $\mathbf{X}^+$ and $\mathbf{X}^-$ represent the key positive and negative instances in source domain, α and β are the parameters that control the sparsity of $\mathbf{X}^+$ and $\mathbf{X}^-$, if $\mathbf{X}^+$ and $\mathbf{X}^-$ are over-sparse, its contribution cannot be much more better. y_* is the label of x that is:

$$y_* = \begin{cases} 1, x = x_i^+ \\ -1, x = x_j^- \end{cases}.$$

To solve (3) directly is difficult, the decision function in pre-classification process (4.1) is used as auxiliary approach to solve this optimization problem. The value of decision function is positively correlated with the distance between all instances and plane P. Thus, solving (3) equals to select all the instances that satisfied:

$$\max_{x \in X_S} \left| sgn(\sum_{i=1}^{m} y_i \theta_i K(x_i, x) + \gamma) \right|, \tag{4}$$

where $K(.)$ is RBF kernel function, m is the number of all the instances in source domain, theta and gamma are relative parameters to control the scale of variables' value (Here we constraint the number of selected x in source domain via the number of key instances N). $sgn(.)$ is a signal function such like sigmoid function.

Here we can adapt heuristic solution: calculate the decision function value for each instance and sort them in descending order. In all the positive instance set, the instance of maximum decision function value corresponding to is the key positive instance u^+ for positive instance set. And the key negative instance u^- is the instance with minimum decision function value in negative instance set.

4.3   Upper Problem: Similarity Measurements Cross Domains

Transforming the unlabeled data into labeled data and then training classifier with the labeled data can improve classification performance very much. The measurement between instance pairs $(\mathbf{x}, \mathbf{y})$ is defined firstly. To keep more useful information, we consider not only similarity but also relativity:

$$SIM(x, y) = \frac{\mathbf{x} \cdot \mathbf{y}}{\|\mathbf{x}\| \|\mathbf{y}\|} + \frac{1}{(\mathbf{x} - \mathbf{y})^2} = \frac{\sum_{i=1}^{d} \mathbf{x_i} \times \mathbf{y_i}}{\sqrt{\sum_{i=1}^{d} (\mathbf{x_i})^2} \times \sqrt{\sum_{i=1}^{d} (\mathbf{y_i})^2}} + \frac{1}{\sum_{i=1}^{d} (\mathbf{x_i} - \mathbf{y_i})^2}, \tag{5}$$

here the cosine similarity is adapted as the similarity measurement and the reciprocal of Euclidian di-stance is considered as the relativity of structural and contents of instances distribution between source domain and target domain, we allot the different coefficients to adjust the weights of similarity and relativity like:

$$SIM(\mathbf{x_s}, \mathbf{x_T}) = \frac{\mathbf{x_s} \cdot \mathbf{x_T}}{\|\mathbf{x_s}\| \|\mathbf{x_T}\|} + \frac{\rho}{(\mathbf{x_s} - \mathbf{x_T})^2}$$
$$= \frac{\sum_{i=1}^{d} x_S^i \times x_T^i}{\sqrt{\sum_{i=1}^{d} (x_S^i)^2} \times \sqrt{\sum_{i=1}^{d} (x_T^i)^2}} + \frac{\rho}{\sum_{i=1}^{d} (x_S^i - x_T^i)^2}, \tag{6}$$

where $\mathbf{x_s}$ and $\mathbf{x_T}$ represent the instances in source domain and target domain respectively. d is the dimension of features for each instance. Here we extract the same dimension feature vector as the instance. ρ is the parameter that keep the balance magnitude of two items.

Pseudo-labeling the target instance positive label or negative label according to which similarity. The larger similarity means the positive label and the smaller similarity means the negative label.

Now the sign classifier can be trained with labeled source domain data and labeled target domain data and then predict other unlabeled data in target domain.

5 Evaluation Experiments

Five datasets are adapted in evaluating the proposed model: Epinions (note as EPN) [16], Slashdot (not as SLD) [17], bitcoinalpha (note as ALP) [18], bitcoinotc (note as OTC) [19] and Wiki-Vote (note as WKV) [20, 21]. The distribution information of these datasets is given in Table 1.

Table 1. Distribution information of the experimental datasets

	OTC	ALP	EPN	SLA	WKV
Number of nodes	5881	3783	131828	82140	7118
Number of links	35592	24186	841372	549202	103747
Average degree	12.104	12.787	13.372	12.765	29.151
Number of negative links	11981	8890	123705	124130	22497
Negative link ratio	33.66%	36.76%	14.7%	22.6%	21.68%

5.1 Experiments Setting

Pointed to different source domain and target domain, here are 60 groups in these data sets. For efficiency, we use 6 representative groups in testing experiments.

All the experiments can be two main parts: fixing the ratio of positive and negative links in networks and comparing its performance in different ratio of source instances and target instances. Second part is to fix the ratio of source and target.

For different link labels ratio experiment, the number ratio of source domain and target domain is set to be 1:2. The number of key instances N in all experiments is 30. The evaluating indicator is that accuracy and F1-Score.

5.2 Baselines

Self-taught learning (STL) [6]: this method is an unsupervised transfer learning method to predict unlabeled target domain by source domain. TrAdaboost (TRA) [11]: It is a preventative and efficient ensemble transfer learning method to obtain accurate target label information in complex networks. Transfer component analyze (TCA) [12]: this method is an important way that combining the supervised learning and unsupervised learning. Adversarial learning (AL): this method is modified by [7], which makes the model adjust to complex networks. Only source (OS): it trains the classifier with source instances directly and then use target domain instances to test the model performances.

Closed Triple Micro-Structure (CTMS) [8]: CTMS extracts all the possible closed micro triple structures (here are 96 categories for the micro triple structures) around a link to predict the label of the link.

5.3 Prediction Performance

The Influence of the Ratio of Positive Links and Negative Links
In this section, we control the number of instances in source domain and target domain is 1:2. The model parameter is 30. At the beginning, the negative links in complex networks is 20% (except WKV, it begins at 25%, because it has less negative links in original data set.), and the last test ratio is 50%, which is the situation for the maximum of cross-entropy between each instances in the same domain. Test results are shown in Fig. 2.

According to the results, the performance tend of all methods is decreasing with the increasing of negative links. This is reasonable because the uncertainty of the networks is more and larger, which is more difficult to ensure the labels for unknown instances. And this is also can prove the value of our model pointed this more realistic situation. It can overcome the uncertainty of instances in the most situation.

The Influence of the Ratio of X_S and X_T
In this section, we main test the factor that different scales of source domain and target domain instances. Here we start from source domain: target domain = 1:1, then increasing the ratio to 1:10 to observe the performances in all the methods. The parameter N in TCSP is set to be 30.

Note that the CTMS needs triangle structures to predict signs so that it depends on sign ratio very much, and its performance is influenced seriously in this section. The ability of all the methods is shown in Fig. 3.

Here the efficiency of TCSP model can be obviously observed. For the most situations, TCSP is better than other baselines and this means that TCSP is much more general for complex network in link prediction task via transfer learning method.

5.4 Parameter Analyze

Here we test the influence of the range of N in TCSP. Here for fairness, the negative link ratio is set to be 40% and the number ratio of source domain instances and target domain instances is set to be 1:2, 1:3 and 1:4 respectively. Because of the space of the paper, we choose a group of experiment to test the performance of different N. The results are shown in Fig. 4.

For the most common situation that is the negative links ratio closed to 50%, the trend of the performance is a stable and little decreasing as shown in Fig. 4. The ratio of the source domain instances and target domain instances has little difference with the same range of N. With the increasing of N, the real distribution may be changed much to cause negative influence on prediction performance. And the N is suggested to be set as 35–35 to fit the TCSP model.

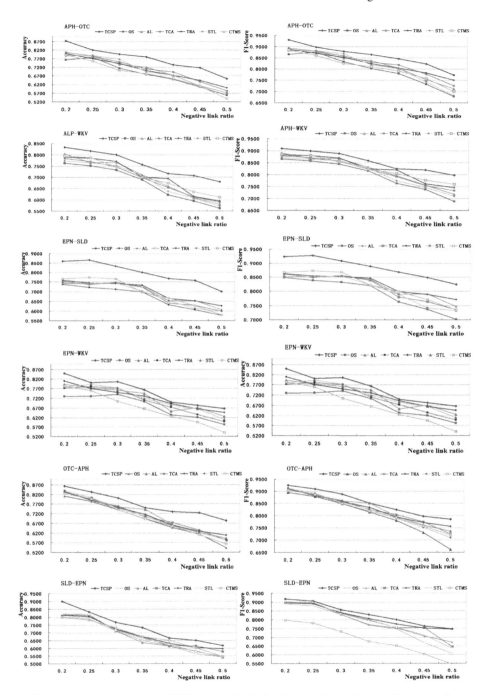

Fig. 2. The performances of different methods for sign prediction in complex networks.

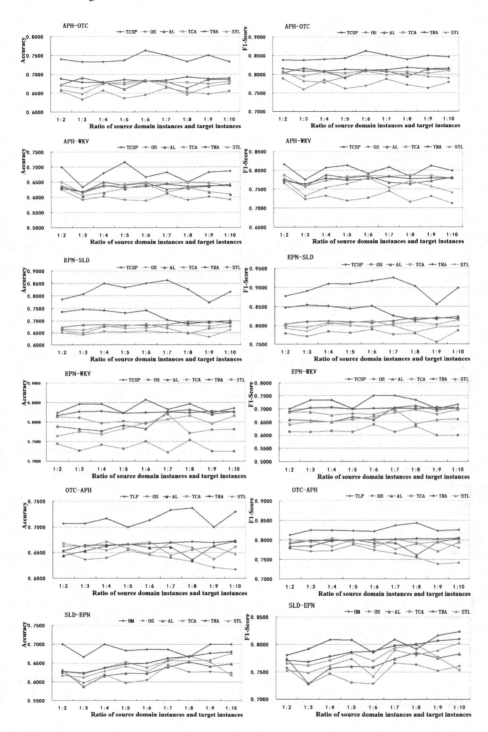

Fig. 3. The performances of different methods for sign prediction in complex networks.

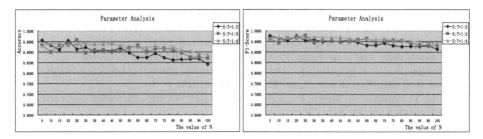

Fig. 4. The prediction performance of different N in the proposed model.

6   Conclusions and Future Works

In this paper, the tri-level program based sign prediction model (TCSP) is proposed, which transfers knowledge from source domain to target domain with pseudo-labels. The classifier with the insufficient source domain and a small part of "pseudo-labeled" instances in target domain can be trained. After training, the classifier can predict the rest of unlabeled target domain instance. Considering the efficiency and accuracy, the unsupervised sign prediction problem can be solved comprehensively by three inter-constrained programs. Because the intersection of the constrained conditions in every program ensures all the solution in the results is optimal in every level.

The future work of this paper is to improve the performance of the proposed model by decreasing the influence of negative transferring and optimizing the strategy of measuring the similarity and relativity of instances between source domain and target domain. And we also explore whether the constraints in each level can be relaxed.

Acknowledgement. This research was supported by Nature Science Foundation of China (Grant No. 61672284), Natural Science Foundation of Jiangsu Province (Grant No. BK20171418), China Postdoctoral Science Foundation (Grant No. 2016M591841), Jiangsu Planned Projects for Postdoctoral Research Funds (No. 1601225C).

References

1. Ye, J., Cheng, H., Zhu, Z., et al.: Predicting positive and negative links in signed social networks by transfer learning. In: Proceedings of the 22nd International Conference on World Wide Web, pp. 1477–1488. ACM (2013)
2. Raina, R., Battle, A., Lee, H., et al.: Self-taught learning: transfer learning from unlabeled data. In: Proceedings of the 24th International Conference on Machine learning. pp. 759–766. ACM (2007)
3. Saito, K., Watanabe, K., Ushiku, Y., et al.: Maximum classifier discrepancy for unsupervised domain adaptation. In: Proceedings of the IEEE Conference on Computer Vision and Pattern Recognition, pp. 3723–3732 (2018)
4. Khodadadi, A., Jalili, M.: Sign prediction in social networks based on tendency rate of equivalent micro-structures. Neurocomputing **257**, 175–184 (2017)

5. Rout, J.K., Choo, K.K.R., Dash, A.K., et al.: A model for sentiment and emotion analysis of unstructured social media text. Electron. Commer. Res. **18**, 181–199 (2018)
6. Chen, W., Zhang, Y., Yeo, C.K., et al.: Unsupervised rumor detection based on users' behaviors using neural networks. Pattern Recogn. Lett. **105**, 226–233 (2018)
7. Kakisim, A.G., Sogukpinar, I.: Unsupervised binary feature construction method for networked data. Expert Syst. Appl. **121**, 256–265 (2019)
8. Dutta, S., Chandra, V., Mehra, K., et al.: Ensemble algorithms for microblog summarization. IEEE Intell. Syst. **33**, 4–14 (2018)
9. Kudugunta, S., Ferrara, E.: Deep neural networks for bot detection. Inf. Sci. **467**, 312–322 (2018)
10. Mohammadrezaei, M., Shiri, M.E., Rahmani, A.M.: Identifying fake accounts on social networks based on graph analysis and classification algorithms. Secur. Commun. Networks **2018**, 8 (2018)
11. Yao, Y., Doretto, G.: Boosting for transfer learning with multiple sources. In: 2010 IEEE Computer Society Conference on Computer Vision and Pattern Recognition, pp. 1855–1862 (2010)
12. Pan, S.J., Tsang, I.W., Kwok, J.T., et al.: Domain adaptation via transfer component analysis. IEEE Trans. Neural Networks **22**, 199–210 (2010)
13. Noroozi, M., Vinjimoor, A., Favaro, P., et al.: Boosting self-supervised learning via knowledge transfer. In: Proceedings of the IEEE Conference on Computer Vision and Pattern Recognition, pp. 9359–9367 (2018)
14. Wang, L., Geng, X., Ma, X., et al.: Crowd flow prediction by deep spatio-temporal transfer learning (2018). arXiv preprint arXiv:1802.00386
15. Schuldt, C., Laptev, I., Caputo, B.: Recognizing human actions: a local SVM approach. In Proceedings of the 17th International Conference on Pattern Recognition, 2004, ICPR 2004, vol. 3, pp. 32–36. IEEE (2004)
16. Richardson, M., Agrawal, R., Domingos, P.: Trust Management for the Semantic Web. In: Fensel, D., Sycara, K., Mylopoulos, J. (eds.) ISWC 2003. LNCS, vol. 2870, pp. 351–368. Springer, Heidelberg (2003). https://doi.org/10.1007/978-3-540-39718-2_23
17. Leskovec, J., Lang, K.J., Dasgupta, A., et al.: Community structure in large networks: natural cluster sizes and the absence of large well-defined clusters. Internet Math. **6**, 29–123 (2009)
18. Kumar, S., Hooi, B., Makhija, D., et al.: Rev2: fraudulent user prediction in rating platforms. In: Proceedings of the Eleventh ACM International Conference on Web Search and Data Mining, 333–341. ACM (2018)
19. Kumar, S., Spezzano, F., Subrahmanian, V.S., et al.: Edge weight prediction in weighted signed networks. In: 2016 IEEE 16th International Conference on Data Mining (ICDM), pp. 221–230 (2016)
20. Leskovec, J., Huttenlocher, D., Kleinberg, J.: Predicting positive and negative links in online social networks. In: Proceedings of the 19th International Conference on World Wide Web, pp. 641–650 (2010)
21. Leskovec, J., Huttenlocher, D., Kleinberg, J.: Signed networks in social media. In: Proceedings of the SIGCHI Conference on Human Factors in Computing Systems, pp. 1361–1370 (2010)

An Efficient Mining Algorithm of Closed Frequent Itemsets on Multi-core Processor

Huan Phan[1,2(✉)]

[1] Division of IT, University of Social Sciences and Humanities – VNU-HCMC,
Ho Chi Minh City, Vietnam
huanphan@hcmussh.edu.vn
[2] Faculty of Mathematics and Computer Science,
University of Science – VNU-HCMC, Ho Chi Minh City, Vietnam

Abstract. In this paper, we improved a sequential **NOV-CFI** algorithm mining closed frequent itemsets in transaction databases, called **SEQ-CFI** and consisting of three phases: *the first phase*, quickly detect a **Kernel_COOC** array of co-occurrences and occurrences of kernel item in at least one transaction; *the second phase*, we built the list of **nLOOC-Tree** base on the **Kernel_COOC** and a binary matrix of dataset (*self-reduced search space*); *the last phase*, the algorithm is a fast mining closed frequent itemsets base on **nLOOC-Tree**. The next step, we develop a sequential algorithm for mining closed frequent itemsets and thus parallelize the sequential algorithm to effectively demonstrate the multi-core processor, called **NPA-CFI**. The experimental results show that the proposed algorithms perform better than other existing algorithms, as well as to expand the parallel **NPA-CFI** algorithm on distributed computing systems such as Hadoop, Spark.

Keywords: Co-occurrence items · Closed frequent itemsets · Multi-core processor · Parallel NPA-CFI algorithm

1 Introduction

There are variously foundational and necessary problems in the applications of data mining (e.g. the discovery of association rules, strong rules, correlations, multi-dimensional pattern, and many other essential discovery tasks). Among of them, mining frequent itemsets (**FI**) [1] is an important one. The formulation of this problem is being given a transactional database, then finding all frequent itemsets, where a frequent item occurs in *at least a user-specified percentage* of transaction databases. When we are mining association rules in transaction database, a *huge number* of frequent itemsets will be generated. Authors around the world proposed mining for closed frequent itemsets (**CFI**) [8]; **CFI** are non-redundant representations of all frequent itemsets.

Most mining algorithms for closed frequent itemsets, proposed by various authors around the world, are based on lattice framework (A-CLOSE) [2], IT-Tree (CHARM) [3], FP-Tree (CLOSET+, CFIM-P) [4, 5]. Algorithms generated candidate using a breadth-first search, with tidset format. Besides, the algorithms improve upon a depth-first search,

© Springer Nature Switzerland AG 2019
J. Li et al. (Eds.): ADMA 2019, LNAI 11888, pp. 107–118, 2019.
https://doi.org/10.1007/978-3-030-35231-8_8

diffset format. The main limitation of algorithms based on lattice framework, IT-Tree a major advance developed using pattern-growth based on FP-Tree.

Simultaneously to speed up the implementation of the mining closed frequent itemsets, authors worldwide propose the parallelization of algorithms based on the IT-Tree [6] and FP-Tree [7]. In this paper, we improved a novel sequential NOV-CFI [9] algorithm that mines closed frequent itemsets, and then, parallelizing the sequential algorithm to demonstrate the multi-core processor in an effective way as follows:

- **Algorithm 1:** Computing Kernel_COOC array of co-occurrences and occurrences of kernel item in at least one transaction;
- **Algorithm 2:** Building list nLOOC_Tree based on Kernel_COOC array;
- **Algorithm 3:** Generating closed frequent itemset based on list nLOOC_Tree;
- Parallel **NPA-CFI** algorithm quickly mining closed frequent itemsets from transactional databases implemented on the multi-core processor.

This paper is organized as follows: in Sect. 2, we describe the basic concepts for mining closed frequent itemsets and data structure for transaction databases. Some theoretical aspects of our approach relies, are given in Sect. 3. Besides, we describe our sequential algorithm to compute closed frequent itemsets on transactional databases. After that we parallelize the improved sequential algorithm. Details on implementation and experimental tests are discussed in Sect. 4. Finally, we conclude with a summary of our approach, perspectives and extensions of this future work

2   Background

In this section, we represent the basic concepts for mining closed frequent itemsets and efficient data structure for transaction databases.

2.1   Closed Frequent Itemsets Mining

Let $I = \{i_1, i_2,..., i_m\}$ be a set of m distinct items. A set of items $X = \{i_1, i_2,..., i_k\}$, $\forall i_j \in I$ $(1 \leq j \leq k)$ is called an itemset, an itemset with k items is called a k-*itemset*. D be a dataset containing n transaction, a set of transaction $T = \{t_1, t_2,..., t_n\}$ and each transaction $t_j = \{i_{k1}, i_{k2},..., i_{kl}\}$, $\forall i_{kl} \in I$ $(1 \leq k_l \leq m)$.

Definition 1. The support of an itemset X is the number of transaction in which occurs as a subset, denoted as $sup(X)$.

Definition 2. Let *minsup* be the threshold minimum support value specified by user. If $sup(X) \geq minsup$, itemset X is called a frequent itemset, denoted **FI** is the set of all the frequent itemset.

Definition 3. Itemset X is called a closed frequent itemset: If $sup(X) \geq minsup$ and for all itemset $Y \supset X$ then $sup(Y) < sup(X)$, denoted **CFI** is the set of all the closed frequent itemset.

See an example transaction database $\mathcal{D}$ in Table 1.

Table 1. The transaction database $\mathcal{D}$ used as our running example

TID	Items						TID	Items					
t1	A	C		E	F		t6				E		
t2	A	C				G	t7	A	B	C	E		
t3				E		H	t8	A		C	D		
t4	A	C	D		F	G	t9	A	B	C	E		G
t5	A	C		E		G	10	A		C	E	F	G

2.2 Data Structure for Transaction Database

The binary matrix is an efficient data structure for mining frequent itemsets [9]. The process begins with the transaction database transformed into a binary matrix BiM, in which each row corresponds to a transaction and each column corresponds to an item. Each element in the binary matrix BiM contains 1 if the item is presented in the current transaction; otherwise it contains 0.

3 The Proposed Algorithms

3.1 Generating Array Contain Co-occurrence Items of Kernel Item

In this section, we illustrate the framework of the algorithm generating co-occurrence items of items in transaction database.

Definition 4 [9]. Project set of item i_k on database $\mathcal{D}$: $\pi(i_k) = \{t_j \in \mathcal{D} \mid i_k \subseteq t_j\}$ is set of transaction contain item i_k. According to Definition 1.

$$sup(i_k) = |\pi(i_k)| \tag{1}$$

Definition 5 [9]. Project set of itemset X = $\{i_1, i_2,..., i_k\}$, $\forall i_j \in I$ $(1 \leq j \leq k)$: $\pi(X) = \pi(i_1) \cap \pi(i_2)... \pi(i_k)$.

$$sup(X) = |\pi(X)| \tag{2}$$

Definition 6 [9] (Reduce search space). Let $\forall i_k \in I$ $(i_1 \prec i_2 \prec ... \prec i_m)$ items are ordered in support ascending order, i_k is called a kernel item. Itemset $X_{lexcooc} \subseteq I$ is called co-occurrence items with the kernel item i_k, so that satisfy $\pi(i_k) \equiv \pi(i_k \cup i_j)$, $i_k \prec i_j$, $\forall i_j \in X_{lexcooc}$. Denoted as $lexcooc(i_k) = X_{lexcooc}$ (Table 2).

Definition 7 [9] (Reduce search space). Let $\forall i_k \in I$ $(i_1 \prec i_2 \prec ... \prec i_m)$ items are ordered in support ascending order, i_k is called a kernel item. Itemset $Y_{lexlooc} \subseteq I$ is called occurrence items with kernel item i_k in as least one transaction, but not co-occurrence items, so that $1 \leq |\pi(i_k \cup i_j)| < |\pi(i_k)|$, $\forall i_j \in Y_{lexlooc}$. Denoted as *lexlooc* $(i_k) = Y_{lexlooc}$.

Algorithm Generating Array of Co-occurrence Items

This algorithm is generating co-occurrence items of items in transaction database and archive into the *Kernel_COOC* array and each element have 4 fields:

- Kernel_COOC[k].*item*: kernel item k;
- Kernel_COOC[k].*sup*: support of kernel item k;
- Kernel_COOC[k].*cooc*: co-occurrence items with kernel item k;
- Kernel_COOC[k].*looc*: occurrence items kernel item k in least one transaction.

The framework of Algorithm 1 is as follows:

Algorithm 1. Generating Array of Co-occurrence Items

        Input : Dataset $\mathcal{D}$
        Output: *Kernel_COOC array, matrix BiM*
1:    **foreach** Kernel_COOC[k] **do**
2:       Kernel_COOC[k].item = i_k; Kernel_COOC[k].sup = 0
3:       Kernel_COOC[k].cooc = $2^m - 1$; Kernel_COOC[k].looc = 0
4:    **foreach** $t_j \in T$ **do**
5:       **foreach** $i_k \in t_j$ **do**
6:          Kernel_COOC[k].sup ++
7:          Kernel_COOC[k].cooc = Kernel_COOC[k].cooc **AND** vectorbit(t_j)
8:          Kernel_COOC[k].looc = Kernel_COOC[k].looc **OR** vectorbit(t_j)
9:    sort Kernel_COOC array in ascending by support
10:   **foreach** $i_k \in t_j$ **do**
11:      Kernel_COOC[k].cooc = lexcooc(i_k)
12:      Kernel_COOC[k].looc = lexlooc(i_k)

We illustrate Algorithm 1 on example database in Table 1.

Table 2. Kernel_COOC array are ordered in support ascending order (line 1 to 9) [9]

Item	H	B	D	F	G	E	A	C
sup	1	2	2	3	5	7	8	8
cooc	E	A, C, E	A, C	A, C	A, C		C	A
looc		G	F, G	D, E, G	B, D, E, F	A, B, C, F, G, H	B, D, E, F, G	B, D, E, F, G

Execute command line 10, 11 and 12 in Algorithm 1:

We have $looc(G) = \{B, D, E, F\}$, where B, D $\prec$ F $\prec$ G $\prec$ E, so *lexlooc*(G) = {E}. Execute command line 12, 13 and 14 has result on Table 3.

Table 3. The Kernel_COOC array are co-occurrence items ordered in support ascending order.

Item	H	B	D	F	G	E	A	C
sup	1	2	2	3	5	7	8	8
cooc	E	A, C, E	A, C	A, C	A, C	∅	C	∅
looc	∅	G	F, G	G, E	E	A, C	∅	∅

3.2 Generating List nLOOC-Tree

In this section, we describe the algorithm generating list *nLOOC-Tree* based on *Kernel_LOOC* array. Each node within the *nLOOC_Tree*, 2 main fields:

- nLOOC_Tree[k].*item*: kernel item k;
- nLOOC_Tree[k].*sup*: support of item k;

The framework of Algorithm 2 is as follows:

Algorithm 2. Generating list nLOOC-Tree (*self-reduced search space*)

      Input : Kernel_COOC array, matrix BiM
      Output: *List nLOOC-Tree*
1:   **foreach** Kernel_COOC[k] **do**
2:      nLOOC_Tree[k].*item* = *Kernel_COOC*[k].*item*
3:      nLOOC_Tree[k].*sup* = *Kernel_COOC*[k].*sup*
4:   **foreach** $i_j \in t_l$ **do**
5:      **foreach** $i_j \in Kernel\_COOC[k].looc$ **do**
6:         **if** $i_j \notin child\ node\ of$ nLOOC_Tree[k] **then**
7:            Add child node i_j to nLOOC_Tree[k]
8:      **else**
9:         Update support of child node i_j on nLOOC_Tree[k]
10: **return** list nLOOC_Tree

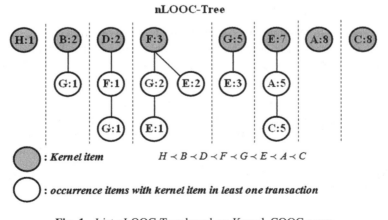

Fig. 1. List nLOOC-Tree based on Kernel_COOC array

Each **nLOOC-Tree** has the characteristics following Fig. 1:

- The height of the tree is less than or equal to the number of items that occurrence at least in one transaction with the kernel item (*items are ordered in significance support ascending order*).
- Single-path is an *ordered pattern* from the root node (*kernel item*) to the leaf node and the support of a pattern is the support of the leaf node ($i_k \rightarrow i_{k+1} \rightarrow ... \rightarrow i_\ell$).
- Sub-single-path is part of *single-path* from the root node to any node in an ordered pattern and the *sub-single-path* support is the support of the child node at the end of the *sub-single-path*.

Example 4. Consider *kernel item F*, we observe **nLOOC-Tree**(*F*) generating *single-path* {$\underline{F} \rightarrow G \rightarrow E$}, *sup*($\underline{F}GE$) = 1; *sub-single-path* {$\underline{F} \rightarrow G$}, *sup*($\underline{F}G$) = 2.

3.3   Algorithm Generating All Closed Frequent Itemsets

In this section, we illustrate the framework of the algorithm generating DIRECT all closed frequent itemsets bases on the nLOOC-Tree and Kernel_COOC array.

Lemma 1. (Generating DIRECT closed frequent itemset from co-occurrence items) $\forall i_k \in I$, if $sup(i_k) \geq minsup$ and itemset $X_{lexcooc}$ is set of for all element of $lexcooc(i_k)$ then $sup(i_k \cup X_{lexcooc}) \geq minsup$ and itemset $\{i_k \cup X_{lexcooc}\} \in$ **CFI**.

Proof. According to Definition 6, (1) and (2): itemset $X_{lexcooc}$ is set of co-occurrence items with the kernel item i_k, so that satisfy $\pi(i_k) \equiv \pi(i_k \cup i_j)$, $i_k \prec i_j$, $\forall i_j \in X_{lexcooc}$ and obviously $\pi(i_k) \equiv \pi(i_k \cup X_{lexcooc})$. Therefore, we have $sup(i_k) = sup$ ($i_k \cup X_{lexcooc}) \geq minsup$ and according to Definition 7: $\nexists X' \supset X_{lexcooc}$, $sup(X') = sup(i_k)$∎.

Example 5. See Table 3. Consider the item D as kernel item (*minsup* = 2), we detect co-occurrence items with the item D as $lexcooc(D) = \{A, C\}$ then *sup* (DAC) = 2 $\geq minsup$ and itemset *DAC* is closed frequent itemset.

Lemma 2. $\forall i_k \in I$, $X_{lexcooc} = lexcooc(i_k)$, generating single-paths/sub-single-paths from nLOOC-Tree(i_k) have the longest and $sup(i_k \rightarrow i_{k+1} \rightarrow ... \rightarrow i_\ell) \geq minsup$ then {ik $\cup ... \cup i_\ell \cup X_{lexcooc}\} \in$ **CFI**.

Proof. According to Definition 6, 7 and Lemma 1: we have $|\pi(i_k \cup y_{lexlooc})| < |\pi(i_k)|$ $\equiv |\pi(i_k \cup X_{lexcooc})|$ ($y_{lexlooc}$ contain items of single-paths/sub-single-paths, $y_{lexlooc} \in lexlooc(i_k)$) and $sup(i_k \cup y_{lexlooc}) \geq minsup$. Therefore, we have $sup(i_k \cup y_{lexlooc} \cup X_{lexcooc}) \geq minsup$ and $\{i_k \cup y_{lexlooc} \cup X_{lexcooc}\} \in$ **CFI**∎.

Example 6. See Table 3 and Fig. 1. Consider the item G as kernel item (*minsup* = 2), we detect co-occurrence items with item G as $X_{lexcooc} = lexcooc(G) = \{A, C\}$; we observe **nLOOC-Tree**(*G*) generating *single-path* {$\underline{G} \rightarrow E$}, $sup(\underline{G}E) = 3 \geq minsup$ then $sup(\underline{G}EAC) = 3 \geq minsup$ and itemset $\underline{G}EAC$ is closed frequent itemset.

Property 1. (Reduce generated space) If $sup(i_{k-1}) = sup(i_k) \wedge i_k \in lexcooc(i_{k-1})$ then $i_{k-1} \equiv i_k$ (generating closed frequent itemset from item i_{k-1} then not consider item i_k).

The framework of Algorithm 3 is presented as follows:

Algorithm 3. Generating all closed frequent itemsets satisfy *minsup*

Input : *minsup, Kernel_COOC array*, nLOOC_Tree
Output: **CFI** consists all closed frequent itemsets

1:   **foreach** Kernel_COOC[k].sup ≥ *minsup* **do**
2:       **if** NOT((Kernel_COOC[k-1].sup = Kernel_COOC[k].sup) AND
             (Kernel_COOC[k].item ∈ Kernel_COOC[k-1].cooc)) **then** //*property 1*
3:           CFI[k] = CFI[k] ∪ {i$_k$ ∪ Kernel_COOC[k].cooc} //*lemma 1*
4:           **if** (Kernel_COOC[k].sup > *minsup*) AND (Kernel_COOC[k].looc ≠ {∅})
5:               SSP = GenPath (nLOOC_Tree(Kernel_COOC[k].item))
6:               **foreach** *ssp$_j$* ∈ SSP **do**
7:                   **if** (*sup(ssp$_j$*) ≥ *minsup*)//*long frequent itemset*
8:                       CFI[k] = CFI[k] ∪ {i$_k$ ∪ Kernel_COOC[k].cooc ∪ *ssp$_j$*}//*lemma 2*

3.4   The Sequential Algorithm SEQ-CFI

In this section, we represent the diagram of **SEQ-CFI** algorithm for mining closed frequent itemsets, as shown in Fig. 2.

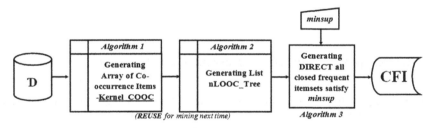

Fig. 2. The diagram of sequential algorithm for mining CFI (SEQ-CFI).

We illustrate Algorithm 3 on example database in Table 1 and *minsup* = 2. After the processing Algorithm 1 result the *Kernel_COOC* array in Table 3 and Algorithm 2 presented the list **nLOOC_Tree** in Fig. 1.

Line 1, consider items satisfying *minsup* as kernel items {B, D, F, G, E, A, C};

Consider *kernel item* B, *sup*(B) = 2 = *minsup* (*Lemma 1- line 3*) generating closed frequent itemset with *kernel item B* as CFI$_{[B]}$ = {(**B**EAC, 2)} (not satisfy line 4).

Consider *kernel item* D, *sup*(D) = 2 = *minsup* (similarly *kernel item B*) generating closed frequent itemset with *kernel item D* as CFI$_{[D]}$ = {(**D**AC, 2)} (not satisfy line 4).

Consider the *kernel item* F, *sup*(F) = 3 > *minsup* (*Lemma 1- line 3*): generating frequent itemsets CFI$_{[F]}$ = {(**F**AC, 3)}; *(from line 4 to 8)* – we observe **nLOOC-Tree** (F) single-path {**F**→E}: *sup*(FE) = 2 ≥ *minsup* generating closed frequent itemsets CFI$_{[F]}$ = {(**F**EAC, 2)} ∪ {(**F**AC, 3)} and single-path {**F**→G→E}, *sup*(FGE) = 1 < *minsup* has *sub-single-path* {**F**→G}, *sup*(**F**G) = 2 ≥ *minsup* generating closed frequent itemsets CFI$_{[F]}$ = {(**F**GEAC, 2)} ∪ {(**F**EAC, 2), (**F**AC, 3)}.

Consider the *kernel item* G, *sup*(G) = 5 > *minsup* (similary *kernel item F*): generating closed frequent itemsets CFI$_{[G]}$ = {(G̲AC, 5)}; (*from line 4 to 8*) – we observe **nLOOC-Tree**(G) have single-path {G̲→E}: *sup*(GE) = 3 ≥ *minsup* generating closed frequent itemsets CFI$_{[G]}$ = {(G̲EAC, 3)} ∪ {(G̲AC, 5)}.

Consider the *kernel item* E, *sup*(E) = 7 > *minsup* (similary *kernel item F*): generating closed frequent itemsets CFI$_{[E]}$ = {(E̲, 7)}; (*from line 4 to 8*) – we observe **nLOOC-Tree**(E) have single-path {E̲→A→C}: *sup*(EAC) = 5 ≥ *minsup* generating closed frequent itemsets CFI$_{[E]}$ = {(E̲AC, 5)} ∪ {(E̲, 7)}.

Consider the *kernel item* A, *sup*(A) = 8 > *minsup* (similary *kernel item F*): generating closed frequent itemsets CFI$_{[A]}$ = {(A̲C, 8)} (not satisfy line 4).

The *kernel item* C is not consider – NOT satisfy *line 2*. (*Property 1*)

Table 4 shows the closed frequent itemsets at *minsup* = 2.

Table 4. CFI satisfy *minsup* = 2 (example database in Table 1).

Kernel item	Closed frequent itemsets - **CFI**		
B	(B̲EAC, 2)		
D	(D̲AC, 2)		
F	(F̲ACG, 2)	(F̲ACE, 2)	(F̲AC, 3)
G	(G̲ACE, 3)	(G̲AC, 5)	
E	(E̲AC, 5)	(E̲, 7)	
A	(A̲C, 8)		

3.5 Parallel NPA-CFI Algorithm Generating All Closed Frequent Itemsets

In this section, we illustrate parallel algorithms and experimental setup on the multi-core processor (MCP). We proposed a parallel **NPA-CFI** algorithm for because it quickly detects closed frequent itemsets on MCP.

The parallel **NPA-CFI** algorithm for generating all closed frequent itemsets, including 3 phases:

– *Phase 1*: Computing *Kernel_COOC* array by parallelization Algorithm 1;
– *Phase 2*: Building list *nLOOC_Tree* by sequential Algorithm 2;
– *Phase 3*: Generating all **CFI** by parallelization Algorithm 3;

Phase 1 - Parallelization Algorithm 1 is shown in the diagram:

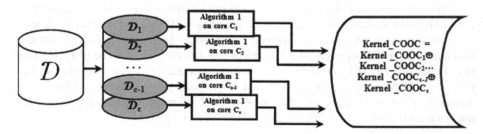

Fig. 3. The diagram parallelization Phase 1.

In Fig. 3, we split the transaction database $\mathcal{D}$ into c (*number of core on CPU*) parts $\mathcal{D}_1, \mathcal{D}_2, \ldots, \mathcal{D}_c$. After that, the core j^{th} executes Algorithm 1 with input transaction database $\mathcal{D}_j$ and output the $Kernel\_COOC_{\mathcal{D}_j}$ array. The $Kernel\_COOC_{\mathcal{D}}$ array for the transaction database $\mathcal{D}$, we compute the following equation:

$$Kernel\_COOC_D = Kernel\_COOC_{D_1} \oplus Kernel\_COOC_{D_2} \oplus \ldots \oplus Kernel\_COOC_{Dc} \tag{3}$$

$\oplus$ denoted as **sum** for *sup*, **AND** for *cooc*, **OR** for *looc* field of each element array. The next step, we sort the $Kernel\_COOC$ array in ascending order by supporting, executing commands line 10, 11 and 12 of the Algorithm 1.

Example 7. See Table 1. We split the transaction database $\mathcal{D}$ into 2 parts: the database $\mathcal{D}_1 = \{t_1, t_2, t_3, t_4, t_5\}$ and database $\mathcal{D}_2 = \{t_6, t_7, t_8, t_9, t_{10}\}$.

The processing of Algorithm 1 on database $\mathcal{D}_1$

Item	A	B	C	D	E	F	G	H
sup	4	0	4	1	3	2	3	1
cooc	10100000	11111111	10100000	10110110	00001000	10100100	10100010	00001001
looc	10111110	00000000	10111110	10110110	10101111	10111110	10111110	00001001

The processing of Algorithm 1 on database $\mathcal{D}_2$

Item	A	B	C	D	E	F	G	H
sup	4	2	4	1	4	1	2	0
cooc	10100000	11101000	10100000	10110000	00001000	10101110	10101010	11111111
looc	11111110	11101010	11111110	10110000	11101110	10101110	11101110	00000000

Results of (3), we have the $Kernel\_COOC$ array as presented in Table 3.
Phase 3 – Parallelization of Algorithm 3 is shown in the diagram:

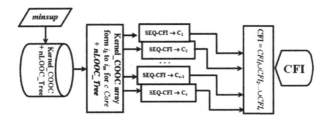

Fig. 4. The diagram parallelization Phase 3.

In Fig. 4, we split the $Kernel\_COOC_{\mathcal{D}}$ array from element i_k to i_m ($sup(i_k) \geq minsup$) into c parts. After that, the core j th execute Algorithm 3 with input $Kernel\_COOC_{\mathcal{D}}$ array from $k + (j-1)*((m-k+1) \; div \; c)$ to $k + j*((m-k+1) \; div \; c)$ element, returns results

116   H. Phan

frequent itemsets $CFI_{\mathcal{D}_j}$. The frequent itemsets $CFI_{\mathcal{D}}$ for the transaction database $\mathcal{D}$, we compute the following equation:

$$CFI_{\mathcal{D}} = CFI_{\mathcal{D}_1} \cup CFI_{\mathcal{D}_2} \cup \ldots \cup CFI_{\mathcal{D}_c} \qquad (4)$$

Example 8. See Table 1. Generating all closed frequent itemsets satisfy *minsup* = 2, the transaction database $\mathcal{D}$ split into 2 parts as Example 7. Results of phase 1 parallelization, we have the *Kernel_COOC*$_{\mathcal{D}}$ array as Table 3.

The processing of Algorithm 3 on the *nLOOC_Tree* form *item* B to F:

Kernel item	Closed Frequent itemsets - $CFI_{\mathcal{D}_1}$		
B	(**B**EAC, 2)		
D	(**D**AC, 2)		
F	(**F**ACG, 2)	(**F**ACE, 2)	(**F**AC, 3)

The processing of Algorithm 3 on the *nLOOC_Tree* form *item* G to A:

Kernel item	Closed Frequent itemsets - $CFI_{\mathcal{D}_2}$		
G	(**G**ACE, 3)	(**G**AC, 5)	
E	(**E**AC, 5)	(**E**, 7)	
A	(**A**C, 8)		

Results of (4), we have closed frequent itemsets as presented in Table 4.

4 Experiments

All experiments were conducted on a PC with a Core Duo CPU T2500 2.0 GHz (*2 Cores, 2 Threads*), 4 Gb main memory, running Microsoft Windows 7 Ultimate. All codes were compiled using C#, Microsoft Visual Studio 2010, .Net Framework 4.

We experimented on two instance types of datasets:

- Two real datasets are both *dense* form of UCI Machine Learning Repository [http:// archive.ics.uci.edu/ml] as **Chess** and **Mushroom** datasets.
- Two synthetic *sparse* datasets are generated by software of IBM Almaden Research Center [http://www.almaden.ibm.com] as **T10I4D100K** and **T40I10D100K** datasets.

Table 5. Datasets description in experiments

Name	#Trans	#Items	#Avg. length	Type	Density (%)
Chess	3,196	75	37	Dense	49.3
Mushroom	8,142	119	23	Dense	19.3
T10I4D100K	100,000	870	10	Sparse	1.1
T40I10D100K	100,000	942	40	Sparse	4.2

We improved a sequential **NOV-CFI** [9] algorithm mining closed frequent itemsets on transaction databases, called **SEQ-CFI**. We have compared the parallel **NPA-CFI** algorithm with sequential algorithms **SEQ-CFI** and **CHARM** [3].

Performance implementation parallel **NPA-CFI** algorithm on MCP:

$$P = 1 - \left(T_{Npa} - \frac{T_{Seq}}{c} \right) / \left(\frac{T_{Seq}}{c} \right) \tag{5}$$

Where: - T_{Seq}: executing time of the *sequential algorithm*;
- T_{Npa}: executing time of the *parallel algorithm*;
- c: number of the core on CPU.

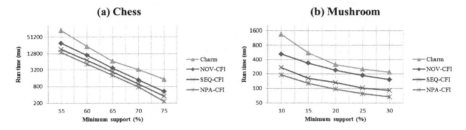

Fig. 5. Running time of the four algorithms on **Chess** and **Mushroom** datasets.

Figure 5(a) and (b) show the running time of the compared algorithms on datasets **Chess** and **Mushroom**. **SEQ-CFI** runs faster **NOV-CFI** and **CHARM** algorithm under all minsup; **NPA-CFI** runs faster **SEQ-CFI** algorithm. Average performance of the parallel **NPA-CFI** algorithm in turn: **Chess** as $\overline{P}$ = 75%; σ = 3.3% and **Mushroom** as $\overline{P}$ = 74%; σ = 3.1%.

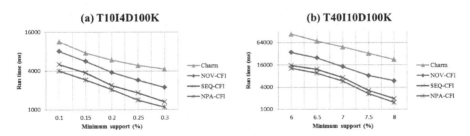

Fig. 6. Running time of the four algorithms on **T10I4D100K** and **T40I10D100K** datasets.

Figure 6(a) and (b) show the running time of the compared algorithms on sparse datasets **T10I4D100K** and **T40I10D100K**. **SEQ-CFI** runs faster among two algorithms **NOV-CFI** and **CHARM** under all minimum supports; **NPA-CFI** runs faster **SEQ-CFI** algorithm. Average performance of the parallel **NPA-CFI** algorithm in turn: **T10I4D100K** as $\overline{P}$ = 80%; σ = 3.6% and **T40I10D100K** as $\overline{P}$ = 81%; σ = 2.1%.

In summary, experimental results suggest the following ordering of these algorithms as running time is concerned: **SEQ-CFI** runs faster **NOV-CFI** and **CHARM** algorithm; **NPA-CFI** runs faster **SEQ-CFI** algorithm. Average performance of the parallel **NPA-CFI** algorithm on datasets experimental is $\overline{P} = 77\%$; $\sigma = 4.1\%$.

5   Conclusion

In this paper, we improved a sequential algorithm mining **CFI** on transaction databases [9], consisting of three phases: *the first phase*, quickly detect a **Kernel_COOC** array of co-occurrences and occurrences of kernel item in at least one transaction; *the second phase*, we built the list of **nLOOC-Tree** base on the **Kernel_COOC** (*self-reduced search space*) and a binary matrix of dataset; *the last phase*, the algorithm is proposed for fast mining **CFI** base on **nLOOC-Tree**. Besides, when using mining **CFI** with *other minsup value* then the proposed algorithm only performs mining **CFI** based on the **nLOOC-Tree** that is calculated previously (*the second phase - Algorithm 2*), reducing the significant processing time. The next step, we develop a sequential algorithm for mining **CFI** and thus parallelize the sequential algorithm to effectively demonstrate the multi-core processor called **NPA-CFI**. The experimental results show that the proposed algorithms perform better than other algorithms.

The results from the algorithm proposed: In the future, we will expand the algorithm to be able to mining **CFI** on weighted transaction databases, as well as to expand the parallel **NPA-CFI** algorithm on distributed computing systems.

References

1. Agrawal, R., Imilienski, T., Swami, A.: Mining association rules between sets of large databases, pp. 207–216. ACM SIGMOD International Conference on Management of Data, Washington, DC (1993)
2. Pasquier, N., Bastide, Y., Taouil, R., Lakhal, L.: Discovering frequent closed itemsets for association rules. In: 7th International Conference on Database Theory, pp. 398–416 (1999)
3. Zaki, M. J., Hsiao, C.: CHARM: An efficient algorithm for closed association rule mining. In: 2nd SIAM International Conference on Data Mining, pp. 457–473 (2002)
4. Wang, J., Han, J., Pei, J.: CLOSET+: searching for the best strategies for mining frequent closed itemsets. In: ACM International Conference on Knowledge Disc and Data Mining, pp. 236–245 (2003)
5. Binesh, N., Amiya, K.T.: Accelerating closed frequent itemset mining by elimination of null transactions. J. JETCIS **2**(7), 317–324 (2011)
6. Wang, S., Yang, Y., Gao, Y., Chen, G., Zhang, Y.: MapReduce-based closed frequent itemset mining with efficient redundancy filtering. In: IEEE 12th ICDM, pp. 449–453 (2012)
7. Wang, F., Yuan, B.: Parallel frequent pattern mining without candidate generation on GPUs, pp. 1046–1052. IEEE ICDM Workshop, Shenzhen (2014)
8. Prabha, S., Shanmugapriya, S., Duraiswamy, K.: A survey on closed frequent pattern mining. Int. J. Comput. Appl. **63**(14), 47–52 (2013)
9. Huan P.: NOV-CFI: a novel algorithm for closed frequent itemsets mining in transactional databases. In: ICNCC 2018, pp. 58–63. ACM, NY (2018)

TSRuleGrowth: Mining Partially-Ordered Prediction Rules From a Time Series of Discrete Elements, Application to a Context of Ambient Intelligence

Benoit Vuillemin[1,2]([✉]), Lionel Delphin-Poulat[1], Rozenn Nicol[1], Laetitia Matignon[2], and Salima Hassas[2]

[1] Orange Labs, Lannion, France
`benoit.vuil@gmail.com`
[2] Univ Lyon, Université Lyon 1, CNRS, LIRIS, UMR5205, 69622 Lyon, France

Abstract. This paper presents TSRuleGrowth, an algorithm for mining partially-ordered rules on a time series. TSRuleGrowth takes principles from the state of the art of transactional rule mining, and applies them to time series. It proposes a new definition of the support, which overcomes the limitations of previous definitions. Experiments on two databases of real data coming from connected environments show that this algorithm extracts relevant usual situations and outperforms the state of the art.

Keywords: Rule mining · Ambient intelligence · Habits · Automation · Support · Time series

1 Introduction

Searching for prediction rules in a time series is a major problem in data mining. Used in stock price analysis and recommendation of items for consumers among other fields, this problem has been studied increasingly as the field of ambient intelligence (AmI) expands. AmI is the fusion between artificial intelligence and the Internet of Things, and can be described as: "A digital environment that proactively, but sensibly, supports people in their daily lives" [2]. This work falls within the field of AmI: we want to make a system that finds the habits of users in a connected environment, i.e. an environment in which connected objects are present, in order to provide users with automation.

This paper describes TSRuleGrowth, a new algorithm used in our AmI system, that searches for prediction rules over a time series. Here, this time series represents events sent by connected objects. These prediction rules will then be proposed to users as automation possibilities. TSRuleGrowth uses the principles of a rule mining algorithm on transactions, TRuleGrowth, while adapting them to time series. Also, a new definition of support on time series is described, which overcomes the limitations of the state of the art. In the scope of this paper, the

© Springer Nature Switzerland AG 2019
J. Li et al. (Eds.): ADMA 2019, LNAI 11888, pp. 119–134, 2019.
https://doi.org/10.1007/978-3-030-35231-8_9

time series is composed only of categorical values, rather than continuous, that can occur at any time, i.e. there is no fixed sampling frequency in the time series. The structure of these rules is described, as well as the state of the art of the fields concerned, which will explain the choices made for this algorithm.

2 Context and Definitions

2.1 Input of Our Ambient Intelligence System

There are two types of connected objects: sensors and actuators. **Sensors** monitor environmental variables. A sensor returns events, corresponding to changes in the state of the observed variable. For example, for a door opening sensor, opening and closing events are sent over time. Sensors can measure **categorical** or **continuous** variables. For example, the temperature of a room, expressed in degrees, can be considered as a continuous variable, while the selection of a radio station, or the opening of a door are categorical variables. A discretization process can convert continuous data into categorical data. **In this paper, only sensors that monitor categorical variables are considered. Actuators** act on the environment. An actuator returns an event when it has made an action. For example, a connected shutter will return an event when it closes or opens. Actuators can perform categorical actions, such as opening a shutter, or continuous actions, like increasing the temperature to a certain value. **As with sensors, only actuators that make categorical actions are considered.**

Each object, whether it is a sensor or an actuator, sends elementary events. In this paper, they are referred to as **elements**. All the elements sent by all the objects are gathered in a set noted E. Let us take the example of a room containing two connected objects: a presence sensor, used to define whether a person is in the room or not, and an actuator: a radio. The presence sensor can detect the following: "Present" and "Absent". The radio can act in two ways: its power status can be: "Radio on" or "Radio off", and it can select one of the following stations: "Music", "News", "Talk". Therefore, the set of all elements is $E = \{$Present, Absent, Radio on, Radio off, Music, News, Talk$\}$.

Our proposed AmI system collects data streams from several connected objects. Each data stream is composed of a succession of elements, each of which may occur once or several times. Each occurrence is time stamped. Thus, each element is potentially associated with several time data corresponding to its multiple occurrences. For further processing, all collected data from the various objects are aggregated into one single **time series**. In other words, a time series is obtained by a time-ordered concatenation of elements provided by all the individual objects. It is noted $TS=\langle(t_1, I_1), ..., (t_n, I_n)\rangle, I_1, ..., I_n \subseteq E$, where:

- t_i is a **time stamp**. It defines a fixed point in time.
- $I_i \subseteq E$ is called an **itemset**. It is the set of individual elements of E which are observed at time stamp t_i

Please note that a given element can only be seen once in an itemset. Also, time stamps are not necessarily equally distributed. The Fig. 1 is an example of a time series created from the environment mentioned in Sect. 2.1. Its mathematical representation is: $TS = \langle$(10:00 am, {Present}), (10:44 am, {Radio on, Music}), (11:36am, {Radio off}), (12:11 am, {Absent}), (2:14 pm, {Present}), (2:52 pm, {Radio on, News}), (3:49 pm, {Music}), (5:14 pm, {Radio off}), (5:57 pm, {Absent})$\rangle$. TS represents activities of a user in the environment. The following section details what the system must find from a time series.

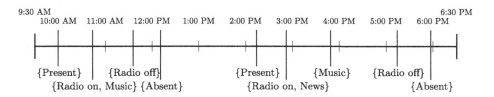

Fig. 1. Representation of a time series

2.2 Output of Our Ambient Intelligence System

The proposed system needs to find **prediction rules**, to express the user's observed habits. A prediction rule is noted $R : E_c \Rightarrow E_p$, where $E_c \subseteq E$ is the **condition**, and $E_p \subseteq E$ is the **prediction** of the rule. R states that if E_c is observed, E_p will be observed after a certain time. A rule must be frequent and reliable to be validated. One could also search for rules in the context of anomaly detection, i.e. very infrequent but highly interesting rules, but this does not fall within the scope of this paper. In the proposed use case, we want to limit the search for rules **for which the prediction part E_p must only be composed of elements originating from actuators**. Indeed, the rule search process being highly combinatorial, this makes it possible to limit this aspect while being adapted to the use case: the system's goal is to propose automatic actions according to situations. According to the time series example in Sect. 2.1, a rule can be {Present} $\Rightarrow$ {Radio on}. This is a **basic rule**, where condition and prediction are composed of a single element. It should be noted that we do not want, for example, to find the {Radio off} $\Rightarrow$ {Absent} rule because its prediction part, {Absent}, comes from a sensor (the presence sensor) and not from actuators (the radio). Several types of prediction rules are possible [7]:

- **Fully-ordered sequential rules**, where the condition E_c and the prediction E_p are sequences, i.e. time ordered successions of elements
- **Partially-ordered sequential rules** [8], where E_c and E_p are both unordered, but an order still exists as E_p comes after E_c. Two mathematical structures are possible for E_c and E_p: **sets**, where an element can only appear once, and **multisets**, where multiple instances of elements are allowed. The number of instances of an element in the multiset is called the **multiplicity**. For example, the multiplicity of the element x in the multiset $\{x, x, y\}$ is 2.

After experimenting with each of them, we chose to use **partially-ordered sequential rules containing multisets**. The problem with fully-ordered sequential rules is that multiple rules can characterize the same situation. Partially-ordered rule mining generates fewer candidates, and fewer rules, by definition. Furthermore, they are described as more general, with a higher prediction accuracy than fully-ordered sequential rules, and they have been used in real applications [7]. In the proposed use case, describing a situation does not necessarily require an order, but the multiplicity of an element can be important. To explain this choice, we can take the example of a sound detection lamp: when one claps twice, i.e. when one makes the same sound twice, the lamp lights up.

3   Related Work

As said before, the system must search for partially-ordered prediction rules over a time series of elements coming from sensors and actuators. Thus, in the state of the art, two major areas of research should be considered: rule mining on time series and partially-ordered rule mining. Let us first recall some definitions. A prediction rule $R : E_c \Rightarrow E_p$ must be frequent and reliable. In rule mining, to check that a rule is frequent, its **support** is calculated. The notion of support depends on the structure of the input, but estimates the frequency of a rule, a set of elements, or an element. To ensure that a rule is reliable, its **interest** is calculated. Several measures can estimate the interest of a rule. The most known is confidence [3], but alternatives exist, such as conviction [3], lift [3] or netconf [1]. These measures depend on the supports of R, E_c and E_p.

3.1   Rule Mining on Time Series

[5] proposes a system mining basic rules on a sequence of elements, where one element predicts another. Those elements represent simple variations of stock market data. It can also search for more complex rules, where the condition is a sequence. This system therefore makes it possible to mine prediction rules over a time series. However, it seeks fully-ordered prediction rules, rather than partially-ordered ones. Also, the prediction part of the rules is limited to a single element, a limitation that we want to avoid in our AmI system. [11] can be considered as an improvement over [5], because this system looks for rules where the prediction is not limited to a single element. But, since it seeks fully-ordered rules, this system cannot be applied in our case. [10] introduces a notion of support for a time series, via a sliding window with a determined duration. The support of an element, a set of elements or a rule is the number of windows in which this element, set or rule appears. This algorithm finds partially-ordered rules, first finding sets of elements that are frequent, then combining these sets to generate rules. Other algorithms use this notion of support, including [6] which finds rules whose prediction is composed of one single element. The algorithm presented in [10] can therefore be applied in our case. But this definition of the support can be problematic: the elements of E_p being strictly later than E_c, the number of windows covering the rule R will be strictly lower than the number covering E_c. Even if E_p always appears after E_c, the support of the rule will be lower than

that of E_c, reducing its interest. Also, since the search is structured in two steps (mine frequent sets, then search for rules), the algorithm is not fully efficient.

3.2   Partially-Ordered Rule Mining

To our knowledge, few algorithms of partially-ordered sequential rule mining exists. The most known are RuleGrowth [8], and its variations, TRuleGrowth (TRG) [8] and ERMiner [7]. These algorithms take as input a set of transactions. A transaction is a time-ordered sequence of itemsets, but, unlike time series, without associated time stamp. RuleGrowth searches directly for prediction rules, unlike [10] that searches for frequent itemsets and then searches for rules on these itemsets. In addition, the incremental architecture of this algorithm allows to limit the size of the searched rules, and to limit the elements in which rules are searched. In our use case, we want to mine rules whose predictions are made only of elements from actuators. RuleGrowth allows this limitation directly during the search, reducing the total computation time. TRG is an extension of RuleGrowth that accepts the constraint of a sliding window, determined by a number of consecutive itemsets. It allows to limit the search to rules that can only occur in this window. ERMiner is presented as a more efficient version of RuleGrowth, but without an extension that accepts a sliding window. But those algorithms have a major problem in the proposed use case: they take transactions instead of a time series. The notion of support depends directly on the structure of transactions, and cannot be applied on a time series. Despite the advantages of these algorithms, they cannot be applied directly to our input data.

3.3   Scientific Problems

To our knowledge, the state of the art algorithms are not satisfactory enough to solve the initial problem. Two major issues need to be solved:

1. How to define the support of a rule in a time series that avoids the problem encountered in Sect. 3.1?
2. How to build a rule mining algorithm upon this new support measure?

In addition, this algorithm must address the following:

3. How to limit the duration of the found rules?
4. How to limit the search to certain elements in the condition or prediction?
5. How to avoid that a rule is found twice?

RuleGrowth answers points 4 and 5, but only takes transactions as input. Its extension, TRG, uses a sliding window that can be used to answer to the third problem with some modifications. The following section describes an adaptation of the AmI data to be accepted by TRG, and raises limitations of this adaptation. After, we describe our algorithm: TSRuleGrowth. It uses the principles of TRG, but applies them to time series, to deal with the first two problems.

3.4 Adapting Time Series to TRuleGrowth

To solve the problem of the input data of these algorithms, one can simply convert the time series into a list of transactions, as in Fig. 2. To do this, this time series is divided (1 in the figure) into smaller ones with a defined duration noted Δ_{tr} (2 and 3 in the figure). Then the notion of time of the small time series is removed, to keep only the order of appearance of the elements (4 in the figure). Without this notion of time, they are no longer time series, but rather sequences of elements, in other words, transactions.

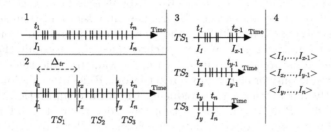

Fig. 2. Example of conversion of a time series into transactions

But the main problem of this implementation is the calculation of the support of a rule. Let us take the following example with three transactions:

$$\langle \{x\}, \{x\}, \{y\}, \{x\}, \{x\} \rangle$$
$$\langle \{x\}, \{y\}, \{x\}, \{x\}, \{x\} \rangle$$
$$\langle \{x\}, \{x\}, \{y\}, \{x\}, \{x\} \rangle$$

Here, $x \Rightarrow y$ is considered valid, because its support is 3, the same as x and y. As long as a rule has only been seen once in a transaction, it is considered valid throughout that transaction, even if it could have been invalidated, as in the example: x can be seen without y after, in all the transactions. Cutting a time series into transactions can lead to rules that are validated by mistake. There are other problems, inherent in Δ_{tr}. Having a small Δ_{tr} can increase the risk of a rule being "split in two", i.e. whose occurrence is separated between two transactions, which reduces interest. Having a large Δ_{tr}, over a time series, can reduce the absolute support of the rules the system is looking for.

Converting a time series into a set of transactions can be applied in the proposed use case. However, the above limitations have led us to create a new algorithm, inspired by TRG, which is fully adapted to time series.

4   TSRuleGrowth

4.1   Inputs, Outputs

This paper outlines the proposed rule mining algorithm on a time series of discrete elements : TSRuleGrowth, for "Time Series RuleGrowth", abbreviated to

TSRG. This algorithm is incremental, and can limit the search to certain elements in the condition and prediction. TSRG takes as inputs:

- $TS = \langle (t_1, I_1), ..., (t_n, I_n) \rangle, I_1, ..., I_n \subseteq E$: A time series of discrete elements
- min_{sup}: The minimum absolute support for a rule to be frequent
- min_{int}: The minimum interest for a rule to be reliable
- $window$: A time frame in which the rules must occur

TSRG produces partially-sequential prediction rules using multisets, detailed in Sect. 2.2. In the proposed use case, the prediction part of the rules is only composed of elements coming from actuators. Since TSRG takes a time series as input instead of a list of transactions, some notions need to be redefined: the support, the interest, and how to record the occurrences of a rule.

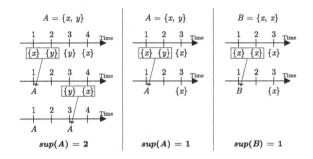

Fig. 3. Support calculation examples. Each column represents a step-by-step example of support calculation

---

Algorithm 1: Count : support counting algorithm

Data: A: multiset, $TS = \langle (t_1, I_1), ..., (t_n, I_n) \rangle$, $I_1, ..., I_n \subseteq E$: time series, $window$: duration
 // Initialization
1 Assign a blacklist $b(a)$ to every unique element $a \in A$;
2 $sup(A) \leftarrow 0$;   // Support of A
 // Sliding window through the time series
3 **while** *the window has not reached the end of* TS **do**
4 found $\leftarrow$ True;
5 Scan the window, record the time stamps of $a \in A$ in $T(a)$;
6 **foreach** *element* $a \in A$ **do**
7   $T(a) \leftarrow T(a) \setminus b(a)$;
8   **if** $|T(a)| <$ *multiplicity of* a *in* A **then**
9   found $\leftarrow$ False ;   // No distinct occurrence
10 **if** *found is True* **then**
11   $sup(A)$ += 1;
12   **foreach** *element* $a \in A$ **do**
    // Add the earliest time stamps of $T(a)$ to the blacklist of a
13    $m \leftarrow$ multiplicity of a in A;
14    $b(a) \leftarrow b(a) \cup m$ earliest time stamps of $T(a)$;
15 Slide the window by one itemset;
16 **Return** $sup(A)$;

4.2 Metrics

Support. For a time series TS noted $\langle (t_1, I_1), ..., (t_{n_s}, I_{n_s}) \rangle$ where I_i is an itemset and t_i is an associated time stamp, the support of element x, noted $sup(x)$, is defined as the number of itemsets containing x (Eq. 1).

$$sup(x) = \left| (t_z, I_z) \in TS | x \in I_z \right| \tag{1}$$

The absolute support of a multiset of elements A is the number of distinct occurrences of all elements of A within the time window. If an occurrence of an element of A has contributed to an occurrence of the multiset A, it can no longer contribute to other occurrences of A. The examples in Fig. 3 can help to understand this concept more easily. The support counting algorithm, Count (Algorithm 1), scrolls a window on the time series. If all elements of A are seen, their occurrences will be blacklisted to prevent them from being involved in another occurrence of A. This ensures that the definition of the support is respected. If several occurrences of the same element of A are seen in the same window, only the earliest ones are blacklisted. It leaves newer ones the possibility to contribute to a future occurrence of A. The absolute support of $R : E_c \Rightarrow E_p$ is the distinct number of occurrences where all the elements of E_c are observed, followed by all the elements of E_p. The elements of E_c and E_p also have blacklists, grouped into two sets: one for the elements of E_c, and one for those of E_p. The relative support of an element x, a multiset A or a rule R, noted $relSup$, is its absolute support divided by the total number of itemsets in the time series (Eq. 2). This support can be applied to partially-ordered rules, unlike [5,11], and avoids the case expressed in Sect. 3.1.

$$relSup(R) = \frac{sup(R)}{|(t_z, I_z) \in TS|} \tag{2}$$

Interest. In TSRG, one can compute the interest of a rule through its confidence, conviction or lift as mentioned in Sect. 3.2. In the proposed use case, we chose netconf [1]. Unlike confidence, netconf tests the independence between occurrences of E_c and those of E_p. Also, unlike conviction and lift, it is bounded between -1 et 1, 1 showing that E_p has a high chance of appearing after E_c, -1 that E_p has a high chance of not appearing after E_c, and 0 that this chance is unknown. For a rule $R : E_c \Rightarrow E_p$:

$$netconf(R) = \frac{relSup(R) - relSup(E_c) \times relSup(E_p)}{relSup(E_c) \times (1 - relSup(E_c))} \tag{3}$$

4.3 Recording of Rule Occurrences

Let us take the example of $R : \{a, b, c\} \Rightarrow \{x, x, y\}$. An occurrence of R is decomposed as the occurrence of E_c and E_p. Indeed, an element can be found in both E_c and E_p, and it is necessary to distinguish the occurrences of this element in E_c from those in E_p. An occurrence of a multiset is recorded in an associative array, where the keys are the distinct elements of the multiset, and their values are the set of time stamps where the elements are observed. In Fig. 4, the occurrence of E_c is $\{a{:}\{2\}, b{:}\{2\}, c{:}\{1\}\}$ and the occurrence of E_p is $\{x\{5,6\},\ y{:}\{4\}\}$. Two time stamps are recorded for x, because it is present twice in E_p. To lighten the memory, an occurrence of a multiset can also be stored on a list of time stamps, provided that the multiset is ordered. On the list, the index of a time stamp is the same one as the index of the linked element in the multiset. In the previous example, the occurrence of $E_p = \{x, x, y\}$ is $[5, 6, 4]$. The recording of multiple occurrences of a multiset is a list of these structures. All occurrences of the rule are recorded in two lists, for E_c and E_p.

Fig. 4. Rule and time series example   **Fig. 5.** Rule and time series example

4.4   Principles

Principles Shared with TRuleGrowth. TSRG takes the principles of TRG and applies them to time series. The algorithm uses a sliding window, to limit the search. But, unlike TRG where the window is a number of consecutive itemsets, TSRG has a time sliding window. It allows to restrict the search, and to have an estimate of the lifetime of a rule. Also, this algorithm will find basic rules, where one element can predict another. Then, recursively, it will extend them, by adding an element in E_c or E_p, via ExpandCondition and ExpandPrediction. This mechanism allows, if necessary, to limit the maximum length of the rules to be searched, i.e. the maximum number of elements in E_c and E_p. Then, TSRG applies two principles of TRG to avoid finding duplicate rules. First, Expand-Prediction cannot be called by ExpandCondition. Second, ExpandCondition and ExpandPrediction can add an element only if it is larger than all the elements of E_c or E_p, according to the lexicographic order.

New Principles. Let us take the example in Fig. 5. For this rule R, even if $sup(R) = 1$, two occurrences of the rule are possible: $\{x{:}\{1\}, y{:}\{3\}\}$ and $\{x{:}\{2\},\ y{:}\{3\}\}$. This problem is inherent in time series: we cannot know *a priori* which occurrence will be useful for an extension of this rule. To do this, TSRG tries to extend all seen occurrences of this rule. In addition, TSRG does not use the same rule structure as TRG: instead of being sets, E_c and E_p are multisets. Therefore, a principle coming from TRG needs to be modified: ExpandCondition and ExpandPrediction can add an element if it is larger than all the elements of E_c or E_p, but also if it is equal to the greatest element of E_c or E_p, according to the lexicographic order. But a new problem of duplication arises. In Fig. 5, if we try to grow $\{x\} \Rightarrow \{y\}$ to $\{x, x\} \Rightarrow \{y\}$, the same occurrence will be found twice. $\{x:\{1\}, y:\{3\}\}$ will extend to $\{x:\{1, \mathbf{2}\}, y:\{3\}\}$, by adding the time stamp 2, and $\{x:\{2\}, y:\{3\}\}$ will extend to $\{x:\{\mathbf{1}, 2\}, y:\{3\}\}$, by adding the time stamp 1. To avoid this, TSRG does the following: if the rule extends to the greatest element of E_c or E_p, it should only record the time stamps of that element that occur **strictly later** than the last time stamp of that element in the base rule. Thus, in the previous example, the first occurrence is recorded, not the second.

4.5   Algorithm

Main Loop. Like TRG, the main loop (Algorithm 2) tries to find basic rules, i.e. rules whose conditions and predictions are composed of only one element. To do this, it computes the support for all basic rules that can be created in the time series. If one of these rules has a support higher than min_{sup}, it tries to make it grow, by adding an element in E_c (ExpandCondition), and in E_p (ExpandPrediction). Finally, it computes its interest for validation. As mentioned earlier, the algorithm computes all distinct occurrences of the rule for its support, but also all possible occurrences for the expansion of the rule. To do this, TSRG uses a blacklist system to discern occurrences. Multiprocessing can be added to TSRG, by treating all basic rules in parallel, to reduce the execution time.

Algorithm 2: TSRuleGrowth

    Data: TS: time series, min_{sup}: minimum support, min_{int}: minimum interest, *window*: duration

1 Scan TS once. For each element e found, record the time stamps of the itemsets that contains e in $T(e)$;

    // Creation of basic rules

2 **foreach** *pair of elements i, j* **do**

3      $sup(i \Rightarrow j) \leftarrow 0$;   // Support of the rule

4      $O_c(i \Rightarrow j), O_p(i \Rightarrow j) \leftarrow []$;   // Occurrences of the condition and the prediction

5      $b(i), b(j) \leftarrow \emptyset$;   // Blacklists

6   **foreach** t_i *in* $T(i)$ **do**

7   **foreach** t_j *in* $T(j)$ **do**

8   **if** $0 < t_j - t_i \leq window$ **then**

                // New occurrence of the rule

9   Add t_i to $O_c(i \Rightarrow j)$;

10   Add t_j to $O_p(i \Rightarrow j)$;

11   **if** $t_i \notin b(i)$ **and** $t_j \notin b(j)$ **then**

                    // New distinct occurrence

12                    $sup(i \Rightarrow j) += 1$;

13                    $b(i) \leftarrow b(i) \cup \{t_i\}$;

14                    $b(j) \leftarrow b(j) \cup \{t_j\}$;

      // Growth of basic rules

15   **if** $sup(i \Rightarrow j) \geq min_{sup}$ **then**

16   Run ExpandCondition and ExpandPrediction on the rule $i \Rightarrow j$;

17   **if** $netconf(\frac{|T(i)|}{|TS|}, \frac{|T(j)|}{|TS|}, \frac{sup(i \Rightarrow j)}{|TS|})) \geq min_{sup}$ **then** output rule

---

Algorithm 3: ExpandPrediction

Data: TS: time series, $E_c \Rightarrow E_p$: rule, $sup(E_c)$, occurrences of $E_c \Rightarrow E_p$, min_{sup}: minimum support, min_{int}: minimum interest, $window$: duration

```
    // Growth of the original rule E_c ⇒ E_p
1   for each occurrence of the rule E_c ⇒ E_p do
2       foreach element k seen in the search area do
3           if k has never been seen before then
4               Create a new rule E_c ⇒ E_pk, its lists of occurrences and its blacklists;
5               sup(E_c ⇒ E_pk) ← 0;
6           foreach time stamp of k t_k inside the window (ascending order) do
7               if k > max(e), e ∈ E_p or t_k > occurrences of k in the prediction part of the
                rule then
8                   Create a new occurrence of E_c ⇒ E_pk;
9                   if time stamps are not in the blacklists then
10                      sup(E_c ⇒ E_pk) += 1;
11                      Add the time stamps to the blacklists;
    // Growth of the new rules found
12  foreach item k where sup(E_c ⇒ E_pk) ≥ min_sup do
13      sup(E_pk) ← Count(E_pk, TS, window);
14      Run ExpandCondition and ExpandPrediction;
15      if netconf(sup(E_c)/|TS|, sup(E_pk)/|TS|, sup(E_c⇒E_p)/|TS|) ≥ min_int then output rule
```

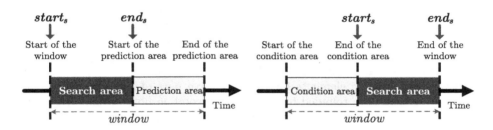

Fig. 6. ExpandCondition search area   **Fig. 7.** ExpandPrediction search area

Expanding the Rules. ExpandCondition (Algorithm 3) tries to expand a rule by adding an element to its condition. It goes through all the possible occurrences of the rule, from the earliest to the most recent. To respect the time constraint imposed by $window$, the condition of a rule can only expand between two time stamps, noted $start_s$ and end_s, as seen in the Fig. 6. As for ExpandCondition, ExpandPrediction searches for new elements for E_p in the area described in Fig. 7. After having found new rules, ExpandCondition and ExpandPrediction try to grow them again, and verify their interest. Here, the simplified pseudocodes of TSRG and ExpandPrediction are described.

5   Experiments and Results

5.1   Results of TSRuleGrowth on Two Databases

We tested this algorithm on two databases: ContextAct@A4H (A4H) [9] and Orange4Home (O4H) [4]. Both databases contain daily activities of a single occupant. The characteristics of these databases and the parameters applied to TSRG

Table 1. Database characteristics, and parameters applied to TSRuleGrowth

	ContextAct@A4H	Orange4Home
Recording period	7 days in July and 21 days in November	4 consecutive weeks
Number of connected objects	213	222
Data records	35634	746745
TSRuleGrowth parameters		
min_{sup}	7	20
min_{int}	0.9	0.9
$window$ (in seconds)	1,2,5,20,40,60,80,100,120, 140,160,180	1,2,5,10,15,20,25,30

are described in Table 1. The A4H database is located on the same physical location as O4H, but it has differences: the objects, as well as their names, are not the same. Also, the observed person is different, as is the observation period. Thus, the observed habits are different from one database to another. Some objects were specified manually to be actuators: shutters, doors, and lights for example. In addition, an amplitude discretization process was carried out on objects that reported continuous data, such as a temperature sensor. As a reminder, only actuators can provide elements for the predictive part of the rules. Also, the timestamps have been rounded to the nearest second on both databases. TSRG has been implemented in Python with multiprocessing[1]. First, let us look at TSRGs results on the two databases. Two aspects of the algorithm are evident in Fig. 8. The execution time and the number of rules increase exponentially with the window size. Indeed, when the window is larger, so is the search space. Thus, TSRG considers more and more elements, exponentially increasing the number of possible rules. For example, on the O4H database, 43 rules are observed on a one-second window, and 57103 on a 30-s window. This is explained by two complementary reasons. In a connected environment, several objects can be used to characterize a situation. For example, a person's entry into their home can be observed by a presence, noise, or door opening sensor. Thus, the rules can be formed from a combination of elements of these three objects. The larger a window is, the more combinations are possible, thus increasing the number of rules. Also, the rules discovered on a given window will, for the most part, be found again on larger windows, which also contributes to the increase in the number of rules. It is mentioned "for the most part" in the previous sentence, as some rules can be invalidated from one window to another. The invalidation of these rules does not come from their support, which can only increase from one window to another, but rather from their interest.

---

[1] CPU: Intel(R) Xeon(R) Gold 5118 @ 2.30 GHz, RAM: 128 GiB, Ubuntu 18.04.2 LTS.

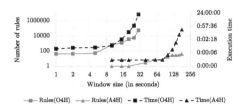

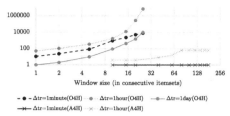

Fig. 8. Number of rules and execution time, TSRuleGrowth on O4H and A4H

Fig. 9. Number of rules for TRule-Growth on O4H and A4H

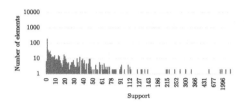

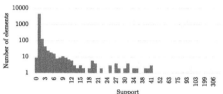

Fig. 10. Histogram of the elements grouped by their support in O4H

Fig. 11. Histogram of the elements grouped by their support in A4H

Indeed, the interest of a rule $R : E_c \Rightarrow E_p$ is calculated according to the support of R, E_c and E_p. In some cases, the support of E_c or E_p may increase more than R, reducing the interest enough to invalidate R. For example, the rule {'bathroom light 1: on, bathroom switch top left: off'} $\Rightarrow$ {'bathroom door: closed'}, discovered on O4H, has been validated on a window of 5 s. The supports are 38 for the rule, 42 for E_c and 91 for E_p. Its interest is therefore 0,904. By passing over a window of 10 s, the supports are still at 38 for the rule and 91 for E_p, but change to 44 for E_c. This is typically the case explained above, where the support of the rule increases less than that of its components. As a result, its interest drops to 0.863, invalidating the rule for this window. These invalidated rules represent only a fraction of the total number of discovered rules. Indeed, on O4H, by passing from a window of 10 to 15, 3 rules were invalidated, while 694 rules were observed on the window of 10 s, and 1170 on 15 s. In Fig. 8, we have explained the overall results curve of TSRG. However, this figure shows a very clear difference in results between O4H and A4H, although the physical environment and most of the connected objects are the same between these two databases. Two factors explain this. First, there is much less input data in A4H than O4H, as seen in Table 1: 35634 vs 746745. The less input data there is, the lower the probability of finding rules. Second, of all the elements in the database, very few are frequent in A4H. It can be observed by comparing Fig. 10 and 11. On A4H, there are 63 elements with an absolute support larger or equal to 20, unlike 395 on O4H. That is why we lowered min_{sup} to 7 on A4H, to have enough frequent elements (here, 132). This is reflected in the results reported by TSRG: even with min_{sup} lowered to 7, far fewer rules are found on A4H than on O4H

(1 vs 3689 for a 20 s window), and the execution is also faster (1 s vs 14 min for a 20 s window).

Let us now look at the rules themselves, first from the O4H database. On small windows (less than 5 s), straightforward rules are discovered, mostly the actions of switches in the environment. For example, {'bedroom switch bottom left: on'} ⇒ {'bedroom shutter 1: closed', 'bedroom shutter 2: closed'} and {'bedroom switch top right: on'} ⇒ {'bedroom light 1: off', 'bedroom light 2: off'}, seen in a 1 s window, indicate the different functions of the connected switches of the bedroom. Then, by increasing the window size, more complex rules are observed, characterizing the user's usual situations. {'office door: open', 'office presence: on', 'office switch left: on'} ⇒ {'office door: closed'}, seen in a 30 s window, indicates the user's entry into his office, by considering several different objects. For the A4H database, many fewer rules are observed in general, but some interesting rules are emerging. For example, {'fridge door: open'} ⇒ {'fridge door: closed'} describes that the fridge door will be closed within 40 s of being opened. As users, this rule may seem trivial to us. However, it should be remembered that the system has no preconceptions about the objects to which it is connected. With TSRG, the system learns the rules that govern the environment, and the habits of users. Thus, for O4H as for A4H, TSRG reports interesting results. Let us now compare these results with those of TRG.

5.2   Comparison Between TRuleGrowth and TSRuleGrowth

In this section, we compare TSRG with TRG. To do this, we use the same input databases, O4H and A4H. These data have been converted into transactions through the process detailed in Sect. 3.4. Three sets of transactions were made, with $\Delta_{tr} = 1$ min, 1 h and 1 day. The same parameters were applied between TRG and TSRG for min_{sup}, min_{int}, and $window$ sizes. TRG uses netconf as a measure of interest, and min_{sup} is absolute instead of relative, but no other changes are made to this algorithm: the window used is still a consecutive number of itemsets, instead of a duration for TSRG. This difference implies that for TRG, it is possible to find rules whose duration can go up to Δ_{tr}. This explains why TRG can find more rules than TSRG in some cases. For example, on O4H, for a window of 25 itemsets/seconds, and with $\Delta_{tr} = 1$ h, TRG finds 267007 rules, and TSRG only 5677. Figure 9 shows that, like TSRG, TRG finds more rules exponentially as the window expands. However, this figure also shows the impact that the size of Δ_{tr} has on the number of found rules. On O4H, and for a window of 25 consecutive itemsets, TRG finds 8028 rules if $\Delta_{tr} = 1$ min, 7052216 rules if $\Delta_{tr} = 1$ h, and 9851 rules if $\Delta_{tr} = 1$ day. These results can be interpreted as follows: when $\Delta_{tr} = 1$ min, the number of rules is limited by the short duration of the transactions. When $\Delta_{tr} = 1$ day, fewer transactions are made. This reduces the absolute support of the rules and thus limits the search of the latter. Figure 9 shows that the number of rules made with $\Delta_{tr} = 1$ day catches up with that of $\Delta_{tr} = 1$ min as the window grows, until it exceeds it when window = 25. Many identical rules are observed by both TRG and TSRG. For a 1 s window/itemset, and a 1-h Δ_{tr}, 42 rules are common to these two algorithms. This represents

84% of the rules found by TRG and 98% of TSRG's rules. For the same Δ_{tr}, and a window of 10 itemsets/15 s, 1000 rules are common, i.e. 73% of the TRG rules, and 85% of the TSRG rules. But Δ_{tr} can also limit the number of rules common to TRG and TSRG. Of all the possible window combinations, only 194 common rules are found at most for $\Delta_{tr} = 1$ day, 2061 for $\Delta_{tr} = 1$ min, and 8806 for $\Delta_{tr} = 1$ h.

Why does Δ_{tr} influence these results so much? The principles of Sect. 3.4 can explain this. The rules found with $\Delta_{tr} = 1$ min are limited by the size of the transactions, while those with $\Delta_{tr} = 1$ day are limited by their absolute support. Also, some rules can be validated by mistake. For example, {'staircase switch left: on'} ⇒ {'walkway light: off'} is seen with Δ_{tr} of 1 h and 1 day, but not on $\Delta_{tr} = 1$ min nor TSRG. Instead, the rule {'walkway switch 2 top right: on'} ⇒ {'walkway light: off'}, discovered by TSRG, is more coherent, because the two involved objects are in the same room. Δ_{tr}'s limitations are more visible on A4H. With $min_{sup} = 7$, and a Δ_{tr} of 1 h or 1 day, TRG does not find any rule, for any window. If $\Delta_{tr} = 1$ min, TRG finds a single rule, which is also observed by TSRG. Thus, in the case of A4H, TRG finds much fewer rules than TSRG for the same min_{sup}. By lowering min_{sup} to 6, TRG finds more rules: if $\Delta_{tr} = 1$ day, no rule is found, if $\Delta_{tr} = 1$ min, only 1 rule, also found by TSRG. This number can be up to 64 if $\Delta_{tr} = 1$ h. It is higher than TSRG can find (maximum 40), but few rules are common to both TRG and TSRG (maximum 16). This is explained by the difference in the window concept between TRG and TSRG, giving unique rules to TRG, and the decrease in absolute support caused by Δ_{tr}, giving unique rules to TSRG.

We can therefore confirm that converting a time series into transactions can severely limit the search for rules and can create rules validated by mistake. TSRG, considering directly a time series, overcomes those shortcomings.

6   Conclusion

This paper described two contributions: a new notion of absolute and relative support over a time series, and an algorithm for searching partially-ordered prediction rules on a time series of discrete elements. The notion of support is freed from the limitations expressed in the state of the art, and the algorithm also distinguishes itself by its features: first, an incremental architecture, inspired by TRuleGrowth, allowing to limit the search to certain elements if necessary, as in the proposed use case; secondly, a sliding window, allowing to limit the duration of the searched rules; finally, the use of multisets in the rule structure, instead of sets in TRuleGrowth. TSRuleGrowth was tested on real data, from two databases of connected environments. The observed rules characterize short-term predictions, such as the action of a switch, and mid-term predictions, characterizing habits. These prediction rules make it possible to offer relevant automation possibilities to users of an AmI system. A comparison with TRule-Growth has been made, highlighting problems and limitations of transactional rule mining algorithms on time series, which are not encountered on TSRule-Growth. TSRuleGrowth finds prediction rules through connected objects data, and can evolve to take into account spacial aspects of the objects for example. But for an AmI system to be truly customized, it must consider the needs of users. A future version of such a system could therefore take into account their tastes to choose and classify the found rules, in order to display them in a way that is useful to them. Combined together, the relevance and usefulness of the rules will form a solid foundation for an AmI system.

References

1. Ahn, K.I., Kim, J.Y.: Efficient mining of frequent itemsets and a measure of interest for association rule mining. J. Inf. Knowl. Manage. **03**(03), 245–257 (2004). https://doi.org/10.1142/S0219649204000869
2. Augusto, J.C., McCullagh, P.: Ambient intelligence: concepts and applications. Comput. Sci. Inf. Syst. **4**(1), 1–27 (2007)
3. Azevedo, P.J., Jorge, A.M.: Comparing rule measures for predictive association rules. In: Kok, J.N., Koronacki, J., Mantaras, R.L., Matwin, S., Mladenič, D., Skowron, A. (eds.) ECML 2007. LNCS (LNAI), vol. 4701, pp. 510–517. Springer, Heidelberg (2007). https://doi.org/10.1007/978-3-540-74958-5_47
4. Cumin, J., Lefebvre, G., Ramparany, F., Crowley, J.L.: A dataset of routine daily activities in an instrumented home. In: 11th International Conference on Ubiquitous Computing and Ambient Intelligence (UCAm I), November 2017
5. Das, G., Lin, K.I., Mannila, H., Renganathan, G., Smyth, P.: Rule discovery from time series. In: Proceedings of the Fourth International Conference on Knowledge Discovery and Data Mining, KDD 1998, pp. 16–22. AAAI Press (1998)
6. Deogun, J., Jiang, L.: Prediction mining – an approach to mining association rules for prediction. In: Ślęzak, D., Yao, J.T., Peters, J.F., Ziarko, W., Hu, X. (eds.) RSFDGrC 2005. LNCS (LNAI), vol. 3642, pp. 98–108. Springer, Heidelberg (2005). https://doi.org/10.1007/11548706_11
7. Fournier-Viger, P., Gueniche, T., Zida, S., Tseng, V.S.: ERMiner: sequential rule mining using equivalence classes. In: Blockeel, H., van Leeuwen, M., Vinciotti, V. (eds.) IDA 2014. LNCS, vol. 8819, pp. 108–119. Springer, Cham (2014). https://doi.org/10.1007/978-3-319-12571-8_10
8. Fournier-Viger, P., Wu, C.W., Tseng, V.S., Cao, L., Nkambou, R.: Mining partially-ordered sequential rules common to multiple sequences. IEEE Trans. Knowl. Data Eng. **27**(8), 2203–2216 (2015). https://doi.org/10.1109/TKDE.2015.2405509
9. Lago, P., Lang, F., Roncancio, C., Jiménez-Guarín, C., Mateescu, R., Bonnefond, N.: The ContextAct@A4H real-life dataset of daily-living activities. In: Brézillon, P., Turner, R., Penco, C. (eds.) CONTEXT 2017. LNCS (LNAI), vol. 10257, pp. 175–188. Springer, Cham (2017). https://doi.org/10.1007/978-3-319-57837-8_14
10. Mannila, H., Toivonen, H., Inkeri Verkamo, A.: Discovery of frequent episodes in event sequences. Data Min. Knowl. Discov. **1**(3), 259–289 (1997). https://doi.org/10.1023/A:1009748302351
11. Schlüter, T., Conrad, S.: About the analysis of time series with temporal association rule mining. In: 2011 IEEE Symposium on Computational Intelligence and Data Mining (CIDM), pp. 325–332, April 2011. https://doi.org/10.1109/CIDM.2011.5949303

HGTPU-Tree: An Improved Index Supporting Similarity Query of Uncertain Moving Objects for Frequent Updates

Mengqian Zhang[1(✉)], Bohan Li[1,2,3(✉)], and Kai Wang[1]

[1] College of Computer Science and Technology,
Nanjing University of Aeronautics and Astronautics, Nanjing, China
{mengqianz,bhli}@nuaa.edu.cn, hxyrqxl23@sina.com
[2] Collaborative Innovation Center of Novel Software Technology
and Industrialization, Nanjing, China
[3] Jiangsu Easymap Geographic Information Technology Corp, Ltd,
Yangzhou, China

Abstract. Position uncertainty is one key feature of moving objects. Existing uncertain moving objects indexing technology aims to improve the efficiency of querying. However, when moving objects' positions update frequently, the existing methods encounter a high update cost. We purpose an index structure for frequent position updates: HGTPU-tree, which decreases cost caused by frequent position updates of moving objects. HGTPU-tree reduces the number of disk I/Os and update costs by using bottom-up update strategy and reducing same group moving objects updates. Furthermore we purpose moving object group partition algorithm STSG (Spatial Trajectory of Similarity Group) and uncertain moving object similar group update algorithm. Experiments show that HGTPU-tree reduces memory cost and increases system stability compared to existing bottom-up indexes. We compared HGTPU-tree with TPU-tree, GTPU-tree and TPU^{2}M-tree. Results prove that HGTPU-tree is superior to other three state-of-the-art index structures in update cost.

Keywords: Position uncertainty · Moving objects · HGTPU-tree · Group partition · Update cost

1 Introduction

In the era of mobile computing, effective management of moving objects is a guarantee of high-quality location services. Due to the inaccurate data collection, the delayed updating of moving objects and privacy protection, position uncertainty of moving objects is widespread [1]. Since the position of moving object changes with time, the specific position of the storage space object in the traditional spatial index structure cannot adapt to the updating operation of a large number of spatial objects. Thus it is not suitable for storage and retrieval of moving object [2].

In order to obtain more accurate query results, moving object position information needs to be updated frequently [3]. The existing position update strategies are mainly divided into the following two types: 1. Periodic update: updating the position

J. Li et al. (Eds.): ADMA 2019, LNAI 11888, pp. 135–150, 2019.
https://doi.org/10.1007/978-3-030-35231-8_10

information of the moving object every n cycles; 2. Speculative positioning update [4]: the position information of the moving object is updated as long as the actual position of the moving object and the position recorded in the database exceed a certain threshold. However, the above strategies are focused on managing the position of a single moving object, instead of the relationship of the moving objects.

The motion trajectories of some moving object sets in the real scene often have certain similarity and regularity. If the trajectories of moving objects are similar, they can be divided into a group. For the members in the same group, because the position information of the moving objects is similar to each other, only one moving object's position needs to be updated. Real-time explicit updates of the position information of each moving object are not required. Through this update strategy, the number of updates of moving objects is reduced, thereby decreasing the update cost of moving objects. The main contributions of our work are as follows:

1. We develop an index structure HGTRU-tree that supports moving object group partition on the basis of the existing index TPU-tree supporting moving object uncertainty;
2. We propose the moving object group partition algorithm STSG by comparing and analyzing the historical trajectories of moving objects. STSG uses Spatial Trajectory of Similarity (STS) to describe the similarity of moving objects trajectories;
3. We use hash table as the primary index to support the HGTPU-tree bottom-up query. When the moving objects positions update, hash function is first used to query hash table. The group number of moving object is used to find the leaf node where the moving object is stored;
4. We propose a hybrid trajectory-dependent moving object position update strategy, which combines the update strategy of periodic update and speculative positioning update.

The remainder of the paper is organized as follows: Sect. 2 provides the related work. Our proposed HGTPU-tree is presented in Sect. 3. Section 4 proposes experimental results. Section 5 concludes the paper. Frequently used symbols are listed in Table 1.

Table 1. Symbol description.

Symbol	Explanation
th	Threshold
M_i, M_j	Moving objects
L	Label of moving objects
RD	Relative Direction
SR	Speed Ratio
SD	Spatial Distance
$flag$	Leaf node mark
MBR	Minimum Boundary Rectangles
ptr	Pointers to the next layer

(*continued*)

Table 1. (*continued*)

Symbol	Explanation
G_i	Group
g_id	Group mark
ptr_r	Space layer leaf pointers
ptr_g	Data layer pointers
$time\_update$	Next position update time
oid	Mark of the moving object Mi
$PCR(p_i)$	Position recorded in the database
v	Velocity
pdf_ptr	Probability density distribution function
$next\_flag$	Token of whether there is a next leaf node
n	Number of moving objects
m	Number of moving object groups
H	Height of index tree
L	Number of leaf nodes in index tree

2   Related Work

2.1   Moving Object Index

In order to solve the problem of how to efficiently manage the precise position information of moving objects in real time, a series of index structures were proposed. For example, TPR* tree [5], STAR [6] tree, and R^{EXP} tree [7] are all parameterized indexing methods that manage current and future position information. The top-down update mode of TPR* tree leads to a large I/O cost. R^{EXP} tree improves the update performance of the invalid data by adding data time valid attributes on the node. The historical position, current position and future position information are combined to propose index models such as $PPFN^x$ tree [8] and R^{PPF} tree [9]. In [10], R-tree-based bottom-up update idea is proposed. The update process starts from the leaf node of the tree, which saves the query time. However, the disadvantage lies in the maintenance of the index. [11] proposed the first SFC-based packing strategy that creates R-trees with a worst-case optimal window query I/O cost. The above index models can't deal with the problem of the frequent position updates of the moving object.

Tao [12] et al. proposed a U-tree index model. U-tree has a good dynamic structure. But U-tree is only suitable for static moving object uncertainty indexing. [13] proposed a U-tree-based TPU-tree for efficient current and future uncertain position information retrieval. TPU-tree adds a data structure for recording the uncertain state of moving objects on the U-tree structure. In [14], based on TPU-tree, an update memo (UM) memory structure for recording the state characteristics of uncertain moving objects is added. An uncertain moving object indexing strategy TPU^2M-tree supporting frequent position updates and an improved memo (MMBU/I) based update/insert algorithm are proposed. However, TPU^2M-tree needs extra memory space to store the information of the memo (UM).

The above index structures only consider one single moving object when the position of moving objects changes. The motion trajectories between moving objects are not considered. In addition, most of the uncertain moving object index structures adopt the traditional top-down. It causes a large disk I/O cost. Even if partial index structures have a bottom-up update idea, it needs to sacrifice a large amount of memory resources, resulting in low system stability.

2.2 Trajectory Similarity Calculation

The trajectory data of moving object in the environment is usually discrete. In this paper, the historical position and velocity are used to describe the moving parameters of object, and moving objects are grouped by analyzing the trajectories of moving objects by moving parameters.

The spatio-temporal coordinate of the moving object Mi is a quad (l, x, y, t). In the case where the labels of two moving objects Mi and Mj are known, if Mi and Mj have the same semantic label, they can be directly divided into one group. But in many cases, the semantic label of the moving object Mi cannot be directly obtained. In this situation, the trajectory data of the moving object needs to be analyzed. x, y, t means that the spatial coordinate of the moving object Mi is (x, y) at time t.

The position information of the moving object Mi at time $t0$ is $(l, x0, y0, t0)$, and after ΔT the coordinate of the time $t1$ becomes $(l, x1, y1, t1)$. Let $\Delta x, \Delta y$ be the change amount of motion in the direction of x, y, the moving speed be v, and the moving direction be θ:

$$v = \frac{\sqrt{\Delta x^2 + \Delta y^2}}{\Delta T} \tag{1}$$

$$\theta = \begin{cases} \varphi.\text{sgn}(\Delta y) & \Delta x > 0 \\ \pi/2.\text{sgn}(\Delta y) & \Delta x = 0 \\ (\pi - \varphi).\text{sgn}(\Delta y) & \Delta x < 0 \end{cases} \tag{2}$$

$$\Delta x = x1 - x0, \Delta y = y1 - y0, \Delta T = t1 - t0, \tan(\varphi) = |\Delta y/\Delta x|, \theta \in (-\pi, \pi)$$

For the moving characteristics of moving objects, some researches have focused on Relative Direction (RD) [15] and Speed Ratio (SR) [16]. We propose Spatial Distance (SD) and the Spatial Trajectory of Similarity (STS).

$$RD(M_i, M_j, t) = \cos\left(\theta_{M_i}(t) - \theta_{M_j}(t)\right) \tag{3}$$

The relative direction RD of the moving objects Mi and Mj at time t is calculated as Eq. 3, which is defined as the cosine of the angle of the velocity.

$$SR(M_i, M_j, t) = \frac{\min\left(v_{M_i}(t), v_{M_j}(t)\right)}{\max\left(v_{M_i}(t), v_{M_j}(t)\right)} \tag{4}$$

The calculation of the speed ratio *SR* of the moving objects *Mi* and *Mj* at time *t* is shown in Eq. 4, which is defined as the ratio of the minimum speed to the maximum speed. *SR* reflects the speed difference between *Mi* and *Mj*.

The *SD* of the moving objects *Mi* and *Mj* at time *t* is defined as the spatial distance difference between the two moving objects, and is calculated by Euclidean Distance. The calculation formula for *SD* is as follows:

$$SD(M_i, M_j, t) = \sqrt{\left(M_i.x(t) - M_j.x(t)\right)^2 + \left(M_i.y(t) - M_j.y(t)\right)^2} \qquad (5)$$

STS describes the spatial trajectory of similarity between moving objects, and the value of *STS* depends on *SR*, *RD*, and *SD*. From the previous formula, the more consistent the velocity and direction of moving objects, the larger the value of *RD* and *SR*, and vice versa. The *STS* is positively correlated with *SR* and *RD* and is negatively correlated with *SD*, and its calculation formula is as follows:

$$STS(M_i, M_j, t) = \frac{RD(M_i, M_j, t) * SR(M_i, M_j, t)}{SD(M_i, M_j, t)} \qquad (6)$$

3 HGTPU-Tree

3.1 Model

HGTPU-tree implements a bottom-up update with a zero-level index hash table and the entire index structure is divided into three layers: a space layer, a group layer, and a data layer.

Hash Table. HGTPU-tree implements bottom-up query with a hash table. When moving object performs position update, it first queries hash table to find the address of the group where moving object is stored, and then directly locates leaf node, and determines whether the updated position exceeds the MBR range of leaf node. If the range is not exceeded, the leaf node is updated directly.

The hash function takes the group number of the moving object as input. The record in the hash table contains 2 parts, one part is the output value of the hash function, and the remaining part is the address corresponding to the group number *Gi*. The hash table in HGTPU-tree ensures that the address of group object is recorded in real time by adopting a synchronous update with leaf node.

The Space Layer. The space layer describes the position of the space in which moving object is stored. The record form of the node in the space layer is *<flag, MBR, ptr>*. Since the position of the moving object changes at any time, the spatial position of the group in which the moving object is stored also changes. When the spatial distance between the moving object of the group *Gi* in the group layer and the position of the currently recorded leaf node is larger than the threshold *th*, a position update operation is performed. The pointer of the group layer and the leaf node is disconnected, so that the group layer points to the leaf node where the current moving object is actually located.

The Group Layer. The record form of the HGPTU-tree node in the group layer is <*g_id, ptr_r, ptr_g, MBR, th, time_update*>. HGTPU-tree adopts a hybrid update strategy combining periodic update and speculative positioning update. When the position information *MBR* and the space layer node indicated by *ptr_r* in the group layer exceeds the threshold *th*, the data is updated and *ptr_r* is reassigned. In order to make the motion trajectory of moving object in the same group as consistent as possible, it is necessary to periodically update the grouping. Update strategy determines whether the trajectory of the group members can still be divided into a group by *ptr_g* in the past.

The Data Layer. The form of each HGTPU-tree leaf node in the data layer is <*oid, ptr, PCR(pi), MBR, v, pdf_ptr, next_flag*>. The moving objects in the same group in the HGTPU-tree are continuously stored with each other. When the moving objects in the group are periodically detected, it is not only judged whether the spatial position and the speed deviation of the moving object exceed the threshold, but also needs to update the probability-restricted area of the moving object *Mi*.

3.2   Spatial Trajectory of Similarity Group

In the HGTPU-tree, moving objects with similar motion trajectories in a historical period are divided into one group, and then the moving objects in the same group are stored in the same leaf node in the HGTPU-tree. Regarding the group partition of moving object, a Spatial Trajectory of Similarity Group (STSG) algorithm is proposed. Some definitions in the STSG algorithm are as follows:

Definition 3 (directly reachable): The minimum spatial trajectory of similarity STSMin is the judgment threshold of the direct reach of the node and it is a constant. When STS (*Mi, Mj, t*)>STSMin, it is considered that *Mi* and *Mj* are directly reachable at time *t*, which is recorded as $M_i \leftrightarrow M_j$, otherwise, *Mi* and *Mj* are not directly reachable, and are recorded as $M_i \nleftrightarrow M_j$.

Definition 4 (dependency reachable): For any two nodes *Mi* and *Mj* satisfy $M_i \nleftrightarrow M_j$ but there is M_k, let $M_i \leftrightarrow M_k$ and $M_i \leftrightarrow M_k$ then *Mi* and *Mj* are dependency reachable, denoted as $M_i \simeq M_j$, otherwise *Mi* and *Mj* are not dependency reachable and is recorded as $M_i \npreceq M_j$.

Definition 5 (connection): For any two nodes *Mi* and *Mj* satisfy $M_i \nleftrightarrow M_j$ and $M_i \npreceq M_j$, but there is a node set $S(M_1,\ldots, M_n)$, $n > 1$, so that *Mi* and *Mj* can be reached by S dependence, then *Mi* and *Mj* are connected, which is denoted as $M_i \approx M_j$, otherwise *Mi* and *Mj* are not connected which is recorded as $M_i \npreceq M_j$.

Definition 6 (group): Divide moving objects with similar motion trajectories into a group denoted as g, if and only if g satisfies the following two conditions:

(1) Any node *Mi* and *Mj*, if $M_i \in g$ and $M_i \leftrightarrow M_j \mid M_i \simeq M_j$, then $M_j \in g$;
(2) Any node *Mi* and *Mj*, if $M_i \in g$ and $M_j \in g$, then $M_i \approx M_j$.

The goal of the STSG algorithm is to divide all moving objects that are dependency reachable or directly reachable into the same group, and then store them in the same leaf node in the HGTPU-tree.

As shown in Algorithm 1. First, the vertex array V and the adjacency matrix E (lines 2–3) are initialized. And secondly, in the moving object array M, the spatial trajectory of similarity relationships between any two moving objects are calculated, and the results are recorded in V and E and an undirected graph (lines 4–10) is constructed. Then find the moving object *Mi* of the group and initialize a group g for *M*. Add these objects to g (rows 13–17) by traversing all objects that are dependency reachable or directly reachable by *Mi* through breadth-first traverse. Objects and finally return the group set *G*.

Algorithm 1 STSG

Input: Moving object set M, The minimum spatial trajectory of similarity STSMin
Output: Group set G (g1, g2, ... gn)
Sub-function description: The Judge (Mi, Mj, STSMin) function is to determine the spatial trajectory of similarity between the two object Mi and Mj. BFS (V, E, Mi) is to add all objects that are dependency reachable or directly reachable to the object Mi to g
Variable description: M_num : number of moving objects, V : vertex array, E : adjacency matrix, g : a group
1. STSG(M,STSMin)
2. Init V;
3. Init E;
4. **for** $i \leftarrow 0$ **to** M_num
5.   **for** $j \leftarrow 0$ **to** M_num
6.   edgs←Judge(M_i,M_j,STSMin);
      // Calculate the spatial trajectory of similarity of Mi and Mj
7.   E.add(edgs);
8.   **end for** j
9.   V.add(Mi);
10. **end for** i
11. Init G;
12. **for** $i \leftarrow 0$ **to** M_num
13.   **if** $M_i \notin G$ **then**   // Find object Mi that are not yet grouped
14.   Init g;   // Initialize a group g for Mi
15.   g.sons←BFS(V,E,Mi);
      // Find all objects that are dependency reachable and directly reachable to Mi
16.   g.id←Get_Id();
17.   G.add(g);
18.   **end if**
19. **end for** i
20. **return** G;

3.3   HGTPU-Tree Update Algorithm

When the moving object issues a position update request, the new record information is inserted into the HGTPU-tree, and the old position information needs to be deleted. HGTPU-tree synchronizes the update mechanism of the hash table and the space layer to ensure that the latest group address information is stored in the hash table in real time without saving old records.

At the space layer, update is performed by speculative positioning update. When the positional deviation of actual and the recorded position of moving object in the HGTPU-tree exceed the threshold *th*, an update operation is performed. As shown in Algorithm 2, the algorithm is mainly divided into three steps: 1. Substitute the group number of the moving object *Mi* into a hash function to obtain the address of the group in the hash table (lines 1–3); 2. Determine whether the updated position exceeds the *MBR* range of the leaf node. If the range is not exceeded, the leaf node is directly updated. Otherwise, the update process is equivalent to deleting and inserting new records in the HGTPU-tree (lines 4–16); 3. After the space layer data is updated, the address of the group in which *Mi* is stored is synchronously written back to the hash table (line 17).

Algorithm 2 UpdateTree

Input: Uncertain moving object Mi, HGTPU_tree
Output: updated HGTPU_tree'
Sub-function description: FindLeaf finds the leaf inserted by Mi in the space layer according to the address. CondenseTree deletes the leaf node and compresses the tree. AdjustTree performs structural adjustment operation on the tree after the node is split.

1. key←G_i
2. address←hash_fun(key);
3. L←FindLeaf(address)
4. **if** MBR(M_i) **not** beyond MBR(L)
5.   delete L
6.   CondenseTree(HGTPU_tree)
7.   L'←ChooseLeaf(HGTPU_tree,M_i) // Leaf node to be inserted
8.   **if** L' have free space **then**
9.   L'.add(M_i)   // If there is free space, insert directly
10.   **else**
11.   SplitNode L' **to** L' **and** LL
// The split node divides the L' node into L' and LL
12.   AdjustTree L' **and** LL
13.   **end if**
14 **else**
15   update L // Directly update the L node
16 **end if**
17 write address(G_i) back to hash table
// Write the new group address back to the hash table
18. **return** HGTPU_tree'

The moving trajectory of the moving object that was divided into the same group, after the motion for a period of time, changes. And some moving objects deviate from the group. At this time, the group needs to be re-divided. HGTPU-tree uses a periodic detection strategy to detect moving objects in the data layer. As shown in Algorithm 3, first, the current time *t_now* (line 1) of the system is obtained, and the next update time recorded in each group in the HGTPU-tree is compared with *t_now*. If a group needs to be updated, all the objects of the group are stored in the set *M*. The STSG algorithm is called to re-group *M* (lines 2–5), compare the new group *G'* and the old group *G*. If a change occurs, the new group *G'* is added as the data layer to HGTPU-tree (lines 6–7). Finally, update the time of the next update (line 9).

Algorithm 3 Update_Group

Input: HGTPU_tree before update
Output: updated HGTPU_tree'
Sub-function description: Adjust_Group adds a new group to the index tree when a group changes
Variable description: G_num : the number of groups, update_time : records the next update time, T : update cycle.
1. t_now ← Get_localtime
2. **for** *i* ← 0 **to** G_num
3.   **if** t_now=G$_i$.time_uodate **then**
// Get system time compared to update time recorded in the group
4.   M ← G$_i$
5.   G'=STSG(M,STSMin)// Regrouping
6.   **if** G < > G'
7.   HGTPU_tree' ← Adjust_Group(HGTPU_tree,G')
// Insert the regrouped group into the HGTPU-tree
8.   **end if**
9.   update_time ← update_time+T
10. **end if**
11. **end for** *i*
12. **return** HGTPU_tree'

3.4 Update Cost Analysis

The cost analysis of 3 different update strategies for one update of n moving objects is given in turn: top-down update, bottom-up update, and disk I/O times required for group-based update. As shown in Table 2, the top-down update cost consists of two parts: (1) the cost of querying and deleting old records; and (2) the cost of inserting new records. Since there is a possibility of overlapping of regions between the nodes of the index, querying a record requires accessing H nodes in the best case, and in the worst case, accessing L*(L-1)/4 nodes. The old record position is searched for deletion and written back to the disk. At least one disk write operation is required in the absence of a node overflow. Before inserting a new record, at least H nodes need to be accessed to find a suitable leaf node for insertion. As a consequence, an update using the top-down update strategy requires 2n*(H+1) disk reads and writes in the best case, and nL2/4+nH +2n disk reads and writes in the worst case.

There are two cases for the bottom-up update strategy. When the new record can be directly inserted into the original leaf node where the old record is stored, the best case requires 3n disk I/O: read the secondary index (1) to locate the original leaf node, then read the leaf node (1) and write back the node (1). When the new record conflicts with the MBR of the old record, it is the worst case that H+6 disk I/O is needed: read the secondary index (1) to locate the original leaf node, then read (1) and write back (1).

Access H nodes to find the appropriate leaf node for insertion, then read (1) and write back (1) the leaf node, and finally update the secondary index (1), a total of n* (H+6).

The bottom-up update strategy based on group partition is improved on the existing bottom-up update strategy. By updating only one representative object for the moving objects of the same group, the number of updates is reduced. Consequently, for the cost of one update of n moving objects, the best case requires m*3 disk I/O, and the worst case requires m*(H+6) disk I/O. Since n is generally much larger than m, the bottom-up update strategy based on group partitioning has a minimal update cost.

Table 2. Disk I/O times for 3 update policies.

Update strategy	Number of disk I/Os updated by n moving objects at one time		
	Best case	Worst case	Average situation
Top-down	$2n(H+1)$	$nL^2/4+nH+2n$	$nL^2/8+1.5nH+2n$
Bottom-up	$3n$	$n(H+6)$	$nH/2+4.5n$
Group partition	$3m$	$m(H+6)$	$mH/2+4.5m$

4   Experimental Evaluation

Our experiments used Gist [17] to compare the algorithmic efficiency of index structures based on HGTPU-tree, GTPU-tree, TPU-tree and TPU^2M-tree, and gave evaluation and analysis. The experimental data set is a real-world large scale taxi trajectory dataset from the T-drive project [18, 19]. It contains a total of 580,000 taxi trajectories in the city of Beijing, 5 million kilometres of distance travelled, and 20 million GPS data points. We randomly pick 100,000 taxi trajectories from this dataset to be the query trajectories. Experimental hardware environment: CPU Intel Core i5 1.70 GHz, memory 6 GB; operating system Windows7, development environment VS2010.

4.1   Impact of STSMin on Group Partitioning and Updating

The algorithm STSG utilizes the size of STS to measure the similarity of historical trajectories of moving objects. In the STSG algorithm, the minimum spatial trajectory of similarity STSMin size directly affects the effect of group partitioning. As STSMin increases, the number of divided groups increases positively with STSMin. This is because as STSMin increases, the number of directly reachable and dependency reachable of moving objects is reduced, so that the number of groups in the dividing result increases.

A good group partition should have the characteristic that the number of deviations from the group is small for a long period of time in the future. As the STSMin increases, the number of deviations from the group gradually decreases. As the number of STSMins increases, the number of moving objects of the group increases, but the closer the historical motion trajectory of the moving object of the group is. Therefore, the probability that moving objects will remain similar increases, and the number of moving objects that deviate from the group gradually decreases.

When STSMin is between [6, 8], the STSMin value in this interval reduces the number of divided groups and the number of moving objects that deviate from the group. Considering comprehensively, the minimum spatial trajectory of similarity STSMin is set to 6 in subsequent experiments.

4.2   Effect of the Number of Moving Objects on Node Relocation

HGTPU-tree implements bottom-up update with zero-level index hash table. When the number of moving objects increases, the number of moving objects that need to be relocationed after position updating is gradually increased. Especially at 50 K, the rate of increasing is the biggest. And finally it tends to be stable.

The space layer of HGTPU-tree is based on the R-tree. As the number of moving objects increases, the number of nodes in the index tree increases. The number of child nodes in each non-leaf node has a limit, so the MBR of each non-leaf node gradually decreases. When the MBR of the node decreases, the probability that the newly inserted node exceeds the MBR where the original record is stored increases, so the probability that the updated node needs to be relocationed increases.

4.3   Query Performance

Range query is one of the most common queries in moving object data management. We examine the query performance of HGTPU-tree through range query. The average query time of HGTPU-tree is slightly higher than that of R-tree. This is because the entire index structure of HGTPU-tree is divided into three layers. And the index tree of HGTPU-tree has more levels, so the query performance will be reduced. However, the query performance of HGTPU-tree is still roughly equivalent to R-tree on the basis of reducing the update cost.

4.4   Insertion Performance

For the moving objects of different numbers, the insertion time of HGTPU-tree, GTPU-tree, TPU-tree and TPU^2M-tree is shown in Fig. 1. With the increase of the number of moving objects, the required time for these four increases steadily. HGTPU-tree takes less time than TPU-tree and TPU^2M-tree, indicating that the insertion performance of HGTPU-tree is better than TPU-tree and TPU^2M-tree. This is because as the number of moving objects increases, the space layer level in the HGTPU-tree gradually increases and the free space in the index increases. Compared with the pre-grouping operation of TPU-tree and TPU^2M-tree, the moving objects of the same group in HGTPU-tree can be directly inserted into the nodes of the group layer, avoiding the one by one-insertion of TPU-tree and TPU^2M-tree. HGTPU-tree not only needs to insert it into the index tree but also needs to record it into the secondary index structure when inserting a new node. As a result, the insertion performance of GTPU-tree is slightly better than that of HGTPU-tree.

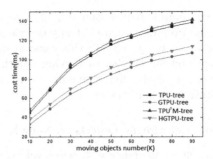

Fig. 1. Performance comparison of insert.

4.5 Update Cost

In order to ensure the accuracy of query results, it is necessary to simultaneously update the data in the database and the index. The update cost of moving objects with frequently updated positions is huge. Disk I/O and CPU are two major concerns when considering the update cost. The number of update times and the number of moving objects are the main reasons that affect the update cost of uncertain moving objects.

As illustrated in a of Figs. 2 and 3, HGTPU-tree greatly reduces the number of node access times compared to the other three index structures, regardless of whether it is trajectory stability or frequent group deviation. And the number of node access times directly affects disk I/O, which shows that HGTPU-tree has good performance in reducing disk I/O for moving objects with frequent position updates. HGTPU-tree improves the moving object grouping processing compared with TPU-tree and TPU^{2}M-tree, and saves the moving object of the same group in the same leaf node in the data layer. When update positions, only one moving object needs to be updated for the moving objects of the same group, reducing the number of update times. Moreover, HGTPU-tree reduces the disk I/O required for the query compared with GTPU tree, because the HGTPU tree implements bottom-up node access strategy by means of a hash table, thereby improving the update efficiency.

Comparing b of Figs. 2 and 3, we can find that the CPU calculation cost of HGTPU-tree is slightly higher than that of TPU-tree and GTPU-tree, and accounts for a larger proportion of the overall update cost. But when the moving object group trajectory is stable, the CPU calculation cost of HGTPU-tree is lower than that of TPU^{2}M-tree. This is because when the node update is performed, TPU^{2}M-tree needs to query the memo first. Furthermore, when the number of records in the memo increases, additional space cleaning operations are required, which increases the CPU calculation cost. In HGTPU-tree, the moving objects of same group maintain the same motion trajectory before the next group update. However, for the moving object trajectory is uncertain, periodic regroups are required in order to ensure the similarity of the moving object trajectory of same group, which increases the CPU calculation cost. HGTPU-tree has higher CPU cost than GTPU-tree. This is because HGTPU-tree needs to read and query the hash table when performing position update, and needs to update to the hash table synchronously, which increases CPU cost.

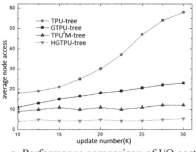
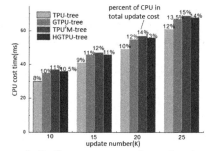

a. Performance comparison of I/O cost   **b.** Performance comparison of cost

Fig. 2. Compare I/O+CPU cost with group trajectories stable.

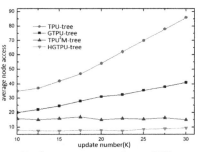
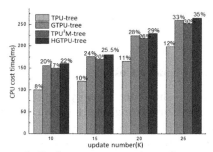

a. Performance comparison of I/O cost   **b.** Performance comparison of cost

Fig. 3. Compare I/O+CPU cost with group frequent updates.

As Figs. 4 and 5 show, the HGTPU-tree overall update cost is smaller than the other three index structures whether it is in the scene where the moving object group trajectory is stable or the group frequently deviates. With the increase in the number of moving object pairs, the advantages of HGTPU-tree are more obvious.

For TPU²M-tree with bottom-up update, as the number of moving objects increases, the number of nodes in the index tree increases and the MBR of each non-leaf node gradually decreases. When the MBR of the node decreases, the probability that the newly inserted node exceeds the MBR where the original record is stored increases. If the new node exceeds the original recorded MBR, it is equivalent to inserting a new record in the index tree, and the update efficiency is reduced. Compared with GTPU-tree that is also based on group partition, HGTPU-tree reduce disk I/O and the update cost by means of hash table.

For HGTPU-tree, when the number of moving objects increases, the number of moving objects of each group increases correspondingly, which is more conducive to the overall update. Especially in the case of stable group trajectory, the advantage of HGTPU-tree is more obvious. Because the update period T of group re-partition can be appropriately increased in the case where the trajectory of the moving object group is stable compared to the frequent deviation of the group. Therefore, in the same time period, the group trajectory is stable, which can reduce the CPU cost caused by group re-partition, thereby reducing the overall update cost.

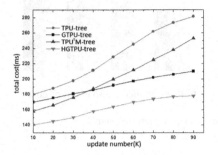 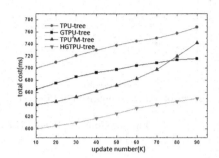

Fig. 4. Total cost with trajectories stability.   **Fig. 5.** Total cost with trajectories deviation.

4.6 Memory Cost

Figure 6 shows the memory cost of HGTPU-tree and TPU^{2}M-tree under the different numbers of moving object. As the number of moving objects increases, the memory cost of TPU^{2}M-tree fluctuates periodically. TPU^{2}M-tree is based on the UM structure. The old records are retained when the moving object updates position. Meanwhile, TPU^{2}M-tree cleans up old records periodically. HGTPU-tree uses synchronize update mechanism with the index tree to update the address content in the hash table every time the moving object is updated, thus there is no need to save the old record. Moreover, HGTPU-tree only records the address of one single object for the same group of moving objects. Therefore, HGTPU-tree can greatly reduce the memory cost and improve the system stability.

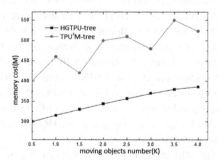

Fig. 6. The performance of memory cost.

5 Conclusion

In this paper, we developed an index structure HGTPU-tree that supports moving object group partition and bottom-up group update strategy. We proposed a group partition algorithm STSG and a moving object group update algorithm. Experiments based on real dataset analyzed the performance comparison of HGTPU-tree, GTPU-tree, TPU-tree and TPU^{2}M-tree in different situations. The results show that HGTPU-tree is better than TPU-tree and TPU^{2}M-tree in insertion performance. In terms of update cost, the update cost of HGTPU-tree is lower than other three index structures, especially when the moving object group trajectory is stable. HGTPU-tree increases the complexity of the index structure in terms of query performance. However, the query performance can still be approximately equivalent to the traditional index. HGTPU-tree solves the problem of the high memory cost of existing bottom-up update indexes with synchronous update mechanism.

References

1. Li, J., Wang, B., Wang, G., et al.: A survey of query processing techniques over uncertain mobile objects. J. Front. Comput. Sci. Technol. **7**(12), 1057–1072 (2013)
2. Saltenis, S., Jensen, C.S., Leutenegger, S.T.: Indexing the Positions of Continuously Moving Objects. ACM SIGMOD 2000, Dallas, Texas, USA (2000)
3. Li, B., et al.: Algorithm, reverse furthest neighbor querying, of moving objects. In: ADMA 2016, Gold Coast, QLD, Australia, pp. 266–279 (2016)
4. Güting, R.H., Schneider, M.: Moving Objects Databases, pp. 220–268. Elsevier (2005)
5. Tao, Y., Papadias, D., Sun, J.: The TPR*-Tree: an optimized spatio-temporal access method for predictive queries. In: VLDB, pp. 790–801 (2003)
6. Procopiuc, Cecilia M., Agarwal, Pankaj K., Har-Peled, S.: STAR-tree: an efficient self-adjusting index for moving objects. In: Mount, David M., Stein, C. (eds.) ALENEX 2002. LNCS, vol. 2409, pp. 178–193. Springer, Heidelberg (2002). https://doi.org/10.1007/3-540-45643-0_14
7. Saltenis, S., Jensen, C.S.: Indexing of moving objects for location-based services. In: ICDE, p. 0463 (2002)
8. Fang, Y., Cao, J., Peng, Y., Chen, N., Liu, L.: Efficient indexing of the past, present and future positions of moving objects on road network. In: Gao, Y., Shim, K., Ding, Z., Jin, P., Ren, Z., Xiao, Y., Liu, A., Qiao, S. (eds.) WAIM 2013. LNCS, vol. 7901, pp. 223–235. Springer, Heidelberg (2013). https://doi.org/10.1007/978-3-642-39527-7_23
9. Pelanis, M., Saltenis, S., Jensen, C.S.: Indexing the past, present, and anticipated future positions of moving objects. ACM Trans. Database Syst. (TODS) **31**(1), 255–298 (2006)
10. Lee, M.L., Hsu, W., Jensen, C.S., et al.: Supporting frequent updates in R-trees: a bottom-up approach. In: Proceedings of the 29th International Conference on Very large data bases-Volume 29. VLDB Endowment, pp. 608–619 (2003)
11. Qi, J., Tao, Y., Chang, Y., Zhang, R.: Theoretically optimal and empirically efficient r-trees with strong parallelizability. Proc. VLDB Endowment (PVLDB) **11**(5), 621–634 (2018)
12. Tao, Y., Cheng, R., Xiao, X., et al.: Indexing multi-dimensional uncertain data with arbitrary probability density functions. In: Proceedings of 31st International Conference, VLDB 2005, pp. 922–933. Morgan Kaufmann Publishers, Inc. (2005)

13. Ding, X., Lu, Y., Pan, P., et al.: U-Tree based indexing method for uncertain moving objects. J. Softw. **19**(10), 2696–2705 (2008)
14. Ding, X.F., Jin, H., Zhao, N.: Indexing of uncertain moving objects with frequent updates. Chin. J. Comput. **35**(12), 2587–2597 (2012)
15. Sadahiro, Y., Lay, R., Kobayashi, T.: Trajectories of moving objects on a network: detection of similarities, visualization of relations, and classification of trajectories. Trans. GIS **17**(1), 18–40 (2013)
16. Ra, M., Lim, C., Song, Y.H., Jung, J., Kim, W.-Y.: Effective trajectory similarity measure for moving objects in real-world scene. In: Kim, Kuinam J. (ed.) Information Science and Applications. LNEE, vol. 339, pp. 641–648. Springer, Heidelberg (2015). https://doi.org/10.1007/978-3-662-46578-3_75
17. Stamatakos, M., Douzinas, E., Stefanaki, C., et al.: Gastrointestinal stromal tumor. World J. Surg. Oncol. **7**(1), 61 (2009)
18. Yuan, J., Zheng, Y., Xie, X., Sun, G.: Driving with knowledge from the physical world. In: Proceedings of the KDD, pp. 316–324 (2011)
19. Yuan, J., et al.: T-drive: Driving directions based on taxi trajectories. In: Proceedings of the GIS, pp. 99–108 (2010)

Robust Feature Selection Based on Fuzzy Rough Sets with Representative Sample

Zhimin Zhang[1,2], Weitong Chen[2], Chengyu Liu[3], Yun Kang[4],
Feng Liu[2], Yuwen Li[3(✉)], and Shoushui Wei[1(✉)]

[1] School of Control Science and Engineering, Shandong University,
Jinan 250100, China
zmzsdu@gmail.com, sswei@sdu.edu.cn
[2] School of Information Technology and Electrical Engineering,
The University of Queensland, Brisbane, QLD 4072, Australia
uqwchel2@uq.edu.au, feng@itee.uq.edu.au
[3] School of Instrument Science and Engineering, Southeast University,
Nanjing 210096, China
chengyu@seu.edu.cn, liyuwen2012@163.com
[4] College of Information Science and Engineering, Hunan Normal University,
Changsha 410081, China
kangyun1225@163.com

Abstract. Fuzzy rough set theory is not only an objective mathematical tool to deal with incomplete and uncertain information but also a powerful computing paradigm to realize feature selection. However, the existing fuzzy rough set models are sensitive to noise in feature selection. To solve this problem, a novel fuzzy rough set model that is robust to noise is studied in this paper, which expands the research of fuzzy rough set theory and broadens the application of feature selection. In this study, we propose a fuzzy rough set model with representative sample (RS-FRS), and it deals better with noise. Firstly, the fuzzy membership of the sample is defined, and it is added into the construction of RS-FRS model, which could increase the upper and lower approximation of RS-FRS and reduce the influence of the noise samples. The proposed model considers the fuzziness of the sample membership degree, and it can approximate other subsets of the domain space with the fuzzy equivalent approximation space more precisely. Furthermore, RS-FRS model does not need to set parameters for the model in advance, which helps reduce the model complexity and human intervention effectively. At the same time, we also give a careful study to the related properties of RS-FRS model, and a robust feature selection based on RS-FRS with sample pair selection is designed. Extensive experiments are given to illustrate the robustness and effectiveness of the proposed model.

Keywords: Feature selection · Fuzzy rough sets · Representative sample

© Springer Nature Switzerland AG 2019
J. Li et al. (Eds.): ADMA 2019, LNAI 11888, pp. 151–165, 2019.
https://doi.org/10.1007/978-3-030-35231-8_11

1 Introduction

Data usually contains a large number of features, and some features are redundant or irrelevant for a particular learning task. Redundant features may lead to high computational complexity and "the curse of dimensionality". Irrelevant features may confuse the learning algorithm and reduce the learning performance. On the premise of ensuring classification accuracy, feature selection is used to find relevant and indispensable features from the original feature set to form an optimal feature subset. Feature selection can mitigate the impact of "the curse of dimensionality" and improve classification performance. Compared with feature extraction, feature selection can not only retain the most useful information in the dataset but also preserve the physical meaning of the original feature set to provide better model readability and explanatory power. Therefore, feature selection (or attribute reduction) is necessary before classification learning [1, 2]. Also, feature selection is one of the key research problems of rough set theory [3–7] and its applications [8–10]. At the same time, rough set theory is also an effective tool to deal with uncertain and incomplete data. It has been widely applied in data mining, machine learning, pattern recognition and other fields [11–13].

Feature selection based on rough set theory can remove redundant and irrelevant features under the condition of keeping the same ability of data classification. The biggest advantage is that it can effectively process data by only using the information of data itself without prior knowledge and additional information. However, the classical rough set theory is based on the indiscernibility relation of equivalence relation, so the classical rough set can only deal with symbolic data. This defect makes it restricted in some practical applications, but it also promotes the further development of rough set theory.

Because classical rough set models cannot effectively deal with real-valued features, fuzzy rough set [14, 15] (FRS) is proposed as an extension of the rough set model, and it has been widely applied in recent studies [16, 17]. FRS can effectively deal with the fuzziness and ambiguity of data sets. However, merely the nearest sample of the given target sample is used in the upper and lower approximation calculation for classical FRS models. As a result, subjected to the constraint of the nearest sample, the classical FRS model is extremely sensitive to noise.

To improve the robustness of classical FRS and reduce the influence of noise samples in the lower approximation, many robust FRS models have been proposed [18–25]. The existing robust FRS models can be roughly divided into two categories. Firstly, the samples located at the classification boundary are directly regarded as noise samples. The upper and lower approximations of this kind of model are calculated by ignoring these samples, like β-precision fuzzy rough set (β-PFRS) [18], soft fuzzy rough set (SFRS) [19], soft minimum enclosing ball (SMEB)-based fuzzy rough set (SMEB-FRS) [20], data-distribution-aware fuzzy rough set (PFRS) [21] and K-trimmed fuzzy rough set (K-trimmed FRS) [22]. The other kind of models replaces the maximum and minimum statistics with robust approximation operators to reduce the influence of the nearest noise samples, such as K-means fuzzy rough set (K-means FRS) [22], K-median FRS [22], vaguely quantified rough set (VQRS) [23], fuzzy variable precision rough set (FVPRS) [24] and the ordered weighted average fuzzy rough set (OWA-FRS) [25].

This paper proposes a novel fuzzy rough set model, namely fuzzy rough set with representative sample (RS-FRS) model. It can find representative samples for each label of a given data set. By calculating the distance between the target sample and each representative sample, the fuzzy memberships of the target sample concerning all labels are determined. Therefore, in calculating the upper and lower approximation, RS-FRS can not only consider the distance between the target sample and the nearest different classes' sample but also take into account fuzzy membership degree of the nearest different classes' sample. One of the most important reasons for such processing is that the samples in the actual data located in the classification boundary may be mislabeled and become noise samples. These samples are easily selected as the nearest different classes' sample to be used to calculate the lower approximation of samples, which leads to a too small lower approximation of samples, thus seriously affecting the learning performance of feature selection algorithm. Consequently, RS-FRS could reduce the effects of noise samples by increasing the upper and lower approximation. In this model, we introduce the fuzzy information granule to define the non-parametric fuzzy membership and propose a robust feature selection based on RS-FRS with sample pair selection. Finally, extensive experiments were performed to verify the effectiveness of the proposed algorithm.

2   Preliminaries

Given a non-empty universe U, R is a fuzzy equivalence relation if it satisfies reflexivity, symmetry, and sup-min transitivity. The fuzzy equivalence class $[x]_R$ is generated by a fuzzy equivalence relation R concerning sample $x \in U$. $[x]_R$ is a fuzzy set on U, which is also referred as the fuzzy neighbourhood of x, i.e., $[x]_R(u) = R(x, u)$ for all $u \in U$.

Definition 1 (The Lower and Upper Approximations of Classical FRS) [14]: Given a non-empty universe U, $A(U)$ is the fuzzy power set of U and R is a fuzzy binary relation on U. Let $A \in A(U)$ be a fuzzy set, and the lower and upper approximations of x concerning A can be defined as

$$
\begin{cases}
\underline{R}A(x) = \inf_{u \in U} \max\{1 - R(x, u), A(u)\} \\
\overline{R}A(x) = \sup_{u \in U} \min\{R(x, u), A(u)\}
\end{cases}
\tag{1}
$$

In Eq. (1), $1 - R(x, u)$ reveals the dissimilarity between x and u. $A(u)$ is the membership of u belonging to A. $\underline{R}A(x)$ indicates the certainty that x belongs to a class, and $\overline{R}A(x)$ indicates the possibility that x belongs to a class. The predictive ability of a sample is proportional to its lower approximation membership.

Let $\langle U, A \cup D \rangle$ be a fuzzy decision system, where the sample set $U = \{x_1, x_2, \cdots, x_n\}$ has m attributes $A = \{a_1, a_2, \cdots, a_m\}$. The decision attribute D divides the sample set U into r crisp equivalent decision classes $U/D = \{D_1, D_2, \cdots,$ $D_i, \cdots, D_r\}(1 \leq i \leq r)$. The lower and upper approximations can be degenerated as

$$
\begin{cases}
\underline{R}D_i(x) = \inf_{u \notin D_i} \{1 - R(x, u)\} \\
\overline{R}D_i(x) = \sup_{u \in D_i} \{R(x, u)\}
\end{cases}
\tag{2}
$$

3   Fuzzy Rough Set Model with Representative Sample

According to Definition 1 and Eq. (1), the upper approximation of the sample $x \in U$ is determined by $R(x, u)$ and $A(u)$. The lower approximation of the sample $x \in U$ is determined by $1 - R(x, u)$ and $A(u)$, where $A(u)$ is the membership of the sample $u \in U$ with respect to the equivalent class $A \in F(U)$.

Existing FRS models all consider that the decision attribute D divides the sample set U into several crisp decision classes, so the membership degree in the upper and lower approximation based on FRS model is a binary function with a value of 0 or 1. Then, the upper and lower approximation of the classical FRS model degenerates as Eq. (2). FRS model is extremely sensitive to the noise samples. When noise samples exist, sample membership $A(u)$ has fuzziness and uncertainty. If $A(u)$ is defined by a binary function with 0 or 1, it does not meet the needs of the practical application, and cannot well reflect the relations between samples and each equivalence class. Therefore, determining the samples membership is another important challenge of FRS model.

3.1   Representative Sample

To reduce the influence of noise samples on the upper and lower approximation of the classical FRS model, we design an effective method to calculate the fuzzy membership of samples. To be specific, the corresponding representative samples are found for each label. Then, the fuzzy membership degree of the target sample concerning each label is calculated according to the distance between the target sample and the representative sample, so as to design a robust FRS model.

Definition 2 (Representative Sample): Let $\langle U, A \cup D \rangle$ be a fuzzy decision system, where the sample set $U = \{x_1, x_2, \cdots, x_n\}$ has m attributes $A = \{a_1, a_2, \cdots, a_m\}$. The decision attribute D divides the sample set U into r crisp equivalent decision classes $U/D = \{D_1, D_2, \cdots, D_i, \cdots, D_r\}(1 \leq i \leq r)$. The Representative Sample RS_i of the class D_i is defined as:

$$
RS_i = \arg_{x \in D_i} \min \sum_{y \in D_i} d(x, y)
\tag{3}
$$

where $d(x, y)$ is the distance between two samples in the class D_i. In this paper, Euclidean distance is used as a basic implementation of $d(x, y)$.

Definition 2 provides a method for finding representative samples of each class. For all samples belonging to this class, the sample with the smallest sum of distances from all samples is selected as the representative sample. As shown in Fig. 1, red circles belong to class 1, and blue triangles belong to class 2. We calculate the sum of the distances between each sample x in class 1 and the other samples in class 1 and define the sample that minimizes the sum of the distances as the representative sample of class 1.

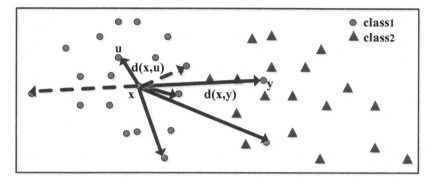

Fig. 1. Illustration on representative samples. (Color figure online)

Definition 3 (Membership Degree): Let $\langle U, A \cup D \rangle$ be a fuzzy decision system, where the sample set $U = \{x_1, x_2, \cdots, x_n\}$ has m attributes $A = \{a_1, a_2, \cdots, a_m\}$. The decision attribute D divides the sample set U into r crisp equivalent decision classes $U/D = \{D_1, D_2, \cdots, D_i, \cdots, D_r\}(1 \leq i \leq r)$. The representative sample of the class D_i is RS_i. The membership degree of the sample $x \in U$ with respect to class D_i is defined as:

$$D_i(x) = 1 - \frac{d(x, RS_i)}{\sum_{k=1}^{r} d(x, RS_k)} \tag{4}$$

where $d(x, RS_i)$ is the distance between sample x and representative sample RS_i.

According to Definition 3, we can determine the membership degree of sample x with respect to each equivalence class by calculating the distance between sample x and the representative samples of each equivalence class. The membership degree $D_i(x)$ meets $D_i(x) \in (0, 1)$ and $\sum_{i=1}^{r} D_i(x) = 1$. It can be seen that $D_i(x)$ can fully reflect the fuzziness of sample membership. The larger the value of $D_i(x)$, the higher the degree of sample x belonging to class D_i. The smaller the value of $D_i(x)$, the lower the degree of sample x belonging to class D_i. In the data set, the samples located in the boundary region may be the noise samples that have been mislabeled. By calculating the fuzzy membership, the degree of the boundary samples belonging to each class can be determined.

3.2   Fuzzy Rough Set Model with Representative Sample

Based on Definitions 2 and 3, we propose a fuzzy rough set model with representative samples (RS-FRS).

Definition 4 (The Lower and Upper Approximations of RS-FRS): Let $\langle U, A \cup D \rangle$ be a fuzzy decision system, where the sample set $U = \{x_1, x_2, \cdots, x_n\}$ has m attributes $A = \{a_1, a_2, \cdots, a_m\}$. The decision attribute D divides the sample set U into r crisp equivalent decision classes $U/D = \{D_1, D_2, \cdots, D_i, \cdots, D_r\}(1 \leq i \leq r)$. R is a fuzzy equivalence relation on U. The representative sample of the class D_i is RS_i. The upper and lower approximation of RS-FRS model is defined as:

$$\underline{R^{RS}}D_i(x) = \inf_{u \in U} \max\{1 - R(x, u), D_i(u)\}$$
$$\overline{R^{RS}}D_i(x) = \sup_{u \in U} \min\{R(x, u), D_i(u)\} \qquad , \qquad (5)$$

where $D_i(u) = 1 - \frac{d(u, RS_i)}{\sum_{k=1}^{r} d(u, RS_k)}$.

The samples of data set located in the classification boundary region are most likely to be noise samples. Because these samples are close to the samples of other classes, these noise samples are often used to calculate the lower approximation of the classical FRS model. This process causes the lower approximation to get smaller. In the proposed RS-FRS model, we consider not only the distance between the target sample and the nearest different classes' sample but also the fuzzy membership of the nearest different classes' sample. The fuzzy membership degree is calculated to expand the lower approximation of the model and reduce the influence of noise sample on the lower approximation, thus RS-FRS is robust.

3.3   Related Properties of Fuzzy Rough Set Model with Representative Sample

For the standard max operator $S(x, y) = \max(x, y)$, standard min operator $T(x, y) = \min(x, y)$ and standard complement operator $N(x) = 1 - x$, some properties of RS-FRS model are discussed. If other fuzzy operators are used [13, 14], the relevant conclusions can be similarly generalized.

Proposition 1: For $\forall A \in F(U)$, the following statements hold.

$$(1)\ \underline{R^{RS}}A = N(\overline{R^{RS}}(A)), \quad (2)\ \overline{R^{RS}}A = N(\underline{R^{RS}}(A)). \qquad (6)$$

Proof. $\forall x \in U$

$$N(\overline{R^{RS}}(A(x))) = N(\sup_{u \in U} \min\{R(x, u), A(u)\}) = \inf_{u \in U}(N(\min\{R(x, u), A(u)\}))$$
$$= \inf_{u \in U} \max\{1 - R(x, u), A(u)\} = \underline{R^{RS}}A$$

$$N(\underline{R^{RS}}(A(x))) = N(\inf_{u \in U} \max\{1 - R(x,u), A\,(u)\}) = \sup_{u \in U} N(\max\{1 - R(x,u), A\,(u)\})$$

$$= \sup_{u \in U} \min\{R(x,u), A\,(u)\} = \overline{R^{RS}}A$$

4 Feature Selection Based on Fuzzy Rough Set Model with Representative Sample

An important application of FRS is feature selection, also known as attribute reduction. In general, there are two main types of feature selection methods based on FRS, including a heuristic method based on dependency [26–28] and a structured method based on a discernibility matrix [29–33]. In this section, we will propose the feature selection algorithm based on RS-FRS model.

Let $\langle U, A \cup D \rangle$ be a fuzzy decision system, where the sample set $U = \{x_1, x_2, \cdots, x_n\}$ has m attributes $A = \{a_1, a_2, \cdots, a_m\}$. Each conditional attribute $a_t \in A$ induces a fuzzy relation $R_{\{a_t\}}$. The decision attribute D divides the sample set U into r crisp equivalent decision classes $U/D = \{D_1, D_2, \cdots, D_i, \cdots, D_r\}(1 \leq i \leq r)$. Attribute subset $B \subseteq A$ induces the fuzzy relation $R_B = \cap_{a_t \in B} R_{\{a_t\}}$. The discernibility matrix of this decision system is a $n \times n$ matrix, denoted by $M_D(U, A)$, and the element of discernibility matrix is c_{ij}:

$$\begin{aligned}&(1)\, c_{ij} = \{a_t : 1 - R_{\{a_t\}}(x_i, x_j) \geq \lambda_i\}, \quad \lambda_i = \underline{R_A}[x_i]_D(x_i), \text{if } x_j \notin [x_i]_D;\\ &(2)\, c_{ij} = \emptyset, \text{ otherwise.} \end{aligned} \quad (7)$$

where λ_i is the lower approximation of x_i with respect to $[x_i]_D$.

From Eq. (7), it can be seen that the elements of the discernibility matrix are one feature subset, and sample x_i and sample x_j can be distinguished according to these features. Because of the reflexivity and symmetry of the fuzzy equivalence relation, we can only calculate the lower or upper triangular matrix of the discernibility matrix.

Given a fuzzy decision system $\langle U, A \cup D \rangle$, c_{ij} is an element of the discernibility matrix $M_D(U, A)$, and discernibility function $f_D(U, A)$ is defined as:

$$f_D(U, A) = \wedge \{\vee(c_{ij}) : c_{ij} \neq \emptyset\} \quad (8)$$

$f_D(U, A)$ contains all feature subsets of the original feature set after feature selection. To obtain the disjunction of $f_D(U, A)$, we have to do the absorption operation. The other elements in $M_D(U, A)$ are absorbed by these minimum elements. The minimum elements refer to the element in the discernibility matrix that cannot be absorbed by other elements. Minimal elements are the key to feature selection based on the discernibility matrix. If the minimum elements in the discernibility matrix can be calculated directly, the storage space and computational space will be greatly compressed. Notice that each of these minimum elements is determined by at least one sample pair, so these sample pairs for minimum elements are determined before feature selection.

In this paper, the sample pair selection algorithm (SPS) is adopted as feature selection method. Based on SPS [32, 33], minimal elements of discernibility matrix can be obtained. Based on this, we propose a feature selection algorithm based on RS-FRS model with SPS.

In RS-FRS model, the relative discrimination relation of the conditional attribute a_t with respect to decision attribute D is defined as a binary relation, which is calculated by the following equation:

$$\text{DIS}'(R_{\{a_t\}}) = \{(x_i, x_j) \in U \times U \mid 1 - R_{\{a_t\}}(x_i, x_j) \geq \lambda_i, x_i \notin [x_i]_D\}, \qquad (9)$$

where $\lambda_i = \underline{R_A}^{SR}[x_i]_D(x_i)$ and $\text{DIS}'(R_A) = \cup_{a_t \in A} \text{DIS}'(R_{\{a_t\}})$.

We obtain the following results by finding the relationship between $\text{DIS}'(R_{\{a_t\}})$ and element c_{ij} in the discernible matrix $M_D(U, A)$. If $c_{ij} \neq \emptyset$, $(x_i, x_j) \in \text{DIS}'(R_{\{a_t\}}) \Leftrightarrow a_t \in c_{ij}$. $N_{ij} = |\{a_t | (x_i, x_j) \in \text{DIS}'(R_{\{a_t\}})\}|$, where N_{ij} is the number of conditional attributes that are satisfied $(x_i, x_j) \in \text{DIS}'(R_{\{a_t\}})$. Obviously, $N_{ij} = |c_{ij}|$.

According to the above definitions and analysis, a feature selection algorithm based on RS-FRS model with SPS can be described by Algorithm 1.

Algorithm 1 Feature selection algorithm based on RS-FRS model with SPS

Input: a set of condition attributes A ; a set of samples U .

Output: Selected feature subset S

1: $\forall x_i \in U$, according to Equation (5), the lower approximation λ_i of RS-FRS model is computed;

2: Compute every $\text{DIS}'(R_{\{a_t\}})$ and $\text{DIS}'(R_A)$;

3: Sort $(x_i, x_j) \in \text{DIS}'(R_{\{a_t\}})$ according to N_{ij} ;

4: **while** $\text{DIS}'(R_A) \neq \emptyset$ **do**

5:     Selected the first sample pair $(x_{i0}, x_{j0}) \in \text{DIS}'(R_A)$;

6:     Select one a_t such that $(x_i, x_j) \in \text{DIS}'(R_{\{a_t\}})$ and add a_t into S ;

7:     $\text{DIS}'(R_A) = \text{DIS}'(R_A) - \text{DIS}'(R_{\{a_t\}})$;

8: **end while**

9: return S

---

5 Experiments

In this section, RS-FRS model is compared with some existing robust fuzzy rough set model, including FRS [14], β-PFRS [18], K-trimmed FRS [22], K-means FRS [22], K-median FRS [22] and SFRS [19] model. Firstly, this experiment presents the comparison results of all FRS models classification accuracy under the original and noise data sets. Then, the robustness of each model is analyzed and compared.

5.1 Data Sets

We conduct experiments on 12 data sets from the UCI database [34]. Table 1 summarises the detailed characteristics of the data sets.

Table 1. Descriptions of 12 data sets.

No	Data sets	Samples	Features	Classes
1	Glass	214	9	6
2	Wine	178	13	3
3	Heart	270	13	2
4	Segment	2310	18	7
5	Hepatitis	155	19	2
6	ICU	200	20	3
7	German	1000	20	2
8	Soy	47	21	4
9	Horse	368	22	2
10	Wdbc	569	30	2
11	Wpbc	198	33	2
12	Sonar	208	60	2

5.2 Experiment Settings

In this experiment, K-nearest neighbour (KNN, K = 3) [35] is used to test the performance of all FRS models in feature selection because KNN is the most common classifier.

To verify the robustness and effectiveness of RS-FRS model, we compare it with other FRS models, including FRS, β-PFRS, K-trimmed FRS, K-means FRS, K-median FRS and SFRS model. Also, we set the corresponding parameters of the existing FRS models respectively according to the corresponding literature. To be specific, k is set to 5 in K-trimmed FRS, K-means FRS and K-median FRS, β = 0.5 in the β-PFRS, and the parameter is 0.1 in SFRS.

5.3 Experiment Results

In our experiment, the classification accuracy of 10-fold cross validation based on all FRS models is used as an evaluation index to compare the performance of feature selection.

Comparison of Classification Accuracy
In this section, we compare the robustness of different FRS models with the noise data of 0%, 5% and 10% respectively. We assume that the original data in the UCI data set does not contain any noise; that is, the noise level is 0%. Noise level equals 5% (or 10%) means there are 5% (or 10%) samples mislabeled randomly. To ensure the objectivity of the evaluation, we add the random label noise for ten times and conduct experiments ten times accordingly. Finally, the average accuracy of 10 experiments is taken as the experimental result. Table 2 shows the classification accuracy under KNN based on FRS, β-PFRS, K-trimmed FRS, K-means FRS, K-median FRS, SFRS and RS-FRS model. Bold indicates the optimal performance among all FRS models, and italic indicates the average classification accuracy of each model under all data sets.

It can be seen from the results in Table 2 that the average classification accuracy of RS-FRS model is higher than that of other FRS models under KNN. In most data sets, the classification accuracy based on RS-FRS model is significantly higher than that of other models. In the 12 original data sets, we can observe that the classification performance of RS-FRS model is superior on 8 out of 12 original data sets with KNN, as shown in Table 2. For the original data sets of Wine, Soy, Hepatitis, ICU and WPBC, the seven FRS models have the same or similar performance. This is because if there is no noise in the data set, for a given target sample, these seven models can select the same nearest sample in the feature selection process, and then calculate the same lower approximation.

In Table 2, we can obtain that the classification accuracy based on RS-FRS model is significantly higher than that of other FRS models in most data sets with two noise levels. In the 24 noisy data sets, we can observe that the classification performance of RS-FRS model is superior on 15 out of 24 noisy data sets with KNN. In this experiment, it can be seen from Table 2 that all FRS models are affected by noise, and the classification accuracy decreases with the increase of noise level, because the noisy sample may be regarded as the nearest sample of the given target sample when these models calculate the lower approximation of the target sample. Therefore, the classification accuracy of these FRS models will be reduced. However, the classification performance of RS-FRS model is relatively better than other models in these noisy data sets.

Robustness Analysis
Also, we compare the robustness of FRS, β-PFRS, K-trimmed FRS, K-means FRS, K-median FRS, SFRS and RS-FRS model to analyse the sensitivity of all models against noise. Figure 2 is graphical representations of the average classification accuracy of the original data set and noisy data set in Table 2. The numbers 1, 2, …, 6, 7 denote seven models, i.e., FRS, β-PFRS, K-trimmed FRS, K-means FRS, K-median FRS, SFRS and RS-FRS model, respectively.

Table 2. Performance comparison of all FRS models using KNN in original and noisy data sets.

Data sets	Noise level	FRS	β-PFRS	K-trimmed FRS	K-means FRS	K-median FRS	SFRS	RS-FRS
Glass	0%	**0.678 ± 0.134**	0.650 ± 0.068	0.631 ± 0.061	0.650 ± 0.078	0.655 ± 0.099	**0.678 ± 0.134**	0.668 ± 0.031
	5%	0.629 ± 0.061	0.649 ± 0.027	0.630 ± 0.037	0.647 ± 0.091	0.648 ± 0.043	0.655 ± 0.096	**0.656 ± 0.029**
	10%	0.628 ± 0.098	0.647 ± 0.066	0.626 ± 0.110	0.645 ± 0.019	0.644 ± 0.068	0.648 ± 0.089	**0.649 ± 0.015**
Wine	0%	**0.931 ± 0.072**	0.926 ± 0.054	0.926 ± 0.054	**0.931 ± 0.072**	**0.931 ± 0.072**	**0.931 ± 0.072**	**0.931 ± 0.072**
	5%	0.892 ± 0.069	0.910 ± 0.045	0.925 ± 0.059	**0.930 ± 0.059**	0.924 ± 0.062	0.920 ± 0.073	0.928 ± 0.086
	10%	0.876 ± 0.058	0.909 ± 0.038	0.924 ± 0.035	0.912 ± 0.072	0.908 ± 0.054	0.919 ± 0.071	**0.926 ± 0.044**
Heart	0%	0.744 ± 0.069	**0.759 ± 0.082**	0.741 ± 0.105	0.730 ± 0.078	0.730 ± 0.078	0.744 ± 0.069	0.744 ± 0.069
	5%	0.735 ± 0.071	0.739 ± 0.059	0.740 ± 0.110	0.728 ± 0.080	0.727 ± 0.013	0.741 ± 0.067	**0.742 ± 0.038**
	10%	0.719 ± 0.082	0.733 ± 0.086	0.734 ± 0.044	0.726 ± 0.019	0.727 ± 0.078	0.736 ± 0.054	**0.736 ± 0.025**
Segment	0%	0.946 ± 0.109	0.949 ± 0.109	0.953 ± 0.109	**0.955 ± 0.109**	0.953 ± 0.109	0.946 ± 0.033	0.946 ± 0.109
	5%	0.944 ± 0.038	0.948 ± 0.036	0.949 ± 0.032	0.951 ± 0.092	**0.952 ± 0.034**	0.945 ± 0.055	0.945 ± 0.010
	10%	0.941 ± 0.040	0.947 ± 0.032	0.946 ± 0.053	**0.949 ± 0.039**	0.947 ± 0.037	0.944 ± 0.071	0.944 ± 0.104
Hepatitis	0%	**0.765 ± 0.107**	**0.765 ± 0.107**	**0.765 ± 0.107**	**0.765 ± 0.107**	**0.765 ± 0.107**	**0.765 ± 0.107**	**0.765 ± 0.107**
	5%	0.763 ± 0.092	0.764 ± 0.108	0.763 ± 0.045	0.764 ± 0.099	0.760 ± 0.123	0.764 ± 0.092	**0.764 ± 0.062**
	10%	0.750 ± 0.118	0.759 ± 0.075	0.760 ± 0.075	**0.764 ± 0.081**	0.753 ± 0.077	0.750 ± 0.028	0.762 ± 0.104
ICU	0%	0.868 ± 0.162	0.879 ± 0.183	0.879 ± 0.183	0.868 ± 0.129	0.868 ± 0.129	0.868 ± 0.162	**0.880 ± 0.042**
	5%	0.856 ± 0.176	0.859 ± 0.087	0.860 ± 0.158	0.857 ± 0.162	0.855 ± 0.146	0.861 ± 0.054	**0.863 ± 0.107**
	10%	0.850 ± 0.023	0.855 ± 0.126	0.853 ± 0.101	0.856 ± 0.023	0.852 ± 0.176	0.856 ± 0.010	**0.862 ± 0.093**
German	0%	**0.716 ± 0.037**	0.712 ± 0.061	0.713 ± 0.045	0.713 ± 0.032	0.713 ± 0.032	**0.716 ± 0.037**	**0.716 ± 0.037**
	5%	0.708 ± 0.038	0.710 ± 0.046	0.710 ± 0.059	0.709 ± 0.037	0.712 ± 0.041	0.713 ± 0.063	**0.714 ± 0.031**
	10%	0.706 ± 0.033	0.710 ± 0.035	0.708 ± 0.042	0.708 ± 0.091	0.709 ± 0.032	0.710 ± 0.025	**0.713 ± 0.088**
Soy	0%	**0.850 ± 0.141**	0.825 ± 0.134	**0.850 ± 0.141**	**0.850 ± 0.141**	**0.850 ± 0.141**	**0.850 ± 0.141**	**0.850 ± 0.141**
	5%	0.790 ± 0.062	0.819 ± 0.077	0.818 ± 0.025	0.818 ± 0.018	0.816 ± 0.050	**0.820 ± 0.041**	0.820 ± 0.112
	10%	0.760 ± 0.046	0.818 ± 0.082	0.810 ± 0.082	0.806 ± 0.087	0.809 ± 0.246	0.816 ± 0.092	**0.818 ± 0.070**

(continued)

Table 2. (*continued*)

Data sets	Noise level	FRS	β-PFRS	K-trimmed FRS	K-means FRS	K-median FRS	SFRS	RS-FRS
Horse	0%	**0.864 ± 0.056**	0.845 ± 0.051	0.834 ± 0.060	0.834 ± 0.060	0.840 ± 0.061	0.845 ± 0.051	**0.864 ± 0.056**
	5%	**0.830 ± 0.042**	0.829 ± 0.061	0.823 ± 0.072	0.830 ± 0.055	0.825 ± 0.073	0.828 ± 0.052	0.828 ± 0.081
	10%	0.815 ± 0.056	0.825 ± 0.048	0.818 ± 0.065	**0.829 ± 0.061**	0.824 ± 0.074	0.826 ± 0.014	0.827 ± 0.099
Wdbc	0%	0.937 ± 0.036	0.955 ± 0.019	**0.956 ± 0.023**	0.946 ± 0.034	0.952 ± 0.034	0.937 ± 0.028	0.937 ± 0.036
	5%	0.928 ± 0.032	0.933 ± 0.041	0.951 ± 0.020	0.941 ± 0.037	**0.952 ± 0.029**	0.936 ± 0.071	0.936 ± 0.111
	10%	0.920 ± 0.027	0.927 ± 0.021	0.949 ± 0.038	0.940 ± 0.034	**0.951 ± 0.067**	0.935 ± 0.083	0.935 ± 0.027
Wpbc	0%	**0.757 ± 0.050**	0.727 ± 0.083	0.721 ± 0.101	0.711 ± 0.095	0.721 ± 0.082	0.726 ± 0.101	**0.757 ± 0.050**
	5%	0.721 ± 0.087	0.721 ± 0.066	0.712 ± 0.114	0.711 ± 0.098	0.711 ± 0.069	0.722 ± 0.081	**0.751 ± 0.114**
	10%	0.720 ± 0.089	0.720 ± 0.053	0.710 ± 0.095	0.709 ± 0.108	0.706 ± 0.101	0.719 ± 0.077	**0.747 ± 0.093**
Sonar	0%	0.731 ± 0.067	0.774 ± 0.060	0.779 ± 0.083	0.769 ± 0.098	0.769 ± 0.098	0.731 ± 0.067	**0.780 ± 0.091**
	5%	0.730 ± 0.063	0.750 ± 0.055	0.763 ± 0.064	0.765 ± 0.106	0.764 ± 0.077	0.729 ± 0.013	**0.772 ± 0.123**
	10%	0.728 ± 0.067	0.744 ± 0.089	0.726 ± 0.070	0.726 ± 0.075	0.730 ± 0.059	0.728 ± 0.088	**0.761 ± 0.105**
Average		*0.798 ± 0.072*	*0.805 ± 0.069*	*0.804 ± 0.074*	*0.804 ± 0.074*	*0.804 ± 0.080*	*0.804 ± 0.068*	*0.812 ± 0.073*

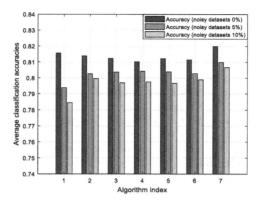

Fig. 2. Illustration of representative samples.

As shown in Fig. 2, each model is affected by noise, and the classification accuracy decreases with the increase of noise. After adding noise, the average classification accuracy of the classical FRS model changes the most. This is because the lower approximation of the classical FRS model depends on the nearest different classes' sample, which is extremely sensitive to noise. Therefore, under KNN, the influence of noise on the classical FRS model is greater than that on other models. This also indicates that other FRS models are more robust than the classical FRS models. In particular, the average classification accuracy based on the RS-FRS model has the smallest reduction after adding noise. Thus, the robustness of RS-FRS model is the strongest. Moreover, the RS-FRS model has the best average classification performance in both the original data set and the noisy data set.

6 Conclusions

The extension of the robust fuzzy rough set is a hot topic in fuzzy rough set theory. In this paper, the non-parametric fuzzy membership degree is defined by fuzzy granular calculation, and RS-FRS model is proposed. Firstly, the distance between the target sample and each representative sample is calculated by finding representative samples of each label. Then, the fuzzy membership degree of the target sample with respect to all labels is determined. On this basis, a robust feature selection algorithm based on RS-FRS model is designed. The experimental results show that RS-FRS model and the proposed feature selection algorithm in this paper are feasible, effective and robust in the processing of uncertain information systems with noises. RS-FRS model expands the research on fuzzy rough sets and the application of feature selection.

Acknowledgement. This work was supported by Shandong Province Key Research and Development Plan (2018GSF118133) and China Postdoctoral Science Foundation (2018M642144).

References

1. Murthy, C.A.: Bridging feature selection and extraction: compound feature generation. IEEE Trans. Knowl. Data Eng. **29**(4), 757–770 (2017)
2. Chen, X.J., Yuan, G.W., Wang, W.T., Nie, F.P., Chang, X.J., Huang, J.Z.: Local adaptive projection framework for feature selection of labeled and unlabeled data. IEEE Trans. Neural Netw. Learn. Syst. **29**(12), 6362–6373 (2018)
3. Chen, H.M., Li, T.R., Fan, X., Luo, C.: Feature selection for imbalanced data based on neighborhood rough sets. Inf. Sci. **483**, 1–20 (2019)
4. Zhou, P., Hu, X.G., Li, P.P., Wu, X.D.: Online streaming feature selection using adapted Neighborhood Rough Set. Inf. Sci. **481**, 258–279 (2019)
5. Wang, C.Z., Huang, Y., Shao, M.W., Chen, D.G.: Uncertainty measures for general fuzzy relations. Fuzzy Sets Syst. **360**, 82–96 (2019)
6. Liu, K.Y., Yang, X.B., Yu, H.L., Mi, J.S., Wang, P.X., Chen, X.J.: Rough set based semi-supervised feature selection via ensemble selector. Knowl.-Based Syst. **165**, 282–296 (2019)
7. Zhou, P., Hu, X.G., Li, P.P., Wu, X.D.: OFS-density: a novel online streaming feature selection method. Pattern Recogn. **86**, 48–61 (2019)
8. Pawlak, Z.: Rough sets. Int. J. Comput. Inform. Sci. **11**, 341–356 (1982)
9. Pawlak, Z., Skowron, A.: Rough sets and boolean reasoning. Inf. Sci. **177**, 41–73 (2007)
10. Pawlak, Z., Skowron, A.: Rough sets: some extensions. Inf. Sci. **177**, 28–40 (2007)
11. Lin, Y.J., Hu, Q.H., Liu, J.H., Chen, J.K., Duan, J.: Multi-label feature selection based on neighborhood mutual information. Appl. Soft Comput. **38**, 244–256 (2016)
12. Li, Y.W., Wu, S.X., Lin, Y.J., Liu, J.H.: Different classes' ratio fuzzy rough set based robust feature selection. Knowl.-Based Syst. **120**, 74–86 (2017)
13. Li, Y.W., Lin, Y.J., Liu, J.H., Weng, W., Shi, Z.K., Wu, S.X.: Feature selection for multi-label learning based on kernelized fuzzy rough sets. Neurocomputing **318**, 217–286 (2018)
14. Dubois, D., Prade, H.: Rough fuzzy sets and fuzzy rough sets. Int. J. Gen. Syst. **17**, 191–209 (1990)
15. Dubois, D., Prade, H.: Putting rough sets and fuzzy sets together. Intell. Decis. Support **11**, 203–232 (1992)
16. Wu, W.Z., Leung, Y., Shao, M.W.: Generalized fuzzy rough approximation operators determined by fuzzy implicators. Int. J. Approx. Reason. **54**, 1388–1409 (2013)
17. Wu, W.Z., Mi, J.S., Zhang, W.X.: Constructive and axiomatic approaches of fuzzy approximation operators. Inf. Sci. **159**, 233–254 (2004)
18. Salido, J.M.F., Murakami, S.: Rough set analysis of a general type of fuzzy data using transitive aggregations of fuzzy similarity relations. Fuzzy Sets Syst. **139**, 635–660 (2003)
19. Hu, Q.H., An, S., Yu, D.R.: Soft fuzzy rough sets for robust feature evaluation and selection. Inf. Sci. **180**, 4384–4400 (2010)
20. An, S., Hu, Q.H., Yu, D.R., Liu, J.F.: Soft minimum-enclosing-ball based robust fuzzy rough sets. Fundam. Inf. **115**, 189–202 (2012)
21. An, S., Hu, Q.H., Pedrycz, W., Zhu, P.F., Tsang, E.C.C.: Data-distribution-aware fuzzy rough set model and its application to robust classification. IEEE Trans. Cybern. **99**, 1–13 (2015)
22. Hu, Q.H., Zhang, L., An, S., Zhang, D., Yu, D.R.: On robust fuzzy rough set models. IEEE Trans. Fuzzy Syst. **20**, 636–651 (2012)
23. Cornelis, C., De Cock, M., Radzikowska, A.M.: Vaguely quantified rough sets. In: An, A., Stefanowski, J., Ramanna, S., Butz, C.J., Pedrycz, W., Wang, G. (eds.) RSFDGrC 2007. LNCS (LNAI), vol. 4482, pp. 87–94. Springer, Heidelberg (2007). https://doi.org/10.1007/978-3-540-72530-5_10

24. Zhao, S.Y., Tsang, E.C.C., Chen, D.G.: The model of fuzzy variable precision rough sets. IEEE Trans. Fuzzy Syst. **17**, 451–467 (2009)
25. Verbiest, N., Cornelis, C., Herrera, F.: OWA-FRPS: a prototype selection method based on ordered weighted average fuzzy rough set theory. In: Ciucci, D., Inuiguchi, M., Yao, Y., Ślęzak, D., Wang, G. (eds.) RSFDGrC 2013. LNCS (LNAI), vol. 8170, pp. 180–190. Springer, Heidelberg (2013). https://doi.org/10.1007/978-3-642-41218-9_19
26. Hu, Q.H., Yu, D.R., Liu, J.F., Wu, C.X.: Neighborhood rough set based heterogeneous feature subset selection. Inf. Sci. **178**, 3577–3594 (2008)
27. Wang, C.Z., et al.: A fitting model for feature selection with fuzzy rough sets. IEEE Trans. Fuzzy Syst. **25**, 741–753 (2017)
28. Hu, X.H., Cercone, N.: Learning in relational databases: a rough set approach. Int. J. Comput. Intell. **11**, 323–338 (1995)
29. Yao, Y.Y., Zhao, Y.: Discernibility matrix simplification for constructing attribute reducts. Inf. Sci. **179**, 867–882 (2009)
30. Jensen, R., Tuson, A., Shen, Q.: Finding rough and fuzzy-rough set reducts with SAT. Inf. Sci. **255**, 100–120 (2014)
31. Liang, J.Y., Xu, Z.B.: The algorithm on knowledge reduction in incomplete information systems. Int. J. Uncertainty Fuzziness Knowl.-Based Syst. **12**, 651–672 (2004)
32. Chen, D.G., Zhao, S.Y., Zhang, L., Yang, Y.P., Zhang, X.: Sample pair selection for attribute reduction with rough set. IEEE Trans. Knowl. Data Eng. **24**, 2080–2093 (2012)
33. Chen, D.G., Zhang, L., Zhao, S.Y., Hu, Q.H., Zhu, P.F.: A novel algorithm for finding reducts with fuzzy rough sets. IEEE Trans. Fuzzy Syst. **20**, 385–389 (2012)
34. Asuncion, A., Newman, D.J.: UCI Machine Learning Repository. School of Information and Computer Science, University of California, Irvine (2007). http://www.ics.uci.edu/mlearn/MLRepository.html
35. Aha, D.W., Kibler, D., Albert, M.K.: Instance-based learning algorithms. Mach. Learn. **6**, 37–66 (1991)

Classification and Clustering Methods

HUE-Span: Fast High Utility Episode Mining

Philippe Fournier-Viger[1]([⊠]), Peng Yang[2], Jerry Chun-Wei Lin[3], and Unil Yun[4]

[1] School of Humanities and Social Sciences, Harbin Institute of Technology (Shenzhen), Shenzhen, China
philfv8@yahoo.com
[2] School of Computer Science and Technology, Harbin Institute of Technology (Shenzhen), Shenzhen, China
pengyeung@163.com
[3] Department of Computing, Mathematics and Physics, Western Norway University of Applied Sciences (HVL), Bergen, Norway
jerrylin@ieee.org
[4] Department of Computer Engineering, Sejong University, Seoul, Republic of Korea
yunei@sejong.ac.kr

Abstract. High utility episode mining consists of finding episodes (subsequences of events) that have a high importance (e.g high profit) in a sequence of events with quantities and weights. Though it has important real-life applications, the current problem definition has two critical limitations. First, it underestimates the utility of episodes by not taking into account all timestamps of minimal occurrences for utility calculations, which can result in missing high utility episodes. Second, the state-of-the-art UP-Span algorithm is inefficient on large databases because it uses a loose upper bound on the utility to reduce the search space. This paper addresses the first issue by redefining the problem to guarantee that all high utility episodes are found. Moreover, an efficient algorithm named HUE-Span is proposed to efficiently find all patterns. It relies on a novel upper-bound to reduce the search space and a novel co-occurrence based pruning strategy. Experimental results show that HUE-Span not only finds all patterns but is also up to five times faster than UP-Span.

1 Introduction

Frequent Episode Mining (FEM) [1,4–6,12,15] is a fundamental data mining task, used to analyze a sequence of discrete events. It consists of identifying all episodes having a support (occurrence frequency) that is no less than a user-defined minimum support threshold. An *episode* (also known as serial episode) is a totally ordered set of events (a subsequence). Though FEM has been well-studied, it assumes that each event cannot appear more than once at each time point and that all events have the same importance (e.g. in terms of weight, unit profit or value). But for many real-life applications, this assumption does not hold [17]. For example, for market basket analysis, a sequence of customer transactions may contains non binary item purchase quantities at each time point,

© Springer Nature Switzerland AG 2019
J. Li et al. (Eds.): ADMA 2019, LNAI 11888, pp. 169–184, 2019.
https://doi.org/10.1007/978-3-030-35231-8_12

and purchased items may have different importance in terms of unit profits. On such data, FEM algorithms may discover a large amount of frequent episodes that yield a low profit and discard profitable episodes that are less frequent. Hence, to find interesting episodes in sequences, other aspects can be considered such as a measure of importance (e.g. profit).

To address this issue, FEM was generalized as *High Utility Episode Mining* (HUEM) [17] to consider the case where events can appear more than once at each time point and each event has a weight indicating its relative importance. The goal of HUEM is to find *High-Utility Episodes* (HUEs), that is sub-sequences of events that have a high importance as measured by a utility measure (e.g. profit). HUEM has many applications such as website click stream analysis [2], cross-marketing in retail stores [11,16], stock investment [13] and cloud workload prediction [3]. However, HUEM is more difficult than FEM because the *downward-closure property* used in FEM to reduce the search space using the support measure does not hold for the utility measure. That property states that the support of an episode is anti-monotonic, that is a super-episode of an infrequent episode is infrequent and sub-episodes of a frequent episode are frequent. But the utility of an episode is neither monotonic or anti-monotonic, that is a high utility episode may have a super-episode or sub-episode with lower, equal or higher utility [17]. Hence, techniques designed for reducing the search space in FEM cannot be directly used for HUEM. To mine HUEs in a complex sequence (where some events may be simultaneous) without considering all possible episodes, Wu et al. [17] proposed the UP-Span algorithm. It relies on an upper-bound on the utility that is anti-monotonic, named *EWU* (*Episode Weighted Utilization*), which is inspired by the *TWU* measure used in high utility itemset mining [8]. Another HUEM algorithm named T-Span [11] was then proposed but appears to be incomplete and is reported to provide a marginal performance improvement over UP-Span (up to about 25% faster).

Although HUEM is useful, it has two major limitations. First, as this paper will explain, the traditional way of performing utility calculations for episodes, which can underestimate their utility. As a consequence, current HUEM algorithms may miss several HUEs [11,17]. The reason for this underestimation is that an episode may be supported by multiple timestamps in a time interval but traditional HUEM algorithms only consider the timestamps that follow a specific processing order, and ignore other timestamps where the episode may yield a higher utility. This simplifies the design of HUEM algorithms but can lead to discarding high utility patterns. Second, the state-of-the-art UP-Span algorithm utilizes the loose *EWU* upper bound on utility. This upper bound is ineffective for reducing the search space of HUEM in large databases.

This paper addresses these limitations by presenting a new framework for mining HUEs in complex event sequences. Contributions are as follows:

– The problem of HUEM is redefined to fix the utility calculation of episodes to guarantee that all high utility episodes are found.

- An efficient algorithm named HUE-Span (**H**igh **U**tility **E**pisodes mining by **Span**ning prefixes) is proposed for mining the complete set of HUEs in complex event sequences.
- The proposed algorithm integrates the concept of *remaining utility* [8,14] with the *EWU* model to derive a tighter upper bound on episode utility, named *ERU*. HUE-Span applies novel search space reduction strategies based on the *ERU* to reduce the number of candidate episodes.
- To reduce the cost of episode *spanning* (extending an episode with a single event to generate a larger episode), a novel pruning strategy is proposed, named *EEUCP* (Estimated Episode Utility Cooccurrence Pruning). It can eliminate low utility episodes before a pattern is extended (spanned).
- The performance of the proposed HUE-Span algorithm is compared with the state-of-the-art UP-Span algorithm on both synthetic and real datasets. Results show that the proposed HUE-Span algorithm discovers all HUEs for the redefined HUEM problem, while UP-Span can miss up to 65% of them. Moreover, HUE-Span generates less candidates and is up to five times faster.

The rest of this paper is organized as follows. Section 2 introduces HUEM and explains why the traditional HUEM model can miss HUEs. Section 3 presents the revised HUEM problem. Then, Sects. 4, 5 and 6 respectively presents the proposed HUE-Span algorithm, the experimental evaluation and the conclusion.

2   Frequent and High Utility Episode Mining

The first studies on episode mining focused on finding frequent episodes in a sequence of discrete events with timestamps. FEM is defined as follows [12,15].

Definition 1 (Complex event sequence). Let $\varepsilon = \{e_1, e_2, \cdots, e_m\}$ be a finite set of events. A complex event sequence $CES = \langle (tSE_{t_1}, t_1), (tSE_{t_2}, t_2), \cdots, (tSE_{t_n}, t_n) \rangle$ is an ordered sequence of simultaneous event sets, where each $tSE_{t_i} \subseteq \varepsilon$ consists of all events associated with a time stamp t_i, and $t_i < t_j$ for any $1 \leq i < j \leq n$.

For example, Fig. 1 (left) shows a complex event sequence $CES = \langle ((A), t_1), ((BD), t_2), ((BC), t_3), ((AC), t_4), ((D), t_5) \rangle$, that will be used as running example. Such sequence can represents various types of data such as customer transactions [1,4–6], alarm sequences [15], stock data [13] and cloud data [3].

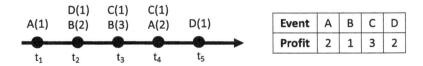

Fig. 1. A complex event sequence (left) and external utility values (right)

The goal of FEM is to find all frequent episodes [12,15]. The support (occurrence frequency) of an episode is measured by counting its minimal occurrences in the input sequence. These concepts are defined as follows.

Definition 2 (Episode containing simultaneous event sets). An episode α is a non-empty totally ordered set of simultaneous events of the form $\langle SE_1, SE_2, \cdots, SE_k \rangle$, where $SE_i \subseteq \varepsilon$ and SE_i appears before SE_j for $1 \leq i < j \leq k$.

Definition 3 (Occurrence). Given an episode $\alpha = \langle SE_1, SE_2, \cdots, SE_k \rangle$, a time interval $[t_s, t_e]$ is called an occurrence of α if (1) α occurs in $[t_s, t_e]$, (2) SE_1 occurs at t_s, and (3) SE_k occurs at t_e. The set of all occurrences of α is denoted as $occSet(\alpha)$.

For instance, the set of all occurrences of $\langle (B), (C) \rangle$ is $occSet(\langle (B), (C) \rangle) = \{[t_2, t_3], [t_2, t_4], [t_3, t_4]\}$.

Definition 4 (Minimal occurrence). Given two time intervals $[t_s, t_e]$ and $[t'_s, t'_e]$ of occurrences of episode α, $[t'_s, t'_e]$ is a *sub-time interval* of $[t_s, t_e]$ if $t_s \leq t'_s \leq t'_e \leq t_e$. The time interval $[t_s, t_e]$ is called a *minimal occurrence* of α if (1) $[t_s, t_e] \in occSet(\alpha)$, (2) there is no alternative occurrence $[t'_s, t'_e]$ of α such that $[t'_s, t'_e]$ is a sub-time interval of $[t_s, t_e]$. The complete set of minimal occurrences of α is denoted as $moSet(\alpha)$.

For example, the episode $\langle (B), (C) \rangle$ has two minimal occurrences that are $moSet(\langle (B), (C) \rangle) = \{[t_2, t_3], [t_3, t_4]\}$.

Definition 5 (Support of an episode). *The support of an episode is its number of minimal occurrences.*

For example, the support of episode $\langle (B), (C) \rangle$ is $|moSet(\langle (B), (C) \rangle)| = 2$. FEM consists of finding all episodes that have a minimum support. To consider that events can appear more than once at each time point and that events may have different importance (utility), FEM was generalized as HUEM [17] by introducing the concepts of internal and external utility.

Definition 6 (Internal and external utility of events). Each event $e \in \varepsilon$ of a CES is associated with a positive number $p(e)$, called its *external utility*, representing its relative importance (e.g. unit profit). Moreover, each event e in a simultaneous event set tSE_i at a time point t_i is associated with a positive number $q(e, t_i)$, called its *internal utility* indicating its number of occurrences at time t_i (e.g. purchase quantity).

For example, Fig. 1 (left) shows a complex event sequence with internal utility values. At time point t_2, events B and D have an internal utility (quantities) of 2 and 1, respectively. Figure 1 (right) indicates that the external utility of A, B, C and D are 2, 1, 3 and 2, respectively. The goal of HUEM is to find high utility episodes, where the utility of an episode is calculated as follows [17].

Definition 7 (Utility of an event at a time point). The *utility* of an event e at a time point t_i is defined as $u(e, t_i) = p(e) \times q(e, t_i)$.

For example, $u(B, t_2) = p(B) \times q(B, t_2) = 1 \times 2 = 2$.

Definition 8 (Utility of a simultaneous event set at a time point). The utility of a simultaneous event set $SE = \{e_{f(1)}, e_{f(2)}, \cdots, e_{f(l)}\}$ at a time point t_i is defined as $u(SE, t_i) = \sum_{j=1}^{l} u(e_{f(j)}, t_i)$.

For example, $u((BD), t_2) = u(B, t_2) + u(D, t_2) = 2 + 2 = 4$.

Definition 9 (Utility of a minimal occurrence of an episode). The utility of a minimal occurrence $[t_s, t_e]$ of an episode $\alpha = \langle SE_1, SE_2, \cdots, SE_k \rangle$ is defined as $u(\alpha, [t_s, t_e]) = \sum_{i=1}^{k} u(SE_i, t_{g(i)})$.

For example, the utility of the minimal occurrence $[t_2, t_3]$ of $\alpha = \langle (B), (C) \rangle$ is $u(\alpha, [t_2, t_3]) = u(B, t_2) + u(C, t_3) = 2 + 3 = 5$. And $u(\alpha, [t_3, t_4]) = 6$.

Definition 10 (Utility of an episode in a complex event sequence). The *utility of an episode α in a complex event sequence* is the sum of the utility of its minimal occurrences, that is $u(\alpha) = \sum_{mo \in moSet(\alpha)} u(\alpha, mo)$.

For example, the utility of $\langle (B), (C) \rangle$ in the running example is $u(\langle (B), (C) \rangle) = u(\langle (B), (C) \rangle, [t_2, t_3]) + u(\langle (B), (C) \rangle, [t_3, t_4]) = 5 + 6 = 11$.

Definition 11 (High utility episode mining). An episode is a *high utility episode*, if and only if its utility is no less than a user-specified *minimum utility threshold (minUtil)*. The task of HUEM is to find all HUEs [17].

A major problem with the traditional definition of HUEM is that the utility of an episode is calculated without considering all the timestamps of its minimal occurrences. Hence, utility can be underestimated and it can be argued that some HUEs are missed. This problem is illustrated with an example. Let $minUtil = 9$. The utility of episode $\langle (A), (B), (A) \rangle$ in the CES is calculated as $u(\langle (A), (B), (A) \rangle) = u(\langle (A), (B), (A) \rangle, [t_1, t_4]) = u(A, t_1) + u(B, t_2) + u(A, t_4) = 2 + 2 + 4 = 8$. Thus, this pattern is considered as a low utility episode by HUEM algorithms, and is discarded. But it can be observed that this pattern is a HUE for other timestamps in the same minimal occurrence $[t_1, t_4]$. In fact, $\langle (A), (B), (A) \rangle$ also appears at timestamps t_1, t_3 and t_4 with a utility of $9 \geq minUtil$. The reason why current HUEM algorithms calculate the utility of that episode as 8 in $[t_1, t_4]$ rather than 9 is that the pattern $\langle (A), (B), (A) \rangle$ is obtained by extending $\langle (A), (B) \rangle$ with (A), and that the timestamps of $\langle (A), (B), (A) \rangle$ are obtained by combining those of the minimum occurrence of $\langle (A), (B) \rangle$, i.e. $[t_1, t_2]$ with the timestamp t_4 of (A). In other words, timestamps used for calculating the utility of a minimal occurrence of an episode are determined by the processing order, and other timestamps are ignored. This can lead to underestimating the utility of episodes in time intervals of their minimal occurrences, and hence to discard episodes that should be considered as HUEs.

3   Redefining High Utility Episode Mining

To fix the above issue of utility calculation in HUEM, and ensures that all HUEs are found, this paper proposes to consider all timestamps that match with an episode in each of its minimal occurrence. This is done by using the maximum of the utility values. Definition 9 is redefined as follows.

Definition 12 (Redefined utility of a minimal occurrence of an episode). Let $[t_s, t_e]$ be a minimal occurrence of an episode $\alpha = \langle SE_1, SE_2, \cdots, SE_k \rangle$, in which each middle simultaneous event set $SE_i \in \alpha$ and $i \in [2, k-1]$ is associated with some (at least one) time points $t_{g(i)1}, t_{g(i)2}, \cdots, t_{g(i)j}$. The *utility* of the episode α w.r.t. $[t_s, t_e]$ is defined as $u(\alpha, [t_s, t_e]) = u(SE_1, t_s) + \sum_{i=2}^{k-1} max\{u(SE_i, t_{g(i)x}) | x \in [1, j]\} + u(SE_k, t_e)$.

For example, the redefined utility of the minimal occurrence $[t_1, t_4]$ of $\langle (A), (B), (A) \rangle$ is $u(\langle (A), (B), (A) \rangle, [t_1, t_4]) = u(A, t_1) + max\{u(B, t_2), u(B, t_3)\} + u(A, t_4) = 2 + max(2, 3) + 4 = 9$. Thus, that episode is a HUE for $minUtil = 9$.

Moreover, to avoid finding some very long minimal occurrences which may not be meaningful, the concept of *maximum time duration* is used in the proposed problem, as in previous work [12].

Definition 13 (Maximum time duration). Let $maxDur$ be a user-specified *maximum time duration*. A minimal occurrence $[t_s, t_e]$ of an episode α is said to satisfy the *maximum time duration* if and only if $t_e - t_e + 1 \leq maxDur$.

The redefined HUEM problem is defined as follows.

Definition 14 (Redefined High Utility Episode Mining). Given $minUtil$ and $maxDur$ thresholds, the redefined problem of HUEM is to find all HUEs when considering only minimal occurrences satisfying the $maxDur$ constraint, and calculating the utility using Definition 12.

4   The HUE-Span Algorithm

This subsection introduces the proposed *HUE-Span* algorithm to efficiently discover HUEs in a complex event sequence. HUE-Span adopts the prefix-growth paradigm [17], starting from patterns containing single events and then recursively concatening events to obtain larger patterns.

Definition 15 (Simultaneous and serial concatenations). Let $\alpha = \langle SE_1, SE_2, \cdots, SE_x \rangle$ and $\beta = \langle SE_1', SE_2', \cdots, SE_y' \rangle$ be episodes. The *simultaneous concatenation)* of α and β is defined as $simul\text{-}concat(\alpha, \beta) = \langle SE_1, SE_2, \cdots, SE_x \cup SE_1', SE_2', \cdots, SE_y' \rangle$. The *serial concatenation* of episodes α and β is defined as $serial\text{-}concat(\alpha, \beta) = \langle SE_1, SE_2, \cdots, SE_x, SE_1', SE_2', \cdots, SE_y' \rangle$.

To reduce the search space, the *EWU* upper bound on the utility was proposed [17]. It is presented, and then a tighter upper bound is proposed.

Definition 16 (Episode-Weighted Utilization of a minimal occurrence of an episode). Let there be a minimal occurrence $[t_s, t_e]$ of an episode $\alpha = \langle SE_1, SE_2, \cdots, SE_k \rangle$ satisfying $maxDur$, where simultaneous event sets are associated with some time points $t_{g(1)}, t_{g(2)} \cdots t_{g(k)}$, respectively. The *episode-weighted utilization* (EWU) of the minimal occurrence $[t_s, t_e]$ of α is $EWU(\alpha, [t_s, t_e]) = \sum_{i=1}^{k-1} u(SE_i, t_{g(i)}) + \sum_{j=t_e}^{t_s+maxDur-1} u(tSE_j, j)$, where tSE_j is the simultaneous event set at time point j in CES.

Definition 17 (Episode-Weighted Utilization of an episode). The *episode-weighted utilization* of α is the sum of the EWU of its minimal occurrences, that is $EWU(\alpha) = \sum_{mo \in moSet(\alpha)} EWU(\alpha, mo)$.

For example, if $maxDur = 3$, $EWU(\langle (A), (D) \rangle) = \{u(A, t_1) + [u((BD), t_2) + u((BC), t_3)]\} + \{u(A, t_4) + u(D, t_5)\} = \{2 + [4+6]\} + \{4+2\} = 18$. The EWU is an anti-monotonic upper bound on an episode's utility and can be used to reduce the search space [17]. To be more effective, a tighter upper bound is proposed in this paper, inspired by the concept of *remaining utility* [8,9,14].

Definition 18 (Episode-Remaining Utilization of a minimal occurrence of an episode). Let $\succ$ be a total order on events from ε. The *episode-remaining utilization* of a minimal occurrence $[t_s, t_e]$ of an episode α is $ERU(\alpha, [t_s, t_e]) = \sum_{i=1}^{k} u(SE_i, t_{g(i)}) + u(rSE_{t_e}, t_e) + \sum_{j=t_e+1}^{t_s+maxDur-1} u(tSE_j, j)$, where $u(rSE_{t_e}, t_e) = \sum_{x \in tSE_{t_e} \wedge x \succ SE_k} u(x, t_e)$.

Definition 19 (Episode-Remaining Utilization of an episode). For an episode α, its *episode-remaining utilization* is the sum of the ERU of its minimal occurrences, that is $ERU(\alpha) = \sum_{mo \in moSet(\alpha)} ERU(\alpha, mo)$.

For example, if $maxDur = 3$, $ERU(\langle (A), (D) \rangle) = \{[u(A, t_1) + u(D, t_2)] + 0 + u((BC), t_3)\} + \{u(A, t_4) + u(D, t_5)\} = \{[2+2] + 0 + 6\} + \{4+2\} = 16$.

Lemma 1 (Anti-monotonicity of the ERU). *Let α and β be episodes, and $\gamma = simult\text{-}concat(\alpha, \beta)$ or $\gamma = serial\text{-}concat(\alpha, \beta)$. It follows that $u(\gamma) \leq ERU(\gamma) \leq ERU(\alpha) \leq EWU(\alpha)$.*

Proof. Let $moSet(\alpha) = [mo_1, mo_2, \cdots, mo_x]$, $moSet(\gamma) = [mo'_1, mo'_2, \cdots, mo'_y]$. Because $\gamma = simult\text{-}concat(\alpha, \beta)$ or $\gamma = serial\text{-}concat(\alpha, \beta)$, $|moSet(\alpha)| \geq |moSet(\gamma)|$. Based on Definitions 16 and 18, $EWU(\alpha) \geq ERU(\alpha) = \sum_{i=1}^{x} ERU(\alpha, mo_i) \geq \sum_{i=1}^{y} ERU(\gamma, mo_i) \geq \sum_{i=1}^{y} ERU(\gamma, mo'_i) = ERU(\gamma) \geq u(\gamma)$.

Theorem 1 (Search space pruning using ERU). For an episode α, if $ERU(\alpha) < minUtil$, then α is not a HUE as well as all its *super-episodes* (obtained by concatenations). Proof. This follows from Lemma 1.

The proposed algorithm uses the EWU and ERU to eliminate candidate episodes during the search for HUEs. However, the ERU and EWU cannot be used to remove events from the complex sequence, and it is costly to calculate these upper bounds. To remove events, we introduce a measure called AWU of events. If the AWU of an event is less than $minUtil$, it can be removed. The rationale for pruning using the AWU will be explained after.

Definition 20 (Action-Window Utilization of an episode). Let $moSet(\alpha) = [t_{s1}, t_{e1}], [t_{s2}, t_{e2}], \cdots, [t_{sk}, t_{ek}]$ be the set of all minimal occurrence of the episode α. Each minimal occurrence $[t_{si}, t_{ei}]$, must be a *sub-time interval* of $[t_{ei} - maxDur + 1, t_{si} + maxDur - 1]$. Hence, the *action-window utilization* of α is defined as $AWU(\alpha) = \sum_{i=1}^{k} \sum_{j=t_{ei}-maxDur+1}^{t_{si}+maxDur-1} tSE_j$.

For example, let $maxDur = 3$. The $AWU(\langle (A) \rangle) = [0 + 0 + 2 + 4 + 6] + [4 + 6 + 7 + 2 + 0] = 31$. The $AWU(\langle (AC) \rangle) = [4 + 6 + 7 + 2 + 0] = 19$. The $AWU(\langle (A), (B) \rangle) = [0 + 2 + 4 + 6] = 12$.

Algorithm 1: The HUE-Span algorithm

   input : CES: a complex event sequence,
              $minUtil$ and $maxDur$: the user-specified thresholds.
   output: The complete set of high utility episodes

1   Scan CES once to calculate the AWU of each event, and remove events such that their $AWU < minUtil$ from the CES, let $\varepsilon*$ be the events that their $AWU \geq minUtil$. Let $\succ$ be the total order of AWU ascending values on $\varepsilon*$;
2   Scan the updated CES to build $EEUCS_{Simul}$ and $EEUCS_{Serial}$;
3   **foreach** *event* $\alpha \in \varepsilon*$ *such that* $ERU(\alpha) \geq minUtil$ **do**
4 | $MiningHUE(\alpha, moSet(\alpha), minUtil, maxDur)$;
5   **end**
6   **Procedure** $MiningHUE(\alpha, moSet(\alpha), minUtil, maxDur)$:
7 | **if** $u(\alpha) \geq minUtil$ **then** Output α
       | $MiningSimultHUE(\alpha, moSet(\alpha), minUtil, maxDur)$;
8 | $MiningSerialHUE(\alpha, moSet(\alpha), minUtil, maxDur)$;
9   **EndProcedure**

The HUE-Span Algorithm. The pseudocode is shown in Algorithm 1. It takes as input a complex event sequence CES with utility values, and the $minUtil$ and $maxDur$ thresholds. The algorithm first scans the CES to calculate the AWU of each event. The algorithm removes events having AWU values that are less than $minUtil$ from CES, and identifies the set $\varepsilon*$ of all events having AWU values that are no less than $minUtil$. The AWU values of events are then used to establish a total order $\succ$ on events, which is the order of ascending AWU values. A second sequence scan is then performed to build a new structure, named $EEUCS$ (Estimated Episode Utility Co-occurrence Structure) used by a novel strategy named $EEUCP$ (Estimated Episode Utility Co-occurrence Pruning) to reduce the number of EWU and ERU calculations. The $EEUCS$ structure is defined as a set of triples of the form (x, y, c), where a triple (x, y, c) indicates that $AWU(\langle (xy) \rangle) = c$ (where $y \succ x$), or that $AWU(\langle (x), (y) \rangle) = c$. A $EEUCS$

of the first type is called $EEUCS_{simult}$, while a $EEUCS$ of the second type is called $EEUCS_{serial}$. The $EEUCS_{simult}$ and $EEUCS_{serial}$ structures can be implemented as two matrices as shown in Fig. 2. But in HUE-Span, they are implemented as hashmaps of hashmaps where only tuples of the form (x, y, c) such that $c \neq 0$ are stored. This representation is more memory efficient because on real data, few events typically co-occur with other events in $EEUCS_{simult}$.

Event	A	D	B	C
A		0	0	19
D			19	0
B				21
C				

Event	A	D	B	C
A	0	27	12	12
D	17	0	19	19
B	36	15	19	38
C	19	30	0	19

(a) $EEUCS_{simult}$ (b) $EEUCS_{serial}$

Fig. 2. $EEUCS_{simult}$ and $EEUCS_{serial}$ for the sequence of Fig. 1 and $maxDur = 3$

Then, the algorithm considers extending each episode $\alpha \in \varepsilon*$ such that $ERU(\alpha) \geq minUtil$ by calling the $MiningHUE$ procedure. Other episodes are not extended, based on Theorem 1. The $MiningHUE$ procedure spans a prefix α (Line 6–10) by calling two procedures $MiningSimultHUE$ and $MiningSerialHUE$. The former first considers concatenating simultaneous events to α according to $\succ$, while the latter first considers concatenating serial events to α.

The $MiningSimultHUE$ procedure (Algorithm 2) is applied as follows. For each occurrence $[t_s, t_e] \in occSet(\alpha)$, the algorithm considers each event e that occurs at t_e and such that e is greater than all events in the last event of α according to $\succ$. For each such event, the algorithm performs a simultaneous concatenation of α with e to obtain an episode β (Line 4). Then, $[t_s, t_e]$ is added to $occSet(\beta)$ (Line 5). If $[t_s, t_e]$ is a minimal occurrence, $[t_s, t_e]$ is added to $moSet(\beta)$ (Line 6). Then, β is added to a set β-Set. After $occSet(\alpha)$ has been traversed, the algorithm considers each episode $\beta \in \beta$-Set. If the episode does not pass the $EEUCP$ pruning conditions, it is ignored (Line 11). Let y be the last added event to β. The pruning conditions are that there is no tuple (x, y, c) such that $c \geq minUtil$ (1) in $EEUCS_{simult}$ for an event x appearing at the same time point as y, and no such tuple (2) in $EEUCS_{serial}$ for an event x followed by y. If the conditions are verified, then β and all its super-episodes are not HUEs and are ignored. Otherwise, $ERU(\beta)$ is calculated by using $moSet(\beta)$, and if $ERU(\beta) \geq minUtil$, the procedure $MiningHUE$ is called to further concatenate events to β to find larger HUEs (Line 11).

The $MiningSerialHUE$ procedure (Algorithm 3) is applied as follows. For each minimal occurrence $[t_{s1}, t_{e1}]$ of $occSet(\alpha)$, the algorithm finds the next minimal occurrence $[t_{s2}, t_{e2}]$ (Line 2–3). Then, the algorithm processes each event e occurring at a time point t in interval $[t_{e1} + 1, \min(t_{s1} + maxDur - 1, t_{e2})]$ (Line 4). For each such event e, a serial concatenation of α with e is done to

---

Algorithm 2: *MiningSimultHUE*

---

    input : α: an episode, $occSet(\alpha)$: possible occurrences of α,
              $minUtil$, $maxDur$: the user-specified thresholds.
    output: The set of high utility simultaneous episodes w.r.t prefix α
1 Let $lastEvent$ be the last event of α, and initialize $\beta\text{-}Set \leftarrow \emptyset$;
2 **foreach** occurrence of α $[t_s, t_e] \in occSet(\alpha)$ **do**
3   **foreach** event e that occurs at t_e and $e \succ lastEvent$ **do**
4             $\beta = simult\text{-}concat(\alpha, e)$;
5             $occSet(\beta) \leftarrow occSet(\beta) \cup [t_s, t_e]$;
6   **if** $[t_s, t_e]$ is a minimal occurrence of β **then**
                 $moSet(\beta) \leftarrow moSet(\beta) \cup [t_s, t_e]$
7   Add β to $\beta\text{-}Set$;
8   **end**
9 **end**
10 **foreach** episode $\beta \in \beta\text{-}Set$ **do**
11   **if** $\forall(x, y) \in \beta, EEUCS_{simult}(x, y) \geq minUtil \wedge EEUCS_{serial}(x, y)$
      $\geq minUtil$ **and** $ERU(\beta) \geq minUtil$ **then**
      $MiningHUE(\beta, occSet(\beta), minUtil, maxDur)$
12 **end**

---

obtain an episode β (Line 7). Here, it is important to note that existing HUEM algorithms [11,17] ignore the fact that t cannot exceed the end time point of the next minimal occurrence (or the largest time point of CES). If t exceeds the end time point of the next minimal occurrence ($t > t_{e2}$), then $[t_{s1}, t]$ cannot be a minimal occurrence because $[t_{s2}, t]$ is a *sub-time interval* of $[t_{s1}, t]$. Hence, this technique reduces the search space. Then, the next operations are the same as *MiningSimultHUE* with the only difference being that only $EEUCS_{serial}$ is used in *MiningSerialHUE* (Line 12). This is because no events are simultaneous events with the last added event y in β.

The $EEUCP$ strategy is correct (only prunes low-utility episodes) because the AWU considers a larger window than ERU, and ERU is an upper bound on the utility (Theorem 1). Because HUE-Span starts from single events and considers larger episodes by recursively performing simultaneous and serial concatenations, and only prunes the search space by Theorem 1 and using $EEUCP$, HUE-Span is correct and complete to discover all HUEs.

5   Experimental Evaluation

We performed experiments to assess the performance of the proposed algorithm. Experiments were performed on a computer having a 64 bit Xeon E3-1270 3.6 Ghz CPU, running Windows 10 and having 64 GB of RAM. We compared the performance of HUE-Span with the state-of-the-art UP-Span algorithm for high-utility episode mining. Both real and synthetic datasets were used to compare the algorithms' performance. The real *Retail* and *Kosarak* datasets are

---

Algorithm 3: *MiningSerialHUE*

---

input : α: an episode, $occSet(\alpha)$: possible occurrences of α,
         $minUtil$, $maxDur$: the user-specified thresholds.
output: The set of high utility serial episodes w.r.t prefix α

1 Let β-$Set \leftarrow \emptyset$;
2 **foreach** minimal occurrence $[t_{s1}, t_{e1}] \in occSet(\alpha)$ **do**
3   Let $[t_{s2}, t_{e2}]$ be the next minimal occurrence;
4   **foreach** event e occurring at a time point t in
         $[t_{e1} + 1, \min(t_{s1} + maxDur - 1, t_{e2})]$ **do**
5          $\beta = serial\text{-}concat(\alpha, e)$;
6          $occSet(\beta) \leftarrow occSet(\beta) \cup [t_{s1}, t]$;
7   **if** $[t_{s1}, t]$ is a minimal occurrence of β **then**
         $moSet(\beta) \leftarrow moSet(\beta) \cup [t_{s1}, t]$
8   Add β to β-Set;
9   **end**
10 **end**
11 **foreach** episode $\beta \in \beta$-Set **do**
12   **if** $\forall(x, y), EEUCS_{serial}(x, y) \geq minUtil$ **and** $ERU(\beta) \geq minUtil$ **then**
     $MiningHUE(\beta, occSet(\beta), minUtil, maxDur)$
13 **end**

---

commonly used in the pattern mining literature and were obtained from the SPMF library website (https://www.philippe-fournier-viger.com/spmf/), while synthetic datasets were generated using the IBM data generator. The IBM generator has four parameters: T is the average size of a simultaneous event set at a time point; I is the average size of event sets in frequent episodes; N is the number of distinct events; D is the total number of time points. Internal utility and external utility values were then generated using the SPMF generator. It has two parameters: Q is the maximum internal utility (quantity) of each event at a time point; F is the average external utility of each event. The obtained *Retail* and *Kosarak* datasets have unit profits (external utility) and purchased quantities (internal utility). Note that these three datasets are sometimes considered as transaction databases but they also can be considered as a single complex event sequence by regarding each item as an event and each transaction as a simultaneous event set. Characteristics of the datasets are presented in Table 1.

Table 1. Characteristics of the datasets

Dataset	#Time Point	#Event	Avg. length
T25I10N1KD10KQ10F5	9,976	929	24.8
Retail	88,162	16,470	10.3
Kosarak	990,002	41,270	8.1

In the experiments, UP-Span is compared with three versions of the proposed algorithm: HUE-Span(ERU) only uses *ERU* for search space pruning; HUE-Span(EEUCP) only uses *EEUCP* for search space pruning; HUE-Span(ERU+EEUCP) uses both *ERU* and *EEUCP* for pruning. In the following, an algorithm name followed by a star * means that it applies the proposed redefined utility (Definition 12) to find all HUEs by calculating the maximum utility for each minimal occurrence of an episode. In the following experiments, *minUtil* is expressed as *a percentage* of the total utility of the complex event sequence.

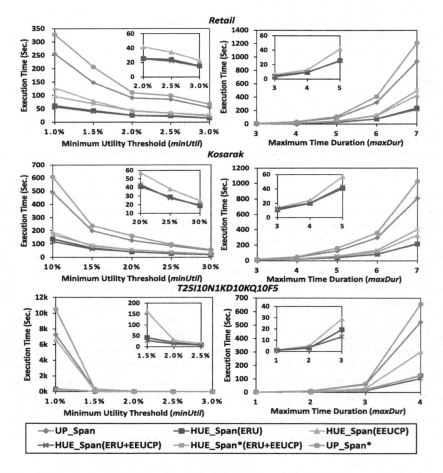

Fig. 3. Comparison of execution times for various *minUtil* and *minDur* values

Figure 3 compares the runtimes of HUE-Span and UP-Span for different *minUtil* and *maxDur* values on these three datasets respectively. In the leftmost figures from top to bottom, *maxDur* was set to 5, 5 and 3 respectively.

In the rightmost figures from top to bottom, $minUtil$ was set to 2%, 20% and 2% respectively. It is observed that HUE-Span(ERU+EEUCP) is up to 5 times faster than UP-Span on all datasets. Moreover, for the dense dataset (T25I10N1KD10KQ10F5), HUE-Span(ERU+EEUCP) is up to 20 times faster than UP-Span. This is because pruning using ERU is more effective for dense datasets. Six sub-figures show enlarged parts of the charts to better show the runtime differences between ERU pruning and $EEUCP$. It can be observed that ERU pruning is better than $EEUCP$. The reason is that $EEUCP$ uses the AWU of an episode, and this latter considers a larger window than the ERU.

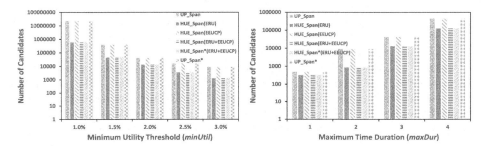

Fig. 4. Number of candidates on T25I10N1KD10KQ10F5 for various $minUtil$ and $minDur$ values

Figure 4 shows the number of candidates generated by different algorithms on T25I10N1KD10KQ10F5 using a log scale. In the left figure, $maxDur = 3$ and in the right figure, $minUtil = 2\%$. It is observed in Fig. 4 that the number of candidates grows rapidly when $minUtil$ decreases or $maxDur$ increases. It is also seen that using ERU pruning reduces the number of candidates by a large amount compared to if only EWU pruning or $EEUCP$ are used. For example, in Fig. 4 (left), HUE-Span(ERU+EEUCP) generates 10 times less candidates than UP-Span when $minUtil$ is set to 1%.

Memory consumption of the algorithms was also evaluated. Figure 5 (left) compares the memory consumption of the algorithms on the Retail dataset for different $minUtil$ values. It is observed that HUE-Span with pruning strategies uses less memory than UP-Span since the proposed pruning strategies reduce the number of candidates. Figure 5 (right) compares memory consumption of the algorithms on the Kosarak dataset for different $minUtil$ values. It is found that HUE-Span(ERU) sometimes uses less memory than HUE-Span(ERU+EEUCP) because the $EEUCS_{simult}$ and $EEUCS_{serial}$ require memory. Overall, results show that the HUE-Span(*) algorithm is better than the UP-Span(*) algorithm.

The number of patterns found was also compared for different $minUtil$ and $maxDur$ values. Results for Retail and Kosarak are shown in Table 2. The column #HUE^{*} indicates the number of HUEs found using the proposed redefined utility (calculated as the maximum utility for each minimal occurrence of an episode). The column #HUE indicates the number of HUEs found by

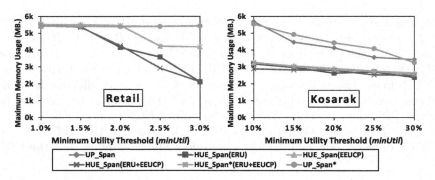

Fig. 5. Memory consumptions of the algorithms

UP-Span. The column $\#HUE^-$ indicates the number of patterns for which the utility is underestimated by UP-Span. It can be observed that UP-Span finds much less HUEs than the proposed HUE-Span* algorithm, missing up to 65% of the HUEs found by HUE-Span*. Moreover, UP-Span underestimates the utility of up to 79% of the HUEs that it outputs in terms of redefined utility.

Table 2. Number of patterns found by the algorithms

Dataset	$minUtil$	$maxDur$	$\#HUE^*$	$\#HUE$	$\#HUE^-$
Retail	1%	5	1,556	1,174	745
	1.5%	5	523	422	196
	2%	5	179	170	98
	2%	6	730	439	296
	2%	7	2,084	1,077	858
Kosarak	10%	5	105	73	29
	15%	5	27	22	5
	20%	5	3	2	0
	20%	6	21	8	1
	20%	7	81	28	16

6   Conclusion

This paper demonstrated that the traditional HUEM model can underestimate the utility of episodes and thus miss HUEs. To address this issue, this paper has adapted the HUEM model to consider the highest (maximal) utility for each minimal occurrence. Moreover, to mine HUEs efficiently, an algorithm named HUE-Span was proposed. It relies on a novel ERU upper bound to reduce the search space and a novel pruning strategy based on event co-occurrences. Extensive experiments on both synthetic and real datasets have shown that HUE-Span not only discovers all HUEs but is up to five times faster than the state-of-the-art UP-Span algorithm. The source code of HUE-Span and datasets can be downloaded from the SPMF website. For future work, we will design other optimizations for high utility episode mining and consider using high utility episodes to derive high utility episode rules [5,6], peak episodes [10] and significant patterns [7].

References

1. Achar, A., Laxman, S., Sastry, P.S.: A unified view of the apriori-based algorithms for frequent episode discovery. Knowl. Inf. Syst. **31**(2), 223–250 (2012)
2. Ahmed, C.F., Tanbeer, S.K., Jeong, B.S.: A framework for mining high utility web access sequences. IETE Tech. Rev. **28**(1), 3–16 (2011)
3. Amiri, M., Mohammad-Khanli, L., Mirandola, R.: An online learning model based on episode mining for workload prediction in cloud. Future Gener. Comput. Syst. **87**, 83–101 (2018)
4. Ao, X., Luo, P., Li, C., Zhuang, F., He, Q.: Online frequent episode mining. In: Proceedings of 31st IEEE International Conference on Data Engineering, pp. 891–902 (2015)
5. Ao, X., Luo, P., Wang, J., Zhuang, F., He, Q.: Mining precise-positioning episode rules from event sequences. IEEE Trans. Knowl. Data Eng. **30**(3), 530–543 (2018)
6. Fahed, L., Brun, A., Boyer, A.: DEER: distant and essential episode rules for early prediction. Expert Syst. Appl. **93**, 283–298 (2018)
7. Fournier-Viger, P., Li, X., Yao, J., Lin, J.C.W.: Interactive discovery of statistically significant itemsets. In: Mouhoub, M., Sadaoui, S., Mohamed, O., Ali, M. (eds.) Proceedings of 31st International Conference on Industrial, Engineering and Other Applications of Applied Intelligent Systems, pp. 101–113. Springer, Cham (2018)
8. Fournier-Viger, P., Chun-Wei Lin, J., Truong-Chi, T., Nkambou, R.: A survey of high utility itemset mining. In: Fournier-Viger, P., Lin, J.C.-W., Nkambou, R., Vo, B., Tseng, V.S. (eds.) High-Utility Pattern Mining. SBD, vol. 51, pp. 1–45. Springer, Cham (2019). https://doi.org/10.1007/978-3-030-04921-8_1
9. Fournier-Viger, P., Wu, C.-W., Zida, S., Tseng, V.S.: FHM: faster high-utility itemset mining using estimated utility co-occurrence pruning. In: Andreasen, T., Christiansen, H., Cubero, J.-C., Raś, Z.W. (eds.) ISMIS 2014. LNCS (LNAI), vol. 8502, pp. 83–92. Springer, Cham (2014). https://doi.org/10.1007/978-3-319-08326-1_9
10. Fournier-Viger, P., Zhang, Y., Wei Lin, J.C., Fujita, H., Koh, Y.S.: Mining local and peak high utility itemsets. Inf. Sci. **481**, 344–367 (2019)
11. Guo, G., Zhang, L., Liu, Q., Chen, E., Zhu, F., Guan, C.: High utility episode mining made practical and fast. In: Luo, X., Yu, J.X., Li, Z. (eds.) ADMA 2014. LNCS (LNAI), vol. 8933, pp. 71–84. Springer, Cham (2014). https://doi.org/10.1007/978-3-319-14717-8_6
12. Huang, K., Chang, C.: Efficient mining of frequent episodes from complex sequences. Inf. Syst. **33**(1), 96–114 (2008)
13. Lin, Y., Huang, C., Tseng, V.S.: A novel methodology for stock investment using high utility episode mining and genetic algorithm. Appl. Soft Comput. **59**, 303–315 (2017)

14. Liu, M., Qu, J.: Mining high utility itemsets without candidate generation. In: Proceedings of the 21st ACM International Conference on Information and Knowledge Management, pp. 55–64 (2012)
15. Mannila, H., Toivonen, H., Verkamo, A.I.: Discovery of frequent episodes in event sequences. Data Min. Knowl. Discov. **1**(3), 259–289 (1997)
16. Rathore, S., Dawar, S., Goyal, V., Patel, D.: Top-k high utility episode mining from a complex event sequence. In: Proceedings of the 21st ACM International Conference on Management of Data, pp. 56–63 (2016)
17. Wu, C., Lin, Y., Yu, P.S., Tseng, V.S.: Mining high utility episodes in complex event sequences. In: Proceedings of 19th ACM SIGKDD International Conference on Knowledge Discovery, pp. 536–544 (2013)

Clustering Noisy Temporal Data

Paul Grant$^{(\boxtimes)}$ and Md Zahidul Islam

School of Computing and Mathematics, Charles Sturt University,
Bathurst, NSW 2795, Australia
{pgrant,zislam}@csu.edu.au

Abstract. Clustering time series data is frequently hampered by various noise components within the signal. These disturbances affect the ability of clustering to detect similarities across the various signals, which may result in poor clustering results. We propose a method, which first smooths out such noise using wavelet decomposition and thresholding, then reconstructs the original signal *(with minimised noise)* and finally undertakes the clustering on this new signal. We experimentally evaluate the proposed method on 250 signals that are generated from five classes of signals. Our proposed method achieves improved clustering results.

Keywords: Clustering · Time series · Wavelets · Smoothing · Threshold

1 Introduction

Time series data is becoming evident in a wide range of areas. Traditional data mining methods typically do not readily provide accurate results when applied to time series data, possibly owing to the high dimensionality, inherent noise and correlation between the features [1]. Nevertheless it is often necessary to cluster time series data. Clustering is a commonly used data mining task for grouping similar data objects in a cluster and dissimilar data objects in different clusters [2]. As a result clustering provides a succinct overview of the data and helps in knowledge discovery [3]. Clustering is used in a various fields including market segmentation, medical imaging, anomaly detection, data compression and computer graphics [4].

In this paper we propose a method based on wavelet decomposition and thresholding/denoising to improve the clustering accuracy for time series data. Existing techniques may return accurate clustering results provided the signals are smooth, have low levels of noise and are distinct from each other. We use five different classes of signals to produce 250 signals that we then use to demonstrate that the clustering accuracy of two existing techniques deteriorates when the signals have increased levels of embedded noise. It is not uncommon to have noise in signals in real life.

This method applies the Discrete Wavelet transform (DWT) to extract the wavelet coefficients, soft thresholding on the wavelet coefficients, inverse wavelet

© Springer Nature Switzerland AG 2019
J. Li et al. (Eds.): ADMA 2019, LNAI 11888, pp. 185–194, 2019.
https://doi.org/10.1007/978-3-030-35231-8_13

transform on the thresholded coefficients to obtain smoothened signals and then finally apply an existing clustering technique on the smoothened signals. Our experimental results demonstrate that the proposed wavelet based method improves the clustering accuracy when applied to the noisy signals. The software used extensively in this study was **R** [5] and the **R** package **wmtsa** [6].

2   Related Work

Smoothing is a statistical technique that helps spot trends in noisy data and to compare trends between two or more different time series. It is a useful visualization tool that is available in many statistical packages, inherent in their graphical output systems. Time series smoothing methods to reduce inherent noise in the signal are widely used and many such methods exist including: moving average, exponential smoothing, kalman filter and smoothing spline. This may be seen in various articles combined with different methods to smooth *(remove noise)* in digital images [7], as well as smoothing *or feature extraction* of a time series to reduce noise prior to clustering [8]. An overview of wavelet based signal processing and denoising are available in the literature [9], together with clustering via Wavelet Decomposition and Denoising on standard test signals [10].

2.1   Wavelets

Wavelets are functions that segment the data into different frequency components, where it is possible to then study such components at the resolution level that are matched to its scale. avelets have been applied in various areas such as image compression, turbulence, human vision, radar and digital signal processing [11]. A wavelet transform is the representation of a function by wavelets. If we use a wavelet that is discretely sampled then we have a Discrete Wavelet transform (DWT). The DWT returns a data vector of the same length as that of the input. Usually, in this new vector many data points are almost zero.

Wavelet transform provides:

– A way for analyzing waveforms, bounded in both frequency and duration.
– Enable better approximation of real-world signals.
– Well-suited for approximating data with sharp discontinuities [12].

2.1.1   Wavelet Decomposition

The decomposition process of the DWT may be represented as a tree of low and high pass filters (LPF & HPF), see Fig. 1, with each step transforming the low pass filter. The original signal is successively decomposed into components of lower resolution, while the high frequency components (H_i) are not analysed any further after each decomposition step. The maximum number of levels that may be derived is dependent upon the input size (*length*) of the data to be analysed. A signal of n points in length may be decomposed by the DWT to J levels (*Crystals*) where $2^J = n$.

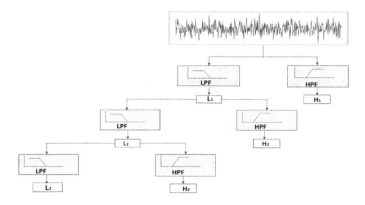

Fig. 1. DWT decomposition. (from www.wavelet.org/tutorial/wbasic.htm)

Given a sequence $\{X : x_1, \ldots, x_n\}$, where $n = 2^J$, the DWT is a linear transform of X producing n DWT coefficients. In vector notation with X as a column vector of n times series values, then the DWT gives $\mathbf{W} = \mathcal{W}X$ where

– $\mathbf{W}$ is a vector of $J + 1$ levels and n DWT coefficients
– $\mathcal{W}$ is a $n \times n$ *orthonormal* transform matrix.

$$\mathbf{W} = \begin{bmatrix} W_1 \\ W_2 \\ W_3 \\ V_3 \end{bmatrix} = [\mathcal{W}]\, X \tag{1}$$

DWT transforms X into 2 different types of coefficients; W_i being the detail wavelet coefficients and V_J the scale coefficients; with $i : 1, \ldots, J$.

The number of coefficients at each level is:

– at finest scale W_1 there are $\frac{n}{2}$ coefficients, each labeled $d_{1,k}$, $k = 1, \ldots, \frac{n}{2}$
– at next scale W_2 here are $\frac{n}{2^2}$ coefficients, each labeled $d_{2,k}$, $k = 1, \ldots, \frac{n}{2^2}$
– at coarsest scale W_J and V_J both contain $\frac{n}{2^J}$ coefficients, each labeled $d_{J,k}$, $S_{J,k}$ respectively, $k = 1, \ldots, \frac{n}{2^J}$

Each of these single coefficients is called an "atom" and all of the coefficients at each scale are called a "crystal".

Referring to Fig. 1: The DWT is composed of the detail wavelet coefficients. contained in $\{H_1, H_2 \text{ and } H_3\}$, while the scaling coefficients come from $\{L_3\}$. If X is 1024 index points in length, and we apply the DWT to decompose the signal into 3 levels, we have 512, 256 and 128 + 128 coefficients in each of the crystals at each level, 1 to 3 respectively. The DWT of the Doppler signal, decomposed using 3 levels is seen in Fig. 2.

The "finer" scales (d1, d2: Fig. 2) identify with the higher frequency components within the Doppler signal and the coarser levels (higher numbered crystals) have ties with the lower frequency part of the signal. The relationship between crystal scale and frequency within a signal is outlined in the literature [13, 14].

2.1.2 Wavelet Reconstruction

The DWT can be used to analyze signals, the process is called decomposition. Similarly the components may be assembled back into the original signal without loss of information. This process is called reconstruction, or synthesis. Diagrammatically, this may be considered as reversing the direction of arrows in Fig. 1, synthesis of the crystals in the relevant order to arrive back with the original signal X, see Fig. 3.

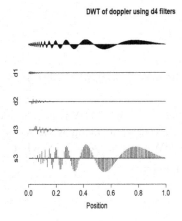

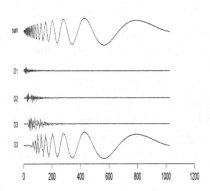

Fig. 2. Doppler decomposition.   **Fig. 3.** Reconstruction of doppler.

2.1.3 Wavelet Thresholding

Within a signal, various levels of energy may be apparent at different frequency ranges. If we define the energy within a signal X as the squared norm $||X||^2$, then following on from Eq. 1,

$$||\mathbf{W}||^2 = W^T W = (\mathcal{W}X)^T \mathcal{W}X$$
$$= X^T \mathcal{W}^T \mathcal{W}X$$
$$= X^T I_N X = X^T X = ||X||^2 \qquad (2)$$

Hence energy is conserved under the wavelet transform.

Simply removing entire crystals will considerably alter the original wave upon reconstruction., In Fig. 3 where decomposition is only to 3 levels, D3 contains approx 1.5% of signal energy. Instead of elimination of entire crystals we could place a threshold value on various wavelet coefficients, affecting those that may contain higher values of unwanted noise. There exists many methods to apply such thresholding [15].

2.1.4   Thresholding Methods

The most common threshold technique is *Universal* thresholding where the noise level σ in the signal is estimated by $\hat{\sigma}$, derived from the standard deviation of the wavelet coefficients at the finer scales. [16] The threshold is then calculated as $\lambda^\mu = \sigma\sqrt{2\log n}$. where n is the number of observations. This threshold value may then be applied to all wavelet coefficients or on subset of the crystal levels. We may apply this *noise* threshold value via different functions, i.e.

$$W_{j,k}^{(ht)} = \begin{cases} 0 & |W_{j,k}| \leq \lambda^\mu \\ W_{j,k} & otherwise \end{cases} \tag{3}$$

which is Hard Thresholding or similarly;

$$W_{j,k}^{(st)} = sign(W_{j,k})\big(|W_{j,k}| - \lambda^\mu\big)_+ \tag{4}$$

where

$$sign(W_{j,k}) = \begin{cases} +1 & if \quad W_{j,k} > 0, \\ 0 & if \quad W_{j,k} = 0, \\ -1 & if \quad W_{j,k} < 0. \end{cases} \qquad (x)_+ \equiv \begin{cases} x & if \quad x \geq 0, \\ 0 & if \quad x < 0. \end{cases}$$

which is Soft Thresholding.

3   Our Approach

While these thresholding functions attempt to smooth out or reduce the noise within the original signal, there are indeed some issues Applying the Universal threshold (λ^μ) value to the wavelet coefficients may cause *over smoothing* of the final estimated signal. This could result in the transform being unrepresentative of the original signal [16].

While λ^μ may eliminate a vast majority of the noise, if we apply λ^μ through the hard thresholding method then any non-zero wavelet coefficient of a fixed value will eventually be set to 0 as $n \to \infty$, where n is the length of the series.

To overcome these problems, the approach taken in this paper is to determine a threshold value λ, that is data-adaptive.

Use of Stein's Unbiased Risk Estimation (SURE), permitted development of a method to estimate a level dependent threshold value [16]. Here by minimising the threshold value λ as a result of SURE, a value is likely to be found on the interval $[0, \sqrt{2\log n}]$. This SURE threshold value is calculated separately for each crystal level. The option to use this threshold calculation and application to the wavelet coefficients via the Soft Thresholding method see Eq. 4, is available in the **wmtsa** R package under the function waveShrink [6]. The intention here is to not *over-smooth* the original signal but provide enough elimination of noise caused signal variation. Our method entails;

– taking the DWT of the signal,

- thresholding the wavelet coefficients using Soft thresholding with an adaptive SURE level based threshold value,
- use the inverse wavelet transform on the thresholded coefficients to reconstruct a smoothed original signal,
- clustering the smoothed signal using an existing technique.

3.1 Advantages

Our approach; while requiring some additional computation as opposed to applying the clustering techniques to the raw noisy signals; is simple in construction and coding, with the software used [5] being freely available together with detailed on-line instruction and support. We are able to target likely noise components within signals, and provide steps to eliminate or reduce such noise.

Section 4 highlights the gain in node purity of our approach compared to: the clustering of either, the raw noisy data or the raw (*unthresholded*) wavelet coefficients.

3.2 Clustering Methods Used

Although our technique may be suitable to be applied to many clustering techniques, in this study we use two standard clustering methods as part of the experimentation. Both of these methods are implemented here using **R** [5].

- **k-means** takes a user input on the number of clusters k and then (generally) randomly selects k different data objects as initial seeds which are the initial centers of k clusters [17].
- **Hierarchical** Agglomerative in structure and uses the Ward method for weighting the distances between clusters as they are formed [18].

3.2.1 Distance Measure

For these clustering methods the manhattan distance is chosen as it places less emphasis on outliers [19].

Manhattan distance; between two vectors **p**, **q** in an n-dimensional real vector space with fixed Cartesian coordinate system, is the sum of the lengths of the projections of the line segment between the points onto the coordinate axes, or;

$$d_1(\mathbf{p}, \mathbf{q}) = ||p - q|| = \sum_{i=1}^{n} |p_i - q_i|$$
$$where\ (\mathbf{p}, \mathbf{q})\ are\ vectors:$$
$$\mathbf{p} = (p_1, p_2, \ldots, p_n)\quad and\quad \mathbf{q} = (q_1, q_2, \ldots, q_n)$$

$$(5)$$

4 Experiment

From the **R** package wmtsa; 5 signals have been generated, as shown in Fig. 4, i.e. Doppler, Level change, Jump Sine, Quadratic and Cubic. Taking multiple copies of these signals, 50 of each class, then selecting in random order, both k-means and hierarchical clustering appear to have no issue in clustering such groups and return expected results, outlined in Sect. 4.1.1.

4.1 Initial Clustering of Raw Signals

First we define a clustering metric; *Similarity measure:*

$$Sim(G, A) = \frac{1}{k} \sum_{i=1}^{k} \max_{1 \leq j \leq k} Sim(G_i, A_j) \tag{6}$$

where

- $Sim(G_i, A_j) = \frac{2|G_i \cap A_j|}{|G_i| + |A_j|}$.
- $G = \{G_i, \ldots, G_k\}$ is the original clustering.
- $A = \{A_i, \ldots, A_k\}$ is the calculated/derived clustering.

4.1.1 Initial Data, Results

Using k-means (with manhattan distance) to cluster the original data (before noise added) we can successfully map the signals into 5 distinct classes as expected, $Sim(G, A) = 1$, Table 1[1]. Using the hierarchical clustering technique, Sect. 3.2, we also map the signals into 5 distinct classes. The evaluation of the hierarchical clustering returns the same results as shown in Table 1.

4.2 Noise Generation

To each of the 250 signals a random noise component is then added for the experimentation purpose. This is achieved via adding a random value to every point x_i in the signal as:

$$Z_i = x_i + rnorm \times \frac{\sqrt{var(X)}}{snr} \tag{7}$$

where:

- Z_i = new value in noisy signal.
- x_i = value from original signal.
- $rnorm$ = random number selected from normal distribution, $\mu = 0$, $\sigma = 1$.
- $var(X)$ = variance of the original signal.
- snr = random number selected from a uniform distribution,
        with a minimum = 2 and a maximum = 8.

This provides us with 50 signals per class with varying random noise added, Fig. 5 shows an one sample of the signals with added noise.

---

[1] Given we know the class that a signal belongs to, we first ignore the class label of a signal to simulate a real life clustering scenario where the class labels are unknown. After clustering the signals we use the class labels as ground truth for the purpose of clustering evaluation.

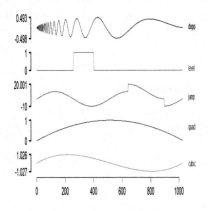

Fig. 4. Initial signals

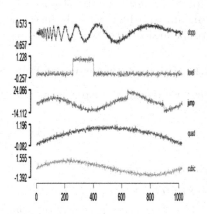

Fig. 5. Noise added to signals, snr = 4.

Table 1. Clustering raw data by k-means using manhattan distance

Class/G_i	\multicolumn{5}{c}{k-means/A_i}				
	1	2	3	4	5
1	50	0	0	0	0
2	0	50	0	0	0
3	0	0	50	0	0
4	0	0	0	50	0
5	0	0	0	0	50

Table 2. Clustering noisy data using k-means [17].

Class	\multicolumn{5}{c}{k-means}				
	1	2	3	4	5
1	50	0	0	0	0
2	0	0	0	0	50
3	0	0	50	0	0
4	0	0	0	50	0
5	0	0	0	0	50

Table 3. Clustering noisy data using the hierarchical method [18].

Class	\multicolumn{5}{c}{Hierarchical}				
	1	2	3	4	5
1	50	0	0	0	0
2	50	0	0	0	0
3	0	2	48	0	0
4	0	0	0	50	0
5	0	0	0	0	50

Table 4. Clustering wavelet thresholded data using k-means.

Class	\multicolumn{5}{c}{k-means}				
	1	2	3	4	5
1	50	0	0	0	0
2	0	50	0	0	0
3	0	0	50	0	0
4	0	0	0	50	0
5	0	0	0	0	50

Table 5. Clustering wavelet thresholded data, hierarchical method.

Class	\multicolumn{5}{c}{Hierarchical}				
	1	2	3	4	5
1	50	0	0	0	0
2	0	50	0	0	0
3	0	0	50	0	0
4	0	0	0	50	0
5	0	0	0	0	50

4.2.1   Clustering Signals with Noise Added

The situation from Sect. 4.1.1 changes once we add random noise to the original signals; clustering using k-means and the hierarchical method, appear to be confused. Table 2 shows us that k-means confuses class G_2 (level change) with class G_5 (cubic), resulting with 100 elements in A_5, $Sim(G, A) = 0.867$.

For hierarchical clustering, Table 3 where $Sim(G, A) = 0.863$, here the clustering confuses the class G_1 (doppler) with class G_2 (level change), as well as splitting the jump sine signal across two clusters.

4.2.2   Our Approach: Clustering the Smoothed Signals

We apply the clustering techniques on the "smoothed" signals, as described in Sect. 3. The results are shown in Tables 4 and 5. The application of k-means on the wavelet transformed and thresholded signals obtained through our proposed method achieves perfect clustering results as shown in Table 4. Here $Sim(G, A) = 1.0$, a considerable improvement over clustering of the raw noisy data. Similarly clustering using the hierarchical clustering technique, results in Table 5, also achieves perfect results when applied on the smoothened signal obtained according to our proposed method.

Table 6. Clustering results; Similarity measure $Sim(G, A)$

	Raw noisy	Mov Av 3	Hard thresh	Soft thresh	Wave coeff	Our approach
	Sim	Sim	Sim	Sim	Sim	Sim
k-means	0.867	0.867	0.65	0.662	1.0	**1.0**
Hierarchical	0.863	0.865	0.865	0.865	0.514	**1.0**

Table 6 outlines the overall result of our experiment using the noisy data, comparing clustering methods on Raw Noisy data, Simple Moving Average[2] order 3, using hard or soft thresholding (then signal reconstruction/clustering), as opposed to simply clustering the raw wavelet coefficients and Our approach.

5   Conclusion

While additional thresholding of the wavelet coefficients, reconstruction via the inverse transform, requires even further computation than simply clustering the raw data, our results show that such data pre-processing is worthwhile when clustering signals with possible higher levels of embedded noise. The data adaptive SURE method of thresholding has enabled us to achieve better clustering accuracy, compared to other standard thresholding techniques as well as a simple moving average smoother of the raw noisy data.

---

[2] Clustering result tables for Simple Moving Average order 3, Hard and Soft thresholding not shown, similarly for clustering using raw wavelet coefficients.

References

1. Vlachos, M., Lin, J., Keogh, E., Gunopulos, D.: Wavelet-based anytime algorithm for k-means clustering of time series. In: Proceedings of Workshop on Clustering High Dimensionality Data and Its Applications (2003)
2. Rahman, M.A., Islam, M.Z.: A hybrid clustering technique combining a novel genetic algorithm with k-means. Knowl. Based Syst. (KBS) **71**, 345–365 (2014)
3. Beg, A.H., Islam, M.Z.: A novel genetic algorithm-based clustering technique and its suitability for knowledge discovery from a brain dataset. In: Proceedings of IEEE Congress on Evolutionary Computation (IEEE CEC), Vancouver, Canada, 24–29 July 2016, pp. 948–956 (2016)
4. Härdle, W.K., Simar, L.: Applied Multivariate Statistical Analysis. Springer, Heidelberg (2015). https://doi.org/10.1007/978-3-662-45171-7
5. R Core Team, R: A language and environment for statistical computing. R Foundation for Statistical Computing, Vienna, Austria (2013). http://www.R-project.org/
6. Constantine, W., Percival, D.: wmtsa: Wavelet Methods for Time Series Analysis. R package version 2.0-3 (2017). https://CRAN.R-project.org/package=wmtsa
7. Goyal, A., Bijalwan, A., Chowdhury, K.: A comprehensive review of image smoothing techniques. Int. J. Adv. Res. Comput. Sci. Technol. **1**(4), 315–319 (2012)
8. Warren Liao, T.: Clustering of time series data-a survey. J. Pattern Recogn. Soc. **38**, 1857–1874 (2005)
9. Sidney Burrus, C., Gopinath, R., Guo, H.: Introduction to Wavelets and Wavelet Transforms. Prentice Hall, New Jersey (1998)
10. Guo, H., Liu, Y., Liang, H., Gao, X.: An application on time series clustering based on wavelet decomposition and denoising. In: Fourth International Conference on Natural Computation (2008)
11. Graps, A.: An introduction to wavelets. IEEE Comput. Sci. Eng. **2**(2), 50–61 (1995)
12. Polikar, R.: The Engineers Ultimate Guide to Wavelet Analysis: The Wavelet Tutorial Part I (2006)
13. Percival, D.B., Walden, A.T.: Wavelet Methods for Time Series Analysis, Cambridge Series in Statistical and Probabilistic Mathematics. Cambridge University Press, Cambridge (2006)
14. Nason, G.P.: Wavelet Methods in Statistics with R. Use R!. Springer, New York (2008). https://doi.org/10.1007/978-0-387-75961-6
15. Downie, T., Silverman, B.: The discrete multiple wavelet transform and thresholding methods. IEEE Trans Signal Process. **46**, 2558–2561 (1998)
16. Donoho, D., Johnstone, I.: Adapting to unknown smoothness via wavelet shrinkage. Am. Stat. Asoc. **90**, 1200–1224 (1995)
17. MacQueen, J.: Some methods for classification and analysis of multivariate observations. In: 5-th Berkeley Symposium on Mathematical Statistics and Probability, pp. 291–297 (1967)
18. Murtagh, F.: Multidimensional clustering algorithms. In: COMPSTAT Lectures 4. Wuerzburg: Physica-Verlag (1985)
19. Aggarwal, C.C., Hinneburg, A., Keim, D.A.: On the surprising behavior of distance metrics in high dimensional space. In: Van den Bussche, J., Vianu, V. (eds.) ICDT 2001. LNCS, vol. 1973, pp. 420–434. Springer, Heidelberg (2001). https://doi.org/10.1007/3-540-44503-X_27

A Novel Approach for Noisy Signal Classification Through the Use of Multiple Wavelets and Ensembles of Classifiers

Paul Grant$^{(\boxtimes)}$ and Md Zahidul Islam

School of Computing and Mathematics, Charles Sturt University,
Bathurst, NSW 2795, Australia
{pgrant,zislam}@csu.edu.au

Abstract. Classification of time series signals can be crucial for many practical applications. While the existing classifiers may accurately classify pure signals, the existence of noise can significantly disturb the classification accuracy of these classifiers. We propose a novel classification approach that uses multiple wavelets together with an ensemble of classifiers to return high classification accuracy even for noisy signals.

The proposed technique has two main steps. In Step 1, We convert raw signals into a useful dataset by applying multiple wavelet transforms, each from a different wavelet family or all from the same family with differing filter lengths. In Step 2, We apply the dataset processed in Step 1 to an ensemble of classifiers. We test on 500 noisy signals from five different classes. Our experimental results demonstrate the effectiveness of the proposed technique, on noisy signals, compared to the approaches that use either raw signals or a single wavelet transform.

Keywords: Signal classification · Wavelets · DWT · Ensembles

1 Introduction

A common approach in machine learning is decision tree induction for decision making or classification. Decision trees can attribute symbolic decisions to new samples. Automatic rule induction systems for inducing classification rules have already proved valuable as tools for assisting in the task of knowledge acquisition for expert systems [1].

Classification is a data mining technique that assigns categories to a collection of data and which permits the analysis of very large datasets. The aim is to create a set of classification rules that will aid in decision making and/or behaviour prediction.

Classification problems containing noise are complex problems and accurate solutions may be quite difficult to achieve, particularly if the classifier is noise-sensitive [2]. In this paper we propose a novel approach using wavelet decomposition to a build set of attributes composed of wavelet coefficients from different wavelets.

© Springer Nature Switzerland AG 2019
J. Li et al. (Eds.): ADMA 2019, LNAI 11888, pp. 195–203, 2019.
https://doi.org/10.1007/978-3-030-35231-8_14

2   Related Work

The use of wavelet coefficients for classification, in preference to raw data has been previously mentioned [3], where a single wavelet filter was used, called the Haar wavelet. This particular wavelet may not be an optimal transform in signals with higher levels of varying noise, as the Haar Wavelet is a square shaped function.

Wavelets can be used to reduce noise in time series data, so that better classification performance may be achieved after conducting a wavelet transform on the original data [4].

It has been claimed that simultaneously using classifiers of different types, complementing each other, improves classification performance on difficult problems, such as image classification, fingerprint recognition and foreign exchange market prediction. Types of multiple classifier systems have been traditionally associated with the capability of working accurately with problems involving noisy data [2]. Also multiple Wavelets have been previously mentioned [5], which highlights the possibility of the superior performance of Multiple wavelets applied to image compression applications and ECG data compression.

2.1   Wavelets

Wavelets have been applied in various areas such as human vision, radar and digital signal processing [6]. If we use a wavelet that is discretely sampled then we have a Discrete Wavelet Transform, (**DWT**). The DWT allows us to analyse *(decompose)* a time series into DWT coefficients **W**, from which we may synthesise *(reconstruct)* our original series [7]. The DWT[1] returns a data vector[2] of the same length as that of the input.

2.1.1   DWT

Let a sequence $X_1, X_2, \ldots, X_n$ represent a time series of n elements, denoted as $\{X_t : t = 1, \ldots, n\}$ where $n = 2^J$: $J \in \mathbb{Z}$, $X_t \in \mathbb{R}$, the discrete wavelet transform is a linear transform which decomposes X_t into J levels giving n DWT coefficients; the wavelet coefficients are obtained by premultiplying X by $\mathcal{W}$

$$\mathbf{W} = \mathcal{W}X \tag{1}$$

- **W** is a vector of DWT coefficients (jth component is W_j)
- $\mathcal{W}$ is $n \times n$ orthonormal transform matrix; i.e.,
  $\mathcal{W}^T \mathcal{W} = I_n$, where I_n is $n \times n$ identity matrix
- inverse of $\mathcal{W}$ is its transpose, $\implies \mathcal{W}\mathcal{W}^T = I_n$
- $\therefore \mathcal{W}^T \mathbf{W} = \mathcal{W}^T \mathcal{W}X = X$

---

[1] The DWT in principle provides more information than the time series raw data points in classification because the DWT locates where the signal energies are concentrated in the frequency domain [3].

[2] In this new vector many data points are almost zero, a sparse representation.

$\mathbf{W}$ is partitioned into $J + 1$ subvectors

- $\mathbf{W}_j$ has $n/2^j$ elements [3]
- $\mathbf{V}_J$ has one element [4]

the synthesis equation for the DWT is:

$$X = \mathcal{W}^T \mathbf{W} = [\mathcal{W}_1^T, \mathcal{W}_2^T, \dots, \mathcal{W}_J^T, \mathcal{V}_J^T] \begin{bmatrix} \mathbf{W}_1 \\ \mathbf{W}_2 \\ \vdots \\ \mathbf{W}_J \\ \mathbf{V}_J \end{bmatrix} \tag{2}$$

Equation 2 leads to additive decomposition which expresses X as the sum of $J + 1$ vectors, each of which is associated with a particular scale $\mathcal{T}_j$

$$= \sum_{j=1}^{J} \mathcal{W}_j^T \mathbf{W}_j + \mathcal{V}_J^T \mathbf{V}_J \equiv \sum_{j=1}^{J} \mathcal{D}_j + \mathcal{S}_J \tag{3}$$

- $\mathcal{D}_j \equiv \mathcal{W}_j^T \mathbf{W}_j$ is portion of synthesis due to scale $\mathcal{T}_j$, called the jth 'detail'.
- $\mathcal{S}_J \equiv \mathcal{V}_J^T \mathbf{V}_j$ is a vector called the 'smooth' of the Jth order [7].

3 Our Approach

Our approach is to apply a wavelet transform to the signal data and then apply that transformed data to classification methods. Here our wavelet transform consists of a number of different wavelets, a Multiple Discrete Wavelet transform, (**MDWT**). The rationale for using multiple wavelets in the transform is, we may include wavelets that are either symmetric, have short support, provide higher accuracy and be orthogonal. No single wavelet may provide all such properties simultaneously [8].

The wavelet coefficients resulting from our MDWT, form the attributes on which the classification methods derive their rule set from. For a transform consisting of a single wavelet we obtain the same number of data points (*here wavelet coefficients*) as provided in the original signal. For the MDWT consisting of N wavelets we would have N times the number of original data points, which could be considered as attributes. It has been shown that the inclusion of new attributes in the attribute space increases the prediction capacity of the decision trees [9].

---

[3] note: $\sum_{j=1}^{J} \frac{n}{2^j} = \frac{n}{2} + \frac{n}{4} + \cdots + 2 + 1 = 2^J - 1 = n - 1$.
[4] If we decompose X_t to level $I \leq J$ then $\mathbf{V}_I$ has $n/2^I$ elements.

3.1 Advantages

Our methodology does require some additional computation as opposed to applying raw signals to the classification methods. However results returned via the MDWT highlight that the extra computation is worthwhile, especially when the signal contains high levels of noise. The construction of the MDWT is not a complicated procedure.

While we are providing a larger set of attributes for the classifiers where most of the energy in the signal is then concentrated into a small of number of components, the classification methods with MDWT tend to return smaller sets of decision rules (or smaller less complex trees) to arrive at their final rule set, as compared to when using raw data with higher levels of embedded noise.

The software used is freely available on-line together with detailed instruction and support: R [10], the R package WMTSA [11] and WEKA [12].

3.2 MDWT

To construct the MDWT from a time series $\{X_t : t = 1, \ldots, n\}$ where $n = 2^J$: $J \in \mathbb{Z}$, $X_t \in \mathbb{R}$, choose N different DWTs and apply to X_t sequentially. From Eq. 3 this results in:

$$\sum_{i=1}^{N} \left[\sum_{j=1}^{J} \mathcal{D}_{ij} + \mathcal{S}_{iJ} \right] \tag{4}$$

giving a sequence of vectors, where $\mathcal{D}_{ij}$, $\mathcal{S}_{iJ}$ contains $n/2^j$ elements *(which are the wavelet coefficients at level j)*

$$\mathcal{D}_{11}, \mathcal{D}_{12}, \ldots, \mathcal{S}_{1J}, \mathcal{D}_{21}, \mathcal{D}_{22}, \ldots, \mathcal{S}_{2J}, \ldots, \mathcal{D}_{N1}, \mathcal{D}_{N2}, \ldots, \mathcal{S}_{NJ}$$

This has N times as many elements as in X_t.

3.3 Technique

Our method entails;

Step 1. From a set of Time series

$$\{X_{t_i} : t = 1, \ldots, n, \, i = 1, \ldots, K\}$$

construct a new set of transformed data

(1a) For each single time series X_{ti} take the DWT of the signal multiple times, using a different wavelet filter for each of the transforms.
(1b) Construct a new data series, placing each of the individual vectors of the wavelet coefficients (from each DWT) in a continuous sequence, one after each other. (which is our MDWT, as shown in Eq. 4).
(1c) Stack each MDWT resulting from each transformed signal, to form a data array *or matrix* which is shown in Table 1.

Step 2. Build a classifier.

(2a) Using the new data as generated by the MDWT, apply to ensemble classifiers.[5]

Table 1. Array of transformed data as developed by MDWT

$\text{MDWT}(X_{t_1})$: $\mathcal{D}_{11_1}$, $\mathcal{D}_{12_1}$, ..., $\mathcal{S}_{1J_1}$, $\mathcal{D}_{21_1}$, $\mathcal{D}_{22_1}$, ..., $\mathcal{S}_{2J_1}$, ..., $\mathcal{D}_{N1_1}$, $\mathcal{D}_{N2_1}$, ..., $\mathcal{S}_{NJ_1}$
$\text{MDWT}(X_{t_2})$: $\mathcal{D}_{11_2}$, $\mathcal{D}_{12_2}$, ..., $\mathcal{S}_{1J_2}$, $\mathcal{D}_{21_2}$, $\mathcal{D}_{22_2}$, ..., $\mathcal{S}_{2J_2}$, ..., $\mathcal{D}_{N1_2}$, $\mathcal{D}_{N2_2}$, ..., $\mathcal{S}_{NJ_2}$

$\qquad\vdots \qquad\qquad\qquad \vdots \qquad\qquad\qquad \vdots \qquad\qquad\qquad \vdots$

$\text{MDWT}(X_{t_K})$: $\mathcal{D}_{11_K}$, $\mathcal{D}_{12_K}$, ..., $\mathcal{S}_{1J_K}$, $\mathcal{D}_{21_K}$, $\mathcal{D}_{22_K}$, ..., $\mathcal{S}_{2J_K}$, ..., $\mathcal{D}_{N1_K}$, $\mathcal{D}_{N2_K}$, ..., $\mathcal{S}_{NJ_K}$

4 Experiment

From the **R** package wmtsa; 5 signals have been generated, as shown in Fig. 1 i.e. Doppler, Level change, Jump Sine, Quadratic and Cubic. We call this Raw data. Taking multiple copies of these signals[6], 100 of each class, with a length of 512 index points.

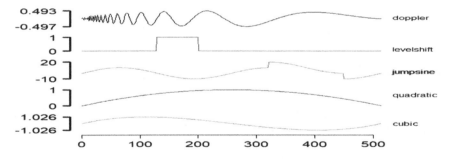

Fig. 1. Generated signals, before noise added.

Using three classification methods, *(Ten-fold Cross-Validation used for evaluation)*, returned 100% accuracy[7] when classifying these *clean* raw signals,[8] which is to be expected for a trivial exercise on such relatively smooth signals.

---

[5] Initially we applied the MDWT data to a single Decision tree classifier as a baseline and then to ensemble classifiers, which are outlined in Sect. 4.1.
[6] With these generated signals we attached class labels and such labels were used as the attribute for Class within the classification methods.
[7] Here Accuracy is defined as the number of correctly Classified Instances (*with respect to our initial Class labels*).
[8] Result tables not shown for this exercise.

4.1   Classification Methods Used

- **J48** a decision tree is an extension of ID3 [13].
- **ForestPA** Decision forest algorithm, with penalised attributes [14].
- **SysFor** Decision forest algorithm, a systematically developed forest [15].

4.2   Noise Generation

To each of the 500 test signals a random noise component is then added for experimentation purposes. This is achieved via adding a random value to every point x_i in the signal as:

$$Z_i = x_i + rnorm \times \frac{\sqrt{var(x)}}{snr} . \tag{5}$$

where:

- Z_i = new value in noisy signal
- x_i = value from original signal
- $rnorm$ = random number selected from normal distribution, $\mu = 0$, $\sigma = 1$.
- $var(x)$ = variance of the original signal
- snr = random number selected from a uniform distribution, varying between
     a specified minimum and maximum value.

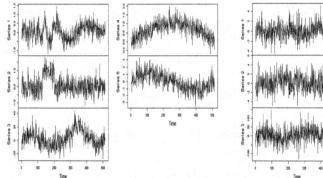 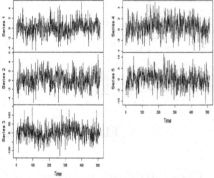

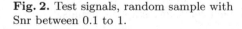

Fig. 2. Test signals, random sample with Snr between 0.1 to 1.

Fig. 3. Test signals, random sample with Snr between 0.1 to 0.2.

4.3 Multiple Discrete Wavelet Transform

Initially construct a MDWT, being **Step 1** in our approach. For data we implement the addition of varying noise to the Generated signals seen in Fig. 1, using the method as shown in Sect. 4.2, this provides 500 noise enhanced signals used for testing, Test Signals.

We alter the variation in noise added to the signal by maintaining the same minimum vale of *snr* and reducing the maximum value in steps[9]. The intention here is to ensure each range of *snr* chosen should have at least some extremely noisy signals, as examples see Figs. 2 and 3.

4.3.1 MDWT with Ensemble Tree Methods

Combining the MDWT with ensemble methods, SysFor and Forest PA: being **Step 2** from our proposed approach in Sect. 3.3. The resulting classification output[10] shown in Tables 2 and 3 respectively, highlight that the two different MDWT[11] provide a better outcome than using raw data with these classifiers and

Table 2. Classifier Accuracy% & Kappa, 80%/20% data split

SNR	SysFor							
	Raw data		Wavelet LA8		MDWT Diff		MDWT Same	
	Acc	Kappa	Acc	Kappa	Acc	Kappa	Acc	Kappa
0.1 to 0.2	82	0.77	92	0.90	94	0.92	94	0.92
0.1 to 0.3	70	0.63	97	0.96	98	0.97	98	0.97
0.1 to 0.5	82	0.77	97	0.96	98	0.97	99	0.99
0.1 to 1.0	78	0.73	98	0.97	98	0.97	96	0.95

Table 3. Classifier Accuracy% & Kappa, 80%/20% data split

SNR	ForestPA							
	Raw data		Wavelet LA8		MDWT Diff		MDWT Same	
	Acc	Kappa	Acc	Kappa	Acc	Kappa	Acc	Kappa
0.1 to 0.2	90	0.87	96	0.95	96	0.95	98	0.97
0.1 to 0.3	92	0.89	95	0.94	97	0.96	100	1.0
0.1 to 0.5	93	0.91	99	0.99	99	0.99	99	0.99
0.1 to 1.0	96	0.95	99	0.99	99	0.99	99	0.99

[9] We maintain 500 noise enhanced signals at each step.
[10] For evaluation here, we use 80% data to form the training set and 20% of data for testing with 100 trees used for each classifier.
[11] The MDWT comprising of four wavelets from different families, we have labelled as "MDWT Diff", similarly for the MDWT with four wavelets from the same family, as "MDWT Same".

in each case a slight improvement, or at least equal to, using a single wavelet filter. For these tables, accuracy is defined as correct classification in regards to as our initial class labels and the Kappa coefficient, calculated as the ratio of the observed excess over chance agreement to the maximum possible excess over chance, this takes into account the possibility of the agreement occurring by chance.

5   Conclusion

The accuracy of the classifiers diminish as amount of introduced noise increases. Classification using the wavelet coefficients from a single wavelet transform, provide higher levels of accuracy, compared to using raw data. However, when using the MDWT; they maintain accuracy as amount of noise increases, if only slightly (approx 2%) better when compared to using a single wavelet transform, but over 8% increase when compared to using the raw data *at the higher levels of embedded noise*. This improvement is similarly noted also in the respective Kappa coefficient. The similar performance of both MDWT in each classifier is likely to be a consequence of the actual wavelet transforms chosen.

References

1. Clark, P., Niblett, T.: Induction in noisy domains. In: Progress in Machine Learning (from the Proceedings of the 2nd European Working Session on Learning), pp. 11–30. Sigma Press, Bled (1987)
2. Saez, J.A., Galar, M., Luengo, J., Herrera, F.: Tackling the problem of classification with noisy data using multiple classifier systems: analysis of the performance and robustness. Inf. Sci. **247**(2013), 1–20 (2013). https://doi.org/10.1016/j.ins.2013.06.002
3. Fong, S.: Using hierarchical time series clustering algorithm and wavelet classifier for biometric voice classification. J. Biomed. Biotechnol. **2012**, Article ID 215019 (2012)
4. Li, D., Bissyand'e, T.F., Klein, J., Traon, Y.L.: Time series classification with discrete wavelet transformed data: insights from an empirical study. In: The 28th International Conference on Software Engineering and Knowledge Engineering (2016)
5. Moazami-Goudarzi, M., Moradi, M.H., Abbasabadi, S.: High performance method for electrocardiogram compression using two dimensional multiwavelet transform. In: IEEE 7th Workshop on Multimedia Signal Processing (2006)
6. Graps, A.: An introduction to wavelets. IEEE Comput. Sci. Eng. **2**(2), 50–61 (1995)
7. Percival, D.B., Walden, A.T.: Wavelet Methods for Time Series Analysis. Cambridge University Press, Cambridge (2000)
8. Nason, G.P.: Wavelet Methods in Statistics with R. Springer, New York (2008). https://doi.org/10.1007/978-0-387-75961-6
9. Adnan, M.N., Islam, M.Z.: A comprehensive method for attribute space extension for random forest. In: 17th International Conference on Computer and Information Technology, ICCIT 2014 (2014). https://doi.org/10.1109/ICCITechn.2014.7073129
10. R Core Team: R: A language and environment for statistical computing. R Foundation for Statistical Computing, Vienna, Austria (2013). http://www.R-project.org/

11. Constantine, W., Percival, D.: wmtsa: Wavelet Methods for Time Series Analysis. R package version 2.0-3 (2017). http://CRAN.R-project.org/package=wmtsa
12. Frank, E., Hall, M.A., Witten, I.H.: The WEKA Workbench. Online Appendix for "Data Mining: Practical Machine Learning Tools and Techniques", 4th edn. Morgan Kaufmann (2016)
13. Quinlan, R.: C4.5: Programs for Machine Learning. Morgan Kaufmann Publishers, San Mateo (1993)
14. Adnan, M.N., Islam, M.Z.: Forest PA: constructing a decision forest by penalizing attributes used in previous trees. Expert Syst. Appl. **89**, 389–403 (2017)
15. Islam, M.Z., Giggins, H.: Knowledge discovery through SysFor: a systematically developed forest of multiple decision trees. In: Proceedings of the Ninth Australasian Data Mining Conference (AusDM 2011) (2011)

12. ...
13. ...
14. ...
15. ...

Recommender Systems

Reminder Care System: An Activity-Aware Cross-Device Recommendation System

May S. Altulyan[1]($\boxtimes$), Chaoran Huang[1]($\boxtimes$), Lina Yao[1]($\boxtimes$), Xianzhi Wang[2], Salil Kanhere[1], and Yunajiang Cao[1]

[1] UNSW Sydney, Kensington, NSW 2052, Australia
m.altulyan@student.unsw.edu.au,
{chaoran.huang,lina.yao,yuanjiang.cao}@unsw.edu.au
[2] University of Technology, Ultimo, NSW 2007, Australia
xianzhi.wang@uts.edu.au

Abstract. Alzheimer's disease (AD) affects large numbers of elderly people worldwide and represents a significant social and economic burden on society, particularly in relation to the need for long term care facilities. These costs can be reduced by enabling people with AD to live independently at home for a longer time. The use of recommendation systems for the Internet of Things (IoT) in the context of smart homes can contribute to this goal. In this paper, we present the Reminder Care System (RCS), a research prototype of a recommendation system for the IoT for elderly people with cognitive disabilities. RCS exploits daily activities that are captured and learned from IoT devices to provide personalised recommendations. The experimental results indicate that RCS can inform the development of real-world IoT applications.

Keywords: Smart home · Internet of Things · Recommender systems · Activity recognition

1 Introduction

Alzheimer's disease (AD) is an incurable degenerative disease that affects the brain cells and has serious implications for large numbers of elderly people worldwide. In the United States, for instance, 6.08 million older people had mild cognitive impairment or clinical AD in 2017 and this figure is projected to increase to 15.0 million by 2060 [7]. AD can be broadly categorised into three stages: mild (which can last around 3 years); moderate (also around 3 years); and the final severe stage. During the mild stage, patients begin to lose short-term memory, which affects their ability to remember people's names or recent events. In the moderate stage, patients may experience acute memory loss, which renders them unable to handle simple tasks without help from others, as well as language problems, confusion about time, personality change and emotional lability. In the

J. Li et al. (Eds.): ADMA 2019, LNAI 11888, pp. 207–220, 2019.
https://doi.org/10.1007/978-3-030-35231-8_15

severe stage, patients lose the ability to talk, understand, swallow and walk and require intensive care from professional or family caregivers [1,11].

Despite advances in medical technology, AD remains incurable and its aetiology is not fully understood. As a result, long-term care for Alzheimer's patients is a major financial burden for society. In 2018, the total cost of caring for Americans with Alzheimer's disease and other dementia was estimated at \$277 billion [4]. One approach to addressing this issue is to deploy recent advances in sensor network technologies, in particular, the emerging Internet of Things (IoT). These technologies have the computing ability to support a wide range of smart home applications that may enable people with AD to live independently for a longer time, thus reducing the costs associated with institutional care, particularly in the early stages. Most currently available smart home applications focus on monitoring the elderly with cognitive disabilities by providing intelligent ambient environments that can detect accidents or symptoms [3,6,16,20,26,28]. However, less attention has been paid to developing smart applications that support Alzheimer's patients by recommending the sequences of tasks needed to complete activities of daily living. Recommendations system (RS) in the IoT environment can play a crucial role in helping Alzheimer's patients to live independently in their own homes. The following scenario presents an example of how such a system could operate by tracking the person's daily activities.

Motivating Scenario. Alice is a 79-year- elderly women with Alzheimer's disease who lives alone in a house. She is making a cup of coffee in her smart kitchen. Motion sensors monitor her every move and track each coffee-making step. If she pauses for too long, a reminder application reminds her what to do next. Also, if she tries to prepare a cup of coffee late at night, the system will remind her of the time and recommend her to go back to bed. In order to provide reminder recommendations to Alice, we need to exploit three major sources of information: simple human activities, localization, and object usage detection. This is the motivation for our research. While the idea of designing a recommender system specifically for Alzheimer's patients is certainly not new, our approach is unique because we explicitly consider multi-source data instead of relying exclusively on people's direct interaction with the technologies [18]. The existing recommendation models cannot be directly applied to our scenario, because they either overlooked the context, or they only include the contextual signals in a fixed combination of physical environments with ignorance of contemporary user's activity [9,22,25].

In this case, the key challenges are to effectively disambiguate the associations among these sources and to identify an algorithm that exploits this relationship to produce reminder recommendations. In this paper, we present the design and development of a prototype system, RCS, for a smart home monitoring process that produces remind recommendations. RSC has the ability to automatically learn the contexts in a smart home environment, such as object usage and daily human activity, by analysing the motion sensor data generated from human movements and interactions with objects. It enhances Alzheimer's patients' awareness of their surroundings and provides better recommendations.

In addition, the proposed system enables users to create personal rules. Several IoT applications can benefit from the architecture and implementation of our system. The main contributions of this paper are summarised as follows:

- We utilize DeepConvLSTM for elementary activities recognition with wearable sensors, which later been used as one of the features for complex activity prediction in our end-to-end reminder recommendation system.
- We build ontological models to considering spatial, artifactual and environmental contextual information, to boost our complex activity recognition by producing rules.
- We adapt Non-negative Matrix Factorization(NMF) for our reminder recommendation system based on the recognised complex activities. Also we take advantage a prior knowledge from existing study to alleviate cold-start issue.

The remainder of the article is structured as follows. Section 2 briefs related existing work; Sect. 3 introduces and explains our proposed system in details; Sect. 4 presents experiment set-up and results evaluation; Finally Sect. 5 concludes this work with remarks.

2   Related Work

In this section, we provide an overview of (1) smart home applications that aim to provide assistance for older adults, and (2) recommender systems for IoT that are closely related to our approach.

In smart home applications, a great deal of research has sought to identify and exploit Activities of Daily Living (ADLs) in the smart environment to help elderly people to complete their activities or reach their goal. The authors in [25] present an end-to-end web based in home monitoring system, namely WITS, for convenient and efficient care delivery. The system exploits both the data and knowledge driven techniques to enable a real-time multi level activity monitoring in a personalised smart home. In [2], exploit a fuzzy temporal data-driven technique to design an anomalies recognition and assistance provision system. The work in [11] propose a SmartMind system to monitor the activity of Alzheimer's patients. However, this system has several limitations in addition to cost where the patient still depends on the assistance of a caregiver to guide them to complete their activities or reach their goal.

Oyeleke et al. [18] propose a system, SML, to track the indoor daily activities of elderly people with mild cognitive impairment. It aims to recommend the correct sequence of tasks for each activity to ensure that the users can reach their goal. Latfi et al. [12] propose an ontological architecture which consists of seven ontologies for the Telehealth Smart Home. It aims to build high-level intelligent applications, particularly for older people suffering from loss of cognitive autonomy.

In our work, in addition to exploiting the interaction between user and things, we extend the model to the relational network of three main data sources: localization, user and thing interaction and simple activities. This improves performance in detecting latent features from the relational network of these sources that can be used to define complex activities.

Recommender system (RS) for the IoT provides a critical platform for demonstrating the benefits of the Internet of Things (IoT). However, it faces several challenges that are more complex than those associated with the conventional recommender approach, for three main reasons: (1) it deals with and analyses a massive amount of extremely heterogeneous data; (2) it needs to exploit rich contextual information; and (3) the data have to pass through several layers for extensive processing over the entire life cycle.

Accordingly, numerous studies have proposed various methods for recommender systems for the IoT. Hwang et al. [9] propose a method for generating automatic rules and recommending the best rule based on things that are installed in smart homes. So, the user has the opportunity to add new rules based on any new devices that are connected to the home without extra efforts. To investigate this goal, the authors applied two steps, designed three ontology models and applied data pipeline based on open data. Salman et al. [22] exploit context aware to build a proactive multi type context aware recommender system which provides different kinds of recommendations. This system has two main phases: identifying the situation of the user and the type of recommendations, and recommending the item. Sewak and Singh [23] design the Optimal State based Recommender (OSR) System by exploiting some machine learning algorithms such as Distributed Kalman Filters; Distributed Mini-Batch SGD (Stochastic Gradient Descent); and Distributed Alternating Least Square (ALS) method. It shifted the conventional recommendations that are based on user/item preferences only into accurate recommendations dealing with real-time.

The most important feature of such a RS for the IoT is its ability to exploit knowledge of human behaviour and the relationships between things as sources to produce accurate recommendations [27]. Massimo [15] propose inverse reinforcement learning (IRL) to model user behaviour to improve the quality of recommendations. The use of IRL in recommender systems has two main features: it learns user decision behaviour by observing the user's actions; and it can learn even from a few samples by grouping its observations. As well, providing personal recommendations makes the user more interested in continuing, especially since most of the recommender systems are smart phone applications. Concerns about limited battery capacity might lead users to turn off this application if its recommendations do not match their preferences. The authors in [5,10] build recommender systems to conduct personalised recommendations by exploiting several data sources. Yao et al. [27] propose a unified probabilistic factor based framework by fusing social, temporal and spatial relations across heterogeneous entities of IoT to make more accurate recommendations.

Our proposed approach has two obvious advantages over the related work discussed above: (1) the context in a smart home environment can be learnt automatically by the system (2) users have ability to create personal rules through a graphical interface by exploiting the interaction with user, objects and, contextual events.

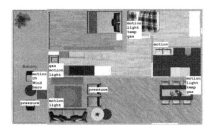

Fig. 1. Example of sensor deployment in home environment

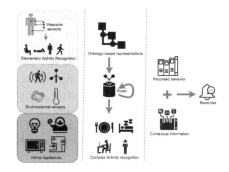

Fig. 2. Overview of the proposed methodology

3   Reminder Recommender Care System

In this section we describe the three major part (see Fig. 2) of our proposed system for reminder recommendation: (1) *Correlation analysis of devices*, where we construct a general ontological model for representing human domestic activities, domain concepts and objects; (2) *Rule-based orchestration*, where strategy will be developed based on a semantic distance-based rule matching method and rule generation; and (3) *Activity-triggered Recommendation*, which utilized non-negative matrix factorization technique to exploit information learnt in the previous two steps, to give reminder recommendations to users.

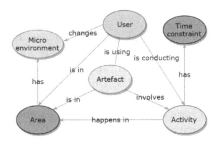

Fig. 3. Activity area modeling

Table 1. Example of activities

Elementary activities	Complex activities
Lying	Sleeping
Sitting	Watching TV
Standing	Preparing tea
Walking	Cooking
Running	Calling phone
	Eating
	Taking medicine

3.1   Correlation Analysis of Devices

Intuitively, as a system to recommend reminders to user, we need to firstly understand what activity or activities our user is undertaking in relatively high level, that is, a Human Activity Recognition (HAR) task.

Studies on HAR has been studied extensively, yet the most ones are still simple or elementary activity recognition, especially with wearable sensors. And elementary activity recognition often only reveal limited information about the user, which can hardly meet the requirements of complex practical applications. Thus, there emerging studies on complex activities recently. And some [14,25] have shown that decomposing complex activities into basic or elementary activities works well. Here we also adapt this strategy, to exploit the recognized elementary activities as one source of our input, along with environmental sensory (see Fig. 1) data and the usages of home appliances, to reveal the correlations of devices.

Definitions. Our input sensory data is continuously streaming, with a certain sample rate limited by hardware. We denote the data reading d from sensor σ at timestamp t as a tuple $r = <t, \sigma, d>$. Accordingly we denote a recent set of reading of sensor σ in a duration between timestamp t_1 and t_2 as $R^{\sigma}_{t_1,t_2} = \{r_1, r_2, ..., r_n\}$, $n \in \mathbb{R}$, is the number of timestamps.

Given a recent set of sensory data readings $R^{\mathcal{S}}_{t_1,t_2}$ where $\mathcal{S} = \{\sigma_1, \sigma_2, ..., \sigma_m\}$ denotes a set of sensors in this reading, our task is now firstly recognize complex activities set $\mathcal{A} = <A_1, A_2, ..., A_k>$ happened within the time range (t_1, t_2), and then make recommendations of reminders $\Gamma = <\gamma_1, \gamma_2, ..., \gamma_l>$.

Elementary Activity Recognition. Here we assume to follow the set up of PAMAP2 [19], using 3 wearable inertial measurement units(IMUs) as data source. The IMUs in the setting can collect 3D-acceleration data, 3D-gyroscope data, and 3D-magnetometer data. Also as illustrated in left upper part of Fig. 2, the IMUs are deployed on the chest, wrist, and ankle of our subject. Here we considering first 5 status related elementary activities in PARMAP setup, namely: lying, sitting, standing, walking, running (see Table 1).

Given a series of readings $R^{\mathcal{S}_{\mathcal{IMU}}}_{t_1,t_2} = \{r_1, r_2, ..., r_j, ..., r_n\}$, $r_j \in \mathbb{R}^K$, where K is the number of IMU sensory data we collect at one timestamp, in this step we require an series output of elementary activities $\alpha = \{a_1, a_2, ..., a_bs\}$ accordingly. As here the input is time series signals from multiple IMUs, DeepConvLSTM [17] classifiers have been proved powerful in handling such data. Note that for such a classifier, the input is a batch of n, and here we set it to be the number of data we collect at one certain time duration with an overlap.

DeepConvLSTM is a state-of-the-art of deep neural networks which combines convolutional, recurrent and softmax layers. The ReLU Convolutioanl layers firstly take the size-n sequential batch inputs over time $[t_1, t_2)$, and they produce a 2D feature map of size $\eta \times K \times f$. Here f denotes the number of filters. The feature map is then received by 2 dense recurrent layers, which in here is made up with LSTM cells, and finally a softmax layer outputs the prediction results.

More details of our settings for this classifier can be found in the Experiment section later (Fig. 4).

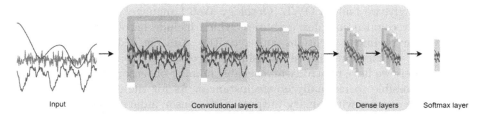

Fig. 4. The structure of DeepConvLSTM

Ontology for Complex Activity Recognition. To our knowledge, it is Yamada et al. [24] firstly come out the idea to apply ontology model in HAR, that involves interactions, i.e., subject performs activities that involves interactions with certain things. And such interactions often result in changing in status of things and environment, produce some contextual information. For example, boiling water can result in (1) local environmental changes like motion(IR radiation by human) and locally high humidity in the kitchen, (2) triggering the usage status of the kettle, (3) time constraint as such activity is highly unlike to happen in early morning before sunrise. In this example we can observe firstly spatial contexts: motion detected in kitchen, that is the place this activity happens; secondly artifactual context: the kettle has been used; thirdly the environmental contexts: the risen in humidity.

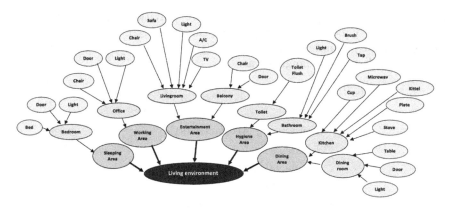

Fig. 5. Example of living area ontology

Noted that in our settings there are some more context information that can help further, in Subsect. 3.1, we utilised wearable IMUs and DeepConvLSTM recognized elementary activities of our subject, and in this example, it outputs some activities include while not limited to standing and arm motions. This basic model of activity with area, environment and time constraint can be presented as Fig. 3, and Fig. 5 shows the relationships between artefacts and area.

Accordingly, we build a OWL (Ontology Web Language[1]) ontological models to help recognize complex activities, which include ontological models for *artefacts, environment, locations,* and *activities*. And Fig. 5 shows the ontology for location, which represents relationships between artefacts and area.

Noted here we have relatively manageable number of sensors deployed, which makes us possible to manually create instances. As for the collected data, we largely have sensors with binary outputs: PIR sensor indicates the absence or presence of human, i.e. user, in certain area with a 0 or 1 readings; electronic valves status indicates if water tap is running. Even sensors with complex value, we can still using simple rules to map the reading into standard semantic presentation. For example, UV meter with reading less than 3 stands for low, between 3 and 5 can be interpret moderate, etc.; Temperature/barometer sensors indicates temperature/pressure rise or fall.

3.2   Rule-Based Orchestration

This part is mainly use previous collected sensory data and ontological models, to recognize the complex activities the user is performing. It contains set of rules, which is extended from the ontological models and combined constraints. The rules response accordingly with set of inputs, and output recognized activities, following the knowledge carried by ontological models and semantically represented sensory data, along with elementary activities within the sensed duration.

Given our ontological models built, rules to recognize complex activities can be produced accordingly, which includes artefacts involved in this activity, area that the activity taken in place, key elementary activities that this activity contains, local environmental changes and the time constraint.

Following the example of activity *boiling water* above, we can set the ontological rule in descriptive language as:

$$boilingWater$$
$$\sqsubseteq \ Cooking$$
$$\sqcap \exists \ involving \ \text{Artefact.Kettle}$$
$$\sqcap \exists \ user\_is\_is \ \text{Area.Kitchen}$$
$$\sqcap \exists \ user\_is\_conducting \ \text{Activity.Standing}$$
$$\sqcap \exists \ risen \ \text{Micro\_environment.Humidity}$$
$$\sqcap \neg \exists \ has \ \text{Time\_constraint.EarlyMorning}$$

Similarly, by traversing the ontological models, we can build rules for all defined activities.

---

[1] https://www.w3.org/standards/techs/owl.

3.3   Activity-Triggered Reminder Recommendation

Early works for activity-triggered reminder recommendation usually using Fuzzy Logic to make decision. While studies show these approaches can work adequately, they can still be improved. One shortcoming is the logic is basically predefined and they may either unable to handle undefined scenarios or the system can be too complex to deal with unpredicted scenarios.

Collaborative Filtering technique, especially Matrix Factorization, has been widely applied in recommender systems, while limited works in reminder recommendation can be identified. Here we propose to use Non-negative Matrix Factorization(NMF) [13] as our predictor for reminder recommendation.

Activity A is already been recognized in previous steps, in addition to the descriptive ontology O for activity A with properties set P, and now for reminder γ, user have a rating ρ. After certain period of time, we can easily collect a set of activities records $\mathcal{A}$, related ontologies $\mathcal{O}$ with properties $\mathcal{P}$ and accordingly for a set of reminder Γ with ratings ϱ. For simplification, we note the matrix $[A; \Gamma; P; \varrho]$ as M, the NMF has goal to decompose M so that $M \approx VH$, which can be achieved by minimizing the error function:

$$min_{VH}||M - VH||_F, \text{ subject to } V, H \geq 0 \tag{1}$$

For $M' = VH$, we restore activities $\mathcal{A}$, reminders Γ and learned ratings ϱ', where the rank ρ's to $[A; \Gamma]$ is the list of our recommendations of reminders. According to the rounded ρ's, we issue the users with high priority reminders.

However, the system still struggles with cold-start. Common solution will be let the user give ratings for random reminders for a certain period of time, which is arguably undesirable. Here we exploit a previous study by Zhou et al. [29], where a survey is done and they have some ground truth on certain ratings under 20 different scenarios. This provision can help to boost our system in cold-start. We derived the data presented in their paper[2], and Table 2 shows the data.

4   Evaluation

In this section we present systematic evaluation of our proposed reminder recommender system, via experiments on public datasets. As the proposed system consists of 3 major parts (see Fig. 2), the evaluation is conducted accordingly.

We will first introduce datasets used for evaluation, and then presents experiment settings and evaluation and result analysis.

4.1   Dataset

We evaluate the proposed system on well-benchmarked public dataset. Firstly we evaluated our elementary activity recognition module, since the recognized

---

[2] Here we use "user expectation level of reminder (UEL)" as rating and 5 levels converted to numbers (5 stand for "very high" and respectively).

Table 2. Default reminders with rating (derived from Zhou et al. [29] (see footnote 2))

ID	Current activity	Triggered reminder	Rating
1	Sleeping	Taking medicine	4
2	Sleeping	Washing clothes	1
3	Sleeping	Turning off gas	5
4	Sleeping	Cooking	2
5	Answering phone	Taking medicine	2
6	Answering phone	Washing clothes	2
7	Answering phone	Turning off gas	5
8	Answering phone	Cooking	2
9	Watching TV	Taking medicine	4
10	Watching TV	Washing clothes	2
11	Watching TV	Turning off gas	5
12	Watching TV	Cooking	4
13	Wandering	Taking medicine	4
14	Wandering	Washing clothes	4
15	Wandering	Turning off gas	5
16	Wandering	Cooking	4

elementary activities are used as one of the inputs of our second process stage, it is essential to ensure its performance. This is evaluated with both PAMAP2 dataset [19] by UC Irvine and also the PUCK dataset [8,21] in Washington State University (WSU) CASAS project in 2011.

After that, the system proceed to complex activity recognition, and this is mainly evaluated on the PUCK dataset, as it contains both smart home environmental sensors and wearable sensory data from smartphones, which match exactly our needs.

PAMAP2 Dataset. The PAMAP2 dataset contains 9 participants performing 12 daily living activities including both basic actions and sportive exercises. The activity sensory data is collected from 3 Inertial Measurement Units (IMUs) attached to three different positions, namely the dominant wrist, the chest and the dominant side's ankle. Each IMU contains two 3-axis accelerometers, two 3-axis accelerometers, one 3-axis gyroscopes, one 3-axis magnetometers and one thermometer with sampling rate of 100 Hz.

PUCK Dataset. The PUCK dataset[3] is collected in Kyoto smart home testbed in Washington State University, and it is a two-story apartment with one living

---
[3] http://casas.wsu.edu/datasets/puck.zip.

room, one dining area, one kitchen, one bathroom and three bedrooms. Various environmental sensors are installed in this testbed, including motion sensors on ceilings, door sensors on room entrances, kitchen cabinet doors as well as microwave and refrigerator doors, temperature sensors in rooms, power meter, burner sensor, water usage sensors, telephone usage sensors and some item sensors for usage monitoring.

Table 3. Baseline test of elementary activity recognition

Method	PAMAP2	PUCK
SVM	58.7	63.4
KNN	69.3	71.8
Random forest	62.8	72.1
LSTM	71.9	**77.4**
DeepConvLSTM	**73.4**	77.2

It is worth mentioning that there is also mobile wearable sensor data available for some subjects, in similar settings of PAMAP2, although less in the numbers of sensors. And in this work, the annotated ground truth is rather rare, we combined subject 3, 8 and 10, because they are the only source of data where environmental and wearable sensor both available publically. We identified 5 complex activities in this dataset, namely 16 instances of *Making phone call*, 4 instances of *Washing hands*, 4 instances of *Cooking*, 4 instances of *Eating* and 4 instances of *Cleaning kitchen*. Noted that with our ontology based rules, some more activities such as *Sleeping*, *Wandering* can be easily identified as well, yet not quite suitable for evaluation.

4.2 Elementary Activity Recognition

As mentioned, firstly we studied the effectiveness of DeepConvLSTM on our tasks, to identify the gesture of subject, that is the elementary activities. We tested several baselines, including SVM, kNN (k = 3), Random Forest (128 trees) and ordinary LSTM with 3 layers and 64 cells. As for the DeepConvLSTM, we adapted a common configuration, where there are 4 convolutional layers with feature maps, 2 LSTM layer with 128 cells. All above tests are conducted with the same settings on both PAMAP2 and PUCK datasets. The above results(in Table 3) prove that our choice of DeepConvLSTM, which outperform all tested baselines on PAMAP2 and adequate on PUCK, where the gap is so small that can be arguably ignored.

4.3 Complexity Activity Recognition

Given our ontology based rules ready, we can perform complex activities recognition. The tests result is reported in Fig. 6.

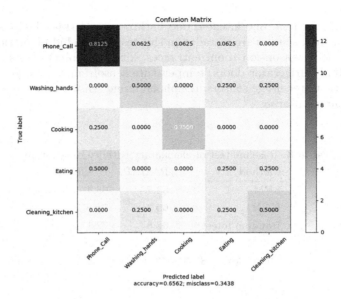

Fig. 6. The confusion matrix of complex activity recognition

Here we can easily read that the overall accuracy for complexity activity recognition is of 65.625%, which is quite reasonable, especially considering that this is based on elementary activity recognition, where our accuracy is around 77.2%, as well as the sample is still quite rare. Also we can tell our framework tend to mis-classify *Phone call* and *Eating*, *Washing hands* and *Cleaning kitchen*. This may be caused by the sharing characteristics of those activities where similar places and devices are being used.

5   Conclusion

In this work, we explored the feasibility of combining environmental sensors and wearable sensors, to recommend reminders to the people need extra care, especially Alzheimer's patient, in an activity-aware and cross-devices basis. We take advantage of one state-of-the-art HAR recognition approaches, DeepConvLSTM to identify the gestures of subject, combining which with predefined ontology representations the environmental sensory data, to produce rules for complexity activity recognition. And this output of subject behaviours are feed into a proposed recommendation engine, and output reminders to the user accordingly. The proposed recommeder system also will retrain itself given appropriate feedback from the user. Experiments demonstrated that our behaviour recognition part is effective and hence the recommendation engine practicable.

However, our evaluations of this system is still not comprehensive enough to prove the premium of this framework, mainly due to lack of test data sources to fit our complex experiments need. In the future, we will build a running system with a sensor enabled test-bed, to collect inclusive and adequate data, and test our framework in reallife use case.

References

1. Alzheimer's society. https://www.alzheimers.org.uk/about-dementia/types-dementia/alzheimers-disease-symptoms#content-start. Accessed 07 Jan 2019
2. Amirjavid, F., Bouzouane, A., Bouchard, B.: Intelligent temporal data driven world actuation in ambient environments: Case study: Anomaly recognition and assistance provision in smart home. In: 2013 IEEE/ACIS 12th International Conference on Computer and Information Science (ICIS), pp. 287–293. IEEE (2013)
3. Aramendi, A.A., et al.: Smart home-based prediction of multi-domain symptoms related to Alzheimer's disease. IEEE J. Biomed. Health Inform. **22**, 1720–1731 (2018)
4. Association, A., et al.: 2018 Alzheimer's disease facts and figures. Alzheimer's Dement. **14**(3), 367–429 (2018)
5. Asthana, S., Megahed, A., Strong, R.: A recommendation system for proactive health monitoring using IoT and wearable technologies. In: 2017 IEEE International Conference on AI & Mobile Services (AIMS), pp. 14–21. IEEE (2017)
6. Blount, M., et al.: Real-time analysis for intensive care: development and deployment of the artemis analytic system. IEEE Eng. Med. Biol. Mag. **29**(2), 110–118 (2010)
7. Brookmeyer, R., Abdalla, N., Kawas, C.H., Corrada, M.M.: Forecasting the prevalence of preclinical and clinical Alzheimer's disease in the united states. Alzheimer' Dement. **14**(2), 121–129 (2018)
8. Das, B., Cook, D.J., Schmitter-Edgecombe, M., Seelye, A.M.: PUCK: an automated prompting system for smart environments: toward achieving automated prompting-challenges involved. Pers. Ubiquit. Comput. **16**(7), 859–873 (2012)
9. Hwang, I., Kim, M., Ahn, H.J.: Data pipeline for generation and recommendation of the IoT rules based on open text data. In: 2016 30th International Conference on Advanced Information Networking and Applications Workshops (WAINA), pp. 238–242. IEEE (2016)
10. Kamal, R., Lee, J.H., Hwang, C.K., Moon, S.I., Hong, C.S.: Autonomic inferring of M2M-IoT service-usage from user-emotion and environmental information. In: Proceedings of the Korea Information Science Society, pp. 1034–1036 (2013)
11. Lam, K.Y., Tsang, N.W.H., Han, S., Ng, J.K.Y., Tam, S.W., Nath, A.: SmartMind: activity tracking and monitoring for patients with Alzheimer's disease. In: 2015 IEEE 29th International Conference on Advanced Information Networking and Applications (AINA), pp. 453–460. IEEE (2015)
12. Latfi, F., Lefebvre, B., Descheneaux, C.: Ontology-based management of the telehealth smart home, dedicated to elderly in loss of cognitive autonomy. In: OWLED, vol. 258 (2007)
13. Lee, D.D., Seung, H.S.: Learning the parts of objects by non-negative matrix factorization. Nature **401**(6755), 788 (1999)
14. Liu, L., Cheng, L., Liu, Y., Jia, Y., Rosenblum, D.S.: Recognizing complex activities by a probabilistic interval-based model. In AAAI, vol. 30, pp. 1266–1272 (2016)
15. Massimo, D.: User preference modeling and exploitation in IoT scenarios. In: 23rd International Conference on Intelligent User Interfaces, pp. 675–676. ACM (2018)

16. Nelson, T.W.H., Kam-Yiu, L., Joseph, N.K.Y., Song, H., Ioannis, P.: Tracking indoor activities of patients with mild cognitive impairment using motion sensors. In: 2017 IEEE 31st International Conference on Advanced Information Networking and Applications (AINA), pp. 431–438. IEEE (2017)
17. Ordóñez, F., Roggen, D.: Deep convolutional and lstm recurrent neural networks for multimodal wearable activity recognition. Sensors 16(1), 115 (2016)
18. Oyeleke, R.O., Yu, C.Y., Chang, C.K.: Situ-centric reinforcement learning for recommendation of tasks in activities of daily living in smart homes. In: 2018 IEEE 42nd Annual Computer Software and Applications Conference (COMPSAC), pp. 317–322. IEEE (2018)
19. Reiss, A., Stricker, D.: Creating and benchmarking a new dataset for physical activity monitoring. In: Proceedings of the 5th International Conference on PErvasive Technologies Related to Assistive Environments, p. 40. ACM (2012)
20. Rialle, V., Duchene, F., Noury, N., Bajolle, L., Demongeot, J.: Health "smart" home: information technology for patients at home. Telemed. J. E-Health 8(4), 395–409 (2002)
21. Sahaf, Y.: Comparing sensor modalities for activity recognition. Ph.D. thesis, Washington State University (2011)
22. Salman, Y., Abu-Issa, A., Tumar, I., Hassouneh, Y.: A proactive multi-type context-aware recommender system in the environment of internet of things. In: 2015 IEEE International Conference on Computer and Information Technology; Ubiquitous Computing and Communications; Dependable, Autonomic and Secure Computing; Pervasive Intelligence and Computing (CIT/IUCC/DASC/PICOM), pp. 351–355. IEEE (2015)
23. Sewak, M., Singh, S.: IoT and distributed machine learning powered optimal state recommender solution. In: International Conference on Internet of Things and Applications (IOTA), pp. 101–106. IEEE (2016)
24. Yamada, N., Sakamoto, K., Kunito, G., Isoda, Y., Yamazaki, K., Tanaka, S.: Applying ontology and probabilistic model to human activity recognition from surrounding things. IPSJ Digital Courier 3, 506–517 (2007)
25. Yao, L., et al.: WITS: an IoT-endowed computational framework for activity recognition in personalized smart homes. Computing 100(4), 369–385 (2018)
26. Yao, L., Sheng, Q.Z., Dustdar, S.: Web-based management of the internet of things. IEEE Internet Comput. 19(4), 60–67 (2015)
27. Yao, L., Sheng, Q.Z., Ngu, A.H.H., Li, X.: Things of interest recommendation by leveraging heterogeneous relations in the internet of things. ACM Trans. Internet Technol. 16(2), 9:1–9:25 (2016)
28. Yao, L., et al.: RF-care: device-free posture recognition for elderly people using a passive RFID tag array. In: Proceedings of the 12th EAI International Conference on Mobile and Ubiquitous Systems: Computing, Networking and Services on 12th EAI International Conference on Mobile and Ubiquitous Systems: Computing, Networking and Services, pp. 120–129. ACM (2015)
29. Zhou, S., Chu, C.H., Yu, Z., Kim, J.: A context-aware reminder system for elders based on fuzzy linguistic approach. Expert Syst. Appl. 39(10), 9411–9419 (2012). https://doi.org/10.1016/j.eswa.2012.02.124

Similar Group Finding Algorithm Based on Temporal Subgraph Matching

Yizhu Cai, Mo Li, and Junchang Xin[✉]

School of Computer Science and Engineering, Northeastern University,
Shenyang, China
xinjunchang@mail.neu.edu.cn

Abstract. The similar group search is an important approach for the recommendation system or social network analysis. However, there is a negligence of the influence of temporal features of social network on the search for similarity group. In this paper, we model the social network through the temporal graph and define the similar group in the temporal social network. Then, the T-VF2 algorithm is designed to search the similarity group through the temporal subgraph matching technique. To evaluate our proposed algorithm, we also extend the VF2 algorithm by point-side collaborative filtering to perform temporal subgraph matching. Finally, lots of experiments show the effectiveness and efficient of our proposed algorithm.

1 Introduction

With the continuous development of computer technology, people face increasing amounts of data every day. Many of these historical data are based on graph representation data. For example, the relationship structure of social networks, the main data of Facebook website is the graph data composed of about 800 million vertices and 104 billion edges. There is also a hyperlink structure between web pages, and the coverage and connection of the Internet can be represented based on a graph. In recent years, the research of graph data presents two trends: First, due to the increasing amount of data, more and more researchers hope to find effective methods for mining data of graph in the context of big data; second, because in practical the edges in the application diagram are usually time-varying, and more and more researchers have introduced time dimensions based on static graphs, thus evolving the temporal graph. A temporal graph is a graph that the edges and vertices can change over time. It can be represented by a snapshot of a series of static graphs, or by adding a timestamp to the edge. Compared to ordinary graph data, the temporal graph allows it to simulate many real-world situations because of its unique structure of time information. For example: In a protein interaction network, the interaction of various protein molecules has a queue order, which makes the entire protein interaction process sequential in time; in the social network, the interaction between various groups of people also change over time; in transportation networks, the time and cost of

© Springer Nature Switzerland AG 2019
J. Li et al. (Eds.): ADMA 2019, LNAI 11888, pp. 221–235, 2019.
https://doi.org/10.1007/978-3-030-35231-8_16

passing each road changes over time as traffic jams occur. Therefore, the management of temporal graph has important practical research significance. The temporal graph can reflect the data generated in real life more vividly because it introduces the time dimension based on the static graph. Therefore, the management of temporal graph has important practical research significance. Especially in social networks, the interactive information between users is constantly changing and may show certain rules, so it is important to study social networks on the temporal graph. However, most of the research on social networks still stays on the static graph data, and the proposed method can not effectively solve various problems on the temporal graph. This requires us to propose a method based on temporal graph processing to explore more practical information in social networks based on the use of temporal graph to represent social networks. By mining the groups with specific interaction patterns, we can find the target groups for further processing. For example, public security personnel may use the interactive data of existing criminal gangs to query similar criminal groups that may exist in social networks. Some merchants can also query the potential customer groups in the social network based on the interaction data of existent group customers. In the paper [14,15], the social network is analized by static subgraph isomorphism, but the time factor is not considered. In this paper, the social network is modeled by temporal graph, and the target group is searched by the isomorphism of the temporal subgraph. The result is more precise.

To summarize, the contribution of our paper are,

- Establish a temporal graph model for social networks, introduce time dimensions in the similar group search problem of social networks, and define the temporal subgraph query semantics that are more suitable for the characteristics of social networks, so that the search results are more accurate.
- The T-VF2 algorithm is proposed. This algorithm is based on the depth-first search of the graph to match, and the vertex-edge collaborative filtering rules are proposed to reduce the complexity of the algorithm.
- The correctness and efficiency of the algorithm have been verified by lots experiments.

The rest of our paper is organized as follows. In Sect. 2, we formally define the minimum temporal paths, and in Sect. 3, we show our storage structure, Adjacency Interval List. Then in Sect. 3, we describe our improving algorithms for computing minimum temporal paths in detail. We report our experimental results and corresponding analysis in Sect. 4. Section 5 discusses related work and Sect. 6 concludes our work.

2   Problem Definition

In order to make the description of the social network more vivid and the similar group search is more accurate, the social network is modeled in this paper by temporal graph. The vertices of the temporal graph represent users in the social network, and the edges represent interactions between users and are directed, representing the direction in which the interaction occurs. There are multiple timestamps on the edge, recording the time each interaction occurs between users. The temporal graph query semantics proposed in this paper not only requires exact matching of nodes, but also requires matching of timestamps on the edges. There are two matching rules for the timestamp on the edge. One is the limitation of the time window, which limiting the time range of the edges in the subgraph, that is, limiting the interaction time interval between users. The other one is temporal relationship that limits the order in which the edges in the temporal subgraph occur, i.e., the order in which interactions between users occur. The relevant definitions in this article are as follows:

Definition 1 (Temporal Graph). $G = (V, E, L, T_e, f)$, where V represents the set of vertices, E represents the set of edges, and T_e represents the set of timestamps on edge e where e $=< v, v' >$ is a directed edge. L represents the label of the vertex, and f represents the mapping relationship of the node to the label, $f(V) = L$.

Definition 2 (Temporal Subgraph). $g = (V', E', L', W, T_r, f)$, where V' represents a set of vertices. E' represents the edge set. L' represents the set of labels for the vertices. f' represents the mapping relationship of the node to the label, $f'(V') = L'$. W is the time window of the entire subgraph, and the range of occurrence time of all the edges in the subgraph is within the time window. $T_r = (e, e', flag)$ indicates the order in which e, e' occurs, where

$$
flag = \begin{cases} 1 & e \text{ occurs before } e' \\ 0 & e \text{ and } e' \text{ occur at same time} \\ -1 & e \text{ occurs after } e' \\ 9 & e \text{ and } e' \text{ no temporal relationship} \end{cases} \tag{1}
$$

Definition 3 (Similar Group). *The interaction model of the target group is established through the query graph, and the same interaction rule group as the query graph is searched in the social network modeled by the temporal graph, that is, the similar group.*

Definition 4 (Temporal Subgraph Isomorphism). *Given a target graph $G = (V, E, L, T_e, f)$, a query graph $g = (V, E, L, w, T_r, f)$, a temporal subgraph isomorphism is a bijective function M such that:*

1. $\forall u \in V', L'(u) \subseteq L(M(u))$
2. $\forall e, e' \in E', (e, e', flag) \in T_r, \exists M(e), M(e') \in E$ and $\exists t \in T_{M(e)}, t' \in T_{M(e')}$, the relationship of t, t' is same as flag.
3. $\forall e, e' \in E', \exists M(e), M(e') \in E and \exists t \in T_{M(e)}, t' \in T_{M(e')}, |t - t'| \leq W.$

Example 1. Fig. 1(a) shows a query graph. A vertex represents a user and an edge denotes interactions between two users. t_1 is the id of edge of AB, t_2 is the id of edge of AC. $t_1 > t_2$ means edge AB occurs before edge AC. $W = 4$ means the time interval of subgraph is 4. Figure 1(b) shows a social network. Each edge

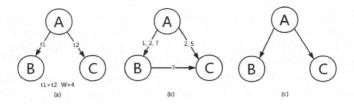

Fig. 1. Adjacency interval list

is associated with a list of timestamps which denotes the time of interaction occurred of the two vertexes. Figure 1(c) shows the result of temporal subgraph search.

Matching process: Starting from node A, the matching criterion for matching nodes is that the node degree is the largest and the number of occurrences in the target graph is the least. The neighboring vertex of A enters the nodes set which to be matched. After the node A matches successfully, the node is selected from the set to be matched to continue matching. When the node is matched, it is necessary to verify that the target graph is to be matched. The neighboring nodes in the matched node set are more than the subgraph, and the neighboring nodes outside the matched node set are more than the subgraph. After node B is successfully matched, AB is the matched edge. When node C matches, it is necessary to balance the edge matching, because $t_1 > t_2 \&\& W = 4$, so the timestamp on the edge AC is checked to satisfy the condition, because the timestamp 7 on AB is greater than the timestamps 5 and 2 on AC and $7 - 5 < 4$ is less than the time window W, so the AC edge meets the matching condition, and the node C matches successfully. Because it is looking for a similar group, the timestamp has no practical meaning in the subgraph that is queried, so the output is a subgraph with no timestamp.

3   Algorithm

This section will detail the T-VF2 algorithm. The algorithm is based on VF2 matching, and through vertex-edge collaborative filtering, it achieves the goal of simultaneously matching the points and edges to reduce the complexity of the algorithm.

3.1   Vertex-Edge Collaborative Filtering on Temporal Subgraphs Matching

In this paper, the VF2 algorithm is extended by the point-side collaborative filtering strategy, and the T-VF2 algorithm is proposed to perform sub-graph query processing on the temporal graph.

Algorithm 1 outlines the VF2 algorithm referenced in this paper. First, if state s is a complete mapping vertex set, set the flag of s as true, then return

---

Algorithm 1. VF2

---

input : target graph $G = (V, E, L)$, query graph $g = (V, E, L)$, state s
output: $stateSet \leftarrow \{subgraphg = (v, e, l) \,|\, g \in G\}$

1 **if** s *is a complete mapping vertex set* **then**
2   s.match=true
3   **return** *true*

4 **else**
5   candidatepairs←genCandidatePairs(s,G,g)
6   **for** *each pair in candidatePairs* **do**
7   **if** *cheakFeasibility(s, pair)=true* **then**
8   s.exthendMatch(pair)
9   **if** *matchRecurisive(s,G,g)=true* **then**
10   **if** *s.match=true* **then**
11   stateSet← s
12   **else**
13   s.match=false
14   s.backtrack(pair)

---

true (line 1–3). Obtain candidate vertex pairs by calling gencandidatePairs (line 4). For each candidate vertex pair cheak if it meet the match requirementif so, extend mapping state s, then recursively call matchRecurisive algorithm. When the match flag od state s is ture, put s to stateSet (line 5–10). If candidate vertex pair dont meet the match requirementset the match flag of s as false and backtrack state s (line 11–12).

The T-VF2 algorithm mainly implements the following extensions to the VF2 algorithm.

First, the node to be matched is selected in the pool of nodes to be matched by the degree of the vertex and the neighboring point. The node selection rules proposed in this paper are as follows: In order to reduce the complexity of the matching, the nodes in the query map to be matched with less matching and large degrees in the target graph are preferentially matched. This is because the fewer recursive nodes in the target graph during the depth-first search process. When the nodes with larger degrees are matched, the more nodes to be selected in the predecessor node set and the successor node set, the more accurate the result is. And when selecting the matching node in the target graph, the node is required to have greater than the query graph node, and for each different node label, the number of adjacent nodes with the same label is greater than the subgraph node. After the pair of nodes to be matched is generated, you need to add the check of the opposite edge. Because the timestamp is added on the edge, and the matching needs to meet the requirements of the subgraph in the time dimension, it is necessary to increase the processing of the edge matching.

Algorithm 2. gencandidatePairs

---

input : target graph $G = (V, E, L, T_e)$, query graph $g = (V, E, L, w, T_r, f)$,
state s

output: set of candidatePairs

1 Initialize pairList $\leftarrow \emptyset$
2 **if** *s.T1out not empty and s.T2out not empty* **then**
3 | queryNode$\leftarrow$rank(s.T2out,G,g) **for** v *in T1out* **do**
4 | | pairList$\leftarrow$pair(queryNode, v)
5 | **else**
6 | | **if** *s.T1in not empty and s.T2in not empty* **then**
7 | | | queryNode$\leftarrow$rank(s.T2in,G,g) **for** v *in T1in* **do**
8 | | | | pairList$\leftarrow$pair(queryNode,v)
9 | **else**
10 | | queryNode$\leftarrow$rank(s.unmapped2,G,g)
11 | | **for** v *in s.unmapped1* **do**
12 | | | pairList$\leftarrow$pair(queryNode,v)

13 **return** pairList

Algorithm 2 shows a matching node pair selection algorithm, gencandidatePairs. First, initialized pair list (line 1). If the set of precursor nodes of the query graph and the target graph are not empty, the matching nodes in the query graph are selected by the rank function in the precursor node set (line 2∼3). The rank function selects a large number of nodes with fewer labels in the target graph. The formula: ((degree of v) d)/the number of nodes n in the target graph that are the same as the label of v. The set of precursor nodes of the target graph is traversed, and the pair of nodes to be matched with the query graph node are generated (line 4–5). If the set of precursor nodes of the query graph or the target graph is empty, the nodes are selected in the subsequent node set (line 6–9). If the predecessor node set and the successor node set of the query graph or the target graph are both empty, a pair of nodes to be matched is generated in the unmatched node set (line 10–13).

For the temporal relationship requirements and time window requirements in the query graph, first establish the temporal relationship of each two edges according to the chronological order of the edges given in the query graph. For example, if the edge time order requirement in the query graph is $t_1 < t_2$, $t_2 < t_3$, three time-sequence matching is performed when matching, that is, $t_1 < t_2$, $t_2 < t_3$, $t_1 < t_3$. This is because the time window is limited while the edges are matched. Only the time window limit is met for every two matches to ensure that the resulting subgraph also meets the time window requirements. The specific matching method for the time window and the order in which the edges occur is as follows: (1) If the time window is W and the order of occurrence of edge e is less than e'. It is then required that at least one timestamp on the edge e satisfies the maximum timestamp less than the edge e' and the difference from the smallest timestamp on the edge e' that is greater than the timestamp is less than the time window. (2) If the time window is W and the order of occurrence of edge e is greater than e'. It is then required that at least one timestamp on the edge e satisfies the minimum timestamp greater than the edge e' and the difference between the largest timestamp on the edge e' that is less than the timestamp is less than the time window. (3) If the time window is W and the order of occurrence of edge e is equal to e'. It is then required that at least one timestamp on the edge e is equal to the timestamp on the edge e'. (4) If the time window is W and the order of occurrence of edge e is independent of e'. It is then required that at least one timestamp on edge e satisfies the difference between the maximum and minimum timestamps on edge e' that is less than the time window.

The reason for this is that for a similar group search of a social network, only the group that meets the requirements is required, and the order of interaction of the found groups and the specific time of the interaction are not required. Therefore, it is only necessary to ensure that the found subgraph is satisfying the requirements of the query graph, and does not accurately filter the time stamp on the edge. So, as long as any timestamp on the edge satisfies the time requirement of the query graph, the edge can be regarded as satisfying the matching condition, and a matching relationship can be established.

Algorithm 3. checkFeasibility

---

    input : state s, to be matched pair (targetNode v, queryNode v)

1 **if** *label of v not same as label of v* **then**
2 | **return** false
3 **if** *checkPredAndSucc(s, v, v)==false* **then**
4 | **return** false
5 **if** *checkInAndOut(s, v, v)==false* **then**
6 | **return** false
7 **if** *checkNew(s, v, v)==false* **then**
8 | **return** false
9 **return** true

Algorithm 3 shows the check rules of T-VF2. First, check if the labels of the matching nodes are the same (line 1–2). Then check whether the predecessor and successor nodes of the matching nodes are consistent in the matched node set, and whether the edge formed by the matching nodes and the predecessor or successor node satisfies the temporal restriction by calling checkingPredAndSucc (line 3–4). Then check whether the indegree and outdegree of the node in the predecessor and successor node set meet the requirements (line 5–6). Then, check whether the indegree and outdegree of the node in other nodes set meets the requirements (line 7–8). Returns true if everything meets the requirements (line 9).

Algorithm 4. checkPredAndSucc

---

input : state s, to be matched pair (targetNode v, queryNode v)

1 initialize matched edges set $qEdgeIds$
2 **for** *each edge e in inEdges of v* **do**
3 | **if** *the source node of e has been matched* **then**
4 | | **if** *no corresponding edge in the target graph* **then**
5 | | | **return** false;
6 | **else**
7 | | UnTimes←timeofEdge(e)
8 | | Obtain the matched edge set $qEdgeIds$
9 | | **for** *each edge e in qEdgeIds* **do**
10 | | | rela←getTemRela(e, e)
11 | | | minTime←getMinTime(e)
12 | | | maxTime←getMaxTime(e)
13 | | | **if** *rela is 1* **then**
14 | | | | **for** *time t of UnTimes* **do**
15 | | | | | Get the minimum timestamp greater than t maxTimeSec on the matched edge
16 | | | | | **if** $t<minTime||t\geq queryGraph.W+maxTimeSec$ **then**
17 | | | | | | UnTimes.remove(t)
18 | | | | | | **if** *UnTimes is Empty* **then**
19 | | | | | | | **return** false
20 | | | **if** *rela is 0* **then**
21 | | | | **for** *time t of UnTimes* **do**
22 | | | | | **if** *getFeasTimeofEdge(e) dont contains t* **then**
23 | | | | | | UnTimes.remove(t)
24 | | | | | | **if** *UnTimes is Empty* **then**
25 | | | | | | | **return** false
26 | | | **if** *rela is 1* **then**
27 | | | | **for** *time t of UnTimes* **do**
28 | | | | | Get the minimum timestamp smaller than t maxTimeSec on the matched edge
29 | | | | | **if** $t<minTime||t\leq queryGraph.W+maxTimeSec$ **then**
30 | | | | | | UnTimes.remove(t)
31 | | | | | | **if** *UnTimes is Empty* **then**
32 | | | | | | | **return** false
33 | | | **if** *rela is −1* **then**
34 | | | | **for** *time t of UnTimes* **do**
35 | | | | | **if** $Math.abs(minTime-t)>queryGraph.W$ ── $Math.abs(maxTime-t)>queryGraph.W$ **then**
36 | | | | | | UnTimes.remove(t)
37 | | | | | | **if** *UnTimes is Empty* **then**
38 | | | | | | | **return** false
39 | | s.feasTimeofEdge.put(e, UnTimes)

Algorithm 4 shows the check rule of the predecessor of the matching node. First, initialize the query graph matched edge set $qEdgeIds$. For the inbound edge of the node to be matched with the query graph, determine whether the target graph node is to be matched with the corresponding entry edge, and if there is no corresponding edge, the match fails (line 3–5). Get all the timestamps on the edge to be matched (line7). Traverse the edges of the query graph and find all the matched edges to join qEdgeIds (line 8). For each matched edge, obtain the feasible maximum timestamp and minimum timestamp on the edge, and the relationship with the edge to be matched (line 9–12). When the query graph requires that the edge to be matched occurs earlier than the matched edge. Then the timestamp on the edge to be matched should be greater than the minimum timestamp of matched edge and the difference from the largest timestamp on edge matched edge which is less than the timestamp is less than the time window. If a timestamp on the edge does not meet the requirement, the timestamp is deleted. If all timestamps on the edge are deleted, the edge does not meet the requirements and the match fails (line 13–19). When the query graph requires that the edge to be matched occurs at the same time as the matched edge. The timestamp on the edge to be matched should be the same as the matched edge. Delete the timestamp on the edge to be matched that is different from the matched edge. If all the timestamps on the edge are deleted, the edge does not meet the matching requirements and the match fails (line 20–25). When the query graph requires that the edge to be matched occurs later than the matched edge. The timestamp on the edge to be matched should be less than the maximum timestamp of matched edge and the difference from the smallest timestamp on matched edge which is greater than the timestamp is less than the time window. If a timestamp on the edge does not meet the requirement, the timestamp is deleted. If all timestamps on the edge are deleted, the edge does not meet the requirements and the match fails (line 26–32). When the edge to be matched is independent of the matched edge, it is confirmed that the difference between the timestamp on the edge to be matched and the largest and smallest timestamp on the matched edge is less than the time window. If a timestamp on the edge does not meet the requirement, the timestamp is deleted. If all timestamps on the edge are deleted, the edge does not match the match and the match fails (line 33–38). If the edge passes the check, record all feasible timestamps on the edge that have not been deleted (line 39). The outbound edge of the vertex to be matched also needs to be verified, which is the same judgment logic, and will not be described in detail herein.

Algorithm 5 outlines Check logic for node access. First, initialize the collection $queryPredCnt$, $targetPredCnt$ (line 1). For the query graph to be matched node, traverse its predecessor node, if it is in the predecessor or successor node set, the corresponding label count of the node is $+1$ (line 3–6). The same processing step is also performed for the target graph to be matched(line 7–11). For each record label, if the count in the target graph is less than the count in the query graph, the match fails (line 12–14). The same check logic is also used for the successor nodes of the node, and will not be described in detail herein.

Algorithm 5. checkInandOut

---

    input : targetNode v, queryNode v

1 Initialize set $queryPredCnt$, $targetPredCnt$
2 **for** *each u belonging to predecessor nodes of v* **do**
3   **if** *u in $s.T2in$ or $s.T2out$* **then**
4   **if** *$queryPredCnt$ has label of u* **then**
5   Count of label(u) +1
6   **else**
7   queryPredCnt.put(label(u), 1)

8 **for** *each u belonging to predecessor nodes of v* **do**
9   **if** *u in $s.T1in$ or $s.T1out$* **then**
10   **if** *$targetPredCnt$ has label of u* **then**
11   Count of label(u) +1
12   **else**
13   targetPredCnt.put(label(u), 1)

14 **for** *each label l of $queryPredCnt$* **do**
15   **if** *$queryPredCnt.count$ of l > $targetPredCnt.count$ of l* **then**
16   **return** false

17 **return** true

For the algorithm checkNew, the predecessor and successor nodes of the pair of nodes to be matched in the unmatched node set are calculated, which is the same as the calculation method of the algorithm 6. This article will not go into details.

4   Experimental Evaluation

In this section, we first describe the experimental environment and datasets in Sect. 4.1, then we analysis the results in Sect. 4.2.

4.1   Experimental Environment and Datasets

The algorithms are implemented in java, and the experiments are performed on a Windows 10 machine with Inter Core i7-6700 3.40 GHz CPU and 8 GB memory. The time costs reported here are calculated by system clock.

    The experiment used two data sets, wiki-talk temporal network and CollegeMsg temporal network. The data comes from the Stanford University Large Network Dataset. Wiki-speak temporal network is a temporal network represents Wikipedia users editing each other's Talk page. A directed edge (u, v, t) means that user u edited user v's talk page at time t. CollegeMsg temporal network is comprised of private messages sent On an online social network at the University of California, Irvine. Users could search the network for others and then initiate conversation based on profile information. An edge (u, v, t) means that user u sent a private message to user v at Time t. The wiki-talk temporal network and CollegeMsg temporal network dataset node labels are manually generated, and the artificially generated virtual labels are evenly distributed throughout the network. The node label indicates the user's job position. Detailed statistical information of the processed data set is shown in Table 1.

Table 1. Dataset

	Wiki_talk	CollegeMsg
Nodes	100	1000
Edges	1073	21843
Labels	10	40

In order to test the validity of the T-VF2 algorithm, the subgraphs ran out of the VF2 algorithm are compared with those of temporal matching rules. It is mainly compared by matching different size query graphs and target graphs of different sizes.

4.2 Results

By performing multiple sets of experiments and averaging, the experimental results in the real data set are shown:

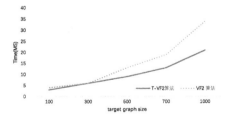

Fig. 2. Size of target graph   **Fig. 3.** Size of query graph

By comparison, it is found that the proposed algorithm is more efficient than the VF2 algorithm in processing temporal subgraph matching problems. In Experiment 1, the size of the subgraph is fixed to two sides of three nodes, and the two time limits are added to the subgraphs limited by the time window. As the target graph expands, both algorithms take longer and longer, but the growth rate of the T-VF2 algorithm is significantly smaller than the VF2 algorithm. This is because as the target map expands, the number of nodes to be matched

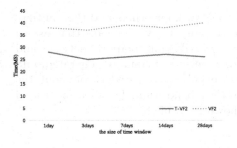

Fig. 4. Size of time window

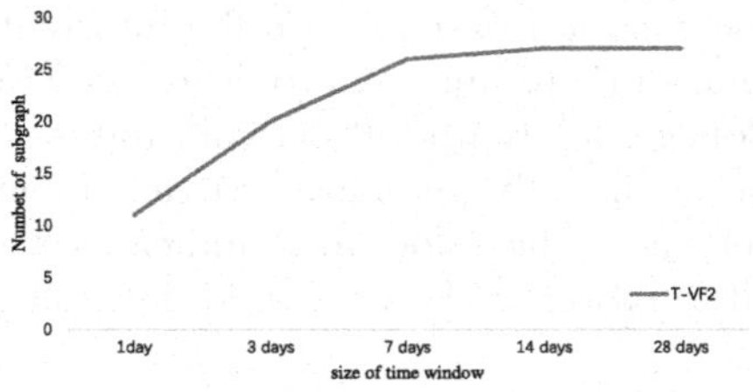

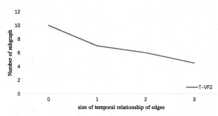

Fig. 5. Size of time window

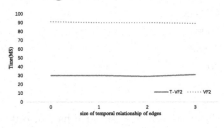

Fig. 6. Size of temporal relationship of edge

Fig. 7. Size of temporal relationship of edge

increases, and the number of deep traversals increases. In the T-VF2 algorithm, through vertex-to-edge collaborative filtering, more nodes are filtered out during the matching process, and the traversal complexity is reduced.

In Experiment 2, the target map size was fixed to 1000 nodes. With the expansion of the subgraph, the time of the two algorithms increases, but the growth rate of the T-VF2 algorithm is significantly smaller than that of the VF2 algorithm. This is because as the target map expands, the recursive depth of the depth traversal at the time of matching increases, which leads to an increase in time. However, because the T-VF2 algorithm uses vertex-to-edge collaborative filtering to filter most of the mismatched node pairs early, it is not necessary to continue deep traversal, reducing the complexity of the algorithm.

In Experiment 3, the size of query graph is 3 nodes. The size of target graph is 1000 nodes. With the expansion of the time window of query graph, the efficiency of the two algorithms not change much. And the number of subgraph is increase.

In Experiment 4, the size of query graph is 5 nodes. The size of target graph is 1000 nodes. With the expansion of the temporal relationship of edges in query graph, the efficiency of the two algorithms not change much. And the number of subgraph is decrease.

This four experiments can prove that the T-VF2 algorithm is accurate and efficient in processing temporal subgraph matching problems.

5   Related Work

In the aspect of static graph subgraph matching, The Ullmann algorithm [19] is the earliest known index-free matching method. The latter representative algorithms include VF2 [5], GraphQl [7], GADDI [21], Spath [20], etc. These algorithms mainly add pruning and other auxiliary information to improve the search strategy based on the Ullmann algorithm. Last few years, the [6] proposed a resource-constrained query processing strategy for dynamic graph reduction, which improved the efficiency of data local query and non-data local query processing; Zhao Chang et al. [3] first based on k The -Automorphism privacy model converts the original image into a graph that preserves the privacy relationship, and then uses the transformation graph symmetry to implement the subgraph matching query, which not only saves the query space but also ensures the query efficiency. In [17], the subgraph isomorphic query acceleration method Boost-Iso is proposed, which uses the relationship between vertices to eliminate the repeated calculation of the isomorphic query of the subgraph in the large image. The [9] designs and implements the hard disk based large-scale graph single machine parallel subroutine. The graph enumeration method, the dual method of subgraph enumeration is designed, and the subgraph matching is effectively realized. The [13] studies the subgraph query problem in which the data graph is public and the query structure is confidential, and the query is realized by using the encrypted aggregate grouping. The query coding method of privacy matrix operation; [10] proposed the Left-Deep-Join-based subgraph enumeration algorithm TwinTwigJoin in MapReduce environment, and proposed three optimization strategies and compression graph structure considering vertex equivalence relation. Improve query processing efficiency.

In the subgraph matching of the timing diagram, Bogdanov et al. [2] defined the high-sequence subgraphs in the time series, proved that it is NP-hard, and proposed a fast heuristic approximation algorithm to solve, while using the approximate upper limit narrowing search Space to improve the speed of query processing; the literature [18] studied the dynamic subgraph query in the time series diagram, gave the definition of the query model, and proposed the query processing method of finding the associated edge set and then generating the dynamic subgraph, and proposed the waveform. And the binary tree two index methods accelerate the search of the associated edges; Kansal et al. [8] proposed a Graph-Coarsening-based index to accelerate the subgraph query in the dynamic graph database, which not only does not require parameters, resident memory, but also can deal with the change of database.

Graphical pattern matching plays an important role in social network analysis, which has been widely used in, for example, expert discovery, social community mining, and social location detection. In [15], the authors mine patterns that emerge frequently in the social graph, and show that such patterns possess enough discriminative power to accurately predict the relationships among social network users. In [14], Software tools for Social Network Analysis (SNA) are being developed which support various types of analysis of social networks extracted from social media websites (e.g., Twitter). In [12] first conceptually

extends bounded simulation to multi-constraint simulation (MCS) and proposes
a new NP-complete multi-constraint graph matching (MC-GPM) problem. Then
a new concept called Strong Social Component (SSC) is proposed, and then a
method for identifying SSC is proposed. A new SSC indexing method and graph
compression method are proposed. In addition, a heuristic algorithm is designed
to effectively identify MC-GPM results without decompressing graphics. In [11],
a multi-threaded heuristic algorithm, called M-HAMC, is designed based on the
literature [12] to search for MC-GPM results in parallel. [16] propose a novel combination of sub graph matching queries which have been studied extensively in
the context of both RDF and social networks, and scoring functions. [4] propose
a novel parameter-free contextual community model for attributed community
search. [1] propose a new hashtag recommendation model which predicts the
top-y hashtags to the user based on a hierarchical level of feature extraction
over communities, users, tweets and hashtags.

6   Conclusion

This paper represents the social network through the time series diagram, and
analyzes the social network through the time series subgraph matching technology to find similar groups. In this paper, the VF2 algorithm is extended, and the
T-VF2 algorithm is proposed. The point-side collaborative filtering rule is proposed to make the sequential subgraph search efficient and efficient. Finally, the
effectiveness and efficiency of the T-VF2 algorithm are proved by experiments.

Acknowledgement. This work was supported in part by the National Natural Science Foundation of China (Nos. 61472069, 61402089 and U1401256), China Postdoctoral Science Foundation (Nos. 2019T120216 and 2018M641705), the Fundamental Research Funds for the Central Universities (Nos. N161602003, N180408019 and
N180101028), the Open Program of Neusoft Institute of Intelligent Healthcare Technology, Co. Ltd. (No. NIMRIOP1802) and the fund of Acoustics Science and Technology
Laboratory.

References

1. Alsini, A., Datta, A., Huynh, D.Q., Li, J.: Community Aware Personalized Hashtag
   Recommendation in Social Networks. In: Islam, R., Koh, Y.S., Zhao, Y., Warwick,
   G., Stirling, D., Li, C.-T., Islam, Z. (eds.) AusDM 2018. CCIS, vol. 996, pp. 216–
   227. Springer, Singapore (2019). https://doi.org/10.1007/978-981-13-6661-1_17
2. Bogdanov, P., Mongiovi, M., Singh, A.K.: Mining heavy subgraphs in time-evolving
   networks. In: ICDE, pp. 81–90 (2011)
3. Chang, Z., Zou, L., Li, F.: Privacy preserving subgraph matching on large graphs
   in cloud. In: SIGMOD, pp. 199–213 (2016)
4. Chen, L., Liu, C., Liao, K., Li, J., Zhou, R.: Contextual community search over
   large social networks. In: ICDE, pp. 88–99 (2019)
5. Cordella, L.P., Foggia, P., Sansone, C., Vento, M.: A (sub)graph isomorphism algorithm for matching large graphs. IEEE Trans. Pattern Anal. Mach. Intell. **26**(10),
   1367–1372 (2004)

6. Fan, W., Wang, X., Wu, Y.: Querying big graphs within bounded resources. In: SIGMOD, pp. 301–312 (2014)
7. He, H., Singh, A.K.: Graphs-at-a-time: query language and access methods for graph databases. In: SIGMOD, pp. 405–418 (2008)
8. Kansal, A., Spezzano, F.: A scalable graph-coarsening based index for dynamic graph databases. In: CIKM, pp. 207–216 (2017)
9. Lai, L., Qin, L., Lin, X., Chang, L.: Scalable subgraph enumeration in mapreduce. Very Large Data Bases **8**(10), 974–985 (2015)
10. Lai, L., Qin, L., Lin, X., Chang, L.: Scalable subgraph enumeration in mapreduce: a cost-oriented approach. Very Large Data Bases **26**(3), 421–446 (2017)
11. Liu, G., et al.: MCS-GPM: multi-constrained simulation based graph pattern matching in contextual social graphs. IEEE Trans. Knowl. Data Eng. **30**(6), 1050–1064 (2018)
12. Liu, G., et al.: Multi-constrained graph pattern matching in large-scale contextual social graphs. In: ICDE, pp. 351–362 (2015)
13. Meng, X., Kamara, S., Nissim, K., Kollios, G.: GRECS: graph encryption for approximate shortest distance queries. In: ACM, pp. 504–517 (2015)
14. Ogaard, K., Kase, S.E., Roy, H., Nagi, R., Sambhoos, K., Sudit, M.: Searching social networks for subgraph patterns. In: Proceedings of SPIE, vol. 8711 (2013)
15. Papaoikonomou, A., Kardara, M., Tserpes, K., Varvarigou, T.A.: Predicting edge signs in social networks using frequent subgraph discovery. IEEE Internet Comput. **18**(5), 36–43 (2014)
16. Park, N., Ovelgonne, M., Subrahmanian, V.S.: SMAC: subgraph matching and centrality in huge social networks. In: SocialCom, pp. 134–141 (2013)
17. Ren, X., Wang, J.: Exploiting vertex relationships in speeding up subgraph isomorphism over large graphs. Very Large Data Bases **8**(5), 617–628 (2015)
18. Rong, H., Ma, T., Tang, M., Cao, J.: A novel subgraph k^+-isomorphism method in social network based on graph similarity detection. Soft Comput. **22**(8), 2583–2601 (2018)
19. Ullmann, J.R.: An algorithm for subgraph isomorphism. J. ACM **23**(1), 31–42 (1976)
20. Zhao, P., Han, J.: On graph query optimization in large networks. Very Large Data Bases **3**(1), 340–351 (2010)
21. Zou, L., Chen, L., Yu, J.X., Lu, Y.: A novel spectral coding in a large graph database. In: EDBT, pp. 181–192 (2008)

Traditional PageRank Versus Network Capacity Bound

Robert A. Kłopotek[1]([✉])[ID] and Mieczysław A. Kłopotek[2][ID]

[1] Faculty of Mathematics and Natural Sciences, School of Exact Sciences,
Cardinal Stefan Wyszyński University in Warsaw, Warsaw, Poland
r.klopotek@uksw.edu.pl
[2] Computer Science Fundamental Research Institute, Polish Academy of Sciences,
Warsaw, Poland
mieczyslaw.klopotek@ipipan.waw.pl

Abstract. In a former paper [10] we simplified the proof of a theorem
on personalized random walk that is fundamental to graph nodes clustering and generalized it to bipartite graphs for a specific case where the
probability of random jump was proportional to the number of links of
"personally preferred" nodes. In this paper, we turn to the more complex
issue of graphs in which the random jump follows a uniform distribution.

Keywords: Bipartite graphs · PageRank · Uniform jump probability ·
Flow limits · Graph mining

1 Introduction

The PageRank is widely used as a (primary or supplementary) measure of the
importance of a web page since its publication in [15]. Subsequently, the idea was
explored with respect to methods of computation [3], application areas (web page
ranking, client and seller ranking, clustering, classification of web pages, word
sense disambiguation, spam detection, detection of dead pages etc.) and application related variations (personalized PageRank, topical PageRank, Ranking
with Back-step, Query-Dependent PageRank, Lazy Walk Pagerank etc.), [11].

The traditional PageRank reflects the probability that a random walker
reaches a given webpage. The walker, upon entering a webpage, follows with
uniform probability one of the outgoing edges unless he gets bored or there are
no outgoing edges. If so, he jumps to any web page with uniform probability.

One of the application areas of PageRank is the creation of new clustering
methods especially for graphs, including undirected[1] graphs in which we are
interested in this paper. One of the clues for clustering of graphs assumes that
a good cluster has low probability to be left by a random walker. Though the
concept seems to be plausible, it has been investigated theoretically only for

---

[1] Unoriented graphs have multiple applications as a means to represent relationships
spanned by a network of friends, telecommunication infrastructure or street network.

© Springer Nature Switzerland AG 2019
J. Li et al. (Eds.): ADMA 2019, LNAI 11888, pp. 236–249, 2019.
https://doi.org/10.1007/978-3-030-35231-8_17

a very special case of a random walker (different from the traditional walker), performing the "boring jump" with the probability being proportional to the number of incident edges (and not uniformly) – see e.g. [4, 10].

In this paper, we will make an attempt to extend this result to the case when the "boring jump" is performed uniformly (as in case of traditional walker) (Sect. 2 with some variants described in Sect. 3) and to generalize it to bipartite graphs (Sect. 4).

PageRank computation for bipartite graphs was investigated already in the past in the context of social networks, e.g. when concerning mutual evaluations of students and lecturers [13], reviewers and movies in a movie recommender systems, or authors and papers in scientific literature or queries and URLs in query logs [7], recommendations [9], food chain analysis [1], species ranking [8], economy [16], social net analysis [6], or performing image tagging [2]. Akin algorithms like HITS were also generalized for bipartite graphs, [14]. As pointed at in [10], the bipartite graphs have a periodic structure explicitly while PageRank aims at graph aperiodicity. Therefore a suitable generalization of PageRank to a bipartite structure is needed and we will follow here the proposals made in [10].

2   Traditional PageRank

One of the many interpretations of PageRank views it as the probability that a knowledgeable (knowing addresses of all the web pages) but mindless (choosing next page to visit without regard to any content hints) random walker will encounter a given web page. So upon entering a particular web page, if it has no outgoing links, the walker jumps to any web page with uniform probability. If there are outgoing links, he chooses with uniform probability one of the outgoing links and goes to the selected web page, unless he gets bored. If he gets bored (which may happen with a fixed probability ζ on any page), he jumps to any web page with uniform probability. One of the modifications of this behavior (called personalized PageRank) was a mindless page-u-fan random walker who is doing exactly the same, but in case of a jump out of boredom he does not jump to any page, but to the page u. Also, there exist plenty of possibilities of other mindless walkers between these two extremes. An unacquainted reader is warmly referred to [12] for a detailed treatment of these topics.

Let us recall the formalization of these concepts. With $\mathbf{r}$ we will denote a (column) vector of ranks: r_j will mean the PageRank of page j. All elements of $\mathbf{r}$ are non-negative and their sum equals 1.

Let $\mathbf{P} = [p_{ij}]$ be a matrix such that if there is a link from page j to page i, then $p_{i,j} = \frac{1}{outdeg(j)}$, where $outdeg(j)$ is the out-degree of node j[2]. In other words, $\mathbf{P}$ is column-stochastic matrix satisfying $\sum_i p_{ij} = 1$ for each column j. If a node had an out-degree equal 0, then prior to construction of $\mathbf{P}$ the node is replaced by one with edges outgoing to all other nodes of the network. Hence

---

[2]   For some versions of PageRank, like TrustRank $p_{i,j}$ would differ from $\frac{1}{outdeg(j)}$ giving preferences to some outgoing links over the other. We are not interested in such considerations here.

$$\mathbf{r} = (1 - \zeta)\cdot\mathbf{P}\cdot\mathbf{r} + \zeta\cdot\mathbf{s} \tag{1}$$

where $\mathbf{s}$ is the so-called "initial" probability distribution (i.e. a column vector with non-negative elements summing up to 1) that is also interpreted as a vector of web page preferences.[3] For a knowledgeable walker for each node j of the network $s_j = \frac{1}{|N|}$, where $|N|$ is the cardinality of the set of nodes N constituting the network. For a page-u-fan we have $s_u = 1$, and $s_j = 0$ for any other page $j \neq u$. For a uniform-set-U-fan[4] we get

$$s_j = \begin{cases} \dfrac{1}{|U|} & \text{if } j \in U \\ 0 & \text{otherwise} \end{cases} , \quad j = 1, \ldots |N| \tag{2}$$

and for a hub-page-preferring-set-U-fan we obtain

$$s_j = \begin{cases} \dfrac{outdeg(j)}{\sum_{k \in U} outdeg(k)} & \text{if } j \in U \\ 0 & \text{otherwise} \end{cases} , \quad j = 1, \ldots |N| \tag{3}$$

The former case is the topic of this paper, the second was considered in our former paper [10].

Instead of a random walker model, we can view a web as a pipe-net through which the authority is flowing in discrete time steps. In single time step a fraction ζ of the authority of a node j flows into so-called *super-node*, and the fraction $\frac{1-\zeta}{outdeg(j)}$ is sent from this node to each of its children in the graph. After the super-node has received authorities from all the nodes, it redistributes the authority to all the nodes in fractions defined in the vector $\mathbf{s}$. Note that the authority circulates lossless (we have a kind of a closed loop here). Besides this, as was proven in many papers, we have to do here with a self-stabilizing process. Starting with any stochastic vector $\mathbf{r}^{(0)}$ and applying the operation

$$\mathbf{r}^{(n+1)} = (1 - \zeta)\cdot\mathbf{P}\cdot\mathbf{r}^{(n)} + \zeta\cdot s$$

the series $\{\mathbf{r}^{(n)}\}$ will converge to $\mathbf{r}$ being the solution of the Eq. (1) (i.e. to the main eigenvector corresponding to eigenvalue 1).

Subsequently let us consider only connected graphs (one-component graphs) with symmetric links, i.e. unoriented graphs. Hence for each node j the relationships between in- and out-degrees are: $indeg(j) = outdeg(j) = deg(j)$. In a former paper we have proven [10].

Theorem 1. *For the preferential personalized PageRank we have*

$$p_o\zeta \leq (1 - \zeta)\frac{|\partial(U)|}{Vol(U)}$$

where $\partial(U)$ is the set of edges leading from U to the nodes outside of U (the so-called "edge boundary of U"), $|\partial(U)|$ is the its cardinality, and $Vol(U)$, called volume or capacity of U is the sum of out-degrees of all nodes from U.

---

[3] We will denote the solution to the Eq. (1) with $\mathbf{r}^{(t)}(\mathbf{P}, \mathbf{s}, \zeta)$.

[4] We will call the set U "fan-pages" or "fan-set" or "fan-nodes".

Let us discuss now a uniform-set-U-fan defined in Eq. (2). Consider the situation where U is only a proper subset of N, and assume that

$$r_j^{(t)} = \begin{cases} \dfrac{1}{|U|} & \text{if } j \in U \\ 0 & \text{otherwise} \end{cases} , \quad j = 1, \dots |N| \tag{4}$$

in a moment t. To find the distribution $\mathbf{r}^{(t')}$ for $t' > t$ we state that if in none of the links the passing amount of authority will exceed $\gamma = (1-\zeta)\frac{1}{|U|\min_{k \in U} deg(k)}$, then at any later time point $t' > t$ the inequality $r_j^{(t')} \le deg(j) \cdot \gamma + \frac{\zeta}{|U|}$ holds at any node $j \in U$, because if a node $j \notin U$ gets via links $l_{j,1}, \dots, l_{j,deg(j)}$ the authority amounting to $a_{l_{j,1}} \le \gamma, \dots, a_{l_{j,deg(j)}} \le \gamma$ then it accumulates

$$\mathfrak{a}_j = \sum_{k=1}^{deg(j)} a_{j,k} \le \gamma \cdot deg(j)$$

of total authority, and in the next time step the following amount of authority flows out through each of these links:

$$(1-\zeta)\frac{\mathfrak{a}_j}{deg(j)} \le \gamma(1-\zeta) \le \gamma$$

If a node $j \in U$ gets via incoming links $l_{j,1}, \dots, l_{j,deg(j)}$ the authority amounting to $a_{l_{j,1}} \le \gamma, \dots, a_{l_{j,deg(j)}} \le \gamma$ then, due to the authority obtained from the super-node equal to $\mathfrak{b}_j = \zeta\frac{1}{|U|} \le deg(j)\gamma\frac{\zeta}{1-\zeta}$, in the next step through each link the authority amounting to

$$(1-\zeta)\frac{\mathfrak{a}_j}{deg(j)} + (1-\zeta)\frac{\mathfrak{b}_j}{deg(j)} \le \gamma(1-\zeta) + \gamma\frac{\zeta}{1-\zeta}(1-\zeta) = \gamma$$

flows out. So if already at time point t the authority flowing out through any link from any node did not exceed γ, then this property will hold (by induction) forever, especially for the equation solution $\mathbf{r}$ which is unique. Let us denote by p_o the total mass of authority contained in all the nodes outside of U. We ask: "How much authority from outside of U can flow into U via super-node at the point of stability?" This question concerns the quantity $p_o\zeta$. We claim that

Theorem 2. *For the uniform personalized PageRank we have*

$$p_o\zeta \mathrel{<=} (1-\zeta)\frac{|\partial(U)|}{|U|\min_{k \in U} deg(k)}$$

Proof. Let us notice first that, due to the closed loop of authority circulation, the amount of authority flowing into U from the nodes belonging to the set $\overline{U} = N \backslash U$ must be identical with the amount flowing out of U to the nodes in $\overline{U}$. But from U only that portion of authority flows out that flows out through the boundary of U because no authority leaves U via super-node (it returns from there immediately). As at most the amount $\gamma|\partial(U)|$ leaves U, then

$$p_o\zeta \leq \gamma|\partial(U)| = (1-\zeta)\frac{1}{|U|min_{k\in U}deg(k)}|\partial(U)| = (1-\zeta)\frac{|\partial(U)|}{|U|min_{k\in U}deg(k)}$$

When you compare the above two Theorems 1 and 2, you will see immediately that the bound in case of "preferential" Theorem 1 is lower than in case of "uniform" Theorem 2. If we look more broadly at the s vector with $s_j > 0\ \forall_{j\in U}$ and $s_j = 0\ \forall_{j\notin U}$, we will derive immediately by analogy the relation.

Theorem 3. *For the personalized PageRank with arbitrary s vector such that $s_j > 0\ \forall_{j\in U}$ and $s_j = 0\ \forall_{j\notin U}$ we have*

$$p_o\zeta <= (1-\zeta)\frac{|\partial(U)|}{min_{k\in U}\frac{deg(k)}{s_k}}$$

3 Variants of the Theorems

In this section, our attention is concentrated on some versions of PageRank related to a random walk with a distinct semantic connotation.

3.1 Lazy Random Walk PageRank

A variant of PageRank, so-called *lazy-random-walk-PageRank* was described e.g. by [5]. It differs from the traditional PageRank in that the random walker before choosing the next page to visit he first tosses a coin and upon heads he visits the next page, and upon tails, he stays in the very same node of the network. Recall that for the lazy walker PageRank we have:

$$\mathbf{r}^{(l)} = (1-\zeta)\cdot(0.5\mathbf{I}+0.5\mathbf{P})\cdot\mathbf{r}^{(l)} + \zeta\cdot\mathbf{s} \qquad (5)$$

where $\mathbf{I}$ is the identity matrix.[5] Rewriting reveals relation to traditional one.

$$\mathbf{r}^{(l)} = \frac{1-\zeta}{1+\zeta}\cdot(\mathbf{P})\cdot\mathbf{r}^{(l)} + \frac{2\zeta}{1+\zeta}\cdot\mathbf{s} \qquad (6)$$

So $\mathbf{r}^{(l)}$ for ζ is the same as $\mathbf{r}^{(t)}$ for $\frac{2\zeta}{1+\zeta}$ ($\mathbf{r}^{(l)}(\mathbf{P},\mathbf{s},\zeta) = \mathbf{r}^{(t)}(\mathbf{P},\mathbf{s},\frac{2\zeta}{1+\zeta})$) Hence

Theorem 4. *For the preferential lazy personalized PageRank we have*

$$p_o\zeta \leq \frac{1-\zeta}{2}\frac{|\partial(U)|}{Vol(U)}$$

Theorem 5. *For the uniform lazy personalized PageRank we have*

$$p_o\zeta \leq \frac{1-\zeta}{2}\frac{|\partial(U)|}{|U|\,min_{k\in U}deg(k)}$$

---

[5] We will denote the solution to the Eq. (5) with $\mathbf{r}^{(l)}(\mathbf{P},\mathbf{s},\zeta)$.

3.2 Generalized Lazy Random Walk

Let us generalize this behavior to *generalized-lazy-random-walk-PageRank* by introducing the laziness degree λ. It means that, upon tossing an unfair coin, probability of tails is λ (and heads $1-\lambda$). For the generalized lazy walker PageRank we have:

$$\mathbf{r}^{(g)} = (1-\zeta)\cdot(\lambda\mathbf{I} + (1-\lambda)\mathbf{P})\cdot\mathbf{r}^{(g)} + \zeta\cdot\mathbf{s} \tag{7}$$

where $\mathbf{I}$ is the identity matrix.[6] Rewrite it to relate to the traditional PageRank.

$$\mathbf{r}^{(g)} = \frac{(1-\zeta)\cdot(1-\lambda)}{1-\lambda+\zeta\lambda}\mathbf{P}\cdot\mathbf{r}^{(g)} + \frac{\zeta}{1-\lambda+\zeta\lambda}\cdot\mathbf{s} \tag{8}$$

So $\mathbf{r}^{(g)}$ for ζ is the same as $\mathbf{r}^{(t)}$ for $\frac{\zeta}{1-\lambda+\zeta\lambda}$ ($\mathbf{r}^{(g)}(\mathbf{P},\mathbf{s},\zeta,\lambda) = \mathbf{r}^{(t)}(\mathbf{P},\mathbf{s},\frac{\zeta}{1-\lambda+\zeta\lambda})$) Therefore

Theorem 6. *For the preferential generalized lazy personalized PageRank we have*

$$p_o\zeta \le (1-\lambda)(1-\zeta)\frac{|\partial(U)|}{Vol(U)}$$

Theorem 7. *For the uniform generalized lazy personalized PageRank we have*

$$p_o\zeta \le (1-\lambda)(1-\zeta)\frac{|\partial(U)|}{|U|\min_{k\in U} deg(k)}$$

4 Bipartite PageRank

Some non-directed graphs occurring e.g., in social networks are in a natural way bipartite graphs. That is there exist nodes of two modalities, and meaningful links may occur only between nodes of distinct modalities (e.g., clients and items purchased by them). Literature exists already for such networks attempting to adapt PageRank to the specific nature of bipartite graphs, e.g., [7]. Regrettably, no generalization of Theorem 2 was formulated. The one seemingly obvious choice would be to use the traditional PageRank like it was done in papers [2,13]. However, this would be conceptually wrong because the nature of the super-node would cause authority flowing between nodes of the same modality, which is prohibited by the definition of these networks. Therefore in this paper, we intend to close this conceptual gap using Bipartite PageRank concept created in our former paper [10] and will extend the Theorem 2 to this case.

So let us consider the flow of authority in a bipartite network with two distinct super-nodes: one collecting the authority from items and passing them to clients, and the other the authority from clients and passing them to items.

$$\mathbf{r}^p = (1-\zeta^{kp})\cdot\mathbf{P}^{kp}\cdot\mathbf{r}^k + \zeta^{kp}\cdot\mathbf{s}^p \tag{9}$$

$$\mathbf{r}^k = (1-\zeta^{pk})\cdot\mathbf{P}^{pk}\cdot\mathbf{r}^p + \zeta^{pk}\cdot\mathbf{s}^k \tag{10}$$

The following notation is used in these formulas

---

[6] We will denote the solution to the Eq. (7) with $\mathbf{r}^{(g)}(\mathbf{P},\mathbf{s},\zeta,\lambda)$.

- $\mathbf{r}^p$, $\mathbf{r}^k$, $\mathbf{s}^p$, and $\mathbf{s}^k$ are stochastic vectors, i.e. the non-negative elements of these vectors sum to 1;
- the elements of matrix $\mathbf{P}^{kp}$ are: if there is a link from page j in the set of *Clients* to a page i in the set of *Items*, then $p_{ij}^{kp} = \frac{1}{outdeg(j)}$, otherwise $p_{ij}^{kp} = 0$;
- the elements of matrix $\mathbf{P}^{pk}$ are: if there is a link from page j in the set of *Items* to page i in the set of *Clients*, then $p_{ij}^{pk} = \frac{1}{outdeg(j)}$, otherwise $p_{ij}^{pk} = 0$;
- $\zeta^{kp} \in [0,1]$ is the boring factor when jumping from *Clients* to *Items*;
- $\zeta^{pk} \in [0,1]$ is the boring factor when jumping from Items to Clients.

Definition 1. *The solutions $\mathbf{r}^p$ and $\mathbf{r}^k$ of the equation system (9) and (10) will be called item-oriented and client-oriented bipartite PageRanks, resp.*

Let us assume first that $\zeta^{pk} = \zeta^{kp} = 0$ i.e. that the super-nodes have no impact. Let $K = \sum_{j \in Clients} outdeg(j) = \sum_{j \in Items} outdeg(j)$ mean the number of edges leaving one of the modalities. Then for any $j \in Clients$ we have $r_j^k = \frac{outdeg(j)}{K}$, and for any $j \in Items$ we get $r_j^p = \frac{outdeg(j)}{K}$. Because the same amount of $\frac{1}{K}$ authority is passed through each channel, within each bidirectional link the amounts passed cancel out each other. So the $\mathbf{r}$'s defined this way are a fix-point (and solution) of the Eqs. (9) and (10). For the other extreme, when $\zeta^{kp} = \zeta^{pk} = 1$ one obtains, that $\mathbf{r}^p = \mathbf{s}^p$, $\mathbf{r}^k = \mathbf{s}^k$.

In analogy to the traditional PageRank let us note at this point that for $\zeta^{kp}, \zeta^{pk} > 0$ the "fan"-nodes of both the modalities (the sets of them being denoted with U^p for items and U^k for clients), will obtain in each time step from the super-nodes the amount of authority equal to ζ^{pk} for clients and ζ^{kp} for items, resp. Let us now think about a fan of the group of nodes U^p, U^k who jumps uniformly, Assume further that at the moment t we have the following state of authority distribution: node j contains $r_j^k(t) = \frac{1}{|U^k|}, r_j^p(t) = \frac{1}{|U^p|}$ (meaning analogous formulas for r^p and r^k). Let us consider now the moment $t+1$. From the item node j to the first super-node the authority $\zeta^{pk} \frac{1}{|U^p|}$ flows, and into each outgoing link $(1 - \zeta^{pk}) \frac{1}{|U^p|deg(j)}$ is passed. On the other hand the client node c obtains from the same super-node authority $\zeta^{pk} \frac{1}{|U^k|}$, while from link ingoing from j $(1 - \zeta^{pk}) \frac{1}{|U^p|deg(j)}$. The authority from clients to items passes in the very same way.

We have a painful surprise this time. In general, we cannot define a useful state of the authority of nodes, analogous to that of traditional PageRank from Sect. 2, so that in both directions between U^p and U^k nodes the same upper limit of authority would apply. This is due to the fact that in general capacities of U^k and U^p may differ. Therefore a broader generalization is required.

To find such a generalization let us reconsider the way how we can limit the flow of authority in a single channel. The amount of authority passed consists of two parts: a variable one being a share of the authority at the feeding end of the channel and a fixed one coming from a super-node. So, by increasing the variable part, we come to the point that the receiving end gets less authority that was there on the other end of the channel.

Let us seek the amount of authority d such that multiplied by the number of out-links of a sending node will be not lower than the authority of this node and that after the time step its receiving node would have also amount of authority equal or lower than d multiplied by the number of its in-links. That is we want to have that:

$$d \cdot (1 - \zeta^{pk}) + \frac{\zeta^{pk}}{\sum_{v \in U^k} outdeg(v)} \leq d$$

The above relationship corresponds to the situation that on the one hand if a node in *Items* has at most d amount of authority per link, then it sends to a node in *Clients* at most $d \cdot (1 - \zeta^{pk})$ authority via the link. The receiving node j on the other hand, if it belongs to U^k, then it gets additionally from the super-node exactly $\frac{\zeta^{pk}}{|U^k|deg(j)}$ authority per its link. We seek a d such that these two components do not exceed d together.

If we look from the perspective of passing authority from *Clients* to *Items*, then, for similar reasons at the same time we have

$$d \cdot (1 - \zeta^{kp}) + \frac{\zeta^{kp}}{|U^p|deg(j)} \leq d$$

This implies immediately, that

$$d \geq \frac{1}{|U^k| \min_{j \in U^k} deg(j)} \text{ and } d \geq \frac{1}{|U^p| \min_{j \in U^p} deg(j)}$$

so we come to a satisfactory d when

$$d = \max\left(\frac{1}{|U^k| \min_{j \in U^k} deg(j)}, \frac{1}{|U^p| \min_{j \in U^p} deg(j)}\right)$$

$$= \frac{1}{\min(|U^k| \min_{j \in U^k} deg(j), |U^p| \min_{j \in U^p} deg(j))}$$

Now we are ready to formulate a theorem for bipartite PageRank analogous to the preceding Theorem 2.

Theorem 8. *For the uniform personalized bipartite PageRank we have*

$$p_{k,o} \zeta^{kp} \leq \frac{(1 - \zeta^{pk}) \partial(\frac{U^p}{U^k})}{\min(|U^k| \min_{j \in U^k} deg(j), |U^p| \min_{j \in U^p} deg(j))}$$

and

$$p_{p,o} \zeta^{pk} \leq \frac{(1 - \zeta^{kp}) \partial(\frac{U^k}{U^p})}{\min(|U^k| \min_{j \in U^k} deg(j), |U^p| \min_{j \in U^p} deg(j))}$$

244   R. A. Kłopotek and M. A. Kłopotek

where

- $p_{k,o}$ *is the sum of authorities from the set* $Clients \backslash U^k$,
- $p_{p,o}$ *is the sum of authorities from the set* $Items \backslash U^p$,
- $\partial(\frac{U^k}{U^p})$ *is the set of edges outgoing from* U_k *into nodes from* $Items - U_p$ *(that is "fan's border" of* U^k*)*,
- $\partial(\frac{U^p}{U^k})$ *is the set of edges outgoing from* U^p *into nodes from* $Clients \backslash U^k$ *(that is "fan's border" of* U^p*)*,

$\square$

The proof is analogous as in case of classical PageRank, using now the quantity d we have just introduced.

Proof. Let us notice first that, due to the closed loop of authority circulation, the amount of authority flowing into U^k from the nodes belonging to the set $\overline{U^p} = Items \backslash U^p$ must be identical with the amount flowing out of U^p to the nodes in $\overline{U^k}$. The same holds when we exchange the indices $p < - > k$.

But from U^p only that portion of authority flows out to $\overline{U^k}$ that flows out through the boundary of U^p because no authority leaves the tandem U^p, U^k via super-nodes (it returns from there immediately). As the amount $d|\partial(\frac{U^p}{U^k})|$ leaves at most the U^p not going into U^k, then

$$p_{k,o}\zeta^{kp} \leq d(1 - \zeta^{pk})\partial(\frac{U^p}{U^k}) = \frac{(1 - \zeta^{pk})\partial(\frac{U^p}{U^k})}{min(|U^k|min_{j \in U^k}deg(j), |U^p|min_{j \in U^p}deg(j))}$$

The convergence can be verified in an analogous way as done for the HITS (consult e.g., [12, Ch. 11]).

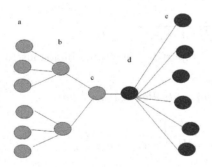

Fig. 1. Unoriented tree-like network

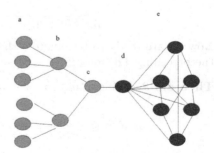

Fig. 2. Unoriented complex network

5   Experimental Exploration of the Limits

With the established limits, we can pose the question how tight the limits are or rather whether we can construct networks for which the limits are approached sufficiently close.

For this purpose we will use a family of networks depicted in Figs. 1 and 2. Each network is divided into three *zones* of nodes. Zones d and e belong to the set of fan-nodes.

Zones a, b, c are not fan-sets. There is only one node in zones c and d so that the edge connecting d to c is the channel through which the authority flows out

Table 1. PageRanks for network Fig. 1. Boring factor = 0.1

	Zone a	Zone b	Zone c	Zone d	Zone e
Traditional uniform	0.012479	0.055464	0.072565	0.370274	0.061892
Traditional preferential	0.013019	0.057864	0.075705	0.386296	0.057358
	Outflow	Limit	Rel.left		
Traditional uniform	0.025837	0.128571	0.799		
Traditional preferential	0.026955	0.069230	0.610		

Table 2. PageRanks for network Fig. 2. Boring factor = 0.1

	Zone a	Zone b	Zone c	Zone d	Zone e
Traditional uniform	0.006094806	0.027088026	0.0354401	0.1808376	0.1154962
Traditional preferential	0.006306085	0.028027043	0.0366687	0.1871064	0.1137223
	Outflow	Limit	Rel.left		
Traditional uniform	0.0126185	0.032142	0.6074242		
Traditional preferential	0.013055	0.029032	0.5502957		

Table 3. PageRanks for enlarged network Fig. 2 by factor in the first column. Boring factor = 0.1. Traditional PageRank with preferential authority re-distribution.

Factor	Zone a	Zone b	Zone c	Zone d	Zone e
10	1.737833e−05	7.723703e−05	7.073624e−04	2.438616e−02	1.620532e−02
100	1.969998e−08	8.755548e−08	7.674967e−06	2.494130e−03	1.662448e−03
1000	1.995495e−11	8.868865e−11	7.739489e−08	2.499416e−04	1.666249e−04
10000	1.998069e−14	8.880307e−14	7.745988e−10	2.499942e−05	1.666625e−05
100000	1.998323e−17	8.881436e−17	7.746628e−12	2.499994e−06	1.666662e−06
Factor	Outflow	Limit	Rel.left		
10	0.0003294802	0.0003657049979	0.0990544634		
100	3.700605208e−06	3.740632831e−06	0.01070076246		
1000	3.745018664e−08	3.749062578e−08	0.0010786466		
10000	3.749501576e−10	3.749906250e−10	0.000107915		
100000	3.749943936e−12	3.749990625e−12	1.245027547e−05		

Table 4. PageRanks for enlarged network Fig. 2 by factor in the first column. Boring factor = 0.1. Traditional PageRank with uniform authority re-distribution.

Factor	Zone a	Zone b	Zone c	Zone d	Zone e
10	1.679439e−05	7.464174e−05	6.835939e−04	2.356675e−02	1.622082e−02
100	1.904272e−08	8.463432e−08	7.418903e−06	2.410918e−03	1.662589e−03
1000	1.928972e−11	8.573209e−11	7.481482e−08	2.416095e−04	1.666263e−04
10000	1.931466e−14	8.584294e−14	7.487786e−10	2.416610e−05	1.666626e−05
100000	1.931710e−17	8.585376e−17	7.488401e−12	2.416661e−06	1.666663e−06
1000000	1.931896e−20	8.586206e−20	7.488419e−14	2.416666e−07	1.666666e−07

Factor	Outflow	Limit	Rel.left		
10	0.0003184092239	0.0003688524590	0.1367572		
100	3.577140044e−06	3.743760399e−06	0.04450614810		
1000	3.620173279e−08	3.749375104e−08	0.03445956209		
10000	3.624516929e−10	3.749937501e−10	0.03344604329		
100000	3.624940904e−12	3.749993750e−12	0.033347481127		
1000000	3.625220796e−14	3.74999937e−14	0.033274293139		

Table 5. PageRanks for densified network from last line of previous table - the zone e node degrees as in the first column

e node deg.	Zone a	Zone b	Zone c	Zone d	Zone e
5000000	1.572210e−20	6.987602e−20	6.094048e−14	1.966666e−07	1.666666e−07
5500000	1.440820e−20	6.403644e−20	5.585813e−14	1.803030e−07	1.666666e−07
5900000	1.352272e−20	6.010099e−20	5.242307e−14	1.692090e−07	1.666666e−07
5990000	1.333886e−20	5.928383e−20	5.171155e−14	1.669171e−07	1.666666e−07
5999000	1.331915e−20	5.919623e−20	5.163832e−14	1.666916e−07	1.666666e−07
5999900	1.332161e−20	5.920716e−20	5.163986e−14	1.666691e−07	1.666666e−07

e node deg.	Outflow	Limit	Rel.left		
5000000	2.950251336e−14	2.999999500e−14	0.01658272402		
5500000	2.703801851e−14	2.727272272e−14	0.0086058227330		
5900000	2.537613978e−14	2.542372457e−14	0.00187166895		
5990000	2.503123889e−14	2.504173205e−14	0.00041902692587		
5999000	2.4994569e−14	2.500416319e−14	0.0003836900900		
5999900	2.49983829e−14	2.500041250e−14	8.117929671e−05		

of the fan-node set and we seek the upper limit of authority lost via this link. The zones are symmetrically constructed. The number of nodes in a is a multiple of the number of nodes in b. All nodes in e are connected to d, and otherwise, they constitute a regular subgraph. In Fig. 1 this subgraph is of degree zero, and in Fig. 2 it is of degree 3. Because of symmetry, the PageRanks in each of the zones are identical.

Table 1 shows the PageRanks for the graph in Fig. 1. Table 2 shows the PageRanks for the graph in Fig. 2. In each table the columns *zone a,...,zone e* show the PageRank attained by each node in the respective zone. *outflow* column shows the amount of authority flowing out from the fan-set of nodes to the rest of the network. *limit* column is the upper limit derived theoretically in the

Table 6. PageRanks for various network structures with the same upper limit of authority passing - the preferential redistribution. Zone a and b both 60000 nodes each.

e node deg./count	Zone a	Zone b	Zone c	Zone d	Zone e
511/1024	6.092727e−11	1.353939e−10	5.370716e−06	1.953285e−03	9.746382e−04
255/2048	6.095403e−11	1.354534e−10	5.373075e−06	3.906379e−03	4.863655e−04
127/4096	6.096742e−11	1.354832e−10	5.374255e−06	7.812567e−03	2.422291e−04
63/8192	6.097412e−11	1.354980e−10	5.374845e−06	1.562494e−02	1.201609e−04
31/16384	6.097746e−11	1.355055e−10	5.375140e−06	3.124970e−02	5.912678e−05
15/32768	6.097914e−11	1.355092e−10	5.375287e−06	6.249920e−02	2.860973e−05
7/65536	6.097997e−11	1.355110e−10	5.375361e−06	1.249982e−01	1.335121e−05
3/131072	6.098038e−11	1.355119e−10	5.375397e−06	2.499961e−01	5.721944e−06
1/262144	6.098056e−11	1.355124e−10	5.375413e−06	4.999919e−01	1.907314e−06

e node deg./count	Outflow	Limit	Rel.left		
511/1024	1.714998913e−06	1.716610495e−06	0.0009388162095		
255/2048	1.715752081e−06	1.716610495e−06	0.0005000635487		
127/4096	1.716128933e−06	1.716610495e−06	0.0002805306660		
63/8192	1.71631741e−06	1.716610495e−06	0.0001707321858		
31/16384	1.716411644e−06	1.716610495e−06	0.0001158392913		
15/32768	1.716458707e−06	1.716610495e−06	8.842327961e−05		
7/65536	1.716482125e−06	1.716610495e−06	7.478124133e−05		
3/131072	1.716493600e−06	1.716610495e−06	6.809630427e−05		
1/262144	1.716498849e−06	1.716610495e−06	6.503878422e−05		

previous sections for the respective case. *rel.left* is computed as 1-*outflow/limit*. The lower the value, the closer the actual outflow to the theoretical limit.

The obvious tendency to keep authority is observed when the network of connections is densified between fan nodes. Also, the outflow of authority gets closer to the theoretical bound.

How close can it go? In Tables 3 and 4 we increase by the factor of 10,100 etc. the number of nodes in zones *a*, *b* and *e* and also the number of connections between the nodes in zone *e* (enlarging the network of Fig. 2, results in Table 5).

We see that in case of preferential attachment, we quickly approach the bounds. In case of uniform authority redistribution, we get a stabilization. The situation changes for the uniform case, however, if we densify the connections in zone *e*. For the network of the last line, we increase the density of connections in zone *e*. Last not least, let us observe that the relationship between the upper limit and the actual amount of authority passed is a function of the structure of the network. In the Tables 6 (for preferential redistribution) and 7 (for uniform redistribution) we see this effect. For preferential redistribution, we see that the lower degrees the nodes are, the bigger part of the authority is flowing out. For the uniform redistribution, the tendency is in the other direction.

Table 7. PageRanks for various network structures with the same upper limit of authority passing - the uniform redistribution Zone a and b both 60000 nodes each.

e node deg./count	Zone a	Zone b	Zone c	Zone d	Zone e
4/131071	4.480253e−11	9.956117e−11	3.949326e−06	1.836718e−01	6.228041e−06
8/65535	4.933356e−11	1.096301e−10	4.348734e−06	1.011236e−01	1.371576e−05
16/32767	5.196287e−11	1.154730e−10	4.580507e−06	5.325655e−02	2.889275e−05
32/16383	5.339301e−11	1.186511e−10	4.706573e−06	2.736115e−02	5.936787e−05
64/8191	5.416866e−11	1.203748e−10	4.774947e−06	1.387931e−02	1.203889e−04
128/4095	5.468880e−11	1.215307e−10	4.820796e−06	7.006293e−03	2.424855e−04
256/2047	5.545008e−11	1.232224e−10	4.887903e−06	3.551911e−03	4.867770e−04
512/1023	5.783015e−11	1.285114e−10	5.097705e−06	1.852184e−03	9.756907e−04

e node deg./count	Outflow	Limit	Rel.left		
4/131071	1.261114759e−06	1.716613769e−06	0.2653474055		
8/65535	1.388655573e−06	1.716613769e−06	0.1910494961		
16/ 32767	1.462666077e−06	1.716613769e−06	0.147935252		
32/16383	1.502922183e−06	1.716613769e−06	0.1244843712		
64/8191	1.524755444e−06	1.716613769e−06	0.1117655749		
128/4095	1.539396343e−06	1.716613769e−06	0.1032366329		
256/2047	1.560825131e−06	1.716613769e−06	0.09075345911		
512/1023	1.627819998e−06	1.716613769e−06	0.05172612086		

6   Concluding Remarks

In this paper, we have proposed limits for the flow of authority in ordinary unoriented and in the bipartite graph under uniform random jumps. We have empirically demonstrated tightness of some of these limits.

The obtained limits can be used for example, when verifying the validity of clusters in such graphs. It is quite common to assume that the better the cluster, the less authority flows out of it when treating the cluster as the set on which a fan concentrates while a personalized PageRank is computed. The theorem says that the outgoing authority has a natural upper limit dropping with the growth of the size of the sub-network so that the outgoing authority cluster validity criterion cannot be used because it will generate meaningless large clusters. So a proper validity criterion should make a correction related to the established limits in order to be of practical use.

As a further research direction, it is obvious that finding tighter limits are needed. This would improve the evaluation of e.g., cluster quality.

References

1. Allesina, S., Pascual, M.: Googling food webs: can an eigenvector measure species' importance for coextinctions? PLoS Comput. Biol. **5**, e1000494 (2009)
2. Bauckhage, C.: Image tagging using PageRank over bipartite graphs. In: Rigoll, G. (ed.) DAGM 2008. LNCS, vol. 5096, pp. 426–435. Springer, Heidelberg (2008). https://doi.org/10.1007/978-3-540-69321-5_43
3. Berkhin, P.: A survey on PageRank computing. Internet Math. **2**, 73–120 (2005)

4. Chung, F.: PageRank as a discrete green's function. In: Ji, L. (ed.) Geometry and Analysis, I, Advanced Lectures in Mathematics (ALM), vol. 17, pp. 285–302. International Press of Boston, 15 July 2011
5. Chung, F., Zhao, W.: PageRank and random walks on graphs (2008). http://www.math.ucsd.edu/~fan/wp/lov.pdf
6. De Domenico, M., Sole-Ribalta, A., Omodei, E., Gomez, S., Arenas, A.: Ranking in interconnected multilayer networks reveals versatile nodes. Nat. Commun. **6**, 6868 (2015)
7. Deng, H., Lyu, M.R., King, I.: A generalized co-hits algorithm and its application to bipartite graphs. In: Proceedings of the 15th ACM SIGKDD, pp. 239–248, Paris (2009)
8. Dominguez-Garcia, V., Munoz, M.A.: Ranking species in mutualistic networks. Sci. Rep. **5**, 8182 (2015)
9. He, X., Gao, M., Kan, M.Y., Wang, D.: Birank: towards ranking on bipartite graphs. IEEE Trans. Knowl. Data Eng. **29**(1), 57–71 (2017). https://doi.org/10.1109/TKDE.2016.2611584
10. Kłopotek, M.A., Wierzchoń, S.T., Kłopotek, R.A., Kłopotek, E.A.: Network capacity bound for personalized bipartite PageRank. In: Matwin, S., Mielniczuk, J. (eds.) Challenges in Computational Statistics and Data Mining. SCI, vol. 605, pp. 189–204. Springer, Cham (2016). https://doi.org/10.1007/978-3-319-18781-5_11
11. Langville, A.N.: An annotated bibliography of papers about Markov chains and information retrieval (2005). http://www.cofc.edu/~langvillea/bibtexpractice.pdf
12. Langville, A.N., Meyer, C.D.: Google's PageRank and Beyond: The Science of Search Engine Rankings. Princeton University Press, Princeton (2006)
13. Link, S.: Eigenvalue-based bipartite ranking. Bachelorarbeit/bachelor thesis (2011)
14. Liu, C., Tang, L., Shan, W.: An extended hits algorithm on bipartite network for features extraction of online customer reviews. Sustain. MDPI Open Access J. **5**(10), 1–15 (2018)
15. Page, L., Brin, S., Motwani, R., Winograd, T.: The PageRank citation ranking: bringing order to the web. Technical Report 1999-66, Stanford InfoLab, November 1999. http://ilpubs.stanford.edu:8090/422/
16. Tacchella, A., Cristelli, M., Caldarelli, G., Gabrielli, A., Pietronero, L.: A new metrics for countries' fitness and products' complexity. Sci. Rep. **2**, 723 (2012)

RecKGC: Integrating Recommendation with Knowledge Graph Completion

Jingwei Ma[1(✉)], Mingyang Zhong[2], Jiahui Wen[3], Weitong Chen[1],
Xiaofang Zhou[1], and Xue Li[1,4]

[1] The University of Queensland, Brisbane, Australia
{jingwei.ma,w.chen9}@uq.edu.au
{zxf,xueli}@itee.uq.edu.au
[2] Central Queensland University, Brisbane, Australia
m.zhong@cqu.edu.au
[3] National University of Defense Technology, Changsha, China
wen_jiahui@outlook.com
[4] Neusoft Institute of Information, Dalian, China

Abstract. Both recommender systems and knowledge graphs can provide overall and detailed views on datasets, and each of them has been a hot research domain by itself. However, recommending items with a pre-constructed knowledge graph or without one often limits the recommendation performance. Similarly, constructing and completing a knowledge graph without a target is insufficient for applications, such as recommendation. In this paper, we address the problems of recommendation together with knowledge graph completion by a novel model named RecKGC that generates a completed knowledge graph and recommends items for users simultaneously. Comprehensive representations of users, items and interactions/relations are learned in each respective domain, such as our attentive embeddings that integrate tuples in a knowledge graph for recommendation and our high-level interaction representations of entities and relations for knowledge graph completion. We join the tasks of recommendation and knowledge graph completion by sharing the comprehensive representations. As a result, the performance of recommendation and knowledge graph completion are mutually enhanced, which means that the recommendation is getting more effective while the knowledge graph is getting more informative. Experiments validate the effectiveness of the proposed model on both tasks.

Keywords: Big data · Visualization · Information retrieval

1 Introduction

In many applications, the data sources, such as social networks, on-line video platforms and public health systems, contain a large number and various types of individual entities interacting with each other. Many approaches have been proposed toward a better understanding of data sources, among which are two

© Springer Nature Switzerland AG 2019
J. Li et al. (Eds.): ADMA 2019, LNAI 11888, pp. 250–265, 2019.
https://doi.org/10.1007/978-3-030-35231-8_18

prominent ones: *recommender system* (RS) and *knowledge graph* (KG). On one hand, RS evaluates entities of datasets based on some scoring functions, such as ranking and similarity, that mathematically shows the characteristics of entities. On the other hand, KG collects triples of facts that denote entities and the semantic relation among them. However, applying either of them over a dataset often leads to incomplete or sometimes rather biased results. For example, the accuracy of recommending videos based on selected modalities, such as item profile [14,22], is usually limited. Alternatively, completing KG can be further enhanced by considering target applications, such as recommendation. Integrating the two techniques leads to more effective and comprehensible results for both of them.

In RS domain, many previous works have been proposed to model user-item interactions. Collaborative Filtering, as one of the conventional and widely-applied methods, assumes that users with similar preferences in the past are supposed to make similar choices in the future [11]. However, this type of methods suffer from data sparseness and cold start problems [29] (***Problem 1: Sparseness***). Existing works, to alleviate *Problem 1*, incorporate additional information such as social relation for point-of-interest recommendation [27], and text and image for video recommendation [10]. However, the requirement of additional information limits the applicability of these methods, as the information is usually difficult to acquire in real applications (***Problem 2: Applicability_RS***). Thus, other works [8] investigate the implicit information carried by one dataset, and extract features/embeddings/representations that capture latent semantics among the users and the items in the dataset for recommendation. However, the features in these method are empirically selected, which may potentially limit the recommendation performance (***Problem 3: Empiricism***).

KG, as one of the most effective data modelling techniques, has been spotlighted in many applications, such as question answering [12] and information retrieval [19]. KG is naturally a solution for the aforementioned problems in RS. Few works have applied KG to recommendation [25,28]. For example, Wang et al. [25] extend users' potential interests by propagating user preferences along links in the KG. However, these KG based recommenders rely on the quality of the pre-defined KG that are simply constructed based on the dataset (***Problem 4: Quality***). To cope with this problem, many knowledge graph completion (KGC) models have been proposed for KGC tasks including link prediction and triple classification, such as traditional translational models (e.g. TransE [1]) and compositional models using a tensor/matrix product (e.g. ProjE [23]). However, these completed KGs that are designed for general purposes often limit the performance on specific tasks (***Problem 5: Applicability_KG***). For example, the Google Knowledge Graph[1] has been constructed and managed for many practical tasks, such as Google search, in which more than 70 billion facts are available. However, the performance of applying this general KG on health-related applications was limited, thus in 2015, Google announced the Google Health Knowledge

---

[1] https://developers.google.com/knowledge-graph/.

Graph for health-related applications [21]. Furthermore, there are still a lot of missing and incorrect facts even in manually constructed KGs [16].

In this paper, to approach all the aforementioned research problems, we propose RecKGC, a novel model that seamlessly integrates recommendation and KGC by learning and sharing comprehensive representations. Given a dataset, our model directly generates a completed KG for recommendation as well as recommends items to target users. In recommendation domain, we leverage a KG in which items are associated with various entities, and generate attentive embeddings of items to discriminate the importance of different characteristics of items among entities for recommendation. As a KG has been incorporated in recommendation which means various types of entities are modelled, it naturally mitigates **Problem 1** and **Problem 2**. Furthermore, rather than empirically selecting features, we jointly embed different types of entities to address **Problem 3**. In KGC domain, we extract high-level representations of entities and relations in a KG, which defers the interaction among different dimensions and improves the quality of the generated KG for **Problem 4**. In addition, learning shared embeddings further enhances the quality and the applicability of the KG for recommendation, which addresses both **Problem 4** and **Problem 5**. Our study demonstrates that RecKGC advances the effectiveness of both tasks, compared with the state-of-the-art methods. The main contributions of this work are listed below:

- We propose a novel RecKGC model in which recommendation and KGC are seamlessly integrated. To the best of our knowledge, our work is the first that makes use of recommendation and KGC simultaneously for both tasks.
- We propose attentive embeddings that integrate tuples in a KG for recommendation. We validate that recommendation and KGC can mutually enhance each other.
- We perform a thorough evaluation on real datasets in comparison with the state-of-the-art methods, and the experimental results demonstrate the power of RecKGC.

2   Related Work

In recommendation domain, deep learning techniques have been widely applied in recent years. Most of them employ multi-layer neural networks to model deep user-item interactions. For example, He et al. [8] combine generalize matrix factorization and multi-layer perceptron to model user-item similarities, instead of using the inner product of users and items. The non-linear transformations in the perceptron is demonstrated to be effective for capturing user preferences. Cheng et al. [3] leverage item contexts (i.e. user historical ratings) to compensate the interaction function, and jointly model item-item similarities and recommend items based on these historical ratings. However, one major drawback of those models is that they mainly rely on the interaction data and suffer from data sparseness (*Problem 1*). Existing works alleviate this drawback by incorporating additional information from different modalities, and this auxiliary information discriminates the interests/characteristics of users/items. For example, Ma et al. [13] extract features from different modalities individually, such as user/item embeddings and visual/textual features of micro-videos, and then latent categories of micro-videos are learned based on the visual and textual features that are empirically selected (*Problem 3*). Furthermore, information of many modalities can be missing, such as the historical ratings in [3] and the textual information of micro-videos in [13] that is users' descriptions/comments on micro-videos (*Problem 2*).

In KGC domain, few recent KGC models exploit rich context information associated with facts to improve the expressiveness of embeddings. For example, MPME [2] embeds textual information, entities and relations into a same vector space, while CACL [18] utilizes k-hop neighbourhood information to map entities and relations to a linear space. However, as these models are not designed for any target application, when applying KGs constructed by these models, the performance of the applications can be limited (*Problem 5*). In other words, these KGC models use cross validation and statistical metrics to evaluate the quality of the completed KGs, but for unseen entities and relations, they are hard for evaluation.

3   Preliminaries

As for recommendation, we denote a user set as $U = \{u_1, u_2, \cdots, u_m\}$ and an item set as $V = \{v_1, v_2, \cdots, v_n\}$, where m and n are the number of users and items, respectively. Interactions between users and items can be reflected by rating behaviours, resulting a rating matrix $\boldsymbol{R} \in \mathbb{R}^{m \times n}$. Each element R_{ij} in $\mathbf{R}$ indicates the interaction between the user u_i and the item v_j, representing the user's explicit (e.g. 5-star rating) or implicit preference over the item. In this work, we focus on user's implicit feedback on items, and predict the interactions (e.g. viewing) between users and items.

Beside the rating matrix, we integrate a KG $G = (E, R)$ that encodes the structural information of entities and relations in a dataset, where $E = \{e_1, e_2, \cdots, e_{|E|}\}$ is the entity set and R is the relation set. The topology of a KG can be representation by a set of triples $T \subset E \times R \times E$, and a triple is denoted as (e_h, r, e_t), where e_h and e_t are two linked head and tail entities, and r is the type of link between them. The task of knowledge graph completion is to find missing but valid triples.

Given a $\mathbf{R}$ and a G, we aim to jointly predict the missing values in $\mathbf{R}$ and find the valid triples in G. We represent users, items, entities and relations as vectors in a low-dimensional space, and the joint optimization of both recommendation and KGC can be bridged by sharing this embedding space.

3.1   Neural Collaborative Filtering

Latent factor models such as Matrix Factorization embed each user/item into a low-dimensional feature vector, and estimate the rating score of a user over an item with the inner product of their respective latent vectors. Recently, many works such as Neural Collaborative Filtering [8] propose to replace the inner product with multiple-layer neural networks for capturing complex user-item interactions. Formally, assume $\mathbf{u}_i$ and $\mathbf{v}_j$ are the embeddings of the user u_i and the item v_j respectively, and then the corresponding estimated rating score $\hat{R}_{ij}$ can be calculated as follows:

$$
\begin{aligned}
\hat{R}_{ij} &= sigmoid(\mathbf{w}_{uv}^T \mathbf{h}_{ij} + b_{uv}) \\
\mathbf{h}_{ij} &= \phi_L(...\phi_2(\phi_1(\mathbf{z}_0))...) \\
\phi_l &= \sigma_l(\mathbf{W}_l^T \mathbf{z}_{l-1} + \mathbf{b}_l), \quad l \in [1, L] \\
\mathbf{z}_0 &= [\mathbf{u}_i; \mathbf{v}_j]
\end{aligned}
\tag{1}
$$

where $[;]$ is the concatenation operation. ϕ_l is the l-th layer neural network, and $\sigma_l, \mathbf{W}_l, \mathbf{b}_l$ are the corresponding activation function, weight matrix and bias vector, respectively. $\mathbf{h}_{ij}$ is the deep representation of the $(u_i$-$v_j)$ pair. $sigmoid = \frac{1}{1+exp(-x)}$ is the softmax function parametrized by weight vector w_{uv} and bias term b_{uv}. In this paper, we propose an integrated model for both recommendation and KGC.

4   RecKGC Model

In this section, we describe our proposed model RecKGC for both recommendation and KGC tasks, by which the performance of both tasks are mutually enhanced.

4.1   Knowledge Graph Completion

KGC includes three subtasks, namely head entity prediction (i.e. predict e_h given r, e_t), relation prediction (i.e. predict r given e_h, e_t) and tail entity prediction (i.e. predict e_t given e_h, r). In this work, we focus on tail entity prediction. However, the methodology can be easily extended to relation prediction task by changing the input. We employ neural networks for this task. Specifically, given two input embeddings (e.g. $\mathbf{e}_h, \mathbf{r}$) and a candidate embedding (e.g. $\mathbf{e}_t$), their respective deep representations are obtained through matrix combination operators. The deep representations are interacted with each other in a latent space for predicting the validity of the triple. We define the combination operation as follows:

$$
\begin{aligned}
\mathbf{e}_h \oplus \mathbf{r} &= \mathbf{w}_h \circ \mathbf{e}_h + \mathbf{w}_r \circ \mathbf{r} + \mathbf{b}_{hr} \\
\mathbf{h}_{hr} &= f(\mathbf{e}_h \oplus \mathbf{r})
\end{aligned}
\tag{2}
$$

where $\circ$ is the element-wise product. $\mathbf{w}_h$ and $\mathbf{w}_r$ are the global weight vectors for an head entity e_h and a relation r. $\mathbf{b}_{hr}$ is the combination bias, and f is the activation function (e.g. $tanh$). The element-wise product defers the interaction among different dimensions, as it is unnecessary to have interactions at early stages [23]. Similarly, the deep representation for a candidate entity can be defined:

$$\mathbf{h}_t = f(\mathbf{w}_t \circ \mathbf{r} + \mathbf{b}_t) \tag{3}$$

where $\mathbf{w}_t$ and $\mathbf{b}_t$ are the weight and bias vectors, respectively.

The deep representations are then fed into feedforward neural networks to obtain the high-level interaction representations:

$$\begin{aligned} \mathbf{h}_{hrt} &= \phi_L(...\phi_2(\phi_1(\mathbf{z}_0))...) \\ \phi_l &= \sigma_l(\mathbf{W}_l^T \mathbf{z}_{l-1} + \mathbf{b}_l) \\ \mathbf{z}_0 &= [\mathbf{h}_{hr}; \mathbf{h}_t] \end{aligned} \tag{4}$$

where $[;]$ is the concatenation operation, and ϕ_l is the l-th layer neural network parametrized by activation function σ_l, weight matrix $\mathbf{W}_l$ and bias vector $\mathbf{b}_l$. $\mathbf{h}_{hrt}$ can be viewed as the interaction representation of a tuple, and it can be used to predict the validity of the tuple:

$$\hat{R}_{hrt} = sigmoid(\mathbf{w}_{kgc}^T \mathbf{h}_{hrt} + b_{kgc}) \tag{5}$$

where $\mathbf{w}_{kgc}$ and b_{kgc} are the weight vector and bias term, respectively.

Compared with previous neural models such as [4], we defer the interaction among different dimensions, which is demonstrated to be superior to earlier interactions [23]. Some other works such as [23] define matrix combination operators to combine entities and relations, and calculate the inner product between the combination and candidate embedding for entity prediction. By contrast, we extract high-level representations of two input embeddings and a candidate embedding, and model their deep interactions with neural networks for the prediction task.

4.2   Recommendation with KG

In a KG, an item can be viewed as an entity, and the associated tuples involve other entities that describe the characteristics of the item from different views, and they can be exploited to uncover the true factors underlying user preferences over the item. Taking the tuple *(movie, hasActor, actor)* as an example, a user's interest in the movie can be explained by his favor over the actor. In practice, each item can be associated with numerous entities, and different users could pay attention to different characteristics of an item in the rating process.

To address this problem, we propose an attention mechanism to integrate the tuples in a KG for boosting recommendation performance. Formally, we define the entities associated with an item v_j as $E(j) = \{e | (v_j, r, e) \in \vee (e, r, v_j) \in T\}$, and the attentive embedding of the entities associated with an item can be obtained as follows:

$$\beta_{e_j} = \mathbf{v}^T tanh(\mathbf{w}_e^T \mathbf{e}_j + \mathbf{w}_u^T \mathbf{u}_i + \mathbf{b}); \quad e_j \in E(j)$$

$$\alpha_{e_j} = \frac{exp(\beta_{e_j})}{\sum_{e_j \in E(j)} exp(\beta_{e_j})} \tag{6}$$

$$\mathbf{e}_{v_j}^{u_i} = \sum_{e_j \in E(j)} \alpha_{e_j} \mathbf{e}_j$$

where $\mathbf{e}_j$ is the embedding of e_j, and β_{e_j} is the intermediate scalar measuring the interaction between the user u_i and the entity e_j associated with the item v_j. $\mathbf{w}_e, \mathbf{w}_u$ are the weight matrices and $\mathbf{b}$ is the bias vector, and $\mathbf{v}$ is the parameter vector. α_{e_j} is the softmax normalization of β_{e_j}, and $\mathbf{e}_{v_j}^{u_i}$ is the weighted sum of the entities associated with v_j. Note that, $\mathbf{e}_{v_j}^{u_i}$ attends differently to the associated entities given different users, as users show various interests to different characteristics of an item. In this work, we apply attentive embeddings on items, and it can be similarly extended to users.

By incorporating the knowledge from the KG for recommendation, the estimated rating score $\hat{R}_{ij}$ in Eq. (1) can be re-written as follows:

$$\hat{R}_{ij} = sigmoid(\mathbf{w}_{uv}^T \mathbf{h}_{ij} + \mathbf{w}_{ue}^T \mathbf{h}_{ij}^{ue} + b_{uv})$$
$$\mathbf{h}_{ij}^{ue} = \phi_L(...\phi_2(\phi_1(\mathbf{z}_0^{ue}))...)$$
$$\phi_l = \sigma_l(\mathbf{W}_l^T \mathbf{z}_{l-1} + \mathbf{b}_l), \quad l \in [1, L] \tag{7}$$
$$\mathbf{z}_0^{ue} = [\mathbf{u}_i; \mathbf{e}_{v_j}^{u_i}]$$

where $\mathbf{h}_{ij}^{ue}$ is the hidden representation of the interaction between the user u_i and the entities associated with the item v_j. As shown in Eq. (7), we model both user-item and user-entity interactions. Therefore, an item can be ranked higher in the recommendation list as long as the user preference can be properly captured in any one of the interactions.

4.3 Integrating Recommendation with KGC

To advance both recommendation and KGC, we propose a joint model that addresses the two tasks simultaneously, and its architecture is illustrated in Fig. 1. Recommendation and KGC are assumed to be complimentary with each other by learning comprehensive representations. These representations are learned in each respective domain and serve as auxiliary knowledge to the other. Furthermore, Integrating recommendation with KGC can mitigate data sparseness. As shown in the figure, we joint the tasks of recommendation and KGC by sharing an embedding layer. In each domain, we take a tuple as input ((u_i, v_j) in recommendation and (e_h, r, e_t) in KGC). In recommendation domain, user-item pairs, including the entities associated with the items, are interacted with each other for estimating the rating score, while in KGC domain, deep representations of input and candidate embeddings are extracted independently, and then they

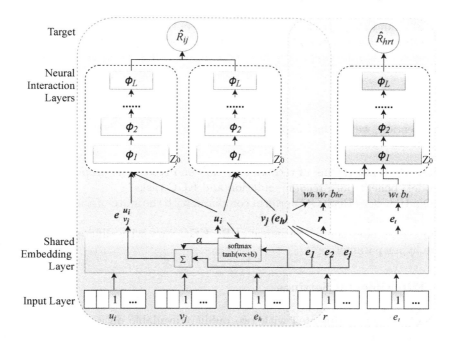

Fig. 1. Architecture of the proposed RecKGC model.

are interacted for predicting the validity of the tuple. The joint objective of the proposed model is defined as follows:

$$
\begin{aligned}
\mathcal{L} &= \mathcal{L}_{rec} + \alpha \mathcal{L}_{kgc} \\
&= \sum_{(u_i,v_j) \in \mathcal{D}_{rec}} [R_{ij} log \hat{R}_{ij} + (1 - R_{ij}) log(1 - \hat{R}_{ij})] \\
&\quad + \alpha \sum_{(e_h,r,e_t) \in \mathcal{D}_{kgc}} [R_{hrt} log \hat{R}_{hrt} + (1 - R_{hrt}) log(1 - \hat{R}_{hrt}))]
\end{aligned}
\tag{8}
$$

where $\mathcal{D}_{rec}$ and $\mathcal{D}_{kgc}$ are the training sets for recommendation and KGC, respectively. α is the trade-off between the two learning objective. Due to the nature of implicit feedback, we adopt negative sampling [15] to constitute the training sets $\mathcal{D}_{rec}$ and $\mathcal{D}_{kgc}$. For a given u_i (or (e_h, r)), we only sample a subset of negative items (or candidate entities) for uniform distribution. Therefore, the learning objectives can be re-written as follows:

$$
\begin{aligned}
\mathcal{L}_{rec} &= - \sum_{(u_i,v_j) \in \mathcal{D}^+_{rec}} \left\{ log \hat{R}_{ij} + \sum_{n} \mathbb{E}_{k \sim P} log(1 - \hat{R}_{ik}) \right\} \\
\mathcal{L}_{kgc} &= - \sum_{(e_h,r,e_t) \in \mathcal{D}^+_{kgc}} \left\{ log \hat{R}_{hrt} + \sum_{n} \mathbb{E}_{k \sim P} log(1 - \hat{R}_{hrk}) \right\}
\end{aligned}
\tag{9}
$$

where $\mathcal{D}^+_{rec}$ and $\mathcal{D}^+_{kgc}$ are the implicit feedbacks of the two tasks, respectively. n is the number of negative samples, and P is the uniform distribution. The objective function can be minimized with stochastic gradient descent or its variants.

5   Experiments

In this section, we conduct experiments with the aim of answering the following research questions:

- RQ1: Does integrating of recommendation and KGC (the proposed RecKGC model) benefit both recommendation and KGC tasks?
- RQ2: How does RecKGC perform compared with the state-of-the-art methods on both tasks?
- RQ3: How does the performance of RecKGC vary with different settings of the hyper-parameters?

5.1   Experimental Settings

Datasets. We experimented with two publicly available datasets: MovieLens[2] and Amazon Music[3]. Following previous work [8], we transformed the explicit rating data in both datasets into implicit data, where each entry is marked as 0 or 1 indicating whether the user has rated the item. We also filtered the datasets to retain users with at least 20 interactions. We consider users, items and their attributes as entities to construct tuples in KGs. For example, a tuple in the KG of MovieLens can be (*"Persuasion"*, *"categorized_into_genre"*, *"Romance"*). To evaluate the performance of both recommendation and KGC, we adopted the widely-used leave-one-out evaluation protocol [8]. Note that, the statistics of the datasets can be referred to [3].

Evaluation Metrics. As for recommendation, since it is time-consuming to rank all items for every user during evaluation, we followed the common strategy [5] that randomly samples 100 items that are not interacted with users. Each test item is ranked among the 100 samples to compute a ranked list. We applied Hit Ratio (HR) and Normalized Discounted Cumulative Gain (NDCG) as metrics [9]. The ranked list is truncated at 10 for both metrics. As for KGC, two widely-used metrics are adopted, including Mean Reciprocal Rank (MRR, the average of the reciprocal ranks of the test entities/relations from all the test triples) and Hits@k. Although Hits@k is equivalent to HR@k, we kept separate notations for differentiating the two tasks. Mean rank (MR) is not used, as it is sensitive to outliers [17].

---

[2] https://grouplens.org/datasets/movieLens/1m/.
[3] http://jmcauley.ucsd.edu/data/amazon/.

Parameter Settings. We implemented our proposed method based on Tensorflow. We randomly sampled one interaction for each user as the validation data, and tuned all the hyper-parameters on it. We sampled four negative instances per positive one, and used the batch size of 256 and the learning rate of 0.001. The size of the last hidden layer is similarly termed as predictive factors, and three hidden layers are employed. We adopted ReLU as the activation function by default if not specified, which is proven to be non-saturated and yields better performance than others (e.g. *tanh* and *sigmoid*) in deep networks [6].

5.2   Performance Comparison (RQ1 and RQ2)

To evaluate the performance of RecKGC in both recommendation and KGC domains, we compare our model with the state-of-the-art methods in both domains. We demonstrate the advantage of integrating recommendation and KGC by comparing RecKGC with two variants: **RecKGC_rec** (this recommendation model utilizes a KG pre-constructed by TransE [1], designed in Subsect. 4.2) and **RecKGC_kgc** (this KGC model does not learn the shared embedding with recommendation, designed in Subsect. 4.1).

- **Compared Recommendation Methods.** We compared our methods with the following methods:

  - BPR [20]: This method applies a pairwise ranking criterion, where the latent factors of users, items, and tags are jointly optimised for recommendation.
  - CDL [24]: This method jointly performs deep representation learning for the content information and collaborative filtering for the ratings matrix.
  - NeuMF [8]: This latent factor model learns a non-linear interaction function via a multi-layer perceptron to predict the final preference score.
  - DELF [3]: This method learns user/item embedding and user-item interaction embedding obtained by an attentive neural network.

As shown in Fig. 2, we compare the proposed models (RecKGC and RecKGC_rec) with the state-of-the-art recommenders in terms of top-k recommendation where k ranges from 1 to 10, and the size of predictive factors is set to 64. First, we can see that RecKGC achieves the best overall performance on both datasets for all the values of k, and improvements become significant for k larger than 3. Specifically, in terms of top-10 recommendation, RecKGC outperforms the best baseline, DELF, with a relative improvement of 6.2% (HR@10) and 3.1% (NDCG@10) on MovieLens, and 5.6% (HR@10) and 4.2% (NDCG@10) on Amazon, respectively. The reason that RecKGC outperforms other baselines is that, we integrate recommendation with KGC by sharing an embedding layer, and the learned comprehensive representations serve as auxiliary knowledge and enhance both tasks. For example, besides users, items and user-item interactions, KG naturally contains additional knowledge such as user's gender and movie's genre in MovieLens. This also validates the contributions of RecKGC to

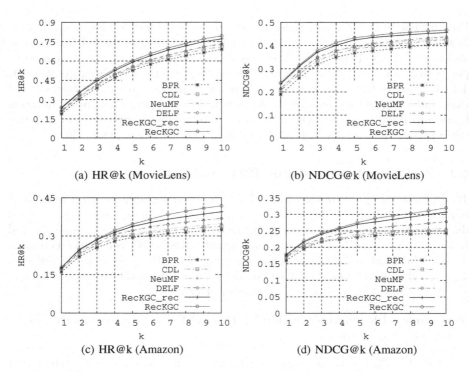

(a) HR@k (MovieLens)   (b) NDCG@k (MovieLens)

(c) HR@k (Amazon)   (d) NDCG@k (Amazon)

Fig. 2. Evaluation of Top-k item recommendation where k ranges from 1 to 10 on the two datasets

Problem 2, *Problem 3* and *Problem 5* described in Sect. 1. Second, DELF outperforms other baselines, such as NeuMF and BPR, as DELF models the characteristics/similarity of users and items besides user-item interactions, which is consistent with previous works [3,8].

Furthermore, RecKGC_rec outperforms other baselines, as we incorporate a pre-constructed KG that models multiple types of entities and relation as a whole, rather than extracting features of each type separately in other baselines such as DELF. However, this KG is generated by TransE based on the datasets. By contrast, the KG in RecKGC is learned and improved along with recommendation, thus integrating recommendation with KGC is able to enhance recommendation.

Compared KGC Methods. We compared our methods with the following methods:

- TransE [1]: This translation based method views valid triples as translation operations of entities for learning the embeddings of entities and relations, then uses the triples with high scores to complete the KG.
- DistMult [26]: This method adopts a multiplication operator among head/tail entity vectors and relation diagonal matrix to define the score function.

- R-GCN [26]: This method replaces random initialization by entity embeddings using neural networks.
- SENN [7]: This method adopts shared embeddings of entities and relations, and unifies the prediction tasks of head entities, relations and tail entities into a neural network based framework.

Table 1. Evaluation of KGC in terms of Hits@10 and MRR

Method	MovieLens		Amazon	
	Hits@10	MRR	Hits@10	MRR
TransE	0.939	0.582	0.862	0.507
DistMult	0.936	0.894	0.913	0.835
R-GCN	0.976	0.893	0.964	0.833
SENN	0.977	0.963	0.964	0.952
RecKGC_kgc	0.985	0.972	0.978	0.964
RecKGC	0.989	0.974	0.982	0.965

As shown in Table 1, we compare our RecKGC and RecKGC_kgc with the state-of-the-art KGC methods, in terms of Hits@10 and MRR. First, RecKGC outperforms all the baselines across all metrics, similar to recommendation, which indicates the advantage of integrating recommendation with KGC. Compared with the best baseline SENN, RecKGC yields a relative improvement of 1.2% (Hits@10) and 1.1% (MRR) on MovieLens, and 1.8% (Hits@10) and 1.3% (MRR) on Amazon, respectively. This also validates the contributions of RecKGC to *Problem 4*. Second, SENN outperforms other baselines, as SENN integrates the three KGC tasks, mentioned in Subsect. 3.1, by sharing the embeddings of them in a fully-connected neural network, which is consistent with previous works [7].

Furthermore, RecKGC_kgc outperforms other baselines. The possible explanation is that extracting high-level representations of the input and the candidate embeddings and modeling their deep interactions with neural networks are effective for KGC. As MovieLens and Amazon datasets are commonly used in recommendation domain, we conduct an other set of experiments to evaluate the performance of our model. However, the datasets used in KGC domain are not suitable for item recommendation, thus we only compare RecKGC_kgc with the baselines on two commonly-used datasets for KGC, including WN18 and FB15k [1]. The statistics of the two datasets can be also referred to [1]. In our experiments on all four datasets, RecKGC_kgc is able to outperform the baselines in terms of Hits@10 and MRR, and we plot the results of MRR as an example, shown in Fig. 3. The performance on FB15k is generally lower than that on other datasets, as the relation set of FB15k is relatively large.

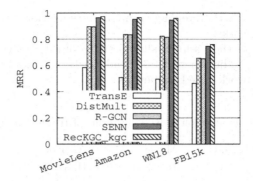

Fig. 3. Evaluation of MRR on 4 datasets

- **Stand-alone v.s. Integration.** Our previous experiments illustrate the effectiveness of the proposed RecKGC in recommendation and KGC domains, separately. In other words, RecKGC that integrates the two techniques is able to advance the performance of both recommendation and KGC.

5.3   Hyper-parameter Study (RQ3)

We first evaluate the performance of our proposed model with respect to different numbers of predictive factors, taking recommendation as example. Table 2 shows that larger numbers of predictive factors yield better performance of HR@10 and NDCG@10, indicating the effectiveness of using factor models for recommendation. Furthermore, the margin of the improvement on Amazon is larger than that on MovieLens when increasing the number of factors, which indicates that RecKGC can handle the data sparseness problem as Amazon dataset is more sparse than MovieLens dataset.

We demonstrate the impact of negative sampling ratio for RecKGC in Fig. 4. One negative sample per positive instance is insufficient while employing more than one negative samples is beneficial to recommendation performance. As for MovieLens, the sampling ratio larger than 4 helps RecKGC to achieve better results. By contrast, the optimal negative sampling ratio for Amazon is between 3 to 8. The results are consistent with previous works [3,8]. As RecKGC outperforms other baselines with respect to all numbers of predictive factors and negative samples, we only plot the results of RecKGC. Similar performance of RecKGC on experiments of KGC are also observed.

Table 2. Performance of RecKGC w.r.t number of predictive factors

Factors	MovieLens		Amazon	
	HR@10	NDCG@10	HR@10	NDCG@10
8	0.763	0.446	0.346	0.288
16	0.772	0.450	0.357	0.291
32	0.786	0.461	0.385	0.299
64	0.794	0.467	0.418	0.32

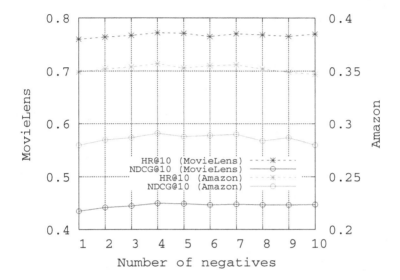

Fig. 4. Performance of RecKGC w.r.t number of negative samples per positive instance (predictive factor = 16)

6   Conclusion

In this paper, we propose a novel RecKGC model that integrates recommendation with KGC. An attention mechanism is proposed to learn attentive embeddings of items for recommendation, while high-level interaction representations of entities and relations are learned for KGC. We jointly model both recommendation and KGC tasks by learning the shared embeddings in neural networks. As a result, the performance of recommendation and KGC are mutually enhanced, which means that the recommendation is getting more effective while the knowledge graph is getting more informative. Thorough evaluation validates the effectiveness of our model.

References

1. Bordes, A., Usunier, N., Garcia-Duran, A., Weston, J., Yakhnenko, O.: Translating embeddings for modeling multi-relational data. In: Proceedings of NIPS, pp. 2787–2795 (2013)
2. Cao, Y., Huang, L., Ji, H., Chen, X., Li, J.: Bridge text and knowledge by learning multi-prototype entity mention embedding. In: Proceedings of ACL, vol. 1, pp. 1623–1633 (2017)
3. Cheng, W., Shen, Y., Zhu, Y., Huang, L.: Delf: a dual-embedding based deep latent factor model for recommendation. In: Proceedings of IJCAI, pp. 3329–3335 (2018)
4. Dong, X., et al.: Knowledge vault: a web-scale approach to probabilistic knowledge fusion. In: Proceedings of SIGKDD (2014)
5. Elkahky, A.M., Song, Y., He, X.: A multi-view deep learning approach for cross domain user modeling in recommendation systems. In: Proceedings of WWW, pp. 278–288 (2015)
6. Glorot, X., Bordes, A., Bengio, Y.: Deep sparse rectifier neural networks. In: Proceedings of AIStats, pp. 315–323 (2011)
7. Guan, S., Jin, X., Wang, Y., Cheng, X.: Shared embedding based neural networks for knowledge graph completion. In: Proceedings of CIKM, pp. 247–256 (2018)
8. He, X., Liao, L., Zhang, H., Nie, L., Hu, X., Chua, T.: Neural collaborative filtering. In: Proceedings of WWW, pp. 173–182 (2017)
9. He, X., Chen, T., Kan, M.Y., Chen, X.: Trirank: review-aware explainable recommendation by modeling aspects. In: Proceedings of CIKM, pp. 1661–1670 (2015)
10. Hu, L., Jian, S., Cao, L., Chen, Q.: Interpretable recommendation via attraction modeling: learning multilevel attractiveness over multimodal movie contents. In: Proceedings of IJCAI, pp. 3400–3406 (2018)
11. Koren, Y., Bell, R.: Advances in collaborative filtering. In: Ricci, F., Rokach, L., Shapira, B. (eds.) Recommender Systems Handbook, pp. 77–118. Springer, Boston, MA (2015). https://doi.org/10.1007/978-1-4899-7637-6_3
12. Lukovnikov, D., Fischer, A., Lehmann, J., Auer, S.: Neural network-based question answering over knowledge graphs on word and character level. In: Proceedings of WWW, pp. 1211–1220 (2017)
13. Ma, J., Li, G., Zhong, M., Zhao, X., Zhu, L., Li, X.: LGA: latent genre aware micro-video recommendation on social media. Multimedia Tools Appl. **77**(3), 2991–3008 (2018)
14. Ma, J., Wen, J., Zhong, M., Chen, W., Zhou, X., Indulska, J.: Multi-source multi-net micro-video recommendation with hidden item category discovery. In: Li, G., Yang, J., Gama, J., Natwichai, J., Tong, Y. (eds.) DASFAA 2019. LNCS, vol. 11447, pp. 384–400. Springer, Cham (2019). https://doi.org/10.1007/978-3-030-18579-4_23
15. Mikolov, T., Sutskever, I., Chen, K., Corrado, G., Dean, J.: Distributed representations of words and phrases and their compositionality. In: Proceedings of NIPS (2013)
16. Min, B., Grishman, R., Wan, L., Wang, C., Gondek, D.: Distant supervision for relation extraction with an incomplete knowledge base. In: Proceedings of NAACL-HLT, pp. 777–782 (2013)
17. Nickel, M., Rosasco, L., Poggio, T., et al.: Holographic embeddings of knowledge graphs. In: Proceedings of AAAI, vol. 2, pp. 3–2 (2016)
18. Oh, B., Seo, S., Lee, K.H.: Knowledge graph completion by context-aware convolutional learning with multi-hop neighborhoods. In: Proceedings of CIKM, pp. 257–266 (2018)

19. Ren, X., et al.: Cotype: joint extraction of typed entities and relations with knowledge bases. In: Proceedings of WWW, pp. 1015–1024 (2017)
20. Rendle, S., Freudenthaler, C., Gantner, Z., Schmidt-Thieme, L.: BPR: bayesian personalized ranking from implicit feedback. In: Proceedings of UAI, pp. 452–461 (2009)
21. Rotmensch, M., Halpern, Y., Tlimat, A., Horng, S., Sontag, D.: Learning a health knowledge graph from electronic medical records. Sci. Rep. **7**(1), 5994 (2017)
22. Sarwar, B., Karypis, G., Konstan, J., Riedl, J.: Item-based collaborative filtering recommendation algorithms. In: Proceedings of WWW, pp. 285–295 (2001)
23. Shi, B., Weninger, T.: ProjE: embedding projection for knowledge graph completion. In: Proceedings of AAAI (2017)
24. Wang, H., Wang, N., Yeung, D.Y.: Collaborative deep learning for recommender systems. In: Proceedings of SIGKDD, pp. 1235–1244 (2015)
25. Wang, H., et al.: Ripplenet: propagating user preferences on the knowledge graph for recommender systems. In: Proceedings of CIKM, pp. 417–426 (2018)
26. Yang, B., Yih, W.T., He, X., Gao, J., Deng, L.: Embedding entities and relations for learning and inference in knowledge bases. arXiv preprint arXiv:1412.6575 (2014)
27. Yang, C., Bai, L., Zhang, C., Yuan, Q., Han, J.: Bridging collaborative filtering and semi-supervised learning: a neural approach for POI recommendation. In: Proceedings of SIGKDD, pp. 1245–1254 (2017)
28. Yu, X., Ma, H., Hsu, B.J.P., Han, J.: On building entity recommender systems using user click log and freebase knowledge. In: Proceedings of WSDM, pp. 263–272 (2014)
29. Zheng, L., Noroozi, V., Yu, P.: Joint deep modeling of users and items using reviews for recommendation. In: WSDM, pp. 425–434 (2017)

PRME-GTS: A New Successive POI Recommendation Model with Temporal and Social Influences

Rubai Mao, Zhe Han, Zitu Liu, Yong Liu$^{(\boxtimes)}$, Xingfeng Lv,
and Ping Xuan

HeiLongJiang University, Harbin, China
liuyong123456@hlju.edu.cn

Abstract. Successive point-of-interest (POI) recommendation is an important research task which can recommend new POIs the user has not visited before. However, the existing researches for new successive POI recommendation ignore the integration of time information and social relations information which can improve the prediction of the system. In order to solve this problem, we propose a new recommendation model called PRME-GTS that incorporates social relations and temporal information in this paper. It can models the relations between users, temporal information, points of interest, and social information, which is based on the framework of pair-wise ranking metric embedding. Experimental results on the two datasets demonstrate that employing temporal information and social relations information can effectively improve the performance of the successive point-of-interest (POI) recommendation.

Keywords: Social networks · POI recommendation · Metric embedding

1 Introduction

With the rapid development of location-based social networks, users can share their location and visit point-of-interest (POI) experience through check-in behavior.

Successive POI recommendations are an extension of traditional POI recommendations and have attracted a lot of attention since their introduction in 2013. Feng et al. [1] first defined the new successive POI recommendation problem and proposed a personalized metric embedding method to model the user's check-in sequence. Cheng et al. [2] solved the successive POI recommendation problem by using Markov chain and local region partitioning. However, all of these methods do not take into account how to incorporate time and social relationships to improve the performance of the new successive POI recommendation model.

In this paper, we will tackle this challenge and try to advance the baseline in POI recommendation method. We propose a new recommendation model named PRME-GTS to recommend the most likely successive POI sequence for users to visit based on the user's current check-in sequence, check-in timestamp and user's social relationship. The experimental results show that the proposed method can effectively carry out

© Springer Nature Switzerland AG 2019
J. Li et al. (Eds.): ADMA 2019, LNAI 11888, pp. 266–274, 2019.
https://doi.org/10.1007/978-3-030-35231-8_19

the state-of-the-art new successive POI recommendation method. The main contributions of this paper are as follows:

1. We model time intervals in a metric embedded based framework, which presents a novel perspective on successive POI recommendation model.
2. We also incorporate the influence of social relationship on POI recommendation, and integrate user's social relationship factors into the framework, which promotes the performance of social prediction of the model.
3. Experimental results in two datasets show that our PRME-GTS model is effective and clearly outperform the state-of-art methods.

2   Related Work

Ye et al. [3] first incorporated the distance factor between geographical locations into the traditional commodity recommendation method. Later, Lian et al. [4] used kernel density estimation to obtain spatial clustering information checked by users and combined it with weight matrix decomposition model. Recently, Ying et al. [5] proposed that PGRank algorithm integrates user's geographic preferences into Bayesian Personalized Ranking (BPR [6]). In addition, some work [7, 8] have studied the influence of social network information on POI recommendation.

Currently, there is but a small portion of research work recommended for successive POI. Snag et al. [9] proposed a probabilistic model to integrate the category transition probability of interest points and the popularity of points-of-interest to solve the continuous POI recommendation problem. However, this method relies on the categories of points-of-interest and personal attributes of users, such as age and home address, which involve personal privacy issues of users and are difficult to obtain. Cheng et al. [2] extended the current mainstream context-aware Markov chain decomposition method, FPMC [10]. Zhao et al. [11] proposed the model named STELLAR, which includes the time feature vector Bayesian personalized sorting, but only considers the time factor in this model. The difference between this paper and the current research work is as follows: (1) Our model incorporate time feature vector into a metric learning based method and add a time constraint term to prevent timing overfitting. (2) The current metric-based learning personalized ranking methods only consider geographic information and does not take into consideration social relations. This paper utilizes social relations and geographic information simultaneously in the metric-based learning personalized ranking method.

3   Model Formulation

3.1   The Definition of New Successive POI Recommendation

Definition 1. Let $\mathcal{U}$ denote a set of users and $\mathcal{L}$ is the location collection. $\mathcal{L}_u$ represents a collection of places that user u has visited. We used $\mathcal{T}$ to represent the user check-in timestamp set, and $\mathcal{L}_u^t$ to represent the user u check-in set in timestamp t, where $t \in \mathcal{T}$. Given a set of check-in sequences for users, $\mathcal{L}_u^1, \ldots, \mathcal{L}_u^t$, and the latitude and longitude of each location, the new successive POI recommendation problem is to recommend a new set of points-of-interest S_u^{t+1} that may be preferred for user u at time $t + 1$. $S_u^{t+1} = \{l \in \mathcal{L} \backslash \mathcal{L}_u\}$. Since it is difficult to predict potential new POIs for users based on sparse historical records, successive new POI recommendations are more challenging than successive POI recommendations.

3.2   Pairwise Ranking Metric Embedding

Metric Embedding Model. We utilize the Markov chain model to learn the transition probability between check-ins and use the Euclidean distance to represent the transition probability between the point pairs l_i and l_j as the form of Eq. 1:

$$\widehat{P}(l_j|l_i) = \frac{e^{-\|X(l_j)-X(l_i)\|^2}}{z(l_i)} \tag{1}$$

Where $\|X(l_j) - X(l_i)\|^2 = \sum_{k=1}^{K} \|X_k(l_i) - X_k(l_j)\|^2$, K is the number of dimension of the latent space and $z(l_i) = \sum_{n=1}^{|L|} e^{-X\|(l_n)-X(l_i)\|^2}$ is a normalization term.

Ranking Based Metric Embedding. Due to the sparseness of user check-in data, we will use the ranking method to learn the transfer relationship between POI and user's position in the potential space. The observed POI is more relevant to the user's current POI than the unobserved POI. For example, given the user's current location l^c, the transition sequence $l^c \rightarrow l_i$ has been observed, and $l^c \rightarrow l_j$ has not been observed, then we rank point l_i before l_j. We represent this sorting relation as:

$$l_i >_{l^c} l_j \Leftrightarrow \widehat{P}(l_i|l^c) > \widehat{P}(l_i|l^c) \tag{2}$$

In this way, the purpose of the POI recommendation becomes to provide the user with a ranking of all check-in locations and recommend the top ranked locations for the user. Since we focus on the ordering between POIs, we only reserve the Euclidean distance $\|X(l_j) - X(l_i)\|^2$ (abbreviated as D_{l_i,l_j}) in the potential space for POI sorting.

$$\begin{aligned} \widehat{P}(l_i|l^c) > \widehat{P}(l_j|l^c) &\Rightarrow e^{-X\|(l_i)-X(l^c)\|^2} > e^{-X\|(l_j)-X(l^c)\|^2} \\ &\Rightarrow X\|(l_i) - X(l^c)\|^2 < X\|(l_j) - X(l^c)\|^2 \\ &\Rightarrow D_{l^c,l_j} - D_{l^c,l_i} > 0 \end{aligned} \tag{3}$$

4 Our Proposed Model

This section we first introduce how to integrate time and social information in the proposed model PRME-GTS, and then give a learning method of model parameters.

4.1 Incorporating Time Influence (PRME-GT)

We divide the 24 h of the day into 4 segments and distinguish whether the day is a working day, so that the time is divided into 8 segments ($|\mathcal{T}| = 2 \times 4$). We define $D_{t,l}^T = ||X^T(t) - X^T(l)||^2$ represents the distance between the timestamp t and the location l in the potential temporal space. Where $X^T(t)$ and $X^T(l)$ are the location in the potential space. The model we define the integration time regular as follows:

$$
Du, t, l^c, l = \begin{cases} D_{u,l}^P & \text{if} \Delta(l, l^c) > \tau \\ w_{l^c,l} \cdot (\alpha D_{u,l}^P + \beta D_{l_i,l_j}^S + (1 - \alpha - \beta)D_{t,l}^T) & \text{otherwise} \end{cases} \tag{4}
$$

Since each timestamp t has its adjacent timestamps t_{-1} and t_{+1}, we define $A_{t,t_{-1}}$ as the similarity of check-in behavior between adjacent timestamps formulated by (5):

$$
A_{t,t_{-1}} = \frac{\sum_{i=1}^{|\mathcal{L}_u|} P(u,t,i).P(u,t_{-1},i)}{\sqrt{\sum_{i=1}^{|\mathcal{L}_u|} P(u,t,i)^2} \cdot \sqrt{\sum_{i=1}^{|\mathcal{L}_u|} P(u,t_{-1},i)^2}} \tag{5}
$$

Where, $P(u,t,i) = \{0,1\}$ indicates whether user u has visited the place i under time t.

4.2 Integrating Social Relationship Information Model (PRME-GS)

Since Ma et al. [12] found that users will have similar sign-in behavior to their friend that in the same social circle, we add a social relationship regular term C_s to the objective function. We define the social relationship regular term function as follows:

$$
C_s = \sum_{u \in U} \left\| X^P(u) - \frac{1}{\sum_{u' \in S(u)} B_{u,u'}} \sum_{u' \in S(u)} B_{u,u'} X^P(u') \right\|^2 \tag{6}
$$

Where, $S(u)$ is the set of friends of user u, and $B_{u,u'}$ is the similarity between user u and friend u' s check-in behavior. We use $S_{u,i}$ to indicate whether user u has visited location i. If yes, the value is 1; otherwise, the value is 0. We define $B_{u,u'}$ as:

$$
B_{u,u'} = \frac{\sum_{i=1}^{|\mathcal{L}_u|} S_{u,i} S_{u',i}}{\sqrt{\sum_{i=1}^{|\mathcal{L}_u|} (S_{u,i})^2} \sqrt{\sum_{i=1}^{|\mathcal{L}_u|} (S_{u',i})^2}} \qquad \text{if } u' \in S(u) \tag{7}
$$

4.3   Parameter Learning

Similar to the standard of Bayesian personalized ranking BPR in literature [12], we used the method of maximum likelihood posteriori probability to construct the objective function and fused the previously mentioned time information and social information. The derivation process of the optimization objective function of the model is as follows:

$$
\begin{aligned}
\mathcal{O} &= \underset{\Theta}{\mathrm{argmax}} \log \prod_{u \in \mathcal{U}} \prod_{l^c \in \mathcal{L}} \prod_{l_i \in \mathcal{L}} \prod_{l_j \in \mathcal{L}} \prod_{t \in \mathcal{T}} P(>_{u,t,l^c} | \Theta) P(\Theta) \\
&= \underset{\Theta}{\mathrm{argmax}} \sum_{u \in \mathcal{U}} \sum_{l^c \in \mathcal{L}} \sum_{l_i \in \mathcal{L}} \sum_{l_j \in \mathcal{L}} \sum_{t \in \mathcal{T}} \log \sigma \big(D_{u,t,l^c,l_j} - D_{u,t,l^c,l_i} \big) - \lambda \|\Theta\|^2
\end{aligned}
\tag{8}
$$

Where, $\Theta = \{X^S(l), X^P(l), X^P(u), X^T(t), X^T(l)\}$ is the model parameters to be learned. In order to add the time regular term and the social relation regular term, we minimize the negative logarithmic likelihood probability and write the final optimization objective function in the form of formula (9).

$$
\begin{aligned}
\mathcal{O} &= \underset{\Theta}{\mathrm{argmax}} \sum_{u \in \mathcal{U}} \sum_{l^c \in \mathcal{L}} \sum_{l_i \in \mathcal{L}} \sum_{l_j \in \mathcal{L}} \sum_{t \in \mathcal{T}} - \log \sigma \big(D_{u,t,l^c,l_j} - D_{u,t,l^c,l_i} \big) \\
&+ \mu \sum_{u \in U} \left\| X^P(u) - \frac{1}{\sum_{u' \in S(u)} B_{u,u'}} \sum_{u' \in S(u)} B_{u,u'} X^P(u') \right\|^2 \\
&+ \varepsilon \sum_{u \in U} \sum_{t \in \mathcal{T}} A_{t,t-1} \left\| X^T(t) - X^T(t_{-1}) \right\|^2 \\
&+ A_{t,t+1} \left\| X^T(t) - X^T(t_{+1}) \right\|^2 + \lambda \|\Theta\|^2
\end{aligned}
\tag{9}
$$

Where, $\mu, \varepsilon, \lambda$ are the regularization parameters used to optimize the experimental results.

The parameter update method is shown in formula (10):

$$
\Theta \leftarrow \Theta - \gamma \frac{\partial \mathcal{O}}{\partial \Theta}
\tag{10}
$$

Where, γ is learning rate. The learning algorithm of PRME-GTS is summarized in Algorithm 1:

Algorithm1:PRME-GTS

Input : regularization parameters: μ, ε, λ, weigh parameters α,β,time threshold: τ

Output : parameters, $\Theta = \{X^S(l), X^P(l), X^P(u), X^T(t), X^T(l)\}$

1.   Initializing the model parameters Θ with a normal distribution $\mathcal{N}(0, 0.01)$
2.   **repeat**
3.   **for each** Observation set$\langle u, t, l^c, l_i \rangle$
4.   Randomly generate an unobserved POI l_j;
5.   **if** $\Delta(l, l^c) < \tau$ **then**
6.   Update $X^P(u), X^P(l_i), X^P(l_j)$;
7.   Update $X^S(l^c), X^S(l_i), X^S(l_j)$;
8.   Update $X^T(t), X^T(l_i), X^T(l_j)$;
9.   **if** $\Delta(l, l^c) \geq \tau$ **then**
10.   Update $X^P(u), X^P(l_i), X^P(l_j)$;
11.   **until** convergence;
12.   **return** $\Theta = \{X^S(l), X^P(l), X^P(u), X^T(t), X^T(l)\}$

---

5 Experiment

5.1 Experiment Setup

We use two public datasets to evaluate the performance of our proposed model. The first dataset is the Brightkite check-ins within Singapore [10] while the second one is the Gowalla check-ins dataset within California [13]. To make our experiments repeatable, we make our dataset and codes publicly available at website[1].

5.2 Evaluated Methods

In the experiment, we compare PRME-GTS with the following methods:

PRME-G [1]: The model proposed by Feng et al. [1] that measures the embedding of personalized ranking and incorporates geographic information factors to solve the continuous new POI recommendation problem.

PRME-GT: The model we integrated time regular factors into the PRME-G model.

PRME-GS: The model we added social relationship terms into PRME-G model.

---

[1] https://github.com/cython1995/PRME-GTS.

5.3   Experimental Result

The comparison results are shown in Figs. 1 and 2. First, we compare the PRME-G model with the PRME-GT model and the PRME-GS proposed in this paper. We can see that both PRME-GT model and PRME-GS model are better than PRME-G model obviously. This results indicate that time regular and social regular have positive effects on new successive POI recommendation respectively. Then, we compare the PRME-GT model with the PRME-GS model. The figures show that the PRME-GS model is slightly better than the PRME-GT model, which means that the social relationship factor plays an important role in the metric embedded personalized ranking method than the time factor. Finally, comparing PRME-GTS with other models, we can see that the model performance is higher than all the other models, which are indicating that time factors and social factors can be well integrated into the model of personalized learning ranking.

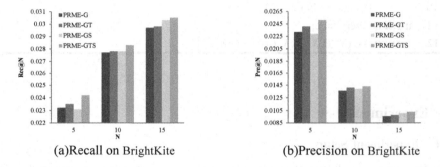

(a)Recall on BrightKite   (b)Precision on BrightKite

Fig. 1. The result methods on BrightKite

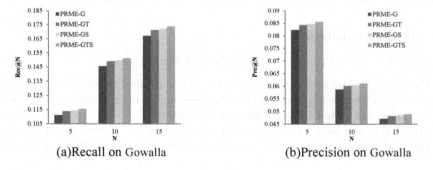

(a)Recall on Gowalla   (b)Precision on Gowalla

Fig. 2. The result methods on BrightKite

The results of this set of experiments show that time factors and social relationship factors can indeed improve the performance of continuous new POI recommendations. Our proposed PRME-GTS model is indeed better than the PRME-G model.

6   Conclusion

In this paper, we first integrated the time factor and social relationship factor into the personalized ranking method based on metric learning, and proposed a new POI recommendation model PRME-GTS. Experimental results show that the personalized ranking method of which integrates the time factor and social relationship factor can effectively improve the recommendation performance of new successive POI.

Acknowledgement. This work was supported by the National Natural Science Foundation of China (No. 61972135, No. 61602159), the Natural Science Foundation of Heilongjiang Province (No. F201430), the Innovation Talents Project of Science and Technology Bureau of Harbin (No. 2017RAQXJ094, No. 2017RAQXJ131), and the fundamental research funds of universities in Heilongjiang Province, special fund of Heilongjiang University (No. HDJCCX-201608, No. KJCX201815, No. KJCX201816).

References

1. Feng, S., Li, X., Zeng, Y., Cong, G., Chee, Y.M., Yuan, Q.: Personalized ranking metric embedding for next new POI recommendation. In: IJCAI 2016, pp. 2069–2075 (2015)
2. Cheng, C., Yang, H., Lyu, M.R., King, I.: Where you like to go next: successive point-of-interest recommendation. In: IJCAI 2013, pp. 2605–2611 (2013)
3. Ye, M., Yin, P., Lee, W.C., Lee, D.L.: Exploiting geographical influence for collaborative point-of-interest recommendation. In: ACM SIGIR 2011, pp. 325–334 (2011)
4. Lian, D., Zhao, C., Xie, X., Sun, G., Chen, E., Rui, Y.: GeoMF: joint geographical modeling and matrix factorization for point-of-interest recommendation. In: ACM SIGKDD 2014, pp. 831–840 (2014)
5. Ying, H., Chen, L., Xiong, Y., Wu, J.P.: PGRank: personalized geographical ranking for point-of-interest recommendation. In: WWW 2016, pp. 137–138 (2016)
6. Rendle, S., Freudenthaler, C., Gantner, Z., Schmidt-Thieme, L.: BPR: Bayesian personalized ranking from implicit feedback. In: Proceedings of the Twenty-Fifth Conference on Uncertainty in Artificial Intelligence, pp. 452–461 (2009)
7. Hu, B., Ester, M.: Social topic modeling for point-of-interest recommendation in location-based social networks. In: ICDM 2014, pp. 845–850 (2014)
8. Li, H., Ge, Y., Hong, R., Zhu, H.: Point-of-interest recommendations: learning potential check-ins from friends. In: ACM SIGKDD 2016, pp. 975–984 (2016)
9. Sang, J., Mei, T., Sun, J.T., Xu, C., Li, S.: Probabilistic sequential POIs recommendation via check-in data. In: Proceedings of the 20th International Conference on Advances in Geographic Information Systems, pp. 402–405 (2012)
10. Rendle, S., Freudenthaler, C., Schmidt-Thieme, L.: Factorizing personalized markov chains for next-basket recommendation. In: WWW 2010, pp. 811–820 (2010)

11. Zhao, S., Zhao, T., Yang, H., Lyu, M.R., King, I.: STELLAR: spatial-temporal latent ranking for successive point-of-interest recommendation. In: AAAI 2016, pp. 315–321 (2016)
12. Zhu, J., Ma, H., Chen, C., Bu, J.: Social recommendation using low-rank semidefinite program. In: AAAI 2011, pp. 158–163 (2011)
13. Cho, E., Myers, S.A., Leskovec, J.: Friendship and mobility: user movement in location-based social networks. In: ACM SIGKDD 2011, pp. 1082–1090 (2011)

Social Network and Social Media

Social Network und Social Media

Precomputing Hybrid Index Architecture for Flexible Community Search over Location-Based Social Networks

Ismail Alaqta[1,2]([✉]), Junhu Wang[1], and Mohammad Awrangjeb[1]

[1] School of Information and Communication Technology, Griffith University,
Brisbane, Australia
ismail.alaqta@griffithuni.edu.au,
{j.wang,m.awrangjeb}@griffith.edu.au
[2] Department of Computer Science, Jazan University, Gizan, Saudi Arabia
ialaqta@jazanu.edu.sa

Abstract. Community search is defined as finding query-based communities within simple graphs. One of the most crucial community models is minimum degree subgraph in which each vertex has at least k neighbours. Due to the rapid development of location-based devices; however, simple graphs are unable to handle Location-Based Social Networks LBSN personal information such as interests and spatial locations. Hence, this paper aims to construct a Precomputed Hybrid Index Architecture (PHIA) for the sake of enhancing simple graphs to store and retrieve information of LBSN users. This method consists of two stages; the first is precomputing, and the second is index construction. Numerical testing showed that our hybrid index approach is reasonable because of its flexibility to combine different dimensions by adapting the wide used community model $k - core$.

Keywords: Community search · $k - core$ · Indexing · Spatial graph

1 Introduction

Recent statistics showed that over 1.75 billion of Facebook users are monthly active.[1] The graph data model is widespread to represent social networks. More specifically, the number of on-line social network users has been growing exponentially due to the spread of mobile internet access. Most of the work on social networks is concerned the community retrieval. Thus, It is essential to define what the community is. One of the most common definition is that the community is a subset of nodes which have more dense connections among themselves compared to the other subsets of the graph (Shang et al. 2017). Community retrieval can generally be classified into community detection (CD) and community search (CS). However, our research interest focuses on the second type of

---

[1] http://www.statisticbrain.com/facebook-statistics.

© Springer Nature Switzerland AG 2019
J. Li et al. (Eds.): ADMA 2019, LNAI 11888, pp. 277–287, 2019.
https://doi.org/10.1007/978-3-030-35231-8_20

community retrieval, which is the community search that aims to return dense communities involving query vertices (Sozio and Gionis 2010).

The community search has been utilised in various applications within a different type of graphs. The general definitions of attributed graphs and spatial graphs are outlined as follow:

Attributed Graph: Is fundamentally a graph whose vertices or edges have text or keywords. For example, Fig. 1 shows that each social network user, represented by a vertex in this graph, has different attributes to describe users' interests. Furthermore, the attributes can handle other personal information of the user, such as gender, education, relationship, etc. As a result, attributed graphs can make social network sites service-oriented, e.g. marketing. Technically, the node and edge attributes of simple graph model increase the possibilities of finding more cohesive groups due to the available information added by the attributes (Galbrun et al. 2014).

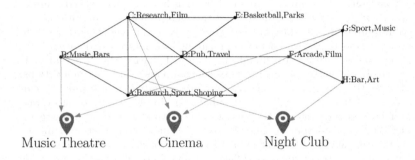

Fig. 1. Example of spatial graph

Spatial Graph: Clear examples of a spatial graph are Twitter, Facebook and Foursquare, which have become standard for their users to share locations. Due to the emergence of LBSN, lots of attention have been paid. In these LBSNs, a user has geo-locations information which can be used to indicate where the user is as shown in Fig. 1. This type of network is generally defined as spatial graphs. The social graph in Fig. 1 has a group of people with three different places as each person checked in a specific point.

This paper has adapted one of the most common community models named $k - core$ to construct a Precomputed Hybrid Index Architecture (PHIA) for the sake of enhancing simple graphs to store and retrieve information of LBSN users. It also experimented on an LBSN dataset in order to create an efficient hybrid index that can handle different types of data. The experiment demonstrated that PHIA could be more efficient in term of retrieving meaningful query-based-communities.

In the rest of this paper, we discuss the related works in Sect. 2 and define the problem of our communities in Sects. 3 and 4. Section 5 presents the Precomputed Hybrid Index Architecture (PHIA) as well as experimental results are presented, and finally, we conclude the paper in Sect. 6.

2   Related Works

The attributed community that has been conducted by many works of literature is characterised by vertices associated text or keyword-named attributes. More features, for instance, interpretation and personalisation can be provided effectively by using these attributes (Fang et al. 2017). The same authors studied attributed community search by combining a cohesive structure and keyword. Similar work was conducted by (Shang et al. 2017), who employed an attributed community search method that improved and enhanced by (Huang et al. 2014). Their research was aimed to construct the graph based on topology-based and attribute-based similarities – the constructed graph in this study named TA-graph. From TA-graph structure, an index called AttrTCP-index based on TCP-index (Huang et al. 2014) was created. Hence, queries that can be found on the new index AttrTCP-index return to communities that satisfy the queries. Another leading dimension of community search is spatial, which refers to an online social network. In this dimension, internet users can share their location information, i.e. position during check-ins. There are considerable works conducted to study a spatio-social community search, as previously reviewed works assume non-spatial graphs (Cui et al. 2014; Huang et al. 2014; Li et al. 2015; Sozio and Gionis 2010). A recent study named spatial-aware community (SAC) was undertaken by (Fang et al. 2016). This study has adopted the concept of minimum degree using the k-core technique.

By the reviewed literature, K-core has been found one of the most significant graph theory techniques to model communities, especially social ones. (Li et al. 2016) argued that two significant reasons that have made the $k - core$ a sufficient model to measure the level of the user group's social acquaintance. The first reason is that $k - core$ has the minimum degree constraints which consider in social science, an important measure of group cohesiveness. The second reason is that the k-core has been extensively used in the graph problems research. Indeed, in this research, we used the k-core because of its flexibility and effectiveness to capture suitable communities within LBSN.

3   Preliminaries and Problem Statement

We model a location-based social network (LBSN) as an undirected graph $G = (V, E)$, where each node $u \in V$ represents a user, and the edges represent relationships between users. Each user u is associated with a tuple (l_u, W_u)

where l_u is the geo-location of the user, and W_u is a set of keywords that represent the interests of the users, e.g., movie, music, martial arts. The user interests are obtained by the places she visited, i.e., the check-in information, and we assume each place has a set of interests.

Given an interest $w \in W_u$ and a user u, we define

$$RS(w, u) = \frac{f_{w,u}}{\Sigma_{w_i \in W_u} f_{w_i, u}}$$

where $f_{w,u}$ is the frequency of w that occurs in the places visited by user u. Intuitively $RS(w, u)$ represents the weight of interest w in user u.

Given a connected subgraph H of G and a node u in U, we use $nbr(u, H)$ and $deg(u, H)$ to denote the the set of neighbors of u in H and the degree of u in H respectively. Let H be a connected subgraph of G. Given an interest w, we define

$$KRS(w, H) = \frac{\Sigma_{u \in H} RS(w, u)}{|H|}$$

4 Problem Statement

Given a LBSN $G = (V, E)$, an interest w, a user $u \in V$, an integer $k > 0$, and a radius $r > 0$, our problem is to find a maximal subgraph H of G such that

1. $deg(v, H) \geq k$ for all $v \in H$.
2. $d(u, v) \leq r$ for all $v \in H$, where $d(u, v)$ is the geological distance between u and v.
3. $KRS(w, H)$ is maximal among all subgraphs of G that satisfy the above conditions 1 and 2.

Intuitively, the conditions 1, 2, and 3 represent structural cohesiveness, location cohesiveness and interest cohesiveness respectively.

5 Precomputing and Index Architecture

In this section, the design of precomputing architecture is presented. First, An overview of the architecture is given. Then each section elaborates each component, (1) indexing, (2) Precomputed results structure and (3) Query processing.

5.1 Indexing

Here we propose our index structure to solve a community search problem over LBSN effectively and efficiently. Our approach consists of two stages, precomputing and query processing. In the precomputing stage, the attributed social

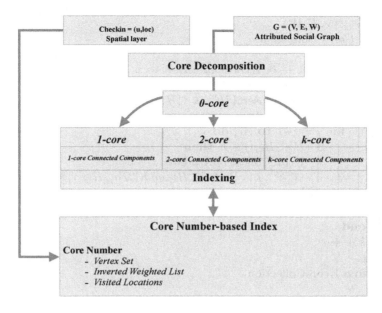

Fig. 2. Core-based index

graph is the input that needs to be processed offline in order to decompose and store subgraphs, which interestingly, can be employed when processing a query. Secondly, the index construction.

Precomputing Stage. The precomputing stage of our proposed index structure depends on an interesting relationship between query-based community and core decomposition. Moreover, a key observation that makes our index structure relies on k-$core$ is that cores are nested. Thus, in this stage, it is straightforward to decompose the graph recursively. Specifically, as illustrated in Fig. 2, the 0-$core$, which is basically the whole graph, is generated. Then, the $(k+1) - cores$ are consequently generated. The idea behind precomputing the core decomposition of the input graph is to sort the $k - cores$ in order to efficiently locate the $k - core$, which includes answers to the issued queries. Moreover, this phase is crucial to extract our final hybrid index named *Attri-Spatial Core-based Index*.

In following Algorithm 1, the k-$core$ decomposition is precomputed and stored in an oriented-document database. In an iterative manner, our algorithm starts with initialising $k = 0$ and an empty collection to host the decomposed k-$cores$. Each k-$core$ is stored in a document whose key holds k and the value of k represents a k-$core$ subgraph. Each subgraph has connected components. Each component of vertices C_i^k is represented by an array as demonstrated by (Line 3).

Data: $G = (V, E, W)$
Result: *Cores Collection*
begin
1 | Initialization: $k \leftarrow 0$, $KcoreCollection \leftarrow \phi$
2 | **while** $k_{max} \geq k$ **do**
3 | | KcoreCollection.insert$\{"k" : k : [H(V)] \leftarrow CoreComp(k, G)\}$
4 | | **for** $i = 0$ **to** $|H|$ **do**
5 | | | **for** $j = i+1$ **to** $|H|$ **do**
6 | | | | **if** $(H[i], H[j]) \in E$ **then**
7 | | | | | KcoreCollection.Update
    | | | | | $(\{"k" : k\}, \{"H_E" : H_E.add((H[i], H[j]))\})$
    | | | | **end**
    | | | **end**
    | | **end**
8 | | $k++$
    | **end**
9 | **return** KcoreCollection
end

Algorithm 1. k-core Precomputation

In following Algorithm 2, the connected components are precomputed for each $k - core$ subgraph.

Data: *Cores Collection*
Result: List of Connected Components for each *k-Core*
1 Initialization: $CCList[\ ] \leftarrow \phi, Subgraph\ H = (V_H, E_H)$ **begin**
2 | **while** K **do**
3 | | $k \leftarrow K.pop()$
4 | | **for** $cc \in H.CC$ **do**
5 | | | **for** $u \in cc$ **do**
6 | | | | CCList.append(u)
    | | | **end**
7 | | | $ColCores.update(\{"k" : k\}, \{"CC\_Users" : CCList\})$
8 | | | $CCList.clear()$
9 | | | $H.clear()$
    | | **end**
10 | | **return** Updated Cores Collection
    | **end**
end

Algorithm 2. K-Core Connected Components Precomputation

Index Construction. After the core decomposition occurred $C = \{C_1, \cdots, C_k\}$, we utilise the core number as an index for those users who have the same core order in the graph G which is already decomposed into $k - cores$. In other words, the core number for each user is kept as $C(u) = k$ as the following:

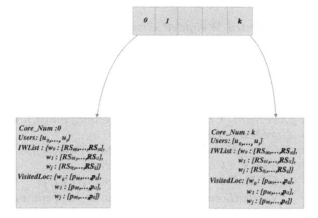

Fig. 3. Attri-spatial core-based index

- For all users $u \in V$, the core index $C(u)$ of u, that is as the index of the highest order core containing u: $C(u) = max\{k \in [0 \cdots k] \,|u \in C_k\}$.

Underneath each core index as illustrated in Fig. 3, we encapsulate the other core-based index components to make our hybrid index more effective by employing the inverted weighted index for the graph attributes. To summarise, each index, which is referred to as a core number, contains three elements:

- *VertexSet*: a set of graph vertices that represent users;
- *InvertedWeightedList*: a list of $\langle key, value \rangle$ pairs, where the *key* is a keyword that is contained by *VertexSet* and the *value* is an array of weights. Each element represents a weight, given by Eq. 3, which corresponds to each user in *VertexSet*.
- *VisitedLocations*: a set of coordinates $\langle x, y \rangle$ of places that have been visited by u. More effectively, all spatial objects, that contain the interest w, are mapped to the interest w.

The main idea of the structure in Fig. 3 is to enhance query processing by taking the advantages of the inverted index data structure. After the precomputing process, Algorithm 3 is proposed to construct our index named Attri-Spatial Core-based Index. To tackle this proposed algorithm, the technique of the inverted index has been adopted inside the MongoDB. Specifically, users V, interests W and places P are grouped into a single collection called $CoreNum\_Col$. In details, for each interest $w_j \in W$ we build an inverted weighted list whose elements represent weights RS_{ij} that correspond to $Users$. Besides, the places P, which has been visited by users, are also inverted by each interest w_j.

1 **Data:** *CoresCol C,*
         Social Attributed Weighted Graph Col,$CK = \{\langle u_i, p_k \rangle\}$
2 **Result:** *Core-based Index*
   begin
3 $\quad$ Initialization: $CoreNum\_Col \leftarrow \phi, Core\_num \leftarrow 0$
4 $\quad$ **foreach** $w_j \in W$ **do**
5 $\quad\quad$ **foreach** $u_i \in V$ **do**
6 $\quad\quad\quad$ **if** $|CoreNum\_Col| < |KcoreCollection.find(u_i)|$ **then**
7 $\quad\quad\quad\quad$ $CoreNum\_Col.insert($
                  $"Core\_Num" : |KcoreCollection.find(u_i)|,$
                  $"Users" : VertexSet[\ ].append(u_i),$
                  $"IWList"\{: w_j : weight[\ ].append(RS_{ij})\},$
                  $"VisitedLocations" : \{w_j : places[\ ].append(p_{k_u})\})$
         $\quad\quad\quad$ **end**
8 $\quad\quad\quad$ **else**
9 $\quad\quad\quad\quad$ $CoreNum\_Col.update(\ "Users" : VertexSet[\ ].append(u_i),$
                  $"IWList" : w_j : \{weight[\ ].append(RS_{ij})\},$
                  $"VisitedLocations" : \{w_j : places[\ ].append(p_{k_u})\})$
         $\quad\quad\quad$ **end**
      $\quad\quad$ **end**
   $\quad$ **end**
10 $\quad$ **return** Core-based Index
   end

Algorithm 3: Attri-Spatial Core-based Index

5.2 Dataset and Numerical Testing

Weeplaces is a dataset (Liu et al. 2014) that has been collected from a website named Weeplaces, in which users' check-in activities can be visualised in LBSN. It has been integrated using the API of other well-known LBSNs, e.g. Facebook Places, Foursquare, and Gowalla. The dataset contains more than 7.5 million check-ins by 15,799 users across 971,309 geolocations.

Core	k	H_E	CC_Users
[163 elements]	15	[2026 elements]	[1 elements]
[119 elements]	14	[472 elements]	[1 elements]
[188 elements]	13	[707 elements]	[3 elements]
[206 elements]	12	[654 elements]	[6 elements]
[202 elements]	11	[337 elements]	[15 elements]
[415 elements]	10	[1329 elements]	[9 elements]
[327 elements]	9	[489 elements]	[23 elements]
[626 elements]	8	[1173 elements]	[33 elements]
[803 elements]	7	[1356 elements]	[61 elements]
[912 elements]	6	[1090 elements]	[98 elements]
[1252 elements]	5	[1207 elements]	[171 elements]
[1613 elements]	4	[1281 elements]	[229 elements]
[2367 elements]	3	[1385 elements]	[421 elements]
[3251 elements]	2	[1359 elements]	[597 elements]
[3578 elements]	1	[481 elements]	[387 elements]

Fig. 4. The pre-computation collection structure

In Fig. 4, Algorithms 1, 2 have been implemented and then stored inside a MongoDB collection called Col_cores. This collection has four fields named Core, k, H_E, and CC_Users. For instance, at $k = 1$, there are 3578 users stored in field Core and 387 connected components of users stored in CC_Users. These components belong to the subgraph edges H_E.

Core_num		1	Int32
▶ Core_Users		[3578 elements]	Array
IWLL		[474 elements]	Array
▼ 0		{ 2 fields }	Object
kw		Hot Dogs	String
▼ Score		[3 elements]	Array
0		[6 elements]	Array
0		daniel-poulsen6	String
1	$C(u) = max\{k \in [0 \cdots k] \mid u \in Ck\}$	doug-hanna	String
2		john-moccia	String
3		justin-street	String
4		joe-landor	String
5		marc-ribo	String
1		[6 elements]	Array
0		0.08038326515710895	Double
1	list of (key, value) pairs, where the key is a keyword kw	0.05749636327298755	Double
2	that is contained by VertexSet and the	0.017920944396498314	Double
3	value is an array of weights	0.11499272654419751	Double
4		0.0025982543706074	Double
5		0.029359845075114258	Double
2		[8 elements]	Array
▶ 0		[2 elements]	Array
▶ 1	a set of coordinates (x, y) of places that	[2 elements]	Array
▶ 2	have been visited by u w.r.t the keyword kw	[2 elements]	Array
▶ 3		[2 elements]	Array
▶ 4		[2 elements]	Array
▶ 5		[2 elements]	Array
▶ 6		[2 elements]	Array
▶ 7		[2 elements]	Array

Fig. 5. Attri-spatial core-based index inside MongoDB

In Fig. 5, Algorithm 3 has been implemented in order to index our LBSN graph G by employing the core number as illustrated in Fig. 3.

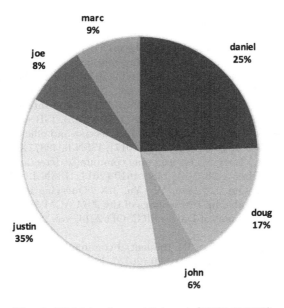

Fig. 6. Weights of users' Interest (HOT DOGS)

The pie chart in Fig. 6 shows the result of weights for interest (HOT DOGS) in which users can be retrieved at core number $k = 1$ as illustrated in Fig. 5. From the pie chart it is clear that user named *justin* is highly interested in *HOT DOGS* compared with other users in the core number $k = 1$.

6   Conclusion and Future Work

This paper has discussed the possibilities of spatio-attributed community search to enrich the simple graphs model. It can be done by constructing a precomputed Hybrid Index Architecture method (PHIA) which could assist for the sake of enhancing simple graphs to retrieve and store users' information over LBSN. The proposed method has consisted of two phases; the first is precomputing, where the second is index construction. In both stages, the attributed social graph is the input that needs to be processed offline to store and compose and then the hybrid index can be employed when processing a query. Together, Numerical testing showed that our hybrid index approach is promising due to its flexibility to combine different dimensions by adapting the wide used community model $k - core$. Future research will focus on conducting extensive experiments on an LBSN dataset in order to enhance the efficiency of the developed hybrid index that can handle different types of data in order to demonstrate that PHIA can be more efficient in term of retrieving meaningful query-based-communities. Moreover, the query processing, which is involved of two elements, a retrieval and ranking function algorithm, will be further designed; hence, the PHIA will be efficiently utilised.

References

Cui, W., Xiao, Y., Wang, H., Wang, W.: Local search of communities in large graphs. In: Proceedings of the 2014 ACM SIGMOD International Conference on Management of Data - SIGMOD 2014, vol. 1, pp. 991–1002 (2014). ISSN 07308078

Fang, Y., Cheng, R., Tang, W., Maniu, S., Yang, X.: Scalable algorithms for nearest-neighbor joins on big trajectory data. In: 2016 IEEE 32nd International Conference on Data Engineering, ICDE 2016, pp. 1528–1529 (2016). ISBN 9781509020195

Fang, Y., Cheng, R., Chen, Y., Luo, S., Hu, J.: Effective and efficient attributed community search. VLDB J. 26(6), 803–828 (2017). ISSN 0949877X

Galbrun, E., Gionis, A., Tatti, N.: Overlapping community detection in labeled graphs. Data Min. Knowl. Discov. 28(5–6), 1586–1610 (2014). ISSN 13845810

Huang, X., Cheng, H., Qin, L., Tian, W., Yu, J.X.: Querying k-truss community in large and dynamic graphs. In: Proceedings of the 2014 ACM SIGMOD International Conference on Management of Data - SIGMOD 2014, vol. 2, pp. 1311–1322 (2014). ISSN 07308078

Li, R.-H., Qin, L., Yu, J.X., Mao, R.: Influential community search in large networks. Proc. VLDB Endowment 8(5), 509–520 (2015). ISSN 2150–8097

Li, Y., Chen, R., Xu, J., Huang, Q., Hu, H., Choi, B.: Geo-social K-cover group queries for collaborative spatial computing. In: 2016 IEEE 32nd International Conference on Data Engineering, ICDE 2016, vol. 27(10), pp. 1510–1511 (2016). ISSN 10414347

Liu, Y., Wei, W., Sun, A., Miao, C.: Exploiting geographical neighborhood character-istics for location recommendation. In: Proceedings of the 23rd ACM International Conference on Conference on Information and Knowledge Management, CIKM 2014, pp. 739–748. ACM, New York (2014). https://doi.org/10.1145/2661829.2662002. ISBN 978-1-4503-2598-1

Shang, J., Wang, C., Wang, C., Guo, G., Qian, J.: An attribute-based community search method with graph refining. J. Supercomput. 1–28 (2017). ISSN 1573–0484

Sozio, M., Gionis, A.: The community-search problem and how to plan a successful cocktail party. In: Proceedings Of The ACM SIGKDD International Conference on Knowledge Discovery and Data Mining, pp. 939–948 (2010)

Expert2Vec: Distributed Expert Representation Learning in Question Answering Community

Xiaocong Chen[1](✉), Chaoran Huang[1], Xiang Zhang[1], Xianzhi Wang[2],
Wei Liu[1], and Lina Yao[1]

[1] University of New South Wales, Sydney, NSW 2052, Australia
{xiaocong.chen,chaoran.huang,wei.liu,lina.yao}@unsw.edu.au,
xiang.zhang3@student.unsw.edu.au
[2] University of Technology Sydney, Sydney, NSW 2007, Australia
xianzhi.wang@uts.edu.au

Abstract. Community question answering (CQA) has attracted increasing attention recently due to its potential as a de facto knowledge base. Expert finding in CQA websites also has considerably board applications. Stack Overflow is one of the most popular question answering platforms, which is often utilized by recent studies on the recommendation of the domain expert. Despite the substantial progress seen recently, it still lacks relevant research on the direct representation of expert users. Hence hereby we propose *Expert2Vec*, a distributed Expert Representation learning in question answering community to boost the recommendation of the domain expert. Word2Vec is used to preprocess the Stack Overflow dataset, which helps to generate representations of domain topics. Weight rankings are then extracted based on domains and variational autoencoder (VAE) is unitized to generate representations of user-topic information. This finally adopts the reinforcement learning framework with the user-topic matrix to improve it internally. Experiments show the adequate performance of our proposed approaches in the recommendation system.

Keywords: Stack Overflow · Expertise finding · Question answering · Embedding · Recommendation system · Reinforcement learning

1 Introduction

Recommender Systems are software applications that support users in finding items of interest within a larger number of objects in a personalized way. Community question answering (CQA), such as Quora, Stack Overflow and so on, is a type of web application which contains a large number of open-end questions and answers. The major challenge existing on CQA is that the question can not be answered on time and as such users can not get the expected answers very soon. The expert recommendation problem, which recommends some expert users to

© Springer Nature Switzerland AG 2019
J. Li et al. (Eds.): ADMA 2019, LNAI 11888, pp. 288–301, 2019.
https://doi.org/10.1007/978-3-030-35231-8_21

an unsolved question such that the question can be answered in an acceptable time block after it was proposed, is a problem which fits this scenario.

The challenge existing on the CQA is that there exist many questions which can not be answered in a reasonable time, meaning that it lacks a sufficient algorithm to make the match between users and questions. The common strategy that is used to solve this problem is to find previous questions which may be similar to the new question and make recommendations, or to make recommendation by using user's browsing history. However, there still exists the problem that it may not have similar problems previously [14]. For example on Stack Overflow website, assume there is a user who clicks a question named "Why is it faster to process a sorted array than an unsorted array?". The system behind will record this action and analyse the topic. It will extract the key word "sorted array", "unsorted array" and "fast". Based on these keywords, it makes a recommendation to a new question which is "Is '==' in sorted array not faster than unsorted array". This strategy has the same problem which was mentioned before; there may not be any other questions with the same keywords, and so the recommendation system may not work properly.

In recent years, reinforcement learning has achieved many impressive processes in learning representation [4], improving generative adversarial network [5] and so on. Reinforcement learning can be applied in many areas such as recommendation system [7], general game playing and many other areas. In this work, we adopted the reinforcement learning into our model to improve the accuracy of our embedding. The normal reinforcement learning based recommendation systems treat the recommendation system as sequential actions between the users and the system (agent) and try to figure out a optimal strategy to maximise the reward [27]. Different from the normal reinforcement learning based recommendation system, we use the reinforcement learning to determine the best policy to optimize our embedding instead of finding a optimal recommending strategy. The major contributions we made in this paper present as follows:

- We acquire some idea about the distributed representation from word2vec which is applied on the CQA problem as well as the expert recommendation. Based that, we propose a new distributed representation for user expertise which does not have many research before.
- Evolution on the big and complex data set - Stack Overflow where we got a acceptable result on several measure metrics among a few state-of-art models.
- We apply the reinforcement learning to improve the embedding so that it can get a better performance in recommendation.

The remainder of this paper has the following structure. It will follow the related work which discusss the history and recent year's progress on expert recommendation. After discussing the related work, we explain the methodology in detail. Which includes how to pre-process the data, how to utilize the data set to get the input and the learning step of the distributed representation. The result analysis is presented, as well as the conclusion and the future work at the end.

2 Related Work

2.1 CQA and Expert Recommendation

As the expert recommendation acquire some good research works and the CQA problem can gain the experience from the expert recommendation [24]. So that apply expert recommendation on CQA problem comes more common in recent years [20]. Query likelihood language (QLL) is most popular learning model which used on this question which use the hidden markov model [16]. After the QLL model which get a good result on CQA problem, Zheng et al. [30] proposed a expertise-aware QLL model which based on QLL and combine the answers quality to increase the recommend accuracy. The QLL model are focus on the language side which is majority on natural language processing.

Another type of models were focus on the topic, those models try to mine the information behind the topic such as Latent Dirichlet Allocation (LDA), Probabilistic Latent Semantic Analysis (PLSA) and so on [22]. Segmented Topic Model is a hierarchical topic model based on LDA which proposed by Du et al. [6]. Also, there is type of method is network-based which build a user-user network and try to use the relation between users to make recommendation such as PageRank [2].

As the expert recommendation is a type of recommendation problem, there are some models which are based on collaborative filtering (CF) or matrix factorization (MF). Yang et al. proposed a model which uses the probabilistic matrix factorization (PMF) [23], an extension of the basic MF. As the neural network acquires outstanding results on many areas including expert recommendation. Liu et al. proposed a model which combine the QLL and the LDA to compute the relevance and make recommendation by assuming that good respondents will give better answers [13]. Zheng et al. find that the convolutional neural network (CNN) can be used to combine the user features and question features together to make recommendation [28] more accurate. There are some hybrid methods which can combine topic model and apply the classification methods [10] or Network-based method with clustering [3]. However, the accuracy is still lower than expectation, the reason is that the NLP technique still needs be improved and the dataset used in CQA is extremely sparse.

2.2 Auto-Encoder

Autoencoder is a type of neural network which is normally used in dimension reduction and feature learning [21,26]. Autoencoder is a multi-layer neural network which has an encoding layer, hidden layer and a decoding layer. It uses backpropagation to make the output as same as the input. There are many works that show that the autoencoder can get a good result in sentence encoding, image encoding and many other areas [12,17]. Sarath et al. state that the autoencoder can do the feature learning from the word representation [1].

2.3   Reinforcement Learning Based Recommendation System

Reinforcement learning (RL) in recommendation systems attracts many interests
in recent years. Yash et al. proposed a new way to represent the actions during
the learning process to improve RL's training efficiency and robustness [4]. As the
generative adversarial network (GAN) obtains a promising result on computer
vision and recommendation system area, Chen et al. proposed a GAN model
for RL based recommendation system [5] which combines the GAN and the
RL by cascading. Zhao et al. proposed a model-based deep RL for a sequential
recommendation especially in whole-chain recommendation [27] which uses user's
feedback as the reward and adopting the auto-encoder. Zheng et al. proposed
a deep reinforcement learning framework for the news recommendation which
based on the deep Q-learning [29]. Expert recommendation is similar with the
normal recommendation, but more specific. Traditional recommendation system
aims to recommend users some items based on users' purchase history or browse
history. The common strategy is: assign an id to a user and label the items with
id as well, then the recommendation system will based on this two-dimension
user-item matrix to make recommendation. There are some works which attempt
to add more temporal information to boost the performance like review [25] and
had some improvement. However, expert recommendation requires a focus on
the answers which will be a higher dimension vector than the normal items. If
we follow the common strategy to construct a user-item matrix, it will have an
extremely high dimension matrix and the traditional recommendation system
will get stuck on it.

3   Background

Recommendation system can recommend k items to users in a single page, the
user can provide some feedback by clicking one of those choices or switch the
pages. After the feedback is provided, the system will record it and recommend
another k items based on user's feedback. RL have two different branches which
are model-based RL and model-free RL. The model-free RL based recommendation systems require a big dataset which contain a large number of user actions
so that it can figure out a good policy. A larger sized dataset may lead to problems such as the model being hard to converge, recommendation system needing
to be complex enough to handle those information and so on. RL initially comes
from the Markov decision process (MDP), which defined as:

$$\mathcal{M} = (\mathcal{S}, \mathcal{A}, P, R) \text{ Where } P \in [0, 1]$$

Where $\mathcal{S}$ represents the set of states, $\mathcal{A}$ represents the set of actions, P is
the probability of transition which is normally written as $P(s_{t+1}|s_t, a_t)$ where
$s_{t+1}, s_t \in \mathcal{S}, a_t \in \mathcal{A}$ which represents the probability of action a_t transfer from
state s_t to state s_{t+1} from a certain timestamp t to timestamp $t+1$, the R is the
reward function. If we consider the discount factor γ, the MDP can be written
as $\mathcal{M} = (\mathcal{S}, \mathcal{A}, P, R, \gamma)$.

However, the model-based RL methods will suffer from the computation difficulty when the $\mathcal{S}, \mathcal{A}$ becomes large. So we prefer to use the model-free RL methods. The model-free RL methods have two different approach which are value-based methods and policy-based methods. The traditional value-based RL methods is the Temporal difference (TD) which are trying to find the optimal value V^* by iteration:

$$V(s) = (1 - \eta)V(s) + \eta(R(s) + \gamma V(s_{t+1}))$$

In some cases, the value will depend on both states and actions, so we have the Q-learning. In Q-learning, we use the Q-value $Q(s, a)$ to determine the optimal policy π^*, different from the MDP, the Q-value baed on the pair of action a and state s instead of using state s only. The definition of π^* can be written as:

$$\pi^*(s) = \arg\max_{a \in \mathcal{A}} Q^*(s, a)$$

the Q^* is the optimal Q-value where can be defined as:

$$Q^*(s, a) = R(s) + \gamma \sum_{s_{t+1} \in \mathcal{S}} P(s_{t+1}|s_t, a_t) \max_{a_{t+1} \in \mathcal{A}} Q^*(s_{t+1}, a_{t+1})$$

This formula was used when known the certain state-action pair (s, a), and the γ is the discount factor which used in a long-term RL. During the training process the Q-value will be updated iteratively based on:

$$Q(s, a) \leftarrow (1 - \eta)Q_o(s, a) + \eta(R(s) + \gamma \max_{a \in \mathcal{A}} Q(s_{t+1}, a))$$

The Q-learning is an off-policy learning which means it will learn from different policy and try to learn the value. However, the TD method is the on-policy learning which means it can only learn different values in the same policy. Benefiting from the neural network, the Q-learning was extended to the deep Q-learning (DQN). The DQN will pass the state s into a neural network and find out many q-values at once. The DQN have a similar target with the normal Q-learning, the DQN try to do:

$$\min[R(s) + \gamma \max_{a'} Q_w(s_{t+1}, a') - Q_w(s_t, a_t)]^2$$

where the $Q_w(s, a)$ is parametrized by the neural network weight w. During the optimizing the neural network, we only need to apply the gradient descent into the term $Q_w(s_t, a_t)$ which is the current q value for current state s_t and action a_t. In addition, to help the converge, the DQN uses the technique called experience replay that can store recent j experience pairs $(s_t, a_t, R(s), s_{t+1})$ with a replay batch with size j. The DQN will choose action based on the greedy algorithm from the reply batch and the current value.

We will use the Q-learning in our proposed model, here are some key aspects used in our model:

– **Environment**: Is the system which user can select on the top k items which provided by the recommendation system.
– **State** $s \in \mathcal{S}$: will defined as the match from the recommended items and user's exactly choose, in simple it represent the value changed in the embedding matrix which will detailed discussed in Sect. 4.3.
– **Action** $a \in \mathcal{A}$: is defined as a subset $\mathbb{A} \subset k$ which those k items is the possible experts/topics show to the user. Also, the $\mathcal{A} \in (\begin{smallmatrix} I_t \\ k \end{smallmatrix})$ where the I_t is the whole possible topics/experts which may be recommended, the $(\begin{smallmatrix} I_t \\ k \end{smallmatrix})$ means that we select top k items from the item-set I_t at timestamp t.
– **State Transition Probability** $P(s_{t+1}|s_t, a_t) : \mathcal{S} \times \mathcal{A} \times \mathcal{S} \mapsto [0, 1]$:it corresponds to a user behavior a_t which will give a probability from current state s to next state s_{t+1} at the timestamp t.
– **Reward Function** $R(S) :\in [0, 1]$: Unlike the normal RL method, we do not have a mapping function used for reward. The reward value used in our model is the accuracy between the decoded embedding and the original data as we are aiming to use the RL to improve our embedding.
– **Policy** $\pi(s)$: is defined as the strategy on how to optimize our embedding which generated by the auto-encoder.
– **Discount Factor** γ **and Learning Rate** $\eta : \eta, \gamma \in [0, 1]$: is the hypeparameter in this model, and need to be adjusted manually depends on the measure metric. Where when the $\gamma = 0$ which means the long-term reward will not be considered, only the current reward will be take into account. In opposite, $\gamma = 1$ means all the reward from previous can be fully considered in current state s.

The overview of a simple RL based recommendation system is (where the recommend agent represent the whole recommendation system) (Fig. 1):

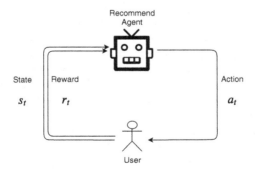

Fig. 1. Flaw chart for RL

4   Methodology

In this section, we will briefly illuminate our approach and the model structure. We will discuss the pre-processing step, how to obtain the original representation, how to get the embedding we are looking for, how to measure the accuracy between the embedding and the original representation, how reinforcement learning works in our model and how to used in a recommendation system.

4.1   Pre-process of the Data

The original dataset provided by Stack Overflow contain all questions and the corresponding answers which are plain text. We use the *SEWordSim* [19] which is a word similarity database for the Stack Overflow dataset which can make it more reliable and reduce some edge effects. In addition, we delete the questions which have zero response to overcome the cold-start problem for recommendation system. After deleting the unnecessary words, we extract all the users and users' answered questions and its corresponding vote received. Furthermore, the sentences are in higher dimension space, in order to reduce the dimension, we would convert all the topics and answers into vectors by using word2vec [15]. As the word2vec is a distributed representation of words which can retain the relation in the sentence, so we can use the vector form directly in the following steps.

4.2   Generate the User-Topic Matrix

After the pre-processing of the data, we get the formatted data which is needed for the matrix generation and the vector for each word. To keep all the information which is needed for ranking, we store all the voting and its corresponding user and topic together. As the topic is vector based and has high dimension which is hard to put it together with the topic information into the matrix. We build a hashing function $f : \mathbb{R} \mapsto \mathbb{R}$ which can simply map the topicID to its corresponding original vector, and we initialise a hash table to store all the mapping relations based on our hash function f. Thus our user-topic matrix can contain all the voting information by ordering. If user don't have action with specific topic, the value of this cell with be null. In some cases the userId may not be continuous, and we convert all the userId with a list of continuous id so that it can easily determine the size. Also, it's easy to roll back to the original id. In addition, the userId is not important in the user-topic matrix as we only need to know the relationship between user and the topic.

The most important thing is how to rank the topic for each user. We cannot use the original voting information because less-popular questions may have very small view counts which can lead to a good answer receiving only one or zero vote. Also, the number of answers is varied for different questions which means we are unable to compare those answers through the same measurement metric due to the different number of competing answers. Therefore, we require a consistent measurement metric to help us determine the order, which means we need to make sure the votes in popular questions and less-popular questions are equivalent. To overcome this problem, we use the percentage vote (PVote) to compare answers, where we transfer all the votes receive for a certain answer j in a question q into a percentage mark:

$$\text{PVote}_q^j = \frac{V_j}{\sum_{i=0}^n V_i}$$

Where V_j means the vote that jth answer get on question q, n means number of answers we have on the question q. The denominator is the sum of all answers' vote. In addition, PVote can restrict the value in range $[0, 1]$ which means we do not need further processing or normalization. We do not need to consider about the case which denominator is zero as we delete all the topics which have zero response. Then, we convert all the topicId back to it's vector form as we need the topic information. After those operations we get a User-Topic Matrix $M : U \times \vec{T} \in \mathbb{R}^{T \times U}$, where U, T is the number of users and topics, $\vec{T}$ is the ranked topics.

4.3   AutoEncoder

As the user-topic matrix R has already been generated, the dimension of R is acceptable but the size $U \times T$ is relatively large. So we use the matrix R as the input of the variational autoencoder (VAE) [11]. Then, the VAE can learn a lower-dimension representation during the training which is the embedding E. The reason why we use the VAE is that the autoencoder is used widely on dimension reduction and features learning. Our user-topic matrix R have a high dimension topic embedding, we need to figure out a way to reduce the dimension and retain the necessary information to conduct analysis. The representation E we get from the autoencoder is the rough version of the embedding we are looking for. Then we need to calculate the similarity of the representation E. We pass the E into the decoder so that we can get a decoded matrix D_e which is supposedly the as same as the original matrix R. We use the "accuracy" to measure the similarity between D_e and R:

$$accuracy = \frac{\sum_i^n D_e^i \odot R^i}{n}$$

where n is the number of elements inside matrix R and D_e. The $\odot$ is the XNOR which used to calculate how many elements are exactly same the D_e^i, R^i is the i-th element in matrix D_e and R. The XNOR operator has following property:

$$a \odot b = \begin{cases} 0 & \text{if } a \neq b \\ 1 & \text{if } a == b \end{cases}$$

4.4   Reinforcement Learning and Recommendation

As the accuracy was defined in previous section, we will use this accuracy as the reward in our reinforcement learning framework. We use the Q-learning here, the training algorithm was described in the Algorithm 1. We will use the Q-learning to allow our model to improve the embedding E by itself. The n in algorithm refers to the number of episode. The strategy is to find a best direction of the value change in the embedding E which can acquire the highest Q-value. Once the optimal Q-value reached, it means we have figured out an optimal policy π^* which can improve our embedding representation E. Finally, we obtain an optimal embedding E^* which we can use in the recommendation system. In the real recommendation system, what we will use is the optimal embedding E^*. The embedding cannot be used for recommendation directly as the embedding does not have any valuable information for recommendation system. So, we need to recover the embedding E^*, through the decoder, into a matrix R' that contains the user-topic information and the ranking information. The recommendation method we used is the collaborative filtering (CF). So, the overall structure for our proposed model in Fig. 2.

Algorithm 1: Q-learning

Initialize Q-table,Q(s,a) randomly;
Initialize embedding E comes from the VAE;
Initialize $\eta \leftarrow \eta_{init}, \gamma \leftarrow \gamma_{init}$;
for $i = 0$ *to n* **do**
    Initialize s;
    $r = \text{accuracy}(E,R)$;
    for *each step in episode i* **do**
        choose a from s using policy derived from Q ;
        $Q(s_t,a) \leftarrow Q(s_t,a) + \eta(r + \gamma \max_a Q(s_{t+1},a))$;
        use the q-value find the policy: $\pi \leftarrow Q(s,a)$;
        $s_t \leftarrow s_{t+1}$
    end
    use the policy update the embedding: $E \leftarrow E'$;
end

---

5 Experiment

5.1 Experiment Setup

The data set used for experiment is the Stack Overflow which was flattened by removing all the XML markups and converted into the json format. The original data set contained 14,768,990 records including answers and questions. After filtering, the dataset was changed as 'userID:Topic' format that was described in Sect. 4.1. After that, we had 99,220 users and 118,320 questions in total. As we conduce some data cleaning technique with the dataset, it leads to the userID not being consecutive as some users are considered inactive users. If we use the original userId as the axis it will make our matrix extremely big as the userID comes from 0 to 6,454,151, but we only need the 99,220 active

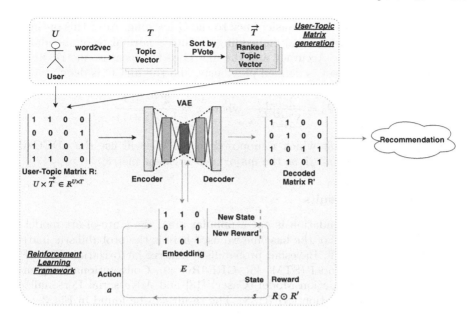

Fig. 2. Model structure, where the red line represent the work flow of RL. The new state is s_{t+1}, new reward is $R_{t+1} \odot R'$, t is the timestamp (Color figure online)

users. Using the original userId as the index of matrix will get a matrix with shape [6454151,118320] which will take a huge amount of memory of computer. To overcome this problem, we replace the normal userId with our customised userId by using a hash table can map from [1,99220] to the [1,6454151]. By using the customised userId we can save $\frac{6454151-99220}{6454151} = 98.5\%$ run-time memory. So we have a user-topic matrix R which has shape [99,220,118,320] with the values 1, meaning have action, and 0, meaning no action. Also, topic we used in R is the topic id which is mapped as well (See Sect. 4.2 for detail). The methodology we used for getting the vector is the word2vec, we use the pre-trained word2vec to transfer the topic into vector. What we do is that we firstly generate all single word's vector by using word2vec, so we get two lists which have word name and its vector. After that, the topic will be convert into vector with the dimension of 300. As the data is pretty big for training, to vertify the correctness of our approach, we just select top 20% of the samples from the dataset based on the reputation which still have over 2,000,000 records.

After finished the pre-process step, we just put the user-topic matrix R into the VAE to get a reconstructed representation E. To verify this representation is valid and have the necessary information we need, we recover it back to user-topic matrix R' by using the decoder. Then we calculate the accuracy between R and R' by using the formula mentioned in Sect. 4.3. Then we put the embedding E and the accuracy R into the Q-learning framework to improve it. For each episode i, we take the improved embedding E_i and compare with the original matrix R

to get the new accuracy and transfer back to the Q-learning. After this optimize process, we passing the optimal embedding E' into a normal recommendation system. Then, using the Accuracy and the nDCG as the measure metric in our model where the accuracy is defined previously, and the nDCG is defined as:

$$nDCG_p = \frac{\sum_{i=1}^{p} x}{\sum_{i=1}^{|REL|} x} \text{ where } x = \frac{2^{rel_i} + 1}{\log_2(i+1)}$$

the rel_i is the real result which i supposed to be. We will use the nDCG@k, accuracy@k and the recall@k as the major measurement metric.

5.2 Experiment Results

As the expert recommendation is not a popular area, the state-of-art model is hard to figure out [20]. So, the baseline we used here is the probabilistic matrix factorization (PMF) [23], Bayesian probabilistic matrix factorization (BPMF), the segmented topic model (STM) [6], GRE4Rec [9], Convolutional Sequence Embedding Recommendation Model (Caser) [18] and Adversarial Personalized Ranking for recommendation (APR) [8]. The result can be found in Fig. 3.

5.3 Evaluation

It is obvious that when the accuracy increases the nDCG increases as well, which means the reinforcement learning is improving the embedding E by itself. However the nDCG@k is still not good enough which the highest value can reach 0.4767834. The reason is due to data sparsity. Even if the number of records are reduced and all the active users in the dataset are selected, it is still too sparse for the recommendation system to recommend a topic for a user. But we can see that our model is better than the others. The accuracy which is passed into the reinforcement learning is stable after a few episodes and it is stable at around 0.3, which means much information is lost during the encoding and decoding process. However, we still obtain a competitive result on the recommendation which means that our model meets the expectation. The caser is a state-of-art model which used in recommendation system area, it's sensitive with the sparsity data which we can find that the result is not good enough.

5.4 Possible Improvement and Future Work

As discussed in Sect. 4.1, we mentioned that in some questions they only have one answer which means user can only vote this answer or answer one. It may lead to some edge effects which will make the recommendation less efficient. Furthermore, due to the limitation of NLP technique, we may still lose information during the word2vec, and the answers are normally a paragraph which contains many sentences. We need a more efficient way to capture the relation between the word in word level and sentence level. That is the possible improvement can be done in the dataset side. From the model perspective, we can make some

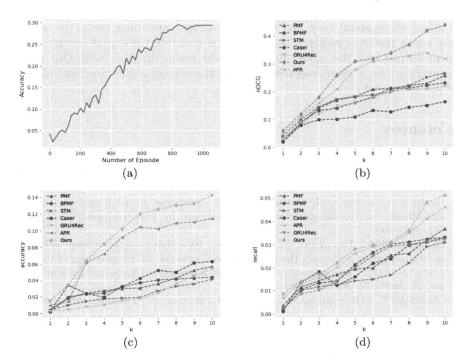

Fig. 3. Graph (a) is the accuracy during the RL process. (b) is the model comparison result in nDCG, (c) is the comparison result in accuracy, (d) is the comparison result in recall.

improvements in the recommendation system and the reinforcement learning system. For example, we can change the CF to the matrix factorization (MF) based recommendation system or a more complex model. But the challenge is that all the state-of-art recommendation systems are not working properly in CQA, in the future we may can adopt the state-of-art recommendation systems to the CQA problem so that it can make recommendation through our embedding.

As the neural network get some surprising result on reinforcement learning, we may change our reinforcement learning framework to deep reinforcement learning. One typical example is that change the Q-learning to DQN which discussed in Sect. 3. But consider about the dataset's complexity, it will be tough to employ the complex recommendation system and the DQN framwork.

6   Conclusion

In this study we proposed a new distributed representation (expert2vec) for expert which is used on solving the CQA problem and the expert recommendation problem. Expert2vec is the distributed representation which contain the information about user and topic and its corresponding rank. We innovatively adopt the reinforcement learning framework into the expert recommendation problem to let the model to improve the embedding by itself. Our model (Expert2Vec) got a promising result among the current expert recommendation state-of-art model.

References

1. Sarath Chandar, A.P., et al.: An autoencoder approach to learning bilingual word representations. In: Advances in Neural Information Processing Systems, pp. 1853–1861 (2014)
2. Borodin, A., Roberts, G.O., Rosenthal, J.S., Tsaparas, P.: Link analysis ranking: algorithms, theory, and experiments. ACM Trans. Internet Technol. (TOIT) **5**(1), 231–297 (2005)
3. Bouguessa, M., Dumoulin, B., Wang, S.: Identifying authoritative actors in question-answering forums: the case of yahoo! answers. In: Proceedings of the 14th ACM SIGKDD International Conference on Knowledge Discovery and Data Mining, pp. 866–874. ACM (2008)
4. Chandak, Y., Theocharous, G., Kostas, J., Jordan, S., Thomas, P.S.: Learning action representations for reinforcement learning. In: International Conference on Machine Learning (2019)
5. Chen, X., Li, S., Li, H., Jiang, S., Qi, Y., Song, L.: Generative adversarial user model for reinforcement learning based recommendation system. In: International Conference on Machine Learning, pp. 1052–1061 (2019)
6. Du, L., Buntine, W., Jin, H.: A segmented topic model based on the two-parameter poisson-dirichlet process. Mach. Learn. **81**(1), 5–19 (2010)
7. Dulac-Arnold, G., et al.: Deep reinforcement learning in large discrete action spaces. arXiv preprint arXiv:1512.07679 (2015)
8. He, X., He, Z., Du, X., Chua, T.S.: Adversarial personalized ranking for recommendation. In: The 41st International ACM SIGIR Conference on Research & Development in Information Retrieval, pp. 355–364. ACM (2018)
9. Hidasi, B., Karatzoglou, A., Baltrunas, L., Tikk, D.: Session-based recommendations with recurrent neural networks. arXiv preprint arXiv:1511.06939 (2015)
10. Ji, Z., Wang, B.: Learning to rank for question routing in community question answering. In: Proceedings of the 22nd ACM International Conference on Information & Knowledge Management, pp. 2363–2368. ACM (2013)
11. Kingma, D.P., Welling, M.: Auto-encoding variational bayes. arXiv preprint arXiv:1312.6114 (2013)
12. Li, J., Luong, M.T., Jurafsky, D.: A hierarchical neural autoencoder for paragraphs and documents. arXiv preprint arXiv:1506.01057 (2015)
13. Liu, M., Liu, Y., Yang, Q.: Predicting best answerers for new questions in community question answering. In: Chen, L., Tang, C., Yang, J., Gao, Y. (eds.) WAIM 2010. LNCS, vol. 6184, pp. 127–138. Springer, Heidelberg (2010). https://doi.org/10.1007/978-3-642-14246-8_15
14. Liu, Q., Agichtein, E., Dror, G., Maarek, Y., Szpektor, I.: When web search fails, searchers become askers: understanding the transition. In: Proceedings of the 35th International ACM SIGIR Conference on Research and Development in Information Retrieval, pp. 801–810. ACM (2012)

15. Mikolov, T., Sutskever, I., Chen, K., Corrado, G.S., Dean, J.: Distributed representations of words and phrases and their compositionality. In: Advances in Neural Information Processing Systems, pp. 3111–3119 (2013)
16. Miller, D.R., Leek, T., Schwartz, R.M.: A hidden markov model information retrieval system. In: SIGIR, vol. 99, pp. 214–221 (1999)
17. Pu, Y., et al.: Variational autoencoder for deep learning of images, labels and captions. In: Advances in Neural Information Processing Systems, pp. 2352–2360 (2016)
18. Tang, J., Wang, K.: Personalized top-n sequential recommendation via convolutional sequence embedding. In: Proceedings of the Eleventh ACM International Conference on Web Search and Data Mining, pp. 565–573. ACM (2018)
19. Tian, Y., Lo, D., Lawall, J.: SEWordSim: software-specific word similarity database. In: Companion Proceedings of the 36th International Conference on Software Engineering, pp. 568–571. ACM (2014)
20. Wang, X., Huang, C., Yao, L., Benatallah, B., Dong, M.: A survey on expert recommendation in community question answering. J. Comput. Sci. Technol. 33(4), 625–653 (2018)
21. Wang, Y., Yao, H., Zhao, S.: Auto-encoder based dimensionality reduction. Neurocomputing 184, 232–242 (2016)
22. Xu, F., Ji, Z., Wang, B.: Dual role model for question recommendation in community question answering. In: Proceedings of the 35th International ACM SIGIR Conference on Research and Development in Information Retrieval, pp. 771–780. ACM (2012)
23. Yang, B., Manandhar, S.: Tag-based expert recommendation in community question answering. In: 2014 IEEE/ACM International Conference on Advances in Social Networks Analysis and Mining (ASONAM 2014), pp. 960–963. IEEE (2014)
24. Yao, L., Wang, X., Sheng, Q.Z., Benatallah, B., Huang, C.: Mashup recommendation by regularizing matrix factorization with API co-invocations. In: IEEE Transactions on Services Computing (2018)
25. Zhang, S., Yao, L., Sun, A., Tay, Y.: Deep learning based recommender system: a survey and new perspectives. ACM Comput. Surv. (CSUR) 52(1), 5 (2019)
26. Zhang, X., Yao, L., Yuan, F.: Adversarial variational embedding for robust semi-supervised learning. In: Proceedings of the 25th ACM SIGKDD International Conference on Knowledge Discovery and Data Mining KDD 2019, pp. 139–147. ACM, New York (2019)
27. Zhao, X., Xia, L., Zhao, Y., Yin, D., Tang, J.: Model-based reinforcement learning for whole-chain recommendations. arXiv preprint arXiv:1902.03987 (2019)
28. Zheng, C., Zhai, S., Zhang, Z.: A deep learning approach for expert identification in question answering communities. arXiv preprint arXiv:1711.05350 (2017)
29. Zheng, G., et al.: DRN: a deep reinforcement learning framework for news recommendation. In: Proceedings of the 2018 World Wide Web Conference on World Wide Web, pp. 167–176. W3C (2018)
30. Zheng, X., Hu, Z., Xu, A., Chen, D., Liu, K., Li, B.: Algorithm for recommending answer providers in community-based question answering. J. Inf. Sci. 38(1), 3–14 (2012)

Improving the Link Prediction by Exploiting the Collaborative and Context-Aware Social Influence

Han Gao[1(✉)], Yuxin Zhang[1], and Bohan Li[1,2,3(✉)]

[1] College of Computer Science and Technology, Nanjing University of Aeronautics
and Astronautics, Nanjing, China
{gh,bhli}@nuaa.edu.cn
[2] Collaborative Innovation Center of Novel Software Technology and
Industrialization, Nanjing, China
[3] Jiangsu Easymap Geographic Information Technology Corp., Ltd, Nanjing, China

Abstract. The study of link prediction has attracted increasing attention with the booming social networks. Researchers utilized topological features of networks and the attribute features of nodes to predict new links in the future or find the missing links in the current network. Some of the works take topic into consideration, but they don't think of the social influence that has potential impacts on link prediction. Hence, it leads us to introduce social influence into topics to find contexts. In this paper, we propose a novel model under the collaborative filter framework and improve the link prediction by exploiting context-aware social influence. We also adopt the clustering algorithm with the use of topological features, thus we incorporate the social influence, topic and topological structure to improve the quality of link prediction. We test our method on Digg data set and the results of the experiment demonstrate that our method performs better than the traditional approaches.

Keywords: Link prediction · Social networks · Social influence · Context

1 Introduction

With the popularity and development of social networks, online social networks such as Facebook, Twitter and Weibo are playing an increasingly significant role in people's lives, as well as changing the way that people communicate with each other. Social networks contain a wealth of information, provide researchers an unprecedented opportunity to explore human behavior patterns. Link prediction, as the basic research problem of social networks, is to look for potential links from existing networks or to predict the links that may appear or break in future networks [1]. Because of its practical value, link prediction has become an effective computational tool for many real-world applications. It can be applied in many fields. The most typical application is the recommendation system,

© Springer Nature Switzerland AG 2019
J. Li et al. (Eds.): ADMA 2019, LNAI 11888, pp. 302–315, 2019.
https://doi.org/10.1007/978-3-030-35231-8_22

for instance, friend recommendation in the social network [2] and commodity recommendation in online shopping website [3]. It is obvious that effective link prediction can improve user experience and user stickiness to the application.

Existing link prediction methods mainly utilize network topological features and node attribute features. Lin [4] proposed a method based on node attributes such as the number of common features shared by them. Leicht et al. [5] proposed the method based on graph-topological features. Tylenda et al. [6] used topological and node feature both by including the temporal information. However, as a matter of fact, there is a lot of useful information that is not considered in social networks. Some works consider topics [7], nevertheless, it is essential to think of social influence when introducing the topics. Social Influence reflects the interaction pattern of individual behaviors in social networks, the role of which has been demonstrated in many previous works [8,9]. In fact, the influence of the same user may vary greatly under different topics. Li et al. [10] investigated the problem of the personalized influential topic search, which is to find the top-k q-related topics that are most influential for the query user. Nguyen et al. [11] presented a method to find meaningful context (a collection of topics) with similar influence patterns, which in turn means that these user have similar behavior patterns. That is the reason motivated us to use context for tackling link prediction problem.

In addition, we also use the topological structure characteristics of social networks, which has been applied in many works. And we employ clustering algorithm to classify user nodes and the collaborative filtering framework is adopted to incorporate topological feature with context, so as to improve the effect of link prediction. The main contributions of this paper are:

• We take the context into consideration for link prediction and introduce context as a user node feature where user's social influence performs as the same pattern.

• We present a novel model for link prediction, incorporate social influence, topic and topological features to improve the performance under the collaborative filter framework.

• We verify our model through experiments on a real-world dataset and the results demonstrate the effectiveness and accuracy for link prediction.

The rest of the paper is organized as follows. In Sect. 2, we introduce the related work including link prediction in the social network, social influence, node clustering, and collaborative filter. In Sect. 3, we formulate our model in detail from three parts. The experiment and results are shown in Sect. 4. Finally, in Sect. 5, we make a conclusion for this paper and draw future research directions.

2   Related Work

2.1   Link Prediction in Social Networks

Link prediction has a huge development in recent years and is applied in many fields, especially in social networks. It can be represented as a graph when dealing with link prediction problem: $G(V, E)$ where V is the node representing a user and E is the edge representing there is a relationship between two users. Traditional methods can be divided into three categories: similarity-based method, which is also the most commonly used method, probability-based method and machine learning-based method [12].

The first one is to calculate the similarity of each pair of nodes to determine whether they may be connected. Similarity can be divided into two kinds, one is measured by node attributes, such as location, age, gender, etc. The other is to measure similarity by the topological features, like common neighbors [13]. These methods are based on the principle that the comparison of node pairs with large similarity tends to have potential relations. The calculation of such kind of methods is simple, which can infer the potential links quickly. However, these methods still have obvious defects. Firstly, it regards node attributes and topological features as independence. Therefore, it lacks consistency and appropriate ways to define similarity by using these two types of related features both. The prediction ability of the model may vary greatly due to different nodes.

In order to overcome this weakness, some strategies based on probability are presented, such as Bayesian probability model [14], in which node attributes and topological feature attributes were regarded as random variables to learn the probability distribution model of links from the observation network, and the potential structure assumed in the Bayesian method is used to estimate the link relationship. But it may be difficult to know the distribution of the appearance of links in advance in the real-world application which is necessary for the probabilistic-based model.

Meanwhile, in recent years, some other methods that used machine learning have been proposed. Pujari et al. [15] presented a supervised classification aggregation method for link prediction in complex networks. Ahmed et al. [16] used a supervised learning strategy for link prediction which takes structural metrics as features.

2.2 Social Influence

In social networks, a particular area of interest is the study of social influence. Social ties between users play an important role in dictating their behavior [17]. In simple terms, a user's actions are not only influenced by other users but also affect other users meanwhile. Many previous works have demonstrated the existence of influence in social networks [18,19], and then researchers focused on modeling it appropriately. The independent cascade model (IC) and the linear threshold model (LT) [20] are the two basic models that have been widely studied. Tang et al. [21] proposed Topical Affinity Propagation (TAP) to model the topic-level social influence on large networks. A variety of probabilistic models of influence between users in a social network are presented by Goyal et al. [22]. Xiang et al. [23] proposed an unsupervised potential variable model based on behavior and similarity of users to learn the strength of the relationship between users, and in this way to measure the social influence. However, traditional approaches didn't consider social influence under different contexts. As we all know, a user in different context prone to have different social influence.

Nguyen et al. [11] introduce the novel problem of finding the meaningful context of social influence, and the social influence performs similarly in the same context. The problem raised in this work motivates us to consider context which can be used in link prediction.

2.3   Node Clustering

It is a laborious and time-consuming task to measure the similarity of all nodes of the whole graph. Moreover, some redundant information in the full graph often has a negative impact on the results of prediction. Therefore, it is necessary to cluster the nodes of the whole graph before conduct link prediction. In this way, we can obtain the cluster of each node, and use it as a measurement of potential links [13]. On the premise of preserving the key information, node clustering extract subgraphs from the whole graph, which not only guarantee the effect of prediction but also reduced the calculation cost greatly. In our paper, we require the graph structure and the node attributes for node clustering.

2.4   Collaborative Filter

Collaborative filter (CF) is an effective method that is widely used in recommendation systems. It takes advantage of collective intelligence, i.e. it uses the preferences of users who have similar interests or experience to recommend information for another user [24]. Tapestry is the first developer who coined the phrase "collaborative filter" [25]. Memory-based CF methods that contain user-based and item-based algorithms are extensively applied in commercial systems because of easy-to-implement and highly effective [26,27]. Nevertheless, this kind of method encounters two obvious shortcomings: matrix sparsity and the expansion problem caused by limited computer resources. Under the circumstances, model-based techniques are investigated, including Bayesian-based model [28], latent-based model [27] and SVM-based model [29], etc. In fact, from the perspective of practice, each kind of method has its own weakness, a good recommendation system usually uses Hybrid CF techniques such as combine CF and content-based with each other to make up for disadvantages [30,31]. In this paper, the model we proposed is based on the collaborative filter framework.

3   Proposed Model for Link Prediction

In this section, we illustrate the notations and concepts used in this paper and formulate the problems of link prediction formally. For our research problem, we assume that the social network is static, and we define it as an undirected graph $G = (U, E)$, where $U = \{u_1, u_2, ..., u_N\}$ is the set of users and $E \subseteq \{e = (u, v) \mid u, v \in U\}$ is the set of undirected edges representing the relationships between users. For example, if we have an edge (u, v) which means user u is a friend of user v (i.e. there is a link between user u and user v). Furthermore, for every user, there is a set of actions $A = \{a_1, a_2, ..., a_M\}$, and for every action, there is a corresponding topic $T = \{t_1, t_2, ..., t_P\}$. Our purpose is to improve link prediction by integrating the context-aware social influence with topological features. We will introduce the model in detail in the next following subsection.

3.1   Context-Aware Social Influence

In [11], Jennifer H proposed a problem with finding meaningful contexts where users influence each other similarly. Based on this, we present our context-aware social influence module and give some related definitions. In this module, we gather the statistics of all actions that users perform and calculate the weight of social influence respectively according to their topic. Finally, we determine the context-aware vector of all edges in the network by calculating the weight difference of social influence under different context classifications.

Given a data set, I is a set of items denoted as $I = \{i_1, i_2, ..., i_M\}$, and every user u has a set representing all actions they performed during a certain time span, which is denoted as $A_u = \{a_1^i, a_2^i, ..., a_N^i\}$. Each element in A_u is denoted as $a_u^i = (u, i, d_u^i)$, where d_u^i is the time of the action and $i \in I$. a_u^i means user u perform an action on item i at time stamp d_u^i. In our model, we assume that each user can only perform one action per item, which means $a_u^i \leq 1$, For the accuracy and efficiency of the model in later prediction, we only consider those users who have one action at least. Users who have never made any action is negative to our prediction and are meaningless in the real world.

In the social network, each user performs an action on an item at a certain time. If there is a edge $e = (u, v)$, and both u and v perform an action on item i, then we compare the time stamp of them. We can infer that the user whose time stamp is prior to another is the initiator of social influence, that is to say, the other user is the one who is influenced. Hence, we regard the process as an item adoption if $d_u^i < d_v^i$. And the set of all items adopted by v from u are denoted as $IA_e = \{i \mid a_u^i \in A_u \wedge a_v^i \in A_v \wedge d_u^i < d_v^i\}$.

Our model implements the context-aware module via including social influence, so we need to quantify the social influence. For each edge $e = (u, v) \in E$ and topic $t \in T$, the social influence weight is defined as follows:

$$w_e^t = \begin{cases} \frac{|IA_e^t|}{|A_u^t|} & \text{if } |A_u^t| \neq 0 \\ undefined & \text{if } |A_u^t| = 0 \end{cases}, \qquad (1)$$

where $A_u^t = \{a_u^i \in A_u \mid i \in t\}$. The weight of edge e concerning topic t is simply measured by calculating the ratio of the number of actions that user u exert influence on topic t to the number of all actions user u performs. If a user does not have any actions, its influence cannot be measured (i.e. undefined).

By measuring each edge under each topic, we obtain a $|E|$-dimensional vector to represent the topic's influence signature. Each element in the vector denote the topic's weight of each edge, which is as follows:

$$t = (w_{e1}^t, w_{e1}^t, ..., w_{e|E|}^t) \in R^{|E|}.$$

The topic is quantified via influence signature, as such, we can divide the topics into groups. Besides, we guarantee the topics in the same group are highly similar, while the topic in different groups has few similarities. We denote C as a subset of the topics T. In the next, we are going to introduce how to obtain these vectors. For each context C, we define the context centroid μ as $\mu = (\mu_1, \mu_1, ..., \mu_{|E|}\}$ where

$$\mu_e = |W_e|^{-1} \sum_{\substack{t \in C \\ w_e^t \neq undef}} w_e^t, e = 1, 2, ..., |E| \tag{2}$$

and $W_e = \{t \in C \mid w_e^t \neq undef\}$.

For each pair of influence signatures (s, t), the distance between them is computed as

$$Dist(s, t) = |N|^{-1} \sum_{e \in E} diff(w_e^s, w_e^t), \tag{3}$$

where

$$diff(x, y) = \begin{cases} |x - y| & x, y \text{ both } defined \wedge (x \neq 0 \cup y \neq 0) \\ 0 & otherwise \end{cases}$$

and

$$N = \{e \in E \mid w_e^s, w_e^t \text{ both } defined \wedge (w_e^s \neq 0 \cup w_e^t \neq 0)\}$$

We use the distance between two influence signatures to measure the difference of each context classification. Finally ,we divide the topics into groups by minimizing the distance between groups. The formula for calculating the distance between groups is as follows:

$$Q_k(C) = \sum_{k=1}^{k} \sum_{t \in k} Dist(t, \mu_k) \tag{4}$$

where k is the number of context categories, and $\forall_{i,j} : C_i \cap C_j = \emptyset \wedge \bigcup_{k=1}^{k} C_k = t$. Through the above steps, we realize the context-aware module which classifies the topics based on social influence and construct the context-aware vector for each user, which is shown below:

$$CV_u = (c_1, c_2, ..., c_k, |Au|)$$

$$c_i = \frac{|A_u^{C_i}|}{|A_u|} \tag{5}$$

where $A_u^{C_i}$ denote the number of actions that user u performs on context C_i. At last, we use the context-aware vector as a significant feature of user nodes, which reflect the user's social influence and interest toward different topics or fields.

3.2 Node Clustering

The topological structure of the graph is an important attribute in the social network, which can help us to make a better performance for link prediction. We can get the potential link prediction for each node by learning the original graph topology. Therefore, using topology information of the graph can not only improve the accuracy of prediction effectively, but also improve the efficiency of the algorithm greatly. Below, we formulate a node clustering method based on topological features.

For each user node, we assume that all its possible linked neighborhood nodes aggregate as a cluster. Topological structure is also a reflection of node feature, hence we deem that two nodes sharing a link have certain similarities. For each user node i, the set of neighborhood node cluster is denoted as $\{N_i\}_{i=1}^k$, the topological feature vector is denoted as F_i. And we set a personalized weight W_i for each user. The cluster of N_i is estimated by the following formula:

$$\delta_i = \min_{W_i} \frac{1}{k} \sum_{j=1}^{k} ||W_i \otimes F_j - F_i|| \tag{6}$$

where δ_i is the topological feature radius of cluster of each N_i. Personalized weight can minimize the node topological feature radius, and mirror user's attention preference and potential habit in the real world.

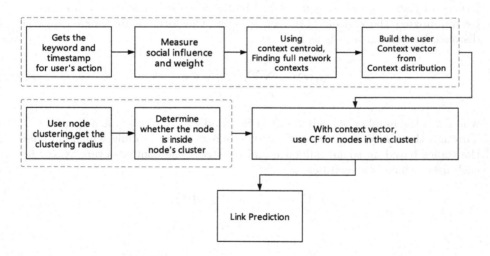

Fig. 1. The flowchart of proposed model

3.3 Collaborative Filter

After completion of the above work, we obtain the context-aware vector and the node clustering radius based on the topology of each user node. When we conduct link prediction for the missing link, the cluster radius of nodes is used to judge whether the user node is inside the cluster of N_i at first.

$$\delta_{ij} = \|W_i \otimes F_j - F_i\|,$$

if $\delta_{ij} > \delta_i$, we regard user j is outside the cluster of N_i, which means the probability of user j have a link with user i is low. We only consider nodes that satisfy the condition of $\delta_{ij} \leq \delta_i$, because there is a higher probability for these nodes to have a link with the center node compare to other nodes. On account of their topology feature is similar, they are the potential links. After we find the potential link nodes, we need to combine them with a context-aware vector for collaborative filtering. The similarity of nodes is calculated as follows:

$$Sim(i, j) = \frac{1}{|CV_i - CV_j|} \tag{7}$$

Finally, we can use our model to find the missing links in social networks based on the similarity above. The overall structure of our model is shown in Fig. 1.

4   Experiments

In this section, we test our model on Digg social network dataset to evaluate the performance for link prediction and compare it with some existing link prediction methods. Besides, we analyze the data used in each module of the model as well.

4.1   Data

The dataset we use is from Digg social network as of 2008, and we will introduce it briefly at first in this subsection. At the beginning of the experiment, we need to pre-process the original data to remove a large amount of redundant information. The original data set includes digg stories, users and their actions (submit, digg, comment and reply) to the stories. Firstly, we remove two kinds of data that are valueless in social networks from the original data set: the users who have no neighbors or any actions and the items which no user has performed on. Besides, we change the directed graph in the original dataset to the undirected graph. Figure 2 shows the statistics of the Digg social network after pre-processing briefly, from which we can see that 7921 users have 47149 relationships and performed 848218 actions in total. There are 2.98 neighbors for each user on average, and most users have neighbors from 10 to 99 while only a small part of users have neighbors over 100. We can also know from the Digg dataset that the average number of actions per user is 930, and the amount of users actions is exponentially distributed (i.e. most items are only "digg" by a few users). At the same time, we count the number of common topics of each edge in Digg dataset which turn out is normally distributed, and the average number of common topics for each edge is 56.11. A majority of edges have the number of common topics in the range of 50 to 100, which is higher than the pairs of users without edges. This further illustrates that context is an important attribute for user nodes. In addition to the above work, we statistically analyzed the distribution about the number of items users acted on and the distribution about types of users' actions(i.e. the number of actions of different types from users), and find that the distribution of these attributes is roughly same without obvious further information.

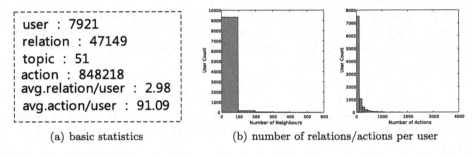

(a) basic statistics   (b) number of relations/actions per user

Fig. 2. Statistics of Digg dataset

4.2   Context Analysis

In the absence of ground truth for the contexts, we present a qualitative analysis of the contexts as [11]. Figure 3 shows the results of the contexts learned by the model in the different cases when $K = 4, 6, 8, 10$. When the value of K is different, the performance of the model is different correspondingly. In the case of $K = 4$, the classification granularity of context is large, and the difference between contexts is large too. We can see that the number of topics in each context varies hugely. In this situation, the information of context attribute is relatively less, which can not greatly improve the performance for link prediction. It is vague to the model and difficult to understand when a context contains too many topics, which results in valueless. For $K = 6$, the situation has no significant change, there is still a context that has an obvious bigger number of topics than others. While $K = 8$, we can see more clearly that the composition of each context and the clarity of classification increases. In this situation, the interval between contexts is appropriate and the number of topics contained in each context is consistent. As a result, the amount of information contained in each context is greatly increased. As for $K = 10$, multiple single topic categories appear in the contexts, which contains the largest amount of information. However, because of the granularity is too fine, it will not only greatly increase the calculation consumption of the model, but also lead to the decline of stability, making it easy to be affected by noise.

We hope that the results of context classification can be both stable and contain sufficient information. A good context classification will improve the

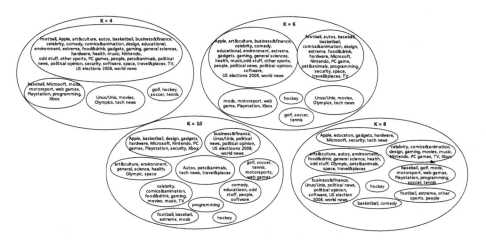

Fig. 3. Context classifications

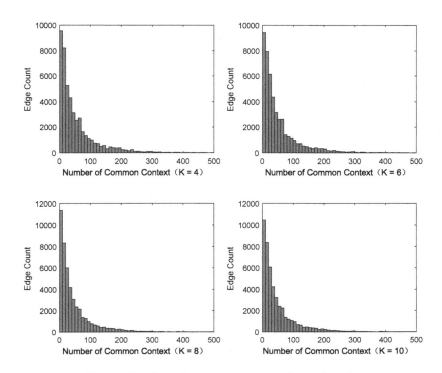

Fig. 4. Number of common contexts for node pairs

accuracy of link prediction tremendously. As shown in Fig. 4, we counted and analyzed the number of common contexts of each context classification.

During the process, we find that there are some actions in the Digg social network dataset that the corresponding user involved in many different contexts. For example, there are 459 actions as "digg" for each user on average. One of the reasons is that "digg" is a very simple and cheap action, which means it doesn't take much effort or risk. But the opposite situation occurs when we consider "comment" which require more efforts and a certain degree of professionalism, consequently users tend to perform this action according to the topic they are interested in, so we can obtain a higher quality context-aware vector via adopting the data of "comment". Thus, we only selected the data about the "comment" action as the data source of the context-aware vector in the experiment.

4.3 Link Prediction

To evaluate the performance of our proposed method, we use the following evaluation metrics and compare them with some traditional link prediction methods. We use AUC score, precision, recall to assess the quality of the results of link prediction.

AUC (Area Under the Receiver Operating Characteristic Curve): It can regards as the probability of the score of an existing randomly picked link being higher than that of a randomly chosen non-existent one. The value of AUC is defined as follows: $AUC = \frac{(p+0.5q)}{r}$, where p is the number of times the existing edges that have a higher score, q is the number of times they score the same, and r denotes the number of independent comparison [32].

Precision: It measures as the ratio of the number of links predicted correctly to the number of total predicted links. The formula is shown as follows: $Precision = \frac{n}{H}$, where n represents the number of true predicted links, H represents the number of total links predicted by our method.

Recall: It measures as the ratio of the number of links predicted correctly to the number of all links which should be observed. The formula is shown as: $Recall = \frac{n}{N}$, where n is the same definition as Precision and N represents the total number of existing edges.

The above metrics are used to compare the performance of our method with the following three traditional methods, and the results are shown in Fig. 5.

R&M [33]: Links are predicted by the number of retweets and mentions per pair of users.

CN [34]: The similarity of users is measured by the number of common neighbors per pair of users, and conduct link prediction based on this. This method is widely used for its simpleness and efficiency.

PA [35]: The more friends two users have, the more likely they are connected. Based on this idea, PA scores link prediction using the product of the user's friend.

We find that our model performed well in all measures, especially in terms of recall, which means that our model can predict well the missing edges in the

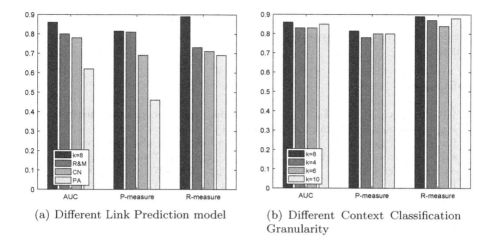

(a) Different Link Prediction model

(b) Different Context Classification Granularity

Fig. 5. Comparison of experiment results

existing social networks. To improve the stability of our model, we set different corruption fractions for the clustering radius of nodes and compared their performance of prediction. The results are shown in Table 1. Finally, we get the best prediction of the model when the corruption fraction is $\delta = 5\%$. The validity of our model is proved through the experiments and compared with the traditional methods for link prediction our model has a better performance.

Table 1. Mean recall of our model with different corruption fraction.

δ	K			
	4	6	8	10
0%	0.87	0.84	0.89	0.88
5%	0.88	0.86	0.89	0.91
10%	0.87	0.86	0.88	0.89

5 Conclusion

In this paper, we proposed a novel model for link prediction, which mainly contains two modules: context-aware social influence module and node clustering module. We apply the collaborative filter framework to integrate the modules, accordingly, we can take advantage of features such as topics, social influence and topological structure all to improve the performance of link prediction, and the experimental results demonstrate that our model is effective and prior to the traditional methods. We focus on the user's actions rather than other private information of users that is not easy to obtain in the real social networks, which is a prominent advantage of our method. In future work, we will further consider the situation in dynamic social networks, which are more complex and challenging.

References

1. Wang, P., Xu, B.W., Wu, Y.R., et al.: Link prediction in social networks: the state-of-the-art. Sci. China Inf. Sci. **58**(1), 1–38 (2015)
2. Barbieri, N., Bonchi, F., Manco, G.: Who to follow and why: link prediction with explanations. In: Proceedings of the 20th ACM SIGKDD International Conference on Knowledge Discovery and Data Mining, pp. 1266–1275. ACM (2014)
3. Backstrom, L., Huttenlocher, D., Kleinberg, J., et al.: Group formation in large social networks: membership, growth, and evolution. In: Proceedings of the 12th ACM SIGKDD International Conference on Knowledge Discovery and Data Mining, pp. 44–54. ACM (2006)
4. Lin, D.: An information-theoretic definition of similarity. In: Icml, vol. 1998, no. 98, pp. 296–304 (1998)
5. Leicht, E.A., Holme, P., Newman, M.E.J.: Vertex similarity in networks. Phys. Rev. E **73**(2), 026120 (2006)
6. Tylenda, T., Angelova, R., Bedathur, S.: Towards time-aware link prediction in evolving social networks. In: Proceedings of the 3rd Workshop on Social Network Mining and Analysis, p. 9. ACM (2009)
7. Aslan, S., Kaya, M.: Topic recommendation for authors as a link prediction problem. Future Gener. Comput. Syst. **89**, 249–264 (2018)
8. Bakshy, E., Karrer, B., Adamic, L.A.: Social influence and the diffusion of user-created content. In: Proceedings of the 10th ACM Conference on Electronic Commerce, pp. 325–334. ACM (2009)
9. Yang, Y., Jia, J., Wu, B., et al.: Social role-aware emotion contagion in image social networks. In: Thirtieth AAAI Conference on Artificial Intelligence (2016)
10. Li, J., Liu, C., Yu, J.X., et al.: Personalized influential topic search via social network summarization. IEEE Trans. Knowl. Data Eng. **28**(7), 1820–1834 (2016)
11. Nguyen, J.H., Hu, B., Günnemann, S., et al.: Finding contexts of social influence in online social networks. In: Proceedings of the 7th Workshop on Social Network Mining and Analysis, p. 1. ACM (2013)
12. Sharma, P.K., Rathore, S., Park, J.H.: Multilevel learning based modeling for link prediction and users' consumption preference in online social networks. Future Gener. Comput. Syst. (2017)
13. Wang, X., He, D., Chen, D., et al.: Clustering-based collaborative filtering for link prediction. In: Twenty-Ninth AAAI Conference on Artificial Intelligence (2015)
14. Wang, C., Satuluri, V., Parthasarathy, S.: Local probabilistic models for link prediction. In: Seventh IEEE International Conference on Data Mining, ICDM 2007, pp. 322–331. IEEE (2007)
15. Pujari, M., Kanawati, R.: Supervised rank aggregation approach for link prediction in complex networks. Proceedings of the 21st International Conference on World Wide Web, pp. 1189–1196. ACM (2012)
16. Ahmed, C., ElKorany, A., Bahgat, R.: A supervised learning approach to link prediction in Twitter. Soc. Netw. Anal. Min. **6**(1), 24 (2016)
17. Anagnostopoulos, A., Kumar, R., Mahdian, M.: Influence and correlation in social networks. In: Proceedings of the 14th ACM SIGKDD International Conference on Knowledge Discovery and Data Mining, pp. 7–15. ACM (2008)

18. La Fond, T., Neville, J.: Randomization tests for distinguishing social influence and homophily effects. In: Proceedings of the 19th International Conference on World Wide Web, pp. 601–610. ACM (2010)
19. Singla, P., Richardson, M.: Yes, there is a correlation:-from social networks to personal behavior on the web. Proceedings of the 17th International Conference on World Wide Web, pp. 655–664. ACM (2008)
20. Kempe, D., Kleinberg, J., Tardos,É.: Maximizing the spread of influence through a social network. In: Proceedings of the Ninth ACM SIGKDD International Conference on Knowledge Discovery and Data Mining, pp. 137–146. ACM (2003)
21. Tang, J., Sun, J., Wang, C., et al.: Social influence analysis in large-scale networks. In: Proceedings of the 15th ACM SIGKDD International Conference on Knowledge Discovery and Data Mining, pp. 807–816. ACM (2009)
22. Goyal, A., Bonchi, F., Lakshmanan, L.V.S.: Learning influence probabilities in social networks. In: Proceedings of the Third ACM International Conference on Web Search and Data Mining, pp. 241–250. ACM (2010)
23. Xiang, R., Neville, J., Rogati, M.: Modeling relationship strength in online social networks. In: Proceedings of the 19th International Conference on World Wide Web, pp. 981–990. ACM (2010)
24. Su, X., Khoshgoftaar, T.M.: A survey of collaborative filtering techniques. Adv. Artif. Intell. **2009**, 1–19 (2009)
25. Goldberg, D., Nichols, D., Oki, B.M., et al.: Using collaborative filtering to weave an information tapestry. Commun. ACM **35**(12), 61–71 (1992)
26. Linden, G., Smith, B., York, J.: Amazon. com recommendations: item-to-item collaborative filtering. IEEE Internet Comput. **2003**(1), 76–80 (2003)
27. Hofmann, T.: Latent semantic models for collaborative filtering. ACM Trans. Inf. Syst. (TOIS) **22**(1), 89–115 (2004)
28. Su, X., Khoshgoftaar, T.M.: Collaborative filtering for multi-class data using belief nets algorithms. In: 18th IEEE International Conference on Tools with Artificial Intelligence, ICTAI 2006, vol. 2006, pp. 497–504. IEEE (2006)
29. Su, X., Khoshgoftaar, T.M., Zhu, X., et al.: Imputation-boosted collaborative filtering using machine learning classifiers. In: Proceedings of the 2008 ACM Symposium on Applied Computing, pp. 949–950. ACM (2008)
30. Melville, P., Mooney, R.J., Nagarajan, R.: Content-boosted collaborative filtering for improved recommendations. In: Aaai/iaai, vol. 23, pp. 187–192 (2002)
31. Pavlov, D.Y., Pennock, D.M.: A maximum entropy approach to collaborative filtering in dynamic, sparse, high-dimensional domains. In: Advances in Neural Information Processing Systems, pp. 1465–1472 (2003)
32. Aslan, S., Kaya, M.: Topic recommendation for authors as a link prediction problem. Future Gener. Comput. Syst. **89**, 249–264 (2018)
33. Cha, M., Haddadi, H., Benevenuto, F., et al.: Measuring user influence in Twitter: the million follower fallacy. In: Fourth International AAAI Conference on Weblogs and Social Media (2010)
34. Liben-Nowell, D., Kleinberg, J.: The link-prediction problem for social networks. J. Am. Soc. Inf. Sci. Technol. **58**(7), 1019–1031 (2007)
35. Newman, M.E.J.: Clustering preferential attachment in growing networks. Phys. Rev. E **64**(2), 025102 (2001)

A Causality Driven Approach to Adverse Drug Reactions Detection in Tweets

Humayun Kayesh[ID], Md. Saiful Islam[(✉)][ID], and Junhu Wang[ID]

School of Information and Communication Technology,
Griffith University, Gold Coast, Australia
humayun.kayesh@griffithuni.edu.au,
{saiful.islam,j.wang}@griffith.edu.au

Abstract. Social media sites such as Twitter is a platform where users usually express their feelings, opinions, and experiences, e.g., users often share their experiences about medications including adverse drug reactions in their tweets. Mining and detecting this information on adverse drug reactions could be immensely beneficial for pharmaceutical companies, drug-safety authorities and medical practitioners. However, the automatic extraction of adverse drug reactions from tweets is a nontrivial task due to the short and informal nature of tweets. In this paper, we aim to detect adverse drug reaction mentions in tweets where we assume that there exists a cause-effect relationship between drug names and adverse drug reactions. We propose a causality driven neural network-based approach to detect adverse drug reactions in tweets. Our approach applies a multi-head self attention mechanism to learn word-to-word interactions. We show that when the causal features are combined with the word-level semantic features, our approach can outperform several state-of-the-art adverse drug reaction detection approaches.

Keywords: Adverse drug reaction detection · Causality · Neural network · Multi-head self attention

1 Introduction

Adverse Drug Reaction (ADR), which is considered to be responsible for millions of fatalities every year, is the harmful and unwanted reaction caused by the usage of a medical product [17]. The pharmaceutical companies use ADR information to inform patients about any potential side effects of their products. The identification of ADRs is critical not only for pharmaceutical companies but also for health care management authorities. The accurate and automatic identification of ADRs can save a huge amount of money spent every year by the health care management authorities for treating patients affected by ADRs.

Ideally, adverse drug reactions are identified by lab experiments. Patients are also encouraged to report ADRs through self-reporting systems. However, both of these techniques have limitations. Lab tests are often conducted on a

© Springer Nature Switzerland AG 2019
J. Li et al. (Eds.): ADMA 2019, LNAI 11888, pp. 316–330, 2019.
https://doi.org/10.1007/978-3-030-35231-8_23

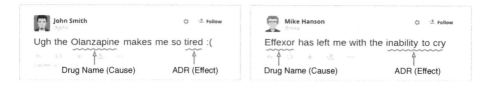

Fig. 1. ADRs in tweets with the cause-effect relationship

limited number of subjects and run for a limited period whereas an ADR may accrue after a long time of using a drug. This issue is partially solved by the self-reported ADR collections where patients voluntarily report adverse reactions of drugs. However, the steps of self-reporting systems are often too complex and time-consuming, hence the patients who experience severe adverse reactions on medicines do not feel the urge to go through all standard steps to report an ADR. This contributes to the rise of unknown or unidentified ADRs.

Nowadays, social media platform such as Twitter has become a popular source of ADRs-related information. Users often tweet for seeking information about different health conditions or just to share their medication experiences. Tweets often include drug names and ADR mentions. Consider the two example tweets as visualized in Fig. 1. The first example mentions an ADR where the name of the drug is *Olanzapine* and the adverse reaction is *tired*. The second example shows that the patient is unable to cry after taking *Effexor*. Due to the availability of a huge volume of data and potentiality of patient-reported hidden ADRs, pharmacovigilance researchers are now interested in automatic ADR detection from tweets. However, automatic detection of ADRs from tweets is a nontrivial problem. There are several challenges in the task of detecting ADRs from tweets. Firstly, tweets are highly informal; sometimes, the posts contain grammatically incorrect sentences, misspellings, and emojis. Secondly, the posts are often short and the adverse reactions are vaguely described. Thirdly, a variety of expressions are used by different twitter users to explain the same thing.

The existing approaches [16,17] that detect ADRs from tweets exploit co-occurrence information as a signal to detect the ADR relationship between a drug and an adverse reaction. However, the co-occurrence of a word with a drug name may not always suggest that the word is an ADR. For example in the tweet "Thank god for vyvanse or I would be sleeping on the cash register right now", the word *sleeping* is used with a drug name *vyvanse*, but it is not an ADR. Other approaches such as [3] apply word embeddings as features but word embeddings cannot detect the relationship between drug names and ADRs as the drug names are not regular English words. Hence, it is important to take the causal relationship between drug and ADRs into consideration rather than co-occurrence of words or word embeddings only.

In this paper, we aim to detect ADRs from tweets by extracting causal features between drug name (cause) and adverse reaction (effect). Causal features are extracted for every word by splitting a tweet into segments such as prefix, midfix, and postfix depending on the position of the word and calculating tf-idf from each segment. The causal features are then combined with word features, which are extracted from word embeddings. Finally, we propose to apply a multi-head self attention (MHA) mechanism on the combined features to detect ADRs from tweets. The main contributions of this paper are given below.

- We propose a novel method to extract causal features for a sequence labeling-based ADR detection.
- We propose a causality driven ADR detection framework that combines causality features and word-level semantic features and applies multi-head self attention to detect ADRs in tweets.
- We compare our proposed ADR detection approach with several existing ADR detection approaches and show that our approach produces relatively stable and robust results on two benchmark datasets.

The rest of the paper is organized as follows. Section 2 reviews the existing approaches from the literature. Section 3 presents our causality driven approach to adverse drug reaction detection. Section 4 demonstrates the superiority of our approach by conducting extensive experiments with two benchmark datasets. Finally, Sect. 5 concludes our work and presents future research direction.

2   Related Work

The existing approaches to automatic ADR detection from social media short text including tweets can be grouped into two broad categories: ADR Signal detection and sequence labeling-based ADR detection.

2.1   ADR Signal Detection

The approaches in this category aim to detect signals that indicate an ADR mention in a text. Yang et al. [17] propose an approach to detect ADR signals from tweets. In this approach, the authors apply the association mining technique to detect ADRs. In association rule mining, the frequently co-occurring words are considered to be an indication of association with each other. The authors also used proportional reporting ratios (PPR) [4,9] which is a statistical approach to calculate the association strength of a drug and an ADR. A major drawback of the approach is that it only considers the co-occurrence of drugs and adverse reactions irrespective of any semantic relation conveyed between them. Another association rule mining-based approached is proposed in [13]. This approach proposes an end-to-end multi-drug ADR detection system. Firstly, the authors apply an association rule mining technique to generate drug-ADR signals. Then, a pruning technique is used to discard unimportant associations. Finally, a contextual association clustering technique is used to detect multi-drug ADRs.

Some recent approaches apply machine learning (ML) techniques to detect ADR signals. Huynh et al. [8] propose a neural network (NN) based approach to detect ADRs from the text. The authors propose Convolutional Recurrent NN and Recurrent Convolutional NN, where word embeddings are used as features for learning. Bollegala et al. [1] propose another ML-based technique to extract causality patterns to detect ADR signals in Tweets. In this approach, a set of lexical patterns are extracted from a set of manually annotated tweets using the skip-gram technique. The lexical patterns are then used to generate feature vectors. Finally, a linear SVM model is trained on the feature vectors to detect the causal relationship between a drug and an adverse reaction. However, this approach cannot detect more than one drug-ADR relations in a single post.

2.2 Sequence Labeling-Based ADR Detection

Some approaches in the literature aim to detect the exact locations of the ADR words in a text. These approaches consider ADR detection as a sequence labeling problem. Song et al. [14] propose a sequence labeling-based ADRs detection approach. The authors consider adverse reactions as named entities and they apply conditional random field (CRF) [10] to label ADRs in tweets. The CRF model is trained on the lexical features and the contextual features such as n-grams and part-of-speech (POS) tags. However, this approach does not identify the drug-ADR relationships.

Many recent approaches apply a neural network-based technique to detect ADRs. Chowdhury et al. [2] propose a multi-task framework to detect both ADR and indications. The framework, which is based on Recurrent Neural Network (RNN), contains a binary classifier to predict whether a text has ADR or not. Additionally, the framework contains two sequence labeling models to label ADRs and indications. Another neural network-based approach [3] aims to label ADRs on tweets. The proposed method in this approach includes a Bidirectional Long Short-Term Memory (BLSTM) [6], which uses a forward RNN and a reverse RNN in its core. However, the experiments are performed on a small dataset.

3 Our Approach

This section presents our causality driven approach to adverse drug reaction detection from tweets in detail.

3.1 Problem Formulation

We consider an adverse drug reaction (ADR) as an event that is caused by another event of taking one or many drugs. We assume that there exists a causal relationship between taking drugs and ADRs. In the following example: "I was sucking on this Lozenge that's supposed to numb sore throats and now I can't feel my mouth", *can't feel my mouth* is an adverse reaction of the drug *Lozenge*. We aim to detect such ADRs in a sequence of text in a tweet by applying causal inference. Our research question is as follows:

RQ: *How can we apply causal inference to extract ADRs from tweets?*

Words	Ugh	the	Olanzapine	makes	me	so	tired	:(
Labels	O	O	O	O	O	O	I-ADR	O

Fig. 2. The words in a tweet are labeled with 'I-ADR' and 'O' labels

Let us denote a tweet as τ which contains a sequence of words $W = [w_0, w_1, ..., w_{n-1}]$, where n is the number of words in τ. We aim to develop a function f that will take W as input and detect corresponding labels for each word. Formally, we define the problem studied in this paper as follows.

$$f(W) = L \tag{1}$$

$$\forall L_i \in L : L_i = \begin{cases} \text{I-ADR} & \text{if } w_i \text{ is an ADR,} \\ \text{O} & \text{otherwise} \end{cases} \tag{2}$$

where L is an output sequence generated by f that contains a sequence of labels of the corresponding words in W. The labels 'I-ADR' (Inside-ADR) and 'O' (Outside-ADR) denote the ADR words and the non-ADR words respectively. For example, consider the words in the first tweet as given in Fig. 1, the corresponding labeling of the words in this tweet is illustrated in Fig. 2.

3.2 Proposed ADR Detection Model

In this section, we describe our ADR detection model that combines both causal features and word-level features and apply a multi-head self attention (MHA) mechanism in four modules including the label prediction module as follows.

- **Causal Features Extraction Module:** This module captures the causal features for each candidate ADR word in a tweet. Here, we assume that a drug name in a tweet is the *cause* and other words are candidate ADR words (i.e., effect of the cause).
- **Word Features Extraction Module:** This module extracts the local contextual features by applying BLSTM on the word-level semantic features. We exploit word embeddings to extract word-level semantic features from the words in a tweet.
- **Attention Mechanism Module:** The features extracted by the first two modules are combined and used as input to the third module. This module aims to detect ADR words by capturing the interactions between them via multi-head self attention mechanism.
- **Label Prediction Module:** The labels for a sequence of words in a tweet is generated by this module. The output of the attention mechanism module is used as the input to this module.

The internal procedures of each of the module are described in detail below.

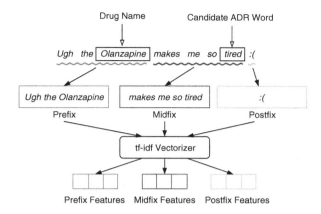

Fig. 3. Split of a tweet into segments: prefix, midfix and postfix, and the corresponding prefix tf-idf based prefix, midfix and postfix features extraction

Causal Features Extraction Module. We assume that when a tweet has a drug name, any other word in the tweet can be an ADR word for that drug. In other words, we consider every word except the drug name as a candidate ADR word. Also, a drug name is considered to be the cause and all other words are considered to be the potential effect in our approach. To detect such relationships, we aim to extract patterns from the occurrence of words around drug names and the candidate ADR words.

- First, we split a tweet into three segments: prefix, midfix, and postfix. Prefix contains the words starting from the beginning of the tweet until the drug name or the candidate ADR word whichever comes first. Midfix contains the words between the drug name and the candidate ADR words. Postfix contains the words after the drug name or the candidate ADR words, whichever comes last, until the end of the tweet. Assume that w_i is a drug name and w_j is a candidate ADR word in a tweet τ with n number of words, where the words are represented as $W = [w_0, w_1, ..., w_{n-1}]$. For the candidate ADR word w_j, the prefix $W_{pre} = [w_0, w_1, ..., w_i]$, midfix $W_{mid} = [w_{i+1}, w_{i+2}, ..., w_j]$, and postfix $W_{post} = [w_{j+1}, w_{j+2}, ..., w_{n-1}]$. For example, consider the words in the first tweet as given in Fig. 1, the corresponding prefix, midfix and postfix segmentation of this tweet is illustrated in Fig. 3.
- Then, we convert W_{pre}, W_{mid}, and W_{post} into tf-idf feature vectors v_{pre}^d, v_{mid}^d, and v_{post}^d respectively, where d is the size of the dictionary. The vectors are then concatenated together to prepare a single feature vector $v_{c_j}^m$, where $m = 3d$. Similarly, every word in a tweet τ is represented as a vector v_c^m. The vectors are then combined together to prepare a matrix $M_c \in R^{n' \times m}$, where n' is the maximum length of word sequence in the dataset. If the number of words $n < n'$, then we add padding to avoid generating variable length matrices. We pass M_c to a one dimensional convolutional neural network (CNN) followed by a ReLU activation layer, which generate a causal feature

matrix $M'_c \in R^{n' \times m'}$ as follows:

$$M'_{c\{i,j\}} = ReLU(I_{i,j} \times K_r + b_r) \tag{3}$$

where I is the output from CNN; m', K_r and b_r are the dimension of the causal features, the kernel and the bias parameters, respectively.

Word Features Extraction Module. We use word embedding features generated by a publicly available pre-trained Word2vec model [5] to capture the word-level semantic features. The model is trained on more than 400 million domain-independent tweets.

- First, a tweet τ is tokenized into word sequences. The word sequences are then padded by a default token if $n < n'$, where n is the number of words in τ and n' is the maximum length of the sequence in the dataset. The padding is essential to avoid generating a variable-length feature matrix. The word sequences are then replaced by their corresponding indices by looking up in a dictionary. The dictionary contains the words in our dataset and the corresponding indices. Using this dictionary, τ is converted to a vector $v_w^{n'}$. In the next step, the index vector is used to extract word embeddings from a pretrained Word2vec model [5] and the tweet τ is converted into a matrix $M_w \in R^{n' \times l}$, where l is the dimension of the word embeddings.
- The word embeddings feature matrix M_w is then passed to a BLSTM to extract local contextual features from the word sequence. The output of the BLSTM layer is another matrix $M'_w \in R^{n' \times l'}$, where l' is the length of word-level features.

Attention Mechanism Module. In our model, we use a Multi-head self attention (MHA) layer to detect ADR labels. We apply the MHA mechanism proposed by Vaswani et al. [15] that can capture word to word interactions in a word-sequence. We combine the causal features M'_c, word-level contextual features M'_w to create an augmented matrix by concatenating them together as follows:

$$M \in R^{n' \times k} = (M'_c \mid M'_w) \tag{4}$$

where $k = m' + l'$. This combined feature matrix M is passed to the MHA layer. In general, not every word in a word sequence contributes equally to decide whether a particular word is an ADR or not. MHA mechanism allows us to capture the interactions between words. This feature allows us to learn what other words to focus on while predicting the label for a word. This layer produces another matrix $M' \in R^{n' \times k}$, which is passed to the label prediction module where the ADR labels are predicted.

Label Prediction Module. This module consists of a fully connected layer with softmax as the activation function. The matrix M' of the attention mechanism module is passed to this layer where the softmax function finally outputs

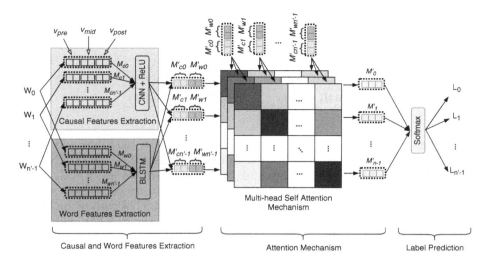

Fig. 4. Architecture of the proposed ADR detection system

label L_i of each word w_i as follows:

$$L_i = softmax(M'_i k_s + b_s) \tag{5}$$

where k_s and b_s are the learnable parameters.

The overall architecture of our proposed ADR detection system in tweets consisting of the above modules is illustrated in Fig. 4.

4   Experiment

This section presents our experimental results and demonstrates the superiority of our approach to ADR detection from tweets.

4.1   Dataset and Experimental Settings

We use two benchmark datasets to evaluate our approach. The first dataset, we refer to it as ASU_CHUP, is published by Cocos et al. [3]. This dataset is an updated version of the Twitter ADR Dataset (v1.0) [12]. The other dataset, we refer to it as SMM4H, is used in Shared Task 2 of Social Media Mining for Health Applications (SMM4H) Workshop & Shared Task 2019[1]. Both of the datasets are labeled by human annotators. We use 75% data for training and 25% data for the test as experimented in [3]. We also use 10% of the training data as the validation data similar to [3]. The validation data is used for the hyperparameter optimization of the ADR detection models experimented in this paper. Table 1 presents the summarized statistics of the tested datasets.

---

[1] https://healthlanguageprocessing.org/smm4h/challenge/.

Table 1. Test datasets statistics

Datasets	Tweets(ADRs)	
	Training set	Test set
ASU_CHUP dataset	585(492)	206(172)
SMM4H dataset	1487(1368)	496(464)

In the causal feature extraction, we apply a CNN with 120 filters and kernel size 5. We use ReLU as the activation function in the CNN. The CNN layer is followed by a fully collected layer of 16 nodes where we use ReLU as the activation function in each node. In the word-level features extraction, we use 400-dimension pretrained word embeddings [5] and a BLSTM with 80 units. We set tanh as the activation function and dropout to 0.1 in the BLSTM model. The multi-head self attention model has 41 heads, which is the maximum number of words in a tweet in our dataset $(n' - 1)$. We optimize the combined model using the RMSprop optimizer [7] function and the categorical crossentropy loss function [11]. We also use *accuracy* as the metric to optimize the model during training. We evaluate our approach by calculating the approximate match score [12], which is used for evaluating sequence labeling-based methods [3]. We report average precision, recall, and f1-score for 5 runs with different random seeds.

4.2 Performance Evaluation

We evaluate our causality-driven ADR detection approach against several benchmarks methods. The benchmark approaches that we have implemented in our experiments are described below.

- **CRF** [10]: We implement a conditional random fields (CRF) model on 400-dimension word-embedding features.
- **Cocos et al.** [3]: This approach applies a BLSTM to predict ADR labels, where the word embedding is used as the feature set.
- **BLSTM**: This benchmark approach applies a BLSTM on the word embeddings features to generate the word-level features. Additionally, character features and causal features are used in this approach. To generate the character features, we convert each word into a one-hot-vector of characters and generate embeddings of 100 dimensions. We apply a CNN on the word embeddings and the hidden state output of the CNN model is used as the character features. The schematic diagram of the approach is illustrated in Fig. 5. The causal features are extracted as described in Sect. 3.2. Finally, the character features, word features, and causal features are concatenated together and passed to a fully connected layer.
- **BLSTM+CharMHA**: This approach concatenates word features and character features and then applies an MHA layer.
- **BLSTM+CharCausalMHA**: In this approach, word features, character features, and causal features are concatenated together and then an MHA layer is applied.

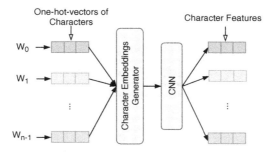

Fig. 5. Generating character features from each word in a tweet

- **BLSTM+MHA**: This is the closest variant of our proposed model, which applies an MHA model on the word features but it does not use the causality features.
- **BLSTM+CausalMHA**: This is our approach as described in Sect. 3.2.

Parameter Optimization. We optimize loss function while training using the training data and the validation data. We run our models for a maximum of 30 epochs and store each model but stop training as soon as the model starts to overfit. The best model in terms of f1-scores on the validation data is used on the test data. Figure 6 displays training loss, validation loss and f1-scores for different epochs of Cocos et al., BLSTM, BLSTM+MHA and BLSTM+CausalMHA approaches. For Cocos et al., the model starts overfitting after the $3rd$ epoch, whereas for all of the other approaches, the model starts overfitting after the $4th$ epoch as the validation loss and training loss starts diverging.

Results. Table 2 shows that our proposed method BLSTM+CausalMHA outperforms the benchmark approaches on the SMM4H dataset in terms of recall and f1-scores while keeping the precision comparable. We report that our approach achieves more than 5% improvement in terms of recall and more than 1% improvement in terms of f1-score over the closet performing benchmark BLSTM+MHA. In the smaller datasets ASU_CHUP, our approach is comparable to the top-performing existing approach *Cocos et al.* in terms of f1-score. However, this approach performs poorly on the SMM4H dataset as its f1-score is significantly less than our approach. We also compare our proposed approach BLSTM+CausalMHA with *Cocos et al.* and BLSTM+MHA on the reduced training data of the SMM4H dataset to show that the improvement of recall and f1-score is consistent. While keeping the test set the same, we reduce the number of training data to 25% and 50% of the original training data. Figure 7 demonstrates that our approach BLSTM+CausalMHA outperforms these two benchmark approaches in terms of both recall and f1-score.

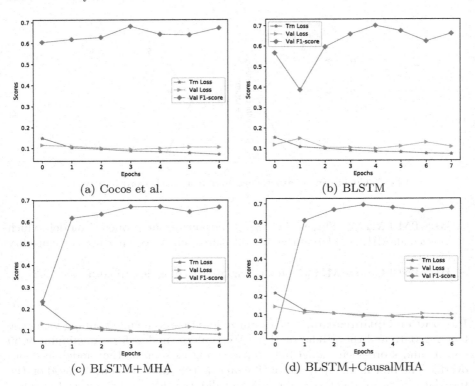

(a) Cocos et al.

(b) BLSTM

(c) BLSTM+MHA

(d) BLSTM+CausalMHA

Fig. 6. Optimization of loss function

Effectiveness of Causal Features. We find that the application of causal features improves ADR detection performances on both ASU_CHUP and SMM4H datasets. The results between BLSTM+MHA and BLSTM+CausalMHA, where the only difference is causal features, are reported in Table 2. Table 2 demonstrates that we get higher f1-scores on both of the tested datasets if causal features are used with word-level semantic features. Additionally, Fig. 7(b) shows that the f1-scores of BLSTM+CausalMHA is higher than BLSTM+MHA for 25%, 50% and 100% training sets. These verify the consistency of the effectiveness of causal features in different sizes of the training sets.

We also investigate the effectiveness of causal features when combined with both character features and word features in ADR detection. In Table 2, we compare BLSTM+ CharCausalMHA and BLSTM+CausalMHA, where BLSTM+ CharCausalMHA applies character features in addition to causal and word features. We observe that the character features negatively impact the results. This is because, character features seems to add more noise than useful information.

Case Study. To demonstrate the effectiveness of our proposed approach BLSTM+ CausalMHA which applies causal features in addition to word-level

Table 2. Comparison of results of our approach BLSTM+CausaMHA with existing approaches

Approaches	ASU_CHUP dataset			SMM4H dataset		
	Precision	Recall	F1-score	Precision	Recall	F1-score
CRF	**0.8224**	0.5175	0.6348	**0.5510**	0.4218	0.4771
Cocos et al.	0.6610	**0.8313**	0.7242	0.5459	0.5568	0.5447
BLSTM	0.6869	0.7500	0.7119	0.5466	0.5851	0.5600
BLSTM + CharMHA	0.7226	0.5725	0.6037	0.5357	0.6561	0.5882
BLSTM + CharCausalMHA	0.7324	0.6688	0.6563	0.5337	0.6600	0.5829
BLSTM + MHA	0.7197	0.7550	0.7162	0.5091	0.7211	0.5950
BLSTM + CausalMHA	0.7287	0.7250	**0.7241**	0.5037	**0.7777**	**0.6077**

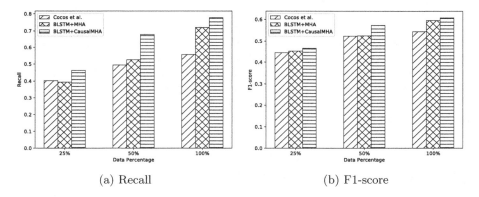

(a) Recall   (b) F1-score

Fig. 7. Evaluation of Cocos et al., BLSTM+MHA and BLSTM+CausalMHA (our approach) on the reduced training sets

features to detect ADRs from tweets, we present several tweets labeled by BLSTM+MHA, Cocos et al. and our approach BLSTM+CausalMHA. We preserve user privacy by replacing usernames by the '<user>' tag. We also replace the names of the medicine by the '<medicine>' tag. We present two tweets below for which our approach BLSTM+CausalMHA can detect the ADR words correctly but BLSTM+MHA and Cocos et al. cannot capture the ADRs.

- **Tweet 1:** *<user>: playing league while on <medicine> is too damn stressful. back to public i go!*
  True Tags: ['O', 'O', 'O', 'O', 'O', 'O', 'O', 'O', 'O', 'O', 'I-ADR', 'O', 'O', 'O', 'O', 'O', 'O', 'O']
  Cocos et al.: ['O', 'O', 'O', 'O', 'O', 'O', 'O', 'O', 'O', 'O', 'O', 'O', 'O', 'O', 'O', 'O', 'O', 'O']
  BLSTM+MHA: ['O', 'O', 'O', 'I-ADR', 'O', 'O', 'O', 'O', 'O', 'O', 'O', 'O', 'O', 'O', 'O', 'O', 'O', 'O']

328   H. Kayesh et al.

BLSTM+CausalMHA: ['O', 'O', 'O', 'O', 'O', 'O', 'O', 'O', 'O', 'O', 'I-ADR', 'O', 'O', 'O', 'O', 'O', 'O', 'O']
ADR: stressful

– **Tweet 2:** *<medicine> gives me a head high but it makes me feel like throwing up after. ugh . #thestruggle*
True Tags: ['O', 'O', 'O', 'O', 'O', 'O', 'O', 'O', 'O', 'O', 'I-ADR', 'I-ADR', 'I-ADR', 'I-ADR', 'O', 'O', 'O', 'O', 'O']
Cocos et al.: ['O', 'O', 'O', 'O', 'O', 'O', 'O', 'O', 'O', 'O', 'O', 'O', 'I-ADR', 'I-ADR', 'O', 'O', 'O', 'O', 'O']
BLSTM+MHA: ['O', 'O', 'O', 'O', 'I-ADR', 'I-ADR', 'O', 'O', 'O', 'O', 'O', 'O', 'I-ADR', 'I-ADR', 'O', 'O', 'O', 'O', 'O']
BLSTM+CausalMHA: ['O', 'O', 'O', 'O', 'O', 'O', 'O', 'O', 'O', 'O', 'I-ADR', 'I-ADR', 'I-ADR', 'I-ADR', 'O', 'O', 'O', 'O', 'O']
ADR: feel like throwing up

In Tweet 1, our approach can correctly detect the ADR word *stressful* because we applied causal features to capture the causal relationship between the drug name and the ADR words. However, the approaches that apply only word features, cannot detect the relationship, hence these approaches labeled the ADR words incorrectly. In Tweet 2, our approach can detect the whole phrase *feel like throwing up* as the ADR but BLSTM+MHA and Cocos et al. can only detect the ADR phrase partially.

– **Tweet 3:** *bedtime. hopefully the headache and nausea from the <medicine> will be gone leaving me with only the more common side effects of antibiotics.*
True Tags: ['O', 'O', 'O', 'O', 'O', 'O', 'I-ADR', 'O', 'O', 'O', 'O', 'O', 'O', 'O', 'O', 'O', 'O', 'O', 'O', 'O', 'O', 'O', 'O', 'O']
Cocos et al.: ['O', 'O', 'O', 'I-ADR', 'O', 'I-ADR', 'O', 'O', 'O', 'O', 'O', 'O', 'O', 'O', 'O', 'O', 'O', 'O', 'O', 'O', 'O', 'O', 'O', 'O']
BLSTM+MHA: ['O', 'O', 'O', 'O', 'I-ADR', 'O', 'I-ADR', 'O', 'O', 'O', 'O', 'O', 'O', 'O', 'O', 'O', 'O', 'O', 'O', 'O', 'O', 'O', 'O', 'O']
BLSTM+CausalMHA: ['O', 'O', 'O', 'O', 'O', 'O', 'I-ADR', 'O', 'O', 'O', 'O', 'O', 'O', 'O', 'O', 'O', 'O', 'O', 'O', 'O', 'O', 'O', 'O', 'O']
ADR: nausea

In Tweet 3, all three approaches were able to correctly label the ADR word *nausea*. However, BLSTM+MHA and Cocos et al. also labeled *headache* as an ADR word. Although headache is a word that describes an undesirable health condition, in this tweet, it is not used as an ADR word. Rather *headache* was the reason for undertaking the drug. In this scenario, only our approach was able to predict a word as a non-ADR word. The next two tweets are examples where our approach struggles to capture ADRs.

– **Tweet 4:** *<user> <user> ugh. my partner was on <medicine> for a while. it made him hide in the apartment. :/*
True Tags: ['O', 'O', 'O', 'O', 'O', 'O', 'O', 'O', 'O', 'O', 'O', 'O', 'O', 'O', 'O', 'I-ADR', 'I-ADR', 'I-ADR', 'I-ADR', 'O', 'O']

Cocos et al.: ['O', 'O', 'O', 'O', 'O', 'O', 'O', 'O', 'O', 'O', 'O', 'O', 'O', 'O', 'O', 'O', 'I-ADR', 'O', 'O', 'O', 'O', 'O']

BLSTM+MHA: ['O', 'O', 'O', 'O', 'O', 'O', 'O', 'O', 'O', 'O', 'O', 'O', 'O', 'O', 'O', 'O', 'I-ADR', 'O', 'O', 'I-ADR', 'O', 'O']

BLSTM+CausalMHA: ['O', 'O', 'O', 'O', 'O', 'O', 'O', 'O', 'O', 'O', 'O', 'O', 'O', 'O', 'I-ADR', 'O', 'O', 'I-ADR', 'O', 'O']

ADR: *hide in the apartment*

- **Tweet 5:** *<medicine> is definitely kicking my ass but my skin lools great.*
  True Tags: ['O', 'O', 'O', 'I-ADR', 'I-ADR', 'I-ADR', 'O', 'O', 'O', 'O', 'O', 'O']
  Cocos et al.: ['O', 'O', 'O', 'O', 'O', 'O', 'O', 'O', 'I-ADR', 'O', 'O', 'O']
  BLSTM+MHA: ['O', 'O', 'O', 'O', 'O', 'O', 'O', 'O','I-ADR', 'O','O', 'O']
  BLSTM+CausalMHA: ['O', 'O', 'O', 'I-ADR', 'O', 'O', 'O', 'O', 'I-ADR', 'O', 'O', 'O']
  ADR: *kicking my ass*

Tweet 4 contains a sequence *hide in the apartment* as ADRs which contains a preposition *in* and an article *the*. Both BLSTM+CausalMHA and BLSTM+MHA can detect the words *hide* and *apartment* as the ADR while Cocos et al. can only detect *hide* as the ADR word. One reason behind this is that causal features and word features for prepositions and articles are less informative, which makes it difficult for the models to decide in which context the words should be labeled as ADR. In Tweet 5, the ADR words are *kicking my ass*. Only our approach detected *Kicking* as an ADR, although it misses the other two words, where there is a pronoun *my*. Whereas, all three approaches incorrectly label *skin* as an ADR. From this analysis, we can conclude that capturing the long ADR phrases with less meaningful words, such as articles, prepositions and pronouns is a challenging task and it could be a possible future extension of this work.

5 Conclusion

In this paper, we propose a sequence labeling based ADR detection approach which applies causal features with word-level semantic features to detect ADRs from tweets. The causal features are extracted for every word after splitting a tweet into prefix, midfix, and postfix. The causal features are combined with word-level semantic features, which is extracted from word embeddings, and then a Multi-head self attention mechanism is applied in our approach to detect ADRs from tweets. We show that the proposed approach works for both small and large size of datasets. The proposed approach can only label whether a word is an ADR but it cannot identify the boundary or hierarchical structure of ADRs in text, e.g. whether an ADR word inside another ADR. We consider this an important research direction for the future work of this paper.

References

1. Bollegala, D., Maskell, S., Sloane, R., Hajne, J., Pirmohamed, M.: Causality patterns for detecting adverse drug reactions from social media: text mining approach. JMIR Public Health Surveill. **4**(2), e51 (2018)
2. Chowdhury, S., Zhang, C., Yu, P.S.: Multi-task pharmacovigilance mining from social media posts. In: WWW (2018)
3. Cocos, A., Fiks, A.G., Masino, A.J.: Deep learning for pharmacovigilance: recurrent neural network architectures for labeling adverse drug reactions in Twitter posts. JAMIA **24**(4), 813–821 (2017)
4. Evans, S., Waller, P.C., Davis, S.: Use of proportional reporting ratios (PRRS) for signal generation from spontaneous adverse drug reaction reports. Pharmacoepidemiol. Drug Saf. **10**(6), 483–486 (2001)
5. Godin, F., Vandersmissen, B., De Neve, W., Van de Walle, R.: Multimedia lab @ acl wnut ner shared task: named entity recognition for Twitter microposts using distributed word representations. In: Proceedings of the Workshop on Noisy User-Generated Text, pp. 146–153 (2015)
6. Graves, A., Schmidhuber, J.: Framewise phoneme classification with bidirectional LSTM and other neural network architectures. Neural Netw. **18**(5–6), 602–610 (2005)
7. Hinton, G., Srivastava, N., Swersky, K.: Neural networks for machine learning lecture 6a overview of mini-batch gradient descent. Neural networks for machine learning, Coursera lecture 6e (2012)
8. Huynh, T., He, Y., Willis, A., Rüger, S.: Adverse drug reaction classification with deep neural networks. In: COLING, pp. 877–887 (2016)
9. Ji, Y., et al.: A potential causal association mining algorithm for screening adverse drug reactions in postmarketing surveillance. IEEE Trans. Inf Technol. Biomed. **15**(3), 428–437 (2011)
10. Lafferty, J., McCallum, A., Pereira, F.C.: Conditional random fields: probabilistic models for segmenting and labeling sequence data. In: ICML, pp. 282–289 (2001)
11. LeCun, Y., et al.: Handwritten digit recognition with a back-propagation network. In: Advances in Neural Information Processing Systems, pp. 396–404 (1990)
12. Nikfarjam, A., Sarker, A., O'Connor, K., Ginn, R., Gonzalez, G.: Pharmacovigilance from social media: mining adverse drug reaction mentions using sequence labeling with word embedding cluster features. JAMIA **22**(3), 671–681 (2015)
13. Qin, X., Kakar, T., Wunnava, S., Rundensteiner, E.A., Cao, L.: Maras: signaling multi-drug adverse reactions. In: KDD, pp. 1615–1623 (2017)
14. Song, Q., Li, B., Xu, Y.: Research on adverse drug reaction recognitions based on conditional random field. In: International Conference on Business and Information Management, pp. 97–101 (2017)
15. Vaswani, A., et al.: Attention is all you need. In: Advances in Neural Information Processing Systems, pp. 5998–6008 (2017)
16. Yang, C.C., Jiang, L., Yang, H., Tang, X.: Detecting signals of adverse drug reactions from health consumer contributed content in social media. In: Proceedings of ACM SIGKDD Workshop on Health Informatics. ACM (2012)
17. Yang, C.C., Yang, H., Jiang, L., Zhang, M.: Social media mining for drug safety signal detection. In: International Workshop on Smart Health and Wellbeing, pp. 33–40 (2012)

Correlate Influential News Article Events to Stock Quote Movement

Arun Chaitanya Mandalapu[1], Saranya Gunabalan[1], Avinash Sadineni[1],
Taotao Cai[1(✉)], Nur Al Hasan Haldar[2(✉)], and Jianxin Li[1]

[1] Deakin University, Melbourne, Australia
{acmandal,sgunaba,asadinen,taotao.cai,jianxin.li}@deakin.edu.au
[2] The University of Western Australia, Perth, Australia
nur.haldar@research.uwa.edu.au

Abstract. This study is to investigate the digital media influence on financial equity stocks. For investment plans, knowledge-based decision support system is an important criterion. The stock exchange is becoming one of the major areas of investments. Various factors affect the stock exchange in which social media and digital news articles are found to be the major factors. As the world is more connected now than a decade ago, social media does play a main role in making decisions and change the perception of looking at things. Therefore a robust model is an important need for forecasting the stock prices movement using social media news or articles. From this line of research, we assess the performance of correlation-based models to check the rigorousness over the large data sets of stocks and the news articles. We evaluate the various stock quotes of entities across the world on the day news article is published. Conventional sentiment analysis is applied to the news article events to extract the polarity by categorizing the positive and negative statements to study their influence on the stocks based on correlation.

Keywords: Correlation · Sentiment analysis · Name entity recognition

1 Introduction

In the digital age, people are connected more than ever in human history. The evolution of media articles in the past decade has changed the way investors forecast the stock market. Investors can potentially utilize the real-time user opinion from the media feeds by leveraging machine learning techniques. Predicting the stock market using micro blogging is becoming mainstream in recent years. "Social media has completely changed the way traders engage with consumers". Predicting the stock prices using the media news will eventually reduce the risk and provides a better financial plan. In this research, it is investigated that, whether the user sentiments are affecting the equity stocks. All the media articles are unstructured data, such data can provide valuable perception on the stock prices, but it is difficult to analyze and interpret correctly. To deal with

© Springer Nature Switzerland AG 2019
J. Li et al. (Eds.): ADMA 2019, LNAI 11888, pp. 331–342, 2019.
https://doi.org/10.1007/978-3-030-35231-8_24

such type of unstructured data, a novel approach for data extraction. The combination of structured stock price data and unstructured media data provides an improved prediction model in the financial domain. Sentiment analysis is applied to the news article data to find the correlation and the relevant economic indicators. The main reason for choosing social media news to predict the stock price is due to the following characteristics: 1. Information Content, 2. Reachability, and 3. Quality and source of truth in information.

In order to control the dissemination of the content, social media, plays an essential role in reaching the broad range of audience. Social media can prioritize the information during the announcement and influence by targeting a group of people, which had its direct influence on the stock prices. Social media is found to be one of the pushing mediums for information to the audience. However, it pushes the information to the audience directly and can target people with respective information, which builds a strong network effect. In this study, the unstructured data of news articles are being analyzed to know the impact of that news on the stock price equity market. Also, the stock prediction has three phases, which involve Name Entity Recognition, Sentiment Analysis, and Correlation models.

2   Related Work

This study is to investigate the social media influence on financial equity stocks. Social media does play a leading role in making decisions and change the perception of looking at things. Keeping this as a precedent, the intended to study the correlation and relate the hidden behaviour of financial equity stock markets with social media events.

By applying conventional sentiment analysis on news event-media data polarity of the news events is being identified. By extracting the polarity of the events, the articles can be categorized into positive and negative statements and their influence. The stock data set is cleansed and prepared to perform time series analysis. After categorizing the data, the stock movement is correlated with social media events on the day news articles is published in the media. As the opinions are spreading virally and the availability is in the reach for the stock investors to adopt the opinion or sentiment on the stock when the social media or news has been put out [5].

A Social-Media-Based Approach to Predicting Stock Co-movement: Stock return co-movement is inversely associated with economic resources allocation. Nguyen et al. [4] proposed a novel method to identify homogeneous stock groups to predict the stock co-movement for specific social media metrics. They analyzed samples from NASDAQ and NYSE and found that firms with official Twitter accounts have much higher co-movement that those without such accounts [4]. By using micro blogging metrics, they classify firms into the homogeneous group. The major drawback in this paper is that they have not used text and sentiment analysis to explore the impact the public opinions on predicting stock movement. They have only used quantitative metrics. However, they were the first to reveal the impact the social media metrics on stock return co-movement returns.

Sentiment Analysis on Social Media for Stock Movement Prediction: Goyal et al. [1] aims to build a novel model for predicting and integrating the stock price movement using the sentiment from social media. Also, Goyal et al. have shown the evaluation of the effectiveness of the sentiment analysis in the stock prediction. To handle the high dimensional data, they have used the support vector machine algorithm. The demerit of this model is that they can predict only when the stock price is up or down. However, the drastic movement of the stock market will be more effective. This model can be extended to predict the degree of the change by fine-grained classes. Also, they have considered only the historical prices and sentiments from social media [1]. One of the merits in the proposed method is that it can predict the stock price movement with more than 60 percent accuracy.

Stock Price Movement Following Financial News Article Release: Lee et al. [3] elaborated the implementation of linear regression estimate statistical model in order to establish the correlation between the stock price moment after the publication of the new article. This article is only checking the slope of a ration of change in the price of a stock to a new article published by different news outlets. Sentiment analysis applied differently after finding the deviation of stock. With sentiment analysis and linear regression applied separately, this method of approach may create a misalignment of the news article and the effect of new articles on readers. In this article, the time taken to stock is only confined to 20 Min's after and before the news article is published [3]. Considering the reachability of the news to individual readers of 20 Min's time window gap is insignificant. This article has not mentioned entity recognition for the news articles, which is essential to identify the stock of a particular entity.

3   Methods and Methodology

System configuration Research in proposed framework starts with building up a hypothetical framework structure that will be pursued and later form a framework engineering that comprehends framework plan and produce expected results. The system framework design as follows (Fig. 1):

Methodology. Data pre-processing, sentiment analysis, name entity recognition and econometric correlation analysis is implemented for research is discussed in this section. It has two stages and the following are discussed below

1. Qualitative approach: Executes data pre-processing tasks.
2. Quantitative approach: Stock price movement prediction with the help of correlation values.

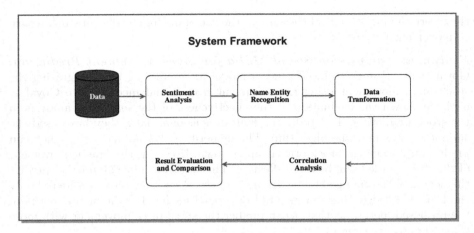

Fig. 1. Overview of system architecture.

Data Set

News Articles: In the implementation, two different data sets are being used. one is news articles and another one is stock data set. The news article data set consists of title, summary and time.

The data types of the attributes are discussed below:

- Title: Headline of the news article.
- Summary: News article information in more context.
- Time: The day when the article is published.

Stock Data: The stock price data set consists of the symbol of the entity, open and close quote of the stock entity on the day the news article is published. '*percentagechange*' is calculated with open and close quotes to understand the movement of the entire stock on the day the news article published.

- *Symbol*: The stock market listed symbols in the respective stock markets.
- *Openquote*: Price of stock when the market opened on the day news article published.
- *Closequote*: Price of stock when the market closed on the day news article published.
- *Percentagechange*: Change in stock with respect to open and close of the stock of the day.
- Movement: A categorical variable to describe the percentage change of stock with negative and positive categories.

In order to evaluate the correlation model, the two different datasets are combined to form single news and stock dataset. In which from the news article dataset, the summary attribute is selected to extract entities mentioned in the news using Name Entity Recognition and sentiment analysis is performed on the summary attribute of new dataset to understand the polarity of a statement. After performing both NER and Sentiment analysis, the stock percentage in change is calculated with the open and close quote of the stock dataset. With the combination of the polarity of article and percentage in the change of stock of entities listed in news article, further data transformation and analysis are performed.

Data Pre-processing. The data collected for both news articles and the stock data have a different range of datasets. In stock dataset, the variation of the stock price is range from -30 to $+30\%$ in change. Using this data would cause a lot noisy when performing analysis. In order to eliminate this, an underlying cleansing mechanism is implemented to reduce the range. Most of the outliers of the stock data set are identified as Investment fund group or related to a non-equity fund. Elimination of values in percentage change has been handled with checking the percentage value not equal to zero. This is primarily because, on the data news article published, the stock may be closed, or the entity is no more on the stock. Most of the articles are having multiple entities mentioned. To track the multiple entities stock in one percentage change is not a feasible solution to correlate. In order to track individual entity listed in the news article, the news article data is made redundant with unique entity symbols.

Eliminating Outliers: Most of the data outliers are handle by using inter-quartile change. With the elimination of data outliers and the data, the range has been confined to -3 to $+4\%$ of change.

Data Normalization: Data normalization helps to extract better insights in an analysis by bring the different scale of numerical data into a uniform scale without distorting the values. The data collected in the real world may not be uniformly distributed or consistent. An analysis is always better to perform on the uniformly distributed data or the data in which the features are selected should be on the same scale. In the dataset of news articles and stock, the range of polarity is $[-1, +1]$ and the range of change in stock percentage is around $[-30, +20]$. This outliers and noisy data in the data will result in inappropriate results (Figs. 2 and 3).

Data Statistics: The data collected initially is having around 15000 articles. After performing named entity recognition, the data has been filtered out empty entities. A refined data is made around 11000 articles with unique entity yet redundant articles after getting the stock symbols and quotes of entities (Fig. 4).

Sentiment Analysis. Sentiment analysis is carried out using Text Blob, which aims in providing access to everyday text processing operations through a familiar interface. Text Blob is a python library Since python is used for implementation python strings has learned how to do Natural Language Processing. Part

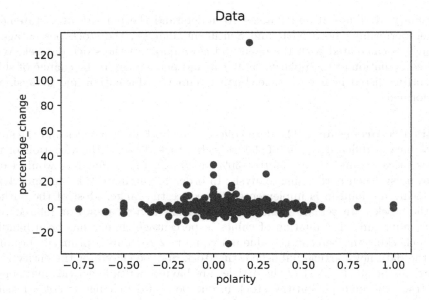

Fig. 2. Data distribution before data pre-processing.

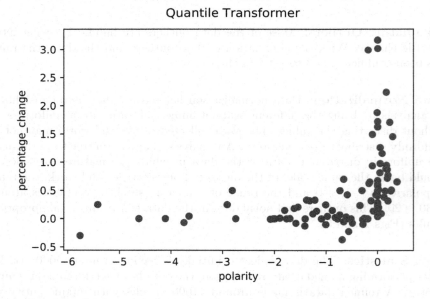

Fig. 3. Data distribution after data pre-processing and applying quantile transformer.

of speech tagging involves marking words present in a text based on its definition and context with noun, adjective or verb and more. Sentiment property returns a named tuple of the form sentiment such as polarity and subjectivity.

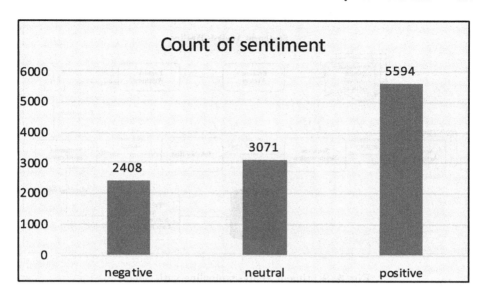

Fig. 4. Refined news article data set.

The range of polarity ranges from −1.0 to 1.0, and the subjectivity is a float the value ranges from 0.0 to 1.0. In which 1.0 is said to very subjective, and 0.0 is very objective based on the word in the sentence.

The articles are labelled with positive, negative, and neutral based on the polarity value, higher than zero are marked as positive and values less than zero are marked negative. In this research activity data of subjectivity is ignored considering as neutral. Polarity plays a pivotal role in order to correlate the stock change with respective on the day new article is published (Fig. 5).

Name Entity Recognition. Name Entity Recognition is an information extraction process which seeks out and categories specified entities in a body of texts. Through which identity extraction is done. Spacy is used in NER, which is an open source library in python. Since the data set is enormous in volume, Spacy is specifically designed for the production use and understands the data set. Spacy will assign the labels to groups of tokens which are contiguous. Entities like organization, event, or a person are separated in the default model, which can be recognized using spacy parts of speech tagging and classification. After tagging the data is filtered out for 'ORG' tagged sets. An arbitrary class can also be added in spacy by training the model to update it with newer trained samples (Fig. 6).

Stock Data Extraction. The stock price data on the day news article is fetched from Yahoo Finance historical data. Those data cover financial services of many companies and industrial sectors over two years. Entities stock opening

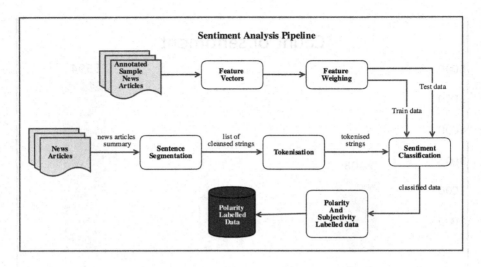

Fig. 5. Sentiment analysis pipeline with Spacy.

and closing price each day as the daily stock price to calculate the percentage in change of stock. Furthermore, transformation is applied to stock percentage in change because the sentiment data ranges from 0 to 1 [2]. The percentage change of a company's stock price can be found using the log of stock price depending upon the news articles sentiment level.

4   Econometric Correlation Analysis Model

To predict the stock movement of percentage in change accurately, various types of correlation model have been used in the research. The correlation is carried out between the polarity and the percentage change of the stock price, which

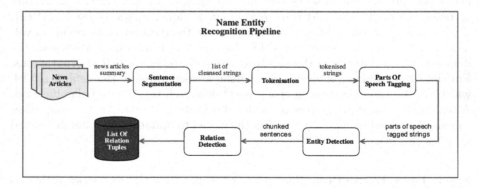

Fig. 6. Name entity recognition pipeline with Text Blob.

is obtained through the log. It has limited ability in predicting returns in the stock market. The correlation coefficient is a statistical measurement of the relationship between how stocks move in tandem with respective other values, as well as of the strength of that relationship. Correlation model can be used to mitigate the risk. The correlation coefficient is measured on a scale from -1 to $+1$, Whereas the positive correlation is indicated by coefficient 1, and the negative correlation is indicated by -1. The positive correlation indicates that the movement of the stocks always moves in the same direction, and the negative correlation indicates that the historical stock movements in the opposite direction. The correlation is calculated by taking the co-variance of the stocks against the mean returns for each stock divided by the product of the standard deviation of the returns of each stock. The correlation is calculated using the following formula.

$$ r_{xy} = \frac{\sum (x_i - \overline{x})(y_i - \overline{y})}{\sqrt{\sum (x_i - \overline{x})^2 \sum (y_i - \overline{y})^2}} $$

Where

- $r_x y$ - The correlation coefficient of the linear relationship between variables x and y i.e. polarity and percentage change.
- x_i - The value of polarity in the sample.
- $\overline{x}$ - Mean value of polarity.
- y_i - The value of percentage change in the sample.
- $\overline{y}$ - The mean of percentage change obtained using descriptive statistics.

This research is to find out the best econometric correlation model for finding the relationship between the variable polarity and *percentagechange*. The following correlation model has been used for the evaluation.

1. Pearson correlation model: It measures the strength of a linear association between polarity and *percentagechange* variables and it is by r. The R value ranges from $+1$ to -1. In which the value 0 indicates that there is no association between the two variables. If the value greater than 0 it indicates that there is positive association between the variables. The main drawback in Pearson correlation is it cannot classify whether the variable is a dependent or independent variable. Also, it cannot explain the cause and effect relationship.

$$ \gamma = \frac{N \sum xy - \sum(x)(y)}{\sqrt{[N \sum x^2 - \sum(x^2)][N \sum y^2 - \sum()y^2]}} $$

2. Kendall correlation model: It is non-parametric test which measures the strength of dependence between two variables. By considering two variable samples polarity and *percentagechange* with the sample size 100 then we know that the total number of pairings with percentage size is $100(100-1)/2$. The following formula is used to calculate the Kendall rank correlation.

$$ \tau = \frac{n_c - n_d}{\frac{1}{2}n(n-1)} $$

The main disadvantage of using Kendall's rank correlation is in terms of observing the probabilities the concordant and discordant is very indirect.

3. Spearman's Rank correlation: It is denoted by Rho. Spearman's Rank correlation is used when there are no tied ranks and it tends to give sufficiently good approximations in case of fewer number of tied ranks. The following is the formula for spearman's rank correlation.

$$\rho = 1 - \frac{6 \sum d_i^2}{n(n^2 - 1)}$$

Where,

- d_i - represents the difference in the ranks given to the values of the variable for each item of the data.
- n - number of observations.

Also, it does not depend on the assumptions of various distributions, that is it free from the data distribution. The variable is said to be concordant pairs when both the variables of one observation is more significant than their respective variables of other observations. Also, if two variables in one observation differ in the opposite direction, it is said to be discordant pairs. In Spearman's correlation, the data must be least ordinal, and the scores on one variable must be monotonically related to another variable. Spearman's correlation shows the significance of the data and accurately approves or disapproves the correlation. It does not assume for normal distribution (Table 1).

Table 1. Correlation - results

Correlation model	Correlation coefficient	Strength
Pearson correlation	0.478	Less positive correlation
Kendall correlation	0.483	Moderate positive correlation
Spearman correlation	0.700	Strong positive correlation

5 Results and Evaluation

The strong positive correlation between the polarity and percentage change is 0.700. This value indicates that there is a robust uphill correlation between the variables. Spearman correlation is not restricted to linear relationships, and it expresses the monotonic relationship between the polarity and relies on the rank order of the variables. Since the data set consists of both continuous and discrete value, applying Spearman's correlation model would be most appropriate as it depends only on the relative order of values for each variable.

Hence, Spearman's correlation is the best model for defining the relationship between the variables in stock movement coefficient correlation of Spearman's model is found to have reasonably positive strong relationship as the value obtained is 0.700 which is very much close to the correlation value $+1$ (positive correlation). Spearman's correlation shows a monotonic and non-linear relationship between the variables, whereas the Pearson correlation model shows the partial linearity of the relationship, thus reduces the relationship strength between the variables. In the case of Kendall's correlation model, it shows a good association between the variables only if the variables are discrete, which again affects the strength of the association. Considering all these factors, It can be concluded saying that Spearman's correlation model is the best in defining the relationship between the polarity and percentage change in stock movement.

Confirmatory Data Analysis. A confirmatory data analysis i.e., Hypothesis testing, is done for Spearman's correlation to check whether the assumption made is True or False with statistical proof of it. Here the two variables form the data set is taken to check whether the samples of those variables are correlated or not. Hence the hypothesis can be defined by the following:

- H_Θ = samples are uncorrelated (Null hypothesis)
- $H_1 \neq$ samples are correlated (Alternate hypothesis)

Listing 1.1. Hypothesis Testing

```
# Spearman's correlation - Hypothesis testing
from scipy.stats import spearmanr
# prepare data
polarity = data_sample["polarity"]
change = data_sample["change"]
# calculate spearman's correlation
coef, p = spearmanr(polarity, change)
print('P-value_is:_' %p)
# level of significance
alpha = 0.05
if p > alpha:
    print('Samples_are_uncorrelated__p=%.3f' % p)
else:
    print('Samples_are_correlated_p=%.3f' % p)

Result:
    P-value is: 3.20135823077835e-13
    Samples are correlated p=0.000
```

After defining the hypothesis, the test statistic is calculated from descriptive measures of the two variables in the data sets. Then the sample size is decided where $n = 100$. The default significance level is taken as 0.05.

Then the p-value is calculated using a permutation test and re-sampling. Also, then it is compared with the significance level. Since the P-value < significance level, the null hypothesis is rejected.

6   Conclusion

After evaluating the results, it can be concluded that,

– Dataset sourced from Yahoo Finance and Reuters websites with higher authenticity. This dataset contains both structured and unstructured data where the veracity of the dataset is not assured.
– Name entity recognition is the pivotal part of the research as stock data is entirely depended upon the data extract from the news article. Spacy an NLP pipeline is used as part of NER. Spacy provides a better context of the parts of speech tagging by classifying entities as an organization. As news is not always about private entities, other irrelevant information is filtered out with cleansing.
– In sentiment analysis, news articles are labelled with polarity with Text blob NLP pipeline. Polarity is considered as the most significant attribute in the sentiment analysis. Subjectivity is considered as insignificant for this research as news is about reporting not the view of each person.
– Data transformation and cleansing techniques applied in order to eliminate any noisy or outlier from the data set.
– Different Correlation analysis methods are applied on 'polarity' and 'percentage change' to understand the interdependence, on a sample data. Also, among all the models, Spearman's correlation model gave the best correlation results with the $R = 0.700$, which is very much close to the coefficient range +1.
– A confirmatory analysis is performed using Hypothesis testing on a sample data set, and the analysis shows that data is well correlated and establishes a strong relationship between the polarity and percentage change.

References

1. Goyal, A., Gupta, V., Kumar, M.: Recent named entity recognition and classification techniques: a systematic review. Comput. Sci. Rev. **29**, 21–43 (2018)
2. He, W., Guo, L., Shen, J., Akula, V.: Social media-based forecasting: a case study of tweets and stock prices in the financial services industry. J. Organ. End User Comput. **28**, 10 (2016)
3. Lee, T.K., Cho, J.H., Kwon, D.S., Sohn, S.Y.: Global stock market investment strategies based on financial network indicators using machine learning techniques. Expert Syst. Appl. **117**, 228–242 (2019)
4. Nguyen, T.H., Shirai, K., Velcin, J.: Sentiment analysis on social media for stock movement prediction. Expert Syst. Appl. **42**(24), 9603–9611 (2015)
5. Zhang, X., Zhang, Y., Wang, S., Yao, Y., Fang, B., Philip, S.Y.: Improving stock market prediction via heterogeneous information fusion. Knowl.-Based Syst. **143**, 236–247 (2018)

Top-N Hashtag Prediction via Coupling Social Influence and Homophily

Can Wang[1], Zhonghao Sun[2], Yunwei Zhao[2(✉)], Chi-Hung Chi[3],
Willem-Jan van den Heuvel[4], Kwok-Yan Lam[5], and Bela Stantic[1]

[1] School of ICT, Griffith University, Gold Coast, Australia
[2] CN-CERT, Beijing, China
zhaoyw@cert.org.cn
[3] CSIRO, Hobart, Australia
[4] Tilburg University, Tilburg, Netherlands
[5] Nanyang Technological University, Singapore, Singapore

Abstract. Considering the wide acceptance of the social media social influence starts to play very important role. Homophily has been widely accepted as the confounding factor for social influence. While literature attempts to identify and gauge the magnitude of the effects of social influence and homophily separately limited attention was given to use both sources for social behavior computing and prediction. In this work we address this shortcoming and propose neighborhood based collaborative filtering (CF) methods via the behavior interior dimensions extracted from the domain knowledge to model the data interdependence along time factor. Extensive experiments on the Twitter data demonstrate that the behavior interior based CF methods produce better prediction results than the state-of-the-art approaches. Furthermore, considering the impact of topic communication modalities (topic dialogicity, discussion intensiveness, discussion extensibility) on interior dimensions will lead to an improvement of 3%. Finally, the joint consideration of social influence and homophily leads to as high as 80.8% performance improvement in terms of accuracy when compared to the existing approaches.

Keywords: Top-N hashtag adoption · Behavior interior dimensions · Social influence · Homophily

1 Introduction

In the area of information diffusion, the change in behavior that one person causes in another is predominant over its competing hypothesis, i.e. homophily [1]. Homophily, also known as the compositional effect in social experiments [2], has long been treated as the confounding factor for social influence. It is often applied to explain the phenomenon of individuals' large-scale almost identical behaviors. This is known as the "correlated unobservable problem" [3]. Techniques, such as the linear threshold model, are developed to measure the social

© Springer Nature Switzerland AG 2019
J. Li et al. (Eds.): ADMA 2019, LNAI 11888, pp. 343–358, 2019.
https://doi.org/10.1007/978-3-030-35231-8_25

influence in users' adoption decisions. Nevertheless, we observe that the previous research efforts in social influence are mostly not investigated together with the homophily. Yang et al. [4] proposed a method that works to improve the performance of recommendations by integrating sparse rating data given by users and sparse social trust network among these same users. However, the user relation (e.g. the interaction and the following relation) is not addressed in their work. For example, see Table 1, when predicting the preference of user u_1 on the hashtag i_4 ("#smart speaker"), the user u_1's neighbors from which the model learns u_1's potential preferences, are largely limited to the users who have already adopted the same hashtags as u_1. As a result, the hashtag i_4 will not get recommended through the traditional collaborative filtering (CF) models, since u_1's neighbor (e.g. the user u_2) has not used i_4 before. Even though u_1 has never got a chance to adopt i_4, however, u_1 may expect to have similar preferences as the user u_3. Their tweets may both reveal happy, excited emotions and enthusiasms about high-tech products. Through these interior dimensions (e.g. sentiment and disturbance), i_4 could be recommended to the user u_1, because of the closeness between u_1 and u_3 via those implicit dimensions, as well as the adoption of i_4 by the user u_3. It is highly probable to happen that the sets of hashtags adopted by two users sharing similar interests, are intersected with rather a small proportion, or even non-overlapping at all, due to the multitude of hashtags existing in Twitter.

Table 1. An instance of hashtag recommendation problem

	i_1 (#iphone8)	i_2 (#huawei mate10)	i_3 (#galaxy)	i_4 (#smart speaker)	i_5 (#the avengers)
u_1	✓	✓		?	?
u_2	✓	✓	✓		
u_3				✓	
u_4					✓

On the other hand, suppose there is a following relation between the users u_1 and u_4. The hashtag i_5 ("#the avengers") still does not get recommended to u_1, through the above method. However, it is most likely that u_1 might get influenced by u_4, and posts a tweet "gonna watch off work!!" under this hashtag. In this scenario, simply considering the homophily is not sufficient, as there seems be no direct textual connection between the discussions on the movie "The avengers" and the IT products, like cell phones and smart speakers. If we take into account such social influence via following (follower) relations, i_5 might be recommended to u_1, due to the social connection between u_1 and u_4, as well as the use of the hashtag i_5 by u_4. Therefore, jointly considering the homophily and the social influence will lead to a more comprehensive recommendation candidate set.

Despite the interior dimensions are addressed in above mentioned studies the focus is either unidimensional without considering the interdependence, or static without considering the temporal dependence. Recently, there has been an increasing trend to use the sophisticated domain knowledge based transformation functions to integrate multiple interdependent data sources [5,6] for deeper understanding about entity behaviors. We refer these measures as the behavior interior dimensions (or features). In real-world scenarios these multiple dimensions usually appear simultaneously and therefore considering jointly those multiple effects is both necessary and important. In this work, we address above mentioned shortcomings and focus on how to apply the interior dimensions based approach to enhance the prediction of users' hashtag adoption behavior, aiming at a better understanding of user preferences.

We also propose to investigate how both social aspects (i.e. influence and homophily) can be used together in the prediction of hashtag adoption frequency in Twitter. When experimentally compared with the state-of-the-art social influence identification area there is an increasing impact of the homophily in social media analysis, due to the following two reasons. Firstly, while most traditional product diffusion scenarios focus on a single product with a fairly long life-cycle and widespread impact, the social media is with multiple threads of various life-cycles and varied scales of reach in the network. For example, a hashtag life-cycle could last for several months or only a few days. The impact also ranges from the network-wide distribution (e.g. #FollowFriday and #shoutOutTo) to the circulation only within a few people, with the distribution heavy-tailed towards the latter. Secondly, the ease of hashtag accessibility increases the potentials of applying the homophily for the hashtag adoption prediction. This is because of the multiple hashtag usages in a single tweet, and the direct hashtag searching in Twitter.

In this paper, therefore, we introduce an effective coupling mechanism that integrates the linear threshold model and the neighborhood CF model via the behavior internal dimensions. We summarize the main contributions as follows:

- We enrich the CF models by capturing the temporal dynamics of homophily via using the user-oriented and the topic-oriented behavior interior dimensions.
- We propose an integrating model to couple the social influence and the homophily for the prediction of the top-N hashtag adoption frequency, which considers the impact of topic communication modalities on behavior interior dimensions as well.
- Our proposed models are evaluated against the state-of-the-art algorithms on Twitter data in terms of prediction accuracy, dynamic evolution, and parameter sensitivity, with demonstrated superiority in performance.

The structure of this paper is as follows. We review the related work in Sect. 2. In Sect. 3, we formalize the problem statement and preliminaries, then describe the behavior interior dimensions captured for both users and topics. In Sect. 4, we present the proposed models in detail. Experiments are extensively evaluated on Twitter data in Sect. 5. Finally, we conclude this paper and present future research directions in Sect. 6.

2   Related Work

Understanding the interior aspect of behaviors is a pivotal issue in various fields [10,11]. Behavior interior dimensions are also investigated on a user generated content (e.g. Twitter, Facebook) basis in political elections, stock market trending, etc.

The simplest hashtag recommendation methods are heuristic-based, i.e. Hashtag Average Adoption Times and Top Popularity [12]. The former approach recommends top-N items with the highest average adoption times. The latter adopts a similar prediction schema, recommending top-N items with the highest popularity, which is the greatest number of users that adopted this hashtag.

Homophily related hashtag recommendation methods are collaborative filtering (CF) [13,14] and content-based (CB) approaches [15]. The major difference between them lies in the role of users in seeking recommendations and providing preference to peer seekers. In CB methods, the recommendation is based on the seeker's self-preference: users do not need to provide preferences to peer seekers as in the case of CF approaches [16]. These traditional methods capture homophily through exterior rating/adoption times and term frequencies. In this sense, our method extends the neighborhood based model by measuring the similarity between users/items and neighbors with multiple interior dimensions.

Our previous work [8] focuses on the pros and cons between the behavior interior dimensions based approach and the exterior dimensions based approach. The proposed work in this paper conducts an in-depth study of behavior interior dimensions based user-hashtag adoption prediction w.r.t the integration sensitivity of homophily and social influence, and the interaction between topic communication modalities and behavior interior dimensions.

3   Problem Statement and Preliminaries

3.1   Problem Statement

The task of top-N hashtag recommendation is to find a few (top-N) specific hashtags (topics) which are supposed to be most appealing to a particular user. A large number of users with potential hashtags can be organized by an information table $<U, I, \Gamma, D, F>$, where $U = \{u_1, u_2, \cdots, u_m\}$ and $I = \{i_1, i_2, \cdots, i_n\}$ denote the set of m users and the set of n hashtags, respectively. $\Gamma(u, i) = \{r_{ui}\}$ is an $(m \times n)$ matrix, recording the exterior statistics of hashtag usage. $D = <D_u, D_i>$ stands for the interior dimensions. For each user u, $D_u = \{d_1(u), d_2(u), \cdots, d_k(u)\}$ denotes the user interior dimensions, where each component $d_x(u)$ is a time-series. For example, the component $d_x(u)$ can be $Act(u, t)$ or $Sent(u, t)$, as shown in the upper half of Table 2. Similarly, for the hashtag i, $D_i = \{d_1(i), d_2(i), \cdots, d_k(i)\}$ denotes the topic interior dimensions, where each component $d_y(i)$ is a time-series. For example, the component $d_y(i)$ can be $Sent(i, t)$ or $Contro(i, t)$, as displayed in the latter half of Table 4. F is a

$m \times m$ matrix, where each entry $F(x, y) = \{f_{u_x u_y}\}$ stores the following relation between users u_x and u_y.

The hashtag recommendation problem is to predict the adoption likelihood $p(u, i)$ of item i to user u, then give the top-N recommendations with the highest likelihood. Following the example in Table 1, $U = \{u_1, u_2, u_3, u_4\}$, $I = \{i_1, i_2, i_3, i_4, i_5\}$, $\Gamma = \{r_{u_1 i_1}, r_{u_1 i_2}, r_{u_2 i_1}, r_{u_1 i_2}, r_{u_2 i_3}, r_{u_3 i_4}, r_{u_4 i_5}\}$, $F = \{f_{u_4 u_1}\}$. The example in Table 1 is to calculate the adoption likelihood of $p(u_1, i_4)$ given the above described quintuple $<U, I, \Gamma, D, F>$.

3.2 Behavior Interior Dimensions

To figure out behavior interior dimensions, we apply both "top-down" and "bottom-up" approaches from multiple literatures, as introduced in our previous work [8] in detail. On one hand, it needs to be rooted from domain knowledge and on the other hand, these dimensions have to be automatically

Table 2. Behavior interior dimensions: user self-oriented

Dimensions	Definition	Measurement in our study
Activeness	Continually being engaged	$Act(u,t) = n_t$, n_t is tweet count at time t
Sentiment [7]	Observable manifestations of a subjectively experienced emotion	$Sent(u,t) = \sum Sent(p_j^{u,t})/n_t$, $p_j^{u,t}$ is a user's j^{th} tweet at time t, n_t is tweet count at time t, $Sent(p_j^{u,t})$ is valence value in ANEW of u's j^{th} tweet at time t.
Disturbance [7]	Degree of emotional stability	$Disturb(u,t) = \sum avg(Anx(p_j^{u,t}) + Sad(p_j^{u,t}))/n_t$, $Anx(p_j^{u,t})$ and $Sad(p_j^{u,t})$ denotes the anxiety and sadness value in LIWC of u's j^{th} tweet at time t
Openness [10]	Preference for novelty and variety	$Open(u,t) = 0.5 \times n_h + 0.5 \times avg\Delta_i$, n_h is number of hashtags adopted, measuring hashtag usage variety, Δ_i $(i = 1, \cdot, n_h)$ is hashtag adoption latency, i.e. time difference between first encounter of a hashtag and the first use

Table 3. Behavior interior dimensions: peer-oriented

Dimensions	Definition	Measurement in our study
Activeness	Continually being engaged	$Act(u,t) = n_t$, n_t is tweet count at time t
Dominance [7]	Tendency to control others	$Dom(u,t) = \sum Dom(p_j^{u,t})/n_t$, $Dom(p_j^{u,t})$ is the dominance value in ANEW of u's j^{th} tweet at week t
Reciprocity [10]	Agreeableness, altruism	$Rp(u,t) = n_f$, n_f is friend count.
Sociability [10]	Extraversion reflected in text writing	$Soc(u,t) = \sum Soc(p_j^{u,t})/n_t$, $Soc(p_j^{u,t})$ is the social process value in LIWC
Influence [11]	Tendency to influence others	$Inf(u,t) = avg(n_r(u) + n_m(u))$, $n_r(u)$ and $n_m(u)$ is retweet count and mention count
Passivity [11]	Difficulty for a person to get influenced	$Pas(u,t) = n_{uH}/n_H$, n_{uH} is unadopted hashtag count, n_H is the number of hashtags a user encounters
Popularity [7]	Tendency to be widely accepted	$Pop(u,t) = in - degree(u)$
Gregariousness	Tendency to interact with others	$Gre(u,t) = out - degree(u)$

Table 4. Behavior interior dimensions: topic-oriented

Dimensions	Definition	Measurement in our study
Sentiment	Valence- positive or negative	$Sent(i,t) = \sum Sent(p_j^{i,t})/n_t$, $p_j^{i,t}$ is hashtag i's j^{th} tweet, n_t is number of tweets at time t.
Controversy	Sentiment variation	$Contro(i,t) = \sum |Sent(p_j^{i,t}) - Sent(p_{j-1}^{i,t})|/(n_t - 1)$
Content richness	content volume (Number of unique words) and content diversity (Non-redundancy of the words)	$CR(t) = CV(t) + CD(t)$, $CV(t)$ is the word length within a tweet at time t, $CD(i,t) = avgld(p_{j1}^{i,t}, p_{j2}^{i,t})/max(length(p_{j1}^{i,t}), length(p_{j2}^{i,t}))$, $ld(p_{j1}^{i,t}, p_{j2}^{i,t})$ is the Levenshtein distance, i.e. the minimum number of the single-word edits required to change tweet j_1 into j_2
Hotness	Transmission times and reach of impact	$H(i,t) = \alpha CC(i,t) + \beta CovP(i,t)$, $CC(i,t)$ and $CovP(i,t)$ is communication count and coverage of people at time t
Trend momentum	Absolute hotness difference in successive time windows	$TM(i,t) = \alpha TM_{CC}(i,t) + \beta TM_{CovP}(i,t)$, $TM_C C(i,t) = |CC(i,t) -^* (i, t-1)|$

measured or approximated. Hence, we come up with the set (see Tables 2 and 3) of user-oriented dimensions based on the principle whether they can be measured practically and are not redundant in concept [8]. This classification serves as a rough criterion to measure each dimension from multiple data sources. It reflects the data coverage involved, i.e., the data sources that describe the users' own behaviors and their peer's behaviors.

The case is relatively simpler for the topic-oriented interior behavior dimensions, since it covers less concept hierarchy in the related domain knowledge [8]. The selection is displayed Table 4. Moreover, we note that there exists a nonnegligible divergence between topic groups w.r.t communication modalities [9]. Topic communication modality refers to the way people interact and exchange messages on social networks. It comprises of three main constructs: "Topic Dialogicity", i.e. the topic is monological or conversational; "Discussion Intensiveness", i.e. the topic is simply replicated or proceeds with changing comments; "Discussion Extensibility", i.e. whether multiple hashtags co-exist within a topic. Table 5 summarizes the topic communication modality related variables under study in this work.

4   Top-N Hashtag Adoption Prediction

In Sects. 4.1 and 4.2, we present the interior dimensions based homophily model and social influence based model, respectively. Section 4.3 introduces the coupled model of these two factors.

4.1   Homophily Based Model

Traditionally neighborhood models capture homophily through exterior adoption times, see Eq. (1). In this sense, our method extends the neighborhood based model by measuring the similarity s_{uv} between user u and neighbor v with multiple interior dimensions, see user-oriented models below. There are two types [19,20]: user-based and item-based. We will explicate in detail below.

Table 5. Behavior interior dimensions: communication modalities

Dimensions	Definition	Measurement in our study
Is_Conversational	Presence of topic t as a conversational topic	Indicator variable $I_{CT}(t)$
Dialogicity Strength	Number of paths of t's dialogue composition	$DLS(t) = normalized(|DC(t)|)$
Is_Discussion Intensive	Presence of topic t as a discussion intensive topic	Indicator variable $I_{DIT}(t)$
Discussion Intensiveness	Number of paths of t's discussion-intensive composition	$DIS(t) = normalized(|DIC(t)|)$
Discussion Hotness	Average attention paid to the content-changed discussion	$DH(t) = \sum_{j=1,\ldots,DIC(t)} (\alpha avg \Delta cc(p_j(t))+ \beta avg \Delta covp(p_j(t)))/|DIC(t)|$
Information Addition	Average information supplemented in the content-changed discussion	$IA(t) = \sum_{j=1,\ldots,DIC(t)} avg \Delta info Add(p_j(t))/|DIC(t)|$
Emotion Attachment	Average emotion attached to the content-changed discussion	$EA(t) = \sum_{j=1,\ldots,DIC(t)} avg \Delta affect(p_j(t))/|DIC(t)|$
Is_Discussion Extensible	Presence of topic t as a discussion extensible topic	Indicator variable $I_{ET}(t)$
Discussion Extensibility Strength	Number of paths of t's extensible composition	$DES(t) = normalized(|EC(t)|)$, $EC(t)$ is the extensible composition [9]

User-Oriented Models. Equation (1) shows the case for user-based model. The recommendation is based on the ratings/adoptions by similar users or given to similar items, after removing global effect and habitual rating.

$$\hat{r}_{ui} = \mu + b_u + b_i + f(u,i), \tag{1}$$

where $\hat{r}_{ui}$ is the recommendation for user u of a certain item/hashtag i, μ is the global average and b_u and b_i denote the user- or item- specific habitual rating difference from μ, $f(u,i) = (\sum_{v \in S_{u;i}^k} s_{uv}(r_{vi} - b_v - b_i))/(\sum_{v \in S_{u;i}^k} s_{uv})$, s_{uv} measures the similarity between user u and u's neighbor v, $S_{u;i}^k$ denotes the set of u's k-nearest neighbors. The user- and item- based neighborhood models are dubbed as "$Ngbr_{Corr}^U$" and "$Ngbr_{Corr}^T$" respectively. These will serve as the base model for behavior interior dimension based improvements.

The similarity between two users (topics) in Eq. (1) is computed based on behavior interior dimensions from both static and dynamic perspectives. Static analysis measures the similarity with the Frobenius form of the difference in the empirical mean amplitude of the users' interior dimensions (see Eq. (2)). For clarity's sake, this model is dubbed as "$Ngbr_{EpM}^U$".

$$s_{uv} = \sqrt{\sum_k (\bar{d}_{uk} - \bar{d}_{vk})^2}, \tag{2}$$

where $\bar{d}_u = <\bar{d}_{uk}>$ is the empirical mean amplitude of the users interior dimensions, and k is the dimension number.

Then, three dynamic patterns are extracted [17,18], we dub these three user-oriented models as "$Ngbr_{DFT}^U$", "$Ngbr_{DWT}^U$", and "$Ngbr_{PCA}^U$":

- The first one is DFT (i.e. Discrete Fourier Transform) based global shape feature $\theta_u^{ac} = \theta_{ukl}^{ac}$, $s_{uv} = \sqrt{\sum_{k,l}(\theta_{ukl}^{ac} - \theta_{vkl}^{ac})^2}$, where $theta_{uk}^{ac} = <\theta_{ukl}^{ac}>$ is the alternating current (AC) components or the non-zero frequency coefficients, k is the dimension index, and l indexes the largest non-zero frequency coefficients and is set to 4 as the subsequent coefficients of most topics are zero.
- The second one is DWT (i.e. Discrete Wavelet Transform) based local shape $\theta_u^s = \theta_{ukl}^s$, $s_{uv} = \sqrt{\sum_{k,l}(\theta_{ukl}^s - \theta_{vkl}^s)^2}$, where $theta_{uk}^s = <\theta_{ukl}^s>$ is the vector representing the shape signatures, k is the dimension index, and l is set to 7 (i.e. the $2^{nd} - 8^{th}$ DWT coefficients, the 1st one is average amplitude), considering the 41 weeks coverage.
- The third one is PCA (i.e. Principal Component Analysis) based co-occurrence pattern, i.e. eigenvector, $s_{uv} = \sum_{k=1}^{n_d} w_k \sum_i o_{ik}^u o_{ik}^v$, where $o_k^u = o_{ik}^u$ is the eigenvector of the co-variance matrix for the multiple behavior interior dimensions.

Topic Oriented Models. Similarly, for topic-oriented enhanced neighborhood models, we have "$Ngbr_{EpM}^T$", "$Ngbr_{DFT}^T$", "$Ngbr_{DWT}^T$", and "$Ngbr_{PCA}^T$".

The Interaction Between Communication Modality and Behavior Interior Dimension. In addition, we note that the way in which users interact with hashtags, e.g. attractive or aversive, content rich or lean, merely repeating or vividly discussing, etc., may lead to difference in topic behavior interior dimensions [9]. Thus, we give a finer adjustment to the topic-oriented models as follows. As shown in Table 4, we have a 9-element vector c to describe a topic's communication modalities, as given in Eq. (3).

$$c = <I_{CT}(t), I_{DIT}(t), DIS(t), DH(t), IA(t), EA(t), I_{ET}(t), DES(t)> \qquad (3)$$

where dummy variables (a.k.a., indicator variable) $I_{CT}(t)$, $I_{DIT}(t)$ and $I_{ET}(t)$ denote the presence of topic t as a conversational topic, discussion-intensive topic and discussion extensible topic, $DLS(t)$ denotes the dialogicity strength, $DIS(t)$ denotes the discussion intensiveness strength, $DH(t)$ denotes the discussion hotness $DH(t)$, $IA(t_i)$ denotes the information addition, $EA(t)$ denotes the emotional attachment, and $DES(t)$ denotes the discussion extensibility strength.

The integrating model is given in Eq. (4).

$$\hat{r}_{ui} = \frac{\sum_{j \in S^k(i;u)} d_{ij}^p (r_{uj} - b_{uj})}{\sum_{j \in S^k(i;u)} d_{ij}^p} + \hat{r}_{ui}^* \qquad (4)$$

where the first term is neighborhood, d_{ij}^p corresponds to the similarity function as given above, and p denotes the four patterns of the multiple interior dimension time series under analysis, i.e. Empirical Mean, DFT-based global shape, and

DWT-based local shape, PCA-based co-occurrence pattern. The second term corresponds to the estimation model in Eqs. (5) and (6).

$$\hat{r}^*_{ui} = \mu + b_u + b_i + \sum_k p^d_{uk} \bar{d}^i_k + \sum_j p^c_{uk} c_{ij} \qquad (5)$$

$$\hat{r}^*_{ui} = \mu + b_u + b_i + \sum_k p^d_{uk} \bar{d}^i_k + \sum_j p^c_{uk} \bar{c}_{ij} + \sum_j \sum_k p + ujk^{d'} c_{ij} \bar{d}^i_k \qquad (6)$$

where $c = <c_{ij}>$ denotes the 9-element vector of topic i.

To clearly show the impact of topic communication modalities on topic behavior interior dimensions in hashtag adoption prediction, we decompose the user-hashtag adoption matrix with the 9-element communication modality feature as well as the interior dimensions. We dub this model as "SVD^1_{CmEpM}", see Eq. (5). Similarly, we have "SVD^1_{CmDFT}", "SVD^1_{CmDWT}", "SVD^1_{CmPCA}". Then we include a multiplicative term in factorizing the user hashtag usage matrix, see Eq. (6), which specifies the hashtag usage estimation through multiple behavior interior dimensions conditional on the communication modality feature. Thus, we expect this to deliver better prediction accuracy. The model specified in Eq. (6) is dubbed "SVD^2_{CmEpM}", Similarly, we have "SVD^2_{CmDFT}", "SVD^2_{CmDWT}", "SVD^2_{CmPCA}", respectively.

4.2   Social Influence-Based Model

The model capturing the social influence effect in hashtag adoption is developed based on Linear Threshold Models ("LT") [1]. In "LT", the probability of a given user to turn active is a function $p(a)$ of the number a of friends being active. The challenges of applying "LT" model in top-N hashtag adoption frequency prediction setting lie in: (a) there is a shift of focus from single item to multiple items, and (b) it may produce very low prediction accuracy if we take all the non-adoption event into consideration, due to the fact that social media is a noisy and asynchronous environment for user interaction. Thus, we have Multiple Thread Linear Threshold Model where the differences for each individual topic/hashtag are considered, dubbed as "MTLT" (see Eq. (7)).

$$ln(\frac{p(u,i,t)}{1-p(u,i,t)}) = \alpha ln(a+1) + \beta, \qquad (7)$$

where $p(u,i,t)$ is proportional to the number of active friends, i.e. $p(u,i,t) = p(a)$, a is friend count, α measures social influence, i.e. a large value of α indicates a large degree of influence, β is to reduce the possibility of overfitting. The optimization goal is to maximize the likelihood of hashtag adoption prediction at each t, see Eq. (8).

$$O = \prod_i \prod_t p(u,i,t)^{Y_{i,t}}, Y_{i,t} = \sum_u I_{u,i,t}, \qquad (8)$$

where $p(u,i,t)$ is the probability of user u adopting hashtag i at time t $Y_{i,t}$ is the adoption event count of topic i at time t, and $I_{u,i,t}$ is an indicator variable denoting that user u adopts topic i at time t.

352   C. Wang et al.

4.3 Coupled Model

Now we have the probability of user u adopting hashtag i that considers both homophily and social influence, see Eq. (9). Following the example of calculating the recommendation likelihood of u_1 and i_5 in Table 1, we now have $\hat{r}_{u_1 i_5} = 0$, $p(u, i, t_l) > 0$, suppose $\gamma = 0.5$, then we have $p(u_1, i_5) = 0.5 * p(u, i, t_l)$. Note that the range of these two components in Eq. (9) is as different, as the homophily model predicts future user hashtag adoption times that can reach as high as 2000+, i.e. $\hat{r}_{ui} \in [0, 2000+]$, while the threshold model predicts the probability of adopting the hashtag, i.e. $p(u, i, t) \in [0, 1]$. Therefore, considering the highly skewed distribution, a non-linear normalization is needed to integrate these two models, see Eq. (9).

$$p(u, i) = a(1 - \gamma) \cdot (1 - \epsilon^{\hat{r}_{ui}}) + \gamma \cdot p(u, i, t_l), \tag{9}$$

where a and ϵ are normalization coefficients, t_l denotes the last week in the observation period, $\gamma \in [0, 1]$, $\gamma = 0$ implies the homophily based model, and $\gamma = 1$ implies the influence based model.

The models are dubbed as "$Intgr_{Exter}^U$", "$Intgr_{Inter}^U$", "$Intgr_{DFT}^U$", "$Intgr_{DWT}^U$", and "$Intgr_{PCA}^U$" in accordance with the homophily models used. The same applies to topic-oriented models.

5 Empirical Study

5.1 Experimental Setting

Dataset. We used our existing Twitter data with the total size of 70 GB, which contains 488,411 hashtags and 112,044 users. The behavior interior dimensions are extracted for each user and topic on a weekly basis, (specifically 41 full weeks). In extraction of data we followed the procedure mentioned in literature and adoption frequency prediction is evaluated on a 5-core dataset S in which every user has adopted at least 5 hashtags and every hashtag has been adopted at least by 5 people. The 5-core dataset S is then spitted into two sets: a training set S_{train} and a testing set S_{test}. Denote the splitting time point as t_{split}, consider the 10-month data set ($2^{nd} \sim 42^{nd}$ weeks of 2010), t_{split} is set at the last month, i.e. 38th week. In total, we have $|U_{train}| = 22849$, and $|T_{train}| = 32727$. The statistics are summarized in Table 6.

Table 6. Statistics of training set and test set

Train set (S_{train})			Test set (S_{test})	
$|U_{train}|$	$|T_{train}|$	Event count	$|U_{test}|$	$|T_{test}|$
22,849	32,727	753,859	19,138	4,806

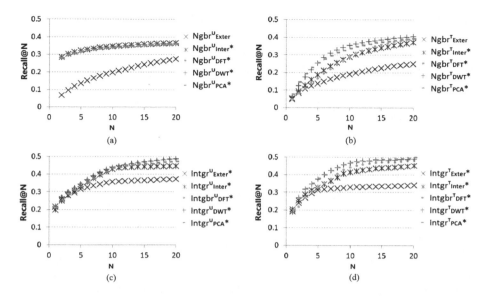

Fig. 1. Prediction accuracy based on user/topic homophily. (The methods tagged with
* are our proposed models)

Evaluation Metric and Method: The prediction accuracy is measured by
recall rate/hit rate of the top-N adoption frequency prediction, $recall(N) = \frac{\#hits}{|U_{test}|}$, where a hit is deemed as occurred if the N hashtags generated for user
u contains u's most probably adopted hashtag (i.e. hidden hashtag/withheld
hashtag) [19]. The most probably adopted hashtag is with the highest frequency.
A confounding factor, 1000 random hashtags, are added for each true adoption.

In addition to the user- and item- based neighborhood baseline models,
dubbed as $Ngbr_{Corr}^{U}$ and $Ngbr_{Corr}^{T}$ [19,20] (see Eq. (1)), the proposed methods
are also evaluated against two competing models developed based on heuristics: Hashtag Average Adoption Times ("AvgAdoption") and Top Popularity
("TopPopular") [12], see Sect. 2.

5.2   Experiment Results and Analysis

Interior Behavior Dimensions Enhanced CF Model. Figure 1(a) and (b)
show the results of homophily based models with user-oriented and topic-oriented
interior dimensions, respectively. Figure 1(c) and (d) present the results of integrating social influence with the enhanced homophily-based recommendations
in Fig. 1(a) and (b) through Eq. (9). Note that the normalization coefficients are
set as $a = 10$, and $\epsilon = 0.9$.

We observe that for user-oriented behavior interior dimensions (see Fig. 1(a)
and (c)), models with static interior dimensions features and dynamic interior
dimensions features are similar in the recall rate based prediction accuracy.

Table 7. The impact of communication modality

Method	Recall@1	Recall@5	Recall@10	Recall@20
SVD^1_{CmEpM}	10.5%	25.7%	32.1%	38%
SVD^1_{CmDFT}	10.5%	36.1%	31.4%	38.2%
SVD^1_{CmDWT}	9.2%	24.9%	31.2%	37.3%
$\boldsymbol{SVD^1_{CmPCA}}$	17%	32%	37.8%	42.6%
SVD^2_{CmEpM}	10.6%	24%	30.8%	36.9%
SVD^2_{CmDFT}	11.2%	26.3%	32.2%	38.1%
SVD^2_{CmDWT}	9.3%	25%	31.2%	37.4%
$\boldsymbol{SVD^2_{CmPCA}}$	19.8%	32.2%	37.8%	42.9%

The prediction accuracy curves for both types of models are in convex shape: it increases very fast for small N and then starts to level off. The turning point occurs at about 5 for user-oriented models, and 10 for topic-oriented models. It indicates the homophily based models perform equally badly for small N ($N = 1$). Thus, the homophily based models perform fairly well for recommending a set of hashtags that people are most likely interested in, not a precise prediction of the exact hashtag a user may adopt. For topic-oriented behavior interior dimensions (see Fig. 1(b) and (d)), we can observe a similar pattern. However, different from the user-oriented case, models with dynamic interior dimension features can achieve better results, with DWT based local shape the best prediction accuracy, followed by PCA-based pattern.

Furthermore, the gap difference between user and topic-oriented enhanced models (e.g. $Ngbr^{U/T}_{Inter}$) and their corresponding baseline model (i.e. $Ngbr^{U/T}_{Exter}$) indicates that user and topic-oriented enhanced models have their own "best bets" range. More specifically, the gaps are large for user-oriented models but almost zero for topic-oriented models at a small range of N, whereas at a large range of N, the gaps for topic-oriented models are much larger than those of user-oriented models. Therefore, in utilizing interior dimensions for hashtag recommendation, it is better to use user-oriented models for small N recommendation, and use topic-oriented models for large N recommendation.

The Interaction Between Communication Modality and Behavior Interior Dimension. From Table 7, we can see that including communication modality will deliver better accuracy. In particular, at a small value of N, the recall rate of SVD^2_{CmPCA} at top-1 recommendation is 19.8%, higher than SVD^1_{CmPCA}–17%. This is also the highest accuracy that we achieve at top-1 recommendation. At a large value of N, for example, $N = 20$, the recall rate of SVD^2_{CmPCA} at top-20 recommendation is 42.9%, higher than SVD^1_{CmPCA}–42.6%. The observation with respect to the static and time-sensitive features also applies here. The PCA-based co-occurrence pattern that considers the interdependence between multiple dimensions still wins over other features.

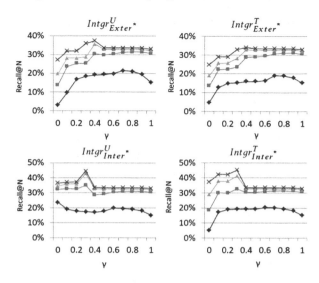

Fig. 2. Sensitivity of integration parameter γ. (The methods tagged with $*$ are our proposed models)

Coupling Homophily and Social Influence. The sensitivity analysis of integration parameter γ is shown in Fig. 2. The top-left figure is the integration model with homophily based on user-oriented behavior exteriors; top-right figure is the integration model with homophily based on topic-oriented behavior exteriors; bottom-left figure is the integration model with homophily based on user-oriented behavior interiors; bottom-right figure is the integration model with homophily based on topic-oriented behavior interiors. As γ increases, the accuracy first increases, then levels off; when γ gets close to 1, the accuracy decreases. The integration of social influence and homophily performs robustly between $\gamma \in [0.2, 0.8]$. Thus, it provides a basis to implement this strategy in making recommendations of hashtags to Twitter users. The highest coupling result occurs when $\gamma \in [0.3, 0.4]$ for a larger N (e.g. $\in [5, 20]$), and $\gamma \in [0.6, 0.8]$ for a smaller N (e.g. top-1).

Generally speaking, coupling social influence and homophily in hashtag recommendations in Twitter will lead to around 10%-20% improvement compared with adopting each of them separately. The only exception happens for $Intgr_{Inter}^{U}$ when N = 1 where the model performs best when $\gamma = 0$, i.e. homophily-based model, and deteriorates almost all the way down to influence based model. This indicates users' interior dimensions based CF model is less robust in for Top-1 hashtag recommendation. Moreover, Top-1 recommendation puts a much harsher requirement for all the recommendation methods studied in this paper. It requires the dimensions highly condense all the information so as to capture user and hashtag preference and thereby make a precise recommendation. However, in practice, normally top-20 hashtags will be pushed

Table 8. Prediction accuracy (with N = 1, 5, 10, 20)

Method		Recall@1	Recall@5	Recall@10	Recall@20
Baseline	SVD	17.6%	25.7%	28.4%	31.2%
	AvgAdoption	0%	0%	0.1%	0.3%
	TopPopular	8.3%	19.8%	21%	24.9%
Homophily					
Exterior	$Ngbr_{Exter}^{U}$	3.2%	13.6%	19.7%	27.4%
Usage	$Ngbr_{Exter}^{T}$	4.8%	13.6%	19%	25%
Interior	$Ngbr_{Inter}^{U*}$	**23.8%**	32.3%	34.5%	36.5%
Dimension*	$Ngbr_{Inter}^{T*}$	5.3%	18.5%	28.9%	37.3%
Influence*	MTLT*	15.1%	30.6%	32.2%	33%
Coupled*	$Intgr_{Exter}^{U*}$	**21.5%**	31.4%	35.7%	37.2%
	$Intgr_{Exter}^{T*}$	19.1%	31.2%	32.9%	34%
	$Intgr_{Inter}^{U*}$	19.8%	**32.8%**	**42.8%**	**44.6%**
	$Intgr_{Inter}^{T*}$	20.4%	**32.6%**	**41.3%**	**45.2%**

to users for reference, the coupling method performs fairly good in this circumstance based on the analysis above with a significant improvement for all the four methods studied. Note that $Intgr_{Exter}^{U}$ and $Intgr_{Exter}^{T}$ are based on the exterior dimensions, and $Intgr_{Inter}^{U}$ and $Intgr_{Inter}^{T}$ are based on the interior dimensions.

Table 8 summarizes the recall rate of the methods proposed in Sect. 4. The models are trained with learning rate 0.007, $\lambda = 0.002$. Our proposed models are marked with *. The two largest recall scores are highlighted in bold for each group. We have the following findings: First, we see that capturing homophily through behavior interior dimensions has better performance (the recall rate for top-20 recommendation is 36.5% and 37.3% for $Ngbr_{Inter}^{U}$ and $Ngbr_{Inter}^{T}$) than those based purely on usage statistics (27.4% and 25% for $Ngbr_{Exter}^{U}$ and $Ngbr_{Exter}^{T}$). This supports our assumption that interior dimensions capture latent similarity between users and topics in addition to the extrinsic user-hashtag adoption frequency. Second, we observe that coupling social influence and homophily leads to a higher recall rate, with $Intgr_{Inter}^{T}$ the highest: 45.2%. In this case, the improvement rate achieves the highest: 80.8%. The recall rate of the two coupling components, $Ngbr_{Inter}^{T}$ and MTLT, are 37.3% and 33%, respectively. Hence, the complementary property of these two factors: (a) social influence-driven contagion through followers' posts or other people's posts in the same topic; and (b) homophily in interests, where hashtag prediction is supported.

In summary, the experiment results reveal that (i) for both the user-oriented and the topic-oriented homophily based hashtag recommendations, the interior dimensions based homophily models have better performance than the exterior statistics based models, with a more prominent improvement for the user-oriented models; (ii) the integration of social influence and homophily in hashtag recommendations leads to better accuracy. For a larger N (e.g. $\in [5, 20]$), the highest result occurs when the integration is weighted towards the homophily side. For a smaller N (e.g. top-1), it occurs when weighted towards the social influence side. The highest result reaches as high as 45.2%, which is around 10%-20% better than simply considering one factor.

6   Conclusion

In this paper, we study the problem of how to integrate the social influence and homophily for the top-N hashtag adoption frequency prediction. We propose a method that couples the social influence and homophily: two complementary mechanisms in information propagation. We test a series of models on the real-world Twitter data, and the results demonstrate that jointly considering these two aspects leads to higher recall rate with better performance. Another main contribution is to apply the domain knowledge to capture as much data inter-dependence as possible. The interdependence between multiple data sources is captured in two levels. Firstly, the interdependence is teased out in terms of the user-oriented and topic-oriented aspects, respectively. In particular, the impact of topic communication modalities on behavior interior dimensions are captured, with an improvement of $\sim 3\%$. Secondly, the social influence and homophily are two interior dimensions specific for the purpose of top-N hashtag recommenda-tion. As for future work, one direction could be to extend the current algebraic calculation based integration method, and explore the kernel method to unveil the interaction of social influence and homophily in hashtag recommendation.

References

1. Anagnostopoulos, A., Kumar, R., Mahdian, M.: Influence and correlation in social networks. In: SIGKDD, pp. 7–15 (2008)
2. McPherson, M., Smith-Lovin, L., Cook, J.M.: Birds of a feather: homophily in social networks. Ann. Rev. Sociol. **27**(1), 415–444 (2001)
3. Soetevent, A.R.: Empirics of the identification of social interactions: an evaluation of the approaches and their results. J. Econ. Surv. **20**(2), 193–228 (2006)
4. Yang, B., Lei, Y., Liu, J., et al.: Social collaborative filtering by trust. PAMI **39**(8), 1633–1647 (2017)
5. Wang, C., Dong, X., Zhou, F., et al.: Coupled attribute similarity learning on categorical data. IEEE Trans. Neural Netw. Learn. Syst. **26**(4), 781–797 (2015)
6. Wang, C., Chi, C., Zhou, W., et al.: Coupled interdependent attribute analysis on mixed data. In: AAAI, pp. 1861–1867 (2015)
7. Azucar, D., Marengo, D., Settanni, M.: Predicting the Big 5 personality traits from digital footprints on social media: a meta-analysis. Pers. Individ. Differ. **124**, 150–159 (2018)
8. Wang, C., Bo, T., Zhao, Y., et al.: Behavior-interior-aware user preference analysis based on social networks. Complexity **2018** (2018). Article ID 7371209
9. Zhao, Y., Wang, C.: Beyond the power of mere repetition: forms of social commu-nication on twitter through the lens of information flows and its effect on topic evolution. IJCNN (2019, to be published)

10. Marbach, J., Lages, C.R., Nunan, D.: Who are you and what do you value? Investigating the role of personality traits and customer-perceived value in online customer engagement. J. Mark. Manag. **32**, 502–525 (2016)
11. Romero, D.M., Galuba, W., Asur, S., Huberman, B.A.: Influence and passivity in social media. In: Gunopulos, D., Hofmann, T., Malerba, D., Vazirgiannis, M. (eds.) ECML PKDD 2011. LNCS (LNAI), vol. 6913, pp. 18–33. Springer, Heidelberg (2011). https://doi.org/10.1007/978-3-642-23808-6_2
12. Lu, H., Lee, C.: A Twitter hashtag recommendation model that accommodates for temporal clustering effects. IEEE Intell. Syst. **30**(3), 18–25 (2015)
13. Song, Q., Cheng, J., Yuan, T., et al.: Personalized recommendation meets your next favorite. In: CIKM, pp. 1775–1778 (2015)
14. He, X., Chen, T., Kan, M., et al.: TriRank: review-aware explainable recommendation by modeling aspects. In: CIKM, pp. 1661–1670 (2015)
15. Chu, W., Tsai, Y.: A hybrid recommendation system considering visual information for predicting favorite restaurants. World Wide Web **20**(6), 1313–1331 (2017)
16. Lee, J., Hwang, W.-S., Parc, J., et al.: l-Injection: toward effective collaborative filtering using uninteresting items. TKDE **31**(1), 3–16 (2019)
17. Si, G., Zheng, K., Zhou, Z., et al.: Three-dimensional piecewise cloud representation for time series data mining. Neurocomputing **316**, 78–94 (2018)
18. Qahtan, A., Alharbi, B., Wang, S.L., et al.: A PCA-based change detection framework for multidimensional data streams: change detection in multidimensional data streams. In: KDD, pp. 935–944 (2015)
19. Aggarwal, C.C.: Neighborhood-based collaborative filtering. In: Aggarwal, C.C. (ed.) Recommender Systems, pp. 29–70. Springer, Cham (2016). https://doi.org/10.1007/978-3-319-29659-3_2
20. Portugal, I., Alencar, P.S.C., Cowan, D.D.: The use of machine learning algorithms in recommender systems: a systematic review. Expert Syst. Appl. **97**, 205–227 (2018)

Unfolding the Mixed and Intertwined: A Multilevel View of Topic Evolution on Twitter

Yunwei Zhao[1], Can Wang[2], Han Han[1(✉)], Willem-Jan van den Heuvel[3], Chi-Hung Chi[4], and Weimin Li[5]

[1] CNCERT/CC, Beijing, China
hanh@cert.org.cn
[2] School of ICT, Griffith University, Gold Coast, Australia
[3] Tilburg University, Tilburg, The Netherlands
[4] CSIRO, Hobart, Australia
[5] School of Computer Engineering and Technology,
Shanghai University, Shanghai, China

Abstract. Despite the extensive research efforts in information diffusion, most previous studies focus on the speed and coverage of the diffused information in the network. A better understanding on the semantics of information diffusion can provide critical information for the domain-specific/socio-economic phenomenon studies based on diffused topics. More specifically, it still lacks (a) a comprehensive understanding of the multiplexity in the diffused topics, especially with respect to the temporal relations and inter-dependence between topic semantics; (b) the similarities and differences in these dimensions under different diffusion degrees. In this paper, the semantics of a topic is described by sentiment, controversy, content richness, hotness, and trend momentum. The multiplexity in the diffusion mechanisms is also considered, namely, hashtag cascade, url cascade, and retweet. Our study is conducted upon 840, 362 topics from about 42 million tweets during 2010.01–2010.10. The results show that the topics are not randomly distributed in the Twitter space, but exhibiting a unique pattern at each diffusion degree, with a significant correlation among content richness, hotness, and trend momentum. Moreover, under each diffusion mechanism, we also find the remarkable similarity among topics, especially when considering the shifting and scaling in both the temporal and amplitude scales of these dimensions.

Keywords: Information diffusion · Topic evolution · Twitter · Multivariate time-series

1 Introduction

Information diffusion is a substantial part in social media research. In the diffusion process, multi-faceted aspects are captured through "human sensors",

© Springer Nature Switzerland AG 2019
J. Li et al. (Eds.): ADMA 2019, LNAI 11888, pp. 359–369, 2019.
https://doi.org/10.1007/978-3-030-35231-8_26

including news, public opinions, and customer reviews of goods as well as services, and etc. Some researchers aptly described it as "diamond in the rough" [1]. A large amount of research has been conducted in both computer science and domain-specific studies. In particular, diffused information is usually taken as a central starting point from which to investigate a number of issues, including the topic evolution that studies the process by which a topic is developed from its emergence to disappearance, and the domain-specific analytics, such as the stock market trend as well as the potential success of a candidate in a political election [1]. However, these studies have several limitations:

Firstly, there has been a predominant focus on the exterior transactional statistics (e.g. tweet amount) in the traditional computer science area. For example, the current topic evolution research mostly focuses on the topic popularity and the trending [2,3], etc., rather than the behavior interior dimensions (the semantic meanings, e.g., sentiment) [4]. Secondly, even though it addresses the behaviour interior dimensions in utilizing the diffused topic to interpret the related phenomenon in domain-specific studies, the focus in those studies is usually on the individual interior dimension, much less effort is devoted to the correlations and co-occurrence patterns between multiple dimensions in the evolution [5]. Thirdly, domain-specific studies are often validated only on the highly diffused topics. However, the heuristic based on the topic popularity may not necessarily mean a proportional relation in other dimensions as well. Highly diffused topics may be repeated as ad posts and involve few people, and may not be very useful sources for domain-specific areas such as viral marketing. A full spectrum analysis with respect to the similarity and difference is thereby necessitated from the least to the most popular ones.

Therefore, there is a lack of understanding in the diffused topics along the behaviour interior dimensions time series, in particular with respect to (a) the temporal relations and inter-relations of the multiple behaviour interior dimensions, (b) the similarity and difference in these characteristics of topics across different diffusion degrees. Following our previous work [4], the behavior interior dimensions that we use to study the topics are "Sentiment", "Controversy", "Content Richness", "Hotness" and "Trend Momentum". The major research questions of this study are as follows:

RQ1. How does each topic behavior interior dimension evolve at different diffusion degrees with respect to the amplitude and the shape of each interior dimension time series? How does it vary along the different diffusion degrees?

RQ2. What are the co-occurrence patterns between the multiple dimensions? How does it vary along the different diffusion degrees?

RQ3. Are the topic behavior interior dimensions similar in terms of shifting and scaling in temporal dimensions within the same diffusion degree level? How about scaling in the amplitude across different diffusion degrees?

RQ4. Are the results in RQ1-3 exhibiting the same pattern or different patterns under different diffusion formation ways, i.e. hashtag, url, retweet?

The remainder of this paper is organized as follows. Section 2 reviews the related work. Section 3 presents the hypothesized framework that guides our empirical studies. Section 4 introduces the multivariate time series approach that we have used to extract the temporal and inter-dimensional relations in the weekly time series of the multiple interior dimensions, followed by the experiments and result discussions. Section 7 concludes this paper.

2   Related Work

Two strands of literature contribute to the research work in this paper: first, the literature pertaining to user-generated content (UGC) based socio-economic event analysis; second, the literature pertaining to the dynamic temporal analysis in topic evolution research.

The potential of user generated content in making sense of an event in near real-time attracts wide attention from tracking public attitudes to predicting certain socio-economic events. A number of interior dimensions have already been incorporated in these studies, here we follow the research conducted in [4]. However, there are two major limitations: first, they usually approach from a uni-dimensional view with a lack of their inter-relations. For example, one recent work in stock microblogs [5] studies how to predict the stock market features based on bullishness, level of agreement between postings and message volume; however, the interdependence between these determinants is missing. Second, these studies usually focus on the magnitude of the dimensions, but neglect the associated temporal features, such as shape patterns (e.g. spikes, rises, etc.) and temporal dependences (e.g. decays, etc.).

On the other hand, the majority of current topic evolution research focuses on topic popularity and trending [2,3]. Some work studies the persistence and decay of the attention given to a specific topic [3]. Some other work investigates the predictors for the speed–whether and when the first diffusion instance will take place, scale–the number of affected instances at the first degree, and range–how far the diffusion chain can continue on in depth of the diffusion. However, research on the inter-dependence relationship between multiple interior dimensions under the topic evolution environment will be even less. Moreover, despite its predominant focus on the topic popularity, most are only validated partially on the popular topics, e.g. in the 1, 000 most frequently mentioned hashtags and urls [6], a holistic view is lacking on both popular and non-popular topics. Thereby, a comprehensive analysis of the topic evolution at a full spectrum of diffusion degrees with respect to the temporal and inter-relations between the multiple behaviour interior dimensions is particularly important for understanding the related socio-economic phenomena.

3   Theoretical Framework

The reproduced information r (also usually used to denote the topic) includes the following three main types in literature, namely, a hashtag, a url or a tweet. The diffusion degree of a topic is the total transmission times its tweets are spread over the entire social network.

Definition 1 (Information Diffusion). Information diffusion in Twitter is a reproduction process in the form of a sequence of "infection" events: $\psi(r) = (r, u_0, c_0, w_0), (r, u_1, c_1, w_1), \ldots, (r, u_N, c_N, w_N)$, where the quadruple (r, u_i, c_i, w_i) represents the ith reproduction event where user u_i posted content c_i that reproduced r in the ways denoted in w_i.

Definition 2 (Topic). Given time interval T, a topic $t(r)$ is a sequentially indexed set of all the content that is reproduced from r since it first surfaced in content c_0 within the entire observation time interval T.

The hypotheses are developed at different granularities, from within-topic to across topic level, along different diffusion degree levels and different diffusion mechanisms. Before we introduce the details, we will first define the diffusion degree level of a topic. As noted in the literature [7], the information transmitted in social media follows a long-tail distribution. However, it is the highly diffused topics that receive the most widespread attention. Based on these considerations, we use a logarithmic function (see Eq. (1)) to determine the diffusion degree level, where CC_i represents the communication count of topic i. Accordingly, the hashtag-, url-, and retweet-based topics are segmented into 11 levels, 9 levels, and 6 levels, respectively (see Table 2 for greater details). Figure 1 presents selective hashtag-based topics at different levels.

$$Level(i) = \lfloor ln(CC_i) \rfloor \qquad (1)$$

Our hypotheses are mainly formulated from intuitions based on an integration of what is observed in news reports and in day-to-day experience centered on this research aim.

Within Topic: At the within-topic level, there are two sets of hypotheses: the first set of hypotheses corresponds to RQ 1, focusing on the magnitude and temporal features of individual dimensions. In particular, for magnitude features, we focus more on the comparison across topic diffusion degree level and diffusion mechanisms; for temporal features, besides the smooth or spiky shape and ascending or descending trend, we focus more on the temporal dependence of the topic hotness, i.e., whether the hot topics tend to get hot over the next several moments and the period this trend lasts for.

H1. The behavior interior dimensions decrease as diffusion degree reduces, and they vary across hashtag-based, url-based and retweet-based topics.

H1a: Hashtag-based topics have higher sentiment and controversy than url- and retweet-based topics.

H1b: Hashtag-based topics have the highest content richness, and retweet-based topics have the lowest content richness, with url-based topics in the middle.

H1c: Hashtag-based topics have a higher degree of hotness than url- and retweet-based topics.

H2v: Topic hotness is temporally dependent and differs w.r.t. diffusion degree.

H2a: The higher the diffusion degree of the topics, the higher the probability of forecasting future hotness trend based on current observation.

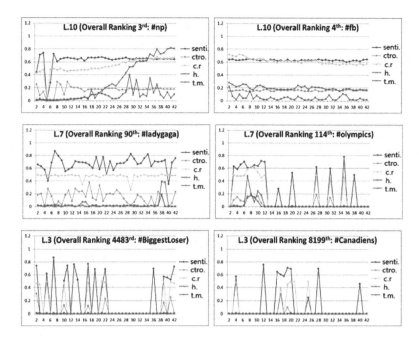

Fig. 1. An illustration of the temporal and amplitude shifting and scaling in the behavior interior dimensions of hashtag-based topics w.r.t. different diffusion degrees.

H2b: The higher the diffusion degree of the topics, the longer the forecasting interval of future hotness trend based on current observation with regard to a certain threshold.

The second set of hypotheses corresponds to RQ 2, focusing on the interdependence between the multiple behavior interior dimensions. Positive content is more likely to be widely shared out of the users' motives of self-preservation. The same applies to content richness, it is noted that content that bears practical utility tends to be more exploited [8]. Additionally, controversial content tends to receive more attention [9]. In particular, the topics relating to event significance and information authenticity, where users have greater emotional input, tend to go viral, due to feelings of personal involvement at times of social crises, e.g. personal health concern in a pandemic outbreak [10]. In our daily life, we also come across such news from time to time, e.g., natural disasters, pandemic outbreak, and death hoaxes. Thus, we have the following hypotheses under all three diffusion mechanisms, i.e. hashtag cascade, url cascade, and retweet:

H3. The topic behavior interior dimensions are not mutually independent.

H3a: Sentiment and hotness has a positive correlation with each other.

H3b: Controversy and hotness has a positive correlation with each other.

H3c: Content richness and hotness has a positive correlation with each other.

Across Topics: At the cross-topic level (RQ 3), we note that temporal shifting and scaling are pervasive in Twitter topics. Temporal shifting refers to the average lag in the time series between the effective(non-vacant) coverage of two topics during the sampling period. The effective coverage dramatically varied from several days to the entire sampling period (41 weeks). For example, compared with "#Olympics" at L.7 in Fig. 1, the topic "#Canadiens" at L.3 shifts to the right, but the amplitudes and the shapes of the two multi-variate time series are similar. Temporal scaling refers to the variation degree between different topic time series length, such as "#ladygaga" and "#olympics" at L.7 in Fig. 1. The former covers the entire sampling period (41 weeks), while the latter mainly lasts only 10 weeks. Amplitude shifting and scaling, on the other hand, is defined on each dimension. Note that the amplitude shifting is trivial as each dimension is already normalized to [0, 1]. Amplitude scaling refers to the variation degree in the average values in the effective period. Different dimensions may have different scaling features. For example, compared with the topic "#now playing" at L.11, all the five dimensions of the topic "#fb" at L.10 have decreased at a certain degree, but with hotness the greatest. Thus, we hypothesize as follows,

H4. The behavior interior dimensions, namely, sentiment, controversy, content richness, hotness, and trend momentum, have various temporal and amplitude shifts and scales.

H4a: At each diffusion degree, the behavior interior dimensions are similar with regard to temporal shifting and scaling.

H4b: From high diffusion degree to low diffusion degree, the amplitude scales down. The behavior interior dimensions, i.e. sentiment, controversy, content richness, hotness varies across hashtag-based, url-based and retweet based topics.

4   A MTS Approach

To address the research questions, we resort to multivariate time series (MTS) clustering techniques [11] to analyze the similarities and differences in topic dimension time series on each diffusion degree w.r.t. the temporal and inter-dimensional relations. Table 1 presents an overview of the methods used to address the research questions. There are two considerations from the research question that guide us in the technique selection: (a) the magnitude or the shape focus of the time series, (b) the assumption that the multiple dimensions are independent or correlated. We note that there are two features of Twitter topic time series that pose great challenges to MTS methods: (i) dramatically varying life cycles, and (ii) pervading temporal shifting in similar topic time-series[1].

5   Experiment Settings

5.1   Data

The dataset is crawled within 2010.01-2010.10 containing about 78 million tweets from 112,044 users. The sentiments of the tweets are evaluated based on ANEW

---

[1] The magnitude is calculated over non-vacant values.

Table 1. An overview of the MTS methods

Analytic focus of the methods	Features of the methods			
	MTS or STS Extension	Similarity or Model-based	Future Value Forecasting	Fuzzy or Crisp Clustering
RQ 1 (Within topic: Evolutionary features of individual dimension)				
Magnitude Perspective: $m_d^i = avgm_d^i(t)$, $m_d^i(t)$ is the dth dimension at time t.				
Shape Perspective				
DFT [12] (Global shape)	STS	Similarity	N	Crisp
Temporal Dependence				
ACF [13] (Temporal dependence)	STS	Similarity	N	Crisp
RQ 2 (Within topic: Inter-dependence of multiple dimensions)				
CCF [11] (Cross-correlation)	MTS	Similarity	N	Crisp
PCA [11] (Co-occurrence pattern)	MTS	Similarity	N	Crisp
RQ 3 (Across topic: Shape similarities in shifting and scaling)				
SpAde [14] based method$p_l = (\theta_{tsh}, \theta_{tsc}, \theta_{asc}^d)$, where $\theta_{tsh} = avg(tl_{i1} - tl_{i2})$, $\theta_{tsc} = <min(lc_i/\overline{lc}^l), max(lc_i/\overline{lc}^l)>$, $\theta_{asc}^d = <min(m_i^d/\overline{m}_d^l), max(m_i^d/\overline{m}_d^l)>$				

with emoticons[2] and slangs[3] replaced with the corresponding text. We have 42,475,140 tweets and 840, 362 topics. Table 2 presents the statistics at each segmented diffusion degree level based on Eq. 1.

Table 2. Segmentation of Twitter data set according to diffusion distribution

Diffusion degree L.x	Communication count range	Number of topics within diffusion degree $L.x^1$		
		Hashtag cascade	Url cascade	Retweet collection
L.11	[59875, 162754]	2	–	–
L.10	[22027, 59874]	2	–	–
L.9	[8104, 22026]	6	6	–
L.8	[2981, 8103]	28	18	–
L.7	[1097, 2980]	81	41	–
L.6	[404, 1096]	342	94	1
L.5	[149, 403]	1049	404	8
L.4	[55, 148]	2582	1488	78
L.3	[21, 54]	5930	5002	754
L.2	[8, 20]	14259	17726	6476
L.1	[3, 7]	37857	97163	47753
L.0	[1, 2]	290243	215220	95749

5.2 Evaluation Methods

To decide the optimal number of clusters, we have considered the Silhouette method [15] and the "jump" method, deciding in the end to use the Silhouette method as it considers both the within-cluster and cross-cluster distance, while the "jump" method only focuses on within-cluster distance.

---

[2] See webpage http://cool-smileys.com/text-emoticons, containing 938 text emoticons.

[3] See webpage http://www.noslang.com/, containing 5396 slangs and abbreviations.

Table 3. Magnitude of the topic interior dimensions across different diffusion degrees and topic diffusion mechanisms

	Hashtag						Url						Retweet					
	$\overline{Ic}$	S.	C.	C.R.	H.	T.M.	$\overline{Ic}$	S.	C.	C.R.	H.	T.M.	$\overline{Ic}$	S.	C.	C.R.	H.	T.M.
L.11	41	0.67	0.16	0.88	0.91	0.16												
L.10	41	0.63	0.17	0.58	0.25	0.06												
L.9	30	0.59	0.14	0.48	0.12	0.07	31	0.58	0	0.34	0.4	0.04						
L.8	30.14	0.57	0.15	0.47	0.07	0.08	20.78	0.55	0.02	0.34	0.33	0.14						
L.7	26.63	0.59	0.13	0.44	0.03	0.07	12.44	0.55	0.04	0.36	0.23	0.13						
L.6	19.46	0.55	0.12	0.4	0.02	0.07	12.8	0.59	0.05	0.31	0.15	0.14	5	0	0	0.13	0.51	0.43
L.5	14.98	0.52	0.1	0.36	0.01	0.04	8.34	0.54	0.04	0.27	0.08	0.09	13.75	0.24	0.02	0.33	0.28	0.28
L.4	8.64	0.48	0.08	0.32	0.01	0.02	5.88	0.5	0.04	0.24	0.04	0.05	5.18	0.36	0	0.19	0.34	0.38
L.3	4.53	0.44	0.06	0.26	0	0.01	4.19	0.49	0.04	0.22	0.02	0.03	2.4	0.4	0	0.17	0.21	0.21
L.2	2.37	0.41	0.04	0.22	0	0	2.32	0.47	0.03	0.2	0.01	0.02	1.39	0.41	0	0.16	0.11	0.11
L.1	1.4	0.36	0.03	0.18	0	0	1.36	0.44	0.02	0.19	0.01	0.01	1.1	0.38	0	0.16	0.05	0.05
L.0	1	0.28	0	0.02	0	0	1.09	0.4	0.01	0.19	0.01	0.01	1.02	0.33	0	0.18	0.03	0.03

6 Results

This section presents the results at three scales: (i) within-topic individual dimension, (ii) within-topic across dimensions, and (iii) across topics.

Within-Topic: Evolutionary Features of Individual Dimension. We can see from Table 3 that the sentiment range is 0.55–0.67 from L.6–L.11 for hashtag-based topics, 0.55–0.58 for url-based topics and almost zero for retweet-based topics. The measure of controversy would not be high, as it is not realistic for each consecutive pair of tweets to have almost exactly the opposite extreme values in sentiments. We could still observe the same trend: the controversy is above 0.1 at L.5–L.11 in hashtag-based topics but almost zero in url- and retweet-based topics. Therefore, H1a is supported. Hashtag-based topics have the highest content richness (0.88 in L.11), retweet-based topics have the lowest content richness (0.13 in L.6), with url-based topics in the middle (0.34 in L.9). Therefore, H1b is supported. Note that in contrast with other dimension measurements, hotness is not directly comparable across different topic diffusion mechanisms as it is normalized within each mechanism (Table 3).

As to the temporal dependence relations for each individual dimension, the auto-correlation results show that the forecasting interval (without loss of generality, suppose the threshold is set at 0.4) is 8 at L.11 and, 8 at L.9 and 2 at L.7 in hashtag-based topics, 8 at L.9, 3 at L.7, and 1 at L.5 in url-based topics. Therefore, H2a and H2b are supported in hashtag- and url-based topics, but not in retweet-based topics. As the topics are more explosive and transient in retweet-based type, the average lifecycle even for the highly diffused retweet-based topics is much shorter (around 10 weeks) than hashtag- and url-based topics (above 30 weeks).

Within-Topic: Inter-dependence of Multiple Dimensions. For the inter-dependence of multiple dimensions, the PCA results show there is a clear co-occurrence pattern between the five dimensions. There are at most two principal

Table 4. Shifting and scaling features in temporal and amplitude dimensions of hashtag-based topics

	Temporal Shifting(θ_{tsh})	Temporal Scaling(θ_{tsc})	Amplitude Scaling (θ_{asc}^d)				
			Sent.	Contro	C.R.	H.	T.M.
L.11	0	(1.0, 1.0)	(0.96, 1.04)	(0.88, 1.12)	(0.88, 1.12)	(0.93, 1.07)	(0.96, 1.04)
L.10	0	(1.0, 1.0)	(1.0, 1.0)	(0.97, 1.03)	(0.93, 1.07)	(0.8, 1.2)	(0.66, 1.34)
L.9	5.33	(0.53, 1.37)	(0.84, 1.13)	(0.65, 1.29)	(0.79, 1.14)	(0.55, 1.31)	(0.47, 1.97)
L.8	5.91	(0.07, 1.36)	(0.37, 1.2)	(0.22, 1.46)	(0.55, 1.15)	(0.28, 3.96)	(0.22, 4.62)
L.7	7.43	(0.08, 1.54)	(0.23, 1.35)	(0.12, 1.65)	(0.5, 1.15)	(0.19, 4.31)	(0.07, 6.75)
L.6	9.32	(0.05, 2.11)	(0, 1.46)	(0.0, 3.3)	(0.2, 1.35)	(0.05, 9.93)	(0.06, 11.84)
L.5	10.37	(0.07, 2.74)	(0.03, 1.69)	(0.0, 3.25)	(0.1, 1.68)	(0, 11.94)	(0.01, 14.75)
L.4	12.31	(0, 4.05)	(0, 1.81)	(0, 6.13)	(0, 1.65)	(0.0, 17.61)	(0, 16.56)
L.3	13.14	(0, 5.08)	(0, 1.98)	(0, 9.24)	(0, 1.94)	(0.0, 26.63)	(0, 23.96)
L.2	14.2	(0, 5.9)	(0, 2.13)	(0, 14.23)	(0, 2.34)	(0.0, 48.03)	(0, 19.13)
L.1	13.01	(0, 4.98)	(0, 2.41)	(0, 25.17)	(0, 2.86)	(0, 950.38)	(0, 18.8)
L.0	11.7	(0, 1.99)	(0, 3.15)	(0, 546.31)	(0, 27.26)	(0, 0)	(0, 16.69)

Table 5. Main hypotheses and results summary

	Diffusion mechanisms		
	Hashtag cascade	Url cascade	Retweet collection
Within topic:			
Single dimension–magnitude (across diffusion mechanisms)			
H1a (Sentiment and controversy)		S	
H1b (Content richness)		S	
H1c (Hotness and trend momentum)		S	
Single Dimension–Temporal Dependence			
H2a	S	S	S
H2b	S	S	NS
Multi-dimension Interdependence			
H3a	NS	NS	NS
H3b*	NS	NS	NS
H3c*	S	CS	CS
Across topics:			
Shape similarity in shifting and scaling			
H4a	S	S	S
H4b	S	S	S

components (capturing the most variances in the original series) since there are only two non-zero eigenvalues (i.e. non-zero projection strength). As diffusion degree level changes, the values in the principal eigenvectors tend to get more evenly distributed for all three diffusion mechanisms. Therefore, H3 is supported. There is barely a correlation between sentiment, controversy and hotness under all three diffusion mechanisms. However, there is a significant correlation between content richness and hotness in highly diffused topics in hashtag-based type. Therefore, H3a and H3b are not supported, but H3c is supported in hashtag-based topics and conditionally supported in url- and retweet-based topics[4].

Across-Topic: Shape Similarities in Shifting and Scaling. Table 4 presents the temporal and amplitude shifting and scaling features across different topics within each different diffusion degree. We can see that the average temporal shifts between topics at each level increase as the diffusion degree reduces, as the lifecycle is getting shorter. For the same reason, the temporal scaling span also increases, from <1.0, 1.0> at the top diffusion degree level to <0, 5.9>, <0, 8.63>, and <0, 8.77> at about the third bottom diffusion degree level for each of the three diffusion mechanisms, respectively. The amplitude scales are homogeneous for more diffused topics as the amplitude scaling feature between topics at each level stables around 1 ($\geq$L.7 in hashtag-based). We have similar observations in url-based and retweet-based topics. Therefore, H4a is supported. Then the magnitude scales get more diverse as topic diffusion degree increases. We can see from Table 3 that the amplitude of hotness, content richness and sentiment are generally scaling down from higher diffusion degrees to lower ones. As mentioned above, the content richness of the greatest diffused url-based topics can be much less (e.g. horoscope stays around 0.35 in its whole lifecycle) than that of the less diffused ones. Therefore, H4b is also supported.

7 Conclusion

This paper has embarked on a systematic exploration of the topic evolution, covering the full spectrum of diffusion degrees from the most- to the least-popular, w.r.t. the temporal relations and inter-relations of the behavior interior dimensions. The results show that the multiple behavior interior dimensions exhibit a unique pattern at each diffusion degree, with a significant correlation among the content richness, the hotness, and the trend momentum. Moreover, we find the remarkable similarity in the evolutionary features across topics, especially when taking the temporal and amplitude shifting and scaling into consideration. The observation similarity leads us to conclude that the multiple behavior dimensions are not randomly distributed in the Twitter space, but exhibiting a co-occurrence pattern affected by diffusion degrees and topic diffusion mechanisms.

---

[4] There are some exceptions in url-based topics and retweet-based topics (the abnormally low correlation in the most diffused level): (a) the content richness is not positively correlated with hotness and trend momentum for the url- and retweet-based topics that are content self-replicating; (b) the content richness is positively correlated with hotness and trend momentum for the url- and retweet-based topics that have various subjects ongoing. For example, the 12th most diffused url-based topic http://faxo.com/t include "Harry Potter vs. Twilight", "Top YouTube Musician", "Musician of the Month", etc.

References

1. Diakopoulos, N.A., Shamma, D.A.: Characterizing debate performance via aggregated Twitter sentiment. In: CHI 2010, Atlanta, Georgia, USA, pp. 1195–1198 (2010)
2. Budak, C., Agrawal, D., Abbadi, A.E.: Structural trend analysis for online social networks. Proc. VLDB Endowment **4**(10), 646–656 (2011)
3. Sitaram, A., Bernardo, A.H., et al.: Trends in social media: persistence and decay. In: ICWSM 2011, Barcelona, Spain, pp. 434–437 (2011)
4. Wang, C., Bo, T., Zhao, Y., et al.: Behavior-interior-aware user preference analysis based on social networks. Complexity **2018**, Article ID 7371209 (2018). https://www.hindawi.com/journals/complexity/2018/7371209/cta/
5. Sprenger, T.O., Tumasjan, A., et al.: Tweets and trades: the information content of stock microblogs. Eur. Fin. Manag. **20**(5), 926–957 (2013)
6. Yang, J., Leskovec, J.: Patterns of temporal variation in online media. In: WSDM 2011, Hong Kong, China, pp. 177–186 (2011)
7. Cremonesi, P., Koren, Y., Turrin, R.: Performance of recommender algorithms on top-n recommendation tasks. In: RecSys 2010, Barcelona, Spain, pp. 39–46 (2010)
8. Boyd, D., Golder, S., Lotan, G.: Tweet, Tweet, Retweet: Conversational aspects of retweeting on Twitter. In: HICSS 2010, Honolulu, HI, pp. 1–10 (2010)
9. Guerini, M., Strapparava, C., Ozbal, G.: Exploring text virality in social networks. IN: ICWSM 2011, Barcelona, Spain, pp. 506–509 (2011)
10. Chew, C., Eysenbach, G.: Pandemics in the age of Twitter: content analysis of tweets during the 2009 H1N1 outbreak. PLoS ONE **5**(11), e14118 (2010)
11. Yang, K., Shahabi, C.: A PCA-based similarity measure for multivariate time series. In: MMDB 2004, Washington D.C, US, pp. 65–74 (2004)
12. Morchen, F.: Time series feature extraction for data mining using DWT and DFT. Department of Mathematics and Computer Science, University of Marburg (2003)
13. Galeano, P., Pena, D.: Multivariate analysis in vector time series. Resenhas **4**(4), 383–403 (2000)
14. Chen, Y., Chen, K., Nascimento, M.A.: Effective and efficient shape-based pattern detection over streaming time series. TKDE **24**(2), 265–278 (2012)
15. Rousseeuw, P.J.: Silhouettes: A graphical aid to the interpretation and validation of cluster analysis. J. Comput. Appl. Math. **20**, 53–65 (1987)

Behavior Modeling and User Profiling

DAMTRNN: A Delta Attention-Based Multi-task RNN for Intention Recognition

Weitong Chen[1]([✉]), Lin Yue[2]([✉]), Bohan Li[3], Can Wang[4], and Quan Z. Sheng[5]

[1] The University of Queensland, Brisbane, QLD, Australia
w.chen9@uq.edu.au
[2] Northeast Normal University, Changchun, Jilin, China
yuel031@nenu.edu.cn
[3] Nanjing University of Aeronautics and Astronautics, Nanjing, Jiangsu, China
[4] Griffith University, Gold Coast, QLD, Australia
[5] Macquarie University, Sydney, NSW, Australia

Abstract. Recognizing human intentions from electroencephalographic (EEG) signals is attracting extraordinary attention from the artificial intelligence community because of its promise in providing non-muscular forms of communication and control to those with disabilities. So far, studies have explored correlations between specific segments of an EEG signal and an associated intention. However, there are still challenges to be overcome on the road ahead. Among these, vector representations suffer from the enormous amounts of noise that characterize EEG signals. Identifying the correlations between signals from adjacent sensors on a headset is still difficult. Further, research not yet reached the point where learning models can accept decomposed EEG signals to capture the unique biological significance of the six established frequency bands. In pursuit of a more effective intention recognition method, we developed DAMTRNN, a delta attention-based multi-task recurrent neural network, for human intention recognition. The framework accepts divided EEG signals as inputs, and each frequency range is modeled separately but concurrently with a series of LSTMs. A delta attention network fuses the spatial and temporal interactions across different tasks into high-impact features, which captures correlations over longer time spans and further improves recognition accuracy. Comparative evaluations between DAMTRNN and 14 state-of-the-art methods and baselines show DAMTRNN with a record-setting performance of 98.87% accuracy.

Keywords: Attention network · Multi-task learning · Human intention recognition

This research is partially funded by Fundamental Research Funds for the Central Universities (Grant No. 2412017QD028), China Postdoctoral Science Foundation (Grant No. 2017M621192), Scientific and Technological Development Program of Jilin Province (Grant No. 20180520022JH).

© Springer Nature Switzerland AG 2019
J. Li et al. (Eds.): ADMA 2019, LNAI 11888, pp. 373–388, 2019.
https://doi.org/10.1007/978-3-030-35231-8_27

1   Introduction

The human brain is a complex system that has enticed researchers to explore its mysteries for centuries. Thankfully, the advent of electroencephalography (EEG) means we no longer need trepanning to gain insight into this "masterpiece of creation" as Nicolaus Steno described it in 1669. Rather, we can rely on more non-invasive techniques to examine brain functions. For example, we can use EEGs and brain-computer interfaces (BCI) to reveal neuron activity in the mind when a subject is performing specific tasks. This type of study is called intention recognition and, in recent years, it has become one of several essential research topics in brain exploration [4,5,12,23]. Many valuable inventions have arisen out of examining the correlations between EEG signals and non-muscular controls/communications, such as brain-controlled wheelchairs [6], intention-controlled input [37], and EEG wavelet-controlled exoskeletons [7]. These innovations have the ability to restore the faculties of individuals suffering from even very high degrees of motor disability or locked-in syndrome.

1.1   Motivation

Deep learning is, arguably, regarded as the future champion of machine intelligence, promising much to almost every domain of computer science. And human intention recognition is not excluded from this group. For example, deep learning models have already been used to examine EEG signal streams and intention [18,26,36]. However, it is commonly known that EEG signals can also be divided into multiple data streams according to frequency ranges, with each band having its own biological significance [6,27]. Yet, to date, most existing deep learning models only accept EEG signals as a single time series; researchers have not yet begun to explore the correlations between individual bandwidths and intention with deep models. Doing so may greatly improve the accuracy of predictions.

More specifically, EEG data can reflect neuron activity in the range of 0.5 Hz to 28 Hz. This spectrum can be divided into bandwidths known as *Delta, Theta, Alpha, Beta1, Beta2,* and *Beta3* and each frequency range has a unique biological significance. For instance, delta wavelets are highly correlated to mental attention states, while theta wavelets reflect motor behaviors [10]. By analyzing EEG signals in different bandwidths separately, these transient features can be accurately captured and localized. The insights this additional data provide contribute to better predictions of intention [39]. For instance, Moore et al. [16], achieved around 60% accuracy in emotion recognition by considering alpha rhythms, while Chen et al. [4], Korik et al. [13] and Kim et al. [12] produced incredibly precise predictions when they considered the temporal correlations between frequency bands.

1.2   Challenges

Although many applications of EEG signals for human intention recognition have achieved promising results, EEGs have several limitations. (1) EEG signals are typically very noisy. Unlike invasive techniques that communicate directly with neurons, EEGs acquire their data from sensors placed over the scalp. The distance between sensor and neuron, and what fills that distance, typically lead to variations in signal strength and a mass of noise. (2) EEGs are poor measures of neural activity, and the relationships between EEG wavelets and many possible intentions over time is difficult to model. Obviously, this affects model performance, even in supervised settings. Hence, most studies on intention recognition have only involved binary classifications. (3) Current thinking is that one's mental state greatly influence the shape of the EEG signals, even when an individual has the same intention [28]. Therefore, EEG signals tend to have large intra-class variations.

1.3 Solution

In answer to the challenges above, we have developed a delta attention-based multi-task recurrent neural network. Called DAMTRNN, the model considers the temporal features in multivariate time series data when constructing the feature representations as shown in Fig. 1). Plus, it captures the biological significance of each frequency band by taking decomposed EEG signals as separate inputs. Using divided signals as inputs both reduces the influence of noise and generates more robust feature representations. The separate EEG signals are learned by a single long-short term memory (LSTM) unit as a discrete task. To highlight the most prominent features associated with a particular intention, we designed a delta attention mechanism with an adjustable time span. This means feature correlations can be exploited over a wider temporal range for each learning task. To improve the model's performance even further, the spatial and temporal correlations across different tasks are fused into high-impact features, thus capturing both synchronous and asynchronous interactions. As a result, the network can automatically search for the parts of measures that are most relevant to human intention to achieve the best prediction results. Lastly, DAMTRNN is not only capable of identifying a specific intention, it can also accurately recognize multiple motion intentions.

1.4 Contribution

In brief, our research makes the following contributions to the literature:

- A novel multi-task RNN and delta attention network for human motion intention recognition tasks that concurrently learns the individual frequency bands of EEG wavelets. Hence, the biological significance of each signal band and the temporal correlations between tasks over time can be used to generate more accurate predictions of motor intention.
- A novel multi-task RNN and delta attention network for human motion intention recognition tasks that concurrently learns the individual frequency bands of EEG wavelets. Hence, the biological significance of each signal band and the temporal correlations between tasks over time can be used to generate more accurate predictions of motor intention.

- Extensive experiments that compare DAMTRNN to eight state-of-the-art methods on the publicly-available EEGMMID benchmark dataset. DAMTRNN's results set a new record for human intention recognition with 98.87% accuracy.

The rest of this paper is organized as follows. Related works are reviewed in Sect. 2. In Sect. 3, we present the details of our method, followed by the experimental evaluations and related discussions in Sect. 4. We conclude the paper in Sect. 5 with a summary of our contributions.

2   Related Work

Intention recognition can be treated as a classification problem – that is, as the problem of predicting a person's multiple and subjective intentions based on EEG traces rather than from actions triggered by events or their environment. Brain-like computing places its focus on devices, models, and methods that simulate the type of learning we experience through physiological structures – in other words, in the same ways our human brains process information. The goal is to create a brain-like computer with brain-like intelligence. Unlike the systematic routes to learning we see in artificial intelligence, such as classic symbolism, connectionism, and behaviorism, or the statistical approaches we see in machine learning, brain-like computing follows an emulationist pedagogy, where structural hierarchies mimic the brain, devices approximate the brain, and intelligence levels transcend the brain – at least that is the hope. As such, brain-like computing tends to lean on autonomous learning and training rather than manual programming.

Deep neural networks fit neatly into this learning paradigm, and therefore have already been applied to different EEG-based intention identification tasks with reasonable success. Applications that support people with social disorders and motion disabilities are especially thriving [12,32]. Unlike many invasive methods, EEG signals measure neuron activity through a simple sensor cap over the scalp, so data is relatively easy to acquire. Hence, EEG signals have been widely used in human intention research [8,14,18,36]. Generally speaking, most of this research has centered on ways to improve either the feature representations or the efficacy of the learning model.

EEG signals are complex and highly dimensional. Therefore, most current intention recognition methods reduce the data to a fairly simple set of features, which in turn reduces accuracy. By way of examples. Vizard et al. [30] achieved a prediction accuracy of 71.59% on a binary classification of alertness states using a common spatial pattern (CSP) procedure to extract the features. Similar to Vizard et al., Meisheri et al. [15] and Shiratori et al. [24] leveraged multi-class CSP techniques for EEG feature extraction, only achieving 54.63% and 56.7% accuracy, respectively By utilising features extracted from the Mu and Beta rhythms separately, Kim et al. [12] achieved a higher accuracy of 80.5%. Unfortunately, the potential of these methods has its limits because they underuse the temporal information inherent in time series data, which can be very beneficial to prediction tasks.

As mentioned, EEG signal shapes from the brain constantly change according to one's mental state, which gives rise to very high intra-class variations given the same intention [28]. Hence, a classifier must be able to capture the hidden consistencies in EEG signals to accurately predict an intention. Inspired by the broad success of deep neural networks. Kang et al. [11] reached 70% classification accuracy by constructing a shared latent subspace over multiple subjects with a Bayesian CSP model and an Indian buffet process. Bashivan et al. [3] and Zhang et al. [36] both took advantage of deep recurrent neural networks (DRNNs) in slightly different ways to capture the nature of time-series features over time, Bashivan et al. [3] achieved 85.05%, while Zhang et al. [36] reached 95.5% of accuracy. By taking the spatial and temporal information into consideration, Chen et al. [4] and Zhang et al. [34] yielded 97.8% and 98.3% of accuracy, respectively. One of the few drawbacks of these methods is that "time" and "space" information is processed in a heuristic manner, which may result in over- or under-parameterization when modeling time intervals [38].

Attention mechanisms are a relatively recent development in deep learning that are showing in solid success with many different learning tasks across many research disciplines [4,20,33]. Bahdanau et al. [2] for example, integrated an attention mechanism and an underlying encoder-decoder design to select the most essential features for a given prediction task, achieving quite competitive performance. In [31], attached weights to attention to reflect how much emphasis should be given to an input vector as a technique to improve performance with large-scale datasets. Sharma et al. [22] applied a location-based softmax function to the hidden states in LSTM layers. As a result, the model could identify high-impact elements within sequential inputs for action recognition tasks. The downside of all these techniques is that they only consider nearby features; they cannot capture the temporal correlations within time series data over long time-spans.

3   Methods and Technical Solutions

In this section, we outline the architecture of our proposed method to precisely recognize human motion intentions based on raw EEG signals. The conceptual framework of the approach is illustrated in Fig. 1 and each step of the framework is explained in detail in the sections that follow.

3.1   Data Acquisition

The framework begins with EEG signals captured by a BCI system via a wearable headset over the scalp comprising multiple electrodes. When a motor movement is performed by the test subject, the electrodes record the fluctuations in voltage generated by neurons. Thus, a raw EEG reading r at time

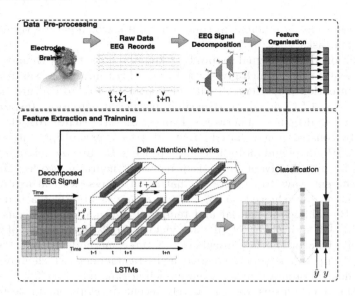

Fig. 1. The workflow of the proposed model. After pre-processing the data and optimizing the fast Fourier transform filters, the EEG signal is transformed into a matrix and fed into the DAN model for motion intention recognition.

t ($t \in \{1, 2, \cdots, T\}$) time can be represented as a single dimensional vector $r_t^i = [r_t^1, r_t^2, r_t^3, \cdots, r_t^{i-1}, r_t^i]$, where i is an electrode channel.

The raw EEG readings cover the full spectrum of power bands, which can be broken down into multiple time series that correspond to different frequency ranges. There are six established frequency ranges – alpha, betas 1–3, gamma, and delta. Recall that an individual's brain state may make certain frequencies more dominant; therefore, each frequency range has a unique biological significance [6,27], as shown in Table 1. Using a Fourier transform to convert and divide the raw signals into individual bandwidths, an EEG reading R from the i-th channel at time step t can be represented as a linear combination c, ($c \in C = \{\delta, \theta, \alpha, \beta_1, \beta_2, \beta_3\}$, of a particular set of wavelets,

$$R_t^{c,i} = \left[r_t^{\alpha,i}, r_t^{\beta_1,i}, r_t^{\beta_2,i}, r_t^{\beta_3,i}, r_t^{\theta,i}, r_t^{\delta,i} \right] \tag{1}$$

Table 1. Correlations between EEG bandwidth spectrums and brain functions

Bandwidth	Rhythm	Notation	Function
0.5–3.5 Hz	Delta	δ	Continuous-attention tasks
3.5–8 Hz	Theta	θ	Inhibition of elicited responses
8–12.5 Hz	Alpha	α	Relaxed and closing the eyes
12.5–16 Hz	Beta 1	β_1	Mental and physical stress
16.5–20 Hz	Beta 2	β_2	Sustained attentional processing
20.5–28 Hz	Beta 3	β_3	Mental alertness power

To acquire EEG singles from specific frequency range "on the fly", we designed a bandpass array consisting of multiple bandpass filters. In general, a bandpass filter only allows signals in a specific frequency range to pass through, rejecting all frequencies outside the specified range. Therefore, each filter is actually a highpass filter and a lowpass filter in series. The highpass filter $h[m]$, only passes signals with a frequency higher than the threshold m. The low-pass filter, $l[n]$, only attenuates signals with a frequency higher than the threshold n. The procedure for dividing an EEG signal s_t into bandwidths is schematically illustrated in Fig. 2a, where $\{m, n\} = \{x \in \mathbb{Q} \mid 0 < x < 28\}$. The downsampled output of the first filter becomes the r_t^θ and the input for the next filter. Figure 2b illustrates how the embedded features in the EEG signal are identified and divided through band-pass filtering. In short, the EEG signals are divided by comparing the filtered signal $r_t^{\beta_2, i}$ and the original signal r_t^i from the same channel at the same time point. In the figure, $i = 3$ and $t = 1.8$ million seconds.

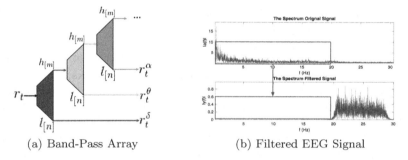

(a) Band-Pass Array   (b) Filtered EEG Signal

Fig. 2. EEG signal sub-division: (a) Filtering the raw EEG signal r_t filtering. The $h[m]$ and $l[n]$ denote the upper and lower limits of the band filter, respectively. (b) A visualization of the EEG signal from the band-pass filter.

3.2 The Delta Attention-Based Multi-Task RNN (DAMTRNN)

DAMTRNN comprises a series of LTSM networks [9] and a delta attention network. LSTMs were designed as a solution to the difficulties RNNs have with learning long-range dependencies involving transition functions. Often, the components of the gradient vectors can vanish or explode exponentially over long sequences, but LSTMs address this problem by incorporating gating functions. The activation function f of the current hidden state $\mathbf{h}_t$ at t time step can be computed as followings:

$$\mathbf{h}_t = \begin{cases} 0 & t = 0 \\ \int (\mathbf{h}_{t-1}, r_t^c) \; otherwise \end{cases} \tag{2}$$

At each time step t, an LSTM cell [9] includes i, f, o, c, and h, which denote the input gate, forget gate, output gate, memory cell, and hidden state respectively. The forget gate controls the amount of memory in each unit to be "forgotten", the input gate governs the update of each unit, and the output gate checks the exposure of each internal memory state. In our multi-task architecture, the divided EEG wavelets are each learned through an LSTM, and each learning procedure is treated as a separate learning task. The update equations for j-the task can be written as:

$$i_t^{(j)} = \sigma(W_{r^c i}^{(j)} r^{c(j)}_t + W_{hi}^{(j)} h_{t-1}^{(j)} + W_{ci}^{(j)} c_{t-1}^{(j)} + b_i^{(j)}),$$
$$f_t^{(j)} = \sigma(W_{r^c f}^{(j)} r^{c(j)}_t + W_{hf}^{(j)} h_{t-1}^{(j)} + W_{cf}^{(j)} c_{t-1}^{(j)} + b_f^{(j)}),$$
$$o_t^{(j)} = \sigma(W_{r^c o}^{(j)} r^{c(j)}_t + W_{ho}^{(j)} h_{t-1}^{(j)} + W_{co}^{(j)} c_{t-1}^{(j)} + b_o^{(j)}), \qquad (3)$$
$$c_t^{(j)} = k_t^{(j)} c_t^{(j)} + (1 - k_t^{(j)}) c_{t-1}^{(j)},$$
$$h_t^{(j)} = k_t^{(j)} h_t^{(j)} + (1 - k_t^{(j)}) h_{t-1}^{(j)}$$

where r_t^c is the input, i.e., a EEG wavelet division, at time t, ($t \in \{1, 2, \cdots, T\}$), Ws are weights(e.g., W_{ri} corresponds to the weight matrix for the hidden-input gate); bs are bias terms (e.g. b_i is the bias term for the input gate); and $\sigma(\cdot)$ denotes the logistic sigmoid function. Unlike the LSTM in [9], the MTRNN's final output is a concatenation of the hidden states of all tasks.

The delta attention network consists of a set of attention frameworks that capture the temporal correlations between tasks over time. It is worth noting that delta attention has more flexibility to exploit feature correlations over long temporal ranges. Our delta attention structure $h_{t+\Delta}$, has a variable length and can exploit asynchronous feature correlations over quite a long temporal range. Consequently $h_{t+\Delta}$ is applied to a hidden state in the sub-task neural network $\mathcal{N}_a$ so as to highlight high-impact features (see Eq. 5). Once applied, the hidden states in the LSTMs can be calculated by:

$$\hat{h}_{t+\Delta} = \mathcal{N}_a(h_{t+\Delta}) \odot h_{t+\Delta}, \qquad (4)$$

where $\odot$ denotes the element-wise product.

To fuse the synchronous and asynchronous interactions across tasks, a fusion attention structure Nu transforms $\mathcal{N}_u$ is used to transform $\hat{h}_{t+\Delta}^J$ into a unified attended result at time t: $\bar{h}_{t+\Delta}^J = \{h_{t+\Delta}^1 \oplus h_{t+\Delta}^2, \cdots, h_{t+\Delta}^J\}$. Then, the final hidden output of the LSTM is updated with the following rule::

$$\bar{h}_{t+\Delta} = \mathcal{N}_u(\bar{h}_{t+\Delta}^J) \odot \bar{h}_{t+\Delta}^J, \qquad (5)$$

3.3   Complexity

The complexity of our framework is asymptotic, and therefore offers a higher degree of parallelism than frameworks with only single-task LSTMs. For example, consider a framework with the following specifications: the hidden dimensions are d-dimensional and the length of the input sequence is T. Since the framework is implemented in a parallel fashion, we only need to focus on the most complex task, which is the feature correlation with attention. According to Parikh et al. [17], the time complexity of the LSTM is $O(T * d^2)$, and, from Vaswani et al. [29] the complexity of calculating the dot-product with attention is $O(T^2 d)$. Since attention layers only consider nearby time steps $\pm \delta$, they process data more quickly than recurrent layers when the sequence length T is smaller than the dimensionality of the representation d. Thus, the overall complexity of the framework is $O(Td^2 + T^2 d)$, which is $O(d^2)$. when simplified. Hence, the complexity of DAMTRNN is identical to a basic LSTM model.

4 Experiment

To evaluate DAMTRNN, we first benchmarked its accuracy on the publicly-available EEG Motor Movement/Imagery Dataset *(eegmmidb)*[1]. Then we conducted extensive experiments to examine and analyze the influence of multi-resolution wavelets. Lastly, we investigated the model's robustness on an open dataset developed by our research group. The source code and sample data are available at GitHub[2].

4.1 Dataset

We compared eight state-of-the-art methods and several baselines using 10-fold cross-validation on two datasets. The datasets were:

- EEGMMIDB [21], which contains EEG signals captured through a BCI 2000 system[3], from 64 electrodes, each sampled at a rate of 160 per second. The recordings also include an annotation channel. The dataset contains more than 1500 one-to-two-minute experiment runs of 109 subjects. Each subject performed 14 experiments across five different imagery tasks. Table 2 shows the details.
- emotiv[4], is a dataset of EEG signals collected using an EMOTIV Epoc+ 14 channel headset. The recordings cover 7 subjects, aged from 23 to 27, each with 80,640 48-s samples at a sampling rate of 128 MHz. Of those, 46080–76800 samples belong to one of five classes as shown in Table 2. Totally 240 s collection data.

Table 2. Class annotations in the two different datasets

Dataset	Class 1	Class 2	Class 3	Class 4	Class 5
EEGMMID	eye closed	left hand	right hand	both hands	both feet
emotiv	confirm	up	down	left	right

---

[1] https://physionet.org/pn4/eegmmidb/.
[2] https://github.com/AnthonyTsun/DAN/.
[3] http://www.schalklab.org/research/bci2000.
[4] shorturl.at/gqB78.

In terms of the baselines, we made no changes to the structures or settings of the model. Rather, we extracted different features from the data to evaluate the influence of signals in various bandwidths. A brief description of the eight benchmark methods we compared follows:

- Alomari et al. [1]: A support vector machine based method is used for binary classification, along with features extracted from multi-resolution EEG signals.
- Shenoy et al. [23]: A regularisation-based method to improve the robustness and accuracy of CSP estimation for feature extraction. Fisher's linear discriminant is used to perform binary classification tasks.
- Rashid et al. [19]: A neural network for binary classification tasks that decomposes raw EEG data to extract significant features.
- Kim et al. [12]: A prediction method based on a random forest classifier in which mu and beta rhythms are extracted from nonlinear EEG signals..
- Sita et al. [25]: A multiple classification method solved by LDA with features extracted from open source EEG data.
- Zhang et al. [34]: A deep recurrent neural network (DRNN) for multiple classification, tested on an open EEG database.
- Chen et al. [4]: An MTRNN, called MTLEEG, for motion intention recognition based on EEG signals.
- Zhang et al. [35]: A cascaded convolutional recurrent neural network (Cas-RNN) for multiple classification.

4.2   Experiment Result

The results, as reported in Table 3, show DAMTRNN as the clear frontrunner in accuracy of all the state-of-the-art and baseline methods with a 1.01% improvement of over the next best method and a new record in accuracy of 98.87% [4]. In other observations, we note that method #1–3 focuses on relative scenarios, so it is unsurprising that DAMTRNN had substantially better performance. Also, the RNN with $r^{\alpha,\beta,raw}$ multi-resolution signals achieved a relatively competitive result, which provides support for the importance of signal segregation.

Receiver operating characteristic (ROC) curves measure the discriminative capability of a classifier by plotting the true positive rate against the false positive rate over a range of threshold values. The area under the ROC curve (AUC) is a measure of accuracy. Typically, ROC curves are used to evaluate binary classification problems. So, to evaluate our multi-class classification scenario, we binarized the output by considering each task separately (i.e., one task vs. the others). Figure 3a, along with Table 4, show ROC curves of above 0.99% in all categories, which indicates very high performance by our classifier. The results also show that accuracy improves as the number of training iterations increases during the feature learning phase. Figure 3b shows that performance stabilized at 55 epochs ($\geq$90%). The length of the time span is another of the factors that affect DAMTRNN's performance, and specifically the delta attention network. To examine this influence, we tested DAMTRNN's accuracy with varying Δ

Table 3. Accuracy of DAMTRNN vs. the comparators on the EEGMMID dataset

Index	Method	Class	Accuracy
1	Almoari [1]	Binary	0.7500
2	Shenoy [23]	Binary	0.8206
3	Rashid [19]	Binary	0.9199
4	Kim [12]	Multiple (3)	0.8050
5	Sita [25]	Multiple (3)	0.8500
6	DRNN [34]	Multiple (5)	0.9558
7	MTLEEG [4]	Multiple (5)	0.9753
8	CasRNN [35]	Multiple (5)	0.9287
9	RNN	Multiple (5)	0.9327
10	CNN	Multiple (5)	0.8401
11	RNN-r^{α}	Multiple (5)	0.8834
12	RNN-r^{β}	Multiple (5)	0.8938
13	RNN-$r^{\alpha,\beta,raw}$	Multiple (5)	0.9323
14	RNN-ATT	Multiple (5)	0.9337
15	**DAMTRNN**	Multiple (5)	**0.9887**

settings. The results appear in Fig. 3c, showing that performance is positively correlated to the time span of attention. $\Delta = 4$ produced the highest accuracy at 90.76%.

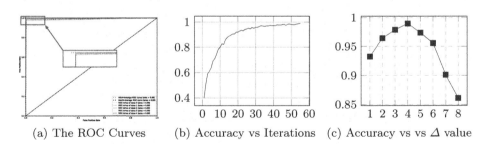

(a) The ROC Curves   (b) Accuracy vs Iterations   (c) Accuracy vs vs Δ value

Fig. 3. Performance evaluation. Panel (a) shows the discriminative ability of the classifier (x-axis = false positive rate; y-axis = true positive rate). Panel (b) shows the effectiveness of the normalising method (x-axis = iterations; y-axis = accuracy). Panel (c) shows the prediction accuracy with different values of Δ Performance evaluation. Panel (a) shows the discriminative ability of the classifier (x-axis = false positive rate; y-axis = true positive rate). Panel (b) shows the effectiveness of the normalising method (x-axis = iterations; y-axis = accuracy). Panel (c) shows the prediction accuracy with different values of Δ (X-axis = Δ value; y-axis = accuracy).

Table 4. The influence of the decomposed EEG signals for all methods

	Method	Class1	Class2	Class3	Class4	Class5	Average
Precision	RNN-r^{α}	0.9742	0.8895	0.8378	0.8700	0.8457	0.8834
	RNN-$r^{\beta 2}$	0.9755	0.8242	0.8903	0.9022	0.8767	0.8938
	RNN-$r^{\alpha,\beta 2}$	0.9807	0.9030	0.8931	0.9134	0.9154	0.9211
	RNN-$r^{\alpha,\beta 2,raw}$	0.9660	0.9315	0.8942	0.9304	0.9392	0.9323
	DRNN	0.9618	0.9618	0.9574	0.9732	0.9396	0.9588
	MTLRNN	0.9824	0.9721	0.9687	0.9796	0.9735	0.9753
	CassRNN	0.9795	0.8645	0.9336	0.9319	0.9338	0.9287
	RNN-ATT	0.9856	0.9393	0.9168	0.8935	0.9333	0.9337
	DAMTRNN	**0.9991**	**0.9855**	**0.9933**	**0.9854**	**0.9916**	**0.9887**
Recall	RNN-r^{α}	0.9505	0.7823	0.8844	0.8907	0.9199	0.8856
	RNN-$r^{\beta 2}$	0.9755	0.8242	0.8903	0.9022	0.8767	0.8938
	RNN-$r^{\alpha,\beta 2}$	0.9604	0.8900	0.8994	0.9201	0.9489	0.9237
	RNN-$r^{\alpha,\beta 2,raw}$	0.9512	0.9273	0.8949	0.9532	0.9457	0.9345
	DRNN	0.9380	0.9084	0.9257	0.9028	0.9392	0.9228
	MTLRNN	0.9919	0.9573	0.9687	0.9805	0.9869	0.9771
	CassRNN	0.9667	0.9277	0.8932	0.9302	0.9260	0.9288
	RNN-ATT	0.9581	0.8819	0.9338	0.9706	0.9497	0.9388
	DAMTRNN	**0.9937**	**0.9823**	**0.9885**	**0.9908**	**0.9947**	**0.9900**
F1-Score	RNN-r^{α}	0.9622	0.8325	0.8605	0.8802	0.8813	0.8833
	RNN-$r^{\beta 2}$	0.9755	0.8242	0.8903	0.9022	0.8767	0.8938
	RNN-$r^{\alpha,\beta 2}$	0.9704	0.8964	0.8962	0.9167	0.9318	0.9223
	RNN-$r^{\alpha,\beta 2,raw}$	0.9596	0.9308	0.9088	0.9341	0.9348	0.9336
	DRNN	0.9497	0.9241	0.9413	0.9413	0.9394	0.9392
	MTLRNN	0.9822	0.9643	0.9687	0.9800	0.9801	0.9751
	CassRNN	0.9667	0.9277	0.8932	0.9302	0.9260	0.9288
	RNN-ATT	0.9717	0.9097	0.9252	0.9305	0.9414	0.9357
	DAMTRNN	**0.9937**	**0.9823**	**0.9885**	**0.9908**	**0.9947**	**0.9900**
AUC	RNN-r^{α}	0.9622	0.8325	0.8605	0.8802	0.8813	0.8833
	RNN-$r^{\beta 2}$	0.9702	0.9149	0.9196	0.9315	0.9406	0.9354
	RNN-$r^{\alpha,\beta 2}$	0.9758	0.9346	0.9393	0.9520	0.9643	0.9532
	RNN-$r^{\alpha,\beta 2,raw}$	0.9935	0.9947	0.9932	0.9964	0.9973	0.9950
	DRNN	0.9982	0.9977	0.9990	0.9990	0.9987	0.9985
	MTLRNN	0.9989	0.9987	0.9990	0.9996	0.9996	0.9992
	CassRNN	0.9667	0.9277	0.8932	0.9302	0.9260	0.9288
	RNN-ATT	0.9717	0.9097	0.9252	0.9305	0.9414	0.9357
	DAMTRNN	**0.9966**	**0.9896**	**0.9926**	**0.9941**	**0.9964**	**0.9939**

To explore the influence of divided EEG signals, we transformed our model into a single-task RNN with an attention network (RNN-ATT), and conducted a series of evaluations on the same data but in different resolutions. The four baselines for comparison were: RNN-r^α, which learnt the alpha band α; RNN-$r^{\beta2}$, which learnt $\beta2$; RNN-r learnt raw non-segregated EEG signals r; and RNN-$r^{\alpha,\beta2,r}$ learnt all the three rhythms α, $\beta2$, and r separately and concatenated all three features into a feature vector. In addition to DAMTRNN, the three best counterparts from the main comparison (Table 3) were also included in this evaluation. These were DRNN [36], MTLRNN [4], CassRNN [35]. Performance was measured in terms of precision, recall, F1 score, and AUC. The results provided in Table 4 illustrate that DAMTRNN consistently outperformed all the methods and baselines, which provides strong support for considering the correlations between rhythms over time. It also proves that incorporating a shared layer into the framework improves performance.

In a last experiment, we tested DAMTRNN's robustness with a real-world application using the emotiv dataset. The task was to recognize which of four keys the subjects will press on a keyboard: *up, down, left, right*, and *confirm (eye closed)*. We removed the *alpha* rhythm and the *beta2* signals because of their high relevance to typing gestures. 70% of the data samples were used for training, and the remaining records were used for testing and validation. The parameter settings were the same as in previous experiments. Again, we also included the three best performers from Table 3 in the evaluation (DRNN [36], MTLRNN [4], CassRNN [35]. The results are reported in Tables 5 and 7 with the specific results for each class in Table 6. We attribute the overall decrease in performance from 98.87% in the comparison with EEGMMID down to 89.97% with the emotiv dataset to 14 of 64 low-resolution sensor signals recorded by EMOTIV EPOC + V.S.BCI2000). However, even with sub-par signals, DAMTRNN was still able to robustly recognize human intentions.

Table 5. Accuracy of DAMTRNN vs. the comparators on the emotive dataset

Index	Method	Class	Accuracy
1	RNN-r	Multi(5)	0.6751
2	RNN-$r^{\alpha,\beta2,r}$	Multi(5)	0.8103
3	MTLRNN	Multi(5)	0.8847
4	DRNN	Multi(5)	0.7980
5	CasCNN-α,β	Multi(5)	0.8064
6	CasCNN-α	Multi(5)	0.7931
7	CasCNN-β	Multi(5)	0.7793
8	DAN	Multi(5)	0.8852
9	**DAMTRNN**	Multi(5)	0.8997

Table 6. Model evaluation

Class	Precision	Recall	F1-Score	AUC
1	0.956398	0.946445	0.966008	0.97018758
2	0.84697	0.897992	0.871735	0.931446027
3	0.896508	0.872904	0.889388	0.92775921
4	0.89444	0.930211	0.915086	0.955631739
5	0.892162	0.926773	0.91941	0.953103725
Avg	0.8972956	0.914865	0.9123254	0.947625656

Table 7. Confusion matrix

	Class 1	Class 2	Class 3	Class 4	Class 5
Class 1	**0.9464**	0.0198	0.0135	0.0104	0.0099
Class 2	0.0137	**0.8980**	0.0273	0.0233	0.0378
Class 3	0.0035	0.0706	**0.8729**	0.0247	0.0282
Class 4	0.0046	0.0376	0.0129	**0.9302**	0.0147
Class 5	0.0023	0.0282	0.0183	0.0244	**0.9268**

5 Conclusion

In this paper, we introduced a novel delta attention-based multi-task RNN called DAMTRNN for recognizing human motor intentions. The DAMTRNN framework consists of a series of LSTMs and a delta attention network. The LSTMs separately learn the six different bandwidths in an EEG, and the delta attention network captures the temporal correlations within and across tasks. The result is a framework that captures the biological significance of each band and the correlations between signals and actions over longer time spans to significantly improve the accuracy of predictions. A comparative evaluation of DAMTRNN against 14 state-of-the-art methods and baselines on a public benchmark data set shows the framework with a record-setting accuracy of 98.87%. A similar comparison with a real-world task yielded reduced accuracy due to low-quality signals but with a performance that still substantially exceeded the comparison methods.

References

1. Alomari, M.H., Abubaker, A., Turani, A., Baniyounes, A.M., Manasreh, A.: EEG mouse: a machine learning-based brain computer interface. Int. J. Adv. Comput. Sci. Appl. **5**, 193–198 (2014)
2. Bahdanau, D., Cho, K., Bengio, Y.: Neural machine translation by jointly learning to align and translate. arXiv (2014)
3. Bashivan, P., Rish, I., Yeasin, M., Codella, N.: Learning representations from EEG with deep recurrent-convolutional neural networks. arXiv preprint arXiv:1511.06448 (2015)
4. Chen, W., et al.: EEG-based motion intention recognition via multi-task RNNS. In: Proceedings of the 2018 SIAM International Conference on Data Mining, pp. 279–287. SIAM (2018)
5. Dai, M., Zheng, D., Na, R., Wang, S., Zhang, S.: EEG classification of motor imagery using a novel deep learning framework. Sensors **19**, 551 (2019)
6. Fiala, P., Hanzelka, M., Čáp, M.: Electromagnetic waves and mental synchronization of humans in a large crowd. In: 11th International Conference on Measurement. IEEE (2017)
7. Frolov, A.A., Húsek, D., Biryukova, E.V., Bobrov, P.D., Mokienko, O.A., Alexandrov, A.: Principles of motor recovery in post-stroke patients using hand exoskeleton controlled by the brain-computer interface based on motor imagery. Neural Netw. World **27**, 107 (2017)

8. Graves, A.: Generating sequences with recurrent neural networks. arXiv preprint arXiv:1308.0850 (2013)
9. Hochreiter, S., Schmidhuber, J.: Long short-term memory. Neural Comput. **9**, 1735–1780 (1997)
10. Kaiser, A.K., Doppelmayr, M., Iglseder, B.: EEG beta 2 power as surrogate marker for memory impairment: a pilot study. Inter. Psychogeriatr. **29**, 1515–1523 (2017)
11. Kang, H., Choi, S.: Bayesian common spatial patterns for multi-subject EEG classification. Neural Netw. **57**, 39–50 (2014)
12. Kim, Y., Ryu, J., Kim, K.K., Took, C.C., Mandic, D.P., Park, C.: Motor imagery classification using mu and beta rhythms of EEG with strong uncorrelating transform based complex common spatial patterns. Comput. Intell. Neurosci. **2016**, 13 (2016)
13. Korik, A., Sosnik, R., Siddique, N., Coyle, D.: 3D hand motion trajectory prediction from EEG mu and beta bandpower. Prog. Brain Res. **228**, 71–105 (2016)
14. Major, T.C., Conrad, J.M.: The effects of pre-filtering and individualizing components for electroencephalography neural network classification. In: SoutheastCon. IEEE (2017)
15. Meisheri, H., Ramrao, N., Mitra, S.K.: Multiclass common spatial pattern with artifacts removal methodology for EEG signals. In: 4th International Symposium on ISCBI. IEEE (2016)
16. Moore, M.R., Franz, E.A.: Mu rhythm suppression is associated with the classification of emotion in faces. Affect. Behav. Neurosci. Cogn. **17**, 224–234 (2017)
17. Parikh, A.P., Täckström, O., Das, D., Uszkoreit, J.: A decomposable attention model for natural language inference. arXiv preprint arXiv:1606.01933 (2016)
18. Pinheiro, O.R., Alves, L.R., Romero, M., de Souza, J.R.: Wheelchair simulator game for training people with severe disabilities. In: International Conference on TISHW. IEEE (2016)
19. or Rashid, M.M., Ahmad, M.: Classification of motor imagery hands movement using Levenberg-Marquardt algorithm based on statistical features of EEG signal. In: 3rd International Conference on ICEEICT. IEEE (2016)
20. Rocktäschel, T., Grefenstette, E., et al.: Reasoning about entailment with neural attention. arXiv (2015)
21. Schalk, G., McFarland, D.J., Hinterberger, T., Birbaumer, N., Wolpaw, J.R.: BCI 2000: a general-purpose BCI system. IEEE TBE (2004)
22. Sharma, S., Kiros, R., Salakhutdinov, R.: Action recognition using visual attention. arXiv (2015)
23. Shenoy, H.V., Vinod, A.P., Guan, C.: Shrinkage estimator based regularization for EEG motor imagery classification. In: ICICS. IEEE (2015)
24. Shiratori, T., Tsubakida, H., Ishiyama, A., Ono, Y.: Three-class classification of motor imagery EEG data including "rest state" using filter-bank multi-class common spatial pattern. In: 3rd International Winter Conference on BCI. IEEE (2015)
25. Sita, J., Nair, G.: Feature extraction and classification of EEG signals for mapping motor area of the brain. In: International Conference on ICCC. IEEE (2013)
26. Tabar, Y.R., Halici, U.: A novel deep learning approach for classification of EEG motor imagery signals. J. Neural Eng. **14**, 016003 (2016)
27. Tatum, W.O.: Ellen R. grass lecture: extraordinary EEG. Neurodiagn. J. **54**, 3–21 (2014)
28. Vaadia, E., Birbaumer, N.: Grand challenges of brain computer interfaces in the years to come. Frontiers Neurosci. **3**, 151–154 (2009)
29. Vaswani, A., et al.: Attention is all you need. In: Advances in Neural Information Processing Systems (2017)

30. Vézard, L., Legrand, P., Chavent, M., Faïta-Aïnseba, F., Trujillo, L.: EEG classification for the detection of mental states. Appl. Soft Comput. **32**, 113–131 (2015)
31. Vinyals, O., Kaiser, Ł., Koo, T., Petrov, S., Sutskever, I., Hinton, G.: Grammar as a foreign language. In: NIPS (2015)
32. Wairagkar, M., Zoulias, I., Oguntosin, V., Hayashi, Y., Nasuto, S.: Movement intention based brain computer interface for virtual reality and soft robotics rehabilitation using novel autocorrelation analysis of EEG. In: 6th IEEE International Conference on BioRob. IEEE (2016)
33. Yang, Z., Yang, D., Dyer, C., He, X., Smola, A., Hovy, E.: Hierarchical attention networks for document classification. In: HLT (2016)
34. Zhang, D., Yao, L., Zhang, X., Wang, S., Chen, W., Boots, R.: EEG-based intention recognition from spatio-temporal representations via cascade and parallel convolutional recurrent neural networks. arXiv preprint arXiv:1708.06578 (2017)
35. Zhang, D., et al.: Cascade and parallel convolutional recurrent neural networks on EEG-based intention recognition for brain computer interface. In: Thirty-Second AAAI Conference on Artificial Intelligence (2018)
36. Zhang, X., Yao, L., Huang, C., Sheng, Q.Z., Wang, X.: Intent recognition in smart living through deep recurrent neural networks. arXiv (2017)
37. Zhang, X., Yao, L., Sheng, Q.Z., Kanhere, S.S., Gu, T., Zhang, D.: Converting your thoughts to texts: enabling brain typing via deep feature learning of EEG signals. arXiv (2017)
38. Zheng, K., Gao, J., Ngiam, K.Y., Ooi, B.C., Yip, W.L.J.: Resolving the bias in electronic medical records. In: Proceedings of the 23rd ACM SIGKDD. ACM (2017)
39. Zhu, X., Huang, Z., Yang, Y., Shen, H.T., Xu, C., Luo, J.: Self-taught dimensionality reduction on the high-dimensional small-sized data. Pattern Recogn. **46**, 215–229 (2013)

DeepIdentifier: A Deep Learning-Based Lightweight Approach for User Identity Recognition

Meng-Chieh Lee[1], Yu Huang[1], Josh Jia-Ching Ying[2], Chien Chen[1],
and Vincent S. Tseng[1(✉)]

[1] National Chiao Tung University, Hsinchu, Taiwan, ROC
{jeremy08300830.cs06g,yuvisu.cs04g}@nctu.edu.tw,
{chienchen,vtseng}@cs.nctu.edu.tw
[2] National Chung Hsing University, Taichung City, Taiwan, ROC
jcying@nchu.edu.tw

Abstract. Identifying a user precisely through mobile-device-based sensing information is a challenging and practical issue as it is usually affected by context and human-action interference. We propose a novel deep learning-based lightweight approach called *DeepIdentifier*. More specifically, we design a powerful and efficient block, namely funnel block, as the core components of our approach, and further adopt depthwise separable convolutions to reduce the model computational overhead. Moreover, a multi-task learning approach is utilized on *DeepIdentifier*, which learns to recognize the identity and reconstruct the signal of the input sensor data simultaneously during the training phase. The experimental results on two real-world datasets demonstrate that our proposed approach significantly outperforms other existing approaches in terms of efficiency and effectiveness, showing up to 17 times and 40 times improvement over state-of-the-art approaches in terms of model size reduction and computational cost respectively, while offering even higher accuracy. To the best of our knowledge, *DeepIdentifier* is the first lightweight deep learning approach for solving the identity recognition problem. The dataset we gathered, together with the implemented source code, is public to facilitate the research community.

Keywords: Identity recognition · Convolutional neural networks · Model reduction · Biometric analysis

1 Introduction

With the rapid growth of IoT technologies and the proliferation of mobile devices, many ubiquitous services (e.g., healthcare and fitness applications) can be improved significantly. These ubiquitous services are usually designed in a user-centered manner. In other words, a mobile device usually belongs to a single user, and most ubiquitous services are always designed in personalized manner.

© Springer Nature Switzerland AG 2019
J. Li et al. (Eds.): ADMA 2019, LNAI 11888, pp. 389–405, 2019.
https://doi.org/10.1007/978-3-030-35231-8_28

Such personalized manner would learn user's preference and improve the user experience of the human-device interaction. As a result, user identification is required to recognize whether the current user is owner of the mobile device.

In fact, user identity recognition can be categorized into two types, obtrusive recognition and unobtrusive recognition. The obtrusive recognition requires that users take part in, such as FaceID [11] and fingerprints [9], which are not continuous and need re-authentication. On the other hand, the unobtrusive recognition that identifies user based on their biometric patterns are usually mined from the data crawled from the sensors of users' mobile devices. Owing to the mounting of sensors embedded in mobile devices, including accelerometers [3], gyroscopes and photoplethysmography (PPG) sensors [4], those biometric patterns can be recognized easily through the data collected from these devices. Unobtrusive recognition can be applied to passive security mechanisms. For example, in daily life scenarios, the smart devices are popularly used for paying the bills, with passive security mechanisms, the users can directly walk through the gate while shopping in self-service stores or buying tickets for the underground, without any participation to the authentication; this process of which is unobtrusive and continuous. Furthermore, unobtrusive recognition can also be utilized against the theft of mobile devices, which can lock the devices or send out alerts as soon as they sense the user is not their owner.

The identification of people based on biometric patterns plays a crucial role and has attracted many studies over the last decade [1,6,7,14,16]. Most of the existing works are limited by the extremely restrictive setup [1], neglecting the issue of under different contexts and human-action interference. In real-world applications, the authentication task is usually affected by the user's daily activities, such as walking, running, and going up stairs. The quality of the signal data may also suffer from human-action interference, for example, there exists differences between the data of running on a treadmill and running to catch the train, even though the user performs the same activity. To solve the aforementioned issues, some existing works intuitively adopted a two-phase framework [6], which highly relies on the personal labeled activity data. Other existing works used cumbersome deep learning-based model [14] to enhance the performance, consuming considerable model memory and substantial computation overheads. However, a user-identification model should execute on the mobile devices in real-time with limited resources. It not only needs to be compressed within a reasonable size in order to be deployed on the mobile devices, but also requires low latency and power consumption. As a result, it is desired to build an energy-efficient and accurate model for user identity recognition such that the model can be contiguously performed on a mobile device since being activated.

In this paper, we address the problems of identification recognition based on sensor data (as recorded by an accelerometer and a gyroscope) under different contexts and human-action interference, as well as reduction of the recognition model for deployment on mobile devices. As aforementioned, there are two major issues in this problem: (1) Accurate identification of the user under different contexts and human-action interference through a single model, and (2) Reduction of the model into a reasonable size for mobile devices. To deal with these two issues, we propose a novel deep learning approach named *DeepIdentifier*, which offers high accuracy on identity recognition with highly-reduced model size and computation cost. To encode the time-series data under different contexts into the latent variables, we propose a new breed of multi-scale block, namely funnel block, which extracts the features in a more comprehensive view. To increase the robustness of the model, we adopt multi-task learning to avoid interference of human-action. The reconstruction loss generated by feeding the latent variable to an additional decoder and the classification loss is both used in the training phase. The contributions of our research are four-fold:

- We propose the *DeepIdentifier* approach, a lightweight deep learning-based approach for recognizing the identity of users under contexts and the human-action interference. To the best of our knowledge, *DeepIdentifier* is the first lightweight deep learning approach for solving the identity recognition problem.
- To accurately recognize the user identity under different contexts through only one model, *DeepIdentifier* learns the mutual information with funnel blocks. Moreover, it is trained based on multi-task learning to deal with the data under human-action interference, enhancing the model robustness.
- To allow the model for deploying on mobile devices, we design a fully-utilized framework and further compress it with depthwise separable convolutions. It not only abates the needed memory and computation resource for more than 10 times and 40 times respectively, but also empowers the model to work in real-time manner with low power consumption.
- Based on two real-world datasets, the experimental results show that our proposed approach outperforms state-of-the-art research in terms of efficiency and effectiveness. The dataset we gathered, together with the implemented source code, is public to facilitate the research community, at https://github.com/jeremywahaha/DeepIdentier.

The rest of this paper is organized as follows: We briefly review the related work on identity recognition with different approaches and methods. Next, we introduce the problem statement and detail our novel approach. Experimental results are then presented. Finally, we conclude with discussions.

2   Related Work

In recent years, the deep learning-based approach has been widely used in various fields including identity recognition. In 2016, IDNet [1] is proposed, the first deep learning approach for identity recognition, which combines a convolutional neural network (CNN) and a support vector machine (SVM). It uses the CNN as a feature generator to extract the features from the accelerometer and gyroscope data. Then, the features are input to the SVM to recognize the user identity. IDNet is not accurate enough to deal with the identity recognition issue, but it provides a new path for the research community. To increase the accuracy of the deep learning-based approach, a preprocessing method is introduced for the CNN input [16]. In a real-world scenario, data collection always produces some noise with the orientation issue of sensors while putting the device in trouser pocket. They detect each gait from raw data and encode them into an angle-embedded gait dynamic image (AE-GDI) to correct the orientation bias. A multi-region size convolution neural network [7] is used to perform the authentication task on mobile sensor data. The model reports a better effectiveness than other approaches, but it does not take different contexts into consideration. DeepSense [14] is a powerful deep learning framework that deals with the sensor data-classification problem; it conducts the convolutional neural networks and recurrent neural networks to catch the spatial and temporal dependencies. This model is accurate to solve the identity recognition problem, but it is highly cumbersome. DeepSense consists of six convolutional layers and two recurrent layers, with a huge number of parameters and computations, and is difficult to deploy in mobile devices.

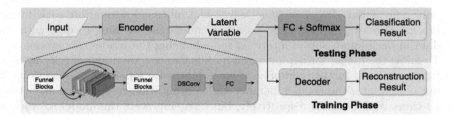

Fig. 1. The architecture of *DeepIdentifier* approach.

3   Problem Definition

In this section, we provide the formal definition of the problem addressed by our proposed *DeepIdentifier* approach. Before introducing the problem definition, we first detail the input data format for *DeepIdentifier* approach.

Definition 1 (Sensor Data). *Suppose there are U different input sensors (e.g., accelerometer and gyroscope) and each can produce a series of readings over time. The readings of each sensor can be represented in a $d \times t$ matrix called S_u, where d is the dimension of each reading (e.g., readings along the x-, y-, and z-axes of the sensor) and t is the total length of readings.*

Definition 2 (Input Data Format). *According to the real-world scenario, we should set a period of time w over which to recognize the user identity. Then, we split S_u into small matrices of $X_u \in \mathbb{R}^{d \times w}$. To this end, we stack these matrices into a set of $X = \{X_1, \ldots, X_i\}, i \in \{1, \ldots, U\}$, where each set corresponds to a label y.*

The normalization process is done on all matrices in X. Afterwards, we concatenate them as a single matrix χ such that the matrix χ can be feed into the neural network. (i.e., $\chi = [X_1...X_u]^T$) Accordingly, the problem we addressed in this manuscript can be formulated as follows:

Given the matrix χ which is extracted from the sensors with a specific time period w, recognize whether the data is generated by an genuine or an imposter.

4 *DeepIdentifier* Approach

We introduce *DeepIdentifier*, a lightweight deep learning-based approach for identity recognition with sensor data inputs. In this section, we divide our description into three parts. The first is preprocessing, in which we present how to deal with the input data. The last two parts, approach architecture and model training, are the core descriptions of our proposed method.

4.1 Approach Architecture

The architecture of our proposed approach is as shown in Fig. 1. The structure of *DeepIdentifier* differs between the training and testing phases. In the training phase, the input signal data is embedded into latent variables, encoded by an encoder consisting of two funnel blocks to capture the high-level features from raw signal data, and four depthwise separable convolutions to deal with low-level features. Then, the latent variables are used to perform the classification task by feeding to the softmax layer, and to reconstruct the output by feeding to the decoder separately. Finally, the training phase learns the input data and updates the network based on the combination of the two loss functions by multi-task learning; it is capable of balancing the trade-off between the classification and reconstruction views. In the testing phase, only the classification part is reserved for recognizing the signal data.

Depthwise Separable Convolutions. Inspired by MobileNets [2], we adopt depthwise separable convolutions as the core blocks in the *DeepIdentifier* approach.

For *DeepIdentifier*, the depthwise separable convolutions consist of two layers, depthwise convolution and pointwise convolution. The depthwise convolution adopts independent kernels to each of the channels. Then, the pointwise convolution combines the outputs from the depthwise convolution by applying 1×1 convolutions. These two layers are followed by a batch normalization layer and an activation function ReLU.

Recall the standard convolution; it filters and combines inputs to the outputs in one step, which leads to substantial computations $K_1 \cdot K_2 \cdot M \cdot N \cdot F_1 \cdot F_2$, where K_1 and K_2 denote the kernel size of the convolution, F_1 and F_2 denote the size of the input feature map, M denotes the input channels and N denotes the output channels. In contrast, the depthwise separable convolution reduces the computations and model size by the concept of factorization, reducing the computation to $K_1 \cdot K_2 \cdot M \cdot F_1 \cdot F_2 + M \cdot N \cdot F_1 \cdot F_2$. So the total reduction in computation of the depthwise separable convolutions is $\frac{1}{N} + \frac{1}{K_1 \cdot K_2}$.

Funnel Block. In the real-world scenario, the characteristics of signal data differ considerably with various contexts. For instance, the frequency of walking data is much lower than that of the running data, so the kernel with too small size is not able to catch the exact patterns of walking. To deal with this problem, we propose an novel block, named funnel block, which aims to extract features by using convolutions with multi-scale kernels.

Figure 2 shows the architecture of the funnel block in detail. The funnel block contains P paths, consisting of $P-1$ depthwise separable convolutions with a kernel size of $(i \cdot K_1) \times K_2, i \in \{1, ..., P-1\}$, and a $K_1 \times K_2$ max pooling followed by a 1×1 standard convolution. To avoid decreasing the model efficiency, the number of channels from $P-1$ depthwise separable convolutions and max pooling is $\frac{N}{M}$ and $M - (M-1) \cdot \frac{N}{M}$ respectively, which the summation is the same as the number of output channels. Afterwards, the outputs of all the paths are concatenated into a single tensor on channel dimension, forming the input for the next layer.

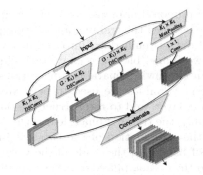

Fig. 2. A funnel block contains P paths, where $P-1$ paths are depthwise separable convolutions, and 1 path is a max pooling layer followed by a 1×1 convolution.

The value of P highly depends on data characteristics, such as frequency and sliding window size; the higher the value of P is, the larger receptive field would scan by convolutional layers, and the lower frequency patterns can be caught. In addition, a pooling layer is added to prevent the loss of information from the original input, and the followed 1×1 convolution aims to integrate the information among channels. To avoid impeding the information flow, using concatenation instead of summation is able to reserve all the information from different frequencies along the channel dimension, and it will be used in the next convolutional layer. To sum up, funnel blocks not only extract comprehensive features from different frequencies, but also adhere to keep model lightweight simultaneously.

4.2 Model Training

Based on aforementioned architecture, we present the detail of training procedure of our model in this section. As stated in the section of Problem Statement, the input signal contains complex contexts and human-action interference, which are the key factors affecting the model performance.

To conquer this challenge, we adopt the concept of multi-task learning. Regarding our proposed approach, the latent variables from the encoder can be treated as the features for the classifier (dense layer). In this case, the model can learn the hidden features for the recognition task by optimizing the classification error. In the other view, we can reconstruct the inputs and minimize the bias to encode the context information into latent variables, which makes the data with the same activity under different human-action interference closer after encoded. During the training phase, we pass the latent variables into the fully connected layer to perform classification and the decoder to reconstruct the inputs.

For the classification task, the latent variables are fed into a fully connected layer following a softmax layer. The output of the softmax layer is $\hat{y}$, which contains the probability for each class, corresponding to a label y. For the reconstruction task, the latent variables are input into an additional decoder. The decoder output is denoted as $\hat{\chi}$, which is the reconstruction result of the input χ. However, $DeepIdentifier$ is trained to minimize the loss by combining these two criteria, which can then be defined as follows:

$$\mathcal{L} = -\sum_{i=1}^{n} y_i \log \hat{y}_i + \frac{\alpha}{n} \sum_{i=1}^{n} (\chi_i - \hat{\chi}_i)^2 \tag{1}$$

where α is the coefficient to balance these two tasks. By default, during the test phase, we remove the decoder and use the classification result as final output.

5 Experiments

In this section, we present the results from a series of experiments to evaluate the performance of $DeepIdentifier$ using two real-world datasets, UIR dataset and HHAR dataset. We first describe the preparation of the experiments, and then introduce the evaluation methodology. Finally, we present and discuss our experimental results.

5.1 Data Description

We use two real-world datasets UIR and HHAR [10] to conduct a series of experiments to evaluate the performance of $DeepIdentifier$.

- **UIR:** UIR dataset is a realistic dataset we collected from ten subjects with seven activities: running, walking, going up stairs, going down stairs, jumping, rope jumping, and cycling. Each subject performs each activity with the same time duration, so the data is balance on both subjects and activities. Unlike those data collected in highly restricted environments by laboratory-quality devices, we adopted commercial mobile phone products for collection. We set the sampling rate to 100 Hz. To restore the real-world scenario, we performed multiple activities in one record from 2-min to 7-min. For example, we walked for 2-min and then ran for 3-min on the playground, and continued this cycle. The dataset contains more than a total of 30 h of sensor data, which is much longer than that provided by any other data. Moreover, our data is publicly available and free to download.

– **HHAR:** HHAR dataset is collected from nine subjects, and each subject wears twelve devices and performs six activities: biking, sitting, standing, walking, stair up and stair down, which are widely used in human activity recognition research [5, 8, 13]. To collect this data, eight smartphones are kept in a bag on the waist, and there are two smartwatches worn on each arm. Each device contains two sensors, accelerometer and gyroscope. The devices have different sampling rates, which are around 50 Hz to 200 Hz. Each subject was asked to perform each activity for 5-min, which means the total length of data is no more than 5 h.

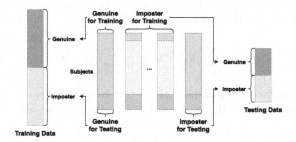

Fig. 3. The experimental setting is revisited as followed: one of the subjects is chosen as the genuine subject for both training and testing, one subject is chosen as the imposter for testing, and others are chosen as the imposters for training.

Unlike previous works [6,12], we consider some imposters' data should not be utilized for model training. As a result, we choose one of the subjects as the genuine subject for both training and testing, one subject as the imposter for testing, and others as the imposters for training as shown in Fig. 3. For example, suppose we have subjects A to J, if A is selected as genuine, B is selected as the imposter in first turn of model testing, and the remaining subjects (i.e., C to J) are treated as the imposter in first turn of model training. Then, C would be selected as the imposter in second turn of model testing, and so on. To sum up, in UIR dataset, we run nine experiments by different imposters for each subject and totally 9 × 10 = 90 tests in each turn of evaluation. Moreover, random sampling 1/8 samples from each imposter can inherently avoid data imbalance issue for model training.

Accordingly, we divide the records in our dataset into training and testing at a ratio of 8:2. To balance the activities for both training and testing, we set the same cut ratio to the records. The records with the same activity in training phase are from different days with the ones in testing phase, ensuring the human-action interference of each subject would be generated due to their changed status. Each record is split into sliding windows with an overlap percentage of 50% to conduct the data augmentation. The sliding window size w is set to 500, approximately 5 s, which is a very short period. A moving average filter is added to denoise the data. We use two sensors to perform the experiment, namely the accelerometer and gyroscope, on separate x-, y-, and z-axes.

In the HHAR dataset, each subject is only asked to perform each activity once, and a record only contains one activity. For each subject, we select front 80% of each record as the training data, and the remaining record as the testing data. To reveal a user's daily life, we focus on the accelerometer and gyroscope data collected from only one smartphone in our experiment, which DeepSense [14] used eight smartphones and four smartwatches in their experiment. We only use the data with activities are biking, walking, stair up and stair down, because there are no biometric patterns while sitting and standing. The sliding window size w is set to 500, approximately 5 s. The remaining experimental setting of this dataset is as the same as we done on UIR dataset.

5.2 Evaluation Metrics

The main metric for measuring the effectiveness of identity recognition is accuracy, which is formally defined as follows:

$$Accuracy\ (Acc) = \frac{TP + TN}{TP + FP + FN + TN},\tag{2}$$

where TP is the true positive of the identity recognition results, FP the false positive, FN the false negative, and TN the true negative.

Besides accuracy, genuine precision also plays an important role for measuring the fraction of genuine subjects in the retrieved genuine subjects. In other words, high genuine precision can ensure the robustness of the approach. Meanwhile, the genuine recall denotes that how many times a genuine have been accepted by his mobile device while using. The genuine precision and genuine recall are formally defined as follows:

$$Genuine\ Precision\ (GP) = TP/(TP + FP)\tag{3}$$

$$Genuine\ Recall\ (GR) = TP/(TP + FN)\tag{4}$$

Imposter recall is the fraction of total imposters that have been retrieved, which is the opposite view of the genuine precision. It reflects the model would not treat imposter as genuine. The imposter precision means the proportion of correct recognition on imposter, otherwise will reject the genuine. The imposter precision and imposter recall are formally defined as follows:

$$Imposter\ Precision\ (IP) = TN/(TN + FN) \tag{5}$$

$$Imposter\ Recall\ (IR) = TN/(TN + FP) \tag{6}$$

To evaluate the efficiency of identity recognition, we consider two aspects, the number of parameters (PARMs) and the number of floating-point operations (FLOPs), which have been widely used in deep learning-based model reduction domian [2,15]. The number of PARMs determine the memory used by the model. The update speed usually depends on the model size during the download process. In addition, the bigger the model, the slower the devices during activation of the recognition application due to memory access cost. The number of FLOPs nearly represents the recognition process speed of the model. It is a very important criterion when the model is positioned in a real-time system. Moreover, less computational resources are occupied in systems with fewer FLOPs, reducing the power consumption of mobile device. However, different devices may have their own hardware optimization for deep learning-based method, making execution time not be reliable to consider as the model efficiency metric.

The PARMs and FLOPs of 2-dimensional convolution layers can be calculated as:

$$PARMs = (K_1K_2C_{in} + 1)C_{out} \tag{7}$$

$$FLOPs = 2F_1F_2W(K_1K_2C_{in} + 1)C_{out} \tag{8}$$

where F_1, F_2 and C_{in} denote the height, width and number of channels of the input feature map, K_1 and K_2 denote the height and width of kernel, and C_{out} denotes the number of output channels.

The PARMs and FLOPs of fully connected layers can be calculated as:

$$PARMs = (F_{in} + 1)F_{out} \tag{9}$$

$$FLOPs = (2F_{in} - 1)F_{out} \tag{10}$$

where F_{in} denotes the input dimension and F_{out} denotes the output dimension.

Table 1. Impact of number of latent variables

Latent variables	Acc	GP	GR	IP	IR	KPARMs	MFLOPs
5	94.0%	**93%**	**96%**	**96%**	92%	42	9.9
10	**94.2%**	**93%**	**96%**	**96%**	93%	50	9.9
15	93.8%	92%	**96%**	95%	92%	58	9.9
20	93.5%	92%	**96%**	95%	91%	66	9.9
25	93.5%	92%	**96%**	95%	91%	74	9.9
30	93.7%	92%	95%	95%	92%	82	9.9
35	93.3%	**93%**	94%	94%	93%	90	9.9
40	92.9%	**93%**	92%	92%	**94%**	98	9.9

Table 2. Impact of number of kernels in funnel blocks

Kernels in funnel block	Acc	GP	GR	IP	IR	KPARMs	MFLOPs
2	93.2%	91%	95%	95%	91%	47	8.6
3	93.7%	92%	**96%**	**96%**	92%	48	9.1
4	**94.2%**	**93%**	**96%**	**96%**	**93%**	50	9.9
5	93.7%	92%	**96%**	**96%**	92%	51	10.8

5.3   Baseline Approaches

We compare our proposed *DeepIdentifier* with the following six baselines:

- **MobileNets** [2]: This is a lightweight deep learning framework with fourteen convolution layers for CIFAR10 image classification task, which is based on depthwise separable convolutions to build lightweight deep neural networks on image classification task.
- **ShuffleNets** [15]: This is a lightweight deep learning framework with seventeen convolution layers for CIFAR10 image classification task, which utilizes pointwise group convolution and channel shuffle to greatly reduce computation cost while maintaining accuracy.
- **DeepSense** [14]: This is a deep learning framework on identity recognition that integrates six-layer CNN and two-layer RNN, which shows the state-of-the-art results for deep learning identity recognition tasks.
- **Enc:** This is a CNN model which has three convolution layers. The decoder that we use to calculate the reconstruction loss is its exact reverse.
- **Enc-DSC:** This model has the same architecture as Enc, but the standard convolutions are replaced with depthwise separable convolutions.
- **DeepEnc-DSC:** This model has the same architecture as *DeepIdentifier* without using funnel blocks.

5.4   Internal Experiments

In this section, we evaluate our proposed *DeepIdentifier* on the UIR dataset under various number of latent variables, number of kernels in funnel blocks, reconstruction loss, time interval, and generality.

Number of Latent Variables. We evaluate the impact of the number of latent variables. Table 1 shows that the number of parameters (i.e., KPARMs) increases as that of latent variables increases. We can also observe that the highest accuracy, genuine precision, and imposter recall occurs while the number of latent variables is set as 10. As a result, we have sufficient confidence to say that 10 latent variables are enough to cover and distinguish these contexts.

Table 3. Impact of reconstruction loss

Model	with $loss_r$	Acc	GP	GR	IP	IR
Enc	No	91.4%	89%	95%	94%	88%
Enc-DSC	No	89.5%	87%	92%	92%	87%
DeepEnc-DSC	No	92.0%	90%	94%	94%	89%
DeepIdentifier	No	93.6%	92%	96%	95%	92%
Enc	Yes	89.1%	86%	93%	92%	85%
Enc-DSC	Yes	89.8%	88%	93%	92%	87%
DeepEnc-DSC	Yes	92.8%	91%	95%	95%	90%
DeepIdentifier	Yes	**94.2%**	**93%**	**96%**	**96%**	**93%**

Table 4. Impact of generality

Subject	Gender	Height (cm)	Weight (kg)	Acc	GP	GR	IP	IR
A	M	177	75	92.9%	88%	94%	94%	87%
B	F	158	68	97.0%	90%	98%	98%	90%
C	M	174	62	89.4%	93%	93%	93%	93%
D	F	155	46	90.2%	91%	94%	94%	90%
E	M	180	73	93.2%	90%	93%	93%	89%
F	F	165	49	96.1%	88%	98%	98%	87%
G	M	180	78	95.6%	90%	99%	99%	90%
H	M	171	55	93.7%	93%	99%	99%	93%
I	M	175	66	96.6%	91%	98%	98%	90%
J	M	181	72	93.2%	90%	94%	94%	89%
Standard Deviation	\	8.83	10.56	2.46%	1.6%	2.4%	2.4%	1.9%

Number of Kernels in Funnel Blocks. In this section, we evaluate the impact of the number of kernels in the funnel blocks. Table 2 shows that the effectiveness increases as the number of the kernels in the funnel blocks increases. On the contrary, the efficiency decreases as the number of the kernels in the funnel blocks increases. Thus, the number of the kernels in the funnel blocks is the pivot between effectiveness and efficiency. Intuitively, adding more kernels in the funnel blocks increases the computational overhead and learns the signal data in more detail. Another observation is that if we increase the number of different kernel to 5, the effectiveness exhibits a reducing trend. The kernel size controls the number of extracted features according to the context frequency. In our case, there is no activity with such a low frequency in the UIR dataset, and thus increasing the kernel size is useless in terms of improving the effectiveness. Besides, increasing the number of paths disperses the number of channels for each convolution, which is another reason for the loss in model accuracy.

Impact of Reconstruction Loss. Table 3 shows the impact of the reconstruction loss between each model in the model-training phase, where $loss_r$ denotes the reconstruction loss. Here, we set $\alpha = 10$ to ensure classification loss and reconstruction loss at the same scale. The top half of Table 3 shows the models without the addition of reconstruction loss, and the bottom half of the table presents either. The results indicate that additional reconstruction loss is useful for improving the model performance in terms of accuracy, precision, and recall simultaneously. The reason why the performance of Enc decreases with combining reconstruction loss is that Enc is built without any model reduction. While the number of parameters of Enc is large, it is more likely to get overfitting on both classification and reconstruction tasks. However, due to low data variety of UIR dataset, the improvement scale is limited.

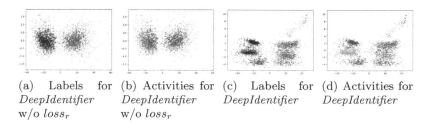

(a) Labels for *DeepIdentifier* w/o $loss_r$

(b) Activities for *DeepIdentifier* w/o $loss_r$

(c) Labels for *DeepIdentifier*

(d) Activities for *DeepIdentifier*

Fig. 4. Illustration regarding how data is clustered in the latent space by *DeepIdentifier*. Different colors in (a) and (c) indicate different ground-truth classes. The colors in (b) and (d) denote different activities collected in the dataset. (Color figure online)

To deeply investigate the impact of the additional reconstruction loss, we perform a further experiment with our data. We train two models, *DeepIdentifier* without reconstruction loss, and *DeepIdentifier*. First, we feed the training data into two models to obtain the latent variables. Then, we perform dimensionality reduction using principle component analysis (PCA) to encode the latent variables into two dimensions, in order to visualize the resulting distribution. As shown in Fig. 4a, the results of *DeepIdentifier* without reconstruction loss can be divided into two groups, genuine and imposter. However, in Fig. 4b, the activities are slightly mixed in each group, which means that the context features are useless in this model. The results of *DeepIdentifier* are as shown in Fig. 4c and d. *DeepIdentifier* with multi-task learning is able to clearly classify the genuine and imposters into two groups. Moreover, the activities, which are gathered in the same activity clustering, can also be recognized. In other words, the model with reconstruction loss has tackled the problem of under different contexts as the activities can be projected into the different context space (cluster), which helps the model to recognize the different subjects' biometric patterns in the same context space. Besides, this also ensures that similar samples are closer after encoded, even if they are affected by human-action interference. These results demonstrate that *DeepIdentifier* actually learns the data from different views, and the context features are helpful to perform the recognition task. To conclude, the robustness of the model is improved by combining the reconstruction and classification losses with multi-task learning in the training phase.

Impact of Generality. To seek optimum setting of the generality, we perform an experiment to examine the effectiveness of each subject. The subjects' physical capacities, such as gender, height and weight, are varied in UIR dataset, so it is important to find out whether our model performs well on both different and similar types of subject. As shown in Table 4, the experimental results of each subject are highly close to those of other subjects. The standard deviation of accuracy is about 2.46%, the standard deviation of genuine precision is 1.6%, and the standard deviation of imposter recall is 1.9%. Moreover, although the subject E, G and J have similar physical capacities, we observe that the model is still capable of distinguishing them from others well, gaining over 93% on accuracy. The mean accuracies of male and female subjects are 93.5% and 94.4% respectively, presenting no difference between gender. This experiment proves that the diversity issue of subjects does not affect the effectiveness of our model, and our model is able to handle both people with different and similar physical capacities, demonstrating the generality of our model.

Table 5. Effectiveness on UIR dataset and HHAR dataset

Model	UIR dataset					HHAR dataset				
	Acc	GP	GR	IP	IR	Acc	GP	GR	IP	IR
MobileNets	91.8%	90%	95%	94%	89%	84.2%	80%	91%	89%	78%
ShuffleNets	92.2%	91%	94%	94%	90%	85.9%	83%	91%	90%	81%
DeepSense	88.8%	85%	94%	93%	84%	84.5%	81%	90%	89%	79%
Enc	91.4%	89%	95%	94%	88%	83.5%	79%	91%	90%	76%
Enc-DSC	89.8%	88%	93%	92%	87%	82.6%	78%	90%	88%	75%
DeepEnc-DSC	92.8%	91%	95%	95%	90%	82.1%	79%	88%	86%	76%
DeepIdentifier	**94.2%**	**93%**	**96%**	**96%**	**93%**	**87.9%**	**84%**	**93%**	**93%**	**82%**

Table 6. Model efficiency

Model	KPARMs	MFLOPs
MobileNets	320	197.7
ShuffleNets	863	144.5
DeepSense	419	403.1
Enc	405	31.9
Enc-DSC	47	1.4
DeepEnc-DSC	48	7.1
DeepIdentifier	**50**	**9.9**

5.5   External Experiments

In terms of effectiveness, our proposed method clearly outperforms all of the baselines on both metrics on UIR dataset. Table 5 shows the details of the comparison between our proposed method, *DeepIdentifier*, MobileNets [2], ShuffleNets [15] and the DeepSense architecture [14]. Specifically, *DeepIdentifier* shows 6.1%, 9.4% and 10.7% improvements over the state-of-the-art deep learning approach on identity recognition (DeepSense) in terms of accuracy, genuine precision, and imposter recall, respectively. *DeepIdentifier* also outperforms the other five baselines, Enc, Enc-DSC, DeepEnc-DSC, MobileNets, and ShuffleNets.

As we mentioned before, DeepEnc-DSC can be seen as a simple version of *DeepIdentifier* without the funnel blocks; it is found to be inferior to *DeepIdentifier* as the lack of ability to extract patterns from different frequencies. In addition, the accuracy of Enc appears to be sufficient, but the genuine precision and imposter recall is relatively low compared to that of *DeepIdentifier*, because the excessive parameters make model overfitting. However, as mentioned in the evaluation metrics section, it is especially important to enhance the effectiveness of genuine precision and imposter recall, which is achieved with *DeepIdentifier*. Another interesting result is that MobileNets and SuffleNets outperform DeepSense, as the network architecture of them are deeper than DeepSense, and the data scale of UIR dataset is large enough to train these models. DeepSense is not able to perform well as long as the experiment settings become more practical, and the validation becomes more rigorous. *DeepIdentifier* is able to outperform MobileNets and ShuffleNets with the shallow architecture, which ensures the effectiveness and efficiency simultaneously, demonstrating the necessity of designing a model specifically for identity recognition task.

Table 5 also shows the experimental results on HHAR dataset, *DeepIdentifier* still outperforms the other baselines on this dataset. The effectiveness of all models is lower than the results from UIR dataset because the data scale of HHAR is much smaller than UIR dataset; it further proves that DeepIdentitfier is able to handle the small dataset well. We can see that the effectiveness of Enc is better than DeepEnc-DSC as the model is easy to overfit on this data, which is different from the result on UIR dataset. The reason is that the distribution of training and testing data in HHAR dataset is very similar; as shown in the section of experimental setting, on the HHAR dataset, the front 80% of record is split as training, and the back 20% is split as testing data, unlike UIR dataset, which split is according to the records, containing human-action interference. Moreover, DeepSense outperforms the MobileNets, because the scale of data is not large enough to train such deep networks well. However, *DeepIdentifier*, being robust enough, still outperforms DeepSense even when the data scale is smaller. *DeepIdentifier* shows 4.0%, 3.7% and 3.8% improvements over DeepSense in terms of accuracy, genuine precision, and imposter recall, respectively.

To evaluate the efficiency, we compare the number of parameters and FLOPs of each approach; the results are shown in Table 6. Enc-DSC is the lightest model in our experiment; however, according to the previous experiment, it is not good enough to perform the identity recognition task. DeepEnc-DSC is slightly lighter than *DeepIdentifier*, but the effectiveness is worse. DeepSense combines CNN and RNN, which makes the model extremely cumbersome. MobileNets and ShuffleNets are designed for image classification task, so their models are much larger while they need the network going deeper, which is not useful and efficient for identity recognition task. To summarize, the experimental results show that our model parameters are 8× smaller than those of DeepSense. Moreover, the FLOPs of *DeepIdentifier* are 41× smaller than those of DeepSense. Our model even outperforms both MobileNets and ShuffleNets on efficiency.

6   Conclusion

In this work, we have proposed a novel lightweight deep learning-based model named *DeepIdentifier* for recognizing the identity of mobile device users based on sensor data. To deal with the issues of different underlying contexts and human-action interference, we designed a novel convolution block called funnel blocks, which can accurately recognize the user identity in different contexts through a single model. In addition, we adopted depthwise separable convolutions as the core blocks to our proposed approach in order to reduce the model size and computations. Moreover, the multi-task learning concept is applied in *DeepIdentifier*, where it learns to recognize the identity and reconstruct the signal of the input sensor data simultaneously during the training phase. To the best of our knowledge, *DeepIdentifier* is the first lightweight deep learning approach for the identity recognition problem. We evaluated our model using the data collected by commercial mobile devices and the experimental results show that *DeepIdentifier* reduces the model size and computation cost by more than 10 times and 40 times respectively. To conclude, *DeepIdentifier* is validated as promising solution that offers high accuracy and feasibility for identity recognition with wearable and mobile devices. The dataset we gathered, together with the implemented source code, is public to facilitate the research community.

Acknowledgement. This research was partially supported by Ministry of Science and Technology, Taiwan, under grant no. 107-2218-E-009-005.

References

1. Gadaleta, M., Rossi, M.: Idnet: Smartphone-based gait recognition with convolutional neural networks. arXiv preprint arXiv:1606.03238 (2016)
2. Howard, A.G., et al.: Mobilenets: efficient convolutional neural networks for mobile vision applications. arXiv preprint arXiv:1704.04861 (2017)
3. Huang, Y., Lee, M.C., Tseng, V.S., Hsiao, C.J., Huang, C.C.: Robust sensor-based human activity recognition with snippet consensus neural networks. In: 2019 16th International Conference on Wearable and Implantable Body Sensor Networks (BSN 2019), pp. 1–4. IEEE (2019)
4. Kavsaoğlu, A.R., Polat, K., Bozkurt, M.R.: A novel feature ranking algorithm for biometric recognition with PPG signals. Comput. Biol. Med. **49**, 1–14 (2014)

5. Kwapisz, J.R., Weiss, G.M., Moore, S.A.: Activity recognition using cell phone accelerometers. ACM SIGKDD Explor. Newsl. **12**(2), 74–82 (2011)
6. Lee, W.H., Lee, R.B.: Sensor-based implicit authentication of smartphone users. In: 2017 47th International Conference on Dependable Systems and Networks (DSN), pp. 309–320. IEEE (2017)
7. Nguyen, K.-T., Vo-Tran, T.-L., Dinh, D.-T., Tran, M.-T.: Gait recognition with multi-region size convolutional neural network for authentication with wearable sensors. In: Dang, T.K., Wagner, R., Küng, J., Thoai, N., Takizawa, M., Neuhold, E.J. (eds.) FDSE 2017. LNCS, vol. 10646, pp. 197–212. Springer, Cham (2017). https://doi.org/10.1007/978-3-319-70004-5_14
8. Preece, S.J., Goulermas, J.Y., Kenney, L.P., Howard, D.: A comparison of feature extraction methods for the classification of dynamic activities from accelerometer data. IEEE Trans. Biomed. Eng. **56**(3), 871–879 (2009)
9. van der Putte, T., Keuning, J.: Biometrical fingerprint recognition: don't get your fingers burned. In: Domingo-Ferrer, J., Chan, D., Watson, A. (eds.) Smart Card Research and Advanced Applications. IFIP, vol. 52, pp. 289–303. Springer, Boston, MA (2000). https://doi.org/10.1007/978-0-387-35528-3_17
10. Stisen, A., et al.: Smart devices are different: assessing and mitigatingmobile sensing heterogeneities for activity recognition. In: 2015 13th ACM Conference on Embedded Networked Sensor Systems (SenSys), pp. 127–140. ACM (2015)
11. Turk, M.A., Pentland, A.P.: Face recognition using eigenfaces. In: 1991 IEEE Computer Society Conference on Computer Society Conference on Computer Vision and Pattern Recognition, pp. 586–591. IEEE (1991)
12. Xu, W., Shen, Y., Zhang, Y., Bergmann, N., Hu, W.: Gait-watch: a context-aware authentication system for smart watch based on gait recognition. In: 2017 2nd International Conference on Internet-of-Things Design and Implementation (IoTDI), pp. 59–70. IEEE/ACM (2017)
13. Yang, J.: Toward physical activity diary: motion recognition using simple acceleration features with mobile phones. In: 2009 1st International Workshop on Interactive Multimedia for Consumer Electronics, pp. 1–10. ACM (2009)
14. Yao, S., Hu, S., Zhao, Y., Zhang, A., Abdelzaher, T.: Deepsense: a unified deep learning framework for time-series mobile sensing data processing. In: 2017 26th International Conference on World Wide Web (WWW), pp. 351–360. International World Wide Web Conferences Steering Committee (2017)
15. Zhang, X., Zhou, X., Lin, M., Sun, J.: ShuffleNet: an extremely efficient convolutional neural network for mobile devices. ArXiv e-prints, July 2017
16. Zhao, Y., Zhou, S.: Wearable device-based gait recognition using angle embedded gait dynamic images and a convolutional neural network. Sensors **17**(3), 478 (2017)

Domain-Aware Unsupervised Cross-dataset Person Re-identification

Zhihui Li[1], Wenhe Liu[2], Xiaojun Chang[3(✉)], Lina Yao[1], Mahesh Prakash[4],
and Huaxiang Zhang[5]

[1] School of CSE, University of New South Walesa, Kensington, Australia
[2] School of Computer Science, Carnegie Mellon University, Pittsburgh, USA
[3] Faculty of Information Technology, Monash University, Melbourne, Australia
cxj273@gmail.com
[4] Data61, Csiro, Australia
[5] School of Information Science and Engineering, Shandong University, Jinan, China

Abstract. We focus on the person re-identification (re-id) problem of
matching people across non-overlapping camera views. While most existing works rely on the abundance of labeled exemplars, we consider a
more difficult unsupervised scenario, where no labeled exemplar is provided. One solution for unsupervised re-id that attracts much attention in the recent researches is cross-dataset transfer learning. It utilizes knowledge from multiple source datasets from different domains to
enhance the unsupervised learning performance on the target domain.
In previous works, much effect is taken on extraction of the generic and
robust common appearances representations across domains. However,
we observe that there also particular appearances in different domains.
Simply ignoring these domain-unique appearances will misleading the
matching schema in re-id application. Few unsupervised cross-dataset
algorithms are proposed to learn the common appearances across multiple domains, even less of them consider the domain-unique representations. In this paper, we propose a novel domain-aware representation
learning algorithm for unsupervised cross-dataset person re-id problem.
The proposed algorithm not only learns a common appearances across-
datasets but also captures the domain-unique appearances on the target
dataset via minimization of the overlapped signal supports across different domains. Extensive experimental studies on benchmark datasets
show superior performances of our algorithm over state-of-the-art algorithms. Sample analysis on selected samples also verifies the ability of
diversity learning of our algorithm.

Keywords: Unsupervised person re-identification · Cross-dataset
Re-ID · Domain-aware

1 Introduction

Research on person re-identification (re-id) draws much attention in recent years
[10,11,18]. The primary target of person re-identification is re-identifying a

© Springer Nature Switzerland AG 2019
J. Li et al. (Eds.): ADMA 2019, LNAI 11888, pp. 406–420, 2019.
https://doi.org/10.1007/978-3-030-35231-8_29

person from camera shots across pairs of non-overlapping camera views. In Computer Vision field, person re-id is evaluated as an image *retrieval* task. Given a *probe* image of a person of one camera view, it is required to identify images of the same person from a *gallery* of images taken by other non-overlapping camera views.

Most existing re-id methods are supervised algorithms. They require labeling pairwise images across camera views for training re-id model. However, manually labeled re-id data is hard to produce. On the one hand, it is a tough task even for the human to annotate the same person in different camera views among a huge number of imposters [9,19]. Meanwhile, camera numbers are increasingly large in today's world, e.g. over a hundred in an underground station. It makes the labeling cost becoming prohibitively high because supervised re-id methods require sufficient label information for each pair of camera views. As a result, the scalability of supervised re-id methods is severely limited and hard to applied to practical re-id applications.

To overcome the limitation of supervised re-id methods, one solution is to perform the identification with unsupervised learning algorithms, which utilizes only unlabeled data. However, typical unsupervised methods often are proposed for a single dataset. Without labels for matching information, unsupervised re-id methods sometimes are unable to recognize persons across camera views because of the uncontrollable and/or unpredictable variation of appearance changes across camera views, such as body pose, view angle, occlusion and illumination conditions [8,19,24], etc. As a result, most of the single-dataset unsupervised re-id methods report much weaker performance than supervised methods.

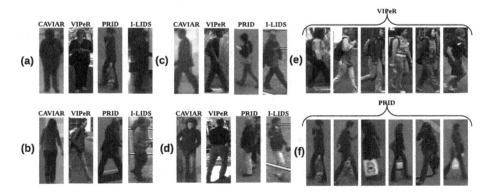

Fig. 1. Examples of common and unique appearances on four datasets. Better being watched in color. **Common appearances** shared by four datasets: (a) wearing dark coat and pants; (b) wearing red upper cloth; (c) walking forward; (d) wearing dark cloth and light color pants. The images in (a) to (d) from different datasets and they are belong to the different persons. **Unique appearances**: (e) VIPeR: carrying backpack; (f) PRID: carrying bags in hand. Notice (Color figure online)

Few recent works are proposed to address unsupervised person re-identification problem via cross-dataset transfer learning methods [17–19]. They intend to capture dataset-invariant and discriminative representations across multiple datasets. Different from single-dataset works, cross-dataset transfer learning brings an incredible challenge in re-id. First, it requires completely different learning task under different domains, i.e. identifying sets of non-overlapped persons under different camera networks. Second, they are also required to learning discriminative presentations on the target dataset, which may be heavily affected by the source datasets. In the research, we observe that among the re-id datasets there are not only shared common appearances [19, 22, 24] but also domain-unique appearances.

As presented in Fig. 1, we illustrate some instances of re-id datasets VIPeR [5], PRID [7], iLIDS [28] and CAVIAR [3]. First, as shown in Fig. 1(a) to (d), there are common appearances across domains, such as 'wearing black cloth' or similar pose such as 'walking forward'. Second, domain-unique appearances also be observed. As shown in Fig. 1(e) and (f), many individuals are carrying backpacks in VIPeR dataset while many persons are captured carrying a handbag in PRID dataset. The reason is that cameras are setting in the different scenes, such as shopping mall, campus, and airport. Therefore, simply ignore or disregard the importances of domain-unique features definitely will degraded the re-id performance. As we will show in the experiments, previous algorithms relying on the common appearance will mismatch the lady to other person wear dark cloth even they clearly not carrying a pink handbags.

However, previous works do not value the importances of domain-unique appearances [19]. To overcome the mentioned limitations and improve the re-id performance, we propose our algorithm. It is an domain-aware unsupervised cross-dataset multi-task learning algorithm. Our algorithm not only can obtain shared appearances across datasets via multi-task dictionary learning but also captures the domain-unique appearances. Rather than using Euclidean distances, we bring discriminative overlapping support as the metric of inter-dataset similarity. The importance of common and domain-unique appearances are valued simultaneously and jointly contribute to the representation learning for re-id task. We illustrate the procedure of our algorithm in Fig. 2. The main contributions of our algorithm states in three folds as following:

- We propose a novel unsupervised cross-dataset learning algorithm with support discriminative regularization for person re-id. To our knowledge, it is the first attempt to leverage the common and domain-unique representations across datasets in the unsupervised re-id application.
- We introduce an iterative re-weights optimization scheme to solve our problem. Our algorithm simultaneously optimizes the common representation and minimizes the overlapping supports across datasets to enrich the domain-unique representations.
- Extensive experimental studies on benchmark datasets show superior performances of our algorithm over state-of-the-art algorithms.

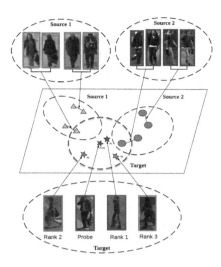

Fig. 2. Overview of our algorithm for person re-id. Source datasets are datasets with labels, target dataset is a dataset with no label. A dictionary is learned with all datasets. With the dictionary, all images are encoded in one low dimensional space. The linked samples in the source dataset are labeled as the same person.

2   The Proposed Framework

Notation. Let the superscript $^\top$ denote the transpose of a vector/matrix, $\mathbf{I}$ be an identity matrix. Let $\mathrm{Tr}(\mathbf{A})$ be the trace of matrix $\mathbf{A}$. Let $\mathbf{a}_i$ and $\mathbf{a}^j$ be the i-th column vector and j-th row vector of matrix $\mathbf{A}$ respectively. Let $\mathrm{diag}(\mathbf{v})$ be a diagonal matrix with diagonal elements equal to $\mathbf{v}$, $\langle \mathbf{A}, \mathbf{B} \rangle = \mathrm{Tr}(\mathbf{A}\mathbf{B}^\top)$ be the inner product of $\mathbf{A}$ and $\mathbf{B}$, and $\|\mathbf{v}\|_p$ be the ℓ_p-norm of a vector $\mathbf{v}$. The Frobenius norm of an arbitrary matrix $\mathbf{A}$ is defined as $\|\mathbf{A}\|_F = \sqrt{\langle \mathbf{A}, \mathbf{A} \rangle}$. The ℓ_2-norm of a vector $\mathbf{a}$ is denoted as $\|\mathbf{a}\|_2 = \sqrt{\mathbf{a}^T\mathbf{a}}$ and the $\ell_{2,1}$-norm of matrix $\mathbf{A} \in \mathbb{R}^{n \times m}$ is denoted as $\|\mathbf{A}\|_{2,1} = \sum_{i=1}^{n} \sqrt{\sum_{j=1}^{m} a_{ij}^2} = \sum_{i=1}^{n} \|\mathbf{a}^i\|_2$, where a_{ij} is the (i,j)-th element of $\mathbf{A}$ and $\mathbf{a}^i$ is the i-th row vector of $\mathbf{A}$. For the analytical consistency, $\ell_{2,0}$-norm of a matrix $\mathbf{A}$ is denoted as the number of the nonzero rows of $\mathbf{A}$. We denote $\mathcal{G}$ as a weighted graph with a vertex set $\mathcal{X}$ and an affinity matrix $\mathbf{S} \in \mathbb{R}^{n \times n}$ constructed on $\mathcal{X}$. The (unnormalized) Laplacian matrix associated with $\mathcal{G}$ is defined as $\mathbf{L} = \mathbf{D} - \mathbf{S}$, where $\mathbf{D}$ is a degree matrix with $\mathbf{D}(i,i) = \sum_j S(i,j)$. Let $\mathbf{a} \circ \mathbf{b}$ represent the Hadamard (element-wise) product between two vectors $\mathbf{a}$ and $\mathbf{b}$. Let $\mathbf{a}^{\odot 2} = \mathbf{a} \circ \mathbf{a}$ be the element-wise square of $\mathbf{a}$.

2.1   Formulation

We focus on the cross-dataset person re-identification problem that the datasets are collected from several different camera networks. In multi-task learning, we are able to learn and transfer knowledge of the labeled source datasets to the unlabeled target dataset and therefore overcome the limitations of unsupervised re-id problem. Such kind of algorithm is claimed as an unsupervised [18,19] and asymmetric [26] multi-task leaning algorithm.

Let $\mathbf{X} = \{\mathbf{X}_{S_1}, \cdots, \mathbf{X}_{S_N}, \mathbf{X}_T\} \in \mathbb{R}^{d \times \{n_1, \cdots, n_N, n_T\}}$ be the $T = N+1$ datasets with N *source* datasets and one *target* dataset. Each datasets has d features and n_t instances. We denote the dictionary shared by all datasets as $\mathbf{D} \in \mathbb{R}^{d \times k}$. With the dictionary $\mathbf{D}$, every image with feature vector $\mathbf{x}_{t,i}$, i.e. person appearance in original datasets, can be encoded as a sparse column atom in the coefficient matrix $\mathbf{A} = \{\mathbf{A}_{S_1}, \cdots, \mathbf{A}_{S_N}, \mathbf{A}_T\} \in \mathbb{R}^{k \times \{n_1, \cdots, n_N, n_T\}}$ in one lower k-dimensional subspace. Notice these corresponded representations are invariant to the camera view changes or camera network differences, makes it suitable for person re-identification.

Generally, we formulate the person re-identification task as the following multi-task dictionary learning problem:

$$\min_{\mathbf{D}, \mathbf{A}} \sum_{t=1}^{T} R(\mathbf{X}_t, \mathbf{D}, \mathbf{A}_t) + \Omega(\mathbf{A}), \tag{1}$$

where T is the number of tasks. $\mathbf{D}$ is a dictionary shared by all tasks. We denote the reconstruction loss $R(\mathbf{X}_t, \mathbf{D}, \mathbf{A}_t)$ as the Frobenius norm:

$$R(\mathbf{X}_t, \mathbf{D}, \mathbf{A}_t) = \|\mathbf{X}_t - \mathbf{D}\mathbf{A}_t\|_F^2. \tag{2}$$

We denote $\Omega(\mathbf{A})$ as is the regularization term of $\mathbf{A}$. In our work, we specified the regularization term of our algorithm as a combination function of three regularization terms for person re-identification:

$$\Omega(\mathbf{A}) = \alpha g(\mathbf{A}) + \beta l(\mathbf{A}) + \gamma f(\mathbf{A}), \tag{3}$$

where α, β, γ are leverage parameters.

Structure Sparsity. For the first regularization term, we bring in the structure sparsity by defining

$$g(\mathbf{A}) = \sum_{t=1}^{T} \|\mathbf{A}_t\|_{2,1} = \sum_{t=1}^{T} \sum_{k=1}^{n_t} \|\mathbf{a}^{(tk)}\|_2, \tag{4}$$

where $\mathbf{A}_t$ is the coefficient matrix for the t-th task and $\mathbf{a}^{(tk)}$ denotes the k-th row of matrix $\mathbf{A}_t$. We use a $\ell_{2,1}$-norm rather than ℓ_1 norm in typical dictionary works [6,10] to gain row sparse representations. Such that, the proposed algorithm can find the shared nonzero supports shared all tasks automatically [16]. Moreover, as discussed in [28], $\ell_{2,1}$-norm can enhance the robustness and suppresses the affect of outliers. Outliers are widely appeared in re-id [9].

Pairwise Relationship Preserving. The second regularization term is defined as a Graph Laplacian term:

$$l(\mathbf{A}) = \sum_{t=1}^{T} \sum_{i,j=1}^{n_t} w_t(i,j) \|a_{t,i} - a_{t,j}\|^2 = Tr(\mathbf{A}_t \mathbf{L}_t \mathbf{A}_t^\mathsf{T}). \tag{5}$$

where $\mathbf{a}_{t,i}$ and $\mathbf{a}_{t,j}$ are column atoms of $\mathbf{A}_t$ and $\mathbf{L}_t = \mathbf{S}_t - \mathbf{W}_t$ is the Laplacian matrix of $\mathbf{W}_t$. In $\mathbf{W}_t$, each element $w_t(i,j)$ is the indicator of relationship of samples in task t. Specifically, in our task, we follow previous work in [19] to set $w_t(i,j) = 1$ if $\mathbf{x}_{t,i}$ and $\mathbf{x}_{t,j}$ are of the same person across views and $w_t(i,j) = 0$ otherwise. For the target task we initialize $w_t(i,j)$ as all zeros because the target dataset does not provide any label information. The Graph Laplacian term preserves the pairwise relationships of images across camera views. Minimization of $l(\mathbf{A})$ will force the images of the same person across views being closed to each other and therefore enhance the performance of re-id.

Algorithm 1. Multi-task Dictionary Learning with support discrimination term for Person Re-ID

Input: T training Data sets $\mathbf{X} = \{\mathbf{X}_1, \cdots, \mathbf{X}_T\}$, regularization leverage parameters α, β and γ.

1: Initialize dictionary $\mathbf{D} \in \mathcal{R}^{d \times k}$, iteration index i = 0.
2: **while** not converge **do**
3:      Update $\mathbf{A}^{i+1}$ with $\mathbf{D}^i$ according to Algorithm 2.
4:      Update $\mathbf{D}^{i+1}$ with $\mathbf{A}^{i+1}$ by solving (17).
5:      Update i = i+1;
6: **end while**

Output: Dictionary $\mathbf{D}$.

Algorithm 2. Sparse Code Learning using ADMM for (14)

Input: T training Data sets $\mathbf{X} = \{\mathbf{X}_1, \cdots, \mathbf{X}_T\}$, regularization leverage parameters α, β and γ, penalty parameter u, learning step size η,

1: Initialize dictionary $\mathbf{D} \in \mathcal{R}^{d \times k}$ with $\mathbf{A}^0 = \mathbf{0}$ and $\Lambda^0 = 0$
2: **for** t = 1:T **do**
3:    Initialize iteration index i = 0;
4:    **while** not converge **do**
5:        Compute $\boldsymbol{\Phi}_t^i$ according to (10).
6:        Update $\mathbf{Z}^{i+1} = Shrink(\mathbf{A}_t^i, \Lambda^i, u, \gamma)$.
7:        Update $\mathbf{A}^{i+1}$ by each of its column a_t^{i+1} according to (16).
8:        Update $\Lambda^{i+1} = \Lambda^i - \eta u (\mathbf{Z}_t^{i+1} - \mathbf{A}_t^{i+1})$.
9:        Update i = i+1;
10:   **end while**
11: **end for**

Output: Estimated sparse code $\mathbf{A}$.

Domain-Aware Representation Learning. Furthermore, in order to learn the domain-unique appearances in the schema, we aim to emphasize the dissimilarity of representations across different datasets. We introduce a support discriminative term:

$$f(\mathbf{A}) = \sum_{t=1}^{T} \sum_p \sum_q \|\mathbf{a}_{t,p} \circ \mathbf{a}_{/t,q}\|_0. \qquad (6)$$

where $\mathbf{a}_{t,p}$ and $\mathbf{a}_{/t,q}$ are the p-th column vector of $\mathbf{A}_t$ and q-th column vector of $\mathbf{A}_{/t}$ receptively. $\mathbf{A}_i$ is the coefficient matrix for the t-th task and $\mathbf{A}_{/t}$ is the sub-matrix of $\mathbf{A}$ with columns of $\mathbf{A}_i$ removed. The ℓ_0 norm $\|\mathbf{a}_{t,p} \circ \mathbf{a}_{/t,q}\|_0$ presents the number of shared supports of sparse representation $\mathbf{a}_{t,p}$ and $\mathbf{a}_{/t,q}$ of feature vectors $\mathbf{x}_{t,p}$ and $\mathbf{x}_{/t,q}$ [16]. In our task, they represents the camera shots of persons between task t and other tasks. Therefore, minimizing $f(\mathbf{A})$ will decrease the overlapping supports between different datasets, such that will enlarge the dissimilarity of representations between different tasks (datasets). As a result, our algorithm can learn the domain-aware representations simultaneously in dictionary learning.

Finally, we propose our re-id algorithm as a unsupervised multi-task dictionary learning optimization problem as following:

$$\min_{\mathbf{D},\mathbf{A}} \sum_{t=1}^{T} \{\|\mathbf{X}_t - \mathbf{D}\mathbf{A}_t\|_F^2 + \alpha\|\mathbf{A}_t\|_{2,1} + \beta Tr(\mathbf{A}_t\mathbf{L}_t\mathbf{A}_t^{\mathsf{T}}) + \gamma \sum_p \sum_q \|\mathbf{a}_{t,p} \circ \mathbf{a}_{/t,q}\|_0\}. \quad (7)$$

2.2 Optimization

We propose an iterative algorithm to optimize the objective function in (7). We describe the optimization algorithm in Algorithm 1. The details of the proposed algorithm are as following:

Optimize A. When fixed $\mathbf{D}$ and $\mathbf{L}_t$, we optimize A_t by solving each task as a subproblem of (7):

$$\min_{\mathbf{A}_t} \|\mathbf{X}_t - \mathbf{D}\mathbf{A}_t\|_F^2 + \alpha\|\mathbf{A}_t\|_{2,1} + \beta Tr(\mathbf{A}_t\mathbf{L}_t\mathbf{A}_t^{\mathsf{T}}) + \gamma \sum_p \sum_q \|\mathbf{a}_{t,p} \circ \mathbf{a}_{/t,q}\|_0. \quad (8)$$

However, minimizing the last term $\|\mathbf{a}_{t,p} \circ \mathbf{a}_{/t,q}\|_0$ is an NP-hard problem. Following the iterative reweighting schemes in [1,2,16,23], we use the iterative reweighted ℓ_2 minimization to approximate the ℓ_0 norm, which is able to produce more focal estimates in optimization progresses [16]. Specifically, in each iteration $i(i > 1)$ the objective value of $f(\mathbf{A}_t)^{(i)}$ is updated by the reweighted $\ell_{2,1}$-norm $f(\mathbf{A}_t)^{(i)} = \sum_p \sum_q \|\phi_{t,p,q}^{(i)}\mathbf{a}_{t,p} \circ \mathbf{a}_{/t,q}\|_2$, where $\phi_{t,p,q}^{(i)}$ is the weight calculated according to the previous iteration. When updating $f(\mathbf{A}_t)^{(i)}$ in each task t, the vector of other tasks $\mathbf{A}_{/t} = \{\mathbf{a}_{/t,q}\}_{q=1}^{n_t}$ are fixed. In our algorithm, the pairwise weight is estimated as following:

$$\phi_{t,p,q} = \frac{1}{(\mathbf{a}'_{t,p} \circ \mathbf{a}'_{/t,q})^{\odot 2} + \epsilon}. \quad (9)$$

where $\mathbf{a}'_{t,p}$ and $\mathbf{a}'_{/t,q}$ are coefficients from the previous iteration. ϵ is a regularization factor decreasing to zero when iteration number increases. Notice computing each pairwise weight is time consuming. Indeed, affected by $\ell_{2,1}$ structure sparsity norm $g(\mathbf{A})$, coefficients in the same task will high probably present a similar sparse structure. Therefore, we approximate the self-squared

Hadamard product of each atom by the average of all atoms in the task t as $\forall p,\ (\mathbf{a}'_{t,p})^{\odot 2} \approx (\tilde{\mathbf{a}}'_t)^{\odot 2} = \sum_p (\mathbf{a}'_{t,p})^{\odot 2}/n_t$. Thus the approximated weight shared by all atoms in task t is rewritten as $\tilde{\phi}_{t,q} = \frac{1}{(\tilde{\mathbf{a}}'_t)^{\odot 2} \circ (\mathbf{a}'_{/t,q})^{\odot 2} + \epsilon}$. We can verify that $\sum \tilde{\phi}_{t,p,q} \circ (\mathbf{a}_{t,p} \circ \mathbf{a}_{/t,q})^{\odot 2} = \mathrm{diag}((\tilde{\phi}_{t,p,q} \circ \mathbf{a}_{/t,q})^{\odot 2} \cdot \mathbf{a}_{t,p}^{\odot 2})$. Overall, we define

$$\boldsymbol{\Phi}_t = \mathrm{diag}(\sqrt{\sum_q (\sqrt{(\tilde{\phi}_{t,q})} \circ \mathbf{a}_{/t,q}^{\odot 2})}), \tag{10}$$

and thus $f(\mathbf{A})$ can be rewritten as

$$f(\mathbf{A}) = \sum_{t=1}^{T} \sum_p \|\boldsymbol{\Phi}_t \mathbf{a}_{t,p}\|_{2,1} = \sum_{t=1}^{T} \|\boldsymbol{\Phi}_t \mathbf{A}_t\|_F^2. \tag{11}$$

Finally (8) can be rewritten to

$$\min_{\mathbf{A}_t} \|\mathbf{X}_t - \mathbf{D}\mathbf{A}_t\|_F^2 + \alpha \|\mathbf{A}_t\|_{2,1} + \beta Tr(\mathbf{A}_t \mathbf{L}_t \mathbf{A}_t) + \gamma \|\boldsymbol{\Phi}_t \mathbf{A}_t\|_F^2. \tag{12}$$

Alternating direction method of multipliers (ADMM) can be used to solve (12). First, by introducing an auxiliary variable $\mathbf{Z}_t = \mathbf{A}_t \in \mathbb{R}^{k \times n_t}$, the problem can be reformulated to

$$\min_{\mathbf{A}_t, \mathbf{Z}_t} \|\mathbf{X}_t - \mathbf{D}\mathbf{A}_t\|_F^2 + \alpha \|\mathbf{Z}_t\|_{2,1} + \beta Tr(\mathbf{A}_t \mathbf{L}_t \mathbf{A}_t) + \gamma \|\boldsymbol{\Phi}_t \mathbf{A}_t\|_F^2,$$
$$s.t.\ \mathbf{A}_t - \mathbf{Z}_t = 0. \tag{13}$$

Then the augmented Lagrangian function w.r.t $\mathbf{A}_t$ and $\mathbf{Z}_t$ can be formed as

$$\begin{aligned} L_u(\mathbf{A}_t, \mathbf{Z}_t) &= \|\mathbf{X}_t - \mathbf{D}\mathbf{A}_t\|_F^2 + \alpha \|\mathbf{Z}_t\|_{2,1} + \beta Tr(\mathbf{A}_t \mathbf{L}_t \mathbf{A}_t) \\ &+ \gamma \|\boldsymbol{\Phi}_t \mathbf{A}_t\|_F^2 - \boldsymbol{\Lambda}_t^T (\mathbf{Z}_t - \mathbf{A}_t) + \frac{u_t}{2} \|\mathbf{Z}_t - \mathbf{A}_t\|_2^2, \end{aligned} \tag{14}$$

where $\boldsymbol{\Lambda}_t \in \mathbb{R}^{k \times m}$ is the Lagrangian multipliers and $u_t > 0$ is a penalty parameter. The objective function (14) can be minimized by alternately updating $\mathbf{A}_t$ and $\mathbf{Z}_t$. We also use a row shrink function [19] when updating $\mathbf{Z}_t$ which is represented as

$$\mathbf{z}^r = max\{\|\mathbf{q}^r\|_2 - \frac{w_t}{u_t}, 0\} \frac{\mathbf{q}^r}{\|\mathbf{q}^r\|_2}, \quad r = 1, \cdots, k, \tag{15}$$

where $\mathbf{q}^r = \mathbf{a}^r + \frac{\lambda_t^r}{u_t}$ and $\mathbf{z}^r$, $\mathbf{a}^r$, λ_t^r represent the r-th row of matrix $\mathbf{Z}_t$, $\mathbf{A}_t$, $\boldsymbol{\Lambda}_t$ respectively. When $\mathbf{Z}_t$ is fixed, we can update $\mathbf{A}_i$ by each column $\mathbf{a}_i$. Optimal solution $\mathbf{a}_t^\star$ can be obtained by setting derivative of L_u w.r.t $\mathbf{a}_t$ to zero, which is similar as in [6, 16, 19]:

$$\begin{aligned} \mathbf{a}_{t,k}^\star &= (\mathbf{D}^T \mathbf{D} + \beta \boldsymbol{\Phi}_t^T \boldsymbol{\Phi}_t + 2\beta l_{ii} \mathbf{I} + u_1 \mathbf{I})^{-1} \\ &\times (\mathbf{D}^T \mathbf{x}_{t,k} - 2\beta \sum_{k \neq i} \mathbf{a}_{t,k} l_{ki} + u_1 \mathbf{Z}_i^{k+1} - \frac{1}{2} \lambda_{t,k}) \end{aligned} \tag{16}$$

where l_{ii} is the (i, i) element of $\mathbf{L}$, $\mathbf{a}_{t,k}$ is the k-th column vector of $\mathbf{A}_t$, $\mathbf{x}_{t,k}$ is the k-th column vector of $\mathbf{X}_t$, $\lambda_{t,k}$ is the k-th column vector of $\mathbf{\Lambda}_t$. The Algorithm solve (8) is detailed in Algorithm 2.

Optimize $\mathbf{D}_t$. When given fixed $\mathbf{A}$ and $\mathbf{L}_t$, the optimization problem in (7) is equal to

$$\|\mathbf{X}_t - \mathbf{DA}\|_F^2, \quad s.t. \quad \|\mathbf{d}_i\|_2^2 = 1, \tag{17}$$

which is a standard dictionary learning task. We can solve it by updating $\mathbf{d}_i$ column by column. When updating $\mathbf{d}_i$, all the other columns $\mathbf{d}_j$, $j \neq i$ are fixed. Generally, it is required that each column $\mathbf{d}_i$ of $\mathbf{D}$ is a unit vector. It is a quadratic programming problem and it can be solved by using the K-SVD algorithm [20].

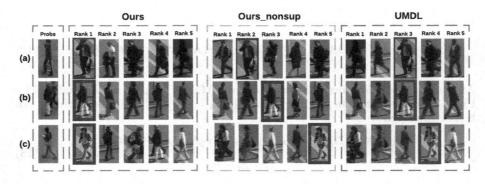

Fig. 3. Performances of UDML and Ours algorithm on PRID dataset. Probe images are provided in the left column. Top-5 candidate images are sorted in descent order according to their score. The ground truth images are marked with red bounding boxes. (Color figure online)

Update $\mathbf{W}_t$. Following [19], we update the affinity matrix $\mathbf{W}_t$ the algorithm obtains optimal $\mathbf{A}$ and $\mathbf{D}$. Recall that in the initialization stage, $\mathbf{W}_t$ of source datasets are constructed with labeled information, and $\mathbf{W}_T$ of target dataset in set as zero matrix. After operating Algorithm 2, $\mathbf{W}_t$ for all the source and the target datasets are recomputed with $\mathbf{A}_t$ buy cosine similarity metric $\mathrm{sim}_{\cos}(\mathbf{a}_i, \mathbf{a}_j) = \frac{\mathbf{a}_i \cdot \mathbf{a}_j}{\|\mathbf{a}_i\| \cdot \|\mathbf{a}_j\|}$ where $\mathbf{a}_i$ and $\mathbf{a}_j$ are atoms of coefficient matrix $\mathbf{A}_t$ corresponding to dataset $\mathbf{X}_t$. Specifically, for each $\mathbf{a}_i$, if $\mathbf{a}_j$ is his k-nearest neighborer, the $w_{i,j} = \mathrm{sim}_{\cos}(\mathbf{a}_i, \mathbf{a}_j)$ otherwise $w_{i,j} = 0$. In our work we set $k = 5$. With the renewed $\mathbf{W}_t$, we re-run Algorithm 2 in the next criterion. The termination condition is set as an loose stopping criterion when $\frac{|Lu^{k+1} - Lu^k|}{|Lu^0|} \leq \varepsilon$. In practice, ε is set to 0.1 and the total iteration number is typically under 5 in our experiments.

3   Experiments

3.1   Experimental Settings

Datasets. We compare our algorithm with the state-of-the-art algorithms on four widely referred benchmark dataset of Peron Re-identification. The **ViPeR** [5] dataset contains 1,264 images of 632 persons from two non-overlapping camera views. Two images are taken for each person, each from a different camera. Viewpoint changes and varying illumination conditions have occurred. The **PRID** [7] dataset contains images of 385 individuals from two distinct cameras. Camera B records 749 persons and Camera A records 385 persons, with 200 of them are same persons. The **iLIDS** [28] dataset records 119 individuals captures by three different cameras in an airport terminal. It contains 476 images with large occlusions caused by luggage and viewpoint changes. The **CAVIAR** [3] dataset for re-id contains 72 individuals captured by two cameras in a shopping mall. The amount of image is 1,220, with 10 to 20 images for each individual. The size of images in the CAVIAR dataset vary significantly from 39×17 to 141×72. The **CUHK03** [12] dataset contains images of 1360 different individuals captured in a campus by six cameras. A total number of 13,164 images are recorded and 4.8 images are recorded for each individual on average.

As in [15,19], we scaled all images to 128×48 pixel images and normalized to color+HOG+LBP histogram-based 5138-D feature representations [13]. The size of dictionaries is set to 150 for all experiments. Other parameters are tuned by four-fold cross-validation method.

Algorithms. We first consider the single-task experiments as a baseline. In the single-task experiments, there is no source data for transfer learning. Therefore, we could investigate wether the cross-data transfer learning (the multi-task methods) can improve the performance of unsupervised re-id. (a) *Single-task methods:* **SDALF:** [4] SDALF generates hand-crafted-feature for unsupervised re-id learning by exploiting the property of symmetry in pedestrian images. **eSDC:** [27] eSDC method introduces unsupervised saliency learning for re-id task. **GTS:** [21] GTS is proposed to solve re-id problem by exploring generative probabilistic topic modeling. **ISR:** [14] ISR applies sparse representation recognition model for re-id built on sparse basis expansions. **CAMEL:** [25] CAMEL introduces a cross-view asymmetric metric learning for unsupervised re-id. **UMDL_S:** We also involve unsupervised multi-task dictionary method UMDL [19] method with no source data related term for single task test, which is denoted as UMDL_S. **Ours_S:** For single-task experiment, there is only one dataset. Therefore, the support discriminative term and the Graph Laplacian term are not activated and only the structure sparse term is used.

(b) *Multi-task methods:* There are few unsupervised cross-dataset multi-task learning applied for person re-identification. As in former works [19], we additionally invite several multi-task learning methods as baselines: **AdaRSVM:** [18] AdaRSVM is a cross-domain unsupervised adaptive ranking SVM learning method designed for person re-identification. It permit the information of negative pairs in target training. **SA_DA+kLFDA:** (abbr. SA+kLFDA) In the framework, SA_DA is an unsupervised domain adaptation algorithm that aligns the source and target domain through data distributions. After domain adaptation, the supervised re-id algorithm kLFDA is implemented on labeled source data and then applied to the aligned target dataset [19]. **kLFDA_N:** Furthermore, we provide a transfer learning method baseline. In the framework, kLFDA algorithm is first trained on source datasets and applied directly to target dataset with no model adaptation. We denoted this algorithm as kLFDA_N. **UMDL:** In [19], the authors proposed a multi-task cross-dataset dictionary learning algorithm with a Laplacian regularization term for person re-identification. **Ours:** In the experiments, we denote our algorithm as Ours. For ablation study, we also perform our algorithms without support discriminative term in the test, which is denoted as **Ours_nonsup**.

Settings. In each experiment, one dataset is selected as the target dataset, the other datasets are chosen as the source datasets. For the target dataset, no label information is utilized in training stage; For the source datasets, label information is utilized for initializing the corresponding Laplacian matrix as mentioned in (5). We report the average performance of 20 independent trials. In each trial, we randomly divide each dataset into two equal-sized subsets as training and testing sets, with no overlapping on person identities. For datasets recording two camera views, e.g. VIPeR, PRID, images from one view are selected randomly as probe sets, and images from other views are chosen as gallery sets. For multi-view dataset, e.g. iLIDS, one view is selected randomly as gallery images with others are chosen as probe sets.

3.2   Experimental Analysis

Performance of Person Re-identification. As Shown in Table 1, we display the performance of the investigated algorithms by rank one machining accuracy (%). We observe that: (1) In multi-task learning, our algorithm consistently shown outstanding performance on all the datasets. Specifically, our algorithm and UMDL algorithm performance much better than other algorithms. It indicates that the cross-data dictionary learning can improve the performance of re-id. Moreover, our algorithm presents better performance on all the datasets than UMDL. Especially, our algorithm outperforms others by up to 5% in the experiments. (2) Compared to single-task learning, UMDL and our algorithm report a much better performance than UMDL_S and Ours_S. It indicates that utilizing the knowledge from source domains can improve the re-id performance. (3) In multi-task learning, the results of kLFDA_N reports weaker performance, which indicates directly transfer knowledge from source datasets to target dataset do not help much in re-id. Meanwhile, SA_DA+kLFDA does not report high performance, too. It indicates that unsupervised domain adaptation methods may not be suitable to cross-datasets re-id. The reason is domain adaptation methods assume that all domains have the same classification tasks but in our re-id problem classes of persons are completely different as the persons are non-overlapped.

Table 1. Rank one matching accuracy (%) on unsupervised Re-ID. (a) Single-task methods. (b) Multi-task methods.

	Dataset	VIPeR	PRID	CAVIAR	iLIDS	CUHK03
(a)	SDALF	19.9	16.3	–	29.0	–
	eSDC	26.7	–	–	36.8	8.76
	GTS	25.2	–	–	42.4	–
	ISR	27.0	17.0	29.0	39.5	11.46
	CAMEL	30.9	–	–	–	31.9
	UMDL_S	24.3	14.1	33.5	45.7	13.8
	OURS_S	26.9	19.2	31.6	44.3	16.2
(b)	kLFDA_N	12.9	8.5	32.8	36.9	7.6
	SA+kLFDA	11.6	8.1	32.1	35.8	6.8
	AdaRSVM	10.9	4.9	5.8	–	5.8
	UMDL	31.5	24.2	41.6	49.3	27.1
	OURS_nonsup	24.7	22.52	40.1	48.1	26.8
	OURS	31.9^*	27.9^*	42.5^*	50.3^*	35.2^*

Ablation Study. For the ablation study, we analyze performances of our algorithms (Ours) and our algorithm without the support discriminative term (Ours_nonsup). UMDL is also invited as a baseline as it is also a cross-dataset algorithm report the state-of-the-art performance in previous works.

(1) Numerical analysis. First, We run Ours, Ours_nonsup and UMDL on PRID and CAVIAR datasets. As shown in Fig. 4(a) and (b), the Ours algorithm presents the best performance over UMDL and Ours_nonsup on matching accuracy consistently on the two datasets. It outperforms others very early around 5% from top-10 rank performance on PRID and 3% on CAVIAR until all algorithms meet over 90% matching accuracy on top-50 rank performance. It implies that introducing support discriminative term improves the re-id performance.

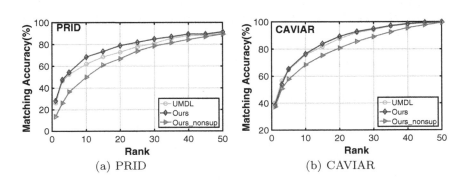

(a) PRID   (b) CAVIAR

Fig. 4. Re-id performance for ablation study.

(2) **Case analysis.** As we shown earlier in Fig. 1, common appearances and domain-unique appearance are observed in re-id datasets. In this section, we aim to test the ability of our algorithms in discovering these domain-unique appearances. We pick up three persons with domain-unique appearances as probe images and select top-5 ranked candidates from the gallery sets the tested algorithms. Candidates are ranked according to their similarities to the probe in descending order. Ground truth person images are marked with red bounding boxes.

As displayed in Fig. 3, UMDL prefers to rank candidates based on the common appearances over the domain-unique appearances. For the person (a), UMDL weights person with 'dark coat and pants' over 'carrying pink handbag'; For the person (b), it orders the person with 'dark color coat and white pants' over 'carrying handbags (or not)', such that the imposters wearing the similar clothes but carrying handbags are ranked over the ground truth person, which does not carrying bags at all. For the person (c) who is taking white bags, because of a heavily viewpoint change, UMDL mismatches the probe to imposters with white coats. Meanwhile, our algorithm can learn the domain-unique appearances and thus successfully matches the probes to the correct candidates. In the top-5 ranked candidates, we observe that our algorithm can select candidates with domain-unique appearances. For the person (a), it selects four candidates carrying handbags; for the person (c), there are four candidates carrying shoulder bags. Moreover, we could verify that the support discriminative term emphasizes the diversity of unique appearance. As shown in Fig. 1, if there is no support discriminative term, our algorithm (denoted as Ours_nonsup) will not be able to recognize the domain-unique feature. The performance of Ours_nonsup degrades dramatically as shown in Table 1.

(3) **Inter-dataset similarity analysis.** In order to verify the ability of our algorithm on discriminative representation learning, we further calculate the *similarity index* of samples inter-datasets. Ideally, higher similarity index indicates that the features of samples between two datasets are more similar. In particular, we define the similarity index of dataset $\mathbf{A}_i$ to dataset $\mathbf{A}_j$ as: $S_{ij} = \sum_p \sum_q \|\mathbf{a}_{i,p} \odot \mathbf{a}_{j,q}\|_0 / n_i$ where $\mathbf{a}_{i,p}$ is the p-th column of $\mathbf{A}_i$ and $\mathbf{a}_{j,q}$ is the q-th column of $\mathbf{A}_j$. Experiments are re-run on PRID dataset with the best performed parameter $\alpha = 1$, $\beta = 10^{-3}$, $\gamma = 3$.

We display the inter-dataset similarity index in Table 2. As shown in the table, UMDL and Ours_nonsup algorithm performances distinctly higher similarity indexes cross datasets w.r.t. PRID then Ours algorithm. It implies the support discriminative term can enhance the discriminative capability of representations across-datasets.

Table 2. Inter-dataset similarity index with target dataset PRID ($\times 10^2$)

	UMDL	Ours_nonsup	Ours
VIPeR w.r.t. PRID	12.50	8.24	0.29
CAVIAR w.r.t. PRID	13.01	7.59	0.27
iLID w.r.t. PRID	12.94	10.59	0.22
CUHK03 w.r.t. PRID	19.33	15.49	0.43

4 Conclusion

In this paper, we proposed a novel domain-aware unsupervised cross-dataset approach on person re-identification. It is able to characterize both the shared and domain-unique representations cross different camera-view network domains. Experiments on four real-world datasets consistently report outstanding performance of our algorithm. Analysis on selected cases also support that our algorithm enhances the re-id performance by utilizing domain-unique representations. Future works are suggested to extend the proposed algorithm to real-world re-id scenario with more source domains with various domain-unique appearances.

Acknowledgments. This paper is based on research sponsored by Air Force Research Laboratory and DARPA under agreement number FA8750-19-2-0501 and ARC DECRA (DE190100626). The U.S. Government is authorized to reproduce and distribute reprints for Governmental purposes notwithstanding any copyright notation thereon. This project is also aligned with and co-sponsored by the Disaster Management and Smart Cities related activities in CSIRO Data61.

References

1. Candes, E.J., Wakin, M.B., Boyd, S.P.: Enhancing sparsity by reweighted ell _1 minimization. J. Fourier Anal. Appl. **14**(5–6), 877–905 (2008)
2. Chartrand, R., Yin, W.: Iteratively reweighted algorithms for compressive sensing. In: IEEE International Conference on Acoustics, Speech and Signal Processing, ICASSP 2008, pp. 3869–3872. IEEE (2008)
3. Cheng, D.S., Cristani, M., Stoppa, M., Bazzani, L., Murino, V.: Custom pictorial structures for re-identification. In: BMVC (2011)
4. Farenzena, M., Bazzani, L., Perina, A., Murino, V., Cristani, M.: Person re-identification by symmetry-driven accumulation of local features. In: CVPR, pp. 2360–2367. IEEE (2010)
5. Gray, D., Brennan, S., Tao, H.: Evaluating appearance models for recognition, reacquisition, and tracking. In: PETS, vol. 3 (2007)
6. Guo, H., Jiang, Z., Davis, L.S.: Discriminative dictionary learning with pairwise constraints. In: Lee, K.M., Matsushita, Y., Rehg, J.M., Hu, Z. (eds.) ACCV 2012. LNCS, vol. 7724, pp. 328–342. Springer, Heidelberg (2013). https://doi.org/10.1007/978-3-642-37331-2_25
7. Hirzer, M., Beleznai, C., Roth, P.M., Bischof, H.: Person re-identification by descriptive and discriminative classification. In: Heyden, A., Kahl, F. (eds.) SCIA 2011. LNCS, vol. 6688, pp. 91–102. Springer, Heidelberg (2011). https://doi.org/10.1007/978-3-642-21227-7_9
8. Karanam, S., Li, Y., Radke, R.J.: Person re-identification with discriminatively trained viewpoint invariant dictionaries. In: ICCV, pp. 4516–4524 (2015)
9. Kodirov, E., Xiang, T., Fu, Z., Gong, S.: Person re-identification by unsupervised ell_1 graph learning. In: ECCV. pp. 178–195. Springer (2016)
10. Kodirov, E., Xiang, T., Gong, S.: Dictionary learning with iterative laplacian regularisation for unsupervised person re-identification. In: BMVC, vol. 3, p. 8 (2015)

11. Li, S., Shao, M., Fu, Y.: Cross-view projective dictionary learning for person re-identification. In: IJCAI, pp. 2155–2161 (2015)
12. Li, W., Zhao, R., Xiao, T., Wang, X.: Deepreid: deep filter pairing neural network for person re-identification. In: CVPR (2014)
13. Lisanti, G., Masi, I., Bagdanov, A., Del Bimbo, A.: Person re-identification by iterative re-weighted sparse ranking. IEEE Trans. Pattern Anal. Mach. Intell. **PP**(99), 1 (2014). https://doi.org/10.1109/TPAMI.2014.2369055
14. Lisanti, G., Masi, I., Bagdanov, A.D., Del Bimbo, A.: Person re-identification by iterative re-weighted sparse ranking. IEEE Trans. Pattern Anal. Mach. Intell. **37**(8), 1629–1642 (2015)
15. Lisanti, G., Masi, I., Del Bimbo, A.: Matching people across camera views using kernel canonical correlation analysis. In: Proceedings of the International Conference on Distributed Smart Cameras, p. 10. ACM (2014)
16. Liu, Y., Chen, W., Chen, Q., Wassell, I.: Support discrimination dictionary learning for image classification. In: ECCV. pp. 375–390. Springer (2016)
17. Lv, J., Chen, W., Li, Q., Yang, C.: Unsupervised cross-dataset person re-identification by transfer learning of spatial-temporal patterns. arXiv preprint arXiv:1803.07293 (2018)
18. Ma, A.J., Li, J., Yuen, P.C., Li, P.: Cross-domain person reidentification using domain adaptation ranking SVMs. IEEE Trans. Image Process. **24**(5), 1599–1613 (2015)
19. Peng, P., et al.: Unsupervised cross-dataset transfer learning for person re-identification. In: CVPR, pp. 1306–1315 (2016)
20. Rubinstein, R., Zibulevsky, M., Elad, M.: Efficient implementation of the K-SVD algorithm using batch orthogonal matching pursuit. Cs Technion **40**(8), 1–15 (2008)
21. Wang, H., Gong, S., Xiang, T.: Unsupervised learning of generative topic saliency for person re-identification. In: Proceedings of the British Machine Vision Conference. BMVA Press (2014)
22. Wang, J., Zhu, X., Gong, S., Li, W.: Transferable joint attribute-identity deep learning for unsupervised person re-identification. In: Proceedings of the IEEE Conference on Computer Vision and Pattern Recognition, pp. 2275–2284 (2018)
23. Wipf, D., Nagarajan, S.: Iterative reweighted ℓ_1 and ℓ_2 methods for finding sparse solutions. IEEE J. Sel. Top. Signal Process. **4**(2), 317–329 (2010)
24. Xiao, T., Li, H., Ouyang, W., Wang, X.: Learning deep feature representations with domain guided dropout for person re-identification. In: CVPR, pp. 1249–1258 (2016)
25. Yu, H.X., Wu, A., Zheng, W.S.: Cross-view asymmetric metric learning for unsupervised person re-identification. In: ICCV (2017)
26. Zhang, Y., Yeung, D.Y.: A convex formulation for learning task relationships in multi-task learning. arXiv preprint arXiv:1203.3536 (2012)
27. Zhao, R., Ouyang, W., Wang, X.: Unsupervised salience learning for person re-identification. In: CVPR, pp. 3586–3593 (2013)
28. Zheng, M., et al.: Graph regularized sparse coding for image representation. IEEE Trans. Image Process. **20**(5), 1327–1336 (2011)

Invariance Matters: Person Re-identification by Local Color Transfer

Ying Niu[1], Chunmiao Yuan[1], Kunliang Liu[1], Yukuan Sun[2], Jiayu Liang[1], Guanghao Jin[1,3], and Jianming Wang[2,4(✉)]

[1] School of Computer Science and Technology, Tianjin Polytechnic University, Tianjin, China
[2] School of Electronics and Information Engineering, Tianjin Polytechnic University, Tianjin, China
wangjianming@tjpu.edu.cn
[3] Tianjin International Joint Research and Development Center of Autonomous Intelligence Technology and Systems, Tianjin Polytechnic University, Tianjin, China
[4] Tianjin Key Laboratory of Autonomous Intelligence Technology and Systems, Tianjin Polytechnic University, Tianjin, China

Abstract. Person re-identification is a complex image retrieval problem. The color of the image is distorted due to changes in illumination, etc., which makes pedestrian recognition more challenging. In this paper, we take the conditional image, the reference image and its corresponding clothing segmentation image as input, and then restore the true color of the person through color conversion. In addition, we calculate the similarity between the conditional image and the image dataset by the chromatic aberration similarity and the clothing segmentation invariance. We evaluated the proposed method on a public dataset. A large number of experimental results show that the method is effective.

Keywords: Color transfer · Similarity · Segmentation · Re-identification

1 Introduction

Person re-identification [24,26,31] is given to monitor a pedestrian image and retrieve the pedestrian image across the device, which can be widely used in video surveillance, intelligent security and other fields. This is still a challenge due to color distortion caused by illumination changes, etc. [25]. A person may appear in camera A with dim light at 6:00 a.m., then in camera B with normal light at 9:00 a.m., and fifinally in camera C with glare light at 12:00 p.m. There is little research on this illumination-adaptive issue. The ReID task under different illumination conditions is named Illumination-Adaptive Person Re-identification

Supported by Natural Science Foundation of Tianjin (Grant No. 16JCYBJC42300, 17JCQNJC00100, 18JCYBJC44000, 18JCYBJC15300) and National Natural Science Foundation of China (Grant No. 6180021345, 61771340).

J. Li et al. (Eds.): ADMA 2019, LNAI 11888, pp. 421–430, 2019.
https://doi.org/10.1007/978-3-030-35231-8_30

422   Y. Niu et al.

(IA-ReID) [29]. In this task, given a probe image under one illumination, the goal is to match against gallery images with several different illuminations.

Some researches investigated the issue of different illuminations in ReID [1, 27]. However, they just consider a situation of two scales of illuminations. They assumed that the probe and the gallery images are respectively captured from two cameras, each with a corresponding illumination condition. In such a controlled setting, they proposed to learn the relationship between two scales of illuminations by brightness transfer functions [1] or the feature projection matrix [27]. IA-ReID is a more practical problem with multiple illuminations. Obviously, constructing the relationships among different scales of iluminations is not a practical solution for this problem. If there are 10 different scales in the dataset, the method needs to construct 10 different relationships, and it cannot be guaranteed the 10 relationships work perfectly.

Removing the effect of illumination is another intuitive idea. One solution is to do image enhancement [3] for the low-illumination images and image reconstruction [7] for the images with high exposure. However, this kind of methods either cannot handle extreme illuminations [6], or are particularly designed for visualization and rely heavily on the data condition and training samples [3,7].

Another solution is to disentangle the illumination information apart from the person feature. Such as Illumination-Identity Disentanglement (IID) [29] network.

The key idea of our approach is to determine the reference image by similarity calculations to improve the accuracy of color conversion for the true color recovery of the garment. More specifically, we calculate the color similarity to determine the reference image range, and then reduce the reference image range by calculating the similarity of the segment layout by dividing the image.

The solution to restore the true color of the garment is to convert the character's clothing color of the conditional image into a reference image based on human parsing [16–19] while maintaining the structure of the conditional image and the generated image unchanged. The effectiveness of the method is verified by experimental results.

2   Related Work

In this section, we first review some of the related work in each ReID, especially those based on deep learning. Then we introduce some style transfer methods related to our methods. Finally, we briefly introduce some human parsing.

Person ReID. Most of the existing methods of Person ReID can be divided into two categories, one is the traditional method and the other is the deep learning based method. For traditional methods, there are usually two phases. First, calculate hand-crafted features such as color histograms [11,28], Ga bor features [14], and dense SIFT [30]. Handcrafted features are expected to contain as much information as possible from different people. The following stages are similarity measure learning. Different metric learning methods have been proposed to determine whether two images match [4,5,10,15]. A suitable metric should indicate the similarity of the two images based on the handcrafted features, i.e. the two images of the same person should have a smaller distance than the images of different people. Some work even uses a collection of different indicators [21]. Since the feature extraction phase and metric learning are two separate components in a traditional approach, optimization of feature and distance metrics may not help each other and eventually become sub-optimal. The approach we propose is very different from all these traditional methods because we work together to learn the features and metrics in deep neural networks.

Style Transfer. Image style conversion is an enduring topic that converts the style of a reference style image into another input image. For example, selecting a reference style image can artistically convert photos taken in different lighting, different time periods, and different seasons into different styles. The global style transformation algorithm uses spatially invariant transformation methods to process images, which has limitations in complex style matching.

Local style transfer algorithms based on spatial color mappings are more expressive and can handle a broad class of applications such as time-of-day hallucination [8,22] and weather and season change [12,22]. Our work is most directly related to the line of work initiated by Gatys et al. [9] that employs the feature maps of discriminatively trained deep convolutional neural networks such as VGG-19 [23]. Our work aims for photorealistic transfer, which, introduces a challenging tension between local changes and large-scale consistency. We introduce an optional guidance to the style transfer process based on human parsing of the inputs (similar to [2]) to avoid the content-mismatch problem, which greatly improves the photorealism of the results.

Human Parsing. Due to low quality and computational cost, very little work introduces segmentation into the person ReID. With the rapid development of image segmentation methods based on deep learning, we can now easily obtain better body parsing images.

3   Methods

Our task is to restore the color of the conditional picture clothes to the color at the same time, and retain the important appearance details of the identity. Our model consists of two main modules: a similarity calculation module and a color conversion module. Our model overview is shown in the figure. We define the problem as follows. We assume that we have conditional images and data sets. There are reference images of people and clothing in the data set that are different from the different lighting conditions in the conditional image. Our goal is to restore the conditional image to the color of the reference image, eliminating the effects of illumination on the reID.

3.1 Similarity Calculation

In order to improve the accuracy of matching the conditional image with the reference image, we propose to select the reference image with the highest similarity in the dataset by matching the color difference similarity between the top and bottom of the image and the invariance of the clothing segment layout structure (Fig. 1).

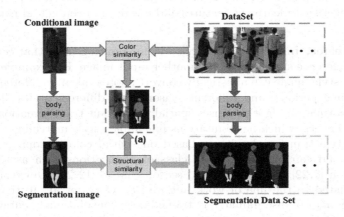

Fig. 1. Similarity calculation module. (a) reference image and segmented image. Given a conditional image and a reference data set, the reference image is determined by the similarity calculation.

Similarity of Chromatic Aberration. Since the conditional image and the reference image should be the same person wearing the same picture under different lighting conditions, the color difference between the top and bottom of the two pictures is similar to that of the bottom. Calculate color difference based on LAB color space:

$$\Delta E_{ab}^* = \sqrt{(L_2^* - L_1^*)^2 + (a_2^* - a_1^*)^2 + (b_2^* - b_1^*)^2} \tag{1}$$

Where L represents Luminosity, a represents a range from magenta to green, and b represents a range from yellow to blue.

Structural Similarity. In the case where the picture color is distorted and the person's posture may be different, the segmentation layout of the clothes remains unchanged, so the structure of the picture changes little. Liang et al. [16]. LIP method can accurately segment the layout of clothes, and it is more convenient to use the segmented picture to calculate structural similarity.

3.2   Color Transfer

Our algorithm uses four images: conditional images, reference images, and their segmented images. The reference image color is transferred to the conditional image while maintaining consistency of the results with the content and structure of the conditional image. Our approach is to use style conversion to learn images from different lighting - image conversion models.

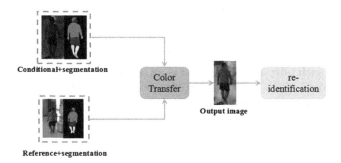

Fig. 2. Color Transfer module. The conditional image is restored to the original color according to the reference image.

Style Transfer. The color conversion algorithm is based on the neural network style algorithm of the paper, and the Neural Style algorithm by Gatys et al. [9] that transfers the reference image S onto the condition image C to produce an output image O by minimizing the objective function:

$$\mathcal{L}_{\text{total}} = \sum_{\ell=1}^{L} \alpha_\ell \mathcal{L}_c^\ell + \Gamma \sum_{\ell=1}^{L} \beta_\ell \mathcal{L}_s^\ell \qquad (2)$$

$$\mathcal{L}_c^\ell = \frac{1}{2N_\ell D_\ell} \sum_{ij} (F_\ell[O] - F_\ell[I])_{ij}^2 \qquad (3)$$

$$\mathcal{L}_s^\ell = \frac{1}{2N_\ell^2} \sum_{ij} (G_\ell[O] - G_\ell[S])_{ij}^2 \qquad (4)$$

where L is the total number of convolutional layers and ℓ indicates the ℓ-th convolutional layer of the deep convolutional neural network. In each layer, there are N_ℓ filters each with a vectorized feature map of size D_ℓ. $F_\ell[\cdot] \in \mathbb{R}^{N_\ell \times D_\ell}$ is the feature matrix with (i, j) indicating its index and the Gram matrix $G_\ell[\cdot] = F_\ell[\cdot] F_\ell[\cdot]^T \in \mathbb{R}^{N_\ell \times N_\ell}$ is defined as the inner product between the vectorized feature maps. α_ℓ and β_ℓ are the weights to configure layer preferences and I is a weight that balances the tradeoff between the content and the style.

Photorealism Regularization. In order to encourage color transfer to maintain the style consistency between input and output, the [20] proposes an image realistic regularization parameter term of the objective function in the optimization process, and constrains the reconstructed image to prevent distortion by local affine color transformation of the input image.

This strategy is to express this constraint not on the output image directly but on the transformation that is applied to the input image. Characterizing the space of photorealistic images is an unsolved problem. Our insight is that we do not need to solve it if we exploit the fact that the input is already photorealistic. Our strategy is to ensure that we do not lose this property during the transfer by adding a term to Eq. 1a that penalizes image distortions. Our solution is to seek an image transform that is locally affine in color space, that is, a function such that for each output patch, there is an affine function that maps the input RGB values onto their output counterparts. Each patch can have a different affine function, which allows for spatial variations. To gain some intuition, one can consider an edge patch. The set of affine combinations of the RGB channels spans a broad set of variations but the edge itself cannot move because it is located at the same place in all channels.

Formally, we build upon the Matting Laplacian of Levin et al. [13] who have shown how to express a grayscale matte as a locally affine combination of the input RGB channels. They describe a least-squares penalty function that can be minimized with a standard linear system represented by a matrix $\mathcal{M}_I$ that only depends on the input image I (We refer to the original article for the detailed derivation. Note that given an input image I with N pixels, $\mathcal{M}_I$ is $N \times N$). We name $V_c[O]$ the vectorized version ($N \times 1$) of the output image O in channel c and define the following regularization term that penalizes outputs that are not well explained by a locally affine transform:

$$\mathcal{L}_m = \sum_{c=1}^{3} V_c[O]^T \mathcal{M}_I V_c[O] \tag{5}$$

Using this term in a gradient-based solver requires us to compute its derivative w.r.t. the output image. Since MI is a symmetric matrix, we have: $\frac{d\mathcal{L}_m}{dV_c[O]} = 2\mathcal{M}_I V_c[O]$.

3.3 Overall Approach

We formulate the color transfer objective by combining all 3 components together:

$$\mathcal{L}_{total} = \sum_{l=1}^{L} \alpha_\ell \mathcal{L}_c^\ell + \Gamma \sum_{\ell=1}^{L} \beta_\ell \mathcal{L}_s^\ell + \lambda \mathcal{L}_m \tag{6}$$

where L is the total number of convolutional layers and ℓ indicates the ℓ-th convolutional layer of the deep convolutional neural network. Γ is a weight that controls the style loss. α_ℓ and β_ℓ are the weights to configure layer preferences. λ is a weight that controls the photorealism regularization. $\mathcal{L}_c^\ell$ is the content loss. $\mathcal{L}_s^\ell$ is the style loss. $\mathcal{L}_m$ is the photorealism regularization.

4   Experiment

4.1   DataSet

For all our experiments, we used the PRDDC data set. The images were collected in a public place, and 12279 frames are included in the data-set. Mainly used to change the clothes after the person ReID. Since this article does not consider the change of clothes, we use the pictures taken at the same time as a training set, and take pictures taken at different times with different darkness of illumination as test1-sets. Convert the pictures with different brightness and darkness in the test set to generate a picture with the same brightness and darkness as the test2-set (Fig. 3).

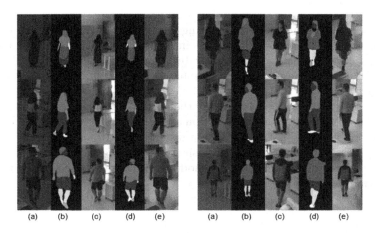

Fig. 3. Color transfer results. Examples of generated images on PRDDC. (a) conditional image; (b) segmented image of the conditional image; (c) reference image; (d) segmented image of the reference image; (e) generation image.

4.2   Evaluation

The results of our color transfer module are shown in Fig. 2. The segmentation image is obtained by the LIP method of the paper, and the reference image is determined by calculating the similarity. The color of the condition image is converted into a reference image based on the guidance of the semantic segmentation image, and finally the generated image is output.

Ablation experiments. To investigate the effectiveness of color conversion on eliminating illumination effects, we performed ablation studies in Table 1. As shown in Table 1 when tested on the PRDDC data set, the color conversion significantly improved the results compared to the baseline. Baseline uses [32] ReID methods to evaluate the accuracy of our methods and baseline methods. Specifically, the R-1 accuracy increased from 47.8% to 56.4%, the mAP increased from 35.8% to 42.6%, and the results of the R-5 accuracy and the R-10 accuracy

Table 1. Re-ID results

Methods	PRDDC			
	R-1	R-5	R-10	mAP
Baseline	47.8%	53.2%	61.8%	35.8%
Ours	56.4%	64.2%	67.2%	42.6%

increased by 11% and 5.4%, respectively. This improvement indicates that the effect of illumination changes on the ReID can be eliminated by color conversion.

5   Conclusion

We propose a new method for restoring the true color of a picture based on color conversion. We designed two specific modules to determine the reference image and color conversion. The generated image is displayed as a color in the reference image environment while keeping the content of the conditional image unchanged.

The results produced are limited by the current database we use. Most of the images included in our training collection are simple backgrounds. Therefore, the learning model is biased towards such a distribution. In fact, we do not assume any constraints or background processing. We believe that if the training set contains more kinds of images, our model can also eliminate the influence of illumination on the recognition.

References

1. Bhuiyan, A., Perina, A., Murino, V.: Exploiting multiple detections to learn robust brightness transfer functions in re-identification systems. In: 2015 IEEE International Conference on Image Processing (ICIP), pp. 2329–2333. IEEE (2015)
2. Champandard, A.J.: Semantic style transfer and turning two-bit doodles into fine artworks. arXiv preprint arXiv:1603.01768 (2016)
3. Chen, C., Chen, Q., Xu, J., Koltun, V.: Learning to see in the dark. In: Proceedings of the IEEE Conference on Computer Vision and Pattern Recognition, pp. 3291–3300 (2018)
4. Chen, D., Yuan, Z., Hua, G., Zheng, N., Wang, J.: Similarity learning on an explicit polynomial kernel feature map for person re-identification. In: Proceedings of the IEEE Conference on Computer Vision and Pattern Recognition, pp. 1565–1573 (2015)
5. Chen, J., Zhang, Z., Wang, Y.: Relevance metric learning for person re-identification by exploiting global similarities. In: 2014 22nd International Conference on Pattern Recognition, pp. 1657–1662. IEEE (2014)
6. Chen, Y.S., Wang, Y.C., Kao, M.H., Chuang, Y.Y.: Deep photo enhancer: unpaired learning for image enhancement from photographs with GANS. In: Proceedings of the IEEE Conference on Computer Vision and Pattern Recognition, pp. 6306–6314 (2018)

7. Eilertsen, G., Kronander, J., Denes, G., Mantiuk, R.K., Unger, J.: HDR image reconstruction from a single exposure using deep CNNs. ACM Trans. Graph. (TOG) **36**(6), 178 (2017)
8. Gardner, J.R., et al.: Deep manifold traversal: Changing labels with convolutional features. arXiv preprint arXiv:1511.06421 (2015)
9. Gatys, L.A., Ecker, A.S., Bethge, M.: Image style transfer using convolutional neural networks. In: Proceedings of the IEEE Conference on Computer Vision and Pattern Recognition, pp. 2414–2423 (2016)
10. Guillaumin, M., Verbeek, J., Schmid, C.: Is that you? metric learning approaches for face identification. In: 2009 IEEE 12th International Conference on Computer Vision, pp. 498–505. IEEE (2009)
11. Koestinger, M., Hirzer, M., Wohlhart, P., Roth, P.M., Bischof, H.: Large scale metric learning from equivalence constraints. In: 2012 IEEE Conference on Computer Vision and Pattern Recognition, pp. 2288–2295. IEEE (2012)
12. Laffont, P.Y., Ren, Z., Tao, X., Qian, C., Hays, J.: Transient attributes for high-level understanding and editing of outdoor scenes. ACM Trans. Graph. (TOG) **33**(4), 149 (2014)
13. Levin, A., Lischinski, D., Weiss, Y.: A closed-form solution to natural image matting. IEEE Trans. Pattern Anal. Mach. Intell. **30**(2), 228–242 (2007)
14. Li, W., Wang, X.: Locally aligned feature transforms across views. In: Proceedings of the IEEE Conference on Computer Vision and Pattern Recognition, pp. 3594–3601 (2013)
15. Li, Z., Chang, S., Liang, F., Huang, T.S., Cao, L., Smith, J.R.: Learning locally-adaptive decision functions for person verification. In: Proceedings of the IEEE Conference on Computer Vision and Pattern Recognition, pp. 3610–3617 (2013)
16. Liang, X., Gong, K., Shen, X., Lin, L.: Look into person: joint body parsing & pose estimation network and a new benchmark. IEEE Trans. Pattern Anal. Mach. Intell. **41**(4), 871–885 (2019)
17. Liang, X., et al.: Deep human parsing with active template regression. IEEE Trans. Pattern Anal. Mach. Intell. **37**(12), 2402–2414 (2015)
18. Liang, X., Shen, X., Xiang, D., Feng, J., Lin, L., Yan, S.: Semantic object parsing with local-global long short-term memory. In: Proceedings of the IEEE Conference on Computer Vision and Pattern Recognition, pp. 3185–3193 (2016)
19. Liang, X., et al.: Human parsing with contextualized convolutional neural network. In: Proceedings of the IEEE International Conference on Computer Vision, pp. 1386–1394 (2015)
20. Luan, F., Paris, S., Shechtman, E., Bala, K.: Deep photo style transfer. In: Proceedings of the IEEE Conference on Computer Vision and Pattern Recognition, pp. 4990–4998 (2017)
21. Paisitkriangkrai, S., Shen, C., Van Den Hengel, A.: Learning to rank in person re-identification with metric ensembles. In: Proceedings of the IEEE Conference on Computer Vision and Pattern Recognition, pp. 1846–1855 (2015)
22. Shih, Y., Paris, S., Durand, F., Freeman, W.T.: Data-driven hallucination of different times of day from a single outdoor photo. ACM Trans. Graph. (TOG) **32**(6), 200 (2013)
23. Simonyan, K., Zisserman, A.: Very deep convolutional networks for large-scale image recognition. arXiv preprint arXiv:1409.1556 (2014)
24. Song, C., Huang, Y., Ouyang, W., Wang, L.: Mask-guided contrastive attention model for person re-identification. In: Proceedings of the IEEE Conference on Computer Vision and Pattern Recognition, pp. 1179–1188 (2018)

25. Sun, X., Zheng, L.: Dissecting person re-identification from the viewpoint of viewpoint. arXiv preprint arXiv:1812.02162 (2018)
26. Sun, Y., et al.: Perceive where to focus: Learning visibility-aware part-level features for partial person re-identification. arXiv preprint arXiv:1904.00537 (2019)
27. Wang, Y., Hu, R., Liang, C., Zhang, C., Leng, Q.: Camera compensation using a feature projection matrix for person reidentification. IEEE Trans. Circuits Syst. Video Technol. **24**(8), 1350–1361 (2014)
28. Xiong, F., Gou, M., Camps, O., Sznaier, M.: Person re-identification using kernel-based metric learning methods. In: Fleet, D., Pajdla, T., Schiele, B., Tuytelaars, T. (eds.) ECCV 2014. LNCS, vol. 8695, pp. 1–16. Springer, Cham (2014). https://doi.org/10.1007/978-3-319-10584-0_1
29. Zeng, Z., Wang, Z., Wang, Z., Chuang, Y.Y., Satoh, S.: Illumination-adaptive person re-identification. arXiv preprint arXiv:1905.04525 (2019)
30. Zhao, R., Ouyang, W., Wang, X.: Person re-identification by salience matching. In: Proceedings of the IEEE International Conference on Computer Vision, pp. 2528–2535 (2013)
31. Zheng, L., Yang, Y., Hauptmann, A.G.: Person re-identification: Past, present and future. arXiv preprint arXiv:1610.02984 (2016)
32. Zheng, L., Zhang, H., Sun, S., Chandraker, M., Yang, Y., Tian, Q.: Person re-identification in the wild. In: Proceedings of the IEEE Conference on Computer Vision and Pattern Recognition, pp. 1367–1376 (2017)

Research on Interactive Intent Recognition Based on Facial Expression and Line of Sight Direction

Siyu Ren[1], Guanghao Jin[1,2], Kunliang Liu[1], Yukuan Sun[3], Jiayu Liang[1], Shiling Jiang[1], and Jianming Wang[3,4(✉)]

[1] School of Computer Science and Technology, Tianjin Polytechnic University, Tianjin, China
[2] Tianjin International Joint Research and Development Center of Autonomous Intelligence Technology and Systems, Tianjin Polytechnic University, Tianjin, China
[3] School of Electronics and Information Engineering, Tianjin Polytechnic University, Tianjin, China
wangjianming@tjpu.edu.cn
[4] Tianjin Key Laboratory of Autonomous Intelligence Technology and Systems, Tianjin Polytechnic University, Tianjin, China

Abstract. Interaction intent recognition refers to the discrimination and prediction of whether a person (user) wants to interact with the robot during the human-robot interaction (HRI) process. Interactive intent recognition is one of the key technologies of intelligent robots. This paper mainly studies the interactive intent recognition method based on visual images, which is of great significance to improve the intelligence of robots. In the process of communication between people, people often make different interactions according to each other's emotional state. At present, the visual-based interactive intent recognition method mainly utilizes the user's gesture, line of sight direction, and head posture to judge the interaction intention, and has not found the interactive intention recognition method based on the user's emotional state. Therefore, this paper proposes an interactive intent recognition algorithm that combines facial expression features and line of sight directions. The experimental results show that the accuracy of the intent recognition algorithm including expression recognition is 93.3%, and the accuracy of the intent recognition algorithm without expression recognition is 83%. Therefore, the performance of the intent recognition algorithm is significantly improved after the expression recognition is increased.

Keywords: Human-robot interaction · Line of sight · Expression recognition · Intentional recognition

Supported by Natural Science Foundation of Tianjin (Grant No. 16JCYBJC42300, 17JCQNJC00100, 18JCYBJC44000, 18JCYBJC15300) and National Natural Science Foundation of China (Grant No. 6180021345, 61771340).

J. Li et al. (Eds.): ADMA 2019, LNAI 11888, pp. 431–443, 2019.
https://doi.org/10.1007/978-3-030-35231-8_31

1   Introduction

Human-robot interaction (HRI) [10] is a study of the methods and approaches of interaction between humans and robots. The ultimate goal of the field is to achieve a more realistic, smooth, and intuitive interaction between people and robots. Human-robot interaction technology is a multidisciplinary research area that includes artificial intelligence, robotics, sensor technology, psychology, and industrial design [5]. In many cases, the research and development of HRI technology draws on and references the interaction and communication between humans, and the human-computer interaction process is also carried out between people (users) and robots, so in a sense, HRI It is the reproduction and extension of the way humans communicate.

The HRI technology based on visual image first uses the camera to capture the user's image or video, and then analyzes and understands the content in the image, thereby realizing the judgment and recognition of the user's intention [9]. Visual information is the main way for humans to obtain external information. According to the analysis, more than 80% of human brain processing information comes from the visual system. Therefore, HRI technology based on visual image is the most important and most research potential in this field [20].

The user interaction intent recognition technology refers to the robot's determination of whether the user wants to communicate with the user, specifically, the limited information that the robot provides from the user (such as voice, gesture [13], head posture, line of sight direction [3], and facial expression). The problem of understanding the user's interaction purpose (expectation, goals, intentions, etc.) within [4,6,11].

Through literature review, it is found that there is a lack of recognition of user's expression information in many previous intent recognition studies [7], and expressions are factors closely related to people's inner thoughts in psychological perspective. Emotion is considered to be a key factor that intuitively reflects what people think and think, so how to use individual emotions to understand the intention becomes necessary and feasible [16].

2   Related Work

Generally speaking, the expression reflects the user's inner activity. Therefore, in view of the problem that the existing human-computer interaction intention recognition research has not utilized the expression information [2], this paper proposes a user interaction intention recognition algorithm based on the combination of expression information and line of sight direction. The research focuses on the influence of expression information on the user's interaction intention recognition, and how to combine the line of sight direction and expression information to identify the user's interaction intention.

2.1   Line of Sight Estimation Method

A 3D eyeball based approach is used herein to estimate the user's line of sight direction [21]. Firstly, the user's facial feature point information is detected from the input video, the user's head posture is calculated according to the facial feature point coordinates, and the user's eyeball center and pupil center are calculated through the facial feature points. The optical axis information is calculated through the eyeball and the pupil, and the user's line of sight direction estimation is obtained. When it is detected that the user's head is deflected, the head needs to be first corrected, and then the above steps are performed.

Calculate the user's eye center O and the eye point N through the eye area coordinates in the user's facial feature points, and the front point N, and connect the ON two points and define the optical axis, and finally calculate the line of sight direction (as shown in Fig. 1).

Fig. 1. Schematic diagram of line of sight direction

Facial Expression Recognition Method. The Facial Action Coding System (FACS) [8] is arguably the most widely used method for encoding facial expressions in behavioral science. The system describes facial expressions based on 46 component movements, roughly corresponding to the movement of individual facial muscles. An example of a partial facial motion area is shown in Fig. 2. FACS provides an objective and comprehensive way to analyze facial states or movements that have been proven to detect a person's emotional state [14]. The FACS can encode any anatomically possible facial expression and break it down to form a specific action unit (AU) to objectively describe the different facial expressions. The system is therefore used herein to identify several specific expressions of the user.

The facial expression is recognized by a plurality of facial action unit combination information. For the problem to be solved in this paper, that is, the type of expression to be recognized, an appropriate facial action unit is selected to remove excess facial action unit information, thereby reducing noise and improving recognition rate. In the next experiment, experiments were performed on

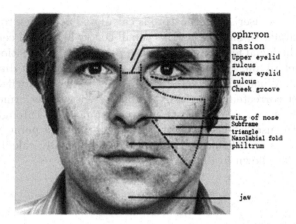

Fig. 2. Example of face decomposition in facial motion coding system

multiple sets of data to screen facial movements, and selected parts were selected as the main action units through the experimental results. The combined screening of action units is described in detail in the experimental section.

3   Our Methods

Facial expressions and gaze directions are the most basic dimensions of human behavioral intentions, and are all related to "approach-oriented" or "avoidance-oriented" [17]. Positive emotions or angry emotions and direct vision are considered to be close to each other, while negative emotions such as fear, sadness, and disgust are the same as the direction of diversion. The "combined signal" hypothesis proposed by Adams and Kleck [1] argues that when the gaze direction and the facial expression's motivation tend to be consistent, the recognition of the gaze direction or emotion will be enhanced, and the user's approaching or avoiding tendency intention will be more apparent.

Specifically, happy and angry expressions are considered to be "close to the trend" emotions, which can be considered as having strong interactive intents when looking directly at them. Fear and sad expressions are considered to be "avoidance trends" and can be considered as no interaction intention when combined with non-direct line of sight.

3.1   Interaction Intent Discrimination Rules

Based on the related content of the approaching trend and avoidance trend in psychology, the rules for discriminating the interaction intentions studied in this paper are shown in Table 1.

Table 1. Classification of interactive intention recognition

Gaze direction	Emotion				
	Angry	Happy	Fear	Sad	Disgusting
Gaze Forward	Have interaction Intention	Strong interactive Intention	No interaction Intention	No interaction Intention	No interaction Intention
Not Gaze Forward	No interaction Intention	No interactive Intention	No interaction Intention	No interaction Intention	No interaction Intention

3.2   Implementation Plan

Firstly, it is initially determined whether the user's gaze area is the robot head by the line of sight direction of the user, and a preliminary determination is made as to whether the user wants to interact with the robot, and the user's facial expression unit information combination is used to identify the user's expression at the same time. The user's interactive intention is further discriminated by determining whether the user's expression is close to the trending expression or avoiding the trending expression, and finally determining whether the user has an intention to interact with the robot. The algorithm flowchart is shown in Fig. 3.

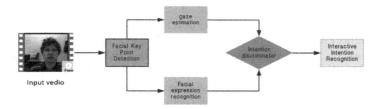

Fig. 3. Algorithm flowchart

First, the video V is captured by the camera of the robot head, and the n-frame image in the video is obtained by detecting the video V, and then the user facial feature point Fi of each frame (Ii) in the video is detected:

$$F_i = Face(F_i) \quad i = (1L\ n) \tag{1}$$

By detecting the mapping relationship between the user's facial two-dimensional feature point Fi2D and the three-dimensional feature point Fi3D, the user's head posture Hi is calculated by the SolvePnp function, and the user's facial feature point is corrected by the head posture to obtain the user's line of sight. Direction Ei:

$$E_i = Eye(F_i, H_i) \quad i = (1L\ n) \tag{2}$$

The action unit AUj of the user's face is detected using the detected facial feature point information while estimating the user's line of sight direction, and is used for the user's expression recognition:

$$AU_j = ActionUnites(F_i) \quad i = (1L\ n) \tag{3}$$

In this paper, all the action unit feature sets in the single frame picture data are set to Ai:

$$A_i = AU_j \quad i = (1L\ n) \tag{4}$$

After obtaining the user's eye line of sight direction feature Ei and the face action unit feature set AUi, the two types of features are combined to estimate whether the user wants to interact with the robot (R):

$$R = Intention(E_iL\ E_n; A_iL\ A_n) \quad i = (1L\ n) \tag{5}$$

Finally, the user's expression and the line-of-sight direction feature information are used to determine whether the user has an intention to interact with the robot. In the identification of the interaction intention, it is first determined whether the user's line of sight direction is in the direct view robot, and if it is determined to be direct view, it is initially determined to have an interactive intention, and if it is not directly viewed, it is determined to have no interaction intention. After preliminary determination of whether there is an interaction intention by the direction of the line of sight, the expression information is added for further interaction intention determination. If the emotion is close to the trend emotion, that is, positive emotion (happy) or anger, the user is determined to have a strong interactive intention to the robot, and the emotion When it is determined that the negative emotion (fear, sadness, disgust) is avoided, the user is determined that the intention to interact with the robot is extremely low, and thus it is determined that there is no interaction intention.

4   Experiment

4.1   DataSet

This paper builds a new first-person video dataset with the context of the interaction between the user and the observer (robot). Video information is collected using a webcam installed under the robot's head; testers are required to simulate interactions and interact with the robot. In this study, the main focus is on the problem of robots' identification of user interaction intentions. Therefore, the dataset is based on the robot as the first perspective. The line of sight direction, expression information, and interaction intent information in the data are marked. The collection scheme is shown in Fig. 4.

A total of 120 consecutive video sequences were constructed. Each type of video data is taken in a different environment and/or by different testers. Each participant is required to interact with the robot with five expressions (anger, happiness, fear, disgust, sadness). The line of sight of the participants is divided

Fig. 4. Data collection scheme.

into direct vision robot and non-direct vision. Testers are also divided into two types: no glasses and glasses. Each type of intent video contains multiple video data, and each video data is shot at least twice. The video uses the 640×480 24-bit True Color (RGB) AVI format.

The annotation of the expression information in this dataset is performed by four people who are not involved in the dataset, and the artificial image recognition and real value annotation are performed on the captured video data.

In addition, in order to increase the amount of training data that the robot intends to identify, this paper also makes a segmented version of the data set: the video in the data set is segmented, and each video segment contains a medium type, providing at least 7 for each group. In order to verify the robustness of the algorithm, three station modes were adopted during shooting to test the accuracy of the algorithm when the user is in different orientations within the visible range of the camera. The tester's station position is shown in Fig. 5. The tester's station position is shown in Fig. 5:

It should be emphasized that the first person video in this article is different from the public activity identification data set in the third person perspective. It is also different from previous gesture recognition datasets that use Kinect sensors because the video in this dataset involves human-observer (robot) inter-action behavior.

In addition, this article uses JPL interaction [19] to expose some data in the dataset for experimental verification. A new data annotation is performed on the selected data as part of the validation set to validate the framework. The data set is a first-person data set containing a video of the interaction between a person and an observer. They attached the GoPro2 camera to the head of the humanoid model and asked human participants to interact with the humanoid robot by performing activities. To mimic the mobility of the real robot, wheels

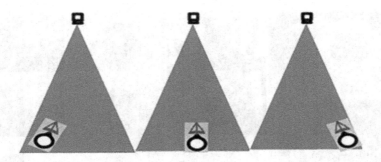

Fig. 5. Three different station data capture modes (where the blue arrow represents the main face of the face and the gray triangle is the range of the robot camera view) (Color figure online)

are placed underneath the humanoid robot and the operator moves the humanoid robot by pushing the humanoid robot from behind. This paper selects the data in the data set handshake, hug and beckoning behavior to fully recognize the face, as the data with interactive intent for the verification set for experimental verification.

4.2 Experimental Verification

Facial Action Unit Screening. In order to understand the detection results of the relevant facial action units of different expressions in the action unit detection algorithm used in this paper, in the experiment, various expression pictures in the public data set. The Extended Cohn-Kanade Dataset (CK+) [12] are input into the algorithm respectively. A test is performed to observe which action units are detected in each expression data, and each expression is individually trained and tested. The detection results of each facial action unit reveal the relationship between each action unit and the expression in the algorithm. Here, we mainly verify the five types of expressions of anger, happiness, fear, sadness and disgust that need to be identified in this paper. The recognition probability of facial movements with different expressions is shown in Fig. 6.

In this experiment, we choose the facial action unit that is most easily detected to represent the expression. According to Fig. 6, The highest probabilistic action units detected in angry expressions are AU1, AU2, AU4, AU7, AU26. The highest probabilistic action units detected in happy expressions are AU6, AU12. There are many action units related to fear expression. This paper chooses AU1, AU4, AU5, AU7, AU20 and AU26 to identify fear expression. Facial action units AU9, AU15 and AU16 were selected to recognize the sad expressions of users. The highest probabilistic action units detected in disgusting expressions are AU9, AU15.

It is also found in the above experimental results that a single action unit may have a high degree of correlation with multiple expressions, so it is extremely important to use a combination of multiple action units to recognize expressions.

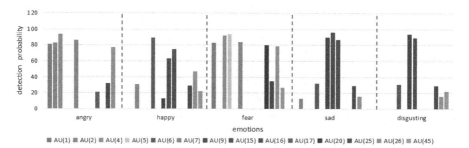

Fig. 6. The recognition probability of facial movements with different expressions. Legends represent different action units. 1: Raise the inner corner of eyebrow 2: Raise the outer corner of eyebrow 4: Frown 5: Wrinkle nose 6: Outer ring of orbicularis oculi muscle 7: Inner ring of orbicularis oculi muscle 9: Wrinkle nose 15: Pull the angle of mouth down 16: Push the lower lip up 17: Push the lower lip up 20: Push the lower lip up 25: Lip micro-tension 26: Mandible down 45: Blink

The optimal combination of action units for the expressions used herein in the experimental results is given in Table 2.

Table 2. Expression related facial action unit combination

Emotion	Relevant action unit combination
Angry	AU1+AU2+AU4+AU7+AU26
Happy	AU6+AU16
Fear	AU1+AU4+AU5+AU7+AU20+AU26
Sad	AU9+AU15+AU16
Disgusting	AU9+AU15

Through the above experiment, the facial action units (AU1, AU2, AU4, AU5, AU6, AU7, AU9, AU15, AU16, AU20, AU26) included in the desired recognition expression are selected for the identification of the expression information in the intention recognition of the present invention. Verification to reduce the effects of unwanted noise affecting the intent to identify.

Sight Estimation Accuracy Test. In this experiment, it is mainly to test the accuracy of the line of sight when the user directly views the robot in the self-built data set, randomly select the data of the four participants, and according to the three stations of the user in the self-built data set (Fig. 5) They were verified separately. The experimental results are shown in Table 3.

Through the above results, the line-of-sight direction estimation algorithm can be obtained, and the user's line of sight direction can be effectively estimated in this experiment, and the more accurate the face is, the higher the estimation accuracy is. The final comprehensive accuracy can reach 94.3%.

Table 3. Sight line direction detection accuracy of different stations

User	Position			Average
	Left of robot	Front of robot	Rigth of robot	
User1	93.8%	95.5%	92.7%	94%
User2	94%	95.2%	94.1%	94.4%
User3	93.2%	96.1%	93.5%	94.3%
User4	93.4%	96.7%	93.3%	94.5%
Average	93.6%	95.9%	93.4%	94.3%

Expression Recognition Accuracy Experiment. In this paper, some existing expression recognition methods based on facial action unit combinations are selected in the self-built data set of this paper. The experimental results are shown in Fig. 7.

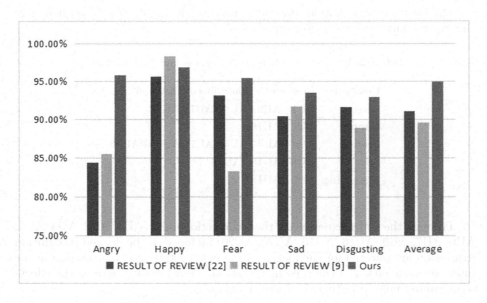

Fig. 7. Different methods of expression recognition results

After verifying the user's line of sight direction information and expression information, it can be concluded that the feature information for user interaction intent recognition can be effectively detected.

Intent Recognition Experiment. In this experiment, the accuracy of user intention recognition algorithm proposed in this paper is verified by experiments, and the recognition accuracy of two kinds of intentions, i.e. interactive intent and non-interactive intent, is counted separately. The results are shown in Table 4.

Table 4. User intent recognition accuracy

User	Have interactive intension	No interactive intension	Average
User1	94.1%	93.6%	93.85%
User2	94.6%	91.7%	93.2%
User3	93.7%	92.4%	93.1%
User4	93.5%	93.1%	93.3%
User5	94.1%	92.6%	93.4%
User6	93.6%	92.8%	93.2%
User7	94.7%	93.2%	94%
User8	94%	92.8%	93.4%
Average	93.9%	92.8%	93.3%

After obtaining the above experimental results, the algorithm was evaluated by the accuracy, recall and F-Measure indicators in all the data. The accuracy rate refers to the ratio between the data that correctly classifies the two types of interaction intentions and the total data in the experiment; the recall rate is accurately determined as the ratio between the data with interaction intention and the data with all interaction intentions; F-Measure is the weighted harmonic average of Precision and Recall. The results are shown in Table 5.

Table 5. Algorithm evaluation

Algorithm	Accuracy rate	Recall rate	F value
No expression information	83%	84.6%	83.8%
Have expression information	93.3%	93.9%	93.6%

Table 6. Algorithm comparison

	Interactive intention recognition using reference [22]	Ours
No expression information	86.3%	92.8%
Have expression information	85.9%	93.3%

It is not difficult to see from the above experimental results that the user intent recognition algorithm based on line of sight direction and expression information proposed in this paper can effectively identify the user's interaction intention.

In addition, the expression recognition algorithm in the algorithm is replaced by the algorithm in the literature [22], and the interaction intention is identified. The results of the comparison with the algorithm are shown in Table 6.

5   Conclusion

This paper presents an interactive intention recognition algorithm which combines facial expression features and line-of-sight direction. The experimental results show that the performance of intention recognition algorithm is significantly improved after adding expression recognition. The method proposed in this paper is limited to single person's interactive intention discrimination, and does not discriminate multi-person scenarios. The next step is to improve the method of human-computer interaction intention discrimination in multi-person scenarios and complex environments.

References

1. Adams Jr., R.B., Kleck, R.E.: Perceived gaze direction and the processing of facial displays of emotion. Psychol. Sci. **14**(6), 644–647 (2003)
2. Adolphs, R.: Recognizing emotion from facial expressions: psychological and neurological mechanisms. Behav. Cogn. Neurosci. Rev. **1**(1), 21–62 (2002)
3. Argyle, M., Ingham, R.: Gaze, mutual gaze, and proximity. Semiotica **6**(1), 32–49 (1972)
4. Armentano, M.G., Amandi, A.: Plan recognition for interface agents. Artif. Intell. Rev. **28**(2), 131–162 (2007)
5. Baxter, P., Kennedy, J., Senft, E., Lemaignan, S., Belpaeme, T.: From characterising three years of HRI to methodology and reporting recommendations. In: 2016 11th ACM/IEEE International Conference on Human-Robot Interaction (HRI), pp. 391–398. IEEE (2016)
6. Charniak, E., Goldman, R.P.: A bayesian model of plan recognition. Artif. Intell. **64**(1), 53–79 (1993)
7. Dutta, V., Zielinska, T.: Predicting the intention of human activities for real-time human-robot interaction (HRI). In: Agah, A., Cabibihan, J.-J., Howard, A.M., Salichs, M.A., He, H. (eds.) ICSR 2016. LNCS (LNAI), vol. 9979, pp. 723–734. Springer, Cham (2016). https://doi.org/10.1007/978-3-319-47437-3_71
8. Ekman, P., Friesen, W.V., Hager, J.C.: Facial action coding system: The manual on CD-ROM. A Human Face, Salt Lake City, pp. 77–254 (2002)
9. Goldin-Meadow, S.: The role of gesture in communication and thinking. Trends Cogn. Sci. **3**(11), 419–429 (1999)
10. Goodrich, M.A., Schultz, A.C., et al.: Human-robot interaction: a survey. Found. Trends Hum. Comput. Interact. **1**(3), 203–275 (2008)
11. Heinze, C.: Modelling intention recognition for intelligent agent systems. Technical report, defence science and technology organisation salisbury (Australia) systems... (2004)

12. Lucey, P., Cohn, J.F., Kanade, T., Saragih, J., Ambadar, Z., Matthews, I.: The extended cohn-kanade dataset (ck+): a complete dataset for action unit and emotion-specified expression. In: 2010 IEEE Computer Society Conference on Computer Vision and Pattern Recognition-Workshops, pp. 94–101. IEEE (2010)
13. McNeill, D.: Hand and Mind: What Gestures Reveal About Thought. University of Chicago Press, Chicago (1992)
14. Menne, I.M., Lugrin, B.: In the face of emotion: a behavioral study on emotions towards a robot using the facial action coding system. In: Proceedings of the Companion of the 2017 ACM/IEEE International Conference on Human-Robot Interaction, pp. 205–206. ACM (2017)
15. Ming, G.: Research on Oriental Emotion Recognition Based on Dynamic Facial Expressions. Master's thesis, University of Electronic Science and Technology (2016)
16. Novikova, J., Watts, L.: Towards artificial emotions to assist social coordination in HRI. Int. J. Social Robot. 7(1), 77–88 (2015)
17. Nurmi, J.E., Toivonen, S., Salmela-Aro, K., Eronen, S.: Optimistic, approach-oriented, and avoidance strategies in social situations: three studies on loneliness and peer relationships. Eur. J. Pers. 10(3), 201–219 (1996)
18. O'Haire, H.E.: The influence of gaze direction on approach-vs. avoidance-oriented emotions. Inquiries J. 3(03) (2011)
19. Ryoo, M.S., Matthies, L.: First-person activity recognition: What are they doing to me? In: Proceedings of the IEEE Conference on Computer Vision and Pattern Recognition, pp. 2730–2737 (2013)
20. Sigalas, M., Pateraki, M., Trahanias, P.: Visual estimation of attentive cues in HRI: the case of torso and head pose. In: Nalpantidis, L., Krüger, V., Eklundh, J.-O., Gasteratos, A. (eds.) ICVS 2015. LNCS, vol. 9163, pp. 375–388. Springer, Cham (2015). https://doi.org/10.1007/978-3-319-20904-3_34
21. Wood, E., Baltrusaitis, T., Zhang, X., Sugano, Y., Robinson, P., Bulling, A.: Rendering of eyes for eye-shape registration and gaze estimation. In: Proceedings of the IEEE International Conference on Computer Vision, pp. 3756–3764 (2015)
22. Yang, P., Liu, Q., Metaxas, D.N.: Exploring facial expressions with compositional features. In: 2010 IEEE Computer Society Conference on Computer Vision and Pattern Recognition, pp. 2638–2644. IEEE (2010)

Text and Multimedia Mining

Mining Summary of Short Text with Centroid Similarity Distance

Nigel Franciscus[✉], Junhu Wang, and Bela Stantic

Institute for Integrated and Intelligent Systems, Brisbane, QLD, Australia
{n.franciscus,j.wang,b.stantic}@griffith.edu.au

Abstract. Text summarization aims at producing a concise summary that preserves key information. Many textual inputs are short and do not fit with the standard longer text-based techniques. Most of the existing short text summarization approaches rely on metadata information such as the authors or reply networks. However, not all raw textual data can provide such information. In this paper, we present our method to summarize short text using a centroid-based method with word embeddings. In particular, we consider the task when there is no metadata information other than the text itself. We show that the centroid embeddings approach can be applied to short text to capture semantically similar sentences for summarization. With further clustering strategy, we were able to identify relevant sub-topics that further improves the context diversity in the overall summary. The empirical evaluation demonstrates that our approach can outperform other methods on two annotated LREC track dataset.

Keywords: Text summarization · Short text · Word embeddings

1 Introduction

With the growth and advances of Web 2.0, people can share and obtain textual information quickly from many sources. The abundance of textual data on the internet, in particular, short text, creates a large scale information overload. With too much information to digest, there is an increasing demand to provide an efficient tool to enable readers to quickly identify and summarize the important events around their area of interest. Summarization in the short text domain such as social media, forums, and blogs, can be considered as a special case of text summarization due to its broad contexts. It is conventionally defined as discovering the primary 'gist' or core synopsis by generating short, concise, and informative summaries covering important information from the content of documents.

In the past, automatic summarization of longer documents has been researched extensively. However, when applied to the short text, the summary oftentimes is of poor quality due to its sparsity nature. One common approach in handling short text is to concatenate short text into a collection of (longer)

© Springer Nature Switzerland AG 2019
J. Li et al. (Eds.): ADMA 2019, LNAI 11888, pp. 447–461, 2019.
https://doi.org/10.1007/978-3-030-35231-8_32

text, and process them using traditional summarization method such as MEAD centroid [18], Graph-based - LexRank [7] and TextRank [14], and SumBasic [23]. While these approaches yield good results with longer texts, they do not always work well with short text. Some approaches consider the metadata information such as temporal signals, author influential score, and network information [4,10]. However, these approaches can only be applied to texts having those attributes.

When relying on pure text, there is a need to represent words and sentences into computable information. Word Embeddings [15,17] introduce a solution by projecting words in a semantic space based on their relationship with each other using a shallow neural network. Word embedding represents a continuous vector representation that can capture syntactic and semantic information of a word. For example, the nearest neighbor of a word frog are "[toad, litoria, leptodactylidae, rana, lizard, and eleutherodactylus]". Figure 1 shows another example where word embeddings can capture word similarity according to its categories, such as cities and governmental entities. Based on this information, sentences that have the same topic can be clustered automatically.

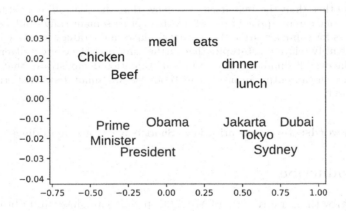

Fig. 1. Capturing similarity from word embeddings

Based on the assumption that words share a similar topic tend to appear closer in the embedding space, we propose CEmbed: a simple but effective short text summarization technique based on the embeddings centroid. The idea of utilizing word embeddings centroid for extractive summarization was first introduced in [20]. The primary hypothesis is that the centroid represents a pseudo-document which condenses the meaningful information of a document. However, the original method is not suitable when applied to short text. The most notable issue is that in short text the sentences are more scattered into many sub-topics where a single centroid is not sufficient to represent the summary. Thus, we need to improve the diversity in summaries by considering multiple centroids to represent sub-topics.

Contribution. We propose a short text summarization method by exploiting the centroid assumption in combination with word embeddings. We were able to detect multiple topics/sub-topics to improve diversity in summary. We conduct an empirical evaluation using two annotated short text datasets to compare our approach with the existing popular techniques. The experiment validated our method by an improvement in summarization evaluation metrics.

Organization. The rest of the paper is organized as follows: in Sect. 2, we present some related work; in Sect. 3, we explain the summarization method proposed; in Sect. 4, we provide the experiment results along with the evaluation discussion; and finally in Sect. 5 we conclude the findings and indicate the future work.

2 Related Work

2.1 Short Text Summarization

One way of handling short text is to concatenate short text into a collection of (longer) text, and then process them using traditional summarization methods such as MEAD, LexRank, or SumBasic. These techniques are practical and suitable for a longer article where many words are overlapping but do not work well due to sparsity issue in short text. Phrase Reinforcement with Hybrid TF-IDF algorithm was introduced to overcome the sparsity by considering each short text as a single document [21]. More recent approaches explore to utilize microblog social features such as number of replies, number of retweets, author popularity (i.e., number of followers or influential score), and temporal signals [4]. Similarly, the work in [10] exploits the network information between user posts. In contrast, our work considers text without metadata information (e.g., temporal, user info) since not all short text has rich properties and are networked. For example, news blog [2], meetings reconstruction [24], or blog/microblogs comments with low interconnected network like reviews [28].

2.2 Word Embeddings

Word embeddings stands for a continuous vector representation that can capture syntactic and semantic information of a word. The use of word embeddings for short text can be tracked back to text similarity [5,11]. In [20], the centroid is computed directly from the embeddings with the help of tf-idf based on the selected topic. However, it is not clear whether it can identify the sub-topics that may exist. Multi-document bag-of-words [13] shows that sentence embeddings with Distributed Bag of Words (DBOW) outperformed the Distributed Model (DM) on longer DUC article dataset. Finally, The work in [22] measures ROUGE performance on different word embeddings approaches where it suggests that further layer on top of embeddings may be required. On top of these previous work, we fit the centroid-based method with a distributed representation of sentences where we employ clustering to generate multiple centroids and overcome the limitation of sub-topics diversity. We confirm that DBOW also works well with the short text.

2.3   Short Text Clustering

To this date, a large number of clustering algorithms have been proposed with KNN (K-Nearest Neighbours) and K-Means as some of the most famous ones. Among those, given the problem of clustering short documents, Dirichlet multinomial mixture clustering model [27], Biterm Topic Modeling (BTM) [25] have been shown to perform well on short text. These approaches acknowledge that as the number of words in short documents is limited, and each word in the same document can be assigned to one topic. Then documents assigned to the same topic are in the same cluster. Topic models often correlate with text clustering as the objective is quite similar. Some other relevant topic models applied to short text are including [26,29,30]. The purpose of topic modeling is to discover the hidden thematic structure in a collection of documents, and it is quite limited when it comes to a deeper understanding of the content.

3   Method

In this section, we present our proposed method. Here, we refer to each short text or tweet as a sentence and a collection of sentences as a document. A document usually has a main topic. The overall processing consists of three steps. First, we conduct the preprocess filtering to remove noise and redundancy from the text. Then, we use the word vector to represent sentences. The vector can be trained manually or can be retrieved from the pre-trained corpus. Finally, sentences are clustered and selected based on the distance from the centroid.

3.1   Preprocess Filtering

Preprocessing is the most important part of the pipeline due to the noise in the text. First, for each document, we apply the standard procedure such as removing non-alphanumeric elements (e.g., URL, username, punctuation) and inconvertible ASCII characters. We observed that summaries tend to have multiple entities. For example, Fig. 2 shows samples of annotated summary from

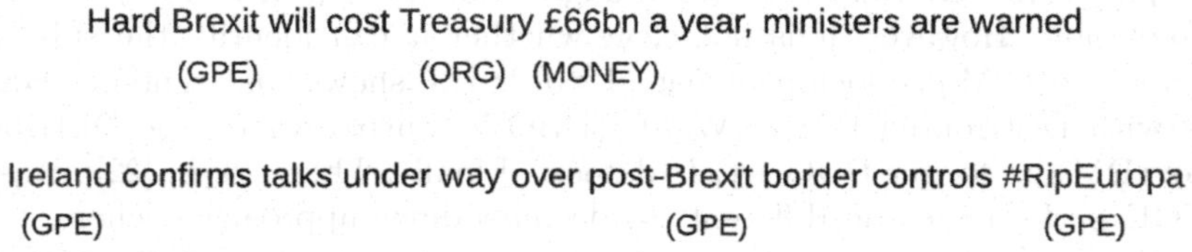

Hard Brexit will cost Treasury £66bn a year, ministers are warned
(GPE)   (ORG) (MONEY)

Ireland confirms talks under way over post-Brexit border controls #RipEuropa
(GPE)   (GPE)   (GPE)

Fig. 2. Extracting named entity recognition

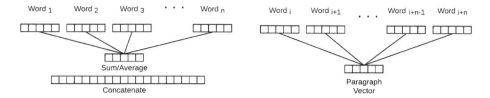

Fig. 3. Pretrained word embeddings   **Fig. 4.** DBOW paragraph vector

Brexit Topic. After applying named entity recognition, we can extract tokens that are classified as entities such as Geopolitical (GPE) or Organization (ORG). Subsequently, we filter out sentences that do not have at least two entities. This process also helps to remove the unimportant sentences when building the sentence embeddings in the next step. Finally, in building the vocabulary, we remove words that have a frequency of less than two.

3.2 Sentence Representation

Traditionally, sentences or documents are represented as a bag of words with TF-IDF, in which a one-hot vector represents a word. In this work, we use word embeddings as the building block to represent texts. There are two ways to use the embeddings vector. First, by using the pre-trained corpus and second, by training the input corpus.

Intuitively, one may use pre-trained word embeddings since it is trained from large amount of corpus. This approach avoids manual training and is suitable when the corpus are updated frequently. To generate the sentence representation, a straightforward method is to aggregate (summing/averaging) or concatenate words that belong to their respective sentence. For example, in Fig. 3, each word w represents a vector which collectively are able to produce its sentence $S = (w_1, w_2, ..., w_n)$. Aggregating embeddings $S = \frac{w_1 - \sum_{i=2}^{n} w_i}{n}$ is the simplest method which yields a same n-dimension vector. On the other hand, concatenating word vectors $S = (w_1 \oplus w_2 \oplus ... \oplus w_n)$ preserves the word order but in return will generate $1 \times n * m$ vector where m is the number or words. In the experiment, we tested different pre-trained embeddings for different dataset.

Another option is to train the word embeddings based on the input dataset. Since we want to represent sentence, instead of computing the word vector from scratch, the better option is to build the paragraph vector [12] directly. Paragraph vector resembles the word vectors, except that a classifier uses an additional paragraph identifier to predict words. During training, paragraph vectors are randomly initialized and updated by sampling the word vector in a skip-gram window. In short text, sentences usually have an average length of 10 words after preprocessing. As such, the paragraph vector or the sentence vector samples their own words at least once. As suggested in [13] we use the distributed bag-of-words (DBOW) implementation approach since it is more suitable for short text.

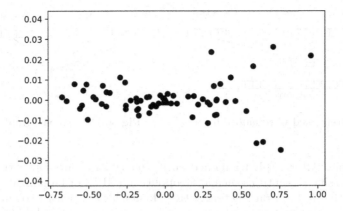

Fig. 5. Sample of sentence projection with PCA

3.3   Embeddings Centroid

The diversity of the sentences are visible through the scattered points when they are mapped into Euclidean space (Fig. 5). If we compute the centroid directly, some of the important sentences will not be selected. Semantically related terms that co-occur together should be captured through density. To solve this problem, we divide the sentences into their own group and categorize using a simple clustering algorithm.

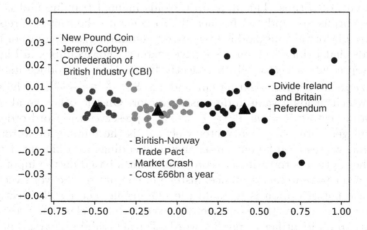

Fig. 6. Generating multiple centroid with clustering (Color figure online)

We use the clustering algorithm to split the 'topic distribution' further and to maximize the diversity in summary. Initially, we compared k-means with faster implementation of density-based clustering HDBSCAN [3]. However, in practice, the epsilon parameter is sensitive and difficult to tune. We opt for k-means as the most straightforward method with only one input parameter. To approximate the initial number of k, we use the elbow approach or sum of squared error (SSE) method. Given a range of 1 to 10 as the possible number of k, we iterate the k-means several times to find the most suitable k. Then, we remove clusters with low silhouette score to get the best possible sentence selection. Silhouette score is measured as $\frac{(b-a)}{max(a,b)}$ where a is the mean intra-cluster distance and b is the mean of nearest-cluster (minimum) distance for each sample. A high silhouette score often indicates a dense cluster where the sentences are semantically more similar. The remaining clusters will most likely capture some sub-topics that represent each of them. For example, based on Brexit parent topic Fig. 6 reveals three sub-topics each with its centroid. The first (red) and second (yellow)

Algorithm 1: EMBEDDINGCENTROID

Input: a collection of preprocessed document D, maximum sentence selection k, minimum sentence length len, minimum entity occurence ent, silhouette threshold ϕ

Output: Summaries $Summ$

1   List $L \leftarrow \emptyset$

2   **for** *each* sentence $s_i \in D$ **do**

3   **if** $Length(s_i) > len$ **and** $Entity(s_i) > ent$ **then**

4   add s_i to L

5   **end**

6   **end**

7

8   Embeddings Vector Space $E \leftarrow \emptyset$

9   Train Paragraph Vector PV

10   $E \leftarrow PV(L)$

11

12   Candidate $R \leftarrow \emptyset$

13   Clusters $C = \text{KMeans}(E)$

14   **for** *each cluster* $c_i \in C$ **do**

15   **if** $SilhouetteScore < \phi$ **then**

16   continue

17   **end**

18   Compute *centroid*

19   **while** *argmin sort (centroid distance)* $< k$ **do** // closest from centroid

20   **if** *sim(s$_i$, s$_{i+1}$)* > 0.85 **then** // similarity score

21   add $s_i \in c_i$ to R

22            $k++$

23   **end**

24   **end**

25   **end**

26   merge R into $Summ$

27   **return** $Summ$

sub-topic talk about Jeremy Corbyn with CBI and the Brexit impact on European market respectively. Similarly, the third sub-topic (blue) talks about Ireland and Britain referendum, although it indicates a weaker relationship between sentences compared to the previous two where the points are more scattered.

The overall process can be represented in Algorithm 1. On average, a good number of clusters (number of k) generated should not be more than three which is usually validated by SSE. In the case of a higher number of cluster, we increase the silhouette threshold (Line 15). Often, this means that the input document has a higher level of diversity in topic/sub-topics where additional filtering might be necessary.

Sentence Scoring. After we establish the centroid vector for each cluster, we select the closest top-k sentences from each of the centroids. In the experiment, we vary the number of k; on average, the best selection is around the range of four to six sentences. For each sentence selection, standard cosine similarity (threshold > 0.85) is used to remove nearly similar sentences (Line 20). Note that in the benchmark comparison, we record the time after building the paragraph vector.

4   Experiments

4.1   Datasets and Preprocessing

One common problem in evaluating short text summarization is the availability of a standard benchmark dataset. In the experiment, we use two types of annotated datasets from the LREC track; one is Twitter while the other one consist of BBC and Guardian news live blog. The Twitter dataset [16] comprises parent topics such as Brexit, ISIS, and the presidential election. Each topic consists of several child-topics; for example, Brexit has immigration and political parties as the sub-topics. In the experiment, we process each child topic independently and later aggregate the score. For the second dataset, we include the live blog from [2]. A live blog is a dynamic news article providing rolling textual coverage of an ongoing event and is continuously updated by journalists. In the end, the author will generate a summary for the respective article.

Initially, Any non-ASCII characters, URLs, and metadata (e.g., author, hashtags) were removed to reduce the noise. We notice that the hashtags are often abused and hampered the word position when building the word graph. Standard Cosine similarity without embedding (threshold $= 0.9$) was also used to remove duplicate tweets (overlapping words). Finally, we apply tokenization with stopwords removal to build the dictionary. The average length after preprocessing is approximately ten tokens for each tweet and 60–100 tokens for each snippet in the news blog. For the pre-trained word embeddings, we choose word2vec implementation of Google News corpus with 3 million unique vocabularies[1]. While for the Twitter dataset, we use the Glove implementation based on Twitter corpus[2].

---

[1] https://code.google.com/archive/p/word2vec/.
[2] https://nlp.stanford.edu/projects/glove/.

Parameter Setting. For the paragraph vector, we use the DBOW model with vector size of 300. A window size of sampling follows the average length of sentences, which is 12. The minimum frequency for vocabulary construction is two tokens, and the total iteration to train vector is set to 100. For k-means, we initialise the centroid with k-means++ [1] with maximum iteration set to 100. Implementation is written in Python by relying on scikit-learn[3], gensim [19] and SpaCy[4] libraries.

4.2   Baselines

We performed a comparison with the widely used extractive text summarization. In particular, we compare our approach with other techniques that rely on pure text without additional metadata information. We tested our approach with two types of word embeddings; one is by using pre-trained corpus and the other one with DBOW paragraph vector.

1. **LexRank** [7], which computes sentence importance based on the concept of eigenvector centrality in a graph representation.
2. **TextRank** [14], a graph-based ranking algorithm for phrases and sentence extraction.
3. **LSA** (Latent Semantic Analysis) [6] is an old but popular approach involving a dimensionality reduction of the term-document matrix with singular value decomposition.
4. **KL-Greedy** [9] minimizes the Kullback-Leibler (KL) divergence between the word distributions in summary and the documents.
5. **h-TFIDF** [21] a modified TF-IDF to compensate short text sparsity by considering each short text as a single document.
6. **ICSI** [8] a global linear optimization that extracts a summary by solving a maximum coverage problem using the most frequent bigrams in the source documents.

We can feed the input to these techniques directly since all documents are aggregated based on their particular topic. For comparison, we calculate two upper bounds as suggested in [2]. The upper bound for extractive summarization is measured by solving the Integer Linear Programming (ILP) based on maximum coverage of n-grams from the reference summary. Similarly, we use the size of 1-gram and 2-grams with the maximum length of summary according to the annotation. The upper bound can be seen as the optimum value of overlapping words, the closer to the upper-bound the better.

---

[3] https://scikit-learn.org.
[4] https://spacy.io/.

Table 1. ROUGE metrics evaluation for text summarization on several approaches compared to the extractive upper bounds baseline.

Systems	Twitter	BBC			Guardian		
	R1	R1	R2	SU4	R1	R2	SU4
UB-1	.525	.484	.229	.228	.379	.158	.156
UB-2	.512	.471	.275	.247	.363	.210	.172
TF-IDF	.325	.219	.046	.070	.137	.019	.034
LexRank	.431	.259	.068	.092	.179	.032	.048
TextRank	.474	.203	.039	.065	.150	.024	.039
LSA	.443	.210	.030	.058	.123	.010	.027
KL	.382	.225	.047	.072	.157	.024	.040
h-TFIDF	.455	.262	.069	.095	.184	.035	.048
ICSI	.475	**.289**	**.087**	.105	.199	.047	.052
CEmbed (Pretrained)	.439	.253	.058	.091	.201	.045	.058
CEmbed (PV-DBOW)	**.509**	.286	.063	**.115**	**.226**	**.059**	**.066**

4.3 Evaluation Metrics

We run the ROUGE (Recall-Oriented Understudy for Gisting Evaluation) metrics which measures summary quality by counting overlapping units such as n-grams word sequences and word pairs between the system generated summary and the gold standard summary (annotated). ROUGE precision is calculated as:

$$ROUGE - N = \frac{\sum_{s \in M} \sum_{n-grams \in s} match(n - gram)}{\sum_{s \in M} \sum_{n-grams \in s} count(n - gram)}$$

We choose ROUGE-N and ROUGE-SU4 in our experiments. To be specific, ROUGE-N is an n-gram recall (1-gram and 2 grams) and ROUGE-SU4 is a unigram plus skip-bigram match with maximum skip distance of 4 between a system generated summary and a set of model summaries. Only ROUGE-1 is used for Twitter since the summaries are in the form of tweets and we only compare the precision of summaries and the original tweets.

4.4 Quantitative Evaluation

We report the ROUGE metrics on several techniques as a comparison in Table 1. Based on the observation, we can conclude the following findings:

- When combined with word embeddings, centroid technique is still a competitive approach in handling short text. When properly tuned, word embeddings help to cluster semantically similar terms to discover sub-topics further.
- Training corpus appears to outperform the pre-trained corpus by a small margin. We also observed that the preprocessing plays a significant part,

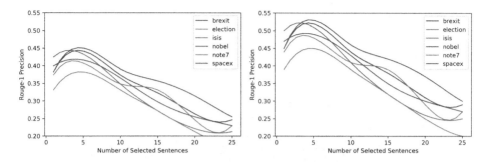

Fig. 7. Effect of sentence selection on Twitter rouge-1 precision. Pre-trained embeddings (left), paragraph vector (right)

especially in eliminating noise. As mentioned previously, we only include the sentences contain at least three entities. The summaries produced by annotator are more inclined to the facts where there are likely to have subjects and objects.

- Among all methods, ICSI shows a comparable performance where it outperformed other approaches, especially on news dataset, although by a small margin compared to the popular TextRank and LexRank. Small margins improvements indicate that short text is still a challenging task.

Number of Sentence Selection. We vary the number of sentence selection from each cluster and compare the effect of ROUGE precision. The number of cluster was kept small around 3 to 4 cluster for each topic - the closer to the centroid, the more relevant the sentences to the sub-topic. On average, optimal selections are shown to be between 4 to 6 sentences (Fig. 7). A higher selection should improve the recall but may overlap with other clusters. Note that if the similarity between sentences during selection is high, the latter selection should be discarded to maximize diversity. Training corpus has a slightly better correlation with ROUGE performance compared to pre-trained as reflected in the overall performance evaluation.

Efficiency in Generating Summary. In Fig. 8 we measure the time to produce a summary for each document. Since the length of each document differs in each dataset, we report the average time. The longest approach was ICSI due to ILP optimization. Both TextRank and LexRank have similar computation time followed by centroid (CEmbed), KL, LSA, and TF-IDF. For our approach, we use the one with the best ROUGE score which is the PV-DBOW. Surprisingly, once the documents are trained, the centroid computation time is quite similar to other approaches. K-means with silhouette score does not take too much time when the inputs are small. We also observed that ICSI and KL are fluctuating, especially when the document input is large.

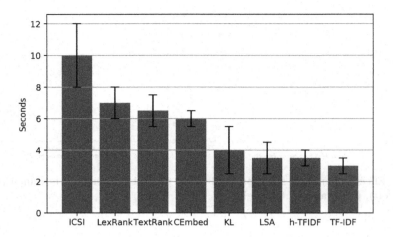

Fig. 8. Time spent generating summary per document

4.5   Qualitative Evaluation

To further investigate the quality of the summary, we select one of the system generated summaries as the use case. For example, in Fig. 9 a summary was taken from the Brexit topic where the related keywords or phrases are highlighted in blue and red. We can observe that most of the critical event such as 'Brexit could cost £66bm a year', 'JCB leaves CBI', and 'Norway rejects post-Brexit trade pact with UK' are directly mentioned. While other events such as 'Brexit may cause market crash' and 'sovereignty in the referendum' are partially mentioned and still relevant. Some relevant events such as Britain and Ireland and the new pound coin are mentioned although still not clear to interpret. Furthermore, the system was able to pick up the important events but were not considered in the reference, for example, 'Theresa May totalitarian approach'.

Overall, most of the important events or keywords are mentioned in the summary. We expect the system to benefit from the sub-topics sampling after the clustering process. The ROUGE score above 0.5 should indicate half of the overlapping words. However, most selected sentences are relevant and have a higher degree of similarity.

It is worth mentioning that most extractive approaches generate summaries by selecting important keywords with or without the word order. After that, they find a sentence or tweet that best represent the important keywords, usually by maximizing the most overlapping words. This is indeed similar to selecting meaningful sentences or tweets to generate summaries as it constructs the original document. In the end, it remains challenging to preserve grammatical structure in short text summarization, especially for microblogs. We observed that users tend to write in a compressed, informative news headline style. We expect the combination of both extractive and abstractive should provide a better summary in terms of keywords and grammatical aspect.

Reference	System Generated
Hard Brexit will cost Treasury up to £66bn a year, ministers are told..	TIMES FRONT PAGE 'Hard Brexit could cost £66bn a year' #skypapers.
Parliament is not sovereign but Brexit will restore its sovereignty.. 'Taking the Fear out of Brexit' (full length) #EU #brexit #referendum #voteleave..	Crazy Tory #Brexit notion that 'bringing back sovereignty' equals bypassing parliament Scrutiny accountability and role o....
Norway rejects post-Brexit trade pact with UK via #Sterling..	Brexit May Crash 2017's Market - The GuardianBrexit May Crash 2017's Ma... #market #news.
JCB leaves CBI 'over Brexit stance'..	Liam Fox approached Norway on a new free trade deal - Norway said no. #Brexit.
Leave voters are losers too.. BBC News - Peter Lilley on #Brexit: Remain voters are 'bad losers'..	"We will reject any attempt to keep Britain in the EU by the back door" rejects calls for a parliamentary....
Hard #Brexit risks damaging UK's open economy, says CBI chief..	JCB leaves CBI 'over Brexit stance': The construction firm JCB has left the business lobby group, the CBI...
To celebrate Brexit, Britain is producing a new pound coin.. "We will reject any attempt to keep Britain in the EU by the back door" rejects calls for a parliamentary v.....	#Brexit plan 2 divide Britain + Ireland.
Brexit Chief Says the Pound's Fall Is Good for U.K..	Brexit Chief Says the Pound's Fall Is Good for U.K. Exporters - Bloomberg: BloombergBrexit Chief Says the Pou....
Ireland's government is promising to "Brexit-proof" the economy when it delivers its Budget tomorrow..	Norway rejects post-Brexit trade pact with UK via #Sterling.
Any 'Brexit' is worse than simple economic vandalism; in addition, the sovereignty of parliament, one might consider, is being.....	#Brexit terms belong to All British people -The public will not accept Theresa May's totalitarian approach #bbcnews.
Consumers are being warned that shop prices may have to rise substantially following Brexit..	

Fig. 9. Reference and sample generated summary. Related keywords are highlighted (Color figure online)

5 Conclusion

We presented the centroid method for short text summarization using word embeddings. Within the scheme, we investigated the text similarity distance, in particular using both training or pre-trained corpus to generate clusters. Overall, training the documents with paragraph vector produced better clusters due to better interpretation with the current dataset. By using a simple clustering such as k-means, we were able to detect sub-topics through each cluster and aggregate them to improve the overall summary. Through the practical implementation and evaluation in our experiments and by using two annotated dataset, we showed the effectiveness of the centroid of the cluster, especially for the short text. Some future works include an effective way to handle social media hashtags as they tend to be abused by users. We also plan to test the ROUGE metrics using word

embeddings to improve the judgement when there are no overlapping words but
semantically similar.

References

1. Arthur, D., Vassilvitskii, S.: k-means++: the advantages of careful seeding. In:
   Proceedings of the Eighteenth Annual ACM-SIAM Symposium on Discrete Algorithms, pp. 1027–1035. Society for Industrial and Applied Mathematics (2007)
2. Avinesh, P., Peyrard, M., Meyer, C.M.: Live blog corpus for summarization. In:
   Proceedings of the Eleventh International Conference on Language Resources and
   Evaluation (LREC) (2018)
3. Campello, R.J.G.B., Moulavi, D., Sander, J.: Density-based clustering based on
   hierarchical density estimates. In: Pei, J., Tseng, V.S., Cao, L., Motoda, H., Xu, G.
   (eds.) PAKDD 2013. LNCS (LNAI), vol. 7819, pp. 160–172. Springer, Heidelberg
   (2013). https://doi.org/10.1007/978-3-642-37456-2_14
4. Chang, Y., Tang, J., Yin, D., Yamada, M., Liu, Y.: Timeline summarization from
   social media with life cycle models. In: IJCAI, pp. 3698–3704 (2016)
5. De Boom, C., Van Canneyt, S., Demeester, T., Dhoedt, B.: Representation learning
   for very short texts using weighted word embedding aggregation. Pattern Recogn.
   Lett. **80**, 150–156 (2016)
6. Deerwester, S., Dumais, S.T., Furnas, G.W., Landauer, T.K., Harshman, R.: Indexing by latent semantic analysis. J. Am. Soc. Inf. Sci. **41**(6), 391–407 (1990)
7. Erkan, G., Radev, D.R.: Lexrank: Graph-based lexical centrality as salience in text
   summarization. J. Artif. Intell. Res. **22**, 457–479 (2004)
8. Gillick, D., Favre, B.: A scalable global model for summarization. In: Proceedings
   of the Workshop on Integer Linear Programming for Natural Langauge Processing,
   pp. 10–18. Association for Computational Linguistics (2009)
9. Haghighi, A., Vanderwende, L.: Exploring content models for multi-document summarization. In: Proceedings of Human Language Technologies: the 2009 Annual
   Conference of the North American Chapter of the Association for Computational
   Linguistics, pp. 362–370. Association for Computational Linguistics (2009)
10. He, R., Duan, X.: Twitter summarization based on social network and sparse recon-
    struction. In: Thirty-Second AAAI Conference on Artificial Intelligence (2018)
11. Kenter, T., De Rijke, M.: Short text similarity with word embeddings. In: Proceed-
    ings of the 24th ACM International on Conference on Information and Knowledge
    Management, pp. 1411–1420. ACM (2015)
12. Le, Q., Mikolov, T.: Distributed representations of sentences and documents. In:
    International Conference on Machine Learning, pp. 1188–1196 (2014)
13. Mani, K., Verma, I., Meisheri, H., Dey, L.: Multi-document summarization using
    distributed bag-of-words model. In: 2018 IEEE/WIC/ACM International Confer-
    ence on Web Intelligence (WI), pp. 672–675. IEEE (2018)
14. Mihalcea, R., Tarau, P.: Textrank: Bringing order into text. In: Proceedings of the
    2004 Conference on Empirical Methods in Natural Language Processing (2004)
15. Mikolov, T., Sutskever, I., Chen, K., Corrado, G.S., Dean, J.: Distributed repre-
    sentations of words and phrases and their compositionality. In: Advances in Neural
    Information Processing Systems, pp. 3111–3119 (2013)
16. Nguyen, M.-T., Lai, D.V., Nguyen, H.T., Le Nguyen, M.: Tsix: a human-involved-
    creation dataset for tweet summarization. In: Proceedings of the Eleventh Inter-
    national Conference on Language Resources and Evaluation (LREC) (2018)

17. Pennington, J., Socher, R., Manning, C.: Glove: Global vectors for word representation. In: Proceedings of the 2014 Conference on Empirical Methods in Natural Language Processing (EMNLP), pp. 1532–1543 (2014)
18. Radev, D.R., Jing, H., Styś, M., Tam, D.: Centroid-based summarization of multiple documents. Inf. Process. Manag. **40**(6), 919–938 (2004)
19. Řehůřek, R., Sojka, P.: Software framework for topic modelling with large corpora. In: Proceedings of the LREC 2010 Workshop on New Challenges for NLP Frameworks, pp. 45–50. ELRA, Valletta, May 2010. http://is.muni.cz/publication/884893/en
20. Rossiello, G., Basile, P., Semeraro, G.: Centroid-based text summarization through compositionality of word embeddings. In: Proceedings of the MultiLing 2017 Workshop on Summarization and Summary Evaluation Across Source Types and Genres, pp. 12–21 (2017)
21. Sharifi, B.P., Inouye, D.I., Kalita, J.K.: Summarization of twitter microblogs. Comput. J. **57**(3), 378–402 (2013)
22. Templeton, A., Kalita, J.: Exploring sentence vector spaces through automatic summarization. In: 2018 17th IEEE International Conference on Machine Learning and Applications (ICMLA), pp. 55–60. IEEE (2018)
23. Vanderwende, L., Suzuki, H., Brockett, C., Nenkova, A.: Beyond sumbasic: task-focused summarization with sentence simplification and lexical expansion. Inf. Process. Manag. **43**(6), 1606–1618 (2007)
24. Wang, L., Cardie, C.: Domain-independent abstract generation for focused meeting summarization. In: Proceedings of the 51st Annual Meeting of the Association for Computational Linguistics (Volume 1: Long Papers), vol. 1, pp. 1395–1405 (2013)
25. Yan, X., Guo, J., Lan, Y., Cheng, X.: A biterm topic model for short texts. In: Proceedings of the 22nd International Conference on World Wide Web, pp. 1445–1456. ACM (2013)
26. Yang, Y., Wang, F., Zhang, J., Xu, J., Philip, S.Y.: A topic model for co-occurring normal documents and short texts. World Wide Web **21**(2), 487–513 (2018)
27. Yin, J., Wang, J.: A dirichlet multinomial mixture model-based approach for short text clustering. In: Proceedings of the 20th ACM SIGKDD International Conference on Knowledge Discovery and Data Mining, pp. 233–242. ACM (2014)
28. Yu, N., Huang, M., Shi, Y., et al.: Product review summarization by exploiting phrase properties. In: Proceedings of COLING 2016, the 26th International Conference on Computational Linguistics: Technical Papers, pp. 1113–1124 (2016)
29. Zuo, Y., et al.: Topic modeling of short texts: a pseudo-document view. In: Proceedings of the 22nd ACM SIGKDD International Conference on Knowledge Discovery and Data Mining, pp. 2105–2114. ACM (2016)
30. Zuo, Y., Zhao, J., Xu, K.: Word network topic model: a simple but general solution for short and imbalanced texts. Knowl. Inf. Syst. **48**(2), 379–398 (2016)

Children's Speaker Recognition Method Based on Multi-dimensional Features

Ning Jia[1]([⊠]), Chunjun Zheng[1,2], and Wei Sun[1]

[1] Dalian Neusoft University of Information, Dalian, Liaoning, China
jianing@neusoft.edu.cn
[2] Dalian Maritime University, Dalian, Liaoning, China

Abstract. In life, the voice signals collected by people are essentially mixed signals, which mainly include information related to speaker characteristics, such as gender, age and emotional state. The commonality and characteristics of traditional single-dimensional speaker information recognition are analyzed, and children's individualized analysis is carried out for common acoustic feature parameters such as prosodic features, sound quality features and spectral-based features. Therefore, considering the temporal characteristics of voice, combined with the Time-Delay Neural Network (TDNN) model, Bidirectional Long Short-Term Memory model and the attention mechanism, the multi-channel model is trained to form a speaker recognition problem solution for children's speaker recognition. A large number of experimental results show that on the basis of guaranteeing the accuracy of age and gender recognition, higher accuracy of children's voiceprint recognition can be obtained.

Keywords: Children's speaker recognition · Bidirectional Long Short-Term Memory · Time delay neural network · Attention mechanism

1 Introduction

Speech is a unique way for human beings to communicate with information, thoughts, emotions and opinions. It is one of the fastest and most effective communication tools for human beings. Most current automatic speech recognition systems focus on adult speech recognition, and these systems have different performance degradations for children's speech recognition. Therefore, on the basis of existing identification technologies, it is particularly important to study children's speech recognition related technologies.

It is well known that while listening to a voice signal, it is possible to acquire multi-dimensional voice information such as who is speaking, what is being spoken, and the voice of the surrounding environment when speaking. This is because the voice signal collected in the daily environment is actually a mixed signal. The mixed signal usually contains three types of information: the content which contained in the voice, the information which related to the speaker characteristics (including gender, age, identity, and emotion) contained in the voice and the background environment sound information which mixed with the voice. Therefore, people have generalized speech recognition technology, including speech content recognition, speaker identification,

© Springer Nature Switzerland AG 2019
J. Li et al. (Eds.): ADMA 2019, LNAI 11888, pp. 462–473, 2019.
https://doi.org/10.1007/978-3-030-35231-8_33

speaker emotion recognition, language recognition, voice search, speech scoring and many other recognition tasks.

At present, speech recognition is the recognition of single information or content, such as speaker recognition, semantic recognition or emotional recognition. There are few models of multi-task interaction and co-promotion. This is due to the different characteristics selected between different tasks, which leads to some obstacles in communication between tasks.

However, if all kinds of speech recognition tasks work independently, they will not be conducive to understanding the emotions of speech expression, promoting the development of voice communication and dialogue system, recognizing personal information related to speakers, and improving the robustness of speech recognition, especially for children, because they are special voices. Identify groups [1].

Children's voice characteristics are significantly different from those of adults. With the increase of age, the difference of different acoustic characteristics is also changing, and this change is divergent. Therefore, the task of speaker recognition based on multi-dimensional information is difficult. If it is applied to children's age group, it will be more difficult.

Therefore, a children speaker recognition model based on multi-dimensional speech information is proposed. Multidimensional voice information mainly comes from age, gender and identity of the speaker. Through children's voiceprint information, the speaker's age and gender can be recognized jointly. On the basis of ensuring the accuracy of the two information, the accuracy of voiceprint recognition can be further improved. In this way, the synchronization and high-precision discrimination of multiple tasks can be realized through a voice input.

2   Related Work

Speaker identification, which is also named voiceprint recognition, is a voice parameter that reflects the physiological and behavioral characteristics of the speaker according to the voice waveform. It is a recognition technology that automatically identifies the speakers by the machine. The theoretical basis is the unique characteristic of the feature [2]. Its theoretical basis is the unique characteristic of human voiceprint features [3]. Speaker recognition focuses on the individualized differences between different speakers' voice channels, vocal organs and vocal habits, but has nothing to do with the speech content, i.e. therefore, speaker recognition can be considered as a research topic that integrates many disciplines [4].

The parametric models commonly which was used in speaker recognition are: Hidden Markov Model, Gaussian Model and Gaussian Mixture Model-Universal Background Model (GMM-UBM). Based on Joint Factor Analysis, Dehak and Kenny proposed a more simplified method based on factor analysis (FA) for speaker recognition, which is called i-vector [5].

Speaker recognition technology has developed several research directions in the development process [6]. For different environmental needs, it tends to improve the performance of some aspects of the system. For example, in order to extract more speaker voiceprint features from voice, a voiceprint recognition system is implemented based on a large amount of sufficient voice data to improve the system recognition rate.

In order to enhance the practicability of the system, a real-time speaker recognition system based on scarce data is designed. It is a direction of research on voiceprint recognition technology to achieve a satisfactory recognition effect of voiceprint recognition system under different requirements [7].

Therefore, how to quickly extracting accurate, stable and unique information characterizing voice is a key point in voiceprint recognition research.

By combining multiple modeling methods with researching new modeling methods, proposing more reliable decision strategies is another important difficult in the research of speaker recognition technology.

Gender identification aims at identifying the gender of speakers. It is a technique for automatically discriminating the gender of a speaker by analyzing the waveform signal effectively by computer. It is also a basic subject in the field of speech recognition [8]. In the early days, it was a sub-subject in the field of speaker recognition. Gender recognition of voice signals and speaker recognition based on male and female categories can significantly reduce search space and time, and have great significance in improving the accuracy and processing speed of speaker recognition. Therefore, gender recognition can also be considered as a special task of feature extraction and recognition of acoustic signals.

In the traditional recognition system, the recognition effect of the training corpus with the phoneme or unit sound as the gender recognition in the pure voice environment can reach 88%, and the gender recognition for the telephone voice is as high as 85%.

The recognition rate applied to children's voice is greatly reduced. This is because the fundamental frequency range of male voice is 80–170 Hz, the fundamental frequency range of female is 150–260 Hz, while for children, it is up to 300–500 Hz [9]. Because of the large span and wide range of high frequency, there are always some errors in recognition and judgment. Because of the difference of pitch and base frequency between children and adults, the research on gender recognition of children's voice often has some difficulties. Now, more attention and research are gradually started [10, 11]. Finding a new method for the centralized fusion and the gender recognition, age and region in speech [12] is an important issue for children's voice gender recognition and speaker recognition.

3   Acoustic Characteristics of Children's Voice

During the development of children, the acoustic characteristics of children's voice mainly include the duration of children's voice, pitch, and formants.

3.1   Duration

For children aged 5–8, the vowel pronunciation time is the longest, and the pronunciation time is more variable. After 8 years old, the duration of children's vowel pronunciation tends to be the same as adult. For consonants, children's pronunciation duration and pronunciation time variability tend to be adult at around 11–12 years old.

3.2   Pitch

For children, there is little correlation between baseline frequency and gender, and the baseline frequency is about 240 Hz.

3.3   Formants

The frequency of the Formants (F1, F2, F3) decrease as the child ages. Before the age of about 11, there is a little difference in the resonance peaks between boys and girls. Between 11 and 15 years old, the frequency of formant frequencies of the male children decreased faster than that of the female children. Changes in vocal tract length (or changes in age) are consistent for changes in male and female resonance peaks, and the consistent linear trend is not affected by different vowel pronunciations. For the female children, the different formants have different trends with age, although it is a down-ward trend, not a linear decline. Because of the non-linear relationship between formant and age, some obstacles have been brought to children's acoustic feature recognition.

3.4   Spectral Envelope

For the two repetitions of the same vowel, the spectrum variability of young children is larger than that of adults, and the variability of formants has the same characteristics. This means that the child has not established an optimal vowel pronunciation target in a given context.

For the first half and the second half of the same vowel, the spectrum change of young children is larger than that of adults. It may be because young children have poor co-pronunciation ability, and the pronunciation of vowels is greatly affected by the consonant pronunciation behind it.

Considering that the temporal variability of children's pronunciation in sentences is also close to the adult level at around 12 years old, the time and frequency domain of the voice of the younger children are changeable and not well coordinated, which is not conducive to the generation of the spectrum.

In summary, compared to adults, children's voice has along vowel duration, a high pitch frequency and a formant frequency, and the dynamic range of these parameters is large. The magnitude and variability of these acoustic parameters began to stabilize and mature around the age of 12.

The changing characteristics of these acoustic characteristics are mainly depending on the anatomical maturation of the vocal organs and the voice-related speech motor control, as well as the physiology and social psychology factors also have an impact on changes in acoustic characteristics.

Similar findings have been made in the study of domestic children's voice. Both the fundamental frequency and the formant have a tendency to decrease with age. The children's fundamental frequency and formant value change trend is relatively close, and at the age of 18, it almost reaches the adult level.

If the bandwidth of the output voice signal is too low, the information about the high frequency formant in the voice signal is probably lost. Thus, the formant information of the corresponding acoustic unit (such as a note) in the voice signal spectrum may be reduced.

The formant of children's voice is higher than the formant of adult voice. Therefore, if the recognizer adopts the bandwidth standard of adult voice signals, the high-frequency formant information about the acoustic unit in the spectrum of the children's voice signal will be lost, which is result in a decline in the rate of speaker recognition for children.

Therefore, the emphasis of voice signal spectrum recognition should be different in different age groups. With the increase of the bandwidth of voice signal, the recognition rate of voice signal is improved accordingly. Therefore, it is difficult to identify young children with low bandwidth.

4   Design of Children's Speaker Recognition Model

The traditional speaker recognition process generally uses GMM-UBM, i-vector and other methods to obtain effective features directly in the traditional model, or uses the Deep Neural Network (DNN) to train the original audio signal by using spectrograms or audio features. However, for the specific frequencies of children's speak, such as fundamental frequency and formant, it is difficult to use traditional models to achieve accurate speaker recognition for children's speech.

Based on this, combined with the characteristics of children's voice, such as age, gender, etc., multidimensional information is prejudged. On this basis, considering the temporal characteristics of voice, the neural network model is combined with TDNN for the children's speaker recognition. The design process of the joint model is shown in Fig. 1.

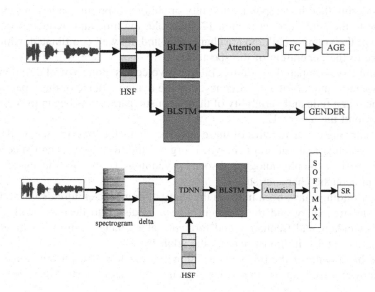

Fig. 1. Joint model of HSF and CRNN

The model is divided into two stages. The first one realizes the recognition of age and gender, and the second one mainly completes the recognition of children's speakers. Using the results of age and gender recognition provided in the first stage, the salient features of children's voice are obtained, and different tasks are effectively combined.

The main work of the two phases is explained separately below.

4.1 Identification Task of Age and Gender

As the first stage of child speaker recognition, the main purpose of age and gender recognition task is to further improve the accuracy of child speaker recognition on the basis of ensuring accurate age range and gender classification.

The age and gender recognition model uses the original feature signal as the basic input. Based on the extraction of the original feature signals, combined with BLSTM, a new neural network model is designed: the attention mechanism is seamlessly integrated into the BLSTM network.

Original Feature Signal. Through a lot of scientific analysis, there are many characteristics that can reflect the results of age and gender.

Combining them with the respective advantages, Durations, formants, spectral envelopes, MFCC, fundamental frequency, energy characteristics, and pitch are commonly used. In order to effectively solve the problem of excessive dimensionality of voice features, it may be considered to select the features of the parameters that have the greatest contribution to age and gender recognition, as shown in the Table 1.

Table 1. The combination of the features

Features	
LLD	Duration, Pitch ,Formants(1–3), energy, Spectral Envelope, zero-crossing rate, Loudness, spectralFlux, MFCC1-13, F0 frequency, shimmer, jitter, logMelFreqBand1-6
HSF	Mean, variance, min, max, range, median, quartiles, sma, stddev,

Age and Gender Identification Model. The model is composed of 2 channels, which are used for age recognition and gender recognition tasks respectively. The inputs of the model are the same, which are the original feature signals mentioned above.

For the task of the age recognition, the first channel is consists of a bidirectional LSTM layer, an attention layer, a fully connected layer, and an output layer. The strategy adopted is designed inside: the input gate, the output gate, and the forget gate. The weight information of error function feedback is selected.

Through the forgetting door, it is determined whether the memory unit is saved or cleared. The fully connected layer is used to form all the results of the previous form into global features. The output layer uses the Softmax function to map the input to the space of 0 and 1, and normalizes it to ensure the sum of them is 100%.

At the same time, the threshold is set, and the probability value within the threshold range is taken as the type of the identified obstacle. Figure 2 shows the BLSTM model structure.

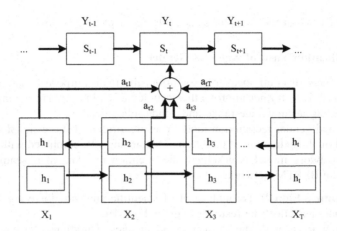

Fig. 2. The structure of BLSTM

The model does not only contains process long-term and short-term sequences, but also extracts effective and valuable information from the sequence through the attention mechanism. The key of the structure is adding the attention gate to the internal unit of the LSTM, which is equivalent to the attention mechanism operation of the sequence in each time step, so as to increase the learning ability of the model.

In order to improve the validity of the model and prevent over-fitting, the characteristics of the model can be constrained by sparse regularization optimization.

The second channel is used for the gender recognition, which is mainly composed of the BLSTM structure. Due to its sub-classification problem, the features are more obvious. The model simplified the previous channel by having a higher success rate of recognition.

Significant Feature Selection for Children's Speakers. According to the age and gender characteristics of the children that have been acquired, some targets related to age and time and gender are selected. The characteristics are sorted, and the top 40% feature sets are selected.

The characteristics related to age and gender is highlighted. The related features is consist of 2 parts which are called LLD and HSF. There are 10 groups of LLDs involved: Duration, Pitch, Formants (1–3), Spectral Envelope, MFCC (1–2), Loudness, logMelFreqBand. For each LLD, the mean, variance, sma, median, and stddev of the relevant features are extracted. For all the pieces of the audio data, 50-dimensional features related to the child's age and gender characteristics are obtained.

For all the children of different ages and genders, the importances of 50-dimensional features are not exactly the same. Based on a large number of experiments, the children's education and scientific research data, a list of features based on different conditions is obtained, as shown in Table 2. The content of each data item is a ranking of a set of children's voice characteristics.

Table 2. Sorting the importance of children's voice features

Age	Gender	
	Male	Female
5–8	T11	T11
9–11	T21	T22
12–14	T31	T32
15–18	T41	T42

As shown in the Table 2, in the voice characteristics of children aged 5–11, the influence of the gender is very small, almost negligible, and in the voice characteristics of adolescents aged 12–18, the proportion of gender is gradually increasing. Tij in Table 2 represents a set of voice feature rankings under the conditions which are different, where i is the number of different age ranges, and j is 0 or 1, which means male or female. Each dataset has a total of 50 dimensions characteristics.

Taking T11 as an example, Duration, Pitch, Formants (1–3), and Spectral Envelope have a great effect, while MFCC (1–2), Loudness, and logMelFreqBand are ranked lower. For T41 and T42, the role of MFCC is greater, but the ordering of features such as Pitch and Formants (1–3) is different.

4.2 Recognition Tasks for Children's Speaker

Spectrogram. A spectrogram is a representation of a voice time-frequency visualization that contains a large amount of voice information. When people using different speeds, tone levels, etc. to express different emotions, the spectrum of different emotions will show obvious differences.

The spectrograms are different. For example, the energy of disgusting emotions is more dispersed; on the contrary, the spectrum energy of sad emotions is more concentrated. For the emotions of sad and disgusting, the duration of spectral energy is similar.

When analyzing the spectrum of voice signal, the voice signal is first segmented, then each segment of the voice signal is windowed, and the waveform under the sliding window is subjected to frame by using short-time Fourier transform. The energy spectral density of the frame signal is calculated and converted into labels.

Finally, the energy spectrum data obtained from the frame by frame is stored in a matrix according to the column, and the matrix is mapped into a two-dimensional image to obtain a spectral map of the original voice signal. The generation process of the spectrogram is shown in Fig. 3.

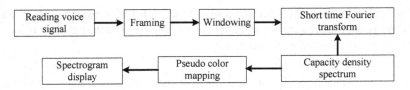

Fig. 3. The generation process of the spectrogram

TDNN. In the speaker recognition tasks, in order to capture long-term dependencies between voices, a time-invariant acoustic model that acquires this relationship is usually required. Time-Delay Neural Network (TDNN) is a network model that meet the requirement.

TDNN is a feedforward neural network that is calculated by interconnected layers of multiple clusters. The network structure inside is shown in the Fig. 4. The input is a j-dimensional vector, $D1 \sim DN$ is a delay vector, and Wi is a connection weight. By sum the delay number N is 2, the input layer dimension $j = 10$, the adjacent of 2 frame vectors, plus the current frame, a total of 3 frame vectors are spliced together as a batch of the input in the layer.

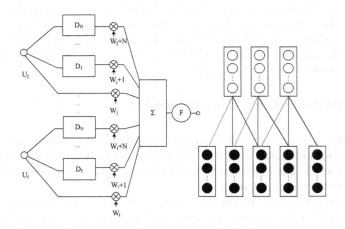

Fig. 4. Neural network structure of TDNN

An important idea of time-delay neural networks is weight sharing, the connection weights of the same location are the same. When the delay is level 2, there are 3 sets of weights in the network, D1 is for the current frame and D2 is for the delay frames. Different colors have different weights and the same position shares the weight. The training method uses the traditional BP learning method.

In the TDNN network structure, the first few hidden layers are learned from the context of shorter steps. As the levels of neurons increase, the learning ability becomes stronger and stronger, so the deep hidden layer needs to learn from the later steps of the wider step.

Unlike the traditional forward-propagating neural networks, TDNN can capture the long-term dependence of time-series-related feature pairs. It is because the features which are chosen by TDNN as the method for extracting speaker representation vectors. Multi-frame training data is stitched together in different network layers for learning, by obtaining long-term features between voice frames.

In the network, the input layer is recorded as the inputs, and the hidden layer is recorded as hidden_i, i $\in$ [1, 8]. It is assumed that the input layer inputs the current frame at time t, and the frames at the three moments before and after the hidden layer are connected as the inputs before.

Hidden 2 and hidden 3 respectively connect the outputs of the first 3 moments and the last 3 moments as the current inputs. Hidden 4 and hidden 5 combine 4 frames before and after as the inputs. Hidden 6 and hidden 7 directly receive the output of the previous layer as input, without increasing the context of the upper and lower frames.

After the TDNN model, a BLSTM layer is added, which can process and predict timing-related voice features in the time series. The mechanism of 2-way communication further aggravates the influence of the time series.

Besides, an attention layer is added, which can be described as a "selection mechanism" for assigning the processing capabilities of the limited informations. For each vector in the input sequence, the attention weight is calculated according to the scoring function.

The last layer of the output layer is the Softmax layer. The output layer is used only during the training process, and the output result is the probability corresponding to the speaker category.

Original Acoustic Feature Channel. The input of the TDNN network is consist of 3 parts, the first and second one are the spectrogram and its delta processed segmentation data.

After the whitening operation, the mean value of each dimension of each audio is calculated to form a full sentence spectral feature of 1 * 512 dimensions.

After gender and age recognition, the third part is the top 40% of the 50-dimensional features of the outstanding features which are obtained.

The features are combined in a series and fed together into the TDNN network model for training.

5   Experiment and Result Analysis

In the paper, the data in the children's spoken speech corpus provided by the "Words Flow" software is used to test the effect of the voice evaluation model. The 400 volunteers (aged to 16 years old, with an average age of 10 years, 50% for men and women) are recruited. After reading the specified text, each volunteer read the content aloud in a quiet environment. At the same time, the various voice signals are recorded in time.

The Tensorflow framework is used to construct the network model structure, and the Children's speaker signal is judged on the audio signal. Using the i-vector model as the baseline, model 1: TDNN, model 2: TDNN + Attention mechanism, model 3:

current system (multi-channel joint representation), respectively calculate the accuracy of speaker judgment. The results are shown in Table 3.

Table 3. The accuracy comparison of children's speaker recognition under different models

Model	Accuracy
Baseline: i-vector Model	73%
Model 1: TDNN	77%
Model 2: TDNN + Attention	79%
Current System: Multi-Channel Joint Representation	83%

In order to highlight the validity of the model for children's voice data, the comparison between children's and adult's voice speaker recognition is carried out. The self-built speech emotion corpus of the whole age is used as the adult corpus, and the age and gender distribution is uniform.

The results of the speaker recognition, as shown in Table 4, under the condition of using the same model, the model proposed in the paper can improve the success rate of children's speaker recognition based on the level of adult speaker recognition.

Table 4. Accuracy comparison of speaker recognition at different age levels

Model	The accuracy of adult recognition	The accuracy of children recognition
Baseline: i-vector Model	78%	73%
Model 1: d-vector Model	79%	71%
Model 2: TDNN Model	77%	79%
Current System: Multi-Channel Joint Representation	79%	83%

6 Conclusion

Based on the children's reading speech corpus provided by the "Words flow " software, the model of TDNN combined with BLSTM network is designed, and the attention mechanism is added to train the multi-channel models for solving a speaker identification problem solution.

The experimental results show that the proposed model has higher accuracy and the mean square error value is easy to converge.

In the future work, the processing of the children's voice data will be further completed, more authoritative data will be obtained, a large number of children's spoken speech database will be set up, and corresponding interfaces will be provided. At the same time, the model optimization is further completed for the existing neural network to reduce the error rate between the model score and the true value.

Acknowledgment. This paper is funded by the "Dalian Key Laboratory for the Application of Big Data and Data Science".

References

1. Phapatanaburi, K., Wang, L., Sakagami, R.: Distant-talking accent recognition by combining GMM and DNN. Multimedia Tools Appl. **75**(9), 5109–5124 (2016)
2. Wang, J., Yang, Y., Mao, J., et al.: CNN-RNN: a unified framework for multi-label image classification. In: Proceedings of IEEE Conference on Computer Vision and Pattern Recognition, pp. 2285–2294 (2016)
3. Jiang, H., Lu, Y., Xue, J.: Automatic soccer video event detection based on a deep neural network combined CNN and RNN. In: Proceedings of the 28th IEEE International Conference on Tools with Artificial Intelligence, pp. 490–494 (2016)
4. Schmidhuber, J.: Deep learning in neural networks: an overview. Neural Netw. **61**(3), 85–94 (2014)
5. Abdullah, H., Garcia, W., Peeters, C., et al.: Practical hidden voice attacks against speech and speaker recognition systems (2019)
6. Mary, L.: Significance of Prosody for Speaker, Language, Emotion, and Speech Recognition (2019)
7. Wang, Y., Fan, X., Chen, I.F., et al.: End-to-end anchored speech recognition (2019)
8. Lakomkin, E., Zamani, M.A., Weber, C., et al.: Incorporating end-to-end speech recognition models for sentiment analysis (2019)
9. Harb, H., Chen, L.: Vlice-based gender identification in multimedia applications. Int. J. Pattern Recogn. Artif. Intell. **19**(2), 63–78 (2005)
10. Liu, Z., Wu, Z., Li, T., et al.: GMM and CNN hybrid method for short utterance speaker recognition. IEEE Trans. Ind. Inform. **14**(7), 3244–3252 (2018)
11. Ravanelli, M., Bengio, Y.: Speech and speaker recognition from raw waveform with SincNet (2018)
12. Parthasarathy, S., Busso, C.: Predicting speaker recognition reliability by considering emotional content. In: International Conference on Affective Computing & Intelligent Interaction (2017)

Constructing Dictionary to Analyze Features Sentiment of a Movie Based on Danmakus

Jie Li[1] and Yukun Li[1,2(✉)]

[1] Tianjin University of Technology, Tianjin 300384, China
liyukun_tjut@163.com
[2] Tianjin Key Laboratory of Intelligence Computing and Novel Software
Technology, Tianjin, China

Abstract. As a new commenting mode, danmaku not only shows the subjective attitude or emotion of the reviewer, but also has instantaneity and interactivity compared with traditional comments. In order to improve the existing film evaluation mechanism of mainstream film rating websites, this paper trains the word vector model based on movies' danmaku and builds the movie feature word lexicon iteratively. And then, through the Boson (https://bosonnlp.com/dev/resource) sentiment dictionary and TF-IDF algorithm, we set up the feature-sentiment dictionary. Finally, we use the feature-sentiment dictionary and combine the dictionary of the degree words to calculate the sentiment score of each feature based on the movie danmaku. Our experimental results are compared with the scores of a film rating website "Mtime" (http://www.mtime.com/). The comparison proves that our method of analyzing and computing sentiment of movie features is not only novel but also effective.

Keywords: Sentiment analysis · Sentiment dictionary · Danmaku

1 Introduction

Movie is a kind of regret art, there is not a perfect movie. A people criticizes a movie doesn't mean he or she hates all aspects of it. Meanwhile, praising a movie doesn't mean it has no flaws. Today, many of us habitually open some movie rating websites to see score or reviews of a movie before watching it. If the movie score is too low, it may be excluded of our viewing range. Therefore, the evaluation of rating website has a butterfly effect on a movie. At present, similar to douban, almost all mainstream websites adopt the average of all reviewers' scores as the scores of a movie. But this kind rating mechanism has three disadvantages. First, every audience's score actually is the holistic and comprehensive score of a movie, which cannot reflect how they feel about various aspects of the film. It will miss some unique highlights of the movie or overlook some deficiencies in details. It is difficult to judge fully the movie according to one score of a movie. Second, users only grade or comment a film after watching the whole film or even after a period of time usually. They may not remember the features or details of the film clearly and profoundly, which will affect the accuracy and objectivity of the grading or reviewing data. Last but not the least, there are many scandals about the biased scores of some film rating websites and there are two reasons

© Springer Nature Switzerland AG 2019
J. Li et al. (Eds.): ADMA 2019, LNAI 11888, pp. 474–488, 2019.
https://doi.org/10.1007/978-3-030-35231-8_34

for this phenomenon. One is somebody are hired to rate a movie many times in order to get a higher score or belittle a movie deliberately. The employer may be the producers of the film or someone has an opposing relationship to them. Another one is some websites probably does some changes on the movie data out of self-interest. As a result, more and more users have doubt objectivity and authenticity of these movie rating sites.

However, the danmaku is based on video time point. Viewers have volunteered to send danmaku in real time when they look the video. As a result, the rating method based on the danmaku can overcome the above disadvantages. Therefore, we design the crawlers to obtain 20,000 movies' danmaku data form bilibili3 (the biggest danmaku video website in China) as corpus first, then we use corpus to train word vector by Word2vec model, then we iteratively build feature word lexicon of film by calculation of feature word similarity. After building feature word lexicon, we design the crawler again to obtain film reviews from the douban. It is the most popular film website. At last, we grab 230,000 positive reviews and 180,000 negative reviews as positive corpus set and negative corpus set. Then, through the TF-IDF algorithm, we use the feature word lexicon and combine the Boson sentiment dictionary to construct the feature-sentiment dictionary. Finally, combining the feature word lexicon, the feature-sentiment dictionary and the degree words dictionary, we calculate the sentiment score of each feature for movies based on their danmaku data. Our experimental results are compared with the scores of "Mtime", we find our results are closer to the real evaluation of users on various aspects of the film. The comparison proves that our method of analyzing and computing sentiment of movie features is not only novel but also effective.

2 Related Works

2.1 Research and Work of Danmaku

Danmaku ("danmu" in Chinese) is a short commentary based on video time point. At present, it is only popular in China, Japan and other Asian countries, so the related work on danmaku is limited. Early studies are usually based on simple statistical methods, such as Wu et al. [6] analyzed the correlation between some common danmaku (e.g. "2333", etc.) and the number of plays of video to predict and analyze the popularity of video. Murakami et al. [1] expanded scope and proposed the sorting algorithm of danmaku to carry out emotional analysis on video contents; they apply the results to the video retrieval system.

Since danmaku is highly correlated with video time point, many researchers study danmaku to realize automatic marking or fragment extraction of video. Such as, Wu et al. [5] applied danmaku into the video marking for the first time in 2014. They first computed similarity of danmaku video segment and user. They obtained the correlation of video fragment in time and the users' preference of sending danmaku in their research. According to the LDA theme model, Xian et al. [7] focused on the potential semantic information of danmaku. For the first time, they realized the extraction of video highlights from the perspective of text with the help of danmaku sentiment, so as to avoid image processing. Zhang et al. [11] proposed a novel temporal summarization model SJTTR and T-SJTT of danmaku video based on the data reconstruct principle. Zhuang et al. [10] analyzed the LSTM network model and the AT-LSTM model based on attention model, and then proposes an SIS-LSTM sentiment analysis model that combines video importance scoring and LSTM network model to research the danmaku. Deng et al. [8] analyzed the classification of danmaku based on LDA topic model, evaluated the emotional vector of the words in this kind of time-sync comments to analyze the emotion relationships among the video shots for video shots recommendation.

To sum up, the research based on danmaku mainly focus on estimating the tendency of comment according to the existing emotional dictionary or some machine learning model, and the results are mainly applied in the following three aspects, prediction and analysis of video popularity, extraction of video highlights, and video markers or abstracts.

2.2   Sentiment Analysis Research on the Film Reviews and Other Text

Text Sentiment Analysis, also known as opinion mining, mainly by emotion dictionary and machine learning methods. A traditional method of sentiment analysis is manually or automatically setting up a sentiment dictionary based on emotion knowledge and domain knowledge and then estimating the emotional tendency of subjective texts by the dictionary. At present, the main sentiment dictionary resources include Opinion Finder subjective sentiment dictionary, Bing Liu dictionary, Word- Net, NTUSD, a Chinese emotion polarity dictionary developed by Taiwan University, and HowNet of CNKI. Specially, BosonNLP sentiment dictionary is automatically constructed from microblog, news, BBS and other tagged data. This dictionary includes many network terms and informal abbreviations, and has a high coverage rate for non-standard texts. However, the growth rate of the Internet text was so high and new special words appeared constantly. The existing emotional dictionaries are difficult to meet the requirement of sentiment analysis. Therefore, the researchers tend to use method of combining the knowledge base and corpus, add the expanded sentiment knowledge and sentiment words extracted from corpus into the sentiment dictionary to enrich the emotion dictionary. Such as, Yang et al. [12] use word2vec to train a set of word vector from the corpus, after comprehensive screening NTUSD, HowNet and the sentiment ontology library of Dalian university of technology. They set up the Senti-Ruc dictionary. Their dictionary has achieved good results in the field of general data sets. Zhou et al. [9] compared the sentiment dictionary and machine learning, aiming at the shortcomings of the two methods. They extended the microblog sentiment dictionary by computing the SO-PMI between sentiment words, and proposed a microblog sentiment analysis method based on sentiment dictionary and sentence pattern classification.

In addition, the supervised and semi-supervised sentiment analysis methods are more popular at present, which depend on a large number of marked texts to train the classification model. Researchers used different machine learning algorithms to classify the target text or predict the sentiment tendency of the target text. Soelistio et al. [3] proposed a simple model based on Naive Bayes to analyze the emotional polarity of digital newspapers and applied it to obtain positive or negative emotion of politicians from digital news articles. Wikarsa et al. [4] paid attention on the users' tweets to study an application of Naive Bayes sentiment classification to classify the Twitter users. The most representative research is Pang et al. [2] use Naive Bayes, SVM and Maximum Entropy classifier to classify sentiment in English movie reviews. Huang et al. [13] made a sentiment analysis of the user-generated text of the financial sector by using the SVM classification method combined with the Stanford language depend- ency. For the film reviews, Song et al. [14] utilized movie reviews of douban to train their lexicon-based model. They introduced a lexical updating algorithm based on a widely used lexicon. Cui et al. [15] use film website comments to analyze film features. They can analyze users' interests according to users' historical comment information. When recommending films to users, they proposed a personalized recommendation algorithm that integrates emotional analysis and feature expansion of LDA theme model. Considering the theme factors of film comments and potential semantic relations be- tween film themes.

A large number of manually annotated corpora are needed in training the model of supervised text sentiment analysis research. However, with the explosive development of online data, there are more and more irregular, colloquial and short data that need to be analyzed for sentiment. It will take an unimaginable amount of manpower to label these data. Meanwhile, the existing sentiment dictionaries perform well or poorly in different fields' sentiment analyzing works. Therefore, it is not the best choice whether to merely use the existing sentiment dictionary or only rely on ma- chine learning method to mine sentiment information. In this paper, we combine the external knowledge base and corpus to construct the feature and sentiment dictionary to judge the emotional tendency and calculate the multiple features emotional value of a movie.

3 Constructing Feature-Sentiment Dictionary for Danmaku Movie

This section introduces the whole process of constructing feature sentiment dictionary. Section 3.1 propose crawling and pre-processing process of danmaku data in advance; Sect. 3.2 describes how to build a feature word lexicon based on danmaku corpus by the word vector model; in Sect. 3.3, the feature sentiment dictionary is built based on the external film review corpus and the feature word lexicon from Sect. 3.2.

3.1 Danmaku Crawling and Pre-processing

First of all, we design crawlers to obtain 20,000 movies' danmaku files in form of XML from bilibili, each XML file contains all danmaku of the film, each row in the xml file is a barrage of information, which including video ID, danmaku contents, appearing time in the video (from the starting time of the video, in seconds) and the user ID and so on. Several detailed data are shown in the Table 1. The table header is the label in the XML file. In this paper, we only use the commenting contents in the label "d" after crawling XML files.

Table 1. A part of danmaku data

Chatid	d	Timestamp(s)	Uid
6110167	The appearance is so good!	427.52	e64668eb
2041696	Welcome back to here	4.25	7b09cf48
4810659	What the fuck of fearful music	356.59	7e58cc69

To integrate all movies' danmaku into a TXT file, using jieba segmentation tools and adding some stop words. Moreover, considering there is some network language or danmaku language in our corpus, we set up a custom dictionary on the basis of jieba dictionary, we add some common network or danmaku special words in order to assure these words will not be separated. Table 2 shows some words and description of the custom dictionaries. At the same time, because they have emotional tendency, they are used in supplementing the feature sentiment dictionaries later.

Table 2. Some words of customized dictionary

Special word	Explanation
2333	Showing something is very funny
666	Showing something is amazing
bgm	Abbreviation of background music
BE/HE	Abbreviation of bad ending and happy ending
prprpr	Lick screen, often appears when attractive people shows up

3.2   Building Feature Word Lexicon Based on Word Vector Model

The feature word lexicon is the basis of follow-up work of building feature sentiment dictionary and calculating emotional values of danmaku. This section describes how to build a feature word lexicon based on danmaku corpus through the word vector model. The main idea is using a large scale danmaku data set to train word vector model, and through the calculation of similarity to add associated words with the target feature words into the lexicon and regard these associated words as target word to iteratively compute similarity. Until all words are in the lexicon, we have finish building the feature word lexicon.

The Word2vec is used in our method. It was developed by Google in 2013 with the idea of deep learning, which can represent a large number of training corpora as n-dimensional space vectors. With the help of Word2vec, everyone can obtain some semantic knowledge form corpus. The CBOW and the Skip-Gram is main model of Word2vec. The Skip-Gram model predict the context $S_{w(t)} = (w_{(t-k)}, \ldots, w_{(t-1)}, w_{(t+1)}, \ldots, w_{(t+k)})$ by inputting word $w_{(t)}$, k is the size of the context window of $w_{(t)}$, that is the number of selected words in left and in right. The CBOW model is contrary to Skip-Gram model, it predict $w_{(t)}$ through context $S_{w(t)}$. The training objective optimization functions of Skip-Gram and CBOW are shown in formulas (1) and (2) respectively. For the given w(t) or Sw(t), Word2Vec adopts random gradient ascent to maximize the result of the formulas (1) and (2).

$$L_{\text{Skip-Gram}} = \sum_{w_{(t)} \in C} \sum_{-k \leq j \leq k, j \neq 0} \log p(w_{(t+j)} \mid w_{(t)}) \qquad (1)$$

$$L_{\text{CBOW}} = \sum_{w_{(t)} \in C} \log p(w_{(t)} \mid S_{w_{(t)}}) \qquad (2)$$

The parameter C is all word in corpus, the parameter k is the size of $w_{(t)}$ context. The input of Skip-Gram is $w_{(t)}$ and output is $S_{w(t)}$, CBOW is opposite of Skip-Gram, they are shown in Fig. 1.

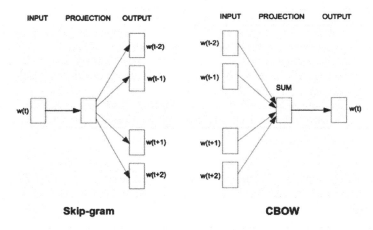

Fig. 1. Skip-gram model and CBOW model of Word2vec

We use the gensim package of python to implement Word2Vec. In order to train model, the model input is processed 20,000 movies danmaku corpus. Considering most of the danmaku are relatively short, we set the parameter "window" at 5 (the default is 10) the parameter "min_count" at 3 (defaults is 5), and set the default value 100 to the feature vector dimension. The model outputs the related words with target feature through calculating the similarity between the feature words and others words of corpus.

Take "story" for example, Table 3 lists five most similar words with "Story", and then manually filters out similar words that are not feature words. For example, "Campy", "Farfetched" and other emotional words are not feature words, while "Plots" and "Logic" in the table will continue to be used as target words to calculate the similarity. This process is repeated until all the feature words are added into the lexicon, the iterative construction is completed.

Table 3. Five most similar words with "Story"

Word	Similarity with "Story"
情节(Plots)	0.720615327
狗血(Campy)	0.646508098
牵强(Farfetched)	0.643559575
逻辑(Logic)	0.617229521
紧凑(Compact)	0.612514317

Table 4. The words describing a feature

Feature	Words
Story	剧中(in story) 主题(theme) 片中(in movie) 讲述(narrate) 走向(progress) 剧情(story) 情节(plot) 段落(plot) 这段(plot) 逻辑(logic) 这剧(this story) 剧本(script) 编剧(scriptwriter) 故事(story) 改编(recompose) 片段(fragment) 桥段(plot) 设定(setting) 设计(setting) 内容(content) 发展(development) 对白(dialogue) 结局(ending) 结尾(ending) 高潮(climax)
Acting	演技(acting skill) 演绎,饰演,演的/得,演,演出,出演,表演,拍戏,演戏(perform) 塑造(shape) 诠释(interpret) 眼神(eyes) 表情(facial expression) 动作(posture)

The detailed process of setting up feature word lexicon based on Word2vec is shown in Algorithm 1. The final result of construction for "Story" and "Acting" are shown in Table 4.

Algorithm 1. Setting up Feature Word Lexicon Based on Word2vec

```
Input: word2vec.model and five initial feature words
Output: feature_lexicon
1.  model  = load(word2vec.model)
2.  similar_word[] = model.most_similar(feature)
3.  for feature in five initial feature words:
4.      for word in similar_word[]:
5.          if word belong to feature
            and  word is not in feature_lexicon:
6.              feature_lexicon.append(word)
7.              most_similar(word)
8.          end if
9.      End for
10. End for
11. return feature_lexicon
```

3.3 Construction of Feature Sentiment Dictionary Based TF-IDF

This section mainly introduces the construction of the feature sentiment dictionary. Firstly, showing the acquisition and pre-processing of douban film reviewing data set. Next, we pay more attention on describing the process of constructing feature sentiment dictionary by Boson emotion dictionary and TF-IDF algorithm.

First of all, because danmaku data is a kind of data without pre-marked emotional label, it is not suitable to be used as corpus of building the emotional dictionary. However, when posting reviews for a movie on the douban, users can grade the movie with one star to five stars. This rating data can represent user attitude to the movie. For these truths, we design the crawler to obtain reviews and corresponding rating data from the douban. According to the "Rating", we divided all reviews into the positive reviews set (Rating > 3) and negative reviews set (Rating < 3). According to the feature word in Table 4, the positive and negative reviews that only involving one type of feature would be filtrated and recombined next. So all positive and negative reviews with same feature will be list in one reviews set respectively. After classifying tendency and filtrating feature, some movies' reviews were shown in Table 5.

Table 5. Douban comments of movie with feature and sentiment label

Rating	Content	Tendency	Feature	Word of feature
2	Mediocre story and chaotic logic	Neg	Story	Story; Logic
4	Nino' acting skill is fantastic	Pos	Acting	Acting skill

Table 6. A part of Boson sentiment dictionary

Word	Score
精湛(Exquisite)	3.025328886
mlgb	-4.408225468
脑残(Brain dead)	-1.802233555

Take positive reviews set of each feature for example, after cutting sentence and taking out stop words, we take all positive words(value is greater than zero) of Boson sentiment dictionary to match and output all words in positive reviews sets. The words and their value of Boson sentiment dictionary was shown in Table 6. And then, through the TF-IDF algorithm, we select the positive emotional and estimated words matching various features.

TF-IDF is a classical statistical method for calculating the weight of words, which is composed of term frequency (TF) and inverse document frequency (IDF). The word frequency calculation is shown in formula (3) $tf_{i,j}$ represent the frequency of word w_i in document d_j, $n_{i,j}$ are the frequency of word w_i in document d_j, the denominator is the sum of the frequency of all words in document d_j, k is the number of different words in document d_j. The inverse document frequency calculation is shown in formula (4) idf_i is the inverse document frequency of word w_i in the text library d, n_d is the total number of documents in the text library d, df (d, w_i) is the number of documents containing word w_i in the document library d, plus 1 is to prevent the situation that df (d, w_i) is zero. Finally, the calculation of the normalization of TF-ID is shown in formula (5).

$$\text{tfi,j} = \frac{n_{i,j}}{\sum_{k=1}^{k} n_{k,j}} \tag{3}$$

$$\text{idfi} = \log \frac{n_d}{df(d, w_i) + 1} \tag{4}$$

$$\text{tf - idfi,j} = \frac{\text{tf}_{i,j} \times idf_i}{\sqrt{\sum w_i \in d_j [\text{tf}_{i,j} \times idf_i]^2}} \tag{5}$$

According to the formula (5), the importance of word w_i to document d_j is directly proportional to the frequency of word w_i in document d_j, and inversely proportional to the number of documents containing word w_i in the whole text library d. Based on this and for the purpose of extracting the specific sentiment words largely describing one certain future, we select the TF-IDF to obtain the sentiment words to make feature word lexicon.

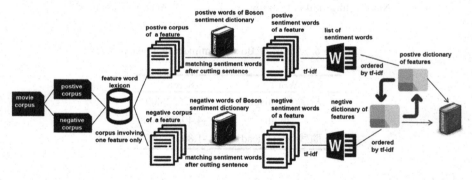

Fig. 2. The detailed process of setting up the five features sentiment dictionary based on the feature word lexicon and movie corpus of douban.

We regard all positive reviews set as the whole text library d and see the different set about every feature as d_j. And then, through calculating tf-idf value of w_i and sorting all words under each feature, we set up the positive feature sentiment dictionary. The steps of setting up the negative sentiment dictionary are exactly same. The whole process of constructing a feature sentiment dictionary is shown in Fig. 2.

4 Computing Feature Score of Danmaku Based on Dictionary

Adding some network words and danmaku words shown in Table 2, these words are collected from Microblog, Post Bar and some related papers in Sect. 4.1. In Sect. 4.2, we calculate the emotional value of each feature based on the movie danmaku by using feature word lexicon, sentiment dictionary and combining the degree dictionary. The dictionary of the degree words was built by us with reference to the degree word magnitude rules in the research of quantity of the modern Chinese adverbs of degree [16].

4.1 Classifying Words of Danmaku

After cutting sentence and taking out stop words, in order to achieve the works of matching sentiment word, feature word and degree word, we change the segment result of danmaku into the dictionary format in python. The key is word, and the value is this word's index of the segment result. Such as, a danmaku is "背景音乐好伤感, 就是外婆出现的不是时候啊, 略扯" the segment result is "背景音乐 (background music) 好 (very) 伤感 (sad) 外婆 (grandma) 出现 (appear) 不是 (not) 时候 (correctly) 略 (somewhat) 扯 (abnormal)". The result in the dictionary format is "{'background music':0, 'very':1, 'sad':2, 'grandma':3, '出现':4, 'no':5, 'correctly':6, 'somewhat':7, 'abnormal':8}".

Algorithm 2. Classifying Words of Processed Danmu Comments

```
Input: word_dict in the form of {w₁:0,w₂:1,…wₙ:n-1}
Output: feature_word,sen_word,degree_word
1.  for word in word_dict.keys():
2.    if word in feature_dic.keys():
3.      feature_word[word_dict[word]] = feature_dic[word]
4.    if word in sen_dic.keys():
5.      sen_word[word_dict[word]] = sen_dic[word]
6.    if word in degree_dic.keys():
7.      degree_word[word_dict[word]] = degree_dic[word]
8.  end for
9.  while sen_word is not null:
10.    return feature_word,sen_word,degree_word
```

The detailed process of classifying words of processed danmaku comments is shown in Algorithm 2. Since our purpose of analyzing emotional tendency of danmaku, the algorithm only returns the word classification results if sen_word is not null. Next section takes this result as input to compute the sentiment value of a danmaku. Take last example, the input is {'background music': 0, 'very': 1, 'sad': 2, 'grandma': 3, 'appear': 4, 'no': 5, 'correctly': 6, 'somewhat': 7, 'abnormal': 8} and the output is feature_word: {0: music}, sen_word: {2: '-1@music', 8: '-1@story'}, degree_word: {1:1, 5:-1, 7:1.2}.

4.2   Computing Sentiment Score of Movie Features

The classification results of previous section are taken as the input to calculate the each feature value in this section. The word index is used to determine whether the feature word matches the sentiment word, and whether the sentiment word matches the degree word.

Algorithm 3. Computing Sentiment Values of Features

```
Input: feature_word,sen_word,degree_word
Output: feature_score
1.  for feature in sen_word:
2.    if feature in feature_word:
3.       if sen_word index in (feature index±3):
4.          if degree_word:
5.             fs_weight = 1,feature_score = 1
6.             if degree_index in (sen_word index±2):
7.                fs_weight = fs_weight * word_degree
8.             else: fs_weight = fs_weight * 1
9.          elif no degree_word:
10.              feature_score = score * fs_weight
11.      else: no matched feature
12.   elif not feature_word:
13.      if degree_word:
14.         s_weight = 1, feature_score = 1
15.         if degree_index in (senword index±2)
16.            s_weight = s_weight * word_degree
17.         else: s_weight = s_weight * 1
18.      elif no degree_word:
19.            feature_score = score * s_weight
20. return feature_score
```

For every danmaku of a movie, classifying words and computing feature score, then the final emotion value of each feature was obtained by calculating the average amount. The detailed computing process of feature sentiment value is shown in Algorithm 3. Finally, the output is sentiment score of each feature.

The established goal of sentiment analysis was achieved. The work based on the danmaku to analyzing sentiment tendency of multiple features of the film was completed.

5   Experiment and Analysis

In this chapter, we randomly find 25 danmaku movies from bilibili, including some films of different types, different regions, different eras and qualities. Based on their danmaku data, we use the method proposed in this paper to make sentiment analysis for each feature. "Mtime" is a little famous website of rating films.

The experimental results of this paper are compared with each feature scores in "Mtime". Due to there are some distinctions between our features and aspects of "Mtime", we compare our experimental results to the most related aspects of "Mtime". Two results are shown in Table 7. The first is the score hidden in the character string with "json" format of every film page in the "Mtime" website. We obtained them by a crawler program. The second score is the normalized result based on our computing method. The full mark for each item is ten

In order to investigate which kind of scores is closer to movie viewers' real evaluation of the movie, we invite 20 classmates to verify experimental results. Depending on participant are whether familiar with a movie or not, we asked them select about ten of 25 movies first. The selectance of movies is shown in Fig. 3.

Table 7. Five movies' scores at "Mtime" and our experimental results

Movie	Acting	Picture/Appearance	Music	Quality/director	Story
Léon	9.3/8	8.5/7.9	8.6/9.5	9/9	9/7.2
Yip Man	8/9.4	8/4.6	7.4/5.5	7.9/9.2	7.4/8.7
Your Name	5/6.5	9/4.9	8.4/8.5	6.6/9.1	8/9.2
Train to Busan	5/8.3	8/5.9	7.4/4.9	6.5/8.5	7.7/8.6
Switch	1.7/3	3.1/6.7	2.6/3.9	2.2/3	2.5/3

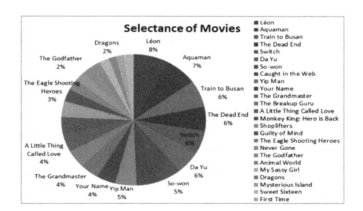

Fig. 3. The selectance of 25 movies.

And then, for every movie selected, participants should compare two scores of the "Mtime" and our method respectively, they need to decide which result is closer to the truth and give feedback to us. We finally counted the results of choosing between the two scores of 25 movies and its features. The partial counting results are shown in Table 8, The "Count" of this table is the number of participants selecting the movie.

We finally counted the results of choosing between the two scores of 25 movies and each of their features. The partial counting results are shown in Table 9. The "Count" of this table is the number of participants selecting the movie. The average accuracy is

58.27%. And the accuracies of five features are 66.43%, 53.39%, 47.64%, 63.41% and 60.51% respectively. The analyzing result verifies the experimental results of our method are closer to the real user evaluation.

Table 8. The ten-point system rules of rating a movie

Rules	Score	Rules	Score
It is impeccable in all aspects and has strong impfunction and great value	10	A mediocre work called Popcorn movie. You can see it when you are boring	6–7
It accords with your personal aesthetics and has broad imagination and audiovisual value	9–10	Its' flaws are obvious. Relying on the reputation of actors or directors to attract spectators	5–6
It is vivid and beautiful result of perfect combination of color, aroma and taste	9	It has great investment but merely shows empty and inane contents	4–5
It has certain status in film history, but not becomes your favorite one	8–9	It is a little boring, but you can stand it	3–4
It has some flaws, but it is fresh or interesting for you	8	You are almost impossible to see it integrally	2–3
Some special-interest works, which have some indetectable merits	7–8	After seeing it, you think it wastes your time	1–2
The work is neat and integrated, but it has no outstanding features	7	You are not interested in it at all	0–1

Table 9. The accuracy of our experimental results of partial movies

Movie	Acting	Appearance	Music	Quality	Story	Count
Léon	22%	67%	89%	56%	50%	18
Aquaman	71%	29%	82%	82%	35%	17
Train to Busan	80%	33%	33%	60%	53%	15
The Dead End	93%	50%	43%	64%	43%	14
Da Yu	100%	77%	77%	62%	62%	13

6 Conclusion

With the popularity of danmaku video, the Chinese mainstream video websites and live streaming platforms and even shopping websites loaded the danmaku functions. Danmaku is highly real-time and interactive, so it can be used as the research object for sentiment analysis, and the analysis results can be applied in many aspects. For example, in this paper, danmaku is used to judge the advantages and disadvantages of a film in some aspects. And the overall emotional change trend of danmaku also could be used to extract highlight of video, etc.

Based on Word2vec and TF-IDF, this paper constructs feature sentiment dictionary for movies, and then uses it to calculate the emotional value of a movie features. Through the actual comparison, our experimental results are closer to the real evaluation of users on various aspects of the film. For two reasons, the first is the danmaku was synchronously sent by a number of viewers when they watching movies, published contents and film contents are highly related. The second is danmaku is a form of textual commentary, compared with a separate score of rating websites, it reflects the attitude from viewers to a movie in the round. On basis of this study, the next step is paying attention on others danmaku, such as making sentiment analysis based on live streaming danmaku, to extract highlights in live streaming and soon.

Acknowledgements.. This research was partially supported by the Natural Science Foundation of Tianjin (No. 15JCYBJC46500), the Natural Science Foundation of China (No. 61170027), the Training plan of Tianjin University Innovation Team (No. TD13-5025), and the Major Project of Tianjin Smart Manufacturing (No. 15ZXZNCX00050)

References

1. Murakami, N., Ito, E.: Emotional video ranking based on user comments. In: iiWAS 2011 - The 13th International Conference on Information Integration and Web-based Applications and Services. ACM, pp. 499–502 (2011) https://doi.org/10.1145/2095536.2095639
2. Bo, P., Lillian, L., Shivakumar, V.: Thumbs up? sentiment classification using machine learning techniques. In: Proceedings of the ACL-02 Conference on Empirical Methods in Natural Language Processing – EMNLP 2002 (2002)
3. Soelistio, Y.E., Surendra, M.R.S.: Simple text mining for sentiment analysis of political figure using Naïve Bayes classifier method (2015)
4. Wikarsa, L., Thahir. S.N.: A text mining application of emotion classifications of Twitter's users using Naïve Bayes method. In: International Conference on Wireless & Telematics. IEEE (2016). https://doi.org/10.1109/icwt.2015.7449218
5. Wu, B., Zhong, E., Tan, B.: Crowdsourced time- sync video tagging using temporal and personalized topic modeling. In: Proceeding KDD 2014 Proceedings of the 20th ACM SIGKDD International Conference on Knowledge Discovery and Data Mining (2014). https://doi.org/10.1145/2623330.2623625
6. Wu, Z., Ito, E.: Correlation analysis between user's emotional comments and popularity measures. In: IIAI 3rd International Conference Advanced Applied Informatics, pp. 280–283. IEEE (2014). https://doi.org/10.1109/iiai-aai.2014.65
7. Xian, Y., Li, J., Zhang, C.: Video highlight shot extraction with time-sync comment. In: Proceedings of the 7th International Workshop on Hot Topics in Planet-Scale Mobile Computing and Online Social Networking (2015). https://doi.org/10.1145/2757513.2757516
8. Yang, D., Chenx, Z., Jiangf, L.: Video shot recommendation model based on emotion analysis using time- sync comments. J. Comput. Appl. **37**, 1065–1070 (2017)
9. Jie, Z., Chen, L.: A study on the emotion classification of network news commentary based on machine learning. J. Computer Appl. **30**(04), 1011–1014 (2010)
10. Xuq, Z., Fang, L.: Emotional analysis of bullet screen comments based on AT-LSTM. J. Digital technology and application. **36**(02), 210–212 (2008)

11. Chao Z.: Research on automatic abstract generation based on video bullet screen comments. D. University of science and technology of China (2017)
12. Xiaop Y., Zhongx Z.: Automatic construction and optimization of an emotion dictionary based on Word2Vec. J. Comput. Sci. **44**(01) (2017)
13. Jin H., Tong R., Ruiq J.: Public opinion analysis in financial field based on SVM and dependency syntax. Computer engineering and application, **51**(23) (2015)
14. Yiw, S., Kaiw, G.: A lexical updating algorithm for sentiment analysis on Chinese movie reviews. In: Fifth International Conference on Advanced Cloud and Big Data (2017)
15. Ping, C., Li, S., Xink, Y.: Personalized movie recommendation system based on LDA theme extension. J. Comput. Sci. Appl. (2018)
16. Shang Q.: The research of quantity of the modern Chinese adverbs of degree. D. Hebei university (2018)

Single Image Dehazing Algorithm
Based on Sky Region Segmentation

Weixiang Li[1,2(✉)], Wei Jie[1,2(✉)],
and Somaiyeh Mahmoudzadeh[1,2(✉)]

[1] Nanjing Tech University, Nanjing 211800, Jiangsu, China
lwxlf@njtech.edu.cn, 1147155464@qq.com
[2] Deakin University, Geelong, VIC 3220, Australia
s.mahmoudzadeh@deakin.edu.au

Abstract. In this paper a hybrid image defogging approach based on region segmentation is proposed to address the dark channel priori algorithm's shortcomings in de-fogging the sky regions. The preliminary stage of the proposed approach focuses on segmentation of sky and non-sky regions in a foggy image taking the advantageous of Meanshift and edge detection with embedded confidence. In the second stage, an improved dark channel priori algorithm is employed to defog the non-sky region. Ultimately, the sky area is processed by DehazeNet algorithm, which relies on deep learning Convolutional Neural Networks. The simulation results show that the proposed hybrid approach in this research addresses the problem of color distortion associated with sky regions in foggy images. The approach greatly improves the image quality indices including entropy information, visibility ratio of the edges, average gradient, and the saturation percentage with a very fast computation time, which is a good indication of the excellent performance of this model.

Keywords: Image haze removal · Atmospheric scattering model · Regional segmentation · Dark channel prior · DehazeNet

1 Introduction

One of the main challenges associated with the outdoor computer vision system in foggy weather is that the captured images show degradation phenomena such as decreased contrast and color distortion [1]. Therefore, having an efficient de-hazing mechanism is a necessary requirement to cope with the raised issues in dimmed or foggy weather conditions [2]. There are two main approaches for image defogging, one is relying on image enhancement methods [3], such as Retinex algorithm [4], wavelet transform [5], etc., and another approach is the image restoration. Image enhancement techniques can effectively improve the contrast of foggy image and boost the visual effect; however, some image information will be lost as the image degradation with fog is not taken into account in these methods.

On the other hand, the image restoration method uses the modeling and analysis of atmospheric scattering to establish a foggy image degradation model, and takes advantage of the prior knowledge captured in fog-free weather to recover the degraded foggy image [6]. Respectively, Tan (2008) applied contrast enhancement to restore the

© Springer Nature Switzerland AG 2019
J. Li et al. (Eds.): ADMA 2019, LNAI 11888, pp. 489–500, 2019.
https://doi.org/10.1007/978-3-030-35231-8_35

structural features of images and improve the Visibility in bad weather condition [7]. In [8], reflectivity of the object surface is assumed to be not correlated with the medium transmission rate. The author applied independent component analysis to obtain the scene reflectivity, while Markov Random Field (MRF) is employed for image restoration. However, for regions with low image signal-noise, the applied method in [8] is not efficient in terms of defogging. Later on, He et al. [9] proposed a dark channel prior image defrosting algorithm, which could achieve reasonable performance in enhancing majority of the foggy images. However, refining the transmission rate in this method relies on soft matting algorithm, which results in excessive time complexity.

The shortcoming with the dark channel prior theory is that applying this method on images with sky region results in color distortion while reducing the defogging effect, which makes it inappropriate for the images with the sky region. To address this issue, a guided filtering method has been applied by [10] to improve the efficiency of dark channel prior fogging and reduce the time complexity associated with soft matting method; however, in some cases the method tends leave defogging phenomenon incomplete or patchy. Liu et al. [11] proposed a fast image defogging algorithm, which could also improve the sharpness and contrast of the restored image, but this method is still not ideal for the defogging effect of the sky region. Later on an integrated pipeline has been introduced by Li et al., in (2017) that could directly reconstruct a fog-free image through an end-to-end Convolutional Neural Networks (CNNs), but still the resultant image tends to be dark and not clear enough [12].

Respectively, a single image defogging algorithm based on region segmentation is proposed in this research, which aims to address the shortcomings associated with the aforementioned defogging algorithms. To this purpose, MeanShift algorithm with embedded confidence is applied in the first stage to segment the sky and non-sky regions of the original image. Afterward an optimized dark channel prior defogging algorithm is adopted to handle defogging of the non-sky area, while the sky region defogging is handled using an improved neural network DehazeNet. Using such a hybrid approach effectively solves the problem of sky region color distortion in the dark channel prior algorithm. Performance of the proposed approach is investigated and compared to some of the previous researches in the area. The captured restored images in this research tend to have supreme contrast and excellent brightness, rich details, where the resultant colors are very natural, which is a good indication of the promising performance of this hybrid approach.

2 Dark Channel Prior Defogging Algorithm

2.1 Atmospheric Scattering Model

The quality reduction process of foggy image is generally represented by the following atmospheric scattering model:

$$I(x) = J(x)t(x) + A(1 - t(x)) \tag{1}$$

where, $I(x)$ is the observed hazy image, $J(x)$ is the real scene to be recovered, A is the global atmospheric light, $t(x)$ is the medium transmission.

2.2   Dark Channel Prior Defogging Principle

He et al. [9] found that in the vast majority of non-sky areas, the color channel brightness value of some pixels is close to 0. For any input image J, Its dark channel J^{dark} satisfies:

$$J^{dark}(x) = \min_{y \in \Omega(x)} \left(\min_{c \in \{r,g,b\}} (J^c(y)) \right) \to 0 \tag{2}$$

In (2), $\Omega(x)$ corresponds to local neighborhood centered on x; J^c denotes an RGB channel of the image J. Accordingly, the given equation in (1) can be transformed to the following:

$$\frac{I^c(x)}{A^c} = t(x)\frac{J^c(x)}{A^c} + 1 - t(x) \tag{3}$$

Assuming the transmission rate as a constant value in the selected window (presented by $\tilde{t}(x)$ here) and applying the *min* function, the given relation in (3) will be turned to the following:

$$\min_{y \in \Omega(x)} \left(\min_{c \in \{r,g,b\}} \frac{I^c(y)}{A^c} \right) = \tilde{t}(x) \min_{y \in \Omega(x)} \left(\min_{c \in \{r,g,b\}} \frac{J^c(y)}{A^c} \right) + 1 - \tilde{t}(x) \tag{4}$$

Given the dark channel prior theory:

$$\min_{y \in \Omega(x)} \left(\min_{c \in \{r,g,b\}} \frac{J^c(y)}{A^c} \right) = 0 \tag{5}$$

Substituting into Eq. (4):

$$\tilde{t}(x) = 1 - \min_{y \in \Omega(x)} \left(\min_{c \in \{r,g,b\}} \frac{I^c(y)}{A^c} \right) \tag{6}$$

In order to express the depth of field for the image, the coefficient ω $(0 < \omega < 1)$ is introduced by the Eq. (6) as follows:

$$\tilde{t}(x) = 1 - \omega \min_{y \in \Omega(x)} \left(\min_{c \in \{r,g,b\}} \frac{I^c(y)}{A^c} \right) \tag{7}$$

Given A, t and I, we can obtain J as follows:

$$J(x) = \frac{I(x) - A}{\tilde{t}(x)} + A \tag{8}$$

According to (8), the $\tilde{t}(x)$ has inverse relation to J, respectively, when the value of transmission $\tilde{t}(x)$ is too small, J will be large, which leads to the overall whitening of the restored image. Therefore, the threshold value of t_0 (usually is set to 0.1) is encountered to obtain the final image restoration formula as follows:

$$J(x) = \frac{I(x) - A}{\max(\tilde{t}(x), t_0)} + A \tag{9}$$

3   Research Methodology

In this research, we employed a hybrid method including three different phases. In the first stage before defogging procedure, the image gets segmented into sky and non-sky regions. In the second stage, the non-sky regions will be defogged using an improved dark channel prior defogging algorithm. Afterward, the sky region gets proceeded using deep learning neural network DehazeNet. Ultimately, the reconstructed image is obtained by combining the processing results of sky and non-sky regions.

3.1   Extract and Segment the Sky Region

This research, sky region segmentation is carried out using an edge detection embedded with confidence measurement strategy along with the mean shift approach. The confidence measurement strategy facilitates more efficient edge detection.

Assuming the x_i, z_i, $(i = 1, 2, \ldots, n)$ respectively represent the d-dimensional input image of the spatial-color domains, which at the same time corresponds to the pixel of the filtered image, and L_i denote the label of the ith pixel of the segmented image, the mean shift segmentation algorithm consists of the following steps:

Step-1: Let $j = 1$, $y_{i,1} = x_i$
Step-2: Use the following formula to calculate $y_{i, j+1}$, until the convergence of $y = y_{i,c}$.

$$y_{j+1} = \frac{\sum_{i=1}^{n} x_i g\left(\left\|\frac{x-xi}{h}\right\|^2\right)}{\sum_{i=1}^{n} g\left(\left\|\frac{x-xi}{h}\right\|^2\right)}, j = 1, 2, \ldots \tag{10}$$

Where, y_1 is the initial center of the core; y_{j+1} is the weighted average value of position $\{y_j\}$, $(j = 1, 2, \ldots, C)$ calculated by Gaussian kernel function.
Step-3: Let $z_i = (x_i^s, y_{i,c}^r)$, where S represents the domain of the eigenvector and r is the color domain information.

Step-**4:** For each z_i in *Step*-3, put the points whose distance with z_i is less than h_r in the color domain, and less than h_s in the airspace domain, into the corresponding category.

Step-**5:** Set the threshold value M to exclude the number of pixels smaller than M.

The whole procedure is depicted by Fig. 1.

(a) The original image   (b) Grayscale image

(c) Sky cognition process   (d)Morphological operations

Fig. 1. Sky segmentation mechanism

As shown in Fig. 1, first the original foggy image is transformed to grayscale image (Fig. 1(b)). The introduced method is then applied to segment different regions of the image (given by Fig. 1(c)). Afterward, morphological expansion along with corrosion operations is conducted to extract the sky area and obtain the binary image given in Fig. 1(d).

3.2   Dark Channel Prior Optimization Algorithm

Acquiring the Atmospheric Light A. Most of the dark channel prior algorithms take the brightest pixels in the image with fog as the value of atmospheric light A. The main issue with this strategy is that if the non-sky region includes a bright area as well, the obtained atmospheric light A will be larger, which will affect the defogging efficiency. To deal with this issue, we need to scan the whole image and take the average of the pixel point's value with their brightness of the first 0.5%, and then assign it to atmospheric light value of A. The atmospheric light obtained by this method has strong robustness and can eliminate noise interference to some extent.

Obtaining the Transmitter t. In this research, the value of dark channel J^{dark} is assumed to be maximized in order to reduce the transmitter t to a particular extent. Therefore, the min operation in (2) is replaced with the average operation as follows:

$$J^{dark}(x) = \underset{y \in \Omega(x)}{avg} \left(\underset{c \in \{r,g,b\}}{\min} (J^c(y)) \right) \tag{11}$$

According to Eqs. (1) and (7), the improved transmitter can be obtained by (12) as follows:

$$\tilde{t}(x) = 1 - \omega \underset{y \in \Omega(x)}{avg} \left(\underset{c \in \{r,g,b\}}{\min} \frac{I^c(y)}{A^c} \right) \tag{12}$$

Finally, guided filtering is used to refine the transmitter.

Brightness Adjustment. The transmitter obtained by dark channel prior algorithm tends to be small, so this cause the resultant defogged image to be dark. Therefore, in order to compensate this issue, current research conducts a nonlinear contrast stretch image enhancement method [13] to adjust the brightness of the restored image, which is formulated as follows:

$$J'(x) = J(x)(2 - \frac{mean(J(x))}{255}) \tag{13}$$

Where, $mean(J(x))$ represents the pixel brightness. The given adjustment through the (13) can improve the total brightness of the restored image.

3.3   Improved DehazeNet Defogging Algorithm

In order to have an efficient defogging, Cai et al. [14] proposed an end-to-end system model DehazeNet based on CNN, which is divided into four stages: feature extraction, multi-scale mapping, local extremum and nonlinear regression.

This research applies the optimized version of the DehazeNet model making the use of full convolution network structure, which effectively preserves the important image information. Consequently, the method is augmented with a multiple feature fusion mechanism facilitating the direct reconstruction of the defogged sky-region image out of the foggy image. So the algorithm follows two steps of multi-scale feature fusion and feature extraction. The operation diagram of the algorithm is depicted by Fig. 2.

Feature Extraction. Feature extraction stage consists of a single convolutional layer and three consecutive three-layer convolutional layers. The output of all convolution operations should be equal to zero to ensure that the output image remains in the same size. The given 9 convolutional layers operate as 3 sets of feature extraction units which can gradually obtain the detailed information of the image. The convolutional operation is formulated as follows:

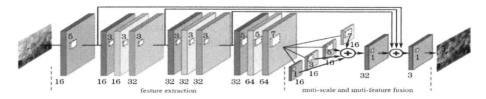

Fig. 2. Improved DehazeNet structure

$$G_l = W_l * F_{(l-i)}(Y) \tag{14}$$

Here, W_l represents the lth convolutional layer and corresponds to the number of parameters calculated through the $n_l \times f_l \times f_l$, where n_l and f_l are the number and size of the convolution kernel, respectively. G_l is the characteristics of the output image, and '*' is the convolution operation.

The PReLU is adopted as the network's activation function in this research. The PReLU function is advantageous to be able to modify the parameters, which improves the model's overall scalability and generalization. Furthermore, PReLU can accelerate the convergence speed of the algorithm. The PReLU function is defined as follows:

$$P_{ReLU}(x_i) = \max(x_i, 0) + a_i \min(0, x_i) \tag{15}$$

Where, x_i is the positive input signal to layer i; a_i is the weight coefficient of the negative interval of the ith layer. Accordingly, output of the final convolutional layer would be:

$$F_l(Y) = P_{ReLU}[W_l * F_{l-1}(Y) + B_l] \tag{16}$$

Here, B_l represents the bias to layer l, and F_l is the final characteristics of the output graph.

Multi-scale Multi-feature Fusion. Since the image of foggy sky contains both color differences caused by different fog concentrations and texture features, this paper adopts multi-scale multi-feature fusion method to further extract the existing features. The model is structured with five trainable convolutional layers, where the output of these multi-scale convolutional layers is fed to three feature extraction units as input.

Table 1. Multi-scale Multi-feature fusion parameter configuration

Layer type	Configuration (padding, Stride, feature map, Kernel)				
Convolution layer	Pad-0	Stride-1	Fm-16	Kernel-1 $\times$ 1	PReLU
Convolution layer	Pad-0	Stride-1	Fm-16	Kernel-3 $\times$ 3	PReLU
Convolution layer	Pad-0	Stride-1	Fm-16	Kernel-5 $\times$ 5	PReLU
Convolution layer	Pad-0	Stride-1	Fm-16	Kernel-7 $\times$ 7	PReLU

Multi-feature fusion is completed with four cores of 1×1, 3×3, 5×5, and 7×7. Multi-scale multi-feature fusion layer parameters are configured as is shown in Table 1.

The multi-scale convolution process is as follows:

$$F_{li}(Y) = P_{ReLU}[W_{li} * F_{l-1}(Y) + B_l] \tag{17}$$

In (17), B_l represents the bias to layer l, F_{l-1} is the characteristics of the output graph, W_{li} ($i = 1, 2, 3, 4$) corresponds to four convolution kernels. Four given sets of convolution kernels process in parallel in order to provide 64 feature graphs. Afterward, the provided 64 feature graphs will be convolved with a convolution kernel size of 1×1. After all, multi-scale feature information gets weighted and fused to obtain the image after defrosting.

4 Simulation Results and Analysis

A number of foggy images are selected for simulation and evaluation of the applied method. The efficiency of the proposed method in this paper is compared to the algorithms applied in the same area by two recent approach [9, 14]. The provided results and the comparisons are depicted in Fig. 3, which is carried out to test and evaluate the applied methods' performance from the various perspective and in different environments. The mainstream deep learning caffe and Matlab R2014a have been used as the simulation platform. The PC used for the experiment was configured as: 64-bit Windows10 operating system, 8 GB of memory, Intel Core(TM)i7-6700K@4.0GHz processor, and NVIDIA QUADRO GP100 GPU.

For training and testing the applied improved DehazeNet model, an experimental data source of 10 foggy images has been used, in which the images are captured under natural scenes and 60 images of foggy images restored by atmospheric scattering model. The images have been rotated for 90°, 180°, and 270°, and then expanded to 2, 3, 4, and 5 times to get 1400 pictures of different resolution and scene. The provided images then have been used as the training and validation sets with of 6:1, respectively.

4.1 Subjective Evaluation

The efficiency of the proposed approaches by He et al. [9] and Cai et al. [14] in defrosting the image of non-sky areas is relatively good as the image clarity and contrast are greatly improved, which is presented by Fig. 3. However, referring to the results depicted in Fig. 3(b)(c) and comparing them to Fig. 3(a)(d), apparently both of the proposed approaches in [9] and [14] do not show the expected efficacious performance in dealing with sky regions. Especially focusing on Figs. 3(b) and 7(b) it is obvious that although the proposed approach in [9] greatly defogs the non-sky areas, but color distortion occurs in non-sky regions. Cai et al. [14] took the advantages of end-to-end CNN model to deal with this issue; however, the method provided poor defogging performance in the natural scene, which is clearly presented by Fig. 4.

Furthermore, referring to Figs. 3, 4, 5, 6 and 7 it can be seen the defogged images by [9] and [14] tend to be dark with low contrast, which negatively affect the visual appearance of the scene. Comparing to the proposed methods by [9] and [14], the introduced hybrid method in this research shows competent performance in defogging the image of both sky and non-sky area, while also improves the overall brightness of the restored image, making the color of the image real and natural. Performance of the proposed hybrid method and the previously applied methods is depicted by Figs. 3, 4, 5, 6 and 7 and the comparison is carried out in different scenes.

Considering the both sky and non-sky regions in Figs. 3 and 5, evidently our proposed approach greatly preserves the images natural of the original scene in the close shot when comparing to [9, 14]. Moreover, defogging effect at the distant shot is greatly improved, and the method tends to show a superior performance in the overall color reduction. Accordingly, the provided comparison and analyses by Figs. 3, 4, 5, 6 and 7 is a good indication of superior performance of the proposed model in this research.

(a)	(b)	(c)	(d)
The original image	Algorithm applied by He et al., [9]	Algorithm applied by Cai et al., [14]	Algorithm proposed by this research

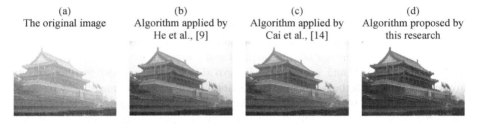

Fig. 3. Comparison of defogging effect in sky/non-sky regions

Fig. 4. Comparison of defogging effect in natural scene

Fig. 5. Comparison of defogging effect in building scene

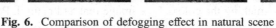

Fig. 6. Comparison of defogging effect in natural scene

Fig. 7. Comparison of defogging effect in city scene

4.2 Objective Evaluation

To further assess the performance of our model, number of important image quality evaluation indices such as entropy information, visibility ratio, average gradient, and pixels' saturation percentage are investigated and compered to [9] and [14].

This investigation and comparison is provided by Table 2, where the entropy information represents the richness of information contained in an image, which should be maximized. Both ratio of new visible edges and the percentage of saturated pixels reflect the degree of local contrast enhancement of foggy images. The ratio of new visible edges needs to be increased in order to improve the clarity of the image and feature recovery of the scene. On the other hand, the saturated pixels' percentage should be reduced in order to achieve a better image restoration. The average gradient reflects the details of the image, which has a direct relation to image contour clarity and should be increased [15].

Given the results in Table 2, it can be seen the entropy information and average gradient of the algorithm in this research tends to be higher that provided values by [9] and [14], which indicates superior color saturation and methods accuracy in detailed image restoration. Fast computation is also an important performance factor that should be taken into account. In terms of algorithm execution time, our propose approach considerably reduces the run time in the two stages of sky region segmentation and defogging comparing to [9] and [14], which also indicates method's competent execution efficiency.

The simulation results show that the proposed algorithm is thoroughly suitable for non-sky region defogging as well. The proposed method in this research provides great level of color restoration, saturation and clarity improvement compared to [9] and [14]. From the objective perspective, the performance indices obtained by the algorithm in this paper are also superior to the results provided by [9] and [14]. Ultimately, it can be inferred from the entire comparisons over the simulation results that our proposed method tends to have excellent operational efficiency and great performance especially in processing of the single foggy image.

Table 2. Comparison of performance indices provided by different algorithms

Image	Applied method	Entropy info	Visibility ratio	Average gradient	Pixels' saturation %	Run time (s)
A 473 × 283	Cai et al. [14]	5.7105	0.0276	3.8103	15.0008%	11.7350 (s)
	He et al. [9]	5.7130	0.1146	3.6574	32.2857%	3.14680 (s)
	This research	5.7706	0.2492	4.0763	12.9594%	2.19860 (s)
B 472 × 317	Cai et al. [14]	6.8610	0.2695	3.6932	18.7260%	13.3360 (s)
	He et al. [9]	6.8488	0.1388	3.1168	16.5730%	4.19320 (s)
	This research	6.8989	0.3346	3.7371	13.8560%	3.30620 (s)
C 470 × 352	Cai et al. [14]	5.4778	0.0710	3.2199	20.3762%	9.53600 (s)
	He et al. [9]	7.4709	0.1475	2.9654	18.2453%	2.74060 (s)
	This research	7.5389	0.1642	3.6061	17.6342%	2.13450 (s)
D 600 × 525	Cai et al. [14]	6.4162	0.2318	5.7956	15.6282%	12.2658 (s)
	He et al. [9]	7.3935	0.3237	5.7364	15.6228%	1.83980 (s)
	This research	8.4941	0.3020	5.8585	14.3758%	2.16740 (s)
E 564 × 399	Cai et al. [14]	7.5322	0.1983	1.9538	15.9823%	12.2486 (s)
	He et al. [9]	8.3514	0.0584	1.7980	14.1240%	2.23650 (s)
	This research	8.4609	0.1874	2.2166	14.0026%	3.07550 (s)

5   Conclusion

In this paper, a single image defogging algorithm based on region segmentation is proposed, which uses the optimized atmospheric dissipation function to defog the sky region. The proposed approach employs DehazeNet algorithm which is based on deep learning convolutional neural network to effectively solve the problem of dark channel prior algorithm in color distortion of sky region in foggy situations. On the other hand, an optimized dark channel prior defogging algorithm is adopted to deal with the non-sky areas, which improves the brightness while preserving the excellent defogging performance of the dark channel prior algorithm. The simulation result indicates the superior performance of our approach comparing to the results provided by two recent researches in the area. The approach has outstanding performance of defogging both sky and non-sky regions, while the restored image has a great level of color reduction and without losing details. The algorithm also perfectly satisfies the performance indices of the image quality such as entropy information, visibility ratio, average gradient, and the saturation percentage, which is a good indication of the excellent performance of this model.

References

1. Dan-Dan, C., Li, C., Yong-Xin, Z.: Fog removal of single image with modified atmospheric dissipation function. Chin. J. Image Graph. **22**(06), 787–796 (2017)
2. Ping, W., Yunfeng, Z., Fangxun, B., Hongwei, D., Caiming, Z.: Optimization of fog removal method based on image quality reduction model in foggy days. Chin. J. Image Graph. **23**(04), 605–616 (2008)

3. Yufei, D., Yan, Y., Biting, C.: Single image depth defogging algorithm based on guidance graph optimization. Comput. Appl. **37**(01), 268–277 (2017)
4. Yang, L., Jie, Z., Hui, Z.: A modified Retinex algorithm for image defogging research and application. Comput. Sci. **45**(S1), 242–251 (2018)
5. Wenchao, J., Haibo, L., Yujie, Y., Jiafeng, C., Aobing, S.: A high similarity image recognition and classification algorithm combining wavelet transform and convolutional neural network. Comput. Eng. Sci. **40**(09), 1646–1652 (2018)
6. Dian-Wei, W., Wei-Chao, Y., Ying, L., Ting-Ge, Z.: Fast single image defogging algorithm based on dark channel prior. Comput. Appl. Res. **01**, 1–7 (2019)
7. Tan, R.T.: Visibility in bad weather from a single image. In: IEEE Conference on Computer Vision and Pattern Recognition, Washington, pp. 1–8 (2008)
8. Fattal, R.: Single Image Dehazing. ACM Trans. Graph. **27**(3), 72 (2008)
9. He, K.M., Sun, J., Tang, X.O.: Single image haze removal using dark channel prior. IEEE Trans. Pattern Anal. Mach. Intell. **33**(12), 2341–2353 (2011)
10. He, K.M., Sun, J., Tang, X.O.: Guided image filtering. IEEE Trans. Pattern Anal. Mach. Intell. **35**(6), 1397–1409 (2013)
11. Jieping, L., Bingkun, H., Gang, W.: A fast algorithm for defogging single image. Acta Electronica Sinica **45**(08), 1896–1901 (2017)
12. Li, B., Peng, X., Wang, Z.: An All-in-One Network for Dehazing and Beyond. arXiv: Computer Vision and Pattern Recognition (2017)
13. Zhang, D., Ju, M., Wang, X.: A fast image defogging algorithm based on dark channel prior. Acta Electronica Sinica **43**(07), 1437–1443 (2015)
14. Cai, B., Xu, X., Jia, K., Qing, C., Tao, D.: DehazeNet: an end-to-end system for single image haze removal. IEEE Trans. Image Process. **25**(11), 5187–5198 (2016)
15. Chengming, R.: Research on defogging algorithm for single fog image. Anhui University (2017)

Online Aggregated-Event Representation for Multiple Event Detection in Videos

Molefe Vicky Mleya[1], Weiqi Li[1], Jiayu Liang[1], Kunliang Liu[1], Yunkuan Sun[2], Guanghao Jin[1], and Jianming Wang[1(✉)]

[1] School of Computer Science and Technology, Tianjin Polytechnic University, Tianjin, China
wangjianming@tjpu.edu.cn
[2] School of Electronics and Information Engineering, Tianjin Polytechnic University, Tianjin, China

Abstract. Event detection is used to locate the frames corresponding to events of interest in given videos. Real-world videos contain multiple events of interest, and they are rarely segmented. Existing online methods can only detect segments containing single event instances, and this is not suitable for processing videos with several event instances. There are multiple event detection methods, but they are all relatively inefficient and offline methods. To handle the online detection of several events, we propose a novel framework with three modules that are: the event proposal generation, aggregated-event representation, and refined detection modules. The first module can locate time intervals that are likely to contain target events, termed as proposals. The second module can aggregate all events before the current time to form a temporal context that will be used to generate initial detection results of multiple events. The refined detection module finally refines the results based on event proposals and object detection. The proposed method achieves a detection accuracy of 24.88% on a multi-event dataset - Charades, which is higher than state-of-the-art methods.

Keywords: Multiple event detection · Online event detection · Aggregated-event representation

1 Introduction

Event detection is the process of locating the frames corresponding to target events in a given video [3,13]. Challenging as it may be, it is an important computer vision task which has a wide range of real-world applications such as live videos, smart surveillance, online video retrieval, and robot perception [2,3,13,14].

Supported by Natural Science Foundation of Tianjin (Grant No. 16JCYBJC42300, 17JCQNJC00100, 18JCYBJC44000, 18JCYBJC15300) and National Natural Science Foundation of China (Grant No. 6180021345, 61771340).

© Springer Nature Switzerland AG 2019
J. Li et al. (Eds.): ADMA 2019, LNAI 11888, pp. 501–515, 2019.
https://doi.org/10.1007/978-3-030-35231-8_36

Based on whether there is a single event or multiple events in a time interval of the given videos, there are single and multiple event detection methods that may be used [5,9,17] (explained in Fig. 1). The event detection methods can either be online or offline methods [5]. The online methods begin to detect the start of an event in a video stream as soon as it happens [5], while the offline methods are not real-time, they detect events after thoroughly observing an entire video.

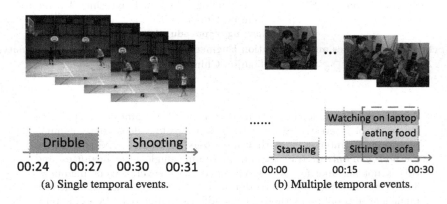

Fig. 1. Different temporal organization of events in videos: (a) only a single event occurring in a temporal interval; (b) multiple events overlap temporally.

Most existing online event detection methods [5,11] perform single event detection, which only assigns a single event label to a particular time interval. De Geest et al. [5] propose an online action detection dataset and an evaluation protocol, while the work by Zheng et al. [11] proposes a new task, i.e., online detection of action start (ODAS) in continuous videos. However, real-world videos typically contain multiple events that are rarely segmented [9]. *The existing online methods are not suitable for handling the detection of multiple, correlated events. Online methods are not able to accumulate the temporal context with multiple events, mainly when multiple events exist in a temporally-overlapping manner.*

In literature, there is a limited number of works related to multiple event detection [9,16]. Yeung et al. [16] in their work, extend the sports video dataset THUMOS to form a new dataset MultiTHUMOS containing dense labels for each video, and propose a new method based on the LSTM (long short-term memory) network for multiple event recognition. Piergiovanni et al. [9] go on to introduce a new concept, termed as a super-event that is a set of events occurring together with a particular temporal organization to assist frame-level event detection. *The major challenge of the two multiple detection methods [9,16] is that they adopt offline frameworks, which we can not use in online applications.* In particular, the method [9] needs to extract the optical flow images in advance to obtain motion information, which is very inefficient and time-consuming.

Based on the above analyses, online multiple event detection on video streams undoubtedly deserves more investigation, and this paper designs a new online method that can detect multiple events. The framework consists of three modules, i.e., the event proposal generation module, aggregated-event representation module, and refined detection module. To be specific, the first module can locate frames that are likely to contain target events, and these are called event proposals. In the second module, we introduce a new concept (termed as aggregated-event representation), based on which the initial detection results (time boundaries on a given video for each target event). The refined detection module finally refines the initial results based on event proposals and object detection.

The main contributions of this paper are as follows:

- It proposes an online framework for multiple event detection for the first time.
- It introduces a new concept called aggregated-event representation - It aggregates past events before current time on a video to form the context information that can be used to improve the detection accuracy on the current frame.
- It achieves state-of-the-art results on challenging multiple event dataset.

2   Related Work

Based on different grouping criteria, there are single or multiple event detection methods [4,16] and also online or offline event detection methods [5,15]. This paper aims to solve online multiple event detection tasks; therefore, in this section, the existing online and multiple event detection methods are reviewed.

2.1   Online Event Detection

Online event detection Online event/action detection aims to detect the start of action in a video as soon as it occurs [11]. It is a challenging task since it only observes a part of the actions, and significant variability exists within and across action classes in real-world videos [5].

De Geest et al. [5] propose an online action detection dataset, containing 27 episodes from 6 TV series, annotated with 30 action classes. An evaluation protocol based on precision is proposed to evaluate the online action detection tasks. They also select three popular baseline methods for action detection on the proposed dataset. None of the selected methods perform well, which reflects that online action detection is challenging and deserves investigation.

Zheng et al. [11] aim to solve a new task, i.e., online detection of action start (ODAS) in continuous videos. They aim to detect the action start with high accuracy and low latency, which is essential in many applications, e.g. timely alert generation for timely security or emergency response. Specifically, three novel methods are proposed to address problems in training ODAS models. Firstly, a GAN (Generative Adversarial Network) is applied to generate difficult negative samples that help to distinguish ambiguous backgrounds. Secondly, they explicitly model the temporal consistency between video intervals around and succeeding action starts. Thirdly, an adaptive sampling strategy, is designed to tackle the scarcity of training data. Experiments on datasets like THUMOS14 and ActivityNet, achieve promising results.

A drawback of these two works is that they are designed to detect single event instances in a segment. However, real-world videos typically contain multiple events that are correlated; unfortunately, the existing online methods cannot handle multiple event detection.

2.2   Multiple Event Detection

In realistic videos, it is common for multiple events to occur in a sequence or a parallel manner [9]. There is only a limited number of event detection works [9,16] that can handle multiple events.

Yeung et al. [16] think that in order to understand human activity in a video comprehensively, it is necessary to use multiple labels to label each frame. They extend the THUMOS video dataset to form a new dataset MultiTHUMOS that contains dense labels over each video. They also propose a new network based on an LSTM (long short-term memory) network to capture temporal relations within and between activity classes, which helps with multiple action recognition. The proposed MultiLSTM outperforms the LSTM on the MultiTHUMOS dataset on multiple action detection. This MultiTHUMOS dataset, however, it is limited to sport categories.

Piergiovanni et al. [9] introduce a concept, called a super-event, which refers to a set of events occurring together in videos. As real-world videos usually contain multiple activities that are rarely separated, learning super-events helps capture the temporal relations of events in videos. Specifically, they design temporal structure filters to capture certain video intervals that are then processed by a soft attention mechanism to learn representations of super-events. Then the super-event representations are incorporated with per-frame features extracted by a CNN to provide frame-level representations. Eventually, the frame representations are input to an activity detector. Note that the proposed method is an end-to-end activity detector that also learns super-event representations too. The results show that the proposed method outperforms existing multiple activity detection methods.

One major drawback of the existing multiple detection methods [9,16] is that they are in offline form, and they use the temporal context of the past and future frames for event detection on the current frame. They are not suitable for online detection when future frames are not available. Moreover, these methods cannot handle events with extended time intervals; thus, the detected events are fragmented and concentrated into shorter event frames within the corresponding ground truth events. In other words, they cannot detect the start and end of events accurately. Therefore, online multiple event detection deserves more investigation, which we have addressed in this paper.

3 Methodology

Figure 2 shows the proposed online event detection method for multiple events. It consists of three modules: the event proposal generation module, the aggregated-event representation module, and the refined detection module. The event proposal generation module and the aggregated-event representation module run simultaneously. The first module can detect and locate time intervals that are likely to contain target events (possible time boundaries for all events). Firstly, the outputs of the proposal generation and aggregated-event modules are analyzed to locate the non-overlapping temporal intervals. Secondly, considering that the non-overlapping intervals are highly likely to contain events, these time regions are re-considered, and labels are given based on the information of event-relevant objects detected in the frames.

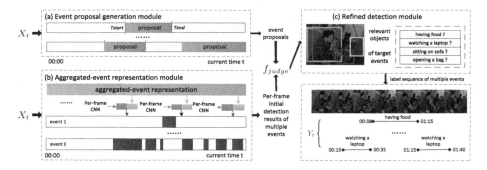

Fig. 2. Framework of the proposed online multiple event detection method (E stands for the number of target events; *Tstart* and *Tend* mean the starting and end time of each proposal respectively).

Input to the Proposed Method: A video stream X_t (shown in Eq. 1)

$$X_t = \{[x_1, x_2, \ldots, x_\delta], \ldots, [x_{(t-1)*\delta+1}, x_{(t-1)*\delta+2}, \ldots, x_{t*\delta}]\}$$
$$= \{\{x_i\}_{i=1}^{\delta}, \ldots, \{x_i\}_{i=(t-1)*\delta+1}^{t*\delta}\} \tag{1}$$
$$= \{\overrightarrow{x_1}, \ldots, \overrightarrow{x_t}\}$$

where X_t is equally separated into t non-overlapping time stamps/intervals (each stamp has δ frames); t stands for the current time stamp; x_i refers to the i_{th} frame of this video stream; $\overrightarrow{x_1}$ is the first time interval with δ frames.

Output of the Proposed Method: A label sequence Y_t with multiple event labels in temporal order. It can be expressed as follows.

$$Y_t = \{\overrightarrow{y_1}, \overrightarrow{y_2}, \ldots, \overrightarrow{y_{t*\delta}}\}$$
$$= \{\overrightarrow{y_i}\}_{i=1}^{t*\delta} \tag{2}$$
$$\overrightarrow{y_i} = \{y_i^j\}_{j=1}^{n}$$

where $\vec{y_i}$ refers to the labels of the multiple events occurring in the i_{th} frame of the input video; y_i^j is the j_{th} event label occurring in the i_{th} frame, and n is the number of event categories.

Specifically, when given the video observations X_t reaches timestamp t (each stamp has δ frames), a new aggregated set of estimated event proposals is produced. The stated estimate Y_t until stamp t is obtained using the following equation through Bayes Rule (the result of the last frame is $\vec{y_{t*\delta}}$ belongs to Y_t):

$$p(Y_t|X_t) = R\{f_{judge}[S_{GRU}(\phi_{C3D}(X_t)), A(\phi_{I3D}(X_t))]\} \tag{3}$$

where the frame sequences X_t are first input to a C3D visual encoding module ϕ_{C3D} to extract the features. Then according to the event proposal generation module, features are processed by a sequence encoding module S_{GRU} to get the proposals output. At each time stamp, they output k variable length proposals, which end at time $t \cdot \delta$. On the aggregated-event module, we use I3D as the feature extractor ϕ_{I3D}. The latent aggregated-event is generated by function A, which is detailed in Sect. 3.2. The output of this module is a per-frame event detection confidence score distribution among n pre-defined event classes. We set a filter threshold $\alpha = 0.1$ to select possible events. After that, we refine frames which are covered by proposals but not detected as events using refiner module R. The refined frames are selected by function f_{judge}.

3.1   Event Proposal Generation Module

Bush et al. [1] propose a method called the Single-Stream Temporal Action Proposal (SST) to detect time intervals that contain events of interest; we term these as event proposals. However, each proposal in the paper [1] only corresponds to a single event. In other words, the SST method can only generate a single proposal at a time.

This paper is a variant of the SST method. It is capable of generating proposals at different time intervals and only needs to iterate over the video once. We increased the length of the anchor during training to include longer-order events, and at the end, we eliminated non-maximum suppression to keep overlapping proposals separate and treat them as individual outputs.

Through these modifications, we improve the SST method to handle multiple co-occurring target events, which can generate event proposals containing multiple events with corresponding confidence scores. The generation of proposals on the current timestamp is only based on past and current video information; thus, this module can be utilized in online applications.

Input to This Module: The input X_t contains the new, current time stamp $\vec{x_t}$ and previous input $\{\vec{x_1}, \ldots, \vec{x_{t-1}}\}$. (details are in Eq. 1).

As shown in Fig. 3, the C3D (a 3D Convolutional network [3]) is applied to extract video features from the current time stamp (described in Eq. 4). Then the C3D features of each time stamp are input temporally to the recurrent sequence model (a Gated Recurrent Unit (GRU) model) S_{GRU} to encode the sequential information between the time stamps.

$$\overrightarrow{v_t} = \{v_i\}_{i=(t-1)*\delta+1}^{t*\delta} \tag{4}$$

where v_i is a feature vector that describes the i_{th} frame.

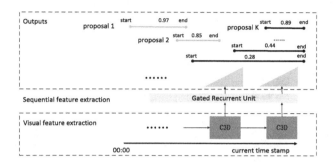

Fig. 3. The framework of the proposal generation module. The black part of the output subgraph represents the candidate proposals generated at the current timestamp. The number indicates the corresponding confidence scores of each proposal, and the red number indicates that the score is too low to be regarded as a proposal; thus, it is excluded. The gray part indicates the retained proposals from the previous timestamp have high confidence scores. It has K proposals after the current timestamp. (Color figure online)

Output of This Module: K proposals with high confidence scores.

Each proposal is a time interval detected as containing target events, and the confidence scores reflect confidence of the proposals being correct. As shown in Fig. 3, a series of candidate proposals generated at the current timestamp may vary in length but share the same temporal ending boundary $x_{t*\delta}$ (the last frame of the current timestamp), but only candidates with higher confidence scores will be considered as proposals. K proposals are composed of current timestamp proposals and previous timestamp proposals, these proposals all have high confidence score. Proposals with low scores are excluded.

3.2 Aggregated-Event Representation

In this section, a new concept termed aggregated-event representation is introduced. It is an online variant of latent super-event representation introduced in the work [9].

The super-event is defined as a longer-term event containing several events of interest; it is the opposite concept of 'sub-events.' Such super-events are 'latent,' meaning that no super-event annotations are provided.

There are some differences between aggregated-events and super-events: (1) The super-event representation is generated in an offline manner and thus requires the whole video for processing. On the other hand, aggregated-event representation does not rely on the complete video being acquired in advance. It, however, can accumulate all events occurring from the beginning to the current time to generate a temporal context representation. (2) In our online form, the aggregated-event can be updated, because as the number of video frames we read increases, the latent context of each event instance changes.

The online aggregated-event representation is introduced to describe the events of interest occurring from the start to the current time.

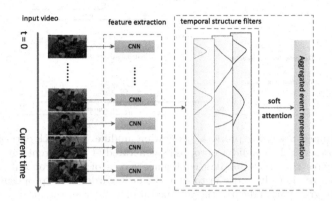

Fig. 4. The framework of the aggregated-event representation module.

As shown in Fig. 4, the input to this aggregated-event representation module comprises of frame sequences from when the video starts to the current timestamp. Since we have already extracted the video features from previous frames before the current timestamp, a pre-trained CNN is applied to only extract features (v_t) on each new frame that comes up, then the features are concatenated.

The temporal structure filters [9] are used to process the CNN features, which can extract information that focuses on particular sub-intervals and select the time frames with possible events. After that, a set of per-event soft-attention weights are learned. These will then concatenate the events to form the aggregated-event representation.

For a set of E target events and M structure filters ($F_m, m = 1, \ldots, M$), the learned weights are $W_{e,m}$ and the soft attention is $S_{e,m}$ (shown in Eq. 5). Based on these, the aggregated-event representation is described by A_e (shown in Eq. 6).

$$S_{e,m} = \frac{\exp(W_{e,m})}{\sum_k^M \exp(W_{e,k})} \tag{5}$$

$$A_e = \sum_m^M S_{e,m} \cdot \sum_{i=1}^{t \cdot \delta} F_m[i] \cdot v_i \tag{6}$$

The learned aggregated-event representation is then used as the temporal context when conducting online event detection on the current frame. Specifically, per-frame binary classification is conducted for each event by incorporating the aggregated-event representation, together with the per-frame CNN representation:

$$p(e|[v_t, A_e]) = \sigma(W[v_t, A_e]) \tag{7}$$

where A_e is the aggregated representation; W is a learnable parameter and σ is the sigmoid function; p stands for probability; v_i refers to the features of the i_{th} frame.

As the number of video frames that we read increases, the latent context of the event of interest to be detected is also changed. That is, the aggregated-event is updated over time, and the previous detection results need to be updated based on current event information. To handle this, we add the current frames as new timestamp frames. Then we treat the new timestamp as new input to this module, and the aggregated-event representation is generated again upon addition of each new timestamp, based on previous frames and current frames.

3.3   Refined Detection Module

In this section, all the event detection results of the aggregated-event module are refined based on the outputs of the proposal generation module and object detection. Firstly, the detection results of the first two modules (i.e., the proposal generation and the aggregated-event modules) are analyzed to locate the non-overlapping time intervals. The frames that need to be refined are filtered by a function f_{judge}. This is done in order to ensure there is no miss-detection in the non-overlapping time intervals. The detection of objects in videos helps with understanding human behaviour/events interaction with surroundings. Object detection based on Faster-RCNN [10] is conducted on the frames of the non-overlapping intervals. If the objects relevant to certain target events in the non-overlapping intervals are detected, it is then believed that events related to these objects occur and they are labelled accordingly.

4   Results and Discussions

4.1   Experiment Preparation

Dataset: The mAP (mean average precision) [9] is applied to evaluate the event detection performance, the higher it is, the better. The benchmark event detection dataset, Charades, is selected. It contains 9848 videos across 157 human activities/events, including "preparing a meal" and "opening a laptop". Additionally, each video contains 6.8 events on average, which often overlap temporally. Each event category name comprises of behavioral verbs to do with human bodily movement (e.g. "close" and "throw"); the object categories are nouns (e.g. "book" and "phone") that interact with the person.

Implementation and Details: In our experiments, we implemented the whole framework in PyTorch. We set the length of a timestamp $\delta = 16$. The framework reads 16 new frames per each timestamp. In the event proposal generation module, we follow the [1] training procedures. In the aggregated-event representation module, we use I3D as part of the base features of the CNN, and the I3D module is fine-tuned to work on the Charades dataset. In the refined detection module, we obtain the pre-trained model on ResNet V1 101; we train it on the COCO dataset [7] which contains 80 object categories. We retrained the object categories that were not included in the COCO dataset but appeared in the charades dataset.

4.2   Results of the Proposal Generation Module

The event proposal generation module localizes the time intervals that are likely to contain target events in a given video. Table 1 shows the results of this module in terms of "recall@1000, tIoU $= m$", which follows the settings of the paper [1]. Specifically, "recall@1000" are the recall at 1000 proposals; "tIoU" stands for temporal Intersection over Union, which means temporal overlap with the ground truth event interval; The higher recall/tIoU the better. Therefore, "tIoU $= 80\%$" is selected for the following experiments. This table shows that the proposal generation module reaches 0.752 in recall when "tIoU $= 80\%$".

Table 1. Results of the event proposal generation module (Recall@1000 means the recall at 1000 retrieved proposals; tIoU is the temporal overlap with ground truth).

tIoU	20%	40%	60%	80%
Recall@1000	0.993	0.987	0.948	0.752

4.3   Results of the Aggregated-Event Representation Module

Aggregated-event representation is introduced to extract context information from past frames for event detection on the current frame. It is a variant of latent super-event representation [9] that is in an offline form. To meet the needs of online processing, we design the proposed aggregated-event representation module without using future frames for event detection on the current frame.

When we observe the videos, we compare the frame-level mAP at different temporal parts. We have shown the top-3 results in Table 2. As shown in Fig. 5, we reach the highest frame-level mAP when the video observation percentage is almost 60%.

Table 2. Top-3 frame-level mAP and its corresponding video observation percentage.

Video observation percentage	mAP
65%	23.1932
60%	23.0266
50%	22.9476

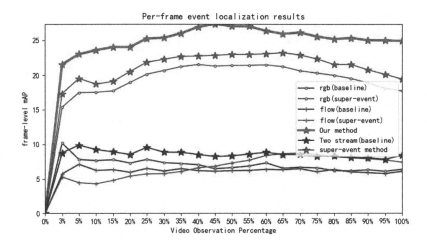

Fig. 5. An example of event detection generated by the proposed method. (Color figure online)

4.4 Results of the Proposed Method with Three Modules

Figure 5 shows the performance of the per-frame localization with our online setting. We follow the original Charades test setting (i.e., Charades v1 localize evaluation) from the dataset website, and we compare our method with state-of-the-art methods. Our method (shown by the red line) obtains the best per-frame event localization results on the Charades dataset. The baseline (shown in blue) shows the two-stream method implemented by [12]. After [12] observes the complete video, the frame-level mAP they achieve is 8.94%. The super-event method (shown in green) represents the method proposed by [9], and we also illustrate its corresponding RGB and flow results, respectively. From Fig. 5, we can see that our method gets state-of-the-art frame-level mAP results, regardless of which part of the video we observe.

Table 3 shows the event detection results when we observe 100% of the videos; thus, we can compare the proposed method with both online methods [12] and offline methods [2, 6, 8, 9, 15]. These referenced methods are all updated event detection methods that achieve state-of-the-art performance. The proposed method reaches 24.88 in mAP, which is the best among all the reference methods. Specifically, when compared with the proposed method, the results from the

"RGB" and "Two-stream" methods [12] are only around one quarter of its mAP value. In addition, the proposed method has a mAP that is also significantly better than the "R-C3D [15], I3D [2], I3D + LSTM [9], I3D + Stacked-STGCN [6] and I3D + Super-events [9]". Moreover, the most updated work [8] proposes "I3D + 3TGMs + Super-events" by introducing a Temporal Gaussian Mixture (TGM) layer to capture temporal structure. It ranks second with its mAP value being around three less than our method.

Table 3. Results on the Charades dataset with full off-line videos observed.

Methods	mAP
RGB [12]	7.89
Two-stream [12]	8.94
R-C3D [15]	12.7
I3D [2]	17.22
I3D + LSTM [9]	18.1
I3D + Stacked-STGCN [6]	19.09
I3D + Super-events [9]	19.41
I3D + 3TGMs + Super-events [8]	21.8
The proposed method	24.88

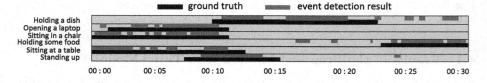

Fig. 6. An example of event detection generated by the proposed method.

Figure 6 illustrates the results of an example of multiple event detection generated by the proposed method. Compared with the ground truth, we see that the detected event intervals are quite accurate since the majority of the detected intervals overlap with the ground truth. Note that true negative and false negative intervals both exist. Considering that multiple event detection is a challenging task, and the Charades dataset is highly varied in event types and backgrounds, the results are still promising.

4.5   Event Detection Results

In this section, we evaluate the performance of our method on both single and multiple event detection. Each frame has a set of event categories it contains. In the Charades test-set, all the events per-frame that are numbered and labeled (in Table 4). Each frame has up to 19 labeled events, which means these events are all present in this frame and together describe the person in the video's current behavior. We can intuitively see that most of the frames have three labeled events in Table 4, and they account for 16.74% of total test video frames ran. This figure is closely followed by that of the frames that have four event labels, which accounts for about 16.57% of total test frames, and only 14.94% have two event labels.

In this part of the experiment, we measure the number of events correctly detected and labeled. Each frame in the charades dataset comes readily marked with a certain number of event labels. In previous settings, we could only consider detection results as correct when the number of event predictions within a particular frame corresponded to the total number of labels in the multi-label set. We, however, change this setting, and in this work, detection will be considered as correct when the N predictions in the detected event set match the N events correctly predicted from the multi-label set. We make the N value variable, which means that we can change it to any whole number.

Table 5 shows the performance results of the proposed method when it performs detection on one, two, and multiple events.

Table 4. Statistic results of charades dataset

Number of events per frame	Percentage of total frames
3	16.74%
4	16.57%
2	14.94%

Table 5. Performance results of single and multiple event detection. When we predict an event, that matches one of the labels in the correct label set; we assume that the detection in this frame is correct. The performance is measured by dividing the number of correctly predicted frames in the entire dataset by the total number of frames.

Number events correctly detected	All	2	1
Detection performance	21.93%	52.99%	70.66%

5   Conclusion

In this paper, we propose an online framework for detecting multiple events, which consists of three modules, i.e., the event proposal generation module, aggregated-event representation module, and the refined event detection module. The event proposal generation module can locate time intervals that are likely to contain target events. The aggregated-event representation module generates the initial detection results of multiple target events. The refined event detection module refines the initial detection results based on the results of the first two modules. Moreover, for the first time, a new concept (aggregated-event representation), which can capture information of past frames to provide context for event detection on the current frame is introduced. We tested the proposed method on a benchmark event dataset, the Charades dataset. Compared with several state-of-the-art event detection methods, the proposed method is significantly better with a mAP value of 24.88.

References

1. Buch, S., Escorcia, V., Shen, C., Ghanem, B., Carlos Niebles, J.: SST: single-stream temporal action proposals. In: The IEEE Conference on Computer Vision and Pattern Recognition (CVPR), July 2017
2. Carreira, J., Zisserman, A.: Quo vadis, action recognition? A new model and the kinetics dataset. CoRR abs/1705.07750 (2017). http://arxiv.org/abs/1705.07750
3. Du, T., Bourdev, L., Fergus, R., Torresani, L., Paluri, M.: Learning spatiotemporal features with 3D convolutional networks. In: IEEE International Conference on Computer Vision, pp. 4489–4497 (2015)
4. Gao, J., Yang, Z., Nevatia, R.: Cascaded boundary regression for temporal action detection. CoRR abs/1705.01180 (2017). http://arxiv.org/abs/1705.01180
5. De Geest, R., Gavves, E., Ghodrati, A., Li, Z., Snoek, C., Tuytelaars, T.: Online action detection. CoRR abs/1604.06506 (2016). http://arxiv.org/abs/1604.06506
6. Ghosh, P., Yao, Y., Davis, L.S., Divakaran, A.: Stacked spatio-temporal graph convolutional networks for action segmentation. CoRR abs/1811.10575 (2018). http://arxiv.org/abs/1811.10575
7. Lin, T., et al.: Microsoft COCO: common objects in context. CoRR abs/1405.0312 (2014). http://arxiv.org/abs/1405.0312
8. Piergiovanni, A.J., Ryoo, M.S.: Activity detection with latent sub-event hierarchy learning. CoRR abs/1803.06316 (2018). http://arxiv.org/abs/1803.06316
9. Piergiovanni, A., Ryoo, M.S.: Learning latent super-events to detect multiple activities in videos. In: The IEEE Conference on Computer Vision and Pattern Recognition (CVPR), June 2018
10. Ren, S., He, K., Girshick, R.B., Sun, J.: Faster R-CNN: towards real-time object detection with region proposal networks. CoRR abs/1506.01497 (2015). http://arxiv.org/abs/1506.01497
11. Shou, Z., et al.: Online detection of action start in untrimmed, streaming videos. In: Ferrari, V., Hebert, M., Sminchisescu, C., Weiss, Y. (eds.) ECCV 2018. LNCS, vol. 11207, pp. 551–568. Springer, Cham (2018). https://doi.org/10.1007/978-3-030-01219-9_33
12. Sigurdsson, G.A., Divvala, S., Farhadi, A., Gupta, A.: Asynchronous temporal fields for action recognition. In: The IEEE Conference on Computer Vision and Pattern Recognition (CVPR), July 2017
13. Simonyan, K., Zisserman, A.: Two-stream convolutional networks for action recognition in videos. CoRR abs/1406.2199 (2014). http://arxiv.org/abs/1406.2199
14. Tang, K., Yao, B., Fei-Fei, L., Koller, D.: Combining the right features for complex event recognition. In: The IEEE International Conference on Computer Vision (ICCV), December 2013

15. Xu, H., Das, A., Saenko, K.: R-C3D: region convolutional 3D network for temporal activity detection. CoRR abs/1703.07814 (2017). http://arxiv.org/abs/1703.07814
16. Yeung, S., Russakovsky, O., Ning, J., Andriluka, M., Mori, G., Li, F.F.: Every moment counts: dense detailed labeling of actions in complex videos. Int. J. Comput. Vis. **126**(2–4), 1–15 (2018)
17. Zhao, Y., Xiong, Y., Wang, L., Wu, Z., Lin, D., Tang, X.: Temporal action detection with structured segment networks. CoRR abs/1704.06228 (2017). http://arxiv.org/abs/1704.06228

Standard Deviation Clustering Combined with Visual Psychological Test Algorithm for Image Segmentation

Zhenggang Wang[1,2,3], Jin Jin[1,2(✉)], and Zhong Liu[1,4]

[1] Institute of Computer Application, Chinese Academy of Sciences,
Chengdu 610041, China
`jinjin@nsu.edu.cn`
[2] University of Chinese Academy of Sciences, Beijing 100049, China
[3] Chengdu Customs District of People's Republic of China, Chengdu 610032, China
[4] Leshan Vocational and Technical College, Leshan 614000, China

Abstract. Detection of the visual salient image area for image segmentation, image recognition, and adaptive compression application is beneficial. It makes an object, a person, or some pixels stand out against the background of the image and provide support for image recognition and target detection. The detection can simplify the process of computer visual image processing and improve the effect and efficiency of computer visual inspection. This paper introduces a kind of salient detection method, without any manual intervention, and uses the method of decomposing brightness, color space, negative map solution, and standard deviation to find the super-distance pixel in the image. The method of clustering is used to separate the region of objects and image background, and output RGB color salient objects image. Moreover, it can accurately highlight the object contour and internal pixels. This method studies the characteristics of the original pixels such as brightness or color and utilizes the image basis features to achieve the image saliency detection. It has high adaptive detection ability, low time complexity and high computational efficiency.

Keywords: Saliency map · Standard deviation · Negative map ·
Clustering · Salient color objects

1 Introduction

Visual Attention Mechanism (VAM) refers to the phenomenon that when faced with a scene, the human automatically processes the regions of interest while selectively ignoring the regions of interest that are not. These regions of interest are called salience regions. In the development of saliency region detection, researchers have been making efforts to reduce human intervention and enhance the processing ability of the computer itself. Due to the diversity of images, founding the saliency areas of the image is still the difficulty in the computer

© Springer Nature Switzerland AG 2019
J. Li et al. (Eds.): ADMA 2019, LNAI 11888, pp. 516–525, 2019.
https://doi.org/10.1007/978-3-030-35231-8_37

vision field. Many saliency detection algorithm models are derived from human intuition, which simulates human intuition to highlight a local anomaly in the image. Some saliency region detection methods use spatial domain processing to detect the sum of Euclidean Distances of each pixel and all other pixels in the image. Zhai *et al.* [1] proposed a fast algorithm of super temporally location detection framework for detecting attention regions and motions of interest in video sequences. Combining temporal and spatial models with dynamic fusion techniques, and summarized a pixel-level saliency map using color histograms. Achanta *et al.* [2, 4, 5] proposed a saliency region detection algorithm based on the maximum symmetrical surround idea for large object images and complex backgrounds, used low-level color and brightness features to generate complete resolution saliency maps. They proposed a method for determining the salient regions of an image using low-order luminance and color features. They generated a saliency map identical to the input image size and resolution and calculated the local contrast between the image region and its neighborhood on different scales. They used the distance between the average eigenvector of the image sub-region pixel and the average eigenvector of the neighborhood pixels as the scale to generate a saliency map for image segmentation. The algorithm complexity is not high, and it was suitable for real-time image processing. They used frequency-domain bandpass filtering for image saliency region detection, but the calculation process of this algorithm was only sensitive to the image with strong background contrast. The successful rate is closely related to the color difference between the target and the background. Cheng *et al.* [3] proposed a saliency calculation method based on global contrast, based on the contrast of the histogram and the spatial information-enhanced region. The unsupervised segmentation algorithm Saliency Cut can automatically segment the most prominent objects in the image. Hou *et al.* [6] proposed a SA algorithm based on the basic principle of suppressing frequent occurring characteristics whereas being sensitive to deviation from common characteristics, and obtaining a saliency map by time-frequency transform. Vikram *et al.* [7] randomly selected rectangular regions to calculate saliency maps, narrowed the range of individual pixel comparisons by focusing on local random rectangular regions, and highlighted salient objects. Goferman *et al.* [8] proposed a Context-aware saliency region detection method that focuses on detecting textures and edges of foreground objects, but not enough to detect internal regions of objects. Otazu *et al.* [9] proposed a color vision sensing process model to detect object saliency. Later, Murray *et al.* [10] optimized the wavelet transform for the scale weighting function based on Otazu's, and extended the color appearance model to the saliency estimation. They provided a common low-level visual front end for different visual tasks. Zhang *et al.* [11–13] proposed a saliency algorithm for online bottom-up, which matches the performance of a more complex state of the algorithms in predicting human fixations during free-viewing of videos. Rahtu *et al.* [14] proposed an explicit object segmentation method based on combining the saliency measure with a conditional random field model for segmenting foreground and background images. Deep learning and convolutional neural networks have been used for image processing and saliency testing [15, 16], Cheng *et al.* [17, 18, 20] proposed DES algorithm, which detected the saliency of the image based on the depth image of 2D image pixels. Wang *et al.* [19], improved Cheng's algorithm and added the light field information to enhance their saliency detection effect. He *et al.* [21] used the super-pixel convolutional neural network to detect salient object detection, which can improve the realism of saliency region detection. The above algorithms can solve the problem of saliency region detection to some extent. They have achieved better results in the target detection field. However, processing all pixels of an image with the same standard makes the edge objects and background cover the saliency of large objects, resulting in false saliency detection. To this end, we propose an unsupervised saliency detection algorithm to select foreground object image and suppress background to get the image of the human saliency attention model. It can segment the saliency object regions of random images directly. This algorithm reduces the pixels of the training set image with the unsupervised algorithm mode. The saliency target in the image is extracted in an unsupervised way to label image training datasets automatically without manual intervention. It can be used as the basis of image segmentation or as the image training pretreatment step of convolutional neural network.

2   Related Work

Saliency maps detection should be fast, accurate, have low memory footprints, and easy to generate to allow processing of large image collections, and facilitate efficient image classification and retrieval. Although many salient region detection algorithms, to a certain extent, to highlight foreground objects, it is still difficult for many saliency region detection algorithms to detect the most important object or position of the object when they simulate the first view of most people. So it is still an urgent need in the field of computer vision to find new fast and low computational complexity algorithms based on human visual attention. We not only focus on bottom-up data-driven highlighting object detection using image contrast, but also consider the use of a function that simulates human attention to a certain extent. Our algorithm adopts different standards to process the image pixels of the approximate object and the approximate background in the Lab space component image. Taking global and local mean, global and local standard deviation as the scale, the spatial components of Lab in the whole image and part of the region we are respectively extracted with features, and the integrated three-space components of Lab generated saliency map. In this paper, a new unsupervised saliency detection algorithm is proposed to select foreground object image and suppress background to get the image of the human saliency attention model and generate a segmentation image which is the maximum close to the grand truth image.

3   Salient Region Detection and Segmentation

This section describes our saliency determination method and its application in dividing the entire object in detail. We get our partition graph using the saliency calculation method described later.

3.1   Generate Binary Masks of the Saliency Map

Image Preprocessing. As is known to all, human vision system (HVS) understands the real world. But, The visual biological characteristics of human eyes determine that our owe eyes mostly pay attention to the central region of the image first, and to the peripheral region of the image [19]. Especially, we will pay special attention to the big color contrast objects, or large bulk objects [25–27]. The two-dimensional Gaussian function is normally distributed, and the value from the center to the edge decreased. So the Gaussian kernel function can be used to add the Gaussian mixture model. The central region of the image is highlighted and the boundary region is suppressed for subsequent calculation. We need to normalize the three-space component image to [0, 1] first. The images of the three spatial components of Lab are dotted by the image of the Gaussian kernel function with the same size to obtain the new images of the three new spatial components.

Generate the Saliency Map. When generating the saliency map, we need to make the pixel value of the foreground object significantly larger than the background, and the background pixels need to be suppressed and flattened. Such saliency map is especially beneficial to the subsequent segmentation clustering and the segmentation. On account of the pixel value of foreground object may be smaller than the background or even tend to be 0 after the decomposition of Lab space, the foreground object cannot be highlighted. We will use the following method to determine whether the L, a, b components needs to be transformed into a negative map. First, we obtain the distance between the value of each pixel of the L, a, b three-space component image and the mean value μ of the spatial component image. Compare this distance with the standard deviation of the spatial component image. Pixels which distance is greater than the standard deviation are called super-distance pixels (here, super-distance pixels fall into two categories: Super-distance pixels larger than the mean are named forward super-distance pixels, super-distance pixels smaller than the mean are named reverse super-distance pixels). The super-distance pixels should be set to this mean value μ. Then we take the mean of the new graph. The total number of forward super-distance pixels is greater than the total number of reverse super-distance pixels, if the mean value of the new image is greater than the mean value of the original image. At this point, negative map is used to replace the original image for detection. Otherwise, we do not have to do anything with the image. Because of the standard deviation is the average measure of the distance from the mean of all pixels in the image, the higher the standard deviation, the more obtrusive the image, and the smaller the standard deviation, the flatter the image. We find the standard deviation of the images of the spatial components of L, a, b, and assign the proportion of the spatial components of L, a, b in the saliency map according to the weight of the standard deviation coefficient. The weighted sum of the spatial components of L, a, b in accordance with the proportion of the standard deviation gives the saliency map. The calculation formula is shown in (1) (Fig. 1):

$$S(x,y) = S_L(x,y)k_L + S_a(x,y)k_a + S_b(x,y)k_b \tag{1}$$

Among it

$$k = \frac{\sigma}{\sigma_L + \sigma_a + \sigma_b}$$

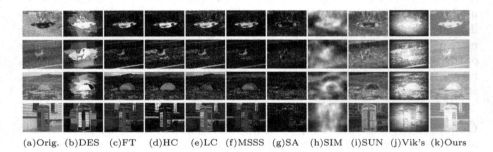

(a)Orig. (b)DES (c)FT (d)HC (e)LC (f)MSSS (g)SA (h)SIM (i)SUN (j)Vik's (k)Ours

Fig. 1. The visual comparison of different methods on the DUT-OMRON and the HKU-IS dataset. (a) the original image. (b–j) comparison charts of 9 algorithms. (k) our algorithm. The pixels value of foreground objects is significantly higher than those of background, and the background tends to be flat and stable.

Salient Region Detection. The forward super-distance pixels in the saliency map S are all directly set to 1, and the other pixels are set to 0. We can get saliency binary image. It contains binary masks that look like salient objects in the space component image, and all other pixels except binary masks are 0. The positions of the salient objects are highlighted to the greatest extent. The calculation formula is shown in (2) and (3).

$$D(x,y) = \sqrt{|(I(x,y) - \mu)^2 - \sigma^2|} \tag{2}$$

$$n_i = \begin{cases} 1, & D_i \geqslant D \& I_i \geqslant \mu \\ 0, & I_i < \mu \end{cases} \tag{3}$$

Adaptive Threshold Denoising. Due to the fact that the original image contains high-frequency noises or some small relatively prominent background objects, the binary saliency object image detected will have some small isolated binary masks (named tiny binary masks) in the image large background. These tiny binary masks affect the speed of the algorithm and are almost not salient objects. We need to decide whether to do the image inflation of binary masks according to the proportion of tiny binary masks to the total image pixels. When the proportion of tiny binary masks is less than 20%, we do the image inflation operation on the binary mask image. The definition of inflation is: when you shift the structural element B by a, you get B_a, and if B_a hits X, we take the point. The set of all points that meet the above conditions is called the result of X being inflated by B. The set of binary pixels of the inflated algorithm is denoted by S_m, as shown in (4).

$$S_m(x,y) = \{a|B_a \uparrow X\} = X \oplus B \tag{4}$$

Among it

$$B = \begin{bmatrix} 0 & 1 & 0 \\ 1 & 1 & 1 \\ 0 & 1 & 0 \end{bmatrix}$$

We take the total number of image pixels m as the scale and determine the area of the tiny binary masks that need to be removed (total number of binary pixels). When e in the formula (5) is less than a constant (The constant in our algorithm is 0.003), it is considered that the isolated regions are tiny binary masks, and the number of the connected region is significantly reduced after removing the tiny binary masks image.

$$e = \frac{\sum_{i=1}^{k_j} n_i}{m} \tag{5}$$

3.2 Clustering

The foreground object will cause the separate image of the binarization masks to appear unconnected after saliency detection due to their texture or color difference. The idea of clustering is needed to distinguish the categories of isolated partitions, and to solve the classification problem between objects and backgrounds, between objects and objects. So far, many clustering algorithms such as K-Means, Fuzz C-Means, Meanshift, DBSCAN [22–24] have been widely used. However, as far as the problem of this paper is concerned, the time complexity of these clustering algorithms is too high. For real-time image processing, especially for high-definition video image processing, the amount of system computation will be very large and affecting the real-time processing effect. Our goal is to control the time complexity of the entire algorithm process in the $O(N)$ range. Thus we propose the $2+1$ clustering method to solve them.

The Unique Independent Partition Standard Deviation Test Cluster.
After Subsect. 3.1, new image binary masks will present two cases: one presents
an isolated, disconnected region, another present several isolated, disconnected
area. When encountering the first kind of circumstance, we need recursive recall
$3.1 - Adaptivethresholddenoising$ and $3.1 - Salientobjectdetection$ steps to calculate the standard deviation of the saliency mask image. If the standard deviation is less than a certain minimum threshold value (The threshold is 0.005 in our
algorithm), it indicates that the color brightness and other saliency of the image
corresponding to the binary mask tends to be consistent. The binary mask is
regarded as the same objects. The binary mask color image is directly captured
to obtain the segmentation image. If the standard deviation is greater than the
threshold value, the binary mask image should be re-clustered. Since most background images have been suppressed, the task of highlighting salient objects has
become simple, and we need to process a few pixel values only. Further, we recall
step $3.1 - Adaptivethresholddenoising$ and $3.1 - Salientobjectdetection$ until it
converges to the threshold. Usually, through 1–2 calls, the segmentation of the
region of binary masks can be completed (The mean and standard deviation of
binary masks images are adopted at this time, and the 0 value regions are not
involved in the calculation).

The Mean Saliency Quadratic Clustering of Independent Block Images.
When the image binary masks present several isolated and disconnected areas,
it is necessary to judge the image saliency comprehensively. Similar to the ideas
mentioned in $3.1 - Imagepreprocessing$, we can associate the Gaussian kernel
function. Our algorithm adds Gaussian mixture model with the same size as the
original image. Therefore, the pixel value of the middle region of the image is mag-
nified, so the middle region is highlighted, and the boundary region is suppressed.
The pixel value of an image is $m \times n$, and the size of the Gaussian kernel function
is $m \times n$ too, sigma is equal to 400. After Subsect. 3.2, we generate k isolated non-
connected binary masks. We use k binary masks to generate an isolated k matrix
$A_i \in (A_1, A_2, \ldots, A_k)$ from k binary masks (The position element of binary mask
is 1, and the rest is 0). Finding the Hadamard product of a and the Gaussian kernel function w to get the image B_i. Sum all the elements of B to get the array
$a_i \in (a_1, a_2, \ldots, a_k)$, as in formulas (6) and (7).

$$B_i = A_i * w \tag{6}$$

$$a_i = \sum_{x=1}^{m} \sum_{y=1}^{n} B_i \tag{7}$$

The saliency priority of binary masks is higher when the a_i value is larger. Thus
we can generate the binary masks saliency sort of image, and get the differences
of saliency binary mask respectively, according to the a_i value. We can generate
the sort of saliency binary masks, and get the differences of saliency binary mask
respectively, according to the a_i value.

4   Algorithm Complexity Analysis

Various algorithms for image calculation require at least frequent traversal of each pixel. The time complexity of them is $O(N^2)$ or more. It is not very useful to real-time image processing applications, because the time complexity is too enormous. Whereas our algorithm iterates the image pixels for constant times, usually 3 to 6 times. In the process of clustering, only some pixels of the image are traversed, and it takes less time. The total time complexity of the algorithm is $O(N)$, and it is suitable for real-time image processing applications (Figs. 2, 3 and 4).

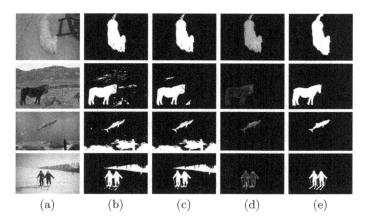

(a)   (b)   (c)   (d)   (e)

Fig. 2. The images of only one salient object region. (a) Original image. (b) Image mask obtained through the detection of salient object region. (c) Image mask obtained through adaptive threshold denoising. (d) Final result graph after the image clustering method. (e) Ground truth image.

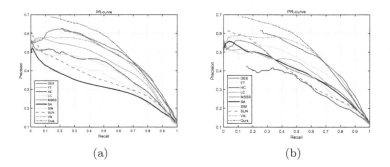

(a)   (b)

Fig. 3. Precision-recall curve of different saliency detection approaches on the DUT-OMRON and HKU-IS image sets. (a) PR-curve on DUT-OMRON dataset. (b) PR-curve on HKU-IS dataset. Our new approach shows better Precision-recall performance.

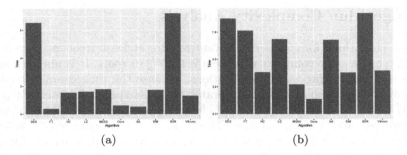

(a)   (b)

Fig. 4. The comparison of the running time of various algorithms. (a) Generation of saliency image time. (b) Average running time of the algorithms. It can be seen that our algorithm has a great advantage in computing time.

5 Conclusion

We have studied a number of salient region detection algorithm and proposed a new standard deviation clustering saliency region detection algorithm. This method is based on the most basic data of image low-level feature brightness and color. We examined 5166 color images from OMRON's DUT-OMRON dataset and 4,447 color images from HKU-IS dataset of HKU. The objects are uniformly highlighting. Noise, small objects and background are completely suppressed. Higher detection rate and less time complexity are obtained, comparing with the ground truth image dataset.

References

1. Zhai, Y., Shah, M.: Visual attention detection in video sequences using spatiotemporal cues. In: Proceedings of the 14th ACM International Conference on Multimedia, pp. 815–824. ACM, October 2006
2. Achanta, R., Sustrunk, S.: Saliency detection using maximum symmetric surround. In: Proceedings of the IEEE Conference on Image Processing, Hong Kong, China, December 2010, pp. 2653–2656. IEEE, Hong Kong, December 2010
3. Cheng, M.-M., Mitra, N.J., Huang, X., Torr, P.H., Hu, S.-M.: Global contrast based salient region detection. IEEE Trans. Pattern Anal. Mach. Intell. **37**(3), 569–582 (2015)
4. Achanta, R., Estrada, F., Wils, P., Süsstrunk, S.: Salient region detection and segmentation. In: Gasteratos, A., Vincze, M., Tsotsos, J.K. (eds.) ICVS 2008. LNCS, vol. 5008, pp. 66–75. Springer, Heidelberg (2008). https://doi.org/10.1007/978-3-540-79547-6_7
5. Achanta, R., Hemami, S., Estrada, F., Susstrunk, S.: Frequency-tuned salient region detection. In: Proceedings of the IEEE CVPR, pp. 1597–1604. IEEE, Miami, June 2009
6. Hou, X., Zhang, L.: Saliency detection: a spectral residual approach. In: Proceedings of the IEEE CVPR, pp. 1–8. IEEE, Minneapolis, June 2007

7. Vikram, T.N., Tscherepanow, M., Wrede, B.: A saliency map based on sampling an image into random rectangular regions of interest. Pattern Recogn. **45**(9), 3114–3124 (2012)
8. Goferman, S., Zelnik-Manor, L., Tal, A.: Context-aware saliency detection. IEEE Trans. Pattern Anal. Mach. Intell. **34**(10), 1915–1926 (2012)
9. Otazu, X., Parraga, C.A., Vanrell, M.: Toward a unified chromatic induction model. J. Vis. **10**(12), 5 (2010)
10. Murray, N., Vanrell, M., Otazu, X., Parraga, C.A.: Saliency estimation using a non-parametric low-level vision model. In: Proceedings of the IEEE CVPR, pp. 433–440. IEEE, Colorado Springs, August 2011
11. Zhang, L., Tong, M.H., Marks, T.K., Shan, H., Cottrell, G.W.: SUN: a Bayesian framework for saliency using natural statistics. J. Vis. **8**(7), 32–32 (2008)
12. Zhang, L., Tong, M.H., Cottrell, G.W.: SUNDAy: saliency using natural statistics for dynamic analysis of scenes. In: Proceedings of the 31st Annual Cognitive Science Conference, pp. 2944–2949. AAAI Press, Cambridge, December 2009
13. Kanan, C., Tong, M.H., Zhang, L., Cottrell, G.W.: SUN: top-down saliency using natural statistics. Vis. Cogn. **17**(6–7), 979–1003 (2009)
14. Rahtu, E., Kannala, J., Salo, M., Heikkilä, J.: Segmenting salient objects from images and videos. In: Daniilidis, K., Maragos, P., Paragios, N. (eds.) ECCV 2010. LNCS, vol. 6315, pp. 366–379. Springer, Heidelberg (2010). https://doi.org/10.1007/978-3-642-15555-0_27
15. He, K., Zhang, X., Ren, S., Sun, J.: Deep residual learning for image recognition. In: Proceedings of the IEEE CVPR, pp. 770–778, June 2016
16. Kar, A., Tulsiani, S., Carreira, J., Malik, J.: Category-specific object reconstruction from a single image. In: Proceedings of the IEEE CVPR, pp. 1966–1974. IEEE, June 2015
17. Cheng, Y., Fu, H., Wei, X., Xiao, J., Cao, X.: Depth enhanced saliency detection method. In: Proceedings of International Conference on Internet Multimedia Computing and Service, p. 23. ACM, July 2014
18. Wang, A., Wang, M., Li, X., Mi, Z., Zhou, H.: A two-stage bayesian integration framework for salient object detection on light field. Neural Process. Lett. **46**(3), 1083–1094 (2017)
19. Wang, A., Wang, M.: RGB-D salient object detection via minimum barrier distance transform and saliency fusion. IEEE Sig. Process. Lett. **24**(5), 663–667 (2017)
20. Li, N., Ye, J., Ji, Y., Ling, H., Yu, J.: Saliency detection on light field. In: Proceedings of the IEEE CVPR, pp. 2806–2813. IEEE, June 2014
21. He, S., Lau, R.W., Liu, W., Huang, Z., Yang, Q.: SuperCNN: a superpixelwise convolutional neural network for salient object detection. Int. J. Comput. Vis. **115**(3), 330–344 (2015)
22. Cebeci, Z., Yildiz, F.: Comparison of K-means and fuzzy C-means algorithms on different cluster structures. JAI **6**(3), 13–23 (2015)
23. Dhanachandra, N., Manglem, K., Chanu, Y.J.: Image segmentation using K-means clustering algorithm and subtractive clustering algorithm. Proc. Comput. Sci. **54**, 764–771 (2015)
24. Rodriguez, A., Laio, A.: Clustering by fast search and find of density peaks. Science **344**(6191), 1492–1496 (2014)
25. W-l, I.: Getting the brain's attention. Science **278**, 35–37 (1997)
26. Kozasa, E.H., et al.: Meditation training increases brain efficiency in an attention task. Neuroimage **59**(1), 745–749 (2012)
27. Gopalakrishnan, V., Hu, Y., Rajan, D.: Random walks on graphs for salient object detection in images. IEEE Trans. Image Process. **19**(12), 3232–3242 (2010)

Fast Video Clip Retrieval Method via Language Query

Pengju Zhang[1], Chunmiao Yuan[1], Kunliang Liu[1], Yukuan Sun[2], Jiayu Liang[1], Guanghao Jin[1,3], and Jianming Wang[2,4(✉)]

[1] School of Computer Science and Technology, Tianjin Polytechnic University, Tianjin, China
[2] School of Electronics and Information Engineering, Tianjin Polytechnic University, Tianjin, China
wangjianming@tjpu.edu.cn
[3] Tianjin International Joint Research and Development Center of Autonomous Intelligence Technology and Systems, Tianjin Polytechnic University, Tianjin, China
[4] Tianjin Key Laboratory of Autonomous Intelligence Technology and Systems, Tianjin Polytechnic University, Tianjin, China

Abstract. The goal of video clip retrieval is to find video clips that match the description of the query in massive video data based on natural language queries. The booming of video-based social media, the increase in the amount of video data and the increasing complexity of video content have created challenges for video retrieval. The existing relevant methods rely on more complex description paragraphs to match corresponding videos then associate each sentence with specifically interest segment, which is need more rich language queries supervision. In this paper, we aim to improve the efficiency by generating proper descriptions from the videos and searching the clips only in the possible videos, which descriptions matches the queries. Specifically, our method is top-down framework, which divides the task into two stages. The upper stage is basically coarse retrieval that selects candidate videos according to the description of the videos. The bottom stage is video clips locating that is done by matching the queries with candidate clips through the matching strategy. We tested our method with the existing methods on Charades-STA dataset and the experimental data shows it improves remarkable performance.

Keywords: Video clip retrieval · Temporal localization · Matching strategy

1 Introduction

With the increasing amount of online media and mobile cameras, the number and complexity of video also grow that make the video clip retrieval a challenge.

Supported by Natural Science Foundation of Tianjin (Grant No. 16JCYBJC42300, 17JCQNJC00100, 18JCYBJC44000, 18JCYBJC15300) and National Natural Science Foundation of China (Grant No. 6180021345, 61771340).

J. Li et al. (Eds.): ADMA 2019, LNAI 11888, pp. 526–534, 2019.
https://doi.org/10.1007/978-3-030-35231-8_38

Locating an activity in the relevant videos is one of the important video clip retrieval problem. Generally, the activity is described by some queries and we should try to find the clips that can match the activity from huge amount of videos. Thus a good searching strategy can improve the efficiency of retrieval while bad one consumes huge computational time.

The existing methods encode the video to feature vectors and retrieve the clips by matching those features with query vectors. Gao et al. [3] first proposed this task in TACoS [12]. They proposed a novel Cross-model Temporal Regression Localizer to combine text query and video clips, and output alignment scores and action boundaries regression results for candidate clips. Shao et al. [14] encode each video with queries to a whole feature vector, and implement matching. Those methods embed natural language queries and video fragments into a common space to calculate visual semantic relevance. When scanning a video using a sliding window, each clip set may contain a large amount of backgrounds that contain meaningless content. Those meaningless clip sets decrease the efficiency of retrieval when the amount of video set is huge.

To address the problem, we proposed a structural framework called fast retrieval method that can localize activity among videos and clips. Our research is similar to the multiple video searching. However, there are only a limited number of studies to this task. Shao et al. [14] proposed a two-stage method FIFO which first made paragraph vs. video matching, and then conducted part-level association to locate single video clips for each sentence in paragraph. However, this method is based on the pre-existing paragraphs, that means it need more natural language queries supervision during training that is inefficient.

Different from the existing methods, our framework is divided into two stages. The first one retrieves the candidate video by matching the key frames of each video with queries. Then the concept of modeling activities combined text, language and visual characteristics of modality, the candidate query statement video clip positioned to give the final fragments. As it is shown in Fig. 1, the natural language query is a input, and coarse positioning is performed from key frames of all videos to find possible candidate videos. Next, the start and end of the clips that can match the query (the description of a activity) are located. Finally, all the results are sorted to get the final output.

Our contributions can be summarized as follows: (1) We proposed a novel method that perform the retrieval in multiple stages to improve the efficiency. (2) We use sample clips instead of natural languages to describe the videos to improve the accuracy.

2   Related Work

Object Detection. The existing object detection methods are mostly based on image recognition. In the picture, the area box that may appear for all objects is exhausted, and after all the areas with successful classification are obtained, the output result is suppressed by the non-maximum value. R-CNN [6] can apply high-capacity convolutional neural networks (CNNs) to bottom-up region

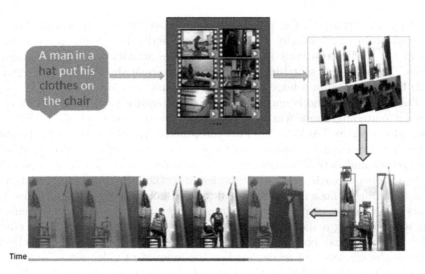

Fig. 1. Overview of our task. Given a natural language query, our goal is to retrieve candidate video and then locate clips from candidate video.

proposals in order to localize and segment objects. Faster-rcnn [13] proposes a full convolutional neural network to implement a complete end-to-end convolutional neural network target detection model.

Natural Language Image/Video Retrieval. Given a set of video/image and sentence queries, the task is to retrieve the video/image that matches the query. Sun et al. [17] proposed to discover visual concepts from image-sentence pairs and apply the concept detectors for image retrieval. Yu et al. [22] proposed to improve the paradigm of video based on concept retrieval through end-to-end learning. Lin et al. [11] parsed the sentence descriptions into a semantic graph which matches the objects in a video and the words in a description via bipartite matching.

For Temporal Action Localization Task. Early methods relied mainly on sliding windows and hand-crafted features [2, 7, 18]. The uses of convolutional networks improves performance. Shou et al. [15] trained C3D [19] with localization loss and achieved state-of-the-art performance on THUMOS 14. Dai et al. [1] extracts the feature sequence from the video using the two-stream network, and then uses the sliding window mechanism to generate multiple proposals of different sizes at each position in the video. Finally, an action classifier and a ranker were trained for each proposal to classify and sort the proposal. Yang et al. [21] can obtain the same size of receptive field without shortening the timing length in the condition of without timing pooling.

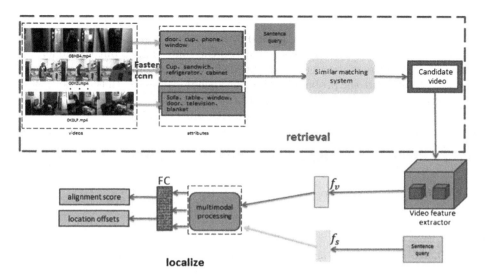

Fig. 2. The framework of faster retrieve and localize system.

3 Methods

Our main goal is to retrieve the corresponding video from a set of untrimmed videos based on a given natural language description, while locating the corresponding time segment in each video. To this end, we designed a model that first retrieves the candidate videos based on the query, then locates the activities in the candidate videos and sorts them according to the results. The framework is shown in Fig. 2.

In this section, we will introduce the candidate proposal generation, clip localization and overall framework in details.

3.1 Candidate Proposal Generation

Conventional method is to encode each video as a whole into an eigenvector and retrieve it simply through feature matching. Because there are a lot of duplicate fragments and unused background clips in a video, it takes a lot of time and memory to encode each frame of the entire video. So we process the input data and capture the key frames of each video to reduce the time data preprocessing, instead of embedding the entire video as input to improve efficiency. In this step we use FFmpeg to extract video keyframes. FFmpeg is a fairly powerful multimedia codec framework, through which we demux multimedia files, separate the audio stream from the video stream to facilitate decoding them, and then read the basic data stream from the video stream. Comparing the thresholds between different frames and select keyframes. Next, the obtained keyframe input area is suggested as a network. The image is input to the convolutional neural network, and a sliding window is placed on the convolution feature graph output by the last convolutional layer. The size of the sliding window is usually $n \times n$. Each sliding window corresponds to a generation anchor that has the same center, but the generated anchors have different aspect ratios and scale factors. Each anchor point calculates a value p to measure the probability that the anchor overlaps with the boundary of the surrounding object region, returns to the bounding box by the position coordinates, and determines whether the region contains the object. Finally, the relevance between the objects contained in the key frame and the query is compared to determine the candidate video.

$$t_x = (x - x_a)/w_a, \quad t_y = (y - y_a)/h_a,$$
$$t_w = \log(w/w_a), \quad t_h = \log(h/h_a),$$
$$t_x^* = (x^* - x_a)/w_a, \quad t_y^* = (y^* - y_a)/h_a,$$
$$t_w^* = \log(w^*/w_a), \quad t_h^* = \log(h^*/h_a),$$

Where w_a, h_a, x_a, y_a are the width, height and centre of anchor and w^*, h^*, x^*, y^* are the ground truth bounding box width, height, center.

3.2 Clip Localization

Feature Extraction. Given a video, follow the method of [4], we first decompose video into a continuous video unit with frame length lu, and extract unit level features by feature extractor Ev. A clip c consists of several consecutive units, $c = \{u_j\}_{su}^{s_u+n_c}$ Where S_u is the index of the starting unit and $e_u = s_u + n_u$ is the index of the ending unit. The final feature of the clip is composed of the current clip and the context clip. In order to obtain the complete feature, we apply the pooling operation P to each unit feature. So the feature of video clip c is $\mathbf{x}_c = P\left(\{\mathbf{x}_i\}_{s_u-1-n_{ctx}}^{s_u-1}\right) \| P\left(\{\mathbf{x}_i\}_{s_u}^{e_u}\right) \| P\left(\{\mathbf{x}_i\}_{e_u+1}^{e_u+1+n_{ctx}}\right)$ Where $\|$ represents a vector connection, and n_{ctx} is a hyperparameter indicating the number of units owned by the context clip. Similar to visual feature extraction, the sentence description is extracted by the sentence embedding extractor Es to extract the sentence-level embedding $\mathbf{f}_s'$, and then the $\mathbf{f}_s'$ is mapped to the $\mathbf{f}_s$ with the dimension $\mathbf{d}_s$ through the linear conversion layer. Following [5], we analyze the semantic activity concept of sentences, verb-obj pairs. Embedding two words conjunctions as active features.

Multi-modal Matching. We use multimodal processing to calculate the visual feature $\mathbf{f}_s$ with the same dimension and the embedded sentence $\mathbf{f}_v$. We use vector element addition (+), vector element multiplication ($\times$), and vector connection ($\|$) to explore the interaction between different modes, and then connect these three operations. The element operation allows interaction between the two modes without changing the feature dimension, so the dimension we get is $4d_t$. We denote the operational connections between the modalities as: $f_t = (f_s \times f_v) \| (f_s + f_v) \| (f_s \| f_v)$, where $\mathbf{f}_t$ is the output of multimode processing.

3.3   Overall Framework

Given a natural language description, we can retrieve the relevance of each video to it by using the clip localization method shown above to find the most relevant part. This approach, however, can be time consuming when dealing with large databases because it requires dynamic proposal generation and resolution of matching problems.

In order to balance retrieval performance and operational efficiency, we propose a framework called fast retrieve and localize activity via language query, as shown in Fig. 2. First, we process the data and replace the lengthy video with the intercepted key frame. In the retrieval stage, we extract the object nouns from the detailed language description. These words are relevant to the scene according to the context, so we take them as our targets. For example, 'A man in a hat put his clothes on the chair.' is a query. The objects of that sentence must exist in the fragment we are looking for (hat, clothes, chair). We perform object detection on each keyframe, sort the results, and find the most relevant ones with our target as candidate proposals, thus effectively narrowing the search scope. In the locating stage, we set the candidate video and query statement obtained in the previous step as input, respectively locate the activity concept time action for each candidate, and output the action time regression boundary of aligned scores and candidate clips. Finally, we combine the results of the two parts and the clips are reordered to get the temporal position of the most relevant clips.

4   Experiment

4.1   DataSet

Charades-STA. Charades-STA is modified by Charades [16]. It contains 9,848 videos across 157 activities. These videos were recorded by people in their own homes based on a provided script. Each video contains temporal activity annotation and sentence descriptions with start and end time to make them suitable for language-based temporal localization task. In total, there are 13898 clip-sentence pairs in Charades-STA training set, 4233 clip-sentence pairs in test set and 1378 complex sentence quires.

Table 1. Results for video retrieval on Charades-STA.

	R@1	R@5	R@10	R@50
Random	0.18	0.56	1.32	6.14
S2VT	3.42	10.70	15.29	30.26
Krishna	6.34	18.52	30.29	47.28
Ours	8.72	21.64	32.58	50.12

Table 2. Comparison of clip localization performance for different proposal methods.

Method	R@1 IoU = 0.7	R@1 IoU = 0.5	R@5 IoU = 0.7	R@5 IoU = 0.5
Random	2.15	5.43	10.02	23.46
DVSA	4.31	11.26	18.39	43.82
CTRL	6.28	17.35	25.20	50.17
ACL	7.04	18.08	31.69	54.93

4.2 Video Retrieval for Proposal

For the video retrieval task, we used *Recall@K* for evaluation, the percentage of the ground truth included in the top K candidates retrieved using a given query. S2VT [20] encodes the video frame using several LSTMs and associates video with the text data. Krishna et al. [10] used a captioning model to encode each paragraph and a proposal model to encode each fragment. Compare our method with them. Table 1 shows the results of video retrieval on the charades-STA dataset.

4.3 Proposal Localization

We compared the performance of different methods in the task of clip location. Firstly, we used the action concept localization method (ACL) to process video clips on the pre-trained C3D network on Sports-1M [9], and extracted the 4096 dimension vector of $fc6$ layer as the visual feature at the unit level. The output of $fc8$ layer as the visual activity concept in video, bidirectional skip-thoughts was used to forward and reverse code the sentences, and 4800 dimensional sentence embedding was obtained. To parse a sentence, select two words as verb-obj pairs, and then process the words with an encoder to embed each word with 300 dimensions. We use a metric $R@n, IoU = m$ similar to [3], which means that the percentage of at least one of the top-n results having Intersection over Union (IoU) larger than $m. R(n, m) = \frac{1}{N} \sum_{i=1}^{N} r(n, m, s_i)$ where N is the total number of queries, $r(n, m, s_i)$ is the recall for a query s_i. During the test, we set the length of the sliding window to $\{128, 256\}$, iou = 0.75. We compare it with DVSA [8] and CTRL [3]. As shown in Table 2, our method can achieve higher accuracy.

5 Conclusion

In this paper, we addressed the problem of clip localization in massive video. We propose a two-stage retrieval and location framework. Based on the relationship between coarse retrieval and fine localization, the time endpoint of video clip can be found and located quickly from massive video according to the description of natural language.

References

1. Dai, X., Singh, B., Zhang, G., Davis, L.S., Qiu Chen, Y.: Temporal context network for activity localization in videos. In: Proceedings of the IEEE International Conference on Computer Vision, pp. 5793–5802 (2017)
2. Gaidon, A., Harchaoui, Z., Schmid, C.: Temporal localization of actions with actoms. IEEE Trans. Pattern Anal. Mach. Intell. **35**(11), 2782–2795 (2013)
3. Gao, J., Sun, C., Yang, Z., Nevatia, R.: TALL: temporal activity localization via language query. In: Proceedings of the IEEE International Conference on Computer Vision, pp. 5267–5275 (2017)
4. Gao, J., Yang, Z., Chen, K., Sun, C., Nevatia, R.: TURN TAP: temporal unit regression network for temporal action proposals. In: Proceedings of the IEEE International Conference on Computer Vision, pp. 3628–3636 (2017)
5. Ge, R., Gao, J., Chen, K., Nevatia, R.: MAC: mining activity concepts for language-based temporal localization. In: 2019 IEEE Winter Conference on Applications of Computer Vision (WACV), pp. 245–253. IEEE (2019)
6. Girshick, R., Donahue, J., Darrell, T., Malik, J.: Rich feature hierarchies for accurate object detection and semantic segmentation. In: Proceedings of the IEEE Conference on Computer Vision and Pattern Recognition, pp. 580–587 (2014)
7. Jain, M., Van Gemert, J., Jégou, H., Bouthemy, P., Snoek, C.G.: Action localization with tubelets from motion. In: Proceedings of the IEEE Conference on Computer Vision and Pattern Recognition, pp. 740–747 (2014)
8. Karpathy, A., Fei-Fei, L.: Deep visual-semantic alignments for generating image descriptions. In: Proceedings of the IEEE Conference on Computer Vision and Pattern Recognition, pp. 3128–3137 (2015)
9. Karpathy, A., Toderici, G., Shetty, S., Leung, T., Sukthankar, R., Fei-Fei, L.: Large-scale video classification with convolutional neural networks. In: Proceedings of the IEEE Conference on Computer Vision and Pattern Recognition, pp. 1725–1732 (2014)
10. Krishna, R., Hata, K., Ren, F., Fei-Fei, L., Carlos Niebles, J.: Dense-captioning events in videos. In: Proceedings of the IEEE International Conference on Computer Vision, pp. 706–715 (2017)
11. Lin, D., Fidler, S., Kong, C., Urtasun, R.: Visual semantic search: retrieving videos via complex textual queries. In: Proceedings of the IEEE Conference on Computer Vision and Pattern Recognition, pp. 2657–2664 (2014)
12. Regneri, M., Rohrbach, M., Wetzel, D., Thater, S., Schiele, B., Pinkal, M.: Grounding action descriptions in videos. Trans. Assoc. Comput. Linguist. **1**, 25–36 (2013)
13. Ren, S., He, K., Girshick, R., Sun, J.: Faster R-CNN: towards real-time object detection with region proposal networks. In: Advances in Neural Information Processing Systems, pp. 91–99 (2015)
14. Shao, D., Xiong, Y., Zhao, Y., Huang, Q., Qiao, Y., Lin, D.: Find and focus: retrieve and localize video events with natural language queries. In: Ferrari, V., Hebert, M., Sminchisescu, C., Weiss, Y. (eds.) ECCV 2018. LNCS, vol. 11213, pp. 202–218. Springer, Cham (2018). https://doi.org/10.1007/978-3-030-01240-3_13
15. Shou, Z., Wang, D., Chang, S.F.: Temporal action localization in untrimmed videos via multi-stage CNNs. In: Proceedings of the IEEE Conference on Computer Vision and Pattern Recognition, pp. 1049–1058 (2016)
16. Sigurdsson, G.A., Varol, G., Wang, X., Farhadi, A., Laptev, I., Gupta, A.: Hollywood in homes: crowdsourcing data collection for activity understanding. In: Leibe, B., Matas, J., Sebe, N., Welling, M. (eds.) ECCV 2016. LNCS, vol. 9905, pp. 510–526. Springer, Cham (2016). https://doi.org/10.1007/978-3-319-46448-0_31

17. Sun, C., Gan, C., Nevatia, R.: Automatic concept discovery from parallel text and visual corpora. In: Proceedings of the IEEE International Conference on Computer Vision, pp. 2596–2604 (2015)
18. Tang, K., Yao, B., Fei-Fei, L., Koller, D.: Combining the right features for complex event recognition. In: Proceedings of the IEEE International Conference on Computer Vision, pp. 2696–2703 (2013)
19. Tran, D., Bourdev, L., Fergus, R., Torresani, L., Paluri, M.: Learning spatiotemporal features with 3D convolutional networks. In: Proceedings of the IEEE International Conference on Computer Vision, pp. 4489–4497 (2015)
20. Venugopalan, S., Rohrbach, M., Donahue, J., Mooney, R., Darrell, T., Saenko, K.: Sequence to sequence-video to text. In: Proceedings of the IEEE International Conference on Computer Vision, pp. 4534–4542 (2015)
21. Yang, K., Qiao, P., Li, D., Lv, S., Dou, Y.: Exploring temporal preservation networks for precise temporal action localization. In: Thirty-Second AAAI Conference on Artificial Intelligence (2018)
22. Yu, Y., Ko, H., Choi, J., Kim, G.: End-to-end concept word detection for video captioning, retrieval, and question answering. In: Proceedings of the IEEE Conference on Computer Vision and Pattern Recognition, pp. 3165–3173 (2017)

Research on Speech Emotional Feature Extraction Based on Multidimensional Feature Fusion

Chunjun Zheng[1,2(✉)], Chunli Wang[1], Wei Sun[2], and Ning Jia[2]

[1] Dalian Maritime University, Dalian, Liaoning, China
zhengchunjun@neusoft.edu.cn
[2] Dalian Neusoft University of Information, Dalian, Liaoning, China

Abstract. In the field of speech processing, speech emotion recognition is a challenging task with broad application prospects. Since the effective speech feature set directly affects the accuracy of speech emotion recognition, the research on effective features is one of the key issues in speech emotion recognition. Emotional expression and individualized features are often related, so it is often difficult to find generalized effective speech features, which is one of the main research contents of this paper. It is necessary to generate a general emotional feature representation in the speech signal from the perspective of local features and global features: (1) Using the spectrogram and Convolutional Recurrent Neural Network (CRNN) to construct the speech emotion recognition model, which can effectively learn to represent the spatial characteristics of the emotional information and to obtain the aggravated local feature information. (2) Using Low-Level acoustic Descriptors (LLD), through a large number of experiments, the feature representations of limited dimensions such as energy, fundamental frequency, spectrum and statistical features based on these low-level features are screened to obtain the global feature description. (3) Combining the previous features, and verifying the performance of various features in emotion recognition on the Interactive Emotional Dyadic Motion Capture (IEMOCAP) emotional corpus, the accuracy and representativeness of the features obtained in this paper are verified.

Keywords: Low-Level Acoustic Descriptors · Convolutional Recurrent Neural Network · Feature Fusion · Speech emotion recognition

1 Introduction

With the development of smart machines and domain applications, the demand for sentiment recognition has grown exponentially. In the field of theoretical science to engineering, emotion recognition has attracted more attention. It turns out that emotions have a great influence on decision-making and social interaction. The field of intelligent machine manufacturing requires an emotional recognition task, because through this task, the machine can interface with humans and conduct emotional and effective communication with normal people. Since emotion is very important in social

© Springer Nature Switzerland AG 2019
J. Li et al. (Eds.): ADMA 2019, LNAI 11888, pp. 535–547, 2019.
https://doi.org/10.1007/978-3-030-35231-8_39

communication, it is hoped that intelligent machines can effectively recognize the emotions of human.

At present, there are many difficulties in accurately identifying emotions. Because the basic emotional model is now inconclusive, the same emotions can only be identified in different ways depending on the situation. Another problem is that the emotions of a particular class may have representations of other classes [1]. Although there are many complexities, researchers are working hard to overcome them. In addition, the set of features used by researchers is not specific, even now there are large differences.

Currently, the most common processing method is to obtain many acoustic and prosodic features from speech. It is possible to detect emotions by using a large number of emotional features, but when the acquired feature dimension is high, the recognition time is long and the efficiency is low. Therefore, it is necessary to screen out the most precise features and minimize the feature dimension, so as to maximize the efficiency of emotion recognition under the premise of ensuring recognition accuracy [2].

In fact, emotional recognition of speech signals is classification problem. In order to develop a system that correctly classifies emotions, the system must be fully trained. The training is depending on a large extent on the quality of the dataset. After selecting the dataset, the main concern is to decide the valid feature. The data of the speech is generally high-dimensional, not all data are equally responsible for emotions [3]. However, the main motivation of the proposed method is to select as few features as possible and to ensure high accuracy. 256 local features are extracted from the speech signal and then merged with the 20-dimensional global features. In this paper, the selection of features is highlighted by combining the results of two forms of feature selection algorithms.

2 Related Work

In recent years, there has been increasing interest in applying cutting-edge technology to automatically learn useful features from emotional speech data. There are two main methods. The first method is to use the deep learning technology to extracting the feature. The authors in [4] applied deep neural networks to traditional discourse-level statistical features. This approach improves recognition accuracy compared to traditional classifiers.

The work in [5, 3] is to use the deep feedforward and Recurrent Neural Networks (RNN) at the frame level to learn short-term acoustic features, and then use the extreme learning machine ELM to map the tradition to a sentence-level representation.

In [6], A convolutional layer and a loop layer is used to learn the mapping directly from the time domain speech signal to the emotional continuous value ring model space. These feature extraction methods and approaches are often influenced by speech data, and even by various factors such as the environment, their robustness is often poor. This is caused by the unexplainability of deep learning.

The second method is to extract emotionally affected acoustic features from short frames of 20 to 50 ms using conventional acoustic features of the original speech signal, commonly referred to as Low Level Descriptors (LLDs). Specifically, common LLDs include fundamental frequency, energy, formant, zero-crossing rate, Mel-Frequency

Cepstral Coefficient (MFCC), Linear Predictive Cepstral Coefficient (LPCC), Shimmer, and Jitter [7].

On the basis of obtaining a large number of low-level descriptors, the global advanced statistical functions are applied to complete the statistics and fusion of features. The High level Statistics Functions(HSF) is calculated as the statistical data of the LLD, such as the average value, the maximum value, the minimum value, the variance, the kurtosis, the skewness, etc., which basically represent the global dynamic change of the LLD.

For example, the GeMAPS Feature Set (The Geneva Minimalistic Acoustic Parameter Set) [8] has a total of 62 features, all of them have HSF features, which are calculated from 18 low-level descriptor features, including 6 frequency-dependent features, 3 energy/amplitude correlation features, and 9 spectral features. eGeMAPS (The external Geneva Minimalistic Acoustic Parameter Set) is an extension of GeMAPS. It adds some features based on 18 low-level descriptors, including 5 spectral features: MFCC1-4, Spectral flux, bandwidth of the second formant and the third formant.

ComParE (Computational Paralinguistics ChallengE) [9] feature set, contains 6373 static features, calculate various functions on the low-level descriptor, it comes from a challenge on INTERSPEECH. The INTERSPEECH 2009 Emotion Challenge feature set has a total of 384 features, including 16 low-level descriptors, and its first-order difference, and then applies 12 statistical functions to the 32 lower-level descriptors to obtain 384-dimensional features.

The representations of these feature sets each have their own unique advantages, because they all describe the characteristics of the phonetic emotion from different angles. However, there are many problems in the feature sets, such as excessive number of features and strong coupling between features. Therefore, using these features directly for model training often fails to achieve excellent results.

Therefore, the features obtained by traditional and deep learning can describe emotional information from different aspects. However, at present, there is still no clear conclusion on the optimal universal feature set of speech and emotional tasks.

Based on this, a feature extraction method combining global features and local features is designed. By adopting this design idea, the advantages of features in sentiment analysis can be improved, and the deficiency of local and global features can be compensated, thus improving the accuracy of emotion recognition.

3   Extraction of Local Features for Speech Emotion

3.1   Spectrogram

For speech signals, time domain analysis and frequency domain analysis are two important methods of speech analysis, but both of them have limitations. Time domain analysis does not have an intuitive understanding of the frequency characteristics of speech signals. There is no relationship between speech signal and time in frequency domain.

A spectrogram is a two-dimensional representation of the speech signal that connects the time domain to the frequency domain and shows how the spectrum of the speech changes over time.

Spectrogram combines the characteristics of spectrum and time domain waveform. It dynamically shows the change of speech spectrum with time. Therefore, the amount of information contained in the spectrogram is larger than that in the time domain or the frequency domain alone.

The vertical axis of the spectrum shows the frequency, the horizontal axis represents time, and the shade of the color represents the amount of signal energy at a given time for a given frequency component. The waveform signal of the speech and the resulting spectrum are shown in Fig. 1.

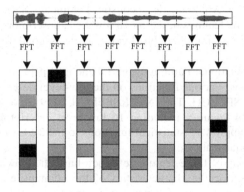

Fig. 1. The generation process of spectrogram

The spectrogram includes a large number of features of the speech signal, including the fundamental frequency, voiced sound, and formant, which have a great effect on emotion recognition. By changing the expression of speech, such as tone, intonation and speed of speech, people express different emotions, and the spectrogram changes accordingly. For different moods and frequency of change, the area of the color in the spectrogram changes frequently, and the horizontal and vertical stripes in the spectrogram also have large fluctuations.

Although speech is a non-stationary time-varying signal, it is found in the research that the speech signal has a smoothness in a short time. Therefore, the preprocessing is generally based on the "short-time stationary technique", based on this, the redundant part of the signal is eliminated, the quality of the speech is improved. Therefore, after obtaining the spectrogram, the relevant preprocessing operations are performed.

Because the dimensionality of the generated map is high, it needs to be processed first to achieve basic dimensionality reduction. Firstly, the Whitening is performed on the newly generated spectrogram, and two kinds of experiments are performed on the generated features. The first type of experiment forms the 1 * 512-dimensional global feature by calculating the mean value of per-dimensional feature. In the experiment, the whitened features are segmented to form shorter equal length clauses with a feature dimension of 30 * 512 dimensions. The remainder that does not exceed the feature dimension is padded with zero until the same dimension information is met. Each clause is assigned an emotional tag corresponding to the entire sentence. After obtaining the clause, the features of the clause are normalized and their values are limited to the range of [0, 1]. In the whole experiment, the processed speech features are used for model training and testing.

In view of the learning ability of Deep Neural Networks (DNN), which can directly model raw data, DNN is used for speech emotion recognition, some use CNN to model the spatial neighborhood features of the spectrogram, and some use RNN to model the temporal features of the spectrogram. However, none of them can comprehensively model the time-frequency two-domain features of the spectrum, and the existing models have some problems, including long training time and low recognition accuracy.

3.2 Extraction of Local Features

Spectrogram is a special form of speech expression. It not only reflects time domain information, but also has frequency domain features. It is particularly important to find a model suitable for the above features.

The CRNN model is composed of two parts: a convolutional neural network and a recurrent neural network. The convolutional neural network is based on the traditional CNN network model, which is used to extract the frequency domain features of the spectrogram. For the temporal domain feature modeling of the profilogram, the CNN part adopts a multi-layer Bidirectional Long Short-Term Memory (BiLSTM) network.

Aiming at the above problems, a speech emotion recognition model based on Convolutional Recurrent Neural Network (CRNN) is proposed. The spatial spectrum pattern representing emotional information can be effectively learned. The network model is shown in Fig. 2.

The recognition performance of deep neural network requires high data volume. In the pre-processing segmentation segment, a large amount of new data is generated, which can minimize the impact on the model due to insufficient data volume. It can speed up the training of the network model and reduce the impact of over-fitting during training on the data sets.

The model takes into account the time and frequency characteristics of the spectrogram, and takes the spectrogram as the input of the network, trains the convolutional layer parameters in the CNN, and reconstructs the feature map output from the convolutional neural network. Take advantage of CNN's advantages in image recognition and the ability of RNN to handle serialized data.

The goal of designing CRNN in this subject is not to directly judge the speech emotion, but to use the model obtained from the training in CRNN for secondary verification. During verification, the result of the penultimate fully connected layer is directly output, and is used as a local feature for subsequent integration.

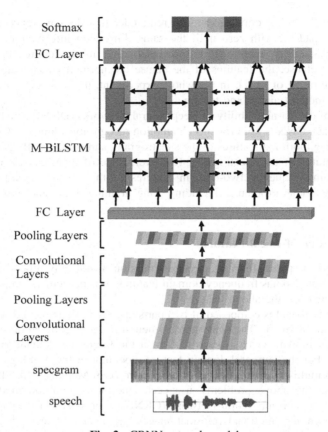

Fig. 2. CRNN network model

3.3 Experiment for Local Features

The models used in this section form a complete functional module for individual model training and model testing. Through experiments, the progress and feasibility of each model are determined, and finally multi-dimensional local features are generated.

Experiments were performed using the IEMOCAP dataset which aims at study multimodal expression binary interactions. It is collected in 5 binary sessions of 10 themes using motion capture and audio/video recording. Each session consists of a different conversation in which one male and one female actor follow the script and participate in spontaneous impromptu conversations triggered by emotional scene cues.

At least three evaluators use the classified emotional tags selected from the collection to annotate each utterance in the dataset. The categories of emotions included are: happy, sad, neutral, angry, surprised, excited, frustrated, disgusted, fearful, and others. Only at least two-thirds of the evaluators who gave the same emotional label were adopts. There are two types of data in the dataset: scripts and impromptu dialogs, which are not broken down in this article.

The related emotions of the standard audios in the dataset are combined and the related samples are removed. Finally, four types of emotional sample data are summarized, and the excited class is merged with happiness to form a new category. In addition, there are also three category which are related with the emotion of sad, angry and neutral. Sample data for the remaining 6 categories was discarded. Now, a total of 5,531 samples were generated (anger: 1,103, happy: 1,636, neutral: 1,708 and sad: 1,084).

On this basis, the batch samples are segmented according to 30 * 512 dimensions, and a total of 28,425 samples are obtained, and the experiment is performed using the ten-fold cross-validation method. 90% of the data is used to train deep neural networks, and the remaining data is used for verification and accuracy testing.

When designing the model, the size of a spectrogram segment is 512 * 30 dimensions. With the CRNN model, the size of the batch is 100 and the maximum number of rounds is 100,000. The learning rate is set to 0.001. Dropout is set to 0.4. Adam is used as an optimizer. The mean square error is used as a loss function.

The CRNN infrastructure consists of two convolutional layers, the first of which has 32 filters of size 3×3. The second layer has 64 filters of size 5×5. Both convolutional layers use the Relu activation function. The two largest pooling layers are 2×2 in size and have a stride of 1. In the HSF channel, the Softmax layer has 4 nodes and uses cross entropy as the objective function for training.

The design idea of this paper is to use the Tensorflow framework to build the network model structure. Two different kinds of experiments were carried out on the processed spectral features, and different emotional classification models were tested. The first type of experiment has a quantity of 5,531 samples + 512 dimensions + CNN model, which serves as a baseline, and each dimension feature is the mean of the characteristics of its corresponding column. Model 1: 5,531 samples + 512 dimensions + CRNN model, the feature processing method is the same as the baseline.

The second type of experiment is mainly to segment the generated features. Model 2: 28425 samples + 30 * 512 dimensions + CNN model, Model 3: Current system (28425 samples + 30 * 512 dimensional features + CRNN model). Through experiments, the accuracy of emotion recognition is calculated separately. Table 1 shows the accuracy of different speech sentiment classifications after experimental verification.

Table 1. Accuracy of speech sentiment classification

Model	Accuracy
Baseline: 5,531 samples +512 dimensions + CNN model	43%
Model 1: 5,531 samples + 512 dimensions + CRNN model	47%
Model 2: 28425 samples + 30 * 512 dimensions + CNN model	50%
Current System: 28425 samples + 30 * 512 dimensions + CRNN model	57%

It can be seen from Table 1 that the proposed strategy has the best classification in all models and has the best accuracy. Followed by Model 2, and the baseline has the lowest accuracy. It can be determined that the combined feature CRNN model after segmentation can effectively improve the recognition accuracy. Based on this, the result of the second-to-last full connection of the model is extracted and used as the optimal set of local features, which is effectively merged with the global features below.

4   Extraction of Global Features for Speech Emotion

In the field of speech emotion recognition, there are many characteristics that can reflect the emotion of the speaker, and the advantages of different speech emotion features can be considered and merged together. Although the recognition performance of speech emotions is improved to a certain extent, it is generally a simple fusion of two speech emotion features. The fusion method leads to an increase in the dimension of the emotional features of the speech, and at the same time makes the whole process of speech emotion recognition cumbersome, which in turn increases the spatial complexity and time complexity of the speech emotion recognition system.

Currently, the common acoustic characteristics are MFCC, Pitch, Energy, and Formants. In order to effectively solve the problem of excessive dimension of speech emotional features, it is necessary to select the features that contribute most to speech emotional recognition rate and integrate them. The list of features is shown in Table 2.

To determine the maximum contribution of the recognition rate of these three-dimensional speech emotion features is a problem that needs to be explored in the following paper.

Table 2. The combination of features

Features	
LLD	Loudness, spectralFlux, MFCC1-2, alpha RatioUV, equivalent Sound Level, F0 semitone, F1 frequency, slopeV0-500, shimmer LocaldB, logMelFreqBand1-6
HSF	sma, sma_de, stddev

4.1   Spectral Feature

Among the spectral features, it is recognized that the characteristic parameters based on the auditory characteristics of the human ear and the mechanism of speech production [10], MFCC are the most accurate and most effective speech emotion features.

According to the human auditory mechanism, the auditory system only focuses on specific frequency components and has different sensitivities to signals with different frequencies. Low-frequency speech below 1000 Hz are sensitive to the human ear, and the perception is proportional to the frequency. In the high frequency part above 1000 Hz, the human ear feels rough, and the perceptual ability is logarithmically related to the frequency. The principle of extracting MFCC is based on the auditory mechanism of human ears, from which relevant speech feature parameters can be obtained (Fig. 3).

The extraction order of MFCC features is shown in the figure below.

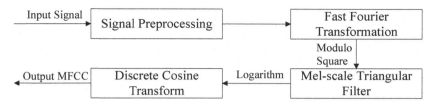

Fig. 3. Steps for extraction of MFCC

First, pre-emphasis, framing, and windowing are performed. Then, in order to convert the time domain signal into the frequency domain for subsequent frequency analysis, Fast Fourier Transformation (FFT) is performed on each frame of the speech signal $x(n)$, Next, the square of the modulo is calculated to obtain the energy spectrum. The logarithmic energy of each filter bank is calculated by a set of Mel-scale triangular filter banks. The coefficients are subjected to Discrete Cosine Transform (DCT) and transformed. Finally, the M-dimensional MFCC parameters are calculated. The detailed calculation formula is shown in Eq. 1.

$$C_{MFCC}(i) = \sqrt{\frac{2}{N}} \sum\nolimits_{j-1}^{Q} m_j \cos\left[\left(j - \frac{1}{2}\right)\frac{\pi_i}{M}\right] \tag{1}$$

The MFCC can be composed of three groups, which are 13 parameters, its delta and the delta of delta. The validity of the MFCC1-2 parameters will be verified experimentally later.

In addition to the MFCC, the Alpha Ratio is obtained by dividing the energy of 50–1000 Hz and the energy of 1–5 kHz, using the Hammarberg Index obtained by dividing the strongest energy peak of 0–2 kHz with the strongest energy peak of 2–5 kHz. Two regions of the linear power spectrum, Spectral Slope 0–500 Hz, the logarithmic power of the Mel band, and features such as Spectral flux, are also extracted as an important part of the feature set.

4.2 Pitch Features

Pitch Features has a certain relationship with personal physiological structure, age, sex and pronunciation habits, which is reflected in the difference of length, thickness and tightness of vocal cords.

Pitch period refers to the period of vocal cord vibration when a person pronounces. When a person pronounces a voiced sound, a quasi-periodic excitation pulse train will be generated, which will lead to vocal cord vibration. At this time, the vibration frequency is also called gene frequency, which is reciprocal to the pitch period.

Since the pitch period has quasi-periodic characteristics, it can only be estimated using the short-term averaging method. The specific expression formula is as follows.

$$R_n(k) = \sum_{m=0}^{N-k-1} s_n(m)s_n(m+k) \tag{2}$$

In the above formula, $s_n(m)$ represents the windowed speech signal, N is the length of the window function, and n represents the nth segment of the speech signal.

4.3 Energy

The energy characteristics are generally related to sound quality, which describes the nature of the glottal excitation signal, including the voice of the vocalist and breathing. Energy is generally used to compensate for channel effects by pulse inverse filtering.

In addition, the performance of energy characteristics varies from emotion to emotion. By evaluating it, the body and mind information of the speaker can be obtained and the emotional state can be distinguished. Energy characteristics mainly include harmonic noise ratio, jitter, Shimmer and Loudness.

The Shimmer and Loudness features are selected. Shimmer represents the difference in amplitude peaks between adjacent pitch periods. Loudness is an estimate of the intensity of the sound that can be obtained from the spectrum. The spectral difference Spectral flux of two adjacent frames can be calculated from the energy.

4.4 Equivalent Sound Level

The Equivalent Sound Level describes the preferred method of sound level over time, which produces a single decibel value, taking into account the total acoustic energy over the time period of the attention zone.

It tracks all fluctuations, keeps them in memory, and calculates the "average energy" at the end of the measurement. However, this is not a simple arithmetic mean because it is a logarithmic value measured in decibels. At the valence level, the feature is more accurate for the description of audio with higher mood fluctuations.

For the LLD feature, an HSF representation is performed to obtain the global characteristics of the segmented audio file. The HSF of sma, sma delta, and stddev is used. Sma represents the smoothed global result by a moving average filter with a window length n, the delta of sma is the product of sma, and stddev represents the standard deviation of LLD.

On the basis of experimental verification, the local features are effectively merged with the global features. Among them, the local features can maximize the feature weights of some important regions. The global feature measures the standard of the audio over the entire time range. The local and the global features have their own characteristics and corresponding emphasis directions. If they are effectively combined, the significant regions can be emphasized at the same time, and the information of all the features can be taken into consideration. Experiments are carried out on the design idea.

5 Experiment for Global Features and Fusion Feature

5.1 Extraction of the Global Feature

In this paper, the results obtained by LLD and HSF are extracted in batches for the global features, so as to obtain the best combination and simplified version of the feature set.

In order to avoid the influence of the imbalance of different emotions, Weighted Accuracy (WA) and Unweighted Accuracy (UA) are used as the evaluation indicators. The tests of the Model are performed for different sets of the emotional features. The baseline is a combination of The INTERSPEECH 2010 Paralinguistic Challenge Feature Set and the LSTM model. The 1582 features that mainly consider in this feature set are obtained from more than 70 LLDs contour values, using more than 20 HSFs.

Due to its wide coverage of LLD and the comprehensiveness of HSF applications, significant effects can be observed with this feature set as the baseline. A lot of work has been done in the process of finding the optimal set of global features. Only some of the commonly used comparison models are listed below:

Model 1: Partial baseline features + HSF (714 dimensions), Model 2: All spectral features (43 dimensions), Model 3: Current system (20 dimensions), all of them are applied in the LSTM models, the WA and UA are respectively calculated for the emotional recognition. The specific information is shown in Table 3.

Table 3. Comparison of results from different global features

Sample sets	WA	UA
Baseline: INTERSPEECH 2010 Paralinguistic Challenge Feature Set	46%	43%
Model 1: 714 dimensions	48%	46%
Model 2: 43 dimensions	50%	47%
Current System: 20 dimensions	57%	54%

It can be seen from Table 3 that the current system proposed in this paper performs the best in all of the models, with the best WA and UA. Followed by Model 2, and the baseline has the lowest accuracy. It can be judged that the global combined features selected by the current system can improve the recognition accuracy.

5.2 Feature Fusion

The optimal set of 256 dimensions of local features is concatenated with the 20 dimensions of the global features, and the adopted model remains unchanged. The experimental results are shown in Table 4.

It can be seen from Table 4 that the local and global feature set performs best, it has the highest accuracy of WA and UA, and the result of this combination exceeds the form of a single feature combination. It can be determined that the combined feature can maximize the recognition accuracy.

Table 4. Comparison of results of fusion features

Feature sets	WA	UA
The local feature (256 dimensions)	57%	52%
The global feature (20 dimensions)	57%	54%
Fusion feature (276 dimensions)	67%	67%

Table 5 is the result of the confusion matrix for the specific sentiment categories in the current system. According to the results, if the emotions has a higher arousal, the recognition accuracy is higher, such as joy, anger, etc., and conversely, for the categories with low arousal such as calmness and sadness, the recognition accuracy is low.

Table 5. Confusion matrix of emotional categories

Recognition accuracy	Sad	Happy	Anger	Calm
Sad	71.5%	5%	5.5%	18%
Happy	6%	75.2%	6.8%	12%
Anger	10.3%	8.9%	74.3%	6.5%
Calm	12.2%	10.9%	13.4%	63.5%

6   Conclusion

Automatic emotion recognition from speech is a challenging task, and the results are depend on the effectiveness of speech features. In this work, the effective set of local and global features is used to automatically discover emotional-related features from speech. The results show that the CRNN is used to learn the local characteristics of emotional correlation, which is more significant. Meanwhile, LLD and the HSF of LLD can effectively learn the global features. The global features with local features is combined to form a new feature set, and is evaluated on the IEMOCAP corpus. Compared with the existing emotional feature set, it can provide higher accuracy of prediction.

Acknowledgment. This paper is funded by the "Dalian Key Laboratory for the Application of Big Data and Data Science".

References

1. Tahon, M., Devillers, L.: Towards a small set of robust acoustic features for emotion recognition: challenges. IEEE/ACM Trans. Audio, Speech Lang. Process. **24**(1), 16–28 (2016)
2. Sarker, M.K., Alam, K.M.R., Arifuzzaman, M.: Emotion recognition from speech based on relevant feature and majority voting. In: International Conference on Informatics (2014)
3. Lee, J., Tashev, I.: High-level feature representation using recurrent neural network for speech emotion recognition. In: Interspeech (2015)

4. Stuhlsatz, A., Meyer, C., Eyben, F., Zielke, T., Meier, G., Schuller, B.: Deep neural networks for acoustic emotion recognition: raising the benchmarks. In: 2011 IEEE International Conference on Acoustics, Speech and Signal Processing (ICASSP). IEEE, pp. 5688–5691 (2011)
5. Han, K., Yu, D., Tashev, I.: Speech emotion recognition using deep neural network and extreme learning machine. In: Interspeech, pp. 223–227 (2014)
6. Trigeorgis, G., et al.: Adieu features? end-to-end speech emotion recognition using a deep convolutional recurrent network. In: IEEE International Conference on Acoustics, Speech and Signal Processing (ICASSP), pp. 5200–5204. IEEE (2016)
7. Anagnostopoulos, C.N., Iliou, T., Giannoukos, I.: Features and classifiers for emotion recognition from speech: a survey from 2000 to 2011. Artif. Intell. Rev. **43**(2), 155–177 (2015)
8. Eyben, F., Scherer, K.R., Truong, K.P., et al.: The geneva minimalistic acoustic parameter set (GeMAPS) for voice research and affective computing. IEEE Trans. Affect. Comput. **7**(2), 190–202 (2017)
9. Schuller, B., Weninger, F., Yue, Z., et al.: Affective and behavioural computing: lessons learnt from the first computational paralinguistics challenge. Comput. Speech Lang. **53**, S0885230816303928 (2018)
10. Tiwari, V.: MFCC and its applications in speaker recognition. Int. J. Emerg. Technol. **1**(1), 19–22 (2010)

Improved Algorithms for Zero Shot Image Super-Resolution with Parametric Rectifiers

Jiayi Zhu$^{(\boxtimes)}$, Senjian An, Wanquan Liu, and Ling Li

School of Electrical Engineering, Computing and Mathematical Sciences,
Curtin University, Kent Street, Bentley, WA 6102, Australia
zhu.jiayi@student.curtin.edu.au

Abstract. Recently, a novel Zero-Shot Super-Resolution (ZSSR) method is proposed to generate high-resolution (HR) images from their low-resolution (LR) counterparts. ZSSR employs a convolutional neural network (CNN) to represent transformations from LR images to HR images and is trained on a single image. ZSSR achieves state-of-the-art performance on both real low-resolution images (i.e., historic images, and images taken with a mobile phone) and several benchmark datasets (e.g., Set 5 and Set 14 to name a few). However, the training of the CNN network of ZSSR is not stable since rectifier is used as the activation function and a custom learning rate adjustment policy is proposed in ZSSR. In this paper, we use parametric rectifier as the activation function and present an improved algorithm for the training of ZSSR. Experimental results demonstrate that the proposed method outperforms ZSSR in terms of both reconstruction accuracy and speed on two benchmark datasets: Set 5 and Set 14, respectively.

Keywords: Single Image Super-Resolution · Unsupervised · Computer vision

1 Introduction

Single image Super-Resolution (SISR) refers to generating a HR image from a LR image so that they resemble the same scene. SISR algorithms have been applied to many fields such as facial recognition [3], dynamic image ranging [28], and digital holography [31]. Although SISR has wide applications, its ill-posed [29] nature makes producing an accurate HR image from its LR counterpart difficult. As a result, a large number of methods have been developed to tackle this problem.

SISR methods can be separated into four categories: interpolation methods, reconstruction methods, learning methods and deep learning (DL) methods [29], and DL-based Methods have been shown superior to all the other competing SISR methods by a significant margin [24].

© Springer Nature Switzerland AG 2019
J. Li et al. (Eds.): ADMA 2019, LNAI 11888, pp. 548–561, 2019.
https://doi.org/10.1007/978-3-030-35231-8_40

Existing DL-based SISR methods include both supervised and unsupervised methods. Supervised SISR algorithms [15,16,19,20,32] require substantial amounts of training data and an extensive period of training time to learn a generic mapping between HR images and their LR variants. Such a mapping is then utilized by supervised SISR algorithms to upscale an input image. However, it is not always feasible to assume the availability of such amounts of data and time in the real life. Moreover, supervised SISR algorithms do not produce satisfactory results when they are used for real LR images [1]. This is because supervised SISR methods are often trained on down-sampled data from external databases with down-sampling kernels that do not emulate real LR image acquisition process [1]. For example, real LR images often come with artifacts resulted from image compression process, which would not present in training data if training data was down-sampled using the bicubic kernel. This fact indicates that the performance of supervised SISR methods depends on the data on which they are trained. There are many factors that can affect the generation of a real LR image, each one of which would need to be emulated by a kernel from some training data, so that supervised SISR methods can be trained to a well-rounded state, which may not be feasible.

To address the issues with supervised methods, numerous unsupervised SISR algorithms [7,8,11] have been developed. Recently, Shocher *et al.* [1] introduced a zero-shot method, namely ZSSR, which is the first CNN-based unsupervised SR method that has achieved performance comparable to that of state-of-the-art *supervised*[1] SR methods on several benchmark databases such as Set5 [2] and Set14 [30], and outperformed state-of-the-art supervised SR methods on real LR images in terms of perceptual quality. More importantly, as a zero-shot SISR method ZSSR does not rely on prior training and it acquires training data from only one input image. This is achieved as follows: ZSSR first creates LR-HR example pairs by down-sampling an input image with gradually increasing factors. ZSSR then utilizes internal recurrence of information and patterns extracted from those LR-HR pairs to train itself. As the name implies, ZSSR combines training and production of HR images in one go in a relatively short amount of time (9 s on Tesla V100 GPU for SR $\times 2$ as reported in the original paper).

Despite the improvements ZSSR has achieved, it has two potential issues that could affect its performance: The use of Rectified Linear Unit (ReLu) where rectifier (i.e., $\max(0, x)$) is the activation function and the use of a custom learning rate adjustment policy along with the Adam [17] optimizer. ReLu neurons can be fragile during the training because of the loss of the information from the negative values. For instance, a large gradient flows through a ReLu neuron and updates the weights in a way that the neuron will never be activated again if the values are negative. If this happens, some of the ReLu neurons will become "dead" because the gradient flows through those neurons will always be zero from that point onward. The use of a custom learning rate adjustment policy in

---

[1] Supervised SISR methods outperform unsupervised SISR methods by a significant margin [29].

tandem with the Adam optimizer could also be a problem because Adam optimizer updates each of its parameters with an individual learning rate, which is learned during the training. Interfering such a learning process may be detrimental to the overall performance.

In this paper, we will develop Improved Zero Shot Super-Resolution (IZSSR): an improved version of ZSSR. IZSSR enhances the performance of the network by employing a different activation function for each convolution layer, dynamically adjusting the gradient flow throughout the entire training process. Moreover, the custom learning rate adjustment policy used in ZSSR is removed, and a simple yet effective algorithm is used to determine the number of training epochs. As a result, IZSSR improves the performance (measured by PSNR) of ZSSR by ~1.1 dB on Set14 and ~0.4 dB on Set5. The removal of the learning rate adjustment policy used in ZSSR also accelerates the convergence of the network.

The rest of this paper is organized as follows. Section 2 presents the existing works that are related to the proposed method. Section 3 discusses the implementation of ZSSR and our methodology. Section 4 demonstrates the experimental results followed by Sect. 5 which concludes our work.

2   Related Works

DL-based SISR methods have made great progress in image super-resolution and have outperformed all other competing SISR methods by a significant margin [24]. Zhang *et al.* [32] presented residual dense network (RDN) that demonstrated state-of-the-art performance with a maximum SR factor of 4. It produced state-of-the-art results when measured by PSNR and SSIM [27] on a suite of databases comprising Set5, Set14, Manga109 [23], and BSD100 [22]. This was achieved by the use of residual dense blocks, which utilizes features from all layers to help with training. Similarly, Ledig *et al.* [19] presented a method that is built on top of DL. The proposed framework showed cutting-edge performance in upscaling photo-realistic [6] images with a SR factor of 4. Their results were evaluated through Set5, Set14, BSD100 based on PSNR and SSIM. They achieved promising results, although not as impressive as that of RDN. However, the authors also conducted a mean-opinion-score (MOS) test [5] that showed significant improvement on perceptual quality, which RDN did not fully address. The improvement on perceptual quality was achieved with a neural network based on Generative Adversarial Network (GAN) [9], and a novel perceptual loss function that uses high-level feature-map produced by VGG [26] rather than plain pixels. The aforementioned methods, being supervised, has a few drawbacks: They rely on prior training and more importantly, the quality of the output depends heavily on if the down-sampling kernel can emulate the input image acquisition process. To address this issue, Shocher *et al.* introduced ZSSR which does not rely on prior training and can *estimate an image-specific kernel* to *emulate the image generation process* directly from an input image using the method proposed in [25], so that training data can accurately reflect the condition in which the input image was created.

3   Methodology

3.1   The Original Zero-Shot Super-Resolution (ZSSR)

The original ZSSR has an image-specific CNN consisting of 8 convolutional layers. Each convolutional layer has 64 channels and is followed by a ReLU layer. The input image is interpolated to the desired output size using the bicubic interpolation, and is added to the residual learned by the network to form the output (global residual learning). The Adam optimizer is used with L_1 loss function. Learning rate is set to 0.001 for the training. The training error of each epoch is monitored and the polynomial fit of training errors is periodically measured. If the standard deviation is greater than the slope of the polynomial fit by a user-defined factor the learning rate is reduced by a factor of 0.1. The training for current intermediate SR factor halts when the learning rate reaches 10^{-6}, and the training for next intermediate SR factor begins. The number of intermediate SR factors is specified by the user. The concept of intermediate SR factors is explained below (Fig. 1).

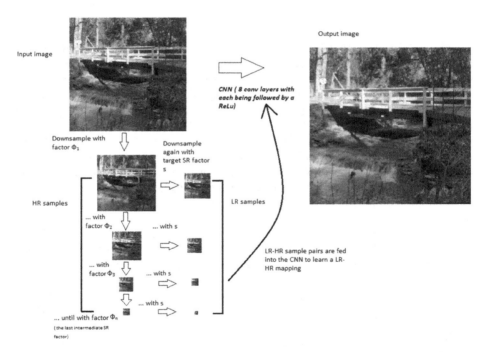

Fig. 1. How ZSSR generates LR-HR pairs from a single input image and learns a LR-HR relation from those pairs. Image adjusted from [1].

The training examples are purely generated from a single image, namely the input image. Specifically, given an input image I, a set of several smaller versions of itself, namely $\hat{I}$, is produced by down-scaling I with a list of user-defined, monotonically increasing SR factors ϕ. Each $\hat{I}_i$ ($i \in [0, k-1]$ where k is the length of ϕ) is used as a HR sample and a LR sample is created by further down-sampling $\hat{I}_i$ by the desired SR factor s (s is the SR factor with which to upscale the input image to the desired output size and is always the last item in ϕ). The bicubic down-scaling filter [13] is used as a default down-scaling filter, and can be substituted by a user-defined filter to emulate the input image acquisition process. Each LR-HR pair is further augmented by a series of affine transformations comprising four rotations ($0°$, $90°$, $180°$, $270°$) and each rotation is followed by two mirror reflections in vertical and horizontal directions. The number of samples in the training set is multiplied by a factor of 8 as a result of augmentations performed on each LR-HR pair. All created LR-HR pairs and their augmentations are utilized by ZSSR to train itself to learn a LR-HR mapping specific to the input image. LR samples in the training set are used as input set to ZSSR and HR samples are used as labels to guide the training. Adding a small amount of noise to LR samples enhances the performance on noisy input images. This is because information specific to an image is likely to recur across different scales of that image whereas noise is not [33]. Thus, adding noise to LR samples helps the network to distinguish between noise and information.

The SR process of ZSSR is performed incrementally to allow SR of tiny images. This is achieved by gradually applying ZSSR to an input image with the user-defined SR factors ϕ. This is to say that ZSSR performs multiple intermediate SR processes before producing the final output. A fixed size of crop of a randomly selected LR-HR pair is taken at each epoch to ensure the training time is independent of the input size. The probability of a LR-HR pair is chosen is proportional to the ratio of the size of a HR sample and that of the input image I. The output of each intermediate SR process and its augmented variants generated during that intermediate SR process are added to the training set as new HR samples to further increase the quantity of the training set. This is repeated until all SR factors in ϕ have been applied in tandem with ZSSR to upscale the input image.

The final output of ZSSR is produced using a slightly modified version of the geometric self-ensemble method presented in [20] (the proposed method produces 8 output images for the 8 augmented variants of the input image I and then merge them) followed by the back-projection method proposed in [12]. In particular, ZSSR takes the median of the 8 generated images instead of taking their mean. A few iterations of back-projection is performed on each of the 8 output images, as well as on the median image to produce the final output.

We emphasize that the use of the ReLU layer after each convolutional layer and the use of a custom learning rate adjustment policy hinder the overall performance of ZSSR. Thus, we will introduce an improved ZSSR, namely IZSSR, in the next section to address these issues.

3.2   Improved Zero-Shot Super-Resolution (IZSSR)

The network architecture of the IZSSR is similar to that of ZSSR. We have 8 convolution layers with the same global residual learning used in ZSSR that adds an input image to the learned residual to form the output. Each convolution layer has 64 channels and is followed by a Parametric Rectified Linear Unit (PReLu) [10] layer instead of a ReLu layer. The input image to IZSSR is also interpolated to the output size using the bicubic filter. The weights of PReLu are initialized with zeros, no regularizer nor constraint for the weights is used. The Adam optimizer is used with the same initial learning rate of 0.001. L_1 loss function is used in tandem to measure the pixel similarity. Unlike ZSSR where a custom learning rate adjustment policy is used to perform learning rate decay and to terminate the training, IZSSR performs no learning rate decay. IZSSR runs a user-defined, fixed number of epochs for the first intermediate SR process. The number of epochs is reduced by half for the next intermediate SR process. This is repeated until all intermediate SR processes are finished. This strategy can be expressed as follows:

$$n_l \approx n_0 \cdot 2^{-l} \tag{1}$$

where l is the index of the lth intermediate SR process, n_l is the number of epochs for the lth intermediate SR process, and n_0 is the number of epochs to run for the first intermediate SR process.

This modification is motivated by our observation that IZSSR converges faster without the custom learning rate adjustment policy used in ZSSR, and the number of epochs required for the network to converge reduces as the training progresses.

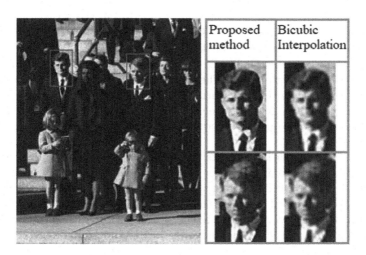

Fig. 2. Comparison of SR result of a real LR image: JFK's funeral. SR was performed with factor 2 on both dimensions. As this is a real LR image no ground truth was provided.

We employ the same training data production and augmentation procedures used in ZSSR to generate LR-HR pairs and their augmented variants, which we feed IZSSR with. The SR process is performed incrementally with a list of user-defined intermediate SR factors which is the same as what ZSSR does. IZSSR uses the same self-ensemble method and back-projection method used in ZSSR to fine-tune the output image.

In summary, the differences between IZSSR and ZSSR are as follow:

○ IZSSR employs a PReLu layer after each convolutional layer whereas ZSSR uses a ReLu layer
○ IZSSR removes the custom learning rate adjustment policy used in ZSSR, and uses algorithm (1) to determine the number of training epochs for each intermediate SR process

Next, we will discuss the main difference between ZSSR and IZSSR.

3.3   Discussion on Activation Functions

The use of PReLu in IZSSR has improved the performance significantly. We attribute this improvement to PReLu's ability to dynamically adjust the gradient flow throughout the training process, and thus effectively alleviate the "dying ReLu" problem.

We have also experimented two more similar activation functions: Leaky Rectified Linear Unit (LeakyReLu) [21] and Exponential Linear Unit (ELU) [4]. The performance improvement gained by employing LeakyReLu is similar but less ideal than that of PReLu, and the use of ELU worsens the performance on Set5 when compared to the original ZSSR. We attribute this phenomenon to the fact that the gradient flow controlled by LeakyReLu and ELU is less optimal than the gradient flow controlled by PReLu. LeakyReLu allows a small, non-zero gradient to flow through the network when the unit is not active [21]. However, such gradient flow is controlled by a hyper-parameter α which stays unchanged throughout the training process. Therefore, in some cases this gradient flow can be detrimental to the overall performance. Similarly, ELU controls its gradient flow with a hyper-parameter α when its input is less than or equal to 0. As α is a constant it cannot adapt to different use cases and needs to be tuned by the practitioner.

PReLu, on the other hand, takes the idea from LeakyReLu and turns α from a hyper-parameter into a parameter that is constantly adjusted as the training progresses. In other words, α is optimized by back-propagation algorithm [18] along with other layers at the same time. As such, PReLu can control its gradient flow in a way that is always positive to the overall performance. Due to this ability to adjust the gradient flow dynamically during the training process, PReLu helps IZSSR to reach a state that is most optimal when the training is complete (Fig. 3).

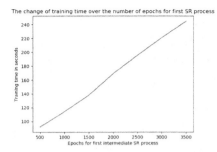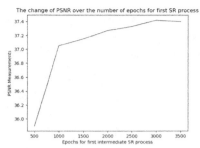

(a) IZSSR: The change of training time over the value of n_0
(b) IZSSR: The change of PSNR measurements over the value of n_0

Fig. 3. Figures generated from the PowerPoint image demonstrated in Fig. 4. 6 intermediate SR factors are used to perform the SR process. With such a setting, ZSSR requires roughly 14000 epochs to converge and 456 s to finish the SR process. The output image of ZSSR has a PSNR measurement of 36.62. IZSSR, on the other hand, converges when n_0 is set to 3000, which means that the total number of training epochs is roughly 6000 according to Eq. (1). The running time for IZSSR is roughly 220 s as can be seen on the figure (a). Furthermore, figure (a) and figure (b) also show that IZSSR can achieve a similar but better performance (PSNR of 36.8) to that of ZSSR 4 times faster (roughly 100 s) when n_0 is set to 800.

Table 1. Comparison of SR results produced by ZSSR, ZSSR with LeakyReLu, ZSSR with ELU, and IZSSR: numerical values are in the format of PSNR/SSIM, downsampling was performed with bicubic kernel.

	Set5	Set14	SR factor
ZSSR	37.37/0.96	33.00/0.91	2
	33.42/0.92	29.80/0.83	3
	31.13/0.88	28.01/0.77	4
ZSSR with LeakyReLu	37.61/0.96	33.98/0.92	2
	33.59/0.92	30.64/0.84	3
	31.37/0.89	28.45/0.78	4
ZSSR with ELU	37.06/0.93	33.35/0.92	2
	33.05/0.90	30.22/0.84	3
	30.51/0.87	28.03/0.76	4
IZSSR (proposed)	37.78/0.96	34.11/0.93	2
	33.91/0.92	30.90/0.87	3
	31.68/0.89	29.13/0.79	4

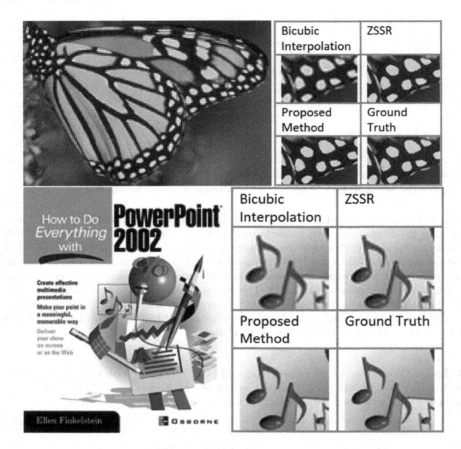

Fig. 4. Comparison of SR results. SR was performed with factor 2 on both dimensions. Left: original LR image. Right: table of small patches cropped from images upscaled by different methods and their ground truths. It can be clearly seen that images produced by the proposed method preserve features to a better extend, and are almost indistinguishable from their associated ground truths.

4   Experiment

4.1   Experiment Setting

All experiments were performed on a Nvidia GTX 1070 GPU on Windows 10 OS. For experiments performed on benchmark datasets with 3 SR factors (x2, x3, x4) we used the "ideal case" described in [1]: A list of gradually increasing intermediate SR factors was supplied for the purpose of gradual SR. The bicubic filter was used for both up-sampling and down-sampling operations. We used algorithm (1) and we set n_0 to 3000 to determine the number of training epochs for each intermediate SR process. We have conducted 10 experiments on both datasets for each method (ZSSR, IZSSR, ZSSR with LeakyReLu, ZSSR with ELU) to minimize the impact of initialization in PReLu.

We used a similar setting for experiments conducted on real LR images: A list of gradually increasing intermediate SR factors were used to perform the SR process. Algorithm (1) was used with n_0 being 3000 to determine the number of epochs for each intermediate SR process. Additionally, we added noise (Gaussian noise with zero mean and standard deviation of 0.0125 when an input image is rescaled to $[0, 1]$) to LR samples and removed the back-projection process, as suggested by [1].

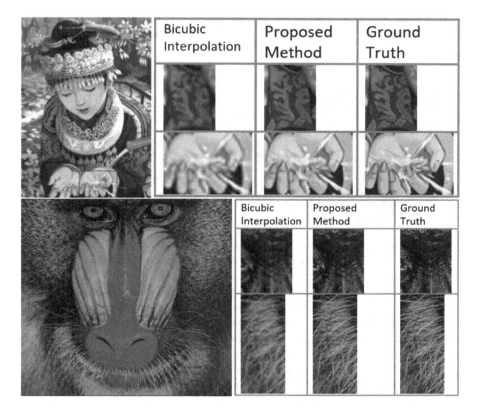

Fig. 5. Comparison of SR results. SR was performed with factor 2 on both dimensions. Left: original LR image. Right: table of small patches cropped from images upscaled by different methods and their ground truths.

4.2 Run-Time Performance

The testing time of IZSSR is almost identical to that of ZSSR with negligible difference (<0.05 s) for a SR factor s where $s \in [2, 4]$. This is because PReLu is equally computationally expensive as ReLu, albeit having more parameters. Therefore, the increased computational cost is trivial and does not pose any issues for employing IZSSR in a production environment.

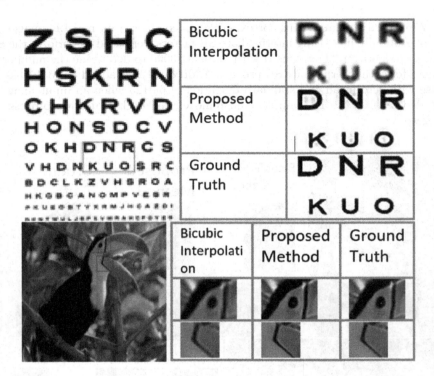

Fig. 6. Comparison of SR results. SR was performed with factor 3 on both dimensions for eye-chart image and with factor 2 on both dimensions for bird image.

The training time of IZSSR is at least 50% shorter than that of ZSSR when n_0 in (1) is set to 3000 and 6 intermediate SR factors are specified. Our observation reveals that ZSSR on average needs 2300 to 2500 epochs to converge in each intermediate SR process. The number of epochs for the entire training process adds up to around 14000. IZSSR requires 3000 epochs to converge in the first intermediate SR process and the number of epochs required to converge in subsequent intermediate SR processes reduces linearly by a factor of 2. This is to say that the total number of epochs IZSSR requires to finish the training process is roughly 6000.

4.3   Experiment Results

We have found out that by replacing ReLu used in ZSSR with PReLu the performance is significantly improved on Set14, and is slightly improved on Set5. The variance of results produced by IZSSR was 0.000046 on Set14 and was 0.0008 on Set5. Those figures revealed that the output of IZSSR is very stable, which is very important for a zero-shot SR method.

PSNRs and SSIMs presented in this paper were mean values calculated from results of experiments we conducted for each method on Set5 and Set14. The calculation of PSNR and SSIM were performed using functions provided in [14]. Please refer to Tabel 1, Figs. 2, 4, 5 and 6 for detailed comparison.

5   Conclusion

We have introduced IZSSR: an enhanced version of ZSSR that achieves state-of-the-art results for unsupervised SISR methods on two datasets: Set14 and Set5. Moreover, the proposed IZSSR requires less time to complete the SR process (training + testing) which is another advantage it has in addition to performance improvement.

The modification introduced in this paper is simple yet effective with improved performance and reduced running-time cost. Other possible alternatives to PReLu are also analyzed to show the advantages of PReLU.

Acknowledgment. This work is supported by a Faculty of Science and Engineering Research and Development Committee Small Grants Program of Curtin University.

References

1. Shocher, A., Cohen, N., Irani, M.: "Zero-shot" super-resolution using deep internal learning. In: The IEEE Conference on Computer Vision and Pattern Recognition (CVPR), June 2018
2. Bevilacqua, M., Roumy, A., Guillemot, C., Alberi Morel, M.L.: Low-complexity single-image super-resolution based on nonnegative neighbor embedding. In: Proceedings of the British Machine Vision Conference, pp. 135.1–135.10. BMVA Press (2012). https://doi.org/10.5244/C.26.135
3. Chowdhuri, D., Sendhil Kumar, K.S., Babu, M.R., Reddy, C.P.: Very low resolution face recognition in parallel environment. Int. J. Comput. Sci. Inf. Technol. **3**, 4408–4410 (2012)
4. Clevert, D.A., Unterthiner, T., Hochreiter, S.: Fast and accurate deep network learning by exponential linear units (ELUs). CoRR abs/1511.07289 (2016)
5. Epstein, J.: Chapter 3 - elements of voice quality. In: Epstein, J. (ed.) Scalable VoIP Mobility, pp. 57 – 72. Newnes, Boston (2009). https://doi.org/10.1016/B978-1-85617-508-1.00003-7, http://www.sciencedirect.com/science/article/pii/B9781856175081000037
6. Ferwerda, J.A.: Three varieties of realism in computer graphics. In: Proceedings of SPIE, Human Vision and Electronic Imaging VIII, vol. 5007 (2003). https://doi.org/10.1117/12.473899
7. Freedman, G., Fattal, R.: Image and video upscaling from local self-examples. ACM Trans. Graph. **30**(2), 12:1–12:11 (2011). https://doi.org/10.1145/1944846.1944852
8. Glasner, D., Bagon, S., Irani, M.: Super-resolution from a single image. In: 2009 IEEE 12th International Conference on Computer Vision, pp. 349–356, September 2009. https://doi.org/10.1109/ICCV.2009.5459271
9. Goodfellow, I., et al.: Generative adversarial nets. In: Ghahramani, Z., Welling, M., Cortes, C., Lawrence, N.D., Weinberger, K.Q. (eds.) Advances in Neural Information Processing Systems, vol. 27, pp. 2672–2680. Curran Associates, Inc. (2014). http://papers.nips.cc/paper/5423-generative-adversarial-nets.pdf
10. He, K., Zhang, X., Ren, S., Sun, J.: Delving deep into rectifiers: surpassing human-level performance on imagenet classification. CoRR abs/1502.01852 (2015). http://arxiv.org/abs/1502.01852

11. Huang, J.B., Singh, A., Ahuja, N.: Single image super-resolution from transformed self-exemplars. In: The IEEE Conference on Computer Vision and Pattern Recognition (CVPR), June 2015
12. Irani, M., Peleg, S.: Improving resolution by image registration. CVGIP: Graph. Models Image Process. **53**(3), 231–239 (1991). https://doi.org/10.1016/1049-9652(91)90045-L. http://www.sciencedirect.com/science/article/pii/104996529190045L
13. Keys, R.: Cubic convolution interpolation for digital image processing. IEEE Trans. Acoust. Speech Sig. Process. **29**(6), 1153–1160 (1981). https://doi.org/10.1109/TASSP.1981.1163711
14. Kim, J., Kwon Lee, J., Mu Lee, K.: Accurate image super-resolution using very deep convolutional networks. In: The IEEE Conference on Computer Vision and Pattern Recognition (CVPR), June 2016
15. Kim, J., Kwon Lee, J., Mu Lee, K.: Deeply-recursive convolutional network for image super-resolution. In: The IEEE Conference on Computer Vision and Pattern Recognition (CVPR), June 2016
16. Kim, J., Lee, J.K., Lee, K.M.: Accurate image super-resolution using very deep convolutional networks. CoRR abs/1511.04587 (2015). http://arxiv.org/abs/1511.04587
17. Kingma, D., Ba, J.: Adam: a method for stochastic optimization. In: International Conference on Learning Representations, December 2014
18. LeCun, Y., et al.: Backpropagation applied to handwritten zip code recognition. Neural Comput. **1**(4), 541–551 (1989). https://doi.org/10.1162/neco.1989.1.4.541
19. Ledig, C., et al.: Photo-realistic single image super-resolution using a generative adversarial network. In: The IEEE Conference on Computer Vision and Pattern Recognition (CVPR), July 2017
20. Lim, B., Son, S., Kim, H., Nah, S., Lee, K.M.: Enhanced deep residual networks for single image super-resolution. CoRR abs/1707.02921 (2017). http://arxiv.org/abs/1707.02921
21. Maas, A.L., Hannun, A.Y., Ng, A.Y.: Rectifier nonlinearities improve neural network acoustic models. In: ICML Workshop on Deep Learning for Audio, Speech and Language Processing (2013)
22. Martin, D., Fowlkes, C., Tal, D., Malik, J.: A database of human segmented natural images and its application to evaluating segmentation algorithms and measuring ecological statistics. In: Proceedings Eighth IEEE International Conference on Computer Vision, ICCV 2001, vol. 2, pp. 416–423 (2001)
23. Matsui, Y., et al.: Sketch-based manga retrieval using manga109 dataset. Multimed. Tools Appl. **76**(20), 21811–21838 (2017). https://doi.org/10.1007/s11042-016-4020-z
24. McCann, M.T., Jin, K.H., Unser, M.: Convolutional neural networks for inverse problems in imaging: a review. IEEE Sig. Process. Mag. **34**(6), 85–95 (2017). https://doi.org/10.1109/MSP.2017.2739299
25. Michaeli, T., Irani, M.: Nonparametric blind super-resolution. In: The IEEE International Conference on Computer Vision (ICCV), December 2013
26. Simonyan, K., Zisserman, A.: Very deep convolutional networks for large-scale image recognition. CoRR abs/1409.1556 (2014)
27. Wang, Z., Bovik, A.C., Sheikh, H.R., Simoncelli, E.P.: Image quality assessment: from error visibility to structural similarity. IEEE Trans. Image Process. **13**(4), 600–612 (2004). https://doi.org/10.1109/TIP.2003.819861

28. Yang, Q., Yang, R., Davis, J., Nister, D.: Spatial-depth super resolution for range images. In: 2007 IEEE Conference on Computer Vision and Pattern Recognition, pp. 1–8, June 2007. https://doi.org/10.1109/CVPR.2007.383211
29. Yang, W., Zhang, X., Tian, Y., Wang, W., Xue, J., Liao, Q.: Deep learning for single image super-resolution: a brief review. IEEE Trans. Multimed. 1 (2019). https://doi.org/10.1109/TMM.2019.2919431
30. Zeyde, R., Elad, M., Protter, M.: On single image scale-up using sparse-representations. In: Boissonnat, J.-D., et al. (eds.) Curves and Surfaces 2010. LNCS, vol. 6920, pp. 711–730. Springer, Heidelberg (2012). https://doi.org/10.1007/978-3-642-27413-8_47
31. Zhang, S.: Application of super-resolution image reconstruction to digital holography. EURASIP J. Adv. Sig. Process. **2006**(1), 090358 (2006). https://doi.org/10.1155/ASP/2006/90358
32. Zhang, Y., Tian, Y., Kong, Y., Zhong, B., Fu, Y.: Residual dense network for image super-resolution. In: The IEEE Conference on Computer Vision and Pattern Recognition (CVPR), June 2018
33. Zontak, M., Mosseri, I., Irani, M.: Separating signal from noise using patch recurrence across scales. In: The IEEE Conference on Computer Vision and Pattern Recognition (CVPR), June 2013

Spatial-Temporal Data

Spatial-Temporal Recurrent Neural Network for Anomalous Trajectories Detection

Yunyao Cheng[1,2], Bin Wu[1,2(✉)], Li Song[1,2], and Chuan Shi[1,2]

[1] Beijing University of Posts and Telecommunications, Beijing, China
{chengyunyao,wubin,shichuan}@bupt.edu.cn
[2] Beijing Key Laboratory of Intelligent Telecommunications Software
and Multimedia, Beijing, China
song200626@gmail.com

Abstract. Aiming to improve the quality of taxi service and protect the interests in passengers, anomalous trajectory detection attracts increasing attention. Most of the existing methods concentrate on the coordinate information about trajectories and learn the similarities between anomalous trajectories from a large number of coordinate sequences. These methods ignore the relationship of spatial-temporal and ignore the particularity of the whole trajectory. Through data analysis, we find that there are significant differences between normal trajectories and anomalous trajectories in terms of spatial-temporal characteristic. Meanwhile Recurrent Neural Network can use trajectory embedding to capture the sequential information on the trajectory. Consequently, we propose an efficient method named Spatial-Temporal Recurrent Neural Network (ST-RNN) using coordinate sequence and spatial-temporal sequence. ST-RNN combines the advantages of the Recurrent Neural Network (RNN) in learning sequence information and adds attention mechanism to the RNN to improve the performance of the model. The application of Spatial-Temporal Laws in anomalous trajectory detection also achieves a positive influence. Several experiments on a real-world dataset demonstrate that the proposed ST-RNN achieves state-of-the-art performance in most cases.

Keywords: Anomaly detection · Recurrent Neural Network · Spatial-temporal sequence

1 Introduction

With the proliferation of global positioning system (GPS) and the reduction of the cost of data transmission and data storage, the increasing trajectory data has been generated. Therefore, many trajectory data mining tasks have been proposed [22], for example, map matching, trajectory compression, stay point detection, POIs recommendation, trajectory classification cation, sensor data

© Springer Nature Switzerland AG 2019
J. Li et al. (Eds.): ADMA 2019, LNAI 11888, pp. 565–578, 2019.
https://doi.org/10.1007/978-3-030-35231-8_41

prediction [11], and anomalous trajectory detection. Anomalous trajectory detection algorithm can improve the quality of taxi service and protect the interests of passengers. Taxi companies can identify these dishonest drivers by anomalous trajectory detection algorithms.

In recent years, many novel methods have been proposed to detect anomalous trajectories [3–5,8,9,19,21,23]. These methods define what anomalous trajectories are and how to solve the problem of anomalous trajectory detection. But they have the following limitations: (1) These methods based on density or isolation can only mine the relationship between points or focus on the characteristics of partial trajectories, but ignore the relationship between whole trajectory sequences. (2) The computational complexity and space complexity of these methods are very high, and a huge history track database needs to be established. Each detection needs to access the entire history database, which reduces the availability of the methods. (3) Spatial-Temporal Law can reflect the characteristics of the trajectory sequence. There are obvious differences in the temporal and spatial characteristics between normal and anomalous trajectories. Most methods focus on spatial attributes or temporal attributes, and cannot combine them effectively.

[17] proposes an anomalous trajectory detection method using the trajectory embedding technology. It proves that the merge of multiple trajectory datasets can enhance the performance of the model. Through data analysis, [7] finds that the anomalous trajectory is significantly different from the normal trajectory in terms of Spatial-Temporal Laws. Inspired by [7,17], we propose an anomalous trajectory detection method named Spatial-Temporal Recurrent Neural Network (ST-RNN). ST-RNN combines the advantages of the two methods mentioned above. It mines Displacement-Distance (D-S) sequence and Displacement-Driving Time(D-T) sequence from the trajectory dataset to construct a neural network. At the same time, the trajectory sequence is input into the RNN part of ST-RNN. Three of these outputs are concatenated for anomalous trajectory detection. We experiment on a real-world dataset and achieve state-of-the-art performance in most cases.

The main contributions to this paper are listed in detail as follows:

(1) ST-RNN uses whole trajectory data instead of isolated points. ST-RNN captures the patterns of sequence information through the RNN and excavates the internal characteristics of trajectories. Therefore, the generalization ability of the model is better. ST-RNN based on the RNN can detect the anomalous trajectory quickly without accessing the historical database, which reduces the computational complexity and space complexity.

(2) In addition to using the traditional recurrent neural network, ST-RNN uses the attention mechanism. When the trajectory vector is long, the accuracy of anomalous trajectory detection will decline. The attention mechanism can automatically mine valuable information on historical trajectories and improve the quality of trajectory representation.

(3) ST-RNN uses spatial-temporal sequence to build a new neural network and improve the utilization of the trajectory dataset. We evaluate ST-RNN on

real-world datasets collected from 442 taxis in Porto for one year. It achieves state-of-the-art detection results from most cases comparing to the other anomalous trajectory detection baselines.

2   Related Work

2.1   Methods of Anomalous Trajectory Detection

In order to improve the efficiency of urban planning, and protect the interests in passengers, many anomalous trajectory detection methods have been proposed. In general, anomalous trajectory detection methods could be divided into three categories.

The first category is based on discrete point information. By analyzing the relationship between the distance and the density of the points, the researchers obtain the internal law of the trajectory. [20] detects anomalous trajectories through a neighbor-based method. It finds outliers by comparing the differences in behavior between moving objects. [12] separates the whole trajectory into segments, then detect outliers of each line segment. [18] also proposes a method to detect outliers by density and distance, but it needs to query the trajectory database. These methods solve the basic problem of anomalous detection, but method based on distance and density unable to learn the particularity of the trajectory pattern, and they need to query the trajectory database. The computing complexity and space complexity are high.

The second category is based on labeled data. [13] uses trajectory segments to build an anomalous detect framework. It identifies suspicious moving and transfers these moving objects into features for classification. [15] mines valuable data from surveillance videos and builds a semi-supervised model to detect anomalous trajectories. [7] combined displacement-distance features and displacement-driving time features to build a supervised learning model, and it realizes the function of online detection. To some extent, these methods reduce the usability when they require huge manpower.

The third category is based on patterns. [21] defines the principles of anomalous trajectory pattern. This method proposes a map function which separates the whole map into squared grids for easy computing. [5] is an enhanced version of Isolated-Based Anomalous Trajectory Detection (IBAT), it extends the function of online detection and improves the accuracy rate of detection. [19] proposes a probabilistic-based model for anomaly trajectory detection, which does not require to access the historical database for detection. [17] proposes the method of trajectory embedding. It converts the trajectory sequence into the embedding vector and then feeds the embedding vector into the RNN. This method greatly improves the accuracy of anomalous trajectory detection. Patterns-based approaches not only to consider the particularity of trajectories but also avoids querying the database. So we adopt this method.

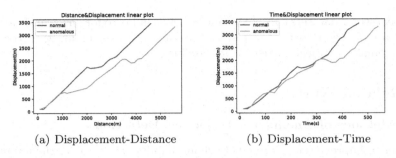

(a) Displacement-Distance   (b) Displacement-Time

Fig. 1. Differences between anomalous trajectory and normal trajectory.

2.2 Spatial-Temporal Laws

[7] based on the temporal and spatial regularity of taxi movement. It proposes an anomalous trajectory detection method called STL. The idea of STL is that for a normal trajectory, there may be a certain relationship between the distance and the displacement generated. STL learns two spatial-temporal models that define two normal ranges from historical taxi trajectories: the D-S model characterizing the relationship between displacement (D) and driving distance (S), and the D-T model characterizing the relationship between displacement and driving time (T). Given two certain range of D-S and D-T. If both of the costs are beyond the normal range, it is more likely to be anomalous.

This method discovered the important role of D-S sequence and D-T sequence in trajectory representation learning through data analysis, as shown in Fig. 1. Anomalous trajectories often cost more than normal trajectories when they reach the same destination point (the displacement is equal). Inspired by this method, we add D-S sequence and D-T sequence to improve the performance of our model.

3 Problem Definition

In this section, we formally define the anomalous trajectory detection problem. In order to aid the understanding of the problem statement, we present the following preliminary concepts.

Definition 1 *(Original Trajectory). An original trajectory is a sequence of coordinate points, it is represented by $T = \{p_1 \rightarrow p_2 \rightarrow \cdots \rightarrow p_n\}$, and each coordinate point p_i is represented by (lon_i, lat_i, t_i), where (lon_i, lat_i) is a geographic coordinate and t_i is the time stamp. p_i and p_n are the source and destination of the trajectory, respectively.*

Definition 2 *(Mapped Trajectory). A map can be split into $n * m$ equal sized grids. Then, a map function $\rho(lon, lat, n, m) = grid_i$ implements a discretization process. A mapped trajectory corresponding to an original trajectory $T = \{p_1 \rightarrow p_2 \rightarrow \cdots \rightarrow p_n\}$ is expressed as $tr = \{grid_1 \rightarrow grid_2 \rightarrow \cdots \rightarrow grid_n\}$, where $grid_i = (lon_i, lat_i, n, m)$.*

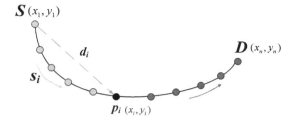

Fig. 2. Example of displacement and distance. (Black spot is the current sampling)

Definition 3 *(Displacement, Driving Distance, Driving Time). As illustrated in Fig. 2, the displacement is the geographical distance d_i between the point p_i obtained in each GPS sampling and the source point p_1. The function of displacement is defined as*

$$d_i = dist(p_i, p_1). \tag{1}$$

The distance s_i is the sum of the geographic distance between current sampling point p_{j+1} and the last sampling point p_j. $S = \{s_1 \rightarrow s_2 \rightarrow \cdots \rightarrow s_{n-1}\}$ is the sequence formed by computing the value of s_i at each sampling of one trajectory. The function of distance is defined as

$$s_i = \sum_{j=1}^{i-1} dist(p_{j+1}, p_j). \tag{2}$$

The driving time t_i is the sum of time cost of each sampling. $T = \{t_1 \rightarrow t_2 \rightarrow \cdots \rightarrow t_{n-1}\}$ is the sequence formed by computing the value of t_i at each sampling of one trajectory. The function of driving time is defined as

$$t_i = \sum_{j=1}^{i-1} time(p_{j+1}, p_j). \tag{3}$$

Definition 4 *(Anomalous Trajectory Detection). Given a set of trajectories $D = \{tr_1, tr_2, \cdots, tr_m\}$, for each trajectory tr_i, we can get the D-S sequence S_i, and the D-T sequence T_i. Anomalous trajectory detection is to use these three sequences to find the trajectory R which is significantly different from the majority of historical datasets.*

4   Methodology

4.1   Overview of ST-RNN

As illustrated in Fig. 3, Our method has three steps. In the step of data preprocessing, we transfer the coordinate sequences of taxis into trajectory embedding, D-S sequence, and D-T sequence. We added D-S and D-T sequence to

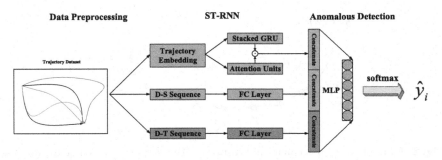

Fig. 3. The architecture of ST-RNN.

enhance the learning ability of the model. In the step of ST-RNN, we feed trajectory embedding into the RNN with an attention mechanism. The RNN will capture the sequential information and the internal characteristics of the trajectories. The attention mechanism will enhance the influence of certain points and improve the quality of the trajectory representation. At the same time, we transfer the D-S sequence and the D-T sequence in two features, then we feed features into two fully connected layers respectively. These two sequences will strengthen the network's understanding of trajectory patterns. All three behaviors are synchronized. After that, we can concatenate these three output vectors. The concatenated vector will flow into the multilayer perceptron layer and a softmax layer. Ultimately, we will get a probability prediction for judging whether the trajectory is an anomalous one.

4.2   Data Preprocessing

We need to preprocess the original trajectory data before feeding data onto ST-RNN for training. To start with, we divide the map into a $n * m$ matrix which the interval of each block is 100 m. Here is the $Haversin$ function (4), R is the radius of the earth, φ_1 and φ_2 are the latitudes of two points, $\Delta\lambda$ is the longitude difference between two points. We transform all coordinate points into $grid_i$ with a unique ID. After that, we acquire mapped trajectories.

$$hav(\frac{d}{R}) = hav(\varphi_2 - \varphi_1) + \cos(\varphi_1)\cos(\varphi_2)hav(\Delta\lambda). \tag{4}$$

Then we pad the missing points in the trajectory to obtain a continuous trajectory sequence [21]. Although the trajectory dataset we used was sampled at a certain sampling rate, the problem of the absence of trajectory points occurred for some reason. Specifically, a taxi travels through many $grids_i$, but the GPS records are not uploaded to the server. As Fig. 4 shows, taxi trajectory is usually a series of non-adjacent points (black units), because of the low sampling rate or sampling failure. For points p_2 and p_3, since they are not adjacent to each other,

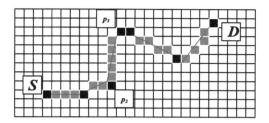

Fig. 4. The method of trajectory padding.

the data sampled by GPS may be different when the taxi passes this trajectory. In order to ensure that the same trajectory is represented equivalently in our system, we need to pad the missing points. We connect point A to point B, the red line through many units which are padded units (gray units). By padding the trajectory, we obtain a continuous trajectory sequence.

Next, we will select SD-Pairs to set up the trajectory dataset. We select the starting point S and the destination point D, and we want to find all the trajectories that start with S and end with D. One problem we face, is that there is not an adequate number of trajectories in a certain SD-Pairs. So we can't train our model sufficiently. To solve this problem, we use the inverted index mechanism [24] to find a sufficient number of trajectories.

To end with, we acquire D-S sequence and D-T sequence from the selected SD-Pairs. When extracting the coordinate sequence, we can get the displacement of the coordinate and the starting point, as well as the sampling time of the coordinate points. The D-S sequence and D-T sequence can be calculated by the method we defined. At this point, we have the required dataset for the experiment.

4.3 ST-RNN

RNN performs well in processing sequential information. It is widely used in sentiment detection [16], speech recognition [10] and other fields. As illustrated with Fig. 5(a), that is the structure of RNN. RNN can capture the relationship between points in the trajectory embedding. The function (5) is the method of update of the hidden state h_t and the output state o_t.

$$
\begin{aligned}
h_t &= f(\boldsymbol{W} \cdot h_{t-1} + \boldsymbol{U} \cdot x_t + b_h), \\
ot &= f(\boldsymbol{V} \cdot + b_o),
\end{aligned}
\tag{5}
$$

where $\boldsymbol{W}$, $\boldsymbol{U}$, $\boldsymbol{V}$ are weight matrices, b_h and b_o are the biases for the hidden state and the output state, respectively. The activation function is f, and x_t is the trajectory embedding.

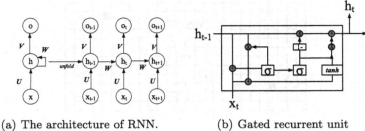

(a) The architecture of RNN.   (b) Gated recurrent unit

Fig. 5. The details of stacked RNN.

GRU is a special RNN cell with the ability to learn long-term dependencies. As Fig. 5(b) shows, the GRU has two gates, the reset gate, and the update gate. The updated approach from these two gates is shown in function (6).

$$
\begin{aligned}
z_t &= \sigma(\boldsymbol{W_z} \cdot [h_{t-1}, x_t]), \\
r_t &= \sigma(\boldsymbol{W_r} \cdot [h_{t-1}, x_t]), \\
\widetilde{h_t} &= tanh(\boldsymbol{W} \cdot [r_t * h_{t-1}, x_t]), \\
h_t &= (1 - z_t)h_{t-1} + z_t\widetilde{h_t},
\end{aligned}
\tag{6}
$$

where $\boldsymbol{W_z}$, $\boldsymbol{W_r}$, $\boldsymbol{W}$ are weight matrices, $\widetilde{h}$ is the state of hidden layer, z_t is the update gate, r_t is the reset gate. σ and $tanh$ refer to the logistic sigmoid and hyperbolic tangent function (7), respectively.

$$
\begin{aligned}
\sigma(z) &= \frac{1}{1 + e^{-z}}, \\
tanh(z) &= \frac{e^z - e^{-z}}{e^z + e^{-z}}.
\end{aligned}
\tag{7}
$$

The attention mechanism was originally applied to the decoding part of the Encoder-Decoder framework [2,14], in order to obtain a better result of machine translation. The attention mechanism enhances the influence of keywords on the whole sentences, enhances the quality of statement representation.

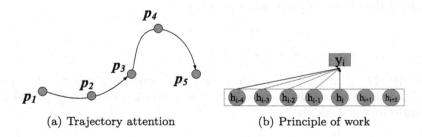

(a) Trajectory attention   (b) Principle of work

Fig. 6. Application of attention mechanism in anomalous trajectory detection.

Trajectory sequences can be regarded as sentences, and each coordinate point can be regarded as a word in one sentence. However, the trajectory sequence is usually longer than sentences, and the problem of gradient vanishing will occur in the process of backpropagation, leading to the failure of model training. As Fig. 6(a) shows, p_2 is connected to p_1 and p_3, and they form an arc with a small radian, so p_2 has less influence on this trajectory. p_4 is connected with p_3 and p_5 respectively, and they form an arc with a large radian, so p_4 has a greater influence on this trajectory. The attention mechanism can assign different weights to different points to enhance the performance of the model.

Figure 6(b) shows how the attention mechanism works for trajectory embedding. The attention mechanism is set in each layer of RNN. At each time step, the output state of the neural unit is determined by the current state and the historical state of the neural network. Taking step i for example, different from the Encoder-Decoder framework, we only encode trajectory embedding, not decode them. The function (8) shows details.

$$
\begin{aligned}
u_i^t &= \boldsymbol{v}^T \tanh(\boldsymbol{W}_a \cdot [h_i^k, c_t^k]), \\
a_i^t &= softmax(u_i^t), \\
h_t' &= \sum_{i=t-B_n}^{t-1} a_i^t h_i,
\end{aligned}
\tag{8}
$$

where $\boldsymbol{W}_a$ and $\boldsymbol{v}^T$ are introduced to learn the weight between the current position and historical state. By this method, the RNN acquires the ability to capture the key points of the trajectory.

4.4   Anomalous Detection

We feed the concatenated trajectory embedding into the multilayer perceptron and reduce the dimension of it.

$$
\boldsymbol{M}_i = \sigma(\boldsymbol{W}_i \cdot \boldsymbol{E}_i + \boldsymbol{b}_i),
\tag{9}
$$

where $\boldsymbol{M}_i$ is the output vector, $\boldsymbol{W}_i$ and b_i are the parameters to be learned by the multilayer perceptron. After that, we input $\boldsymbol{M}_i$ into the softmax layer to generate a predicted probability $\hat{y}_i$. We optimize our model by minimizing cross-entropy:

$$
J = -\sum_{i=1}^{m} [y_i log \hat{y}_i + (1 - y_i) log(1 - \hat{y}_i)].
\tag{10}
$$

5   Experiments

5.1   Dataset and Evaluation Metrics

Our experiments are performed on Porto dataset which contains 442 taxis trajectory data from January 2013 to June 2014. To make a comparison between ST-RNN and baseline methods, we select 5 SD-pairs which have a different number of trajectories. Details of the dataset are shown in Table 1:

Table 1. Details of SD-Pairs

	Trajectories	Anomalousness (%)	avgPointsNum	trainNum	testNum
SD-Pair1	1233	54(4.4%)	32	1150	83
SD-Pair2	765	28(3.7%)	31	693	72
SD-Pair3	617	37(6.0%)	61	537	80
SD-Pair4	1379	44(3.2%)	51	1247	132
SD-Pair5	4973	270(5.4%)	67	4565	408

We use the method of data labeling proposed by [19]. It is a hierarchical clustering algorithm which computes the Jaccard similarity coefficient sim. The clustering algorithm will label all anomalous trajectories.

$$sim = 1 - \frac{len(R_1) \bigcap len(R_2)}{len(R_1) \bigcup len(R_2)} \tag{11}$$

where len is a function to compute the length of trajectories. We use the LCS algorithm to compute the overlap between trajectories, and then compute the value of sim. The smaller sim, the higher similarity between trajectories. Trajectories with high similarity are more likely to be clustered into one class.

Aiming to show the performance of different methods, we use two evaluation metrics: ACC, F_1.

$$ACC = \frac{TP + TN}{TP + TN + FP + FN}$$
$$P = \frac{TP}{TP + FP}$$
$$R = \frac{TP}{TP + FN} \tag{12}$$
$$F_1 = \frac{2PR}{P + R}$$

where TP, TN, FP, FN are true positive, true negative, false positive and false negative in confusion matrix, respectively. ACC refers to the accuracy rate of anomalous trajectory detection. We pay attention to whether the model can accurately classify the normal trajectory and anomalous trajectory in practice. P represents the precision rate. The higher the precision rate is, the fewer negative samples are judged as positive samples. R represents the recall rate. The higher the recall rate is, the fewer positive samples are judged as negative samples. F_1 is the evaluation metrics combining precision rate and recall rate. According to the formula, the larger ACC of F_1 is, the better performance of the model will be.

5.2   Baseline Algorithm

We compare ST-RNN with the methods based on density and distance, pattern and RNN. The baselines are described as follows:

(1) LCS [1] compares the number of points of trajectories. It defines the similarity between the two trajectories and detects anomalous trajectory according to the similarity in the test trajectory. The threshold as the criterion is preset.

(2) XGBoost [6] is a classifier based on the training of features. The trajectory features used in the experiment include the distance, the travel time, the number of key points, the degree of turning angle, and the distance between the two adjacent points.

(3) iBOAT [5] is an anomalous trajectory detection method which based on pattern, it selects subsets randomly from the whole dataset to set up a trajectory tree. The trajectory tree records the number of occurrences of each trajectory in this subset. We repeat this process to set up sufficient trajectory tree to form a trajectory forest, then compare test trajectory and trajectory forest, to find out the anomalous trajectory by computing the support degree.

(4) TOP_EYE [9] is a method which evaluates the degree of the anomaly. It detects anomaly according to the number of occurrences of each point in the dataset and the number of times which turning angle over the threshold.

(5) ATD-RNN [17] is a method based on RNN. It includes ATD-LSTM and ATD-GRU, and it can capture the long term dependencies on points of trajectories. It comes to the conclusion that with an increase in the number of SD-Pairs, the generalization ability of this method is enhanced.

5.3   Results and Analysis

We evaluate the performance of ST-RNN in five SD-Pairs which have a different number of trajectories. The experiment compares the methods based on distance and density, pattern and RNN. The results are shown in Table 2. To reflect the effect of attention mechanism and D-S&D-T sequence respectively, we constructed ST-RNN* and ST-RNN#.

Table 2. Performance of anomalous trajectory detection on different SDPairs.

	SD-Pair1		SD-Pair2		SD-Pair3		SD-Pair4		SD-Pair5	
	Acc	F1	Acc	F1	Acc	F1	Acc	F1	Acc	F1
LCS	0.843	0.780	0.944	0.818	0.963	0.903	0.924	0.706	0.782	0.534
XGBoost	0.880	0.762	0.881	0.444	0.838	0.435	0.947	0.821	0.757	0.447
TOP_EYE	0.963	0.923	0.944	0.857	0.963	0.903	0.947	0.844	0.843	0.812
iBOAT	0.951	0.917	0.958	0.870	0.963	0.828	0.939	0.778	0.875	0.820
ATD-LSTM	0.952	0.917	0.958	0.870	0.988	0.970	0.985	0.955	0.902	0.837
ATD-GRU	0.964	0.941	0.958	0.880	0.975	0.941	0.992	0.977	0.917	0.872
ST-RNN*	0.976	0.960	0.972	**0.917**	0.988	0.970	0.992	0.977	0.919	0.877
ST-RNN#	0.976	0.962	0.972	0.909	0.988	0.970	0.992	0.980	0.931	0.900
ST-RNN	**0.988**	**0.984**	**0.972**	0.909	**0.988**	**0.970**	**0.992**	**0.980**	**0.939**	**0.909**

Analysis. We can observe that, in most cases, ST-RNN achieves the best performance in the anomalous trajectory detection task. Comparing various methods, we have the following analysis:

(1) Compare with the results of LCS, XGBoost, and iBOAT, ST-RNN not only utilizes part of the trajectory sequence information but also makes full use of the complete trajectory sequence information, therefore it has better performance. Although the TOP_EYE algorithm is simple, it also achieves good results when the number of trajectories is less, such as SD-Pair2 and SD-Pair3. However, when the data scale becomes larger, its performance degrades significantly. ST-RNN still performs well in dealing with large-scale data.

(2) We remove the attention mechanism from ST-RNN. ST-RNN* performs best on SD-Pair2 and SD-Pair3, but performs similarly on SD-Pair4 and SD-Pair5 with ATD-GRU. SD-Pair2 with 765 trajectories and SD-Pair3 with 617 trajectories have fewer trajectories than other datasets. SD-Pair4 with 1379 trajectories and SD-Pair5 with 4973 trajectories have a larger data scale. The results show that D-S&D-T sequence can improve the performance of the model when there are few or insufficient data. Although more features are used, models with D-S&D-T sequences are not overfitted on small datasets.

(3) We remove the DS&DT sequence from ST-RNN. Compared with ATD-GRU, ST-RNN# performs better on SD-Pair1, SD-Pair2, and SD-Pair5. These three datasets have a large number of trajectories, thus attention vectors are fully trained. The key points in the trajectory are given higher weights to improve the performance of trajectory embedding.

(4) ST-RNN based on RNN integrates attention mechanism and D-S&D-T sequence. Experiments show that in most cases, ST-RNN which integrates two methods can achieve better results, especially when the number of trajectories is large. But looking at the experiment on SD-Pair2, we found that the F_1 rate decreased. We speculate the reason is that fewer data may affect the performance of attention mechanism leads to overfitting.

6   Conclusions and Future Work

In this paper, we propose a method for anomalous trajectory detection called Spatial-Temporal Recurrent Neural Network (ST-RNN). ST-RNN overcomes the problem that traditional anomalous trajectory detection methods cannot use the whole trajectory effectively. When detecting trajectories, ST-RNN does not require to access the database, which reduces the computational complexity and space consumption. The use of the attention mechanism improves the quality of trajectory representation. When the trajectory is long, RNN will forget the previous information. The attention mechanism enhances the weight of key points, thus avoiding long-term dependence to some extent. With sufficient data, trajectory attention can achieve better performance. Trajectory sequence is not only related to its spatial location, but also to its sampling time. By using D-S&D-T sequences, ST-RNN can obtain better accuracy in anomalous trajectory detection when the scale of data is small or insufficient. Extensive experiments on real-world datasets demonstrate that the combination of attention mechanism and D-S&D-T sequence can improve the performance of our model.

In the future, we will expand the function of ST-RNN in the term of online detection. Online detection means that we can detect anomalous trajectories in real-time, ensuring the safety of passengers. Besides, we will attempt to solve other trajectory data mining tasks and make use of additional information to improve the quality of the trajectory embedding.

Acknowledgement. This work is supported by the National Key Research and Development Program of China (2018YFC0831500).

References

1. Al-Dohuki, S.: SemanticTraj: a new approach to interacting with massive taxi trajectories. IEEE Trans. Vis. Comput. Graph. **23**(1), 11–20 (2016)
2. Bahdanau, D., Cho, K., Bengio, Y.: Neural machine translation by jointly learning to align and translate. arXiv preprint arXiv:1409.0473 (2014)
3. Bu, Y., Chen, L., Wai-Chee Fu, A., Liu, D.: Efficient anomaly monitoring over moving object trajectory streams. In Proceedings of the 15th ACM SIGKDD International Conference on Knowledge Discovery and Data Mining, pp. 159–168. ACM (2009)
4. Chen, C., Zhang, D., Samuel Castro, P., Li, N., Sun, L., Li, S.: Real-time detection of anomalous taxi trajectories from GPS traces. In: Puiatti, A., Gu, T. (eds.) MobiQuitous 2011. LNICST, vol. 104, pp. 63–74. Springer, Heidelberg (2012). https://doi.org/10.1007/978-3-642-30973-1_6
5. Chen, C., et al.: iBOAT: isolation-based online anomalous trajectory detection. IEEE Trans. Intell. Transp. Syst. **14**(2), 806–818 (2013)
6. Chen, T., Guestrin, C.: XGBoost: a scalable tree boosting system. In: Proceedings of the 22nd ACM SIGKDD International Conference On Knowledge Discovery And Data Mining, pp. 785–794. ACM (2016)
7. Cheng, B., et al.: STL: online detection of taxi trajectory anomaly based on spatial-temporal laws. In: Li, G., Yang, J., Gama, J., Natwichai, J., Tong, Y. (eds.) DASFAA 2019. LNCS, vol. 11447, pp. 764–779. Springer, Cham (2019). https://doi.org/10.1007/978-3-030-18579-4_45
8. Ge, Y., Xiong, H., Liu, C., Zhou, Z.-H.: A taxi driving fraud detection system. In: 2011 IEEE 11th International Conference on Data Mining, pp. 181–190. IEEE (2011)
9. Ge, Y., Xiong, H., Zhou, Z.-H., Ozdemir, H., Yu, J., Lee, K.C.: Top-eye: top-k evolving trajectory outlier detection. In Proceedings of the 19th ACM International Conference on Information and Knowledge Management, pp. 1733–1736. ACM (2010)
10. Graves, A., Mohamed, A.-R., Hinton, G.: Speech recognition with deep recurrent neural networks. In 2013 IEEE International Conference on Acoustics, Speech and Signal Processing, pp. 6645–6649. IEEE (2013)

11. Hallac, D., Bhooshan, S., Chen, M., Abida, K., Leskovec, J., et al.: Drive2vec: multiscale state-space embedding of vehicular sensor data. In: 2018 21st International Conference on Intelligent Transportation Systems (ITSC), pp. 3233–3238. IEEE (2018)
12. Lee, J.-G., Han, J., Li, X.: Trajectory outlier detection: a partition-and-detect framework. In: 2008 IEEE 24th International Conference on Data Engineering. IEEE, April 2008
13. Li, X., Han, J., Kim, S., Gonzalez, H.: Roam: rule- and motif-based anomaly detection in massive moving object data sets. In: Proceedings of 7th SIAM International Conference on Data Mining (2007)
14. Luong, T., Pham, H., Manning, C.D.: Effective approaches to attention-based neural machine translation. In: Proceedings of the 2015 Conference on Empirical Methods in Natural Language Processing, pp. 1412–1421, Lisbon, Portugal. Association for Computational Linguistics, September 2015
15. Sillito, R.R., Fisher, R.B.: Semi-supervised learning for anomalous trajectory detection. In: BMVC (2008)
16. Socher, R., et al.: Recursive deep models for semantic compositionality over a sentiment TreeBank. In: Proceedings of the 2013 Conference on Empirical Methods in Natural Language Processing, pp. 1631–1642 (2013)
17. Song, L., Wang, R., Xiao, D., Han, X., Cai, Y., Shi, C.: Anomalous trajectory detection using recurrent neural network. In: Gan, G., Li, B., Li, X., Wang, S. (eds.) ADMA 2018. LNCS (LNAI), vol. 11323, pp. 263–277. Springer, Cham (2018). https://doi.org/10.1007/978-3-030-05090-0_23
18. Vazirgiannis, M., Wolfson, O.: A spatiotemporal model and language for moving objects on road networks. In: Jensen, C.S., Schneider, M., Seeger, B., Tsotras, V.J. (eds.) SSTD 2001. LNCS, vol. 2121, pp. 20–35. Springer, Heidelberg (2001). https://doi.org/10.1007/3-540-47724-1_2
19. Wu, H., Sun, W., Zheng, B.: A fast trajectory outlier detection approach via driving behavior modeling. In: Proceedings of the 2017 ACM on Conference on Information and Knowledge Management, CIKM 2017, pp. 837–846. ACM, New York (2017)
20. Yu, Y., Cao, L., Rundensteiner, E.A., Wang, Q.: Detecting moving object outliers in massive-scale trajectory streams. In: Proceedings of the 20th ACM SIGKDD International Conference on Knowledge Discovery and Data Mining, KDD 2014, pp. 422–431. ACM, New York (2014)
21. Zhang, D., et al.: iBAT: detecting anomalous taxi trajectories from GPS traces. In: Proceedings of the 13th International Conference on Ubiquitous Computing, pp. 99–108. ACM (2011)
22. Zheng, Y.: Trajectory data mining: an overview. ACM Trans. Intell. Syst. Technol. (TIST) 6(3), 29 (2015)
23. Zhu, J., Jiang, W., Liu, A., Liu, G., Zhao, L.: Time-dependent popular routes based trajectory outlier detection. WISE 2015. LNCS, vol. 9418, pp. 16–30. Springer, Cham (2015). https://doi.org/10.1007/978-3-319-26190-4_2
24. Zobel, J., Moffat, A.: Inverted files for text search engines. ACM Comput. Surv. 38(2), 6 (2006)

Spatiotemporal Crime Hotspots Analysis and Crime Occurrence Prediction

Niyonzima Ibrahim$^{(\boxtimes)}$, Shuliang Wang, and Boxiang Zhao

School of Computer Science and Technology, Beijing Institute of Technology,
Beijing 100081, People's Republic of China
nyzbrahim@yahoo.com, slwang2011@bit.edu.cn,
zhaobx9676@gmail.com

Abstract. Advancement of technology in every aspect of our daily life has shaped an expanded analytical approach to crime. Crime is a foremost problem where the top priority has been concerned by the individual, the community and government. Increasing possibilities to track crime events give public organizations and police departments the opportunity to collect and store detailed data, including spatial and temporal information. Thus, exploratory analysis and data mining become an important part of the current methodology for the detection and forecasting of crime development. Spatiotemporal crime hotspots analysis is an approach to analyze and identify different crime patterns, relations, and trends in crime with identification of highly concentrated crime areas. In this paper spatiotemporal crime hotspots analysis using the dataset of the city of Chicago was done. First, we explored the spatiotemporal characteristics of crime in the city, secondary we explored the time series trend of top five crime types, Thirdly, the seasonal autoregressive integrated moving average model (SARIMA) based crime prediction model is presented and its result is compared to the one of the recently developed models based on deep learning algorithms for forecasting time series data, Long Short-Term Memory (LSTM). The results show that LSTM outperforms SARIMA model.

Keywords: Crime prediction · Time series · SARIMA · LSTM

1 Introduction

Ever since laws were first approved crime has been found to be a part of society. It is explained as an act omitted or committed by violating the law, commanding or forbidding it. The punishment is charged upon conviction [1]. Crime is divided into some types like the crime of aggression (homicides, assaults, and rape) and a crime against properties (burglary, theft, and robbery) [2].

There is a huge data in both online and offline in today 's digital world which is associated with what happened happens or what might happen in society. This has enabled law enforcement to gather detailed information on crime data [3]. Crime analysis is required that comprises procedure and measure which intends to lower down the chance of crime to happen [4]. Crime prediction can be done through both quantitative and

© Springer Nature Switzerland AG 2019
J. Li et al. (Eds.): ADMA 2019, LNAI 11888, pp. 579–588, 2019.
https://doi.org/10.1007/978-3-030-35231-8_42

qualitative methods [5, 6]. All these methods are beneficial in the identification of the future criminal activity [7].

Time series forecasting is among the hard areas of machine learning where we need to forecast the numbers of future timestamps by assessing the past data and the correlation between past values and current values, it is actually convenient for predicting the future. In this paper, a historical crime data "Crimes (2001-Present)" for the city of Chicago from Data.gov; from [8] was collected. It contains the reported criminal activities in the different Community Area of the city of Chicago for duration of 18 years. With the help of this historical crime data, we uncovered many patterns by performing the spatiotemporal crime hotspot analysis, then the Seasonal autoregressive integrated moving average model (SARIMA) and recently developed deep learning-based algorithms for forecasting time series data, "Long Short –Term Memory" (LSTM) based crime prediction model is presented for predicting the situation of crime over a period of time.

2   Methodology

2.1   Data Collection

In order to do the crime occurrence prediction models, we collected historical crime data "Crimes (2001-Present)" for the city of Chicago from [8]. The dataset contains more than 6 million rows of data and 22 attributes in CSV comma separated format, its size is 2 GB.

2.2   Data Preprocessing

Natural world datasets are likely to be inconsistent, dirt, and incomplete. Data preprocessing methods are used to enhance the quality of data by that serve to boost the accuracy and effectiveness of the next step which is hotspot analysis and crime occurrence prediction.

There are various number of methods used in data preprocessing, these methods are; data cleaning, data integration, data reduction, as well as data transformation and discretization. These methods intend to reduce some noise, incomplete and inconsistent data.

2.3   Introduction to Time Series

Definition of a Time Series: A time series is defined as a consecutive set of points, computed commonly over sequential times. It is mathematically explained as a collection of vectors x(t), t = 0, 1, 2, wherever t illustrates the time pass by [9]. The variable x(t), is considered as a random variable. The measurements taken throughout an incident in a time series are organized in correct sequential order. A time series accommodating records of one variable is designated as univariate. However, if records contain more than single variable are thought about, it is designated as multivariate.

Time series is commonly employed for predicting future depends on past discovered occurrence or values. Time series observations are often happening upon in several domains like industry, engineering, and science, business as well as economics, etc. [10].

ARIMA has been a regular methodology for time series forecasting for an extended time. While it has considerable limitations. Nowadays, new techniques based on deep learning are developed to overcome these limitations. LSTM (Long Short Memory) is a type of Recurrent Neural Network (RNN) which was originally introduced by [11] to solve these issues. Although it is a comparatively new approach to deal with prediction issues, deep learning-based based approaches have achieved recognition among researchers. For example [12] employed varied kinds of prediction models like deep learning, random forests and gradient-boosted trees to model S&P 500 constitutes.

Components of Time Series: Time series is generally composed of four main components; trend (T), cyclical (C), seasonal (S) and irregular components (I). These components might be separated from the given data. These components are also mixed in several ways. It is typically expected that they're added or multiplied.

$$y_t = T * C * S * I \tag{1}$$

$$y_t = T + C + S + I \tag{2}$$

Strategies for Time Series Forecasting: Time series forecasting is taken into account to be an outstanding area of machine learning with a preeminent aim of predicting the future. It is additionally known as forecasting by exploring the pattern from past data. The required data for time series is grouped into two types: first one is time series data and the second is data with time points.

- **Single step forecasting:** Single-step is appropriate wherever short-term forecasting is needed as an example duration of many minutes, hours or days may all be thought-about short-term. In that state of affairs, calculating a one step ahead is helpful. One step forecasting $(t + 1)$ is accomplished when the current observations. $(t, t - 1, \ldots, t - n)$ is passed to past observations. To a selected model,

$$F(t+1) = M(o(t), o(t-1), o(t-2), \ldots, o(t-n)) \tag{3}$$

Here, $F(t+1)$ is considered to be the forecast for time $(t + 1)$, M is the model, $o(t)$ is an observation at time t.

- **Multi step forecasting:** Multi-step forecasting is helpful wherever the field utilization needs long-term length forecasting. The multiple steps ahead forecasting is explained by five multi-step strategies, among them in our research we decided to use direct H step strategy.

Direct Strategy: Direct strategy develops N distinct forecasting models in order to forecast N steps. As an example, in order to forecast next two point of a scenario employing a direct strategy then the primary forecast point $F(t+1)$ must be computed through a model then a different model would be employed to forecast the second point $F(t+2)$. Nevertheless, significantly, the second point isn't dependent on the first point estimate. Below is the example which explains this.

$$F(t+1) = M_1(o(t), o(t-1), o(t-2), \ldots, o(t-n)) \tag{4}$$

$$F(t+2) = M_2(o(t), o(t-1), o(t-2), \ldots o(t-n)) \tag{5}$$

The direct multi-step strategy is given by the following equation;

$$y_{t+h} = f_h(y_t, \ldots, y_{t-n+1}) \tag{6}$$

Here, h is defined as the number of steps to forecast into the future, n is the defined as the autoregressive order of the model, and f_h is any arbitrary learner.

2.4   Background of Models

SARIMA: Autoregressive Integrated Moving Average, or ARIMA, is one of the most widely used forecasting methods for univariate time series data forecasting. Although the method can handle data with a trend, it does not support time series with a seasonal component. An extension to ARIMA that supports the direct modeling of the seasonal component of the series is called SARIMA.

SARIMA (Seasonal Autoregressive Integrated Moving Average), method for time series forecasting is used on univariate data containing trends and seasonality. SARIMA is composed of trend and seasonal elements of the series. The quality for noting ARIMA model is normally written as ARIMA (p; d; q) p: Trend autoregression order, d: Trend difference order, q: Trend moving average order. The ARIMA model is usually organized as the following formation:

$$Y_t = \alpha + \beta_1 Y_{t-1} + \beta_2 Y_{t-2} + \ldots + \beta_p Y_{t-p} \epsilon_t + \emptyset_1 \epsilon_{t-1} + \emptyset_2 \epsilon_{t-2} + \ldots + \emptyset_q \epsilon_{t-q} \tag{7}$$

Thus, SARIMA model can be specified as: SARIMA (p, d, q) (P, D, Q, m). m is number of observations per year. We use uppercase notation for the seasonal parts of the model, and lowercase notation for the non-seasonal parts of the model. In our model m is equal to 12, which specifies that monthly data suggests a yearly seasonal cycle.

LSTM Model: Long Short-Term Memory (LSTM) [13] is a type of Recurrent Neural Network (RNN) with the potential of memorizing the values from previous stage for the aim of future use. The memorization of previous trend of the data is feasible with the help of some gates together with a memory line integrated in a typical LSTM.

The memory cell is mainly controlled by "the input gate," "the forgetting gate," and "the output gate." The input gate activates the input of information to the memory cell, and the forgetting gate selectively obliterates some information in the memory cell and activates the storage to the next input. Finally, the output gate decides what information will be outputted by the memory cell.

The recognition procedure of LSTM begins with a set of input sequences $x = (x_1, x_2, \ldots, x_t)$ (x_i is a vector) and finally outputs a set of $y = (y_1, y_2, \ldots, y_t)$ (y_i is also a vector), which is calculated according to the following equations:

$$i_t = \sigma(W_{ix}x_t + W_{im}m_{t-1} + b_i) \tag{8}$$

$$O_t = \sigma(W_{ox}x_t + W_{om}m_{t-1} + b_o) \tag{9}$$

$$f_t = 1 - i_t \tag{10}$$

$$tc_t = g(W_{cx}x_t + W_{cm}m_{t-1} + b_c) \tag{11}$$

$$c_t = f_t \odot c_{t-1} + i_t \odot tc_t \tag{12}$$

$$m_t = o_t \odot hc_t \tag{13}$$

$$y_t = \phi(W_{ym}m_t + b_y) \tag{14}$$

For measuring the accuracy of our models, the root mean square (RSME) was used

$$RMSE = \sqrt{\frac{1}{N}\sum_{i=1}^{N}(x_i - \widehat{x}_i)^2} \tag{15}$$

Here, N is the total number of observations, x_i denotes the actual value, and $\widehat{x}_i$ is the predicted value.

3   Experiments and Results

3.1   Spatiotemporal Crime Hotspot Analysis

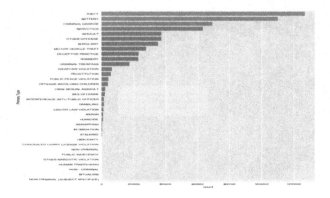

Fig. 1. Frequency of crime categories

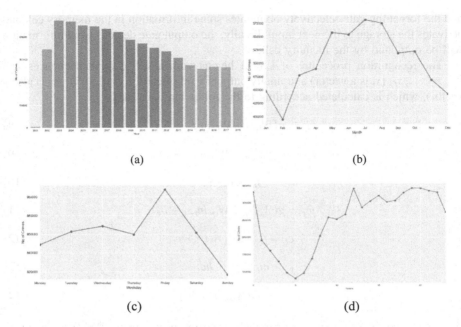

(a)   (b)

(c)   (d)

Fig. 2. Temporal characteristics of crimes.

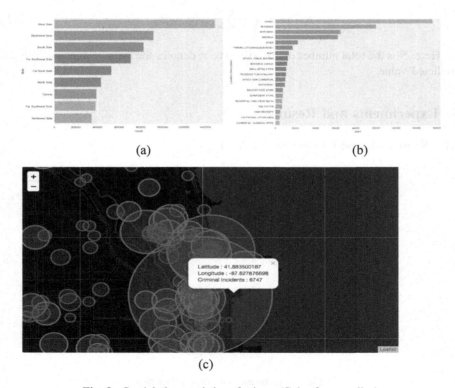

(a)   (b)

(c)

Fig. 3. Spatial characteristics of crimes (Color figure online)

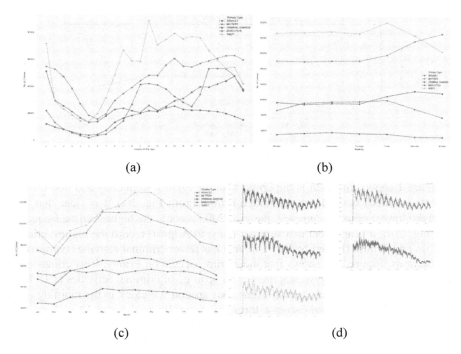

(a)

(b)

(c)

(d)

Fig. 4. Trends of Top 5 crimes.

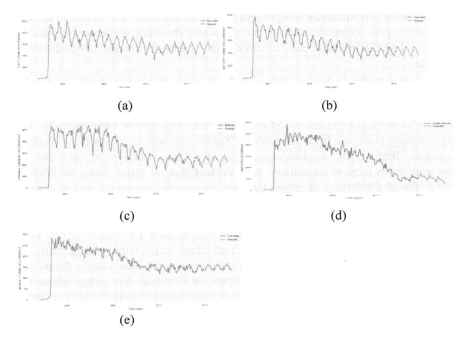

(a)

(b)

(c)

(d)

(e)

Fig. 5. Crime occurrence prediction

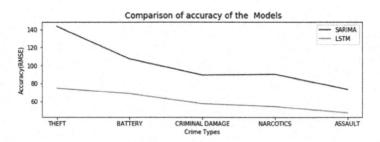

Fig. 6. Comparison of accuracy of the models

Figure 1 shows that theft is the crime with the highest frequency and non-criminal (subject specified) is the least committed crime. From Fig. 2(a) It is clear that 2001 record the lowest crime occurrence, the year 2003 records the highest crime frequency. From Fig. 2(b), it is apparent that summer (June to August) record the highest criminal activities and Winter (December to February) has fewer criminal activities compared to other seasons. Figure 2(c) shows that most crime occurs on Friday; least crimes occur on Sunday. Figure 2(d) shows that there is an upsurge of criminal activities at 18 h and 20 h. Criminal activities are starting to increase around 9 o'clock in the morning and it continues to show a gradual increase throughout the day peaking at 12 o'clock, after which it starts to decrease and increases again at 19 o'clock.

Figure 3(a) shows that the criminal activities on the western side are higher than any other side, northwest side count the lowest crime occurrence. From Fig. 3(b) a huge number of crimes took place on the street followed by residence, the smaller number of crimes occurred on commercial/ business office. The Fig. 3(c) shows crime frequency with corresponding hotspot and cold spots the red circle shows where there are crime hotspots, I considered crime hotspot where the criminal incident is great than or equal to 10000 criminal occurrences in a different area of Chicago using latitude and longitude.

For Fig. 4 trends of top5 crimes shows that theft picks during the mid-day and decreased during the night, Battery starts decreasing from the midnight in order to increase gradually from early morning to afternoon. Narcotics pick during the midday and early in the night and decreased gradually from midnight to early morning. Theft start increases gradually from February to August and start deceases from August to December, Battery also is decreasing gradually from February to July and start decreasing from there to December. It is evident that all crime picks on Friday in general. For all the 5 types of crimes they are showing the lowest number of crimes in 2001, from 2001 for all crime types they started increasing exponentially to have different variation for the following years.

The prediction we produced from Fig. 5 can be used for exploring and understanding the future crime occurrence. Theft (Fig. 5(a)), Battery (Fig. 5(b)), and Criminal damage (Fig. 5(c)) crimes are expected to continue increasing in the next five years. Narcotics crime (Fig. 5(d)) is expected to continue decreasing whereas the forecast shows that assault crime (Fig. 5(e)) is expected to continue to have a constant variation in the next five years. Figure 6 is showing us how LSTM model outperform SARIMA model.

4 Discussion

In this study, two different prediction model's accuracy in crime prediction was compared. The results of the overall difference in error between the models indicate that the LSTM model have higher accuracy than the SARIMA model. The LSTM-model provides considerably more options for fine-tuning compared to SARIMA; this might discredit the SARIMA results. The findings in our study are also in agreement with previous research also comparing LSTM and SARIMA for time-series forecasting problems. Different research compared SARIMA and LSTM on different datasets and their RMSE values favored LSTM. From this we confirm that LSTM will play a big role in the field of crime occurrence prediction.

5 Conclusion and Future Work

In this paper using the Chicago crime dataset the exploratory data analysis was done for exploration of crime pattern, the analysis of spatial and temporal crime hotspot was done, and the results are clearly presented. The time series analysis of top5 crime is also included. Finally, the time series forecasting of these top 5 crimes in Chicago dataset was done and presented in this research. The experimental results achieved with the given dataset on the performance of used models which are SARIMA and LSTM models were also compared. The analysis and the comparison of these two models admit and defends that LSTM model which is based on deep learning has a better performance compared to SARIMA model for predicting future crime occurrence.

In the future the investigation for the improvement of the use of deep learning algorithm and techniques is proposed to be carried out on those problems and other datasets with varied numbers of features. Among these features, dataset about demography, housing, education as well as economic dataset should be combined and analyzed together with crime dataset for improving the result and analyzing the crime time series as multivariate.

Acknowledgement. This work was supported by National Key Research and Development Program of China (2016YFC0803000), Beijing Municipal Science and Technology Projects under Grant (No. Z171100005117002).

References

1. Dubey, N., et al.: Int. J. Eng. Res. Appl. **4**(3), 396–400 (2014). ISSN: 2248-9622 (Version 1)
2. Sathyadevan, S., Devan, M.S., Surya, G.S.: Crime analysis and prediction using data mining. In: International Conference on Networks & Soft Computing, pp. 406–412 (2014)
3. Thongtae, P., Srisuk, S.: An analysis of data mining applications in crime domain. In: International Conference on Computer and Information Technology Workshops, pp. 122–126 (2008)

4. Grover, V., Adderley, R., Bramer, M.: Review of current crime prediction techniques. In: Ellis, R., Allen, T., Tuson, A. (eds.) Applications and Innovations in Intelligent Systems. SGAI 2006, vol. 14, pp. 233–237. Springer, London (2007). https://doi.org/10.1007/978-1-84628-666-7_19
5. Liu, H., Brown, D.E.: Criminal incident prediction using a point-pattern- based density model. Int. J. Forecast. **19**, 603–622 (2003)
6. Vold, G.B.: Prediction methods applied to problems of classification within institutions. J. Crim. Law Criminol. **26**, 202–209 (1951)
7. Babakura, A., Sulaiman, M.N., Yusuf, M.A.: Improved method of classification algorithms for crime prediction. In: International Symposium on Biometrics and Security Technologies (ISBAST), pp. 250–255 (2014)
8. https://catalog.data.gov/dataset/crimes-2001-to-present-398a4
9. Brantingham, P.L., Brantingham, P.J., Vajihollahi, M., Wuschke, K.: Crime analysis at multiple scales of aggregation: a topological approach. In: Weisburd, D., Bernasco, W., Bruinsma, G.J. (eds.) Putting Crime in its Place, pp. 87–107. Springer, New York (2009). https://doi.org/10.1007/978-0-387-09688-9_4
10. Eck, J., Chainey, S., Cameron, J., Wilson, R.: Mapping crime: Understanding hotspots. National Institute of Justice, Washington DC (2005)
11. Hochreiter, S., Schmidhuber, J.: Long short-term memory. Neural Comput. **9**(8), 1735–1780 (1997)
12. Egenhofer, M.J., Franzosa, R.D.: Point-set topological spatial relations. Int. J. Geogr. Inf. Syst. **5**(2), 161–174 (1991)
13. Tseng, F.-M., Tzeng, G.-H.: A fuzzy seasonal ARIMA model for forecasting. Fuzzy Sets Syst. **126**, 367–376 (2002)

Medical and Healthcare Data/Decision Analytics

Fast Bat Algorithm for Predicting Diabetes Mellitus Using Association Rule Mining

Hend Amraoui[1,2(✉)], Faouzi Mhamdi[1,3], and Mourad Elloumi[1]

[1] Laboratory of Technologies of Information and Communication and Electrical
Engineering (LaTICE), National Higher School of Engineers of Tunis (ENSIT),
University of Tunis, Tunis, Tunisia
[2] Faculty of Mathematical, Physical and Natural Sciences of Tunis,
University of Tunis El Manar, Tunis, Tunisia
[3] Higher Institute of Applied Languages and Computer Science of Beja,
University of Jendouba, Jendouba, Tunisia
amraoui.hend@yahoo.fr, faouzi.mhamdi@ensi.rnu.tn,
mourad.elloumi@gmail.com

Abstract. Association Rules (ARs) are the most important tool of Data
Mining (DM) used to extract useful information stored in large databases
during the last years. Motivated by the success of population-based meta-
heuristics dealing with this amount of data, we propose to develop a
faster approach of the Bat algorithm based on ARM. Our approach is
evaluated on a real database of population with or without diabetes. The
proposed algorithm has better optimization accuracy and time complexity compared with the old version of the algorithm.

Keywords: Association Rule Mining · Data Mining · Diabetes
mellitus · ARM Bat · FBat-ARM · Support · Confidence · Fitness

1 Introduction

In recent years, the amount of data stored in the databases has become very
large. This led to a growing interest in the development of tools capable of
extracting knowledge from data [10]. The most important tool for discovering
useful information in databases is Data Mining (DM). DM tasks include classification, regression, clustering and Association Rules (ARs). These latter are
the most used to identify relationships among a set of items in a database [1].
Dealing with large transactional databases, we opted for a metaheuristic with
AR instead of an exact algorithm. Metaheuristic is an optimization algorithm
behave like search algorithms, trying to learn the characteristics of a problem
in order to find an approximation of the best solution [3] which optimizes time
complexity and quality of the generated rules. Our paper is organized as follows: Sect. 2 quotes some previous work related to metaheuristics dealing with

© Springer Nature Switzerland AG 2019
J. Li et al. (Eds.): ADMA 2019, LNAI 11888, pp. 591–604, 2019.
https://doi.org/10.1007/978-3-030-35231-8_43

ARs. A description of the standard version of the Bat algorithm is presented in Sect. 3. Section 4 describes the problem and the technical solutions. Section 5 details our proposed approach. Section 6 presents and discusses different experimental results. Finally, some concluding remarks and future work are presented in Sect. 7.

2   Background and Motivation

Heraguemi et al. [7] proposed a Bat-based Algorithm (BA) for Association Rule Mining (ARM Bat), that aims to maximize the fitness function to generate the best rules in the database. The results are competitive in term of computation speed and memory usage. Neelima et al. [10] proposed a new algorithm called hybrid ABCBAT which minimizes the generation of frequent itemsets and also reduces the time, space and memory. Neelima et al. used a random walk of BAT algorithm in order to increase the exploration. The proposed algorithm has better optimization accuracy, convergence rate and robustness. Djenouri et al. [6] developed a GPU-based Bees Swarm Optimization Miner (GBSO-Miner) where the GPU is used as a co-processor to compute the CPU-time intensive steps of the algorithm. The results of experimentation show that GBSO-Miner outperforms the baseline methods of the literature (GPApriroi, MEGPU, and Dmine) using big textual and graph databases. Talebi and Dehkord [12] developed an electromagnetic field optimization algorithm (EFO4ARH) to hide sensitive association rules. In this algorithm, two fitness functions are used to reach the solution with the least side effects. The proposed algorithm shows a reduction in the side effects and better preservation of data quality. Li and Li [9] adopted an order batching algorithm FPGB based on the Association Rule Mining Algorithm FP-growth to establish the correlation degree of orders in E-commerce. The results of the experiment demonstrate the effectiveness of FPGB which completed order batching in few seconds. Djenouri et al. [5] proposed an approach, which discover useful knowledge at first by using data mining techniques, then swarms use this knowledge to explore the whole space of documents intelligently. The results show that the proposed approach improves the quality of returned documents considerably, with a competitive computational time compared to state-of-the-art approaches.

3   Bat Algorithm

Bat Algorithm (BA) is a metaheuristic method, it was developed for the first time by Yang [13]. BA is inspired from the echolocation or bio-sonar behavior of microbats with varying pulse rates of emission and loudness. Microbats use echolocation to hunt the food, avoid hurdles and to locate their roosting crevices in the dark [10]. Echolocation by bats is characterized by the emission of pulses of some frequency f, loudness A and emission rate R [8]. The exploration capability of the BA is provided by its velocity and position update equations, given by:

$$frequency_i = frequency_{min} + (frequency_{max} - frequency_{min})\beta, \quad (1)$$

$$velocity_i^t = velocity_i^{t-1} + (\gamma_i^t - \gamma_{best})frequency_i, \qquad (2)$$

$$\gamma_i^t = \gamma_i^{t-1} + velocity_i^t, \qquad (3)$$

where $\beta \in [0, 1]$ is a random generated number and γ_{best} is the current best solution which is located after comparing all the solutions among all the bats. For the local search part, once a solution is selected among the current best solutions, a new solution for each bat is generated locally using a random walk.

$$\gamma_{new} = \gamma_{old} + \epsilon A_t \qquad (4)$$

Where $\epsilon \in [-1, 1]$ is a random number, while A_t is the average loudness of all the bats at time t. At each iteration of the algorithm, the loudness A_i is reduced and the rate R_i is increased [7]. *Where*

$$A_i^t = \alpha_{bat} A_i^{t-1} \qquad (5)$$

$$R_i^{t+1} = R_i^0[1 - e^{-\gamma_{bat}^t}] \qquad (6)$$

Where α_{bat} and γ_{bat} are constants. At the initialization step of the algorithm, each bat has a different random loudness A_0 which is $\in [1, 2]$ and a random rate R_0 which is $\in [0, 1]$.

4 Materials and Methods

4.1 Study Population

For experimental evaluation, a benchmark dataset is used as input data https://www.kaggle.com/uciml/pima-indians-diabetes-database.

The studied population is PIMA Indian population, it has been under continuous study since 1965 by the National Institute of Diabetes and Digestive and Kidney Diseases [11]. The dataset is composed of 768 patients, and two classes. The variables are medical measurements of the patient plus age and pregnancy information. The classes are: *C0*, indicates True Diabetic Test (268) and *C1*, indicates False Diabetic Test (500) [4]. Among the factors, d was developed by Smith et al. [11], This function takes into consideration genetic factors inherited from ascendants.

$$d = \frac{\sum_i K_i(88 - ADM_i) + 20}{\sum_j K_j(ALC_j - 14) + 50} \qquad (7)$$

1. i ranges over all relatives, who had developed diabetes by the subject's examination date;
2. j ranges over all relatives, who had not developed diabetes by the subject's examination date;
3. K_x is the percent of genes shared by the relative;
4. ADM_i is the age in years of relative, when diabetes was diagnosed;
5. ALC_j is the age in years of relative j at the last non-diabetic examination;
6. The constants 88 and 14 represent, the maximum and minimum ages at which relatives of the subjects in this study have been developed diabetes;

7. The constants 20 and 50 were chosen such that:
   - A subject with no relatives would have a d value slightly lower than average.
   - The d value would decrease relatively slowly as young relatives free of diabetes joined the database.
   - The d value would increase relatively quickly as known relatives developed diabetes.

Table 1 illustrates an excerpt of data representing medical measures and observations collected after studying a set of (768) patients. The first column contains an ordering number for the patients. The eight next columns represent measures for medical factor: Number of times pregnant: p, Plasma Glucose Concentration at 2 h in an Oral Glucose Tolerance Test: g, Diastolic Blood Pressure (mm Hg): b, Triceps Skin Fold Thickness (mm): s, 2-h Serum Insulin (Uh/ml): i, Body Mass Index ((Weight in kg)/(Weight in m)^2): B, Diabetes Pedigree Function: d, and Age (years): a. The last column describes the fact whether the corresponding patient is actually sick ($C1$) or not ($C0$).

Table 1. Medical measures

	p	g	b	s	i	B	d	a	Out
1	0	100	70	26	50	30.8	0.597	21	$C0$
2	0	100	88	60	110	46.8	0.962	31	$C0$
3	0	101	62	0	0	21.9	0.336	25	$C0$
...	...	...	...	...	...	...	...		...
768	9	184	85	15	0	30	1.213	49	$C1$

4.2 Discretization of Continuous Attributes

In our database, the range of each numeric attribute (factor) is very wide. To overcome this problem, it was decided to turn numeric attributes into discrete ones. The discretization method has been explained in [2]. Table 2 illustrates an excerpt of data after discretization.

Table 2. Discretized medical measures

	p	g	b	s	i	B	d	a	Out
1	11	22	32	43	52	63	73	81	91
2	11	22	33	44	52	65	74	83	91
3	11	22	32	41	51	61	72	82	91
...	...	...	...	...	...	...	...	...	...
768	13	26	33	42	51	63	75	84	92

4.3 Preliminaries and Problem Statement

Given the representation in Table 2 of the patients' database, it is interesting to analyze which combination of criteria ranges implies the most sickness (or no sickness). We may consider combination taking into account all or only subsets of the criteria. To represent a given combination of criteria ranges and the associated desired outcome (sickness or not), we are using an *Association Rule*, defined below.

Definition 1. *Given A a set of integers and c an integer, we define the corresponding Association Rule (or simply Rule), γ, denoted by $A \Rightarrow c$. A is called the antecedent of γ (and denoted by $\mathcal{A}(\gamma)$) and c its consequence (and denoted by $\mathcal{C}(\gamma)$). The size of γ (denoted by $\mathcal{S}(\gamma)$) is the size of its antecedent: $\overline{\mathcal{A}(\gamma)}$.*

An association rule $\mathcal{A}(\gamma)$ represents the logical implication: "if items in A are all observed on medical measures for a patient then the outcome for that patient is c".

Definition 2. *Given an association rule γ, a projection of γ is a rule γ', such that $\mathcal{A}(\gamma')$ is a non-empty subset of $\mathcal{A}(\gamma)$. When γ' is a projection of γ we also say γ is an enrichment of γ'.*

We note that the encoded dataset of Table 2 can be represented by a sequence (array or list) of association rules. Given Definitions 1 and 2 we can now state the problem we propose to investigate.

Problem 1. Given:

- a sequence of association rules $\mathcal{P} = [A_p \Rightarrow c_p]_{p \in I}$, with the same size d, called *population*,
- an objective function f mapping each projection of an association rule in $\mathcal{P}$ to a real value in $[0, 1]$,
- and an integer s between 1 and d.

Compute all the projections of size s of associations rules in $\mathcal{P}$ that maximizes the objective function f.

We propose to solve the Problem 1 for all possible sizes of association rules. As objective function we will use the so-called *fitness*, defined below.

Definition 3. *Given two strictly positive real values α and β, and a set $\mathcal{P}$ of association rules, the fitness function (denoted fit) maps each projection γ of elements in $\mathcal{P}$ to a positive real value $fit(\gamma)$ as described below:*

$$fit(\gamma) = \frac{\alpha \times supp(\gamma) + \beta \times conf(\gamma)}{\alpha + \beta} \tag{8}$$

where : The support of γ denoted by $supp(\gamma)$ is $\frac{y(\gamma)}{\overline{\mathcal{P}}}$, the confidence of γ denoted by $conf(\gamma)$ is $\frac{y(\gamma)}{x(\gamma)}$, $x(\gamma)$ is the number of enrichments of γ in $\mathcal{P}$, and $y(\gamma)$ is the number of enrichments of γ in $\mathcal{P}$, having the same consequence as γ.

We note that for a given association rule γ, $supp(\gamma)$ measures the probability of occurrence of items in $\mathcal{A}(\gamma)$ together with consequence $\mathcal{C}(\gamma)$ in the population, while $conf(\gamma)$ measures the probability of occurrence of the consequence $\mathcal{C}(\gamma)$ having all items in $\mathcal{A}(\gamma)$ appearing in the rules of the population.

5   Fast Bat Algorithm for Association Rule Mining (FBat-ARM)

We propose in this section to use the adaptation of the Bat Algorithm to solve Problem 1. We informally explain the principle of our approach before providing the formal algorithm. In this approach we will solve Problem 1 for a given size s of the rules ($1 \leq s \leq d$). The antecedent of a rule is represented by an array of size d, with possibly null entries. The size of a rule is then the number of entries in the array that are not null.

1. We start with an initial population $\mathcal{P}_0^s$ of n_0 projections of size s extracted (randomly) from the overall rules population $\mathcal{P}$.
2. At iteration $0 \leq i < n$, compute fitnesses for all rules in $\mathcal{P}_i^s$ and pick up the best γ_b^i rules.
3. For each rule γ in $\mathcal{P}_i^s$ create a new empty rule γ' by adjusting frequency $frequency$ and updating velocity $velocity$.
4. For all not null items $\mathcal{A}(\gamma)[j]$ in $\mathcal{A}(\gamma)$, if loudness A is less than a random value, $newItem$ will be increased, else $newItem$ will be decreased.
5. If $\mathcal{S}(\gamma') < s$, replace randomly null items in γ' by not null items in γ, till $\mathcal{S}(\gamma') = s$.
6. If $fit(\gamma') > fit(\gamma)$, replace γ by γ' in $\mathcal{P}_i^s$ to obtain $\mathcal{P}_{i+1}^s$, the new population for next iteration step $i + 1$, adjust velocity $velocity$, pulse rate R and loudness A.
7. If pulse rate R is less than a random value, Generate a new rule by changing randomly just one item in the rule.
8. If $fit(\gamma_b') > fit(\gamma_b)$, replace γ_b by γ_b' in $\mathcal{P}_i^s$, increase pulse rate R and decrease loudness A to obtain $\mathcal{P}_{i+1}^s$, the new population for next iteration step $i + 1$.
9. When iterations are done ($i = n$). Compute and return best fitness in $\mathcal{P}_n^s$ and rules realizing that fitness.

Algorithm 1. GENERATE_INITIAL_POPULATION

Input: $\mathcal{P}, c, s, n_0$
Output: Pop
1    $Pop \leftarrow \emptyset$;
2    $\mathcal{P}' \leftarrow \mathcal{P}$;
3   **for** $i \in [0, n_0[$ **do**
4        $\gamma \leftarrow \mathcal{P}'[\text{RANDOM}(\overline{\mathcal{P}'})]$;
5        $newAntecedent \leftarrow array[\mathcal{S}(\gamma)]$;
6   **for** $j \in \text{RANDOM\_ORDERS}(\{0, \ldots, d-1\}, s)$ **do**
7            $newAntecedent[j] \leftarrow \mathcal{A}(\gamma)[j]$;
8   **end**
9        $\mathcal{P}' \leftarrow \mathcal{P} \setminus \{\gamma\}$;
10       $\mathcal{A}(\gamma') \leftarrow newAntecedent$;
11       $\mathcal{C}(\gamma') \leftarrow c$;
12       $Pop \leftarrow Pop \cup \{\gamma'\}$;
13   **end**
14   **return** Pop;

Algorithm 2. BAT_ASSOCIATION_RULE_MINING

Input: $\mathcal{P}$, c, d, s, N, n_0, A, R, α_{bat}, γ_{bat}
Output: *BestRules, BestFitness*

1   $Pop \leftarrow$ GENERATE_INITIAL_POPULATION($\mathcal{P}$, c, s, n_0);
2   **for** $i \in [1, N]$ **do**
3     $\gamma_b \leftarrow$ BEST_RULE(Pop);
4   **for** $\gamma \in Pop$ **do**
5       $frequency \leftarrow 1+$RANDOM(d);
6       $velocity \leftarrow d - frequency - velocities.get(\gamma)$;
7       $newAntecedent \leftarrow array[\mathcal{S}(\gamma)]$;
8   **for** $j \in [0, d[$ **do**
9         $newItem \leftarrow \mathcal{A}(\gamma)[j]$;
10   **if** $newItem \neq null$ **then**
11   **if** RANDOM_REAL() $\geq A$ **then**
12           $newItem + +$;
13   **end**
14   **else**
15           $newItem - -$;
16   **end**
17   **end**
18         $newAntecedent[j] \leftarrow newItem$;
19   **end**
20       $\mathcal{A}(\gamma') \leftarrow newAntecedent$;
21       $\mathcal{C}(\gamma') \leftarrow \mathcal{C}(\gamma)$;
22   CORRECT_SIZE(γ', γ, s, d);
23   **if** $fit(\gamma') > fit(\gamma)$ **then**
24         $Pop \leftarrow (Pop \setminus \{\gamma\}) \cup \{\gamma'\}$;
25         $velocities.put(\gamma', velocity)$;
26         $R \leftarrow R \times (1 - e^{\gamma_{bat} \times i})$;
27         $A \leftarrow A \times \alpha_{bat}$;
28   **end**
29   **else**
30         $velocities.put(\gamma, velocity)$;
31   **end**
32   **if** RANDOM_REAL() $\geq R$ **then**
33         $\mathcal{A}(\gamma'_b) \leftarrow \mathcal{A}(\gamma_b)$;
34         $\mathcal{C}(\gamma'_b) \leftarrow \mathcal{C}(\gamma_b)$;
35   **while** *true* **do**
36          $randOrder \leftarrow$RANDOM(d);
37   **if** $\mathcal{A}(\gamma'_b)[randOrder] \neq null$ **then**
38           $\mathcal{A}(\gamma'_b)[randOrder] \leftarrow$RANDOM_ITEM($\mathcal{P}$, $randOrder$);
39           $break$;
40   **end**
41   **end**
42   **if** $fit(\gamma'_b) > fit(\gamma_b)$ **then**
43          $Pop \leftarrow (Pop \setminus \{\gamma_b\}) \cup \{\gamma'_b\}$;
44          $velocities.put(\gamma'_b, 0)$;
45          $R \leftarrow R \times (1 - e^{\gamma_{bat} \times i})$;
46          $A \leftarrow A \times \alpha_{bat}$;
47   **end**
48   **end**
49   **end**
50 **end**

Algorithm 3. BEST_RULE

Input: Pop
Output: γ_b
1 $maxFitness \leftarrow 0.0$;
2 $\gamma_b \leftarrow null$;
3 **for** $\gamma \in Pop$ **do**
4     $currentFitness \leftarrow fit(\gamma)$;
5   **if** $currentFitness > maxFitness$ **then**
6        $maxFitness \leftarrow currentFitness$;
7        $\gamma_b \leftarrow \gamma$;
8   **end**
9 **end**
10 **return** γ_b;

Algorithm 4. CORRECT_SIZE

Input: γ', γ, s, d
Output: γ'
1 **if** $\mathcal{S}(\gamma') < s$ **then**
2     $orders \leftarrow \emptyset$;
3   **for** $i \in [0, d[$ **do**
4   **if** $(\mathcal{A}(\gamma)[i] \neq null) \wedge (\mathcal{A}(\gamma')[i] = null)$ **then**
5           $orders \leftarrow orders \cup \{i\}$;
6   **end**
7   **end**
8   **for** $index \in$ RANDOM_ORDERS$(orders, s - \mathcal{S}(\gamma'))$ **do**
9        $\mathcal{A}(\gamma')[orders[index]] \leftarrow \mathcal{A}(\gamma)[orders[index]]$;
10   **end**
11 **end**

Algorithm 5. RANDOM_ORDERS

Input: $orders$, s
Output: $selectedOrders$
1 $selectedOrders \leftarrow \emptyset$;
2 **while** $\overline{selectedOrders} < s$ **do**
3     $selected \leftarrow$ RANDOM$(\overline{orders})]$;
4     $selectedOrders \leftarrow selectedOrders \cup \{orders[selected]\}$;
5     $orders \leftarrow orders \setminus \{orders[selected]\}$;
6 **end**
7 **return** $selectedOrders$;

Complexity. As stated in the paper introducing Bat Algorithm for association rule mining, complexity of Algorithm 2 is: $O(N \times n \times d)$.

5.1 Fitness Computation Improvement

It tackes a costly part of the treatment: the computation of the fitness function itself. We propose to keep track for all computed fitnesses for all analyzed rules. This is efficient for Bat algorithm applied to association rule mining, since fitness is likely to be computed many times for the same rule. *We may also consider other results that reduces computation of the fitness function in the literature.* Computing the fitness for a given rule is a costly task. Indeed we explained in previous sections that it has $O(s \times n)$ complexity, where s is the rule's size and n the population size. We propose to reduce the fitness computation complexity using the following enhancements:

– Provided that we already have computed a mapping $TransactionsByItems$, that sends every item $item$ to the set of the transactions (rules in $\mathcal{P}$) $\Gamma(item)$ where this item appears. We can compute then compute:

$$x(\gamma) = \overline{\bigcap_{item \in \mathcal{A}(\gamma)} TransactionsByItems(item)} \qquad (9)$$

If we extend the definition of $TransactionsByItems$ to the consequences, we can also compute, for a given sequence c:

$$xy(\gamma) = \overline{\bigcap_{item \in \mathcal{A}(\gamma) \cup \{c\}} TransactionsByItems(item)} \qquad (10)$$

Since the complexity of computing the intersection of two sets A and B runs in $O(min(\overline{A}, \overline{B})$. We can infer that the complexity of computing every intersection is $O(s \times Min_{item \in \mathcal{A}(\gamma) \cup \{c\}}(TransactionsByItems(item)))$ and that reduces drastically the fitness computation (time) complexity. We note that pre-computing the mapping $TransactionsByItems$ does not introduce too much cost, since it can be done while parsing rules from the database file.
– We can also keep track of all computed fitnesses so far, using a mapping $ComputedFitnesses$ that sends each already analyzed rule to its fitness value. This is very useful for Bat algorithm, since fitness of a given rule may be used many times during iterations of the algorithm (when computing best rule in a population).

6 Experimental Results

In this paper we have introduced and demonstrated the use of a population-based metaheuristic Algorithm (Bat) with association Rules. we compared our approach to that of Heraguemi et al. [7]. The explanation of the abbreviations used in the Tables below is as follows:

– N: Number of iterations.
– C: The considered consequence (CO or $C1$).
– A.E.T: Average Execution Time.
– A.N.F.1: Average Number of Failures in finding the best solution.

- A.D.F.1: Average Delta between the computed fitness and the actually best fitness.
- A.N.F.2: Average Number of Failures in finding all the rules that realize the best fitness, when the program actually find it.
- A.D.F.2: Average of the ratio

$$\frac{N_{best}^{all} - N_{best}^{returned}}{N_{best}^{all}} \tag{11}$$

where N_{best}^{all} stands here for the number of all rules realizing the best fitness and $N_{best}^{returned}$ for the number of rules realizing the best fitness and actually returned by the program.

All times are measured in millseconds (ms) except when a different unit is explicitly specified.

Table 3. Comparative table of Average Execution Time (A.E.T) provided by ARM Bat Algorithm and FBat-ARM Algorithm

n	N	C	A.E.T ARM Bat	A.E.T FBat-ARM
768	25	91	3995	2658
		92	3565	1858
	50	91	6290	2600
		92	5627	2628
	100	91	11123	3776
		92	10113	3941
	200	91	22306	8210
		92	19876	7781
7680	25	91	33226	5119
		92	28878	5449
	50	91	60775	6835
		92	55178	7384
	100	91	119573	8409
		92	104458	9886
	200	91	224913	12764
		92	195977	14597
76800	25	91	1222114	42200
		92	1111567	54439
	50	91	5068042	53590
		92	2108604	66010
	100	91	7652712	69270
		92	56786280	89684
	200	91	638516	78181
		92	147658	121330

Table 4. Comparative table of Average Number of Failures in finding the best solution (A.N.F.1) provided by ARM Bat Algorithm and FBat-ARM Algorithm

n	N	C	A.N.F.1 ARM Bat	A.N.F.1 FBat-ARM
768	25	91	50,00%	37,50%
		92		
	50	91	62,50%	37,50%
		92	50,00%	
	100	91	62,50%	25,00%
		92	50,00%	37,50%
	200	91		50,00%
		92	62,50%	37,50%
7680	25	91	50,00%	25,00%
		92		50,00%
	50	91	62,50%	37,50%
		92	37,50%	
	100	91	25,00%	00,00%
		92	37,50%	37,50%
	200	91	62,50%	
		92	50,00%	37,50%
76800	25	91	50,00%	25,00%
		92		
	50	91	62,50%	37,50%
		92	50,00%	
	100	91	62,50%	50,00%
		92	50,00%	37,50%
	200	91	50,00%	37,50%
		92		37,50%

Table 5. Comparative table of A.D.F.1 provided by ARM Bat Algorithm and FBat-ARM Algorithm

n	N	C	A.D.F.1 ARM Bat	A.D.F.1 FBat-ARM
768	25	91	0,004443	0,003191
		92	0,000488	0,000407
	50	91	0,004742	0,004167
		92	0,000895	0,000244
	100	91	0,005298	0,003418
		92	0,000407	0,000326
	200	91	0,003662	0,002113
		92	0,000407	0,000244
7680	25	91	0,005607	0,003174
		92	0,000488	0,000488
	50	91	0,004290	0,003153
		92	0,000326	0,000244
	100	91	0,002199	0,000000
		92	0,000488	0,000244
	200	91	0,005450	0,002400
		92	0,000488	0,000244
76800	25	91	0,003516	0,001671
		92	0,000407	0,000244
	50	91	0,004476	0,003679
		92	0,000488	0,000488
	100	91	0,004697	0,004415
		92	0,000407	0,000326
	200	91	0,003906	0,001709
		92	0,000651	0,000407

602   H. Amraoui et al.

Table 6. Comparative table of A.N.F.2 provided by ARM Bat Algorithm and FBat-ARM Algorithm

n	N	C	A.N.F.2 ARM Bat	A.N.F.2 FBat-ARM
768	25	91	0,00%	0,00%
		92	25,00%	25,00%
	50	91	0,00%	0,00%
		92	37,50%	25,00%
	100	91	0,00%	0,00%
		92	37,50%	25,00%
	200	91	0,00%	0,00%
		92	37,50%	12,50%
7680	25	91	0,00%	0,00%
		92	25,00%	25,00%
	50	91	0,00%	0,00%
		92	37,50%	25,00%
	100	91	0,00%	0,00%
		92	37,50%	37,50%
	200	91	00,00%	0,00%
		92	37,50%	25,00%
76800	25	91	0,00%	0,00%
		92	37,50%	12,50%
	50	91	0,00%	00,00%
		92	25,00%	25,00%
	100	91	0,00%	0,00%
		92	25,00%	12,50%
	200	91	0,00%	0,00%
		92	25,00%	25,00%

Table 7. Comparative table of A.D.F.2 provided by ARM Bat Algorithm and FBat-ARM Algorithm

n	N	C	A.D.F.2 ARM Bat	A.N.D.2 FBat-ARM
768	25	91	0,00%	0,00%
		92	18,75%	11,46%
	50	91	0,00%	0,00%
		92	17,71%	16,67%
	100	91	0,00%	0,00%
		92	20,83%	13,54%
	200	91	0,00%	0,00%
		92	20,83%	6,25%
7680	25	91	0,00%	0,00%
		92	16,67%	12,50%
	50	91	0,00%	0,00%
		92	26,04%	14,58%
	100	91	00,00%	0,00%
		92	22,92%	17,71%
	200	91	00,00%	0,00%
		92	15,62%	13,54%
76800	25	91	0,00%	0,00%
		92	17,71%	6,25%
	50	91	0,00%	00,00%
		92	7,29%	7,29%
	100	91	0,00%	0,00%
		92	11,46%	6,25%
	200	91	0,00%	0,00%
		92	12,50%	9,38%

Discussion. From Table 3, we notice that our algorithm FBat-ARM is able to reduce the Average Execution Time (A.E.T) compared to ARM Bat Algorithm even by increasing the size of the dataset. From Table 4, we notice that FBat-ARM encounter less failure to find the best solution compared to ARM Bat for databases with different sizes. From Table 5, we notice that FBat-ARM gets closer to the best fitness compared to ARM Bat for databases with different sizes. From Table 6, FBat-ARM find more most of the rules that trealize the best fitness compared to ARM Bat for databases with different sizes. From Table 7, FBat-ARM return more rules realizing the best fitness compared to ARM Bat for databases with different sizes. Comparing the results of the experimentation, we can deduce that the enhanced approach (FBat-ARM) allows a remarkable improvement on the process even with a raise of the size of the database that goes from 768 to 7680 to 76800 patients. Thanks to our new algorithm, the calculation of the fitness function has been accelerated according to two contributions. In the first one we have already shown that pre-computing the mapping *TransactionsByItems* does not introduce too much cost, since it can be done while parsing rules from the database file and the seconde one by keeping track of all computed fitnesses so far, using a mapping *ComputedFitnesses* that sends each already analyzed rule to its fitness value. According to the experiments, FBat-ARM not only improve the speed a lot, but also improve the quality of the results, this is clear thanks to the measures $A.N.F.1$, $A.D.F.2$, $A.N.F.1$ and $A.D.F.2$.

7   Conclusion

In this paper, we have developed a new fast population-based metaheuristic dealing with ARM (FBat-ARM). Our approach has a complexity of $O(N \times n \times d)$. In order to optimize our algorithm: reducing time complexity and improving the quality of association rules generated, we opted for the reduction of the fitness computation complexity. We realized two improvements: The first one is computing the fitness of intersected sets which reduces drastically the fitness computation (time) complexity. The second one is keeping track of all computed fitnesses of each already analyzed rule. According to the results, we can say that our algorithm is efficient in term of time complexity and optimization accuracy. Our goal in the future is to improve further the algorithm to reach as close as possible the best solution which improves the quality of association rules generated and the prediction of a disease, the Diabetes in our case.

References

1. Agrawal, R., Imieliński, T., Swami, A.: Mining association rules between sets of items in large databases. In: ACM SIGMOD Record, vol. 22, pp. 207–216. ACM (1993)
2. Amraoui, H., Mhamdi, F., Elloumi, M.: Fast exhaustive search algorithm for discovering relevant association rules
3. Amraoui, H., Mhamdi, F., Elloumi, M.: Survey of metaheuristics and statistical methods for multifactorial diseases analyses. AIMS Med. Sci. **4**, 291–331 (2017)
4. Breiman, L.: Bagging predictors. Mach. Learn. **24**(2), 123–140 (1996)
5. Djenouri, Y., Belhadi, A., Belkebir, R.: Bees swarm optimization guided by data mining techniques for document information retrieval. Expert Syst. Appl. **94**, 126–136 (2018)
6. Djenouri, Y., Djenouri, D., Belhadi, A., Fournier-Viger, P., Lin, J.C.W., Bendjoudi, A.: Exploiting GPU parallelism in improving bees swarm optimization for mining big transactional databases. Inf. Sci. **496**, 326–342 (2018)
7. Heraguemi, K.E., Kamel, N., Drias, H.: Association rule mining based on bat algorithm. J. Comput. Theor. Nanosci. **12**(7), 1195–1200 (2015)
8. Jayabarathi, T., Raghunathan, T., Gandomi, A.H.: The bat algorithm, variants and some practical engineering applications: a review. In: Yang, X.-S. (ed.) Nature-Inspired Algorithms and Applied Optimization. SCI, vol. 744, pp. 313–330. Springer, Cham (2018). https://doi.org/10.1007/978-3-319-67669-2_14
9. Li, Y., Li, Y.: E-commerce order batching algorithm based on association rule mining in the era of big data. In: 2018 Chinese Control And Decision Conference (CCDC), pp. 1934–1939. IEEE (2018)
10. Neelima, S., Satyanarayana, N., Krishna Murthy, P.: Minimizing frequent itemsets using hybrid ABCBAT algorithm. In: Satapathy, S.C., Bhateja, V., Raju, K.S., Janakiramaiah, B. (eds.) Data Engineering and Intelligent Computing. AISC, vol. 542, pp. 91–97. Springer, Singapore (2018). https://doi.org/10.1007/978-981-10-3223-3_9
11. Smith, J.W., Everhart, J., Dickson, W., Knowler, W., Johannes, R.: Using the ADAP learning algorithm to forecast the onset of diabetes mellitus. In: Proceedings of the Annual Symposium on Computer Application in Medical Care, p. 261. American Medical Informatics Association (1988)
12. Talebi, B., Dehkordi, M.N.: Sensitive association rules hiding using electromagnetic field optimization algorithm. Expert Syst. Appl. **114**, 155–172 (2018)
13. Yang, X.S.: A new metaheuristic bat-inspired algorithm. In: González, J.R., Pelta, D.A., Cruz, C., Terrazas, G., Krasnogor, N. (eds.) Nature Inspired Cooperative Strategies for Optimization (NICSO 2010), pp. 65–74. Springer, Heidelberg (2010). https://doi.org/10.1007/978-3-642-12538-6_6

Using a Virtual Hospital for Piloting Patient Flow Decongestion Interventions

Shaowen Qin$^{(\boxtimes)}$ ⬤

College of Science and Engineering, Flinders University,
Tonsley, SA 5042, Australia
shaowen.qin@flinders.edu.au

Abstract. It is beyond the capacity of the human mind to process large amounts of interdependent information, such as predicting the dynamic behavior of a complex system and evaluating the short and long term effects of potential interventions aimed to improve its operations. At the same time, it is extremely costly to test these interventions with the real world system subject to improvement. Fortunately, we have moved to an era where advancements in computing and software technology have provided us the capabilities to build virtual complex systems (simulation models), that can serve as risk-free digital platforms for running pilot experiments with potential system interventions and obtain comparative data for decision support and optimization. This paper presents two case studies in a healthcare setting, where a simulation model named HESMAD (Hospital Event Simulation Model: Arrivals to Discharge) was applied to pilot potential interventions proposed by hospital professionals or researchers that are aimed at minimizing hospital patient flow congestion episodes. It was demonstrated that simulation modelling is not only an effective approach to conduct virtual experiments for evaluating proposed intervention ideas from healthcare professionals, but also an ideal vehicle for piloting scientific research outcomes from data science researchers. Some experience-based discussions on various issues involved in simulation modelling, such as validation of the simulation model and interpretation of simulation results are also provided.

Keywords: Simulation modelling · Virtual experiments · Decision support · Optimization · Pilot study · Patient flow

1 Introduction

A complex system consists of many parts that interact directly or indirectly with other parts and the system environment. There are many variables and stochastic events/processes involved in describing the dynamic behaviour of a complex system, and the causes and effects among them are often intertwined and far from obvious. A hallmark of complex systems is often said to be "the whole is more than the sum of its parts". Human mind is limited by its ability to process information and handle complexities [1], hence it is not an exaggeration to say that predicting the dynamics behaviour of a complex system and evaluating the short and long term effects of potential interventions in a quantitative manner is beyond the capacity of the human mind. Quantitative evaluation of the dynamic

© Springer Nature Switzerland AG 2019
J. Li et al. (Eds.): ADMA 2019, LNAI 11888, pp. 605–616, 2019.
https://doi.org/10.1007/978-3-030-35231-8_44

behaviour of complex systems is challenging even for researchers, as closed-form analytic solutions hardly exist and numerical analysis based solutions often involve complicated concepts and procedures that are difficult to understand by non-expert. This in turn increases the difficulties to engage other stakeholders in the solution process. In the past, we have to rely on the wisdom of decision makers to come up with high impact policies/strategies for system improvement, as there was no other means to evaluate the soundness of such decisions. Unfortunately, personal opinions can be egoistic in nature and different perspectives are often dismissed without being carefully examined for merits due to time and other constraints. As a result, costly wrong decisions were often realised after the damages were done. However, we have moved to an era where advancements in computing and software technology provide unprecedented opportunities to aid our problem solving ability. Complex formulae and algorithms become library components that require much less expertise in their applications. Animated visualisations of dynamic processes offer a much improved platform for stakeholder engagement and communication. With these capabilities, we can develop virtual complex systems (simulation models), to explore their dynamic behaviour with relative ease. Built properly, simulation models reveal emergent system level properties, demonstrate short and long term impacts of potential system interventions and offer much more objective reasoning to support management decisions that are data-driven rather than opinion-based.

This paper presents two case studies where a simulation model named HESMAD (Hospital Event Simulation Model: Arrivals to Discharge) [2–4] developed in our research was applied to evaluate interventions to minimize hospital patient flow congestion episodes. The aim is not only to demonstrate the power and benefit of simulation modelling, but also to shed some light, based on our experience, on various issues involved in simulation modelling, such as validation of the simulation model, how detailed a model should be, as well as interpretation of simulation results.

2   The Virtual Hospital

We have developed a patient flow simulation model relating to a large Australian metropolitan hospital with a busy emergency department (ED), named HESMAD (Hospital Events Simulation Model: arrival to Discharge) [2]. HESMAD was created to explore the dynamics of patient flow, and experiment with "what-if" interventions to identify optimal response to congestion episodes as well as general policy changes for patient flow improvement. A modular structure was adopted to represent the hospital where physical units or processes were modeled as modules. The journey of each patient moving through the hospital is captured as a series of discrete events from the time they first present at the ED, or are admitted as elective patients, to the time that they are discharged. HESMAD models all patients in the ED and all specialties, surgical, general medical and overnight elective (surgery & medicine) patients. Patients are characterized by a series of parameters that are assigned at their creation, based on statistics derived from historical data. These parameters include age, arrival mode (ambulance, self-presentation, or elective) and their triage (rating of patients' clinical urgency) status. Modules are also characterized by parameters such as number of beds and processing time.

While an in-depth discussion of the simulation is available elsewhere [2], the following brief summary provides a quick reference. In short, the HESMAS simulation model captured as realistically as possible the macro level behavior of a real Australian metropolitan public hospital. As shown in Fig. 1, the HESMAD simulation model comprises several modules representing emergency, electives, inpatients and discharge. The linked modules capture the various patient flow pathways in the hospital. Fitted distributions based on real hospital data are used throughout the simulation to both represent factors relating to patient condition (used for determining their journey) and specify their length of stay (LOS) throughout various areas of hospital. These fitted distributions are supplemented with strategically placed queues that allow for the representation and capturing of the delay patients might experience due to unavailability of beds in a treatment area or ward. By monitoring the lengths of these queues we are able to investigate the potential impact that changes of arrival patterns or internal practices will have on the operations of the hospital. It is important to note that while focus may be directed to understanding the impacts at the front door of the hospital (i.e., emergency), only though modelling of the entire hospital can we fully capture the ED's behavior due to the bi-directional interplay between emergency and inpatients, which itself is impacted by other factors such as electives and discharge.

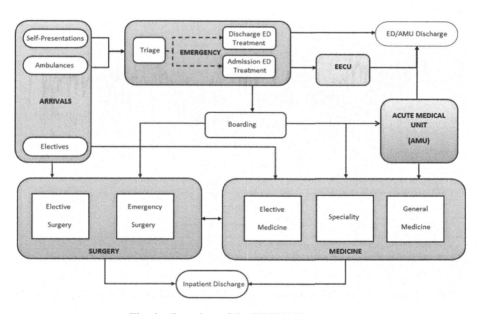

Fig. 1. Overview of the HESMAD structure.

A crucial yet difficult step in developing any simulation model is its validation. Similar to any models for prediction, historical data based validation is usually considered most convincing. However, due to the stochastic nature of the simulation, it is only possible as well as meaningful to compare simulated and historical data metrics at an aggregated level, such as frequency of occupancy or waiting times exceeding certain thresholds. Exact fit of the historical time series data is neither possible nor necessary, as each simulation run will generate a different dataset. This is consistent with real world observation, that is, if history could be repeated, a complex system would not leave an identical trace (data set) to the one left before no matter how hard we try to keep all conditions the same.

An example of validation is presented in Fig. 2 whereby historical midnight occupancy data (in black) is plotted against synthetic midnight occupancy values generated using HESMAD (with data from 100 replications). As can be seen, while there are differences, trend wise the simulation and the historical data closely resemble each other, even for a single simulation replication (in blue). The simulated occupancy has the same prominent weekly trend associated with hospitals and observed in the actual data, and the real data is well bounded by maximum and minimum recorded occupancy values for each day (in gray). A slight discrepancy does occur during the Christmas period which was not explicitly adjusted for within the simulation. It can also be seen in the single realization case that low occupancy events are permissible and, indeed, do occur at times.

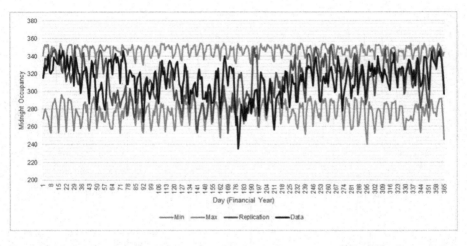

Fig. 2. Simulated vs actual midnight occupancy over a one-year period. (Color figure online)

It is important to mention the advantage of virtual display of the dynamic system behavior in simulation modeling. Figure 3 shows a snapshot of the animation view of HESMAD at run time. This view breaks the barrier of complex computational logics to non-developers and makes the simulation easy to understand, which in turn allows better engagement of all stakeholders and results in more constructive discussion among them. This was indeed our experience during the model development and application processes.

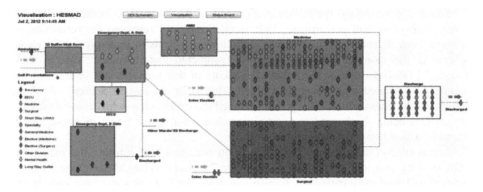

Fig. 3. A snapshot of the animation view of HESMAD at run time.

3   Piloting Heuristic Intervention Strategies

HESMAD has been used to pilot various heuristic decongestion strategies for hospital patient flow improvement and congestion detection and recovery [3, 4]. We briefly present the study on discharge here to emphasize the advantages of using virtual environment for piloting proposed interventions in a risk-free as well as repeated manner that cannot be achieved with its real-world counterpart (the original report of this study was written for medical professions [3]). The timing of a patient's discharge is important and delayed discharges naturally reduce the availability of inpatient beds, hence contributing to patient flow congestions [5]. Delayed discharges occur when a medically stable patient unnecessarily occupies a hospital bed because of usually non-medical reasons rather than patient characteristics [6, 7]. Our research partners at the hospital proposed many intervention ideas for discharge management. These ideas are transcribed into scenarios for testing in HESMAD. The aims are (1) to demonstrate the sensitivity of hospital occupancy to a variety of the delays that can arise when discharging patients; and (2) to identify which discharge impediments, when targeted by hospital-wide policy, might influence hospital occupancy the most. The discharge scenarios consider are summarized in Table 1.

Table 1.   Discharge scenarios considered.

Scenario 0	Standard Hospital Operation – base case
Scenario 1	24 h discharge
Scenario 2	24 h Discharge for patients younger than 65
Scenario 3	Instantaneous discharge
Scenario 4	Scenario 1 & 3 combined
Scenario 5–7	Discharge a % of patient with LOS > 21 days (15, 30 and 100%)
Scenario 8, 9	Reduce LOS by half a day (for LOS > 1 and LOS > 2 days)

Scenario 0 replicated the standard operation of the hospital. It is the baseline for comparison of system performance indicators. Scenario 1 removed the restriction of business hour discharges (7 am–6 pm) and allowed patients to undergo the discharge process at the moment they 'theoretically' completed their treatment, that is, their assigned LOS has expired. Note that all patients in this scenario still underwent the delay/lag associated with being discharged. This is in contrast to Scenario 3 which maintained business hour discharge but removed the 'processing delay' associated with any patient being discharged (e.g. administration, waiting for being picked-up etc.). Scenario 4 is a hybrid of Scenarios 1 and 3.

Scenarios 5–7 investigated the effect upon occupancy of limiting the maximum LOS of long stay outlier patients (LOS over 21 days). While the average LOS of surgical and medical inpatients is four to five days, the LOS of some inpatients in the dataset exceeds a year.

Scenarios 8 and 9 related to potential capacity gains if patient treatment time could be reduced by half a day. Due to the impracticality of reducing all patients' LOS by half a day, we instead focused on those patients whose treatment periods exceeded one or two days. Again, all other aspects of hospital discharges remained as per the base case.

The effectiveness of each strategy was evaluated by an occupancy defined as the number of beds occupied in the hospital plus all admitted patients boarding in the ED at 10 am each simulated day. The period from 7 to 10 am is the busiest time in the hospital and total occupancy frequently exceeds the number of beds available (326 fixed beds and 8 flexi beds for the case study). The average daily occupancy and its standard deviation are presented. Also, we reported the results in context of a color coding (stop-light) system used by SA Health [8] for describing the status of occupancy of the hospital.

- Green means that the hospital has at least 10% of their general base beds available.
- Amber means that the hospital has less than 10% of their general base beds available.
- Red means that the hospital has no fixed bed capacity available.

Simulations results for each scenario including the average occupancy rates and number of days the hospital spent in each color-coded occupancy state over a one-year period are presented in Table 2. For every discharge scenario except for scenarios 2 and 5, a significantly lower mean occupancy at 10 am was obtained with the intervention compared to the base case. Scenario 4, in particular, resulted in the largest reduction in occupancy to an average of only 301 beds occupied. Implementation of most of the discharge strategies produced a reduction in the frequency of red status days and an increase in the number of green status days. As it might be expected, elective surgery cancellations fell as hospital occupancy rates fell.

It is important to mention that Table 2 does not identify the optimal solution out of the potential candidates, as there are multiple criteria to consider and a balanced approach should be applied. For example, although too many red-days are not desirable, too many green-days indicating under-utilization of resources should also be avoided. However, the simulation results provide useful data based evidences for hospital management to reference when decisions need to be made.

Table 2. Summary results of scenario experiments (100 replications).

	Scenario 0: base case	Scenario 1: 24 h discharge	Scenario 2: 24 h discharge for patients younger than 65	Scenario 3: instantaneous discharge	Scenario 4: instantaneous discharge for 24 h	Scenario 5: discharge 15% of patients with LOS > 21 days	Scenario 6: discharge 30% of patients with LOS > 21 days	Scenario 7: discharge 100% of patients with LOS > 21 days	Scenario 8: reduce LOS by 12 h if LOS > 1 day	Scenario 9: reduce LOS by 12 h if LOS > 2 days
Mean occupancy	335	315	332	326	301	333	330	311	314	322
Mean standard dev	11	16	12	12.3	17	12	13	16	17	16
Mean maximum occupancy	353	346	352	348	339	352	352	348	349	351
Mean minimum occupancy	293	263	286	281	248	290	283	259	261	269
Mean red days	282	92	255	193	23	261	223	56	84	153
Mean amber days	82	235	107	165	223	102	138	255	234	192
Mean green days	1	39	3	7	119	2	4	54	47	21
Backlog elective surgery	250	55	213	51	11	211	188	46	7	23
Mean no patients discharged early	0	0	0	0	0	141	258	790	0	0

4   Piloting a Research Based Solution for Congestion Prevention

We present another example where a research based solution for real-time patient flow congestion prevention [9] is piloted to demonstrate its validity and effectiveness. The purpose is to convince hospital management with simulation results so that the solution can be adopted for real-world deployment.

Hospitals are dynamic environments. Each day, some patients are discharged, emergency patients arrive and require admission, and a variable number of elective admissions are planned for the day. The task of balancing these competing demands so as to minimize the risk of congestion will be assisted by access to tools that support decision making. Such tools need to make appropriate allowance for day-by-day variations in patterns of admission and discharge. We have developed an approach [9] for identifying the interaction between the variables that influence the likelihood of the emergence of congestion, and show that the risk of the emergence of congestion can be quantified in relation to the interaction between a limited set of variables: Expected Arrivals; Expected Admissions; Current Occupancy; Expected Discharge; and Maximum Occupancy (a threshold). Specifically, if we define a hospital congestion episode as a situation when the number of new patients needing admission tips the total over the specified threshold, we can estimate the likelihood or risk of congestion in the current day based on recent history of patient movement data. More importantly, this measure of risk exhibits a characteristic sensitivity phenomenon that we have named a hospital's instability wedge (IW, for short). In particular, it is seen that frequently even small changes in the numbers of patients admitted or discharged can dramatically change the risk of exceeding the threshold thereby changing the risk of subsequent congestion episodes. Roughly speaking, it is seen that the thinner is the IW, the more sensitive is the risk. It was demonstrated that relative rates of change in the risk of overcrowding with respect to admission and discharge rates are sensitive to internal, rather than external, factors. This finding is of considerable interest. It shows that, on a day-by-day basis, hospitals have the potential to control their own functioning.

Thus, a real-time decision support tool, based on the finding described above, can be developed that allows a hospital to assess the risk of patient flow congestion on any given day, and, when the risk is deemed high, the relative impact of making minor adjustments to the numbers of admissions or discharges on risk reduction.

Using data from a real hospital, Fig. 4 illustrates the application of the proposed solution for risk calculation implemented using Excel. It's 8.00 am Wednesday September 24th, 2014. The previous day midnight occupancy was 587 patients. The number of elective patients who were scheduled to come and stay for their treatment on that day was 44. Based on statistical analysis of historical data, the expected number of emergency arrivals that day was 266, the average rate of admission was 35.6% and the rate of discharge was 21.4% (typical for a Wednesday). With this information, we should expect 95 admitted patients and 126 discharged patients up to midnight on the 24th. If we set the threshold (maximum occupancy) to be 603 (95% of all beds available in the hospital), the probability of going over this threshold was calculated to be 27.7% (as per the simplified model presented in Sect. 2 of [9]). Note that if the threshold is set to be 600, the risk would increase to 42.5%.

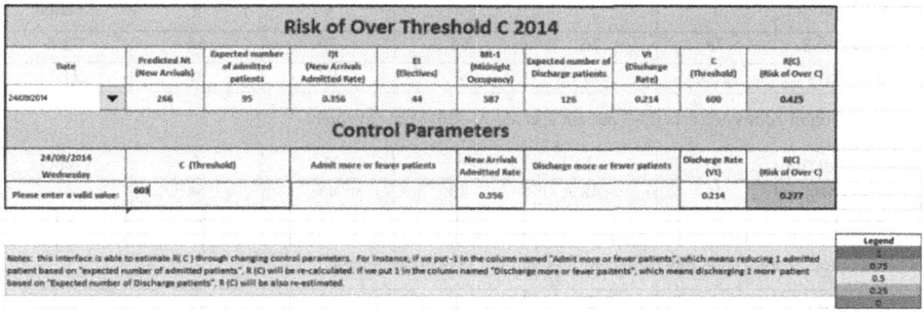

Fig. 4. An example of risk calculation.

If the hospital bed managers were using the tool at 8:00 am, he/she would have been aware that there was a considerable risk of congestion that night. The managers could have chosen to mitigate that risk by reducing a small number of elective admissions (and the impact of delaying 1, 2, 3 or 4 admissions could be calculated) or, during the day, redirecting a small number of emergency admissions. By calculating and then monitoring the risk level during the day, many congestion episodes could have been prevented.

However, the above example used historical patient flow data. How useful and effective the approach would be if applied to the real-world? Piloting in a virtual environment would provide us quantitative evaluation to answer this question. Using HESMAD, a simulation was set up as follows so that evaluation of risk is conducted on a daily basis, and if necessary, a small change to admission rate is made for the day:

- Patient arrivals and admissions are predicted based on historical data (implemented stochastically in HESMAD);
- Previous night's midnight occupancy is taken from simulation;
- Daily discharge based on predicted LOS is taken from simulation;
- Risk threshold C = 317 (90% of the medical and surgical capacity 352);
- Risk (r) prediction is made at 8 am; if $r >= 0.8$, admit a few less patients for the day;
- Each simulate runs for 2 years. Results of the second half of the second year are collected to minimize the impact of the 'warm-up' period;
- Actual red-days are days when midnight occupancy >=345 (98% Maximum capacity).

Table 3 presents some preliminary results of piloting the approach in HESMAD with small percentage of reduction in admission, where r stands for risk of congestion.

The simulation results confirmed that the theoretical research outcome, that is, admitting 2–3 less patients on the day when risk of congestion was predicted high

Table 3. Six months red day count with and without real-time congestion prevention in virtual hospital.

Base Scenario:

Simulation run	1	2	3	4	5	Average
Days $r>0.8$	78	76	65	79	66	72.8
Red Days	103	91	83	92	90	91.8

5% reduction in admission rate (2~3 patient less /day): ~30% improvement

Simulation run	1	2	3	4	5	Average
Days $r>0.8$	44	48	49	45	54	48
Red Days	83	46	69	71	51	64

8% reduction in admission rate (4 patient less /day): ~38% improvement

Simulation run	1	2	3	4	5	Average
Days $r>0.8$	34	33	37	32	27	32.6
Red Days	55	51	63	64	50	56.6

could significantly mitigate the risk and resulting in 30% reduction of red-days comparing with do-nothing; and further reduction in admission rate would not offer as much benefit.

5 Discussion

We have demonstrated that piloting interventions in a virtual environment is an effective approach for healthcare management decision support. These interventions can be heuristics strategies identified by highly experienced healthcare professionals or theoretical solutions developed by researchers. The simulation study does not attempt to propose exact mechanisms for hospitals to achieve these discharge outcomes. Rather, the simulation results demonstrate where greater attention should be paid when addressing patient flow congestions within a hospital if improvements are desired.

This is precisely where modelling can be of assistance: being able to represent the system, to analyze various scenarios, and to understand the outcomes - all without the need to mess up the real system. This provides a definite competitive edge over other decision making approaches.

A fine balance is needed between developing a simulation that is a realistic representation of the system being modelled but not so over parameterized. Unnecessary details often do not contribute to the characteristics of the simulation results. Our experience indicates that a balanced simulation needs to (i) provide reasonable approximation of the macro level flow of patients from arrival to discharge and (ii) be general enough to allow for the analysis and testing of potential interventions and structural alterations.

It is important to keep in mind that the historical data of a healthcare system such as the hospital considered in the case studies is only one instance of the theoretically infinite numbers of possible outcome of a complex stochastic system, that is, a different data set would be generated if we could turn back the clock and rerun the same hospital for the same time period again. Therefore, only behavioral patterns and aggregated data metrics derived from the history data are of value for meaningful validation. Expectation of matching simulation results to observed historical data at lower granularity, such as daily occupancy, is unreasonable and unnecessary. Similarly, simulation results, although quantitative, cannot be taken literally either, as these are the output of a simulation model that can never capture every detail of a real system. However, comparison of the relative pros and cons of simulation results obtained from different scenarios is what we can rely on to make informed decisions. In addition, due to the fact that it is easy to "repeat history" in a virtual environment, simulation can be used for generating big data for reinforcement learning of what works in what context so that, as future work, intelligent tools can potentially be developed to support real time decision making.

6   Conclusion and Future Work

The key message of this paper is that a virtual system based on simulation modelling at the appropriate level of abstraction is an effective approach for conducting quantitative evaluation of impact introduced by proposed changes, being it heuristic change of processes/policies, or adopting a solution based on scientific research.

As demonstrated in this paper, simulation modelling offers the benefits of a more objective and robust means for understanding and testing the possible effects of system change. It allows experimentation of different strategies hence facilitates constructive decision support with data analytics showing performance indicators for all scenarios. Finally, with the animated visualization of system behavior on display, it becomes much easier to communicate with stakeholders and get their buying-in of an optimal decision.

It is envisaged that virtual environment will become not only the laboratory for testing interventions, but also be used by itself to develop Artificial Intelligence based solutions, such as generating synthetic data for reinforcement learning. We have seen similar proposal and early works in the literature [10, 11]. We hope that, in time, virtual testing will be made an integral part of the standard decision evaluation process. This will certainly prevent costly poor decisions from being made and implemented, and convince people to adopt practices that lead to short and long term benefits.

Acknowledgement. The author acknowledges contributions to HESMAD development and the case studies by Dr C. Thompson, Dr D. Ward, Dr T. Bogomolov, Mr. T.Y. Chen and other collaborators.

References

1. Miller, G.A.: The magical number seven, plus or minus two: some limits on our capacity for processing information. Psychol. Rev. **63**(2), 81–97 (1956). https://doi.org/10.1037/h0043158.PMID13310704
2. Ben-Tovim, D., Filar, J., Hakendorf, P., Qin, S., Thompson, C., Ward, D.: Hospital event simulation model: arrivals to discharge-design, development and application. Simul. Model. Pract. Theory **68**, 80–94 (2016)
3. Qin, S., Thompson, C., Bogomolov, T., Ward, D., Hakendorf, P.: Hospital occupancy and discharge strategies: a simulation-based study. Internal Med. J. **47**(8), 894–899 (2017)
4. Hou, W., Qin, S., Thompson, C.: Comparing de-congestion scenarios using a hospital event simulation model. In: 22nd International Congress on Modelling and Simulation. Tasmania, Australia, pp. 1281–1287, December 2017
5. Bryan, K.: Policies for reducing delayed discharge from hospital. Br. Med. Bull. **95**, 33–46 (2010)
6. Watkins, J.R., Soto, J.R., Bankhead-Kendall, B., et al.: What's the hold up? factors contributing to delays in discharge of trauma patients after medical clearance. Am. J. Surg. **208**(6), 969–973 (2014)
7. Challis, D., Hughes, J., Xie, C., Jolley, D.: An examination of factors influencing delayed discharge of older people from hospital. Int. J. Geriatric Psychiatry **29**, 160–168 (2014)
8. SA Health Inpatient dashboard glossary (2016). http://www.sahealth.sa.gov.au/wps/wcm/connect/0659880047b967c7a263fa2e504170d4/Glossary+-+IP+-HSP-+25+oct.pdf?MOD=AJPERES
9. Ben-Tovim, D., Bogomolov, T., Filar, J., Hakendorf, P., Qin, S., Thompson, C.: Hospital's instability wedges. Health Syst. 1–10 (2018)
10. Wang, F.-Y.: Toward a paradigm shift in social computing: the ACP approach. IEEE Intell. Syst. **22**(5), 65–67 (2007). https://doi.org/10.1109/MIS.2007.4338496
11. Shi, J.C., Yu, Y., Da, Q., Chen, S.Y., Zeng, A.X.: Virtual-Taobao: virtualizing real-world online retail environment for reinforcement learning. In: Proceedings of the AAAI Conference on Artificial Intelligence, 17 July 2019. https://doi.org/10.1609/aaai.v33i01.33014902

Deep Interpretable Mortality Model for Intensive Care Unit Risk Prediction

Zhenkun Shi[1,2,3] (ID), Weitong Chen[3], Shining Liang[1,2], Wanli Zuo[1,2(✉)],
Lin Yue[4(✉)], and Sen Wang[3]

[1] Key Laboratory of Symbolic Computation and Knowledge Engineering of Ministry
of Education, Jilin University, Changchun 130012, China
shizk14@mails.jlu.edu.cn
[2] College of Computer Science and Technology, Jilin University,
Changchun 130012, China
Wanli@jlu.edu.cn
[3] School of Information Technology and Electrical Engineering,
The University of Queensland, Queensland 4072, Australia
[4] Northeast Normal University, Changchun 130024, China
yuel031@nenu.edu.cn

Abstract. Estimating the mortality of patients plays a fundamental
role in an intensive care unit (ICU). Currently, most learning approaches
are based on deep learning models. However, these approaches in mortality prediction suffer from two problems: (i) the specificity of causes
of death are not considered in the learning process due to the different diseases, and symptoms are mixed-used without diversification and
localization; (ii) the learning outcome for the mortality prediction is not
self-explainable for the clinicians. In this paper, we propose a Deep Interpretable Mortality Model (DIMM), which employs Multi-Source Embedding, Gated Recurrent Units (GRU), Attention mechanism and Focal
Loss techniques to prognosticate mortality prediction. We intensified the
mortality prediction by considering the different clinical measures, medical treatments and the heterogeneity of the disease. More importantly,
for the first time, in this framework, we use a separate evidence-based
interpreter named Highlighter to interpret the prediction model, which
makes the prediction understandable and trustworthy to clinicians. We
demonstrate that our approach achieves state-of-the-art performance in
mortality prediction and can get an interpretable prediction on four different diseases.

Keywords: Data mining · Missing value · Imputation · Deep
learning · Healthcare

1 Introduction

Accurate assessment of the severity of a patient's condition plays a fundamental
role in acute hospital care especially in ICU, due to the diversity of patients

© Springer Nature Switzerland AG 2019
J. Li et al. (Eds.): ADMA 2019, LNAI 11888, pp. 617–631, 2019.
https://doi.org/10.1007/978-3-030-35231-8_45

who mostly suffer from multiple diseases of various types. It is hard to estimate the severity of a patient's condition in limited time and massive circumstance. However, doctors must give a diagnosis rapidly so that subsequent treatments can be taken.

Traditionally, mortality modeling for ICU patients has been conducted via scoring systems such as the chronic health evaluation (APACHE), sepsis-related organ failure assessment (SOFA) score and simplified acute physiology score (SAPS). All these are adopting fixed clinical decision rules based mainly on physiological data [19]. However, these ICU score systems use only limited measurement indicators to evaluate the mortality risk. For instance, SOFA uses only 11 indicators for scoring. Individually, in MIMIC III [8] there are over 4 thousand indicators. It is obvious that faced with thousands of diseases, these limited indicators are not comprehensive.

Widespread adoption of Electronic Health Record (EHR) and advances in deep learning makes it possible to predict mortality risk more effectively. In fact, several studies using deep learning techniques to forecast in-hospital mortality risk have significantly improved the quality of acute hospital care [20]. However, deep methods are often negotiated as black boxes. While this might not be an obstacle in other more deterministic domains such as image annotation (because the end user objectively validates the tags assigned to the images), in health care, not only the quantity algorithmic performance is necessary but also vital is the reason why the algorithm works. Such model interpretability is crucial for convincing the professionals about actions recommended from the predictive models [11].

By interpreting the mortality risk for the deep model, we mean manifesting textual or visual artifacts that provide the qualitative understanding of the relationship between the clinical measurements, medical treatments, and the model's prediction. The process of interpreting the mortality risk for a single patient is illustrated in Fig. 1. Cooperation and customization with the clinicians highlighter gives an overall rating that indicates the patient's mortality risk and integrates, illustrates, and highlights the related events, items, as well as the diagnosis. With these explanations, clinicians can take further actions based on the results and the explanations. Furthermore, it has been observed, for example, that providing explanations can increase the acceptance of movie recommendations [7].

In this paper, we proposed a Deep Interpretable Mortality Model (DIMM) to predict and interpret the ICU patients' mortality risk. We evaluate the DIMM on MIMIC-III and show that it is highly competitive and outperforms the state-of-the-art traditional methods and commonly used deep learning methods. Furthermore, we can provide evidence for our prediction model in convincing the clinicians to trust the prediction Here is a summary of our contribution: (1) **Multiple Perspectives for ICU Mortality Risk Formulation.** We formulate ICU mortality prediction as a multi-source and multi-task learning problem, where sources correspond to clinical measurements and medical treatment, tasks correspond to diseases. Our model enables us to incorporate disease-specific context into mortality modeling. (2) **Use more inclusive data set.** Use of the entire data set of ICU patients without filtering on length-of-stay. Other similar submission, and previous works heavily filter the data set. (3) **Explainability of the Prediction Outcomes.** We add a highlighter to provide evidence-based trustworthy interpretation to the deep model, and this is very important in real life situations. (4) **Comprehensive Evaluated Experiments.** We demonstrate the effectiveness of our method by using MMIC-III benchmark dataset and achieve the state-of-the-art performance.

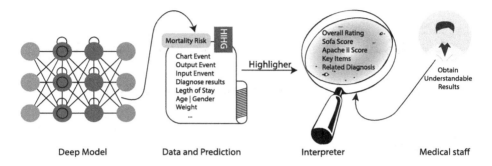

Fig. 1. The process of interpretation.

2   Related Work

Mortality risk prediction has a long history in medical domain, traditional methods for mortality modeling mostly based on scoring systems. However, it is pointed out that these ICU scoring systems are used for only a few patients, namely, 10%–15% of US ICU patients as of 2012 [4]. As information of a more varied, time-evolving nature became available as a form of EHR such as clinical notes and intervention records, data-driven predictive modeling has been explored extensively in recent year [3,6,12,18]. However, these data mining and statistical learning approaches typically need first to perform feature engineering to obtain adequate and more robust features from those data and then build prediction or clustering models on top of them [5,23]. More recently, RNNs provide new effective paradigms to obtain end-to-end learning models from complex data. Harutyunyan [6] and Song [20] used LSTM and Attention Model, respectively, to predict in-hospital mortality and provides the state-of-the-art performance. However, a large body of current works [3,6,20] for mortality prediction mainly focuses on improving the ability of classifiers. Moreover, scarcely any publications think more about the reality in an application scenario, beyond the prediction ability and accuracy; the clinician is caring much about how the model predicted so that they can choose to trust the prediction results or not. What's more, the clinician needs to know the irregular figures and the possible treatment measures. Therefore, low interpretability is a common problem of deep neural networks, but all the works mentioned above have not tackled this problem. Ribeiro *et al.* [14] did some significant work in explaining the prediction, but his work is not evidence-based and is not fully effective in that medical field. Lipton [10] points out that model interpretability in machine learning has multiple definitions but none can be appropriately applied in mortality prediction. Ahmad *et al.* [1] give a comprehensive summary of model interpretability in machine learning. Combining the term of Evidence-based Medicine and previous works, in this paper, the interpretation given evidence and intuitive explanations on how we made the prediction.

Fig. 2. An overview of the proposed GRU-based framework for mortality risk prediction and interpretation.

3 Proposed Approach

In this section, we describe our framework, DIMM.

3.1 Problem Statement

For a given ICU stay of length T hours, it is assumed that we are given a series of regularly clinical actions $\{x_t\}_{t>1}^T$, where x_t is a vector of clinical action at time t. $x_t = a_{ti}\Theta b_{tj}$, where a_{ti} stand for clinical observation vector at time t_i and b_{tj} represent the clinical treatment vector at time t_j, Θ is a joint operation of vector a_{tj} and b_{tj}. Our objective is to generate a sequence-level prediction and give an interpretation of each prediction. The type of prediction depends on the specific task and can be donated as a discrete scalar vector Y for multi-task classification, each discrete vector Y_i for the regression problem. The proposed framework is shown in Fig. 2.

3.2 Input Embedding

Give the R actions for each step t, the first step is to generate an embedding that captures the dependencies across different diseases without the temporal information. Here, N denote the number of diseases. The mortality prediction model is constructed for each disease. The n-*th* disease has P_n patients, and p-*th* patients with n-*th* disease is associated with two feature vectors A_p^n and B_p^n derived from the EHR, where A_p^n donates the clinical measurements and B_p^n donates the medical treatments. The dimension of A and B are α and β, respectively. Combining A_p^n and B_p^n, we generated a new feature vector Φ^n for the n-*th* disease:

$$\Phi^n \equiv [\phi_1^{(n)}, \phi_2^{(n)}, \cdots, \phi_{P_n}^{(n)}]^T \tag{1}$$

$$\phi_p^n = \lambda_1 A_p^n \Theta \lambda_2 B_p^n \tag{2}$$

where Θ is the linear combine operation.

In order to interpret our prediction in the later process, we added a location mask LM to accompany the input embedding process. Because with the process of a series map, transformation and dropout, it is hard to map the result to the original vector space. We define $LM^n = f(\phi_p^n)$, f is the mapping function:

$$f(\phi_p^n) = \begin{cases} 0, & \text{if } \phi_p^n = 0 \\ p, & \text{otherwise.} \end{cases} \tag{3}$$

3.3 Window Alignment

Since our framework contains multiple actions, medical treatments, and clinical measurements. The medical treatments will take a while to take effect and influence the measurement results. Assume $A_p^n \circ t_i$ represent the clinical measurement at time step t_i and $B_p^n \circ t_j$ represents the medical treatment at time step t_j. The alignment is performed by mapping $P(\phi)$ and $P(\phi)$ into a unique time step $P(\phi)$. This strategy is fully competent in our tasks. Besides, in the same time window $P(\phi)$, t_j is usually later than ti, and this accords with the prevailing medical sense.

3.4 Dense Layer

To balance the computational cost as well as the predictable performance, we need to reduce the dimensions before we transfer the raw medical data to the next process step. The typical way is simply to concatenate an embedding at every step in the sequence. However, due to the high-dimensional nature of the clinical features, this causes "cursed" representation which is not suitable for learning and inference. Inspired by the Trask's work [21] in Natural Language Processing (NLP) and Song's [20] in clinical data processing, we add a dense layer to unify and flatten the input features as well as keep the interpretability. To prevent overfitting, we set dropout $= 0.35$ here.

3.5 Task Wise Attention

Inspired by BiDAF [16] in NLP field, after the dense layer, we add a Task wise attention layer to linking and fusing information from the medical treatments and the clinical measurements. The inputs to the layer are treatments vector $P(\phi)$ and measurements vector $P(\phi)$, these two vectors have been flattened in the previous layer. The output clinical action vector $\tilde{\phi}_p^n$ along with the input embeddings from the previous layer. In this layer, we compute attentions in 4 directions: clinical measurements self-attention (M2M); (1) medical treatment self-attention (T2T); (2) measurements to treatments (M2T); (3) treatments to measurements (T2M).

The first two self-attentions can help us focus on the most critical part of their self-vector spaces. For example, cardiotonic can be very helpful in some emergency case, and this treatment is crucial in the whole ICU process. However, this is a discontinuous treatment and usually appears once in the time series; by using self-attention mechanism we are able to capture this vital procedure and raise its weight in the prediction. The M2T and T2M attention are derived from shared similarity matrix $S \in \mathbb{R}^{A \times B}$ between the input embedding of clinical measurements (A) and medical treatment (B), where S_{ab} indicates the similarity between a-th clinical measurement and b-th medical treatment. The similarity matrix is computed by

$$S_{ab} = \ell(A_{:a}, B_{:b}) \tag{4}$$

Where ℓ is a trainable scalar function that encodes the similarity between two input vector, and $A_{:a}$ is the a-th column vector of A, and $B_{:b}$ is the b-th column vector of B. We choose $\ell(A, B) = w_{(S)}^{\mathsf{T}}[A; B; A \circ B]$, where $w_{(S)}^{\mathsf{T}}$ is a trainable weight vector, $\circ$ is elementwise multiplication, [;] is vector concatenation across row, and implicit multiplication is matrix multiplication. By introducing S we can obtain the attention and the attended vectors in both directions.

In addition, this attention mechanism in our work is task wise. We add a tunable switch $S_{w,i}$:

$$S_{w,i} = \begin{cases} 0, & \text{if } can\,improve\,the\,prediction\,performance \\ 1, & \text{otherwise.} \end{cases} \tag{5}$$

where $w \in \{M2M, T2T, M2T, T2M\}$ and i refers the predict task. The motivation why we adopt the task wise mechanism is that the measurements and treatments from different disease categories may hugely different. For instance, the diagnosis and the treatments of the diseases of the respiratory system and the diseases of the genitourinary system are nearly different. So it is hard to share feature spaces between these two kinds of conditions. Therefore, by adopting this mechanism, we not only can reduce the training difficulty but also can avoid inducing noises.

3.6   The Gated Recurrent Unit Layer

The GRU takes the sequence of action $\{x_t\}_{t \geq 1}^T$ from the previous dense layer and then associate p-th patent with a binary class label $y_{n,p}$, donates the class label for the p-th patient with the n-th disease. $y_{n,p}$ is set as follows:

$$y_{n,p} = \begin{cases} 0, & \text{if } dead\,within\,60\,days\,after\,ICU \\ 1, & \text{otherwise.} \end{cases} \tag{6}$$

We create a P_n-dimensional response vector for the n-th disease:

$$y^{(n)} = (y_{n,1}, y_{n,2}, \cdots, y_{n,P_n})^T \tag{7}$$

For the ICU patients' mortality risk prediction, we adopted GRU and represent the posterior probability of the outcome of patient p being death as:

$$\Pr[y_{n,p} = 0|\, \phi_p^{(n)}] = \sigma(\omega^{(n)^N}\phi_p^{(n)}) \tag{8}$$

where $\sigma(a)$ is the sigmoid function $\sigma(a) \equiv (1 + \exp(-a))^{-1}$ and $\omega^{(n)}$ is a $\alpha + \beta$ dimensional model parameter vector for the n-th disease.

To learn the mutual information of data resulting from the customization, we learn models for all diseases jointly, so that we can share the same segment information across the diseases. We represent the trainable parameters of the GRU as a $(\alpha + \beta) \times N$ matrix $W \equiv [\omega^{(1)}, \omega^2, \cdots, \omega^n]$.

3.7 Multi-head Attention and Feedforward

This attention layer is designed to capture dependencies of the whole sequence. In the ICU scenario, the actions closer to the current position are more critical than the farther one. And we should consider information only from positions earlier than the current position being analyzed. Inspired by [22], we use H-heads attention to create multiple attention graphs, and the resulting weighted representations are concatenated and linearly projected to obtain the final representation. Moreover, we also add 1D convolutional sub-layers with kernel size 2. Internally, we use two of these 1D convolutional sub-layers with ReLU (rectified linear unit) activation in between. Residue connections are used in these sub-layers. Unlike [20] and [6] making mortality predictions only once after a specific timestamp, we give prediction and interpretation at each timestamp. This is more helpful for the ICU clinicians because they need to know the patients' mortality risk at any time other than at the particular time. We stack the attention module N times and use the final representations in the mortality risk prediction model.

3.8 Linear and Softmax Layers

The linear layer is designed to obtain the logits from the unified output of attention layer. The activation function used in this layer is ReLU. The last layer is preparing for the output based on different tasks. We use sigmoid for the binary mortality task, the loss function is:

$$Loss\_m = -(y\log(\bar{y})) + (1 - y) \centerdot \log(1 - \bar{y}) \tag{9}$$

where y and $\bar{y}$ denote the true and predicted labels.

We use softmax to distinguish between N different diseases, and the loss function is:

$$Loss\_d = \frac{1}{N}\sum_{n=1}^{N} -(y_k \centerdot \log(\bar{y}_k) + (1 - y_k)). \tag{10}$$

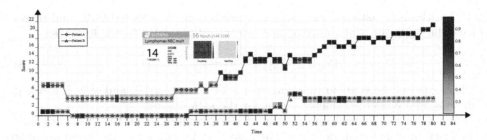

Fig. 3. Deep interpretable mortality prediction framework prediction results showcase. (Color figure online)

3.9   Focal Loss

Due to the distribution otherness of different mortality is very large, and this led to an extreme sample imbalance problem. For example, in MIMIC III dataset "Respiratory distress syn" ICU mortality risk is 3.06% and "Angina pectoris NEC/NOS" ICU mortality risk is 23.2%. This problem is very similar to the sample imbalance problem in text summarization [9]. Therefore, the training difficulty of each disease is different. Moreover, the training difficulty of each action in different diseases is also not the same, represented by $P(\phi)$. The $P(\phi)$ means that an action is an easy training disease where $P(\phi)$ is closed to 1 because the model can predict it with the confidence of one hundred percent, while it will be a difficulty training disease if $P(\phi)$ is small to zero.

Consequently, we need to assign a soft weight to each disease's loss for the model and pay more attention on those whose $P(\phi)$ is small for getting better performance on it. Inspired by the work in NLP [17], we improved our loss function by introducing focal loss. Like Lin's work [9], we do use cross-entropy (CE) to define $P(\phi)$. Let p_f denote the model's estimated probability for the class with the label $y_{n,p} = 0$, and in this work means p-th patient with n-th disease and eventually deadth. We define $P(\phi)$ as:

$$P(\phi) = \begin{cases} -log(p_f), & \text{if } y_{n,p} = 0 \\ -log(1-p_f), & \text{otherwise.} \end{cases} \tag{11}$$

Then we add a modulating factor $(1 - P(\phi))^\gamma$ to the entropy loss, with tunable focusing parameter $\gamma \geq 0$. We define the focal loss as:

$$FL(P(\phi)) = -\lambda_\phi (1 - P(\phi))^\gamma \log(P(\phi)) \tag{12}$$

where λ_ϕ and γ are hyperparameters, which are set as 0.25 and 1 respectively in our experiment.

3.10   Output and Interpretation

Incorporated with the supplementary information from original source, this layer is designed to generate the understandable prediction results. We give the predictions at each time step and the time span can be controlled by the end user. Therefore, the clinician could get the updated patients' mortality risk at any time.

Figure 3 is a showcase of the DIMM prediction with evidence interpretation results. The x-axis is the ICU stay time sequence and the y-axis is the patient's ICU Scoring System score. Here, we plot the SOFA score. *Patient B* is the current patient and *Patient A* represent the similar patient who is like *B*. The color donates the mortality risk of the patient at current time slot, the darker color indicates the higher mortality risk. If we focus on a specific time slot, the Highlighter will give detailed information and the evidence of how we got this prediction. The outputs includes the necessary information about the current patient, the diagnosis, and diagnostic order, the mortality risk, the severity scores from different score systems, the heat map of crucial clinical measurements and, the heat map of adequate medical treatment. Moreover, we also give the most similar patients compared to the current one, and this is very helpful to the clinician.

4   Experiment

4.1   Dataset

We use real-world datasets from MIMIC-III to evaluate the proposed approach. And, we treat each ICU stay as a single case. In other words, different ICU stays of the same patient will be treated as separate cases, and this will help us to get more samples. The diseases choosing standard is like Nori [13]. According to the International Classification of Diseases (ICD) codes, we extracted the following diseases for each patient: the primary diseases that caused the patients admission, and comorbidities the patient had at the time of admission, where the number of comorbidities is at most ten. After filtering the patients aged below 16, we obtained 30508 patients for this study. The total diagnosed diseases in these patients id 5395. For the features, we included 1529 clinical measurement features and 330 medical treatment features. In this study, we picked out the most common four diseases as our prediction tasks, 4019 (Essential hypertension), 41401 (Coronary atherosclerosis), 25000 (Diabetes mellitus), 5849 (Acute renal failure), the sample size of each task is 15561, 9716, 6480, 6270, respectively.

4.2   Prediction Settings

We adopted 30 days mortality as a time window to measure the mortality. That is, if a patient died within 30 days after his or her ICU stay, the outcome is "death" and otherwise "survival". As a measure of different diseases, if the prediction results match one of the main caused diseases, the outcome is "true" otherwise "false". We predict every step. The learning rate we use is 0.001 and epochs size: 30. In our experiment batch size: 32, ADAM dropout to 0.35 and learning rate at 0.001. In the single task process, we set the integrated attention stack time $N = 4$. In the multi-head layer head $= 4$, and, the in the task of 5849, 2500 is $N = 4$, in the task of 41401, 4019 is $N = 2$. In the multitask process, we set $N = 4$.

Table 1. Disease-specific mortality risk prediction tasks

Task	Positive	Negative	Train	Validation	Test
4019	13321	2240	11507	2334	1719
41401	8667	1048	7184	1457	1074
25000	5295	1185	4792	972	716
5849	4433	1837	4637	941	693

4.3 Compared Methods

We compared our proposed method with the following seven methods. Four traditional methods, Logistic Regression with L2 regularization, Random Forest and XGBoost, SVM. Three NN-based methods, *Temporal Convolutional Networks* (TCN) [2], MIMIC-III benchmark tasks (BM) [6], Attend and Diagnosis (SAnD) [20]. To ensure all methods use the same data, we fixed the training and testing dataset. The validation and test data we use is approximately 30% of the whole dataset. The detailed information is shown in Table 1.

4.4 Evaluation Metric

As listed in Table 1, all tasks are facing data unbalancing problem. To comprehensively assess our DIMM framework, we use four different evaluation metrics in our experiment. First, we used Area under Receiver Operator Curve (AUROC) to evaluate our model, which is a combined measure of sensitivity and specificity. The next primary metrics for evaluation is Area under Precision-Recall Curve (AUPRC) because the precision-recall plot is more informative than the Receiver Operating Characteristics (ROC) plot when evaluating binary classifiers on imbalanced datasets [15]. We also considered the Accuracy (ACC).

4.5 Ablation Study

To demonstrate the synergy between different layer modules for DIMM architecture, we trained the different sub-modules of DIMM separately and conducted ablation comparison. The experiment results are shown in Table 2. From the table, we can find that the full DIMM framework can obtain the best result at most of the time. From the columns, we can conclude that the window alignment, the dense layer and the GRU layer composed the backbone of the DIMM. In these four prediction tasks, if we remove some attention layer during the training process, some evaluation metrics may perform better suggesting that not all kinds of attentions are working for many reasons such as different diseases from different categories may prove different in measurements and treatments or history of a patient's diseases is uncorrelated to the current ones. So the task wise attention mechanism is essential. Due to limited space we show only AUROC and ACC here.

Table 2. Ablation study results of different layers

Task	Metric	No-wA	No-dense	No-interact	No-internal	No-TWA	No-GRU	No-STA	FULL
4019	AUROC	0.9009	0.9118	0.9285	0.9284	0.9328	0.8094	**0.9329**	**0.9329**
	ACC	0.8965	0.9086	0.9333	0.9295	0.9299	0.8559	**0.9789**	**0.9789**
41401	AUROC	0.9403	0.9237	0.9487	0.9450	0.9427	0.8406	0.9483	**0.9473**
	ACC	0.9450	0.9264	0.9463	0.9428	0.9386	0.8727	**0.9821**	**0.9821**
25000	AUROC	0.8955	0.9077	0.9354	0.9446	0.9321	0.8044	0.8933	**0.9449**
	ACC	0.8952	0.8785	0.9271	0.9281	0.8893	0.8088	0.9502	**0.9502**
5849	AUROC	0.8934	0.9086	0.9421	0.9403	0.9330	0.8054	0.9247	**0.9421**
	ACC	0.8326	0.8538	0.9017	0.8953	0.9117	0.7686	**0.9763**	**0.9763**

No-wA: eliminate the window alignment. No-dense: eliminate the dense layer. No-interact: eliminate the M2T or T2M attention. No-internal: eliminate the M2M or T2T attention. No-TWA: eliminate the whole task wise attention layer. No-GRU: eliminate the GRU layer. No-STA: eliminate the attention layer after GRU layer. FULL: full DIMM framework.

4.6 Results and Discussion

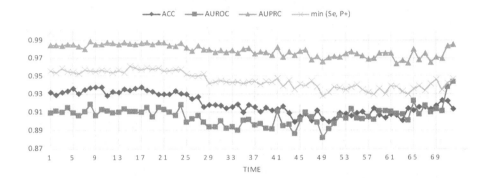

Fig. 4. The performance of the mortality prediction sequence.

Table 3 shows the prediction results. We can see that our model significantly outperformed all the baseline methods. We conducted our experiment for the 30 days mortality risk prediction. To simulate real conditions in ICU, we use all ICU stays. We include all the ICU patients without considering the length of their stay. This is unlike the previous work Harutyunyan et al. [6] and Song et al. [20], who are using measurements from the last 24 h. The performance of different evaluation indicators are as shown in Fig. 4. It is clear that our framework is very stable among all the evaluation metrics.

We can see that NN-based methods are outperforming much better than the LR, SVM, and RF. This suggests that the neural network is much powerful than the traditional methods in our tasks, as we expected. We use the same model and the same settings on different tasks and the results are notably different, suggesting that there exists a notable diversity of the diseases, as we mentioned in

628   Z. Shi et al.

Table 3. Results for mortality risk prediction task

Metrics	Methods									
	LR	RF	XGBoost	SVM	TCN	SAnD	BM-s	BM-m	DIMM-s	DIMM-m
Task1: 4019 Essential Hypertension										
AUROC	0.7601	0.8110	0.8601	0.7702	0.8129	0.8436	0.8906	0.8948	0.9186	**0.9369**
AUPRC	0.9391	0.9546	0.9659	0.9386	0.9518	0.9658	0.9723	0.9727	0.9774	**0.9807**
ACC	0.8402	0.8546	0.8637	0.8406	0.8435	0.8833	0.8888	0.8996	0.9219	**0.9789**
Task2: 41401 Coronary Atherosclerosis										
AUROC	0.8144	0.8313	0.8775	0.7990	0.8356	0.7950	0.9066	0.9088	0.9267	**0.9473**
AUPRC	0.9513	0.9619	0.9676	0.9469	0.9584	0.9635	0.9749	0.9775	0.9806	**0.9854**
ACC	0.8548	0.8691	0.8818	0.8496	0.8678	0.9000	0.9009	0.9015	0.9291	**0.9821**
Task3: 25000 Diabetes Mellitus										
AUROC	0.7414	0.7798	0.8475	0.7907	0.7749	0.8234	0.8581	0.8954	0.8785	**0.9499**
AUPRC	0.8973	0.9217	0.9420	0.9181	0.9094	0.9465	0.9466	0.9616	0.9540	**0.9748**
ACC	0.7796	0.8002	0.8319	0.7820	0.7963	0.8335	0.8535	0.8863	0.8657	**0.9502**
Task4: 5849 Acute Renal Failure										
AUROC	0.8000	0.7900	0.8368	0.7673	0.7201	0.7844	0.8535	0.8639	0.8933	**0.9421**
AUPRC	0.8671	0.8699	0.8989	0.8356	0.8009	0.8811	0.9070	0.9079	0.9235	**0.9741**
ACC	0.7714	0.7563	0.7865	0.7191	0.7091	0.7992	0.8132	0.8258	0.8644	**0.9763**

▨ Non-NN based ▨ NN based ▨ Ours   SAnD: attend and diagnosis, BM: benchmark, -s:single-task, -m: multi-task

the introduction. The fact that all multi-task models can get better performance than the single task models indicates that joint inferencing with multiple related tasks can lead to superior performance in each of the individual tasks, while drastically improving the training. Hence, it is essential to building the mortality prediction model in a multi-task way.

That our single task DIMM outperformed the multi-BM indicates that, diseases specific assessment is helpful in improving the prediction performance. Thus, we can generalize our model to predict ICU mortality risk according to different diseases. More importantly, detailed disease specific predictions are more significant than the disease nonspecific ones, because respiratory physicians are not dealing with the otolaryngology patients and the domain knowledge between respiratory and otolaryngology is different.

In the interpolation process, as shown in Fig. 5, first we show how we made the prediction. The color represents the contribution of current actions; the further from 0, the more significant the contribution is. We can infer from that for the given patient and a specific disease, there are always some critical clinical measurements and medical treatment. Besides evidence-based interpretation figures, we also manifest the textual and visual artifacts to provide the qualitative understanding of the relationship between the clinical measurements, medical treatments, and risk prediction. As shown in Fig. 3: DIMM framework prediction results, this is a showcase that can transfer the information clearly and effectively to the clinicians. So the clinicians can make explicit and judicious

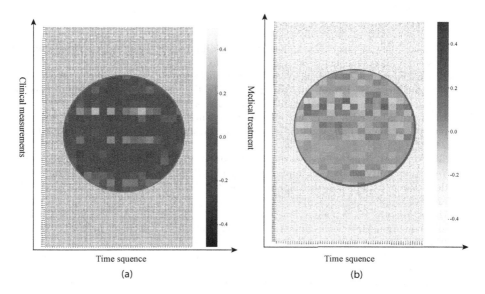

Fig. 5. The evidence-based interpretation of clinical measurements (a) medical treatment (b); mortality prediction. The color represents contribution of the current measurement. (Color figure online)

use of current best evidence in making decisions about the care of individual patients.

5   Conclusion

In this study, we presented a new ICU mortality prediction model, DIMM. The significances of our proposed model can be identified as: (1) We considered the diversity of diseases. This accords with the medical situations. (2) By introducing embedding we can utilize multi-sources for prediction and this has two advantages: improving performance and doing interpretation in the later process. (3) Two attention layers help us capture both the internal correlation between the measurements and the treatments. (4) By using focal loss function, we alleviated problem caused by the unbalanced dataset in the training process. (5) Explainability for the deep model is realized by using the Highlighter. All clinical decisions are based on evidence, we provide a visualization view to the clinicians for our model. This is crucial to the clinical cohort because further medical actions are based on trust chains of the whole prediction process other than a single digit. Nevertheless, how to evaluate the interpretation still remains a challenge in scientific research, and future work can focus on this problem.

References

1. Ahmad, M.A., Eckert, C., McKelvey, G., Zolfaghar, K., Zahid, A., Teredesai, A.: Death vs. data science: predicting end of life. In: AAAI (2018)
2. Bai, S., Kolter, J.Z., Koltun, V.: Convolutional sequence modeling revisited (2018)
3. Bhattacharya, S., Rajan, V., Shrivastava, H.: ICU mortality prediction: a classification algorithm for imbalanced datasets. In: AAAI, pp. 1288–1294 (2017)
4. Breslow, M.J., Badawi, O.: Severity scoring in the critically ill: part 1– interpretation and accuracy of outcome prediction scoring systems. Chest 141(1), 245–252 (2012)
5. Gil, V., et al.: Emergency heart failure mortality risk grade score performance for 7-day mortality prediction in patients with heart failure attended at the emergency department: validation in a spanish cohort. Eur. J. Emerg. Med. 25(3), 169–177 (2018)
6. Harutyunyan, H., Khachatrian, H., Kale, D.C., Galstyan, A.: Multitask learning and benchmarking with clinical time series data. arXiv preprint arXiv:1703.07771 (2017)
7. Herlocker, J.L., Konstan, J.A., Riedl, J.: Explaining collaborative filtering recommendations. In: Proceedings of the 2000 ACM Conference on Computer Supported Cooperative Work, pp. 241–250. ACM (2000)
8. Johnson, A.E., et al.: MIMIC-III, a freely accessible critical care database. Sci. Data 3, 160035 (2016)
9. Lin, T.Y., Goyal, P., Girshick, R., He, K., Dollár, P.: Focal loss for dense object detection. IEEE Transactions on Pattern Analysis and Machine Intelligence (2018)
10. Lipton, Z.C.: The mythos of model interpretability. arXiv preprint arXiv:1606.03490 (2016)
11. Miotto, R., Wang, F., Wang, S., Jiang, X., Dudley, J.T.: Deep learning for healthcare: review, opportunities and challenges. Brief. Bioinform. 19, 1236–1246 (2017)
12. Nori, N., Kashima, H., Yamashita, K., Ikai, H., Imanaka, Y.: Simultaneous modeling of multiple diseases for mortality prediction in acute hospital care. In: Proceedings of the 21th ACM SIGKDD International Conference on Knowledge Discovery and Data Mining, pp. 855–864. ACM (2015)
13. Nori, N., Kashima, H., Yamashita, K., Kunisawa, S., Imanaka, Y.: Learning implicit tasks for patient-specific risk modeling in ICU. In: AAAI, pp. 1481–1487 (2017)
14. Ribeiro, M.T., Singh, S., Guestrin, C.: Why should i trust you? Explaining the predictions of any classifier. In: Proceedings of the 22nd ACM SIGKDD International Conference on Knowledge Discovery and Data Mining, pp. 1135–1144. ACM (2016)
15. Saito, T., Rehmsmeier, M.: The precision-recall plot is more informative than the roc plot when evaluating binary classifiers on imbalanced datasets. PLoS ONE 10(3), e0118432 (2015)
16. Seo, M., Kembhavi, A., Farhadi, A., Hajishirzi, H.: Bidirectional attention flow for machine comprehension. arXiv preprint arXiv:1611.01603 (2016)
17. Shi, Y., Meng, J., Wang, J., Lin, H., Li, Y.: A Normalized Encoder-Decoder Model for Abstractive Summarization Using Focal Loss. In: Zhang, M., Ng, V., Zhao, D., Li, S., Zan, H. (eds.) NLPCC 2018. LNCS (LNAI), vol. 11109, pp. 383–392. Springer, Cham (2018). https://doi.org/10.1007/978-3-319-99501-4_34
18. Shi, Z., Zuo, W., Chen, W., Yue, L., Hao, Y., Liang, S.: DMMAM: deep multi-source multi-task attention model for intensive care unit diagnosis. In: Li, G., Yang, J., Gama, J., Natwichai, J., Tong, Y. (eds.) DASFAA 2019. LNCS, vol. 11447, pp. 53–69. Springer, Cham (2019). https://doi.org/10.1007/978-3-030-18579-4_4

19. Siontis, G.C., Tzoulaki, I., Ioannidis, J.P.: Predicting death: an empirical evaluation of predictive tools for mortality. Arch. Intern. Med. **171**(19), 1721–1726 (2011)
20. Song, H., Rajan, D., Thiagarajan, J.J., Spanias, A.: Attend and diagnose: clinical time series analysis using attention models. In: Thirty-Second AAAI Conference on Artificial Intelligence (2018)
21. Trask, A., Gilmore, D., Russell, M.: Modeling order in neural word embeddings at scale. arXiv preprint arXiv:1506.02338 (2015)
22. Vaswani, A., et al.: Attention is all you need. In: Advances in Neural Information Processing Systems, pp. 5998–6008 (2017)
23. Wang, Y., Kung, L., Byrd, T.A.: Big data analytics: understanding its capabilities and potential benefits for healthcare organizations. Technol. Forecast. Soc. Change **126**, 3–13 (2018)

Causality Discovery with Domain Knowledge for Drug-Drug Interactions Discovery

Sitthichoke Subpaiboonkit[1]([✉])[ID], Xue Li[1,2][ID], Xin Zhao[1][ID], Harrisen Scells[1][ID], and Guido Zuccon[1][ID]

[1] The University of Queensland, Brisbane, Australia
{s.subpaiboonkit,x.zhao,h.scells,g.zuccon}@uq.edu.au
[2] Neusoft University of Information, Dalian, China
lixue@neusoft.edu.cn

Abstract. Bayesian Network Probabilistic Graphs have recently been applied to the problem of discovery drug-drug interactions, i.e., the identification of drugs that, when consumed together, produce an unwanted side effect. These methods have the advantage of being explainable: the cause of the interaction is made explicit. However, they suffer from two intrinsic problems: (1) the high time-complexity for computing causation, i.e., exponential; and (2) the difficult identification of causality directions, i.e., it is difficult to identify in drug-drug interactions databases whether a drug causes an adverse effect – or vice versa, an adverse effect causes a drug consumption. While solutions for addressing the causality direction identification exist, e.g., the CARD method, these assume statistical independence between drug pairs considered for interaction: real data often does not satisfy this condition.

In this paper, we propose a novel causality discovery algorithm for drug-drug interactions that goes beyond these limitations: Domain-knowledge-driven Causality Discovery (DCD). In DCD, a knowledge base that contains known drug-side effect pairs is used to prime a greedy drug-drug interaction algorithm that detects the drugs that, when consumed together, cause a side effect. This algorithm resolves the drug-drug interaction discovery problem in $O(n^2)$ time and provides the causal direction of combined causes and their effect, without resorting to assuming statistical independence of drugs intake. Comprehensive experiments on real-world and synthetic datasets show the proposed method is more effective and efficient than current state-of-the-art solutions, while also addressing a number of drawbacks of current solutions, including the high time complexity, and the strong assumptions regarding real-world data that are often violated.

Keywords: Causality discovery · Bayesian network · Drug-drug interaction

© Springer Nature Switzerland AG 2019
J. Li et al. (Eds.): ADMA 2019, LNAI 11888, pp. 632–647, 2019.
https://doi.org/10.1007/978-3-030-35231-8_46

1   Introduction

An adverse effect is an undesired or harmful event caused by the consumption of a drug, or interactions between drugs. Adverse effects caused by any single drug have been investigated in detail by medical researchers. However, it is often the case that an ill person would consume more than one drug at any given time, e.g., patients with AIDS or cancer usually need to consume a mixture of drugs at the same time [18]. In these cases, adverse effects can be caused by drug-drug interactions. A drug-drug interaction occurs when a consumed drug interacts with another consumed drug, e.g., aspirin consumed together with warfarin may cause excessive bleeding [5]; we denote this with the following notation `aspirin + warfarin →` `bleeding`. Adverse effects caused by drug-drug interactions are often more severe than those from single drugs. This is exemplified in Fig. 1, where the blue drug effectively treats stomach ache with no side effect. The red drug treats knee pain, but it causes a non-severe adverse effect, with a certain likelihood. However, when taken together to treat stomachache and an unrelated knee pain, the likelihood of a severe adverse effect increases due to the drug-drug interaction.

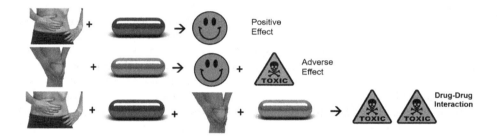

Fig. 1. An example of how two drugs, administered to treat two unrelated conditions, may interact to cause a severe adverse effect. (Color figure online)

Adverse effects caused by drug-drug interactions have a significant impact on public health. Adverse effects cause more than 100,000 deaths and 770,000 injuries per year in the United States alone, costing approximately USD 136.8 billion [9]; and around 30% of adverse effects are reported to be possibly caused by drug-drug interactions [17]. Adverse effects can be prevented if the cause of the drug-drug interaction is known. Unfortunately, it is difficult to perform biological experiments to discover the relation. These experiments in fact are costly, complicated and time-consuming. In addition, it is also impractical, if not impossible, to test all possible combinations of drugs via biological experiments, when more than two drugs are involved in a drug-drug interaction [2]. However, the availability of data related to suspected adverse effects as reported by health care authorities, health care providers, drug manufacturers and patients[1], offers the

---

[1] For example, the Food and Drug Administration (FDA) in the United States has collected this type of data in the FDA Adverse Event Report System (FAERS).

opportunity to study drug-drug interactions causing adverse effects (DDICAE) by using computational methods instead of biological experiments [3].

Most computational methods for discovery of DDICAE are based on statistical association or correlation [6,16,19]; however, they do not guarantee that the discovered relations between multiple drugs and adverse reactions are due to causal reasons. Previous attempts to model causal relations for the DDICAE problem, namely the Causal Association Rule Discovery (CARD) method [3], exist, but they are computationally infeasible, requiring exponential time to run when the number of drugs is considered for each reaction.

In this article, we propose a novel method for DDICAE discovery which extends upon the Bayesian Constraint-based Causality (BCC) model since BCC meaningfully represents causal relationships and effectively handles the large size of data sets, although it also has exponential running time. Our method aims to (1) solve the direction ambiguity problem[2] using conditional independence to prune causal and non-causal relations not involved in DDICAE and without resorting to the V-structure property of BCC[3], and (2) reduce the computational complexity of DDICAE discovery using greedy heuristics to select candidate drugs.

Our method exploits existing domain knowledge. For example, suppose the causal relation between a single drug and an adverse effect is already known (e.g., warfarin causes bleeding, `warfarin` $\rightarrow$ `bleeding`). Then, we can exploit this knowledge to identify which drug that, consumed together with the drug for which an adverse effect is known, increases the likelihood of the adverse effect to occur, e.g., aspirin consumed together with warfarin may increase the chances of excessive bleeding, `aspirin` $+$ `warfarin` $\rightarrow$ `bleeding` $+ +$. This knowledge is used to address the causal direction ambiguity problem because the known causal relation can be used to identify the causal direction within newly discovered causal relations. In addition, the domain knowledge can be exploited to reduce the computational complexity in combination with conditional independence by pruning candidate drugs that are unrelated to the interaction.

2   Related Works

In computational studies of DDICAE, correlations and associations are the key statistics being exploited, e.g., methods based on logistic regression [19], association rules [16] and bi-clustering [6]. These methods only focus on the correlation between drug-drug interactions and adverse effects to predict DDICAE, rather than finding the *causal* relations – which could provide superior insights into the relationship. Note in fact that correlation doesn't necessarily imply causation: causation happens when a change of the causal variable (e.g., consumption of both red and blue drugs) leads to a *direct* change of the effect variable (e.g., bleeding) [15]. In this work, causal variables are drugs, and effect variables are

---

[2] The causal relationship whose direction is unknown.

[3] The V-structure property, in fact, may not identify all causality structures in real-world DDICAE data [18], although it can identify the direction in causality discovery.

adverse effects. If causal relations between combined drug intake and adverse effect were known, then drug prescriptions could be adapted to prevent or mitigate the adverse effects.

Beyond methods that rely just on correlation or associations to discover DDICAE, computational methods that directly model causal relations have been proposed. In Causal Bayesian Network (CBN), causes and effects are modelled using directed acyclic graphs; CBN has been shown to be effective beyond tasks in DDICAE [15,20]. However, for practical purpose, CBN is computationally expensive when more than a few hundred variables are involved. In fact, in this method all possible network paths need to be considered and computation time grows exponentially based on the number of variables (this is an NP-Hard problem) [4]. A popular implementation of CBN is the PC algorithm [13].

The Bayesian Constraint-based Causality (BCC) model extends CBN to feasibly handle data with a large number of variables [1]. To obtain more efficient and scalable performance, BCC limits the discovery of causal relations only to local structures rather than considering the whole Bayesian graph as in CBN. However, in BCC, computation time depends on the number of combinations of variables in the conditional independence tests used to determine a causal relation – these can still be high, thus rendering the method impractical in real situations. In addition, most existing BCC-based approaches, such as Markov Blanket, can find causal relations between variables but cannot identify the direction of the relations (because they rely on measuring conditional independence for a local graph): we name this specific problem as *causality direction ambiguity*. Most BCC approaches can not solve the causality direction ambiguity problem.

Previous work has combined association rules with either partial association test [8] or cohort studies [10] to discover causal relations, including their direction. The partial association test is calculated after discovering association rules to confirm their causality – the key intuition of partial association test is similar to that of conditional independence. In cohort studies, causality relations are found using association rules on observational data fixing the specific control data. These methods are computationally impractical because their run time grows exponentially with respect to the size of variables in the data.

To our knowledge, Causal Association Rule Discovery (CARD) [3] is the only CBN-based method to discover causal relations along with their direction in DDICAE, thus comparable to the method we propose in this work. CARD uses association rules to select significant candidate drugs. Candidate drugs are then iteratively paired and tested for interactions [15] or common-effect relations (or V-structure)[4] [20]. However, this method makes restrictive hypotheses on the relations displayed by the data, and these are often not satisfied by real-world data. In addition, CARD becomes exponential with respect to the number of drugs, because it computes every possible combination – the method we propose, described in Sect. 3, instead offers a polynomial time ($O(n^2)$) solution to the problem of DDICAE discovery.

---

[4] The relationship describing the causes that are marginally independent become dependent when their common effect is given.

3   Proposed Method

The aim of DDICAE discovery is to identify two or more drugs that cause an
adverse effect. Conventional DDI systems typically only consider two interacting
drugs. We introduce Domain-knowledge-driven Causality Discovery (DCD), a
novel constraint-based method that uses conditional independence to discover
causality. DCD is guided by exploiting pre-existing known drug-drug interaction
adverse effect causation contained in domain knowledge resources. Our method is
also made efficient by our novel approach to pruning unrelated candidate drugs.

Our method relies on conditional independence testing because an effective
way to define causation between two variables is to (1) measure statistical dependence between the variables, and (2) ensure no other variables given as the condition eliminate their statistical dependence. Conditional independence can be
exploited by iteratively determining whether to remove drugs that are not a
direct cause of a target adverse effect. These steps are applied in the pruning
stage of DCD to remove drugs that do not meet the necessary criteria to be considered candidate drugs (i.e., interacting drugs causing the target adverse effect).
We define interacting drugs as conjunctive-combined-cause drugs. Finally, DCD
employs a greedy optimisation step in order to find conjunctive-combined-cause
drugs from candidate drugs that have the strongest statistical-dependence score.

Next we formally define the proposed method, and we detail the key steps of
conditional independence testing and pruning; a compendium of the terminology
and acronyms used in this paper is provided in Appendix I.

3.1   Formal Description of Our Method

For the notation in this paper, we use $A \perp B$ to represent statistical independence between A and B. $A \perp B \mid C$ represents the conditional independence of
A and B, given C. The causation between two or more variables is expressed
by $\rightarrow$. The direction indicates which variables cause the other, e.g., $A \rightarrow C$,
and $(A, B) \rightarrow C$ represents multiple causes of A and B causing C. We denote
$D = \{d_1, d_2, ..., d_n\}$ as the drug consumption indicators for a patient, where d_i
is the binary indicator representing whether a patient has consumed drug i (i.e.,
$d_i = 1$ if the patient uses this drug). Similarly, s denotes the binary occurrence
indicator of an adverse effect. We further denote d_m as the drug from a domain
knowledge resource that is known to cause an adverse effect s. Our model is
provided as input a target adverse effect s, the domain knowledge drug d_m as
a given cause, and other drugs D' excluding d_m (i.e., $D' = \{d_1, d_1, ..., d_n\}$ and
$d_m \notin D'$). D' contains the possible drugs that form the conjunctive combined
cause with d_m. Formally, our model identifies $O \subseteq D'$ drugs that are actually
the conjunctive combined cause. Note that O can be empty if no drugs with
significant interactions are found.

$$O = \underset{d_i \in D'}{\mathrm{argmax}}\texttt{Positive Dependence}(d_m, s \mid d_i) \qquad (1)$$

Equation 1 describes how O is obtained. DCD selects O that has the largest dependence value (calculated using the Chi-squared test). Each candidate drug that is added to the combined-cause drugs set provides better positive PMI values than the conjunctive-combined-cause drugs set without that candidate drug. This approach selects the set of DDICAE that is most likely to be causes of the adverse effect.

3.2 Conditional Independence

Our method exploits the conditional independence and the domain knowledge drug and adverse effect to prune the unrelated drugs to the DDICAE (might be correlated or not). Then it uses a greedy algorithm based on Pointwise Mutual Information (PMI) and the Chi-squared statistical hypothesis test to select the highest positive dependence candidate drugs that have high probability to be DDICAE.

In DCD, correlation or dependence is important to screen for possible causal relations. We use the Chi-squared statistical hypothesis test [12] to test for independence. To find combined interacting drugs and the adverse effect, we focus primarily on the positive dependence relation as it accurately represents the co-occurrence DDICAE. We use both the Chi-squared test and Pointwise Mutual Information (PMI) [7] to measure positive dependence between $d_i \in D$ and the d_m which causes s. The Chi-squared test and PMI can solve the drawbacks of each other. The Chi-squared test finds the strength of the dependence when it is divided by the number of observations; however, it cannot discriminate between positive and negative dependence. In contrast, PMI cannot detect the strength of the dependence in sparse datasets where the number of samples with the same variables values is small. However, PMI can differentiate positive dependence from negative dependence. We thus use the Chi-squared test to find which $d_i \in D$ increases dependence strength of co-occurrence of the drug-drug interaction and s, and use PMI to select only positive dependence cases (e.g., $pmi(d_m = 1, d = 1; s = 1) > 0$).

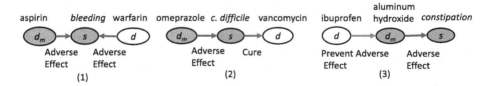

Fig. 2. Three examples of causal dependency (Sub-figures 1–3) that exist among the drugs: (1) domain knowledge drug and the adverse effect, (2) combined cause of s, and (3) consequence or cure of s.

3.3 Pruning

The pruning step aims to eliminate as many unrelated drugs as possible by identifying the drugs that are strongly correlated and positive dependent on d_m. This step also removes any drugs which have opposite causal direction with d_m that cause s. As the result, causal ambiguity (the causal relationship whose causal direction is unknown) is no longer a problem.

There are three possible cases (**C1**, **C2**, and **C3**) of causality existing among the drugs (d), the domain knowledge drug (d_m) and the adverse effect (s):

C1: $d_m \to s \leftarrow d$;
C2: $d_m \to s \to d$; and
C3: $d \to d_m \to s$

As illustrated in Fig. 2.1, **C1** is the conjunctive combined cause (i.e., `aspirin` $\to$ `bleeding` $\leftarrow$ `warfarin` indicates that both aspirin d_m and warfarin d causes bleeding s). In **C2** (Fig. 2.2), the drug is the consequence of an adverse effect instead of a confounded (i.e., `omeprazole` $\to$ `c. difficile` $\to$ `vancomycin` indicates that omeprazole d_m and vancomycin d both cause c. difficile s). In **C3** (Fig. 2.3), the candidate drug is the cause of d_m instead of the confounded of d_m (i.e., `ibuprofen` $\to$ `aluminum hydroxide` $\to$ `constipation` indicates that ibuprofen d is the reason to use aluminium hydroxide d_m, which is the cause of constipation s).

Equation 2 describes our pruning step. Here, the candidate drug d with the structure in **C2** and **C3** are removed from the candidate set D'. Any candidate drugs with any structures in **C2** are removed using conditional independence: $d_m \perp d \mid s = 1$. Any candidate drugs d with **C3** can also be removed using conditional independence: $d \perp s \mid d_m = 1$. In addition, drugs that are independent to d_m and s, or drugs that can be considered as unrelated to d_m and s are also removed when $(d_m \perp d \mid s = 1) \vee (d \perp s \mid d_m = 1)$. In this pruning process, the remaining candidate drugs have a higher probability to cause s. Next, the greedy process of our algorithm is performed to select the most suitable candidate drugs to be the combined causes.

$$D' = \begin{cases} D' - \{d\}, & \text{if } (d_m \perp d \mid s = 1) \vee (d \perp s \mid d_m = 1) \\ D', & \text{otherwise} \end{cases} \quad (2)$$

The pruning step continues each iteration in the greedy method. A candidate drug is removed if it is dependent on O using the conditional independence method as describes in Eq. 3.

$$D' = \begin{cases} D' - \{d\}, & \text{if } (d \perp s \mid d_m, O = 1) \\ D', & \text{otherwise} \end{cases} \quad (3)$$

We next describe algorithmically our iterative pruning algorithm. In each iteration, based on the detected conjunctive combined cause from previous iterations, the drug which has the highest probability to cause s is considered as the candidate drug. If the candidate drug is a correct causal drug, then it is inserted into a conjunctive combined cause for the next iteration. Our pruning algorithm detects a local-optimal solution (the global optimal solution is an NP-hard problem and cannot handle complex data efficiently).

The overall process of our proposed algorithm is illustrated in Algorithm 1.

3.4 Time Complexity Analysis

Next we analyse the time complexity of the proposed algorithm. The pruning step (lines 1–8) costs $O(n)$, where n is the number of drugs considered for DDI (except the drugs contained in the domain knowledge). If at least one drug is not pruned, then we need to consider the greedy step (lines 9–21). Line 10 requires n operations for the worst case in which every candidate drug will be included to form the combined causes, thus contributing $O(n)$ to the algorithm's time complexity. Lines 11 to 18 consider three constant time operations ($O(1)$). These iteration steps (lines 9–21) are considered until all drugs have been discounted (n in the worst case), or the break in line 15 occurs. Thus the greedy step costs $O(n) * [(O(n) + O(1)] = O(n^2)$. The total time complexity of the algorithm is therefore $O(n) + O(n^2) = O(n^2)$.

4 Experiments

Both synthetic and real-world data are used to empirically validate the effectiveness of the proposed method. We use synthetic data to compare our outcome with CARD – other baseline methods for causality discovery such as CBN and BCC are not considered because of the extremely high time complexity for the DDI cases considered in our experiments. Unfortunately, we cannot either compare CARD with our method on real-world data because CARD could not complete its execution due to its exponential time complexity – this highlights the major problem of CARD, which our method aims to resolve. The hardware used for the experiment was a server with an Intel i7-6700 CPU and 16 GB of RAM.

4.1 Domain Knowledge

Our method relies on the availability of domain knowledge about drugs that are known to cause the target adverse effect. We acquire this data from DailyMed, a database of trustworthy adverse effects extracted from official drug labels[5].

4.2 Real-World Data

We use approximately 300,000 patient records collected from FAERS. The extracted data contains missing values and duplicates, as noted previously by others [3,14], and thus we preprocess the data according to previous works.

---

[5] https://dailymed.nlm.nih.gov/dailymed/.

Algorithm 1 Line 1 is the iteration for the validation of **C2** (Line 2) and **C3** (Line 5) mentioned above. Once the relation of a drug, the domain knowledge drug and the adverse effect is classified as **C2** or **C3**, this drug is no longer considered. Line 10 identifies the drug which can most significantly increase the dependence strength between d_m and s based on the conjunctive combined cause detected from previous iterations by using the greedy strategy. Line 11 removes drugs that may not be the direct cause of s. On line 13, if there is no such drug detected, then the current conjunctive combined cause is the final result. On Line 15, PMI is used to identify whether the dependence is positive or negative. For PMI validation, if $d_i \in O$ causes a lower positive dependence than the total combined causes set when not including them in O, then d_i is not considered. However, it may be considered in the future iterations, because the PMI for that drug may change with other conditions.

Input: Domain knowledge drug d_m and adverse effect s
Other drugs $D\prime = \{d_1, d_2, ..., d_n\}$
Threshold of dependency value th = the critical value of Chi-square when significance level $\alpha = x$
Output: Conjunctive combined cause O
$O = \{\}$; //initialise output variable as an empty set
$T = D'$; //temporary variable as a copy of D'
Start
1: **for each** d_i **do**
2:     **if** $chi(d_i, d_m \mid s) < th$ **then**
3:         $D' = D' - \{d_i\}$;
4:         *continue*;
5:     **if** $chi(d_i, s \mid d_m) < th$ **then**
6:         $D' = D' - \{d_i\}$;
7:         *continue*;
8: $T = \{\}$; //temporary variable for the drugs failed in PMI validating
9: **while** true **do**
10:     $d_i = \underset{d \in \mathcal{D}' - \{O, T\}}{\operatorname{argmax}} chi(d_m, s \mid O, d)$
11:     **if** $chi(d_i, s \mid d_m, O) < th$ **then**
12:         $D' = D' - \{d_i\}$;
13:         *continue*;
14:     **if** $chi(d_m, s \mid O, d_i) <= chi(d_m, s \mid O)$ **then**
15:         *break*;
16:     **if** $pmi(d_m, s \mid O, d_i) <= pmi(d_m, s \mid O)$ **then**
17:         $T = T \cup d_i$;
18:         *continue*;
19:     **else**
20:         $O = O \cup d_i$;
21:         $T = \{\}$; //set the temporary variable to the empty set for the next loop
End

Duplicate reports are removed when they contain at least eight drugs or adverse effects, and all drugs, adverse effects and patient demographic information are the same as in [3]. Reports with missing adverse effect are not considered. Only drugs and adverse effects that occur in at least 5 reports are included. Two FAERS attributes are considered in our experiments: 'adverse event' and 'drug name', having approximately 10,000 and 40,000 values, respectively. For drug names, we conflate different names of the same drug to a unique identifier using a method proposed by Banda et al. [2]. We consider all types of adverse effects to provide all available ranges of adverse symptom severity.

In this dataset, a patient may have multiple records indicating that they may take many medicines to cure one or more diseases, and report several adverse effects: it is unclear what drug or combination of drugs has provoked which adverse effect(s). That is, the true causal DDICAE cannot be directly identified from FAERS data. In fact, for each report, the recorded set of drugs usage and adverse effects might be consistent with many possible cases: e.g., (1) some DDIs caused many adverse effects, (2) there are more than one DDICAE, (3) some drugs are used to cure adverse effects that are not the DDI, (4) some drugs do not cause any reported adverse effects, etc. Because of this, the reliance on methods that only depend on correlation between datapoints/features may identify relations between drugs and adverse effects that are actually not causal DDICAE effects – and thus fail to reveal correct insight relationships.

To evaluate on real-world data, the top ten causal drug-drug interactions results discovered using DCD are selected, based on the ranking from the dependence strength of the relations and their positive dependence measurements. To evaluate the prediction correctness, two reliable pharmaceutical drug-drug interaction databases, MedicinesComplete (MedComp)[6] and Drugs.com[7], are selected. The prediction results that do not match with the ground truth in the databases are not necessarily incorrect: the causality might not be confirmed or may have not been yet discovered by clinical or biological methods yet. In our evaluation, the label 'Not Found' is used for a drug-drug interaction that is not found in these databases.

4.3   Synthetic Data

The DDICAE predictions from real-world FAERS data only offer limited ground truth data and thus do not allow for a complete, reliable evaluation. Thus, in addition to FAERS data, we generate synthetic evaluation data using Tetrad[8], a tool widely used in previous studies to generate causal Bayesian graphs for evaluation [1,11]. Tetrad generates the directed acyclic causal Bayesian graph

---

[6] MedicinesComplete published in Pharmaceutical Press and the Royal Pharmaceutical Society: https://www.medicinescomplete.com/mc/alerts/current/drug-interactions.htm.

[7] Data sources from Micromedex, Multum and Wolters Kluwer databases: https://www.drugs.com/drug_interactions.php.

[8] http://www.phil.cmu.edu/tetrad/.

with known causal paths between variables. We generate three groups of graphs, the graphs with 50, 100 and 200 variables, to show the applicability of our method. In our setup, each group contains 10 random graphs and each variable is randomly assigned its directed causal links to connect to other nodes (between 0 to 7 causal links). Each graph contains 10,000 records, no loops, and any two nodes can only have one edge between each other. The conditional probability tables of the causal Bayesian networks are also randomly generated. Binary data for variables in all records are generated based on the conditional probability tables using the Bayesian Instantiated Model. The generated data is preprocessed in the same manner as FAERS data. In the case of domain knowledge from synthetic data, for each child node having at least one parent, one parent is randomly selected as domain knowledge.

To illustrate the effectiveness of our method on the synthetic data, we measure the precision of discovering drug-drug interactions. In our case, precision is defined as $TP/(TP + FP)$, where TP is the number of correct predicted causal links, and FP is the number of incorrectly predicted causal links.

Recall cannot be used for evaluation in both synthetic and real-world data because we do not know which predicted groups of drugs are the true conjunctive combined causes of the adverse events. In place of recall, we use Chi-squared value and PMI. The drug-drug interaction with the highest Chi-squared value and positive PMI is considered significant (with respect to d_m and s). We use this method for a recall-oriented evaluation for both synthetic and real-world data.

5   Results and Discussion

First, we evaluate whether DCD produces a higher quality conjunctive-combined causes compared to inputted domain knowledge and target effects from synthetic data and FAERS. In Table 1, the results of DCD are compared using domain knowledge and the target adverse effects. The evaluation shows that the outcomes have stronger dependence relationship in both synthetic data and causal drug-drug interaction and its adverse effect in FARES measured by the Chi-square. The strength of positive dependence relationships measured with the PMI in our outcomes is also stronger. These results imply that the interaction outcomes causing related effects from both synthetic data and real-world data have a higher probability to be a true cause outcome compared to the domain knowledge and its adverse effect.

Table 2 presents the results of drug-drug interactions and adverse effects from FARES as predicted by DCD. The top ten predictions with the highest positive dependence are selected to be validated with the two pharmaceutical databases, MedComp and Drug.com. Note that DCD can detect DDI cases that have more than 2 drugs (eg. such as LIPITOR + CRESTOR + NEXIUM → *Hypertension*). This table shows that nine out of ten drug-drug interactions and their adverse effect results from FARES predicted by DCD are found in Drugs.com, and three of them are found from both of databases. Only one

Table 1. The average Chi-square (%) and average PMI (log scale) of predicted DDI and the adverse effect compared to d_m and s, by DCD for variable sizes 50,100 and 200 and FARES.

Method	50	100	200	FAERS
Chi-square	1,349.77%	1,167.22%	947.09%	172.22%
PMI (log)	0.13	0.14	0.12	0.42

case, METHOTREXATE + ORENCIA → *Drug ineffective*, is not found in both databases. This outcome can be a candidate for biological tests to validate the causality in the future.

Next, we evaluate the pruning on synthetic data. DCD successfully prunes 96.99% of unrelated interactions, while CARD only removes 17.31%. In addition, the remaining interactions using DCD are more likely to have higher probability

Table 2. Comparison between drug-drug interactions and their adverse effect predicted by DCD and found in selected reliable pharmaceutical databases (D→Drugs.com and M→MedComp).

DDI predicted by DCD	Adverse effect	Found in database
ENBREL + HUMIRA	Sepsis	M, D
PREDNISONE + ENBREL	Infections	D
ENBREL + REMICADE	Drug ineffective	D
ENBREL + HUMIRA	Pain	M, D
METHOTREXATE + ORENCIA	**Drug ineffective**	**Not found**
ENBREL + PLAQUENIL	Drug ineffective	M, D
TEMAZEPAM + GABAPENTIN	Dizziness	D
PREDNISONE + ENBREL	Pain	D
LIPITOR + CRESTOR + NEXIUM	Hypertension	D
ENBREL + METHOTREXATE	Fatigue	D

Table 3. The average precision (%) on synthetic data of DCD compared to CARD for variable sizes 50,100 and 200. Highest values are indicated in **bold**.

Method	50	100	200
DCD	**91.67**	**86.96**	**83.61**
CARD	84.61	76.74	59.01

Table 4. The average computation time (seconds) of DCD compared CARD for variable sizes 50, 100 and 200. Lowest values are indicated in **bold**.

Method	50	100	200
DCD	**0.36**	**2.95**	**10.95**
CARD	55.84	314.17	1,918.78

to be the valid conjunctive combined cause that causes adverse effect or DDI-CAE. The results of these experiments are present in Table 3. Here, the more variables in the synthetic data indicates a higher complexity of the causal graph (i.e., closer to the real-world data). The results of DCD outperform those of CARD in precision using the synthetic data. The computation time of DCD is also lower than that of CARD, which is described in Table 4. When compared to CARD, our method tends to have higher probability to predict causality with higher precision and lower computation time.

To compare the dependence strength of our approach with CARD, Chi-squared value is used to measure dependence strength, and PMI is used to measure the positive dependence relationship, as shown in Table 5. When using synthetic data, we outperform CARD in all measures tested. When using real-world data, DCD also performs effectively; however, the number of variables are too large for CARD to execute because of its exponential time complexity. The results of CARD show the negative dependence (negative value in the bracket) because it uses mutual information to measure the dependence (i.e., it ignores positive and negative dependence). Therefore, CARD tends to be not as effective at discovering causal DDICAE because it cannot identify co-occurrence DDICAE (i.e., it relies on the positive dependence relationship of related drugs).

DCD is the only CBN and BCC method used to discover DDICAE and is state-of-the-art in terms of both effectiveness and efficiency (when compared to CARD). DCD does not only find causality in DDICAE but also confirms the causal direction using domain knowledge and our proposed pruning steps. As highlighted by our evaluation on real-world data, DCD is also more likely to discover true causal DDICAE and to be an effective and efficient method to support decisions for pharmaceutical and medical experts.

Table 5. Average Chi-squared value and PMI of predicted DDI with adverse effect of DCD compared to CARD for variable sizes 50,100 and 200 and FARES.

	Average Chi-squared value				Average PMI			
Method	50	100	200	FARES	50	100	200	FARES
DCD	1,478.84	3,255,886.03	7,192.55	833.34	0.32	0.30	0.20	1.25
CARD	36.31	4,312.94	569.13	-	(−0.21)	(−0.81)	0.02	-

6   Conclusion

Causality discovery in drug-drug interaction and adverse effect is an important task for health care decision support. Traditional methods to confirm causality from drug-drug interaction and adverse effects, such as biological experiments, are difficult, complicated and expensive. Computational methods, such as CBN (e.g., PC-Algorithm), BCC methods (e.g., Markov Blanket), are effective to discovery causality; however, they generally suffer from exponential time complexity, and BCC is affected by the causality direction ambiguity problem. CARD is the only CBN method to effectively discover causality in drug-drug interaction and adverse effect. However, it does not perform well with real-world data and also suffers from its exponential time complexity nature.

In this paper, we have proposed the Domain-knowledge-centred Causality Discovery algorithm (DCD) that can discover causality from drug-drug interactions and adverser effect. Advantages of our algorithm include:

- Domain knowledge is used effectively as a guide to discover causality, and it can confirm the causal direction when used with our proposed pruning steps.
- Computation time is reduced by pruning most of the irrelevant drugs of the target DDICAE (Drug-Drug interaction Causing Adverse Effect) by using the proposed evidence-based DDICAE structure (relating to the domain knowledge) integrated with conditional independence.
- The discovered DDICAEs are meaningful because they are the co-occurrence DDICAEs represented by the positive dependence values (unlike e.g., CARD, that does not exploit such co-occurrence properties).
- The discovered DDICAEs include those that can and cannot be detected using the V-structure property, unlike current state-of-the-art methods such as CARD, that solely rely on the V-structure, whose underlying data assumptions are in fact not necessarily satisfied in real-world data.
- The time complexity of the proposed method is polynomial ($O(n^2)$) because our algorithm applies a greedy algorithm to find causality, and this is a speed-up compared to current state-of-the-art approaches (e.g., CARD).

However, our method provides a locally optimal solution and may not find all drugs in the drug-drug interaction causing the adverse effect. In addition, our method cannot be used when no domain knowledge exists. However, the outcomes are still helpful to reduce the cost of drug-drug interaction discovery and as a decision support for doctors when they prescribe medications to patients.

Acknowledgements. The authors would like to acknowledge Meng Wang from Southeast University, China, and Mingyang Zhong from The University of Queensland, Australia, for their input on the initial stages of this work.

Appendix I: Terminology used in this Paper

BCC: *Bayesian Constraint-based Causality*
CARD: *Causal Association Rule Discovery*
CBN: *Causal Bayesian Network*
DCD: *Domain-knowledge-driven Causality Discovery*
DDICAE: *Drug-Drug Interactions Causing Adverse Effects*
DDI: *Drug-drug interactions*
FAERS: *Food and Drug Administration (FDA) adverse event report system*

References

1. Aliferis, C.F., Statnikov, A., Tsamardinos, I., Mani, S., Koutsoukos, X.D.: Local causal and Markov blanket induction for causal discovery and feature selection for classification part i: algorithms and empirical evaluation. J. Mach. Learn. Res. **11**(Jan), 171–234 (2010)
2. Banda, J.M., Evans, L., Vanguri, R.S., Tatonetti, N.P., Ryan, P.B., Shah, N.H.: A curated and standardized adverse drug event resource to accelerate drug safety research. Sci. Data **3**, 160026 (2016)
3. Cai, R., et al.: Identification of adverse drug-drug interactions through causal association rule discovery from spontaneous adverse event reports. Artif. Intell. Med. **76**, 7–15 (2017)
4. Chickering, D.M., Heckerman, D., Meek, C.: Large-sample learning of Bayesian networks is NP-hard. J. Mach. Learn. Res. **5**(Oct), 1287–1330 (2004)
5. Hansen, M.L., et al.: Risk of bleeding with single, dual, or triple therapy with warfarin, aspirin, and clopidogrel in patients with atrial fibrillation. Arch. Intern. Med. **170**(16), 1433–1441 (2010)
6. Harpaz, R., Perez, H., Chase, H.S., Rabadan, R., Hripcsak, G., Friedman, C.: Biclustering of adverse drug events in the FDA's spontaneous reporting system. Clin. Pharmacol. Ther. **89**(2), 243–250 (2011)
7. He, L., Yang, Z., Lin, H., Li, Y.: Drug name recognition in biomedical texts: a machine-learning-based method. Drug Discov. Today **19**(5), 610–617 (2014)
8. Jin, Z., Li, J., Liu, L., Le, T.D., Sun, B., Wang, R.: Discovery of causal rules using partial association. In: IEEE 12th International Conference on Data Mining, pp. 309–318. IEEE (2012)
9. Lazarou, J., Pomeranz, B.H., Corey, P.N.: Incidence of adverse drug reactions in hospitalized patients: a meta-analysis of prospective studies. JAMA **279**(15), 1200–1205 (1998)
10. Li, J., Le, T.D., Liu, L., Liu, J., Jin, Z., Sun, B.: Mining causal association rules. In: IEEE 13th International Conference on Data Mining (Workshops), pp. 114–123. IEEE (2013)
11. Li, J., Ma, S., Le, T., Liu, L., Liu, J.: Causal decision trees. IEEE Trans. Knowl. Data Eng. **29**(2), 257–271 (2017)
12. McHugh, M.L.: The chi-square test of independence. Biochem. Med. : Biochem. Med. **23**(2), 143–149 (2013)
13. Neapolitan, R.E., et al.: Learning Bayesian Networks, vol. 38. Pearson Prentice Hall, Upper Saddle River (2004)
14. Norén, G.N., Orre, R., Bate, A., Edwards, I.R.: Duplicate detection in adverse drug reaction surveillance. Data Min. Knowl. Discov. **14**(3), 305–328 (2007)
15. Pearl, J.: Causality. Cambridge University Press, Cambridge (2009)
16. Qin, X., Kakar, T., Wunnava, S., Rundensteiner, E.A., Cao, L.: MARAS: signaling multi-drug adverse reactions. In: Proceedings of the 23rd ACM SIGKDD International Conference on Knowledge Discovery and Data Mining, pp. 1615–1623. ACM (2017)
17. Quinn, D., Day, R.: Drug interactions of clinical importance. Drug Saf. **12**(6), 393–452 (1995)
18. Rodrigues, A.D.: Drug-Drug Interactions. CRC Press, Boca Raton (2008)

19. Van Puijenbroek, E.P., Egberts, A.C., Meyboom, R.H., Leufkens, H.G.: Signalling possible drug-drug interactions in a spontaneous reporting system: delay of withdrawal bleeding during concomitant use of oral contraceptives and itraconazole. Br. J. Clin. Pharmacol. **47**(6), 689–693 (1999)
20. Waldmann, M.R., Martignon, L.: A Bayesian network model of causal learning. In: Proceedings of the 20th annual conference of the Cognitive Science Society, pp. 1102–1107 (1998)

Personalised Medicine in Critical Care Using Bayesian Reinforcement Learning

Chandra Prasetyo Utomo[1]([✉]), Hanna Kurniawati[1], Xue Li[1,2], and Suresh Pokharel[1]

[1] The University of Queensland, Brisbane, QLD 4072, Australia
{c.utomo,hannakur,s.pokharel}@uq.edu.au
[2] Neusoft Education Technology Group, Dalian 116023, People's Republic of China
lixue@neusoft.edu.cn

Abstract. Patients with similar conditions in the intensive care unit (ICU) may have different reactions for a given treatment. An effective personalised medicine can help save patient lives. The availability of recorded ICU data provides a huge potential to train and develop the systems. However, there is no ground truth of best treatments. This makes existing supervised learning based methods are not appropriate. In this paper, we proposed clustering based Bayesian reinforcement learning. Firstly, we transformed the multivariate time series patient record into a real-time Patient Sequence Model (PSM). After that, we computed the likelihood probability of treatments effect for all patients and cluster them based on that. Finally, we computed Bayesian reinforcement learning to derive personalised policies. We tested our proposed method using 11,791 ICU patients records from MIMIC-III database. Results show that we are able to cluster patient based on their treatment effects. In addition, our method also provides better explainability and time-critical recommendation that are very important in a real ICU setting.

Keywords: Personalised medicine · Treatment recommendation · Intensive care unit · Time series · Bayesian reinforcement learning

1 Introduction

Personalised treatment recommendation is one of the most desired applications of intensive care unit (ICU) decision support systems. Research in sepsis related patients shows that ICU patients in a similar condition had difference responses to a set of Vasopressor treatments [10]. Some patients responded properly (getting a better condition), other set of patients had complications (getting a worse condition), and the remaining patients did not respond at all. Every four years, ICU community updates their best practise guidelines to deal with sepsis based on recent evidence based medicine research [12]. This process is expensive, time consuming, and possibly has conflicting results.

The availability of ICU database has opened the opportunity to develop a data driven approach for personalised medicine. We aim to develop a personalised

© Springer Nature Switzerland AG 2019
J. Li et al. (Eds.): ADMA 2019, LNAI 11888, pp. 648–657, 2019.
https://doi.org/10.1007/978-3-030-35231-8_47

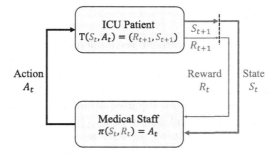

Fig. 1. The interaction between ICU patient and medical staff modeled in reinforcement learning. At a timestamp t, medical staff analyse the current state of patient S_t and reward R_t (scalar value indicating how good the patient condition). Based on a medical policy π, they perform action A_t. The patient response the treatment on current state by revealing the next state S_{t+1} and reward R_{t+1}.

treatment recommendation for sepsis related patients using existing ICU data. We choose sepsis related patients because sepsis is the most frequent cause of death in ICU [13]. In addition, both the definition of sepsis [15] and its effective treatments are still subject of future medical research.

There are two main challenges to do precision medicine in ICU. Firstly, there is no ground truth of best treatments. The current recorded treatments are subject to evaluation for future best practise guidelines. This makes existing supervised learning based recommendation systems [3] are not appropriate. Secondly, the ICU record is a multivariate time series data with common missing values and no proper alignment. Existing recommendation systems [11] were using a fix interval to sequence these data. However, this approach is not applicable as ICU demands a real-time decision making process.

In this paper we proposed personalised medicine based on Bayesian reinforcement learning. Firstly, we developed a real-time multivariate time series sequencing technique called Patient Sequence Model (PSM). Figure 1 illustrates our sequence model. After that, we calculated the likelihood of treatment responses to generate a meaningful feature representation for each patient. Then, we clustered the patient based on their treatment responses. Finally, we define a mathematical model to compute a personalised policy.

There are three main contributions of this paper.

- **Explainable Sequence Model**. We are able to visualise a meaningful state transition diagram represented patient dynamics in ICU.
- **Discovery of Patient Clusters**. We are able to cluster the patients into several groups based on patient responses to the treatments.
- **Personalised Policy Computation**. We define a framework to recommend a personalised treatment as combination of policies from all clusters.

The rest of the paper is organised as follow. Section 2 describes related work. The proposed methods is explained in Sect. 3. Evaluation is provided in Sect. 4. Finally, Sect. 5 gives concluding remark and direction of future work.

2   Related Work

The first set of attempts in treatment recommendation were based on expert systems [1,5]. However, it is difficult and costly to get knowledge from domain expert. As the availability of electronic health records (EHR), data driven method became a reasonable direction. The first set of methods are supervised learning based methods. Hu et al. [6] used similarity method, Cheerla et al. [4] integrated genomics data, and Bajor et al. [3] proposed deep model. However, these methods are not suitable in ICU as ground truth of treatment is unclear. A more reasonable data driven approach is using reinforcement learning. Tsoukalas et al. [16] modeled the treatment recommendation problem as Partially Observable Markov Decision Process (POMDP) while Nemati et al. [9] and Raghu et al. [11] modeled it as deep reinforcement learning. However, these methods sequenced the ICU patients based on a fix length interval, e.g. 4 h. This is not applicable in real ICU setting as it demands real-time decision making. In addition, their models are not explainable to domain expert which is important in this sensitive application.

3   Proposed Methods

Markov Decision Process (MDP) is defined by tuple $(\mathcal{S}, \mathcal{A}, T, R)$ where:

- $\mathcal{S} : S_1 \times S_2 \times \ldots \times S_{ns}$, is the set of states of the system; $S_1, \ldots, S_{ns}$ correspond to the domain of the ns state variables (features). We define qSOFA variables $(ns = 3)$ as state variables. So that, we have $S_1 = ABPSystolic$, $S_2 = RespiratoryRate$, and $S_3 = Mentation$. We added two terminal states *survived* and *dead* to the state space.
- $\mathcal{A} : A_1 \times A_2 \times \ldots A_{na}$, is the set of actions that can be performed by the agent. We define vasopressor treatments $(na = 5)$ as the action set. Here, we have $A_1 = Epinephrine$, $A_2 = Dopamine$, $A_3 = Phenylephrine$, $A_4 = Norepinephrine$, and $A_5 = Vasopression$.
- $T : \mathcal{S} \times \mathcal{A} \times \mathcal{S} \rightarrow [0, 1]$ is the transition function, where $T(s, a, s') = P(s'|s, a)$ represents the conditional probability of moving to state $s' \in \mathcal{S}$ if the agent executes action $a \in \mathcal{A}$ in state $s \in \mathcal{S}$.
- $R : \mathcal{S} \times \mathcal{A} \times \mathcal{S} \rightarrow \mathbb{R}$, the reward function, encodes a reward earned when state s' is reached after executing action a in state s. We defined $R(s, a, survival) = +100$, $R(s, a, death) = -100$, and $R(s, a, s') = -qSOFA(s')$ for all non-terminal states s'.

The goal of the MDP agent is to find an action selection strategy $\pi*$, called a policy, that maximises its long-term expected rewards. The optimal action to take in a state s is defined via the optimal value function V^* representing the return obtained by the optimal policy starting in state s:

$$V^*(s) = \max_{a \in A} \left[R(s, a, s') + \sum_{s' \in S} T(s, a, s')V^*(s') \right]. \tag{1}$$

The optimal action in s is obtained by taking the *argmax* instead of the max in the Eq. 1.

3.1 Sequence Model

We proposed a real-time multivariate time series sequencing called Patient Sequence Model (PSM). Each ICU stay $I^{(i)} = [S_1, A_1, R_2, S_2, A_2, \ldots, R_{T_i}, S_{T_i}]$ is represented by a sequence of states, actions, and rewards. In this model, we did not divide timestep based on a fix length interval, e.g. 4 h. Instead, we extract a new timestep when there is a new observation. We believe that in the real ICU settings, medical staff makes decision based on new observation. They will not wait until a given fix interval to take action.

We discretised both state and action to have a better explainability. We discretised state variables into binary values *normal* and *abnormal*. We followed medical literature to define thresholds for all variables. As we have 3 state variables and 2 values for each variables, we have $2^3 = 8$ states. Since we added 2 terminal states, the total number of states in our state space is 10.

For action variables, we discretised into *true* (if the drug was administered) and *false* (otherwise). As we have 5 action variables and 2 values for each variables, the total number of actions in our action space is $2^5 = 32$. Table 1a and b shows the combination of variables in state and action space, respectively. We left the definition of reward R_t the same.

3.2 Feature Engineering

We want to divide the whole patient cohort into several subgroups. Patients within a same subgroup should have a common responses of a set of treatments. On the other hand, patients from two different subgroups should have different responses. By correctly identifying subgroups of patients, we will be able to deliver a more personalised treatment for a new patient.

We designed a feature that reflects patient responses for all treatments at any given state. For each ICU stay $I^{(i)}$, we calculated feature representation $X^{(i)}$ as

$$X^{(i)} = T(S_t, A_t, S_{t+1}) = P(S_{t+1}|S_t, A_t). \tag{2}$$

$X^{(i)} \in \mathbf{R}^{|S_t| \times |A_t| \times |S_{t+1}|}$ is a transition function of current state S_t, action A_t, and next state S_{t+1}. We can unfold the first dimension into $X^{(i)} = [X_1^{(i)}, X_2^{(i)}, \ldots, X_8^{(i)}]$, where

Table 1. State definition (a) and action definition (b). The reward function is associated with the qSOFA values defined in table (a).

States	ABP Systolic	Respiratory Rate	Mental Status	qSOFA
s_1	normal	normal	normal	0
s_2	normal	normal	abnormal	1
s_3	normal	abnormal	normal	1
s_4	normal	abnormal	abnormal	2
s_5	abnormal	normal	normal	1
s_6	abnormal	normal	abnormal	2
s_7	abnormal	abnormal	normal	2
s_8	abnormal	abnormal	abnormal	3

(a) State space

Actions	Epinephrine	Dopamine	Phenylephrine	Norepinephrine	Vasopressin
a_0	false	false	false	false	false
a_1	false	false	false	false	true
a_2	false	false	false	true	false
a_3	false	false	false	true	true
a_4	false	false	true	false	false
a_5	false	false	true	false	true
a_6	false	false	true	true	false
a_7	false	false	true	true	true
...	...	...	...	...	...
a_{31}	true	true	true	true	true

(b) Action space

$$X_j^{(i)} = P(S_{t+1}|S_t = s_j, A_t). \tag{3}$$

Here, $X_j^{(i)}$ is the conditional probability of ith ICU stay in state s_j. The index j can take value from 1 to 8 because we have $|S_t| = 8$ non-terminal states in our definition (see Table 1a).

For each ICU stay $I^{(i)}$, we calculated the likelihood of conditional probability $\hat{P}(S_{t+1} = s_l|S_t = s_j, A_t = a_k)$ as

$$\hat{P}(s_l|s_j, a_k) = \frac{1}{N(S_t = s_j, A_t = a_k)} \sum_{t=1}^{T} 1(S_t, A_t, S_{t+1} = s_j, a_k, s_l). \tag{4}$$

Figure 3 shows the conditional probability of ICU ID $= 204176$ in state s_4 (abnormal respiratory rate and abnormal mental status). We may see that the patient had been given 7 different treatments when she/he was in this state.

3.3 Personalised Policy

We flattened three dimensional matrix $X^{(i)}$ into a single long vector $\hat{X}^{(i)}$. Number of non-terminal states $|S_t| = 8$ (see Table 1a), number of action states $|A_t| = 32$ (see Table 1b), and number of all possible states $S_{t+1} = 10$ (8 non-terminal states and 2 terminal states). So that, $\hat{X}^{(i)} \in \mathbf{R}^{2,560}$. To have a better visualisation of all patients in the experimental data, we reduced the dimension using PCA and projected in the first three dimensions in Fig. 5a.

The existing methods were calculated a single general policy π_g^* from the whole training data. Then, they applied this policy to the all test data. We believe that the patients can be segmented into some subgroups with a common similarity. We applied k-means clustering to the extracted feature $\hat{X}^{(i)}$ for all patient in training data. The clustering result $(c_1, c_2, \ldots, c_{nc})$ will reflect subgroups of patient with similar responses of treatments.

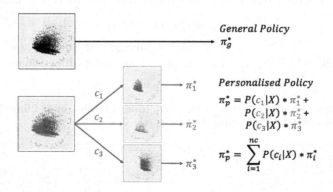

Fig. 2. General policy versus personalised policy

We computed a dedicated policy π_i^* for subgroup c_i. We defined personalise policy π_p^* as

$$\pi_p^* = P(c_1|X) * \pi_1^* + P(c_2|X) * \pi_2^* + \ldots + P(c_{nc}|X) * \pi_{nc}^*. \tag{5}$$

Here, $P(c_i|X)$ is the believe that a new patient X is belong to cluster c_i. Figure 2 illustrates the different between general policy and personalised policy. Suppose we cluster the training data into 3 clusters, then we will have 3 subgroup policies. For n_c number of clusters, we can write the personalised policy as

$$\pi^* = \sum_{i=1}^{nc} P(c_i|X) * \pi_i^*. \tag{6}$$

4   Evaluation

4.1   Dataset

We used real-world ICU dataset from MIMIC-III (Medical Information Mart for Intensive Care) database [8]. We follow six exclusion criteria [7] in order to extract experimental data for optimal treatment recommendation related to sepsis. Firstly, we only considered records of patient admitted from 2008. After that, we excluded non-adults, non-primary admissions, cardiothoracic surgical service admissions, and admissions with missing data. Finally, we removed patient records with suspected of infection more than 24 h before and more than 24 h after ICU admission. The final patient cohort contained 11,791 patients.

4.2   Experimental Design

We divided our experiments into two main parts. Each part serves a dedicated purpose. In the first part, we want to test the explainability of our proposed sequence model. This is the key feature to discuss with domain experts, further our research in the right direction, and increase its applicability. We compute the likelihood of state transition probability $\hat{P}(S_{t+1}|S_t)$ using all dataset. After that, we visualise the result and generate state transition diagram.

In the second part, we want to test the effectiveness of our proposed feature representation. We need to see whether represent each patient based on their response to treatment is useful. We compute pairwise distance of all patients then group them into several number of clusters. We compare the clustering results with existing concepts in medical domain knowledge such as sepsis.

4.3   Result and Analysis

We computed probability of state transition from a current state S_t to a next state S_{t+1}. Figure 4a shows likelihood probability $\hat{P}(S_{t+1}|S_t)$ computed from all patient records in the experimental data. We can see that the diagonal of the figure is mostly dark blue ($\hat{P}(S_{t+1} = s_i|S_t = s_i)$ is close to 1. It suggests

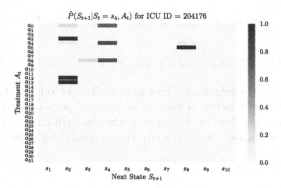

Fig. 3. A conditional probability $\hat{P}(S_{t+1}|S_t = s_4, A_t)$ for a patient (ICU ID = 204176) in current state $S_t = s_4$ (abnormal respiratory rate and mental status).

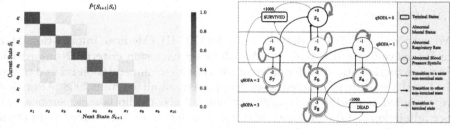

(a) State transition probability $\hat{P}(S_{t+1}|S_t)$.   (b) State transition diagram.

Fig. 4. Patients dynamics in transition probability (a) and diagram (b). (Color figure online)

that most of the time, patient will stay in the same state for several timestamps before changing to another states. State s_3 and s_7 are the two states with greater probability to move to other states. This means, intervention in these states will more likely change patient conditions.

To justify personalised medicine idea, we need to compare the general state transition probability with a particular patient. For that reason, we observed a patient who received the most number of unique treatments as an extreme case. In our experimental data, a patient with ICU ID = 204176 received 18 treatments which is the highest of all patients. Figure 3 shows the conditional probability $\hat{P}(S_{t+1}|S_t = s_4, A_t)$ for the patient in the current state $S_t = s_4$.

We analyse some key features in Fig. 3. The patient received 7 type of treatments $\{a_0, a_3, a_4, a_5, a_8, a_{12}, a_{13}\}$ in state s_4 (abnormal respiratory rate and mental status). The Patient 100% went to a better state s_2 (abnormal respiratory) when given treatments $\{a_3, a_{12}, a_{13}\}$ and 100% went to a worse state s_8 (abnormal blood pressure, respiratory, and mental status) when given treatments $\{a_5\}$. On the other hand, the patient was most probably stay in the state s_4 when give

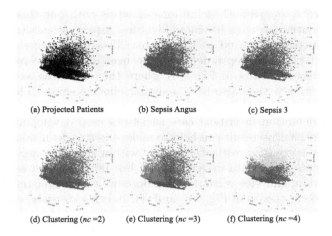

(a) Projected Patients   (b) Sepsis Angus   (c) Sepsis 3

(d) Clustering (*nc* =2)   (e) Clustering (*nc* =3)   (f) Clustering (*nc* =4)

Fig. 5. Patients clustering (Color figure online)

treatments $\{a_0, a_4, a_8\}$ with some small probability moved to other states. These unique features are significantly different with the overall case shown in Fig. 4a where mostly patient in state s_4 are stay in the same state. This suggests that developing treatment recommendation systems using overall dynamics from all patients will not be effective.

We visualise the likelihood of state transition probability into state transition diagram in Fig. 4b. The vertices are eight non-terminal states (circle) and two terminal states (rectangle). The lower the position of a state in the diagram, the worse its condition with respect to qSOFA score. The directed edges represent state transitions. The edge's width is proportional to its conditional probability $P(S_{t+1}|S_t)$. We filtered the edges with $P(S_{t+1}|S_t) < 0.1$. We added three edges with highest probability for each terminal states.

In this filtered diagram, we can see the dynamics such as common survival and mortality models. Most of the survived patients had normal mental status (no blue circle) in ICU discharge. We can also see that most of the patients we getting better during ICU stays. Between non-terminal states, there are 7 edges going up (better qSOFA score) and 4 edges going down (worse qSOFA score). This kind of visualization can be useful for better explainability of proposed method with medical practitioners.

We projected all patients into 3 dimensional space using PCA. Figure 5(a) shows the results. Every single dot in the figure represents a single patient. We color the patients based concepts in medical knowledge. In Fig. 5(b), we used the definition of sepsis by Angus et al. [2]. In Fig. 5(c), we used the third definition of sepsis or sepsis-3 [15] established in 2016. In both definitions, we may see that the sepsis patients (red) are somehow well separated with non-sepsis patients (blue). it means that our feature engineering method based one treatment responses is aligned with medical concept.

We want to compare both definitions of sepsis with our clustering results. The latest definition of sepsis has more identified sepsis patients (more red dots) and visually better separated in the figures. This may suggest that medical knowledge with respect to sepsis definition has been improved. Now, lets compare with the clustering results in Fig. 5(d) where they have the same number of groups. Interestingly, they also have a similar clusters shape. The difference is the clustering result have a lot more red cluster and even better separated.

As sepsis definition in critical care society is keep developing (the next is sepsis-4), the clustering result can help to make a better definition. Our medical collaborator is eager to investigate patients within the same group of majority of sepsis patients using data driven method but not identified as sepsis in the current definition, and vice versa. Furthermore, we can cluster the patients into more than two clusters as in Fig. 5(e) and (f). In other diseases, such as cancer, they are able to identify new subtype of disease [14] using clustering result. Further analysis in our clustering results with domain expert is needed to investigate potential new subtype of sepsis.

5   Conclusion

We proposed the Patient Sequence Model (PSM) to transform multivariate time series patient data into explainable and computable representation. The PSM model is able to generate a meaningful state transition diagram. We developed a reasonable feature extraction method based on probability of treatment effect and clustered all patients based on those high dimensional feature. The clustering result aligns with current medical concept and potentially discovers novel subtypes of sepsis. We proposed a novel Bayesian reinforcement learning method to compute personalised policy based on combination of dedicated policies in each cluster. The future work is discussion with medical collaborator with respect to this clustering results. In addition, we will need to define a medically acceptable performance evaluation criteria to compare our proposed personalised policy with general policy and doctor policy.

Acknowledgements. Chandra Prasetyo Utomo is sponsored by Indonesia Endowment Fund for Education (LPDP). This research is partially supported by Australian Research Council (ARC) project ID: DP160104075 and Universitas YARSI, Jakarta. The authors thank Dr. Robert Boots from Royal Brisbane and Women's Hospital (RBWH) for valuable insight in treatment recommendation research.

References

1. Almirall, D., Compton, S.N., Gunlicks-Stoessel, M., Duan, N., Murphy, S.A.: Designing a pilot sequential multiple assignment randomized trial for developing an adaptive treatment strategy. Stat. Med. **31**(17), 1887–1902 (2012)
2. Angus, D.C., van der Poll, T.: Severe sepsis and septic shock. New England J. Med. **369**(9), 840–851 (2013)

3. Bajor, J.M., Lasko, T.A.: Predicting medications from diagnostic codes with recurrent neural networks. In: Proceeding of the 5th International Conference on Learning Representations - (ICLR 2017), pp. 1–19 (2017)
4. Cheerla, N., Gevaert, O.: MicroRNA based pan-cancer diagnosis and treatment recommendation. BMC Bioinf. **18**(1), 32 (2017)
5. Chen, Z., Marple, K., Salazar, E., Gupta, G., Tamil, L.: A physician advisory system for chronic heart failure management based on knowledge patterns. Theory Pract. Logic Program. **16**(5–6), 604–618 (2016)
6. Hu, J., Perer, A., Wang, F.: Data driven analytics for personalized healthcare. In: Weaver, C.A., Ball, M.J., Kim, G.R., Kiel, J.M. (eds.) Healthcare Information Management Systems. HI, pp. 529–554. Springer, Cham (2016). https://doi.org/10.1007/978-3-319-20765-0_31
7. Johnson, A.E.W., et al.: A comparative analysis of sepsis identification methods in an electronic database. Crit. Care Med. **46**(4), 494–499 (2018)
8. Johnson, A.E., Pollard, T.J., Shen, L., et al.: MIMIC-III, a freely accessible critical care database. Sci. Data **3**, 160035 (2016)
9. Nemati, S., Ghassemi, M.M., Clifford, G.D.: Optimal medication dosing from suboptimal clinical examples: a deep reinforcement learning approach. In: Proceeding of the 38th Annual International Conference of the IEEE Engineering in Medicine and Biology Society (EMBC 2016), Orlando, FL, USA , pp. 2978–2981, August 2016
10. Pollard, S., Edwin, S.B., Alaniz, C.: Vasopressor and inotropic management of patients with septic shock. Pharm. Ther. **40**(7), 438–50 (2015)
11. Raghu, A., Komorowski, M., Ahmed, I., Celi, L., Szolovits, P., Ghassemi, M.: Deep Reinforcement Learning for Sepsis Treatment. In: Proceeding of the 31st Conference on Neural Information Processing Systems (NIPS 2017), Long Beach, CA, USA (2017)
12. Rhodes, A., Evans, L.E., Alhazzani, W., et al.: Surviving sepsis campaign: international guidelines for management of sepsis and septic shock: 2016. Intensive Care Med. **43**(3), 304–377 (2017)
13. Sakr, Y., Jaschinski, U., Wittebole, X., et al.: Sepsis in intensive care unit patients: worldwide data from the intensive care over nations audit. Open Forum Infect. Dis. **5**(12), ofy313 (2018)
14. Shen, R., Olshen, A.B., Ladanyi, M.: Integrative clustering of multiple genomic data types using a joint latent variable model with application to breast and lung cancer subtype analysis. Bioinformatics **25**(22), 2906–2912 (2009)
15. Singer, M., Deutschman, C.S., Seymour, C., et al.: The third international consensus definitions for sepsis and septic shock (sepsis-3). JAMA - J. Am. Med. Assoc. **315**(8), 801–810 (2016)
16. Tsoukalas, A., Albertson, T., Tagkopoulos, I.: From data to optimal decision making: a data-driven, probabilistic machine learning approach to decision support for patients with sepsis. JMIR Med. Inf. **3**(1), e11 (2015)

TDDF: HFMD Outpatients Prediction Based on Time Series Decomposition and Heterogenous Data Fusion in Xiamen, China

Zhijin Wang[1(✉)], Yaohui Huang[2], Bingyan He[1], Ting Luo[2], Yongming Wang[3], and Yingxian Lin[1(✉)]

[1] Computer Engineering College, Jimei University,
Yinjiang Road 185, Xiamen 361021, China
{zhijin,hebingyan,yxlin}@jmu.edu.cn
[2] Chengyi University College, Jimei University,
Jimei Road 199, Xiamen 361021, China
{yhhuang,201641051007}@jmu.edu.cn
[3] China Electronics Technology Group Corporation,
Shandong Middle Road 337, Shanghai 200001, China
ymwang819@gmail.com

Abstract. Hand, foot and mouth disease (HFMD) is a common infectious disease in global public health. In this paper, the time series decomposition and heterogeneous data fusion (TDDF) method is proposed to enhance features in the performance of HFMD outpatients prediction. The TDDF first represents meteorological features and Baidu search index features with the consideration of lags, then those features are fused into decomposed historical HFMD cases to predict coming outpatient cases. Experimental results and analyses on the real collected records show the efficiency and effectiveness of TDDF on regression methods.

Keywords: HFMD prediction · Meteorological factor · Baidu search index

1 Introduction

Hand, foot and mouth disease (HFMD) is a common global infectious disease [4]. This disease is easy to cause fever, oral ulcers, blisters and rashes on hands, feet and buttocks, some serious and potentially fatal complications will lead to serious sequelae and even death [11]. Millions of people, in particular for children less than 5 years old, suffer from HFMD-related disease over the past decade [7,8,16]. The control and prevention of HFMD is a public health issue that receives attentions by government agencies, medical institutions and the public [14]. It became the 38th legally notifiable disease in the China's National Notifiable Disease Reporting and Surveillance System [1,3] on May 2, 2008 [2].

© Springer Nature Switzerland AG 2019
J. Li et al. (Eds.): ADMA 2019, LNAI 11888, pp. 658–667, 2019.
https://doi.org/10.1007/978-3-030-35231-8_48

Auxiliary data are collected to alleviate the uncertainty of disease occurrences and improve the prediction performance. Typically, meteorological factors have been proved to be associated with the incidence of infectious diseases [9,15]. For example, temperature and relative humidity are presented as continuous variables, and connected with HFMD cases using by using linear models. But other weak correlated climate factors are usually ignored, such as dew point and atmospheric pressure. Recently, as an important entry of the Internet, search engines are adopted to track infectious disease epidemics in countries and provinces [6]. These methods commonly use "手足口病" as query keyword, and search engine returns the search indices.

This motivate us to leverage both meteorological factors and search indices to provide predictions for short-term HFMD outpatient visits with respect to feature construction and representation. The challenges of constructing features are: (1) *Weak correlated feature discovery.* Many factors affect infectious disease propagation, and weak correlated factors are usually ignored. (2) *Time concerned feature representation.* There exists a time interval between factors and disease outbreaks. The time interval consists of incubation period and diagnosing duration. Usually, the incubation period is 2–5 days, and it takes another 1–2 days to be diagnosed. In total, it spans 2–7 days from infection time to report time. Hence, the time interval should be taking into consideration for feature representation.

To address the above challenges, the time series decomposition and heterogeneous data fusion (TDDF) method is proposed to enhance the features for a better prediction performance. The TDDF first represent meteorological factor features and Baidu search index features with the consideration of lags, then those features are fused into decomposed historical HFMD cases to predict coming outpatient cases. In the first stage, the related data are collected, organized and count variables in weeks. The correlation between variables and outpatients was analyzed based on bivariate correlation analysis. We try time difference analysis on two observing variables to figure out the connections between current outpatients and the outpatients of several days before. In the second stage, we consolidate a feature matrix based on previous analyses and figures. Thus, outpatients predictions are provided via well trained regression models.

2   Study Area and Auxiliary Data

2.1   Study Area

Xiamen is located in the southeast part of China, and is also an important special economic zone in China. It covers a land area of $1,699.39 \, \text{km}^2$ and a sea area of over $390 \, \text{km}^2$ until 2017. Xiamen has a monsoonal humid subtropical climate, characterised by long, hot and humid summers (but moderate compared to much of the rest of the province) and short, mild and dry winters, the annual mean is $20.7 \, ^\circ\text{C}$ ($69.3 \, ^\circ\text{F}$) [5]. There are 4.01 million permanent residents as of 2018. As the sample of Xiamen's total population is relatively stable between 2012 and 2016, with an annual growth rate between 1.3% and 2.1%, the trend of morbidity during this period can be stipulated by the trend of the number of disease cases. Therefore, the number of HFMD outpatient visits is helpful for monitoring disease status of a city within a period.

2.2 Data Source

HFMD Outpatient Visits. The temporal variation of weekly outpatient cases from January 1, 2012 to December 31, 2016 is collected. It contains 261 weeks data pairs with mean value 113, and ranges from 2 to 435 cases. The cases were all clinical or laboratory-confirmed cases of HFMD and reported by hospital diagnostic.

Meteorological Factor (MF). MF information is provide in days, such as daily average temperature ($°C$), and daily average dew point ($°C$). Therefore, we calculate 261 weekly MF pairs by the downloaded daily records, and their correlations with the variable of HFMD cases can be figured out based on these data pairs.

Baidu Search Index (BSI). The key concern is to find proper query words, to make sure that provided indices are connected to the number of HFMD cases. The commonly used key word "手足口病" is choosed in this work. BSI engine returns daily counts of a given keyword under a given region (e.g., city, province or countrywide) and a given platform (e.g., mobile, PC, or total). Therefore, weekly data pairs are calculated by the returned 6 groups of daily indices.

2.3 Time Difference Analysis

We focus on discovering the autocorrelation of C_{hfmd} and correlations between observation variables (i.e., MF and BSI) and C_{hfmd}. The Pearson Correlation Coefficient (PCC) is adopted to measure degrees of relevance among these continuous variables. All statistical analyses are two-sided and p-value < 0.05 is considered statistically correlated.

Results of statistical analysis are carried out and listed at Table 1. The first 17 rows (from 1st row to the 2nd last row) give time difference correlations between auxiliary variables and HFMD outpatients variable under d lagged weeks. The last row gives the autocorrelation of HFMD outpatients variable under d lagged weeks. These analyses reveal that the lagging period is short, and commonly less than 1 weeks. Technically, weather conditions change 1 week before the disease happen, and people use search engines when disease is occurring or close to it. Possible reasons are: HFMD is quickly onset and its incubation period is short usually 3–5 days. These analyses give suggests of time difference settings to data decomposition and data fusion as well.

Table 1. The results of time difference relevance between variables in auxiliary data and the variable of HFMD cases. The most significant correlated value of each row is in bold type. Symbol "d" denotes the number of weeks of time difference. *: $0.01 <$ p-value < 0.05, correlation. **: p-value < 0.01, significant correlation.

Symbols	$d=0$	$d=1$	$d=2$	$d=3$	$d=4$	$d=5$	$d=6$
T_{max}	**0.4563****	0.4506**	0.4252**	0.3819**	0.3414**	0.2969**	0.234**
T_{min}	**0.4566****	0.4389**	0.3879**	0.3308**	0.2796**	0.2204**	0.1551*
T_{avg}	**0.4694****	0.4559**	0.4060**	0.3512**	0.3051**	0.2508**	0.1853**
D_{max}	0.4937**	**0.5181****	0.4847**	0.4414**	0.4000**	0.3498**	0.2955**
D_{min}	0.4531**	**0.4564****	0.3963**	0.3390**	0.2927**	0.2247**	0.1895**
D_{avg}	0.5064**	**0.5222****	0.4708**	0.4144**	0.3688**	0.3067**	0.2555**
H_{min}	0.3384**	**0.3880****	0.3142**	0.2641**	0.2279**	0.1434*	0.1492*
H_{avg}	0.2968**	**0.3942****	0.3715**	0.3485**	0.3371**	0.3022**	0.3233**
A_{max}	−0.4078**	**−0.4126****	−0.3905**	−0.3494**	−0.3131**	−0.2670**	−0.2190**
A_{min}	−0.2927**	**−0.3201****	−0.2964**	−0.2724**	−0.2825**	−0.2719**	−0.2816**
A_{avg}	−0.3862**	**−0.3969****	−0.3740**	−0.3331**	−0.3097**	−0.2728**	−0.2386**
B_{pc}	**0.5015****	0.4654**	0.4116**	0.3370**	0.2620**	0.1756**	0.0836
B_{mo}	**0.7524****	0.7095**	0.6406**	0.5537**	0.4578**	0.3653**	0.2686**
B_{total}	**0.7551****	0.7105**	0.6396**	0.5488**	0.4501**	0.3519**	0.2489**
B^1_{pc}	**0.6326****	0.5818**	0.5055**	0.4287**	0.3380**	0.2306**	0.1218
B^1_{mo}	**0.7080****	0.6607**	0.5831**	0.5057**	0.4252**	0.3451**	0.2638**
B^1_{total}	**0.7935****	0.7401**	0.6531**	0.5633**	0.4674**	0.3712**	0.2730**
C_{hfmd}	−	**0.9120****	0.7807**	0.6516**	0.5242**	0.4006**	0.2785**

The calculations of these relevant values are formulate as follows. Let $\Omega_m = \{T_{max}, T_{min}, T_{avg}, D_{max}, D_{min}, D_{avg}, H_{min}, H_{avg}, A_{max}, A_{min}, A_{avg}\}$ denote variables of MF, $\Omega_b = \{B_{pc}, B_{mo}, B_{total}, B^1_{pc}, B^1_{mo}, B^1_{total}\}$ denote variables of BSI, and $\Omega = \{\Omega_m, \Omega_b\}$ denote all auxiliary variables. We use $\Omega(1:t)$ to present t data pairs in Ω, N to denote the number of all data pairs. The correlations are formulated as:

$$Corr(\Omega, C_{hfmd}, d) = PCC(\Omega(1:N-d), C_{hfmd}(1+d:N)), s.t., d \quad >= 0;$$
$$Corr(C_{hfmd}, C_{hfmd}, d) = PCC(C_{hfmd}(1:N-d), C_{hfmd}(1+d:N)), s.t., d \quad >= 1.$$
$$(1)$$

3 TDDF and the Development for Prediction

3.1 Time Series Decomposition and Heterogenous Data Fusion (TDDF)

TDDF consists of time difference analysis, time series decomposition, and feature consolidation. For easy presentation, symbol $C_t = \{c_t\}_{t=1}^{N} \in \mathbb{R}^{N \times 1}$ is used to denote the time series of HFMD cases, symbol $\mathbf{M}_t = \{\mathbf{m}_t\}_{t=1}^{N} \in \mathbb{R}^{N \times 11}$ is adopted to describe 11 time series of MF, and symbol $\mathbf{B}_t = \{\mathbf{b}_t\}_{t=1}^{N} \in \mathbb{R}^{N \times 6}$ is employed to describe 6 time series of BSI.

Time Difference Analysis. The degree of time difference relevance is calculated according to Eq. 1, which measures the relevance between variable(s) with d weeks' lagging. The statistical analyses of variables are listed at Table 1.

Time Series Decomposition. Historical infectious disease outbreaks will affect the current status of these diseases. Based on this assumption, the next weeks' cases is formulate as:

$$c_{t+1} \leftarrow (c_{t-d_1}, c_{t-d_1+1}, \cdots, c_t) \quad s.t., \ d_1 \geq 1. \tag{2}$$

We use symbol $\mathbf{c}_{t-d_1} = \{c_i\}_{i=t-d_1}^{t} \in \mathbb{R}^{d_1 \times 1}$ to present historical HFMD cases of previous d_1 weeks. Thus, Eq. 2 is presented as:

$$c_{t+1} \leftarrow \mathbf{c}_{t-d_1} \quad s.t., \ d_1 \geq 1. \tag{3}$$

There are many signal processing methods, which decompose a time-series to extract (or represent) features. Such as, empirical mode decomposition (EMD) [13], wavelets [10], spline methods [6], and ARIMA [12]. In this study, in order to investigate advantages of the auxiliary data in improving prediction performance, we use linear transformation to process $c_t, t \in [1, N]$ and use the mean value of C_t to fill missing values.

Feature Consolidation. Moreover, let $\mathbf{m}_{t-d_2} \in \mathbb{R}^{11 \times 1}$ stand for climate factors of the $t - d_2$ period, and let $\mathbf{b}_{t-d_3} \in \mathbb{R}^{6 \times 1}$ stand for search indices of the $t - d_3$ period. The auxiliary factors are fused and formulated as:

$$c_{t+1} \leftarrow (\mathbf{c}_{t-d_1}, \mathbf{m}_{t-d_2}) \quad s.t., \ d_1 \geq 1 \ and \ d_2 \geq 0, \tag{4}$$

$$c_{t+1} \leftarrow (\mathbf{c}_{t-d_1}, \mathbf{b}_{t-d_3}) \quad s.t., \ d_1 \geq 1 \ and \ d_3 \geq 0, \tag{5}$$

$$c_{t+1} \leftarrow (\mathbf{c}_{t-d_1}, \mathbf{m}_{t-d_2}, \mathbf{b}_{t-d_3}) \quad s.t., \ d_1 \geq 1, \ and \ d_2, \ d_3 \geq 0. \tag{6}$$

Symbol $f_1, \cdots, f_4$ stand for the bridge between features and their target. Thus, we get:

$$c_{t+1} \leftarrow f_4(f_1(\mathbf{c}_{t-d_1}), f_2(\mathbf{m}_{t-d_2}), f_3(\mathbf{b}_{t-d_3})) \quad s.t., \ d_1 \geq 1 \ and \ d_2, \ d_3 \geq 0. \tag{7}$$

According to Eq. 7, abundant of models can be developed for training and prediction. The models include but not limited to neural networks, Adaboost. For better investigation of data-driven improvements and significant correlations of those variables (see Table 1), we adopt linear transformation to carry out $f_1, \cdots, f_4$.

3.2 Performance Evaluation Criteria (PEC)

To date, a variety of performance evaluation criteria (PEC) have been proposed for evaluation and intercomparision of different models, but no single evaluation index is recognized as a universal standard. Therefore, we need to evaluate prediction performance based on multiple PEC and analyze the prediction accuracy performance of different prediction models under multiple metrics.

The disease dataset was divided into two subsets: the first part, from the 1st week of 2012 to the 52nd week of 2015, was used for model training and construction, and the subsequent part, from the 1st to the 52nd week of 2016, for external validity assessment.

4 Experimental Results

4.1 Predictions on the Basis of Historical Cases

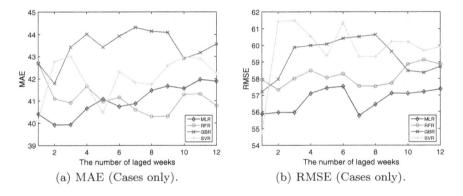

(a) MAE (Cases only).   (b) RMSE (Cases only).

Fig. 1. The performance on historical cases in terms of MAE and RMSE.

Results of predictions on the basis of historical cases (see Eq. 3) in terms of MAE and RMSE are shown in Fig. 1. To observe time-series decomposition parameter d_1 in affecting prediction, we change d_1 from 1 to 12 to measure the performance of regression algorithms. As the results shows, the predicting performance of the 4 algorithms are very unstable, which suggests that predictions on the basis of historical cases are not robust, and have potentials to be improved. When $d_1 = 1$ and $d_1 = 2$, the optimal values of MAE and RMSE are found.

4.2 Predictions Based on Historical Cases and MF

Results of predictions based on historical cases and MF (see Eq. 4) in terms of MAE and RMSE are shown in Fig. 2. To observe time-series decomposition parameter d_1 in affecting prediction, we change d_1 from 1 to 12 while holding

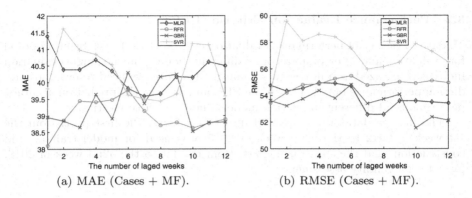

(a) MAE (Cases + MF).   (b) RMSE (Cases + MF).

Fig. 2. The performance on historical cases and MF in terms of MAE and RMSE.

$d_2 = 1$, to measure the performance of regression algorithms. As the results shows, the predicting performance of the 4 algorithms gradually become stable with respect to RMSE in Fig. 2(b), which means the training is well convergent. But the MAE is very unstable in Fig. 2(a). When $d_1 = 2$, 3, and 10, the optimal values of MAE and RMSE are found.

4.3   Predictions Based on Historical Cases and BSI

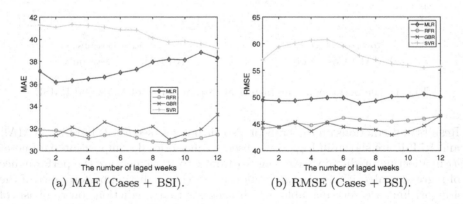

(a) MAE (Cases + BSI).   (b) RMSE (Cases + BSI).

Fig. 3. The performance on historical cases and BSI in terms of MAE and RMSE.

Results of predictions based on historical cases and BSI (see Eq. 5) in terms of MAE and RMSE are shown in Fig. 3. To observe time-series decomposition parameter d_1 in affecting prediction, we change d_1 from 1 to 12, while holding $d_3 = 0$, to measure the performance of regression algorithms. As displayed in Fig. 3(a) and (b), predictions performance become stable, GBR and RFR run better results than other two regressors. When $d_1 = 2$, 3 and 4, the optimal values of MAE and RMSE are found. It should be noted that, SVR's performance becomes worse when compared performance on previous 2 data groups. A possible reason is that few samples can not train a SVR well, either over-fitting or under-fitting.

4.4 Predictions Based on Historical Cases, BSI, and MF

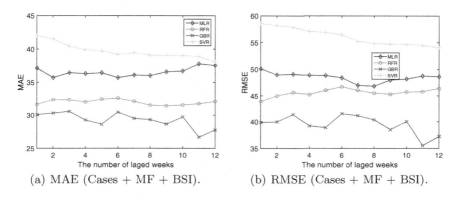

(a) MAE (Cases + MF + BSI).   (b) RMSE (Cases + MF + BSI).

Fig. 4. The performance on historical cases, MF and BSI in terms of MAE and RMSE. (Color figure online)

Results of predictions based on historical cases, MF and BSI (see Eq. 6) in terms of MAE and RMSE are shown in Fig. 4. We change d_1 from 1 to 12, while holding $d_2 = 1$ and $d_3 = 0$, to measure the performance of regression algorithms. As illustrated in Fig. 4(a) and (b), the performance is very stable for all regressors. There are obviously different on regressors: GBR has best predictions (the red line with cross sign), while SVR (the aqua line with plus sign) is worst.

Given that the number of lagged weeks is set to 2, we compare the performance of regressors over the 4 data groups in Fig. 5. The R^2 value in Fig. 5(c) validate the confidence of experimental results. The TDDF (Cases + MF + BSI) outperforms predictions based on other data groups, which shows the effectiveness of our method in heterogenous data fusion for HFMD prediction. Compare Cases with Cases + MF or Cases + BSI, it can be found that MLR, RFR, and GBR benefit from auxiliary data (MF or BSI), but SVR is slightly enhanced. A possible reason is that SVR stacks in few sample training and multiple distribution data, while decision tree based methods perform well at these occasions.

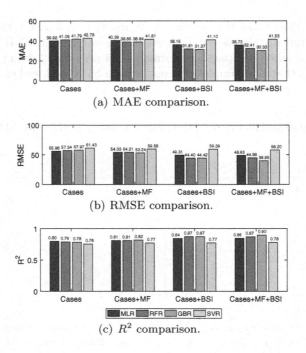

(a) MAE comparison.

(b) RMSE comparison.

(c) R^2 comparison.

Fig. 5. Comparisons of 4 algorithms on 4 data groups in terms of MAE, RMSE, R^2.

5 Conclusion

This paper contributes to the next week HFMD outpatient visits prediction in Xiamen, China. The time difference relevance analysis technique is leveraged to determine the number of lagged weeks for each related factors in meteorological data and Baidu search indices. The statistical model TDDF is proposed to fuse 3 data sources for training and predicting under general regression methods. Extensive experiments of 4 regression algorithms on 4 data groups show the effectiveness of 6 kinds of BSI data, 11 kinds of MF data in decreasing predictive errors, and TDDF in representing these auxiliary data.

The TDDF is a coarse-grained framework, and need to be further studied. One of our future work is windowed time series decomposition using signal processing methods for feature extraction, another is to develop model for windows features in order to better make prediction.

Acknowledgements. This work was supported by the Natural Science Foundation of Fujian Province of China (No. 2018J01539 and No. 2019J01713), and the Xiamen Center for Disease Control and Prevention. The authors would like to thank the editor and anonymous reviewers for their helpful comments in improving the quality of this paper.

References

1. Public Health Emergency Events Emergency Regulations. http://www.nhfpc.gov.cn/yjb/s3580/200804/b41369aac27847dba3e6aebccc72e2f8.shtml/chn (2005)
2. WHO Representative Office China. http://www.wpro.who.int/china/mediacentre/factsheets/hfmd/en/ (2008)
3. National Public Health Emergency Event Information Report and Management Regulations. http://www.nhfpc.gov.cn/mohbgt/pw10601/200804/27519.shtml/chn (2018). Accessed 1 Feb 2016
4. World Health Organization. http://www.who.int/infection-prevention/en/ (2018)
5. Xiamen from Wikipedia. https://en.wikipedia.org/wiki/Xiamen (2019)
6. Chen, S., et al.: The application of meteorological data and search index data in improving the prediction of HFMD: a study of two cities in Guangdong province, China. Sci. Total Environ. **652**, 1013–1021 (2019)
7. Ji, T., et al.: Surveillance, epidemiology, and pathogen spectrum of hand, foot, and mouth disease in mainland of china from 2008 to 2017. Biosaf. Health (2019)
8. Sun, B.J., Chen, H.J., Chen, Y., An, X.D., Zhou, B.S.: The risk factors of acquiring severe hand, foot, and mouth disease: a meta-analysis. Can. J. Infect. Dis. Med. Microbiol. **2018**, 1–12 (2018)
9. McMichael, A.J., Woodruff, R.E.: 14 - climate change and infectious diseases. In: Mayer, K.H., Pizer, H. (eds.) The Social Ecology of Infectious Diseases, pp. 378–407. Academic Press, San Diego (2008)
10. Nourani, V., Alami, M.T., Aminfar, M.H.: A combined neural-wavelet model for prediction of ligvanchai watershed precipitation. Eng. Appl. Artif. Intell. **22**(3), 466–472 (2009)
11. Ooi, M.H., et al.: Identification and validation of clinical predictors for the risk of neurological involvement in children with hand, foot, and mouth disease in sarawak. BMC Infect. Dis. **9**(1), 3 (2009)
12. Shao, Q., Yang, L.: Polynomial spline confidence bands for time series trend. J. Stat. Plann. Infer. **142**(7), 1678–1689 (2012)
13. Torres, M.E., Colominas, M.A., Schlotthauer, G., Flandrin, P.: A complete ensemble empirical mode decomposition with adaptive noise. In: 2011 IEEE International Conference on Acoustics, Speech and Signal Processing (ICASSP), pp. 4144–4147, May 2011
14. Wang, L., Jin, L., Xiong, W., Tu, W., Ye, C.: Infectious disease surveillance in china. In: Yang, W. (ed.) Early Warning for Infectious Disease Outbreak, pp. 23–33. Academic Press, San Diego (2017)
15. Wang, Y., Li, J., Gu, J., Zhou, Z., Wang, Z.: Artificial neural networks for infectious diarrhea prediction using meteorological factors in Shanghai (China). Appl. Soft Comput. **35**, 280–290 (2015)
16. Yang, S., et al.: Epidemiological features of and changes in incidence of infectious diseases in China in the first decade after the sars outbreak: an observational trend study. Lancet. Infect. Dis. **17**(7), 716–725 (2017)

Other Applications

Efficient Gaussian Distance Transforms
for Image Processing

Senjian An[(✉)], Yiwei Liu, Wanquan Liu, and Ling Li

School of Electrical Engineering, Computing and Mathematical Sciences,
Curtin University, Kent Street, Bentley, WA 6102, Australia
s.an@curtin.edu.au

Abstract. This paper presents Gaussian distance transform (GDT) of
images and demonstrates its applications to image partition and image
filtering. The time complexity of the naive implementation of GDT is
quadratic on the image size and is thus computationally intractable for
real time applications and for high resolution images. To address this
issue, we investigate the properties of GDT and show that GDT can
be conducted in linear lime using well known matrix search algorithms.
Experimental results are provided to show the applications of GDT to
image partition and image filtering.

Keywords: Gaussian Distance Transform · Distance transform ·
Image filtering · Image envelopes

1 Introduction

Distance transform (DT) [2] is a popular image processing tool with many applications such as shape analysis [7]. This paper introduces Gaussian distance transform (GDT) of images, an extension to distance transforms of sampled functions
[4] which was developed for efficient object detection. Given an $m \times n$ matrix,
GDT computes the maximum of each entry in its neighbourhood controlled by
a penalty function on the distances. Although the naive implementation takes
quadratic time ($O(m^2 n^2)$) to process images with respect to the matrix size,
we will show that GDT can be computed in linear time (i.e., $O(mn)$) for typical l^p ($1 \leq p < +\infty$) penalties. In particular, when $p = 1$ or $p = 2$, GDT
can be conducted using the lower envelope algorithm [4,5]. The computational
efficiency of the low envelope algorithm enables the well-known deformable part-
based models [3,6] computationally tractable for object detection tasks. In this
paper, we are interested in the applications of GDT to image processing tasks.
Firstly, we will present a novel algorithm which can compute GDT in linear time
for any l_p ($p > 0$) distances. Secondly, we will investigate the spatial properties
of GDT. Finally, we will use GDT and its spatial properties to design image
partition and image filtering algorithms. Furthermore, the image partitions are
determined by penalty levels of the distance. Through different levels of distance
penalties, multi-level image partitions and edge maps can be obtained clearly.

© Springer Nature Switzerland AG 2019
J. Li et al. (Eds.): ADMA 2019, LNAI 11888, pp. 671–680, 2019.
https://doi.org/10.1007/978-3-030-35231-8_49

The major contributions of this paper include the following terms: (1) a new algorithm is developed to compute GDT in linear time for any l_p $(p > 0)$ distance functions; (2) based on the spatial properties of GDT, a multi-scale image partition method is proposed; (3) a novel image filtering method is proposed for specific tasks such as bright scattered noise reduction.

The rest of this paper is organised as follows: In Sect. 2, we provide the definition of GDT and its related spatial properties. Image partition algorithms and the computation of Gaussian extremal envelopes of images are addressed in Sects. 3 and 4 respectively. Section 5 presents a new image filtering method to reduce bright scattered noise and extract dark objects, while Sect. 6 concludes the paper.

2   Gaussian Distance Transform of Images

Let I be an $m \times n$ matrix which represents the intensity values (ranging from 0 to 255 for 8 bit color representation) of an image. Let $x = (x_1, x_2), y = (y_1, y_2)$ denote two points in a 2D rectangular grid $\Omega = \{x : 1 \leq x_1 \leq m, 1 \leq x_2 \leq n\}$. Then image I can be viewed as a function from Ω to an integer set $\{0, 1, 2, \cdots, 255\}$.

The GDT of an image I is defined by

$$VT_\gamma(x) = \max_{y \in \Omega} \left\{ I(y) e^{-\gamma D_p^p(x,y)} \right\}, \tag{1}$$

$$FT_\gamma(x) = \arg\max_{y \in \Omega} \left\{ I(y) e^{-\gamma D_p^p(x,y)} \right\}, \tag{2}$$

and

$$DT_\gamma(x) = D_p\{x, FT_\gamma(x)\}. \tag{3}$$

By performing log function, we have

$$FT_\gamma(x) = \arg\max_{y \in \Omega} \left\{ \log\{I(y)\} - \gamma D_p^p(x,y) \right\}, \tag{4}$$

which is a GDT on the image $\log(I)$. This log transform will enlarge the contrast in the dark area. Note that $\log(0) = -\infty$. Generally speaking, one can conduct any pixelwise nonlinear transform (e.g. $\log(\cdot)$), on an image and get a variant of GDT. The nonlinear transform can be used for specific tasks, say, to enhance the contrast of intensity ranges around some values. In this paper we focus on Gaussian distance transform. Let $J = \log(I)$. Then we have

$$VT_\gamma(x) = \max_{y \in \Omega} \left\{ J(y) - \gamma D_p^p(x,y) \right\}, \tag{5}$$

$$FT_\gamma(x) = \arg \max_{y \in \Omega} \left\{ J(y) - \gamma D_p^p(x, y) \right\}, \tag{6}$$

and

$$DT_\gamma(x) = D_p\{x, FT_\gamma(x)\}. \tag{7}$$

where $D_p(x, y) = (|x_1 - y_1|^p + |x_2 - y_2|^p)^{1/p}$ denotes the L_p distance.

We call (6) feature transform and (7) distance transform in accordance to the conventions in the DT literature.

The optimization problem (5) was called DT of sampled functions in [4]. Here we call it Value Transform to avoid confusion with the traditional DT. So GDT includes three transforms: value transform (to the local maximum with a penalty on distance), feature transform (to the local maximizer) and distance transform (the distance from each pixel to its local maximizer). All these three terms can be obtained by solving the associated optimization problem once.

For l_1 and l_2 (i.e, $p = 1, 2$) distances, GDT can be solved in $O(mn)$ time by the lower envelope algorithm [4]. However, the lower envelope algorithm was specially designed for l_1 and l_2 distances, but does not apply to general l_p metrics when $p \neq 1, 2$. Fortunately, this can still be solved in linear time ($O(mn)$, mn is the number of pixels) by applying the well-known SMAWK algorithm [1]. The details and justification of the proposed algorithm are delegated to the appendix. Here we present the result as a Theorem.

Theorem 1. *The Gaussian distance transform of images, defined as in (5, 6, 7), can be solved in $O(mn)$ time for any image I, any $\gamma > 0$ and any l_p distance measure with $p > 1$.*

3   Image Partition with Gaussian Distance Transform

Let $V_\gamma \subset \Omega$ be the extrema set, i.e.,

$$V_\gamma = \{v = FT_\gamma(x) : x \in \Omega\}, \tag{8}$$

and let L_γ denote the number of points in V_γ and rewrite V_γ as

$$V_\gamma = \{v_i : i = 1, 2, \cdots, L_\gamma\}, \tag{9}$$

For each point v_i in V_γ, we define the patch

$$\Omega_\gamma^{(i)} = \{x : FT_\gamma(x) = v_i\}. \tag{10}$$

Then we have

$$\begin{aligned} \Omega_\gamma^{(i)} \cap \Omega_\gamma^{(j)} &= \emptyset \\ \bigcup_i \Omega_\gamma^{(i)} &= \Omega. \end{aligned} \tag{11}$$

That is, all the patches $\Omega_\gamma^{(i)}$ form a disjoint partition of the whole image.

To give an example, let $0 < \gamma_1 < \gamma_2 < \gamma_3$ be three positive numbers. Then we have

$$
\begin{aligned}
V_{\gamma_1} &= V_1 \\
V_{\gamma_2} &= V_1 \bigcup V_2 \\
V_{\gamma_3} &= V_1 \bigcup V_2 \bigcup V_3 \\
\Omega &= \bigcup_{i=1}^{n_1} \Omega_{\gamma_1}^{(i)} \\
&= \left(\bigcup_{i=1}^{n_1} \Omega_{\gamma_2}^{(i)} \right) \cup \left(\bigcup_{i=n_1+1}^{n_2} \Omega_{\gamma_2}^{(i)} \right) \\
&= \left(\bigcup_{i=1}^{n_1} \Omega_{\gamma_3}^{(i)} \right) \cup \left(\bigcup_{i=n_1+1}^{n_2} \Omega_{\gamma_3}^{(i)} \right) \cup \left(\bigcup_{i=n_2+1}^{n_3} \Omega_{\gamma_3}^{(i)} \right).
\end{aligned}
\tag{12}
$$

It can be seen that: with $\gamma = \gamma_1$, the image is partitioned into n_1 patches. With a larger $\gamma = \gamma_2$, the original n_1 patches shrinks $\Omega_{\gamma_2}^{(i)} \subset \Omega_{\gamma_1}^{(i)}$ and we have more patches. The whole image is partitioned into $n_2(\geq n_1)$ regions.

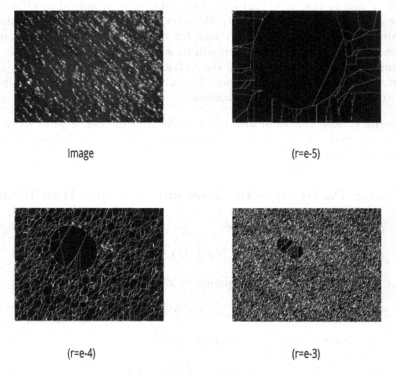

Image   (r=e-5)

(r=e-4)   (r=e-3)

Fig. 1. Multi-scale image partition. White lines are used to show the patch boundaries.

Figure 1 demonstrates an example of multi-level image partition where white lines are used to show the patch boundaries. This partition is based on GDT of the inverse image $((I + \epsilon)^{-1})$, where ϵ is a small number, and the inverse of an image is defined as an image whose intensity at each pixel is the inverse of the intensity at the corresponding pixel of the original image, i.e. $[I^{-1}](i,j) = [I(i,j)]^{-1}$. This transform finds the lower envelop of the image and GDT is used so that the contrast of the dark area is enhanced and the object shark can be found clearly.

From Fig. 1, one can see that the patches are getting smaller with increasing distance penalty level γ. When $\gamma = 0.001$, all the other patches except those around the shark are very small. By setting a threshold on the patch size, one can extract most part of the shark image. However, the boundary of the patches are not tight with the shark boundaries. For a nice foreground/background segmentation, one needs to apply graph cut algorithm with these detected patches as the initial rough guess of the object area.

We can measure the size of the patch by the radius of the patch which is defined as the largest distance of the vertex to its members, that is,

$$r_i = \max\{DT(x) : x \in \Omega_i\}. \tag{13}$$

A large r_i indicates a high contrast and a smooth down area within the patch. Investigate the smoothness of the farthest point in the patch. On the contrary, a small r_i indicates a smooth area around the vertices or a high frequency oscillation.

4 Gaussian Extremal Envelopes of Images

Similar to the extremal envelopes proposed in [8], Gaussian extremal envelopes seek to find a top surface and a bottom surface to bound the image like a sandwich, but in a much more efficient way. The proposed method compute the local extrema and extremal envelop altogether.

Given an $m \times n$ image I, the Gaussian upper envelope of I is defined as

$$\overline{I}(x) = \max_{y \in \Omega} I(y)e^{-D_p(x,y)}. \tag{14}$$

Similarly, the Gaussian lower envelope of I is defined as

$$\underline{I}(x) = \min_{y \in \Omega} I(y)e^{D_p(x,y)}. \tag{15}$$

Let $g(x) = \overline{I}(x) - \underline{I}(x)$ be the gap between the upper and lower envelopes. Let $A(x) = (\overline{I}(x) - \underline{I}(x))/2$ be the average of the two envelopes. The smoothed image is defined by

$$S(x) = \lambda(x)A(x) + (1 - \lambda(x))I(x), \tag{16}$$

where

$$\lambda(x) = e^{-g(x)/(2\sigma^2)}$$

is used to control the smoothing within small variations. When the gap is too large, the envelopes will not fit the image closely and the estimation of the pixel values by averaging the two envelopes is not reliable.

Input Image   Gap Image

Lower Envelope   Upper Envelope

Fig. 2. Gaussian envelopes of images.

5   Downward Image Filtering for Bright Noise Reduction

For downward image filtering, we conduct GDT on the inverse of the image and obtain a lower envelope of the image. Then we push the small patches to their lower envelope values and keep the large size patches unchanged. This can filter bright scattered noises such as the sunlight reflection of waves in the water. One can repeat this procedure by using several different values of γ with increasing order. Note that large patch relates to large scale edges (which are usually the object boundaries). However, the bright scattered noise which are very close to the objects can not be removed without blurring the object area. The very few remaining scattered noise can be removed by row-wise and column-wise median filters which replace the pixel value by the median value of the pixels in its row and column. Figure 3 shows how downward image filtering can be used to remove sun-reflections and make the object more clear.

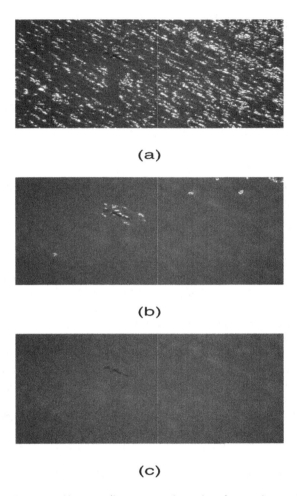

(a)

(b)

(c)

Fig. 3. Downward image filtering (best viewed in the electronic version). (a). Input image; (b). Filtered image with downward filter; (c). Filtered image with downward filter followed by cross median filter.

6   Conclusions

Using matrix search algorithms, a new algorithm is developed to compute Gaussian Distance transforms of images in linear time for any l_p $(p > 1)$ distance functions. Based on the spatial properties of Gaussian Distance transform, a multiscale image partition method is proposed and a novel image filtering method is proposed to remove bright scattered noise and make the dark object clear.

Acknowledgement. This work was supported by a Faculty of Science and Engineering Research and Development Committee Small Grants Program of Curtin University.

Appendix: Proof of Theorem 1

Consider the optimization problem (5)

$$
\begin{aligned}
VT_\gamma(x) &= \max_{y \in \Omega}\{J(y) - \gamma D_p^p(x,y)\} \\
&= \max_{y_1,y_2}\{J(y_1,y_2) - \gamma|x_1 - y_1|^p - \gamma|x_2 - y_2|^p\} \\
&= \max_{1 \le y_1 \le m}\{J(y_1,x_2) - \gamma|x_1 - y_1|^p\} \\
J(y_1,x_2) &\triangleq \max_{1 \le y_2 \le n}\{J(y_1,y_2) - \gamma|x_2 - y_2|^p\}.
\end{aligned}
\tag{17}
$$

The core problem is the following 1D grid optimization with a given sequence $f(i)$ with length l.

$$
g(j) = \max_{1 \le i \le l}\{f(i) - \gamma|j - i|^p\}, 1 \le j \le l.
\tag{18}
$$

Later we will show that this sequence transform problem can be solved in $O(l)$ time. The matrix J can be obtained by calling the sequence transform (18) m times, for $y_1 = 1, 2, \cdots m$, each time setting $f(i) = J(y_1,i)$ where $i = 1, 2, \cdots, n$. This procedure takes $O(mn)$ time. Then based on J, the matrix VT_γ can be obtained by calling (18) n times, for $x_2 = 1, 2, \cdots, n$, each time setting $f(i) = J(i,x_2)$ where $i = 1, 2, \cdots, m$. This procedure takes $O(mn)$ time. So the total time complexity is linear in terms of the matrix size.

Now we show the sequence transform (18) can be solved in linear time. First we prove that this problem is related to a well-known matrix search problem in combinational optimization.

A matrix A is called a *Monge Matrix* if it satisfies the so-called *Monge Property*

$$
A[i,j] + A[k,l] \le A[i,l] + A[k,j], \forall i < k, j < l.
\tag{19}
$$

A is called *Inverse Monge Matrix* if the above the inequalities hold in the reverse directions, i.e.,

$$
A[i,j] + A[k,l] \ge A[i,l] + A[k,j], \forall i < k, j < l.
\tag{20}
$$

An handy property of Monge matrices for us to check its Monge property is that the Monge property (or inverse Monge property) holds if and only if it holds for adjacent rows and adjacent columns, that is, it suffices to check

$$
A[i,j] + A[i+1,j+1] \le A[i,j+1] + A[i+1,j], \forall i, j
\tag{21}
$$

for Monge property, or

$$
A[i,j] + A[i+1,j+1] \ge A[i,j+1] + A[i+1,j], \forall i, j
\tag{22}
$$

for inverse Monge property.

Another property of inverse Monge matrices is that inverse Monge matrices are totally monotone matrices and its row maxima can be found in $O(n + m)$ time by SMAWK algorithm [1]. Note that reversing the order of its rows turns a Monge matrix into an inverse Monge matrix. And therefore, the row maxima of a Monge matrix can also be found in linear time by SMAWK algorithm.

Next, we show that the sequence transform (18) is equivalent to a Monge matrix search problem. Define

$$A(i,j) = f(j) - \gamma |i - j|^p, \qquad (23)$$

then we have

Lemma 2. *Let A be defined as in (23). Then A is an inverse Monge matrix if $p \geq 1$.*

Proof: Let

$$
\begin{aligned}
\delta &\triangleq \{A(i,j) + A(i+1, j+1)\} \\
&\quad -\{A(i, j+1) + A(i+1, j)\} \\
&= |i - j - 1|^p + |i + 1 - j|^p - 2|i - j|^p.
\end{aligned} \qquad (24)
$$

To prove the inverse Monge property of A, it suffices to show $\delta \geq 0$.

When $i = j$, then $\delta = 2 > 0$. Now assume that $i \neq j$ and let $s \triangleq |i - j|$. Note that $s \geq 1$. Then $\delta = (s + 1)^p + (s - 1)^p - 2s^p$. Now let $t = \frac{1}{s}$ and $\xi(t) = \delta/(s^c) = (1+t)^p + (1-t)^p - 2$. Note that $t \in (0, 1]$ and $\text{sign}(\delta) = \text{sign}(\xi)$. Consider the derivative of $\xi(t)$

$$
\begin{aligned}
\xi'(t) &= (p-1)(1+t)^{p-1} - (p-1)(1-t)^{p-1} \\
&= (p-1)\{(1+t)^{p-1} - (1-t)^{p-1}\} \\
&\geq 0, \forall t \in [0, 1].
\end{aligned} \qquad (25)
$$

Note that $\xi(0) = 0$ and $\xi(t)$ is a non-decreasing function in $[0, 1]$. Therefore $\xi(t) \geq 0$ for any $t \in [0, 1]$ and $\delta \geq 0$. So A is an inverse Monge matrix.
□

Lemma 3. *Let A be defined as in (23) except that all diagonals $A(i,i)$ are defined as $-\infty$. Then A is a Monge matrix.*

Proof: Let

$$
\begin{aligned}
\delta &\triangleq \{A(i,j) + A(i+1, j+1)\} \\
&\quad -\{A(i, j+1) + A(i+1, j)\} \\
&= |i - j - 1|^p + |i + 1 - j|^p - 2|i - j|^p.
\end{aligned} \qquad (26)
$$

To prove the Monge property of A, it suffices to show that $\delta \leq 0$.

When $i = j$, $\delta < 0$ since the diagonals are $-\infty$. Now assume that $i \neq j$ and let $s \triangleq |i - j|$. Note that $s \geq 1$. Then $\delta = (s + 1)^p + (s - 1)^p - 2s^p$. Now let $t = \frac{1}{s}$ and $\xi(t) = \delta/(s^p) = (1+t)^p + (1-t)^p - 2$. Note that $t \in (0, 1]$ and $\text{sign}(\delta) = \text{sign}(\xi)$. Consider the derivative of $\xi(t)$

$$
\begin{aligned}
\xi'(t) &= (p-1)(1+t)^{p-1} - (p-1)(1-t)^{p-1} \\
&= (p-1)\{(1+t)^{p-1} - (1-t)^{p-1}\} \\
&\leq 0, \forall t \in [0, 1].
\end{aligned} \qquad (27)
$$

Note that $\xi(0) = 0$ and, when $p \in [0,1]$, $\xi(t)$ is a non-increasing function in $[0,1]$. Therefore $\xi(t) \leq 0$ for any $t \in [0,1]$ and thus $\delta \leq 0$ which implies that A is a Monge matrix.

In summary, the 1D sequence transform problem is equivalent to a Monge matrix search problem which can be solved in linear time, and therefore concluding the proof of Theorem 1.

$\square$

References

1. Aggarwal, A., Klawe, M.M., Moran, S., Shor, P., Wilber, R.: Geometric applications of a matrix-searching algorithm. Algorithmica **60**(2), 195–208 (1987)
2. Fabbri, R., Costa, L.D.F., Torelli, J.C., Bruno, O.M.: 2D euclidean distance transform algorithms: a comparative survey. ACM Comput. Surv. (CSUR) **40**(1), 2 (2008)
3. Felzenszwalb, P., Girshick, R., McAllester, D., Ramanan, D.: Object detection with discriminatively trained part based models. IEEE Trans. Pattern Anal. Mach. Intell. **32**(9), 1627–1645 (2010)
4. Felzenszwalb, P., Huttenlocher, D.: Distance transforms of sampled functions. Technical Report TR2004-1963, Conell Computing and Information Science (2004)
5. Meijster, A., Roerdink, J.B., Hesselink, W.H.: A general algorithm for computing distance transforms in linear time. In: Goutsias, J., Vincent, L., Bloomberg, D.S. (eds.) Mathematical Morphology and Its Applications to Image and Signal Processing, pp. 331–340. Springer, Boston (2002)
6. Pandey, M., Lazebnik, S.: Scene recognition and weakly supervised object localization with deformable part-based models. In: 2011 International Conference on Computer Vision, pp. 1307–1314. IEEE (2011)
7. Ribas, L.C., Neiva, M.B., Bruno, O.M.: Distance transform network for shape analysis. Inf. Sci. **470**, 28–42 (2019)
8. Subr, K., Soler, C., Durand, F.: Edge-preserving multiscale image decomposition based on local extrema. In: ACM Transactions on Graphics (TOG), vol. 28, p. 147. ACM (2009)

Tourist's Tour Prediction by Sequential Data Mining Approach

Lilia Ben Baccar$^{(\boxtimes)}$, Sonia Djebali$^{(\boxtimes)}$, and Guillaume Guérard$^{(\boxtimes)}$

De Vinci Research Center, Pôle Universitaire Léonard De Vinci,
Paris – La Défense, France
`lilia.ben_baccar@edu.devinci.fr`,
{`sonia.djebali,guillaume.guerard`}`@devinci.fr`

Abstract. This paper answers the problem of predicting future behaviour tourist based on past behaviour of an individual tourist. The individual behaviour is naturally an indicator of the behaviour of other tourists. The prediction of tourists movement has a crucial role in tourism marketing to create demand and assist tourists in decision-making. With advances in information and communication technology, social media platforms generate data from millions of people from different countries during their travel. The main objective of this paper is to consider sequential data-mining methods to predict tourist movement based on Instagram data. Rules emerge from those ones are exploited to predict future behaviors. The originality of this approach is a combination between pattern mining to reduce the size of data and the automata to condense the rules. The capital city of France, Paris is selected to demonstrate the utility of the proposed methodology.

Keywords: Sequential pattern mining · Sequential rule mining · Sequence prediction · Big data · Social network · Tourism

1 Introduction

Nowadays, tourism is one of the most prominent areas for the economy in the world. The tourism industry is considered as one of the largest and fastest growing industries [5]. International tourism currently accounts for 7% of world exports of goods with an estimation of $1500 billion of profit earned. The aggregate number of tourists arriving in the world rose from nearly 25 million in 1950 to more than 1.323 billion in 2017 according to the *World Tourism Organization* UNWTO[1]. The prediction of travel behaviour and knowledge of travel motivation play a key part in tourism marketing to create demand and assist tourists in decision-making [14].

Tourism has benefited from the social networks like TripAdvisor, Booking, Facebook, Instagram, etc. Thanks to the increasing number of digital tools, new behaviors have emerged. When photos are add on the web, geographical

---

[1] World Tourism Organization UNWTO. *UNWTO Tourism Highlights: 2018 Edition.*

© Springer Nature Switzerland AG 2019
J. Li et al. (Eds.): ADMA 2019, LNAI 11888, pp. 681–695, 2019.
https://doi.org/10.1007/978-3-030-35231-8_50

information are included. Images and photos represent a tourism and sociological view [2,3].

In this current economic context, being able to anticipate tourist behaviors represents a key asset for the actors of tourism field. The tourism industry must adapt to these new customs, take advantage of them and improve experiences by relevant offers. To answer this issue, many studies have been launched, especially on the analysis of these sharing tools on the internet [4,13]. They face big data's challenges, i.e. enormous volume and heterogeneous data. They purpose two ways to predict a trip: first approach considers some keys locations given by the users to establish a route (also called tour planner); second approach computes behaviors based on the patterns recognized inside the data [12,17–19].

Based on geo-located and time-related information of photographs on Instagram, we propose in this paper an original approach to determine behaviors of tourists by analyzing sequences of places visited during a trip by each tourist. This approach is based on data mining, especially sequential pattern and rule mining. The main idea is to find the most common places and the most reliable route taken by tourists.

The main idea of this study is to determine behaviors of many sets of tourists. Tourist movements may vary in function of its country of origin, age, sex and social class. Since any specific dataset will get their prediction machine, it is easy to compare behaviors between the different set of population. To predict behavior for a specific tourist, one use a suitable dataset to understand its behaviors. In the purpose of this paper, only a dataset established on the country of origin will be used. All the sources are in the GitHub[2].

The paper is organized as follows. Section 2 presents definitions about tourism and how to generate all trips from the Instagram data. Section 3 presents sequential data mining algorithms and how to perform predictions from the results. Section 4 is about the case study while the section Our approach presents the results and future works. Finally, the Sect. 6 concludes this paper.

2   Instagram and Tourism

This section presents the creation of tourist trips thanks to the data on Instagram. Several key points must be clarified:

- From where come the dataset?
- How to define a tourist?
- How to define the country of origin of a tourist?
- How to create tourist trips from the dataset?

2.1   Data

The dataset comes from the photo-sharing website Instagram[3]. In 2017, there were, according to the *BlogDuModerateur*[4] more than 800 million regular active

---

[2] https://github.com/lbenbaccar/SequentialDataMiningforTourism.
[3] https://instagram.com.
[4] https://www.blogdumoderateur.com/chiffres-instagram.

users and more than 500 million of daily users; 95 million photos and videos are posted each day. Instagram is interesting to understand tourism behaviours.

There is a significant correlation between the most visited tourist places in the world and places photographed by Instagrammers. Travelers left digital traces through photos. Those ones contain various metadata as following: idImage, date, location (longitude, latitude), geotag, name of the photo, idUser. All the information of photos on a specific tourism site characterize the satisfaction of tourists about this place; hence their behaviors.

A user is described by his timeline, a representation of a chronological sequence of events (past or future). It defines his route since his first photo posted on the site to the last one. This timeline allows computing intermediate properties: travel time at a destination, number of trips, number of visited countries.

2.2   Tourist

The World Tourism Organization (UNWTO) defines tourism as follows:

> The activities that people undertake during their travels and their trips in places outside their usual environment for a consecutive period not exceeding one year from recreational, business and other purposes.

The term *activities* should be understood here in a general sense of individual occupations.

This study is based on international travelers, i.e. travelers whose country of residence is different from the visited country. All the following kinds of tourism are taken into account:

- International visitors as non-resident visitors transiting (two consecutive nights at most) only for the purpose of traveling to or from another country.
- International day-trippers as non-resident visitors who do not spend a night.
- International tourists as non-resident visitors spending at least one night (and less than one year).

The Instagram data do not allow access to the nationality of a user, this information is not requested at registration. One cannot, at first glance, make a difference between non-resident/foreign tourists and locals. To understand if the user is a foreigner or a local inhabitant, it is worthwhile to known its origin. Since its a lack of information in Instagram metadata, Da Rugna et al. [6] introduce a new paradigm to estimate user's country of residence: one can consider the country of origin of a user is defined by where he stayed the most.

2.3   Tourist Trip

Since the country of origin is obtained, the trip must be defined. A method to generate trips from Instagram's dataset has been implemented.

A trip is a succession of days when a non-resident tourist takes at least one photo per day, i.e. as soon as there is a day when the tourist does not take pictures the trip is considered broken. However, a tourist may not capture pictures during a limited period during the same trip. The break can be canceled between two trips that took place in the similar country by a user. The method consists of merging two trips if they satisfy the following conditions:

$$\Delta B \leqslant \Delta T_i \text{ and } \Delta B \leqslant \Delta T_j \text{ and } L_{T_i} = F_{T_j}$$

with the following variables:

- ΔB: break duration.
- ΔT_i: i^{th} trip duration.
- ΔT_j: j^{th} trip duration.
- L_{T_i}: last country visited during i^{th} trip.
- F_{T_j}: first country visited during j^{th} trip.

The Fig. 1 presents an example of merge two trips **Trip-1** and **Trip-2**.

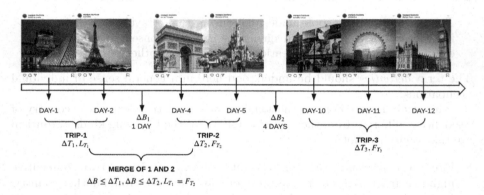

Fig. 1. Example of merge two trips.

From a timeline of a user, several trips are defined as well as the nationality of this user. Each trip is represented by a list of places that the tourist has visited during his trip. Each place corresponds to a photo collected from the timeline, and these places are ordered temporally in a *sequence*. The Table 1 presents the sequences database where each sequence is a trip made by a tourist. For example, the ID_user 2 starts its trip by visiting *Notre-Dame de Paris*, then the *Tour Eiffel* following by the *Arc de Triomphe*, and finishes with the *Louvre's museum*.

3   Our Approach

As explained, the dataset is a set of sequences composed of places in chronological order of appearance on user's timeline, therefore in the order of the trip. The

Table 1. Sequence database example

ID_user	Sequence (trip)
1	Tour Eiffel, Louvre, Sacré Coeur
2	Notre-Dame de Paris, Tour Eiffel, Arc de Triomphe, Louvre
3	Fouquet's, Champs Elysées, Les Halles, Musée d'Orsay
4	Louvre, Pizza Pino, Champs Elysées, Tour Eiffel
5	Champs Elysées, Adagio Hotel, Tour Eiffel
6	Sacré Coeur, Publicis Drugstore, Adidas, Tuileries

purpose of this paper is to use the sequences to understand tourism behaviors. These ones will be exploited to predict future behaviors based on similar data like the beginning of a trip and the knowledge of the country of origin of a tourist.

The proposed approach is composed of three steps as resumed in the Fig. 2:

- DATA PROCESSING: first at all, trips are defined as sequences as explained.
- SEQUENTIAL DATA MINING: secondly, the sequences are analyzed to defined preferences and rules between places thanks to sequential pattern mining algorithms.
- SEQUENCES PREDICTION: in conclusion, those criteria are exploited to predict future behaviors.

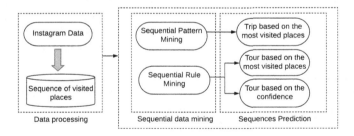

Fig. 2. Our approach steps

3.1 Sequential Pattern Mining

As Viger [9] and Soulet [16] say the task of sequential pattern mining (SPM) is specialized for analyzing sequential data, to discover sequential patterns into, as accurate as possible, a prediction automaton. It detects global trends and local trends which are measured in terms of various criteria like its occurrence, frequency and length.

Two types of descriptive pattern mining methods have been implemented to extract subsequences that appear frequently in the sequence database: *constraint-based* and *preference-based pattern mining.*

Constraint-based pattern mining [21] is designed to extract all the patterns that satisfy a boolean predicate as interestingness criterion. Most often this predicate, called constraint, requires an interestingness measure exceeds a given threshold. The challenge is to achieve an adequate and relevant enumeration despite the huge size of the search space and the complexity of the constraint.

Constraint-based pattern mining algorithms suffer from several issues. Therefore, it is challenging to define its interestingness measure. To be specific, the choice of thresholds may vary in function of the dataset. Sometimes the number of mined patterns is far beyond the size of the original dataset because the size of the language exponentially grows with the number of items. It is then impossible for the user to explore and analyze this collection of patterns.

Preference-based pattern mining [21] is designed to extract the most preferred patterns. This notion of preference relies on a binary relation between patterns specified by the user. For instance, a pattern will be preferred over another if its value for a measure is more significant.

Preference-based pattern mining enjoys many advantages. It reduces the number of mined patterns and focuses on the most preferred patterns. However, although end users no longer have to set a thresholds, it remains problematic to explicitly formulate their preferences.

Several algorithms have been implemented and compared to define the most suitable one to the dataset. Three well-known algorithms are constraint-based: PrefixSpan [15], SPADE [20] and SPAM [1].

The Prefixspan algorithm [15] first scans the database to find the frequent 1-sequences. After that, this algorithm generates the projected database for each frequent 1-sequence. In this way, the Prefixspan algorithm recursively generates the projected database for each frequent k-sequence to find frequent $(k + 1)$-sequences.

PrefixSpan performs better in large sequences; SPADE has a fast discovery patterns; SPAM is better than SPADE in small dataset and better than PrefixSpan in large dataset. Given a particular input, these three algorithms will always produce the same output.

The PrefixSpan algorithm is chosen among the constraint-based methods because it's the best algorithm in terms of memory usage as shown in Table 2 for 3000 explored sequences. Since the dataset is quite small with few similar patterns, PrefixSpan outperforms the more sophisticated algorithms. Indeed, memory management remains a key point of this study when one analyses a dataset.

For preference-based, Viger et al. [7] proposed TKS which uses a vertical bitmap database representation as SPAM and the same candidate generation procedure. It executes several strategies to prune the search space and rely on a data structure named *PMAP* for avoiding costly bit vector intersection operations.

Table 2. SPM algorithms statistics.   **Table 3.** SRM algorithms statistics.

Algorithm	Statistics	
	Runtime	*Max memory*
Minsup = 5%		
PrefixSpan	≈ 66 ms	≈ 2.61 mb
CMSpade	≈ 24 ms	≈ 7.81 mb
CMSpam	≈ 45 ms	≈ 9.77 mb
Preference-based: k = 30		
TKS	≈ 20 ms	≈ 16.93 mb

Algorithm	Statistics	
	Runtime	*Max memory*
Minsup = 1% and minconf = 10%		
RuleGrowth	≈ 22 ms	≈ 13.67 mb
ERMiner	≈ 63 ms	≈ 12.37 mb
Preference-based: k = 30 and minconf = 20%		
TNS	≈ 53 ms	≈ 24.74 mb

3.2   Sequential Rule Mining

Sequential patterns can be misleading. An important limitation of sequential patterns is that there is no assessment of probability that a pattern will be followed. Sequential patterns only indicate how often the pattern appears. They do not provide any indication about the probability of appearance of a pattern following another one. Sequential rule mining (SRM) has been proposed as an alternative to sequential pattern mining to take into account this probability.

A sequential rule is a rule of the form $X \longrightarrow Y$ where X and Y are sets of items (itemsets). A rule $X \longrightarrow Y$ is interpreted as if items in X occurs (in any order), then it will be followed by the items in Y (in any order). To determine sequential rules, two measures are predominantly employed: *support* and *confidence*. The support of a rule $X \longrightarrow Y$ is how many sequences contains the items from X followed by the items from Y, sometimes it is divided by cardinality of the dataset. The confidence of a rule $X \longrightarrow Y$ is the support of the rule divided by the number of sequences containing the items from X.

For constraint-based sequential rule mining algorithms, the following two algorithms have been compared: RuleGrowth and ERMiner. Viger et al. [10] proposed RuleGrowth using the same pattern-growth approach as PrefixSpan. A drawback of RuleGrowth is it repeatedly performs a costly database projection operation, which deteriorates performance for datasets containing dense or long sequences. Viger et al. [8] proposed ERMiner (Equivalence class based sequential Rule Miner) for mining sequential rules, faster than RuleGrowth thanks to a data structure named SCM (Sparse Count Matrix) to prune the search space. However, it generally consumes more memory, so there is a trade-off. The Rule-Growth algorithm has been selected for its performance as shown in Table 3 for 3000 explored sequences.

Constraint-based algorithms can become very slow and generate an extremely large amount of results or generate too few results, omitting valuable information, Viger et al. [11] addressed both of these problems by proposing an preference-based sequential rule mining algorithm named TNS for mining Top-k Non redundant Sequential rules.

3.3   Sequence Prediction

Sequence prediction consists of guessing the next symbols of a sequence based on the previously observed symbols. For example, if a user has visited some places A, B, C, in that order, one may want to predict what is the next places that will be visited by that user.

In this study, three kinds of prediction are operated:

1. To build a trip in function of the most visited places: this prediction presents to the visitor a trip with the most notable locations to visit in a city.
2. To build a tour in function of the most visited places: this prediction presents a sequence of notable locations to visit in a city
3. To build a tour in function of the confidence: this prediction presents a sequence of locations based on the most used city circuits

(1) The first prediction only uses the support since it only gives a set of the most visited locations. This prediction use the SPM constraint-based or preference-based results.
(2) For the second prediction, rules are modeled into an automaton. Each rule is represented as a couple of states where the link contains the symbol of the destination. An initial state linked to all others is added to simplify reading of the sequence. To predict from this automaton, the first steps of the trip is heretofore identified (an empty trip is also possible). To product a prediction, a suffix of any length is created. If a destination has been already visited/picked, it cannot be in the suffix. The second prediction used the SRM constraint-based results.
(3) The last method is a prediction tool which generates a more complete set of results. Based on a probabilistic (but not stochastic) automaton, this prediction not only gives a tour but also the percent of people which may followed this route even if it is an unknown route in the dataset. For this method, the automaton not only includes the symbol of the destination of the rule; it also takes into account the probability of this rule associated with the predecessor, i.e. the confidence. When a tour is build in the automaton, its confidence is computed by multiplying all the confidences of the used rules. That is why having the top k rules ordered by confidence can improve the ultimate value of the tour. The third prediction combines the SRM constraint-based and preference-based results.

To validate the two last method, a metric called **conviction** is used. For a rule $A \longrightarrow B$, conviction can be interpreted as the ratio of the expected frequency that A occurs without B, i.e. an incorrect prediction. Conviction is computed as follows $\frac{1-support(B)}{1-confidence(A \longrightarrow B)}$. Only the conviction of the last rule of the prediction is calculated.

4   Case Study

In this paper, Paris, France, is selected as a case study because it is one of the most tourist-frequented cities in France. Geo-tagged photos are displayed as a density map shown in Fig. 3, with colour brightness representing Instagram photos density (the brighter, the higher density).

Fig. 3. The Paris study area and geotagged Instagram data (Color figure online)

The proposed approach has been concretely experimented with data from Instagram concerning Paris between January 1, 2011, and December 31, 2015. This includes 8 774 users from 114 different nationalities, and 11 645 trips. The Table 4 shows the seven most frequent nationalities in the dataset, i.e. countries for which we have the most trips generated.

Russians tourists are selected among all nationalities since they provide a comparatively large number of trips in Paris with a more prolonged average duration than the other countries. The Table 5 presents the number of trip of Russian in Paris, average number of photos per trip and the best month based on the number of trips between 2011 and 2015.

Table 4. Number of trips in Paris per country

Country	USA	UK	Italy	Russia	Brazil	Spain	Australia
Trips	3 064	1 423	923	742	606	464	330
Average trip duration (days)	≈ 2.64	≈ 2.32	≈ 2.65	≈ 2.91	≈ 2.85	≈ 2.56	≈ 2.77
Average number of photos/trip	≈ 3.76	≈ 3.86	≈ 4.30	≈ 4.87	≈ 4.02	≈ 4.03	≈ 3.70

5   Results

SPM and SRM Results

The Table 6 presents the support of the main locations in Paris. One can observe that the *Tour Eiffel* is in 30.66% of all the trips. This kind of information is valuable to interpret the behaviors of the mass.

Some patterns include several locations as *Louvre's Museum (Musée du Louvre in french)* and *Eiffel Tower*. The latter means that the two places are seen in the same trip in 5.39% of all trips. Since constraint-based and preference-based algorithms are deterministic and analyze the whole dataset, the result are similar. A minor difference is the number of results. Indeed, one kind of algorithm gives all the patterns which verify a constraint while the other one gives the top k patterns among all. For the top 30, the lowest support is equal to 1.8%.

Table 5. Case study: statistics for Russian in Paris

Number of trips		742 trips
Average length of trips		≈ 3 days
Average number of photos per trip		≈ 5 photos
Year	Number of trips in	Best month
2011	1 trip	September (1 trip)
2012	50 trips	September (10 trips)
2013	114 trips	January (15 trips)
2014	253 trips	October (36 trips)
2015	324 trips	September (35 trips)

Table 6. Case study Russia: SPM constraint-based algorithms results

Results: minsup = 5%	
Patterns	*Support*
<Tour Eiffel>	30.66%
<Musée du Louvre>	25.83%
<Cathédrale Notre-Dame de Paris>	16.16%
<Avenue des Champs Elysées>	14.09%
<Sacré-Coeur>	11.89%
<Centre Pompidou (CNAC)>	8.01%
<Jardin du Luxembourg>	6.63%
<Galeries Lafayette>	6.08%
<Musée du Louvre, Tour Eiffel>	5.39%
<Montmartre>	5.39 %

Table 7. Case study Russia: SRM constraint-based algorithms results

Results: minsup = 1% and minconf = 15%		
Rules	*Support*	*Confidence*
Cathédrale Notre-Dame de Paris ⟶ Musée du Louvre	3.59%	22.22%
Musée du Louvre ⟶ Tour Eiffel	5.39%	20.86%
Cathédrale Notre-Dame de Paris ⟶ Tour Eiffel	3.18%	19.66%
Centre Pompidou (CNAC) ⟶ Musée du Louvre	1.52%	18.97%
Tour Eiffel, Musée du Louvre ⟶ Cathédrale Notre-Dame de Paris	1.80%	18.57%
Centre Pompidou (CNAC) ⟶ Tour Eiffel	1.38%	17.24%
Tour Eiffel ⟶ Musée du Louvre	4.97%	16.22%
Tour Eiffel ⟶ Cathédrale Notre-Dame de Paris	4.83%	15.77%
Sacré-Coeur ⟶ Tour Eiffel	1.80%	15.15%
Tour Eiffel, Cathédrale Notre-Dame de Paris ⟶ Musée du Louvre	1.11%	15.09%

The two Tables 7 and 8 presents the results of SRM constraint-based and preference-based algorithms. The rule *Notre-Dame* ⟶ *Louvre*'s museum have a support of 3.59% which means that 3.59% of all the trips contain this transition. The confidence provides the number of trips which spend time at *Notre-Dame* then at *Louvre*'s museum, in this case 22.22%. This kind of information is valuable to predict the following location of a trip.

Table 8. Case study Russia: SRM preference-based algorithms results

Results: k = 15 and minconf = 33%		
Rules	*Support*	*Confidence*
Galerie Emmanuel Perrotin ⟶ Palais de Tokyo - Musée d'Art Moderne, Louis Vuitton Foundation for Creation	0.41%	100%
Colette ⟶ Tour Eiffel	0.55%	66.66%
Tour Eiffel, Musée du Louvre, Centre Pompidou (CNAC) ⟶ Cathédrale Notre-Dame de Paris	0.69%	41.67%
Musée du Louvre, Galeries Lafayette ⟶ Tour Eiffel	0.55%	36.36%
Ladurée ⟶ Avenue des Champs Elysées	0.97%	33.33%
Musée du Louvre, Centre Pompidou (CNAC) ⟶ Tour Eiffel	0.97%	33.33%
L'Avenue ⟶ Avenue des Champs Elysées	0.41%	33.33%
Trocadéro ⟶ Sacré-Coeur, Jardin du Luxembourg	0.41%	33.33%
L'Avenue ⟶ Avenue Montaigne	0.41%	33.33%
Shangri-La Hotel ⟶ Tour Eiffel	0.41%	33.33%

Sequences Prediction Results

Let us remind the three kinds of prediction:

1. To build a trip in function of the most visited places.
2. To build a tour in function of the most visited places.
3. To build a tour in function of the confidence.

For the first prediction, only the SPM algorithm is implemented. A tourist suggests to visit the k most visited place of Paris. The Table 6 seen above illustrates the top 10 most visited places.

For the second prediction, the SRM constraint-based algorithm results is considered. The automaton is built as shown in Fig. 4 with $minsup = 1\%$ and $minconf = 10\%$, i.e. the rules with the most support value and an acceptable confidence. The Table 9 shows the prediction of one and two places from the start location *Sacrée Coeur*, which means that the automaton has already interpreted the transition between the initial state and the state named SC. Like *Sacré Coeur*, the places are represented by their initials. For example, for a prediction of length two, a tourist may visits, after the *Sacré Coeur*, the *Eiffel Tower* and finally the *Notre-Dame* in this order without any places between them. In this case, the conviction is for the rule *Eiffel Tower* ⟶ *Notre-Dame*.

The conviction of the route of the second prediction are close to 1, i.e. the routes behave like a stochastic process. Due to the high support set in the preferences, those route may appear more frequently in the dataset, therefore possess several rules with small confidence. The goal to purpose a realistic route among the mosts visited places is reached.

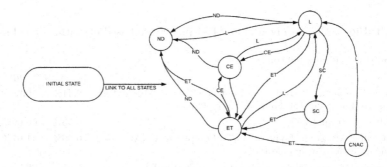

Fig. 4. Automaton created from SRM constraint-based algorithm.

Table 9. Prediction of the tour from SRM constraint-based algorithm from the place Sacré Coeur.

Length	Sequences
1	{SC, ET, $conv = 0.82$}
2	{SC, ET, ND, $conv = 1.01$}; {SC, ET, CE, $conv = 0.99$}; {SC, ET, L, $conv = 1.13$}
3	{SC, ET, ND, L, $conv = 1.21$}; {SC, ET, CE, ND, $conv = 1.09$}; {SC, ET, CE, L, $conv = 1.11$}; {SC, ET, L, ND, $conv = 0.97$}; {SC, ET, L, CE, $conv = 0.99$}

For the third prediction, the automaton is enhanced by the rules from SRM preference-based algorithm. To predict some route in the probabilistic automaton, routes are generated by an increasing order of length, as the second prediction. The automaton of the second prediction has been enhanced to illustrate this method in the Fig. 5. The Table 10 presents the set of predicted routes with the rules in Table 7 and the top 50 results with $minconf = 5\%$. If the example of the second prediction is computed in this one, its confidence is equal to 0.026%. This result means that only 0.026% of tourists that stay in *Sacré Coeur*, *Eiffel Tower* and *Notre-Dame* have made this specific route in this order without any places between them. In this case, the conviction is for the rule *Eiffel Tower* ⟶ *Notre-Dame*.

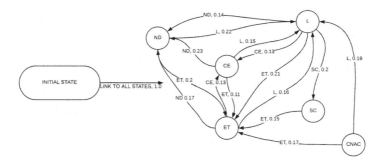

Fig. 5. Probabilistic automaton created from SRM constraint-based algorithm.

Table 10. Confidence of a set of tours from the place Sacré Coeur.

Examples of tours	Confidence of the tour	Latest conviction
{Musée du Louvre, Pont Neuf, Cathédrale Notre-Dame de paris}	13%	7.61
{Saint-Lazare, Galeries Lafayette, Palais Garnier, Musée du Louvre}	11.1%	4.32
{Avenue des Champs Elysées, Arc de Triomphe, Parc Monceau}	9.24%	4.73

The conviction of the route of the second prediction are far above 1, i.e. the routes is more likely used by tourists than others. This is justified to the high confidence developed by the top k algorithm. Also, it is not surprising the highest confidence rule have a low confidence value. The goal to purpose a suitable route in Paris is attained.

5.1 Discussion

The results of these three predictions are to be analyzed with hindsight and understanding tourist dynamics of the city of Paris. The french tourist committee indicates russian tourists prefer activities in the following order: museum, art and prestigious places; gastronomic tour; to visit park and garden. Those preferences suit with the SPM results and SRM preference-based results.

As far as the first prediction is concerned, the sites with the greatest support represent naturally the most notable sites on the international scene and are habitually points of active interest during a first tourist visit. A annually french tourist committee[5] analyse the russian tourist behaviors in Paris. The top places based on the support are similar to the study. The result reinforce the correlation between Instagram photos and tourism behaviors.

---

[5] Comité Régional du Tourisme Paris Ile-de-France. "Clientèle russe Repères" for the years 2011 to 2015.

In the same way, the second prediction gives displacements between these places of exceptionally strong attraction. Tourists staying in the capital for a short time, do not usually take the time to visit less-known places and move directly between points of interest. In addition, Instagram used to display their feat, it is likely that users post only the photos of the most famous monuments for their followers (depending of the profile of the account). Minor change between our study and the french committee occurs; among them the *Louvre*'s museum in below *Notre-Dame* in terms of the most visited places.

The third prediction is to put in relation with the Table 5 which gives the years and the months of the trips. Highly trusted circuits refer to places that are geographically or culturally close. Indeed, the first result of the Table 8 was a common circuit during a great exposition of arts in Paris. The third result of this table presents a very common tourist circuit. Indeed, 32.5% of russian tourists come with a tour operators.

6   Conclusion and Future Works

The main idea of this study is to determine behaviors of many sets of tourists. Patterns and rules may vary in function of the country of origin, the age, the sex, the social class. Considering the presented methods predict the behavior for a specific set of tourists, one may compare to another set of tourists. Once the details of a tourist are known, the method is able to determine a tour that suits to its attributes with an automaton. Those automata will be compared to future works as illustrated below. Those works will focuses on the prediction through Markov Chain. Those methods use inference from a prefix tree like Hidden Markov Chain or CPT+. The results of those methods will be compared to the presented method.

References

1. Ayres, J., Flannick, J., Gehrke, J., Yiu, T.: Sequential pattern mining using a bitmap representation. In: Proceedings of the Eighth ACM SIGKDD International Conference on Knowledge Discovery and Data Mining, pp. 429–435. ACM (2002)
2. Chalfen, R.M.: Photograph's role in tourism: some unexplored relationships. Ann. Tourism Res. **6**(4), 435–447 (1979)
3. Chareyron, G., Cousin, S., Da-Rugna, J., Gabay, D.: Touriscope: map the world using geolocated photographies. In: IGU Meeting, Geography of Tourism, Leisure and Global Change (2009)
4. Chareyron, G., Da-Rugna, J., Raimbault, T.: Big data: a new challenge for tourism. In: 2014 IEEE International Conference on Big Data (Big Data), pp. 5–7. IEEE (2014)
5. Cooper, C., Michael Hall, C.: Contemporary Tourism. Routledge (2007)
6. Da Rugna, J., Chareyron, G., Branchet, B.: Tourist behavior analysis through geotagged photographies: a method to identify the country of origin. In: 2012 IEEE 13th International Symposium on Computational Intelligence and Informatics (CINTI), pp. 347–351. IEEE (2012)

7. Fournier-Viger, P., Gomariz, A., Gueniche, T., Mwamikazi, E., Thomas, R.: TKS: efficient mining of Top-K sequential patterns. In: Motoda, H., Wu, Z., Cao, L., Zaiane, O., Yao, M., Wang, W. (eds.) ADMA 2013. LNCS (LNAI), vol. 8346, pp. 109–120. Springer, Heidelberg (2013). https://doi.org/10.1007/978-3-642-53914-5_10

8. Fournier-Viger, P., Gueniche, T., Zida, S., Tseng, V.S.: ERMiner: sequential rule mining using equivalence classes. In: Blockeel, H., van Leeuwen, M., Vinciotti, V. (eds.) IDA 2014. LNCS, vol. 8819, pp. 108–119. Springer, Cham (2014). https://doi.org/10.1007/978-3-319-12571-8_10

9. Fournier-Viger, P., Chun-Wei Lin, J., Kiran, R.U., Koh, Y.S., Thomas, R.: A survey of sequential pattern mining. Data Sci. Pattern Recogn. 1(1), 54–77 (2017)

10. Fournier-Viger, P., Nkambou, R., Shin-Mu Tseng, V.: RuleGrowth: mining sequential rules common to several sequences by pattern-growth. In: Proceedings of the 2011 ACM Symposium on Applied Computing, pp. 956–961. ACM (2011)

11. Fournier-Viger, P., Tseng, V.S.: TNS: mining top-k non-redundant sequential rules. In: Proceedings of the 28th Annual ACM Symposium on Applied Computing, pp. 164–166. ACM (2013)

12. Fei, H., Li, Z., Yang, C., Jiang, Y.: A graph-based approach to detecting tourist movement patterns using social media data. Cartography Geograph. Inf. Sci. 46(4), 368–382 (2019)

13. Li, J., Lizhi, X., Tang, L., Wang, S., Li, L.: Big data in tourism research: a literature review. Tour. Manag. 68, 301–323 (2018)

14. March, R., Woodside, A.G.: Tourism Behaviour: Travellers' Decisions and Actions. CABI, Wallingford (2005)

15. Pei, J., et al.: Mining sequential patterns by pattern-growth: the prefixspan approach. IEEE Trans. Knowl. Data Eng. 16(11), 1424–1440 (2004)

16. Soulet, A.: Two decades of pattern mining: principles and methods. In: Marcel, P., Zimányi, E. (eds.) eBISS 2016. LNBIP, vol. 280, pp. 59–78. Springer, Cham (2017). https://doi.org/10.1007/978-3-319-61164-8_3

17. Talpur, A., Zhang, Y.: A study of tourist sequential activity patterns through location based social network (LBSN). arXiv preprint arXiv:1811.03426 (2018)

18. Versichele, M., De Groote, L., Bouuaert, M.C., Neutens, T., Moerman, I., Van de Weghe, N.: Pattern mining in tourist attraction visits through association rule learning on bluetooth tracking data: a case study of Ghent. Belgium. Tourism Manage. 44, 67–81 (2014)

19. Yang, L., Lun, W., Liu, Y., Kang, C.: Quantifying tourist behavior patterns by travel motifs and geo-tagged photos from flickr. ISPRS Int. J. Geo-Inf. 6(11), 345 (2017)

20. Zaki, M.J.: SPADE: an efficient algorithm for mining frequent sequences. Mach. Learn. 42(1–2), 31–60 (2001)

21. Zhao, Q., Bhowmick, S.S.: Sequential pattern mining: a survey. ITechnical Report CAIS Nayang Technological University Singapore, 1:26 (2003)

TOM: A Threat Operating Model for Early Warning of Cyber Security Threats

Tao Bo[1,2], Yue Chen[3], Can Wang[4(✉)], Yunwei Zhao[3], Kwok-Yan Lam[5], Chi-Hung Chi[6], and Hui Tian[4]

[1] Key Laboratory of Earthquake Engineering and Engineering Vibration, Institute of Engineering Mechanics, China Earthquake Administration, Beijing, China
[2] Beijing Earthquake Agency, Beijing, China
[3] CNCERT/CC, Beijing, China
[4] School of ICT, Griffith University, Gold Coast, Australia
can.wang@griffith.edu.au
[5] Nanyang Technological University, Singapore, Singapore
[6] CSIRO, Hobart, Australia

Abstract. Threat profiling helps reveal the current trends of attacks, and underscores the significance of specific vulnerabilities, hence serves as the means for providing an early warning of potential attacks. However, the existing approaches on threat profiling models are mainly rule-based and depend on the domain experts' knowledge, which limit their applicability in the automated processing of cyber threat information from heterogeneous sources, e.g. the cyber threat intelligence information from open sources. The threat profiling models based on analytic approaches, on the other hand, are potentially capable of automatically discovering the hidden patterns from a massive volume of information. This paper proposes to apply the data analytic approaches to develop the threat profiling models in order to identify the potential threats by analyzing a large number of cyber threat intelligence reports from open sources, extract information from the cyber threat intelligence reports, and represent them in a structure that facilitates the automated risk assessment, and hence achieve the early warning of likely cyber attacks. We introduce the Threat Operating Model (TOM) which captures important information of the identified cyber threats, while can be implemented as an extension of the Structured Threat Information eXpression (STIX). Both the matrix-decomposition based semi-supervised method and the term frequency based unsupervised method are proposed. The experiment results demonstrate a fairly effectiveness (accuracy around 0.8) and a robust performance w.r.t different temporal periods.

Keywords: Cyber security · Threat operation · Data mining · Classification

This work was supported by BAE Systems.

© Springer Nature Switzerland AG 2019
J. Li et al. (Eds.): ADMA 2019, LNAI 11888, pp. 696–711, 2019.
https://doi.org/10.1007/978-3-030-35231-8_51

1   Introduction

Cyber security analysts study and investigate the behavior and the target system characteristics of various cyber attacks. These analyses are critical in typical cyber operations for various reasons, e.g., providing early warning in order to mitigate hidden costs. Results of the analysis are represented by a threat operating model, which describes how an attack works and what environment it operates in, as well as what impact/damages it causes to the victim. However, the integration of cyber threat-related information from multiple sources (e.g. mainstream cyber security vendors like Symantec[1], and threat detection engines like Threat Expert[2], and online forums, etc.) faces great challenges as it lacks a universally specified identifier to connect different information sources, e.g. different vendors use different naming systems. As a result, the inter-operation on cyber threat related information is limited.

A number of cyber threat ontology models have been proposed in literatures [1,2] to enhance the inter-operation on cyber threat related information and enable automatic cyber threat prediction as well as early-alert, e.g. "diamond model" [1], which includes actors, victims, infrastructure, capabilities, and "Social Dimensional Threat Model" [2] that models the hackers' social motives, such as "Protest against organized events". However, there are two shortcomings in such models that limit their use in the early warning of threats and other cyber operations. Firstly, the current cyber threat ontology focuses primarily on the malware attributes, e.g. memory/file modifications; rather than the behavioral aspects [1], such as the hotness of a threat as a topic and the interests from potential hackers. Secondly, the current cyber threat ontology is constructed in a predefined and static manner based on the knowledge from domain experts. In the fast-changing world of cyber security, nevertheless, it is always desirable for the cyber security analysts to have some dynamic approaches to capture the latest understanding of the threats acquired for cyber threat intelligence. As a result, the effectiveness of the static approaches for the automatic threat warning, the potential hacker/victim detection, and etc., is largely limited. On the other hand, with the increasing capability of capturing the behavioral data [2], recent trends in the cyber security analysis put a lot of emphasis in the information fusion which aims to provide the situation awareness and the threat prediction from a massive volume of sensed data [3].

The goal of this paper is to enable a machine-readable data structure, namely the Threat Operating Model (TOM) model that specifies both the static and dynamic, both the descriptive and behavioral attributes, to apply the data analytic techniques to achieve the automated processing of cyber threat intelligence reports from multiple sources. TOM model can be beneficial to a number of applications. For example, it allows users to determine the likelihood of the threat related events, e.g., whether they are the likely targets of the reported threats. In this study, two types of cyber threat intelligence sources are used for illus-

---

[1] https://www.symantec.com/security-center/writeup/2019-072604-0304-99.
[2] http://threatexpert.com.

Fig. 1. Illustration of Threat Expert malware detection description.

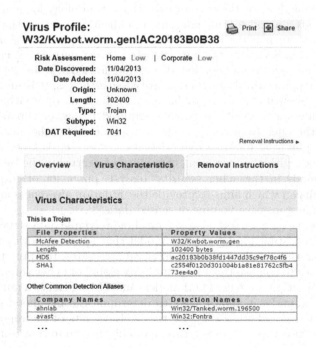

Fig. 2. Illustration of malware reports on Symantec.

trating the feasibility of automatically generating TOM: (i) Type I source, the automatic multi-scanning service providers, e.g. the Threat Expert (see Fig. 1). The users are likely to test out how they bundle the existing malware with different objects, for a new way to spread the malware, which avoids the detection by anti-virus softwares. Reports from this type of sources (i.e. Type I) tend to be more robust but less detailed, probably due to the multi-scanning nature of source. (ii) Type II source, the threat intelligence research sources, e.g. Symantec (see Fig. 2). The details of TOM structure based on the analysis of threat intelligence reports from Type 1 resource, can then be enhanced by analyzing and extracting the information from threat intelligence research sources (i.e. Type II). Reports from the Type II of sources tend to be more detailed, but may have a high false negative rate due to their single scanning nature.

One of the biggest challenges in the task of the automatic creation of TOM Model is to find an efficient and effective means for automatically clustering the threat intelligence reports. In this paper, we investigate two methods for the report clustering: (i) a semi-supervised matrix decomposition-based method, and (ii) an unsupervised term frequency-based method. We manually tag a sample of the reports collected to benchmark the effectiveness of frequency analysis technique, and determine the range of parameters to be used. The contributions of this paper are listed as follows:

- We suggest an automatic approach for analyzing, summarizing, and extracting the information from multiple cyber threat intelligence sources.
- We introduce a type of data structure for storing and representing such information, so that it can be automatically processed for the further Security Operation Center (SOC) operations.
- We validate our approach by integrating two types of cyber threat information sources, and the results illustrate that our approach is robustly effective.

The rest of this paper is organized as follows. Section 2 reviews the related work. We present the proposed Threat Operating Model in Sect. 3, and describe its construction mechanisms in Sect. 4. Section 5 reports the experimental results. Finally, we conclude this paper in Sect. 6.

2   Related Work

Current trends of attacks are revealed by the threat profiling [2], which underscores the significance of specific vulnerabilities. The threat profiling serves as a method to warn potential attacks at an early stage by providing organizations with a clear illustration of the potential threats, helping associate the threats with potential consequences, and enabling them to implement a risk-based prioritized incident management programs proactively.

A number of cyber threat models have been proposed in the literatures. For example, Layered Model [14], Social Dimensional Threat Model [2], etc. There exist two main limitations in terms of their applicability.

Firstly, the current cyber threat ontology addresses the malware infrastructure and capabilities, instead of behavioral aspects. Examples of malware infrastructure [6] include the descriptions of malware attack ways, systems infection ways, consequences, etc. Further, common attack ways [13] cover (i) Denial of service, (ii) Spread of malware, (iii) SQL and code injection. The consequences [13] have (i) Confidentiality (C): The attack leads to the unauthorized access to information, (ii) Integrity (I): The attack results in altering the modification or fabrication of information, (iii) Availability (A): The attack leads to the disruption of services, or the destruction of information. Examples for the threat models that describe the malware capabilities comprise the "Diamond Model" of malicious activity [4] that consists of two families of threat attributes: (i) the commitment attributes that describe the threat's willingness; and (ii) the resource attributes that describe the threat's ability. The commitment attribute family [6] contains intensity (i.e. the degree of damage the attack aims to achieve), stealth (i.e. the level of security in pursuit of launching an attack), and time (i.e. the length of time from the planning to the implementation and the actual execution). In contrast, the resource attribute family [6] contains the technical personnel (directly involved with the actual fabrication of attack weapons), knowledge (level of theoretical and practical proficiency in pursuit of a threat's goal), and access (based on privileges/credentials or not). Greater resources may enable a threat to accomplish an objective/ goal more easily, at the same time achieve greater overall adaptability.

Secondly, the current cyber threat ontology is constructed in a predefined way based on the domain knowledge, rather than an automatic approach of the threat representation. One example is the Social Dimensional Threat Model [2], where social motives include (i) Protest against organized events, (ii) Commemorate historic events, (iii) Commemorate observances, (iv) Human rights abuse, (v) Protest against web filtering/censoring (i.e., alleviate unfavorable conditions). These values are manually annotated, once the news reports are acquired with various factors that are part of an elaborate cyber attack domain model, based on the contents of articles.

In addition, a number of threat information languages have been proposed to represent the threat profiles, so that they are machine-readable. Examples include Cyber Observable Expression (CybOX) [7], Common Attack Pattern Enumeration and Classification (CAPEC) [11], the Malware Attribute Enumeration and Characterization (MAEC) language [7], the CERT Incident Management Body of Knowledge (CIMBOK) [8], the Trusted Automated Exchange of Indicator Information (TAXII) [9], the IP addresses, the x-mailer email fields, and the malware to discover the vulnerabilities and defensive courses of actions. The Structured Threat Information eXpression (STIX) [10] is an extensible XML-based language that describes cyber observables, indicators, incidents, adversary tactics, exploits, and the courses of action, as well as cyber attack campaigns and cyberthreat actors.

3   Notion and Structure of Threat Operating Models

Threat Operating Model (TOM) is a model for describing a group of cyber threats/malwares with similar behaviors. More specifically, TOM describes the behaviors of the attack actors, the system environment (i.e. operating system, networking devices, system softwares and application softwares, as well as their configurations) that the attack is applicable, the observed behaviors of the target systems, and the impacts/damages to the victims, and etc.

TOM consists of two parts: (i) the static component, and (ii) the dynamic component. Static component captures the descriptive attributes of threats (e.g. size, md5 hash value) and descriptions of threat attack methods (e.g. Email, software installation, and etc). Both Threat Expert and Symantec contain information for the static component. Dynamic component captures the behavioral attributes reflected in the potential hackers' activity engaged w.r.t certain threats. This is mainly obtained from the Threatexpert where potential hackers keep uploading malware-obfuscated objects for testing. Such attributes include hack interest and hotness, referring to the degree to which the malware is attacking frequently and lately, respectively (for precise definition, see Sect. 3.2). Moreover, Threatexpert may output more information because it is based on a number of scanners. In this case, we have the non-detectability, referring to the probability of a malware to get away with the detection of the mainstream anti-virus vendors.

3.1   Static Component

The static component of TOM comprises (i) the characteristics of the malwares, including descriptive features (e.g. aliases, file size and type), identity features (e.g. CVE, and cryptographic hash–MD5, SHA), and (ii) the characteristics of the affected party, including affected system, registry key, registry value, file modification, memory modification, and damages. Table 1 summarizes the attributes in the static component and illustrates with an example malware: "W32.Kwbot.Worm".

3.2   Dynamic Component

The dynamic components comprise of three parts, namely the hack interest, hotness, and non-detectability index. As mentioned in the beginning of Sect. 3, potential hackers keep uploading the malware-obfuscated objects for testing on Threat Expert. Therefore, their behaviors provide a good source of information for profiling threats from the perspective of user engagement. For example, the density of malware upload could also be an indicator of the impact of the malware. Figure 3 illustrates two malware examples from the Threat Expert data collected. We can see that these two malwares exhibit different temporal patterns w.r.t number of incidents reported. The upper one increases in an almost linear fashion, while the lower one increases dramatically at first then goes steady. We

Table 1. Static components of TOM and example of malware "W32.Kwbot.Worm"

Static attributes	Meaning	Example
Alias	Aliases used in anti-virus system	Trojan-Dropper.Win32.Loring
FileSize	Size of the file	12,288 bytes
Type	Type of malwares	Trojan Horse; Hack Tool
CVE	Common Vulnerabilities and Exposures-unique and common identifiers for publicly known information-security vulnerabilities	CVE-2012-0158
MD5	A 32-character hexadecimal number that is computed the cryptographic hash function Message Digest algorithm 5	0x2FB0BEA570C92647 DB97293686442F6A
SHA	A 160-bit number that is computed by the cryptographic hash function Secure Hash Algorithm 1	0xEC979C512D39C912 9CC1752E9B856C3E44 CCF95F
Affected System	Operating System	Windows CE; UNIX
RegistryKey	Registry key that gets modified by the attack	HKEY_LOCAL_MACHINE\ SYSTEM\ControlSet001\ Control\MediaResources\msvideo HKEY_LOCAL_MACHINE\ SYSTEM\CurrentControlSet\ Control\MediaResources\msvideo
RegistryValue	Registry value that gets modified by the attacked	[HKEY_LOCAL_MACHINE\ SYSTEM\ControlSet001\Services] ConnectGroup = tbqzs6Y;
File Modification	Processes affected related to file creation, modification, and deletion	The following file was modified:c:\pagefile.sys
Memory Modification	Processes affected related to processes creation, modification, and deletion in memory	There were new processes created in the system:Process NameProcess FilenameMain Module Sizeccuwco.exe%Windir%\ccuwco.exe61,440 bytes
Other Attack Processes	Other attack processes except for previously mentioned (registry key, value, file modification, and memory modification)	Opens port 1025 to send the password information.
Damage	Summary of the damages caused to the system	Force the computer to shut down, restart, or log off; Get a list of running processes; Deliver system and network information to the Trojan's creator, including login names and cached network passwords; Steal cookies associated with PayPal, iFriend, E-Bullion, EZCardin, Evocash, eBay, WebMoney, and various banks

use Hack interest refers to the number of obfuscation trials/incidents detected on Threat Expert for a given malware detected from the start sampling timepoint to t, see Eq. (1).

$$hack\_interest(m_i) = \sum \#incidents(t) \tag{1}$$

where $\#incidents(t)$ denotes the number of incidents of malware m_i detected at time t. In TOM, this dynamic attribute is represented as a triple:

$$< \max_{hack\_interest}, \min_{hack\_interest}, \mathrm{median}_{hack\_interest} >$$

While hack interest describes the impact from an aggregate perspective, a second dynamic attribute – hotness depicts the impact from a differential perspective– the difference of hack interest over the past sampling time points, see Eq. (2).

$$Hotness(m_i) = \#incidents(t) - \#incidents(t-1) \tag{2}$$

where hotness is measured with difference between two consecutive time windows. Similarly, this dynamic attribute is denoted as another triple:

$$< \max_{hotness}, \min_{hotness}, \mathrm{median}_{hotness} >$$

Thirdly, we note that Threat Expert will pass the obfuscation trials to a given list of popular anti-virus scanners (e.g. Symantec, McAfee, and etc.), and the detection rate by these scanners indicates the potential harm that this malware may cause if the latent attacker actually launches this attack. Thus, we use the Non-detectability Index (NDI) to measure the potential damage that a malware might cause. NDI is given in Eq. (3) as below.

$$NDI(m_i) = 1 - n(m_i)/N \tag{3}$$

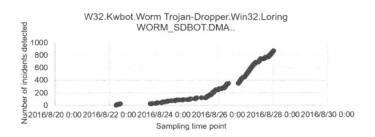

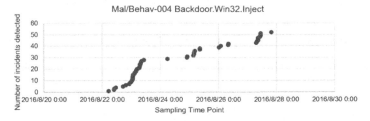

Fig. 3. Illustration of the malware obfuscation trials distribution on Threat Expert, where x-axis is the sampling time point and y-axis is the number of incidents detected.

where $n(m_i)$ denotes the number of anti-virus softwares that successfully detect malware m_i, and N denotes the total number of anti-virus softwares.

4   Automatic Construction of Threat Operating Model

As stated in Sect. 1, TOM is constructed based on the information collected from various cyber threat intelligence sources. In this paper, we conduct our experiments on the data collected from Threat Expert which is multi-scanner based and provides more generic information, and Symantec which is single-scanner based and provides more detail-oriented. Threat Expert reports include the statistical information that is useful to calculate the dynamic attributes. Thus, the TOM construction will be mainly based on the Threat Expert with the Symantec as an enrichment. That is to say, we use the malware name in the Threat Expert to retrieve the threat reports from Symantec and extract the information from Symantec reports, and then fill in as values in the static attributes in the TOM model.

Note that TOM may correspond to multiple malware names, due to different naming systems and the existence of alias. This problem is an unsupervised clustering problem or a semi-supervised problem, since we lack the priori information of TOM. Therefore, two approaches are proposed to solve this problem: (i) a semi-supervised matrix-decomposition based method, (ii) an unsupervised term frequency based clustering method.

4.1   Semi-supervised Matrix Decomposition-Based Method

First, we manually code n malwares into m TOMs ($m < n$), in this way, we have the malware-TOM mapping matrix M. On the other hand, we automatically generate the term-malware mapping matrix A from the processing text in Threat Expert reports by using methods, such as TF-IDF [15]. Let us denote the word frequency (i.e. malware feature)-TOM matrix as B, then by definition we have $M = A \times B$, i.e. $B = A^{-1} \times M$. Afterwards, we apply this sample-based matrix to the entire data set to get the generated TOMs. Note that the manual tag serves as the baseline for evaluating the performance of clustering, i.e. the above described major cluster and sub cluster processes (for details, see Sect. 4.2).

4.2   Unsupervised Term Frequency-Based Method

The construction of TOM consists of two steps. First, establish the correlation between the reports collected from two sources: Symantec and Threat Expert. Note that different systems have different naming mechanisms: for one malware name in Threat Expert, it might refer to multiple malware names in Symantec. For example, "Trojan.Win32.Agent" is also known as "Trojan Horse" and "InfoStealer.Gampass" in Symantec. The correlation is established through calculating the similarity of malware names mentioned in each report (for details, see below). Second, determine TOM from reports clustering based on contents. Then, its attributes can be generated from processing the reports within each corresponding cluster.

Preliminary Threat Expert Report Clustering. This preliminary step establishes the correlation between reports collected from the Threat Expert and the Symantec through the following two steps: (i) Determine name clusters based on string distances, more specifically, we use Jaro-Winkler Distance [12]. The malwares with similar names are considered as a cluster of the same/similar malwares; (ii) Extract the alias names from reports, and use the string distance (Jaro-Winkler Distance) to determine whether aliases are similar. The malwares with similar aliases are considered as a cluster of the same/similar malwares. In the next step, we will apply the content features to determine correlated threat reports within each name and alias cluster.

Jaro-Winkler Distance [12] is a technique widely adopted in name matching. It measures the difference between two strings by the minimum number of single-character transpositions required to change one word into the other. The higher the distance is, the more dissimilar the two strings are. Hence, a transformation with $1-$ Jaro-Winkler distance is normally used to measure the similarity: Jaro-Winkler similarity. After this transformation, the score is normalized, such that 1 equates to the exact match and 0 indicates no similarity.

TOM Construction. Based on the name clusters and the alias clusters obtained from the previous step, we start to construct TOM from the malware reports by using the content-based approach [16]. Given two reports within the name and alias clusters generated, we first enumerate the word frequency in descending order, take the highest n_w words, and choose those words that appear in both reports. After that, we use the cosine distance [16] of reports to determine the correlation. The higher value of cosine distance indicates the greater similarity. K-Means clustering [16] is used to generate the clusters of reports within each name and alias cluster.

In this way, reports are correlated to form a sub-cluster within the name cluster. A TOM model will be created for the sub-cluster by using the union of attributes (i.e. both static and dynamic) in the reports. Once the TOM is obtained, we extract the static attributes, and compute the dynamic attributes, such as hotness and non-detectability in the TOM model.

5   Experiment

In this section, we will first describe the multiple data sources collected for TOM construction in Sect. 5.1, and then specify the evaluation metrics in Sect. 5.2 The experiment results and analyses are then presented in Sect. 5.3.

5.1   Data Description

We collect data from the Threat Expert from August to November in 2016. In total, there are 25,092 incidents reported on the Threat Expert with 3473 unknown malware incidents. There are 1,712 malwares with a skewed distribution of the range of the number of incidents reported $\in [1, 9914]$. From the Symantec, we crawl the report web pages for 16,296 malwares. In addition, 1,081 alias files are collected from the Threat Expert for the clustering of Threat Expert reports.

5.2   Evaluation Metrics

The performance of the TOM construction approach is evaluated with precision and recall rate [17]. The difficulty in developing the precision and recall rates lies in determining the mapping of the labels given by the manual tag and the (semi-)automatic construction approaches. On one hand, the number of TOMs generated may differ. Let us denote the TOMs manually labeled for the test set as $T = t_1, \cdots, t_i$, and the TOMs constructed for the test set by either the matrix-decomposition approaches or the frequency-based clustering approach described in Sect. 4 as $T' = t'_1, \cdots, t'_i$. Note that $|T|$ might differ from $|T'|$. On the other hand, it may happen that for the reports manually tagged as TOM t_i, the labels given by the (semi-)automatic construction approaches comprise a set $S(t_i) = t'_j, \cdots, t'_k$, and vice versa. The label with the most appearances in the set $S(t_i)$ will be deemed as the corresponding mapped label given by the (semi-)automatic construction approaches. Ideally, there is only one dominant tag in each cluster. Note that if messages with the dominant tag is not more than 50% of the number of messages in the cluster, then the clustering algorithm is not reliable.

For each TOM t'_j generated, we denote the mapped manual tag as t_i. The precision and recall of a certain TOM construction approach is then given in Eqs. (4) and (5), respectively.

$$Precision(t) = M(t)/N(t), \tag{4}$$

$$Recall(t) = M(t)/C(t), \tag{5}$$

where $M(t'_j)$ denote the number of reports with the label given by a construction method t'_j, i.e. manual label t_i; $N(t'_j)$ denote the number of reports tagged as t_i in T, and let C denote the number of reports in the generated cluster with label t'_j. Note that the clusters with very small size may lead to an undesirable impact on the evaluation metrics, as they establish the mapping between labels with a very weak correlation (i.e. occurrences of label mapping reflected in a very small number of reports). In the experiments below, we set the threshold as 10, that is to say, we focus on the clusters with more than 10 reports. The small size (<10) clusters are deemed as less important, as it indicates rare attention of potential hackers.

5.3   Experiment Setting

Parameter Calibration in Matrix Decomposition-Based TOM Generation. We adopt the following steps to calibrate the number of reports manually tagged to form the malware-TOM matrix:

1. Manually tag a part of the samples from the original data set with size $3,000$, $4,000$, $5,000$, and 6000. Within each of which, $1,000$ samples are randomly selected as the test set, the remaining data are the training set.
2. For each of the tagged sample data set, the result given by the semi-supervised matrix decomposition-based method is evaluated with, the precision and recall given in Eqs. (4) and (5), respectively.
3. The one leads to the highest precision is used to decide the n (i.e. the number of top frequent words) in parameter calibration in term frequency based TOM construction method.

We then evaluate the effectiveness of matrix on the entire data set by randomly selecting 1000 reports from the remaining data set, to see whether the matrix trained is effective or not, through the precision and recall rates.

Parameter Calibration in Term Frequency-Based TOM Generation. The parameter need to be calibrated is the number of words with the highest frequency in the report used to automatically cluster the malware reports in term frequency based clustering method. Similar to the experiment setting in the matrix decomposition based approach, to determine the appropriate number of words used to automatically cluster the malware reports, the experiment is conducted using: (i) manually tagged sample data set, and (ii) the entire data set.

Robustness w.r.t Time Sensitivity. Furthermore, we collect another two data sets, with time period between 2016.11–2017.01, and 2017.01–2017.03, and randomly select 500 samples from these two time periods and manually tag the TOM, to show the robustness of the proposed approaches. The effectiveness of the proposed two methods are then evaluated on these two newly collected data sets.

5.4   Results and Analysis

Constructed TOM. Fig. 4 shows an illustration of the constructed TOM, in particular, the dynamic component that captures the behavioral aspects of the malwares. In this paper, the constructed TOM is represented in an XML format. Figure 5 displays the distribution of the $\max_{hotness}$, $\max_{hack\_interest}$, and the non-detectability of malwares detected on the Threat Expert.

```
<dynamicAttributes>
  <hackInterestAttribute>
    <sum_hackInterest>9914</sum_hackInterest>
    <max_hackInterest>9913</max_hackInterest>
    <mean_hackInterest>4957.0</mean_hackInterest>
    <hackInterestList>
      <hackInterest id="1" malwareName="Backdoor.Trojan, Backdoor.Win32.Udr.a, Suspect-BN!BCF66BC6D827..">1</hackInterest>
      <hackInterest id="2" malwareName="W32.Kwbot.Worm, Trojan-Dropper.Win32.Loring, WORM_SDBOT.DMA..">9913</hackInterest>
    </hackInterestList>
  </hackInterestAttribute>
  <hotnessAttribute>
    <sum_hotness>149</sum_hotness>
    <max_hotness>149</max_hotness>
    <mean_hotness>74.5</mean_hotness>
    <hotnessList>
      <hotness id="1" malwareName="Backdoor.Trojan, Backdoor.Win32.Udr.a, Suspect-BN!BCF66BC6D827..">0</hotness>
      <hotness id="2" malwareName="W32.Kwbot.Worm, Trojan-Dropper.Win32.Loring, WORM_SDBOT.DMA..">149</hotness>
    </hotnessList>
  </hotnessAttribute>
  <nonDetectabilityAttribute>
    <max_nonDetectability>1.0</max_nonDetectability>
    <mean_nonDetectability>0.75</mean_nonDetectability>
    <min_nonDetectability>0.5</min_nonDetectability>
    <nonDetectabilityList>
      <nonDetectability id="1" malwareName="Backdoor.Trojan, Backdoor.Win32.Udr.a, Suspect-BN!BCF66BC6D827..">1.0</nonDetectability>
      <nonDetectability id="2" malwareName="W32.Kwbot.Worm, Trojan-Dropper.Win32.Loring, WORM_SDBOT.DMA..">0.5</nonDetectability>
    </nonDetectabilityList>
  </nonDetectabilityAttribute>
```

Fig. 4. Example of dynamic component of constructed TOM for malware name "W32.Kwbot.Worm".

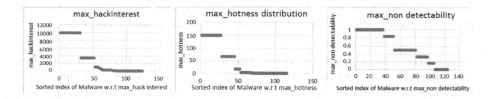

Fig. 5. Distribution of dynamic attributes of TOM detected on Threat Expert.

Matrix-Decomposition Based TOM Generation. In this part, we focus on the accuracy of matrix-based decomposition based TOM generation, and the parameter calibration on the size of the samples manually tagged to train the matrix. We can see from Table 2 that randomly tagging 5000 records manually (i.e. 4000 samples in the training set, and 1000 samples in the test set) out of the total 25092 collected records, lead to a balance between accuracy and time for the manual tagging procedure. The precision and recall rates that reach the highest for the 1000 test samples randomly selected from the manually tagged set are 0.93 and 0.83, respectively; and those reach the second highest are 0.86 and 0.55, respectively. Note that the distribution of mapping label pairs is fairly concentrated. Take the training set size of 4000, and test set size of 1000 as an example, the results show that the major mapping pair of labels takes up at least 62.0%, with the highest reaching 88.6%. Thus, it indicates that for a label generated, we are able to correlate a dominant manually tagged label, which strengthens the effectiveness of the matrix-decomposition based methods.

Term Frequency-Based TOM Generation. Table 3 illustrates the number of matched records between the matrix-decomposition based methods and the frequency-based methods. We can see that when we set the number of top fre-

Table 2. Precision and recall of matrix-decomposition based TOM generation

Trainset size	Manual tagged sample (Testset size: 1000)		Entire Dataset (Testset size: 1000)	
	Max. Precision	Max. Recall	Max. Precision	Max. Recall
2000	0.5	0.24	0.43	0.14
3000	0.83	0.63	0.78	0.41
4000	0.93	0.83	0.86	0.55
5000	0.91	0.8	0.99	0.55

Table 3. Parameter calibration of top n frequent words infrequency-based TOM generation

# of top frequent words	Manually tagged sample (Size: 1000)	Entire dataset (Size: 25092)
20	351	7241
25	358	7387
30	387	7895
35	655	15927
40	655	15921

Table 4. Precision and recall of matrix-decomposition based TOM generation

Trainset period (Train set: 5000)	Manual tagged sample (Test size: 500)	
	Max. Precision	Max. Recall
2016.11–2017.01	1	0.57
2017.01–2017.03	0.72	0.47

quent words as 35, the matched records are the highest, reaching 655 out of 1000 records for the manually tagged sample test set with the training set size of 4000, and 15927 out of 25092 records for the entire data set. The precision and recall rates in this case are 0.6 and 0.3, respectively.

Robustness w.r.t. Time Sensitivity. Tables 4 and 5 illustrates the precision and recall rates of the matrix-based TOM generation and frequency based TOM generation on the two randomly collected samples with sample size of 500 within period: (i) 2016.11–2017.01, and (ii) 2017.01–2017.03. As time goes on, the precision and recall rates of the methods reduce, but still with a fairly acceptable precision and recall rates: 0.72 and 0.47 for period 2017.01–2017.03. This indicates our method performs robustly w.r.t different temporal periods.

Table 5. Precision and recall of frequency based TOM generation

Trainset period (Train set: 5000)	Manual tagged sample (Test size: 500)	
	Max. Precision	Max. Recall
2016.11–2017.01	0.83	0.49
2017.01–2017.03	0.64	0.36

6   Conclusion

In this paper, we report an automated approach for analyzing, summarizing, and extracting the information from those cyber threat intelligence reports available from various sources, such as the Symantec and the Threat Expert. We also propose a type of data structure for storing and representing such information, so that it can be automatically processed for the further SOC operations. The data structure, named the TOM Model, captures both the descriptive aspects of threats, including the target hardware and operating system platform, the vulnerabilities to be exploited, the target industry, and etc.; as well as the behavioral aspects, e.g. hotness and hack interest. Both the matrix-decomposition based semi-supervised method and the term frequency based unsupervised approach are explored to analyze, summarize, and extract the information from multiple sources. The results demonstrate that the highest accuracy can be achieved with the number of top frequent words set at 35.

The availability of the TOM model allows various industry organizations to perform the automated checking to determine whether the IT environment of that organization matches the profile of such cyber threat targets; hence allowing the cyber operations to raise meaningful early warnings. In the future, we will enrich the Structured Threat Information eXpression (STIX) representation by integrating with TOM to enhance its expressive power.

References

1. Obrst, L., Chase, P., Markeloff, R.: Developing an ontology of the cyber security domain. In: STIDS, CEUR Workshop Proceedings, vol. 966, pp. 49–56 (2012)
2. Sharma, A.C., et al.: Building a social dimensional threat model from current and historic events of cyber attacks. In: 2010 IEEE Second International Conference on Social Computing (2010)
3. Yang, S.J., et al.: High level information fusion for tracking and projection of multistage cyber attacks. Inf. Fusion **10**, 107–121 (2009)
4. Ingle, J.: Organizing intelligence to respond to network intrusions and attacks. In: Briefing for the DoD Information Assurance Symposium, Nashville, TN (2010)
5. Burger, E.W., et al.: Taxonomy model for cyber threat intelligence information exchange technologies. In: Proceedings of the 2014 ACM Workshop on Information Sharing & Collaborative Security, pp. 51–60. ACM, Scottsdale (2014)
6. Mateski, M., et al.: Cyber threat metrics, Sandia National Laboratories (2012)

7. Wang, W.: How the small and medium-sized enterprises 'owners' credit features affect the enterprises' credit default behavior. J. Bus. Manage. Econ. **3**, 90–95 (2012)
8. Mundie, D.A., Ruefle, R.: Building an incident management body of knowledge. In: 2012 Seventh International Conference on Availability, Reliability and Security (2012)
9. Bond, G.D., Lee, A.Y.: Language of lies in prison: linguistic classification of prisoners' truthful and deceptive natural language. Appl. Cognitive Psychol. **19**, 313–329 (2005)
10. Barnum, S.: Standardizing cyber threat intelligence information with the structured threat information eXpression (STIX^{TM}), MITRE Corporation (2012)
11. Stein, R.M.: The relationship between default prediction and lending profits: integrating ROC analysis and loan pricing. J. Banking Finan. **29**, 1213–1236 (2005)
12. Cohen, W.W., Ravikumar, P., Fienberg, S.E.: A comparison of string distance metrics for name-matching tasks. In: KDD Workshop on Data Cleaning and Object Consolidation, pp. 73–78 (2003)
13. Shiva, S., Simmons, C., Ellis, C., et al.: AVOIDIT: a cyber attack taxonomy (2009)
14. Burger, E.: A Taxonomy for CyberISE Technology Evaluation. Georgetown University (2014)
15. Lv, B., Wang D., Wang Y.: A hybrid model based on multi-dimensional features for insider threat detection. In: International Conference on Wireless Algorithms, Systems, and Applications, pp. 333–334 (2018)
16. Kumar, V., Srivastava, J., Lazarevic, A.: Managing Cyber Threats: Issues, Approaches, and Challenges. Springer-Verlag, New York (2005). https://doi.org/10.1007/b104908
17. Paredesoliva-Oliva, I., Castell-Uroz, I., Barlet-Ros, P., Dimitropoulos, X., Solé-Pareta, J.: Practical anomaly detection based on classifying frequent traffic patterns. In: International Conference on Computer Communications, pp. 49–54 (2012)

Prediction for Student Academic Performance Using SMNaive Bayes Model

Baoting Jia[1], Ke Niu[1,2](✉), Xia Hou[1], Ning Li[1], Xueping Peng[2], Peipei Gu[3], and Ran Jia[4]

[1] Computer School, Beijing Information Science and Technology University, Beijing 100101, China
jiabaoting96@126.com, niuke@bistu.edu.cn, 15210154586@163.com, ningli.ok@163.com
[2] CAI, School of Computer Science, Faculty of Engineering and Information Technology, University of Technology Sydney, Ultimo, NSW 2007, Australia
xueping.peng@uts.edu.au
[3] Software Engineering College, Zhengzhou University of Light Industry, Zhengzhou 450000, China
gupeipei@zzuli.edu.cn
[4] School of mechanical engineering, Beijing institute of technology, Beijing 100086, China
jiaran89@126.com

Abstract. Predicting students academic performance is very important for students future development. There are a large number of students who can not graduate from colleges on time for various reasons every year. Nowadays, a large volume of students academic data has been generated in the process of promoting education informatization from the field of education. It becomes critical to predict student performance and ensure students to graduate on time by taking the best of these data. Machine learning models that predict students performance are widely available. However, some existing machine learning models still have the problem of low accuracy in predicting students performance. To solve this problem, we proposes a SMNaive Bayes (SMNB) model, which integrates Sequential Minimal Optimization (SMO) and Naive Bayes to make the prediction result more accurate. The basic idea is that the model predicts the performance of students professional courses via their basic course performance in the previous stage. In particular, SMO algorithm is leveraged to predict students academic performance of the first step and produces the results of the prediction; Naive Bayes then makes decision about the inconsistent results of the initial prediction; Lastly, the final results of students professional course performance prediction are produced. To test the effectiveness of our proposed model, we have conducted extensive experiments to compare SMNB against four prediction methods. The experimental results demonstrate that the proposed SMNB model is superior to all the compared methods.

Keywords: Academic prediction · SMNB · MLP · Two-Step

© Springer Nature Switzerland AG 2019
J. Li et al. (Eds.): ADMA 2019, LNAI 11888, pp. 712–725, 2019.
https://doi.org/10.1007/978-3-030-35231-8_52

1   Introduction

In recent years, with the rapid development of education information technology, higher education has entered the era of "big data" [1]. At the same time, it is possible to track, record and analyze students' learning behavior using the application of information technology and learning analysis technology in the field of education. A number of students' academic data has been generated in the process of promoting education informatization. How to exploit useful information from these students' data to predict their academic performance has become an important topic, which is also the main goal of higher education [2]. Therefore, higher education needs to exploit specific methods and processes to capture a large amount of important knowledge from the past and current data sets in order to predict students academic performance [3]. This can effectively help teachers put forward reasonable suggestions for different students, and prevent some of them from dropping out due to poor academic performance, which ensures the education high-quality [4].

Machine learning models that can predict students' academic performance are widely available. Previous studies have shown that machine learning models can identify poor academic performance of students earlier and more accurately than conventional methods [1,5,6]. However, the use of machines learning to predict students' performance in completing college programs still faces new challenges [7]. According to studies from Kabakchieva and Pal [8–10], machines learning was an effective predictor of students academic performance. However, there are not optimization algorithm parameters, resulting in the overall accuracy of the classifier being less than 70%. In addition, it is time-consuming to extract and pre-process students' academic data from database when using machines learning for academic prediction. Oskouei and Saa improved overall accuracy by using machine learning models to predict students performance [11,12]. However, there is a key challenge which the data types are single.

To overcome the aforementioned limitations, we propose a novel two-step prediction model, called "SMNaive Bayes Model (SMNB)". The model is used to predict the performance of college students professional courses. This algorithm is a fusion of the SMO and the Naive Bayes algorithm. In particular, SMO algorithm is first used to make the initial prediction, and produce initial prediction results. Then we leverage Naive Bayes algorithm to predict the inconsistent results of the initial prediction for the improved prediction, and the final prediction results are obtained by ten-fold cross-validation. We used the real students' data of a university to carry out the experiment. Through comparing with four baseline algorithms, which proved that the SMNB algorithm has a higher accuracy in predicting the performance of students professional courses.

The remainders of this paper are organized as follows. Section 2 reviews related studies. Details about our model are presented in Sect. 3. In Sect. 4, we demonstrate the experimental results conducted on two public datasets. Lastly, we conclude our study and outline our future work in Sect. 5.

2   Related Work

Research on student academic performance prediction by using data mining technology and machine learning has been widely used in the development of the new
world [13]. However, there are still some problems with the prediction of students academic performance. Huang et al. [14] used multiple linear regression,
MLP and SVM algorithms to predict students academic performance based on
their performance in compulsory courses and mid-term examinations. The results
showed that SVM had better prediction effect. Lopez et al. [15] used classic classification algorithms and clustering methods to predict students performance in
the course, using data sets on students use of forums and social networking information. The study can predict the students performance, but the experimental
data used is a single type. Zimmermann et al. [16] combined regression models
with variable selection and variable aggregation to analyze how undergraduates
performance predicts graduate performance. Although the data types used are
comprehensive, the accuracy of the prediction results is unsatisfactory. Kulkarni
studied using Naive Bayes, IBK, Kstar and other techniques to track and predict students academic performance, and found that Kstar algorithm has better
classification effect [17]. However, the Kstar algorithm takes more time.

Some common literatures use a single algorithm to predict the academic performance of students. The experimental data used by the algorithm is relatively
simple. It cannot handle different types of students data well, so it cannot better
deal with the issue of students academic prediction. Using a single algorithm to
combine with each other helps to avoid some of the limitations of a single algorithm. For example, in the study of Christian et al. [18], using NBTree model
and students academic data to predict students performance, the experimental
results show that some factors have a significant impact on students academic
performance. Ktona used C4.5 and K-means algorithm to predict students academic performance [19]. In the literature of some hybrid algorithms, some parts
of the two algorithms are merged to predict students academic performance.
However, in the process of algorithm fusion, sometimes mechanical combinations lead to unpredictable prediction results. In our SMNB algorithm, we use
the two-step model to predict the performance of students professional courses.

3   Proposed Model

In order to predict students performance in professional courses, we propose
SMNaive Bayes model, called "SMNB", which is a fusion algorithm based on
SMO and Naive Bayes. The model can modify the first prediction to make the
final result more accurate in the two-step prediction. The basic idea of the proposed model is to use SMO algorithm to predict students' performance to obtain
the inconsistent results in the first step, then to apply Naive Bayes to the inconsistent results from previous step for the second prediction, and finally to conduct
10-fold cross-validation to produce the final result.

SMNB model consists of five parts: (1) Data selection: extracting experimental data from the source data. (2) Data pre-processing: further processing and

optimizing the acquired data related to the experiment. (3) Correlated course selection: select the most relevant course attributes to predict. (4) Two-step prediction: using SMNB algorithm to predict the performance of students professional courses. (5) Results output: output the final result of the prediction. The proposed model framework is shown in Fig. 1.

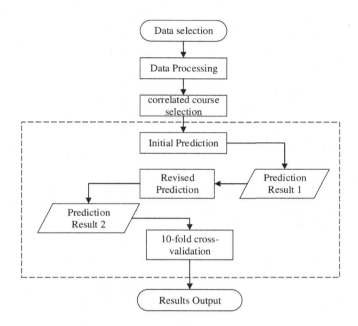

Fig. 1. SMNB model framework.

3.1 Data Selection

The dataset used in this paper is from undergraduate information at a university in Beijing. The data contains basic behavioral information and academic performance information of students. The main types of student data we collected are numeric and character data. The specific attributes of the data are shown in Table 1.

3.2 Data Processing

Due to the data obtained from different sources, they generally are incomplete. Meanwhile, considering the inconsistency of data types, the data have to be normalized. For example, some students are unable to take the exam, choose to go abroad, or drop out of school. For students who fail to take the exam, we use the result of their first makeup exam as the final result. For other students who

Table 1. The specific attributes of the data.

Attribution	Type	Description
Stu_num	Int	Number
Stu_name	Varchar	Name
Stu_sex	Varchar	Sex
Class	Varchar	Class and grade
Course	Varchar	Course name
Score	Float	Course performance
Level	Varchar	Classification
Semester	Varchar	Trimester
Academic_year	Varchar	Academic year
Internet_traffic	Float	Total online traffic
Internet_time	DateTime	Length of Internet access

failed to complete their studies, their data are simply discarded as dirty data. Then we group the students academic performance and the statistical results are shown in Table 2.

Table 2. The statistics of student academic performance.

Performance	Categories (y)
0–59	Fail
60–69	Pass
70–79	Medium
80–89	Good
90–100	Excellent

3.3 Correlated Course Selection

We need to select the most relevant courses to ensure the selected attributes to improve the performance of the prediction model and reduce the over-fitting. Firstly, we use principal component analysis to reduce the dimension of curriculum data. In order to find the most significant feature, we use filter feature selection algorithm [20]. In the selection process, the influence of each course feature C_i on the category label y can be measured. Moreover, we need to consider the difference of the value between different variables, so as to obtain a measure of trends in relevance. Therefore, Pearson correlation coefficient can be used to judge the correlation. The equation is defined as follows:

$$R(i) = \frac{Cov(c_i, y)}{\sqrt{Var(c_i)Var(y)}} \tag{1}$$

The correlation coefficient $R(i)$ satisfies $|R(i)| \leq 1$. The closer $R(i)$ approaches to 1, the higher the similarity between C and y is. For example, $R(i) = 0$ indicates no correlation between courses C and y; $R(i) < 0.5$ indicates a low degree of correlation between course feature C and y; $0.5 \leq R(i) < 0.8$ indicates moderate correlation; $0.8 \leq R(i) \leq 1$ indicates high correlation.

3.4   Two-Step Prediction

The two-step prediction means our proposed model produces an initial prediction result in the first step, and then use the inconsistent result of the initial prediction to perform the second prediction and produce the final result of the prediction. We use the second prediction results to predict students performance, which can correct the results of the initial prediction and improve the accuracy of the final results.

Specifically, a feature vector $x_t(i) = [x_t(1), x_t(2), ..., x_t(n)] \rightarrow Y_t(i)$ for each student. $Y_t(i)$ denotes the activity status of each student i in the t-th semester. A space vector $S_t(i)$ is defined to represent the learning state of the student i in the t-th semester. In the t-th semester, $S_t(i)$ can be expressed $S_t(i) = [S_t(1) \times S_t(2), ..., \times S_t(n)]$. $Z_t(i)$ is the student i-th's performance in the t-th semester of the major course. The prediction of students professional performance depends on the students activity state $Y_t(i)$ and learning state $S_t(i)$. $Y_t(i) \times S_t(i) = Z_t(i)$. Define a loss function weight $w_t(i)$, which represents i-th student performance losses in the t-th semester, and $w_t(i)$ is allocated based on the proportion of each course's credits, course performance, and predicted student performance in professional courses. In the framework of the system, the performance of students in professional courses depends on the performance of the previous semester, that is, in each framework, the performance of students in the t semester is the basis of the $t+1$ semester. The detailed prediction framework is shown in Fig. 2. The specific workflow for predicting the performance of students professional courses using SMNB model is described as follows.

Initial Prediction. The purpose of the initial prediction is to filter the student data by using the SMO which eliminates noise to make the predicted results more accurate. In the initial prediction, according to our actual prediction and the use of student data, we need to forecast the large optimization problem of students academic performance by decomposing large optimization problems into small ones and solving each minimum-scale problem. So we use the SMO algorithm for the first prediction and avoid the iterative algorithm [21]. We need to consider the binary classification problem of datasets $(x_1, y_1), ..., (x_n, y_n)$ where x_i is the input vector, $y_i \subseteq \{-1, 1\}$ is the class label of the vector, and only two values

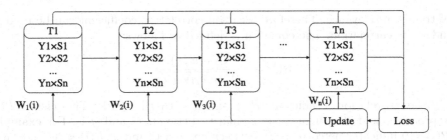

Fig. 2. SMNB prediction framework.

are allowed. The final discriminant method is to directly learn the relationship between feature output y and feature x, that is, all the students professional performance has a corresponding horizontal mapping. Only two variables (α_i, α_j) are optimized in one iteration while the remaining variables are fixed. Override constraints $\alpha_i + \alpha_j = k, \alpha_i \geq 0, \alpha_j \geq 0$. Then α_j is eliminated, and the univariate quadratic programming of α_i is obtained, then $\alpha_i \geq 0$ is obtained, and α_j is obtained from the constraint, and α_i, α_j converge to continuously, thus the vector w is obtained by calculation. For the support variable: $y_i(w^T x_i + b) = 1$, if w is known, the offset b is solved. According to the obtained w and b, the segmentation hyperplane is deduced and the classification is carried out. The distance constraint between the hyperplanes is given as shown in the following equation.

$$f(x) = \begin{cases} w \cdot x_i + b \geq +1, y_i = +1 \\ w \cdot x_i + b \leq -1, y_i = -1 \end{cases} \tag{2}$$

The formula for finding the optimal hyperplane.

$$f(x) = w^t x + b \tag{3}$$

Then find the objective function of optimization, the formula is as follows:

$$min\frac{1}{2}\|w\|^2$$
$$y_i(w^t x_i + b) \geq 1 \tag{4}$$

For some biased data, we introduce the relaxation variable C, which allows the data to be on the wrong side of the hyperplane or between intervals, and the constraint function changes to.

$$C \geq 0$$
$$\sum_{i=1}^{n} a_i y_i = 0 \tag{5}$$

In order to minimize the relaxation variable C, we introduce a penalty factor M to measure the loss caused by ignoring outliers. Finally, we adjust the objective function to.

$$f(w) = \frac{\|w\|^2}{2} + M\left[\sum_{i=1}^{n} \partial\right]^k \tag{6}$$

In the initial prediction, our input values are the students course performance and the students behavioral records, which are considered to be an associated input vector. Students performance in professional courses is regarded as the output variable.

Revised Prediction. After the first prediction, we get the accuracy of the prediction results, and there is room to improve the accuracy, so we make a second prediction. Naive Bayes algorithms have stable classification efficiency and can be used to learn and train Naive Bayes classifiers many times, while some other machine learning methods require the entire training data set to be transmitted at one time. Considering the above considerations, so we use Naive Bayes algorithm to make the second prediction. For the input of the algorithm in the two-step prediction, the data to be trained can be integrated into the vector space T, where $T = \{(x_1, y_1), ..., (x_n, y_n)\}$, x_i presents the student i's professional class performance, and y_i represents the classification result of the student i's professional class performance. $X = (x_{(1)}...x_{(n)})^T$, with a performance of 5, so classification $y = (y_{(1)}...y_{(5)})$. The central idea of the algorithm is that the prior probability and conditional probability must be calculated first, and the formula is as shown in the following equation.

$$P = (Y = c_k) = \frac{\sum_{i=1}^{5} I(y_i = c_i)}{N}, k = 1, 2, ..., k \tag{7}$$

where I (x) is the indicator function. I (ture)=1; I (false)=0; The conditional probability is calculated as follows:

$$P(X^{(j)} = a_{ji} | Y = c_k) = \frac{\sum_{i=1}^{5} I(x_i^{(j)} = a_{ji}, y_i = c_k)}{\sum_{i=1}^{5} I(y_i = c_i)} \tag{8}$$

where $P(x|y_i)$ denotes the level y_i of performance evaluation of students professional courses when the basic course performance of students has been evaluated, and the basic formula is.

$$P(x|y_i) = \frac{P(xy_i)}{P(y_i)} \tag{9}$$

We can obtain a posterior probability $P(y_i|x)$ from a priori probability, as follows:

$$P(y_i|x) = \frac{P(x|y_i)P(y_i)}{P(x)} \tag{10}$$

We regard the inconsistent data as the input value of the second prediction, and then make the second prediction, and then use 10-fold cross-validation. The final output variable is the students performance in professional courses.

3.5   Results Output

We classify the classification items in the data to form a training sample set. In initial prediction, the input is the basic performance of the students, and the output is the training samples of the students professional course performance. In revised prediction, the main work is to calculate the frequency of each students professional performance in the training samples and the classification of each category conditional probability estimation. To use classifier to classify the performance of students professional courses. The input is the classifier and the performance of the students professional courses to be classified. Output item is the mapping relationship of students professional course performance.

4 Experiment

4.1 Experimental Preparation

The performance of students professional courses mainly depends on students academic performance and students behavior. Therefore, the data set we used in the experiment is the data of Grade 13 and Grade 16 undergraduates in the Department of Software Engineering, School of Computer Science and Technology, Beijing Information Science and Technology University. Data for each student include academic performance data (class, course, score, make-up performance) and behavioural information data (internet time and internet traffic). In the experiment, 2000 pieces of academic performance data and 350 pieces of behavioral information of 13th grade students were used as training sets. The purpose is to fit the model and train the classification model. A total of 1026 pieces of performance data and 300 pieces of behavioral information were used as the test sets. We classify the students basic course performance in the data into five categories: fail, pass, medium, good and excellent. The experiment is based on the performance of students basic courses, and the performance of professional courses is regarded as the target category attribute of prediction. The data mining software tool used in the experiment is Weka. The visualization results of the student data after Weka discretization are shown in Table 3.

Table 3. Data visualization.

No.	Label	Count	Weight
1	Excellent	140	140.0
2	Fail	269	269.0
3	Medium	220	220.0
4	Pass	185	185.0
5	Good	211	211.0

4.2 Experimental Settings

SMNB algorithm is a combination of SMO algorithm and Naive Bayes algorithm. From the collected data, we take some of the students professional performance as predictive characteristics. In addition, we also use several algorithms widely discussed in the research of recommendation system as comparative experiments. These include SMO, Naive Bayes, MultiLayer Perceptron (MLP), Locally Weighted Learning (LWL) and IBK algorithms. According to the principles described in the related literature, we tuned the algorithms recommended by each benchmark to produce the best prediction quality.

We conducted 10-fold cross-validation on the collected data and randomly select different training sets and test sets each time, accounting for 80% and 20%, respectively. Finally, we use the results of 10-fold cross-validation to represent the experimental results.

4.3   Results and Analysis

We apply the basic parameters of SMNB algorithm to experiment and compare with other algorithms. The prediction feature used in the experiment is the performance of students professional courses, combining with a variety of algorithms in the weka interface for modeling and model comparison. Transfer SMNB algorithm for experiments, and the experimental results are shown in Table 4.

Table 4. SMNB algorithm results.

Parameter	Results
Correctly classified instances	0.8663
Incorrectly classified instances	0.1337
Kappa statistic	0.8312
Mean absolute error	0.0986
Root mean squared error	0.2159
Relative absolute error	0.3116
Root relative squared error	0.5430

The results show that using the SMNB algorithm to predict the accuracy of students professional courses is 86.6341%. The confusion matrix is shown in Fig. 3.

From the confusion matrix, we can see that 14 of the excellent students were classified as good by mistake. Only one of the students who failed the label was mistakenly classified as passing; 21 of the students with medium labels were mistakenly classified as passing, and 17 students were mistakenly classified as good so on. As what can be seen from Fig. 3 the most accurate predictors of experimental results are the number of students who fail in professional courses. The lowest accuracy rate of predicting results is the number of students who pass the performance test in professional courses. Table 5 shows the detailed results of using the SMNB algorithm to predict students performance in professional courses.

=======Confusion Matrix======

a	b	c	d	e	classified as
108	0	0	0	14	a = Excellent
0	251	0	1	0	b = Fail
0	0	187	21	17	c = Medium
0	18	22	163	1	d = Pass
32	0	11	0	179	e = Good

Fig. 3. The confusion matrix.

Table 5. Detailed accuracy by class.

TP rate	FP rate	Precision	Recall	F-Measure	MCC	ROC area	PRC area	Class
0.885	0.035	0.771	0.885	0.824	0.801	0.960	0.689	Excellent
0.996	**0.023**	**0.933**	**0.996**	**0.964**	**0.952**	**0.983**	**0.901**	Fail
0.831	0.041	0.850	0.831	0.840	0.796	0.933	0.766	Medium
0.799	0.027	0.881	0.799	0.838	0.802	0.919	0.761	Pass
0.806	0.040	0.848	0.806	0.827	0.781	0.944	0.767	Good
0.866	0.033	0.867	0.866	0.865	0.833	0.948	0.789	Weighted avg

We use the area under the ROC curve to measure the performance of each model in predicting students professional courses. Figure 4 shows ROC curve for professional course prediction level using SMNB, MLP, SMO, IBK, and LWL algorithms.

From the ROC curves of each algorithm in the figure above, we can see that the area under the ROC curve of SMNB algorithm is the largest. It can be seen that SMNB algorithm is more accurate than any other algorithms when it is used for prediction. Table 6 shows the comparison results of the various indicators of the six algorithms in the experiment.

With the information above, we can draw conclusions. Compared with the other four algorithms, we using undergraduate data to predict students professional performance, SMNB algorithm with kappa value of 0.8312 has a better prediction result, and the average ROC area of SMNB algorithm is larger, Root mean squared error and Mean absolut error are the lowest, so the prediction accuracy is higher. SMNB algorithm has high scalability and can be applied to multi-type datasets. The result of the algorithm is better when it is used to predict the students performance in professional courses.

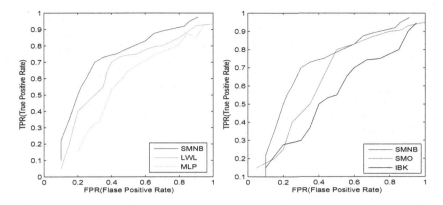

Fig. 4. Comparative ROC curve results for each algorithm.

Table 6. Contrast experimental results.

Algorithm	AVG ROC area	Mean absolute error	Root mean squared error	Kappa statistic	Accuracy
SMNB	**0.948**	**0.0986**	**0.2159**	**0.8312**	**86.6341%**
SMO	0.918	0.2555	0.3396	0.6431	71.6692%
MLP	0.725	0.1809	0.4165	0.4504	55.2833%
LWL	0.922	0.207	0.3222	0.3122	44.8698%
IBK	0.549	0.2881	0.5353	0.1001	28.0245%

5 Conclusion

Predicting students academic performance plays an important role in educational institutions, and it provides reasonable suggestions for students' academic performance. In this paper we proposed an SMNB algorithm based on SMO and Naive Bayes algorithm. The algorithm applies the two-step prediction method to predict the performance of students in professional courses. We use student performance information and student behavior information, and integrate these data into a predictive framework. The experimental results showed that our proposed SMNB algorithm effectively predicts the performance of students professional courses, and verifies that the algorithm has a high accuracy. The theoretical advantage of the combined model is to filter the data through an algorithm in the initial prediction, reducing the noise data in the revised prediction and improve the prediction accuracy. This experiment is conducted on the prediction of Weka software. Weka has certain limitations in data visualization and a certain impact on the results of experimental prediction. In the future, we plan to extract more project features to improve our SMNB algorithm, and we will explore new algorithms and new data mining tools to predict students course performance.

Acknowledgments. This work is supported by the Beijing Information Science and Technology University Teaching Reform Project (No. 2018JGYB13), the Beijing Information Science and Technology University Promote College Discipline Construction Project "Research on Key Technologies of Competitive Intelligence Analysis for Big Data", the National Cultural Heritage Administration "Internet Plus Chinese civilization" Demonstration Project (No. 2018203), the National Natural Science Foundation of China (No. 61672105), the National Key R&D Program of China (No. 2018YFB1004100) and the Teaching and Education Reform Project of Henan Province (No. 2017SJGLX079).

References

1. Hasan, R., Palaniappan, S., Raziff, A.R.A., Mahmood, S., Sarker, K.U.: Student academic performance prediction by using decision tree algorithm. In: 4th International Conference on Computer and Information Sciences (ICCOINS), pp. 1–5. IEEE, Kuala Lumpur (2018)
2. Sorour, S.E., Mine, T., Goda, K., et al.: A predictive model to evaluate student performance. J. Inf. Process. **23**, 192–201 (2015). Information Processing Society of Japan (eds.)
3. Bresfelean, V.P.: Data mining applications in higher education and academic intelligence management. In: Meng, J.E., Yi, Z. (eds.) Theory and Novel Applications of Machine Learning, p. 376. I-Tech, Vienna, February 2009. ISBN 978-3-902613-55-4
4. Asiah, M., et al.: A review on predictive modeling technique for student academic performance monitoring. In: EDP Sciences (eds.) MATEC Web of Conferences 2019, EAAIC, vol. 255, p. 03004. EDP Sciences (2019)
5. Lakkaraju, H., et al.: A machine learning framework to identify students at risk of adverse academic outcomes. In: 21th ACM SIGKDD International Conference on Knowledge Discovery and Data Mining (ACM), pp. 1909–1918. The ACM Digital Library, Sydney (2015)
6. Aguiar, E., et al.: Who, when, and why: a machine learning approach to prioritizing students at risk of not graduating high school on time. In: 5th International Conference on Learning Analytics And Knowledge (ACM), pp. 93–102. The ACM Digital Library, Poughkeepsie (2015)
7. Xu, J., et al.: Progressive prediction of student performance in college programs. In: 31th AAAI Conference on Artificial Intelligence, pp. 1604–1610. AAAI, San Francisco (2017)
8. Kabakchieva, D.: Predicting student performance by using data mining methods for classification. Cybern. Inf. Technol. **13**, 61–72 (2013). Dochev, D., IICT - BAS, Bulgaria (eds.)
9. Yadav, S.K., Bharadwaj, B., Pal, S.: Data mining applications: a comparative study for predicting student's performance. Int. J. Innovative Technol. Creative Eng. IJITCE **1**, 13–19 (2012). Ng, C.K., Simon, S.E.E., Bianchin, M.L. (eds.)
10. Pal, A.K., Pal, S.: Analysis and mining of educational data for predicting the performance of students. Int. J. Electron. Commun. Comput. Eng. IJECCE **4**, 1560–1565 (2013). Chaudhar, V.K., Diwakar, N. (eds.)
11. Oskouei, R.J., Askari, M.: Predicting academic performance with applying data mining techniques (generalizing the results of two different case studies). Comput. Eng. Appl. J. **3**, 79–88 (2014). Lambert-Torres, G., Nurmaini, S. (eds.)
12. Saa, A.A.: Educational data mining students performance prediction. Int. J. Adv. Comput. Sci. Appl. **7**, 212–220 (2016). Arai, K. (eds.)

13. Ashraf, A., Anwer, S., Khan, M.G.: A comparative study of predicting students performance by use of data mining techniques. ASRJETS **44**, 122–136 (2018). Nassar, M.O., Andron, D.R. (eds.)
14. Huang, S., Fang, N.: Predicting student academic performance in an engineering dynamics course: a comparison of four types of predictive mathematical models. Comput. Educ. **61**, 133–145 (2013). Heller, R.S., Nussbaum, M. (eds.)
15. Romero, C., Lpez, M.I., Luna, J.M., et al.: Predicting students' final performance from participation in on-line discussion forums. Comput. Educ. **68**, 458–472 (2013). Heller, R.S., Nussbaum, M. (eds.)
16. Roy, S., Garg, A.: Predicting academic performance of student using classification techniques. In: 94th IEEE Uttar Pradesh Section International Conference on Electrical, Computer and Electronics (UPCON), pp. 568–572. IEEE, Mathura (2017)
17. Kulkarni, P., Ade, R.: Prediction of students performance based on incremental learning. Int. J. Comput. Appl. **99**, 10–16 (2014). Ahmed, A., Mannock, K.L. (eds.)
18. Christian, T.M., Ayub, M.: Exploration of classification using NBTree for predicting students' performance. In: 2014 International Conference on Data and Software Engineering (ICODSE), pp. 1–6. IEEE, Bandung (2014)
19. Mayilvaganan, M., Kalpanadevi, D.: Comparison of classification techniques for predicting the performance of students academic environment. In: 2014 International Conference on Communication and Network Technologies, pp. 113–118. IEEE, Sivakasi (2014)
20. Hall, M.A., Smith, L.A.: Feature selection for machine learning: comparing a correlation-based filter approach to the wrapper. In: 12th International FLAIRS Conference, pp. 235–239. AAAI, Orlando (1999)
21. Hsu, C.W., Lin, C.J.: A comparison of methods for multiclass support vector machines. IEEE Trans. Neural Networks **13**, 415–425 (2002). He, H. (eds.)

Chinese Sign Language Identification via Wavelet Entropy and Support Vector Machine

Xianwei Jiang[1,2(✉)] and Zhaosong Zhu[1]

[1] Nanjing Normal University of Special Education, Nanjing 210038, China
{jxw, zzs}@njts.edu.cn
[2] Department of Informatics, University of Leicester, Leicester LE1 7RH, UK

Abstract. Sign language recognition is significant for smoothing barrier of communication between hearing-impaired people and health people. This paper proposed a novel Chinese sign language identification approach, in which wavelet entropy was adopted for feature reduction and support vector machine was employed for classification. The experiment was implemented on 10-fold cross validation. Our method (WE+SVM) yielded overall accuracy of $85.69 \pm 0.59\%$. The results indicated this method was effective and superior to three state-of-the-art approaches.

Keywords: Chinese sign language · Wavelet entropy · Support vector machine · K-fold cross validation

1 Introduction

Sign language (SL) is an important expression of human body language and is the main way for the hearing impaired to communicate. In areas of learning, work, and life, hearing-impaired people often use sign language as a means of communication in common activities such as education interactivities, medical treatment, shopping, and counseling etc. But sign language is a complex and complete system that contains a series of elements of hand shape, movement, body posture, and even expression. Most people who are hearing are not aware of sign language. Therefore, there are often barriers to communication between the two groups, which is a big challenge for both parties. If these hearing-impaired people are ignored, it will be a waste of social labor resources, because in China alone, the number of deaf people is as high as 27.9 million [1]. And this is also discrimination and disrespect for the hearing impaired. Another solution is to have a sign language interpreter, but this needs to be arranged in advance and at a very high cost. With the development of artificial intelligence, machine learning, especially deep learning, has become more and more popular, which makes it possible to use computer technology to realize sign language recognition. More and more researchers have joined this field.

Chinese Sign Language (CSL) is a form of sign language designed specifically for Chinese hearing-impaired people. According to the universal sign language standard issued by the state on July 1, 2018, Chinese sign language is mainly divided into two

J. Li et al. (Eds.): ADMA 2019, LNAI 11888, pp. 726–736, 2019.
https://doi.org/10.1007/978-3-030-35231-8_53

categories: finger sign language and gesture sign language. The former represents the corresponding Chinese Pinyin letters through the changes and actions of the fingers, and the words are spelled out in order according to the Pinyin rules. It contains 30 sign language letters, 26 of which are single letters (A–Z) and 4 double letters (ZH, CH, SH, NG). Finger sign language has advantages for expressing abstract concepts and terminology, which is easy to learn, has fewer actions, and is accurate in expression [2]. While gesture sign language is difficult to fully and accurately express because of the versatility and ambiguity of Chinese characters. Gesture sign language mainly simulates or gives corresponding meanings through indicative pictographic representations.

Sign Language Recognition (SLR) is defined as follows: using computer technology to interpret or transform sign language information into other information such as text, nature language, audio, which is convenient to understand and communicate. According to the input of data, sign language recognition technology can be divided into two types: sensor-based sign language recognition and computer vision-based sign language recognition. The former employs wearable devices such as data gloves and myoelectric signal armbands, while the latter mainly uses depth cameras. Sign language recognition based on computer vision is free from the constraints of hardware devices, closer to nature and reality, more flexible operation, and lower cost, which makes it the most popular sign language recognition method.

There are several common sign language recognition methods. Many researchers have combined many classification and recognition algorithms including their variants to continuously improve the experimental results. One of these methods is to use statistical analysis techniques to derive various feature vectors of the sample and then classify them. The Hidden Markov Model (HMM) is one of the most typical and commonly used. Grobel et al. [3] combined Hidden Markov Model and color gloves, and then extracted features from the video. The accurate recognition rate of 261 isolated words in their experiment was 91.3%. Mixed HMM, K-means and ant colony algorithm, paper [4] achieved the average recognition rate of 91.3% based on Taiwan sign language which has only 11 vocabularies in the data set. Cao [5] used the framing hidden Markov model to achieve accurate identification of 97.1% in 30 categories of Chinese sign language. The other is to use the template matching technology, that is, pre-establish a defined template, and then match the original data with the template, and complete the recognition with the similarity as a reference. Lichtenauer et al. [6] presented the dynamic time warping (DTW) algorithm and quadratic classification to obtain an average recognition rate of 92.3%. Another is to build on the novel neural network technology, taking advantage of the network's self-learning and organizational capabilities. Wang et al. [7] applied skin color models and convolutional neural networks to identify seven kinds of gesture samples in various test environments, and the recognition results were over 95%. The reference literature [8–10] provided some research on sign language recognition based on deep learning. The introduction of these deep convolutional neural network algorithms achieved high accuracy.

However, there are still shortcomings in these advanced methods. The Hidden Markov Model depends on going through a complicated initialization process and an enormous computational workload. It requires the presence of gesture regions and gesture motion that have been successfully detected, which conditions the robustness of the algorithm. Therefore, it does not meet the requirements of human-computer interaction, and the system has poor real-time performance, which is not conducive to popularization. The traditional template matching method is not accurate, and the identifiable gestures are few, which is only suitable for static gesture recognition. Similarly, although dynamic time warping eliminates nonlinear fluctuations in time and improves the recognition rate, it still demands establishing a template in advance, which has a large amount of calculation and low real-time performance. Novel neural network technology can achieve high accuracy, but the need for large amounts of data and the lengthy training process are its main challenge.

To resolve above issues, in this study, we proposed a method for Chinese sign language identification via wavelet entropy and support vector machine, which had superiorities of reducing the feature number and improving the training speed.

The remainder of the paper is formed as follows: Sect. 2 describes the methodology applied in our study. Here, wavelet entropy (WE), SVM and K-fold cross validation are introduced in details. Section 3 presents the experiments and results. Meanwhile, we seek the wavelet decomposition level against the overall accuracy and compare our method with three state-of-the-art approaches. Finally, conclusion is submitted in Sect. 4.

2   Methodology

2.1   Dataset

As can be seen from Fig. 1, 15 volunteers provided the samples of self-built sign language image dataset, which were divided into 30 categories. A total 450 images of Chinese sign language were preprocessed by software and normalized to 256 * 256. Figure 2 showed part of letters in Chinese sign language, which constructed the materials of our experiment. Deep learning methods [11–17] were not chosen since our dataset only contains 450 images.

Fig. 1. Part of samples

2.2   Wavelet Entropy

Wavelet entropy is a new method that can be used to analyze a certain temporal feature of a complex signal, which includes two parts: discrete wavelet transform (DWT) and entropy calculation [18].

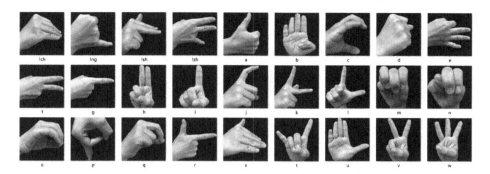

Fig. 2. Part of sign language letters

Discrete wavelet transform is a discrete implementation of continuous wavelet transform based on dyadic scales and positions. Continuous wavelet transform is defined as follows

$$C(m, n) = \int_{-\infty}^{\infty} x(t) \frac{1}{\sqrt{m}} \varphi\left(\frac{t-n}{m}\right) dt \tag{1}$$

Here m indicates the factor of dilation, n represents the factor of translation, which are both real positive numbers.

The following equations give the definition of DWT

$$L(n|j, k) = D_s\left[\sum_n x(n) l_j^*\left(n - 2^j k\right)\right] \tag{2}$$

$$H(n|j, k) = D_s\left[\sum_n x(n) h_j^*\left(n - 2^j k\right)\right] \tag{3}$$

Where $L(n|j, k)$ and $H(n|j, k)$ refer to the coefficients of the approximation and the detailed components, respectively. Separately, j and k denote the scale and translation factors. The D_s indicates the downsampling operation [19–21]. The l and h represent the low-pass and high-pass filter, respectively. The asterisk means the complex conjugate.

DWT technology has the disadvantage of increasing computation time and storage memory, and sometimes even raises the dimensions of the data set. Entropy can not only represent the random metric of image texture but also the uncertainty of information source, which solves this issue efficiently [22]. Shannon entropy, which is redefined from the concept of the traditional Boltzmann/Gibbs entropy, is expressed as follow

$$S = -\sum_{j=1}^{M} p_j \log_2(p_j) \tag{4}$$

Here S indicates the entropy value, j is the grey-level of reconstructed coefficient, M stands for the total number of grey-levels, p_j represents the probability of j.

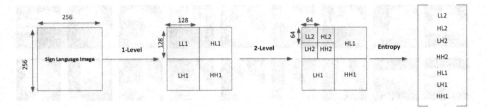

Fig. 3. Diagram of 2D-WE

We employ a 2-level WE as an example to explain this process in Fig. 3. First, for a given 256 * 256 sign language image, four subbands (LL1, HL1, LH1, and HH1) with a size of 128 * 128 are generated by discrete wavelet decomposition through a 1-level DWT. Here, L denotes low-frequency subband and H indicates high-frequency subband. Then, the LL1 is further decomposed, that is, the 2-level DWT is achieved, and four smaller subbands (LL2, HL2, LH2, and HH2) having a size of 64 * 64 are obtained [23–25]. Second, we calculate the entropy of all seven subbands (LL2, HL2, LH2, HH2, HL1, LH1, and HH1) and take it as the input vector for the classifier. In this way, WE accomplishes the reduction of the 256 * 256 sign language image to (3 * n + 1) element vectors, here n is 2, which decreases the feature number, cuts back the memory requirement, and improves the training speed of the classifier [26].

2.3   SVM

Support Vector Machine (SVM) is a common method in classification because of its excellent generalization capabilities. In addition, its advantages include high precision, refined mathematical tractability and direct geometric explanation [27]. The essence of the support vector machine is to find the best hyperplane that can divide the data points in the n-dimensional space based on the value of each feature number for a specific coordinate into two categories [28]. As can be seen in Fig. 4, schematic of linear SVMs is given, here H denotes for the hyperplane, element of S denotes for the support vector.

Suppose there is a n-dimensional M-point training data set which can be formulated as

$$\{(x_i, y_i)|x_i \in R^n, y_i \in \{-1, +1\}\}, i = 1, 2, 3, \ldots, M \qquad (5)$$

Where x_i indicates a n-dimensional training point and y_i is either -1 or $+1$. The value of y_i corresponds class 1 or class 2. Then, a $(n-1)$-dimensional hyperplane is generated as follow

$$w \cdot x - b = 0 \qquad (6)$$

Where w denotes the hyperplane normal vector, $\cdot$ represents the dot product and b is the biases. These values can be optimized to make the distances between the two

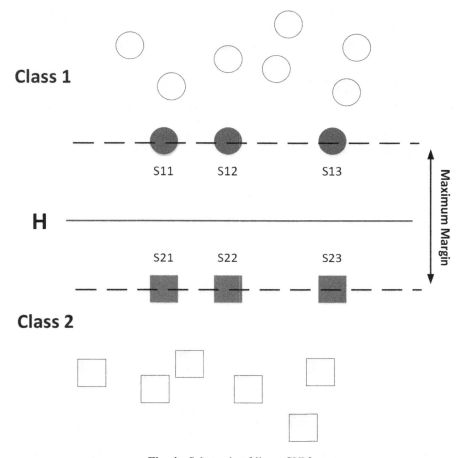

Fig. 4. Schematic of linear SVMs

parallel hyperplanes maximized and make the data separated. In mathematical form, this can be finalized as

$$\min_{w,b} \frac{1}{2} \|w\|^2 \tag{7}$$

$$s.t. y_i(w \cdot x_i - b) \geq 1, i = 1, 2, 3, \ldots, M$$

When the right optimal hyperplane cannot be found, converting the input data set into a higher dimensional space through the kernel function is proposed, which can make data set linearly separable. Therefore, kernel support vector machines are generally superior to linear support vector machines [29–31].

One-versus-one SVM was used as we face the multi-class classification problem. It was constructed of binary classifiers for each distinct pair of classes. Every sample would be included into the class which generated the most positive out [32].

2.4   K-Fold Cross Validation

K-fold cross validation is recommended for ease of use, simple features, and the use of all data during the training and verification phases, which is one of three cross validation methods (another two are leave-one-out validation and random subsampling). Its basic principle is to train with K−1 folds on the data set of the entire K-fold partition and use the left folds for validation. Repeating a total of K times, finally the average error rate of the experiment is granted. As shown in Fig. 5, the classification is implemented on a 10-fold cross validation.

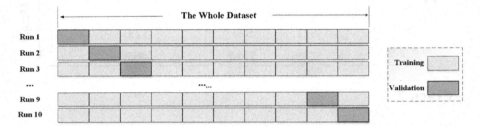

Fig. 5. Diagram of a 10-fold cross validation

Here, the number of folds K is to be focused on. If the value of K is too large, it will lead to the variance of the estimator to be too large, and the calculation will be time consuming. On the contrary, it will result a large deviation of the estimator [33]. As a rule of thumb, it is appropriate to choose a K value of 10 here, which forestalls overfitting and accomplishes out-of-sample estimation.

3   Experiments and Results

We set the wavelet decomposition level to 3, and the wavelet family is set to Haar. The statistical results of 10 runs of 10-fold cross validation were shown in Table 1. Here, overall accuracy was employed to evaluate the results. We can observe that the highest overall accuracy in 10 runs is 86.44% and lowest is 84.89%. We achieved the average overall accuracy of 85.69 ± 0.59%.

We then validated the optimal decomposition level (n). We change it from 1 to 4, and the results were shown in Table 2 and Fig. 6. As can be seen, the average overall accuracy of level (1), level (2), level (3) and level (4) are 84.64 ± 1.17%, 85.04 ± 1.24%, 85.69 ± 0.59%, and 85.20 ± 0.82%, respectively. As far as our experiments are concerned, the value of Mean ± SD raises with increasing of the

Table 1. Statistical results of our WE-SVM approach

Run	Overall accuracy
1	85.11
2	**84.89**
3	**86.44**
4	86.00
5	86.22
6	86.44
7	85.78
8	85.11
9	85.78
10	85.11
Mean ± SD	**85.69 ± 0.59**

decomposition level (n) and then begins to decline when n equals 4. Table 2 indicates that the average overall accuracy reaches the highest and the robustness achieves the best when the decomposition level (n) is 3.

Table 2. Optimal decomposition level

Run	n = 1	n = 2	n = 3	n = 4
1	86.22	84.22	85.11	85.78
2	84.89	85.11	84.89	84.22
3	85.11	84.44	86.44	85.56
4	84.22	84.67	86.00	84.67
5	83.56	84.89	86.22	85.33
6	85.78	83.56	86.44	86.67
7	83.11	86.89	85.78	85.56
8	83.33	87.56	85.11	85.33
9	86.22	84.22	85.78	85.11
10	84.00	84.89	85.11	83.78
Mean ± SD	84.64 ± 1.17	85.04 ± 1.24	**85.69 ± 0.59**	85.20 ± 0.82

Finally, we compared our WE-SVM method with state-of-the-art approaches: HMM [34], SVM-HMM [35], and HCRF [36]. We can find the full names of these abbreviations in their corresponding papers. The results are shown below in Table 3. It illustrates that our method is superior to HMM with 83.77% accuracy, SVM-HMM with 85.15% and HCRF with 78%. The reasons were as follow: Wavelet Entropy, SVM and K-fold cross validation techniques were introduced into our study, which entirely enhanced the performance. Wavelet entropy not only reduced the feature number and improved the training speed of the classifier, which resolved the shortcoming of SVM, but also cut back the requirement of memory. Combined with

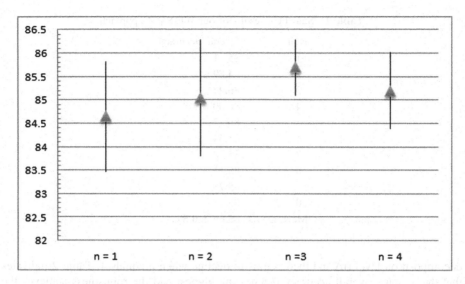

Fig. 6. Overall accuracy against decomposition level (*n*)

Table 3. Comparison with state-of-the-art approaches

Method	# images	Overall accuracy
HMM [34]	2700	83.77
SVM-HMM [35]	300	85.14
HCRF [36]	12960	78
WE-SVM (Ours)	450	85.69 ± 0.59

one-versus-one SVM, the WE-SVM algorithms were optimized. K-fold cross validation avoided overfitting and fulfilled out-of-sample estimation [37]. All of these provided the superiority of our methods.

4   Conclusion

In this study, to recognize the Chinese sign language, we adopted wavelet entropy (WE) for feature extraction and reduction, employed SVM for classification which implemented on 10-fold cross validation. Our methods (WE+SVM) achieved 85.69 ± 0.59% overall accuracy that exceeded other three state-of-the-arts. In terms of the current data set, this effect is pretty good, but it can be further improved. In the future, we shall concentrate on the following areas: (1) enlarging our data set to obtain higher performance; (2) trying other advanced techniques, like PCA [38], PSO, FNN, CNN and etc. (3) applying the WE+SVM method to other fields, such as animal image classification, biomedical imaging, Braille recognition.

Acknowledgement. This work was supported from Jiangsu Overseas Visiting Scholar Program for University Prominent Young & Middle-aged Teachers and Presidents of China.

References

1. Yuan Tiantian, Z. W. Y. X., et al.: Establishment and analysis of large-scale continuous chinese sign language dataset. Comput. Eng. Appl. **11**, 110–116 (2019)
2. Gu Dingqian, S.X., Yuanyuan, Y.: The analysis of Chinese sign language's basic words (basic movements). Chin. J. Spec. Educ. **2**, 65–72 (2005)
3. Grobel, K., Assan, M.: Isolated sign language recognition using hidden Makov model. In: IEEE International Conference on Computational Cybernetics and Simulation, vol. 1, pp. 162–167 (1997)
4. Li, T.S., Kao, M., Kuo, P.: Recognition system for home-service-related sign language using entropy-based K-means algorithm and ABC-based HMM. IEEE Trans. Syst. Man Cybern. Syst. **46**(1), 150–162 (2016)
5. Cao, X.: Development of Wearable Sign Language Translator. University of Science and Technology of China, Hefei (2015)
6. Lichtenauer, J.F., Hendriks, E.A., Reinders, M.J.T.: Sign language recognition by combining statistical DTW and independent classification. IEEE Trans. Pattern Anal. Mach. Intell. **30**(11), 2040–2046 (2008)
7. Long Wang, H.L., Wang, B., et al.: Gesture recognition method based on skin color model and convolutional neural network. Comput. Eng. Appl. **53**(6), 209–214 (2017)
8. Wu, D., Pigou, L., Kindermans, P.J., et al.: Deep dynamic neural networks for multimodal gesture segmentation and recognition. IEEE Trans. Pattern Anal. Mach. Intell. **38**(8), 1583–1597 (2016)
9. Cui, R., Liu, H., Zhang, C.: Recurrent convolutional neural networks for continuous sign language recognition by staged optimization. In: IEEE Conference on Computer Vision and Pattern Recognition, vol. [S.I.], pp. 1610–1618. IEEE (2017)
10. Huang, J., Zhou, W., Li, H., et al.: Attention based 3D-CNNs for large-vocabulary sign language recognition. IEEE Trans. Circuits Syst. Video Technol. **1**, 1 (2018)
11. Muhammad, K.: Image based fruit category classification by 13-layer deep convolutional neural network and data augmentation. Multimedia Tools Appl. **78**(3), 3613–3632 (2019)
12. Pan, C.: Abnormal breast identification by nine-layer convolutional neural network with parametric rectified linear unit and rank-based stochastic pooling. J. Comput. Sci. **27**, 57–68 (2018)
13. Pan, C.: Multiple sclerosis identification by convolutional neural network with dropout and parametric ReLU. J. Comput. Sci. **28**, 1–10 (2018)
14. Huang, C.: Multiple sclerosis identification by 14-layer convolutional neural network with batch normalization, dropout, and stochastic pooling. Front. Neurosci. Original Res. **12** (2018). Art. No. 818, (in English)
15. Xie, S.: Alcoholism identification based on an AlexNet transfer learning model. Front. Psychiatry Original Res. **10** (2019). Art. No. 205, (in English)
16. Lv, Y.-D.: Alcoholism detection by data augmentation and convolutional neural network with stochastic pooling. J. Med. Syst. **42**(1) (2018). Art. No. 2
17. Tang, C.: Twelve-layer deep convolutional neural network with stochastic pooling for tea category classification on GPU platform. Multimedia Tools Appl. **77**(17), 22821–22839 (2018)

18. Gorriz, J.M., Ramírez, J.: Wavelet entropy and directed acyclic graph support vector machine for detection of patients with unilateral hearing loss in MRI scanning. Front. Comput. Neurosci. **10** (2016). Art. No. 160
19. Gorriz, J.M.: Multivariate approach for Alzheimer's disease detection using stationary wavelet entropy and predator-prey particle swarm optimization. J. Alzheimers Dis. **65**(3), 855–869 (2018)
20. Li, Y.-J.: Single slice based detection for Alzheimer's disease via wavelet entropy and multilayer perceptron trained by biogeography-based optimization. Multimedia Tools Appl. **77**(9), 10393–10417 (2018)
21. Han, L.: Identification of Alcoholism based on wavelet Renyi entropy and three-segment encoded Jaya algorithm. Complexity **2018** (2018). Art. No. 3198184
22. Zhou, X.X., Zhang, G.S.: Detection of abnormal MR brains based on wavelet entropy and feature selection. IEEJ Trans. Electr. Electron. Eng. **11**(3), 364–373 (2016). (in English)
23. Phillips, P.: Intelligent facial emotion recognition based on stationary wavelet entropy and Jaya algorithm. Neurocomputing **272**, 668–676 (2018)
24. Li, P., Liu, G.: Pathological brain detection via wavelet packet Tsallis entropy and real-coded biogeography-based optimization. Fundamenta Informaticae **151**(1–4), 275–291 (2017)
25. Li, Y.: Detection of dendritic spines using wavelet packet entropy and fuzzy support vector machine. CNS Neurol. Disord.: Drug Targets **16**(2), 116–121 (2017)
26. Wu, X.: Tea category identification based on optimal wavelet entropy and weighted k-Nearest Neighbors algorithm. Multimedia Tools Appl. J. **77**(3), 3745–3759 (2018)
27. Martiskainen, P., Järvinen, M., Skön, J.P., et al.: Cow behaviour pattern recognition using a three-dimensional accelerometer and support vector machines. Appl. Anim. Behav. Sci. **119**, 32–38 (2009)
28. Bishop, C.M.: Pattern Recognition and Machine Learning. Information Science and Statistics. Springer, New York (2006)
29. Lu, H.M.: Facial emotion recognition based on biorthogonal wavelet entropy, fuzzy support vector machine, and stratified cross validation. IEEE Access **4**, 8375–8385 (2016)
30. Zhou, X.-X.: Comparison of machine learning methods for stationary wavelet entropy-based multiple sclerosis detection: decision tree, k-nearest neighbors, and support vector machine. Simulation **92**(9), 861–871 (2016)
31. Yang, M.: Dual-tree complex wavelet transform and twin support vector machine for pathological brain detection. Appl. Sci. **6**(6) (2016). Art. No. 169
32. Burges, C.J.C.: A tutorial on support vector machines for pattern recognition. Knowl. Discov. Data Min. **2**, 121–167 (1998)
33. Armand, S., et al.: Linking clinical measurements and kinematic gait patterns of toe-walking using fuzzy decision trees. Gait Posture **25**(3), 475–484 (2007)
34. Kumar, P., Saini, R., Roy, P.P.: A position and rotation invariant framework for sign language recognition (SLR) using Kinect. Multimedia Tools Appl. **77**, 8823–8846 (2017)
35. Lee, G.C., Yeh, F., Hsiao, Y.: Kinect-based Taiwanese sign-language recognition system. Multimed Tools Appl. **75**, 261–279 (2016)
36. Yang, H.-D., Lee, S.-W.: Robust sign language recognition with hierarchical conditional random fields. In: 20th International Conference on Pattern Recognition, Istanbul, Turkey, 2010, pp. 2202–2205. IEEE (2010)
37. Wu, L.: An MR brain images classifier via principal component analysis and kernel support vector machine. Prog. Electromagnet. Res. **130**, 369–388 (2012)
38. Artoni, A.D.F., Makeig, S.: Applying dimension reduction to EEG data by Principal Component Analysis reduces the quality of its subsequent Independent Component decomposition. NeuroImage **175**, 176–187 (2018)

An Efficient Multi-request Route Planning Framework Based on Grid Index and Heuristic Function

Jiajia Li[✉], Jiahui Hu, Vladislav Engel, Chuanyu Zong, and Xiufeng Xia[✉]

College of Computer Science, Shenyang Aerospace University, Shenyang, China
{lijiajia,xiaxiufeng}@sau.edu.cn

Abstract. In this paper, we will discuss the recently studied and currently less studied path finding problem, which is multi-request route planning (MRRP). Given a road network and plenty of points of interests (POIs), each POI has its own service lists. User specifies the departure place and destination location as well as request lists, the task of MRRP is to find the most cost-effective route from the user's starting point to the end point and satisfy all the user's requests. At present, only one paper solved MRRP problem. Its method can't be extended to time-dependent road networks directly with time-varying values because it takes up more memory. In this paper, we propose a new framework based on grid file and heuristic functions for solving MRRP problem. The framework consists of three phases. The area arrangement phase compares request lists with service lists contained in the adjacent grid nearby to filter unnecessary regions. In the routing preparation phase, the most profitable POIs are selected to meet the needs of users. And the path finding phase obtains the final shortest path results. Extensive experiments have been conducted to evaluate the performance of the proposed framework and compare with the state-of-the-art algorithms. The results show that the route costs selected by the proposed method are 2–3 times less than those obtained by others under different settings. Meanwhile, the execution time of our algorithm is 2–3 times less than them.

Keywords: Route planning · Multi-request · Heuristic function

1 Introduction

Inexpensive GPS-enabled devices become more and more popular, which gives us the opportunity to collect large amounts of trajectory data and provide route finding service. The key to the route finding problem is to find the best (shortest or cheapest) path by some criteria from source point to destination. In real life, some POIs may provide multi-services. If each POI provide different categories of services and each user has a set of requests, how to choose them to satisfy user's requests so as to minimize the total cost? This is the multi-request route

© Springer Nature Switzerland AG 2019
J. Li et al. (Eds.): ADMA 2019, LNAI 11888, pp. 737–749, 2019.
https://doi.org/10.1007/978-3-030-35231-8_54

planning (MRRP) problem, which has been proposed by [10] recently considering the categories services provided by POIs and was proved NP-hard.

Take Fig. 1 as an example, each POI provides one or more types of services. The user wants to go to D from S, and he also wants to go to KFC for dinner, fill up car, and buy wine. MRRP is to find the most profitable way satisfying the user's requests and reach the destination. Usually, this can be solved by sequential traversal (such as gas stations, drugstores and stores), but this path lacks the requirement of "KFC". Therefore, more strategies should be designed.

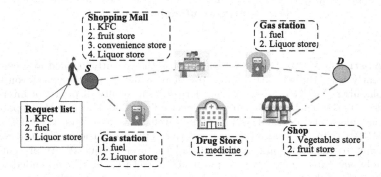

Fig. 1. Example for route planning

As far as we known, there is only one work focusing on solving the MRRP problem [10]. Four approaches for planning route are proposed, but they have some shortcomings if the POIs are far away from the shortest path. Moreover, the proposed method cannot be extended to the time-dependent cases directly where the edge weights changing with time.

The above of example of MRRP is based on the static network, where all the edges have constant weight. However, road network with edge weights changing with time has attracted more and more attention The objective of MRRP in time-dependent road network is to find the fastest path that meets all requests based on the departure time of user. Obviously, it is more difficult under the time-dependent scenario. For the static case, the cost of path can be easily obtained by summing the length of each edge and some pre-computed method can be applied to improve the efficiency of the algorithm.

In this paper, we propose a new framework, named GHMRPF, based on the grid and heuristic function to solve the MRRP problem in both static and time-dependent road networks. GHMRPF includes three important phases: (1) "Area arrangement phase" is to find enough search area utilizing the information stored in the grid file and further reduce the computations. (2) "Routing preparation phase" is to choose profitable POIs from those grids obtained by the first phase to satisfy user's requests. (3) "Path finding phase" is to obtain the final shortest path results. Extensive experiments have been conducted to evaluate the performance of the proposed framework and compare with the state-of-the-art algorithms. The results show that the route costs selected by kA*-MS and kMD-MS are 2–3 times longer than GHMRPF under different setting.

2   Related Work

In this section, we will review the work related to route planning briefly.

Traveling Salesman Problem (TSP) [11] is the well-known problem on route planning for multiple specified POIs. However, MRRP is different from TSP since the route of MRRP is composed of partial nodes instead of all nodes [10]. There are many studies on TPQ [8] and its variants [1,12,15], which are problems similar to MRRP. Li et al. [8] made an introduction to a basic TPQ problem and proposed their solution for static scenario. Given a set of points of interest P in space, where each point belongs to a specific category, a starting point S and a destination D, TPQ retrieves the best trip that starts at S, passes through at least one point from each category, and ends at E. Aljubayrin et al. [2] proposed a new path finding problem which was the skyline trips of multiple POIs category query. They also considered user's requests, and found the path for purchasing all requests where the time-dependency was considered. The difference from MRRP problem is that they find plenty of possible trips with different criteria to satisfy user's interests and they do not consider that each POI can provide several services. Lee et al. [7] proposed a RNET architecture that avoids computing in subnetworks that do not contain any POIs. In [3], the nearest neighbor path problem was studied and an Island-based algorithm was proposed.

In recent years, issuing a routing request under time-dependent scenario has attracted many researchers. Many work [4–6] focus on the nearest neighbor search on time-dependent road network. In addition, Wu et al. [13] studied the reachability and time-based path queries. Yang et al. [14] studied how to find a cost-optimal path with time constraint. Li et al. [9] studied how to find a path with the minimal on-road time which breaks FIFO property.

As far as we know, there is only one work [10] focusing on the MRRP problem. Lu et al. [10] firstly defined the MRRP problem, and proposed four approaches for planning route. k-Minimum Distance with Most Services (kMD-MS) and k-Requests with Most Services (kRA*-MS) algorithms are more efficient ones. (kMD-MS) precomputes distance for a lot of POIs who contain those unserved requests, which takes a long time and uses a lot of memory obviously. And (kRA*-MS) starts expanding the route toward destination blindly without any preliminaries. The expanding holds on until it reaches k POIs, which will take a long time if those k POIs are far away from the shortest path. In the worst case, algorithm may traverse almost all POIs through the map. In addition, these two methods cannot be extended to the time-dependent cases directly.

It can be seen that there are some query type similar to MRRP problem to some extent, but the biggest differences is that the above work consider that a node or a POI only belongs to a category.

3   Problem Definition

In this section, the formal definitions of multi-request route planning based on static and dynamic road networks are given respectively.

Definition 1 (Multi-request route planning, MRRP): *Given a real road network, represented as a graph $G = \{E, V\}$, where $V = \{v_1, v_2, .., v_n\}$ is a set of vertices and $E = \{e_1, e_2, .., e_m\}$ is a set of edges connecting them. There are a set of point of interests $P = \{p_1, p_2, .., p_{|p|}\}$. Each POI has its' own set of provided services $q_i = \{r_1, r_2, .., r_{|q|}\}$. A user specifies a start location S, a destination D and a set of requests $R = \{r_1, r_2, .., r_{|R|}\}$ that he needs. The issue is to find the minimum cost route $F = (S, O, D)$, which starts from S, traverses necessary POIs from O to satisfy user's requests and finishes at D. That is, $F = \{S, O, D\} = L(S, p_1) + \sum_{i=1}^{m-1} L(p_i, p_{i+1}) + L(p_m, D)$, where O is the set of POI objects selected by the algorithm, and $L(p_i, p_j)$ denotes the shortest path from p_i to p_j.*

Definition 2 (Dynamic Multi-request route planning, DMRRP): *Given a real road network, represented as a time-dependent graph $G = \{E, V, T\}$, where $V = \{v_1, v_2, .., v_n\}$ is a set of vertices, $E = \{e_1, e_2, .., e_m\}$ is a set of edges connecting them and T is the time cost function of the departure time for traversing an edge. There are a set of points of interest $P = \{p_1, p_2, .., p_{|p|}\}$. Each POI has its' own set of provided services $q_i = \{r_1, r_2, .., r_{|q|}\}$. A user specifies a start location S, a destination D, a departure time t, and a set of requests $R = \{r_1, r_2, .., r_{|R|}\}$ that he needs. The goal is to find a minimum cost path $F = (S, O, D)$ that takes the shortest time F^c, which starts from S at time t, traverses necessary POIs from O to satisfy user's requests and finishes at D. That is, $F^c = \{S, O, D, t\} = L(S, p_1, t_0) + \sum_{i=1}^{m-1} L(p_i, p_{i+1}, t_i) + L(p_m, D, t_m)$, where O is the set of POI objects selected by the algorithm, and $L(p_i, p_j, t)$ denotes the minimum time cost from p_i to p_j with the departure time from p_i at time t.*

4 GHMRPF Description

In this section, we would like to present our proposed framework "Grid and heuristic based multi-request route planning framework (GHMRPF)" for solving MRRP problem. GHMRPF consists three phases: (1) Preparation phase, or area arrangement phase, where the method prepares network by girds for further search and helps filter the unnecessary areas. (2) Routing preparation phase or choosing POIs phase, where the most profitable POIs are selected based on the heuristic function values. (3) Path finding phase, where the best route is obtained based on the selected POIs utilizing the search algorithm.

4.1 Preparation Phase

When we search the POIs we want from a real road network of certain city, we have to deal with a huge amount of vertices, edges and POIs. Checking all possible POIs to satisfy user's requests is too expensive and not efficient. Actually, we needn't to check the whole map. User specifies his starting and ending points and his requests. We can utilize the above information and search only the surrounding area that will be enough to satisfy user's whole requests, which will require less memory and computation time. To quickly find the smallest area that meets all user requirements, the grid index is utilized to identify the "location" of each POI. The graph is divided into grids of the same size Each grid stores a list of services (requests) provided by those POIs it contains. Based on the location of the starting and ending points, the grid is expanded layer by layer, until the union of these grid services contains the set of user-specified request. At this point, the sub-area is obtained, which is much smaller than the entire map, especially if the starting and ending points are very close.

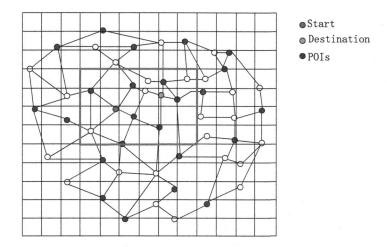

Fig. 2. Arrange area example

Take Fig. 2 as an example, user specified the starting and ending points, we build the area around his probable trip. After building the area we need to ensure whether there are enough POIs to satisfy all requests. For this we store a list of provided services from each POI inside a grid, and then we can get all the lists of services provided inside this area by summarizing grids' services lists. In this case, if the area doesn't contain all the services we can expand the area until we get all needed services.

To obtain the appropriate area, the locations of the start and destination points are used. The grids columns of the two points are obtained to get a "width" of the rectangle and lines to get the "height" of the rectangle. If there are not enough POIs to satisfy user's interests we expand the area by adding one line of grids from each side of rectangle (if it won't reach an edge of the cell), and check services again. The obtained necessary area is denoted as NA.

4.2 Heuristic

Before the description of the second phase, we would like to introduce the heuristic function used here. Calculating the exact distance between two points in the graph is time-consuming. To improve the efficiency, the lower bound of exact distance is estimated, which is more easily calculated and is further used to obtain the heuristic value.

Static Scenario. For static scenario we use Euclidean distance to estimate the lower bound: if the point $S = (x_1, y_1)$ and point $D = (x_2, y_2)$, the E distance between them is:

$$E = \sqrt{(x_1 - x_2)^2 + (y_1 - y_2)^2} \tag{1}$$

The Eq. 1 is the lower bound cost estimated by the classical heuristic function, which will never be higher than the actual cost.

Dynamic Scenario. For dynamic case the strategy is a little bit changed. The cost of the edge changes over time, and it's essentially a change in speed. The minimum cost of going through a edge can be obtained by dividing the length of this edge by the maximum possible speed. Then the lower bound cost between two points in the graph can be estimated by the Euclidean distance and the maximum speed. The heuristic travel cost is:

$$H_t = \frac{\sqrt{(x_1 - x_2)^2 + (y_1 - y_2)^2}}{max(v)} \tag{2}$$

where $max\{v\}$ is the maximum speed on the edges located in this area.

We use a heuristic function to select the POI in the final path. This function calculates the heuristic cost from starting position S to candidate POI p and from p to target D by considering the useful services. We named this function *SPDn*. It is a function that estimates the priority of POI and gives it an evaluation to determine whether it should be calculated. This feature helps to find the POI of the most services in advance and reduces the number of POIs accessed.

The *SPDn* function of a POI depends on:

- Heuristic cost between start point S and destination *D(SD)*, to estimate the lower bound between the start and the destination location.
- Heuristic cost from start point S to point of interest p and from p to destination *D(SPD)*, to estimate the lower bound for the route that starts at start location S, visits POI p and finishes in the destination location D.
- The number of unserved services that this POI can provide.

By combing these factors, the following formula is utilized to rank POIs,

$$SPDn = \frac{SD * n}{SPD} \tag{3}$$

which takes the number of useful services on the POI and the deviation between the POI and the straight route into account.

The parameter n depends on useful services in the moment. What are the useful services? Each POI can provide its own services, one or more, but not necessarily meet the user's requirements. If user requires r_1, r_2, r_3 while a POI provides r_1, r_4, r_{10}, that means there is only one useful service on this POI.

So in the case $n = 1$. Every useful service gains $SPDn$ by several percent. The percentage can be different, e.g., each useful service gives 35% gain. For example, two useful services will gain $SPDn$ by 70%.

Take Fig. 3 as an example. There are two POIs p_1 and p_2. If distances $SD = 10, Sp_1D = 12$ and $Sp_2D = 14$, then $SD/Sp_1D = 0.83$ is higher than $SD/Sp_2D = 0.714$. But if p_1 provides only one useful service ($n = 1$) and p_2 provides two useful services ($n = 2$), $Sp_1D = 0.83$ and $Sp_2D = 1.428$, and as result p_2 will be chosen because now it has a higher priority.

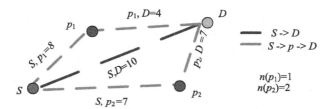

Fig. 3. Heuristic example.

4.3 Choosing POIs Phase

In this phase, the POIs which will form the route are selected. The core content here is $SPDn$ heuristic computing, which is used to select candidate POIs and calculate actual network cost, as well as service comparison, which will select POIs from candidates that will be a part of our route. The strategy of static and dynamic scenarios is similar. The difference is that for dynamic scenarios, dynamic $SPDn$ is used in the first step and time-dependent A* algorithm is used in the second step.

The GHMRPF algorithm selects POIs from the necessary area NA and calculate the heuristic value $SPDn$ for those POIs who provide at least one useful service These calculated values and the corresponding POIs are inserted into temporary set (tmp-set) and sort by $SPDn$ in descending order. Next, GHMRPF chooses the first $k(k$ can be variable) POIs from the tmp-set and calculate the exact sum cost (distance or time) from S to it and from it to D for each POI p_i, denoted as $L_s = (S, p_i, D)$ for static case or $L_d = (S, p_i, D, t)$ for dynamic case. Then, GHMRPF compares k POIs with the smallest L and add the POI with the biggest amount of provided services into the object set O. If more than one POI have the same amount, the one with the smaller L is selected. After adding the candidate POI into the set O, the corresponding requests provided by this POI are deleted from the query request list R. Then GHMRPF cleans the tmp-set and do the same operation again for rest of the requests until all requests from R are satisfied and get the final set O.

4.4 Path Finding Phase

After the previous two main phases, an unordered POIs set O is obtained. To get the valid route $F = (S, O, D)$ with an ordered set O', we use permutation based on same heuristic above. Further we can run search algorithm as follows:

$$TD\_A * route = d(S, p'_1, t_0) + \sum_{i=1}^{n-1} d(p'_i, p'_{i+1}, t_i) + d(p'_n, t'_n, D) \qquad (4)$$

where p'_i is a POI from the ordered set O', t_0 is the given departure time, t_i is the obtained departure time from p'_i and $d(p'_i, p'_{i+1}, t_i)$ is the shortest path computed by time-dependent A* algorithm between any two POIs from departure time t_i.

Take Fig. 4 as an example, TD_A* runs from the start location S toward the first POI p_1 which is from the ordered set O' at the given departure time t_0. When reach the POI p_1, the arrival time t_1 is get. Further, the arrival time t_1 can be used as a departure time from p_1 and run the algorithm toward the second POI p_2. Continue such actions until traversing all the POIs from O'. The last step is to run A* algorithm from the last POI p_n toward the destination D with the departure time t_n.

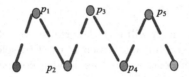

Fig. 4. Running algorithm example

5 Experimental Results

5.1 Environment and Data Set

To evaluate the proposed framework, we use a real road network of Oldenburg. The map contains 6105 nodes and 7035 edges. We randomly generate a set of 600 POIs and 10 different possible services. Each POI has a random amount of services from 1 to 4 and randomly provide services. We divided the Oldenburg network into 122, 256 and 512 grids respectively for testing.

For the dynamic case, the functions of the edges are generated. We divide the day into five parts, namely [22:00, 7:00], [7:00, 9:00], [9:00, 17:00], [17:00, 19:00] and [19:00, 22:00]. Each part has a different range of edge weights. The edge weight is generated randomly every five minutes, and the 288 weights of an edge are fitted into piecewise linear functions.

All results are the average of 100 queries. The kRA*-MS and kMD-MS algorithms proposed in [10] are selected for comparison. All experiments are implemented in Java Intel IDEA with JDK 1.8. The hardware platform is on PC with Intel i7-6700, and 8 GB memory under Windows 10. We tested the route distance (the total distance the result travels, which is the objective of the algorithm, the smaller the better), the number of visited POIs (the number of parking times required, the less the better), and the execution time (the efficiency of the algorithm, the shorter the better) under different query settings (including the amount of requests, and the distance between starting and destination location).

5.2 Evaluation Results of Static Scenario

Figure 5 illustrates the effect of the number of query requests on the route distance of results. As expected, the route distances of both kRA*-MS and kMD-MS are longer than our GHMRPF. That is because both of them choose the POIs with most services only when they have found k POIs, while GHMRPF gives priority to the most services at advance. From this trend, we can see that our heuristic function is more effective. Moreover, kRA*-MS is very close to GHMRPF, since it finds POIs are on the shortest path to destination. But when there aren't such POIs, it loses some accuracy.

Figure 6 illustrate the effect of the number of query requests on the number of visited POIs of results. The fewer POIs we visit, the fewer parking we need, which is preferred by us. GHMRPF shows the smallest number of POIs that we need to purchase through the $SPDn$ function. Because our framework from the beginning gives a priority to the POIs with the largest number of necessary services. As a result, this strategy helps to reduce the number of POIs that we need to visit to satisfy all requests. kRA*-MS and kMD-MS don't calculate the amount of services at advance, but they find some k POIs according to some evaluation firstly and only after give a preference to the most services, they can reduce POIs' number sometimes.

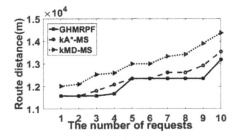
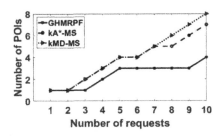

Fig. 5. Route distance vs. number of requests

Fig. 6. Number of POIs vs. number of request

Figures 7 and 8 illustrate the effect of the number of query requests and distance on the execution time respectively. It can be seen that GHMRPF spends the smallest time for computation in both cases. This is because the search area is reduced by the area arrangement strategy which helps to avoid traversing unnecessary areas. In the same area, we reduce the number of POIs that need to be checked, so it takes less time. kMD-MS precomputes distance for a lot of POIs that contain unserved requests. It takes a long time and uses a lot of memory obviously. kRA*-MS starts expanding the route toward destination blindly. The expansion will continue until it reaches k POIs, which will take a long time if those k POIs are far away from the shortest path. In the worst case, algorithm may traverse almost all POIs through the map.

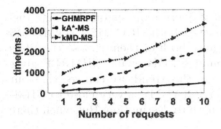 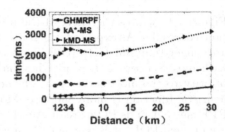

Fig. 7. Execution time vs. number of requests

Fig. 8. Execution time vs. distance

Figure 9 illustrates the effect of the number of grids and the number of requests on the execution time. It can be seen that, with a larger partition, the framework needs less computation time. The partition into 122 grids shows the lowest speed. Because the Oldenburg map isn't big and it doesn't need such large partition. As we can see, 256 and 512 partitions show almost similar result with a small benefit of the 512 partitions.

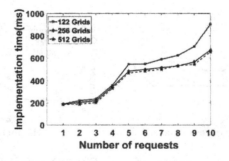

Fig. 9. Execution time vs. number of grids

From these evaluation results, we can see that GHMRPF works better than others with the help of grid and heuristic function. The proposed framework works faster and finds less POIs that need to be traversed to satisfy all requests. As a result, it finds a cheaper route.

5.3   Dynamic Scenario Evaluation

Figures 10 and 11 illustrate the effect of query requests on routing travel time and the execution time of GHMRPF under three different edge functions. The weight of each edge function is generated by dividing the length of the edge by the randomly generated velocity. The Gen-choose code selects one-fifth of the edges, specifies the range of speed changes, and the other four-fifths of the edge velocity is randomly generated. More amounts of user's requests, means that we have to find more services to satisfy the queries. As expected, the travel time of the results and the execution time of GHMRPF both rise as the number of requests increases. It can be seen from Fig. 10 that the travel time doesn't change so dramatically with a bigger number of requests. The reason is that the framework strongly helps to reduce the amount of needed POIs.

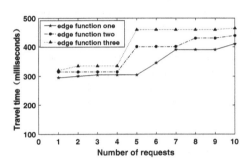

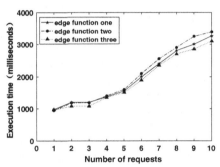

Fig. 10. Travel time vs. number of requests

Fig. 11. Execution time vs. number of requests

The value of k, which determines the number of candidate POIs from the temporary set to be precomputed and impacts on the performance of GHMRPF. Figures 12 and 13 illustrated the effect of k on the routing travel time and the execution time of GHMRPF respectively.

In Fig. 12, with increasing of k, we can get a better accuracy and a better route. However, the accuracy shows explicit growth only for values from 1 to 5, and from 5 to 9 we can observe a constant time. We admit that for different data sets the k value will differ and need to be re-set. But in our case, for Oldenburg map, the value $k = 5$ is enough. The temporary set has been already sorted by $SPDn$ function, which includes the number of n and the maximal deviation from the lower bound. As a result, the POIs in the top of temporary set are not so far away from the fastest route and contain multiple useful services n. That is, POIs with better perspectives are kept in the top of the set, so it doesn't need so high value k to get a high accuracy. It can be seen from Fig. 13 that the execution time increases as the value of k rises. With higher k, we will have more computations and spend longer time as a result.

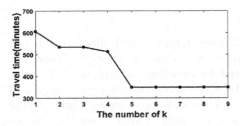
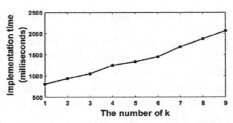

Fig. 12. Travel time vs. value of k **Fig. 13.** Execution time vs. value of k

6   Conclusion and Future Work

We propose a new framework GHMRPF based on grid file and heuristic function to solve the multi-request route planning problem in both static and dynamic scenarios. Extensive experiments have been conducted to evaluate the performance of the proposed algorithm and compare it with two existing algorithms (kRA*-MS and kMD-MS). The experimental results show that the proposed framework can filter the unnecessary areas by comparing the query's requests with the contained types of services in the nearby girds. Specifically, the route costs selected by others are 2–3 times longer than those obtained by us under different settings. Meanwhile, the execution time of our algorithm is 2–3 times less than them.

For future work, we would like to improve time-dependent scenario and develop valid pre-computation strategy for our framework.

Acknowledgement. This research was partially supported by the Natural Science Foundation of Liaoning Province under Grant No. 2019JH3/10300299; National Natural Science Foundation of China under Grant Nos. 61502317, 61802268.

References

1. Ahmadi, E., Nascimento, M.A.: A mixed breadth-depth first search strategy for sequenced group trip planning queries. In: IEEE International Conference on Mobile Data Management (2015)
2. Aljubayrin, S., He, Z., Zhang, R.: Skyline trips of multiple POIs categories. In: Renz, M., Shahabi, C., Zhou, X., Cheema, M.A. (eds.) DASFAA 2015. LNCS, vol. 9050, pp. 189–206. Springer, Cham (2015). https://doi.org/10.1007/978-3-319-18123-3_12
3. Chen, L., Qin, G.: K nearest neighbor path queries based on road networks. TELKOMNIKA Indones. J. Electr. Eng. **11**(11), 6637–6644 (2013)
4. Demiryurek, U., Banaei-Kashani, F., Shahabi, C.: Towards K-nearest neighbor search in time-dependent spatial network databases. In: Kikuchi, S., Sachdeva, S., Bhalla, S. (eds.) DNIS 2010. LNCS, vol. 5999, pp. 296–310. Springer, Heidelberg (2010). https://doi.org/10.1007/978-3-642-12038-1_20
5. Demiryurek, U., Shahabi, C., Banaei-Kashani, F.: Efficient K-nearest neighbor search in time-dependent spatial networks. In: Bringas, P.G., Hameurlain, A.,

Quirchmayr, G. (eds.) DEXA 2010. LNCS, vol. 6261, pp. 432–449. Springer, Heidelberg (2010). https://doi.org/10.1007/978-3-642-15364-8_36
6. Komai, Y., Nguyen, D.H., Hara, T., Nishio, S.: kNN search utilizing index of the minimum road travel time in time-dependent road networks. In: Proceedings of the IEEE Symposium on Reliable Distributed Systems, pp. 131–137 (2014)
7. Lee, K.C., Lee, W., Zheng, B., Tian, Y.: ROAD: a new spatial object search framework for road networks. IEEE Trans. Knowl. Data Eng. **24**(3), 547–560 (2012)
8. Li, F., Cheng, D., Hadjieleftheriou, M., Kollios, G., Teng, S.-H.: On trip planning queries in spatial databases. In: Bauzer Medeiros, C., Egenhofer, M.J., Bertino, E. (eds.) SSTD 2005. LNCS, vol. 3633, pp. 273–290. Springer, Heidelberg (2005). https://doi.org/10.1007/11535331_16
9. Li, L., et al.: Minimal on-road time route scheduling on time-dependent graphs. Proc. VLDB Endow. **10**(11), 1274–1285 (2017)
10. Lu, E.H.C., Chen, H.S., Tseng, V.S.: An efficient framework for multirequest route planning in urban environments. IEEE Trans. Intell. Transp. Syst. **PP**(99), 1–11 (2017)
11. Menger, K.: Das botenproblem. In: Ergebnisse eines mathematischen kolloquiums, vol. 2, pp. 11–12 (1932)
12. Roy, S.B., Das, G., Amer-Yahia, S., Yu, C.: Interactive itinerary planning. In: 2011 IEEE 27th International Conference on Data Engineering, pp. 15–26. IEEE (2011)
13. Wu, H., Huang, Y., Cheng, J., Li, J., Ke, Y.: Reachability and time-based path queries in temporal graphs. In: IEEE International Conference on Data Engineering, pp. 145–156 (2016)
14. Yang, Y., Gao, H., Yu, J.X., Li, J.: Finding the cost-optimal path with time constraint over time-dependent graphs. Proc. VLDB Endow. **7**(9), 673–684 (2014)
15. Zhu, C., Xu, J., Liu, C., Zhao, P., Liu, A., Zhao, L.: Efficient trip planning for maximizing user satisfaction. In: Renz, M., Shahabi, C., Zhou, X., Cheema, M.A. (eds.) DASFAA 2015. LNCS, vol. 9049, pp. 260–276. Springer, Cham (2015). https://doi.org/10.1007/978-3-319-18120-2_16

Nodes Deployment Optimization Algorithm Based on Fuzzy Data Fusion Model in Wireless Sensor Networks

Na Li[1], Qiangyi Li[1,2(✉)], and Qiangnan Li[2]

[1] Nanjing Agricultural University, Nanjing 210095, Jiangsu, China
{cjjl98,cxl979}@yeah.net
[2] Henan University of Science and Technology, Luoyang 471023, Henan, China

Abstract. As an integrated network, wireless sensor networks can connect the logic information world with the real physical world by performing information sensing, gathering, processing and delivering. There are diverse and potential applications for Wireless sensor networks. In recent years, the increasing requisitions of Wireless sensor networks have more and more research dedicated to the question of sensor nodes deployment. As for the nodes deployment of underwater wireless sensor networks, the optimization strategy on node deployment determines the capability and quality of service of Wireless sensor networks as well. There are some key points that should be considered, including the coverage range to be monitored, energy consumption of nodes, amount of deployed sensors, connectivity, and lifetime of the Wireless sensor networks. This paper analyzes the problem of nodes deployment optimization in wireless sensor network. Referring to the fuzzy cognitive model and fuzzy data fusion model, with consideration of certain environmental factors which may affect the detection result, a novel method NAFC is presented in this paper. The simulation model is established by MATLAB software. According to the simulation results, the demonstrated algorithm of underwater sensor node deployment shows its effectiveness, which can fulfill the requisition of network coverage ratio, reduce the number of deployed nodes, prolong the network lifetime and expand the detection range of network, thus the scheme improve the comprehensive detection performance of WSN accordingly.

Keywords: Nodes deployment optimization algorithm · Fuzzy data fusion model · Wireless sensor networks

1 Introductions

Underwater wireless sensor network can set up network automatically referring to a multi-hop, short distance wireless communication technology, utilizing the nodes of the low energy consumption with the self-organizing ability as well [1–6].

Underwater sensor networks deployed in oceans can provide new technology and equipment for, information and data collection platform in many fields, which have extraordinary and extensive application perspectives, with the characteristics of the sensor network, combined with wireless communication technology, network

J. Li et al. (Eds.): ADMA 2019, LNAI 11888, pp. 750–760, 2019.
https://doi.org/10.1007/978-3-030-35231-8_55

technology and information processing technology, to realize real-time monitoring of marine information [7–12].

Underwater wireless sensor network and the marine environment monitoring sensor network management can provide advanced technology equipment and information platform for adverse applications such as resource protection, disaster monitoring, marine engineering, marine production and marine military activities, anti-submarine warfare and so on, thus have obtained great deal of attentions from the academics, research institutions, governmental agencies, military and marine industries, environmental protection organizations etc. At present, the study of underwater wireless sensor network has become a hot issue in the field of wireless sensor network [13–18].

As sensor network nodes are directly related to energy consumption, communication bandwidth of networks, the optimal allocation of limited resources for example computing ability, and affect the lifetime perception, monitoring, communication and other service quality goals of underwater sensor network, consequently, the scheme of sensor nodes deployment affects the cost and performance of the wireless sensor network. A superior deployment strategy can not only effectively enhance sensor networks' perception quality and lifetime, but also reduce the total costs at the same time [19–24]. Therefore, it is the primary problem for underwater sensors networking to adopt a suitable nodes deployment strategy [25–29].

Fuzzy cognitive model and fuzzy data fusion model are presented in this paper, combining with the environmental factors which affect the result of the detection. The algorithm afforded to underwater sensor node deployment can satisfy the demand of coverage quality well, reduce the number of nodes deployed remarkably, extend the network lifetime lastingly, expand the detective network range effectively, and thus improve the detection performance of the network comprehensively.

2 Related Works

Uncertain coverage is a key problem of wireless sensor networks. Currently, the mainstream research method of uncertain cover is usually based on mathematical statistics and probability theory. However, in practice, according to computing the target node distance, the credibility of node detection relates to the credibility values changing between 0 and 1, considering the target characteristics and surrounding environment. As perception degree is not clear and precise at the node's boundary, and perception ability is changeable over time. These phenomena show the fuzzy characteristics of sensors' perception ability. That the paper refers to fuzzy theory to deal with questions with the characteristics of uncertain and fuzzy is unique advantage.

We give the following definitions, consequently.

Factor set: is a set U of objective factors, can be described by Eq. (1), which may affect perception nodes' test results of a certain supposed target point that locates in the detection area of sensor network, within the perception range of a sensor.

$$U = \{u_1, u_2, \cdots, u_n\} \tag{1}$$

As for the factors within set U, we call optimistic (positive) factors which can help network to achieve detecting results, while the factors that can interfere with network's ability to detect are described as pessimistic (negative) factors.

Consequently, the value of factor can be define as follows, if $u_i(0 < i \leq n)$ is a positive factor, the value of u_i equals to 1, and if u_i is a negative factor, the value of u_i equals to 0.

As for as passive sonar sensors, there are some positive factors including the target node source level, target probability distribution function, the frequency of the target, etc. And the pessimistic factors include environmental noise distribution, target directivity index, the target of transmission loss and other interference factors etc.

Factor weight set: is the set of weight values of every factor. The values of weight can affect the detection results of target point while data fusing. It can be described by (2).

$$V = \{v_1, v_2, \ldots v_n\} \tag{2}$$

Define the sum of all factors weight as 1, which is described as follows:

$$v_1 + v_2 + \ldots + v_n = 1 \tag{3}$$

Result evaluation set: Computes the result according to every influence factor and its weight of target point, which can be formulated as follows:

$$W = U \bullet V^T = \{u_1 v_1, u_2 v_2, \cdots, u_n v_n\} \tag{4}$$

The result evaluation set is called the results.

Perception index: Assuming that a certain target point Q is within the detection area, accordingly, its result evaluation set is described as follows:

$$W_Q = \{w_1, w_2, \cdots, w_n\} \tag{5}$$

Define the vector model as the Eq. (6).

$$v(Q) = |W_Q| = \sqrt{w_1^2 + w_2^2 + \cdots w_n^2} \tag{6}$$

Then we call the model as network perception index of point Q.

Fuzzy cognitive model: Due to the randomness and changeability of influence factors, perception index of sensor to the target point is also constantly changing. While the impact of these random factors on perception index is still limited, the perception index is variable within a changeable scope. Thus, we can't get an accurate perception index of the perceptual node to the target point. With the increasing of distance between the target point and sensor node, the perception ability of the sensor node is falling accordingly, forming the "ring" range of fuzzy perception. We can get the fuzzy perception model of the target point after fusing the similar "ring" in fuzzy perception fusion method in terms of detection demands.

Assuming that the target point is in the area of multiple perceptual nodes, the perception index of the target point will increase in fuzzy perception fusion method.

Proving is given as follows. Due to the three sensors' detecting the target point O at the same time, consequently, the effect of positive factors increases at the point O, and its weight also increases after data fusion. So in the circumstances, the perception index of point O increases than that of only one sensor node, after data fusion, sense perception node areas increase accordingly as well. Thus, perception range is equivalent to increasing areas of A single node, namely for the same test area, to achieve the same detection efficiency with reduced the number of nodes.

3 Nodes Deployment Based on Data Fusion

Underwater sensor network system, the data fusion system is mainly of numerical integration level fusion for detection, which are composed of data fusion nodes and detecting nodes. Each detection node can work independently, and deliver the detection results to data fusion node which makes the final decision.

Assume that there are some detection nodes summed up a total of n, existing in a unit of data fusion. The set of factors of detection node i to the target point is described as the factor set U_i. The set of weight values of every factor is described as factor weight set V_i.

In terms of the fuzzy fusion rules, the formulas of the fusion results of target point in the network are as follows,

$$U = U_1 \oplus U_2 \oplus \cdots \oplus U_n = \{u_1, u_2, \cdots, u_m\} \tag{7}$$

$$V = V_1 \oplus V_2 \oplus \cdots \oplus V_i = \{v_1, v_2, \cdots v_m\} \tag{8}$$

Accordingly, the result evaluation set of the target node in network is described as follows,

$$W = U \bullet V^T = \{w_1, w_2, \cdots, w_m\} \tag{9}$$

Perception index of the target node in network is calculated following from (10).

$$v(W) = |W| = \sqrt{w_1^2 + w_2^2 + \cdots + w_m^2} \tag{10}$$

According to the perception index of the target node in network, in terms of fuzzy theory, decision rules of detection nodes in network are as follows.

$$\kappa(W) = P(u_0 = 1|W) = \begin{cases} 1, v(W) \geq t \\ 0, v(W) < t \end{cases} \tag{11}$$

The detection result of target point in network with fuzzy method is computed according to a given vector W, where t is a decision threshold for fusion node.

The emergence of underwater target obeys some natural rules and limited to some factors such as the relationship between migratory habits of fish population and season, the connection between information collection of water quality and ocean current, the contact of overseas routes and channel, etc.

The location of target node and environmental noise may also largely affect the sensor network to detect the target node. Therefore, if we can design deployment algorithm of the sensor nodes, making full use of the location information related to the goal, it will be able to greatly improve the efficiency of network node deployment.

Concerning certain goals such as fish populations, submarine and so on, the paper takes aim at the problem of detecting target points whose position information is usually related to the distribution characteristics, for example, channels, depth, routes, etc. Utilizing the information of the target in the detection area including prior probability, distribution characteristics, influence factors etc., referring fuzzy theory, combining with fuzzy cognitive model and data fusion model, this paper puts forward a node deployment algorithm of fuzzy criterion (NAFC) using fuzzy awareness.

According to the analysis, we make the following assumptions:

(1) All of the nodes are passive sonar sensors, which have the same awareness performance;
(2) All sensor nodes have the abilities of data fusion, communicating with gathering node underwater, self-location and free mobility;
(3) Within a range of detection area, environmental noise relates to the position distribution, however, the environmental noise of the waveform, amplitude, frequency keeps stable in the same location;
(4) The distribution probability about the location of the target node is known;
(5) Node's working state can be divided into two sub-states, namely communication mode and detection mode. In the communication mode node's energy consumption is much higher than that of detection mode.

Algorithm steps are as follows:

Step 1: According to the probability distribution characteristic as well as environmental impact factors of target nodes, we can divide detection area into some regional detection blocks $(V_1, V_2, \ldots, V_l)$; For each detection area block $V_i(0 < i \leq l)$, firstly, we determine the fuzzy perception model M_i of target nodes, then calculate the fuzzy perception radius R_i of detection blocks, the optimal perceived distance D_i and decision threshold t respectively;

Step 2: Accordance with the coverage requirements of each test piece and the optimal perceived distance D_i calculated, determine node deployed density ρ_i and node redundancy γ_i. Then randomly deploy the nodes giving a total of N_i within each detection block $V_i(0 < i \leq l)$;

$$N_i = \rho_i \times V_i \times (1 + \gamma_i) \tag{12}$$

$$N_i' = \rho_i \times V_i \tag{13}$$

Step 3: For each detection block V_i, randomly awaken perceptual nodes summed up a total of N_i', N_i' can be calculated in terms of formula (13). Then set up the marks of these nodes into value of zero. Consequently, the rest nodes enter a dormant state with their flag value marked 1;

Step 4: Randomly choose a perception node in wakened state, setting its flag and ID both equal to 1, then select the nearest perception node, setting its ID equal to 2, recording the distance between the two nodes as D';
Inspired by "fictitious force" principle, the sensor node is quite similar to a molecular. The force between molecules is associated with the distance between molecules. Supposing that the distance between two perception nodes is D', and the optimal perceived distance is D_i, where the threshold value described as t.
When the distance D' between two perception nodes meets

$$D' < D_i - t \qquad (14)$$

The intermolecular force is of repulsion, thus node 2 drifts far away of a unit;
When the distance D' between two perception nodes meets,

$$D' > D_i + t \qquad (15)$$

The intermolecular force is attractive force, which can make node 2 closely of a unit;
Node 2's movement complete until the perception node distance meets

$$D_i - t \leq D' \leq D_i + t \qquad (16)$$

Step 5: Utilizing the greedy algorithm, select the node with minimal perception node distance, meanwhile, whose flag equals to 0, adjusting its position and counting up its ID consequently, until entire node position complete adjustment, therefore, the detection block achieve deployment.
Step 6: Performing steps 4 and 5 iteratively, adjust all the node position within each detection block till all detection areas in the network fulfill a dynamic modulation.
    Each perception node completes the initialization for data fusion task allocation and data fusion node rotation sequence. Nevertheless, the perception sensor nodes act as data fusion nodes and communication nodes in turn.
Step 7: In the stage of dynamic adjustment of network, once a new node is dead, the nearest dormant neighbor node of which will wake up and shift to the suitable location for alternate. The lifetime of network will be over till overall nodes' exhaustion.

4   Simulation Results

We design a simulation platform using MATLAB software to validate NAFC. The parameters of simulation experiment are set up as follows: the target source level, center frequency, the environmental noise level. All performances of passive sonar nodes are the same. As for receiving directivity index, we assume that each single node of passive sonar possesses a sensing radius of 250 m long, in the condition of effective monitoring. The hypothesis detection area is a 3-dimensional bulky space of 8000 m long, 2000 m wide and 1000 m high, ignoring some undersea factors' influence on detection results such as current, environmental ultrasonic and so on. In order to simplify the simulation models, in the detection area, suppose that the influence factors set and the x direction of the target's position obey Gaussian distribution, irrelevant to y and z directions, which is calculated following from (17).

$$f(x) = \frac{1}{\sqrt{2\pi}\sigma} e^{-\frac{(x-\mu)^2}{2\sigma^2}} \tag{17}$$

Where μ is boundary location, and σ is the variance of influence factors.

According to the characteristics of the passive sonar node of underwater sensor networks, in terms of the related definitions, we compare some performance indicators such as coverage ratio of monitoring area, change of detection rate and detection rate of target node of the following simulation deployment algorithms respectively, including target prior probability (VFPP), virtual force algorithm (VFA) and the node deployment algorithm of fuzzy criterion (NAFC). The more effective the network coverage and the higher detection rate of the target node, the superior monitoring performance of the wireless senor network affording, consequently.

In this section, concentrate on some performance indexes comprising detection rate of target node, coverage ratio of monitoring area and total energy remaining, whose changes are analyzed relating to totality of nodes and time consumption in different algorithms including VFPP, VFA and NAFC, respectively. Then contrast results are shown in Figs. 1, 2 and 3:

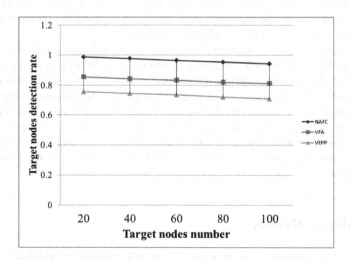

Fig. 1. Change of target detection rate for varying targets number

As that shows in Fig. 1, while deploying the same total of sensors nodes within the same detection area, the target nodes detection rate varies according to the quantity of target nodes.

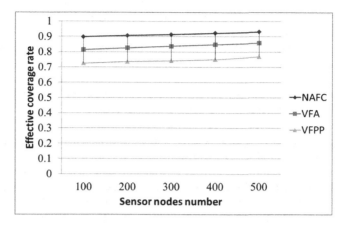

Fig. 2. Relationship between the effective coverage rate and sensor nodes number

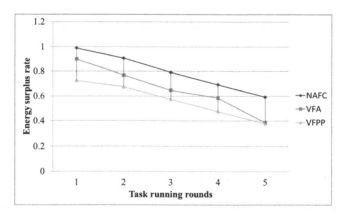

Fig. 3. Lifetimes of wireless sensor networks

Figure 1 illustrates the effective detection rate of target nodes applied algorithm of NAFC is superior to those of VFPP and VFA. The reasons to gain the results of Fig. 1 is as the follows, as the environmental factors which may affect the performance of the network detection have been considered and processed with corresponding adjustment, thus NAFC algorithm presents the best detection rate result. As for VFPP algorithm, which varies the density of nodes deployed in different fields according to the prior probability of the target distribution, thus can obtain better detective performance contrast to VFA.

Figure 2 shows the relationship between the effective coverage rate and sensor nodes' number while applying three different methods in the same detection range. In largely speaking, within a same range of test area, the effective coverage rates of the network grow with the increasing total of sensor nodes for these compared methods. Nevertheless, NAFC algorithm has the most effective coverage range, which has much efficient single node's perception ability and illuminate blind areas, attributing to application of its fuzzy criterion, namely performing an optimal reconstruction of all sensor nodes. Contrasting to VFA, VFPP algorithm reduces the scope of overlapping perception for each senor nodes, enlarge the detection area accordingly.

Figure 3 illustrates the comparisons about survival times of networks constructed using three different algorithms, covering the same number of nodes which owes the same perception performance in the same detection area.

In the initial stage of mobile, for VFPP algorithm and NAFC algorithm, the processing of perceptual node produces a large amount of calculation with much energy consumption. Since both of VFPP algorithm and NAFC algorithm considering the prior probability of deployment target, there're more nodes enter a dormant state. Thus, after fulfilling the deployment VFPP algorithm and NAFC, energy per unit time is less than Random deployment algorithm. As the network redundancy of NAFC algorithm is greater than that of VFPP algorithm, therefore, NAFC algorithm consumes energy faster than VFPP algorithm. Therefore, compared with other algorithm, the network constructed with NAFC algorithm has longer lifetime.

The node deployment algorithm of fuzzy criterion using fuzzy awareness can effectively reduce the number of sensor nodes in underwater sensor network, improve the efficiency of node's awareness, reduce the blind perception area, expand the detection range, improve awareness node redundancy, improve the reliability of the test results, achieving better detection capability of target node and longer network lifetime, verified the validity and superiority of deployment algorithm.

5   Conclusions

This paper concentrates on underwater sensor networks node three-dimensional deployment, using passive sonar probability model, the fuzzy sense perception model and a data fusion model, referring to fuzzy theory, puts forward the node deployment algorithm of fuzzy criterion using fuzzy awareness (NAFC). The effectiveness of the algorithm is verified by simulation experiments. Comparing with the deployment algorithms of using virtual power principle and random deployment, simulation results show that NAFC can effectively reduce the deployed nodes, reduce nodes' energy consumption and prolong network's lifetime, expand the detection range, improve the detection performance of Wireless sensor networks.

The next step we propose to improve, optimize the model demonstrated in this paper, and try to adopt other fusion strategy for optimizing the node deployment algorithm for three-dimensional underwater sensor network to make the Wireless sensor networks more efficient with much superior quality of service.

References

1. Shen, J.Q., Liu, N.Z., Sun, H., Tao, X.L., Li, Q.Y.: Vehicle detection in aerial images based on hyper feature map in deep convolutional network. KSII Trans. Internet Inf. Syst. **13**(4), 1989–2011 (2019)

2. Song, X.L., Gong, Y.Z., Jin, D.H., Li, Q.Y.: Nodes deployment optimization algorithm based on improved evidence theory of underwater wireless sensor networks. Photon Netw. Commun. **37**(2), 224–232 (2019)

3. Cui, M., Mei, F., Li, Q., Li, Q.: Coverage holes recovery algorithm of underwater wireless sensor networks. In: Sun, X., Pan, Z., Bertino, E. (eds.) ICCCS 2018. LNCS, vol. 11067, pp. 191–204. Springer, Cham (2018). https://doi.org/10.1007/978-3-030-00018-9_18

4. Cui, M., Mei, F., Li, Q., Li, Q.: Nodes deployment optimization algorithm based on energy consumption of underwater wireless sensor networks. In: Gan, G., Li, B., Li, X., Wang, S. (eds.) ADMA 2018. LNCS (LNAI), vol. 11323, pp. 428–433. Springer, Cham (2018). https://doi.org/10.1007/978-3-030-05090-0_36

5. Cui, M., Mei, F., Li, Q., Li, Q.: Nodes deployment optimization algorithm of underwater wireless sensor networks. In: Hu, T., Wang, F., Li, H., Wang, Q. (eds.) ICA3PP 2018. LNCS, vol. 11338, pp. 45–50. Springer, Cham (2018). https://doi.org/10.1007/978-3-030-05234-8_6

6. Song, X., Gong, Y., Jin, D., Li, Q., Jing, H.: Nodes deployment optimization algorithm based on improved evidence theory. In: Hu, T., Wang, F., Li, H., Wang, Q. (eds.) ICA3PP 2018. LNCS, vol. 11338, pp. 84–89. Springer, Cham (2018). https://doi.org/10.1007/978-3-030-05234-8_11

7. Song, X.L., Gong, Y.Z., Jin, D.H., Li, Q.Y., Jing, H.C.: Coverage hole recovery algorithm based on molecule model in heterogeneous Wireless sensor networks. Int. J. Comput. Commun. Control **12**(4), 562–576 (2017)

8. Song, X.L., Gong, Y.Z., Jin, D.H., Li, Q.Y., Zheng, R.J., Zhang, M.C.: Nodes deployment based on directed perception model of wireless sensor networks. J. Beijing Univ. Posts Telecommun. **40**, 39–42 (2017)

9. Zhao, M.Z., Liu, N.Z., Li, Q.Y.: Blurred video detection algorithm based on support vector machine of Schistosoma Japonicum Miracidium. In: International Conference on Advanced Mechatronic Systems, pp. 322–327 (2016)

10. Jing, H.C.: Node deployment algorithm based on perception model of wireless sensor network. Int. J. Automation Technol. **9**(3), 210–215 (2015)

11. Jing, H.C.: Routing optimization algorithm based on nodes density and energy consumption of wireless sensor network. J. Comput. Inf. Syst. **11**(14), 5047–5054 (2015)

12. Wu, N.N., et al.: Mobile nodes deployment scheme design based on perceived probability model in heterogeneous wireless sensor network. J. Robot. Mechatron. **26**(5), 616–621 (2014)

13. Zhang, J.W., Li, S.W., Li, Q.Y., Wu, N.N.: Coverage hole recovery algorithm based on perceived probability in heterogeneous wireless sensor network. J. Comput. Inf. Syst. **10**(7), 2983–2990 (2014)

14. Li, Q.Y., Ma, D.Q., Zhang, J.W.: Nodes deployment algorithm based on perceived probability of wireless sensor network. Comput. Measur. Control **22**(2), 643–645 (2014)

15. Li, S.W., Ma, D.Q., Li, Q.Y., Zhang, J.W., Zhang, X.: Nodes deployment algorithm based on perceived probability of heterogeneous wireless sensor network. In: International Conference on Advanced Mechatronic Systems, pp. 374–378 (2013)

16. Li, Q.Y., Ma, D.Q., Zhang, J.W., Fu, F.Z.: Nodes deployment algorithm of wireless sensor network based on evidence theory. Comput. Meas. Control **21**(6), 1715–1717 (2013)

17. Li, Q.Y., Ma, D.Q., Zhang, J.W.: Nodes deployment algorithm based on balance distance of wireless sensor network. Appl. Electron. Tech. **39**(4), 96–98 (2013)

18. Zhang, H.T., Bai, G., Liu, C.P.: Improved simulated annealing algorithm for broadcast routing of wireless sensor network. J. Comput. Inf. Syst. **9**(6), 2303–2310 (2013)

19. Unaldi, N., Temel, S., Asari, V.K.: Method for optimal sensor deployment on 3D terrains utilizing a steady state genetic algorithm with a guided walk mutation operator based on the wavelet transform. Sensors **12**(4), 5116–5133 (2012)
20. Wei, L.N., Qin, Z.G.: On-line bi-objective coverage hole healing in hybrid wireless sensor networks. J. Comput. Inf. Syst. **8**(13), 5649–5658 (2012)
21. Yan, H.L., Ji, C.C., Chen, G.L., Zhao, S.G.: Coverage and deployment analysis of 3D sensor nodes in wireless multimedia sensor networks. J. Comput. Inf. Syst. **8**(15), 6159–6166 (2012)
22. Li, X., He, Y.Y.: A solution to the optimal density of heterogeneous surveillance sensor network in pin-packing coverage condition. J. Comput. Inf. Syst. **8**(17), 7029–7036 (2012)
23. Zhao, X.M., Mao, K.J., Yang, F., Wang, W.F., Chen, Q.Z.: Research on detecting sensing coverage hole algorithm based on OGDC for wireless sensor networks. J. Comput. Inf. Syst. **8**(20), 8561–8568 (2012)
24. Chizari, H., Hosseini, M., Poston, T., Razak, S.A., Abdullah, A.H.: Delaunay triangulation as a new coverage measurement method in wireless sensor network. Sensors **11**(3), 3163–3176 (2011)
25. Ozturk, C., Karaboga, D., Gorkemli, B.: Probabilistic dynamic deployment of wireless sensor networks by Artificial Bee Colony Algorithm. Sensors **11**(6), 6056–6065 (2011)
26. Chen, A., Kumar, S., Lai, T.H.: Local barrier coverage in wireless sensor networks. IEEE Trans. Mob. Comput. **9**(4), 491–504 (2010)
27. Zhang, C.L., Bai, X.L., Teng, J., Xuan, D., Jia, W.J.: Constructing low-connectivity and full-coverage three dimensional sensor networks. IEEE J. Sel. Areas Commun. **28**(7), 984–993 (2010)
28. Ammari, H.M., Das, S.K.: A study of k-coverage and measures of connectivity in 3D wireless sensor networks. IEEE Trans. Comput. **59**(2), 243–257 (2010)
29. Fan, G.J., Wang, R.C., Huang, H.P., Sun, L.J., Sha, C.: Coverage-guaranteed sensor node deployment strategies for wireless sensor networks. Sensors **10**(3), 2064–2087 (2010)

Community Enhanced Record Linkage Method for Vehicle Insurance System

Christian Lu$^{(\boxtimes)}$, Guangyan Huang$^{(\boxtimes)}$, and Yong Xiang$^{(\boxtimes)}$

Deakin University, Burwood 3125, Australia
{luchri,guangyan.huang,yong.xiang}@deakin.edu.au

Abstract. Record linkage is a pivotal data integration stage in the vehicle insurance claims analysis system and serves as a foundation for fraud detection, market promotion and other major business applications. While the traditional method of rules based classification plus clerical review is still in use in the industry, the latest development has advanced into link analysis based collective record linkage which has put the blocking and classification processes under the global context. To apply this method with a fraud detection objective, we have developed a community enhanced record linkage model specially tailored for the requirements of vehicle insurance claim system. A major novel approach is the construction of claim communities linking the claims, customers and vehicles involved and apply probabilistic data matching algorithms integrated with spatio-temporal co-occurrence patterns. In addition, the matched results could be used to identify the outliers in fraud detection analysis.

Keywords: Record linkage · Collective classification · Spatio-temporal co-occurrence · Fraud detection · Vehicle insurance

1 Introduction

Vehicle insurance plays an important role in modern economy with its indispensable role of safeguarding a nation's transport system. Insurance fraud, on the other hand, is threatening the healthy operation of the industry with its ever increasing volume of attack each year. Fraud can be classified into two distinctive types-opportunistic fraud and professional fraud [1]. Professional fraud is committed by veteran criminals often acting in a group to continuously attempt to test and attack the insurance company's anti-fraud defence system aiming to get away with profitable loots through illegal claims [20]. More often than not, professional fraudsters working in groups intentionally modify their personal identities of name, address, vehicle registration or other information to evade the blacklist when lodging a claim [3]. However, being a dynamic transaction system which continuously generates claims transactions the insurance claims system is able to combine people and vehicles into a community together with the coupling of the policy system for the identification of imposters. In

© Springer Nature Switzerland AG 2019
J. Li et al. (Eds.): ADMA 2019, LNAI 11888, pp. 761–776, 2019.
https://doi.org/10.1007/978-3-030-35231-8_56

this respective, the conventional pairwise record linkage methods is inadequate to cope with the data matching task to meet such requirement. More complex record linkage methods needs to be developed to tackle this ambiguous identity resolution problem using the relationship information in the claims transaction system [6]. The record linkage result thus obtained could be used to infer the outliers of matched entities seemingly dissimilar in pairwise comparison for further fraud detection.

Record linkage as a fundamental data integration subject commenced in late 1950's when a major pioneer work of probabilistic data matching model was established by Fellegi and Sunter [8,10]. A standard record linkage system consists of five stages: data prepossessing, blocking, comparing, classification and evaluation as shown in the Fig. 1. Over the years, progress has been made to compare and classify the data based on a broader scope beyond the individual features of the records. Recently collective classification techniques have been proposed to make match decisions in a relational context, which have been shown to significantly outperform the traditional pairwise methods which can also be applied to the vehicle insurance system [6].

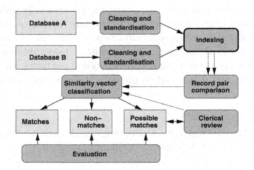

Fig. 1. Record linkage system [6]

The Challenges. The vehicle claims relationship network presents distinctive characteristics which differs significantly with the bibliography reference relationship and social media networks. Two of the major characteristics of automobile insurance claims community are:

a. Opportunistic The link between drivers of a collision is of an accidental nature and thus cannot be treated in the same way as the fixed relationship in social network like family or co-authorships in the above mentioned literatures;
b. Sparsity The structure of the network is relatively sparse with many nodes having low degrees to maintain basic connections.

As a result the existing collective classification methods cannot be directly applied to this scenario. The characteristics of claims system require a distinctive method which takes both the domain specific knowledge as well as the network structure information into consideration to make a valid inference. In this paper we put forward a novel record linkage method using link analysis method integrated with automobile spatio co-occurrence model to assess the similarities of the drivers and their connections in the insurance claims system. In this model, we first construct a claim based community consists of people and entities linked together via connections. We then focus on the spatio pattern of the people actives and calculate the co-occurrence similarity and embed this new feature with the F-S model. A further processing of unsupervised anomaly detection can be performed on the matched results to expose the fraud-suspicious parties.

The structure of the paper is arranged as following. In Sect. 2, we have a review of the most relevant work on collective classification record linkage. In Sect. 3 we formally define the problem setting in sophisticated statistics terminology. In Sect. 4, we present the demonstration of the construction algorithm of the claims community and how the integration with the collision pattern model would help to enhance the matching quality for potential match pairs by introducing the additional weight of the spatio-temporal feature estimated from the co-occurrence model. In Sect. 5 we briefly discuss how to detect suspiciously tempered data using unsupervised anomaly detection methods based on the records' feature similarity vector distribution. Section 6 presents the experiment results and compares it with conventional pair based record linkage and weighted SimRank methods. Finally conclusion and future work directions are stated in Sect. 7.

2 Related Work

The current relationship based record linkage method can be roughly classified into three categories. The first is based on the network topology structure which uses graph theory techniques to construct the similarity feature. A weighted SimRank method is used to compare the similarities of entities in a social network to discover duplicated personnels in references. An iterative process to compute the global weighted SimRank of all the triples between two objects is performed before a manual process to classify the duplicates based on the rankings of the highest similarity scores [4]. In the RelDC approach proposed by Kalashnikov et al., an undirected entity-relationship graph is constructed using feature based similarity on which connection strength is computed to determine the option weights of each equations formed from paths. References of authors is finally resolved after the weights are computed and interpreted [14].

The second category focuses on the semantic information of the relationship graph. A relational clustering algorithm that uses relational information for determining the underlying domain entities is proposed by Bhattacharya and Getoor in which attributes of related references are incorporated as a cluster similarity score into the conventional attribute similarity scores through a linear combination. An entity-relationship graph is constructed where hyper edges are formed between co-authors and reference cluster is constructed. By using a priority queue mechanism, comparison of similarity of clusters is treated as an additional feature to resolve entity reconciliation problem. Negative constraints using domain knowledge is applied to prevent illogical matching of co-authors [11]. A reference reconciliation algorithm is proposed to encompass the attribute values and relationship information in a dependency graph and compute the similarity scores using different domain specific similarity functions [24].

The third category uses sophisticated Bayes network to deal with the similarity reference. A model which incorporates feature similarity, relationship information and logical constraint was proposed by Kouki et al. to infer the personal identities in a familial network using probabilistic soft logic model which is based on Markov random field method. A set of ground rules are defined using evidence and potential matches and is translated into a hinge-loss potential function and in turn define a Markov random field. Each rule is associated with a weight learn through approximate maximum likelihood weight learning algorithm. An optimal threshold is set based on maximized F-score pre-learned [15]. Another novel EM methods based on Markov Logic Networks for message passing between different runs is proposed which is run on several small subsets of entities and thus has achieved scalability [21].

While all these paper give satisfactory solutions to the collective classification problem with relationships taken into account they mostly focus on the structure of the constructed link graph with abundance of fixed relationship bonds. A proper method to address the opportunistic relationship network is therefore needed to handle the specific requirements of vehicle insurance claims system.

3   Overview

Insurance claims system is special kind of transaction database where claim related features is engrossed with personal and vehicle information. The claims table is a transaction log table which tracks on all the essential ingredients to lodge a valid claim. A personal information system can be built by extracting the personnel information from the claims database. Claims and personnel records with synthetic data are shown in the Tables 1 and 2. From the table we can see a claim can consist of multiple persons and their vehicles and one person can be involved in different claims. There is not adequate unique identification field such as driver license number that can distinguish each person so record linkage methods need to be employed to solve the person matching problem.

Table 1. Insurance claims system records

ClaimID	Claim date	CustomerID	Role	Claim value	Vehicle registration	Status
CL23339834	2017-08-16	59018	Insurer	3400	1HOR35	Complete
CL23339834	2017-08-16	524318	Third Party	3400	1HX6BV	Incomplete

While conventional record linkage algorithms in the industry focus on pairwise matching using rule-based classification to deduplicate the persons as well as vehicle registrations, these rules normally are created based on past observations

Table 2. Insurance claims customer records

CustomerID	FirstName	LastName	BirthDate	Address	Email	Phone
s98349	ABC	Smith	06/01/1984	45 ABC St. Cooper Plains, QLD	julie@abc.com	0427466XXX
s12469	DEF	Jones	06/11/1973	12 DEF Road, Hawthorn VIC		0411344577

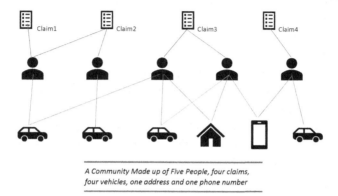

A Community Made up of Five People, four claims, four vehicles, one address and one phone number

Fig. 2. A claim community

and require manual maintenance. Therefore we have developed a probabilistic record linkage system using the community relationship information to deal with the task in a holistic way as stated in the following parts.

3.1 Problem Definition

We consider our problem in a typical insurance claims transaction system where the format of the data records is generic with trivial fields removed. A claims is lodged by an insurer who has experienced an event on his vehicle which may involve one or more third-party persons with their vehicles. A claim thus forms an atomic cluster of at least one person with a unique claim id. Let each claim represented by $c_{id} = \{p_{id\_1}, p_{id\_2}, .., p_{id\_m}\}$ where p_{id_1} is the role of people involved in claim c_{id}, be it claimer or third party. Each party consists of a range of features represented by $p_{id\_i} = \{f^1_{id\_i}, f^2_{id\_i}, ..., f^n_{id\_i}\}$ associated with that person p_{id_1} in this claim system marked by the id. Let $C_i = \{c_a, c_b, ..., c_l\}$ representing a cluster of claims then $C = \{C_1, C_2, ..., C_t\}$ representing all the claims clusters. Let $P = \{p_1, p_2 ..., p_n\}$ denotes the unique true persons involved in the entire claims system. The claim cluster graph can be illustrated by showing different types of entities including claims, drivers, vehicles, phones and addresses. However, in the end it is reduced to an entity-relationship graph where $V = \{p_{id\_1}, p_{id\_2}, ..., p_{id\_n}\}$ is the set of vertices representing the drivers, and $E = \{e_1, e_2, ..., e_m\}$ is the set of edges representing the relationships of the drivers. The goal of the deduplication is to map the p_{id_i} in the claim communities to the unique p_j in the P space, i.e.

to create a mapping table to define the matching pairs $f : p_{id\_i}- > p_j$ for each valid p_{id_i}.

3.2 Proof of Community Enhancement of Data Matching

The inclusion of additional spatio-temporal space similarity can be proved using Bayes Network [2]. We define the field comparison vector

$$\gamma_i^j = \begin{cases} 1 & \text{if field i matches on both of the records of record pair } r_j \\ 0 & \text{otherwise} \end{cases} \tag{1}$$

where $i = 1, 2, \ldots, n$ is the index of field and $j = 1, 2, \ldots N$ is the index of comparison pair[19]. We can summarize the fields to $\gamma^j = \left\{ \gamma_{existing}^j, \gamma_{new}^j \right\}$ as comparison vector of record pair γ^j where $\gamma_{existing}$ is the comparison vector containing the existing conventional fields before the community analysis including name, gender, age,etc, and γ_{new} stands for the newly added feature in our case is the driver's spatio-temporal similarity, as illustrated in the following Fig. 3.

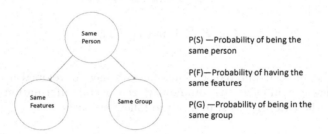

Same
Person

P(S) —Probability of being the
same person

P(F)—Probability of having the
same features

Same
Features

Same Group

P(G) —Probability of being in the
same group

Fig. 3. Bayes network view

Here we use $P(F) = Prob(\gamma_{existing}^j = 1), P(G) = Prob(\gamma_{new}^j = 1)$ to represent the probability of existing and new spatio-temporal group features matching probability. Using Bayes network inference, we can show that the additional feature similarity enhances the prior similarity probability given the empirical fact that drivers sharing a common confined spatio-temporal space are much more likely to be the same person than drivers in different spaces. Empirical estimate shows that two records which are actually identical are more likely to be found in the same spatio-temporal space which is denoted as $P(G \mid S) > P(G \mid \neg S)$.

Proof. This probabilistic graph implies the conditional independence of the existing similarity features and new spatio-temporal feature $\mathcal{F} \perp \mathcal{G}|\mathcal{S}$.

$$P(S \mid F, G) = \frac{P(F, G \mid S)P(S)}{P(F, G)} \qquad \text{[By definition of Bayes Theorem]}$$

$$= \frac{P(G \mid S)P(F \mid S)P(S)}{P(F, G)} \qquad \text{[By Conditional Independence]}$$

$$= \frac{P(G \mid S)P(F \mid S)P(S)}{P(G \mid S)P(F \mid S)P(S) + P(G \mid \neg S)P(F \mid \neg S)P(\neg S)}$$

$$= \frac{P(F \mid S)P(S)}{P(F \mid S)P(S) + \alpha P(F \mid \neg S)P(\neg S)} \qquad [\text{Let } \alpha = \frac{P(G \mid S)}{P(G \mid \neg S)}]$$

$$> \frac{P(F \mid S)P(S)}{P(F \mid S)P(S) + P(F \mid \neg S)P(\neg S)} \qquad [\text{Given } \alpha > 1, P(S) >> P(\neg S)]$$

$$= P(S \mid F)$$

An empirical example would to take $P(S) = 0.04, P(S \mid F) = 0.3, P(S \mid \neg F) = 0.015, P(S \mid G) = 0.2, P(S \mod \neg G = 0.02)$ and after solving a set of equations using the known values, we get posterior probability $P(S \mid F, G) = 0.885 > P(S \mid F) = 0.3$

3.3 System Architecture

The entire system is comprised of three major components which deal with record linkage, community analysis and fraud detection tasks respectively and we are focusing on the former two modules in this paper (Fig. 4).

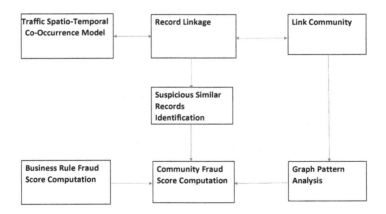

Fig. 4. System architecture overview

In the record linkage part of the system, the first step is to execute a conventional probabilistic record linkage process to match drivers with highly similar features together. This is done using conventional multiple iterations of blocking and comparison methods on names, birthdates and gender features as well as phone number, address and other features if available. A hybrid probabilistic and rule-based classification method is applied where the rules are obtained by year's of manual review experience. The merged personal data provides a solid foundation to link all the entities previously separated in isolated claims.

4   Community Enhanced Algorithm

As above mentioned, a claim community is made up of all the drives interconnected through all kinds of relationships including:

- collision parties
- sharing of a vehicle
- sharing of a mobile phone
- sharing of the same address

as demonstrated in Fig. 2. Served as a *semantic blocking* mechanism, it enables an additional iteration of comparison and classification within the claim community for increased accuracy [12].

4.1   Claim Community Construction

To construct the claim community an iterative SQL procedure is used to engross all entities related to a claim community.

Algorithm 1: Claim Community Construction

Result: data frame of entities and relationships
Initialise the community array;
Sort persons by the number of claims involved into a queue;
while *Queue is not empty* **do**
    Pop the top element from the queue;
    if *the element is not in any community* **then**
        build a new community table in the community array with this element ;
        search all its related parties in all its claims and insert into the community if not already in;
        search all the parties related to its vehicles, mobile phones and addresses and insert into the community if not already in;
        repeat the above two steps for each newly inserted element in the cluster table;
    else
        move to the next person in the queue;
    end
end

The result of the algorithm is the creation of a set of claims communities containing different types of entities.

4.2   Integration with Spatio-Temporal Co-occurrence Pattern

Having constructed the blocking community, the next step is to make use of the relationship information to update matching status within the community. The claim community is in essence an vehicle encounter group constructed by linking the information of claims which are based on road collisions and other types of accidents. Each claim has a geographical collision site which can be used to construct the scope of the encounter group and sequentially the spatio-temporal similarity of two parties in the group. In real life, there is a co-occurrence pattern in human travel with all kinds of transport means including vehicles [9]. Each driver has its own travel spatio-temporal space depending on the nature of his location and work and life patterns. People share the same travel spatio-temporal space may appear in the travel co-occurrence group as experienced by a lot of commuter seen familiar strangers" on their way [18]. The reasoning to use this information for record linkage is based on the logic that drivers within a claim community is linked in a chain of spatio-temporal space and is therefore having a higher probability of being in the same spatio-temporal space and sequentially more likely to be same person.

$$P(p_{id\_m} = p_{id\_n} \mid p_{id\_m}, p_{id\_n} \in ST_i) \sim P(p_{id\_m}, p_{id\_n} \in ST_i \mid p_{id\_m}, p_{id\_n} \in CO_j) \tag{2}$$

Here ST is the spatio-temporal space and CO is the co-occurrence group. A formal modelling of this spatio-temporal co-occurrence space requires complete profile of a person's visit activities which is normally not available to the insurance company [7]. However, a simplified model can be built from the idea of measuring geographical distance on the power law of human travel $P(r) \sim r^{-(1+\beta)}$ which puts the spatio-temporal scope of a human travel into a probability perspective [5]. The reasoning is that two potentially matched people are more likely to co-occur within the same spatio-temporal space and the spatio-temporal similarity value is obviously dependent on the radius of the co-occurrence space and the β value, which can be estimated by the local metropolis traffic data. The radius r is calculated by a linear combination of Manhattan distance in the metropolis zone and Euclidean distance in the rural area indicated by the parameter mr of the geocoding collision locations to reflect the traffic pattern in different traffic zones. Let P, Q be two persons of potential match and denote Path(P,Q) as the set of nodes which makes all the connection paths from P to Q in the community while C is the geocoding centre of all the nodes in the set. Then

$$M = arg \max_{M}\{|M_x - C_x| + |M_y - C_y|\} \quad M \in Path(P,Q) \tag{3}$$

$$r(M,C) = mr * (|M_x - C_x| + |M_y - C_y|) + (1 - mr) * d(M,C), \tag{4}$$

where mr is a coefficient value between 0 and 1 and $d(M,C)$ is the Euclidean distance. When $mr = 0$ the radius is entirely determined by the latter part which reflects the road network of the rural area and when $mr = 1$ indicates a purely a Manhattan distance reflecting city area. In cases of more than two claims involved, the radius is defined as the distance between the centroid and the farthest collision location.

The driver co-occurrence is measured by the overlapping road segments which they are major driver sources(MDS) [16]. The reasoning that two people who have an encounter are more likely to continue their encounter in the next road segment can be described using an affiliation coefficient α. Suppose in the scenario where there are ten road segments for two drivers, each has the equal probability to choose one of the ten roads and therefore their co-occurrence is 1/10. However, if both of them have encounters with a third driver and they are more likely to choose the road segment the third driver has travelled and their chance of encounter is uplifted from 0.1 to $\alpha^2 + 9 * (\frac{1-\alpha}{9})^2 = 0.28$ given $\alpha = 0.8$. When there are more than one intermediate drivers in between, as shown in Fig. 5, the general simplified co-occurrence probability formula for h intermediate drivers is given as:

$$P(Coccur) = (\alpha^{h+1})^2 + (n-1)(\frac{1-\alpha^{h+1}}{n-1})^2 \qquad (5)$$

where $n = kr^2$ is the number of road segments between two locations and k is the coefficient between radius of the community and number of available road segments in the radius area. Obviously the larger the radius the more road segments to choose and thus the smaller probability of encounter. More intermediate drivers in between will cause the chance of continuous encounter to drop as shown in the Fig. 6, which demonstrates the relationship between number of hops and the co-occurrence coefficient.

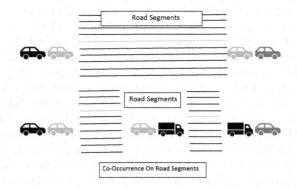

Fig. 5. Co-occurrence relationship

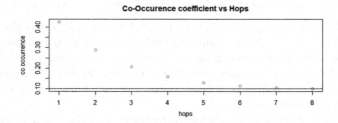

Fig. 6. Co-occurrence relationship

Using this as a foundation, we here establish a spatio-temporal co-occurrence model which makes it distinctive with all other relevant work based on the collective classification. The first step is to calculate the geocoding locations of the collision places and compute the Manhattan distance of two locations. Then using DFS algorithm we find all the paths from person A to person B in the community relationship graph and calculate the number of hops. Notice that in scenarios where persons are linked via sharing common vehicle, address, mobile and phones their hop is not counted as it is assumed they from the same family and have the same spatio-temporal driving pattern. After that the co-occurrence probability is computed using Eq. 5. Here the geocoding is calculated using the hierarchical model as exact address of encounter is sometimes unclear [23]. More complex paths in the community can be calculated using the basic rules (Fig. 7).

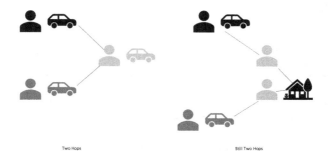

Two Hops   Still Two Hops

Fig. 7. Co-occurrence hops count

After the calculation of the spatio-temporal co-occurrence probability it can be easily integrated with the existing sum of weights in the Fellegi-Sunter model. An EM algorithm is used to iteratively estimate the weight of this new feature. The integration with sophisticated travel co-occurrence models provides a semantic analysis of the relationship network with in-depth insight which greatly enhances the classification accuracy as demonstrated in the next section.

4.3 Community Based Classification Probability Inference

Once te co-occurrence measurement has been converted to a probability value, it can be treated as the distance similarity value like names similarity to be added into the sum of weights for classification [22]. The inference algorithm is listed below as a post processing procedure after the normal pairwise record linkage process has been executed. Here we use an extended Fellegi-Sunter model to allow for approximate field comparison [17]. Binary decision function can be used by adding a threshold if traditional Fellegi-Sunter model is used. The estimate of m_i which should ideally be 1, is estimated using sample training data for the errors. The estimate of u_i is calculated using sampling by blocking [19].

Algorithm 2: Claim Community Weight Update

  Result: Update record classification results
  for *Each claim community* **do**
      Select the potential matches pairs;
      for *Each potential pair* **do**
          Find all the paths between the pair nodes;
          Calculate the radius of the encounter group;
          Calculate the co-occurrence probability of the pair;
          Convert the probability to similarity weights;
          Update the weights of the pairs in the Fellegi-Sunter model;
          if *The updated weights is above the matching threshold* **then**
           | Merge the records
          else
           | Continue to the next pair
          end
      end
  end

---

5   Computing Fraud Scores

After the merge of the potential matches within the community context, a review of the comparison vector using Mahalanobis distance and density based clustering is used to isolate the outliers which could be fraudsters. Here we only focus on exploiting the comparing vector of the obtained match results as defined in Eq. 1. We define $m_j = \left\{ \gamma_i^j = p | r^j \in M \right\}$ to be matching vector for all the pairs that are matched and $M = \{m_1, m_2, \dots, m_n\}$ as the collection of all the fields m_i of all matched pairs. From here Mahalanobis distance of the m_j to the distribution of the overall collection M is computed for each of the recently merged pairs in algorithm 2. After that an unsupervised learning method of density based clustering is run on this vector to detect outliers and assign fraud susceptible scores accordingly. Some of the newly matched pairs are 10 times far away than the normal cluster of matched pairs and clearly show traces of fraudulent modifications of information as illustrated in Fig. 9.

6   Experiment

In the experiments we first performed the new model on a commercial vehicle insurance lower brand customer database with 800,000 claim transactions in a two years' span with over 700,000 non-duplicate personal records derived from the claim transactions. A Linux VM with 30 cores and 128 GB memory is allocated to run the entire program coded in R and Python for parallelism. A rule based classification method using 16 business rules is applied to get over 50,000 merged records. These records, together with a few clerical reviewed pairs from previous fraud detection procedures serve as golden copy for evaluation. An extended Fellegi-Sunter probabilistic record linkage method is used after which the community enhanced classification method is applied on the claim community members. The evaluation result using the common classification metrics of precision, recall and F-score is shown in the Table 3 below.

Table 3. Insurance claims system records

Methods	Matched pairs	Recall rate	Precision	F-Score
Rule-based	55250			
Fellegi-Sunter model	78101	0.91	0.75	0.82
Weighted SimRank model	78780	0.92	0.78	0.84
Community enhanced model	79877	0.95	0.85	0.90

The result shows the improvements on both precision as well as recall rate compared with standard Fellegi-Sunter Model which is the result of the enhanced weight of potentially matching pairs and also the reduction of falsely matched pairs which are now regarded as non-match due to the spatio-temporal co-occurrence low probability as a result of greater geographical distance of the collisions in the close group. Compared with structured based network analysis, the improvement is more evident on the precision result as the integration with geocoding co-occurrence model has significantly reduced the errors of false positives thanks to the exclusion of multiple intermediate drivers as transitive nodes and large spread geographical areas of road network. The pair quality measurement also confirms the advantage of this feature over the conventional and network topology based approaches as it has increased the matched pairs due to additional information gained through the geocoding information from the claims community (Fig. 8).

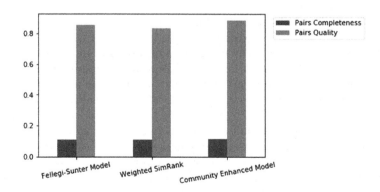

Fig. 8. Matching complexity comparison

The merge could trigger a number of transformations of the community graph including formation of cycles and imbalanced vertices which are extremely useful for fraud mining [13]. In the following graph one can see the power of community enhanced record linkage where persons with multiple modified fields including first and last names, addresses and vehicle registrations are matched due to spatio-temporal co-occurrence. Community enhanced fraud detection will be discussed in additional papers to be followed.

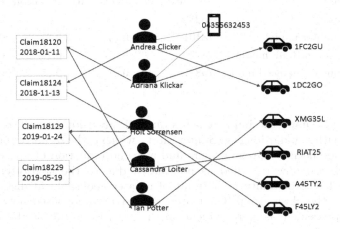

Fig. 9. Matched findings with synthetic names

7   Conclusion and Future Work

In this paper, we have proposed a novel record linkage model using claims community relationship information to enhance the accuracy and efficiency. The integration with spatio-temporal co-occurrence model is a novel realisation of business insight and subsequent breaking- through result has been observed. There are many areas to be extended on this model and the immediate development requirements include the integration of temporal information in the co-occurrence model. The integration with Fellegi-Sunter model could be further improved using the collision location frequency information available. The structure impact of the community graph could be added into the model as sometimes there are complex graphs linked by transferred phone numbers and vehicles which forms cycles and other important structures. Information transitivity coefficient needs to be adjusted in these circumstances. As stated before, the whole work has laid a solid foundation for the next stage of work on link analysis fraud detection. The data matching information collected in this stage will be of great value in the classification of fraud using state-of-the-art statistical learning methods.

References

1. Combating insurance claims fraud. Technical report, SAS (2012)
2. Barber, D.: Bayesian Reasoning and Machine Learning. Cambridge University Press, Cambridge (2010)
3. Bolton, R.J., Hand, D.J.: Statistical fraud detection: a review. Stat. Sci. **17**, 235–255 (2002)
4. Boongoen, T.: Discovering identity in intelligence data using weighted link based similarities: a case study of Thailand (2015)
5. Brockmann, D., Hufnagel, L., Geisel, T.: The scaling laws of human travel. Nature **439**(7075), 462–465 (2006). https://doi.org/10.1038/nature04292. https://www.ncbi.nlm.nih.gov/pubmed/16437114
6. Christen, P.: Data Matching Concepts and Techniques for Record Linkage, Entity Resolution, and Duplicate Detection. Springer, Berlin (2012)
7. David, J., Backstrom, L., Cosley, D., Suri, S., Huttenlocher, D., Kleinberg, J.: Inferring social ties from geographic coincidences. Proc. Nat. Acad. Sci. **107**, 22436–22441 (2010)
8. Fellegi, I.P., Sunter, A.B.: A theory for record linkage. J. Am. Stat. Assoc. **64**, 1183–1210 (1969)
9. Government, Q.: Travel in South-East Queensland an analysis of travel data from 1992 to 2009. Technical report (2012)
10. Newcombe, H.B., Kennedy, J.M., Axford, S.J., James, A.P.: Automatic linkage of vital records. Science **130**, 954–959 (1959)
11. Bhattacharya, I., Getoor, L.: Collective entity resolution in relational data. ACM Trans. Knowl. Disc. Data **1**, 5 (2007)
12. Nin, J., Munt'es-Mulero, V., Martinez-Bazan, N., Larriba-Pey, J.L.: On the use of semantic blocking techniques for data cleansing and integration. In: 11th International Database Engineering and Applications Symposium (IDEAS 2007) (2007)
13. Liu, J., et al.: Graph analysis for detecting fraud, waste and abuse in healthcare data. In: Association for the Advancement of Artificial Intelligence (www.aaai.org) (2015)
14. Kalashinikov, D.V., Mehrotra, S.: Domain-independent data cleaning via analysis of entity-relationship graph. ACM Trans. Database Syst. **31**, 716–767 (2006)
15. Kouki, P., Pujara, J., Marcum, C., Koehly, L., Getoor, L.: Collective entity resolution in familial networks. In: 2017 IEEE International Conference on Data Mining (ICDM), pp. 227–236 (2017). https://doi.org/10.1109/icdm.2017.32
16. Wang, P., Hunter, T., Bayen, A.M., Schechtner, K., González, M.C.: Understanding road usage patterns in urban areas. Sci. Rep. (2012)
17. DuVall, S.L., Kerber, R.A., Thomas, A.: Extending the Fellegi-Sunter probabilistic record linkage method for approximate field comparators. J. Biomed. Inf. **43**, 24–30 (2010)
18. Sun, L., Axhausen, K.W., Lee, D.H., Huang, X.: Understanding metropolitan patterns of daily encounters. Proc. Nat. Acad. Sci. U.S.A. **110**(34), 13774–9 (2013). https://doi.org/10.1073/pnas.1306440110. https://www.ncbi.nlm.nih.gov/pubmed/23918373
19. Herzog, T.N., Scheuren, F.J., Winkler, W.E.: Data Quality And Record Linkage Techniques. Springer, Berlin (2007)
20. Viaene, S., Dedene, G.: Insurance fraud-issues and challenges. In: 2004 The International Association for the Study of Insurance Economics (2004)

776   C. Lu et al.

21. Rastogi, V., Dalvi, N., Garofalakis, M.: Large-scale collective entity matching. Proc. VLDB Endowment **4**, 208–218 (2009)
22. Cohen, W.W., Ravikumar, P., Fienberg, S.E.: A comparison of string distance metrics for name-matching tasks (2003)
23. Christen, P., Churches, T., Willmore, A.: A probabilistic geocoding system based on a national address file (2004)
24. Dong, X., Halevy, A.: Reference reconciliation in complex information spaces (2005)

COEA: An Efficient Method for Entity Alignment in Online Encyclopedias

Yimin Lv[1], Xin Wang[1,2(✉)], Runpu Yue[1], Fuchuan Tang[1], and Xue Xiang[1]

[1] College of Intelligence and Computing, Tianjin University,
Tianjin 300072, China
wangx@tju.edu.cn
[2] Tianjin Key Laboratory of Cognitive Computing and Application,
Tianjin 300072, China

Abstract. Knowledge graph is the cornerstone of artificial intelligence. Entity alignment in multi-source online encyclopedias is an important part of data integration to construct the knowledge graph. In order to solve the problem that traditional methods are not effective enough for entity alignment in online encyclopedias tasks, this paper proposes the Chinese Online Encyclopedia Aligner (COEA) based on the combination of entity attributes and context. In this paper, we focus on (1) extracting attribute information and context of entities from the infobox of online encyclopedias and normalizing them, (2) computing the similarity of entity attributes based on Vector Space Model, and (3) further considering the entity similarity based on the topic model over entity context when the similarity of attributes is between the lower bound and the upper bound. Finally, data sets of entity alignment in online encyclopedias are constructed for simulation experiments. The experimental results, which show the method proposed in this paper outperforms traditional entity alignment algorithms, verify that our method can significantly improve the performance of entity alignment in online encyclopedias in the construction of Chinese knowledge graphs.

Keywords: Entity alignment · Online encyclopedias · Vector Space Model · Topic model · Knowledge graph

1 Introduction

With the continuous development of Web technology, we are moving towards the era of "Web 3.0" based on knowledge interconnection [16]. The Semantic Web [2] as an overall framework for sharing and reusing data between different individuals, is an important feature of "Web 3.0". Building the Semantic Web requires the knowledge base with high quality as the cornerstone [11]. Plenty of large-scale knowledge bases have been constructed, such as FreeBase [5], Yago [3], DBpedia [12], and XLore [17]. Due to the problem of low information coverage and imperfect description of a single knowledge base, and any organization can

© Springer Nature Switzerland AG 2019
J. Li et al. (Eds.): ADMA 2019, LNAI 11888, pp. 777–791, 2019.
https://doi.org/10.1007/978-3-030-35231-8_57

construct the knowledge base according to its own design concept, the data in the knowledge base is diverse and heterogeneous. Efficient and accurate integration of multi-source knowledge bases is the research hotspot currently.

Entity alignment is a key step in integrating the multi-source knowledge bases. Entity alignment, also known as entity matching or entity resolution, is the process of determining whether two entities in the data set correspond to the same entity in the real world [18]. The Web pages of Chinese online encyclopedias contain abundant entity information as shown in Fig. 1. In this paper, unless otherwise specified, we use online encyclopedias to refer to Chinese online encyclopedias. Extracting valuable entity information to perform entity alignment is of great significance for the integration of online encyclopedias knowledge bases. The commonly used traditional method of entity alignment is to judge whether the entity alignment can be performed according to the attribute information of different entities. Extensive experiments show that the performance of this method is not ideal in practical applications. The main reason is that the Web pages of online encyclopedias based on Wiki such as Wikipedia [13] are freely editable. The data from the Web pages is user generated content [15]. As a consequence, the accuracy of judging whether the entity alignment can be achieved through the attribute information depends on data quality. Using the detailed context description of the entity in the Web pages of online encyclopedias, this paper proposes a method of combining the attribute information and the context to comprehensively determine whether the entity can be aligned. Experiments verify that our method effectively improves the accuracy of online encyclopedias alignment and has better generality in entity alignment tasks.

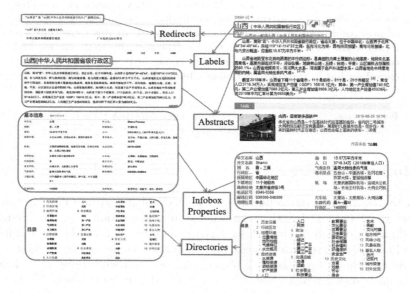

Fig. 1. Sample encyclopedia article pages from Baidu Baike and Hudong Baike

Our main contributions include: (**1**) we propose an efficient method of entity alignment in online encyclopedias. This method improves the efficiency and accuracy of entity alignment; (**2**) To the best of our knowledge, combining attribute similarity and context similarity, the COEA algorithm is the first method of entity alignment in online encyclopedias which takes cnSchema as the unified data standard to regulate the inconsistency of attribute names; (**3**) data sets of entity alignment in online encyclopedias are constructed. The experimental results show that our approach outperforms the traditional methods in entity alignment tasks by a large margin.

The rest of this paper is organized as follows: In Sect. 2, we present some previous works on entity alignment in online encyclopedias. In addition, We describe the implementation of entity alignment in Sect. 3. The experiment is conducted in Sect. 4. Finally, in Sect. 5, we conclude our works and discuss future directions.

2   Related Work

The existing methods of entity alignment in online encyclopedias can be classified as follows:

(1) Rule Analysis

By establishing corresponding rules in specific fields and using the knowledge base dictionary which reflects the semantic co-occurrence relationship between words, the evaluation function is conducted to eliminate ambiguity of entities in [19]. This method works well in specific fields but it is not ideal in the Chinese encyclopedias entity alignment tasks with multiple fields due to the poor generality of the rules in different fields.

(2) Semantic of Web Ontology Language

The Web Ontology Language (OWL) [1] is used to describe ontology construction. Ontology is the formalized world knowledge expressed in different structured forms. Using the classification information in the FreeBase, entity alignment is implemented through the iteration model and discrimination model in [20]. Entity alignment based on OWL Semantics requires complete semantic information. As the generated content of users, entity pages of online encyclopedias refer to different standards when editing. There are no strict standards for the attribute description and context of the same entity. Consequently, semantic information is not unified. Therefore, the entity alignment method based on OWL Semantics is not general in online encyclopedias entity alignment tasks.

(3) Similarity Computation

According to the different contributions of attributes to the final entity similarity, different weights are assigned to the attributes to implement the entity alignment in [7]. The distributions of attributes in online encyclopedias are not uniform and there is no definite rule about the distribution of attribute frequency and value. As a consequence, the contributions of different attributes to the final similarity cannot be taken into consideration appropriately when assigning weights. The experiment shows that the result of entity alignment based on similarity computation highly depends on generic attributes. Therefore, this method is not ideal in online encyclopedias entity alignment tasks.

To sum up, since online encyclopedias contain many fields, entity alignment method based on rule analysis needs to formulate corresponding rules for each new field, which is difficult to meet the requirements of practical applications. The entity information of online encyclopedias based on Wiki is freely edited and the data quality obtained by different users is different. The entity alignment method based on OWL Semantics is restricted by imperfect semantic information. The inconsistency and imperfection of entity attribute information also limit the validity of entity alignment method based on similarity. For the purpose of improving the efficiency and accuracy of entity alignment in online encyclopedias, this paper proposes an entity alignment method based on attribute information and context. The entities from online encyclopedias can be aligned by considering both attribute similarity and context similarity comprehensively.

3   Entity Alignment

This section introduces the overview of the method, unification of attribute names, contextual modeling, similarity calculating, and the algorithm for entity alignment.

3.1   Overview of the Method

The system framework of entity alignment in online encyclopedias designed in this paper is shown in Fig. 2, where the construction of knowledge base and similarity computation are the core parts of entity alignment framework. The process of implementation is as follows: (1) For each new entity, the system extracts its attribute information from the corresponding Web pages. (2) Non-standard attributes are unified according to the community-based data standard cnSchema [10]. (3) Normalized information is stored in the corresponding encyclopedia entity's attribute knowledge databases. (4) The distributed Web crawler is used to extract the context information of the entity in the Web pages. (5) After tokenizing, the potential topic features of the entity are calculated by using the topic model. (6) Topic features are stored in the contextual topic feature database of corresponding encyclopedia entities. (7) For the entity pairs to be aligned from online encyclopedias, the calculation method of attribute similarity based on Vector Space Model is used to determine whether two entities can be aligned or not. Entity alignment can be conducted through the attribute information if the attribute similarity is greater than the upper bound of threshold. (8) The entity alignment algorithm combined with the context information and topic features is further adopted in case that attribute similarity is between the lower bound and the upper bound, to determine whether to output the entity pairs to the set of aligned entities. (**9**) Finally, we obtain the collection of aligned entities. The solid arrows in Fig. 2 indicate the data flow. The dashed arrows denote that the method of entity alignment combined with the context and topic features is further adopted in case that it is difficult to determine whether the entities can be aligned only according to the attribute similarity.

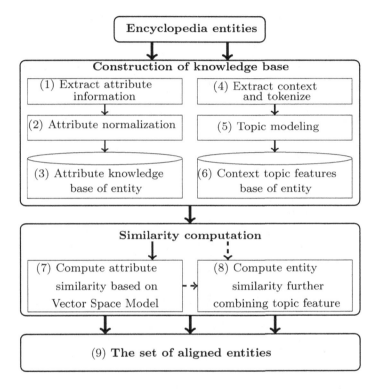

Fig. 2. System framework of entity alignment in online encyclopedias

3.2 Unifying Attribute Names

The infoboxes in the Web pages of online encyclopedias such as Baidu Baike [8] and Hudong Baike [9] spread out the attributes and corresponding values of entities. Structured data can be obtained after preprocessing and data cleansing. Specifically, the information about entities can be expressed as RDF triples. Since Web data from online encyclopedias is user-generated content [15], different users do not refer to the same standards when editing data, which results in diverse attribute names with the same semantics. For instance, "英文名" ("English Name") in Baidu Baike and "外文名" ("Foreign Name") in Hudong Baike refer to the same attribute. Inconsistent attribute names can reduce the accuracy of entity alignment in online encyclopedias to some extent. Therefore, this paper takes cnSchema as the unified attribute standard, counts the high-frequency attributes in the field of *characters* and *movies*, and constructs the attribute word list to regulate the inconsistency of attribute names to improve the accuracy of entity alignment. Part of attribute word list is shown in Table 1. The example of unifying attribute names based on cnSchema is shown in Fig. 3.

Table 1. Examples of attribute word list

Attribute name	Synonymous attributes	URL of attributes
spouse	spouse/wife/husband	http://cnschema.org/spouse
parent	parent/dad/mother	http://cnschema.org/parent
Chinese name	Chinese name/name	http://cnschema.org/name
date of birth	date of birth/year of birth	http://cnschema.org/birthDate
gender	gender	http://cnschema.org/gender

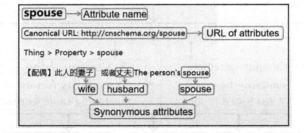

Fig. 3. Unify attribute names based on cnSchema

The Web pages of online encyclopedias contain not only the infobox, but also the context of the entity. The context mentioned in this paper is composed of summaries and descriptions, where "summaries" are centralized generalization of the entity and "descriptions" are comprehensive and detailed representations of almost all aspects of the entity, such as the "early experience" and "personal life" of the character. Because the context with abundant semantics is unstructured text that cannot be directly used in entity alignment, it is necessary to implement contextual modeling and extract topic features from the context.

3.3   Contextual Modeling

The Web pages of the entity contained in the encyclopedia websites such as Baidu Baike and Hudong Baike, generally have comprehensive and exhaustive descriptions of the entity. Unfortunately, these descriptions are often organized in the form of unstructured text that cannot be directly applied on entity alignment. Extracting valuable information from unstructured text for analysis is the key procedure. According to the topic model proposed in [4], topic eigenvectors can be obtained and topic features can be extracted from text after contextual modeling. In LDA, each document may be viewed as a mixture of several topics. It is identified on the basis of automatic detection of the likelihood of term co-occurrence.

If the attribute information is incomplete and it is difficult to determine whether entity alignment can be performed according to the attribute similarity, the context information can be further used to model and extract topic features. Then, the entity can be aligned according to the feature distributions. The implementation of contextual modeling consists of two steps: generating context using Latent Dirichlet Allocation and producing topic features.

Generating Context. For entity e, the process of generating its context c is shown in Fig. 4. The process is described as follows: (**1**) Sample from the Dirichlet distribution α, then generate the distribution vector θ_c over topics of entity context c, where each column of θ_c represents the probability of each topic appearing in the context c. (**2**) Sample from the polynomial distribution θ_c over topics, then generate the topic $z_{c,i}$ of the ith word in context c. (**3**) Sample from the Dirichlet distribution β, then generate the word distribution $\varphi_{c,i}$ of topic $z_{c,i}$ of context. (**4**) Sample from the polynomial distribution $\varphi_{c,i}$ of words and then generate the word $w_{c,i}$ eventually.

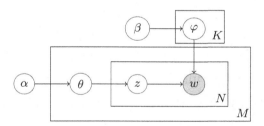

Fig. 4. The process of generating context using the LDA model

where M denotes the number of documents, N is the number of words in a document and K represents the number of topics.

Producing Topic Features. In the LDA model, only word $w_{c,i}$ is the observable variable and the other variables are latent. These latent variables can be solved by Gibbs Sampling proposed in [6]. The process of generating topic features is described as follows:

(1) Computing the topic-word probability matrix φ.

$$\varphi = \begin{bmatrix} p_{11} & p_{12} & \cdots & p_{1v} \\ p_{21} & p_{22} & \cdots & p_{2v} \\ \vdots & \vdots & & \vdots \\ p_{k1} & p_{k2} & \cdots & p_{kv} \end{bmatrix} \tag{1}$$

where k is the number of topics, v represents the number of words and p_{ij} denotes the probability of that the ith word is used to describe the jth topic.

(2) Computing the matrix φ' by sorting each row $(p_{i1}, p_{i2}, \cdots, p_{iv})$ of the topic-word probability matrix φ in reverse order. Each row of the matrix φ' can be represented as $(p_{i1}', p_{i2}', \cdots, p_{iv}')$.

(3) Computing m words with the highest probability under each topic from the matrix φ'. Executing the operation mentioned above under k topics yields the set of feature words W_e and eigenmatrix $F(e)$ as follows:

$$W_e = \{w_0', w_1', \cdots, w_n'\} \tag{2}$$

where n' denotes the number of non-repeating feature words.

$$F(e) = \begin{bmatrix} p_{11}' & p_{12}' & \cdots & p_{1m}' \\ p_{21}' & p_{22}' & \cdots & p_{2m}' \\ \vdots & \vdots & & \vdots \\ p_{k1}' & p_{k2}' & \cdots & p_{km}' \end{bmatrix} \tag{3}$$

(4) Finding out its maximum value in the eigenmatrix $F(e)$ corresponding to each word w_i' in W_e as the eigenvalue of the word. Eigenvector V_e is as follows:

$$V_e = (v_0', v_1', \cdots, v_n') \tag{4}$$

3.4   Similarity Calculating

Attribute Similarity Calculating. The attribute similarity for entity e_1 and e_2 is defined as follows:

$$attribute\_sim(e_1, e_2) = \sqrt{w_n \times sim_n(e_1, e_2)^2 + (1 - w_n) \times sim_d(e_1, e_2)^2} \tag{5}$$

where w_n is the weight of similarity of the name vector. The $sim_n(e_1, e_2)$ is the similarity of the name vector of two entities e_1 and e_2. The $sim_d(e_1, e_2)$ is the similarity of the document vector of two entities e_1 and e_2.

Context Similarity Calculating. The context similarity for entity e_1 and e_2 is defined as follows:

$$context\_sim(e_1, e_2) = \frac{V_{e_1} \cdot V_{e_2}}{|V_{e_1}||V_{e_2}|} \tag{6}$$

where V_{e_1} and V_{e_2} are topic eigenvectors corresponding to entity e_1 and e_2.

The accuracy may decrease in case that only one of attribute similarity and context similarity is considered in entity alignment. In order to improve the performance of entity alignment, the formula of entity similarity can be obtained by combining attribute similarity and context similarity.

Entity Similarity Calculating. The entity similarity is defined as follows:

$$similarity(e_1, e_2) = \frac{attribute\_sim(e_1, e_2) + context\_sim(e_1, e_2)}{2} \tag{7}$$

where $attribute\_sim(e_1, e_2)$ refers to attribute similarity of entities and $context\_sim(e_1, e_2)$ refers to context similarity of entities.

3.5 The Algorithm for Entity Alignment

Algorithm 1: The COEA Algorithm

Input: Two collections of entities from online encyclopedias E_1 and E_2, upper bound λ and lower bound μ of the threshold of attribute similarity of entity, similarity parameter ω of entity.

Output: The collection of alignable entities E_A.

// $size(E)$ refers to the number of elements in the collection E.

1 $E_A \leftarrow \Phi$;
2 **for** *each entity* $e \in (E_1 \cup E_2)$ **do**
3 $\quad$ construct topic-word matrix φ;
4 $\quad$ generate topic-feature vector V_e;

5 $N_1 \leftarrow size(E_1)$;
6 $N_2 \leftarrow size(E_2)$;
7 **for** $i \leftarrow 1$ *to* N_1 **do**
8 $\quad$ **for** $j \leftarrow 1$ *to* N_2 **do**
9 $\quad\quad$ $as \leftarrow attribute\_sim(e_{1_i}, e_{2_j})$;
$\quad\quad$ // e_1 and e_2 are entities from E_1 and E_2, respectively.
10 $\quad\quad$ **if** $as < \mu$ **then**
11 $\quad\quad\quad$ continue;
12 $\quad\quad$ **else if** $as > \lambda$ **then**
13 $\quad\quad\quad$ $E_A \leftarrow E_A \cup \{(e_{1_i}, e_{2_j})\}$;
14 $\quad\quad$ **else**
15 $\quad\quad\quad$ $cs \leftarrow context\_sim(e_{1_i}, e_{2_j})$;
16 $\quad\quad\quad$ $sim \leftarrow similarity(e_{1_i}, e_{2_j})$;
17 $\quad\quad\quad$ **if** $sim \geq \omega$ **then**
18 $\quad\quad\quad\quad$ $E_A \leftarrow E_A \cup \{(e_{1_i}, e_{2_j})\}$;

19 return E_A;

From the pseudocode it is clear that the internal loop is executed N_2 times for each fixed value of i. The value of i ranges from 1 to N_1, which yields a total number of operations roughly on the order of $N_1 N_2$. Overall, the time complexity of the COEA algorithm is $O(n^2)$.

4   Experiments

This section introduces the configuration of experimental environment, descriptions of data sets, experimental details, and analysis of experimental results.

4.1   Configuration of Experimental Environment

In this paper, we use CentOS 7.2, JDK 1.8.0_202, Hadoop 2.5.2, HBase 0.98.8, and Nutch 2.3.1.

4.2   Descriptions of Experimental Data Sets

For the purpose of verifying the effectiveness of the algorithm for entity alignment in online encyclopedias proposed in this paper, we randomly extract entities including the field of *character* and *movie* from Baidu Baike and Hudong Baike. For each entity, the extracted information includes attribute information and its context.

In these two fields, descriptions of popular entities with more editing times and attributes are relatively complete. Nevertheless, the probability of error of attribute values is higher, while ordinary entities have fewer editing times and the possibility of attribute absence is relatively high. The contextual information of entity in the field of *character* is extracted from "character biography", "major achievements" and so on. The context of entity in the field of *movie*, for example, is extracted from "behind-the-scenes footage" and "evaluation of the film". In this paper, the extracted data sets of entity are verified by manual review. The dataset statistics of entity are shown in Table 2.

Table 2. Dataset statistics of entity

Entity class	#Entity pairs	#Alignable entity pairs
character	600	300
movie	400	200

4.3   Analysis of Experimental Results

Evaluation Index. For a binary classification problem, entities can be divided into positive and negative classes with four situations existing: (**1**) an entity can be defined as true positive (TP) if and only if the entity predicted to be positive is positive originally; (**2**) an entity can be defined as false positive (FP) when the entity predicted to be positive is negative initially; (**3**) an entity can be defined as true negative (TN) in the case of the entity predicted to be negative is negative primarily; (**4**) an entity can be defined as false negative (FN) if the entity predicted to be negative is positive originally.

The *precision*, *recall* and *F-measure* are selected as the evaluation standards. The *precision* is defined as:

$$precision = \frac{TP}{TP + FP}. \tag{8}$$

The *recall* is defined as:

$$recall = \frac{TP}{TP + FN}. \tag{9}$$

The *F-measure* is defined as:

$$\text{F-measure} = 2 \times \frac{precision \times recall}{precision + recall}. \tag{10}$$

Corresponding to this paper, meanings of TP, FP, TN, and FN are shown in Table 3.

Table 3. Meaning of variables

Variable name	Meaning in this paper
TP	Alignable entity pairs that are aligned
FP	Nonalignable entity pairs that are aligned
TN	Nonalignable entity pairs that are not aligned
FN	Alignable entity pairs that are not aligned

The *precision* represents the accuracy of correctly aligned entities obtained by entity alignment algorithm, which is used to measure the quality of alignment. The *recall* denotes the total number of correctly aligned entities accounts for the proportion of all aligned entities in the data sets. Moreover, the *F-measure* is a comprehensive index, defined as the harmonic mean of *precision* and *recall*.

Parameter Selection. The parameters to be determined in this paper mainly include upper bound λ and lower bound μ of attribute similarity, topic number K in the topic model, and threshold ω of entity alignment. The method of selecting parameters is as follows:

(1) **Selection of Parameters λ and μ**

After extensive experiments, this paper assigns 0.9 to λ and 0.3 to μ. A pair of entity is nonalignable when the attribute similarity is less than μ and is alignable when the attribute similarity is greater than λ.

(2) **Selection of the Parameter** ω

ω is a significant parameter that affects the accuracy of entity alignment algorithm. Under the specified parameter conditions, the *precision* of entity alignment algorithm is inversely dependent on the *recall*. The *precision* goes up but the *recall* goes down with ω increasing, vice versa. Due to the dependence between *precision* and *recall*, this paper mainly refer to the optimal *F-measure* when selecting the ω. We choose ω that makes the *precision* higher in the case of *F-measure* are nearly identical. According to the Fig. 5, the optimal value of ω in both fields of *character* and *film* is 0.6.

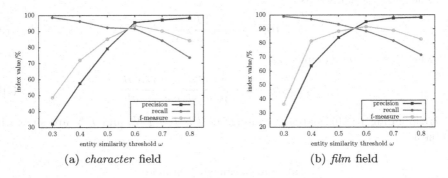

(a) *character* field   (b) *film* field

Fig. 5. Experimental results on different thresholds ω of entity alignment in two fields

(3) **Selection of the Parameter K**

In this paper, the number of different topics is compared and the parameter ω is selected as 0.6. As shown in the Fig. 6, when the number of topics in the field of *character* and *film* is set to 5 and 4, respectively, the overall performance of the algorithm achieves the best.

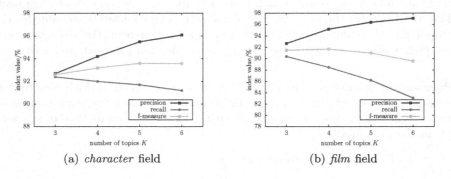

(a) *character* field   (b) *film* field

Fig. 6. Experimental results on different number of topics K in two fields

Compared with Other Algorithms of Entity Alignment. In order to validate the effectiveness of the proposed COEA algorithm, extensive experiments are performed on the basis of constructed data sets of entity alignment. During the experiment, Weighted-LCS algorithm, LCS-TFIDF algorithm, and LDA algorithm is performed on the data sets. The experimental results are shown in Tables 4 and 5. The evaluation of each method is as follows.

Table 4. Results of *character* domain

Algorithm	Precision	Recall	F-measure
LDA	0.898	0.910	0.904
LCS-TFIDF	0.937	0.908	0.922
Weighted-LCS	0.766	0.829	0.796
COEA	**0.955**	**0.917**	**0.936**

Table 5. Results of *film* domain

Algorithm	Precision	Recall	F-measure
LDA	0.877	0.698	0.777
LCS-TFIDF	0.943	0.792	0.783
Weighted-LCS	0.825	0.562	0.669
COEA	**0.952**	**0.885**	**0.917**

(1) LDA Algorithm

This algorithm, which extracts topic features from context information of entities and implements the topic modeling, only uses the context information of entities for entity alignment. The effect is acceptable in the field of *character* with abundantly descriptive information but not ideal in the field of *film* with relatively inadequate descriptions.

(2) LCS−TFIDF Algorithm

This algorithm is one of the effective entity alignment methods in traditional methods, which calculates the value of TF-IDF for each word in the context information of entity [14], constructs the feature vector through the calculation results and then computes the context similarity of the entity by using the cosine similarity of the vector to implement the entity alignment. This algorithm takes only the frequency of word into account without considering the specific semantics. Consequently, this method is slightly less effective than the COEA algorithm.

(3) Weighted−LCS Algorithm

According to the different contributions of attributes to the final entity similarity, this method assigns different weights to the attributes to implement the entity alignment in [7]. The experimental result shows that this method, which weakens the sparse attributes that are significant to encyclopedia entities, highly depends on generic attributes. Therefore, the performance of this method is not ideal in online encyclopedias entity alignment tasks.

(4) **COEA Algorithm**

Taking both attribute information and context with abundant semantics into account, this algorithm outperforms other methods in entity alignment tasks. Assigning 0.6 to the threshold of entity alignment and 5 to the number of topics, the COEA algorithm achieves the optimal effect in the field of *character*. Moreover, the best performance of our proposed method in the field of *movie* can be achieved under the condition of the threshold is 0.6 and the number of topics is 4. The *precision*, *recall*, and *F-measure* of this method in two fields are all the greatest, which verifies the effectiveness of this algorithm in online encyclopedias entity alignment tasks.

5   Conclusion

In order to improve the efficiency and accuracy of entity alignment in online encyclopedias, this paper proposes the COEA method for entity alignment based on attribute information and context information. This method extracts and normalizes attribute information of entity, extracts context information, completes topic modeling, and comprehensively considers attribute similarity and context similarity to implement entity alignment. Compared with the classical entity alignment algorithms, the experimental results show that the method proposed in this paper outperforms the traditional methods of entity alignment in online encyclopedias. In addition, our proposed method has generality in online encyclopedias entity alignment tasks. We will further optimize the algorithm and consider the integration of larger online encyclopedias which is of great significance for constructing integrated and high-quality knowledge graphs of Chinese encyclopedias.

Acknowledgments. This work is supported by the National Natural Science Foundation of China (61572353), the Natural Science Foundation of Tianjin (17JCY-BJC15400), and the National Training Programs of Innovation and Entrepreneurship for Undergraduates (201910056374).

References

1. Antoniou, G., Van Harmelen, F.: Web ontology language: OWL. In: Staab, S., Studer, R. (eds.) Handbook on Ontologies, pp. 67–92. Springer, Heidelberg (2004)
2. Berners-Lee, T., Hendler, J., Lassila, O., et al.: The semantic web. Sci. Am. **284**(5), 28–37 (2001)
3. Biega, J., Kuzey, E., Suchanek, F.M.: Inside YAGO2s: a transparent information extraction architecture. In: Proceedings of the 22nd International Conference on World Wide Web, pp. 325–328. ACM (2013)
4. Blei, D.M., Ng, A.Y., Jordan, M.I.: Latent Dirichlet allocation. J. Mach. Learn. Res. **3**(Jan), 993–1022 (2003)

5. Bollacker, K., Evans, C., Paritosh, P., Sturge, T., Taylor, J.: FreeBase: a collaboratively created graph database for structuring human knowledge. In: Proceedings of the 2008 ACM SIGMOD International Conference on Management of data, pp. 1247–1250. ACM (2008)

6. Griffiths, T.: Gibbs sampling in the generative model of latent Dirichlet allocation (2002)

7. Hai-hua, Z.X.h.J., Rui-hua, D.: Property weight based co-reference resolution for linked data. Comput. Sci. **40**(2), 11 (2013)

8. Baidu Baike Homepage: Line spacing in latex documents. http://baike.baidu.com. Accessed 9 July 2019

9. Hudong Baike Homepage: Line spacing in latex documents. http://www.hudong. com. Accessed 6 July 2019

10. LNCS Homepage: Line spacing in latex documents. http://cnschema.org. Accessed 5 July 2019

11. Huang, J., Li, T., Jia, Z., Jing, Y., Zhang, T.: Entity alignment of Chinese heterogeneous encyclopedia knowledge base. Comput. Appl. **36**(7), 1881–1886 (2016)

12. Lehmann, J., et al.: DBpedia-a large-scale, multilingual knowledge base extracted from Wikipedia. Seman. Web **6**(2), 167–195 (2015)

13. Leuf, B.: The Wiki way: collaboration and sharing on the internet. History **1060**, 12 (2001)

14. Mori, J., Tsujishita, T., Matsuo, Y., Ishizuka, M.: Extracting relations in social networks from the web using similarity between collective contexts. In: Cruz, I., et al. (eds.) ISWC 2006. LNCS, vol. 4273, pp. 487–500. Springer, Heidelberg (2006). https://doi.org/10.1007/11926078_35

15. Nov, O.: What motivates wikipedians? Commun. ACM **50**(11), 60–64 (2007)

16. Sheth, A., Thirunarayan, K.: Semantics empowered Web 3.0 managing enterprise, social, sensor, and cloud-based data and services for advanced applications. Synth. Lect. Data Manag. **4**(6), 1–175 (2012)

17. Wang, Z., et al.: XLore: a large-scale English-Chinese bilingual knowledge graph. In: International Semantic Web Conference (Posters & Demos), vol. 1035, pp. 121–124 (2013)

18. Yan, Z., Guoliang, L., Jianhua, F.: A survey on entity alignment of knowledge base. J. Comput. Res. Dev. **1**, 165–192 (2016)

19. Zheng, J., Mao, Y., Dong, Q.: Department of automation, Tsinghua University Beijing 100084; word sense tagging method based on context. J. Chin. Inf. Process. **5** (2000)

20. Zheng, Z., Si, X., Li, F., Chang, E.Y., Zhu, X.: Entity disambiguation with FreeBase. In: Proceedings of the 2012 IEEE/WIC/ACM International Joint Conferences on Web Intelligence and Intelligent Agent Technology-Volume 01, pp. 82–89. IEEE Computer Society (2012)

Efficient Deployment and Mission Timing of Autonomous Underwater Vehicles in Large-Scale Operations

Somaiyeh MahmoudZadeh$^{(\boxtimes)}$

School of Information Technology, Deakin University,
Geelong, VIC 3220, Australia
S.MahmoudZadeh@deakin.edu.au

Abstract. This study introduces a connective model of routing- local path planning for Autonomous Underwater Vehicle (AUV) time efficient maneuver in long-range operations. Assuming the vehicle operating in a turbulent underwater environment, the local path planner produces the water-current resilient shortest paths along the existent nodes in the global route. A re-routing procedure is defined to re-organize the order of nodes in a route and compensate any lost time during the mission. The Firefly Optimization Algorithm (FOA) is conducted by both of the planners to validate the model's performance in mission timing and its robustness against water current variations. Considering the limitation over the battery lifetime, the model offers an accurate mission timing and real-time performance. The routing system and the local path planner operate cooperatively, and this is another reason for model's real-time performance. The simulation results confirms the model's capability in fulfilment of the expected criterion and proves its significant robustness against underwater uncertainties and variations of the mission conditions.

Keywords: Autonomy · Firefly Optimization Algorithm · Local path planning · Mission routing · Mission time management

1 Introduction

Autonomous Underwater Vehicles (AUVs) are designed to provide cost-effective underwater missions and largely used for different purposes over the past decades [1]. The problem associated with most of the todays AUV's autonomous operation is that they operate with a pre-defined mission outline and require human supervision, in which a set of pre-programmed instructions is fed to vehicle for any specific mission. Considering this deficiency, obtaining a premier autonomy to manage the mission time and autonomous adaption to the environmental changes is a substantial prerequisite in this regard. A vast literature exists on AUVs' routing and motion planning framework. Different deterministic algorithms, such as D* [2], A* [3], and FM* [4], have been used recently to address AUVs' motion planning problem. Deterministic approaches also have been investigated on vehicle's task allocation and routing problems, in which a multiple-target-multiple-agent framework based on graph matching algorithm has

© Springer Nature Switzerland AG 2019
J. Li et al. (Eds.): ADMA 2019, LNAI 11888, pp. 792–804, 2019.
https://doi.org/10.1007/978-3-030-35231-8_58

been studied by Kwok et al., in [5]. Both vehicle routing and path planning are categorized as a non-deterministic polynomial-time problem in which computational burden increases with enlargement of the problem search space. Hence, deterministic and heuristic algorithms cannot be appropriate for real-time applications as these methods are computationally expensive in large spaces [6]. Meta-heuristics are another alternative group of algorithms for solving complex problems that offer near optimal solutions in a very quick computation [7, 8] and is appropriate for the purpose of this study.

There are various examples of evolution-based applications of path planning and routing-scheduling approaches. A Non-Dominated Sorting Genetic Algorithm (NSGA-II) is employed for AUV's waypoint guidance and offline path planning [9]. MahmoudZadeh et al., designed an online Differential Evolution (DE) based path planner for a single AUV's operation in a dynamic ocean environment [10]. A routing-task-assigning framework is also introduced recently for an AUV's mission planning in a large static operating network, in which the performance of genetic algorithm, imperialist competitive algorithm, and Particle Swarm Optimization (PSO) methods are tested and compared in solving the graph complexity of the routing problem [11]. Afterward, they extended their study by modelling a more complex environment where a semi-dynamic operation network is encountered in contrast and subsequently efficiency of the biogeography-based optimization and PSO algorithms are tested and evaluated in solving the dynamic routing and task allocation approach [12, 13].

Indeed, attaining a superior optimization and computationally efficient approach for addressing these complex problems is still an open area for further investigation. Assuming a waypoint cluttered graph-like environment, the AUV must be able to manage its battery lifetime to carry out a mission including specific set of waypoints; hence, a general route planning over the operation network is primary requirement for this purpose. The second essential objective is to adapt the ocean current deformations and safely guide the AUV trough the network vertices. To do so, the system should be computationally efficient to take a real-time trend over the subsea current deformations. Current research constructs a general routing system with a mounted local path planner to provide a reliable and energy efficient maneuver for the AUV. This system takes the meta-heuristics advantages of Firefly Optimization Algorithm (FOA) to meet the requirements of a long-range operation in a turbulent subsea environment. This research conducts a two dimensional turbulent current map generated by a popular predictive model based on superposition of multiple Lamb vortices [14–17].

2   Routing Problem in a Waypoint Cluttered Environment

The operation space is modelled as an undirected weighted graph (G) including a specific number of nodes denoted by P and graph connections/edges (E). The vertices of the network $p_{xyz}^i \in P$ are uniformly distributed in a three dimensional volume of $(x_{10000}, y_{10000}, z_{100})$ that represented as follows:

$$G(P,E) \xrightarrow[\substack{|P|=k \\ |E|=m}]{} \begin{cases} P : \langle p^1, \dots, p^k \rangle \\ E : \langle e^1, \dots, e^m \rangle \\ e^{ij} = \left(p^i, p^j \right) \end{cases} \tag{1}$$

Any edge between p^i and p^j in the graph (e^{ij}) has a corresponding length of (l_{ij}) and approximated traversing time, given by (2). In the given operating graph, the AUV should meet maximum possible nodes in a restricted battery lifetime. Accordingly, the route planner tends to determine a best set of nodes in the graph to guide the AUV toward the target node and to accommodate battery restriction. With respect to given definitions, a route ($\Re$) is mathematically indicated as follows:

$$\forall e^{ij} \quad \exists \quad l_{ij}, t_{ij}$$

$$l_{ij} = \left(\left(p_x^j - p_x^i \right)^2 + \left(p_y^j - p_y^i \right)^2 + \left(p_z^j - p_z^i \right)^2 \right)^{\frac{1}{2}} \tag{2}$$

$$t_{ij} = \frac{l_{ij}}{|v|} + \delta_{ij}$$

$$e^{ij} : \langle p_{xyz}^i, p_{xyz}^j \rangle \Rightarrow \Re = \sum_{\substack{i=1 \\ j \neq i}}^{|E|} S \times e^{ij}; \quad S = \{0,1\}$$

$$\Re : \left\langle \underbrace{e^{si}, \dots, e^{ik}, \dots, e^{kj}, \dots e^{jt}}_{\ell \subseteq \{1, \dots, |E|\}} \right\rangle; \quad \begin{matrix} e^{si} : \langle p_{xyz}^s, p_{xyz}^i \rangle \\ e^{jt} : \langle p_{xyz}^j, p_{xyz}^t \rangle \end{matrix} \tag{3}$$

$$T_\Re = \sum_{\substack{i=1 \\ j \neq i}}^{|E|} S \times e^{ij} \times t_{ij} = \sum_{\substack{i=1 \\ j \neq i}}^{|E|} S \times e^{ij} \left(l_{ij} \times |v|^{-1} \right)$$

here, ℓ is the length of the route which is subset of total number existent edges in the graph ($|E|$). v denotes the vehicle's water referenced velocity in the body frame. S is a selection variable that represents selection of any arbitrary edge in the graph. $T_\Re$ is the route time from start node of p_{xyz}^s to target node of p_{xyz}^t. The battery lifetime denoted by T_τ and is started to counting inversely from the beginning of the operation. The $T_\Re$ should approach the T_τ but should not overstep that. The route should not include non-existent edges, and should not traverse a specific edge for multiple times.

3 Environmental Dynamics and Local Path Planning

In order to deal with environmental impact on vehicles motion, a local path planner is conducted in this study to operate in a smaller operating window between pairs of route nodes. This space reduction leads reducing the computation burden as a smaller window is required to be monitored. Water current is an important environmental factor that influences AUV's motion. The local path planner aims to find a time efficient path while accommodating the current deformations. The current map data in this research is obtained from a popular numerical estimation model based of recursive Navier-Stokes equations [14] as follows:

$$v_c = (v_{c,x}, v_{c,y}) \Rightarrow \begin{cases} v_{c,x} = |v_c| \cos \theta_c \cos \psi_c \\ v_{c,y} = |v_c| \cos \theta_c \sin \psi_c \end{cases} \tag{4}$$

here, the v_c is current velocity vector and the $v_{c,x}$ and $v_{c,y}$ are the $x-y$ components of the v_c. The physical model used by the AUV to diagnose the current velocity field can be found in [18, 19]. AUV's motion in six degree of freedom is provided by state variables of body and NED frames [20], as follows:

$$\eta : (X, Y, Z, \phi, \theta, \psi) \\ v : (v_x, v_y, v_z, p, q, r) \tag{5}$$

where, the η and v denote vehicle's dynamics and kinematic over the time. X, Y, Z denote AUV's position along the path. φ, θ, ψ are the Euler angles of roll, pitch, and yaw, respectively. The v is AUV's velocity vector in the body frame; v_x, v_y, v_z are directional velocities of surge, sway and heave; and p, q, r are the rotational velocities. In this study, the local path $\wp$ is generated using B-Spline curves captured from number of control points while the water current velocity is continuously taken into account. The local path curve $\wp$ is calculated by:

$$\theta_t = tan^{-1} \left(-|\Delta Z_{i,t}| / \sqrt{\Delta X_{i,t}^2 + \Delta Y_{i,t}^2} \right) \\ \psi_t = tan^{-1} \left(|\Delta Y_{i,t}| / |\Delta X_{i,t}| \right) \\ v_{x,t} = |v| \cos \theta_t \cos \psi_t + |v_c| \cos \theta_c \cos \psi_c \\ v_{y,t} = |v| \cos \theta_t \sin \psi_t + |v_c| \cos \theta_c \sin \psi_c \\ v_{z,t} = |v| \sin \theta_t \\ \wp = [X, Y, Z, \psi, \theta, v_x, v_y, v_z] \tag{6}$$

The AUV is presumed with a constant thrust power; hence, the path time $T_\wp$ has a linear relation to path length. The water current deviates the vehicle from its desired trajectory; hence, the resultant path should meet the kinematic constraints of the vehicle in dealing with current force. Therefore, AUV's surge-sway velocities and its yaw-pitch orientation should be constrained to $v_{x,max}$, $[v_{y,min}, v_{y,max}]$, θ_{max}, and $[\psi_{min}, \psi_{max}]$ in all states along the path. Accordingly, the path cost is calculated by (7).

$$\forall \wp_{x,y,z}^i$$

$$T_\wp = \sum_{i=p_{x,y,z}^a}^{|\wp|} \left(\Delta X_{i,t}^2 + \Delta Y_{i,t}^2 + \Delta Z_{i,t}^2\right)^{\frac{1}{2}} \times \left(|v|\right)^{-1}$$

$$C_\wp = T_\wp + \varepsilon_{v_x}\max\left(0; v_{x,t} - v_{x,max}\right) + \dots \qquad (7)$$
$$\dots + \varepsilon_{v_y}\max\left(0; |v_{y,t}| - v_{y,max}\right) + \dots$$
$$\dots + \varepsilon_\theta \max\left(0; \theta_t - \theta_{max}\right) + \dots$$
$$\dots + \varepsilon_\psi \max\left(0; |\dot{\psi}_t| - \psi_{max}\right)$$

The ε_{vx}, ε_{vy}, ε_θ, ε_ψ denote the impact of each constraint violation in determination of the local path cost $C_\wp$.

4 Mission Evaluation Criterion

The generated route ($\Re$) is composed of distances between nodes (l_{ij}) and the path planner generates time efficient trajectory along those distances ($l_{ij} \propto \wp_{ij}$); hence, the path cost of $C_\wp$ directly impacts the route cost of $C_\Re$. As mentioned earlier in Sect. 2, the rout time $T_\Re$ should approach the total battery lifetime T_τ, but should not overstep that. Therefore, the $C_\Re$ gets penalty when the $T_\Re$ for a particular route exceeds the T_τ. The local path may take longer time in dealing with environmental dynamic changes. In such a case, the lost time should be compensated by a proper re-routing process, while its computation cost is considered in total mission cost calculation. Thus, the $C_\Re$ and total mission cost of C_τ in the proceeding research is calculated by (8).

$$C_{\wp_{ij}} \approx T_\wp^{ij} \propto t_{ij} \Rightarrow C_{\wp_{ij}} \propto t_{ij}$$

$$T_\Re = \sum_{\substack{i=0 \\ j \neq i}}^{|E|} s.e^{ij} \times t_{ij}$$

$$C_\Re = |T_\Re - T_\tau| \times \max\left(0, \frac{T_\Re}{T_\tau}\right)$$

$$C_\Re = \left| \sum_{\substack{i=0 \\ j \neq i}}^{|E|} s.e^{ij} \times \left(C_{\wp_{ij}} + \delta_{\wp_{ij}}\right) - T_\tau \right| \times \max\left(0, T_\Re T_\tau^{-1}\right) \qquad (8)$$

$$C_\Re \propto f\left(C_{\wp_{ij}}, T_\tau\right)$$

$$C_\tau = C_\Re\left(C_{\wp_{ij}}, T_\tau\right) + \sum_1^r T_{compute}$$

Where, $T_{compute}$ is the re-routing computation time, and r is the number of re-routing in a mission. $\delta_{\wp ij}$ is the delayed time during the local path planning between p_{xyz}^i and p_{xyz}^j.

5 FOA on Mission Routing and Path Planning

Firefly Optimization Algorithm is a meta-heuristic algorithm inspired from the flashing patterns of fireflies, in which the fireflies attract each other based on their brightness [21]. The fireflies' brightness decreases by distance and the brighter fireflies attract the less bright ones; hence, their attraction is proportional to their brightness and their relative distance. Attraction of a firefly i toward the brighter firefly j is calculated as follows:

$$\partial_{ij} = \|\chi_j - \chi_i\|$$
$$\chi_{i,t+1} = \chi_{i,t} + \beta_0 e^{-\gamma \, \partial_{ij}^2}(\chi_{j,t} - \chi_{i,t}) + \alpha_t \varsigma_i^t \tag{9}$$
$$\alpha_t = \alpha_0 \kappa^t, \quad \kappa \in (0,1)$$

the ∂_{ij} is the distance between fireflies i and j; β_0 is the attraction factor at $\partial = 0$, α_0 and α_t are the initial randomness scaling value and the randomization parameter, respectively. α_t tunes the randomness of fireflies' movement in each iteration. κ is a damping factor. The ς_i^t is a randomly generated vector at time t. The γ light absorption factor. In a case that β_0 approaches zero the movement turns to a simple random walk, while $\gamma = 0$ turns the FOA to a variant of PSO; thus, a proper balance should be set between the engaged parameters [21]. The FOA is efficient due to applying an automatic subdivision approach that enhances convergence rate of the algorithm, and iteratively prevents fireflies from trapping into local optima. This accommodates FOA to efficiently deal with highly nonlinear continuous problems, and makes it flexible in dealing with multimodality [22]. The control parameters in FOA can be tuned iteratively, which is another reason for its fast convergence. Similar to other metaheuristic algorithms, the FA also has two inner loops through the population i_{max} and iteration t_{max}, so at the extreme case the algorithms complexity is $O(i_{max}^2 \times t_{max})$; hence, the computation cost is respectively low as its complexity is linear to time. The cost evaluation is the most computationally complex part of almost all optimization problems. To the purpose of AUV global routing, first step in using the FOA algorithm is to provide the initial population in the format of feasible routes, which has a great impact on algorithms performance. Fireflies in this context are defined as feasible routes in the graph [23, 24].

The solutions take variable length limited to number of vertices in the graph that are generated using graph adjacency information. Accordingly, the algorithm stars to optimize the solutions based on defined cost function for routing problem. In the case of local path planning, the fireflies in the initial population are assigned with candidate local path solutions that are generated by a set of B-Spline control points. Then the FOA tends to efficiently locate the control points of a candidate $\wp$ curve in the solution space according to the defined cost function for the local path. The FOA process of AUV routing, path planning and re-planning is provided by a pseudo-code in Fig. 1.

FOA based Route-Path Planning/Re-planning	Shift Control to the Local Path Planner

FOA based Route-Path Planning/Re-planning

Initialization phase for the **Route Planning System**:

- Set the maximum number of iteration t_{max} and the population size i_{max}.
- Construct global routes $\Re_i$ according to adjacency connections and randomly generated priority vector.
- Initialize solution (Firefly) vectors $\chi_{i,t}^{\Re}$ with the generated route vectors $\Re_i$
- Define light absorption and attraction coefficients for routes $\gamma_\Re, \beta_{\Re 0}$
- Define the randomness scaling factor of $\alpha_{\Re 0}$
- Set the damping and randomization factors of $\kappa_\Re$ and $\alpha_\Re$

For t =1 **to** t_{max}
  Evaluate each candidate Firefly $\chi_{i,t}^{\Re}$ according to route cost function $C_\Re$
  For i =1 **to** i_{max}
    Reconstruct the route $\Re$ according to firefly $\chi_{i,t}^{\Re}$
    Evaluate the $\Re$ by $C_\Re(\chi_{i,t}^{\Re})$
    For j =1 **to** i
      Reconstruct the route $\Re$ according to firefly χ
      Evaluate the $\Re$ by $C_\Re(\chi_{j,t}^{\Re})$
      Update light intensity of $\chi_{i,t}^{\Re}$:
$$\partial_{ij} = \|\chi_{j,t}^{\Re} - \chi_{i,t}^{\Re}\|$$
$$\beta_\Re = \beta_{\Re_0}e^{-\gamma_\Re \partial_{ij}^2}$$
$$\chi_{i,t+1}^{\Re} = \chi_{i,t}^{\Re} + \beta_\Re(\chi_{j,t}^{\Re} - \chi_{i,t}^{\Re}) + \alpha_{\Re,t}\,\varsigma_{i,t}$$
      $if\,(\beta\chi_{j,t}^{\Re} > \beta\chi_{i,t}^{\Re})$,
        Move firefly $\chi_{i,t}^{\Re}$ towards $\chi_{j,t}^{\Re}$
      else
        Move firefly $\chi_{j,t}^{\Re}$ towards $\chi_{i,t}^{\Re}$
      end (**if**)
    end (**For**)
  end (**For**)
  Rank the fireflies and find the current best
end (**For**)
Output the corresponding optimum route $\Re$
Output the corresponding route time $T_\Re$
Output the waypoint sequence
Output expected time (t_{ij}) for passing edge e_{ij}
Send these information to local path planner

Shift Control to the Local Path Planner

Initialization phase for the local path planner:

- Set the maximum iteration t_{max} and population of i_{max}
- Initialize fireflies $\chi_{i,t}^{\wp}$ with the control points along the path $\wp_{xyz}$
- Set the parameters of: $\gamma_\wp, \beta_{\wp 0}, \alpha_{\wp 0}, \kappa_\wp$ and $\alpha_\wp$

For t =1 **to** t_{max}
  For i =1 **to** i_{max}
    Reconstruct the route $\wp$ according to firefly $\chi_{i,t}^{\wp}$
    Evaluate the $\wp_i \approx \chi_{i,t}^{\wp}$ by $C_\wp(\chi_{i,t}^{\wp})$
    For j =1 **to** i
      Reconstruct the route $\wp$ according to firefly $\chi_{j,t}^{\wp}$
      Evaluate the $\wp_j \approx \chi_{j,t}^{\wp}$ by $C_\wp(\chi_{j,t}^{\wp})$
      Update light intensity of $\chi_{i,t}^{\wp}$
$$\partial_{ij} = \|\chi_{j,t}^{\wp} - \chi_{i,t}^{\wp}\|$$
$$\beta_\wp = \beta_{\wp_0}e^{-\gamma_\wp \partial_{ij}^2}$$
$$\chi_{i,t+1}^{\wp} = \chi_{i,t}^{\wp} + \beta_\wp(\chi_{j,t}^{\wp} - \chi_{i,t}^{\wp}) + \alpha_{\wp,t}\,\varsigma_{i,t}$$
      $if\,(\beta\chi_{j,t}^{\wp} > \beta\chi_{i,t}^{\wp})$,
        Move firefly $\chi_{i,t}^{\wp}$ towards $\chi_{j,t}^{\wp}$
      else
        Move firefly $\chi_{j,t}^{\wp}$ towards $\chi_{i,t}^{\wp}$
      end (**if**)
    end (**For**)
  end (**For**)
  Rank the fireflies and find the current best
end (**For**)
Output result the best produced path $\wp$
Output the corresponding path time $T_\wp$

Shift Control to the Re-Planner

INPUT: $\wp$ and $T_\wp$ from the local path planner
INPUT: $\Re, T_\Re$, and t_{ij} from the global route planner
While (Current Waypoint ≠ Destination)
  $if\,(T_\wp^{ij} \le t_{ij})$,
    Continue the current optimum global route $\Re$
    Updated total available time $T_r= T_r - T_\wp^{ij}$
    Send the next pair Waypoints to the path planner.
    Shift the control to the path planner.
  $else\,if\,(T_\wp^{ij} > t_{ij})$,
    Replan Flag ==1
    Eliminate the visited edges from the graph
    Set the current waypoint as a new start point
    Send the new adjacency information to the global route planner
    Updated total available time $T_r= T_r - T_\wp^{ij}$
    Sent the updated T_r to the global route planner
    Shift the control to the global route planner
  end (**if**)
  Calculate the total mission cost C_r
end(While)

Fig. 1. Pseudocode of FOA-based routing, path planning, and re-planning

The battery lifetime T_τ should be managed adaptively. Accordingly, the local path time $T_\wp^{ij}$ gets compared to expected path time of t_{ij} after visiting each node in the route sequence and if it exceeds that, re-routing flag gets triggered. The T_τ gets updated simultaneously. The given process in the pseudo code of Fig. 1 continues until the AUV reaches to the target node.

6 Discussion on Simulation Results

First we turn to evaluate the performance of FOA-based local path planner according to given cost function in (7). The vehicle is assumed to move with a standard thrust power of maximum $\upsilon = 5.5$ (*knots*). The battery consumption for a path is a constant multiple of the path time and path length due to proportional relation of current velocity to the cube root of the thrust. A static current map data is used to evaluate the behaviour of local path planner to water currents deformations. The current map is generated using a Gaussian distribution of 11 vortices in 100×100 grid. The paths' curvature is acquirable by the AUV's directional velocity components and radial acceleration. Figure 2 represents the local path behavior with respect to water current flow.

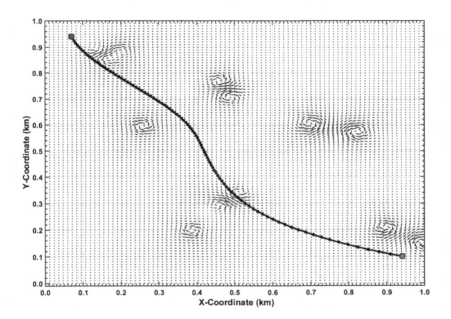

Fig. 2. The local path adaption to current arrows in a static map

As depicted in Fig. 2, it is noteworthy to hint the efficient capability of the FOA-based planner in conforming current arrows either in using accordant current arrows or in avoiding turbulent (vortices). According to path cost function, the path planner aims to determine the shortest battery efficient path between nodes and adapting water current deformations while the actuators boundary conditions and vehicular constraints are considered.

With respect to (7), the path cost function gets penalty when the generated path is violated the boundaries on vehicle's surge, sway, theta rate, yaw rate constraints, which here is defined as follows: $\upsilon_{x,max} = 5.25$ (*knots*); $[\upsilon_{y,min}, \upsilon_{y,max}] = [-0.97, 0.97]$ (*knots*); $\theta_{max} = 20$ (*deg/s*); and $[\psi_{min}, \psi_{max}] = [-17, 17]$ (*deg/s*). Figure 3 presents the local path

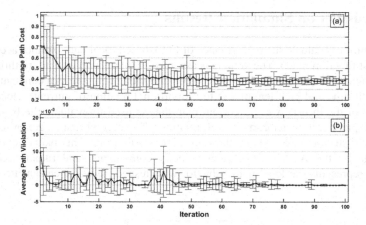

Fig. 3. (a) Cost variations of path population over 100 iterations; (b) Path violation of v_x, v_y, θ, and ψ over 100 iterations;

planner's performance in reducing the path cost and satisfying the above mentioned constraints.

The generated path, as illustrated in plot Fig. 3, shows a great fitness regarding all defined path constraints. The cost variation of path population experiences a moderate convergence to the minimum cost and the variation range narrows down iteratively. It is further outstanding from Fig. 3(b), the FOA-based path planner accurately manages the path toward eliminating the violation factors as the violation of the path population diminishes over the 100 iterations.

On the other hand, the routing model should select an efficient set of nodes restricted to battery life time T_τ to ensure on-time mission termination. A critical factor for concurrency of the routing and path planning models is having a short computational time to keeps any of them from dropping behind the process of the other one. Figure 4 presents the computational performance of the both FOA-based route planner and path planner in 25 simultaneous runs. Moreover, compatibility of the expected time t_{ij} and the path time $T_\wp$ for traversing l_{ij} is another significant performance metric impacts the system synchronism. Hence, there should not be a huge difference between variations of these two parameters. This concurrency also impacts on-time re-routing

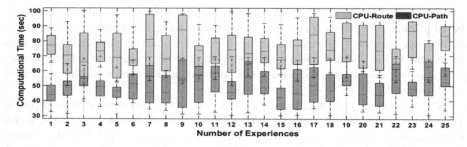

Fig. 4. Computational time variation of route-path planning model over the 25 experiments

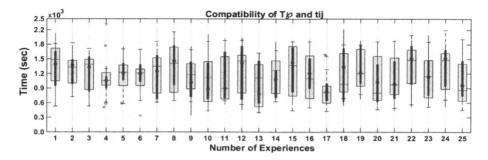

Fig. 5. Compatibility of the value of $T_\wp$ and t_{ij} in a quantitative manner over the 25 experiments

procedure. The concurrency of t_{ij} and $T_\wp$ in 25 experiments is depicted by Fig. 5. Routing and path planning computational time variations, as presented in Fig. 4, are fairly drawn in a narrow range of seconds for all 25 experiments, which hint the real-time performance of the proposed connective FOA-based model in handling the environmental changes.

Analysis of the captured result from multiple experiences, indicates model's consistency in preserving the conformity between t_{ij} (depicted by gray transparent box plot) and $T_\wp$ (depicted by blue compact box plot) as their average variations is relatively close in each experiment. This confirms the accurate synchronization of the routing and path planning system. The whole process of one experiment is illustrated by Fig. 6 for better understanding, in which this single mission includes three re-routing and 11 local path planning passing through the 12 nodes. The routing system provides an initial efficient route. The remained time is initialized with battery life time T_τ and is counted inversely during the mission. The local path planner incorporates local environmental changes and if the $T_\wp$ oversteps the t_{ij} the re-routing flag is triggered and controller shifts to the routing system to compensate the lost time.

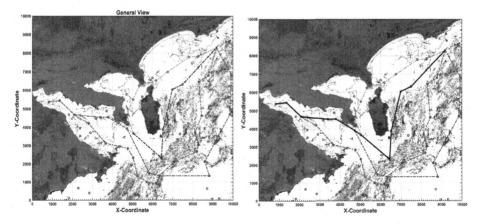

Fig. 6. Routing, path planning, and re-routing procedure by re-arrangement of edges' order in a single mission. (Color figure online)

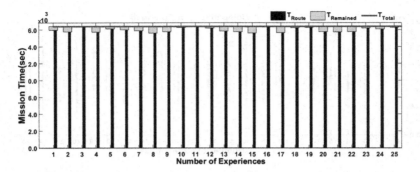

Fig. 7. Statistical analysis of the model's timing performance in 25 missions.

As presented in Fig. 6, the final optimum route (black line) is generated through the three re-planning process, in which the first route (presented by dashed red line) is discarded after passing two nodes; the second one (shown by pink dashed line) is discarded after visiting 5 nodes from the starting point, and the third route (depicted by green dashed line) is discarded in the node 6. These re-planning are carried out to compensate the lost time in the local path planning process.

The most important performance metric in this study is model's accuracy in mission timing and ensuring on-time completion of the mission. Thus, the best outcome of the model is to take a maximum use of battery life time and to fulfill a mission with minimum residual time. The model's capability of mission timing is examined through the 25 individual experiments (missions) presented by Fig. 7, in which the battery life time is set on $T_{\tau} = 7.2 \times 10^{3}$(s) and the terrain is modelled as a realistic underwater environment encountering static ocean current map.

It is outstanding from Fig. 7, the $T_{remained}$ is positive and it is approached to zero in all 25 missions, which means all missions completed before vehicle runs out of battery. Accordingly, the mission time (T_{Route}) maximized to approach upper bound of T_{Total} (presented by pink horizontal line in Fig. 7), but it doesn't overstep the line in any of experiments. It is noted from analyzing the results, the model accurately satisfies mission timing constraints along with other considerations. This is a significant achievement toward having a successful and reliable operation through the excellent mission time management.

7   Conclusion

In this study a connective model of AUV routing and local path planning based on firefly optimization algorithm (FOA) is presented, in which the model is advantaged with a reactive re-routing capability that manages the mission time by re-organizing the order of nodes in a way to be fitted to the battery life time. The local path planner, at the same time, tends to generate energy/time efficient paths along the selected nodes in a route encountering desirable and adverse water current flow. To validate the proposed connective model, the vehicle's operation is simulated in large-scale three-dimensional volume and the static water current map is added to consideration. The FOA performance on the proposed model is tested through the 25 individual mission trials. It is inferred from simulation results that the offered connective model proposes an efficient computational performance (in range of seconds) for both vehicle routing and local path planning that affirms the real-time performance of the model in long range mission management. The local planner also shows a great current resilient efficiency that leads remarkable energy saving in vehicle's continuous deployments. As inferable from the simulation results, the re-planning facilitates the vehicle to have a reliable and energy efficient operation by having an excellent mission timing. The future research will concentrate on expanding the proposed model in terms of upgrading the planners' capabilities and environmental influences on small and long-range missions. It is planned to expand the current study and to prepare a full version as a journal paper.

References

1. Djapic, V., Nad D.: Using collaborative autonomous vehicles in mine countermeasures. In: Oceans'10 IEEE Sydney (2010)
2. Carsten, J., Ferguson, D., Stentz, A.: 3D field D*: improved path planning and replanning in three dimensions. In: IEEE International Conference on Intelligent Robots and Systems 2006, pp. 3381–3386 (2006)
3. Koay, T.B., Chitre, M.: Energy-efficient path planning for fully propelled AUVs in congested coastal waters. The Challenges of the Northern Dimension, Oceans MTS/IEEE Bergen (2013)
4. Petres, C., Pailhas, Y., Patron, P., Petillot, Y., Evans, J., Lane, D.: Path planning for autonomous underwater vehicles. IEEE Trans. Rob. **23**(2), 331–341 (2007)
5. Kwok, K.S., Driessen, B.J., Phillips, C., Tovey, C.A.: Analyzing the multiple-target-multiple-agent scenario using optimal assignment algorithms. J. Intell. Rob. Syst. **35**(1), 111–122 (2002)
6. Roberge, V., Tarbouchi, M., Labonte, G.: Comparison of parallel genetic algorithm and particle swarm optimization for real-time UAV path planning. IEEE Trans. Ind. Inform. **9**(1), 132–141 (2013)
7. Atyabi, A., MahmoudZadeh, S., Nefti-Meziani, S.: Current advancements on autonomous mission planning and management systems: an AUV and UAV perspective. J. Ann. Rev. Control **46**, 196–215 (2018)
8. MahmoudZadeh, S., Yazdani, A., Sammut, K., Powers, D.: Online path planning for AUV rendezvous in dynamic cluttered undersea environment using evolutionary algorithms. J. Appl. Soft Comput. (2017). https://doi.org/10.1016/j.asoc.2017.10.025
9. Ataei, M., Yousefi-Koma, A.: Three-dimensional optimal path planning for waypoint guidance of an autonomous underwater vehicle. Robotics and Autonomous Systems (2014)
10. MahmoudZadeh, S., Powers, D., Sammut, K., Yazdani, A.: Efficient AUV path planning in time-variant underwater environment using differential evolution algorithm. J. Mar. Sci. Appl. (2018). https://doi.org/10.1007/s11804-018-0034-4
11. MahmoudZadeh, S., Powers, D., Sammut, K., Yazdani, A.: Optimal route planning with prioritized task scheduling for AUV missions. In: IEEE International Symposium on Robotics and Intelligent Sensors 2015, pp. 7–15 (2015)

12. MahmoudZadeh, S., Powers, D., Yazdani, A.: A novel efficient task-assign route planning method for AUV guidance in a dynamic cluttered environment. In: IEEE Congress on Evolutionary Computation (CEC), Vancouver, Canada, pp. 678–684. CoRR abs/1604.02524 (2016)

13. MahmoudZadeh, S., Powers, D., Sammut, K., Yazdani, A.: Biogeography-based combinatorial strategy for efficient autonomous underwater vehicle motion planning and task-time management. J. Marine Sci. Appl. **15**(4), 463–477 (2016)

14. Garau, B., Alvarez, A., Oliver, G.: AUV navigation through turbulent ocean environments supported by onboard H-ADCP. In: IEEE International Conference on Robotics and Automation, Orlando, Florida, May 2006

15. MahmoudZadeh, S., Powers, D., Sammut, K.: An autonomous dynamic motion-planning architecture for efficient AUV mission time management in realistic sever ocean environment. Robot. Auton. Syst. **87**, 81–103 (2017)

16. MahmoudZadeh, S., Powers, D., Sammut, K., Atyabi, A., Yazdani, A.: A hierarchal planning framework for AUV mission management in a spatiotemporal varying ocean. J. Comput. Electr. Eng. **67**, 741–760 (2018)

17. MahmoudZadeh, S., Powers, D., Sammut, K., Yazdani, A., Atyabi, A.: Hybrid motion planning task allocation model for AUV's safe maneuvering in a realistic ocean environment. J. Intell. Rob. Syst. **2018**, 1–18 (2018)

18. MahmoudZadeh, S., Powers, D., Sammut, K., Atyabi, A., Yazdani, A.: Hybrid motion planning task allocation model for AUV's safe maneuvering in a realistic ocean environment. J. Intell. Robot. Syst., 1–18 (2018)

19. MahmoudZadeh, S., Powers, K., Atyabi A.: UUV's hierarchical DE-based motion planning in a semi dynamic underwater wireless sensor network. IEEE Trans. Cybern. **99**, 1–14. https://doi.org/10.1109/tcyb.2018.2837134

20. Fossen, T.: Marine control systems: guidance, navigation and control of ships. Rigs Underwater Vehicles. Marine Cybernetics Trondheim, Norway (2002)

21. Yang, X.S.: Nature-Inspired Metaheuristic Algorithms, 2nd edn. Luniver Press, UK (2010)

22. Yang, X.S., He, X.: Firefly algorithm: recent advances and applications. J. Swarm Intell. **1**(1), 36–50 (2013)

23. MahmoudZadeh, S., Powers, D., Sammut, K., Yazdani, A.: A novel versatile architecture for autonomous underwater vehicle's motion planning and task assignment. J. Soft Comput. **20**(188), 1–24 (2016). https://doi.org/10.1007/s00500-016-2433-2

24. MahmoudZadeh, S., Powers, D., Bairam Zadeh, R.: Autonomy and Unmanned Vehicles "Augmented Reactive Mission–Motion Planning Architecture for Autonomous Vehicles", Springer Nature, Cognitive Science and Technology (2019). https://doi.org/10.1007/978-981-13-2245-7, ISBN 978-981-13-2245-7

MLCA: A Multi-label Competency Analysis Method Based on Deep Neural Network

Guohao Qiao[1,2], Bin Wu[1,2(✉)], Bai Wang[1,2], and Baoli Zhang[1,2]

[1] Beijing University of Posts and Telecommunications, Beijing, China
qiaoguohao@yeah.net
{wubin,wangbai,zbaoli}@bupt.edu.cn
[2] Beijing Key Laboratory of Intelligent Telecommunications Software
and Multimedia, Beijing, China

Abstract. The goal of human resource management is to select the right people to the right positions, no matter by recruitment, assessment or promotion. To achieve this goal, competency analysis is an effective way. We can obtain the employee's competency and the position's requirements by the analysis. The competency analysis also provide a strong intellectual support in the downstream works, such as assessing or promoting employees, or establishing employee files. The multi-label text classification model, which is proposed in this paper based on deep neural network, can successfully complete the competency analysis, and its performance is much better than the current text multi-label classification method. We also construct a multi-label classification dataset in human resource field, which is the first one focused on competency analysis, as far as we know.

Keywords: Competency analysis · Multi-label text classification · Deep neural network

1 Introduction

The work scope of human resource management (HRM) involves recruiting, assessing and promoting employees, and making job contents and assessment standards as well. However, the core of HRM is to select the right people to the right positions. Therefore, many researchers have been conducting a lot of researches and modeling works, which can be divided into two directions.

One is Personality-Job Fit Theory (Robbins 2001), which uses six personality types, such as reality, survey, art, society, progress and tradition (Holland 1973). The other is based on the competency model, which analyzes the job-seekers' competency and the matched degree between the job-seeker and the job.

This paper aims at conducting a competency analysis model, inputting text of job description or resume, outputting job requirements and the job-seekers' competency as shown in Fig. 1.

To achieve this goal, the following work has been done:

© Springer Nature Switzerland AG 2019
J. Li et al. (Eds.): ADMA 2019, LNAI 11888, pp. 805–814, 2019.
https://doi.org/10.1007/978-3-030-35231-8_59

Human Resource Assistant

岗位职责：1、执行并完善公司的人事制度与计划，培训与发展，绩效评估，员工社会保障福利等方面的管理工作；2、负责公司各部门的行政后勤类相关工作，做好信息的上传下达。3、协助建立健全公司招聘、培训、工资、保险、福利、绩效考核等人力资源制度建设。4、执行人力资源管理各项务实的操作流程和各类规章制度的实施，配合其他业务部门工作。

任职资格：1、22岁以上，熟悉办公室行政管理知识及工作流程，有经营者优先。2、具有良好的职业道德，踏实稳重，工作细心，责任心强，有较强的沟通、及服务意识，有团队协作精神。3、熟悉使用相关办公软件，具备基本的网络知识；4、工作调理、细微、认真、责任心、办事严谨，对工作有较高的热情，踏实、勤奋、好学、服从上级安排；有效合理的安排工作时间。

General Capability

Professional Ethics, Communication Ability, Service Awareness, Rapid Learning Ability,

Professional Capability

Human Resource Planning, Institutional Optimization, Compensation Management, Performance Management, Employee Training

Fig. 1. An example of model input and output data

– Construct a general and extendible competency analysis model.
– Propose a high-performance multi-label text classification model.
– Manually label more than 20,000 pieces of data, and construct the largest, the best and the most extensive Chinese multi-label classification dataset as far as we know, which can be used in human resource field.

2   Related Work

This section presents some of the technological research, including the works of competency analysis and some research results of text multi-label classification.

2.1   Competency Analysis

By traditional way, the HR experts evaluate the relevant information of the employees, and then judge the employees' competency by their experience and knowledge. The problem of this way lies in: Firstly, it is low efficiency; Secondly, it is lack of uniform standards. Finally, the evaluation result is difficult to qualify, so its accuracy cannot be convinced.

To solve this problem, Zhu proposed a model based on Convolutional Neural Network (PJFNN, Zhu et al. 2018), which separately analyzes the information of both employees and jobs through two different Convolutional Neural Networks, and then matches employees and jobs after full Convolutional extraction feature. However, PJFNN model can only conclude that the employee is fit for a certain job, and it cannot provide the reason, which is very important for both employees and employers.

2.2   Multi-lable Text Classification

A multi-label classification method is required because a job-seeker possesses more than one ability.

In general, there are two methods of multi-label classification: binary method and ranking method (Zhu et al. 2018). The multi-label classification problem is divided into many single label binary classification problem by the binary method, which is simple and efficient. However, the binary method has two disadvantages. One is that the correlation between labels is neglected by separating multi labels. The other is that the number of binary classifiers will increase when the number of label is large, resulting in a decline in classification efficiency. The main idea of the ranking method is to convert the label prediction into a label ranking. Its ultimate goal is to rank the marked label before the unmarked label. The ranking method can avoid the increasing number of the classifiers, but how to select the labels after ranking becomes a new problem.

The multi-label classification model will be introduced specifically in the experience section.

3   Competency Analysis Model

The competency analysis model includes three categories: general capability, management capability and professional capability. The general capability and management capability are shown in Table 1, professional capability is shown in Table 2.

Table 1. General capability and management capability

General capability	Management capability	
Professional ethics	Global vision	Capital operation
Stress resistance	Influence	Creative thinking
Environmental adaptability	Organizational governance	Operation management
Aggressiveness	Resource coordination	Entrepreneurship
Service awareness	Value transmission	Industry sensitivity
Rapid learning ability	Strategic planning	Business judgment
Communication ability	Strategic decomposition	Marketing management
	Human resource management	Negotiation ability
	Talent development	

The general capability contains 7 basic abilities. These abilities apply to all jobs in all industries. Whether recruiting a cashier in supermarket or promoting a CEO of a transnational corporation, we can always use this list of abilities to analyze and evaluate.

Management capability contains 17 management abilities, which are used to measure if an institutional manager is competent. It is noted that there is an

Table 2. Professional capability

Job category	Professional capability	Job category	Professional capability
Human resource	Human resource planning	Business development	Budget assessment
	Recruitment		Strategic analysis
	Employee training		Strategic planning
	Performance management		Operating analysis
	Compensation management	Operation	Business planing
	Labor relationship management		Target tracking
	Institutional optimization		Operational rick management
	Organizational vitality activation		Operational planning
	Business acumen	Manufacture	Production planning
Administrative	Secretarial		Attention to detail
	Board affairs management		Project management
	Security		Innovation
	Branding	Market	Channel planning
	Asset management		Technical knowledge
Legal affairs	Legal expertise		Market information analysis
	Legal risk assessment		Market planning implementation
	Legal advice		Attention to detail
	Legal review		Result-oriented
Finance	Budget management		Leading edge tracking
	Tax management	Sell	Decision making
	Fund management		Market planning implementation
	Business audit		Communication
	Self-regulation		Personal drive
	Information analysis		Performance orientation
Customer service	Customer choice	Invention	Specialized knowledge
	Product display		Personal drive
	Emotional regulation		Thinking ability

inevitable intersection between these abilities in order that all the management abilities in the model can cover the management requires as completely as possible. For example, there is a certain intersection between Strategic Planning and Strategic Decomposition. Therefore, in the following multi-label classification, it is necessary to consider the dependency between the labels.

Professional capability contains 54 abilities in 11 job categories. When the professional capability model was constructed, special attention was paid to maintaining its expandability. So the concept of job category is introduced. Obviously, in a company, the professional requirements for a head of legal department are quite different from those for a head of finance department, although the general and management requirements for them may be the same. For those who use this model, it is easy to meet their needs by adding a new job category to the model.

4   Multi-lable Classification Model

This section introduces the overall architecture of multi-label classification model, and the design ideas of each part as well.

4.1   Model Overview

The model prediction process is shown in Fig. 2. The model can be divided into recurrent structure, convolutional structure and label confirm structure.

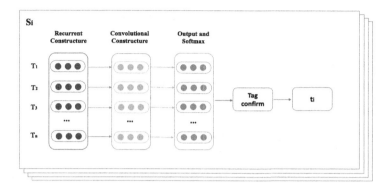

Fig. 2. Each sample is processed by the model, and each box represents a process. For each label, a classifier is constructed separately for recurrent, convolutional, output and softmax processing. Finally, enter the results of all the classifiers into the label confirm layer to summarize the label results. The final output of the model is t.

Define the set of all n samples in the Data Set as S, the ith sample is S_i. Define the set of all m labels in the Data Set as T, the jth label is T_j. Sample S_i is predicted as t_i by the model.

4.2   Recurrent Structure

The recurrent structure is shown in Fig. 3.

Define that there are a total of p words in a sample, then the ith word is w_i. Define its word vector as $v(w_i)$, its left context as $lc(w_i)$, and its right context as $rc(w_i)$. Manually define the left context $lc(w_i)$ of the first word and the right context as $rc(w_i)$ of the last word. Besides, the calculation formulas of the left context and the right context respectively are Eqs. (1) and (2). W_{lc}, W_{rc}, W_{lv}, and W_{rv} used in the equation are all dense matrices involved in training.

$$lc(w_i) = f[W_{lc} \cdot lc(w_{i-1}) + W_{lv} \cdot v(w_{i-1})] \qquad (1)$$

$$rc(w_i) = f[W_{rc} \cdot rc(w_{i-1}) + W_{rv} \cdot v(w_{i-1})] \qquad (2)$$

It is easy to see, for each sample, the left context of a word is calculated from the word itself and all the words on the left of the sample. The right context is the same. Connect the left context, the word embedding, and the right context of a word to form a character representation of the word, as shown in Eq. (3).

$$x_i = [lc(w_i); v(w_i); rc(w_i)] \qquad (3)$$

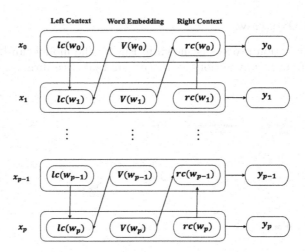

Fig. 3. Recurrent neural network structure

At the end of the recurrent structure, the representation x_i of the word is linearly transformed, as shown in Eq. (4), and enter the result y into the next layer.

$$y_i = ReLU(W^{(1)} \cdot x_i + b^{(1)}) \tag{4}$$

4.3 Convolutional Structure

Convolutional structure is used to summarize textual features. Therefore, the networks should be designed neither too simple nor too complicated. In this paper, a structure consisting of 3 convolutional layers, 1 pooling layer and 1 drop out layer is used. After the convolutional structure, a fully connected layer and a softmax function are respectively connected to obtain the probability of classification, as shown in Eqs. (5) and (6).

$$z_i = W^{(2)} \cdot y_i^{(2)} + b^{(2)} \tag{5}$$

$$P = \frac{\exp(z_i)}{\sum_{i=1}^{n} \exp(z_i)} \tag{6}$$

4.4 Tag Confirm Structure

Finally, enter the classified probability of all samples into the label confirm layer. The classification result of each sample is obtained by the median of 78 sample data.

5   Experiments

The model has been tested on a Chinese multi-label classification dataset in the field of competency analysis, including the comparison with the multi-label classification method which is currently well-performed, and with the classic deep neural network method which is improved as well. The result of experiment shows that the model performs better than these classic methods.

5.1   Data Set

Data comes from the Chinese Recruitment Website 51Job and Liepin. All these recruitment information covers nearly all jobs in all industries and all levels from the year 2017 to 2018. The basic information of multi-label competency analysis data set is shown in Table 3.

If this paper is received, the data set will be open sourced.

5.2   Comparison Method

Multi-label classification has been studied for many years and there are several benchmark algorithms. At the same time, some classic deep neural networks have been modified to achieve the multi-label classification.

MDDM. By projecting raw data into a lower dimensional feature space, it attempts to maximize the dependencies between the original feature description and related labels, in order to achieve the goal of dimensionality reduction (Zhang et al. 2010).

Table 3. Basic situation of multi-label competency analysis data set

	Multi-label competency analysis data set
Class	78
Train	16800
Validation	2100
Test	2100
avg_Length	130
Language	CHN

PMU. It performs multi-label classification by considering the mutual information between the selected feature and the label set (Lee et al. 2013).

MDMR. It combines mutual information with maximum dependencies and minimal redundancy to select a good subset of features for multi-label learning and complete multi-label classification tasks (Lin et al. 2015).

MLMLFS. It eliminates the disrelated and noisy features by adding effective L2, p-norm regularization terms to the feature selection matrix (Zhu et al. 2018).

CNN. It is a convolutional neural network, which classifies features extracted in according to the character level. And it is changed to a multi-label classification model by adding the softmax function and the label confirm structure (Zhang et al. 2015).

RNN. A classic RNN model, similar to CNN, is changed to a multi-label classification model (Socher et al. 2013).

DPCNN. It is a shallow word level CNN model that effectively represents remote associations in text (Johnson and Zhang 2017).

5.3   Performance Experiments

The experimental result is shown in Table 4.

The comparison experiments can be divided into two main types. One is the classic multi-label classification algorithm, which focuses on selecting features and reducing feature dimensions. The other is the multi-label classification algorithm rewritten by the classic single-label text classification algorithm, which pays no attention to the correlation between features. Therefore, the average accuracy is used as a measure index.

The result of these two types of comparison experiment shows that the average accuracy is not much different, which fully demonstrates that there is a low correlation between the labels of the competency analysis model. Therefore, the design goal of the competency analysis model is achieved, that is to make the labels of the competency analysis model as isolated as possible.

Table 4. Experience result

Model	AUC
MDDM (Zhang et al. 2010)	0.485
PMU (Lee et al. 2013)	0.579
MDMR (Lin et al. 2015)	0.561
MLMLFS (Zhu et al. 2018)	0.610
CNN (Zhang et al. 2015)	0.588
RNN (Socher et al. 2013)	0.490
DPCNN (Johnson and Zhang 2017)	0.599
MLCA (Our model)	**0.636**

MLCA Model achieved the best performance on the recruitment information dataset. Competency analysis with more than 60% accuracy is good enough to perform in practice.

6 Conclusion

In this paper, we do the following work:

- Construct a general and extendible competency analysis model, containing 78 abilities in 3 categories.
- Propose a multi-label text classification model based on deep neural network, which can be used to analyze competency in HR field. The model performs better than those multi-label classification model which is currently well-performed.
- Manually label more than 20,000 pieces of data, and construct the largest, the best and the most extensive Chinese multi-label classification dataset as far as we know, which can be used in human resource field.

The results of the work have now been applied to enterprise-level business applications. In the future, we will continue to push the current results downstream.

Acknowledgments. This work is supported by Big Data Research Foundation of PICC.

References

Dai, J., et al.: Deformable convolutional networks. In: Proceedings of the IEEE International Conference on Computer Vision, pp. 764–773 (2017)

Howard, J., Ruder, S.: Universal language model fine-tuning for text classification. arXiv preprint arXiv:1801.06146 (2018)

Huang, W.: Character-level convolutional network for text classification applied to Chinese corpus. arXiv preprint arXiv:1611.04358 (2016)

Johnson, R., Zhang, T.: Deep pyramid convolutional neural networks for text categorization. In: Proceedings of the 55th Annual Meeting of the Association for Computational Linguistics (Volume 1: Long Papers), pp. 562–570 (2017)

Lai, S., Xu, L., Liu, K., Zhao, J.: Recurrent convolutional neural networks for text classification. In: Twenty-Ninth AAAI Conference on Artificial Intelligence (2015)

Lee, J., Kim, D.W.: Feature selection for multi-label classification using multivariate mutual information. Pattern Recogn. Lett. **34**(3), 349–357 (2013)

Lin, Y., Hu, Q., Liu, J., Duan, J.: Multi-label feature selection based on max-dependency and min-redundancy. Neurocomputing **168**, 92–103 (2015)

Lin, Y., Hu, Q., Zhang, J., Wu, X.: Multi-label feature selection with streaming labels. Inform. Sci. **372**, 256–275 (2016)

Mcclelland, D.C.: Testing for competence rather than for "intelligence". Am. Psychol. **28**(1), 1–14 (1973)

Wang, H., Ding, C., Huang, H.: Multi-label Linear Discriminant Analysis. In: Daniilidis, K., Maragos, P., Paragios, N. (eds.) ECCV 2010. LNCS, vol. 6316, pp. 126–139. Springer, Heidelberg (2010). https://doi.org/10.1007/978-3-642-15567-3_10

Wang, L., Wang, L., Lu, H., Zhang, P., Ruan, X.: Saliency Detection with Recurrent Fully Convolutional Networks. In: Leibe, B., Matas, J., Sebe, N., Welling, M. (eds.) ECCV 2016. LNCS, vol. 9908, pp. 825–841. Springer, Cham (2016). https://doi.org/10.1007/978-3-319-46493-0_50

Xiao, Y., Liu, J., Pang, Y.: Development of a competency model for real-estate project managers: case study of China. Int. J. Const. Manag. 1–12 (2018)

Yin, W., Schütze, H., Xiang, B., Zhou, B.: ABCNN: attention-based convolutional neural network for modeling sentence pairs. Trans. Assoc. Comput. Linguist. **4**, 259–272 (2016)

Yu, H.F., Jain, P., Kar, P., Dhillon, I.: Large-scale multi-label learning with missing labels. In: International Conference on Machine Learning, pp. 593–601 (2014)

Zhang, Y., Zhou, Z.H.: Multilabel dimensionality reduction via dependence maximization. ACM Trans. Knowl. Discov. Data (TKDD) **4**(3), 14 (2010)

Zhu, C., Zhu, H., Xiong, H., Ma, C., Xie, F., Ding, P., Li, P.: Person-job fit: Adapting the right talent for the right job with joint representation learning. ACM Trans. Manag. Inf. Syst. (TMIS) **9**(3), 12 (2018)

Zhu, P., Xu, Q., Hu, Q., Zhang, C., Zhao, H.: Multi-label feature selection with missing labels. Pattern Recogn. **74**, 488–502 (2018)

MACCA: A SDN Based Collaborative Classification Algorithm for QoS Guaranteed Transmission on IoT

Weifeng Sun[1], Zun Wang[1(✉)], Guanghao Zhang[1], and Boxiang Dong[2]

[1] School of Software, Dalian University of Technology, Dalian, China
`wfsun@dlut.edu.cn`, `wangzun_ssdut@mail.dlut.edu.cn`,
`zguanghao@163.com`
[2] Montclair State University, Montclair, NJ, USA
`dongb@montclair.edu`

Abstract. Software defined network (SDN) can effectively balance link loads and guarantee QoS for different application categories of data streams on Internet of Things (IoT). To achieve high accuracy and low time consumption for stream classification for SDN, the collaborative methods are considered. By analyzing the data sets of network flows on CyberGIS and IoT, a Misclassification-Aware Collaborative Classification Algorithm named MACCA is proposed. MACCA collaborates the misclassification results judgment module and the decision module to calculate the final classification results, thus it can avoid the reduction of overall accuracy caused by voting to determine the results. The evaluation results show that the MACCA can classify the network data streams efficiently with an average accuracy of 99.66% and a lower time consumption compared to other classification algorithms, which can be implemented on SDN-based networks.

Keywords: Collaborative classification · Misclassification judgment · IoT · CyberGIS · SDN

1 Introduction

On IoT, geographic information data is the basis of location-based service applications such as UAV transportation and disaster rescue. CyberGIS is a distributed computing model for such location-based geographic information data processing. It can meet a variety of different application needs. In CyberGIS, geographic information data can be transmitted by data streams of different applications. However, data flows for different applications have different link requirements and require network load balancing on demand. In the traditional network, it is hard to monitor the global network in real time, and it is unable to achieve link load balancing on demand. SDN can monitor the entire network environment in real time and achieve link load balancing for the data flows on demand.

© Springer Nature Switzerland AG 2019
J. Li et al. (Eds.): ADMA 2019, LNAI 11888, pp. 815–827, 2019.
https://doi.org/10.1007/978-3-030-35231-8_60

In SDN network, we can set different QoS requirements according to the geographic information data flows of different categories of applications [1], and SDN controller can perform link load balancing operation according to the QoS requirements of different data flows. The basis of link load balancing is to classify data flows with high accuracy and low time consumption. The client can classify the data classes and mark priority for the data flow and send priority results to the controller. The controller allocates a path for the data flow based on priority [2]. However, the client can set the highest priority for the data flow without considering the classification result. This situation is not conducive to the realization of link load balancing. So, SDN controller can be used to collect and classify data [3]. At present, there are many classification algorithms, but they cannot achieve high accuracy and low time consumption for stream classification at the same time in SDN network.

In this paper, we concentrate on how to classify data flows with high accuracy and low time consumption in SDN network. By analyzing classification algorithms, we proposed a Misclassification-Aware Collaborative Classification Algorithm (MACCA) for data flow classification in SDN network. MACCA combines C4.5, Naïve Bayesian, and Random Forest algorithms [4]. MACCA does not vote to determine the final classification results. The first stage of MACCA is to use C4.5 and Naïve Bayesian classifiers as basic classifiers in parallel. In the second stage, the two classification results are input into the misclassification results judgment module constructed by the C4.5 algorithm, to determine which of the two algorithms in the first stage is correct. In the last stage, the decision module recalculates or outputs the final classification results according to the results of the misclassification results judgment module.

The rest parts of this paper are arranged as follows: the second part is related work, the third part introduces comparison among classification algorithms, the fourth part introduces MACCA design, and the fifth part is the evaluation results and analysis of MACCA. Finally, it is the summary of this paper.

2 Related Work

CyberGIS [5] is a distributed, scalable geographic information-related data computing model. CyberGIS model requires the network to perform link load balancing on demand, which is not possible with traditional network, but SDN network can solve this problem.

The flexible and dynamic network resource allocation ability of SDN enables it to realize load balancing on demand [6]. In paper [7], a dynamic load balancing method with QoS in SDN was proposed. In this method, controller calculates and chooses the required QoS, and dynamically performs link load balancing according to QoS. In paper [8], authors proposed an application-aware QoS routing algorithm for SDN-based IoT networking. Therefore, how to efficiently classify application data flows to match QoS requirements in SDN has been a hot research issue.

In paper [9], authors used deep packet inspection to classify data flows in SDN network. This DPI-based traffic classification method mainly realized the distinction between programs and services by detecting the application layer load, but the classification process consumed a lot of computing resources. At present, many researchers proposed to use machine learning algorithms to classify streams. In paper [10], authors used SDN controller to collect network traffic, extracted features, and finally used Random Forest algorithm, Stochastic Gradient Boosting and Extreme Gradient Boosting to classify streams respectively. In paper [11], authors proposed a method combining DPI and machine learning. In paper [12], authors proposed a QoS-aware semi-supervised machine learning traffic classification framework, but the accuracy of this framework was lower than 95%.

In SDN network, the controller needs to make decisions quickly [13]. So, for a classification algorithm in the SDN, it is necessary to ensure both high accuracy and low time consumption of classification. In consideration of these problems, we proposed a misclassification-aware collaborative classification algorithm in this paper, which can ensure high accuracy and low time consumption.

3 Feature Selection and Classification Algorithms Comparison

In this paper, we implemented all algorithms using the python programming language. The experimental environment was Windows 10 operating system, with Intel Xeon e3-1230 v3 3.30 GHz CPU, 16 GB memory.

3.1 Dataset Description

In the stream classification experiment in this paper, the selected data set is a subset of the data set which was produced in paper [14]. The data set consists of multiple rows, each row representing a flow. The data set we used is approximately 130,623 rows. We choose TCP data flow as the experiment data set, because TCP is a stable protocol, and its stream has a well-defined start and end, which makes TCP flow a complete flow in theory. The data set described in paper [14] contains a TCP flow that begins with a complete three-way handshake process and ends with a complete handshake process, regardless of the packet loss in the process of transmission network flows, and defines various features of network flows, such as server and client port number, the Ethernet packet length and so on. In this data set, 248 network flow features are defined in total, and the 249th feature is not defined, because it means the application category of this flow which is manually marked. And authors divided the network flows into 10 categories, including WWW, MAIL, FTP, etc.

3.2 Feature Selection Algorithm

In this paper, in order to reduce the data dimension and improve the efficiency of classification algorithm, a feature selection algorithm is proposed, through which, 14 most advantageous features of flow classification can be obtained. In SDN network, the controller only needs to collect or calculate these 14 features, and the flow classification can be completed according to these 14 features.

The feature selection algorithm proposed in this paper is divided into two major steps. In the first step, 248 characteristics are divided into 6 categories. In paper [15], the author divided the characteristics into 9 categories, namely PORTS, PKTS, BYTES, DURATION, PKT THRPT, BYTE THRPT, PKT SIZE, IPAT, TCP FLAG. After the analysis of the paper, we divided the 248 features into 6 categories, such as Port, Packet Numbers, Packet Bytes, Time, TCP Flags and Other. Among them, Port is the Server Port number and the Client Port number. Packet Numbers is associated primarily with the Number of Packets in the network flow. Packet Bytes is mainly related to Byte length in network packet grouping. Time is mainly in the network flow features related to the Time. The feature of the TCP Flags is mainly TCP flow in the process of interaction characteristics related to the sign bit. Other are features cannot be directly obtained from the network flows. In paper [15], the authors also compared the classification results of C4.5, Naïve Bayesian, SVM and KNN algorithms. From the experiment results in paper [15], we found that SVM has a low classification accuracy. In addition, through investigation, we found that the K-Means algorithm is easy to implement. Therefore, in the first step of the feature selection algorithm, we used C4.5, Naïve Bayesian, K-Means and KNN algorithms to classify data according to the 6 categories. For each algorithm, we used 10-fold cross validation to calculate its accuracy. For each category, we calculated and recorded the average accuracy of the four classification algorithms. In the second step, based on the advantages of using Random Forest algorithm for feature selection introduced in paper [16], the Random Forest algorithm is selected to calculate the contribution of each feature in the each feature set to the classification result. Finally, according to the results of the first step, Random Forest algorithm and collectability of features, 14 features are selected. The 14 features are shown in Table 1. We generated a new data set containing the 14 features.

Table 1. The 14 features selected by the feature selection algorithm.

Feature sets	Selected features
Port	Server Port
Packet Numbers	total_packets_a_b, actual_data_pkts_a_b, initial_window_packets_a_b
Packet Bytes	max_data_wire, max_data_ip, var_data_control
Time	max_IAT_a_b, var_IAT_a_b
TCP Flags	SYN_pkts_sent_a_b, FIN_pkts_sent_a_b
Other	ttl_stream_length_a_b, max_segm_size_a_b, min_segm_size_a_b

3.3   Classification Algorithms Comparison

In paper [15, 17, 18], authors used C4.5, Naïve Bayesian, KNN and Random Forest algorithms for comparative experiments. And according to the feature selection algorithm, we finally tested the accuracy and time consumption of the C4.5, Naïve Bayesian, K-Means, KNN, and Random Forest algorithms with the new data set. In our paper, C45, NB, K-means and RF represent the C4.5 algorithm, Naïve Bayesian algorithm, K-Means algorithm and Random Forest algorithm respectively.

In the experiment of accuracy and training time, we randomly selected training set and set up 11 groups of experiments according to the proportion of training set to data set, and randomly selected 13,000 records outside the training set as the test set of each experiment. For each experiment, we recorded the accuracy and training time of the 5 algorithms. In the experiment of classification time, we also randomly selected training set and test set, and the proportion of training set T to the data set is 0.4. We set up 10 groups of experiments according to the proportion of test set to the data set outside the training set. The proportion includes 0.05, 0.1, 0.2, 0.3, 0.4, 0.5, 0.6, 0.7, 0.8, 0.9. The number of streams used for testing ranged from 130623 * 0.6 * 0.05 ≈ 3918 to 130623 * 0.6 * 0.9 ≈ 70535. For each experiment, we recorded the classification time of the 5 algorithms.

3.4 Results Evaluation

According to the experimental description above, we get the experimental results as shown in the Figs. 1 and 2. Figure 1 shows the accuracy of the five algorithms under different training sets. Figure 2(a) shows the training time of the five classification algorithms under different training sets. Figure 2(b) shows the classification time of the five classification algorithms under different test sets.

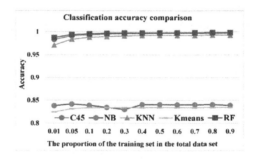

Fig. 1. The comparison of algorithm accuracy.

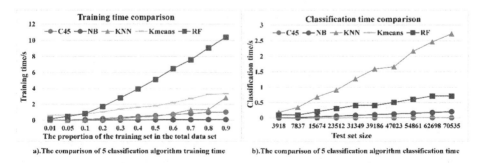

Fig. 2. The comparison of training and classification time.

According to the above experimental results, the average accuracy of Random Forest, C4.5 and KNN algorithms are 99.6%, 99.4%, 98.8%, while the average accuracy of Naïve Bayesian and K-Means algorithms are 83.8%, 83.3%. Random Forest algorithm has the highest average accuracy, but its training time is also the highest in each group of training time experiment. Especially when the proportion of training set to data set is 0.9, its training time is about 10.3 s, much higher than other algorithms. Although C4.5 algorithm has low training time and classification time, its accuracy is lower than Random Forest algorithm 0.1%–0.3% in each group of accuracy experiment. KNN algorithm has the third highest average accuracy. The training time of KNN is much lower than Random Forest in each group of the training time experiment. But in each group of the classification time experiment, the classification time of KNN is much higher than other algorithms. The maximum difference of classification time between KNN and Random Forest is about 2 s. It can be seen that a single classification algorithm cannot meet the requirements of high accuracy and low time consumption at the same time. Therefore, MACCA is proposed in this paper.

4 MACCA Design

In SDN network, we should consider the requirements of high accuracy and low time consumption of flow classification. Therefore, we propose a misclassification-aware collaborative classification algorithm. The process of MACCA is shown in Fig. 3. MACCA is composed of one base classifier module, one misclassification results judgment module and one decision module. In MACCA, classification information data refers to data formed after adding accuracy labels to unclassified data, and classification data refers to unclassified data and classification results of base classifier.

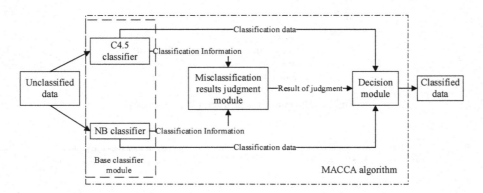

Fig. 3. The process of MACCA.

4.1 Base Classifier Module

The base classifier module contains two base classifiers. The main function of the base classifier module is to provide data support for misclassification results judgment module and decision module. Base classifiers should have low time consumption.

In addition, if two identical classifiers are selected as the base classifiers, their classification results are mostly overlapped, which will not help improve the overall accuracy. Therefore, according to the experiment results in the previous section, Naïve Bayesian and C4.5 algorithms are finally selected as the base classifiers. Although the accuracy of Naïve Bayesian algorithm is low, the error will be corrected by the misclassification results judgment module and the decision module.

4.2 Misclassification Results Judgment Module

In the traditional cooperative classification algorithms, the accuracy of the final result is the product of the accuracy of the base classifiers if the classification results of the base classifiers are the same. For example, if the accuracy of the two base classifiers is 0.97 and 0.98, then the final accuracy may be $0.97 * 0.98 \approx 0.95$, which will reduce the overall accuracy. Therefore, MACCA uses misclassification results judgment module instead of classification results comparison. The input data of the misclassification results judgment module is the classification information of the two base classifiers. After training, the misclassification results judgment module can judge the accuracy of the classification results of the two base classifiers without comparing the results of the base classifiers. If one of the results of two base classifiers is correct or both are correct, then the module will send judgment result to decision module to make it output the correct final result directly. If the results are both wrong, then the classifier will tell the decision module to reclassify data. It can be seen that the misclassification results judgment module is very important in MACCA, which should ensure high accuracy and low time consumption. Since the classification information data is similar to the unclassified data, and training this module requires a large number of training sets, according to the results shown in Figs. 1 and 2, C4.5 algorithm has low time consumption and high accuracy in a large number of training sets, so we choose C4.5 algorithm as the core algorithm of the misclassification results judgment module.

4.3 Decision Module

In the traditional collaborative classifier, when the classification results of the base classifiers are different, the decision module is often used to calculate the final results, which need use complete training set to train the decision module. This process will greatly increase the time consumption of the algorithm. In MACCA, the computational burden of decision module can be reduced by adding a misclassification results judgment module. The decision module only needs to reclassify data if all the results of the base classifiers are wrong. The decision module can directly output right classification result if there is a right classification result in the results of the base classifiers. The decision module only uses the data which base classifiers cannot get the correct classification results by using these data, so as to ensure that the decision module has a high classification accuracy on these data and improve the overall classification accuracy. In MACCA, according to the results shown in Figs. 1 and 2, when the training set is small, Random Forest algorithm has the highest classification accuracy and the lowest time consumption. Therefore, we use Random Forest algorithm as the core algorithm of the decision module.

4.4   The MACCA Algorithm

The pseudo-code of MACCA is roughly shown in Table 2.

Table 2.   The pseudo-code of the MACCA.

MACCA Algorithm
Input: A Data with 14 features
Output: Class label
1.   Label1←C4.5 classifier classification result.
2.   Lable2←Naïve Bayesian classifier classification result.
3.   Base classifier module generates classification information and classification data.
4.   Result←MisclassificationResultsJudgmentModule(classification information)
5.   If   Result ==0 then
6.   Final_result←Decision module recalculates classification result.
7.   Else if   Result ==1 then
8.   Final_result←Label1.
9.   Else if   Result ==2 or Result ==3 then
10.   Final_result←Lable2.
11. Return Final_result.

Lines 1 to 3 show that for the unclassified data, it is classified by two base classifiers, and the category labels Label1 and Label2 are applied. Base classifier module generates classification information data and classification data. Lines 4 shows that the misclassification results judgment module obtains the judgment result according to the classification information data of base classifiers. Lines 5 to 11 show that the decision module decides to recalculate the final classification result or directly output the final result according to the judgment result.

5   Evaluation

In this paper, we implemented MACCA using the python programming language. The experimental environment was Windows 10 operating system, with Intel Xeon e3-1230 v3 3.30 GHz CPU, 16 GB memory.

5.1 Training Process

In the training stage, T represents the total training data set, T_1, T_2, T_3 and T_4 represent the sub-training data sets. The training set T has an application category label. In the experiment of accuracy and training time, the number of training set T is introduced in the first category of experiment in Sect. 5.2. In the experiment of classification time, the number of training set T is introduced in the second category of experiment in Sect. 5.2. And training set T is divided into T_1 and T_2 according to the ratio of 6:4 randomly. First, T_1 is used to train the two base classifiers. Next, we test the two base classifiers using T_2. For each data in T_2, according to two base classifiers' results, if the results of both base classifiers are wrong, we add a "0" at the end of this data. If the result of C4.5 classifier is correct, we add "1" at the end of this data. If the result of Naïve Bayesian classifier is correct, we add "2" at the end of this data. If the results of two base classifiers are correct, we add "3" at the end of this data. After adding an accuracy tag to T_2, we copy T_2 to generate training set T_3. Then we extract the misclassified data of the two base classifiers in T_2 to generate training set T_4. Then, we use T_3 to train the misclassification results judgment module and T_4 to train the decision module.

5.2 Simulation Results

In the test stage, we designed two categories of experiments. For the first category, we randomly selected training set and set up 11 groups of experiments according to the proportion of training set to data set, and randomly selected 13,000 records outside the training set as the test set of each experiment. For each experiment, we recorded the classification accuracy and training time of C4.5, KNN, Random Forest algorithms and MACCA. For the second category, we also randomly selected training set and test set, and the proportion of training set T to the data set is 0.4. We set up 10 groups of experiments according to the proportion of test set to the data set outside the training set. The proportion includes 0.05, 0.1, 0.2, 0.3, 0.4, 0.5, 0.6, 0.7, 0.8, 0.9. The number of records used for testing ranges from $130623 * 0.6 * 0.05 \approx 3918$ to $130623 * 0.6 * 0.9 \approx 70535$. For each experiment, we recorded the classification time of the 4 algorithms.

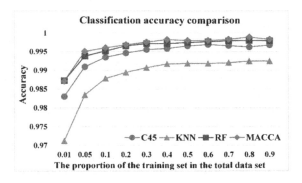

Fig. 4. Classification accuracy comparison.

The Results of Accuracy. As shown in Fig. 4, we tested and recorded the accuracy of C4.5, KNN, Random Forest and MACCA. As can be seen from Fig. 4, the accuracy of the 4 algorithms in each group of experiments is higher than 97%, among which Random Forest algorithm and MACCA's are higher than 98.5%. When the proportion of training set to data set is 0.9, the accuracy of the 4 algorithms is higher than 99%, among which Random Forest algorithm and MACCA's are close to 99.8% and C4.5's is 99.6%. When the training set is small, such as 0.01 (about 1,300 flows), the accuracy of C4.5 and KNN algorithms is lower than 98.5%, while the accuracy of MACCA is close to 98.7%. In conclusion, the accuracy of MACCA is similar to that of Random Forest algorithm, higher than the other two algorithms (C4.5, KNN), and higher than that of Random Forest algorithm in some cases.

The Results of Training Time. We recorded the training time of the four algorithms in 11 groups of experiments, and the results are shown in Fig. 5(a). As can be seen from Fig. 5(a), Random Forest algorithm takes the most time, while MACCA and C4.5 take less time. And with the increase of training set, the training time of each algorithm shows an increasing trend. Among them, Random Forest algorithm training time increases the fastest, followed by KNN algorithm, while MACCA and C4.5 algorithms have low growth rate and low training time. In addition, when the proportion of training set is 0.1–0.9, Random Forest algorithm training time is much higher than the other three algorithms. The maximum difference is 10 s. In conclusion, the training time of MACCA is similar to that of C4.5 algorithm, which is lower than that of KNN and Random Forest algorithms. So, MACCA has low training time.

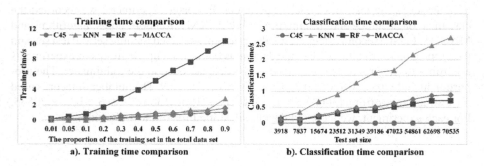

Fig. 5. Training and classification time comparison.

The Results of Classification Time. In the second category of experiments, we recorded the classification time of the four algorithms under different number of test sets, and the results are shown in Fig. 5(b). According to the results, C4.5 algorithm has the lowest classification time in each group of experiments. The classification time of the MACCA is similar to that of Random Forest algorithm, with an average difference of 0.09 s. KNN algorithm has the highest classification time.

In summary, according to the results, the average accuracy of Random Forest algorithm and MACCA are 99.6% and 99.66%. Random Forest algorithm has a high accuracy in different number of training sets, but when the training set is large, the training time is huge, which is not conducive to the realization of flow classification in SDN network. The MACCA is similar to Random Forest algorithm in classification accuracy, better than Random Forest algorithm in some cases, such as 0.05 (about 6,500 flows) and 0.4 (about 52,250 flows). The training time of MACCA is lower than Random Forest algorithm in each group of training time experiments, and close to Random Forest algorithm in classification time. Therefore, MACCA has the advantages of high accuracy and low time consumption.

5.3   Implement MACCA in SDN

There are 10 categories of flows. We use the first 4 bits of IP TOS field in the head field of the flow table to store the class label of the flow. And SDN switches match data flows according to head field in the flow table.

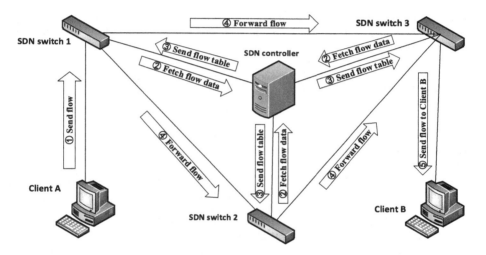

Fig. 6. The description of SDN routing process.

In SDN network, the general process of on-demand load balancing of links using MACCA is shown in Fig. 6. First, SDN controller will calculate the default path for each switch and send the flow table. When client A sends the data flow, client A sets a default IP TOS for the data flow. Then ① the data flow client A sent to client B will arrive at SDN switch 1. The data flow will be routed by default path. And ② the controller will collect the 14 features of this data flow. Then the controller will use MACCA to determine the flow application category and determines the QoS requirements of the flow according to the flow application category. And then, according to the different QoS requirements and current network environment, a routing algorithm can calculate the most appropriate path for this data flow. After that, SDN controller will convert the 14 features of data flow into a 4-bit class label, put 4-bit class label into IP TOS in flow table, and ③ send the flow table to SDN switches in this path. Then, ④ SDN switch 1 will modify IP TOS of the data flow according to the IP TOS in the flow table and SDN switches in this path can forward the data flow according to new flow table. If a link is congested, the controller will reassign the path for the data flow on this link according to priority, thus ensuring on-demand link load balancing. Finally, ⑤ the data will arrive at client B through the most suitable path.

6 Conclusion

Aiming at the problem of data transmission under CyberGIS model and flow classification in SDN network, we selected 14 features through feature selection algorithm and generated a new data set containing these 14 features. And by comparing the five machine learning classification algorithms using the new data set, we found that an ordinary machine learning algorithm cannot meet the requirements of high accuracy and low time consumption at the same time. Therefore, MACCA is proposed. Through a lot of experiments, it is proved that MACCA has higher classification accuracy and lower time consumption, and its average accuracy is up to 99.66%. The MACCA provides theoretical support for realizing link load balancing based on network flow classification in SDN network.

Acknowledgment. This work is supported by National Key R&D Program of China (2018YFB1700100) and the Fundamental Scientific Research Project of Dalian University of Technology (DUT18JC28).

References

1. Fajjari, I., Aitsaadi, N., Kouicem, D.E.: A novel SDN scheme for QoS path allocation in wide area networks. In: IEEE Global Communications Conference, Globecom, pp. 1–7. Institute of Electrical and Electronics Engineers Inc. (2018)
2. Oh, B.H., Vural, S., Wang, N., Tafazolli, R.: Priority-based flow control for dynamic and reliable flow management in SDN. IEEE Trans. Netw. Serv. Manag. **15**, 1720–1732 (2018)
3. Tang, F., Lu, L., Barolli, L., Tang, C.: An efficient sampling and classification approach for flow detection in SDN-based big data centers. In: 31st International Conference on Advanced Information Networking and Applications, pp. 1106–1115. Institute of Electrical and Electronics Engineers Inc. (2017)
4. Gogoi, P., Bhattacharyya, D.K., Borah, B., Kalita, J.K.: A survey of outlier detection methods in network anomaly identification. Comput. J. **54**, 570–588 (2018)
5. Evans, M.R., Oliver, D., Yang, K., Zhou, X., Ali, R.Y., Shekhar, S.: Enabling spatial big data via CyberGIS: challenges and opportunities. In: Wang, S., Goodchild, M. (eds.) CyberGIS for Geospatial Discovery and Innovation. GL, vol. 118, pp. 143–170. Springer, Dordrecht (2019). https://doi.org/10.1007/978-94-024-1531-5_8
6. Yousaf, F.Z., Bredel, M., Schaller, S., Schneider, F.: NFV and SDN - key technology enablers for 5G networks. IEEE J. Sel. Areas Commun. **35**, 2468–2478 (2018)
7. Koryachko, V., Perepelkin, D., Byshov, V.: Approach of dynamic load balancing in software defined networks with QoS. In: 6th Mediterranean Conference on Embedded Computing. Institute of Electrical and Electronics Engineers Inc. (2017)
8. Deng, G.C., Wang, K.: An application-aware QoS routing algorithm for SDN-based IoT networking. In: 2018 IEEE Symposium on Computers and Communication, pp. 186–191. Institute of Electrical and Electronics Engineers Inc. (2018)

9. Li, G., Dong, M., Ota, K., Wu, J., Li, J., Ye, T.: Deep packet inspection based application-aware traffic control for software defined networks. In: Global Communications Conference. Institute of Electrical and Electronics Engineers Inc. (2017)
10. Amaral, P., Dinis, J., Pinto, P., Bernardo, L., Mamede, H.S.: Machine learning in software defined networks: data collection and traffic classification. In: 24th International Conference on Network Protocols. IEEE Computer Society (2016)
11. Suárez-Varela, J., Barlet-Ros, P.: Flow monitoring in software-defined networks: finding the accuracy/performance tradeoffs. Comput. Netw. **135**, 289–301 (2018)
12. Lin, S.C., Wang, P., Luo, M.: A framework for QoS-aware traffic classification using semi-supervised machine learning in SDNs. In: IEEE International Conference on Services Computing, pp. 760–765. Institute of Electrical and Electronics Engineers Inc. (2016)
13. Paliwal, M., Shrimankar, D., Tembhurne, O.: Controllers in SDN: a review report. IEEE Access **6**, 36256–36270 (2018)
14. Moore, A., Zuev, D., Crogan, M.: Discriminators for use in flow-based classification. Queen Mary and Westfield College, Department of Computer Science (2005)
15. Lim, Y.S., Kim, H., Jeong, J., Kim, C.K., Kwon, T.T., Choi, Y.: Internet traffic classification demystified: on the sources of the discriminative power. In: The 6th International Conference on Emerging Networking Experiments and Technologies. Association for Computing Machinery (2010)
16. Chang, Y., Wei, L., Yang, Z.: Network intrusion detection based on random forest and support vector machine. In: IEEE International Conference on Computational Science & Engineering, vol. 1, pp. 635–638. Institute of Electrical and Electronics Engineers Inc. (2017)
17. Gómez, S.E., Martínez, B.C., Sánchez-Esguevillas, A.J., Hernández-Callejo, L.: Ensemble network traffic classification: algorithm comparison and novel ensemble scheme proposal. Comput. Netw. **127**, 68–80 (2017)
18. Shafiq, M., Yu, X., Laghari, A.A., Lu, Y., Abdessamia, F.: Network traffic classification techniques and comparative analysis using machine learning algorithms. In: IEEE International Conference on Computer & Communications, pp. 2451–2455. Institute of Electrical and Electronics Engineers Inc. (2017)

DataLearner: A Data Mining and Knowledge Discovery Tool for Android Smartphones and Tablets

Darren Yates[1(✉)], Md Zahidul Islam[1], and Junbin Gao[2]

[1] Charles Sturt University, Panorama Avenue, Bathurst, NSW 2795, Australia
{dyates, zislam}@csu.edu.au
[2] University of Sydney Business School, The University of Sydney,
Sydney, NSW 2006, Australia
junbin.gao@sydney.edu.au

Abstract. Smartphones have become the ultimate 'personal' computer, yet despite this, general-purpose data mining and knowledge discovery tools for mobile devices are surprisingly rare. DataLearner is a new data mining application designed specifically for Android devices that imports the Weka data mining engine and augments it with algorithms developed by Charles Sturt University. Moreover, DataLearner can be expanded with additional algorithms. Combined, DataLearner delivers 40 classification, clustering and association rule mining algorithms for model training and evaluation without need for cloud computing resources or network connectivity. It provides the same classification accuracy as PCs and laptops, while doing so with acceptable processing speed and consuming negligible battery life. With its ability to provide easy-to-use data mining on a phone-size screen, DataLearner is a new portable, self-contained data mining tool for remote, personalised and educational applications alike. DataLearner features four elements – this paper, the app available on Google Play, the GPL3-licensed source code on GitHub and a short video on YouTube.

Keywords: Knowledge discovery · Data mining · Smartphone · Tablet

1 Introduction

The growing demand for knowledge discovery and data mining has resulted in numerous software tools being developed for PCs and laptops, including the likes of Weka [1] and RStudio [2]. These tools enable users to execute an array of classification, clustering and association rule mining on datasets of the user's choosing.

Meanwhile, since their introduction, smartphones have become the ultimate version of the 'personal' computer, providing multi-core processing power, memory and storage inside a compact battery-powered device. In addition, today's smartphones and tablets are equipped with an array of sensors: temperature, humidity and barometric pressure sensors for environment, accelerometers and gyroscopes for movement, as well as microphone and speaker for audio. Yet, the one device class where general-purpose knowledge discovery and data mining tools remain rare is mobile devices.

© Springer Nature Switzerland AG 2019
J. Li et al. (Eds.): ADMA 2019, LNAI 11888, pp. 828–838, 2019.
https://doi.org/10.1007/978-3-030-35231-8_61

DataLearner is a new open-source data mining and knowledge discovery tool designed for smartphones and tablets running the Android operating system, beginning with Android 4.4 (codenamed 'KitKat'). It includes 40 classification, clustering and association rule mining algorithms and features separate automatically-assigned user interfaces for smartphone and tablet use. DataLearner is fully self-contained – no cloud computing is required to train or 'build' models and no external storage is needed. This presents numerous advantages. First, as no cloud computing or networking connectivity is required, DataLearner enables a smartphone to become a portable data mining tool in remote-location applications where mains power or network connectivity may not be available. Second, by being fully self-contained, the app does not require any data be sent to or received from a server in order to build a model, thus significantly improving data security and privacy. Third, by being able to locally build a model from local data, there is greater scope for personalised feedback, particularly in applications such as personal e-health. Finally, it also provides a practical and compact learning alternative for students studying data science, allowing them to augment their PCs and laptops and build models directly on their Android devices.

1.1   Our Contributions

This paper details the process of developing a mobile application capable of locally-executed data mining and thus, includes a number of contributions:

- To our knowledge, DataLearner is the only application of its type on Google Play, filling a void within the mobile software market.
- DataLearner features a user interface designed to enable easy model-building and evaluation, even on an 800×480-pixel phone screen (see Sect. 3.1).
- DataLearner can be expanded through the inclusion of additional algorithms (Sect. 3.3).
- DataLearner overcomes issues restricting the initial use of the Weka open-source data mining core within the Android platform (Sect. 3.4).
- The DataLearner platform consists of four elements – this research paper, the GPL3-licenced source code available on GitHub[1], a short video tutorial on YouTube[2] and the DataLearner application available on Google Play[3].

Our vision for DataLearner is to enable data mining and knowledge discovery in mobile applications ranging from on-site processing to education. Thus, DataLearner aims to support the end user in need of a compact and easy-to-use data mining tool, but who may have swapped a PC or laptop for an Android smartphone or tablet.

The remainder of this paper continues with Sect. 2 backgrounding previous research efforts in mobile data mining. Section 3 details the techniques and methods behind DataLearner, with Sect. 4 outlining basic usage. Section 5 covers the performance of DataLearner in terms of accuracy and speed on smartphone hardware compared with a

---

[1] https://github.com/darrenyatesau/DataLearner.

[2] https://youtu.be/H-7pETJZf-g.

[3] https://play.google.com/store/apps/details?id=au.com.darrenyates.datalearner.

desktop PC using a range of datasets and algorithms. Section 6 looks at future improvements and research efforts, while Sect. 7 concludes this paper.

2 Related Work

Since their arrival in 2007, smartphones have progressed from mobile phones with basic apps to personal computers with built-in sensors, 3D graphics and multiple wireless communications. Early attempts to incorporate local data mining onto mobile devices included the 'Mobileminer' application [3] that provided a 'general purpose service' for mining frequent patterns, plus the 'acquisitional context engine' (ACE), which was used in identifying user activity on mobile devices through association rule mining [4]. However, with Mobileminer designed for the Samsung Tizen operating system and ACE for Windows Mobile 7.5, neither application is operable on the Android platform. Today, Google's TensorFlow Lite [5] offers reduced-scale neural network processing on mobile devices, but research into more general-purpose data mining and knowledge discovery on Android devices remains limited.

Weka is a graphical user interface (GUI)-based data mining application developed by the University of Waikato to support Windows, Linux and macOS operating systems [1, 6]. It enables the user to build models from training datasets via a range of classification, clustering and association rule algorithms. It is a popular choice in learning institutions, allowing inexperienced users to achieve useful results. However, despite sharing a code base with Linux, Android is not listed as a supported operating system for Weka. Nevertheless, being open-source, Weka features access to its core engine through a Java archive (.jar) file. Attempts to bring Weka to Android have included health-focused mHealthDroid [7] and Weka-for-Android [8], but both now appear deprecated, with neither receiving source code updates since at least 2014.

Moreover, as of June 2019, no applications were found on the Google Play store offering easy-to-use data mining on Android devices. With smartphones increasingly employed in data-gathering from mental health [9] to road maintenance [10], there is real potential for these devices to become self-contained mobile data mining tools not reliant on cloud computing or network connectivity. Thus, a notable gap exists not just in terms of research, but also in the app development of mobile data mining.

Previous research we have conducted has found that the Weka core engine is operable within the Android platform [11]. That research revealed through early testing that Android smartphones present no issues in terms of classification accuracy, delivering the same accuracy performance as personal computers (PCs). Moreover, additional testing found the effect of locally executing data mining algorithms on smartphone battery life is generally negligible. Thus, a general-purpose locally-executed data mining application should be capable of running on Android devices.

3 Our Design Goals and Implementation

Our concept was to develop a general-purpose Android application allowing any user, without requiring programming experience, to load a Weka-compatible dataset, select a suitable algorithm, build a model and test the accuracy of that model using 10-fold cross-validation on any available Android-compatible device. A further goal was to enable the application to expand through the addition of new algorithms as required. This section details these technical decisions in creating the DataLearner application.

3.1 User Interface Design

Two of the design goals for the user interface were ease-of-use by novice data-miners and ease-of-access to all features on a small screen. These were achieved by breaking down the application's functions into key areas designated 'load', 'select' and 'run', shown in Fig. 1 – load a training dataset, select an algorithm, run the algorithm. Each key area is a self-contained Android window or 'fragment', accessible either by swipe-left and right movements, or pressing the appropriate top menu tab option. Human-computer interaction (HCI) research has shown the addition of horizontal swiping has a positive effect on a user's intentions to use mobile content [12].

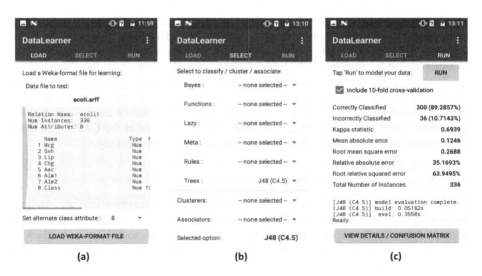

Fig. 1. DataLearner's three user interface screens - (a) Load, (b) Select and (c) Run.

3.2 Algorithm Selection

As the Weka core provides a large number of built-in algorithms, it was decided to implement as many of these as practical within DataLearner. In the first release of the app, this amounts to 37 Weka-based classification, clustering and association rule mining algorithms [13], with the classifiers divided into six subgroups as follows:

- **Bayes** – BayesNet, NaiveBayes
- **Functions** – Logistic, SimpleLogistic
- **Lazy** – IBk (K Nearest Neighbours), KStar
- **Meta** – AdaBoostM1, Bagging, LogitBoost, MultiBoostAB, Random Committee, RotationForest
- **Rules** – Conjunctive Rule, Decision Table, DTNB, JRip, OneR, PART, Ridor, ZeroR
- **Trees** – ADTree, BFTree, DecisionStump, J48 (C4.5), LADTree, Random Forest, RandomTree, REPTree, SimpleCART.

The clusterers include DBSCAN, Expectation Maximisation (EM), FarthestFirst, FilteredClusterer and SimpleKMeans, while the Association Rule algorithms feature Apriori, FilteredAssociator and FPGrowth.

3.3 Adding External Algorithms

DataLearner also allows external algorithms to be compiled into the app. This process has enabled the addition of three further classifiers developed by researchers at Charles Sturt University, namely SysFor [14], ForestPA [15] and SPAARC [16]. This is achieved by replicating the Weka source folder structure within the DataLearner Java application folder. For example, the Weka path for storing decision tree algorithms is/weka/classifiers/trees. By adding a 'weka.classifiers.trees' package to the source code, new decision tree algorithms can be added. Any algorithm conforming to Weka version 3.6.15 is accessible by the core. This technique was used to successfully incorporate the SysFor, ForestPA and SPAARC classification algorithms.

These three algorithms include features well suited to mobile devices – SysFor is an ensemble classifier able to achieve good results from low-dimension datasets, ForestPA aims to improve on Random Forest's accuracy using a sequential attribute-penalising technique, while SPAARC implements time-saving strategies to the CART tree algorithm whilst still maintaining the same overall classification accuracy.

3.4 Solving Integration Issues

To achieve a self-contained application, the Weka core is imported into the Android Studio development environment. However, this revealed some issues during development. First, the latest version 3.8 release of Weka appears to be incompatible with Android, caused by a change first implemented in the previous version that adds a user interface based on Java's Swing/Abstract Window Toolkit (AWT), which is not fully supported by Android. Further investigation revealed that reverting to version 3.6, which implements a standard Java interface, enabled successful operation. Thus, the initial release of DataLearner features the latest 3.6.15 release of the Weka core.

In addition, a separate issue was identified involving J48, Weka's version of the C4.5 decision tree algorithm. This issue resulted in a failure to successfully build and evaluate models from some datasets exceeding 5,000 records. Further troubleshooting identified the issue involved the Android 'stack', a Java memory block for holding active variable data. By dynamically lifting the stack size to 64 KB, the J48 algorithm successfully completed the model build/evaluation process with the same datasets that originally failed. No further J48 issues have since been detected.

DataLearner requires a minimum of Android 4.4, enabling the app to support 96.2% of all devices on Google Play during the week ending May 7, 2019 [17].

4 Basic Usage

The design considerations detailed in Sect. 3 are implemented in this first release of DataLearner. This section will now briefly outline their usage.

4.1 Loading a Dataset

Upon launching the app, the 'Load' screen shown in Fig. 1a greets the user. Pressing the 'Load Weka-Format File' button at the bottom of the screen opens up Android's storage access framework (SAF). This controls file access to internal storage (embedded flash and microSD) for loading suitable files. The user taps the dataset file of interest and it loads into the app. Once the file is loaded, details of the training dataset appear in the Load screen's fully-scrollable summary panel, also shown in Fig. 1a.

Below the summary panel is an option for selecting an alternate class attribute. The class attribute is initially assumed to be the last one listed and the 'Set alternate class attribute' selector is set accordingly. However, this can be set to any attribute index. It is for classification model building only, but may aid in further knowledge discovery.

While DataLearner does not yet include dataset creation features, the ARFF file format is a simple modified CSV (comma-separated variable) text file. This format can be created with any text editor. Details of the ARFF format are available in [18].

4.2 Selecting an Algorithm

With a training dataset loaded, the user either swipes left or taps the 'Select' tab to bring up the algorithm selection fragment shown in Fig. 1b. This menu is divided into two groups – classification algorithms grouped into six subcategories, with clustering and association rule algorithms beneath. Only one algorithm can be selected at any one time by tapping a subgroup and selecting an algorithm from the drop-down list.

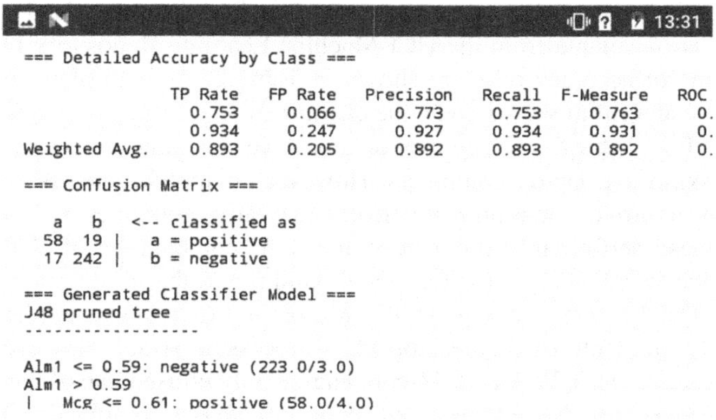

Fig. 2. The 'View Details & Confusion Matrix' button launches a full-screen scrollable view of accuracy by class, confusion matrix and classifier output of the new model.

4.3   Running a Classification Algorithm

Once the dataset and algorithm are selected, the user again swipes left or taps the 'Run' tab. The Run button begins the model training process and toggles into a 'Stop' button. Upon completion, summary results are displayed in the results panel. In addition, run times for build and ten-fold cross-validation processes are shown in the scrollable status panel at the bottom of the results screen (Fig. 1c). If a clustering or association rule algorithm is selected, a customised Run tab window shows the results. Again, the screen is fully-scrollable to enable access to all details.

After completion of the classification build and cross-validation process, the 'View Details and Confusion Matrix' button is enabled. Pressing this button opens a detailed window revealing the accuracy by class, confusion matrix of the model built and classifier output (as appropriate), as shown in Fig. 2. The window is fully-scrollable and can be viewed in portrait (vertical) or landscape (horizontal) mode. Pressing the device's back arrow will return the user to the main DataLearner application screens.

Table 1. Publicly-available training datasets used in testing

Dataset	Instances	Attributes	Attribute type	Missing values
Car eval	1728	6	Categorical	No
Ecoli	336	8	Numeric	No
Mushroom	8124	22	Categorical	Yes
Soybean	683	36	Categorical	Yes
Thyroid	7200	21	Mixed	Yes

5   Accuracy, Speed and Energy Consumption

Smartphones do not feature the same processor architecture as more traditional PCs. However, this does not imply that mobile devices cannot execute data mining algorithms with the same accuracy. Tests comparing the accuracy of classification algorithms and datasets on a quad-core Intel PC and a 2017 Motorola Moto G5 smartphone using DataLearner show this to be the case. The five datasets tested are shown in Table 1 and are available from the UCI Machine Learning Repository [19].

The results of accuracy tests are shown in Table 2. As both platforms ran essentially the same algorithm source code, the classification accuracy results were identical, as expected. By contrast, smartphones do not have the same processor performance levels as desktop and laptop computers. However, as mobile processor development continues to improve, smartphone performance also continues to gain pace. To understand these performance differences, the same combination of algorithms, datasets and devices were again tested for model build times, the results shown in Table 3.

Overall, DataLearner running on the Motorola Moto G5 smartphone delivered approximately one-tenth of the desktop PC's processing speed. However, it must be noted that DataLearner's Weka 3.6.15 core engine only utilised one of the phone's four main processing cores. Nevertheless, all algorithm/dataset combination model builds were completed within half-a-second. Moreover, adding support for multi-core processing into the algorithms should improve processing times considerably. Additionally, testing of DataLearner's energy consumption was conducted, with the J48 (C4.5) algorithm temporarily set to continuously build models from the Thyroid dataset over a 10% range of battery capacity on the Moto G5 phone. This combination completed 7,052 builds within that 10% range. This equates to a single build of this combination using less than 0.000015% of the device's battery capacity.

Table 2. Classification accuracy results comparing a quad-core Intel Core i5-2300 PC using Weka 3.6.15 with a Motorola Moto G5 phone running DataLearner (scores as percentages).

Dataset	3.1 GHz Intel Core i5-2300 PC (running Weka 3.6.15)			Motorola Moto G5 smartphone (running DataLearner)		
	J48 (C4.5)	NaiveBayes	REPTree	J48 (C4.5)	NaiveBayes	REPTree
Car eval	92.3611	85.5324	87.6736	92.3611	85.5324	87.6736
Ecoli	89.2857	85.4167	90.1786	89.2857	85.4167	90.1786
Mushroom	100	95.8272	99.9631	100	95.8272	99.9631
Soybean	91.5081	92.9722	84.7731	91.5081	92.9722	84.7731
Thyroid	99.5758	95.281	99.5758	99.5758	95.281	99.5758

Table 3. Classification model build times comparing a quad-core Intel Core i5-2300 PC using Weka 3.6.15 with a Motorola Moto G5 smartphone running DataLearner (scores in seconds).

Dataset	3.1 GHz Intel Core i5-2300 PC (running Weka 3.6.15)			Motorola Moto G5 smartphone (running DataLearner)		
	J48 (C4.5)	NaiveBayes	REPTree	J48 (C4.5)	NaiveBayes	REPTree
Car eval	<0.001	<0.001	<0.001	0.0479	0.0054	0.0349
Ecoli	<0.001	<0.001	<0.001	0.0115	0.0074	0.0169
Mushroom	0.01	<0.001	0.03	0.2077	0.0554	0.3812
Soybean	0.01	<0.001	0.01	0.1187	0.0079	0.1072
Thyroid	0.03	0.01	0.02	0.2770	0.0814	0.2476

6 Discussion and Further Research

DataLearner's ability to match PC levels of accuracy on smartphone hardware shows that mobile devices present no impediment to data mining model training. Moreover, DataLearner is a useful additional tool for where a PC is inconvenient or unavailable. For training datasets with dimensions similar to those in Sect. 5, the reduced levels of processing speed in most smartphones should not provide a hindrance. Furthermore, having a knowledge discovery tool in a smartphone should provide ample compensation. Add in continuing gains in smartphone processing power and this should allow for larger datasets to be processed into the future. Nevertheless, the single-threaded algorithms in DataLearner are a limitation providing opportunities for further research. More recent Weka versions include multi-core support in some algorithms (including

RandomForest and Bagging). However, as previously noted, Weka versions beyond 3.7 feature a Java Swing/AWT user interface not fully supported by Android. Thus, areas for further improvement of DataLearner include the development of multi-threaded algorithms to take advantage of multi-core processors inside modern smartphones, as well as more-efficient algorithms to achieve faster processing speeds within existing mobile devices. Another feature being considered is a dataset editor to allow users to change individual attribute values within a training dataset.

7   Conclusion

DataLearner turns any smartphone or tablet with Android 4.4 or later into a portable, self-contained, data mining and knowledge discovery tool. It incorporates the open-source Weka data mining engine with minimal modifications to work on Android and provides 40 classification, clustering and association rule mining algorithms.

This paper has discussed the limited research into and examples of general-purpose data mining apps available for mobile devices, as well as the current lack of data mining software available on Google Play. It has detailed the techniques used to incorporate the Weka run-time engine into the Android development platform. It has outlined the implementation and usage of the DataLearner application. Further, performance testing has shown that a smartphone running DataLearner delivers identical levels of accuracy as traditional PCs and despite only using single-threaded code, processing speed is satisfactory and continues to improve. Initial energy consumption testing indicates building a single data mining model on a smartphone using Data-Learner has negligible effect on device battery life. Nevertheless, DataLearner has areas for further improvement, including multi-core support for algorithms and a dataset editor.

7.1   Availability on Google Play, GitHub and YouTube

To our knowledge, DataLearner is the only app of its type currently available on the Google Play store. As outlined in Sect. 1.1, the DataLearner platform consists of four elements – this paper, the app available on Google Play, the GPL3-licensed source code on GitHub, plus a short video on YouTube. If smartphones are the ultimate 'personal' computer, they provide the ultimate platform to explore data mining in a range of applications, including education and personalised e-health. Moreover, having the ability to perform data mining in a pocketable device without the need for network connectivity or mains power should open up an array of opportunities.

Acknowledgments. This research is supported by an Australian Government Research Training Program (RTP) scholarship.

References

1. University of Waikato: Weka 3: Data mining software in Java. http://www.cs.waikato.ac.nz/ml/weka/. Accessed 18 May 2019
2. RStudio: open-source and enterprise-ready professional software for R (n.d.). https://www.rstudio.com/. Accessed 28 May 2019
3. Srinivasan, V., Moghaddam, S., Mukherji, A., Rachuri, K.K., Xu, C., Tapia, E.M.: Mobileminer: mining your frequent patterns on your phone. In: Proceedings of the 2014 ACM International Joint Conference on Pervasive and Ubiquitous Computing. ACM (2014)
4. Nath, S.: ACE: exploiting correlation for energy-efficient and continuous context sensing. In: Proceedings of the 10th International Conference on Mobile Systems, Applications, and Services. ACM (2012)
5. TensorFlow for mobile & IoT – overview (n.d.). https://www.tensorflow.org/mobile/. Accessed 8 June 2019
6. Holmes, G., Donkin, A., Witten, I.H.: WEKA: a machine learning workbench (1994)
7. Banos, O., et al.: mHealthDroid: a novel framework for agile development of mobile health applications. In: Pecchia, L., Chen, L.L., Nugent, C., Bravo, J. (eds.) IWAAL 2014. LNCS, vol. 8868, pp. 91–98. Springer, Cham (2014). https://doi.org/10.1007/978-3-319-13105-4_14
8. rjmarsan: Weka-for-Android. https://github.com/rjmarsan/Weka-for-Android. Accessed 19 May 2019
9. BinDhim, N.F., Shaman, A.M., Trevena, L., Basyouni, M.H., Pont, L.G., Alhawassi, T.M.: Depression screening via a smartphone app: cross-country user characteristics and feasibility. J. Am. Med. Inform. Assoc. **22**(1), 29–34 (2015)
10. Allouch, A., Koubâa, A., Abbes, T., Ammar, A.: RoadSense: smartphone application to estimate road conditions using accelerometer and gyroscope. IEEE Sens. J. **17**(13), 4231 (2017)
11. Yates, D., Islam, Md.Z., Gao, J.: Implementation and performance analysis of data-mining classification algorithms on smartphones. In: Islam, R., et al. (eds.) AusDM 2018. CCIS, vol. 996, pp. 331–343. Springer, Singapore (2019). https://doi.org/10.1007/978-981-13-6661-1_26
12. Dou, X., Sundar, S.S.: Power of the swipe: why mobile websites should add horizontal swiping to tapping, clicking, and scrolling interaction techniques. Int. J. Hum.-Comput. Interact. **32**(4), 352–362 (2016)
13. Hierarchy for all packages (n.d.). http://weka.sourceforge.net/doc.dev/overview-tree.html. Accessed 2 Aug 2019
14. Islam, Z., Giggins, H.: Knowledge discovery through SysFor: a systematically developed forest of multiple decision trees. In: Proceedings of the Ninth Australasian Data Mining Conference, vol. 121. Australian Computer Society, Inc. (2011)
15. Adnan, Md.N., Islam, M.Z.: Forest PA: constructing a decision forest by penalizing attributes used in previous trees. Expert Syst. Appl. **89**, 389–403 (2017)
16. Yates, D., Islam, Md.Z., Gao, J.: SPAARC: a fast decision tree algorithm. In: Islam, R., et al. (eds.) AusDM 2018. CCIS, vol. 996, pp. 43–55. Springer, Singapore (2019). https://doi.org/10.1007/978-981-13-6661-1_4
17. Distribution dashboard. https://developer.android.com/about/dashboards/. Accessed 17 May 2019

18. Weka Wiki: ARFF (stable version). https://urldefense.proofpoint.com/v2/url?u=https-3A__
    waikato.github.io_weka-2Dwiki_&d=DwIGaQ&c=vh6FgFnduejNhPPD0fl_yRaSfZy8CWb
    WnIf4XJhSqx8&r=phx_h-t0CpJpXloE7Nt7XzoVuWOl1rYzfCfuZFItYqZo5lxViGBLk_fC
    3J092Uza&m=0VlfrW45-j_8UJ3daRFYA-iBUnZYvVhEmiM286VE4zE&s=kCsIqb8kbltN
    lMCmBQ0EssRnfhPzWMovPiDMUX57eSA&e=. Accessed 8 June 2019
19. Dheeru, D., Taniskidou, E.K.: UCI machine learning repository. https://urldefense.
    proofpoint.com/v2/url?u=https-3A__archive.ics.uci.edu_ml_datasets.php&d=DwIGaQ&c=
    vh6FgFnduejNhPPD0fl_yRaSfZy8CWbWnIf4XJhSqx8&r=phx_h-t0CpJpXloE7Nt7XzoVu
    WOl1rYzfCfuZFItYqZo5lxViGBLk_fC3J092Uza&m=0VlfrW45-j_8UJ3daRFYA-iBUnZY
    vVhEmiM286VE4zE&s=nemH3VwacqNpBY_mDp5xRbBYN7qbI6KiImLXO4iyOIo&e=.
    Accessed 12 May 2019

Prediction of Customer Purchasing Power of Google Merchandise Store

ZhiYu Ye, AiMin Feng$^{(\boxtimes)}$, and Hang Gao

College of Computer Science and Technology,
Nanjing University of Aeronautics and Astronautics, Nanjing 211106, China
amfeng@nuaa.edu.cn

Abstract. For customer data mining of Google Merchandise Store, ensemble learning models such as LightGBM are popular. However, LightGBM mines the data information once, which has the rough granularity of data mining. So that LightGBM cannot dig into the more potential internal correlation information of Google Merchandise Store's dataset. In this paper, the deep LGB model is proposed to automatically refine the granularity of data mining through sliding window, on this basis, the model is endowed with certain representation learning ability through Deep, so as to dig out deeper association between data. Then, a semi-automatic feature engineering is proposed, which firstly processes some features of the data set automatically, and then generates the final data set with a little manual analysis. The experimental results show that, use customer data of the Google Merchandise Store, the prediction accuracy of the deep LGB model with semi-automatic feature engineering is 6.16% points higher than that of the original data set put into the single LGB model.

Keywords: Data mining · Machine learning · Deep model

1 Introduction

As a branch of the sales forecasting task, prediction of customer's purchasing power of e-commerce platform, which is mainly divided into sequential and non-sequential data's prediction. The prediction of time series data usually refers to the prediction of data changes at future time for the same target individual through its historical data, the major learning model to use are LSTM [1] and its variation [2–4]. Instead of sequential data, non-sequential prediction usually uses the historical data of one group of customers to predict the purchasing situation of another group of customers in the future.

The problem studied in this paper is regarded as non-sequential data prediction, which belongs to regression problem. And the corresponding application scenario means that the relationships between data are more hidden, the shallow network such as SVM and linear regression model [5, 6] are not apply to this problem. Therefore, in order to obtain more associated information between data, the learning model needed to be able to dig deep into user data.

Now the model widely used in regression tasks are LightGBM [8] and Catboost [9]. Both of them are Ensemble-Learning model, which is based on GBDT [7]. With the advantages of the high prediction accuracy, fast training speed and less memory

© Springer Nature Switzerland AG 2019
J. Li et al. (Eds.): ADMA 2019, LNAI 11888, pp. 839–852, 2019.
https://doi.org/10.1007/978-3-030-35231-8_62

consumption, LightGBM and Catboost have become the mainstream solution to the regression problem. However, because they only mine the data associated relationship only once, the mining granularity is rough, and it does not have the ability of deep mining, so they cannot automatically mine the deeper associated relationship between data. The key to solving customer's purchasing power prediction is how to enable models such as LightGBM to automatically obtain depth information. In this paper, we propose two novel techniques towards this goal, as elaborated below.

Sliding Window. We use the window to slide over the original eigenvector, so that the original dataset is split into many subsets. Through the Sliding window operation, our model could not only learn and find information at the whole dataset level, but also at the subset level. Combine these information we could get more accurate predictions.

Deep. This operation make our model become a deep model. Base on the Sliding window operation, we could deepen our model step by step. Through the Deep operation, we could endow our model with certain representation learning ability.

In addition, the semi-automatic characteristic engineering is also proposed to improve the prediction accuracy of the model.

Feature engineering often plays an important role in the field of data mining. A good feature engineering can reveal more relevant information in a dataset, so the machine learning model can get more accurate prediction. But the design of Feature-Engineering [16] relies heavily on manual analysis. When it comes to the manual approach, it can be very time consuming, especially when the amount of data is large. Therefore, if more latent information can be obtained through the combination of automatic feature engineering and manual analysis, it will greatly reduce the manual operation and improve the accuracy of prediction.

2   Relate Work

The proposal of Deep-Forest [13] in 2017 brings a new thinking direction to the deep model that neural networks are not the only models that can be modeled in depth. Drawing on the ideas of the Deep-Forest, this paper makes LightGBM and Catboost become deep model, in order to more accurate predict the customer purchasing power.

First, target of Deep-Forest is classification, the problem studied in this paper belongs to regression. Further, the model used in Deep-Forest is Random-Forest, belongs to bagging [18], which is a branch of Ensemble-Learning [17]. But LightGBM belongs to boosting [19], which is another branch of Ensemble-Learning. Therefore, if we just simply replace the Random-Forest model in the Deep-Forest with other machine learning models, it may not be as good as using the original model alone. Moreover, as the depth increases, the accuracy of the prediction may become lower and lower.

Second, deep form enables the algorithm to automatically extract depth information. The model proposed in this paper adopts Sliding window to automatically extract deep information from the dataset, Sliding window can make the algorithm have situational or structural awareness on the dataset and refine the granularity of information mining. The features in the original feature set are shallow information, which can be obtained without model learning. But the features generated by Sliding window are deep information, these features need to be acquired through model learning.

And, Representation-Learning [20] is recognized as an integral part of the deep neural network. For example, Deep-CNN [10] through multiple convolution operations to achieve Representation-Learning. In order to make the model proposed in this paper can also have this ability, on the basis of features which are generated by Sliding window, add Deep operation to model to make model more powerful. Also the algorithm proposed in this paper has significantly fewer parameters than the deep neural network, the parameters need to be adjusted are only the base model parameters and Sliding window, Deep.

3   Basic Models

3.1   LightGBM

LightGBM is an efficient implementation of GBDT. Although there are already some algorithms for implementing GBDT, such as XGB [11], pGBRT [12], scikit-learn [15] and so on. However, when the feature's dimension is high and the number of samples is large, their performance is not satisfactory. The main reason is that the above implementation algorithm needs to traverse all the data samples and estimate the information gain of all possible partition points, which is very time-consuming. Therefore, LightGBM proposes two solution: ① Gradient-based One-Side Sampling (GOSS); ② Exclusive Feature Building (EFB).

Algorithm 1. Gradient-based One-Side Sampling

input： I: training data, d: iterations, a: sampling ratio of large gradient data, b: sampling ratio of small gradient data, $loss$: loss function, L: weak learner

$$\text{models} \leftarrow \{\}, \text{fact} \leftarrow (1\text{-}a)\,/\,b$$

1. topN $\leftarrow a$ ✗ $len(I)$, randN $\leftarrow b$ ✗ $len(I)$

2. **for** $i = 1$ **to** d **do**

3.   preds $\leftarrow$ models.predict(I)

4.   g $\leftarrow loss(I,$ preds$)$, w $\leftarrow \{1,1,...\}$

5.   sorted $\leftarrow$ GetSortedIndices(abs(g))

6.   topSet $\leftarrow$ sorted[1 : topN]

7.   randSet $\leftarrow$ RandomPick(sorted[topN : $len(I)$], randN)

8.   usedSet $\leftarrow$ topSet + randSet

9.   w[randSet] ✗= fact ▷ Assign weight fact to the small gradient data

10.   newModel $\leftarrow$ L(I[usedSet], -g[usedSet], w[usedSet])

11.   models.append(newModel)

According to GOSS (Algorithm 1), a large number of samples with small gradients were excluded and only the remaining samples were used for information gain estimation. LightGBM [8] has proved that samples with a large gradient play a more important role in calculating the information gain. GOSS can get very accurate information gain calculation through more small-scale data.

Algorithm 2. Greedy Bundling

input: F: features, K: max conflict count

Construct graph G

1. searchOrder ← G.sortByDegree()
2. bundles ← {}, bundlesConflict ← {}
3. **for** i **in** searchOrder **do**
4.   needNew ← True
5.   **for** $j = 1$ **to** len(bundles) **do**
6.   cnt ← ConflictCnt(bundles[j], $F[i]$)
7.   **if** cnt + bundlesConflict[i] ≤ K **then**
8.   bundles[j].add($F[i]$), needNew ← **False**
9.   **break**
10. **if** needNew **then**
11.   Add $F[i]$ as a new bundle to bundles

output: bundles

Algorithm 3. Merge Exclusive Features

input: $numData$: number of data, F: One bundle of exclusive features

1. binRanges ← {0}, totalBin ← 0
2. **for** f **in** F **do**
3.   totalBin += f.numBin
4.   binRanges.append(totalBin)
5. newBin ← new Bin($numData$)
6. **for** $i = 1$ **to** numData **do**
7.   newBin[i] ← 0
8.   **for** $j = 1$ **to** $len(F)$ **do**
9.   **if** $F[j]$.bin[i] ≠ 0 **then**
10.   newBin[i] ← $F[j]$.bin[i] + binRanges[j]

output: newBin, binRanges

EFB (Algorithms 2 and 3) binds mutually exclusive features together to reduce the number of feature. The mutually exclusive features means that they are rarely non-zero at the same time. LightGBM also proves that finding the optimal binding is NP hard, but the greedy algorithm can get very good approximation probability.

3.2 Catboost

First, this model processes and utilizes the classification feature in the training stage rather than in the pre-processing stage. Second, it uses a new model to calculate the value of leaf nodes, thus reducing the overfitting phenomenon. The substitution formula for a classification feature of a sample is as follows:

$$\frac{\sum_{j=1}^{p-1} \left[x_{\sigma_j,k} = x_{\sigma_p,k}\right] Y_{\sigma_j} + a \cdot P}{\sum_{j=1}^{p-1} \left[x_{\sigma_j,k} = x_{\sigma_p,k}\right] + a}$$

4 The Proposed Approach

4.1 The Improved Model

The deep model proposed in this paper consists of two parts: Sliding window and Deep.

Part one, Sliding window extracts new features from the original features, its size is depended on user, step size fixed at 1. Hypothesis, full_cols represents full eigenvector, the size of Sliding window is window_size. The number of Sliding window is len (full_cols)-window_size+1.

Part two, Deep concatenates the predicted results of each window in the part one into a brand new eigenvector, then put these new eigenvector into the chosen basic model for training to produce a prediction. Concatenate the prediction and the input eigenvector as the input of next layer. We can iterate to deepen the model, which is why it's called depth.

4.1.1 Sliding Window

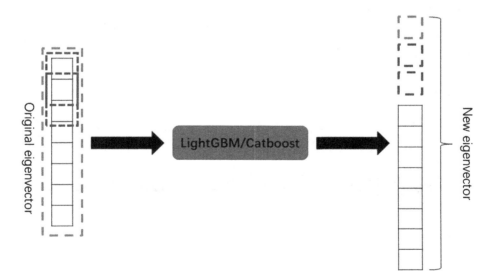

Fig. 1. Sliding window produce new features (Color figure online)

In order to be more granular in the information mining of the data set and make the algorithm have situational or structural awareness on the data set, this paper proposes that concatenate the prediction of Sliding window (correspond to blue and orange dotted boxes in Fig. 1) and original eigenvector as the new eigenvector (Fig. 1). Detail algorithm flow is shown in Algorithm 4. Meanwhile, K-fold cross validation was used to avoid overfitting.

Algorithm 4. Sliding window produce new eigenvector

---

input: Original train set: D, window size: w

1. full_cols = D.columns
2. window_size = len(full_cols)
3. LGB/CAT use data of window_size to train and produce prediction
4. window_size = w
5. **for** i **in range** (len(full_cols)-window_size+1)
6.   each_time_cols = full_cols[i: i + window_size]
7.   LGB/CAT use the data of each_time_cols to train and produce prediction

output: concate full_cols with the prediction of full features and sliding window

---

In the image processing task, the granularity of original feature set is fine, the number of feature is big. So we need to reduce the number of feature. But in this paper, the situation is contrast to the image processing task. What we need is not the dimensionality reduction operation but the dimensionality increase processing, which makes the original rough feature set granularity more exquisite.

We can adjust window_size according to the change of evaluation indexes.

4.1.2 Deep

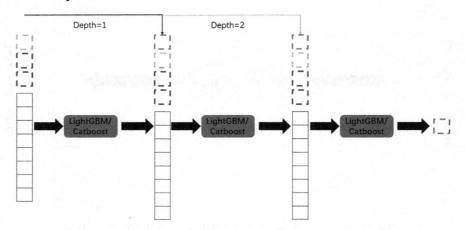

Fig. 2. LGB/CAT deep regression model (Color figure online)

In order to make the model proposed in this paper can have the ability called Representation-Learning [20], on the basis of features which are generated by Sliding window, add Deep operation to model to make model more powerful. Detail algorithm flow is shown in Algorithm 5.

Algorithm 5. LGB/CAT deep regression model

---

input: Output of Sliding window, *Depth*

1. **for** *i* **in range**(*Depth*)
2.   Train LGB/CAT
3.   **if** *i* $= 0$
4.   Concatenate prediction of model with input eigenvector
5.   **else**
6.   Prediction overwrite the corresponding position values in the input
7.   The updated input vector as the input of next layer

output: Final result

In this part, we first use output of Sliding window part as the input vector. Here is the brief explanation about Algorithm 5:

First, we put the input eigenvector into learning model for training by K fold validation. Second, if depth = 1, concatenate the prediction of model and input eigenvector, if depth > 1, overwrite the corresponding position values that are the prediction of previous layer in the input eigenvector. Green dotted box in Fig. 2 represent the prediction of each layer's learning mode. Last but not least, when we arrive at the specified depth, use the prediction of learning model as the output.

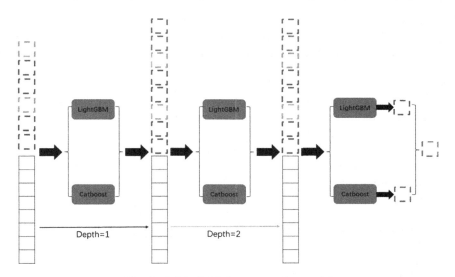

Fig. 3. LGB+CAT deep regression model

Figure 3 shows the model structure when Depth = 2. We can control Depth to adjust the depth of model.

Algorithm 6. LGB+CAT deep regression model

---

input: Output of Sliding window, *Depth*

1. **for** *i* **in range(***Depth***)**
2.   Train LGB and CAT
3.   **if** *i* = 0
4.   Concatenate prediction of two models with input eigenvector
5.   **else**
6.   Prediction overwrite the corresponding position values in the input
7.   The updated input vector as the input of next layer
8. Prediction of LGB and CAT multiply w_{lgb}, w_{cat} respectively, plus two result to produce final prediction

output: Final prediction

Except make LGB and CAT to the deep form, we also make LGB+CAT to deep form.

Before we deepen LGB+CAT, according to Algorithm 4 to produce the full feature prediction and sliding window prediction of LGB and CAT respectively. Hypothesis: full_cols = 100, window_size = 25, then d = full_cols+2+2(len(full_cols)-window_size+1) = 254 that dimension belongs to the output of Sliding window part. The detailed operation about the deep model can be seen in Algorithm 6.

4.2 Feature Engineering

In this part, we will analyze the impact of each feature in LightGBM for feature engineering. In the dataset, each row represents a session, each column represents a feature. Table 1 explains several important features in the original feature set (Table 2).

Table 1. Feature explaining

count_pageviews_per_network_domain	Number of visits per network domain
totals_newVisit	Total number of new visits
sum_hits_per_network_domain	Total number of clicks per network domain
Date_Month	Month when session occurred
count_hits_per_region	Number of visits per geographical area
sum_hits_per_region	Total number of clicks per geographical area
weekday	Weekday when session occurred
totals_bounces	Total number of bounces
count_hits_per_network_domain	Number of visits per geographical area
customDimensions_value	Custom index
device_browser	Browser used
geoNetwork_continent	Continent location

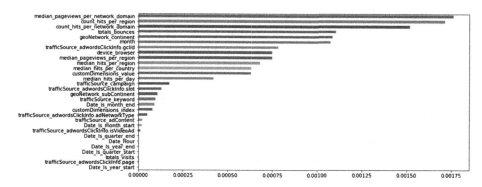

Fig. 4. Original feature

Table 2. Prediction accuracy of different basic models under the original feature

	LGBM	CAT
RMSE	1.0765	1.0326

First, Fig. 4 shows the result of putting original dataset into LightGBM, we can find that pageviews (number of page views per session) has the maximum weight. There are some operations that sum, count, mean to pageviews in original dataset. And pageviews belongs to numerical feature, there have more parameter to numerical calculation.

The feature engineering of this paper automatically processes numerical features, we use sum, count, mean, median, std for statistic analysis. Finally, additional statistical analysis features based on numerical features were obtained.

Except that, we can observe that the weight of totals_newVisits (total number of new visits per session) rank only second to the derivative feature of pageviews. But there have no derivative feature about totals_newVisits, we analyze the derivative feature of pageviews, and group totals_newVisits by network_domain, region. Apply count, sum, mean, median, std on these groups to obtain additional new features.

After doing these two operations, we put the new dataset into LightGBM for training, and we can get the feature weight sorting graph as shown in Fig. 5.

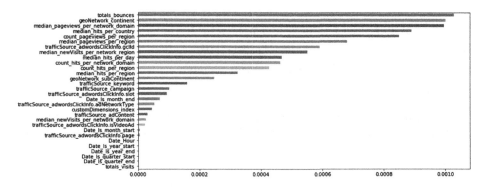

Fig. 5. Additional feature

Table 3. Prediction accuracy of different basic models after adding features

	LGBM	CAT
RMSE	1.0593	1.0331

If we just keep adding features unnecessarily, we will not only increase the running time, but also decrease the prediction accuracy. We can observe from Figs. 4 and 5 that the weight of the first half feature is much greater than that of the second half, and some features have almost zero weight (Table 3).

These features which don't help the learning model are redundant, in this paper, we delete Date_Hour (the hour when session occurred), Date_Is_year_start (whether session occurred at the beginning of year), Date_Is_year_end (whether session occurred at the end of year), Date_Is_quarter_start (whether session occurred at the beginning of quarter), Date_Is_quarter_end (whether session occurred at the end of quarter) and other low weight feature.

Finally, we put the new dataset into LightGBM for training, and we can get the feature weight sorting graph as shown in Fig. 6. We can find that after deleting some redundant feature, the weight distribution of the whole feature is more uniform. And the last few features in the diagram have also contributed to this (Table 4).

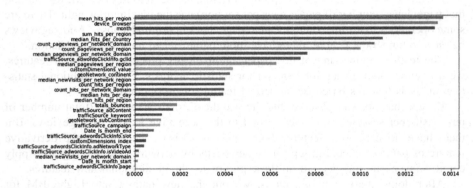

Fig. 6. Delete some feature

Table 4. Prediction accuracy of different basic models under final feature set

	LGBM	CAT
RMSE	1.0571	1.0319

Semi-automatic feature engineering is realized through the above two operations, in which the operation of numerical features belongs to automatic processing, while the deletion of features belongs to manual analysis.

5 Experiments

5.1 Dataset

The dataset used in this paper sources from the Google Analytics Customer Revenue Prediction competition held on the Kaggle website around September 2018. By analyzing dataset about customer of Google Merchandise Store (also known as GStore swag is sold) to predict the purchasing power of each customer in the future. It can ensure the authenticity and validity of data sources, and also prove that the method proposed in this paper has practical application value.

The original data set stated in this paper refers to the data set obtained after data cleaning and some feature engineering operations. Its essential information is shown in Table 5.

Table 5. Original dataset

	Sample size	Feature size
Train set	1708337	86
Test set	401589	85

There is one column represent the forecast target, so the feature size of train set is bigger than test set. The calculation formula of evaluation index RMSE is:

$$RMSE = \sqrt{\frac{1}{n}\sum_{i=1}^{n}\left(y_i - \widehat{y}_i\right)^2}$$

y hat is the natural log of the predicted revenue for a customer and y is the natural log of the actual summed revenue value plus one. A small RMSE represent an accurate prediction.

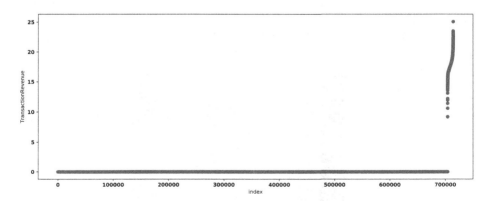

Fig. 7. Customer purchasing power distribution

The 80/20 rule has proven true for many businesses–only a small percentage of customers produce most of the revenue.

By visualizing the data, we can observe that the data of competition accords with the 80/20 rule. Figure 7 shows that customers who have purchased goods are concentrated in no. 700000 or above, but the others almost produce no profit.

5.2   Comparison

This part first shows RMSE scores of different feature engineering under different models, and then shows RMSE scores of improved models and basic models under the same feature engineering.

Table 6 shows the difference between different models and different feature engineering, LightGBM and CAT are used.

Table 6. Different feature engineering

	Original dataset	Additional feature	Delete feature
LGBM	1.0765	1.0593	1.0571
CAT	1.0326	1.0331	1.0319

By observing the experimental results in Table 6, it can be found that the final feature engineering obtained after adding and deleting features is improved in model prediction accuracy, especially the LightGBM model has a significant 2% points improvement. It shows that the semi - automatic feature engineering proposed in this paper is effective for LightGBM.

Table 7. Different models under the same feature engineering

	LGB +sliding window	Deep LGB	CAT +sliding window	Deep CAT	LGB+CAT +sliding window	Deep LGB +CAT
RMSE	1.0410	1.0149	1.0319	1.0334	1.0343	1.0293

The feature engineering used in Table 7 is the beset version in Table 6.

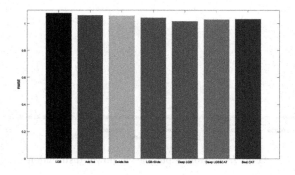

Fig. 8. Model comparison

Final deep model consists of Sliding window and Deep. LightGBM in Fig. 8 represent single LightGBM uses original dataset to train and predict. The adding feature and deleting feature correspond to two feature engineering in Sect. 3.2.

Through Tables 6 and 7, Fig. 8, first, we can observe that base on best feature engineering, the prediction accuracy of LGB+Sliding window is 1.6% points higher than single LightGBM. On this basis, the model is endowed with certain representation learning ability through the Deep step, and the prediction accuracy is improved by 2.6% points. Apply Sliding window and Deep on LightGBM, we can get the Deep LGB model which proposed in this paper.

Last but not least, the prediction accuracy of Deep LGB use dataset that processed by semi-automatic feature engineering is 6.16% points higher than the single LightGBM use original dataset. In conclusion, the Deep LGB and semi-automatic feature engineering proposed in this paper do capture more of the underlying information in the dataset.

6 Conclusion

The experimental results show that the Deep LGB model proposed in this paper has the capability of deep mining and can find deeper correlation between customer data of e-commerce platforms. It also shows that the semi-automatic feature engineering is effective. The Deep LGB model and semi - automatic feature engineering improve the prediction accuracy obviously. And the tree model is particularly explanatory, its if-then logical thinking accords with people's cognition.

Not only can neural networks be made into the deep form, other machine learning models can also be made into the deep form, and currently most of the deep models are neural networks. In addition, the deep model parameters of these non-neural networks are less, the model takes up less space, and the accuracy is almost the same as the deep neural network or even higher. Hopefully, more non-neural network deep models will emerge in the future.

References

1. Hochreiter, S., Schmidhuber, J.: Long short-term memory. Neural Comput. **9**(8), 1735–1780 (1997)
2. Graves, A., Fernández, S., Schmidhuber, J.: Multi-dimensional recurrent neural networks. In: de Sá, J.M., Alexandre, L.A., Duch, W., Mandic, D. (eds.) ICANN 2007. LNCS, vol. 4668, pp. 549–558. Springer, Heidelberg (2007). https://doi.org/10.1007/978-3-540-74690-4_56
3. Bao, W., Yue, J., Rao, Y.: A deep learning framework for financial time series using stacked autoencoders and long-short term memory. PLoS ONE **12**(7), e0180944 (2017)
4. Shao, X.L., Ma, D., Liu, Y., et al.: Short-term forecast of stock price of multi-branch LSTM based on K-means. In: International Conference on Systems and Informatics, pp. 1546–1551. IEEE (2018)
5. Cai, D., He, X., Wen, J.R., et al.: Support tensor machines for text categorization. Int. J. Acad. Res. Bus. Soc. Sci. **2**(12), 2222–6990 (2006)

6. Basak, D., Pal, S., Patranabis, D.C.: Support vector regression. Neural Inf. Process.-Lett. Rev. **11**(10), 203–224 (2007)
7. Friedman, J.H.: Greedy function approximation: a gradient boosting machine. Ann. Stat. **29**(5), 1189–1232 (2001)
8. Ke, G., Meng, Q., Finley, T., et al.: LightGBM: A highly efficient gradient boosting decision tree. In: Advances in Neural Information Processing Systems, pp. 3146–3154 (2017)
9. Dorogush, A.V., Ershov, V., Gulin, A.: CatBoost: gradient boosting with categorical features support (2018)
10. Simonyan, K., Zisserman, A.: Very deep convolutional networks for large-scale image recognition. arXiv:1409.1556 (2014)
11. Chen, T., Guestrin, C.: XGBoost: A scalable tree boosting system. In: Proceedings of the 22nd ACM SIGKDD International Conference on Knowledge Discovery and Data Mining, pp. 785–794. ACM (2016)
12. Tyree, S., Weinberger, K.Q., Agrawal, K., Paykin, J.: Parallel boosted regression trees for web search ranking. In: Proceedings of the 20th International Conference on World Wide Web, pp. 387–396. ACM (2011)
13. Zhou, Z.H., Feng, J.: Deep forest: towards an alternative to deep neural networks (2017)
14. Breiman, L.: Random forests. Mach. Learn. **45**(1), 5–32 (2001)
15. Pedregosa, F., et al.: Scikit-learn: machine learning in Python. J. Mach. Learn. Res. **12**(Oct), 2825–2830 (2011)
16. Scott, S., Matwin, S.: Feature engineering for text classification. In: International Conference on ICML (1999)
17. Oza, N.C.: Online ensemble learning. In: Proceedings of the Seventeenth National Conference on Artificial Intelligence and Twelfth Conference on Innovative Applications of Artificial Intelligence, Austin, Texas, USA, 30 July–3 August 2000. DBLP (2000)
18. Breiman, L.: Bagging predictors. Mach. Learn. **24**(2), 123–140 (1996)
19. Grabner, H., Bischof, H.: On-line boosting and vision. In: IEEE Computer Society Conference on Computer Vision & Pattern Recognition. IEEE (2006)
20. Bengio, Y., Courville, A., Vincent, P.: Representation learning: a review and new perspectives. IEEE Trans. Pattern Anal. Mach. Intell. **35**(8), 1798–1828 (2012)

Research on Short-Term Traffic Flow Forecasting Based on KNN and Discrete Event Simulation

Shaozheng Yu$^{(\boxtimes)}$, Yingqiu Li, Guojun Sheng, and Jiao Lv

Dalian Neusoft University of Information, Dalian 116023, China
{yushaozheng, liyingqiu, shengguojun}@neusoft.edu.cn,
2509662085@qq.com

Abstract. With the rapid development of urban traffic, it is very important to achieve accurate short-term traffic flow forecasting. Firstly, with the problem of short-term traffic flow forecasting, the key features that affect the traffic flow are extracted and the KNN non-parametric regression method is used for forecasting. Secondly, in order to solve the problem of dynamic traffic flow assignment, we build a simulation model and achieved good results. Finally, we use the case of short-term flow forecasting in airport to carry out a data experiment. The experimental results show that the traffic flow of traffic nodes and routes can be forecasted completely by using KNN algorithm combined with discrete event simulation technology, and the results are more credible.

Keywords: Short-term traffic flow forecasting · Nonparametric regression · K nearest neighbor · Discrete event simulation

1 Introduction

The theoretical research and implementation of short-term traffic flow forecasting algorithm is an important part of the implementation of Intelligent Transport System [1]. On the one hand, it provides data support and suggestions for traffic managers in traffic dispatching. Traffic managers can forecast the traffic status of the next period through the data collected in real time and short-term traffic flow. Traffic managers can issue traffic forecasts to travelers and vehicles to avoid pedestrians and vehicles traveling to the traffic congestion section. Usually, if a congestion occurs in a certain location, it may cause chain reaction. The forecasting of a single location is not sufficient to disclose the traffic status of adjacent locations. Short-term traffic flow forecasting takes these situations into full consideration, thus avoiding large-scale road congestion to the greatest extent. On the other hand, it also provides reliable travel reports for travelers. By forecasting the traffic status, traffic managers can make detailed travel suggestions. After getting the travel suggestions from the transportation department, travelers and vehicles can make the optimal travel route, so that the traffic flow on the road can be dispersed in different areas without being too concentrated.

Short-term traffic flow forecasting is a very complicated work, and it is one of the key links that affects the management effect of urban traffic, so this problem has always

© Springer Nature Switzerland AG 2019
J. Li et al. (Eds.): ADMA 2019, LNAI 11888, pp. 853–862, 2019.
https://doi.org/10.1007/978-3-030-35231-8_63

been a hot topic for scholars. The research on short-term traffic flow forecasting based on KNN algorithm has also made some achievements. Yakowitz [2] first applied K-nearest neighbor method to forecasting algorithm in 1988. Davis [3] first introduced K-nearest neighbor non-parametric regression method into the field of traffic flow forecasting in 1991. Based on Davis's research in 1995, Smith [4, 5] collected traffic flow data of a circular highway for five months, and tested K-nearest neighbor non-parametric regression algorithm using historical mean and adjacent time flow as state vectors. Smith compares the forecasting results with the neural network forecasting model. The results show that the average error of K-nearest neighbor non-parametric forecasting algorithm is small. At the same time, he also proved that improving the historical database can improve the forecasting accuracy. Other scholars, such as Clark [6], Turochy [7] and Kindzerske [8], have studied the algorithm from the angle of coefficient selection, K-value selection strategy and feedback of distance metrics.

However, there are still some problems in KNN nonparametric regression algorithm. Firstly, the value of K will affect the forecasting accuracy and efficiency of the algorithm. When using K-nearest neighbor algorithm for regression forecasting, the features of the sample is normalized first, and then the distance between the forecasting vector and the sample vector is calculated. In this way, all the features of the sample have the same weight. However, in a specific short-term traffic flow forecasting problem, different features obviously have different impact on traffic flow, so it should have different weights. In addition, KNN algorithm is difficult to realize dynamic traffic flow assignment in road network. To solve this problem, we introduce a traffic flow dynamic assignment simulation model after forecasting by KNN.

2 KNN Algorithm

2.1 Algorithmic Framework

KNN nonparametric regression is a data-driven heuristic forecasting mechanism. It can forecast future values by searching data which is similar to current observations in historical databases. Generally, it can be divided into three parts: historical data, search mechanism and forecasting function. Thus, the key factors of nonparametric regression are the construction of state vector and forecasting algorithm.

When using KNN non-parametric regression to forecast short-term traffic flow, we first need a large enough capacity and representative historical database. Ideal historical database contains various trends. Data collected in real time can find similar trends among them. However, redundant data will consume the running time of the algorithm. It is particularly important to identify the wrong data when screening the historical databases. At the same time, we should consider the adequacy of the data to reflect as many traffic states as possible. After forming the historical databases, we can forecast the traffic data by observing the real-time traffic data. According to the relevant elements of the non-parametric model set before, including the state vector and distance measurement. The criterion, the selection of K-value and the forecasting algorithm are used to find the nearest neighbors matching the current real-time observation data from the historical database. Finally, the traffic forecasting quantity at the next moment can be obtained by using the forecasting algorithm. The flow of the algorithm can be briefly described in Fig. 1.

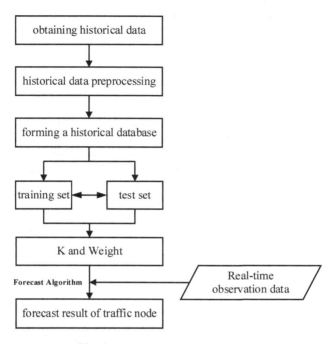

Fig. 1. KNN algorithmic framework

2.2   Definition of State Vector

When comparing the current observation data with the historical database, we need to define a comparison standard, which is described by the state vector. For example, road occupancy, driving speed, weather conditions and so on will affect the traffic flow at the next moment. Even the closest neighboring time and the traffic data of the adjacent section also involve taking several adjacent time intervals and adjacent numbers. The reasonableness of the state vector is directly related to the forecasting accuracy.

There is no uniform criterion for the selection of state vectors. Taking as many factors as possible into account in the state vectors cannot improve the accuracy of forecasting, but will lead to a longer running time of the algorithm. Based on the research results of other scholars and considering the computational efficiency of the algorithm, the state vectors are defined as follows:

$$X(t) = [v(t), v(t-1), v(t-2), v(t-3), w(t), w(t-1), w(t-2), w(t-3)] \quad (1)$$

$$X_h(t) = [v_h(t), \ldots, v_h(t-3), w_h(t), \ldots, v_h(t-3)] \quad (2)$$

Among them, t represents the time serial number. $X(t)$ represents the state vector of the current period, and has two indicators of traffic flow and weather type in the adjacent period to represent the data characteristics. $X_h(t)$ represents the state vector of the same period in history, and the nearest neighbor is generated in the same period in history. We considers four time intervals within the current time, but has two characteristics of traffic flow $v(t)$ and weather $w(t)$, so as to forecast the traffic flow in the next period.

2.3   Distance Metric Criterion

Distance measures the matching degree between real-time data and sample databases. In this paper, the common Euclidean distance is used to calculate the sum of squares of deviations between the components in the state vector and the corresponding points in the historical database. Since the influence of different variables on traffic flow is different, in order to reflect this difference, feature weights are introduced into distance calculation. Distance measurement criteria are as follows:

$$d = \sqrt{\sum_{i=0}^{3} x_{t-i} / (\sum \lambda_{t-i} + \sum \mu_{t-i})} \quad i = 0, 1, 2, 3 \tag{3}$$

$$x_{t-i} = \lambda_{t-i}(v(t-i) - v_h(t-i))^2 + \mu_{t-i}(w(t-i) - w_h(t-i))^2 \tag{4}$$

Among them, λ_{t-i} represents the weight of traffic flow characteristics in the $t-i$ period; μ_{t-i} represents the weight of weather characteristics in the $t-i$ period.

In order to solve the problem that different features have different effects on traffic flow, we use the correlation coefficient between features and traffic flow to represent the weight:

$$r(v(t+1), x(j)) = \frac{Cov(v(t+1), x(j))}{\sqrt{Var[v(t+1)]Var[x(j)]}} \quad j = 1, 2, \ldots, 6 \tag{5}$$

Among them, $v(t+1)$ represents the traffic flow in the forecast period, $x(j)$ represents the j th component of the state vector, Cov represent covariance, Var represent variance.

2.4   Selection of K Value

K value represents the number of neighbors selected from historical databases. The selection of K value is largely related to the specific situation of historical data. There is no established criterion to guide the selection of K. The existing literature also aims at the respective experimental data and finds a better K according to the results of different K values. But too large or too small K value will affect the forecasting. In this paper, the value of K is set between 2 and 20 in the experiment.

2.5 Forecasting Method

At present, the weighted and equal-weighted forecasting algorithms are widely used. The weighted forecasting algorithms take the following forms:

$$v(t+1) = \sum_{i=1}^{K} \theta_i v_{hi}(t+1), \quad \theta_i = \frac{d_i^{-1}}{\sum_{i=1}^{K} d_i^{-1}} \tag{6}$$

The weighted forecasting algorithm considers that if the distance between the observed real-time data and a series of data in the historical database is smaller, the similarity between them will be greater. Correspondingly, in the forecasting algorithm, the traffic flow corresponding to the nearest neighbor with a small distance should have a greater weight in the forecasted value at the next moment. Therefore, the weights are determined by reciprocal distance. The forecasting algorithm takes the following form:

$$v(t+1) = \frac{1}{K} \sum_{i=1}^{K} v_{hi}(t+1) \tag{7}$$

3 Simulation Model

3.1 Components and Events

After using KNN algorithm to forecast the traffic flow of traffic nodes, we establish a dynamic traffic flow allocation simulation model to further forecast the traffic flow of road sections. The main elements of the dynamic traffic flow assignment simulation model include vehicles, road networks, traffic control devices and traffic flow generation and absorption devices. The simulation components and functions used under FlexSim platform are shown in Table 1.

Table 1. Components of simulation model

Components	FlexSim objects	Functions
Generator	Source	Generating traffic flow
Absorber	Sink	Absorbing traffic flow
Path network	NetworkNode	Layout of traffic nodes and paths
Vehicle	TaskExecuter	Traffic flow
Traffic control	TrafficController	Control vehicle speed

The state variables of the simulation model are the number of real-time vehicles in each section of the road network, so there are four discrete events that will affect the state variables as follows:

1. occurrence events of vehicles
2. absorption events of vehicles
3. entry into road section events of vehicles
4. departure from road section events of vehicles

3.2 Simulation Logic

Source generates task executors (vehicles) to enter the traffic network from the starting point, calculates the shortest path and travels to the end according to this path, and calculates the shortest path using Dijkstra. When any task executor enters or leaves any section, it will update the resistance and recalculate the shortest path, and update the current number of vehicles in the section. When the next task executor enters the traffic network, it will select the path according to the latest calculated resistance. This ensures the real-time updating of road resistance and the dynamic distribution of traffic flow.

- Resistance function

$$t = t_0[1 + \alpha(q/c)^\wedge \beta] \tag{8}$$

Among them, t represents the time needed to actually pass the section, t_0 represents the free travel time of the section, q represents the traffic volume passing through the section at that time, c represents the actual capacity of the section, α and β represent the undetermined parameters of the model.

- Vehicle speed

Since in the actual traffic network, the vehicle speed will slow down with the increase of the number of vehicles on the road, so it is necessary to adjust the vehicle speed according to the real-time road conditions.

$$v = v_0 \frac{n}{N} \lambda \tag{9}$$

Among them, v represents the actual speed of the vehicle, v_0 represents the maximum speed of the vehicle, N represents the maximum capacity of the section, n represents the current number of vehicles in the section, λ represents the adjustment coefficient. To sum up, the logical flow chart of the simulation model is shown in Fig. 2.

3.3 Simulation Steps

The dynamic traffic flow distribution simulation model dynamically allocates the generated traffic flow to the traffic network and updates the road resistance in real time. Each unit of traffic is allocated according to the latest road resistance to find the shortest path. After the simulation operation, the traffic volume allocated by each section is counted.

- Step 1: Establish a simulation model, including the components, connections, parameters and code logic of the simulation model, to simulate the traveling process of traffic flow on the traffic network.
- Step 2: Input data, including predicted traffic node flow, zero-flow resistance, resistance function and vehicle travel speed.
- Step 3: Determine the running time of the simulation model and run the simulation model.
- Step 4: Output the statistical results, get the traffic flow allocated by each section, and generate statistical charts.

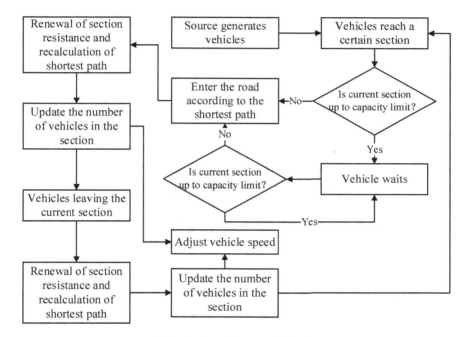

Fig. 2. Simulation model logic

4   Data Experiment

4.1   Forecast Using KNN

Using the data of monthly taxi flow data in an airport, we forecast the number of arriving taxis one day, and compare the forecast results with the actual data. The range of K value selected is from 2 to 20. Different K values have different forecasting effects. Table 2 shows the standard deviation of different K values. According to the error data obtained by cross validation, K value is selected as 3. Table 3 is the result of taxi forecast and Fig. 3 is the comparison between the forecast and actual arrival taxis.

Table 2. Forecasting errors for different K values

K Value	Standard variance of forecast error	K Value	Standard variance of forecast error
2	0.299125693	12	0.326400045
3	0.254261279	13	0.339028401
4	0.324869913	14	0.348673424
5	0.335016384	15	0.350573083
6	0.300311865	16	0.351913000
7	0.296894949	17	0.370527824
8	0.307568453	18	0.350573083
9	0.328284760	19	0.348376289
10	0.324538799	20	0.363547821
11	0.316200582		

Table 3. Forecast results of taxi flow

Time	Forecast	Actual	Error
19:30:00	119	100	0.19
20:00:00	124	110	0.127273
20:30:00	140	120	0.166667
21:00:00	100	130	0.230769
21:30:00	180	150	0.2
22:00:00	121	100	0.21
22:30:00	85	70	0.214286
23:00:00	66	80	0.175
23:30:00	98	80	0.225

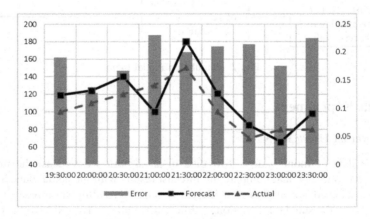

Fig. 3. Contrast chart of forecast results

4.2   Simulation Analysis

In the simulation model, zero-flow resistance and section capacity are input, and the traffic flow of each section is counted. Figure 4 shows the running state of the simulation model and Fig. 5 shows the utilization of six sections in the road network in half an hour after 20 o'clock. Through discrete event simulation, the usage of road sections in a certain period of time in the future can be forecasted.

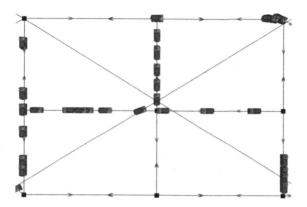

Fig. 4. Running state of simulation model

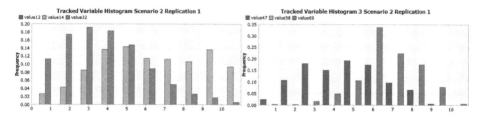

Fig. 5. Simulation statistics of traffic flow

5   Conclusion

KNN non-parametric regression is a non-parametric, portable and high forecasting accuracy algorithm and its error is relatively small. In theory, as long as there is a historical database that meets the requirements, any road condition can be forecasted. The advantage of non-parametric regression forecasting is the most obvious. In addition, the simulation model solves the problems of dynamic traffic flow assignment in road sections.

With the development of computer technology, how to improve the efficiency of the algorithm, accurately identify the optimal combination of state vectors when enlarging the historical database, and apply the construction method of forecasting interval to the historical data for many years remain to be further studied in the future.

Through continuous improvement, a complete and mature system can definitely meet the needs of short-term traffic flow forecasting.

References

1. Chuan, L.: Short-term traffic flow forecasting algorithm based on K-nearest Neighbor Nonparametric Regression (2015)
2. Yakowitz, S.: Nearest-neighbor methods for time series analysis. J. Time Ser. Anal. **8**(2), 10–26 (1987)
3. Davis, G., Nihan, N.: Nonparametric regression and short-term freeway traffic forecasting. J. Transp. Eng. **117**(2), 178–188 (1991)
4. Smith, B.L., Demetsky, M.J.: Traffic flow forecasting: comparison of modeling approaches. J. Transp. Eng. **123**(4), 261–266 (1997)
5. Smith, B.L., Williams, B.M.: Comparison of parametric and nonparametric models for traffic flow forecasting. Transp. Res. Part C **10**, 303–321 (2002)
6. Clark, S.: Traffic forecasting using multivariate nonparametric regression. J. Transp. Eng. **129**(2), 161–168 (2003)
7. Turochy, R.E.: Enhancing short-term traffic forecasting with traffic condition information. J. Transp. Eng. **132**(6), 469–474 (2006)
8. Kindzerske, M.D., Ni, D.H.: Composite nearest neighbor nonparametric regression to improve traffic forecasting. J. Transp. Res. Board **1993**, 30–35 (2007)

Application of Weighted K-Means Decision Cluster Classifier in the Recognition of Infectious Expressions of Primary School Students Reading

Dongqing Zhang$^{(\boxtimes)}$ and Zhenyu Liu[iD]

Dalian Neusoft University of Information,
Dalian 116023, Liaoning, People's Republic of China
zhangdongqing@neusoft.edu.cn

Abstract. In this paper, a new classification algorithm for infectious expressions of reading is proposed. This algorithm called weighted K-means decision cluster classifier (WKDCC) is based on the establishment of decision tree model, but four improvements are proposed: (1) using anchor partition instead of heuristic information such as information gain to search (2) feature weighting; (3) using k-means clustering center instead of centroid as anchor point; (4) asymmetric partition. WKDCC is used for recognize infectious expressions of students reading. The results show that WKDCC performed better in accuracy than decision tree, and its time complexity is lower than that of the classical decision tree algorithm. WKDCC is particularly suitable for large data with many samples such as audio data.

Keywords: Cluster classifier · Weighted K-means · Infectious expression · Asymmetric partition

1 Introduction

1.1 A Subsection Sample

The application of information technology in elementary education is more and more. The automatic discrimination of reading texts, poems of primary school students has been realized by machine learning. At present, most of the interfaces provided by voice platforms can achieve the recognition and scoring of reading accuracy, speech speed, intonation and other indicators, but the scoring for infectious expressions of reading has not been achieved. Many of the comprehensive indicators got high scores of reading audio by machine learning can not be very appealing listened by human experts, and there will be a clear "singing-reading" phenomenon.

This paper will study the indicators of the infectious expressions of reading, extract the Mel-Frequency Cepstral Coefficients [1] (MFCC) from the reading audio, and use one of the most explanatory method, decision tree, to model and recognize.

Decision tree is a common inductive learning method, which essentially learns from a layer of if/else problems and builds models, which can be used for classification and regression [2]. Although the decision tree algorithm has been one of the first machine

© Springer Nature Switzerland AG 2019
J. Li et al. (Eds.): ADMA 2019, LNAI 11888, pp. 863–870, 2019.
https://doi.org/10.1007/978-3-030-35231-8_64

learning approaches, it remains an actively researched domain [3–7], and has been widely used in knowledge discovery, pattern recognition and other fields. Its main advantages include: (1) understandability; (2) robustness against noise; (3) low computational cost; (4) irrelevant and redundant attributes; (5) unaffected by data scaling [2]. In addition, the model generated by decision tree has better generalization ability and can prevent over-fitting through pre-pruning strategy.

A good machine learning model should not only have strong generalization ability, but also be as concise as possible, because simple models are easier to understand. For decision trees, fewer nodes often mean simpler models. The process of constructing optimal decision tree has been proved an NP-complete problem. To avoid falling into local optimal solution, some researchers use evolutionary algorithm to derive decision tree. However, consider of the complexity of computing, most decision trees are deduced by greedy method, top-down and recursive partition, among which Quinlan's ID3 [8] and C4.5 [9] and Breiman et al.'s CART [10] are the most famous. In order to complete the construction of the tree faster, these algorithms use some kinds of impurity measure as heuristic information. When dividing nodes, searching the attribute and threshold of purity decreasing the most. For example, ID3 uses information gain [8], C4.5 uses information gain rate [9], and CART uses Gini coefficient [10]. Weighted K-means Decision Cluster Classifier proposed in this paper does not use evolutionary algorithm and heuristic information, so it has faster computation speed. At the same time, the resulting decision tree has similar or better generalization ability and interpretability to classical algorithms such as C4.5 and CART.

The traditional decision tree algorithm divides nodes into k-forks. K is the number of categories in the current set of node samples. When dividing, the centroid of each category is found as the anchor point (continuous features use mean, discrete features use mode). Each sample is divided into corresponding child nodes according to the anchor point nearest to it. The dividing line (or separating hyperplane) is the middle sag (or mid-vertical hyperplane) of the two anchor points. In the feature selection, the greedy algorithm is adopted essentially, and each sub-node is dealt with recursively. Each child node is processed recursively. There are two termination conditions for complete growth (without pre-pruning): (1) 100% purity or (2) all samples have no discrimination on the feature set.

2   Weighted K-Means Decision Cluster Classifier

In this paper, the proposed method based on weighted K-means decision cluster classifier is still the establishment of decision tree model, but four improvements are proposed: (1) using anchor partition instead of heuristic information such as information gain to search (2) feature weighting; (3) using k-means (for pure continuous attribute data set), k-modes (for pure discrete feature data set) or K-Prototype (for continuous discrete feature mixed data set) clustering center instead of centroid as anchor point; (4) asymmetric partition.

2.1   Why Use Anchor Partitioning Instead of Heuristic Information for Search

The core problem of decision tree generation is splitting features, which usually uses linear splits. In feature space, one or more hyperplanes are selected to divide the feature space into two or more regions. Samples in non-leaf nodes are divided according to their regions, thus forming the next layer of nodes. According to the direction and number of hyperplanes and the selection method, Tin classifies the division methods into three categories [11]: axis-parallel linear splits, oblique linear splits and piecewise linear splits. Among them, the most common and relatively least time complexity is the axis-parallel linear partition. Because the algorithm of generating the optimal decision tree is NP-complete, actually decision tree generation algorithms all adopt some heuristic algorithm. The time complexity of the algorithm is O (N * M * D), where N is the number of samples, M is the number of features, and D is the depth of the tree, equivalent to logM. For the speech data to be studied in this paper, the time complexity is still high. In this paper, another processing method is used to divide the samples according to the distance from the samples to the anchor, which is the centroid of each category of samples in the training set.

2.2   Why Weighting Feature

When calculating distance, all features will be treated equally under normal circumstances, that is, the contribution of strong correlation features, weak correlation features and uncorrelated features to distance is indistinguishable. But in fact, the degree of association between each feature and the classification results is different. Some features are strongly related to the classification results, while others are weakly related to or even not related to the classification results. Therefore, this paper uses relief_f algorithm to weigh all features, which are strongly related to classification gets high score and weakly related gets low score.

Formula 1 is used to calculate the distance after weighting features.

$$d_i = \sum_{j=1}^{n} w_i ||x_{ij} - \mu_i|| \tag{1}$$

Figure 1 illustrates the role of weighting. The line of the small circle is the unweighted centroid dividing line, and the line of the small rectangle is the weighted

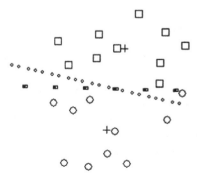

Fig. 1. The role of weighting

centroid dividing line (x-axis attribute 0.2, Y-axis attribute 0.8, that is, Y-axis attribute is more important).

2.3   Why Using Clustering Centers Instead of Centroids as Anchors

When a category of samples does not conform to the Gauss distribution, the centroid of the category does not represent the approximate direction of the category samples very well.

For example, the rectangular samples in Fig. 2 are divided into two clusters. According to the centroids, the demarcation line is the line with small circle (dividing the two kinds of samples into upper and lower parts, the basic purity is not improved), but if using clustering centers, the line with small rectangle in the graph separates at least five samples on the left side.

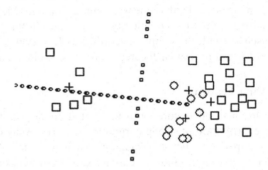

Fig. 2. Cluster center replaces centroid

2.4   Why Use Asymmetric Split

There are many category imbalances in real classification problems. Even for the Iris data set, which is a balanced sample (every category has 50 samples), the root node is splitted once, the category in sub-nodes imbalances will occur. For example, when using kmeans to cluster 150 iris samples into three categories, three sub-nodes (1:50 pure) (2:38, 3:14) (2:12, 3:36), sub-node 2 and sub-node 3 are obviously unbalanced, and the less categories sample is basically on the edge of the boundary at the last split.

3   Data Preprocessing

For the 800 audio data collected, five primary school teachers and broadcasters scored the highest emotional 5 points and the lowest 1 points respectively. Then the average score of each audio was taken by five people and rounded as the final score of the audio.

For each audio, MFCCs are extracted from the data of each frame, but only the MFCCs are used as features, the number of features is too small relative to the number of samples. Therefore, the minimum, maximum, average, median, 1/4 quantile, 3/4 quantile, standard deviation and other indicators are calculated. All of them are features.

4 Algorithm Description

```
Input : Training Set D, minparent: the Minimum Threshold
of Sample Number, mingini: the Minimum Threshold of Gini
exponential
        D={x1 y1,x2 y2…xn yn}, n is the number of samples
        A={a1,a2…ad}, d is the number of features
        L={l1 , l2…lk}, k is the number of categories
        Xi={xi1,xi2,….xid}
        Yi ∈L
Output : Decision tree T with NODE as root
Function TreeCenerate(D, minparent, mingini)
Generate the root node NODE
if the number of samples in D less than minparent OR the
Gini exponentail of samples in D less than mingini OR
sample set is inseparable (That is to say, there are con-
tradictory data in the sample set. All features are the
same but the categories are different. )   Then
    mark NODE as leaf , its category is the category with
the largest number of samples in D
    return
end if
Define k d-dimensional vectors: c1,c2…ck, saving centers
of k category
for i =1 to k do
   for j=1 to d do
      cij=center(ci,aj)
   end for
end for
Define K subsets: D1…Dk, all initialized to empty set
for i=1 to n do
   min=select_near(xi,C)
   Add xi to the collection Dmin
end for
for i=1 to k do
   for j=1 to d do
      cij=center(Di,aj)
   end for
end for
for i=1 to k do
  if ( Di not empty )
    Use the root node of the subtree returned by
TreeCenerate (Di) as the branch node of the current node
NODE
  end if
end for
return NODE
```

5   Performance Analysis of Algorithms

The proposed algorithm can be divided into three stages. Phase 1 calculate the centroid of each category. To complete the calculation, it needs to traverse d features of n samples. Therefore, the time complexity is O (d * n). Phase 2 select the nearest anchor for all samples. It needs to calculate the distance between each sample and each anchor. The determination of anchor needs 1 rounds using k-means algorithm. The time complexity is O (k * d * n * l). Phase 3 calculate the center of each sample subset. The time complexity is O (d * n), so the time complexity of the whole algorithm is O (k * d * n * l). Usually, l has a very small value (less than 10), and when the number of categories k is small, the time complexity of this algorithm is lower than that of the classical decision tree algorithm.

6   Analysis of Experimental Results

For a single decision tree, using WKDCC, C4.5 and CART algorithms, in WKDCC, the depth of decision tree greater than 5, the accuracy is stable, and in C4.5 and CART, the depth greater than 8, the accuracy can be stable. The accuracy and time spent by using 10 fold crossover are shown in Table 1.

Table 1. Comparison of accuracy and time length of three algorithms

Algorithm	Accuracy (%)	Depth of tree	Time length (hours)
WKDCC	78.1	5	2.3
C4.5	75.3	8	4.1
CART	76.1	8	3.8

Then, three different ways are used to construct decision trees and generate random forests. The relationship between accuracy and the number of decision trees is shown in Fig. 3.

Figure 4 shows the relationship between the time required to achieve the same accuracy. In our experiment environment, CPU is Intel Core i7-6500U, 2 Cores, each is 2.5 GHz, RAM is 16 GB.

From the above results, WKDCC algorithm can get better results than C4.5 and CART algorithm, and it takes less time to generate a single decision tree or a random forest. However, the overall accuracy of any algorithm is still not particularly high. Analyzing the data of classification errors in the three algorithms is mainly concentrated in the classification of grade 1 and grade 5. Because the original data scored 1 and 5 points are very few (especially 1 point data, only less than 10 items), their common characteristics are not so uniform and obvious, and the accuracy of scoring 3 and 4 points is almost 100%, also because the original data scored the most, the sample is the most abundant.

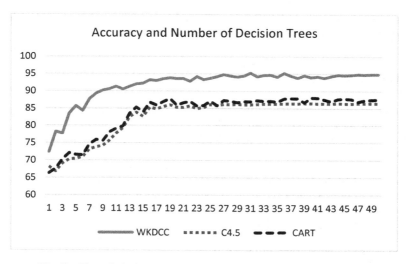

Fig. 3. The relation between accuracy and number of decision trees

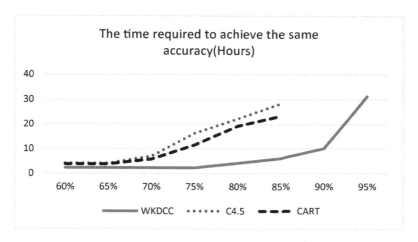

Fig. 4. The time required to achieve the same accuracy

7 Conclusions

In this paper, we have proposed a new classification method called weighted K-means decision cluster classifier (WKDCC) to recognize infectious expressions of primary school students reading. WKDCC is based on decision tree, but four improvements are proposed: (1) using anchor partition instead of heuristic information such as information gain to search (2) feature weighting; (3) using k-means clustering center instead of centroid as anchor point; (4) asymmetric partition.

The experiments show WKDCC performed better in accuracy than decision tree. And WKDCC is suitable for large data with many samples.

References

1. Müller, M.: Information Retrieval for Music and Motion, 65. Springer, Heidelberg (2007). https://doi.org/10.1007/978-3-540-74048-3
2. Müller, A.C., Guido, S.: Introduction to Machine Learning with Python. O'Reilly Media (2016)
3. Wang, Y., Song, C., Xia, S.T.: Improving decision trees by Tsallis Entropy Information Metric method. In: International Joint Conference on Neural Networks (2016)
4. Guan, X., Liang, J., Qian, Y., et al.: A multi-view OVA model based on decision tree for multi-classification tasks. Knowledge-Based Systems (2017). S0950705117304641
5. Gutierrez-Rodríguez, A.E., Martínez-Trinidad, J.F., García-Borroto, M., et al.: Mining patterns for clustering on numerical datasets using unsupervised decision trees[J]. Knowledge-Based Systems, 2015, 82:70–79
6. Tanha, J., Someren, M.V., Afsarmanesh, H.: Semi-supervised self-training for decision tree classifiers. Int. J. Mach. Learn. Cybern. 8(1), 355–370 (2017)
7. Katuwal, R., Suganthan, P.N.: Enhancing multi-class classification of random forest using random vector functional neural network and oblique decision surfaces (2018)
8. Quinlan, J.R.: Induction of decision trees. Mach. Learn. 1, 81–106 (1986)
9. Quinlan, J.R.: C4.5: programs for machine learning (1992)
10. Buntine, W.: Learning classification trees. Stat. Comput. 2(2), 63–73 (1992)
11. Ho, T.K.: The random subspace method for constructing decision forests. IEEE Trans. Pattern Anal. Mach. Intell. 20(8), 1–22 (1998)

An Anti-fraud Framework for Medical Insurance Based on Deep Learning

Guoming Zhang[1,2], Shucun Fu[3], Xiaolong Xu[3], Lianyong Qi[4], Xuyun Zhang[5], and Wanchun Dou[1(✉)]

[1] State Key Laboratory for Novel Software Technology, Nanjing University, Nanjing, China
kelvinzhang@smail.nju.edu.cn, douwc@nju.edu.cn
[2] Health Statistics and Information Center of Jiangsu Province, Nanjing, China
[3] School of Computer and Software, Nanjing University of Information Science and Technology, Nanjing, China
shucunfu@gmail.com, njuxlxu@gmail.com
[4] School of Information Science and Engineering, Qufu Normal University, Qufu, China
lianyongqi@gmail.com
[5] Department of Electrical Computer Engineering, The University of Auckland, Auckland, New Zealand
xuyun.zhang@auckland.ac.nz

Abstract. Given rising medical costs, medical expense control has become an important task in the healthcare domain. To solve the shortage of medical reimbursement mechanisms based on medical service items, single-disease payment models have been extensively studied. However, the approach of payment via a single-disease model is also flawed, and fraud may occur. Herein, we present an anti-fraud framework for medical insurance based on deep learning to automatically identify suspicious medical records, ensure the effective implementation of single-disease charges, and reduce the workload of medical insurance auditors. The framework first predicts the probabilities of diseases according to patients' chief complaints and then evaluates whether the disease codes written in medical records are reasonable via the predicted probabilities; finally, medical records with unreasonable disease codes are selected as abnormal cases for manual auditing. We conduct experiments on a real-world dataset from a large hospital and demonstrate that our model can play an effective role in anti-fraud for medical insurance.

Keywords: International Classification of Diseases (ICD) · Electronic Medical Record (EMR) · Anti-fraud · Deep learning

1 Introduction

Given rapid developments in medical informatization and the widespread use of IoT devices [1,2], the healthcare industry has entered the big data era. Massive

© Springer Nature Switzerland AG 2019
J. Li et al. (Eds.): ADMA 2019, LNAI 11888, pp. 871–878, 2019.
https://doi.org/10.1007/978-3-030-35231-8_65

amounts of medical data bring great value to the healthcare domain, which has attracted great interest from academics and industry [3]. Medical expense control is an important research direction in healthcare big data application.

In the past, reimbursement of medical insurance was based on medical service items, resulting in excessive medical treatment. To solve problems related to the item payment mechanism, single-disease charging based on Diagnosis-Related Groups (DRGs) was extensively studied [4]. The single-disease payment model refers to the scientific determination of a fixed payment standard for each disease through a unified classification of disease diagnoses; this standard is legal and can reduce medical cost consumption [5]. The social security agency pays the hospitalization fee to the designated medical institution according to this standard. In short, the single-disease model specifies how much a certain disease should cost, thereby avoiding the abuse of medical service projects.

However, the approach of payment by single-disease is flawed, and fraud may occur. For example, when determining a code for discharge diagnosis, the hospital may change the actual cost of the disease to that of a more expensive disease, thereby obtaining more insurance benefits. A large number of hospitalized patients means a large amount of manpower could be spent if manual audit is performed for each discharge diagnosis. To solve this problem, we present an anti-fraud framework for medical insurance based on deep learning [6]. The framework predicts the probabilities of the discharge diagnosis according to the chief complaint of a inpatient and then determines whether the diagnosis is reasonable. Identified abnormal disease diagnoses are manually audited. This solution can greatly reduce the workload and improve the efficiency of medical insurance reviews.

To validate our framework, we conducted experiments on the data of 300,000 inpatient admission complaints from a large hospital. The results show that our framework can accurately judge the rationality of the diagnosis and play a good role in anti-fraud.

The remainder of this paper is organized as follows. Section 2 describes the preliminaries and proposes the anti-fraud framework. Section 3 details the deep learning approach for chief complaint classification. Section 4 evaluates the effectiveness of the proposed framework. Section 5 reviews previous related work. Finally, Sect. 6 summarizes our study.

2   Preliminaries

2.1   Notations

We first provide the definitions of two key medical terms to elaborate on our proposed framework clearly.

Definition 1: Chief complaint [7]. The chief complaint is a concise statement written by a doctor according to a patient's description when the patient is admitted to the hospital; it includes the symptoms, problem, condition, duration of symptom, or other healthcare needs of the patient.

Definition 2: International Classification of Diseases (ICD) [8]. The ICD is an internationally harmonized disease classification system developed by the World Health Organization that provides a hierarchy encoding specifications for disease diagnosis. It classifies diseases according to their etiology, pathology, clinical manifestations, and anatomical location. The global 10th revision of this classification, referred to as the ICD-10, is used in most Chinese hospitals.

2.2 Problem Statement

The goal of this study is to find suspicious medical records by evaluating whether the first ICD code of a medical record is reasonable. The proposed framework is described in Fig. 1.

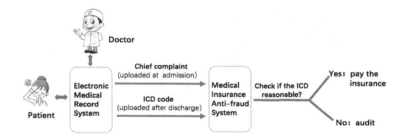

Fig. 1. The proposed anti-fraud framework.

When a patient is admitted to the hospital, the EMR system uploads the patient's chief complaint to the medical insurance anti-fraud system, and the patient's medical record is assigned an ICD code upon discharge from the hospital. The code is then uploaded to the medical insurance anti-fraud system, which judges the rationality of the ICD code based on the patient's chief complaint. If the ICD code is reasonable, the insurance is paid; otherwise, the medical record is audited manually.

3 Methodology

To judge whether a diagnosis is a fraudulent medical record, we must determine whether the disease diagnosis is reasonable according to the chief complaint. To this end, we transform the problem into a text classification problem, that is, to predict which ICD-10 code the chief complaint belongs. Furthermore, we obtain the predicted probability of each ICD-10 code and then sort the resulting ICD-10 codes by probability in descending order. If the prediction result is one of the top-k ICD-10 codes, it is considered reasonable; otherwise, fraudulent behavior may be indicated, and manual auditing is conducted. Text classification is a problem related to natural language processing (NLP). Approaches based on deep learning achieve state-of-the-art in many NLP tasks. To realize the classification of chief complaints, we use the Text-CNN algorithm [9].

3.1   Inputs and Outputs

In the proposed framework, the inputs are the Chinese characters of chief complaints, and the outputs are the probabilities of 130 ICD-10 codes used in the experimental dataset.

3.2   Text-CNN Model Structure

The overall network architecture of the Text-CNN model is shown in Fig. 2. The whole model consists of five layers: an input layer, a convolution layer, a pooling layer, a fully connected layer, and a Softmax layer [9].

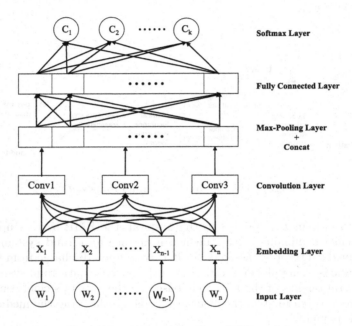

Fig. 2. Structure of the Text-CNN model.

The one-hot encoding of each Chinese Character is fed to the embedding layer. Three convolution kernels of different sizes (3, 4, 5) are used in the Convolution layer. Then the Max-over-time Pooling method is applied in the pooling layer to produce a one-dimensional vector for each sentence. The output of the sentence vectors are then passed to a fully connected layer with dropout.

4   Experiments

4.1   Dataset and Preprocessing

We apply our solution to a dataset containing 300,000 patient admission complaints from a large, grade 3, and first-class hospital in Jiangsu Province, China.

We extract chief complaints and patients' first diagnostic codes from admission records and the medical record home page respectively. In addition, we only obtain the first three digits or letters from the ICD-10 codes, which describe a total of 1,089 diseases.

The counts of ICD-10 codes are unbalanced, and many ICD-10 codes are assigned to a few inpatients only. To address the sparsity problem, we first preprocess the dataset and filter out ICD-10 codes whose counts are less than 500. After filtering out of these data, 198,810 records with 130 ICD-10 categories, covering nearly 80% of the inpatients, are obtained. The average length of all chief complaints is 12 Chinese characters; the longest and shortest complaints contain 38 and 2 Chinese characters, respectively. The vocabulary is generated by all of the experimental data, the sizes of which are 1,456 and 6,760 at the Chinese-character and word levels, respectively. We take the popular toolkit JieBa to segment words with a self-defined dictionary. In the experiment, we split the dataset into a training set, a validation set, and a test set by ICD-10 category at a ratio of 70:15:15.

4.2 Baseline Methods

To evaluate the effectiveness of the proposed framework, we conduct experiments with the following algorithms commonly used for text classification.

- **Text-CNN.** The approach used in our anti-fraud framework. We conduct experiments on Text-CNN at the Chinese-character level and word levels, separately.
- **Text-RNN.** Recurrent Neural Network (RNN) is widely used for sequence learning. It can model natural language sequences of variable length well and capture the inherent sequential nature present in language [10].
- **DPCNN.** Deep Pyramid CNN (DPCNN) is a deep word-level CNN for text classification. It increases the depth of CNN to capture the long-range associations and global representations of a text [11].
- **FastTex.** FastTex is an efficient model for text categorization proposed by Facebook. The model embeds each word in a sentence and then averages the word representations into a text representation, which, in turn, is fed to a linear classifier to obtain the probability distribution over the predefined classes [12].

We tune the parameters on the validation dataset. Our experiments show that the dataset used in this paper is not sensitive to the parameters, and the results of different parameters revealed only slight differences.

4.3 Results and Analysis

To evaluate the performances of the baseline methods, the average macro-precision, average macro-recall, and average macro-F1-score are used as comparative metrics. As mentioned earlier, a chief complaint may result in several diseases; for instance, the diagnosis of "fever" may indicate pneumonia or encephalitis. Therefore, we propose a new evaluation method. If the truth-label of a chief complaint is in the top-k predicted ICD-10 codes arranged in descending order of prediction probability, we assume the prediction result is correct. The value of k is set to 1, 5, or 10 in the experiments. We run each algorithm five times and compute the average score as the final result. The experimental results of different methods are shown in Table 1.

Table 1. Average macro precision, recall, and F1-score for prediction

Methods	Average macro (Top-1)			Average macro (Top-5)			Average macro (Top-10)			Average training time
	Precision	Recall	F1-score	Precision	Recall	F1-score	Precision	Recall	F1-score	
Text-CNN character-level	65.36	58.89	58.94	94.03	89.13	90.86	97.61	95.71	96.55	280 s
Text-CNN word-level	64.40	58.47	58.60	93.29	88.47	90.15	97.15	95.21	96.07	350 s
DPCNN	65.28	58.77	58.80	94.06	89.07	90.75	97.60	95.59	96.47	305 s
Text-RNN character-level	63.27	58.47	57.88	93.46	88.70	90.27	97.28	95.48	96.27	2300 s
Text-RNN word-level	63.38	58.32	57.91	92.85	88.27	89.86	96.87	95.13	95.90	2300 s
FastText	58.13	52.73	52.31	92.53	84.46	86.58	96.71	93.02	94.50	180 s

Table 1 demonstrates that approaches based on CNN are superior to those based on RNN; FastTex, a shallow model, proves to be the least effective method. Text-CNN, which is used in the proposed anti-fraud framework, outperforms all other approaches, and the Chinese-character level Text-CNN experiment yields the best performance. While DPCNN involves a deeper network, its performance decreases slightly compared with that of Text-CNN. In general, the classification performances of the word-level experiments are not as good as those of the character-level experiments, possibly because Chinese medical words are not correctly recognized in the proposed framework. In terms of training time, FastText is completed the fastest; approaches based on CNN are completed nearly 10 times faster than those based on RNN.

5 Related Work

As a branch of NLP, text classification has been widely studied in recent years [12–14]. Yang et al. [13] proposed the Han model, which basically divides text into three layers of words, sentences, and texts by hierarchy and then uses two Bi-LSTM models to model the word-sentence and sentence-doc models. The FastText model [12] proposed by Facebook is very similar to the word2vec model. Its speed is several orders of magnitude higher than other deep learning models, however, the model is less accurate. Lai et al. [14] proposed the RCNN model to solve representations of the left and right context of each word based on word embedding and then combine the three together as the representation of the word.

Several studies to classify and predict ICD codes have been published [15–17]. Li et al. [15] proposed a deep learning framework called DeepLabeler to automatically assign ICD-9 codes. DeepLabeler combines convolutional neural networks with "Document to Vector" technology to extract and encode local and global features. Shi et al. [16] proposed a hierarchical deep learning model with an attention mechanism that could automatically assign ICD diagnostics for a given written diagnosis. Zeng et al. [17] proposed a deep transfer learning framework for automatic ICD-9 encoding that uses knowledge of the transfer MeSH domain to improve automatic ICD-9 encoding. However, few studies have focused on possible fraud in the chief complaints and ICD codes.

6 Conclusion

In this paper, we propose an anti-fraud framework for medical insurance based on deep learning. Our framework predicts the probabilities of diseases according to a patient's chief complaint and then determines whether the resulting ICD-10 code written in the medical record is reasonable and adequate to provide an abnormal disease diagnosis, thereby greatly reducing the workload and improving the efficiency of medical insurance auditors. We conduct numerous experiments on a real-world dataset from a large hospital, and results show that our model can play an effective role in anti-fraud for medical insurance.

Acknowledgment. This work was supported in part by the National Science Foundation of China under Grant No. 61672276, the New Zealand Marsden Fund under Grant No. 17-UOA-24, the University of Auckland FRDF fund under Grant No. 3714668, the National Key Research and Development Program of China under Grant No. 2017YFB1400600, Jiangsu Natural Science Foundation of China under Grant No. BK20171037, Jiangsu Commission Health Research Program No. X201601, and the Collaborative Innovation Center of Novel Software Technology and Industrialization, Nanjing University.

References

1. Xu, X., et al.: An IoT-oriented data placement method with privacy preservation in cloud environment. J. Netw. Comput. Appl. **124**, 148–157 (2018)
2. Xu, X., et al.: A computation offloading method over big data for IoT-enabled cloud-edge computing. Future Gener. Comput. Syst. **95**, 522–533 (2019)
3. Esteva, A., et al.: A guide to deep learning in healthcare. Nat. Med. **25**(1), 24 (2019)
4. Mathauer, I., Wittenbecher, F.: Hospital payment systems based on diagnosis-related groups: experiences in low-and middle-income countries. Bull. World Health Organ. **91**, 746–756A (2013)
5. Gao, F., Tao, Y., Yuan, Z., Li, T.: Discussion on the implementation of single disease payment. Chin. Med. Rec. Engl. Ed. **1**(1), 8–10 (2013)

6. Qi, L., et al.: Finding all you need: web APIs recommendation in web of things through keywords search. IEEE Trans. Comput. Soc. Syst. **6**, 1063–1072 (2019)
7. https://en.wikipedia.org/wiki/Presentingproblem
8. https://www.who.int/classifications/icd/en/
9. Kim, Y.: Convolutional neural networks for sentence classification. arXiv preprint arXiv:1408.5882 (2014)
10. https://nlpoverview.com/
11. Johnson, R., Zhang, T.: Deep pyramid convolutional neural networks for text categorization. In: Proceedings of the 55th Annual Meeting of the Association for Computational Linguistics (Volume 1: Long Papers), vol. 1, pp. 562–570 (2017)
12. Joulin, A., Grave, E., Bojanowski, P., Douze, M., Jégou, H., Mikolov, T.: FastText. zip: compressing text classification models. arXiv preprint arXiv:1612.03651 (2016)
13. Yang, Z., Yang, D., Dyer, C., He, X., Smola, A., Hovy, E.:. Hierarchical attention networks for document classification. In: Proceedings of the 2016 Conference of the North American Chapter of the Association for Computational Linguistics: Human Language Technologies, pp. 1480–1489 (2016)
14. Lai, S., Xu, L., Liu, K., Zhao, J.: Recurrent convolutional neural networks for text classification. In: Twenty-Ninth AAAI Conference on Artificial Intelligence (2015)
15. Li, M., et al.: Automated ICD-9 coding via a deep learning approach. IEEE/ACM Trans. Comput. Biol. Bioinform. **16**(4), 1193–1202 (2018)
16. Shi, H., Xie, P., Hu, Z., Zhang, M., Xing, E.P.: Towards automated ICD coding using deep learning. arXiv preprint arXiv:1711.04075 (2017)
17. Zeng, M., Li, M., Fei, Z., Ying, Y., Pan, Y., Wang, J.: Automatic ICD-9 coding via deep transfer learning. Neurocomputing **324**, 43–50 (2019)

Demos

BSI: A System for Predicting and Analyzing Accident Risk

Xinyu Ma[1(✉)], Yuhao Yang[1], and Meng Wang[2]

[1] School of Software Engineering, Southeast University, Nanjing, China
{xinyu,yuhao}@seu.edu.cn
[2] School of Computer Science and Engineering, Southeast University, Nanjing, China
meng.wang@seu.edu.cn

Abstract. In recent years, the rapid growth of motor vehicle ownership brings great pressure to the road traffic system and inevitably leads to a large number of traffic accidents. Therefore, it is a demanding task to build a well-developed system to identify the high-risk links, i.e., black spots, of a road network. However, most of the existing works focus on identifying black spots in a road network simply based on the statistic data of accidents, which leads to low accuracy. In this demonstration, we present a novel system called BSI, to predict and analyze the high-risk links in a road network by adequately utilizing the spatial-temporal features of accidents. First, BSI predicts the trend of accidents by a spatial-temporal sequence model. Then, based on predicted results, K-means method is utilized to discover the roads with the highest accident severity. Finally, BSI identifies the central location and coverage of a high-risk link by a modified DBSCAN clustering model. BSI can visualize the final identified black spots and provide the results to the user.

Keywords: Black spots · Spatial-temporal sequence · Clustering

1 Introduction

In recent years, road construction is becoming unable to keep up with the rapidly increasing motor vehicles and population. Given this trend, traffic accidents occur frequently and result in a wide variety of adverse consequences such as traffic delays, economic losses, travel time unreliability, increased noise/air pollution, as well as injuries and deaths. Road safety has emerged as a priority issue for road safety management and forecasting practices.

In a road network, the sections or intersections that inherently have high accident risk are usually called **black spots** [1]. Conventional approaches to black spot identification utilize historical records of accident occurrences to find sections or intersections with high accident frequency. In addition to accident frequency, recent clustering based methods utilize other statistical information, e.g., frequencies of deaths and injured people, to form the multi-features of road sections and intersections. Then, they discover similar roads with similar features and finally identify black spots by clustering method.

© Springer Nature Switzerland AG 2019
J. Li et al. (Eds.): ADMA 2019, LNAI 11888, pp. 881–885, 2019.
https://doi.org/10.1007/978-3-030-35231-8_66

However, the occurrence of accidents is often highly related to the temporal and spatial conditions at that time while existing methods [2,5,7] ignore that. Obviously, taking into account the statistical, temporal and spatial features of accidents together will provide a promising way to identify black spots more accurately and obtain more comprehensive analyzing results. Moreover, policymakers can further make more effective strategies and measures to reduce accidents. Based on the above problems and requirements, in this study, we developed a new system called BSI (**B**lack **S**pots **I**dentification), which can accurately predict and analyze black spots based on a spatial-temporal sequence model and a modified DBSCAN clustering algorithm.

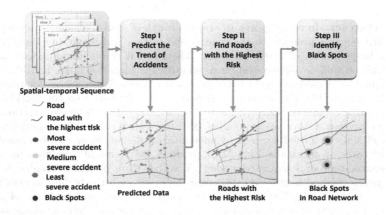

Fig. 1. Pipeline overview of BSI.

In a nutshell, the main contributions of this demonstration are threefold:

- We propose a novel system, BSI, which differs from existing black spot identifying systems and provides more accurate, comprehensive predicting and analyzing results.
- We design a sequence model and leverage spatial-temporal features to predict the trend of accidents, and utilize a modified DBSCAN clustering algorithm to identify black spots over the road network.
- We implement BSI as a web-based interactive visual system for timely exploring, analyzing and downloading black spot results.

2   BSI Overview

BSI will identify black spots in a road network by employing a three-steps pipeline, as shown in Figure 1.

2.1   Predict the Trend of Accidents

In the first step, the BSI system predicts the trend (i.e., the number of accidents, deaths, and injuries) of accidents based on the non-statistical features, e.g., temporal and spatial features of the accident, so that the predicted data can be used in the next analysis. BSI utilizes the STARIMA model in this step [6] which is a space-time autoregressive integrated moving average model. In this step, BSI predicts four features of each road and obtain the trend of accidents.

2.2   Find Roads with Highest Risk

In the second step, BSI integrates the predicted feature values and the statistical features of each road to discover high-risk roads. BSI uses the K-means [3] to cluster the roads as k clusters by iterations. In this step, the road set with the highest risk level is determined.

2.3   Identify Black Spots

In the third step, BSI utilizes a modified DBSCAN clustering method [4] based on the cumulative frequency curve to identify the black spots for each high-risk road.

We use the cumulative frequency curve method to determine a cumulative frequency, which represents the maximum proportion of the total number of roads covered by black spots. Then, BSI employs a modified DBSCAN algorithm to spatially cluster the black spots, which avoids the road segmentation of the road in advance and makes up for the shortcomings of the cumulative frequency curve method. In this step, we identify the final black spots for the road network.

3   Demonstration

BSI provides interactive and visual interfaces to support following functions for users.

(1) The system provides the function of identifying urban black spots. After the user selects a city, the system will timely process the analysis results stored in the database to display the accidents trend (distribution), high-risk roads and black spots to the user. As shown in Fig. 2(a), BSI provides the trend prediction of urban accidents. And Figure 2(b), the black spot identification result is shown. The system also supports a download function for users to obtain the outputs.

(2) The system supports the identification function of black spots in a simulated road network input by users. The system predefines the fixed format of simulating road networks and accident information. Users can generate files of simulating road networks according to the format, upload the files to the system and obtain black spot identification results.

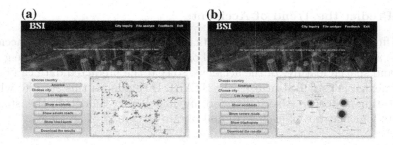

Fig. 2. (a): Screenshot on trend prediction of urban accidents. (b) Screenshot on urban black spots identification.

The BSI system is implemented as a Python Web application. Baidu Map API SDK is incorporated into BSI for creating interactive map visualizations. Demonstration is available online[1]. The source code and data can be found in our Github repository[2].

4   Conclusions

We present an easy-to-use system called BSI in this demo. BSI utilizes a spatial-temporal sequence model and a modified DBSCAN clustering algorithm to identify black spots over the road network. We implemented BSI as a web-based interactive visual system for exploring, analyzing and downloading black spot results. The system also supports to analyze analogue road networks with great flexibility. In the future, the BSI system can be extended by considering more features for black spots identification, e.g., road brightness and road structure, not just the accident itself.

References

1. De Oña, J., López, G., Mujalli, R., Calvo, F.J.: Analysis of traffic accidents on rural highways using latent class clustering and Bayesian networks. Accid. Anal. Prev. **51**, 1–10 (2013)
2. Debrabant, B., Halekoh, U., Bonat, W.H., Hansen, D.L., Hjelmborg, J., Lauritsen, J.: Identifying traffic accident black spots with poisson-tweedie models. Accid. Anal. Prev. **111**, 147–154 (2018)
3. Kanungo, T., Mount, D.M., Netanyahu, N.S., Piatko, C.D., Silverman, R., Wu, A.Y.: An efficient K-means clustering algorithm: analysis and implementation. IEEE Trans. Pattern Anal. Mach. Intell. **7**, 881–892 (2002)
4. Kisilevich, S., Mansmann, F., Keim, D.: P-DBSCAN: a density based clustering algorithm for exploration and analysis of attractive areas using collections of geo-tagged photos. In: Proceedings of the 1st International Conference and Exhibition on Computing for Geospatial Research & Application, pp. 38–41. ACM (2010)

---

[1] http://39.108.119.231:8000/index.html.
[2] https://github.com/Raaabbit/HazardousRoadLocations.

5. Liao, Z.G., Liu, B.M., Guo, Z.Y.: Road black spot identification method based on information assignment. Zhongguo Gonglu Xuebao **20**(4), 122–126 (2007)
6. Pfeifer, P.E., Deutsch, S.J.: A starima model-building procedure with application to description and regional forecasting. Trans. Inst. Br. Geogr. **5**, 330–349 (1980)
7. Vijay, G., Ramesh, A., Kumar, M.: Identification of black spot location for providing improvement measures on selected stretch of a national highway in hyderabad, india. i-Manager's J. Civ. Eng. **7**(3), 6 (2017)

KG3D: An Interactive 3D Visualization Tool for Knowledge Graphs

Dawei Xu[1,2], Lin Wang[1], Xin Wang[2(✉)], Dianquan Li[1], Jianpeng Duan[1], and Yongzhe Jia[1]

[1] TechFantasy Co., Ltd., Tianjin 300387, China
{xudawei,linwang,lidianquan,duanjianpeng,jia}@techfantasy.cn
[2] College of Intelligence and Computing, Tianjin University, Tianjin 300072, China
wangx@tju.edu.cn

Abstract. With the emerge of knowledge graphs in different scales like DBpedia, YAGO, and WikiData, they have become the cornerstone to support many artificial intelligence tasks. However, it is difficult for end-users to query and understand those knowledge graphs consisting of hundreds of millions of nodes and edges. To help end-users better retrieve information from RDF data and explore the knowledge graph without SPARQL or knowing the relation types, we developed an interactive visual query tool, called KG3D, which can realize connection query and pattern matching. Our tool can view the knowledge graph in 3-dimensional space and automatically convert the query to the SPARQL statement. In this paper, we present the superiority of KG3D over other tools, discuss the design motivation, and demonstrate various use cases.

Keywords: Knowledge graph · Semantic web · Visualization · RDF · SPARQL · WebGL

1 Introduction

The Resource Description Framework (RDF) is a standard model for describing resources and exchanging data on the Web [1], which has a feature that facilitates data integration in different schemas. These features make RDF widely developed and accumulated a large number of knowledge graphs like DBpedia, YAGO, and WikiData [2]. SPARQL has emerged as the standard RDF query language by the World Wide Web Consortium. SPARQL is a SQL-like query language able to retrieve and manipulate data stored in RDF. With this language, users can pull values from structured and semi-structured data and explore data by querying unknown relations [3]. However, it is unrealistic to ask end-users to learn SPARQL to query the information they need, which reduces the availability of knowledge graphs for most users. For example, we want to find people born in London with the given name "Jack" before 1900. To issue this query, we have a SPARQL and the corresponding results as shown in Fig. 1.

© Springer Nature Switzerland AG 2019
J. Li et al. (Eds.): ADMA 2019, LNAI 11888, pp. 886–889, 2019.
https://doi.org/10.1007/978-3-030-35231-8_67

```
PREFIX dbo: <http://dbpedia.org/ontology/>
PREFIX xsd: <http://www.w3.org/2001/XMLSchema#>
PREFIX foaf: <http://xmlns.com/foaf/0.1/>
PREFIX : <http://dbpedia.org/resource/>

SELECT ?name ?birth ?death ?person
WHERE {
?person dbo:birthPlace :London .
?person dbo:birthDate ?birth .
?person foaf:name ?name .
?person foaf:givenName "Jack"@en .
?person dbo:deathDate ?death .
FILTER (?birth < "1900-01-01"^^xsd:date) .
} ORDER BY ?name
```

Fig. 1. SPARQL statements and the corresponding results.

In the example, we can find the following problems: First, the SPARQL query is difficult for end users to learn to express their query demands. Second, SPARQL WHERE clauses, abbreviations with prefixes, and full URIs are verbose in the statements. Third, users are supposed to know what relations a specific entity has before the query. The tool should prompt a list of possible relations before the input. Last, most of the visualization tools present results in 2-dimension. Due to space constraints, entities and relations in large number have a high probability of overlapping, which may affect visualization effects. Thus, there is a massive gap between end users and understanding RDF data.

Our research focuses on the design and implementation of a new interactive method of visualization and query for the RDF knowledge graphs. Named KG3D, our demo prototype overcomes the deficiencies above.[1] Our tools can view the knowledge graph in 3-dimensional space by changing the angle of view from overview to details. So the vast spatial and physical force settings ensure that overlap does not occur. The query can automatically convert to SPARQL and full URI to the endpoints, with a heuristic relation prompt function.

2   Demonstration

The data shown in this demo are collected from the SPARQL endpoint of DBpedia. We demonstrate the tool by the following use cases based on the European politics dataset, which contains European cities, the political parties in their local governments, and their ideologies.

Use Case 1: Entity Visual Query. This tool can be used as DBpedia that users are allowed to search for an entity and get its neighbors. When it comes to multiple types of relations, a query can become complicated. This tool as well provides a function that queries a node's neighboring entities by its relation types. For example, "How many cities in France?" To find an answer, we first need to find France, then find those cities in connection with it. We can input

---

[1] GitHub repository: https://github.com/selenesoft/kg3d.

the name in the search box and click the search button. The entity returns as the query result. To find neighbor nodes, user can click on the entity's circular menu and select the explore button, and a pop-up window shows all possible relation types. Select the types by the checkboxes, then execute the query. As shown in Fig. 2, linked nodes and directed edges are shown as user selected. We can repeat this operation to all nodes on the screen.

Fig. 2. Querying entity and its neighbours.

Use Case 2: Connection Query. An important aspect of exploratory search over graph data is to understand what paths connect a given pair of nodes. For example, we want to know how Greece and Germany have parties that share the same ideology. This question can be converted to a problem that determines whether there exists a path between two countries via parties and ideologies. A user starts from a click on one entity's circular menu and selects the path query button on the upper left. We should fill the detail conditions in the text box. The node clicked is automatically set as the object of the first clause. Another entity's name can be input as the second clause, which is the terminal of the path. The query results are shown as Fig. 3.

Fig. 3. Finding a path from France to Greece.

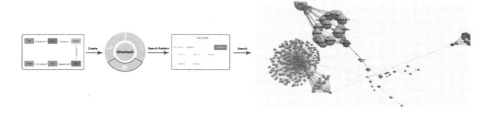

Fig. 4. The process of the complete pattern query.

Use Case 3: Pattern Exploration. If there exists only one type of "Father-Son" relation, we can find someone's grandfather by his father's father. That is a set of conditional clauses or a pattern. This function provides a method to help users complete a set of conditional clauses to query all qualified entities and relations. For example, if we want to know which country share the same ideology with the city Altenbuch's governing party, then the query pattern should be the party that runs the city, party's ideologies, other parties with the same ideology, those parties' governing cities, and corresponding countries. Thus, open the pattern design box. First, drag and drop a city node from the left panel of the screen as the object of the first clause. Then we can click the node to add a relation, which should point to a party node. These operations should be repeated to add more condition clauses until we finish building the pattern, as shown in Fig. 4. We can apply the pattern to the city node named Altenbuch to get the query results. Users can also change the view of the results from a graph to the table if they do not want to see a complex graph with too many nodes.

3   Conclusion

We proposed an interactive visualization tool for presenting RDF data in 3-dimensional space. This tool can help users better retrieve information from RDF data and explore the knowledge graphs without being trained to use SPARQL or knowing the relation types. To enhance usability, we also introduced advanced functions including connection query and pattern matching.

References

1. Wang, X., Wang, J.: ProvRPQ: an interactive tool for provenance-aware regular path queries on RDF graphs. In: Cheema, M.A., Zhang, W., Chang, L. (eds.) ADC 2016. LNCS, vol. 9877, pp. 480–484. Springer, Cham (2016). https://doi.org/10.1007/978-3-319-46922-5_44
2. Yang, C., Wang, X., Xu, Q., Li, W.: SPARQLVis: an interactive visualization tool for knowledge graphs. In: Cai, Y., Ishikawa, Y., Xu, J. (eds.) APWeb-WAIM 2018. LNCS, vol. 10987, pp. 471–474. Springer, Cham (2018). https://doi.org/10.1007/978-3-319-96890-2_41
3. Gómez-Romero, J., et al.: Visualizing large knowledge graphs: a performance analysis. Future Gener. Comput. Syst. **89**, 224–238 (2018)

Author Index

Al Hasan Haldar, Nur 331
Alaqta, Ismail 277
Altulyan, May S. 207
Amraoui, Hend 591
An, Senjian 548, 671
Awrangjeb, Mohammad 277

Ben Baccar, Lilia 681
Bo, Tao 696

Cai, Taotao 331
Cai, Yizhu 221
Cao, Yunajiang 207
Chang, Xiaojun 406
Chen, Chien 389
Chen, Jing 63
Chen, Weitong 151, 250, 373, 617
Chen, Xiaocong 288
Chen, Yue 696
Cheng, Yunyao 565
Chi, Chi-Hung 17, 343, 359, 696

Delphin-Poulat, Lionel 119
Djebali, Sonia 681
Dong, Boxiang 815
Dou, Wanchun 871
Duan, Jianpeng 886

Elloumi, Mourad 591
Engel, Vladislav 737

Feng, AiMin 839
Fournier-Viger, Philippe 169
Franciscus, Nigel 447
Fu, Shucun 871

Gao, Han 302
Gao, Hang 839
Gao, Junbin 828
Gimenez, Judit 79
Grant, Paul 185, 195
Gu, Peipei 712
Guan, Donghai 34, 95

Guérard, Guillaume 681
Gunabalan, Saranya 331

Hackman, Acquah 3
Han, Han 17, 359
Han, Yun 34
Han, Zhe 266
Hassas, Salima 119
He, Bingyan 658
Hou, Xia 712
Hu, Jiahui 737
Huang, Chaoran 207, 288
Huang, Guangyan 761
Huang, Yaohui 658
Huang, Yu 3, 389

Ibrahim, Niyonzima 579
Islam, Md Zahidul 185, 195, 828
Islam, Md. Saiful 316

Jia, Baoting 712
Jia, Ning 462, 535
Jia, Ran 712
Jia, Yongzhe 886
Jiang, Shiling 431
Jiang, Xianwei 726
Jie, Wei 489
Jin, Guanghao 421, 431, 501, 526
Jin, Jin 516

Kang, Yun 151
Kanhere, Salil 207
Kayesh, Humayun 316
Kłopotek, Mieczysław A. 236
Kłopotek, Robert A. 236
Kurniawati, Hanna 648

Labarta, Jesus 79
Lam, Kwok-Yan 343, 696
Lee, Meng-Chieh 389
Li, Bohan 135, 302, 373
Li, Dianquan 886
Li, Jiajia 737

Li, Jianxin 331
Li, Jie 474
Li, Ling 548, 671
Li, Mo 48, 221
Li, Na 750
Li, Ning 712
Li, Qiangnan 750
Li, Qiangyi 750
Li, Weimin 359
Li, Weiqi 501
Li, Weixiang 489
Li, Xue 250, 632, 648
Li, Yingqiu 853
Li, Yukun 474
Li, Yun 63
Li, Yuwen 151
Li, Zhihui 406
Liang, Jiayu 421, 431, 501, 526
Liang, Shining 617
Lin, Jerry Chun-Wei 169
Lin, Yingxian 658
Liu, Chengyu 151
Liu, Feng 151
Liu, Huilin 48
Liu, Kunliang 421, 431, 501, 526
Liu, Wanquan 548, 671
Liu, Wei 288
Liu, Wenhe 406
Liu, Yiwei 671
Liu, Yong 266
Liu, Zhenyu 863
Liu, Zhong 516
Liu, Zitu 266
Lu, Christian 761
Luo, Ting 658
Lv, Jiao 853
Lv, Xingfeng 266
Lv, Yimin 777

Ma, Jingwei 250
Ma, Xinyu 881
Mahdavi, Kaveh 79
Mahmoudzadeh, Somaiyeh 489
MahmoudZadeh, Somaiyeh 792
Mandalapu, Arun Chaitanya 331
Mao, Rubai 266
Matignon, Laetitia 119
Mhamdi, Faouzi 591
Mleya, Molefe Vicky 501

Nicol, Rozenn 119
Niu, Ke 712
Niu, Ying 421

Pang, Jiali 95
Peng, Tao 17
Peng, Xueping 712
Phan, Huan 107
Pokharel, Suresh 648
Prakash, Mahesh 406

Qi, Lianyong 871
Qiao, Guohao 805
Qin, Shaowen 605

Ren, Siyu 431

Sadineni, Avinash 331
Scells, Harrisen 632
Sheng, Guojun 853
Sheng, Quan Z. 373
Shi, Chuan 565
Shi, Zhenkun 617
Shu, Min 17
Song, Li 565
Stantic, Bela 343, 447
Subpaiboonkit, Sitthichoke 632
Sun, Wei 462, 535
Sun, Weifeng 815
Sun, Yukuan 421, 431, 526
Sun, Yunkuan 501
Sun, Zhonghao 343

Tang, Fuchuan 777
Tian, Hui 696
Tseng, Vincent S. 3, 389

Utomo, Chandra Prasetyo 648

van den Heuvel, Willem-Jan 343, 359
Vuillemin, Benoit 119

Wang, Bai 805
Wang, Can 17, 343, 359, 373, 696
Wang, Chunli 535
Wang, Fei 63
Wang, Jianming 421, 431, 501, 526
Wang, Junhu 277, 316, 447
Wang, Kai 135

Wang, Lin   886
Wang, Meng   881
Wang, Sen   617
Wang, Shuliang   579
Wang, Xianzhi   207, 288
Wang, Xin   777, 886
Wang, Yongming   658
Wang, Zhenggang   516
Wang, Zhijin   658
Wang, Zhiqiong   48
Wang, Ziheng   63
Wang, Zun   815
Wei, Shoushui   151
Wen, Jiahui   250
Wu, Bin   565, 805

Xia, Xiufeng   737
Xiang, Xue   777
Xiang, Yong   761
Xin, Junchang   48, 221
Xu, Dawei   886
Xu, Jiajie   63
Xu, Xiaolong   871
Xuan, Ping   266

Yang, Peng   169
Yang, Yuhao   881
Yao, Lina   207, 288, 406
Yates, Darren   828
Ye, ZhiYu   839
Ying, Josh Jia-Ching   389

Yu, Philip S.   3
Yu, Shaozheng   853
Yu, Yonghong   17
Yuan, Chunmiao   421, 526
Yuan, Weiwei   34, 95
Yue, Lin   373, 617
Yue, Runpu   777
Yun, Unil   169

Zhang, Baoli   805
Zhang, Dongqing   863
Zhang, Guanghao   815
Zhang, Guoming   871
Zhang, Huaxiang   406
Zhang, Mengqian   135
Zhang, Pengju   526
Zhang, Xiang   288
Zhang, Xuyun   871
Zhang, Yuxin   302
Zhang, Zhimin   151
Zhao, Boxiang   579
Zhao, Xin   632
Zhao, Yunwei   17, 343, 359, 696
Zheng, Chunjun   462, 535
Zhong, Mingyang   250
Zhou, Xiaofang   250
Zhu, Jiayi   548
Zhu, Zhaosong   726
Zong, Chuanyu   737
Zuccon, Guido   632
Zuo, Wanli   617

Printed in the United States
By Bookmasters